Clapham, J. H.
An economic history
of modern Britain

AN
ECONOMIC HISTORY
OF MODERN BRITAIN

FREE TRADE AND STEEL
1850–1886

AN ECONOMIC HISTORY OF MODERN BRITAIN

FREE TRADE AND STEEL
1850–1886

By

SIR JOHN CLAPHAM

CAMBRIDGE
AT THE UNIVERSITY PRESS
1967

PUBLISHED BY
THE SYNDICS OF THE CAMBRIDGE UNIVERSITY PRESS

Bentley House, 200 Euston Road, London, N.W.1
American Branch: 32 East 57th Street, New York, N.Y. 10022

First Edition 1932
Reprinted 1952
1963
1967

First printed in Great Britain at the University Press, Cambridge
Reprinted by offset lithography by Billing & Sons Limited
Guildford and London

PREFACE

THIS volume has not followed quite so quickly on the heels of the first as I had hoped, mainly, I think, because the material is not very well suited for quick handling. It is at once heavy and incomplete; and much of it has been imperfectly sifted. Then, the further one advances towards the present age of full social and economic statistics, the more difficult does the writing of certain sections of the narrative become. As Britain gets more deeply involved in a 'world economy' the treatment must be something more than insular. After 1870, Alfred Marshall used to say, you cannot write *English* economic history: he might have given an earlier date. How far the adjustment of statistics to narrative, and of England to the world, has been successful is for readers to decide. The attempt to make it has certainly taken time.

Material is incomplete partly because the Mid-Victorians, living in a world which was demonstrably getting more comfortable and was running without too much friction, did not appoint so many Commissions and Committees of Inquiry as the Early Victorians. It has been said that reliance on these accumulated inquiries, concerned as they were primarily with economic and social pathology, has warped our view of the early nineteenth century. I rather think it has, sometimes. But the reports, carefully read, tell almost as much about normal as about diseased social tissue. For instance; one of the comparatively few reports of the earlier type from the Mid-Victorian era, that on child labour in the 'sixties of which Karl Marx made so much use, is full of incidental information about the organisation of industry. So is the trade union inquiry of the same decade. Fortunately the Late-Victorians of the 'eighties and 'nineties became socially and economically anxious, and resumed inquiry into all sorts of things on a scale so huge as to be almost daunting. There is ample retrospective information in the four or five folios on the *Depression of Trade and Industry* of the 'eighties; more still in the sixty-seven folio parts of the *Report of the Royal Commission on Labour* of the 'nineties—beautifully indexed, to the student's great advantage—or in the nine volumes of Charles Booth's *Life and Labour of the People in London*.

Where official and other strictly original sources fail, the lack of enough first-rate local and trade monographs is acutely felt. I have in mind books of the class of G. I. H. Lloyd's *The Cutlery Trades* (1913), C. Wright and C. E. Fayle's *History of Lloyd's* (1928) or G. C. Allen's *Industrial Development of Birmingham and the Black Country* (1929). The appearance of the last two, and of many other books and articles used, including 'the Webbs' on the Poor Law, since my first volume was published, shows how much the second might have gained by—shall we say?—another ten years at a finishing school. But I cannot afford ten years; and I believe that the material which I have used is trustworthy, if still incomplete.

For this volume I owe a special debt to Alfred Marshall. Some years before he died he entrusted to me the bound files of the *Economist*, from the 'forties to the 'seventies, to be kept until I had written beyond them and then transferred to the Marshall Library. It is an uncommon privilege to stroll about the business world of the 'sixties and 'seventies with Walter Bagehot, the editor of those years, literally at one's elbow. He is more vivacious than most economists, trade historians, or secretaries of Commissions; and wiser too.

For procuring information in Glasgow, Liverpool, and Grimsby I am indebted to Mr A. M. Stephen, Mr J. H. Hubback and Mr Joseph Bennett. I owe to Mr A. H. Moberly information about the suburban architecture of the 'eighties used and quoted on p. 498. Of my colleagues at King's, I must thank Professor Pigou, for loans of books and for—what he has quite forgotten—encouragement when the economist in me got impatient with the task of his much bulkier room-mate the historian; Mr John Saltmarsh, for information extracted for my use from our muniments; Mr W. H. Macaulay, who allowed me to draw on his hunting memories and on his complete knowledge of the works of Surtees; and Mr Hamilton McCombie, who checked my references to the chemical industries. I owe special thanks to the last-named because I hold, with conviction, that a writer whose habit is tiresomely detailed has no right to plague his friends with his proof-sheets, but should take his own risks of blundering. For all other passages, and for these, I hereby take mine.

I have decided not to be deterred from thanking my wife for some very heavy work on the Index by the appearance of a monograph entitled *1066 and All That*. English contemporaries will understand the reference; and should my book keep afloat for half a generation, foreigners and learned posterity may profitably inquire into it.

J. H. CLAPHAM

Cambridge
1 May, 1932

CONTENTS

BOOK III

FREE TRADE AND STEEL

Chapter I. BRITAIN AND THE NATIONS 1848–53 *page*

Chapter II. THE INDUSTRIAL FIELD IN 1851

Chapter III. THE COURSE OF INDUSTRIAL CHANGE

Chapter IV. THE DEVELOPMENT OF INDUSTRIAL ORGANISATION

Chapter V. COMMUNICATIONS

Chapter VI. OVERSEAS TRADE AND COMMERCIAL POLICY

Chapter VI. OVERSEAS TRADE AND COMMERCIAL POLICY, *contd*

Chapter VII. AGRICULTURE

Chapter VIII. THE ORGANISATION OF COMMERCE

Chapter IX. MONEY, PRICES, BANKING AND INVESTMENT

Chapter X. THE ECONOMIC ACTIVITIES OF THE STATE

Chapter XI. LIFE AND LABOUR IN INDUSTRIAL BRITAIN

Chapter XI. LIFE AND LABOUR IN INDUSTRIAL BRITAIN, *contd*

Chapter XII. THE FACE OF THE COUNTRY, 1886–7

PLATES AND DIAGRAMS

BOOK III

FREE TRADE AND STEEL

This is no longer the age of mystery. No longer the age of artificial protection to national industry.

PROF. LEONE LEVI, 1863

The ferruginous temper...which...has changed our Merry England into the Man in the Iron Mask.

JOHN RUSKIN, 1880

August 18, 1865. The Atlantic cable has snapped. The Great Eastern is fishing about for the ends.

March 18, 1878. Off to see the telephone and phonograph. The former is nothing to compare with the latter for wonderfulness. *Diary of Mary Gladstone*

Progress and Poverty, by Henry George (New York, 1879: London, 1881).

CHAPTER I

BRITAIN AND THE NATIONS, 1848–53

"OUR Parliament is to be prorogued on Tuesday and dissolved the same day," Victoria wrote to her Belgian uncle on June 29, 1852. "Lord Derby himself told us, that he considered Protection as quite gone. It is a pity they did not find this out a little sooner; it would have saved so much annoyance, so much difficulty."[1] Fourteen months earlier she and her Consort and England had held their triumph of industry and peace under the "blazing arch of lucid glass" at the Great Exhibition. All three felt confident and generous towards the world, as they walked among the exhibits.

> Look yonder where the engines toil:
> These England's arms of conquest are,
> The trophies of her bloodless war:
> Brave weapons these.
> Victorious over wave and soil,
> With these she sails, she weaves, she tills,
> Pierces the everlasting hills,
> And spans the seas.[2]

Let the engines and the engine-minders be fed, and let the art and wealth of the nations come into England—freely. "Albert's name is immortalised, and the wicked and absurd reports of danger of every kind, which a set of people, viz. the *soi-disant* fashionables and the most violent Protectionists, spread, are silenced."[3]

What had "quite gone" in 1852 was the prospect of a reversal of Peel's economic policy as carried forward by the Whigs since 1846, the policy which, in spite of the survival of long lists of dutiable articles in the tariff, had disposed of effective protection to the staples of agriculture, the extractive industries and nearly all manufactures. Ships imported to be broken up paid 25 per cent. *ad valorem* and artificial flowers also 25 per cent.; but the most favoured British manufacture of importance, silk,

[1] Martin, Theodore, *The Life of His Royal Highness The Prince Consort*, II. 451.

[2] Thackeray, W. M., *May-Day Ode*.

[3] Martin, *op. cit.* II. 368.

had now no more than a 15 per cent. duty to shelter it, as against absolute prohibition thirty years earlier. No other manufacture had more than 10 per cent.; and many industries, or parts of industries, had none at all. Iron, wool and hides could come in free; so could coal had anyone wished to send it; also litharge and "live creatures illustrative of natural history," with "magna grœcia ware," manna and manures. Colonial timber could come at 1*s*. a load, or about 2 per cent. *ad valorem* for the commoner sorts; wheat at 1*s*. a quarter, or slightly more than 2 per cent. at the prices current in 1850–52[1]. In effect Britain was an open market for nearly everything which she produced except alcohol; and home-made alcohol had to carry the excise. The last of those export duties on which the kings of medieval England had lived vanished, as a corollary to the repeal of the Navigation Laws, in 1850. It was the duty on coal exported in a foreign ship.

The opened market had done its work well throughout the Irish famine; although during the years 1850–52 farmers were dissatisfied with the prices of grain[2]. Imports of grain and flour of all sorts into the United Kingdom had been at their maximum in 1849, when the Irish potato area had not recovered from the blight and something like 1,400,000 people in Ireland, nearly a quarter of the surviving population, were still in receipt of poor relief[3]. The course of the import trade as conditions became more normal was as follows. The figures are those of the Board of Trade for 'Grain, Flour and Meal as Grain,' entered for home consumption, in millions of quarters[4]:

1849	11·9	1852	7·8
1850	9·1	1853	10·1
1851	9·7	1854	7·8

Except in 1849, when shipments of the maize with which the famine had been stanched were still abnormally large, rather more than half the imports were of wheat or wheaten flour. The

[1] For the customs of this period see *Customs Tariffs of the United Kingdom from* 1800 *to* 1897 (c. 8706 of 1897), p. 717 *sqq*. There were a number of specific duties on silk goods: 15 per cent. was the general maximum rate when levied *ad valorem*. Prices are in Tooke and Newmarch, *History of Prices*, vol. v and in the weekly price-current of the *Economist*.

[2] See vol. I. p. 455.

[3] Pauperism figures are in the *Statistical Abstracts for the United Kingdom*.

[4] All figures are from the Board of Trade's monthly and annual statements. It has not seemed necessary to give references for each from the *Accounts and Papers* of the various years. The statements are also available in full in the files of the *Economist*.

rest was principally oats and maize, neither of which was much eaten by the people of Britain. What the import of a yearly average of about 4,900,000 quarters of wheat, for the triennium 1850–52[1], meant in terms of dependence on the foreigner statisticians were not certain: they did not know how much wheat was grown at home or how much oat and barley meal was eaten. But their calculations went to suggest that perhaps so many as from 5,000,000 to 6,000,000, out of the 21,185,000 people alive in Britain in the year of the census and the Great Exhibition, already 'lived on foreign bread,'[2] or that about a quarter of every one's bread was foreign. The heavy imports and high prices of 1853 showed how desperate the position might have been had the foreign share been excluded.

Whenever wheat had been imported at all, at any time during the previous fifty years and more, some had come as flour. Barrelled flour from America was a standard commodity, especially in the Liverpool trade. A very sharp—though, as it proved, short-lived—rise in the imports of this half-manufactured foodstuff occurred in 1851, provoking some anxious discussion among protectionists and millers[3]. In 1849 the wheat flour imported into the United Kingdom for home consumption had not risen above the figure, already considerable, of 197,000 tons. In 1850 it was rather less. In 1851 the figure jerked up to 270,000 tons. Quite early in the year there was noted "a suspension to some extent of the mill power in this country, but especially in Ireland."[4] Irish mills often bought English and other wheat, and sent the flour to England. Now they were being cut out of this trade by very efficient millers in Rouen and Paris. The comment of the free traders was apposite and prophetic. They admitted "some difficulty which flour mills will have to encounter, placed far from any port, without a local supply of wheat," like those of Ireland; they said it was "generally admitted that the French millers" were "superior to the English...in their mode of management"; but they argued that our "large steam flour mills," with their cheap coal and good machinery, would learn their lesson—were in fact already learn-

[1] It was a triennium of rather poor harvests. Tooke and Newmarch, *History of Prices*, v. 223–5. In 1853 wheat prices rose steadily from 45*s*. to 80*s*.

[2] See the estimates, in Porter, G. R., *Progress of the Nation* (edition of 1851), p. 143. Lawes, J. B. and Gilbert, J. H., in the *J.R.A.S.* 1880, estimated that for the years 1852–9 imported wheat formed 26·5 per cent. of the consumption.

[3] See the article in the *Economist*, quoted below.

[4] The *Economist*, March 29, 1851.

ing it—and would beat the French[1]. Free trade was producing its normal results—tiresome but wholesome stimulus for all; for the weak and ill-placed, the gulf that lies beyond 'the margin' of the economists; for the powerful and adaptable, more power. A fall in the imports of wheat flour, to an annual average of 180,000 tons for the five years 1852–6, came in support of the free traders' argument[2].

Compared with the imports of wheat, those of other essential and competitive foodstuffs were still relatively insignificant. True, the live cattle of all kinds imported rose from 66,000 in 1850 to 127,000 in 1853, and the sheep from 135,000 to 249,000; but Britain had several millions of cattle and many millions of sheep, and she drew from 150,000 to 200,000 of each yearly out of Ireland, with plenty of butter[3]. With the recovery of Ireland after the famine, imports of taxed foreign butter, which had reached 15,000 tons in 1847, remained stationary until 1853, when they rose to 20,000 tons. The imports of cheese were growing even more slowly; those of salted and preserved meat were trifling; and the five taxed foreign eggs per head of the population per annum, which was about the consumption of the early 'fifties, cannot have affected much the market for British and Irish eggs. Nearly all the foreign livestock, with the farm-yard and dairy produce, came by steamer across the Channel and the North Sea; and most of it went into the Thames to feed London. Lancashire and the Clyde had Ireland close at hand. In 1852 the total imports of foreign livestock—cattle, sheep and swine—were returned at 334,000. The weekly reports of arrivals on the London market give a total of no less than 268,000 of these delivered there[4]. Holland was perhaps the most important single source of cattle and dairy produce: her Friesland butter was the standard London quotation. Few animals came from north of the Skaw or south of Finisterre: the arrival of some "very superior oxen" from Oporto was a matter for comment in a market report, usually jejune, of February, 1854[5].

The opening of the British grain market had made the grain

[1] The *Economist*, as above.

[2] There had been no important change in the sources for the supply of wheat and wheat flour given in vol. I. p. 500 for the year 1847.

[3] The imports from Ireland are in a return of 1854, *Accounts and Papers* LXV. 367. The cattle in Great Britain may have been 6,000,000 or rather less, the sheep 28,000,000 or rather more. Regular agricultural returns had not begun.

[4] Reckoned from the weekly Smithfield Market reports in the *Economist*.

[5] *Economist*, February 11, 1854.

imports almost rival in bulk what had been the only regular bulk import trade thirty years earlier, that in timber. So far had British forestry declined very long ago; so insistent had been the demands of the Royal Navy, whose official spokesmen were saying in 1851 that "iron does not appear to be applicable for ships of war,"[1] that there had not been any real question of protecting home-grown timber for years. The issue had been between the foreign and the imperial. Peel had left a duty of 15*s*. a load, which would often work out at over 20 per cent. *ad valorem*, on foreign hewn timber: in 1851 this duty was halved, but it remained an obstacle to trade. Nevertheless the natural convenience of supply from Scandinavia and the Baltic was re-asserting itself[2]. By 1853, out of the total import of 2,404,000 loads of timber into the United Kingdom, very little more than half came from British possessions.

What weight of timber was felled at home is not known: all told it must have been great. Many estates, perhaps most, were nearly self-sufficing for ordinary estate purposes. British ash had no rival for hafts and handles. British oak and beech had many recognised uses. Oak, ash, beech, and the hard-working elm, against which house carpenters had long been turning in favour of soft-working fir timber, each held unchallenged that place in the country wheelwrights' and waggon-builders' scheme which it was not even to begin to lose for another thirty years[3]. There was an immense consumption of wood, much of it no doubt home grown, for railway carriages and waggons. The plantations of young larch and spruce which had angered Cobbett might, when conveniently placed, be felled for pit props, though the larger pitwood often came from overseas. The naval authorities still kept some sort of watch, at least in the remainder royal forests, on the great timber of oaks planted during the American War of Independence and now ripening for use. Yet in spite of its stubborn prejudice in favour of English oak, the Admiralty, which had almost cleared the country of 'navy oak' during the French wars, was now filling up its yards more and more with substitute woods—teak, Baltic oak, Italian oak, pitch pine and fir. Deptford yard in 1855 had in store 4596 loads of these

[1] Captain Washington in the 1851 *Exhibition Lectures*, I. 563.

[2] For the diversion of the trade to British North America since 1800 see vol. I. p. 237–8.

[3] See Sturt, George, *The Wheelwright's Shop* (1923), for the position in the 'eighties.

substitutes against only 1868 of English oak[1]. The railways were mostly laid on sleepers of imported fir. Little else was used in town building. The commercial shipbuilder, though he still used plenty of British timber, had taught the Admiralty the value of the substitutes. For none of the major uses was the British timber essential; which was as well, for there was not enough of it well placed for bulk felling to meet any of them, and apparently nobody thought it likely that there ever would be.

In wool the open market continued to work smoothly for producer, consumer and dealer, and to illustrate beautifully the territorial division of labour and the principles of a free international trade as lately restated by John Mill. Certain classes of wool were regularly sold by the United Kingdom to its continental neighbours, particularly the French. The weight in 1850 was 12,000,000 lbs., and the declared value £624,000—the highest figures ever recorded[2]. This came from an annual clip (including the skin wool from slaughtered sheep) which was estimated by one authority at 157,500,000, and by another at 228,000,000 lbs.—estimates which reveal the real ignorance[3]. Foreign and colonial wool imported had risen in 1850 to 73,000,000 lbs. of which over 14,000,000 lbs. was re-exported, again mainly to France. Every continent and almost every country sent some wool to England, but by 1850 more than half came from Australia, which had taken the place of Germany as the main source of fine wool since 1835. The best 'Electoral' (Saxon) wool still fetched the highest prices, and Spanish wool was quoted first in the antiquated ritual of market reports; but the import from Spain was nearly dead, and the import from all Germany in 1850 was not half what it had been in 1840, and only a third of what it had been in 1830. In 1835 more than half the imported wool had been German: by 1855 the proportion was barely one-sixteenth, as the figures, taken at five-year intervals, show[4].

The growth of the re-export trade between 1845 and 1855 marks the final establishment of London as the distributing centre for Australian wool[5]. Competition of French buyers in

[1] Albion, R. G., *Forests and Sea Power* (1926), p. 403.

[2] A very small amount of the wool was Irish: no figures are available.

[3] The first is that of Prof. Low quoted in James, J., *History of the Worsted Manufacture* (1857), p. 542; the second that of Southey, a London wool-broker, in Forbes, H., *The Worsted Manufacture*; 1851 *Exhibition Lectures*, II. 321.

[4] See Table, p. 7.

[5] See Shann, E., *An Economic History of Australia* (1930), book I, especially ch. VI, "John Bull's Greater Woolsack."

London kept up the prices, both of imported and of British wools. Lincoln long wool rose by more than 22 per cent. between January, 1851 and January, 1853, and good Southdown wool, the nearest in character to the Australian, by 25 per cent. Here was nothing to tempt anyone to reverse a patently successful policy.

	Exports of British wool in millions of lbs.	Total imports in millions of lbs.	Imports from Germany.	Imports from Spain.	Imports from Australia.	Re-exports of wool.
1835	4·6	42·2	23·8	1·6	4·2	4·1
1840	4·8	46·9	21·8	1·3	9·7	1·0
1845	9·1	75·5	18·5	1·1	24·2	2·6
1850	12·0	75·3	9·2	·4	39·0	14·4
1855	16·2	99·3	6·1	·07	49·1	29·4

Nor was there anything in the state of the extractive industries to suggest that the free traders were wrong. Indeed no protectionist said they were; and some extractive industries, copper and tin mining for instance, were still lightly protected[1]. The Cornish mines were splendidly active. Though some 5000 tons of copper, unwrought and part-wrought, and over 40,000 tons of copper ore, were imported annually in 1850 and 1851, more than 6500 tons were exported raw 'in bricks and pigs'; nearly 12,000 tons in sheets, nails and other simple forms; and beyond that all the copper and brass manufactures. Lead was like copper; the exports still greatly exceeded the imports. Tin was not in quite so strong a position, viewed crudely. A few hundred more tons were imported in the ingot, and retained for home consumption, than were exported unwrought; but the tinplate trade raised its exports to £1,000,000 worth in 1851. Tin also entered into many manufactured exports. The prices of English tin were good and they were rising, and employment in Cornwall and Devon grew. In coal and iron Britain was supreme. The position won in the first quarter of the century was retained and improved. Coal exports were growing slowly —they fluctuated between 3,250,000 and 4,000,000 tons in the early 'fifties—but of coal import there was never any question. Exports would have grown rather quicker, but for the protective policies of some other nations. France not only laid a heavy

[1] Copper duties were now negligible: copper ore paid 1*s*. a ton, and raw copper 2*s*. 6*d*. The price rose to above £100 a ton in 1853. Down to 1848 the duty had been protective, working out at about 10 per cent. *ad valorem*. The duty on foreign tin was still about 6 per cent. *ad valorem* (£6 a ton) in the early 'fifties.

duty on all coal, but gave a tariff preference to the land-borne coals of Belgium[1]. The considerable import of iron—30,000 to 40,000 tons—was rather a measure of the prosperity of Sheffield than of effective foreign competition with the British iron-masters: it was the charcoal bar from Sweden or Russia, specially suitable for cutlery; and its value in 1850–53 was much less than that of the steel, largely made out of it, which Britain was exporting unwrought, over and above the edge tools and cutlery.

The produce of British blast and puddling furnaces and rolling mills was pouring abroad in what seemed impossible quantities, as country after country entered the railway age. A shipment of 554,000 tons of the cruder forms of iron—pig, cast and wrought—had been remarkable enough in 1849; for in 1839 the figure had been only 191,000 tons[2]. By 1853 shipments had reached 1,260,000 tons, and of this two-thirds was not pig or cast iron but the more valuable puddled iron—bar, bolt, rod and wrought of all kinds. America remained the great buyer: Yankee clippers left the Mersey heavy with Staffordshire bar[3]. Exports of finished iron and steel goods grew less rankly, yet healthily. There were no imports of manufactured iron, none at least which were inserted in the regular trade returns of the early 'fifties. The customs officials now added from time to time items to the list of commodities described as 'principal articles of foreign and colonial merchandise.' They inserted a number of headings between 1848 and 1853, as the character of the imports changed with the changes in the productive capacities of the nations, and in the British tariffs. But they did not think it necessary to add to the two traditional iron categories—'iron in bar, unwrought' and 'steel unwrought.' The former contained the record of the charcoal bar for Sheffield; the latter, once very important[4], was now almost empty.

That geological variety and geographical lay-out which have made the small area of Britain an almost complete show-case of the geological formations, ringed about by the near sea, are

[1] The French coal tariff was very complex: there were different rates for land and sea-borne coal, and short-haul sea-borne coal paid more than long-haul. See Dunham, A. L., *The Anglo-French Treaty of Commerce of* 1860 *and the Progress of the Industrial Revolution in France* (1930), p. 9, 19.

[2] See the diagram in vol. I. p. 483.

[3] From the memories of an iron-merchant who arranged some of the shipments.

[4] See vol. I. p. 150.

particularly favourable to her extractive industries. Much of her iron lies close to her coal, or close to the sea, or both. Copper lies deep by the sea which washes the edge of the Welsh coalfield. The salt of the Keuper beds in the trias of Cheshire, Stafford and Worcester—about Northwich, Shirleywich and Droitwich—is all near to coal measures[1]. Easily worked at every successive level of civilisation, it had been worked and moved with special ease in the new age of canals, steam and railways. A little salt still came in from 'the Bay,' but the export grew steadily. It was nearly twice as great in 1852–3 as it had been in 1842–3, though worth only some £250,000 a year. On the shoulders of the salt trade stood, very literally, the trade in soda, with its headquarters in South Lancashire and on the Clyde. The exports, from very small beginnings about twenty-five years earlier, had grown to nearly £500,000 a year by 1853. They were associated with other, though less valuable, exports of the heavy chemicals and industrial acids, whose raw materials were home-extracted pyrites and salt, with some imported pyrites and sulphur.

Provided she could count on her regular food supplies from Ireland, Britain was still reasonably self-sufficient in the narrow commissariat sense, when corn crops were pretty good, in spite of the millions who in average years now ate foreign bread. She could have kept alive for the best part of a year, with an effort perhaps from harvest to harvest, even if she had lost control of the outer seas. But as the world then was, and indeed essentially, this is a most unimportant conclusion. Her control of the outer seas was almost as complete as her control of the Solent. A coalition which might have threatened it was unthinkable in 1851. What naval dangers there were—some there were bound to be, with a Napoleon rising again—were almost all localised in the Channel. Had some unthinkable coalition completely mastered the seas, south, east and west, she would have been forced to peace for lack of cotton, hemp, timber, sugar, tobacco, saltpetre, markets and empire some time before she might have been forced to it by a shortage of meat or bread. It is easy to overrate the value of the corn laws as insurance policies. Insurance against a mere interruption in British control of the sea was hardly necessary: at nearly every season of the year there were bread and meat in Britain for months.

[1] Woodward, H. B., *The Geology of England and Wales*, p. 240.

Insurance against the ultimate, and very remote, dangers of a desperate war was to be found only in an overwhelming fleet, a shrewd balance-holding diplomacy, or a consistently pacific policy. The free traders believed that what had lately been done under their inspiration was a contribution to such a policy.

Some of the leaders were no doubt too sanguine in their estimate of the strength of a good international precedent. Even the cautious Peel, who had "no guarantee to give that other nations will immediately follow our example," was convinced that it would "ultimately prevail." He saw "symptoms of it already" in 1846[1]. But the free-trade leaders did not suppose that Britain, with her new cheap food, her coal and iron and machines and capital, had entered on an eternity of industrial and commercial leadership. An age of leadership, yes, but how long? They knew about America, as their master Adam Smith had known, when he faced the possibility of a transfer of the capital of the Empire across the Atlantic "in the course of little more than a century."[2] "Here," Cobden, not yet a politician, had thought in 1835 as he looked from Laurel Hill over the valley of the Monongahela where it flows north towards Pittsburg, "here will one day centre the civilisation, the wealth, the power of the entire world."[3]

"The people there," his newspaper ally, the *Economist*, wrote in 1851, "have our knowledge, our skill, and more than our activity...they have an immense continent at their command, and they continually receive accessions of capital and population from England and from every country in Europe. From the relative progress of the two countries within the last sixty years, it may be inferred that the superiority of the United States to England is ultimately as certain as the next eclipse."[4]

"Ultimately": did the economist, in his mind, give the ultimatum seventy years to run or only fifty? Or did he, as is much more likely, think no more about it because it would not run out in his day, and because there was no question about British superiority in 1851? In an earlier article that same year he, or a colleague, had been discussing the balance of trade[5].

[1] Jan. 27, 1846. Hansard, Third Series, LXXXIII. 277–8. The Corn Law repeal speech.

[2] *Wealth of Nations* (ed. Cannan), II. 124.

[3] Morley, J., *The Life of Richard Cobden*, I. 31.

[4] *Economist*, March 8, 1851.

[5] *Ibid.* January 11, 1851. The article is a very early, perhaps the earliest, complete though necessarily unstatistical analysis of the items in the modern balance of trade.

He deplored the lack of relevant statistics. We knew, he wrote, the declared values of our exports. For the imports we had correct quantities, but only the old official values which were "notoriously no indication whatever of the present value." So alarmists could always argue that the balance was against us. He was sceptical of the possibility of ever securing all the necessary information; but his notes on the information lacking are eloquent of British strength. To the declared value of the exports he added a hypothetical eighth for freights, "the great proportion of which are paid...to British shipowners": in spite of the Yankee clippers, Britain did most of her own carrying. Next he referred to a great unknown sum for "the profit, whatever it may be, obtained abroad on those goods, shipped on account of British houses" (Britons handled much of this trade at both ends. There were British firms in all important Baltic towns, and British banks in every Mediterranean port[1].) Then he spoke of the unknown earnings of "the enormous amount of British capital employed in different parts of the world," and of the remittances of unknown amount from profits and from incomes of public servants overseas. "Most of the banks in Australia, the West Indies and Canada, are conducted with British capital"; so is "a considerable part of the cultivation of our colonies." He went on to enumerate loans to America, investments in European railways, and the rest. These were familiar facts, he said, or should have been. But perhaps the most important fact of all bearing on the balance of trade was "too often entirely overlooked." "As a rule England gives credit to all the world and takes none." "In India, China, North America and all our foreign markets, though in a much less degree in our continental trade"—an important qualification—credits "extending over many months" were given when we exported; when we imported, the goods were drawn against at once by the seller abroad, and the drafts were "usually paid about the time or shortly after the arrival of the cargoes. Practically speaking, then, England gives long credits on her exports, while the imports are paid for in ready money."[2] And the commercial life of the planet, he might have added, was therefore dominated by the bill on London, an international

[1] See Jenks, L. H., *The Migration of British Capital to* 1875 (1927), p. 188–9.

[2] For more critical and balanced statements see the evidence of D. B. Chapman, of Overend and Gurney, before the *S.C. on the Bank Acts*, 1857, x. Q. 4840 *sqq.*, especially Q. 5130–46.

currency, and was largely financed through London. "English credit supplied the capital of almost the whole world."[1] He did not quote the blessing in Deuteronomy xxviii. 12–13, but it would spring to the mind of many Victorian merchants who knew their Old Testament: "and thou shalt lend unto many nations, and thou shalt not borrow. And the Lord shall make thee the head, and not the tail."

Undisputed superiority in commerce and in money-lending went with a superiority in manufacturing which was the more marked because it was shown most in the making of those things which the world chiefly needed. That it would be shown at every point was not to be expected. Already the well-informed knew that an American was more likely than an Englishman to get tiresome and expensive handicraft operations done for him by machinery. This, to take an outstanding instance, had been shown long before, though most British manufacturers had not yet noticed it, in connection with a critical stage in the business of wool spinning. The 'condensing' process, in which the gauzy film of carded wool is stripped mechanically from the carding rollers and delivered in loose ropes ready for the mule, had been fully worked out by John Goulding of Massachusetts before 1832[2]. It got rid of the belated handicraft operation of slubbing, *i.e.* preparing the loose ropes on a hand-worked 'billy,' which came in between machine carding and mule spinning and spoilt the team-work of the machinery. It also got rid of the billy roller with which the brutal slubber so often beats the piecers in the early stories of factory cruelty. By 1850 Goulding's condenser, which has been called "almost as great an advance in wool manufacture as the spinning jenny itself,"[3] was widely, if not universally, used in New England; for several years it had been coming into use in Galashiels and Hawick, where its merits had been advertised in the 'thirties by a local

[1] *S.C. on the Bank Acts and the recent Commercial Distress*, 1857–8, v. Evidence of John Ball, Q. 1702.

[2] See Cole, A. H., *The American Wool Manufacture* (1926), I. 102–3. Goulding, like Arkwright, seems to have been more an organiser of inventions than an inventor. He bought important notions from others. Patents for mechanical condensing had been taken out in England in 1834 (see vol. I. p. 144) but had not come into general use.

[3] By Hayes, G. L., *Bulletin of American Wool Manufacturers*, 1894, p. 329, quoted in Cole, *op. cit.* I. 103.

man who had been to America[1]; but it was hardly known elsewhere.

The lag behind America was not only in wool spinning. New types of cotton spindle, the 'cap' and the 'ring' spindles, were of American origin; and the critics of the Ten Hours Act of 1847 were threatening England with the competition of unregulated cotton factories, which "rivalled if they did not exceed" her own[2]. Americans had shown more interest than Englishmen in the devising of machinery for making such things as pins and screws. It was an American reaping machine, McCormick's, which attracted most attention at the Great Exhibition and afterwards, when tried before twelve hundred farmers at Cirencester in September, 1851[3]. A second good American type was shown; of English types, only one and some models. So great a stir was made about the American invention, which was far from new in 1851, that Scotsmen were forced to point out how Bell's machine had really reaped corn in the Carse of Gowrie for fourteen years. Patriotic propaganda gave an impetus to the use and improvement of the Bell type[4]; but there can be little doubt that the American types were better and more readily improved. The world's principal reapers of to-day have evolved from them.

A very different labour-saving machine was also shown in the American section in 1851, but it aroused rather less interest. There is no mention of it in the series of lectures by which eminent men tried to spread the chief results of the Exhibition. But some of the papers noted it. "There is a sewing machine which works with astonishing velocity," said the *Economist*[5] in a long philosophical article on national industrial characteristics as revealed at the Exhibition. This machine was selected, together with a grease-removing soap which could be used either in salt water or fresh, and the "unbounded...uses to

[1] Bremner, D., *The Industries of Scotland* (1869), p. 160–2. And see below, p. 83.

[2] Hume in Hansard, LXXXIX. 1077 (Feb. 10, 1847). For the spindles see Chapman, S. J., *The Lancashire Cotton Industry*, p. 71 n., Priestman, H., *Principles of Worsted Spinning*, p. 23.

[3] *Economist*, September 13, 1851. It is claimed that McCormick used the notions of John Common, of Denwick, Northumberland (Wood, Sir H. T., *A History of the Royal Society of Arts*, p. 129) just as Arkwright used his predecessors' notions.

[4] See 1851 *Exhibition Lectures*, II. 15; Prof. Wrightson in *British Manufacturing Industries* (1876), VIII. 153.

[5] Of June 28, 1851.

which caoutchouc is put," as a representative revelation of the American spirit. "Their agricultural implements, their Daguerrotypes, and other applications of modern discoveries, not behind their Eastern competitors, we pass over." American inventors, impelled by the need for economy of effort in the American home, had been hammering at the sewing machine for years, in succession to and side by side with English, German and French pioneers. America had the responsive demand. In 1850 Isaac M. Singer made in twelve days what "is said to have been the first machine satisfactory to manufacturers."[1]

Inventive as Americans were, their most typical inventions were hardly competitive with British manufacturing industry. They supplemented it; went beyond it; or met needs which it had not yet been called upon to meet. Hitherto the imports of all of them, or of things made by them, had been trifling and had left no mark on the trade returns. This was not true of some European manufactures. A few, a very few, had been able to compete on the British market when tariffs were still high, and without the smugglers' help. "I am of opinion that if the duty on toys were 100 per cent. it would not be a protection; and I find that almost all the toys used in this country...come from Switzerland and Bavaria and the central states of Germany." So John McGregor told the Committee on Import Duties in 1840[2]. He was thinking of the wooden dolls and Noah's Arks and other products of a hard-living peasantry's winter evenings. Many French fancy goods and articles of fashion were in the same category for a different reason. "In all matters of taste the French appear to excel us," said another witness, himself a silk manufacturer[3]. Sometimes taste, fashion and craftsmanship had combined to bring the French article in over a stiff tariff. "I never wear an English boot"—it is McGregor again speaking—"I do not find any that I like; I pay the 30 per cent. duty

[1] Bolles, A. S., *Industrial History of the United States* (1881), p. 245. For the early history see *ibid.* p. 243–5; Levasseur, E., *Hist. des classes ouvrières et de l'industrie en France de* 1789 *à* 1870, II. 550; Leno, J. B., *The Art of Boot and Shoe Making* (1885), p. 160 *sqq.*; Sewell, *The Birth of the Sewing Machine* (1892). It was only by accident that an excellent French machine, Thémonnier's, was not in the 1851 Exhibition: Leno, p. 160. On the whole subject of American machinery see Burn, D. L., "The Genesis of American Engineering Competition," *E.J.* (*Econ. Hist.*), Jan. 1931.

[2] In answer to Q. 186.

[3] T. F. Gibson, Q. 2274.

and import my own boots from Paris, not so much on account of the price, but of the quality of the leather."[1]

When duties on fine goods dropped to a standard 10 per cent., while those on some rougher manufactures disappeared, it became possible, after a time, to gauge their capacity for penetrating the British market. For the first few years there was not much evidence to go on; but, as Europe settled down to work after 1848, a commercial equilibrium appropriate to the new tariff conditions was gradually established. Most of her debts to England the continent, like the rest of the world, paid in food, raw materials and non-competing commodities such as French or Spanish wines and Italian oils. But its fine manufactures came in increasing quantities, mainly from France and Switzerland. With few exceptions, they were not products of some variant of the new machine industry but of cheap, skilled and tasteful handicraft directed and organised by commercial middlemen. There was little or no machinery used in French tanneries or in French shoe-making and glove-making, but, as John McGregor would have anticipated, there was a growing import of French boots, shoes and gloves. By 1853 the imports of "women's boots and calashes; women's shoes with cork or double soles; and women's shoes of silk, satin, stuff, or leather"[2] had risen to 184,000 pairs, nearly all "entered for home consumption." Of men's boots and shoes 84,000 pairs were imported, but these were mostly re-exported. The gloves for home use had reached the figure, astonishing when the probable number of glove-users in a population of some 22,000,000 is considered, of 3,000,000 pairs. An import of 600,000 pairs of what the customs called 'boot fronts' is not self-explanatory. This is the explanation. "It is found by experience," Charles Babbage wrote in 1851[3], "that the upper leather of Boots made in France is better...than the upper leather manufactured in England." Of sole leather the reverse was true, so you imported the uppers, the 'fronts.' Experience had justified McGregor and furnished the economists with another neat illustration of the territorial division of labour under free trade, which memory says they never used.

Cheap French and Swiss clocks and watches, made by an elaborately divided and subdivided handicraft system, formed another important group of imports. Until 1853 the returns are

[1] Q. 152. [2] The customs classifications in the Board of Trade returns.
[3] *The Exposition of* 1851 (2nd ed.), p. 8.

worthless, being the official values; but after Gladstone modified the duties in that year the numbers began to be recorded. In the first seven months (June–December, 1853) 135,000 clocks and 43,000 watches came in. In 1854 the clocks numbered 228,000 and the watches 79,500. As these are the figures for home consumption, it would seem that English mantelpieces were filling up rather rapidly with French clocks and English pockets with Swiss watches.

There was a growing import of foreign glass of many kinds and from many countries—window, plate, flint, but above all cut, coloured and fancy, from France, Italy, Bohemia and Saxony. The customs returns of the early 'fifties do not permit any exact study of the trade: the values remain worthless and the weights, square feet of plate glass and so on, cannot be compared with any figures of domestic output or consumption. But there can be no doubt that this was, at least in some branches, an important competitive, not merely a supplementary, import. In 1840, when the glass duties were so high as to mean prohibition of the ordinary sorts, and the British manufacturer was protected against smugglers because his goods were "of great bulk and precarious carriage," the glass manufacturers were "among the very few" who were really interested in protective duties[1]. At that time their industry was still subject to the excise; and there is no doubt that the working of the excise had stunted it, ossified it, and made it unadaptable. Optical glass, for example, was nearly all imported because the excise rules did not permit the only methods by which it could properly be made[2]. Cooksons of South Shields made some lenses and prisms for lighthouses between 1831 and 1845, but they were not first-rate and the work did not pay. Most manufacturers in 1840 knew little about the foreign industry except its reputation, and feared the unknown. McGregor, no doubt a witness with a free trade bias, thought that they asked "for protection from ignorance of the matter."[3] In 1845 Peel abandoned the excise and lost nearly £600,000 of revenue in so doing. British glass-making sprang forward at once. Chance Bros. of Stourbridge began to produce lighthouse equipment in 1845, and continued previous experiments with optical glass.

[1] *Report on Import Duties*, Q. 80, 82.

[2] Porter, *op. cit.* p. 256; Powell, H. J., *Glassmaking in England* (1923), p. 108, 110.

[3] Q. 83. According to Gladstone, McGregor was "loose minded." See vol. I. p. 491, n. 2.

But it is said that "little progress was made"[1] in either, until Bontemps and Tabouret, French experts, came to England as refugees in 1848 and worked as heads of departments at Stourbridge. So the Chances made, not only the sheets for the "blazing arch" of 1851, but a complete lighthouse equipment and telescope discs for show under it. With the possible exception of the Pilkingtons of St Helens, who made other things, they were the strongest glass firm in the country. Weaker firms contracted output or closed down as foreign competition became keener.

It was in textiles inevitably that competitive imports were most heard of. French silks waited at the door for each fall in the tariff. That was why silk kept its extra 5 per cent. And French skill and taste were not confined to silks. In cottons neither France nor any other country, except perhaps India, could face Lancashire and Clydesdale. East India piece goods to the declared value of £190,000 were still imported in 1853. There were some European cotton gloves and stockings and yarns, most of which were re-exported; also a block of 'other articles' unspecified, worth £75,000 to £100,000 a year. But this was little to set against an export of cotton goods and yarns worth over £30,000,000, distributed over the whole face of the earth; and these insignificant imports were rather complementary than competitive. Manchester and Glasgow did not worry about any of them. The imports of wool manufactures were also in part complementary; but they were complementary in a sense of which England had no reason to be proud—there was a valuable field of manufacturing where she could not stand up to France, and she admitted it. Sometimes her experts gave technical, sometimes fiscal, sometimes commercial and sometimes artistic reasons. Finally a section of them fell back on a mystical or fatalistic one. The goods in question were called *merinos*, because made of French or French and Australian merino wool, and also *mousselines de laine*, colloquially delaines. The wool was combed, power-spun, and hand-woven. The delaines came mainly from Roubaix, Rheims and the St Quentin country, where the firm of Rodier, which rules the trade to-day, started at Bohain precisely in 1853[2], a year in

[1] Powell, *op. cit.* p. 110, on which this account is based. Georges Bontemps of Choisy-le-Roi, author of *Le guide du verrier*, had previously co-operated with the Chances: his stay in England was only short.

[2] Brunhes, J., *Géographie humaine de la France* (1920), II. 545.

which the value of wool manufactures imported into the United Kingdom rose suddenly by nearly 60 per cent.

The technical reasons given for French success were that the wool was worked 'dry,' *i.e.* without oil, and so took the colour better; that after being combed it was 'prepared' for spinning in a specially effective way; that it was spun on the mule and not on the more strenuous throstle and so made softer and more delicate yarn. The fiscal reason was an important one: French policy encouraged the export of these goods. The commercial reason was also important and relevant: "it has always been the rule acted upon by the British manufacturer, rather to produce a large quantity of goods at a small percentage of profit, than a small quantity at a greater percentage"[1]: these fabrics *de luxe* were made in small quantities with necessarily wide margins of profit: they were not his sort, were in fact hardly competitive so long as he had plenty of work for his throstles and power looms, as in the early 'fifties he generally had. The steady increase in the number of worsted mills showed it. The fatalistic reason was given in a report of a Deputation from the Bradford Chamber of Commerce in 1855, as paraphrased by the great Bradford manufacturer Titus Salt.

> The French produce...goods which by their intrinsic beauty of texture and dye leave every competitor hopelessly in the rear. The prices...are such that we have long since abandoned their manufacture; and the Deputation, unable to find out the cause of this undeniable superiority, were obliged to ascribe it to the well-known truth that a trade once established in a certain locality cannot be carried on with the same success at another place, though the latter may, to all appearances, possess even superior advantages[2].

France had applied to these newly devised and expensive combed-wool fabrics the taste, craftsmanship and commercial enterprise which had made her silk industry so formidable. For wool-working she had called in the new machinery. She had, indeed, in Josué Heilmann of Mulhouse[3], the inventor of the combing machine without which the delaines could not have come so "good cheap" to market; but not much fresh machinery had appeared in the Lyons trade since Jacquard's loom, a hand-loom, established itself there between 1810 and 1825. A little

[1] Forbes, H., 1851 *Exhibition Lectures*, II. 325.

[2] James, *op. cit.* p. 526 n. Comments on the report are in the *Economist*, December 8, 1855.

[3] He died in 1848. See Burnley, J., *Wool and Woolcombing* (1899), ch. IX, for his life.

steam-power was used to supplement water-power in the throwing mills. Experiments were made with the power-loom for plain silks in 1843–4; but even thirty years later there were only about 6000 power-looms to 110,000 hand-looms in Lyons and its neighbourhood[1]. This slow adoption of power was England's opportunity. She had in fact been holding off French competition by power ever since Huskisson opened her market—by power, and East India raw silk, and the study of French fabrics, and the 30 per cent. or 15 per cent. duty. English power-driven throwing machinery was believed to be "superior to that of any other country" in 1840[2]. Since the 'thirties, Manchester had woven some cheap silk and mixed fabrics by power[3]. In the 'forties, Macclesfield and other places were turning Bengal silk, of which Britain had "the exclusive possession," into bandanna handkerchiefs, and actually exporting them, with some other silk goods, to France, a fact which seemed to G. R. Porter "not the least surprising of the effects which have followed the total alteration of our system in regard to this manufacture."[4] These shipments to France were only a small, though a very important, part of a general body of exports of silk and part-silk yarns and fabrics, the maintenance and apparent growth of which were most satisfactory to free traders, who had been forced to reply to prophesyings of total ruin for the British industry whenever the old barriers about it had been touched. The export of British manufactured silk and part-silk goods had been worth £736,000 in 1845 and £838,000 in 1846. With raw material at about the same price as in 1845–6[5], the figure for 1852 was £1,156,000 and for 1853 it was £1,595,000. The imports of European manufactured silk for the years 1852–3 may have been worth nearly twice as much; but no figures of values are available, so that the result has to be reached roughly by multiplying the recorded weights in pounds by at least £3, which was Porter's minimum figure for the average value of silk goods per pound, and by making some allowance for smuggling[6]. Evidently French, and some

[1] From estimates for 1873 in the *Enquête sur l'état de l'industrie textile* of 1904, III. 46.

[2] *Report on Import Duties*, Q. 2236.

[3] See vol. I. p. 196, 554.

[4] *Progress of the Nation*, p. 219.

[5] The standard silk quotations were if anything a shade lower in 1852–3 than in 1845–6. The *Economist's* weekly price current, *passim*.

[6] Porter, *op. cit.* p. 573. At £3, the recorded imports for 1852–3 would be worth £3,981,000 against £2,751,000 of exports. As the imports were largely fine French silks £3 is probably too low. There was no doubt some smuggling. Eastern silks, entered not by the pound but by the piece, are excluded from this calculation.

other, continental manufacturers were making full use of their new opportunities and were doing a good business in England. It is equally clear that the British industry was active, more adaptable than it had been under the pre-Huskisson hot-house regime, and in a position to adapt itself further—though probably with trouble and loss—should it be required to sacrifice the special protection which had been assigned to it. From the standpoint of the whole national economy, it was a secondary industry at best; but then so were all those industries with which foreign competition was real; for it was only one section of one division of the wool manufacture which was dominated by France.

Over her chosen ground, the ground where her engines toiled, England's control was in fact almost complete. Engines toiled in America too; but not much on goods for export[1] and hardly at all on goods for export to England. Belgian machinery was abundant and good; but Belgium was very small. French machinery was relatively scantier and worse, all things considered. Holland was hardly thought of as a manufacturing country: she had turned late to the new industrial technique and had no 'heavy' industries[2]. German machinery, and indeed German manufacture generally, was, as a whole, inferior and imitative—such at least was the impression produced on some visitors to the Exhibition who had no anti-German bias. "In machinery—except perhaps field-pieces...the Germans appear very deficient" the *Economist* wrote[3]. It went on to quote a correspondent of the *Allgemeine Zeitung*: "I cannot deny that German industry has no peculiar character. In the Exhibition (from which alone we judge) it appears as if every national characteristic were carefully avoided. Everywhere German industry appears to lean on some foreign industry and to imitate it....Here one beholds the supporting hand of France, there that of England." This is not a complete or final verdict on the German industry of 1850–51[4]. But it was the verdict which Englishmen naturally gave or repeated, and there was truth in it.

[1] American cotton manufactures were exported in fair quantities to considerable distances. It was this that alarmed Lancashire in 1847. There was also a miscellaneous export of manufactures to Canada, Mexico, the West Indies, etc.; but America bought vastly more than she sold.

[2] Baasch, E., *Holländische Wirtschaftsgeschichte* (1927), p. 415 *sqq*. For Belgium and France, Clapham, J. H., *The Economic Development of France and Germany*, p. 59, 63, 70 and *passim*.

[3] June 28, 1851.

[4] See below, p. 111.

The course of America's economic evolution was predicted by men of long sight. That of France was clearly determined by her past, and was predictable. That of Germany was obscure. Of other countries Britain might utilise the products, value the markets, or respect the arts; she did not affect to place them in an economic category with herself.

CHAPTER II

THE INDUSTRIAL FIELD IN 1851

BRITAIN had turned her face towards the new industry—the wheels of iron and the shriek of the escaping steam. In them lay for the future not only her power and wealth but her very existence. She must take the risks of the 'industry state,' which lives by the export of its manufactures, because she could do no other[1]. Many Englishmen bore those risks proudly, like the industrial free traders of the North. Most bore them ignorantly, seeing to-day's cheaper loaf or to-morrow's good balance-sheet. Educated men of the older country stocks were apt to shoulder them with reluctance, regretting that not ill-adjusted life of town and country which was passing away. Those who had followed Peel with open eyes, like Sir James Graham, had done so because population was growing "at the rate of 300,000 per annum."[2] It had been a question of time, a race between life and food. To such men free trade was a need to be faced, not a treasure to be won.

The course was set towards the 'industry state,' but the voyage was not half over. England lived by her ships, but not even yet quite as the Dutchmen of the seventeenth century had lived by their ships—"the which except they stir, the people starve."[3] Agriculture was still by very far the greatest of her industries. Including landowners, agents, farmers and labourers of all sorts, 26 per cent. of the men of twenty years old and upwards were engaged in it directly. The male agricultural labourers of all ages and all kinds numbered 1,284,000 out of a male population above ten years of age of 7,616,000. To these would have to be added most of the 279,000 farmers and graziers and an unknown number of their sons to get an exact estimate of the male working force of agriculture.[4] Out of 10,736,000 women

[1] For the economic conception of the 'industry state' see the German controversies of two generations later when Germany in turn reached the parting of the ways, especially Wagner, A., *Agrar- und Industriestaat* (1901 and 1902).

[2] Graham to Peel, Dec. 30, 1842. Parker, C. S., *Life and Letters of Sir James Graham*, I. 332.

[3] Mun, T., *England's Treasure by Forraign Trade* (ed. Ashley), p. 107.

[4] *Census of* 1851. *Ages and Occupations* (1852–3, LXXXVIII. Parts I and II) for all figures in this section.

71,000 were outdoor agricultural labourers, 128,000 were indoor farm servants, and 28,000 were farmers. Judged merely by numbers, the industry which came next to agriculture was domestic service[1]. The total of domestic servants of all ages was: male, 134,000; female, 905,000, or almost exactly 1 in 9 of all girls and women from ten years old and upwards. These two great groups may be compared with the main groups of the extractive and manufacturing industries and some important groups of handicraft trades, dealers and middlemen, to give a rough picture of the industrial balance of the country on its human side as Britain moved towards the 'industry state.' The groups vary greatly in composition[2]. Coal-mining and cotton are filled mainly with wage-earners; shoe-making and tailoring largely with small masters and shopkeepers; the blacksmiths are nearly all handicraftsmen with their mates and apprentices. The building crafts also contain many small masters, working either as jobbers or as sub-contractors under builders; and so on. The figures for building and railway work, and some other figures to a less degree, are affected by the fact that 367,000 men and 9000 women were returned simply as labourers, many of whom no doubt worked in different industries at different times of the year. Such facts provide the uncertainties always connected with an occupational census. Further, as the census of 1851 was much the most elaborate yet taken, and as Britain still contained a high proportion of illiterates, there is a wider margin of error than is to be expected in a census to-day. There is also a small arbitrary element in the selection of trades for insertion in the groups given on p. 24[3]. But the outline picture is probably a more accurate one of its kind than can be drawn of any country at any earlier date.

The occupations not specially characteristic of the machine age come high on the list, partly because machinery was setting people free to follow them. Coal-miners had increased greatly since 1831—they had not yet passed the shoe-makers, however[4]

[1] Including coachmen, gardeners, inn-servants; excluding charwomen, professional or institutional nurses, male and female, and farm servants.

[2] The census groups contain all persons 'working or dealing in' coal, iron, leather, etc.

[3] Certain groups in the census have been thrown together to get better industrial comparisons. The census figure for seamen, being necessarily defective, is replaced by the figure from the *Statistical Abstract* for 1851 which refers to the United Kingdom. This involves a slight overstatement, but is preferable to the much understated census figure of seamen within reach of the enumerators.

[4] See vol. I. p. 73.

Principal occupation groups in Britain in 1851 in order of size

	Male	*Female*
Total population	10,224,000	10,736,000
Population of ten years old and upwards	7,616,000	8,155,000
Agriculture: farmer, grazier, labourer, servant	1,563,000	227,000
Domestic service (excluding farm service)	134,000	905,000
Cotton worker, every kind, with printer, dyer	255,000	272,000
Building craftsman: carpenter, bricklayer, mason, plasterer, plumber, etc.	442,000	1,000
Labourer (unspecified)	367,000	9,000
Milliner, dress-maker, seamstress (seamster)	494	340,000
Wool worker, every kind, with carpet-weaver	171,000	113,000
Shoe-maker	243,000	31,000
Coal-miner	216,000	3,000
Tailor	135,000	18,000
Washerwoman		145,000
Seaman (Merchant), pilot	144,000	
Silk worker	53,000	80,000
Blacksmith	112,000	592
Linen, flax worker	47,000	56,000
Carter, carman, coachman, postboy, cabman, busman, etc.	83,000	1,000
Iron worker, founder, moulder (excluding iron-mining, nails, hardware, cutlery, files, tools, machines)	79,000	590
Railway driver, etc., porter, etc., labourer, plate-layer	65,000	54
Hosiery worker	35,000	30,000
Lace worker	10,000	54,000
Machine, boiler maker	63,000	647
Baker	56,000	7,000
Copper, tin, lead-miner	53,000	7,000
Charwoman		55,000
Commercial clerk	44,000	19
Fisherman	37,000	1,000
Miller	37,000	562
Earthenware worker	25,000	11,000
Sawyer	35,000	23
Shipwright, boat-builder, block and mast maker	32,000	28
Straw-plait worker	4,000	28,000
Wheelwright	30,000	106
Glover	4,500	25,000
Nailer	19,000	10,000
Iron-miner	27,000	910
Tanner, currier, fellmonger	25,000	276
Printer	22,000	222

—for though a miner fed machinery and was lifted from his work by it, he used none when at the coal face. Cotton workers had not increased very fast in the twenty years in spite of the huge growth of the trade: spinning machinery was far more efficient and the normal weaver now tended two power-looms. If some allowance be made for builders' labourers, the non-mechanical building trade, as might be expected, must have been more important numerically in relation to cotton than in 1831[1]. None of the 340,000 milliners, dress-makers and seamstresses used sewing machines, it may be assumed; nor did the tailors, nor the shoe-makers. Handicraft blacksmiths were more numerous than the men of the great iron works, even though some men returned as blacksmiths were actually smiths in textile mills or strikers in engineering shops. On the figures—which at this point, however, are specially uncertain, though the fact is probable enough—more men were employed about horses on the roads than in all the work of the young railway system. Machine making is vaguely and generally entered in the returns; yet a few of the specialised textile machinery trades separate themselves out—reed-makers; card-makers; shuttle-makers; gill-makers—and the total also contains over 4000 tool-makers[2]. It is rather remarkable how comparatively few tanners and shipwrights served the needs of nearly 21,000,000 people. A good deal of leather was no doubt imported, but not many ships. The nineteen female commercial clerks will not be overlooked, nor the fifty-four female railway servants, nor the twenty-three women sawyers. The latter, together with other small groups of women found in unlikely occupations—of which the units are given in the table—are probably widows carrying on businesses without necessarily labouring in them.

Any geographical picture of the distribution of occupations such as was attempted, on the whole with great success, for the census commissioners in 1851, necessarily suffers from the difficulty of handling those occupations which are distributed in almost exact proportion to population and so have no distinctive homes. These included at that time a majority of the main women's callings together with building, shoe-making, tailoring, blacksmithing, the work of the sawyer, the wheelwright

[1] See vol. I. p. 71–2.

[2] Not makers of machine-tools but of files and so on.

and the printer, and all mercantile, retail and internal transport business. The ingenious map designed by Augustus Petermann to illustrate the report of the census, which omits all these, is therefore less a map of occupations—though that is what it is called—than a map of industries working for other than the local market[1]. Shoe-making, for example, is indicated by Wellington boots in Northamptonshire, which contained 13,000 shoe-makers and worked for 'export,' but not in counties where the trade might be bigger but supplied mainly local needs. Stafford-shire, also something of an 'export' county, is not dotted with boots on the map, presumably because its population of shoe-makers was not much above the normal for the country—1 in 63 of the population against 1 in 76: Northampton had 1 in 16. One graphic method adopted for England and Wales—the in-sertion of a symbol in every Poor Law Union where an industry existed "to any extent"—tended to exaggerate the importance of outliers from a localised industry[2]. The map gives the im-pression that the wool manufacture was of some importance in Cornwall and South Wales, the six counties from Cardigan and Radnor to the Bristol Channel. In fact only about 450 people in Cornwall and about 2500 in the six counties were in any way connected with it; whereas Devon, which does not look much more important than Cornwall on the map, had 4300 wool workers. Fortunately linen is the only industry besides wool for which this method of mapping is likely to mislead. Taken as a whole, Petermann's map is as illuminating as it is ingenious. Supported by the census figures already given, indicating the occupations which were in the first rank numerically, it tells the whole story which it set out to tell—that of the localisation of manufacture about the end of the early railway age.

Nothing is more remarkable than the complete localisation of some textile industries and the attainment by others of a locali-sation which, although not complete, was not to be altered appreciably during the next half-century. Under pressure of bad times in the 'forties, cotton had fallen back on South Lancashire and the adjacent parts of Cheshire and the West Riding, leaving a strong detached force in Clydesdale and various

[1] Reproduced at the end of the volume. Compare with it the full statistical discussion by Day, Clive, "The Distribution of Industrial Occupations in England, 1841–61," *Trans. Connecticut Acad.* 1927.

[2] For Scotland these symbols are inserted for counties and important towns.

weak ones in other districts. From nearly a dozen English and Scottish counties came complaints of local falls in population resulting from the closing down of cotton mills[1]. The area with the better competitive facilities had come best through a spell of bad trade. Of approximately 527,000 cotton workers in the country, some 312,000 were in Lancashire, 55,000 in Cheshire and the West Riding, and 58,000 in Lanarkshire[2].

The most complete concentration was that of the worsted industry into the West Riding. Its oldest home, Norwich, had been losing ground ever since the eighteenth century, but was still a fairly active manufacturing centre in 1831, though it had adopted little modern machinery, if any. By 1841 the trade was nearly dead: during that decade the population of Norwich had stood still. About 1840 a belated attempt to recover the old industry was made by the establishment of spinning mills[3]. Norwich had been buying yarn from Yorkshire and she wished to end this dependence. It was much too late; for in the next few years Yorkshire perfected combing machinery and went ahead again. In 1850 the factory inspectors reported nearly 865,000 worsted spindles and 32,617 power-looms for worsted in England: there were hardly any in Scotland or Wales. Of the spindles 746,000, and of the looms 30,850, were in Yorkshire. Norfolk had 19,216 spindles and 428 looms[4]. The thing was done, a clean decisive defeat. Worsted had become the Yorkshire industry which it would remain.

The woollen manufacture had almost reached the pitch of concentration which it showed in the twentieth century. It was, and is, less concentrated than cotton and much less concentrated than worsted. Of 138,000 people who described themselves as engaged in it in 1851 only 56,000 were in the West Riding; 15,000 in Scotland; 11,000 in Lancashire; 9000 in Gloucestershire; 7000 in Wiltshire—and the rest scattered over the remaining counties of England and Wales as the industries map suggests, Devon being the county next to Wiltshire in order of importance. Fifty years later the West Riding had still only half the woollen spindles in the kingdom, which implies only a

[1] Redford, A., *Labour Migration in England*, 1800–50 (1926), p. 9, 111.

[2] "Cotton worker" is here used in the comprehensive sense adopted in the table on p. 24 above.

[3] Blyth, *The Norwich Guide and Directory*, 1842, p. 62. Clapham, J. H., "The Transference of the Worsted Industry from East Anglia to the West Riding," *E. J.* 1910, p. 195 *sqq*.

[4] *F. J. Reports*, 1851, *A. and P.* XXIII. 117.

slight increase of concentration during that long and economically decisive age[1].

Just as cotton had drawn into Lancashire and wool into the West Riding, so flax was drawing northward into Scotland—and out of Great Britain altogether into Ulster. It had already ceased to be a really important English industry; for of some 103,000 people engaged in it in Britain no less than 77,000 were Scots, largely hand-loom weavers.

Silk still held out against the mechanical and geographical forces which were making for concentration. There were indeed more silk workers in mechanical Lancashire than in any other county[2], whereas Lancashire had hardly been reckoned a silk county at all thirty years earlier. In Cheshire the old nucleus of workers had grown with the aid of machinery to 22,000. But there were many about Coventry, where power was little used: there were still 16,000 in London and from 2000 to 6000 in each of six other counties. In nearly every place where there was any textile manufacturing, some silk was worked and the industry persisted in a few places where there was no other.

It is not easy to exaggerate the importance of the textile manufactures in the industrial life of the country. Although not even that of cotton was completely mechanised—there may have been still 40,000 to 50,000 cotton hand-looms at work[3]—they stood as the representative industries of the age of machinery and power, even though coal-mining and metallurgy had more final significance. Because they were so much mechanised their output was prodigious. Because they were not completely mechanised they carried with them in their march, and often left to fall by the wayside, a host of those who had now become handworking camp-followers. Not counting hosiery and lace, they found employment for—or should we say gave a trade name to?—nearly eleven hundred thousand people.

Their social importance can perhaps be best brought out by a comparison of 1851 with 1901. The comparison is not statistically exact at all points, but is quite exact enough for purposes of illustration[4]:

[1] Clapham, J. H., *The Woollen and Worsted Industries* (1907), p. 20.

[2] But many of them were hand-loom weavers, whose occupation survived to be hurt by French imports under the 'Cobden' Treaty of 1860.

[3] See vol. I. p. 554.

[4] The 1901 figures are from the *Survey of Industrial Relations* (1926) reproduced in the *Eighteenth Abstract of Labour Statistics*, 1926, p. 20. The heading

	1851	1901
Population of Great Britain	20,960,000	37,000,000
Cotton workers (in 1851 with printers, dyers, etc.) .	527,000	544,000
Wool workers	284,000	235,000
Silk workers	133,000	37,000
Linen and hemp workers (in 1901 with jute) . .	134,000	99,000
Textile printers, dyers, etc.		79,000
	1,078,000	994,000

That is to say, the trades, or their nearest equivalents, which at the opening of the twentieth century employed 1 in 37 of the population had employed 1 in 19 in the year of the Great Exhibition. The hand-working camp-followers outside the mills, and the relative imperfection of machinery inside, account for the astonishing figures of 1851. It is to be remembered that, although there were nearly 250,000 power-looms in the cotton industry in 1850, there were less than 33,000 in worsted, less than 10,000 in woollen, barely 6000 in flax and not 1200 in silk[1].

Even in spinning, mechanisation was not complete, though true hand-spinning was dead in the factory districts, and nearly all the decisive inventions had been made. About 1830, American inventors had introduced the cap and the ring spindles[2], which were to become important in the worsted and cotton industries. But neither was economically decisive, for neither affected industrial organisation or greatly extended the empire of the machine; they were just improvements on the flyer spindle which Arkwright had borrowed from the spinning wheel. Nor had either gained a secure footing in Britain by 1850, and thereafter their progress was slow. That of the British-invented self-acting mule had not been quick, nor was it to become so; a fact of special interest because only with the arrival of the self-actor did mule-spinning become completely automatic. In the old 'hand mule,' although power supplied the main motive force, the 'carriage' on which the spindles are ranked was pulled out and pushed back by the spinner, the yarn being drawn out fine and twisted on the outward run and wound on to the bobbin on the return. It was the toil of this pushing and pulling that a deputation of cotton-spinners once

'Linen and Hemp Workers' includes those classes from the 1851 Occupations census (used on p. 24, above) most closely comparable with those under the heading 'Flax, Hemp, Jute, Rope, Canvas and Canvas Goods' in the 1926 *Survey*. Jute was not a distinct industry in 1851. See below, p. 84.

[1] Vol. I. p. 544.

[2] Above, p. 13.

illustrated to Lord Palmerston with a heavy arm-chair in his own drawing-room[1]. The effective self-actor had been invented by Roberts of Manchester in 1825. By 1834 his firm had made 520 self-actors with over 200,000 spindles, and they were hoping to double the number in 1834–5[2]. But like so many new machines, the self-actor was for a long time too rough for the finest work—it did not wind the yarn well on the bobbin, for one thing—and too dear for the smaller spinners. When the great New Lanark mills were sold, for the second or third time, in 1851, they contained 28,900 self-actor spindles, but also 13,600 'hand-mule spindles.'[3] "On account of the excessive cost very few firms were able to purchase the self-actor," a secretary of the Oldham Master Spinners wrote long after, "and therefore hand-mules were the rule and self-actor mules the exception."[4] In the early 'fifties few self-actors were used in fine-spinning districts such as that of Bolton, and they were far from universal in the districts which span the medium and coarse counts[5].

In woollen spinning, as has already been noted, the operation of slubbing, which Andrew Ure had called a handicraft in 1834, had been little changed. The original 'slubbing billy' was a hand-worked machine like the original jenny. Child piecers rubbed together gauzy strips of wool from the carding engine, to be roughly spun on the billy before going to their final spinning on the jenny or mule. By 1850 the billy might be power driven, but the arduous piecing work for it remained. Even eight years later Edward Baines of Leeds, when describing the local industry before the British Association, treated the billy as normal, though he spoke of a "new machine called the condenser" which would cut out billy and piecers and link the carding machine direct to the mule[6].

Precisely in the year 1851 a textile invention perhaps more decisive than that of the self-acting mule was completed for England: Donisthorpe and Lister perfected a wool-combing machine which became at once commercially successful. There

[1] Hodder, *Life of Lord Shaftesbury*, II. 19–21, quoting Grant, P., *The Ten Hours Bill* (1866).

[2] Baines, E., *History of the Cotton Manufacture* (1835), p. 207–8.

[3] Advertisement in the *Economist*, December 27, 1851.

[4] From a paper read before the British Association in 1887, quoted in Chapman, S. J., *The Lancashire Cotton Industry*, p. 69.

[5] Chapman, *op. cit.* p. 70.

[6] From a paper read in 1858 printed in his *Yorkshire Past and Present*, II. 632. Cf. p. 12, above and p. 83, below.

had been combing machines since Cartwright's day, but his Big Ben, though it had alarmed the hand-combers, neither ruined them nor made a fortune for Cartwright. They could still do better work than any machine. Down to about 1840 their position was reasonably safe—safe from machinery if not from themselves; for their trade was easily learned and the immigrant Irish took to it, with other unskilled and half-skilled men[1]. Then came the effective machines. All through the 'forties in England and France the inventors ultimately successful were at work—Donisthorpe, Heilmann, Lister, Holden, Noble. Heilmann succeeded first, and his patents were sold most profitably to English firms for use not only in the worsted but also in the cotton and flax industries. Lister and Donisthorpe adopted one of his central principles; and though Lister claimed that they had mastered all the difficulties connected with the invention "before M. Heilmann's patent was heard of," Heilmann's representatives secured a verdict for infringement against them in 1852. Next year the comb named after Noble—though it seems to have been mainly the work of Donisthorpe—came on the market; and a few years later Holden, a second collaborator with Lister, perfected another type of comb upon which he had first worked in 1847–8 or earlier[2].

These two men were not simple inventors: they were industrial organisers and combatants of the first rank, and Lister, a gentleman born, started with some capital. They had a European view. In conjunction they had started a combing mill at St Denis in 1849. Within a few years Lister dominated the industry. He sold machines to spinners for a royalty of £1000 each. By 1855 he had five English, three French and one German mill combing on commission for spinners. Never before had a factory industry been more quickly born, once the long gestation was over; nor did one ever grow more quickly. By 1857 James, the contemporary historian of the worsted industry, could write that "by far the larger proportion of the wool worked up in the worsted branch is combed by machinery," and could add that "far the greater proportion of all the wool ...now combed is combed by Lister's machine."[3] A single

[1] James, *op. cit.* p. 501.

[2] The technical story of the patents is most fully told in Burnley's *Wool and Woolcombing*. Lister's claim to have anticipated Heilmann is from a public speech quoted by Burnley on p. 221.

[3] *Op. cit.* p. 564, 573: for the Lister and Holden mills, Burnley, *op. cit.* p. 275, 300.

Lister comb would do the work of a hundred skilled men easily, and do it very much better. Thus wool-combing was mechanised.

In the hosiery and lace industries, which rested on the primary textiles, very advanced hand-driven mechanisms had existed for generations. To these power had been applied, but only sporadically and much more often for lace than for hosiery. Lace-making by machine had developed, between 1760 and 1770, out of the making of fancy stockings on the knitting frame[1]. A little later came the 'warp' machine which combined, as its name implies, the longitudinal threads of a loom with the looped stitches of knitting. Many elaborate types of lace and net machine followed. It was fifty-five of these—John Heathcot's 'traverse bobbin net machines'—which Luddites smashed in Heathcot's factory at Loughborough in 1816. James Towle, their leader, was hanged at Leicester for attempted murder, "in presence of an immense multitude...singing a hymn with seeming fervour."[2] Heathcot bought an old mill at Tiverton, where the Devon cloth industry was decaying[3], and drove his new machines by power. His firm employed 1200 workpeople by 1836, and in the 'fifties between that and 2000. Meanwhile a number of other 'bobbin net' manufacturers had imitated his factory methods, especially about Nottingham. By 1831 there were 22 power factories in the country supposed to contain about 1000 machines employing directly about 3000 people. There were also hand-machine factories with some 5000 machines and there was a complicated system of out-work for finishing and embroidering the net[4]. Perhaps the area of power in the early 'fifties was four times what it had been in 1831; but in dealing with so intricate an industry, much subject to fashion, precision is difficult. A factory might use power and be half full of hand-workers. Its goods might be given out by 'finishing houses' to 'mistresses,' who overworked groups of young girls in 'drawing, scalloping, carding'; and as the whole

[1] The general narrative is in Felkin, W., *History of the Machine Wrought Hosiery and Lace Manufactures* (1867). For the early nineteenth century see also Ure, *The Cotton Manufacture*, II. 342 *sqq.*, 420.

[2] Felkin, *op. cit.* p. 238.

[3] See vol. I. p. 45, n. 3.

[4] Felkin, *op. cit.* p. 340. These are the personal estimates of Felkin, who was in the trade. By 1840, in one factory inspector's district the hand machines were to the power machines as 2½ : 1. *S.C. on Mills and Factories*, Q. 3085. In 1843 "above half" of the lace machines were hand-worked. *R. on the...Lace Manufacture* [*and*]..*the Factory Act* (1861, XXII. 461), p. 6.

industry was relatively small the absolute amount of power factory work was inconsiderable.

In hosiery it was still almost negligible. There had long been 'shops of frames'—small factories without power—and a few power-knitting factories existed before 1840[1], but when William Felkin of his own initiative took a frame census in 1844 he found that throughout the whole industry—silk, cotton and wool—"the number of frames under one roof averaged...rather more than three."[2] There were about 15,000 masters to 33,000 journeymen. The masters as a class were not economically independent. Most of them worked for hosiers or hosiers' middlemen, but they were not factory hands. It would have been far better for them had they been. Power was, however, being applied here and there in the late 'forties and early 'fifties, to the 'rotary' frames for knitting wide goods and to the circular knitter which makes a seamless knitted tube, a machine invented by Isambard Brunel the elder in 1816, neglected for thirty years from conservatism and fear of trouble with the knitters, and only introduced effectively after 1847[3].

The very imperfect mechanisation of most of the remaining British industries is shown whenever the capital equipment or the numbers employed can in any way be tested. There were gigantic iron works in which Nasmyth's steam-hammer had now been added to the equipment, and there were integrated firms covering the whole field from the coal and iron mine to the finished article; but the iron business with one or two rather small blast furnaces was more typical[4]. Right through the light metal and cutlery trades in their infinite variety the small non-mechanised, or power hiring, business predominated. A trade here and there was transformed. Twelve steel-pen making firms in 1849 employed an average of 154 workpeople each[5]; but what Léon Faucher wrote of Birmingham industry in 1845 remained generally true of all the industries which lay in and about Birmingham—"like French agriculture" they had "got into a state of parcellation."[6] There and elsewhere mechanical

[1] *S.C. on Mills and Factories*, 1840, x, Q. 3108: "Stocking frames have recently been worked by power." [2] Felkin, *op. cit.* p. 464. [3] *Op. cit.* p. 496–9.

[4] See vol. I. p. 428–30. But in 1848, 22 per cent. of the 'ironworks' made 57 per cent. of the pig-iron. Fong, H. D., *Triumph of Factory System in England* (Tientsin, 1930), p. 140.

[5] *Birmingham and the Midland Hardware District* (1866), p. 49.

[6] Quoted in vol. I. p. 175.

engineering proper was moving swiftly and its greatest firms were growing fast. Yet out of the 677 English and Welsh engine and machine makers who made returns of the number of men they employed at the census of 1851, although 14 each employed more than 350, 537 employed less than 20, and another 72 less than 50[1].

At the ports and in the greatest towns were found the large steam flour mills which the *Economist* relied on to beat French competition[2]. It did not notice that they had neither adopted the French system of 'high grinding' nor tried the grinding rollers which had for some years been successful in Pesth[3]. Nor did it mention the thousand or two local water mills whose sizes and sites had not changed much since Domesday, in which the representative milling firm, the miller, employed one or two men. The demand for railway timber had encouraged the erection or extension of steam-driven sawmills at the ports: a group of timber-merchants and sawyers considerable in proportion to the size of the trade described themselves as employing more than 20 men; but only 4 out of 416 making returns claimed more than 50; and certainly the great sawmill was not a common thing.

The employment returns here quoted must be used with care. "Many employers of labour—in some trades nearly the whole number—omitted to attend to"[4] the instruction to make them; but they cover nearly three-quarters of a million workpeople; they are the only general figures from which exact information about the size of business units other than textile mills in the middle of the century can be derived; and for some important industries the returns are numerous enough to provide a very fair statistical sample. Only those are quoted in the condensed table given on p. 35[5] which do provide such a sample, which relate to trades of first-rate importance, and which agree with the facts of industrial organisation as otherwise roughly known. The figures in the third column are ambiguous. They include both those masters who said they had no workpeople and those who did not trouble to state the number of their

[1] *Census of* 1851. *Ages and Occupations*, I. cclxxvi. The Scottish returns under this head were so defective that they were not tabulated. See vol. I. p. 448.

[2] Above, p. 3.

[3] Bennett, R. and Elton, J., *A History of Corn-Milling* (1898–1904), III. 296 *sqq.* for the early history of roller-milling. There were English patents for it in the eighteenth century.

[4] *Census of* 1851, as above.

[5] The original contains more numerical subdivisions and many more trades.

workpeople. Judging by the trades where the figures of this group are highest and lowest (*e.g.* the shoe-makers and the builders) it seems to be composed mainly of solitary working masters, though the figures under cotton manufacture do not allow of this interpretation. How many of these masters were really outworkers for a giving-out employer the figures do not show. Nor did the employer state whether or not his men worked on his premises. The figures are sign-posts in the field of industrial organisation, not a map of it; but they are useful sign-posts.

Employers making returns and employed in certain trades in England and Wales, 1851

I	II	III	IV	V	VI	VII	VIII	IX
Trade	Masters making returns	No men or number not stated	1 or 2 men	3–9 men	10–19 men	20–49 men	50–99 men	100 and upwards
Tailor	10991	4239	3852	2456	343	80	10	1
Shoe-maker	17665	7311	6016	3644	444	181	38	31
Engine and machine maker	837	160	152	295	90	72	49	34
Builder	3614	292	417	1541	701	498	113	52
Wheelwright	2057	670	982	373	20	11	1	—
Tanner	349	31	41	147	68	39	8	5
Woollen cloth manufacture	1107	131	199	329	156	179	41	82
Worsted manufacture	154	27	14	24	20	26	12	31
Silk manufacture	272	36	30	72	22	37	29	46
Miller	2394	403	1147	722	84	23	13	2
Brewer	776	120	228	319	67	34	3	5
Lace manufacture	317	58	54	123	28	26	9	19
Cotton manufacture	1670	482	81	174	124	216	172	411
Earthenware manufacture	378	68	68	112	31	56	7	36
Blacksmith	7331	2282	4035	967	31	15	1	—

Evidently for some old-fashioned crafts in which the terms master, journeyman, apprentice were still quite clear, the figures though not exhaustive are almost perfectly representative. The blacksmiths' and wheelwrights' figures illustrate this. The tailors' and shoe-makers' are more difficult, for into them the outworking and shopkeeping elements enter; but they show clearly enough the rarity of large tailors' businesses and the co-existence in boot and shoe-making of a fair number of big—in fact outworking—businesses and innumerable cobblers and small handworking retailers. The engineering figures have been discussed already. Those for building are an invaluable contribution to the history of a trade whose movements are particularly hard to follow with any steady vision[1]. They show quite clearly the master bricklayer or master carpenter starting as a builder with his handful of men; often failing or getting no further; sometimes becoming a substantial employer; occasionally rising into the group of great building contractors. Five firms returned themselves as employers of more than 350 men.

The tanners were beginning to move. Thirty years earlier they had been without exception, so far as is known, in a very small way of business[2]. They had not yet come under the influence either of machinery or of change. As Lyon Playfair said facetiously, if Simon the Tanner whose home was by the seashore at Joppa had lived to compete at the Great Exhibition "no doubt he would have carried off a medal."[3] But the demand for leather never slackened, especially in the industrial North, where it was so much used for machine belting and a thousand other purposes. Therefore, although the typical tanner was still an employer of from three to nine men, a few had pushed into the highest groups.

Among the textile figures those for worsted are obviously defective, though probably representative, those for woollen very illuminating when compared with those for cotton. The full woollen columns IV and V contain surviving domestic clothiers, VI and VII the small factories, which are also well represented in cotton. The contrast between woollen VIII and IX and cotton VIII and IX is overwhelming. Cotton IX contains 113 firms with employment figures of 350 and upwards, woollen IX, 21. Hosiery manufacture figures are not given here because the commissioners mixed up manufacturing and retailing hosiers.

Earthenware shows a well-developed factory system, though it was a system which made little use of power owing to the nature of the processes. The figures suggest a slightly greater amount of industrial concentration than in woollen, not so much as in worsted, and not nearly so much as in cotton. In milling the contrast is marked between a very small group of what are

[1] There are some tolerable figures for the London building trades of 1860 in the *Social Science Association's Report on Trade Societies* of that year, p. 53.

[2] See vol. I. p 170.

[3] 1851 *Exhibition Lectures*, I. 175.

clearly large steam mills; a group of about a hundred fair-sized mills, probably all steam driven; a larger, more indeterminate group (V), in which the water drive was probably general; and the mass of the old mills run by the miller, his mate and his lad. In the brewing figures there are evidently important omissions at the top of the scale; but thirty or forty men can work a very considerable brewery of the old type, so that most of the concerns in columns VII to IX might be classed as large units. The high figures in column IV, and perhaps some of those in column V, register the widespread survival of what has been called the handicraft brewer, the victualler who brewed his own beer and had provided most of the beer sold in many parts of the country twenty years earlier[1]. There were, in fact, in 1853 in all England and Wales 2470 brewers, who consumed 21 million bushels of malt, and 31,000 brewing victuallers and beersellers, who consumed 11 million bushels. London had 79 brewers, 1 brewing victualler and 61 brewing beersellers[2]. In this case the sample of the trade given in the 1851 figures is inadequate and tends to underrate the importance of the small concern, probably because many of the victuallers and beersellers did not naturally describe themselves as brewers.

There had been a time, not so many years back, when engineering would have left little trace on an occupational census and might not have been marked on an industrial map such as Petermann's. Similarly, in 1851, a few young industries of special significance for the future had no official memorial, partly because they were numerically weak, but mainly because their importance had not yet impressed the official mind. Chief among them were those which handled waste products hitherto neglected or raw materials hitherto intractable or unknown. There had been waste-product industries since animal refuse was first made into glue or linen rags into paper; and one of them, paper-making, had acquired a certain well-bred eminence in spite of its connection with the dust-bin and the 'rag and bone' man; but it was only in the nineteenth century, and generally speaking only late in it, that waste-product industries came into their own. As the world saw it, two very different figures were working to promote them—the man with the muck rake turning over heaps of garbage in search of cheap substitutes and of

[1] Vol. I. p. 170–1.

[2] Excise returns for 1853, *A. and P.* 1854, LXV. 325.

gain; the man of science seeking the truth and utility of things and believing that none of them is common or unclean. Perhaps the two should seem to the historian only aspects of a single figure, since gain and utility are cousins and the cheapening of things has been the handmaid of cleanliness.

Cheap substitutes, especially in cloth-making, were a reputed abuse against which gilds and government had made laws for centuries. They had been used most in poor outlying districts where gilds were few and laws ran with difficulty. Yorkshire clothiers in Elizabeth's day made their cloth mostly of coarse wool "and ffloxe and thrummes."[1] Before the last of the laws which had tried to make them do something else was repealed, in 1821[2], they had begun to use the modern 'adulterant'—torn-up rags, shoddy. Yorkshire tradition gave the year 1813 as that of the discovery of shoddy, a very appropriate date for the introduction of a cheap substitute—the peak price year of the century[3]. Machines for grinding up rags to make flocks for saddlery had been used before this in London. It is the very plausible conjecture of the first and only historian of shoddy that they were modifications of the rag-grinding machine which had come from the continent into the English paper trade about 1770[4]; or perhaps they were connected with a Scotsman's patent of 1801 "for preparing wove silk...from articles that have been wore," by grinding them up[5]. The first Yorkshire users of the machines, in Batley, Dewsbury and Brighouse, were characteristically secretive.

By 1828 the new 'adulterant' had come within the view of parliament. A London woolstapler told the Lords' Committee on the Wool Trade of that year that there was already a considerable import of foreign rags for use in Dewsbury. The shoddy went, he said, into "low carpets and low druggets," "goods made for sale not for wear." A second witness said that it never went into goods "for outer wear." A third, who used it, admitted that clothes "for workhouse purposes" were

[1] Heaton, H., *The Yorkshire Woollen Industry* (1920), p. 145: see also p. 97, 131.

[2] Vol. I. p. 339.

[3] Jubb, Saml., *The History of the Shoddy Trade* (1860), p. 17: "ten or fifteen years" before 1828, evidence of John Nussey of Birstall before the *Lords' S.C. on the Wool Trade*, 1828, p. 248.

[4] Jubb, *op. cit.* p. 19. For the paper machine, Spicer, A. D., *The Paper Trade* (1907), p. 55–7.

[5] Warner, Sir F., *The Silk Industry of the United Kingdom* (n.d. actually 1921), p. 426.

made of it, and that a proportion of it, with thrums, was blended with the new wool to make cheap "duffil" cloth "for the lower order of people who cannot get better goods." The machine that made it, one of these witnesses explained, was called "the manufacturers' devil."[1]

This name, with its derivative "devils' dust," was a godsend for men of letters out of love with their own day and for Chartist orators. Printers and barristers had devils, and rag-grinding machines made dust. The shoddy, used in reason, was no worse than the other forms of wool-waste which had always gone into cheap cloth, nor than the rag-waste which went into paper. "Duffil" kept "the lower order of people" warmer than its alternatives, cotton fustians, second-hand clothes, or the coarse linens of Thomas Carlyle's "Past." The shoddy was not always used in reason: rag-grinding is an unpleasant and used not to be a healthy job; the word shoddy probably deserved the connotation which it acquired. There was fraud and that 'illicit' profit which presumably there had been when rag-paper displaced vellum. But the thing rag-wool had nothing hellish about it. Had it not been discovered, the later nineteenth century would have been chillier or dirtier, or both.

Between 1828 and 1850 its use, which remained an English monopoly, was spreading obscurely and a little shamefacedly in the 'heavy woollen district' between the valleys of the Calder and the Aire. At first only soft rags such as stockings and flannels had been torn into shoddy. From about the mid 'thirties the devil was put at hard rags of fulled and felted cloth, old uniform coats, broadcloths and tailors' clippings. It tore them more slowly into 'mungo.' The seams and untearable bits, rotted, went with the true devils' dust, the unspinnable residuum, to manure hopyards. By the 'fifties the dust was beginning to be preserved in its separate colours, for use in making 'flock' wall papers. And so, the unique historian wrote, a few years later, "not a single thing belonging to the rag and shoddy system is valueless or useless."[2]

The close and rather secret association of the rag-wool with the pure wool manufacture made factory inspectors and census officials omit it from their statistics. But there was already

[1] *Lords' S.C.* p. 86, 54, 141.

[2] Jubb, *op. cit.* p. 24. Jubb's traditional date for 'mungo' is 1834. The traditional derivation is that, when the workmen said the hard rags would not go, the Yorkshire employer said "they mun go."

a distinct commercial and industrial organisation. By the side of the new railway through Batley, regular rag sales were organised in the early 'fifties, "on a precisely similar plan to the London colonial wool sales."[1] Rags were imported in quantity and were even 'ground' abroad by migrants from Batley and Dewsbury. Special groups of rag-sorting and shoddy-dealing firms had grown up. The latter either owned 'devils' or got rags ground for them on commission. Originally the cloth manufacturer had ground his own, and often he continued to do so; but now much rag-wool was sold and used outside the district where the business had originated; for in the 'fifties 'mungo' was "insinuating itself into the very seats of the fine cloth manufacture."[2] Hence the specialists to purvey it. The bulk of the rag-wool, however, either went without much admixture of new wool into the paddings, druggets, "workhouse cloths," "convict cloths," "slave cloths" and cheap blankets for which it had first been used, or—and perhaps predominantly—with a fair stiffening of new wool into the very serviceable "pilot cloths" which had become the staple manufacture of the district.

As a young waste-product industry the shoddy trade was lonely in its success. The paper-makers had long since adopted cotton rags as a standard high-grade raw material, using linen alone only for such things as bank notes. For their brown and wrapping papers almost any vegetable waste fibre would serve; but there had been no important recent innovation, except perhaps the 'overloading' of some papers with china clay, not a waste product[3]. Since most continental countries now tried to keep their good paper rags at home, the country was very thoroughly searched for suitable materials. No new waste ones had been found, though there had been experimental makings of straw-board. Glue-makers, size-makers, horn and bone workers, lampblack-makers, catgut twisters, plasterers with their cow hair, and the like, had learnt nothing fresh about the standard uses of animal refuse, though bone-manure making as an industry was only of recent growth[4]. For the most part Britain let her waste products run to waste. All the reserved utilities in her tar had not yet been revealed by the chemists.

[1] Jubb, *op. cit.* p. 36. [2] Such as Huddersfield: *ibid.* p. 30.
[3] See Spicer, *op. cit.* p. 13, 26; also vol. I. p. 325–6.
[4] Vol. I. p. 456.

She sent her coal half-consumed in thousands of tons into the air, to blacken the skies and destroy the health and buildings of her cities, as she sent the rich fats from her wool-washing troughs and much of the fertilising domestic refuse of her towns to defile her streams and canals. Some intelligent farmers, however, had irrigated fields near Holyrood, long before 1850, from the Foul Burn which carried "the contents of a large proportion of the sinks, drains and privies" of Edinburgh[1]. Her coke was often made by burning piled coal in the open and never with any regard to economy of heat or by-products[2]. Her blast-furnaces flamed superbly and wastefully into the night. At "scarcely half-a-dozen" of them was any use made of "the waste gases" in 1851[3]. Here at least was a beginning, if a small one; but not of a new industry.

Of the industries dependent on new raw materials, or on materials newly made available, and still young and small enough to slip through the ordinary statistical meshes, that of caoutchouc—as the educated and even the industrialists still wished to call it[4]—was certainly first in importance. Caoutchouc is "now almost a necessity of life" one of the 1851 Exhibition lecturers said[5]. Yet it left no trace on the very elaborate census figures of that year[6], and the foreign trade returns showed an import of this necessary which had only grown from 150 tons in 1846, when the published records first took account of it, through 290 tons in 1848, to 380 in 1850. The industry was then rather more than five and twenty years old. Men of vision had seen the possibilities of the odd substance almost as soon as it became really known to science during the second quarter of the eighteenth century. South American Indians had shown the way. "On en fait des bottines impénétrables à l'eau, des balles qui rebondissent avec beaucoup de force," Turgot wrote in

[1] Chadwick's *Report on the Sanitary Condition of the Labouring Population*, 1842, p. 48.

[2] See Lowthian Bell's protests against this form of waste so late as 1881 in *Trans. Inst. Mech. Eng.* 1881, p. 432; and again in 1884 in his *Principles of the Manufacture of Iron and Steel*, p. 50.

[3] Playfair, Lyon, 1851 *Exhibition Lectures*, I. 169.

[4] See for its early history, Hancock, T., *Personal narrative of the origin and progress of the Caoutchouc or India Rubber manufacture in England*, 1857; also Collins, J., in *British Manufacturing Industries*, 1876, VII. 97.

[5] Solly, E., *India rubber or Caoutchouc*, I. 255.

[6] The numbers employed have always been relatively small: they only rose above 25,000 in the decade 1911–21. 18*th Abstract of Labour Statistics*, p. 27.

1769[1]; elastic bottles, too, which "peuvent servir de seringues." You might make flexible pipes, surgical bandages, valves for "la machine pneumatique," waterproof clothes and tents and a multitude of useful things. Unhappily, he said, "la gomme élastique" was still very rare: he might have added, had he known, that it was mechanically intractable and chemically perverse.

For fifty years a few chemists experimented with it, a few inventors took out vain patents for utilising it, and other people rubbed out pencil marks with it. In 1820 one of the inventors, Thomas Hancock of London, filed a patent for an elastic wrist band. Three years later Charles Macintosh of Glasgow patented his waterproof varnish, based on the fact already known to chemists that caoutchouc would dissolve in naphtha. Hancock really founded the industry by making the caoutchouc mechanically tractable. He could not get the bits of the stuff to unite readily, and so could not get the sizes he wanted, until he had torn them and pressed them in his 'masticator'—a toothed solid cylinder working in a toothed hollow one, not altogether unlike the shoddy-maker's devil. For something like twelve years he kept the creature working for him in secrecy, while he patented things that Turgot had foreseen—surgical bandages, hose pipes, water-beds. Barclays the brewers first took up his pipes after "a vast amount of opposition from the leather hose-makers."[2] One after another the now familiar uses were marked down. By 1835 the rather simple secret of the masticator was out, but the Hancocks still led the little industry.

All this time rubber goods suffered from the chemical defects of a material which became rigid at a rather early point of cold, decomposed at a rather early point of heat, and was dissolved at varying speeds in different kinds of grease including—though here dissolution was slow—human sweat. These facts may help to explain medical opposition to the early macintoshes and rubber shoes. Thomas Hancock was always at work trying every kind of chemical combination with his rubber. From about 1840 he carried on secret experiments with sulphur, and by 1843 he was patenting his process of 'vulcanisation' which yielded—among other things—the rubber statues of the Great Exhibition[3]. He always asserted that it was a mistake to suppose

[1] *Œuvres* (ed. Schelle), III. 103.

[2] The *Personal narrative*, p. 61. Hancock and Macintosh are in the *D.N.B.*

[3] It is said that he examined in 1842 some rubber "cured" by a secret process by his American contemporary, Charles Goodyear, for whom it is customary in

that rubber was not largely used before this last invention. As early as 1837–8, he said, his firm "often" used three to four tons a week[1]. But he did not say how often, and the import figures show when the real rise in consumption began. His 'elastic vulcanised rubber' resisted temperatures, both up and down, which would have ruined plain rubber. Hence its position as a necessary in a mechanical age. Its use for valves, to take a single instance famous at the time, greatly helped the adoption of high-speed screw marine engines[2]. The rigid vulcanised rubbers also, in their various grades, were finding innumerable uses; so that rubber imports, which had stood at 150 tons in 1846, for the years 1850–59 were to be:

	Tons		Tons		Tons
1850	380	1854	1380	1857	1100
1851	760	1855	2230	1858	1250
1852	980	1856	1440	1859	1060
1853	870				

From 1846 the Hancocks had rubber works at Stratford-le-Bow. There they also handled an even newer raw material, gutta-percha[3]. It had only been brought to public notice in England in 1842 by Dr Montgomerie of Singapore, but by 1845 there was demand keen enough to produce reckless tree-felling in Malaya. That was the year of the first regular sales in London. The Hancocks took up the new material, tested it, treated it and began to sample its surgical and other uses. This was the time of experimental under-water telegraphy, and gutta-percha at once commended itself to Werner Siemens as a coating for cables. He used it on a trial cable across the Rhine in 1847 and at Kiel harbour in 1848. It was employed for the Hudson cable of 1849 and the Dover-Calais cables of 1850–51. William Siemens had recommended it to the British Electric Telegraph Company in March, 1850, and had made arrangements for

America to claim the invention (*e.g.* Bolles, A. S., *Industrial History of the United States*, p. 483). There is also a German claimant, Hindersdorf: *British Manufacturing Industries*, VII. 136. It is perhaps safest, with Levasseur, E., *Hist. des classes ouvrières et de l'industrie...de* 1789 *à* 1870, IV. 556 n., to divide the credit between Goodyear and Hancock: though Goodyear certainly used sulphur before Hancock patented its use. It is significant that both machinery and capital for the North British Rubber Co. of 1855 came from America. Bremner, D., *The Industries of Scotland* (1869), p. 363.

[1] *Personal narrative*, p. 140.

[2] 1851 *Exhibition Lectures*, I. 409.

[3] There is a first-hand account of the early use by Collins in *Brit. Man. Industries*, VII. 72 *sqq*. For the Hancock works, *V. C. H. Essex*, II. 495.

its manufacture[1]. Conditions were ripening for the growth of big industrial units. In 1852 S. W. Silver and Co. moved their waterproofing works across the Thames from Greenwich, joined the Hancocks, and began to work rubber and gutta-percha on a great scale. At first their advertisements of 'vulcanised and unvulcanised india-rubber in every form' were issued from 'North Woolwich'; by 1858 the heading was 'Silvertown.'[2]

The rising, indeed the risen, cement industry of the mid nineteenth century can hardly be classed with industries based on raw materials hitherto waste or new or intractable, though there had been an element of intractability. But like shoddy and rubber it was overlooked by the enumerators of 1851, who tabulated what were presumably the smaller industries of die-sinking and dealing in feathers and quills. Like rubber, it borrows from its future an importance out of line with whatever may have been the size of its occupation group, or of its business units, in 1851. Its past and present were those of a rule of thumb, trial and error, rather small, very slightly mechanised industry. It had grown with the new harbour, canal and railway works of the previous sixty years[3]. The eighteenth century knew no 'hydraulic' (water-resisting) cements, though by burning clayey limestones there had been produced what are now called hydraulic limes, some of which came very near to modern Portland cement in composition. On the London clay of the Thames estuary the limey nodules common in that formation must often have gone to the limekilns. Probably some accident showed that, after calcination, they yielded a cement. The clay which had worked into their cracks furnished, with the limestone, that combination of lime, silica and alumina which, when heated to the point of chemical combination and then ground, is the raw stuff of all hydraulic cements. In 1796 James Parker of Northfleet in Kent patented this very simple handling of what came to be called 'cement stones.'[4] With a fine instinct for publicity he had called his product Roman Cement.

[1] Pole, W., *The Life of Sir William Siemens* (1888), p. 86, 113; Jeans, W. T., *Creators of the Age of Steel* (2nd ed. 1885), p. 194; Bolles, *op. cit.* p. 436; Clapham, J. H., *Economic Development of France and Germany*, p. 157.

[2] Advertisement in the *Economist*, *e.g.* March 27, 1858.

[3] Art. "Cement," *Encyc. Britt.* 11th ed.; Butler, D. B., *Portland Cement* (1899). For harbour works, below, p. 520 *sqq.*

[4] *V. C. H. Essex*, II. 405.

The average 'cement stone' of the London clay does in fact contain, along with a good many other things, the essentials of a very quick setting but not very strong cement[1]. So the hunt for cement stones began. They could be dug or, more cheaply, dredged for. The easiest digging was in the clay cliffs of Essex. These suffered much in consequence. Dredging became an important industry on the Thames, the Blackwater and the Stour in the early nineteenth century: about 1850 some hundreds of smacks still lived by it, though by that time the trade was falling off[2].

The demand for 'Roman Cement' declined before the almost equally well named 'Portland Cement,' a name apparently adopted by Joseph Aspdin, a Leeds stonemason who took out his patent in 1824, because Portland stone was a fine thing and so was his cement and looked rather like it[3]. It was originally just an artificial mixture of the materials—lime and clay, calcined and ground—which nature had mixed in the cement stone. Aspdin made a true Yorkshire secret of it; and legend shows his son working at Wakefield behind twenty-foot walls. Meanwhile others had been attacking the rather obvious problem on the Thames. As they solved it while Aspdin was hiding his dusty knowledge in what is not naturally a good cement-making region, the priority of his patent is not historically very important. By about 1830 Major-General Sir C. W. Pasley at Chatham and the firm of Frost at Northfleet had made good cements from the abundant local materials—chalk and Medway mud[4]. Chemical knowledge of the ingredients was incomplete; their calcination and their chemical combination were defective; grinding was very defective; but the process with the controlled materials prevailed in time over that which accepted any cement stone as good enough. By trial and error, the mixture which produced the maximum strength was found out; the cement was made reasonably uniform; and, about 1850, the 'Portland' industry, which was growing in its first natural home on the Medway, began to work for export.

At first the customs authorities made no returns; but it is known that there was an export of 21,000 tons, worth £64,000, in 1853, which had risen to 79,000 tons, worth £215,000, by 1860[5].

[1] Butler, *op. cit.* p. 3.

[2] *V. C. H. Essex*, II. 405.

[3] See the centenary notices in the press of 1924, *e.g. Observer*, Nov. 7, 1924.

[4] Butler, *op. cit.* p. 2–3.

[5] *Annual Statement of Trade*, 1854–5, LI; 1861, LX. The export in the 'fifties was largely to France.

From the side of organisation the cement industry of the mid century falls into line with such plain unskilled-labour industries as chalk-quarrying and lime-burning. Most of the men in it probably returned themselves as simple labourers in 1851. The calcined material, which had been man-handled before calcination, was broken up with hammers by hand; barrowed to the grinding millstones; and barrowed again to the dumps. No important labour-saving device was introduced for another twenty years; the great business unit was far in the future; and the imperfectly calcined and ill-ground product was of a quantity which "the veriest speculative builder"[1] would have rejected forty years later. But such as it was, like much other British produce of the 'fifties, it had no foreign competition to face at home and something like a monopoly of the export market.

[1] Butler, *op. cit.* p. 4. The first important labour-saving device did not come till 1872.

CHAPTER III

THE COURSE OF INDUSTRIAL CHANGE, 1850-86

LOOKING back on English life from the year 1880 over the thirty-one years since he first published *The Seven Lamps of Architecture*, John Ruskin wrote of "the ferruginous temper" which he then "saw rapidly developing itself, and which, since that day, has changed our Merry England into the Man in the Iron Mask."[1] (While he wrote the mask was turning visibly into steel.) The "ferruginous temper" went back far beyond 1849, as he implied and we know. In the 'twenties foreigners had seen it manifested in the "enormous iron cylinders" which rolled English garden walks[2]. In 1848-9, when the temper was only developing, Great Britain made perhaps half the pig iron of the world, and in 1853 doubts were expressed of her power to maintain so huge an output[3]. Yet she almost trebled it during the next thirty years, continuing to make more than the whole of a far more industrial world for eighteen of them. Further, she had passed from an age of empiricism and from a technique which—at least in the primary processes of iron and steel making—had made no important progress since 1828[4] into an age in which irons, slags, cokes, gases, steels and temperatures could be studied by exact methods, and in which the whole range of scientific problems connected with the inventions of Bessemer, Siemens and Thomas was faced, if not many of its peaks had been mastered. Led by Joseph Whitworth, the metal workers were learning precision. Metallurgy and the metal workers have an absolute primacy in the history of modern manufacturing industry. In no generation is that primacy more obvious.

During the twenty years between 1830 and 1850, the West of Scotland, once an insignificant producing area, had become the producer of more than a quarter of Britain's pig iron. In Staffordshire, furnaces had gone out of blast; South Wales had lost its dominating position[5]. But Scotland's best ironstone,

[1] *The Seven Lamps of Architecture* (ed. of 1880), p. 70 n.
[2] Dupin, *The Commercial Power of Great Britain* (Eng. ed. 1825), I. 165.
[3] See vol. I. p. 425.
[4] When Neilson introduced the hot-blast. Vol. I. p. 51, 426.
[5] Vol. I. p. 425-6, 428-30.

the 'blackband,' was known to be limited. It was this knowledge, combined with the instinctive conviction that the headlong pace of the early railway age must be a transitory thing, which made the iron-historian of that age suppose, in 1853, that "we must retrograde"..."unless mineral fields at present unknown come into operation."[1] Yet Scotland managed to increase her 'make' of iron for another seventeen years, though she never again had so large a share of the whole British 'make' as she had when he was writing[2]; and the new mineral fields were already in use. For many years South Wales, where native coal-measure ironstones were limited and not very rich, had drawn upon the 'pockets' of hematite ore in Cumberland and Furness[3]. When official mineral statistics were first collected, for 1854, it appeared that over 500,000 tons of this ore, with an average content of something like 55 per cent. of iron, had been raised in the year, and nearly all shipped away, some to Staffordshire and Scotland, most to Wales[4]. Since 1836 the much poorer lias ironstone of Cleveland—it averages only 30 per cent. of iron—had been regularly worked in the valley of the Esk, above Whitby, and shipped first to the Tyne and then to the Tees, for smelting mixed with the local coal-measure ironstones[5]. By 1850 the iron output of the North-Eastern area had risen to something like 150,000 tons. In that year John Vaughan ascertained that the main seam of the lias ironstone came through the Cleveland hills till it got into touch with tide-water and South Durham coke at Middlesbrough. His firm had built furnaces at Witton Park, near the coke and the clay-band iron ore, four years earlier. To these furnaces Cleveland ironstone began to move in 1851. Soon the furnaces came to Middlesbrough[6]. Thereafter the rise or fall of the main iron areas, as

[1] Scrivenor, *History of the Iron Trade* (ed. of 1854), p. vi.

[2] Lowthian Bell calculated that the Scottish 'make,' which had been 5·52 per cent. of the whole in 1830, was 28·69 per cent. in 1852, 25·74 per cent. in 1855, 20·5 per cent. in 1870, and 13·53 per cent. in 1880. See Table I of his Memorandum to the *Second Report of the R. C. on Depression of Trade and Industry* (1886), part I. p. 320. The Memo. was reprinted as *The Iron Trade of the U.K. compared with that of the other chief iron-producing nations*, 1886, and is quoted below as Bell, *The Iron Trade*, with the paging of the book.

[3] Vol. I. p. 50, 189.

[4] The first mineral returns in *A. and P.* 1856, LV. 469 *sqq.*

[5] Bell, Lowthian, in *The Reign of Queen Victoria*, II. 203–4 and in *The Industrial Resources of the Tyne, Wear and Tees* (1864), p. 79.

[6] Tomlinson, W. W., *Hist. of the North-Eastern Railway*, p. 405, 507; Head, J., "Recent Developments in the Cleveland Iron and Steel Industry," *Trans. Inst. Mech. Eng.* 1893, p. 225.

ore-producers and iron-producers, was in rough outline as follows[1]:

	Tons of	1855	1865	1875	1885
Staffordshire	Ore raised	2,500,000	1,485,000	1,654,000	1,830,000
	Pig iron made	855,000	899,000	712,000	545,000
Wales and	Ore raised	1,665,000	485,000	538,000	68,000
Monmouth	Pig iron made	871,000	917,000	597,000	833,000
Scotland	Ore raised	2,400,000	1,470,000*	2,452,000	1,838,000
	Pig iron made	827,000	1,163,000	1,050,000	1,004,000
Yorkshire:	Ore raised	255,000	575,000	354,000	127,000
West Riding	Pig iron made	91,000	123,000	267,000	166,000
North Eastern	Ore raised	1,155,000	2,882,000	6,182,000	5,972,000
District	Pig iron made	298,000	1,012,000	2,049,000	2,478,000
Shropshire	Ore raised	365,000	274,000	240,000	178,000
	Pig iron made	122,000	117,000	121,000	45,000
Cumberland and	Ore raised	538,000	1,504,000	1,983,000	2,438,000
Lancashire	Pig iron made	17,000	312,000	1,045,000	1,384,000
Derbyshire	Ore raised	409,000	350,000	218,000	18,000
	Pig iron made	117,000	189,000	272,000	361,000
Lincolnshire and	Ore raised	74,000	489,000	1,660,000	2,349,000
Northampton	Pig iron made	—	26,000	192,000	426,000
Foreign iron ore used	—	—	—	738,000	3,313,000

* A possible serious error in this figure.

As the average iron-content of British ores worked in this period varied from about 30 per cent. to about 34 per cent., except the hematite of Cumberland and Furness which averaged 55 per cent., a district which, like Staffordshire or Scotland in 1855, has an ore figure about three times the size of its iron figure is smelting its own ore and not much else. When the iron figure rises well above a third of the ore figure, as in Wales and Monmouth throughout, ore imports from another district are indicated, in this case from Cumberland—or, latterly, from abroad. As the North-Eastern district never exported ore, the fact that its iron was well below 30 per cent. of its ore in 1855 suggests either bad smelting, or ore accumulating to await fresh furnaces, or error in a new and difficult piece of statistical collection. Cumberland and Lancashire had about got to the point of consuming all their own ore (at 55 per cent.) by 1875. Barrow had come into existence[2]. The Lincolnshire and Northamptonshire mines, at Frodingham, about Kettering, and elsewhere, lie on the curve of the lias beds sweeping from Cleveland down to Oxfordshire, Gloucestershire and the South-West.

[1] Bell, *The Iron Trade*, p. 11, and the *Mineral Returns* for 1886.

[2] Stileman, F. C., "On the Docks and Railway Approaches at Barrow-in-Furness," *Trans. Inst. Mech. Eng.* 1880.

Their development followed the rise of the lias ironstone industry at Middlesbrough; but owing to their distance from coke they remained primarily ore-export districts throughout the period, supplying Derbyshire, the West Riding and the Black Country[1]. Foreign ore, which began to arrive in appreciable quantities before 1870, went first to South Wales, for obvious reasons; later to Scotland and the North-East coast, for reasons connected with the history of steel[2].

The rise of the Middlesbrough industry had given opportunity for the application of the best known methods of smelting. A few furnaces in South Wales had already adopted, and improved, the French device of using the waste gases of combustion, not to illuminate the countryside but to raise steam and heat the blast[3]. This practice was introduced at Middlesbrough from the start, with an economy estimated ultimately at nearly a million and a half tons of coal a year. The furnaces first built were not bigger than the best then at work, the height being from 45 to 50 feet and the capacity some 5000 cubic feet[4]; but by utilising waste gases and increasing temperatures they were soon made to yield 220 tons a week, against a maximum of something like 120 tons from a hot-blast furnace elsewhere in the late 'forties. In 1864 John Vaughan tried a 75-foot furnace, with a view to increasing the weekly 'make.' He found that it not only made more iron but had a better iron-fuel ratio than the smaller structures. Soon 80 feet for height, and 20,000 cubic feet for capacity, became standard sizes. "Before long all the small furnaces on the banks of the Tees were demolished."[5] By 1870 the 80-foot monsters had been made yet hotter and their output driven up to between 450 and 550 tons a day, at an expenditure of two tons of coal per ton of iron made. After that, for over twenty years, there was "no great change in the size, form, or performance of the then best designed furnaces."[6]

What might be called Middlesbrough practice was naturally adopted in other new iron smelting areas, such as the Barrow

[1] Dove, G., "The Iron Industry of Frodingham," *Trans. Inst. Mech. Eng.* 1885. See also *J. of Iron and Steel Inst.* 1876.

[2] Bell, *The Iron Trade*, p. 16. The first Spanish ore came to the N.E. coast in 1861. Tomlinson, *op. cit.* p. 576.

[3] Bell, Lowthian, *Principles of the Manufacture of Iron and Steel* (1884), p. 23, quoted below as Bell, *Manufacture of Iron*; also *Reign of Queen Victoria*, II. 215.

[4] Vol. I. p. 428.

[5] Bell, *Manufacture of Iron*, p. 24. Eighty feet remained the standard size in 1907. Bell, Lady, *At the Works, a Study of a Manufacturing Town*, p. 23.

[6] Head, J., in *Trans. Inst. Mech. Eng.* 1893, p. 231.

district and North Lincolnshire. Older areas were more conservative. The gases flared to waste at nearly 90 per cent. of the Black Country furnaces in 1866[1]. In 1869 "the good folks of Coatbridge [still] had their streets lighted without tax or trouble" by "the flames of no fewer than fifty blast furnaces," which could be seen from the steeple of the parish church. "The flames have a positively fascinating effect. No production of the pyrotechnist can match their wild gyrations."[2] In 1876 the writer of a popular handbook on the iron industry spoke of only "the most modern furnaces" utilising their waste gases: his picture of a typical furnace—conceivably borrowed from some earlier work—showed one that did not[3]. In West Yorkshire it was an article of popular faith among ironmasters in the 'eighties that the very best malleable iron could only be made in the old way by the cold blast; though Lowthian Bell was reminding them that no "complete and systematically conducted course of experiments" had ever proved it, and was attributing the undisputed excellence of "best Yorkshire" iron, not to the temperature of the blast but to "the extraordinary care used in the forge and mill."[4]

As for coke-making, Bell wrote in 1884 that "until very recently, no kind of progress had been made in the process for the last fifty years."[5] In Durham, the chief coking county, not only was the yield of coke from the coal nearly 15 per cent. below what it should have been, owing to bad manipulation, but there was a shocking waste of heat accompanying "the immense volumes of smoke and flame which issue from a Durham coke-work, blackening and desolating the country around it."[6] Yet ever since the year 1860, or even earlier, discreditable waste of this kind had been avoided in the scientific and economical coking practice of a few firms in France and Belgium. In 1884, only Bell himself and certain collieries at Wigan were attempting to economise the heat and save the precious by-products of coke-making. The county of Durham was sending 45,000 tons of sulphur into the atmosphere yearly from its coke ovens alone[7].

[1] *Birmingham and the Midland Hardware District*, p. 59–68. Of 170 furnaces, of which 119 were in blast, "about 20" utilised the waste gases.

[2] Bremner, *The Industries of Scotland*, p. 36.

[3] Williams, W. M., in *British Manufacturing Industries*, I. 15.

[4] Bell, *Manufacture of Iron*, p. 148, 154.

[5] *Ibid.* p. 47.

[6] *Ibid.* p. 50; and similar complaints in the *Trans. Inst. Mech. Eng.* 1881, p. 432.

[7] Bell, *Manufacture of Iron*, p. 49–53.

without Fuel" before the British Association at Cheltenham: Aug. 11, 1856[1]. In the interval both Siemens' open-hearth steel-making process and the Thomas-Gilchrist modification of the Bessemer process had been made almost perfect.

The fuel to which Bessemer referred in his challenging title was not that needed for smelting but that used in puddling, cementation, or the making of crucible cast steel; for his original plan was to run fluid iron straight from the blast furnace into a 'converter'; to burn away all the chemical impurities—mainly silicon and carbon—by a powerful air blast driven through the molten mass from below, if he wanted malleable iron; and to burn out all but an appropriate proportion of carbon, if he wanted steel. "At a certain period of the process any quality of metal can be obtained," he told his Cheltenham audience. That iron could be refined with the aid of an air blast was part of the oldest empirical knowledge of the metal worker. The novelty was the pouring of air from below in great quantity and at great speed into the iron when molten. In old-fashioned refining for steel, as in puddling, the iron was at most viscous. In Bessemer's process, the rapid combustion of the silicon and the carbon was to raise the temperature and keep the mass perfectly fluid.

At first, as early critics pointed out, Bessemer forgot the phosphorus, which is very commonly present in British iron. By chance his experiments had been made with an iron remarkably free of it. When repeated with phosphoric irons, his process failed to eliminate the phosphorus, more than a very minute proportion of which makes the metal non-malleable. Failure from such a cause came to him, he said, "as a bolt from the blue."[2] He began to look for non-phosphoric iron, and found what he wanted in the Cumberland hematite, henceforward a 'Bessemer' ore. This problem, with other difficulties, provided him with some three years' work before he was ready to attack the market himself, after nearly all those who had taken out licences to use his first patent had thrown in their hands discouraged. There were two other main difficulties. He found no effective way of ascertaining the moment of 'the blow' at which his metal had in it just enough carbon to be steel. So he purified it completely, and then added iron which contained known

[1] Bessemer, Sir Henry, *Autobiography* (1905), p. 156 *sqq.*: *The Times*, Aug. 14, 1856.

[2] *Autobiography*, p. 170.

quantities of carbon and manganese, or the mixture known as ferro-manganese. The value of manganese in steel-making had long been recognised, if not understood, especially on the continent. "It was a matter of universal knowledge," he wrote later[1]. Another difficulty was mechanical. His first converters were fixed. But to secure exact results he must be able to stop or restart the full blast at will, and during a stoppage under a fixed converter the air-pipes might get clogged. The converter was therefore swung on an axis so that it could be tilted until the pipes led in above the surface of the molten metal.

During the early years (1856–9) Bessemer's mind ran on steel more than on wrought iron, perhaps because steel left the maximum margin of profit to the inventor. His decision to start making it in Sheffield had important technical and economic consequences. Years afterwards he explained why he took that decision[2]. No Sheffield man would try his method or pay the licence fees for his patent; therefore he must go there and "force the trade to adopt it by underselling." He took a partner and went in 1858. They produced some tool steel; but the things which they made most successfully were such as had hitherto been made, not of tool steel and not at Sheffield, but of the finest Yorkshire or Black Country wrought iron—cranks for locomotives, axles, propeller shafts, railway tyres. For these they employed pure Swedish iron. Later they used English 'Bessemer' iron. As neither was smelted in Sheffield, the plan of running the molten iron from blast furnace to converter had to be dropped. They must melt the pigs. So steel was not made "without fuel," though it was made very cheaply. Again, although Bessemer believed from the start that his steel would be fit for plates, rails, joists and all kinds of economical uses—he read a paper on "Cast Steel and its Application to Constructive Purposes" in 1861[3]—his own firm was so "crammed with orders"[4] for things in which there was more profit that they left the plain work for licencees to take up at their own pace. Some continental licencees, such as Krupp, were quicker that the English. Meanwhile Bessemer's own firm, during the fourteen years of the partnership (1858–72), made profits at a rate which, as he conjectured, had never been equalled "in the history of commerce." Including the selling price of the business at the end, but excluding the immensely profitable sales of licences,

[1] *Autobiography*, p. 264.
[2] *Ibid.* p. 175.
[3] *Trans. Inst. Mech. Eng.* July, 1861.
[4] *Autobiography*, p. 225.

the profit on the original capital throughout the fourteen years averaged "nearly cent. per cent. every two months."[1]

The new material had been tried for almost every use in the early days. John Brown and J. D. Ellis, of the Atlas works, the first men in Sheffield to trust it, rolled steel rails in 1860. They were not cutlers but steel-makers with a young and adaptable business[2]. Experimental Bessemer rails, made under licence by the Weardale Company at Tudhoe, were laid on the Newcastle High Level Bridge in April, 1862. In the following May, the London and North-Western tried some Bessemer rails at Camden Town[3]. At the Exhibition of 1862 Bessemer's firm showed, besides every kind of tool and weapon, shafts, tyres, bars, rods, rails and steel wire for ropes. In 1863 the screw steamer *Pelican* of 329 tons was built of steel plates: by the end of 1865 seventeen other steel ships of various sorts had been launched, among them the sailer *Clytemnestra* of 1251 tons. For years Bessemer spent his strength against the iron-bound obstinacy of the War Office and the Admiralty, whilst Napoleon III observed his guns with keen attention, and the French Ministry of Marine investigated the use of his steel for ships of war[4]. But there were obvious limitations to a very rapid extension of the mass uses. First, his high charge for patentee's licences, which settled down at £1 a ton on steel rails and at £2 a ton on steel for all other purposes[5]. Second, the relatively expensive 'Bessemer' raw material, which, with the licence, made the early steel plate or rail much dearer than its iron competitor. Third, the year-long tests of endurance on the permanent way, in the boiler or the ship, necessary to prove that the dearer material was really the more economical[6]. Finally, the gigantic lock-up of capital and human capital skill in puddling, and the as yet undisputed dominance of the British iron industry in the world's markets, were all against rapid change. The loss of this semi-monopolistic position and the accompanying economies in pro-

[1] *Autobiography*, p. 179.

[2] John Brown had originally been a cutlery factor. He became a steel-maker in 1844. From that time forward his firm was always pioneering. In 1860 it made experimental armour plate. Jeans, W. T., *The Creators of the Age of Steel* (1885), p. 275–86.

[3] *Engineering*, Jan. 5, 1866; Bessemer, *Autobiography*, p. 335; Tomlinson, *The North-Eastern Railway*, p. 648.

[4] All from the *Autobiography*.

[5] Jeans, *op. cit.* p. 282.

[6] See evidence of Seymour Clarke, General Manager of the Great Northern, before the *R.C. on Railways*, 1867 (XXXVIII. pts. I. and II.), Q. 12933: "it is a question of cost."

duction—partly enforced—during the decade 1870–80 were the deciding factors in the ultimate transition.

High among the economies came the development of steel-making in association with smelting, as Bessemer had originally proposed, mainly on the Welsh, North-West, and North-East coasts. Intimately connected with this partial shift from Sheffield to tide-water was the growth of the import of ore. The relatively high price of the limited stock of English hematite might have kept down steel production, had not the spread of the Bessemer and allied methods coincided with growing ore imports—mainly of the Spanish 'rubio' ore. When hematite prices rose "speculators of all kinds rushed off to Spain"[1] to get concessions. In 1870 the total import of ore was only 400,000 tons and the make of steel ingots was 240,000 tons; in 1880 the import of ore was 3,060,000 tons and the make of steel 1,250,000 tons. The economies in production, and the now proved merits of steel for heavy work, had led to the mass conversion of the railway companies during the decade. In 1872 the North-Eastern, in spite of its experiments ten years earlier, only used steel rails at points and crossings. By 1877 it had ceased to give orders for iron rails[2]. The final turn over from iron to steel—for new rails—was "virtually complete in three or four years from its commencement."[3] By 1875 all the locomotive boilers on the North-Western were made of steel plates and the Company had its own Bessemer plant at Crewe[4]. Here quality may have been the determining factor; with the rails that factor was price. The North-Eastern reduced its working expenses in the bad trade year 1879 by buying its steel rails dirt cheap; and when, in 1884, Lowthian Bell declared that steel "must be henceforward looked upon as the proper material for railroads," he led up to his declaration by pointing out that new rails could now be made of steel "even from a comparatively expensive hematite ore...more economically than a good quality of rail" could "be produced in iron from the cheaper ironstone of Cleveland."[5]

When the British 'make' of steel stood at about 240,000 tons, in 1870, 225,000 tons are said to have been made in the Bessemer converter and 15,000 by some form of the 'open-hearth'

[1] Lowthian Bell, quoted in Jeans, *op. cit.* p. 300.
[2] Tomlinson, *op. cit.* p. 648; Bell, *Manufacture of Iron*, p. 379.
[3] Head, J., Presidential Address, *Trans. Inst. Mech. Eng.* 1885, p. 309.
[4] Bessemer, *Autobiography*, p. 250. [5] *Manufacture of Iron*, p. 378.

process connected with the name of Sir William Siemens. Late in the 'seventies came Thomas's basic process. The course of production thenceforward was as follows:

	1878	1880	1883	1884	1885
Bessemer	800,000	1,000,000	1,550,000	1,300,000	1,250,000
Open-Hearth	174,000	251,000	455,000	475,000	610,000
Basic	—	?	121,000	179,000	140,000

The steady upward course of the open-hearth steel in so fluctuating an industry is sufficient witness to the efficiency of the process[1].

In his old age Bessemer recalled that he himself had made open-hearth experiments in the 'fifties and had even taken out a patent in October, 1855, for the "fusion of steel in a bath of cast iron," an essential feature of what came to be known as the Siemens-Martin process, patented in England by M. Martin of Sireuil just ten years later. Bessemer said that he doubted his own wisdom in dropping these experiments[2]. Apparently he half foresaw the abandonment of his ingenious but elaborate converter during the thirty years that followed his death[3]. But he was careful not to rob Siemens and Thomas of their honour. For Siemens—a master of applied science, and a general inventor like himself—he had a special regard. Siemens' main contribution to metal working was a by-product of a lifelong preoccupation with the economy of energy[4]. From economy in engines he passed—at the suggestion, it is said, of his brother Frederick—to economy in furnaces. The result of many years work was the regenerative gas furnace first used industrially in 1861 at Lloyd and Summerfield's flint-glass works in Birmingham, and then at Chance's Stourbridge works, where Michael Faraday saw it. In it, a current of burning gas, which may be of many kinds and is always cheap, heats the fire-brick labyrinth of the regenerative chambers: through them the next incoming currents of gas and air go, sucking in heat, to burn at a far higher temperature than the first current: and so on. Currents and

[1] The figures for the earlier years are rather uncertain. Those given in Bell, *Manufacture of Iron*, p. 432, based on reports of the Iron Trade Association, do not always agree with the official Mineral Statistics. I have followed the Mineral Statistics.

[2] Bessemer, *Autobiography*, p. 141.

[3] He died in 1898. Since 1893 more steel had been made on the open-hearth than in the converter. By 1925 only 6 per cent. was made in the converter, which by 1930 had disappeared.

[4] Pole, W., *The Life of Sir William Siemens* (1888); Obach, E., *Sir Wm. Siemens als Erfinder und Forscher* (1884); *D.N.B.*

temperatures can be exactly controlled and as much heat generated as the fabric of the furnace will stand. The principle can be applied to furnaces for every purpose, and was so applied within seven or eight years all over the world. From the first Siemens had suggested that it might be used not only for the melting of steel, for which it was obviously suited, but for its making[1].

Early experiments by licencees failed; but in 1865 the Martins of Sireuil made cast steel successfully by melting scrap steel in a bath of molten pig iron on an open Siemens hearth, and took out their patent. In that year Siemens started his Sample Steel Works in Birmingham to make his process known. Three years later he and a group of supporters founded the Siemens Steel Company at Landore, Swansea, where his own method—more fundamental than the Martins—was adopted. Into the molten pig, at full heat, was fed a pure ore in relatively small quantities. During the resultant combustion, carbon escaped as carbonic oxide and silicon as silica passed into the slag. The perfect control of the gaseous fuel and of the temperature in a Siemens furnace enabled the steel-makers to work very exactly. Ore was fed in so as to keep ebullition constant. The content of the furnace was sampled at intervals. At the right moment, it was 'physicked,' as the old Sheffield steel-makers used to say, with manganese[2].

The Landore works began to make steel about the middle of 1869, and turned out 75 tons a week. Three other important works were using the process that year[3]. By 1873 Landore had its own blast furnaces and collieries and could make 1000 tons a week, using sometimes the pure Siemens, sometimes the Siemens-Martin process. During the remaining ten years of his life Siemens worked hopefully at a still more fundamental process which had long fascinated him—steel-making direct from the ore without any use of previously smelted pig iron. On the face of it, this was a simpler thing than many which he and his generation had mastered. His metallurgical friends treated it most seriously; but Lowthian Bell wrote in 1878—"I have a kind of instinctive opinion that the Blast Furnace will be difficult to exterminate."[4] It still stands. Meanwhile the slow

[1] Pole, *op. cit.* p. 143.
[2] There is a description in Bell, *Manufacture of Iron*, p. 431.
[3] Pole, *op. cit.* p. 154; Jeans, *op. cit.* p. 159.
[4] Quoted in Pole, *op. cit.* p. 199.

extermination of the Bessemer converter had begun, as the steel-making figures show.

Yet it was in a model converter that Gilchrist Thomas, the young clerk in the Thames Police Court with a classical education and a passion for metallurgy, and his cousin Percy Gilchrist, an iron-works chemist in South Wales, tried their experiments with the basic process[1]. The aim was to render phosphoric ores available for the new steel-making. All the metallurgical world knew that there was a fortune in it: there had been innumerable experiments and some patents. The best opinion of the early 'seventies, that of Lowthian Bell, held that the high temperature and short duration of 'the blow' in the Bessemer converter were responsible for the retention of phosphorus in the iron. Thomas tracked the trouble to the silicon in the converter's lining of fire-brick, which would not unite chemically with the phosphorus. He determined to substitute something which would, something calcareous—bricks of powdered limestone or the like. There were great difficulties of manipulation. These were not overcome in the half-size experiments made at Blaenavon, where Gilchrist was working, and at Dowlais in 1877–8. Then E. W. Richards, manager of the Bolckow-Vaughan works at Middlesbrough, put his resources and experience at the inventors' disposal and the thing succeeded—in 1879. For economy's sake, to save wastage of the lining of magnesian limestone in the converters, more basic material, in the form of lime, was mixed with the charge to take up the phosphorus[2].

The world is so full of phosphoric ores, and the problem had been so much before the minds of metallurgists everywhere, that the announcement of its solution was an international incident. "Middlesbrough was soon besieged by the combined forces of Belgium, France, Prussia, Austria and America."[3] Would-be licencees from abroad called on Thomas before breakfast[4]. Operations were started at once, faster abroad than in Britain; for Britain had a fair supply of Bessemer ores of her own, and a fully developed commercial organisation for bringing foreign ore from mines close to the sea in Spain to furnaces close to the sea at Middlesbrough, or at Swansea, or on the Clyde. By 1882 there were twelve converters in Britain adapted to the new process—six of them at the Bolckow-Vaughan works—and ten

[1] Burnie, R. W., *Memoir and Letters of Sidney Gilchrist Thomas* (1891).

[2] See Richards' address to the Cleveland Institution of Engineers, Nov. 15, 1880, quoted at length in Jeans, *op. cit.* p. 307–13.

[3] Bell, *Manufacture of Iron*, p. 407.

[4] Burnie, *op. cit.* p. 128–9.

others were being prepared[1]. Thomas's principles could be applied without great difficulty to the open-hearth method of steel-making, but for some years, in England, basic converters predominated[2]. In the half-year Sept. 30, 1882—March 31, 1883, 281,000 tons of steel were produced by one or other application of the new process[3]. But of this tonnage only 58,000 was British; no less than 152,000 was German. Bad trade kept both Bessemer and basic converters relatively idle in Great Britain during 1884–5. But as he travelled over the world in those years, famous but dying of consumption, Thomas saw what he had accomplished, what he must have known that he would accomplish, for he was no mere trial and error inventor but a fully educated man who apprehended his problem and its implications. To Britain he had given the free use of her almost unlimited phosphoric ores: concurrently he had lowered the value which her insular position gave her in the Bessemer years. To America he had given little: she had such vast non-phosphoric reserves. To France and Central Europe, above all to the debatable land of Lorraine, he had given everything—for there nearly all the most abundant and accessible ores were phosphoric, and the sea was remote.

The remarkable maintenance of the output of puddled iron during the decade 1873–83[4], in face of competition from the converters and the open-hearths, and in spite of the abandonment of iron railway metal by all the great companies before 1879, was due principally to a great expansion of the demand for iron plates and angles in shipbuilding. The change over is well illustrated by output figures collected in 1883 for what was by that time the principal iron-producing and iron-shipbuilding district in Britain, the North-East coast[5]. They are not quite exhaustive but they tell the story:

	1873	1882
Rails	374,000 tons	7,000 tons
Plates	191,000 „	498,000 „
Angle bars	51,000 „	150,000 „

[1] Mineral Returns, *A. and P.* 1884, LXXXV. 535 *sqq*.

[2] The first important application only came in 1888, when Maximilian Mannaberg installed a basic open-hearth plant at Frodingham in Lincolnshire: see the obituary notice of Mannaberg, *The Times*, Dec. 21, 1929. At the time of his death 70 per cent. of the British steel was made in such plants.

[3] Gilchrist's figures supplied to Bell, *op. cit.* p. 407.

[4] Above, p. 52.

[5] Bell, *Manufacture of Iron*, p. 459. In 1872 "no steel of any kind" was made on the N.E. coast: Head, "Recent Developments in the Cleveland Iron and Steel Industry," *Trans. Inst. Mech. Eng.* 1893, p. 226.

Through all the vicissitudes of the years following the boom-year 1873—in 1877 the total output of the three classes of manufactured iron in Cleveland was more than 35 per cent. lower than it had been in 1873—the proportion of plates to the total output rose quite steadily. The situation in the ship-building industry is shown by the numbers of sea-going ships of all kinds, sail and steam, on hand at June 30th, 1882. They were: wooden 55, steel 100, iron 625. Steel was coming rapidly into use in the 'eighties. On September 30, 1875, there had been no steel ships building at all. The tide turned in 1876–7. In 1880 Lloyd's surveyors inspected a steel tonnage of 35,000; in 1885 a steel tonnage of 166,000—but also 934,000 tons of iron shipping[1]. This late arrival of steel is at first sight surprising, for, as has been seen, a number of vessels of various sorts had been built of Bessemer steel in the years 1863–5. The largest of them, the clipper *Clytemnestra*, had come through the Calcutta cyclone of October, 1864, with credit. But the firm which had done the building got into difficulties and, in spite of financial assistance from Bessemer himself, went into liquidation. Steel was dear as compared with iron. If it was to be adopted it must be proved markedly superior. Proof was not forthcoming; and "for the next ten years steel shipbuilding was almost unheard of."[2] No doubt, as Bessemer always and inevitably believed, sheer conservatism in the shipyards explained much. The conservatism of the Admiralty was there to back it. At Chatham, in 1864, elaborate tests of Bessemer steel plates had shown them to be stronger than iron as a rule but more erratic in fracturing. In 1868 Lloyd's surveyors, instructed to classify ships made out of steel "of approved quality," had tested some Bessemer plates—not of Bessemer's make—and had rejected them[3]. Seven years later, at the Institute of Naval Architects, the chief Admiralty constructor made much of the "uncertainties and treacheries" of steel. If makers would give him plates "as regular and precise" as plates of copper, he was ready to build "the entire vessel, bottom plates and all, of steel." Bessemer traversed the whole chain of argument, adducing the *Clytemnestra* and the steel locomotive boilers. Siemens set him-

[1] See Head in *Trans. Inst. Mech. Eng.* 1885, p. 314; *Annals of Lloyd's Register* (1884), p. 123; Holmes, Sir G. C. V., *Ships Ancient and Modern*, II. 40: Cornewall-Jones, R. J., *The British Merchant Service* (1898), p. 120.

[2] Jeans, *op. cit.* p. 100.

[3] Pole, *Siemens*, p. 192; *Annals of Lloyd's Register*, p. 118.

self to meet the Admiralty challenge, and satisfied their most exacting requirements with a uniform mild steel which was adopted for the despatch vessels *Iris* and *Mercury* in 1876: hence what was called in the shipping world the "resurrection" of steel about the year 1877[1].

By the 'eighties steel uniform enough and cheap enough for some mercantile requirements was being made by both processes. By 1885 marine boilers were "scarcely ever built of iron."[2] The general adoption of steel for the hull had become simply a matter of cost. "No one questions the superiority of steel over iron for naval architecture. The only barrier to its exclusive use is one of price, which is due to considerations of a mechanical order in the rolling mill itself." This was Lowthian Bell's opinion in 1884[3]. Next year, his successor in the Presidency of the Institution of Mechanical Engineers was pointing out that "steel bars, angles or plates...of the quality required by Lloyd's ...cost about 46 per cent. more than if of ordinary wrought iron."[4]

The reluctance of shipbuilders to experiment much with steel plates before the mid 'seventies is easily understood. Iron had not been generally adopted for steamers before the decade 1855–65; only for some of the best sailing ships during the decade 1860–70. Quick change to yet another more expensive, more experimental, material was hardly to be expected in so ancient a craft, in view of the policy and rulings of Lloyd's and the Admiralty. There were even a few little wooden steamships on the stocks on September 30, 1875[5].

The iron sailing ship was known twenty-five years earlier. The Liverpool-built *Ironside* of 1830 is generally reckoned the first, because she was the first rated at Lloyd's[6]; but very possibly iron barges had gone under sail before that. The iron steamer was well known. So early as 1844 B. G. Willcox, managing director of the Peninsular and Oriental, had prophesied its victory, and in 1848 Money Wigram of the Blackwall

[1] The phrase is used in the *Annals of Lloyd's Register*, p. 119; for the Admiralty episode see Price, J., "On Iron and Steel as constructive Material for Ships," *Trans. Inst. Mech. Eng.* 1881, p. 553, and the discussion of the paper.

[2] Head in *Trans. Inst. Mech. Eng.* p. 319. [3] *Manufacture of Iron*, p. 460.

[4] Head, as above, p. 311.

[5] In fact six, of an aggregate tonnage of 1065. Cornewall-Jones, *op. cit.* p. 120.

[6] See *e.g.* Lubbock, Basil, *The Colonial Clippers* (1921), p. 200; *Annals of Lloyd's Register*, p. 75.

yard had allowed its great utility for "propeller ships," then recently introduced[1]. But of the 3,400,000 tons of sailing ships and the 170,000 tons of steamers registered under the red ensign in 1850, only a very tiny proportion was iron-built. The best-known steamers were not, except one or two belonging to the Peninsular and Oriental. The British and North American Royal Mail Steam Packets, as they were still officially described, although named popularly after their promoter and director Samuel Cunard, were all built of wood. The government which subsidised them required that they should be: it did not relax its requirement until 1856, when the iron *Persia*—paddle-wheel, 3766 tons—was built and engined by Robert Napier on the Clyde[2]. But, without any such constraint, their chief American rivals from 1850 to 1858, the Collins line of steamships, were also wood-built—of American live-oak and pitch pine[3].

At that time the wooden American clipper packets, the liners under their famous house flags, were still running in competition with steam. In the early years of the Cunard (1840–5) they had held their own without much difficulty, sometimes making their crossings in twelve to fourteen days—their captains, so it was believed in Liverpool, risking *delirium tremens* by keeping awake on black coffee[4]. As steamship competition began to tell, in the later 'forties, some of them were taken off the Liverpool beat and put into the new and immensely profitable trade round the Horn to California and the gold. But one of the most famous in chronicles of the sea, the *Dreadnought* of the Red Cross Line, was only launched in 1853 and only beaten out of the Atlantic trade by steam ten years later[5].

Wooden shipbuilding in Britain, throughout the age in which she won control of the world's seas by war and commerce, has an odd and, until its very last chapter, not a very glorious technical history. It is agreed that French warship design in the eighteenth century was better than English. Even in 1845 a British *Sanspareil* was planned on the lines of the *Sanspareil*

[1] Vol. I. p. 441.

[2] Napier had engined the Cunarders from the first and had helped to raise the original capital of the company in order that they might be as strong as he advised. Of the £270,000 initial capital Cunard had contributed £55,000. Napier, J., *Life of Robert Napier* (1904), p. 124 *sqq.* For the *Persia, ibid.* p. 192 *sqq.*

[3] Cornewall-Jones, *op. cit.* p. 134–5; Holmes, *op. cit.* II. 22, 29.

[4] Personal reminiscences of a Liverpool merchant: Lubbock, Basil, *The Western Ocean Packets* (1925).

[5] Lubbock, *The Colonial Clippers*, p. 12; *The Western Ocean Packets*, p. 59 *sqq.*

captured in 1794 from the French[1]. It has been suggested that American clipper design goes back to French models. Whether it does or not, there is no doubt about the superiority of American builders, at least down to the decade 1840–50. During more than twenty years after Waterloo the British mercantile marine grew little, if at all[2]. Building was for replacement; there was a good deal of replacement by 'colonial builts'; and design made no progress. The East Indiamen were fine bits of shipwrights' work, built expensively of the best materials, but built on old-fashioned lines. The Company's *Waterloo* looks as if she might have driven with Hawke into Quiberon Bay[3]. As the Company gradually ceased to do business in India, there was some falling off in the size and quality of the ships which carried the eastern trade[4]. Meanwhile the large purchases of 'colonial builts' were giving business and experience in design to the yards of Quebec, Nova Scotia and New Brunswick[5]. A few British owners were already building in the United States. James Aiken of Liverpool did so some time before 1833, because prices in Massachusetts were 30*s*. a ton lower than in Liverpool, where, it may be recalled, the shipwrights' union was difficult to deal with[6]. In 1844 another Liverpool owner had said that it was only possible to compete in the North Atlantic trade by "having North American ships....We could not sail British ships in that trade."[7]

There remained, however, the eastward trades—the Mediterranean, the Cape, India, and especially after the gold discoveries the rush trade to Australia. Here was room enough. Some of the finest ships in the Australian trade of the 'fifties were American built for British owners. American-built and American-owned clippers joined in the tea races from China until 1859; but ever since the early 'forties there had been effective British-built competitors. The years between 1837 and 1848 had seen a revival in British design[8],

[1] She was never launched. Clowes, *History of the British Navy*, VI. 191. And see Holmes, *op. cit.* I. 125, 486–7.

[2] Vol. I. p. 1–2.

[3] See her picture in Morse, H. B., *The Chronicles of the East India Co. trading to China* (1926), Vol. IV. frontispiece.

[4] Lubbock, Basil, *The Blackwall Frigates* (1922), p. 44.

[5] For Canadian ship-building see *Cambridge Hist. of the British Empire*, VI. (1930), 569 *sqq.*; Wallace, F. W., *Wooden Ships and Iron Men* (1924); *In the Wake of the Wind Ships* (1927); *Record of Canadian Shipping* (1929).

[6] *S.C. on Commerce and Industry*, 1833 (VI. 1), Q. 7172 *sqq.* For the Union, Vol. I. p. 212–13.

[7] *S.C. on British Shipping*, 1844 (VIII. 1), Q. 770.

[8] See Cornewall-Jones, *op. cit.* p. 233; Lubbock, *The China Clippers*, p. 144 *sqq.*

which had been preceded by the cheapening and improvement of all the innumerable adjuncts of a wooden ship which are not made of wood. A ship is not made all of wood, "like a box," as Cobden used to say to those who argued that the dearness of timber in Britain justified both dear building and protection[1].

Historians of ships date the beginning of the revival from the launch of the *Seringapatam* from Green's Blackwall yard in 1837[2]. She headed the long and glorious line of the Blackwall frigates, built for first-class passenger and cargo traffic and for speed. They were not technically clippers; rather vastly improved East Indiamen. 'Dicky' Green died in 1863. "Whilst he lived iron ships were not even hinted at in the Blackwall yard."[3] Within a few years of the launch of the *Seringapatam*, ships of the same type were being built by Laing and by Marshall, both of Sunderland. The 'Blackwallers' at first were small as compared with the old East Indiamen; well under 1000 tons against the East Indiaman's normal 1300. By the end of the 'fifties a representative group of them averaged 1050 tons. Laing built up to 1500 tons, and the last Blackwaller built on the Thames was of 1857 tons. She was launched in 1875—and she was of iron[4].

As their name implies, Green's ships had points in common with the newer type of Royal Navy frigate, designed for speed since the close of the French wars. The British ships which first challenged the American clippers in style, though not in size, were those built by Hall of Aberdeen in the early 'forties[5]. When the Australian passenger trade suddenly rose into importance in 1851–2 Liverpool owners, with their long experience of American building, placed their principal orders in Massachusetts, Nova Scotia and New Brunswick—above all, Massachusetts[6]. It was Donald McKay, a Nova Scotian domiciled in Boston, who built for James Baines' Black Ball line perhaps the most famous all-wood sailing ships of the 'fifties, among them the *Donald McKay* herself, launched in 1855 while Bessemer was working at his steel problem, a ship which on six consecutive voyages

[1] Speech of June 9, 1848. Hansard, XCIX. 605.

[2] Lubbock, *The Blackwall Frigates*, p. 150; Chatterton, E. K., *The Ship under Sail* (1926), p. 134.

[3] Lubbock, *The Blackwall Frigates*, p. 103.

[4] Lubbock, *ibid.* p. 274, 290; Chatterton, p. 134.

[5] Lubbock, *The China Clippers*, p. 108.

[6] Lubbock, *The Colonial Clippers*, p. 22 *sqq*.

from Liverpool to Melbourne averaged eighty-three days[1]. But some of the Aberdeen clippers of the later 'fifties, of the Aberdeen White Star Line, though smaller, were at least as good. Among them the *Maid of Judah* passed the heads at Sydney seventy-eight days out from London in 1860. From Hall's yard in Aberdeen had come also the first British tea clippers for the China trade, the *Stornoway* and *Chrysolite* of 1851[2].

These are only a few names from the last and the great age of the British sailing ship. How active construction and purchase were are shown by the figures of the shipping register. In the quarter of a century preceding 1850 British sailing tonnage had grown from some 2,400,000 to 3,400,000: during the next fifteen years, in spite of a rapid increase of steamer tonnage, it reached its absolute maximum of 4,936,776 tons, manned by 158,000 seamen (1865). There were important purchases of American clippers from bankrupt American firms after the commercial collapse in the United States in 1857[3], and purchases in British America were continuous; but there was also very great building activity on the Thames, the Mersey, the Wear, the Clyde and the Dee, and on many a lesser estuary and harbour. Shoreham in 1850 could build up to 500 tons, ships "remarkable for swift sailing."[4] There were seventy-one builders of wooden ships at Sunderland in 1857[5]. Rye was still able to launch a 200 tonner in the early 'seventies[6]. In years of active building such as 1863–5, 1868–9, or 1875–6 the United Kingdom could turn out a sailing tonnage of 230,000 and more. The absolute maximum was 275,000 tons in 1864[7].

Since the 'forties there had always been a few iron sailing ships on the register. By 1865, although people did not build with iron at Shoreham or Rye, its use was familiar in the greater places. Iron steamers had shown the way. The difficulty of procuring 'great timbers' for vessels of any size had long harassed the Admiralty[8]. To the mercantile builder of big clipper ships iron came as a cheap and most efficient substitute. Experience showed that an iron-framed ship could be driven

[1] Lubbock, *The Colonial Clippers*, p. 83–4; Cornewall-Jones, *op. cit.* p. 230; McKay, R. C., *Some Famous Sailing Ships and their builder Donald McKay* (1928).

[2] Lubbock, *The China Clippers*, p. 110; *The Log of the Cutty Sark*, p. 46; Cornewall-Jones, *op. cit.* p. 230.

[3] Lubbock, *The Colonial Clippers*, p. 113.

[4] *V.C.H. Sussex*, II. 234–5.

[5] *V.C.H. Durham*, II. 304.

[6] *V.C.H. Sussex*, as above.

[7] *Tables Showing the Progress of Merchant Shipping*, 1902 (Cd. 329), p. 56.

[8] Albion, *Forests and Sea Power*, *passim*.

harder into a head sea, but that copper-sheathed wood fouled less, and so sailed quicker, than the iron-plates of those days. As racing clippers must be driven hard and brought home quick, the composite structure—planks on an iron frame—had much in its favour. The method came in with the new half-century, the first composite on Lloyd's list being the *Tubal Cain* of 1851[1]. Among the earlier composites to acquire notoriety was the *Red Riding Hood* of 1857 built by a Rotherhithe firm[2]. From 1863, a series of composite clippers was ordered by the Aberdeen Orient Line from this same firm and from Hall of Aberdeen. In 1867 came the *Thyatira* of 962 tons, the first composite clipper of the Aberdeen White Star Line. And so to the composite *Cutty Sark*, laid down by a Dumbarton firm that failed, and finished there by Denny in 1869, the surviving memorial of this great shipbuilding era[3].

Composite building was a by-product of the transition from wood to iron, and it became specialised to the racing clippers. Among other groups of high-class sailing vessels the transition went straight forward. By 1855 Lloyd's Register had issued complete and satisfactory rules for the survey and classification of iron ships. The rules were intended for steamers, but they facilitated the building of iron sailing ships. It is significant that the draft on which they were based was sent in by Lloyd's surveyors on the Clyde, now the headquarters of an industry which in earlier years had been more prominent on the Mersey and the Thames[4]. Apart from its cheapness and strength, the iron sailing ship was in far less danger from fire than the old wooden ship; and what that meant in reduction of human misery, and of insurance, a very little acquaintance with the stories of fire on the high seas will show. Plates of a maximum thickness of $1\frac{1}{16}$ ins. and light girder framework gave the iron ship great carrying capacity. In no country could it be built so cheaply and so well as in the United Kingdom.

Although many iron sailing ships were launched in the

[1] *Annals of Lloyd's Register*, p. 84. But the partial use of iron framing went back to 1810–15. Wood, Sir H. T., *A Hist. of the Royal Society of Arts*, p. 255.

[2] Lubbock, *The Colonial Clippers*, p. 147.

[3] Lubbock, *The Log of the Cutty Sark*, p. 31–2.

[4] *Annals of Lloyd's Register*, p. 76; vol. I. p. 439–40. Robert Napier, who at first built only engines, began iron shipbuilding in 1841. *Life*, p. 149. William Denny was his draftsman, John Elder his engine-shop manager; "most of the leading firms on the river were founded by men who had worked with him and his cousin David." *Ibid.* p. 243. Cp. Glover, J., "On the decline of shipbuilding on the Thames," *S.J.* 1869; where the causes are discussed.

'fifties, their great age was the twenty years from 1860 to 1880, and their principal beat the Australian trade. Throughout this period, and much later, they ran the southern wool. But they sailed on all seas. In 1866 Blackwall yard built the *Superb* of iron, 'Dicky' Green being dead[1]. When T. H. Ismay bought the flag of the Liverpool White Star clippers in 1867, he and his partners ran iron sailing ships for a time[2]. The Aberdeen White Star built its first iron clipper in 1869. The Orient Line followed in 1873. In 1875—the year in which the last Sunderland-built wooden ship was launched[3]—there was built on the Clyde what was believed to be the finest sailing ship afloat, the iron *Loch Garry* of 1500 tons, the first of a line of *Lochs* very prominent in the long-haul trades of the late nineteenth century. For about another ten years such vessels were built of iron. Then began the hybrid age of steel and sails; for to the very end of the nineteenth century there were "many branches of commerce in which sailing ships" might "be more profitably employed than steamers."[4] There may still be a few.

Profitable employment for iron ocean steamers was a little uncertain when, in the early spring of 1850, Tod and MacGregor had launched the screw steamer *City of Glasgow* of 1600 tons. Four years later she put to sea with nearly five hundred souls and was heard of no more; but in her short life she had acted as pioneer to the first line of Atlantic iron steamers—the Liverpool, New York and Philadelphia Steamship Company, the creation of William Inman. Built as a speculation, she was bought by the Company late in 1850. Next year, Tod and MacGregor supplied the bigger *City of Manchester*, which was followed by a succession of *Cities*—among them a solitary *Kangaroo*—with clipper bows and bowsprit and square-rigging on the fore and main masts. When the wooden Collins line broke down, under stress of an abnormal series of losses at sea and the American financial crisis of 1857, Inman adopted their sailing days, started a weekly service from New York, and secured the contract for the United States mail. By that time the Cunard was building of iron, but its first iron screw steamer for the Atlantic trade, the *China*, was not ordered until 1862[5].

[1] Lubbock, *The Blackwall Frigates*, p. 282.

[2] Kennedy, J., *The History of Steam Navigation* (1903), p. 301.

[3] *V.C.H. Durham*, II. 304. [4] Cornewall-Jones, *op. cit.* (1898), p. 237.

[5] Kennedy, *op. cit.* p. 106, 107, 227. Kennedy wrote from Liverpool with local knowledge. Holmes, *op. cit.* II. 30.

It is not easy to determine exactly what effect the extraordinary episode of the *Great Eastern*, at once an example and a warning, had on the transition to the iron screw passenger steamer. The designing in 1852–3 of an iron steamer with both paddles and screw, 675 feet long and 83 feet wide as against the *City of Manchester's* 274 by 38 feet, showed what could be dared and accomplished. She was launched in January, 1858, or rather floated off sideways by a spring tide, at the fourth attempt; for her builders had decided to put that huge length into the Thames broadside on[1]. She had a thirty years' life. But she ruined her builder, Scott Russell of Millwall, and a multitude of shareholders who could not pay their calls; and she was sold unfinished, in the year of her launching, for little more than the launching had cost. She was completed with the aid of capital subscribed by "persons in the humblest ranks of life, domestic servants, costermongers, greengrocers and labourers."[2] Her completion had become a point of national honour, a sporting event which must be brought off; but she never paid the costermongers. After eight years of unprofitable uses, ten of considerable utility as a cable layer (1866–75) led to an inglorious old age on the Mersey as a floating signboard for a great retail "department" shop. She was broken up in 1888. "Her owners at this time were probably the only persons who ever realised a handsome profit out of her."[3] During her lifetime, first-rate Atlantic steamers had grown from the 274 × 38 feet of the *City of Manchester* to the 515 × 52 feet of the steel-built Cunarder *Servia*, with compound engines and incandescent electric lamps, the wonder-ship of the early 'eighties[4]. The *Great Eastern* was well before her time; but the mere building of her had been among the chief mechanical feats of the century.

The wooden paddle steamer before 1850 had carried passengers, mails and valuable cargoes, both on the narrow seas and the oceans, but had not touched bulk cargoes. By 1850–51 the new railways were damaging the coal trade between the North-East coast and the Thames. To meet this competition C. M.

[1] This was not a novelty. James Napier, Robert's brother, had prophesied failure on the basis of his own experience with broadside launches. *Life of Robert Napier*, p. 42.

[2] *The Illustrated London News*, Aug. 13, 1859. The *I.L.N.* is one of the best sources for the story of the *Great Eastern*. And see Kennedy, *op. cit.* p. 119 *sqq.*

[3] Kennedy, *op. cit.* p. 127. The shameful end of the *Great Eastern* came almost as a personal disgrace to schoolboys of the 'eighties who had learnt all about her from such books as Kingston, W. H. G., *The Boys' Own Book of Boats*.

[4] Kennedy, *op. cit.* p. 230.

Palmer of Newcastle had an iron screw collier built and named *John Bowes*. In five days' steaming she did work which two sailing colliers could not have done in a month. Neither prejudice nor the vested interests of the very ancient coastwise sailing trade could resist such obvious efficiency. Besides, the screw colliers solved the commissariat problem in the Crimean War. By 1864 they carried over 900,000 tons of coal to London alone, one of them, the *James Dixon*, with a crew of twenty-one, doing in a year work which would have occupied sixteen sailing colliers and 144 men. Iron steamers, Palmer wrote in that year, did "most of the carrying trade of the Baltic and Mediterranean"[1]—a great exaggeration, but true of that coal export business on which the British bulk-cargo steamer trade of the late nineteenth century was founded.

The iron screw liners of the 'fifties and 'sixties, like their wooden paddle predecessors, were primarily passenger and mail boats. But in 1863 the National Steam Navigation Company was started at Liverpool with a special view to cargo—the carrying trade of the seceded Southern States of the American Union. The trade was not as anticipated; but the Company did well; ran the biggest steamers of the 'sixties; and put into one of them, the *Italy* of 1868, the first compound engines ever used on an Atlantic liner[2].

'Compounding,' the use of the expansive power of steam at different pressures in two or more cylinders, had been patented by Jonathan Hornblower in 1781. Boulton and Watt broke him, on a different count, for infringement of patent. In 1810 Arthur Woolf, who had been a millwright under the great Bramah, patented another two-cylinder engine. But compound expansion, "the only great improvement which the steam engine had undergone since the time of Watt,"[3] did not come into general use during the early railway age, on land or sea—partly because of the dangers of high-pressure steam in the weak boilers of those days. For beam engines of the ordinary Watt type it was revived by M'Naught in 1845. Factory and other engines were 'M'Naughted,' made more powerful and more economical, by the addition of a small high-pressure cylinder. Then, in 1854–6, John Elder applied the principle to the marine engine on the Clyde. But this was only a beginning:

[1] *Industrial Resources of the Tyne, Wear and Tees* (1864), p. 247. Palmer's article on iron shipbuilding.

[2] Kennedy, *op. cit.* p. 109, 301.

[3] Ewing, J. A., *The steam-engine and other heat engines* (1894 ed.), p. 24.

great advances in engine and boiler making were necessary before the compound could drive out its predecessors. Boiler-pressures, for example, in the early 'fifties were seldom above 20 or 25 lbs. to the square inch. Twenty years later, when compound engines were really coming in, they ranged from 45 to 65 lbs.; in 1881, with the advent of triple-expansion, a list of typical new engines gives a mean of 77 lbs.[1]

The Peninsular and Oriental Company put compound engines into the *Mooltan* in 1860–1. There was considerable fuel economy and the experiment was repeated. But the engines proved untrustworthy and were all pulled out. Only in 1869 did the Company secure a set of "high and low pressure machinery which could be regarded as thoroughly satisfactory."[2] Between 1863 and 1872, the fuel consumption of good new marine engines was reduced by one half[3]: that left room for cargo. Meanwhile the Suez Canal had offered all the seas of the East to the iron or steel ship and the compound engine.

Movement became swift, and steam took over the heavy carrying on route after route. It is possible that even the 901,000 steamship tons on the British register in 1865 did more transport work than the 4,937,000 sailing tons of the same year; certain that the 1,900,000 steamer tons of 1875 did more than the 4,200,000 sailing tons of 1875. In 1882 the mounting curve of the steamer tonnage crossed the descending curve of the sailing ships. By 1885, the nearly 4,000,000 steamer tons with their 108,000 men may have done from six to seven times the work of the 3,400,000 tons of sailers and their 91,000 men.

While the mercantile marine was being thus transformed, the fishing fleet had changed more in the size, disposition and functions of its units than in their material or motive power. In the 'thirties and early 'forties the British fisheries had, as a whole, been in a poor way. Boats were small; deep-sea work was neglected; fishermen and their advocates were wailing about foreign competition—Frenchmen well within the three mile limit; even dragging our bays for bait at seasons which were closed in their own. In 1833 it was the considered opinion

[1] Marshall, F. C., "On the Progress and Development of the Marine Engine," *Trans. Inst. Mech. Eng.* 1881, p. 449 *sqq.* See also Wyllie, R., *ibid.* 1886, p. 473 for triple-expansion in the early 'eighties. For Elder, the *D.N.B.* He introduced the triple-expansion engine in 1881. For the compound locomotive, below, p. 180.

[2] Kennedy, *op. cit.* p. 54, quoting Sir Thos. Sutherland of the P. and O.

[3] Jeans, *Creators of the Age of Steel*, p. 147.

of a Select Committee that from Yarmouth to the Land's End the fisheries had been gradually declining since the peace[1]. Trawling, well known in the West Country, especially to the men of Brixham, was hardly practised in the North Sea at all, and it was declining in the Channel. At Hull the first trawler was seen in the year of the Reform Bill[2]. The trade had come up from the West by way of Ramsgate. Trawlers were pushing out beyond the Inner Silver Pit and the Sole Pit in the late 'thirties. In the hard winter of 1843 they first worked the Great Silver Pit under the Dogger Bank with amazing results. But they were still few and small. Hull's twenty-one fishing smacks ran only from 23 to 32 tons in 1844–5; by 1883 she had four hundred first-class trawlers, of from 65 to 90 tons, and some hundreds of lesser craft[3]. Grimsby had more, first-class trawlers and line cod-fishing smacks. Trawling only began there in 1858, "when four or five smacks migrated thither from Hull,"[4] the year before the railway to Grimsby was completed; but the deep-sea line fishing was older. From Yarmouth and Lowestoft and many other ports on the East coast, especially Peterhead and Aberdeen, the herring drifters went out in their season as they had long gone. Their numbers and size also increased and their design improved from about 1850, though they never ran so big as the trawlers. Some West coast fisheries also developed, but the great activity and improvement was on the East. By 1878, out of 176,000 tons of fish carried inland by rail in England and Wales, 124,000 came from Grimsby, Hull, Yarmouth and Lowestoft, and 59,000 from Grimsby alone[5].

Apart from the railway, nothing had done more to develop deep-sea trawling than the use of ice, introduced by Samuel Hewett for his trawler fleet based on Yarmouth about 1855[6]. The ice was imported from Norway or stored in ice-houses from English winter supplies. Last came steam; but its work was subsidiary down to the 'eighties. Between 1865 and 1875 the cutter rigged carriers which raced the fish home to market began to be replaced by steamers, and tugs helped drifters and

[1] Vol. I. p. 322: *S.C. on British Channel Fisheries*, 1833 (XIV. 69), an excellent report.

[2] *R.C. on Trawling*, 1885 (XVI. 471). Evidence of A. Rollit for the Hull smack-owners, Q. 8648. See in general Holdsworth, E. W. H., *Deep Sea Fishing and Fishing Boats*, 1874, based on the *Commission on Sea Fisheries* of 1866, of which Holdsworth was secretary.

[3] *R.C. on Trawling*, Q. 8631, 8627.

[4] Holdsworth, *op. cit.* p. 251.

[5] *R.C. on Trawling*, *App.* C IV.

[6] Holdsworth, *op. cit.* p. 244–5.

trawlers out and back. Late in the 'seventies—when trawling had got to the Great Fisher Bank off Jutland, and the trawlers at times could "almost sight the Naze of Norway"[1]—the steam trawler appeared, first in numbers on the Forth, where trawling of any sort was a recent development. Between 1879 and 1883 twelve steam trawlers were registered at Leith; between 1881 and 1883 nine at Granton, where there was a trawler-owning company. By the end of 1883 there were said to be about thirty in all Scotland[2]. Hull, with its four hundred first-class boats, had "none that go by steam except the carriers and cutters," and Grimsby had a single one[3]. Nor was there much progress in the years 1883–6. Prices were falling and boat-building of all sorts was slack. Only four steam trawlers were built in Scotland in 1886; and when an Inspector of the Fisheries for England and Wales issued a first jejune report in the following year, all that he found to say about trawlers and steam was that most of the trawlers were "fitted with steam capstans" for hauling in the nets[4].

The metal-built ship of the 'eighties, with its improved engines, would hardly have been possible, would certainly not have been possible at the price, but for the exact methods and the new ways of handling steel introduced into British engineering by Whitworth, and the extended use of hydraulic machinery which is connected particularly with the name of Armstrong. Whitworth had employed his true planes in his own Manchester workshop in the 'thirties; had made his methods public in 1840; and had communicated to the Institute of Civil Engineers his scheme for standardising screws, screw threads, and other mechanical essentials in 1841; but, ten years later, when his whole series of patented machine tools, his gauges adjusted to the ten-thousandth part of an inch, and his system of standardised screws and machine parts were praised in chorus by the jury of the Great Exhibition, although the jurymen spoke of the "great extension" which his system of standards had "already obtained," what evidently most impressed them was

[1] *R.C. on Trawling*, Q. 8655. [2] *Ibid.* Q. 5410 and *passim.*

[3] *Ibid.* Hull, Q. 8640; Grimsby, Q. 9182. I am informed however that the Grimsby and North Sea Trawling Coy. formed in 1881 had two, the *Aries* and the *Zodiac*, before 1883.

[4] There had been regular Scottish reports for several years and Irish for many. The English and Scottish for 1887 here quoted are in *A. and P.* 1887, XXI. 147 and 245.

the vast field still to be occupied, and the "confusion and delay" of an unstandardised mechanical world. This too was what most impressed Dr Whewell when he was summoned to lecture on the Exhibition to the people[1].

From the height of an established renown Whitworth was preaching to his fellow engineers in the 'fifties. "I cannot impress too strongly on...this institution," he told the Mechanical Engineers in 1856, "and upon all in any way connected with mechanism, the vast importance of possessing a true plane, as a standard for reference. All excellence in workmanship depends upon it....Next in importance to a true plane is the power of measurement,"[2] which his measuring machine and his gauges provided. This is hardly the tone which a preacher uses to the converted. In the matter of the bolts and screws he had eventually a very complete success. "Now," an admirer wrote in 1885, two years before Whitworth's death, "every marine engine and every locomotive in this country has the same screw for every given diameter. His system...has been adopted throughout the world, wherever engines and machinery are manufactured, the dies for producing the whole series having been originally furnished from his works at Manchester."[3] Working to gauge also spread rapidly in the 'fifties and 'sixties, so that in the more advanced sections of the engineering industry, such as textile engineering, machine parts became perfectly interchangeable. It was no longer necessary, as it once had been, to fit each several spindle in a cotton mill into its bolster by hand. Yet so late as 1886, the President of the Institution of Mechanical Engineers, when recapitulating to his colleagues those things which had "impressed themselves strongly upon" them in their recent visits to engineering shops of the first rank, laid special stress on the practice of "working to gauges throughout."[4] Evidently that practice was not yet among the things which no one need mention.

The individualistic and wilful young engineering industry and the users of engines, during the third quarter of the nineteenth century, were willing to accept the standardisation of a few essentials such as screws, but no more. Perhaps this was a

[1] The report is quoted in most accounts of Whitworth, *e.g.* Jeans, *Creators of the Age of Steel*, p. 228. And see vol. I. p. 446. Much of Whitworth's work was based on that of Maudslay, *e.g.* the 'Whitworth' true plane. *James Nasmyth, an Autobiography* (2nd ed. 1885), p. 144.

[2] *Trans. Inst. Mech. Eng.* 1856, p. 127.

[3] Jeans, *op. cit.* p. 224.

[4] *Trans. Inst. Mech. Eng.* 1886, p. 225.

good thing, if premature rigidity of machine types was to be avoided. Yet the multiplicity of types and specialities, natural as it was in an age of development, had great drawbacks. An extreme instance is that of the locomotive. Before 1850, in the hands of Robert Stephenson and others, it had attained a relatively high level of perfection, as the long lives of some early locomotives and the slight differences between an average locomotive of 1845–50 and one of 1880–85 show. Stephenson's *North Star*, sold to the Great Western in 1837, ran, with a new boiler, until 1870. A long-boiler engine built by him for the Great Eastern in 1847, and rebuilt in 1867, worked on into the 'eighties. An engine of Bury's, built in 1838, served the Furness Railway for sixty years. Yet this almost stabilised machine continued to be turned out to innumerable patterns[1]. "Probably five distinct classes of locomotives would afford a variety sufficiently accommodating to suit the varied traffic of railways," an expert wrote in 1855, "whereas I suppose the varieties of locomotive in actual operation in this country and elsewhere are very nearly five hundred." He suggested standardisation of classes but doubted "if such an arrangement could be worked out unless there were entire amalgamation of railway interests."[2] Seventy years later some such arrangement was being discussed in Britain and attained in Germany after the compulsory transfer of old-fashioned locomotives to the victorious allies.

William Armstrong, a lawyer by profession, had already patented an hydraulic crane and made other inventions when he took over the management of the Elswick works in 1847. There he proceeded to develop hydraulic machinery of every kind—cranes, lifts, capstans, swing and draw-bridges, lock-gates and sluices, grain elevators, pumps, pit winding engines, and mechanism for the movement of land and sea turrets[3]. The work was spread over a generation during which, after the first ten years, more of Armstrong's energies were directed towards munitions and ordnance than towards the things of peace. This side of his work culminated in the opening of the Elswick yard for the building of warships in 1882. Whitworth had been brought into official contact with munitions problems by the

[1] Warren, J. G. H., *A Century of Locomotive Building by Robert Stephenson and Coy.* (1923), p. 339, 355, 329.

[2] Clark, D. K., *Railway Machinery*, 1855, p. vii, quoted in Warren, p. 414.

[3] Important papers by or about Armstrong and his works are in the *Trans. Inst. Mech. Eng.* for 1858, 1868, 1869, 1874, 1881. And see the *D.N.B.*

invitation given him in 1854, at the time of the establishment of the government factory at Enfield, to construct rifle-making machinery for the state. He had decided that it was first necessary to find out experimentally what sort of a rifle ought to be made, and had evolved the type that bore his name, which the state did not adopt. From rifles he proceeded to Whitworth guns, which had their earliest, and very successful, field trials on the Confederate side in the American Civil War. By 1868 he had built a gun of position which could throw a shot weighing 250 lbs. to a distance of six miles and a half.

Meanwhile the small-arms demand had quickened mass-production and team work by machines. America began it. The government armouries of the United States had experimented with machine-made interchangeable parts in the 'twenties. About 1840, Blanshard's lathe for cutting irregular forms had been applied to gun-stocks at the Springfield arsenal. Samuel Colt's revolver, invented in the 'thirties, got its first mass demand from the Californian "forty-niners," and fascinated the old Duke of Wellington at the Great Exhibition. Colt used machinery and made his parts interchangeable. After the Exhibition he brought the machinery to England for use in a factory at Pimlico[1]. Before the government small-arms factory was founded at Enfield, a commission of inquiry was sent to the United States. In 1858 the factory was equipped with American machinery[2]. At Leeds a team of twenty-one machines had been installed earlier to meet the Crimean demand for cartridges[3]. Subsequently, at Birmingham, the Small Arms Trade Association of masters in the wonderfully subdivided Birmingham handicraft gun trade set up the first B.S.A. factory, with stock-making machines from America and rifling and boring machines from Leeds[4].

The story of munitions and ships of war is a thing apart; but its significance for industrial history, great at all times and

[1] Nasmyth's *Autobiography* (ed. 1885), p. 348.

[2] Bolles, *Ind. Hist. of the U.S.A.*, p. 254–6. *Birmingham and the Midland Hardware District* (1886), p. 396 *sqq.* Allen, G. C., *The Industrial Development of Birmingham and the Black Country* (1929), p. 188 *sqq.* Burn, D. L., "The Genesis of American Engineering Competition, 1850–70," *E.J.* (*Ec. Hist.*), 1931.

[3] Meysey-Thompson, A. H., "On the History of Engineering in Leeds," *Trans. Inst. Mech. Eng.* 1882, p. 270.

[4] *Birmingham and the Midland Hardware District*, p. 403 *sqq.*; Goodman, J. D., "On the Progress of the Small Arms Manufacture," *S.J.* 1865, p. 494.

in all stages of industrial development[1], was never greater than during the early years of the age of exact workmanship, hydraulic machinery, and steel. The war departments of states were the metal-working inventor's ideal clients, clients whose demand for absolute strength of material and absolute perfection of workmanship was, or at least should have been, completely inelastic at all times, and in war time might become unlimited. As President of the Institute of Mechanical Engineers in September, 1856, Whitworth had welcomed the prospect which Bessemer's recent announcement held out of securing "iron and steel of a better quality."[2] His later experiments with ordnance convinced him that neither any kind of iron, hitherto exclusively used for gun-making, nor the new hard Bessemer steel in its ordinary state was what he required. Throughout the 'sixties he worked at the problem of compressing steel by hydraulic machinery while it was still fluid. His patent was taken out in 1865, but he was not ready to begin work on a commercial scale for another four years. By that time the uniform metal produced by the Siemens-Martin process was just coming on to the market[3]. It was the best material yet offered to be squeezed by Whitworth's hydraulic plungers into a compressed steel with a maximum both of strength and of ductility[4].

Devised primarily for guns, compressed steel soon found other uses. As ships of all kinds grew bigger, better material than wrought iron was needed for engine and propeller shafts. Compressed steel was used for the propeller shafts of the *Inflexible*, then the heaviest ship in the British navy, in 1876. Within a few years, Whitworth's shafting, made hollow like a gun so as to combine lightness with strength, was being employed in the mercantile marine. It was not merely light and strong. "The surface presented by a steel shaft to the bearings," F. C. Marshall of Newcastle wrote in 1881, "is also—it is not too much to say—almost infinitely more perfect than by the forged iron shaft, with its reeds, open texture, and iron cinder, from which engineers suffer so much. The friction must there-

[1] See the argument in Sombart, W., *Krieg und Kapitalismus*, 1913, and the modified argument in his *Moderne Kapitalismus*, 3rd ed. 1919, *passim*, and especially vol. I. p. 750 *sqq*.

[2] *Trans. Inst. Mech. Eng.* 1856, p. 126.

[3] Above, p. 63.

[4] See *inter alia* Carbutt, E. H., "Fifty years progress in Gun Making," *Trans. Inst. Mech. Eng.* 1887, p. 167.

fore be greatly reduced."[1] He spoke from experience, having just finished six pairs of engines with steel shafts. He was still using wrought iron piston and connecting rods, but was of opinion that, for large steamers, "steel-built crank shafts must come more and more into use. The constant failure of iron cranks...is too serious a question for the shipowner to let alone long." The *City of Rome*, the second largest steamship afloat, just launched for the Inman Line, had a hollow built-up crank-shaft of Whitworth compressed steel[2]. So the transition of the 'eighties to the steel ship proceeded alongside of the transition to the all-steel engine within it.

Whitworth died—in 1887—before compressed steel had occupied more than a small part of the available field. He was anxious to see it employed in the construction of railway rolling-stock, because its use would lead to a great reduction in the dead weight hauled. But it was not at this time, nor in Britain, that the compressed steel underbody was generally adopted for railway vehicles[3]. Whitworth did however see in his last years great extensions in that making of machines by machines which his work had done so much to facilitate, even though "working to gauges throughout" was not yet universal. Wood-working machinery of all kinds, stimulated to rivalry by a rush of American machines in the late 'seventies, was making especially rapid progress in the early 'eighties[4]. In some ways it called for more ingenuity in the making, and more skill in the handling, than metal-working machinery; because the cutting tools of the latter move at fairly constant paces, at angles which vary little, through a material tolerably uniform; whereas no two woods are alike in density or grain; they must be cut at different angles; and tool speeds may vary, or rather did vary at that time, from 500 to 8000 feet a minute[4]. In average metal-working shops, although the "leading tools," the lathe and the plane, had

[1] "On the Progress and Development of the Marine Engine," *Trans. Inst. Mech. Eng.* 1881, p. 475.

[2] *Trans. Inst. Mech. Eng.* 1880, p. 341: an account of the ship while building at Barrow.

[3] There were very few in 1885. Head, J., Presidential Address: *Trans. Inst. Mech. Eng.* 1885, p. 321.

[4] Richards, G., "Recent Improvements in Woodcutting Machinery," *ibid.* p. 77 *sqq.* See also the *Trans.* for 1886, p. 275, the Presidential Address. The extensive use of wood-working machinery in America had been reported on by Wallis and Whitworth, commissioners to the New York Exhibition of 1853–4, in 1854; and America continued to lead during the next twenty years. Burn, D. L., in *E. J.* (*Ec. Hist.*), Jan. 1931, p. 294, 299.

been altered very little "from their original forms,"[1] hydraulic machinery was coming in both for flanging and riveting; multiple punching and multiple drilling were becoming common and were displacing labour; and the rapid growth of the cycle industry at Coventry was providing fresh work for that stamping machinery which, in its simpler forms, had long been regularly used by the light metal trades of the Birmingham area[2].

The revolution in steel-making and the more exact engineering of the generation which followed the Great Exhibition reacted continuously on the older mechanised industries. Wood was not used in any new textile mill except for a few special purposes. Driving engines became steadily more powerful and more efficient. By continuous minor improvements, the driven machinery was made more completely automatic. The beautiful accuracy of its steel parts turned out to gauge made quicker running easy, and replacement swift. All through the labour story of these years runs the problem of 'speeding up.' But, in the cotton industry at least, there was no outstanding mechanical innovation, unless the introduction of Heilmann's comb in the early 'fifties, in place of the final carding process for cotton destined for the finest yarns, or that of ring-spinning on the frame, from America in the 'seventies, be so regarded. The comb, once introduced, changed little in thirty years; but it was used for coarser and coarser counts—down to 40's and 30's instead of 200's or 300's as at first—and, like all other machines, it was much speeded up[3]. Ring-spinning of warp yarns, well established in the United States before 1860, was still experimental in Britain in the late 'seventies. We cannot yet say "what is [its] proper position...in the economy of the cotton trade," an expert wrote in 1880[4]. Its really rapid introduction began only with the 'nineties.

Meanwhile the self-acting mule made steady, if slow, progress. "Before the cotton famine (1861–4) some hesitancy existed in people's minds as to whether [it] was a complete

[1] Meysey-Thompson, A. H., in *Trans.* 1882, p. 269.

[2] Head's Presidential Address, 1886; *Trans.* p. 275 *sqq.*

[3] See Platt, J., "On Machinery for the Preparing and Spinning of Cotton," and Spencer, Eli, "Recent Improvements in the Machinery for Preparing and Spinning Cotton"; *Trans. Inst. Mech. Eng.* 1866 and 1880.

[4] Spencer, Eli, as above, p. 527; and see Chapman, S. J., *The Lancashire Cotton Industry*, p. 71 n.

success, and it was only the more venturous spinners who would order a complete concern of self-actors."[1] Thereafter its final conquest of coarse spinning was rapid; of fine spinning long drawn out. "For spinning the finest counts...the hand-mule has been brought to great perfection," Eli Spencer of Oldham wrote so late as 1880[2]. He added that it was becoming more automatic; that the spinner had only "to supply the little power required to control some of the motions"; and that, even so, "men of first class ability as spinners became scarcer year by year." Two years later the operatives' secretary for the Bolton area, a home of the very finest spinning, reported that in the five years since 1877 the number of pairs of hand-mules in his district had fallen from 1300 to 516, and that their ultimate extinction was certain[3]. Extinction is said to have come in Glasgow about 1887. In English Pennine valleys a very few hand-mules could still be found at the opening of the twentieth century[4].

Meanwhile, taking the spinning industry as a whole—mules and frames and all preparing machinery—the changing relation of labour to machines, and the changes in the machines themselves, had produced these results[5]:

	Number of operatives in spinning mills	Yarn produced per operative in lbs.
1844–6	190,000	2,800
1859–61	248,000	3,700
1880–82	240,000	5,500

As an effective element of the industry, the hand-loom had long been extinct. True, even in 1891–2, a German inquirer found a few grey-headed men and women, in well-lighted cellars at Bolton, weaving by hand "counter-panes of peculiar patterns ...with words woven in, mostly Bible verses." They had an "almost fanatically out-spoken determination to be the last of their trade, and to teach their handicraft to no younger person." The grandchildren worked in the factories, where they earned "three times as much" as their grandparents[6]. But so early as 1856 the cotton hand-looms which had survived the turn of the

[1] Andrew, S., *Fifty Years of the Cotton Trade* (1887), quoted in Chapman, *op. cit.* p. 70.
[2] As above, p. 516.
[3] Chapman, *op. cit.* p. 71.
[4] From personal information.
[5] Schulze-Gävernitz, G. von, *The Cotton Trade in England and on the Continent* (Eng. trans. 1895), p. 99, based on Ellison, T., *The Cotton Trade of Great Britain* (1886), p. 66, 68.
[6] Schulze-Gävernitz, *op. cit.* p. 105.

century had fallen to a few thousands; by 1885 it was a matter of hundreds. Between those years, the power looms had increased from 299,000 to 561,000, and they were running far quicker, probably more than 50 per cent. quicker. Whereas in 1850 there had been one weaving operative for 1·6 looms, in 1878 there was one for 2·1; in 1882 one for 2·2. The result, in the form just given for spinning, was:[1]

	Number of operatives in weaving mills	Cloth produced per operative in lbs.
1844–6	210,000	1,700
1859–61	203,000	3,200
1880–82	246,000	4,000

The worsted industry had followed hard after cotton, of which it had almost become a part, because, between about 1840 and 1870, most of its women's dress fabrics had come to be made with cotton warps[2]. Indeed, as soon as it had assimilated the revolution in combing, that is to say from about 1855[3], it was perhaps more completely mechanised even than cotton. It did not use the mule at all, and so had no hand-mule spinners[4]. When John James wrote his *History* of the industry, in 1857, hand-loom worsted weavers were hardly to be found except in places like Wuthering Heights. Some of them hung on into the 'seventies, perhaps later. But even before James's time it had become impossible to quote general figures of their earnings, for they were no longer an industrial class. In the mills, iron looms clanged faster, steel spindles and gill-boxes and combs worked more smoothly, and labour was saved just as in cotton. Minor improvements were continuous—but it would hardly be too much to say that from the 'sixties to the 'eighties leaders of the industry, having got a complete mechanism, were content with it[5].

In the woollen industry, more varied and more scattered, things were different. Down to 1850, the mule itself had been little used in the Cotswold valleys: spinning was done on the

[1] Schulze-Gävernitz, *op. cit.* p. 108, 112, based on Ellison, *op. cit.* p. 66, 69. The 'weaving operatives' figure includes all those who worked in and about the weaving sheds.

[2] See, for example, the evidence of W. H. Mitchell before the *R.C. on the Depression of Trade and Industry*, 1886, Q. 3860. [3] Above, p. 31.

[4] To be exact, it had not used it at all. 'French spinning' with modern mules was coming in a little in the 'eighties. *R.C. on the Depression of Trade, etc.*, 1886, Q. 6731 (Sir Jacob Behrens).

[5] The 'cap' spindle was one of the improvements, or variations; above, p. 13.

hand-jenny[1]. The decisive improvement of mechanical 'condensing' came in very slowly everywhere. The leading districts had adopted it generally by 1870[2]; but, according to the factory inspectors, there were only five 'condensers' in England and Wales, outside Yorkshire, in 1871. Returns of 'billy spindles' were still being made in 1875[3]. At that time in the still numerous company mills of the small Yorkshire clothiers there was much antiquated machinery; more in remote Welsh or Scottish carding and spinning mills. Within a few miles of Leeds, about Calverley and Farsley, a strong body of hand-loom weavers worked right through the 'seventies. "I went out of business in 1876," a retired Calverley manufacturer said in 1902, "and our firm had never had a single piece woven by power."[4] It was the same in the important fancy woollen trade of the Huddersfield district—the district which produced, among other things, the dashing Victorian waistcoats of John Leech's pictures, and which, with the Tweed towns, was the pioneer of all modern fancy fabrics for men's wear, as opposed to the old broadcloths, friezes and pilot-cloths. In 1866 the hand weavers managed about a quarter of the looms in the trade: they still had some importance twenty years later[5]. In the carpet trade of Kidderminster, power came in with disastrous rapidity in 1855–6; and so in 1866 a Power Loom Weavers' Association was founded among the men for defence. But in 1868 the much older English [Handloom] Carpet Weavers' Association had over 3000 members, in Yorkshire and elsewhere, including some in the Kidderminster area; and it was only after 1876 that this union, which in the interval had spread to Scotland, began to decline, with its trade, before the competition of floor-cloth and linoleum and the power-woven carpet[6]. That the hand-loom was at work in Wales, the Highlands, and the Hebrides many years later needs no demonstration here.

In the British flax industry, still more in the jute industry

[1] *V.C.H. Gloucester*, II. 194. Mules had not been adopted even by Gott of Leeds till 1829. Crump, W. B., *The Leeds Woollen Industry*, 1780–1820 (1931), p. 264.

[2] Baines, E., *Yorkshire Past and Present*, II. 665.

[3] For 'condensing' and the hand-worked 'billy' see above, p. 12, 30. The Inspectors' statistics quoted are in *A. and P.* 1871, LXII. 105; 1875, LXXI. 57. In the next series, *A. and P.* 1878–9, LXV. 201, there are no 'condenser' or 'billy' figures.

[4] Personal information.

[5] Clapham, J. H., "The Decline of the Handloom in England and Germany," *Bradford Textile Journal*, June, 1905, p. 45.

[6] Trade Union facts from *Webb MSS.* London School of Economics. Industrial facts, *V.C.H. Worcester*, II. 298 *sqq.*

which was splitting from it after 1850, the power-loom had gained much ground, and machinery for heckling, drawing and spinning had been improved in detail and pace. There had been only 6092 linen power-looms in 1850 against 32,617 for worsted and 249,627 for cotton[1]. The 6092 includes jute looms. Jute had been known since the Great Wars, when the East India Company had imported it experimentally as a substitute for hemp. Tried first in England, it got to Dundee in the 'twenties, but the machinery then running was not well suited to it. Importing merchants pressed it on manufacturers in vain for some years; but between 1833 and 1848 it came gradually into use for weft yarn, with a hemp or linen warp, in the manufacture of sacking and other rough goods. Not until 1848 were the technical difficulties of using it for the warp finally overcome, and the ground cleared for a pure jute industry. By about that time also, the spread of heckling machinery from Leeds into Scotland got rid of the bottle-neck of a handicraft operation in a preliminary process[2]. The jute industry was not yet, however, really distinct from that of flax. The machinery was almost identical; mills built for the older material went over to the new without difficulty; and so late as 1864, their historian was writing, in words which could hardly have been used twenty years later, that "the Linens manufactured in Dundee comprise flax, hemp and jute goods."[3]

After that date the separation became more marked every year[4]. By 1867 the import of jute into Dundee, for the use of the town and of adjacent towns in Forfar, Fife and Perth, was 64,000 tons—against 1100 in 1838—at a time when the whole national import of 'China Grass, Jute, and other Vegetable Substances of the nature of Hemp,' which was the most accurate figure that the national statistics provided, was only 80,000 tons. In that year there were in Scotland alone 20,000 power-looms for flax, jute and hemp, of which 8000 were in Dundee—considerably more than there had been in all Britain seventeen years before. The hand-loom, though by no means yet extinct in Dundee, was "fast disappearing"[5] even from the

[1] Vol. I. p. 554. [2] See vol. I. p. 146.

[3] Warden, A. J., *The Linen Trade Ancient and Modern* (1864), p. 630. For jute origins see *ibid.* p. 50 *sqq.* and Bremner, *The Industries of Scotland* (1869), p. 251 *sqq.*

[4] For the later history the best source is the evidence of three Dundee witnesses before the *R.C. on Depression of Trade*, 1886, Q. 6175 *sqq.*

[5] Warden, *op. cit.* p. 557.

finer industry of Dunfermline, where much table-linen was made. Its disappearance had been heralded there by a short-lived factory hand-loom system. In England there were never many power-looms in this group of trades, because flax weaving was stationary or declining, and a large scale jute industry did not grow up. Even mill spinning of flax was stationary in the 'sixties at Leeds, where it had started[1]. In England as a whole the flax spindles had begun to fall by, or before, 1860. Ulster gained more than all that Britain lost, and Eastern Scotland gained in jute far more than she lost to Ulster in flax. England alone lost absolutely. Her flax power-looms crawled up to a maximum of 5600 in 1875, but had fallen to 4000 ten years later, hand-looms declining all the while. Her factory spindles fell from 442,000 in 1857 to 118,000 in 1885.

In 1885 the balance of power-driven flax machinery in the three sections of the then United Kingdom was as follows:

	England and Wales	Scotland	Ireland
Spindles	118,000	221,000	817,000
Looms	4,000	21,600	22,000

Scotland's flax mills employed 39,000 people to England's 11,000; her jute mills another 36,000 to England's 4400. In addition each had a few thousand factory hemp-workers[2].

While factory conditions were intensifying, and factory location changing, in hemp, flax and jute, hosiery was just becoming a factory industry, and that slowly. In 1850 it had been an outwork industry with central warehouses, a number of non-power 'frame shops,' and a handful of experiments with power[3]. Ten years later, the Nottingham Chamber of Commerce reported that there were only 3000 to 4000 factory workers at all the rotary, circular, or 'warp' machines, against over 50,000 domestic framework knitters of the old sort[4]. In 1862, when the Commissioners on Children's Employment estimated that 120,000 people were connected with the hosiery industry, only 4487 were within the Factory Law. The latter figure was

[1] But Leeds still had 29 factories with 8000 workpeople in 1871. Baines, *Yorkshire Past and Present*, III. 193.

[2] Factory Returns, *A. and P.* 1875, LXXI. 57; 1884–5, LXXI. 1087.

[3] Above, p. 33.

[4] Felkin, W., *History of the Machine wrought Lace and Hosiery Industries*, p. 514.

no doubt exact[1]. In 1866 Felkin, the historian of knitting machinery, said that "even now the absorption of narrow hand-machines into large masses can scarcely be said to have more than commenced." He was speculating on the consequences of an age of power, how it might depopulate villages and "change local residence," much as some public-spirited cotton lord might have speculated seventy years earlier[2]. With the 'seventies, a parliamentary factory group, headed by Joshua Fielden, began to promote bills for checking evils in the hosiery industry incidental to an outwork system, especially the old standing abuses of frame-renting by middlemen hosiers. They were well advised, because the Inspectors had reported only 129 hosiery factories with 9700 workpeople in 1871. Of these factories, 74 were in Leicester, 45 in Nottingham, 3 large ones in Roxburgh. Many of them still contained great numbers of hand-frames, and so far were only glorified frame shops[3]. The success of Fielden and his group in getting on to the Statute Book the Act 37 and 38 Vict. c. 48 of 1874 helped the factories by interfering with the sweating of outworking knitters by the middleman. This is the course of factory development as reported by the Inspectors[4]:

	Hosiery factories in Great Britain	Persons employed in them
1871	129	9,700
1878	185	14,900
1885	227	19,500

The accompanying decline in hand-frames outside the inspected factories has no such exact record; but it is known that, from the reputed 50,000 of 1850, they had fallen to a reputed 5000 in the Midlands by 1892. By that time more of them were in shops than in homes. It appears that, apart from the few making knitted gloves or doing very high grade work, they were kept going mainly because the War Office had an antiquated specification for military pants. The middlemen were still there and the Trade Unions were trying to drive the trade into the factories[5].

[1] It is from the Factory Inspectors' Report, *A. and P.* 1862, LV. 629. The estimate is in *Second Report of the Children's Employment Commission*, 1864, XXII. p. xxxii.

[2] *Op. cit.* p. 464.

[3] Factories and Workshops Return, *A. and P.* 1871, LXII. 105.

[4] *A. and P.* 1871, LXII. 105; 1878–9, LXV. 201; 1884–5, LXXI. 1087.

[5] *R.C. on Labour*, 1892, XXXVI. part 2, Q. 12,668 *sqq.* (machine workers), Q. 13,324 *sqq.* (hand workers). The pants are in Q. 13,358.

In the complex machine lace industry there was no decisive technical revolution. It was necessarily a sort of factory industry, because its machines were big and expensive. But its factories might well be, and often were, less mechanical and more workshop-like than the hosiery mills[1]. They grew in numbers between 1871 and 1885 about as fast as the hosiery mills; but they were on the average a great deal smaller at both dates. They were mostly in and about Nottingham. The figures are

	Lace factories in Great Britain	Persons employed in them
1871	223	8,300
1885	431	15,000

Very prosperous during the decade 1873–83, mainly because of Victorian lace curtains, the English mills did not take up the most remarkable invention of that time, the lace embroidery machine. The period closes with their representatives explaining to a Royal Commission that this machine was at work in St Gall and Plauen, while Nottingham was making the plain net for it to embroider[2].

Silk, the oldest of power-factory textile industries and the last to make effective and extensive use of the hand-loom; whose yarns were combined with Lancashire cotton and Yorkshire worsted; woven on Coventry ribbon looms and knitted on the frames of Leicester and Derby; employed by craftsmen for the richest brocades and hurried by power into cheap handkerchiefs; the industry which believed itself ruined by the 'Cobden' Treaty of 1860, yet survived, if shorn and crippled, doing some of its old work in its old way, even in Spitalfields—silk was both unchanged and changed fundamentally between 1850 and 1885. Coventry millinery ribbons, made much as they always had been, enjoyed a "last really good spell of business" in the late 'eighties[3]; and when the leading firm of Macclesfield first got the order for silk handkerchiefs for the Navy, in 1883, it made them all on hand-looms[4]. But meanwhile the spun-silk industry, a waste-product machine industry, had been created.

[1] Above, p. 32.

[2] *R.C. on Depression of Trade*, 1886, Q. 6595 *sqq.*

[3] Warner, Sir F., *The Silk Industry of the United Kingdom*, p. 125. For the organisation at Coventry see vol. I. p. 197–8, 553–4 and *E.J.* XVII. 352–3.

[4] Warner, *op. cit.* p. 136.

Silk waste had always been too valuable to be thrown away; so the broken ends of thrown silk, and the short fibres from damaged cocoons, had been carded and spun into 'floretta' silk time out of mind in Italy, and to some extent, it would appear, in England before the invention of spinning machinery. In the early machine age the process had been adapted to the new conditions. In the 'forties a number of mills about Manchester span waste silk for cheap shawls on cotton-spinning lines. In 1836 two Glasgow silk throwsters had taken out a patent for handling waste silk—because of the length of its fibres—on flax or worsted, as opposed to cotton, lines[1]. A variant of this process, coupled with many inventions and ingenious modifications in spinning and weaving and the resolute use of the very cheapest waste cocoons, made one of the several fortunes of the effective creator of the English spun-silk industry, Samuel Cunliffe Lister the woolcomber.

In 1855 a silk broker sent Lister some unsaleable waste to see if he could comb it. With the aid of a co-inventor, Warburton, he did so and span it—in two years at a cost of £360,000. The material was so bad that, as Lister wrote later—"a...silk-spinner would at once have said: 'there is plenty of good waste; why bother with this rubbish?'"[2] Its very badness was his strength, for it left a margin for costly experiment and in the end made popular goods. In time, when the original silk comb had been superseded and all processes revised, Manningham Mills became one of the giant factories of Europe—sending silk sewing thread all over the world, making velvets and softly draping silks fitted to the taste of the 'eighties, with imitation sealskins and furs, very popular indeed. The mills were transferred to a Limited Company in 1889 for near £2,000,000[3].

Round about 1850 the world's oldest mechanical industry, corn-milling, comprised in Britain a few big steam units and innumerable little water mills on their ancient sites. But though in the great towns the motive power had changed, the art and craft of milling had not. The stones might be bigger, but the essentials were what Chaucer's miller would have understood. Not that the metal-age notion of grinding with fluted iron rollers had escaped English inventors. Isaac Wilkinson, iron-

[1] Warner, *op. cit.* p. 403, 417.
[2] As quoted in Warner, *op. cit.* p. 227.
[3] Warner, *op. cit.* p. 228.

master of Cartmel, had patented it in 1753; but nothing had come of the patent[1]. After 1820 the system had been tried experimentally on the continent, while the Corn Law protected the British miller. Shortly after 1846, he felt for a time the competitive effects of the system of 'high grinding' first practised—though not with rollers—in Austria-Hungary, and taken up in France. By that time rollers were being used successfully for the primary grinding, but stones for the finishing, in Pesth. However, when British millers began to inquire into the matter, in the late 'fifties and the 'sixties, the system was rather under a cloud. It had been recklessly applied to unsuitable wheats, and was not then making much headway even at Pesth. Also there were still many improvements needed before its general adoption was likely[2].

From 1862 onwards, experiments were being made with imported roller machinery. By 1870 one firm of Liverpool millers had got rid of stones entirely[3]. But the modern mill, fully equipped with steel rollers, 'centrifugal dressers' and other automatic machinery, only came some ten years later. The firm mainly responsible for its introduction dated it from 1881[4]. Automatic machinery was coming in about the same time in the United States, and no doubt there was interchange of notions. From 1881, aided by the growing concentration of corn-milling at the ports and the competition of American flour, the transformation of the industry and the growth of its representative unit, the great waterside automatic mill, went on very swiftly. By 1886 the steel rollers had "superseded almost entirely the use of mill-stones"[5]—in great mills only, it should be added. "The completeness of the revolution," the responsible engineer wrote in 1889, "is exemplified by the fact that practically in less than ten years the machinery and methods of corn-milling have been...entirely altered. The best kind of roller-mills...resemble ...in the accuracy of their construction the highest class of machine-tools."[6] He came from Manchester, where the high-class machine-tool had been developed by Whitworth.

[1] Bennett and Elton, *A History of Corn Milling*, III. 296.

[2] Bennett and Elton, III. 299 *sqq*.

[3] Bennett and Elton, III. 304.

[4] Simon, H. (the head of the firm), "On the latest Developments of Roller Flour Milling," *Trans. Inst. Mech. Eng*. 1889. See also Simon's paper in *Proc. Inst. Civ. Eng*. 1882, and the criticism in Bennett and Elton, III. 307.

[5] Head's Presidential Address, *Trans. Inst. Mech. Eng*. 1886, p. 286.

[6] Simon, *op. cit*. p. 148.

Almost contemporary with the revolution in milling came the industrial and commercial uses of artificial refrigeration. The physics of refrigeration had long been known. Sir John Leslie had actually made a little laboratory ice at Edinburgh about 1810[1]. English patents for ice-making by compression went back to the 'thirties; but artificial ice was not available in 1855. The transformation in the fish trade which set in in that year was based on the use of natural ice, such as any gentleman might have stored in an ice-house in his grounds to cool his summer drink. Only in 1861 came what has been claimed as "probably the earliest application of a refrigerating machine to manufacturing,"[2] and what was almost certainly the earliest in Britain, when a Harrison ether machine, patented in 1857, was used in the extraction of solid paraffin from shale oil. Next year a similar machine was tried for ground freezing, but not in Britain. It was in Germany that Poetsch finally developed the use of ground freezing for sinking coal pits through water-bearing strata, about the year 1880[3].

Refrigeration in its bearing on food problems was much discussed in the 'sixties, and invention went forward[4]. In 1867 came Reece's freezing machine, one of the early ammonia machines, which, as perfected twelve or fifteen years later, could make fifteen tons of clear block ice a day with a ton and a half of coal. Experiments in the freezing of meat were being made early in the decade by T. S. Mort and E. D. Nicolle in New South Wales. Mort certainly started the first freezing works in the world at that time; but it was not until February 2, 1880, that the *Strathleven* brought a cargo of frozen Australian meat into London docks[5]. Just five years earlier the first trial shipment of 'chilled' meat had come from New York. It had been kept cool by natural ice and a hand-worked fan; but that method had soon been improved upon[6]. By 1880, many types of refrigerating machinery were on the market. Windhausen of

[1] See Ewing, J. A., *The Mechanical Production of Cold* (2nd ed. 1921); Lightfoot, T. B., "Refrigerating Machinery," *Trans. Inst. Mech. Eng.* 1881 and 1886; the *D.N.B.* for Leslie; Critchell, J. T. and Raymond, J., *A History of the Frozen Meat Trade* (1912).

[2] Lightfoot, *op. cit.* p. 231. But Critchell and Raymond point out that a Harrison machine was used in a Bendigo brewery in 1851 and was patented in Australia in 1854–5. *Op. cit.* p. 22–3.

[3] *The Engineer*, Nov. 30, 1883, p. 417.

[4] Wood, Sir H. T., *A History of the Royal Society of Arts* (1913), p. 460–3.

[5] Wood, *op. cit.* p. 462; Critchell and Raymond, *op. cit.* p. 19.

[6] Bolles, *Industrial History of the United States*, p. 123.

Berlin had patented a complete vacuum pump type of ice-maker in 1878: it was tried at the Aylesbury Dairy, Bayswater, in 1881, but was not much imitated[1]. Far more important in the general history of refrigeration were a variety of compression machines patented here between 1873 and 1878—Giffard's, the Bell-Coleman, Lightfoot's—for these were the most easily applicable to cold storage on land or sea. The *Strathleven* had a Bell-Coleman installation. The London and St Katherine Dock Company used a Giffard machine for its first little cold store—to hold 500 frozen sheep—in 1882. Four years later, this and other stores had grown enormously, and even "retail butchers" were "now adopting...stores of their own."[2]

In 1866 the Royal Society of Arts had set up a committee to report on the food of the people, with special reference to "the production, importation, and preservation of substances suitable for food."[3] It took evidence not only about refrigeration but about the still rather experimental business of 'canning' or 'tinning' foods. There were no important novelties in the basic tin-plate industry itself between 1850 and 1886, except the introduction in the 'sixties of an efficient and economical device for spreading the tin, and the replacement of charcoal iron for the plates by Siemens steel between 1880 and 1886[4]; but all the time and in all countries the canning industry grew. There was Australian tinned mutton at the Great Exhibition. Foods preserved in tins had been used long before that, but only by soldiers and sailors and explorers. The committee of 1866 tried a navy tin forty-one years old. After turning aside for a few years from mutton and tin to gold, Australia turned back to them; and in the late 'sixties Australian meat extract and tinned meat began to come into general consumption. In the late 'seventies came the 'compressed cooked meats,' as Americans called them, from Chicago—tongues and corned beef and the rest. American fruits had already begun to arrive, and there was now a large consumption of miscellaneous British and European tinned foods. And every single tin plate which Australia or California or Chicago used was British made[5].

[1] Hopkinson, J., *Journ. R.S. of Arts*, 1882, p. 20.

[2] Lightfoot, *Trans. Inst. Mech. Eng.* 1886, p. 234. For the compression machines generally, Critchell and Raymond, *op. cit.* p. 336 *sqq.*

[3] Wood, *op. cit.* p. 461.

[4] Jones, J. H., *The Tinplate Industry* (1914), p. 10, 17; Cowper, E. A., *Trans. Inst. Mech. Eng.* 1881, p. 420.

[5] For Australian tinning, Critchell and Raymond, *op. cit.* p. 9–11; for American, Bolles, *op. cit.* p. 125; for the British tin-plate monopoly, Jones, *op. cit.* p. 20.

When the *Economist*, in June 1851, called public attention to the "astonishing velocity" of an American sewing machine[1], it noted in the journalists' style of the day that this invention threatened "to extinguish the occupation which dwarfs a race into the ninth part of its normal type." The proverbial philosophy here invoked would also have supplied a saying about "threatened men living long." Tailors are not extinct; but mechanical revolution was rightly foreseen in two of the greatest industrial groups in the country, nearly half a million seamstresses and tailors, and more than a quarter of a million of shoemakers. Neither had been even touched by machinery since the dawn of civilisation. There is also the revolution in domestic sewing to be borne in mind; but this the historian cannot easily follow out.

In Leeds, the town which was to become perhaps the most important home of the clothing factory, it is said that machinery was first introduced "to any extent" in 1857[2]. There, as elsewhere, the thing started simply, obviously, but obscurely when some enterprising man bought a batch of hand sewing machines and set girls to work them. By 1863 one of the pioneers at Leeds had 50 girl machinists on his premises and 200–300 female outworkers[3]. From some such simple beginning, at first without any use of power, and in close touch with contemporary developments in America, the complete factory evolved in the course of the next twenty-five years—borrowing devices from other industries and perfecting the uses of its own characteristic implement, the sewing machine. The evolution was slow and halting. In 1871 the Inspectors were aware of only fifty-eight tailoring and clothing factories in Britain. These were fair-sized concerns for they averaged 136 workpeople each; but they were said to have only 65 h.p. of steam between them. Presumably their 2600 sewing machines—not quite forty-five per factory—were hand-driven, a little power being harnessed

[1] Above, p. 13; *Economist*, June 26, 1851.

[2] Meysey-Thompson, "On the Hist. of Engineering in Leeds," *Trans. Inst. Mech. Eng.* 1882, p. 272. See also *V.C.H. Yorkshire*, II. 426; *V.C.H. Essex*, II. 25, for the Colchester industry.

[3] John Barran, *Children's Employment Commission*, 1864 (XXII), p. 2: "I began in a very small way," he said; adding, "in my retail business I only employ men." Not all the early machines were American. "Shortly after 1850" F. W. Harmer, a Norwich merchant, began to use machines "invented by a tailor named Thomas...like large fret-saws worked by treadles." *F W. Harmer and Coy.*, 1825–1925, p. 7.

for heavier jobs such as cutting or pressing[1]. The making of clothes did not become, and has not yet become, a pure factory industry: sub-contractors and individual outworkers always took jobs for which machinery had not yet been devised, or for which a particular firm might not be large enough to carry the appropriate machines; but the leading firms had a very complete mechanical installation by the early 'eighties. The clothes were cut out from innumerable piled up layers of material, on the top layer of which the pattern was chalked, by a power-driven band-knife working vertically. Sewing machines in ranks ran up to a maximum pace of two thousand stitches a minute. An iron set on the end of a jointed mechanical arm needed human guidance but not human driving; the button-holes were button-holed and all the buttons sewed on by machinery[2].

This was for low grade mass-production. As the quality improved, the amount of hand-work put into it, inside or outside the factory, increased. Such was the industry which was replacing what they called the making of slop clothing when Tom Hood wrote his *Song of the Shirt* for *Punch* in 1843. Women still plied needle and thread on market work: the factory had by no means absorbed all the clothes, and by no means all the work of the factory was machine-work; but there was less stitching "in unwomanly rags" than there had been forty years back. Night work had long disappeared from the Leeds trade. "The machines have saved all that," an employer said, even in 1863[3]. It was in the smart 'rush' trade of the West End season that there was most need for reform in the 'seventies and 'eighties.

The wholesale boot trade of 1850 had its factories, but they had neither machinery nor power. A device for riveting the soles to the uppers had been invented during the French wars by D. M. Randolph. Brunel the elder took it up and added other machines in an army boot factory. Once again the standardised demand for the forces had given the stimulus to mass-

[1] *Return of Factories and Workshops*, 1871 (LXII. 105). Harmer's of Norwich were called "The Steam Clothing Factory" apparently in the 'fifties: *op. cit.* p. 7. For American developments see Cole, A. H., *The American Wool Manufacture*, I. 293, and sources there quoted.

[2] Meysey-Thompson, *op. cit.* p. 272–3. Thomas's machine of the 'fifties ran at twenty stitches a minute; *F. W. Harmer and Coy.* as above.

[3] *Children's Employment Commission*, 1864, p. 7.

production. But like his team of block-making machines, Brunel's mass-production methods in boot-making went out of use, and almost out of memory, with the peace[1]. In the factories of the early 'fifties, under the master's eye, uppers might be cut carefully and soles roughly. Goods would be inspected there at the various stages of manufacture, and warehoused there; but nearly all, if not all, the actual making was done by 'binders,' who sewed together the parts of the upper at home, and by out-working master shoe-makers, who took apprentices just like the men in the bespoke trade, and did the heavy work with sole and heel leather by which the boot was 'made.'[2] By 1855–6 the Singer Company of New York was pushing a sewing machine for leather on the British market. It was a clumsy treadle machine and it made slow progress. At Stafford there was a shoe-makers' strike against machine-closed uppers; but with the aid of girl labour, machines got forward everywhere in time, first for light work sewn with a dry thread, then, with the necessary but not easy modifications, for sewing heavy wet-resisting uppers with a waxed thread[3]. About the year 1858, other treadle machines for cutting the butts (sole leather) and for stamping soles out of them were brought from America. Crick of Leicester reintroduced the system of riveting the sole to the upper by machine, a much simpler mechanical proposition than sewing it, and a very important step towards factory production. At Street in Somerset, William Clark devised and worked for a long time "in great privacy" the first simple machinery for building up and attaching the heels[4].

America and the needs of fighting men always set the pace. It has been said that the War of Secession, with its stupendous demand for army boots, "gave an opportunity to the boot-stitching machine which precipitated its introduction by many years."[5] Blake's decisive machine for sewing on the soles, invented in America and known in Britain before the war, only

[1] For the invention see Doolittle, W. H., *Invention in the* [*Nineteenth*] *Century* (1903), p. 367. For Brunel block-making machines, vol. I. p. 153.

[2] An excellent short account in *One Hundred Years' History of Shoes...at Street, Somerset* (Messrs C. and J. Clark), 1925, p. 6.

[3] Clark, *op. cit.* p. 8. For strikes at Stafford and elsewhere see *Trades Societies and Strikes* (*Nat. Ass. for Social Sci.*), 1860, p. 1. For damage done by these strikes to the Northampton trade, *R.C. on Labour*, 1892, XXXVI. part 2, Q. 12,076.

[4] *Op. cit.* p. 7.

[5] Swaysland, E. J. C., *Boot and Shoe Design and Manufacture* (Northampton, 1905), p. 8.

became thoroughly successful as a result of improvements made public during the war, in 1864[1]. It gave its manufacturers "a virtual monopoly of sole-sewing machinery for some years."[2] This, and Crick's riveting machine, were the first machines of importance special to boot-making, the closing of uppers being a fairly straightforward problem in sewing. With the Blake machine as basis, "the full team system of shoe-making was worked out in America" during the next ten years[3]. Leading firms in Britain kept in touch with American practice and imported the machinery. British machine-makers, mainly at Leicester, sometimes improved on it.

Down to the 'eighties—and for that matter much later—factory boot-making was far from being a complete power industry. In 1871 there were only 400 h.p. of steam in 145 boot and shoe factories; more than in clothing, but still not much[4]. Though the gas engine was coming into use during the next decade, steam remained the obvious power; few machines could be made really automatic; and new light ones for all kinds of sub-processes were constantly being tried. So only the heaviest and most certainly permanent machines, such as those for cutting butts or doing very stiff sewing, were as yet regularly power driven. The rest, as shown in contemporary designs, all have handles or treadles[5]. There was a fresh influx of American machines for the various finishing processes from about 1880. Hitherto machinery had helped only 'making,' in the narrowest sense of the word. Now edge-parers, levellers, ironing machines again roused trade union fears, and had to be introduced with discretion. With them came Goodyear's 'sew-round machine,' which produced the first exact replica of a hand-sewn welted boot. Each stage in boot-making had its team of machines, often simple ones easily replaced by hand processes in small factories; each team, of machines or processes, had its specialists with their new names—heel-builder, heel-breaster, heel-attacher, and the like[6].

There was still a vast deal of hand-work and home-work in

[1] Clark, *op. cit.* p. 9. Leno, J. B., *The Art of Boot and Shoe Making* (1885), p. 183. The actual manufacturer was Colonel McKay.

[2] Clark, as above.

[3] Clark, p. 9; Leno, *op. cit.* p. 186.

[4] *Return of Factories and Workshops*, as above.

[5] As, for example, in Leno's book of 1885.

[6] Leno, *op. cit.* p. 186. See *Dictionary of Occupational Terms*, compiled in connection with the census of 1921 (1927).

boot-factory centres, and more in London. So much boot-making was done at home, and by the piece, in 1886, that trustworthy statistics of boot-makers' earnings could not be compiled, even in the great centres[1]. The Kettering Co-operative Boot and Shoe Factory, founded in that year, installed "the ordinary run of machinery—not what is known as the American system though."[2] Even six years later, in the "heavy medium strong" boot trade of Leeds, "nearly half the work" was "done at the people's homes in the finishing department." There had been recent strikes against American machinery. And the whole London trade was "cut up between little employers," with a maximum of hand-work and home-work[3].

There is an odd, half-accidental, connection between the sewing-machine industries and a new industry of mid-Victorian times which had a future—the manufacture of cycles. Engineers of those times "universally accredited" the invention of the cycle to Gavin Dalziel of Lesmahagow, who put cranks in a hobby-horse in 1836. They were not at all clear about the credit for a much more decisive invention, which really started the industry, the suspension wheel; but they found it specified, together with wire-spokes, rubber tyres, and roller bearings, in a patent by E. A. Cowper of 1868[4]. It happened that at this time distress in the silk trade was driving people out of Coventry: population fell by 7 per cent. between 1861 and 1871. Possibly the presence of a large body of trained watch-makers in the town suggested to someone the idea of starting a new light metal industry, the manufacture of sewing machines. This was round about the year 1870. The factories must have had a hard struggle against their large-scale American competitors; but competition did not go on for long. Cycling became a gentlemanly pastime, and soon undergraduates were to return to the Universities pushing their "high bright bicycles" through the crowds at the railway station[5]. The occasion was seized at Coventry: "not only the human but even the mechanical portion of the equipment of the sewing-machine factories was

[1] *Stat. Tables and Report on Trade Unions*, 1886 (1887, LXXXIX. 715), p. 40.

[2] *R.C. on Labour* (1892, XXXVI. part 2), Q. 14,505.

[3] *Ibid.* Q. 11,984–5 and 15,010.

[4] Phillips, R. E., "On the Construction of Modern Cycles," *Trans. Inst. Mech. Eng.* 1885, p. 467.

[5] Anstey, F., *Vice Versa* (1882).

adapted, so far as possible, to the processes of the dawning industry."[1]

According to the census returns of 1881 only 1072 people in the whole country were employed in cycle-making; but this was probably an underestimate and would not include all the makers of accessories and cycle parts. Four years later it was claimed that there were more than 170 firms making cycles only; that there were 500 different types of cycles; that 3000 men in Coventry itself, and at least 5000 in the United Kingdom, got their living by the trade; that 40,000 cycles were turned out yearly; and that the average price of a machine was £20. Division of the output by the number of types, or of the employment figure by the number of firms, yields significant quotients. The expert who made these estimates in 1885[2] also classified the types. In Class 2c he placed "safety [*i.e.* low built, and geared] bicycles with steering wheel in front." He noted that "the steering was rather sensitive and consequently erratic." Type 2c was the machine which, when other types were forgotten and when its average cost had come something below £20, was to spin men down the grooves of change in England and in Uganda and Gwalior. Neither agricultural labourers nor Asiatics, it is believed, ever made a practice of riding high bright bicycles.

Cycle-making was an offshoot from those light metal trades of the Birmingham area which, like Sheffield cutlery-making, had been hardly mechanised at all before 1850, and were only sporadically mechanised during the succeeding generation. It is true that half-way through that generation (in 1865–6) the young, and already prosperous, Joseph Chamberlain wrote of the "revolution" which since 1850 had been "assimilating the town [of Birmingham] to the great seats of manufacture in the North and depriving it of its special characteristic, viz. the number of its small manufacturers."[3] He had particularly in mind his own industry, that of wood-screw-making, in which the introduction of self-acting machinery from America in 1854 had paved the

[1] Leppington, C. H. d'E., "The Evolution of an Industrial Town," *E.J.* 1907, p. 352. For Coventry watchmaking see vol. I. p. 48, 177.

[2] Phillips, *op. cit.*

[3] *Birmingham and the Midland Hardware District* (1866), p. 604. Though the screw-cutting lathe went back to Maudslay (Nasmyth, *Autobiography*, p. 128 and vol. I. p. 153) and had been used in the Midlands (Editor's note to Chamberlain's article, p. 605) wood-screws in 1850 normally had the thread "filed out by hand" (Chamberlain).

way for the final absorption, in 1866, of almost all the business into the factories and firm of Nettlefold and Chamberlain; but he could have given illustrations of big or fair-sized factories from many other trades of the city and district—locks in Wolverhampton, tinned and enamelled hollow ware at Wolverhampton and elsewhere, brass-tube-making and electro-plating in Birmingham itself, the new type of small-arms manufacture, steel-pen-making and the rising metal bedstead and cheap jewellery trades. There were also great concerns in the heavy industries of the Black Country, and in some branches of engineering proper; and there were large makers of railway rolling-stock. But the size of the large concerns was not always intimately connected with decisive mechanical innovations; and these big businesses rose from the Birmingham democratic industrial plain of small businesses with simple mechanism, and small working masters with little or none[1]. Their roots and suckers spread far beneath it. Chamberlain's process of 'assimilation' went on, but not rapidly, during the 'seventies and early 'eighties. In 1885 the speakers of the Birmingham Chamber of Commerce, whilst recording the rise of the great concerns and their recent transformation into private limited companies, were also calling the attention of Royal Commissioners to the still huge numbers of "small workers." "They take a house and commence to work in the upper part and so on," they explained[2].

The machine, aided by foreign competition, had crippled if not killed one bad old Black Country country trade, that of the outworking nailers. There were supposed to have been 50,000 people in it in 1830, a round figure probably too high. The census of 1851 gives 29,000. A Birmingham expert in 1865 thought 20,000. Wire nails, machine-cut nails, and Belgian competition in overseas markets, were the assigned causes of the decline. The decline continued; but the trade, a home of the worst forms of truck and of the blackguardly exploiting 'nail foggers,' was liable to be flooded in times of depression by unemployed colliers and iron-workers who had learnt it when

[1] *Birmingham and the Midland Hardware District, passim.* It is the report on the district prepared for a meeting of the British Association. Compare *Third Report on Children's Employment* (1864, XXII. 319), p. xi, most children hired by adult piece-workers; p. 7, not more than six or seven factories in lock and key trade; in saddlers' ironmongery "a vast number of small shops," etc.

[2] *R.C. on Depression of Trade and Industry*, Q. 1591.

young. So it was in 1878–9. This flooding, with the continued use of hand-made nails for boot soles and other special purposes, kept some 1500 workers in the trade in the Bromsgrove district at the end of the 'eighties[1].

About Sheffield, though great steel works were rising and factory organisation was making headway in the cutlery trade, there was certainly no cutlery revolution. In 1864 most even of the "large cutlery men" had "part of their work done out" and many cutlers who worked in factories—hiring the power—worked "on their own account or for other masters." When the Factory Acts were extended to cutlery in 1867, the inspectors had grave difficulty in finding 'factory owners' among the small master grinders and cutlers who hired power in little doses and employed a journeyman and a lad or two. With the workshop cutler they were not directly concerned. Even in 1901 there was only an average of six adults to each cutlery 'factory' on the inspectors' lists in the United Kingdom, in spite of the introduction of saw-grinding machinery from America in 1858, of file-cutting machinery about 1875, and of various types of mechanical hammer for blade forging before 1885. File-cutting machinery had been in use at Manchester, at Birmingham and abroad long before 1875. It is significant that men from Sheffield were indicting it before the Commissioners in 1886, and that a prominent manufacturer explained that he supplied both the machine-cut and the hand-cut file. No doubt his industry was a mixed factory-outwork, capitalist-small-master trade, like so many in Hallamshire and the Birmingham area[2].

Behind and beneath the technical development of all the industries lay the coal and the technique of collier and mining engineer. To those who, in 1865, spoke of an age of Iron or an age of Steam, Stanley Jevons replied that "coal alone can command in sufficient abundance either the iron or the steam; and coal, therefore, commands this age."[3] In his classical "inquiry concerning the progress of the nation and the probable exhaustion

[1] Ball in *Birmingham and the Midland Hardware District*, p. 110 *sqq*. *Fact. Ins. Rep*. 1868, p. 295–7 (1868–9, XIV. 75); 1879, p. 18 (1880, XIV. 93). *R.C. on Labour* (1892, XXXVI. part 2), Q. 18,378 *sqq*.

[2] *Fourth Report on Children's Employment*, p. 47, 201 for 1864; *Fact. Ins. Rep*. 1868, p. 12–13, for 1867; Lloyd, G. J. H., *The Cutlery Trades* (1913), p. 182, for 1901; *Ibid*. 186–7, 198, for the inventions; *R.C. on Depression of Trade*, Q. 1150 *sqq*., Q. 3333, for 1886.

[3] *The Coal Question*, p. viii.

of our coal supplies,"[1] he argued that the annual consumption of coal, which he believed to have been 57,000,000 tons for 1851 and knew to have been 83,600,000 in 1861, would probably rise to 166,300,000 in 1881 and to 234,700,000 in 1891. In fact, owing to progressive fuel economy in steam raising, smelting and the like, and in spite of a fast growing export, the former figure was not reached until 1888 and the latter not until 1905. This slackening growth was not accompanied by anything very revolutionary in technique down to the 'eighties. Though there were a few important innovations, and everything got bigger or deeper, or stronger, the work of mining engineers was concentrated mainly on the problem of raising coal from the increasing depths, without increasing either the cost or the risk, and on spreading the best practice of the later 'forties[2].

In the years just before 1850 greater depths had been sounded everywhere, and explosions of fire-damp invariably followed. Before 1845, serious explosions had been rare, except in the deep pits of the North, but now (1845–50), in South Wales, Warwickshire, Lancashire, South Yorkshire, a series of terrible disasters—Risca, Rounds Green, Coppal, and the Oaks and Darley Main collieries at Barnsley—kept parliament busy with inquiries and led to the Act of 1850 (13 and 14 Vict. c. 100), the first of a long series which provided for or extended the 'Inspection of Coal Mines in Great Britain.'[3] The Acts had technical as well as preventive effects. The making and maintenance of correct plans of all collieries became a statutory obligation: the inspectorate provided a body of men with wide specialised knowledge and an uncommercial interest in efficient and safe mining practice. J. J. Atkinson, one of the earliest inspectors, to take a single example, in papers read before the North of England Mining Institute between 1854 and 1863, "laid for the English speaking races the scientific basis of modern mine ventilation."[4]

[1] The sub-title of *The Coal Question*.

[2] See vol. I. p. 432 *sqq*. For the slow spread of the best practice in some districts, Lones, *A Hist. of Mining in the Black Country* (1898), quoted in Allen, G. C., *The Industrial Development of Birmingham and the Black Country* (1929), ch. 6.

[3] For the accidents, Galloway, R. L., *History of Coal Mining* (1882; Galloway's later and fuller book, *Annals of Coal Mining*, was not carried beyond 1850), p. 234 *sqq*. Inspection had been provided for in the Act of 1843 (5 and 6 Vict. c. 99; see vol. I. p. 575–6) and Tremenheere had been appointed inspector; but this was inspection of labour, to see that women remained above ground, etc., not of the mine itself.

[4] Bulman, H. F. and Redmayne, R. A. S., *Colliery Working and Management* (2nd ed. 1906), p. 8.

All the deepest sinkings of the period were on the Lancashire and Cheshire coalfield. In 1858 the Astley deep pit at Dukinfield touched 2100 feet—exactly the reputed depth of the deepest pit of the early railway age, the Apedale in North Staffordshire. Near Wigan, 2448 feet was reached in 1869. Twelve years later, the Ashton Moss Colliery near Manchester sank a new pit to the 'great mine' coal at 2688 feet, the deepest sinking of the early 'eighties. Though Lancashire sank deepest, other districts were always deepening[1].

Deep pits needed great winding engines such as the new steel engineering could easily supply. In the 'forties an engine of 175 h.p. had been counted great: by the early 'eighties 1500 h.p. was sometimes required. The wicker corves for hoisting the coal and the miners were everywhere driven out by metal cages made at first of iron; but, "on account of its superior strength and lightness," steel had "come to be employed to a considerable extent...in the construction of winding ropes and cages, as well as for numerous other purposes" by 1882[2].

Urged on by the inspectors and the law, mining engineers took pains with ventilation. In 1850 there had been numberless pits, in those fields where shallow workings were normal, with no ventilating arrangements at all. On the Northern field, furnace ventilation, accompanied by the device of 'splitting the air,' *i.e.* the use of two air-currents, had been carried to a high level of perfection, and had proved superior in practice to Goldsworthy Gurney's device for producing air-currents by the discharge of jets of high-pressure steam. It was arguable in 1859 that no known mechanical device was better than a well-laid-out system of furnace ventilation[3]. Ten years earlier Struve's air-pump and Brunton's fan—devices based on French and Belgian practice—had succeeded simultaneously in South Wales. By 1852 fans had reached South Yorkshire, where they were tried by Biram, the 'viewer' of Earl Fitzwilliam's collieries near Rotherham. In 1858, J. J. Atkinson was defending not only the utility but the economy of the fan system before the mining engineers of the Northern field; and about two years later the first fan was erected there, at Twisdale Colliery, Durham[4].

[1] Galloway, *op. cit.* p. 265; *V.C.H. Lancashire*, II. 354; vol. I. p. 436.

[2] Galloway, *op. cit.* p. 259 and, for the winding engines, p. 266. The corves were not abandoned in one Cumberland pit till 1875. *V.C.H. Cumberland*, II. 353.

[3] See vol. I. p. 438 n. Also Galloway, *op. cit.* p. 150, 152, 251.

[4] Galloway, *Annals*, II. 296; *History*, p. 253.

The inspiration had come from abroad. So did the actual machines which decided the victory of mechanical ventilation all along the line. In 1862, Guibal of Mons patented the fan which finally converted the engineers of the North. Another foreign type, the Schiele, followed immediately. These two, together with one bearing a British name—the Waddle—were the dominant types of the period 1864–85. The first Guibal was tried at Elswick about two years after it had been patented. "Within ten or twelve years no fewer than two hundred were at work...in different parts of the kingdom."[1] In Eastern Scotland there was only one fan of any sort in 1873: there were over ninety in 1879[2]. About the same time Guibals were being installed in place of furnaces in the Earl of Lonsdale's Whitehaven collieries. The 'viewer' responsible for this was also getting rid of corves, and introducing another valuable innovation, already tried on the more fully mechanised fields, compressed air haulage underground[3]. By the 'eighties, although few even of the most primitive mining practices were literally extinct in Britain, most of the coal was raised from pits with a complete mechanical equipment for winding, ventilation and, at least on the main 'roads,' underground haulage. Thus a diminishing return to labour, at increasing depths, at greater distances from the shaft, and under worse atmospheric conditions was counteracted. Even an appreciable increase in return was secured. Yet there was nothing to be compared with the labour economy of a cotton mill. Very much labour was saved on the movement of men and coal from the face to the pit-bank, but hewing remained a handicraft.

Though not for lack of attempts to alter it. Even in the eighteenth century, invention had grappled with the process of 'holing' or 'kirving,' that is undercutting the coal seam so that it shall collapse by its own weight, the job for which the pitman crouches or, in a thin seam, lies on his side. But no coal-cutting machine had even approached success until the compressed-air drive had become practicable—with the aid of rubber. In the early 'sixties, a percussion type of machine, in which a piston instead of a human arm drives a pick, succeeded at the West Ardsley Colliery, Leeds. The patent was of 1861 and stood in the names of Donisthorpe, Firth and Ridley. Some

[1] Galloway, *History*, p. 255. [2] *Ibid.* p. 256.

[3] The 'viewer' was Mr R. F. Martin. *V.C.H. Cumberland*, II. 365. There had long been steam haulage underground: compressed air was dearer but safer.

ten years after the first success, one of the patentees claimed that forty-eight men with the machine could do the work of sixty without it—a useful saving but no revolution[1]. Experiments were conducted systematically with this and other types of machine during the 'sixties and 'seventies. There were successes besides that at Ardsley. Some of the rotary cutters, in which the work is done by a toothed wheel placed parallel and close to the floor, were said to be "well spoken of" in 1876[2]. But there were all kinds of manipulative difficulties, besides those connected with the transmission of the power. Machines are never easily worked on a much tilted, a much faulted, or an uneven lying seam, or in one with a weak roof. A great deal "depends on the care and skill and energy of the men employed with them,"[3] qualities which, for obvious reasons, could not always be counted on. There was no risk of coal imports, and very little competition with British coal in overseas markets as yet. The upshot was that only some very tiny fraction of that coal was cut by machinery in the 'eighties. No important part was so cut even forty years later[4].

Figures of the mining population and of the output of coal at successive dates measure very roughly the extent to which machinery, organisation, and large-scale workings increased the efficiency of the miners' craft from the 'fifties to the 'eighties:

	British Coal Output, tons		Coal-Miners (Census figures)	Tons per Miner
1851	57,000,000	(Jevons' estimate)	216,000	264
1861	84,000,000	(Mineral returns)	280,000	300
1871	117,000,000	,, ,,	314,000	373
1881	154,000,000	,, ,,	382,000	403
1891	185,000,000	,, ,,	517,000	358

The figures neglect changes in the working day and in the intensity of work, and many other matters which would require attention in an exact statistical treatment; but they tell the broad story. A great accession of mechanical and organising efficiency, and a growth of the normal mining business, increase the product of labour by 41 per cent., in spite of nature's

[1] Bulman and Redmayne, *op. cit.* p. 119; Galloway, *History*, p. 262.

[2] Williams, W. M., in *Brit. Man. Industries*, I. 113.

[3] Bulman and Redmayne, p. 114 (written in 1896).

[4] The use of pneumatic picks and drills was reported from only 557 mines even in 1927: most of these were used for driving headings and boring, not for coal-getting. *Seventh R. of the Sec. for Mines* quoted in *Labour Gazette*, Aug. 1928, p. 281. For the 'eighties, Galloway, *History*, p. 263.

reluctance, between 1851 and 1871. There is increase, but slower, for another decade: then retrogression sets in[1].

External conditions were hostile to mechanical progress in the metalliferous mines, except in the iron mines, and of these few were deep or highly organised. Lead-mining was shrinking into the lonelier hills and attracting little capital[2]. Copper, the glory of Cornwall, was still magnificently prosperous in the 'fifties—but not much later. Its mines had been equipped for pumping by Boulton and Watt themselves. Then steam had been applied to winding and stamping the ore, but not to hoisting the men. In the 'forties came Michael Loam's curious 'man engine,' meant to save the men such ladder climbs as the 228 fathoms of Dolcoath. But there were only eight man engines installed by 1862; and in 1881, though the Dolcoath engine went down 240 fathoms, the bottom was now at 362. A mine captain of seventy explained with pride in 1864 that 200 fathoms of ladders gave him no trouble[3].

By that time the shadow was falling on the mines of the Duchy. The best copper ore was giving out: Rio Tinto copper was being worked with British capital: the abundant copper ores of Lake Superior were to come soon. Though there were plenty of tin mines and stream works, Cornwall at that time lived primarily by its copper[4]. The decade 1871–81, in which at least a quarter of the miners emigrated, and the Cornish population fell by nearly 9 per cent., was no time for re-equipment. There were only ladders still for the 266 fathoms of West Wheal Seton in 1887[5]. Engines of Watt's pattern and boilers of Trevithick's remained in position. Some observers, their backward-looking fancies tickled by the simple uncontentious labour conditions

[1] From the census figures women are omitted; also the group 'miner undefined' in the censuses of 1861 and 1871. It was not large in either. The figures for 1881 and 1891 are those used in the *Survey of Industrial Relations* and reproduced in the *Eighteenth Abstract of Lab. Stat.* 1926, p. 22.

[2] For the one really great iron mine, Hodbarrow near Millom, see *V.C.H. Cumberland*, II. 396. By 1881 there were only 871 lead-miners in Derbyshire, and by 1901 only 285. *V.C.H. Derby*, II. 348. In Durham the lead output of 1905 was about one-tenth of what it had been in the 'fifties. *V.C.H. Durham*, II. 352.

[3] Jenkins, A. K. H., *The Cornish Mines* (1927), p. 222, 333. See also Price, L. L. F. R., "West Barbary or Notes on...the Cornish Mines," in *S.J.* 1888.

[4] Jenkins, p. 304. For the high number of tin-mines (82 out of less than 200 mines of all sorts in Cornwall and the South-West generally) *Fact. Ins. Rep.* 1879 (1880, XIV. 93), p. 84.

[5] Jenkins, p. 182.

of the Duchy, were saying that it seemed "to have escaped the disturbing influence of the Industrial Revolution,"[1] whilst, partly because of this happy escape, other revolutions had sent Cornishmen to the ends of the earth, and would send more.

Two allied elemental industries grew without conspicuous change while coal-mining was being re-equipped and copper-mining stunted. Both witnessed to Jevons' saying of 1865 that "coal commands this age." One, the gas industry, had revealed —most imperfectly—what was in coal; the other, the heavy chemical industry, had used coal to extract from salt its component parts and combine them with other elements, principally the carbon of the coal itself. Neither had been important before 1830. Neither was conspicuous as an employing industry in 1851, nor very conspicuous even in 1881; though the coal used in gasworks had grown from perhaps 600,000 tons in 1850 to 8,400,000 in 1885[2]. But their economic and social weights, like those of the rubber and some other industries, had no relation to numbers. Both, when Jevons wrote, had points of contact, but too few, with the fine chemistry of drugs and essences and the growing chemical science of the laboratories. A fresh contact with chemical science had been set up in 1863 when, under the first Alkali Act (26 and 27 Vict. c. 124), the state appointed an inspecting chemist to make soda manufacturers condense the hydrochloric "acid mist" with which some of their works had polluted the country[3]. The state also controlled gas works, their prices and dividends, and the illuminating power of their product—but not their chemistry. The alkali inspector, becoming "rather weary of the monotony as well as of the narrowness"[4] of his sole task, that of testing chimney gases for hydrochloric acid, began to study the general problems of air defilement, national health, and by-product economy. He secured an extended Alkali Act after eleven years (1874; 37 and 38 Vict. c. 43); but it was another seven before his dream of inspection for all 'emitting' industries—chlorine, cement, manure works and so on—was attained[5]. Some of his leisure had been spent in advocating, with little effect, the use of by-product ovens in coke-making, so as to gain such fertilisers as

[1] Price, *op. cit.* p. 498.

[2] For 1850, the estimate in Porter, *Progress of the Nation*, p. 582; for 1885, Thorpe, Sir E., in *Dic. of Applied Chemistry* (ed. 1922), *s.v.* Coal Gas.

[3] First *Rep. of the Alkali Inspector*, 1864 (1865, xx), p. 15.

[4] *Report of* 1872 (1873, XIX).

[5] *Report of* 1882 (1883, XVIII).

sulphate of ammonia[1]. The chemical affinities of the coal industries were at least being made public.

For many years, while gas works had multiplied, gas-work chemistry remained primitive. Far too much sulphur went into the gas. The coke was sold cheap, rich with unextracted hydrocarbons[2]. Coal-tar was a superabundant by-product for which it was hard to find an effective demand. So, for a time, was the hydrochloric acid which the soda makers no longer sent into the air. They found an outlet for some of their acid early by turning it into the bleaching powder (chloride of lime) for which the expanding cotton and paper industries had a sustained demand. Coal-tar meanwhile went unanalysed into the obvious baser uses; and much sulphur and lime waste went to generate sulphuretted hydrogen in the made ground on which part of Widnes was being built[3]. Then, between 1856 and 1870, came the discoveries of William Perkin and others, which were to transform dyeing; reveal the almost infinite chemical contents of coal; and stimulate the coke makers to save and handle their by-products, which contained many things besides chemical fertilisers. Perkin's 'Tyrian purple', vulgarly mauve, of 1856; the fuchsine of 1859, called also 'magenta' as a selling device; and the first alizarin—'turkey red'—which German chemists isolated in 1868, and Perkin more satisfactorily in 1869; these were the initial discoveries on which an industry was gradually based during the 'seventies and early 'eighties, but based more firmly in Germany than in Britain.

The manufacture of heavy chemicals was an industry of large localised units, easy mass output, and rather conservative routine. Owing to the magnificent location of the principal works, near salt, coal and tide-water—when inspection began, of 84 soda-makers, 38 were in South Lancashire and North Cheshire and 19 on Tyneside[4]—they had early secured control of the world's markets. Owing to concentration—nearly half the rock salt 'roasted' at that time was handled by 10 out of the 84[5]—and the huge Lancashire demand, they were able to work cheaply and, if necessary, dump surpluses abroad. From the start they had used the Leblanc process, or chain of processes, to make the sodium carbonate (washing soda), bicarbonate

[1] *Report of* 1878 (1878–9, XVI).
[2] Bone, W. A., *Coal and its Scientific Uses* (1918), p. 272.
[3] *Alkali Report of* 1874 (1875, XVI).
[4] *Alkali Report of* 1864. [5] *Ibid.*

(cooking soda) and hydroxide (caustic soda), from the chloride which is common salt. Down to the 'sixties, when the world-power of the British makers was at its height, this was the only commercial process known. But in 1863 the Belgian chemical manufacturer Solvay borrowed from English laboratory chemists the so-called ammonia process, which turned out purer soda more cheaply. The strength of the main English firms, and their hold of the markets, prevented this competition from telling on them seriously, or forcing them to consider a change of process, for a decade or more. In 1875–6 more salt was 'roasted' for alkali-making in Widnes, a town most of which was only twelve years old, than in all Prussia[1]. But the trade disturbances and the competition of the later 'seventies so shook the British alkali trade that, in 1881–2, many firms were contemplating its abandonment. The next years saw the struggle of the processes begin in Britain itself. The Leblanc still held its own, especially in Lancashire, in 1886, in which year it consumed over four times as much salt as its rival[2].

The gas industry at that moment was approaching its first difficult corner. Consumption and expansion had gone on quite steadily, with continuous improvement in technique but no fundamental change, since William Murdoch lit up Boulton and Watt's Soho works in the year 1800. Throughout, high illuminating power in gas to be consumed on an open burner had been the sole desideratum. Now came the first flickerings of competition from electricity; Welsbach's invention of the incandescent burner in 1885; a rapidly extending use of gas for cooking and heating, and demands for a cheaper gas for use in internal combustion engines. The companies or municipal works with their comfortable monopoly areas, and no Belgians or Germans to fear, began to feel a little wind of change blowing among their retorts and coke heaps.

To the close of the third quarter of the century, electricity, although it had exerted power in the world by way of the telegraph since the middle of the second quarter, was not 'power.' As light it was still only the intense and rather unlovely glare which Faraday and Holmes had thrown out from the South Foreland on the evening of December 8, 1858. Even in 1881, all that the President of the Institute of Mechanical Engineers found to say about a main aspect of the electricity problem was:

[1] *Report for* 1875–6 (1878–9, XVI), p. 14.

[2] *Reports for* 1882 (1883, XVIII) and 1886 (1887, XVII).

"it is possible, and even probable, that one of the great uses to which Electric Force will be applied eventually, will be the simple conveyance of power by means of large wires."[1] Siemens and Halske had already mounted an experimental electric tramway in Berlin (1879). The full-grown 'dynamo machine,' as it was still called, whose principle had been given to the world almost simultaneously by William Siemens, Wheatstone and Varley, in 1867, had for some time been available, and had just (1880) received an important improvement from Siemens[2]. The President of the Engineers, before he began to speak of the transmission of power, had congratulated his colleagues on the recent arrival of "the elegant and steady domestic light of Mr Swan." A little later (1882) Siemens was telling the Society of Arts that electricity "must win the day as the light of luxury."[3] Graham Bell had demonstrated his telephone to Queen Victoria at Osborne, and the first telephone exchange had been opened in America, in January, 1878. Next year there were exchanges in London and about eight other British towns. In several of the towns 'electric light and telephone' companies were being formed in the early 'eighties. The combination is interesting[4]. William Siemens in his last years—he died in November, 1883—was immersed in the experimental application of electricity to metallurgy[5]. Its use in the chemical industries, but for which the world would have had no commercial aluminium, was to come soon. In America, Edison, very far from death, was pushing into field after field of electrical application and invention. In Germany, Emil Rathenau, a retired iron-founder bitten by electricity, had floated in April, 1883, the Deutsche Edisongesellschaft to exploit the carbon filament lamp[6].

Everything, in short, was ready for electrical industries and an electric age, but, apart from the telegraph industries, neither had arrived. Britain, her critics were telling her, was behind America and Germany. The Birmingham telephone exchange had only 312 subscribers in 1886. Telephone apparatus was

[1] *Trans. Inst. Mech. Eng.* 1881, p. 419 (E. A. Cowper).

[2] See *D.N.B.*, Siemens, and Jeans, W. T., *Creator of the Age of Steel*, p. 175–7, 182, 211.

[3] Quoted in Jeans, *op. cit.* p. 178.

[4] Baldwin, F. G. C., *The Hist. of the Telephone in the United Kingdom* (1925), p. 15, 23, 119. The first central electricity station was in Holborn in 1882.

[5] See *inter alia* Geipel, W., "On the Position and Prospects of Electricity as applied to Engineering," *Trans. Inst. Mech. Eng.* 1888, p. 103.

[6] Kessler, W. R., *Walther Rathenau* [Eng. trans. 1929], p. 12.

nearly all turned out by hand, and usually designed and made by each separate company. Although the uses of electricity in collieries seemed obvious; although a Scottish colliery is believed to have been the first in the world to be lighted by electricity and fitted with a telephone, in 1881[1]; and although a pit in the Forest of Dean was even pumped by electricity in 1882[2]; five years later such enterprise remained unusual. At that time two out of the four United Kingdom experiments in electric traction were Irish: on the continent and in the United States there were many more. In contrast with the few and small British electric light works, nearly all in large towns, there was "hardly a city or town of 20,000 inhabitants in the United States which had not a central station for arc or incandescent lamps"; and "on the continent large central stations" were "already in operation in competition with gas."[3]

All the most interesting early experiments in the transmission of power over relatively long distances had been made abroad. Siemens had directed the attention of the Institute of Civil Engineers in 1883 to the way in which M. Marcel Deprez had managed to transmit as much as 3 h.p. to a distance of 25 miles through ordinary telegraph wires[4]. Electric power had been used by foreigners, though without long transmission and through small motors, in a number of industrial processes—for printing, tailoring, and the like at Boston; for the light metal industries at Geneva; and so on[5]. Such things were not unknown in Britain: electromagnetic riveters were installed at Dumbarton shipyards in 1886–7; but it was agreed that Britain was not the pioneer[6]. Electricity and dynamos and motors were expensive. British towns had not the "arrowy Rhone" flowing through them like Geneva. British factories had their steam engines, belts and shafting in good running order. Trade conditions in the early 'eighties were seldom such as to encourage capital expenditure on novelties. Coal was cheap. It had served my father very well. Why should I think of change just yet? The argument for delay was probably sound in more than nine cases out of ten—if a short view was taken.

[1] Baldwin, *op. cit.* p. 9: the Earnock Colliery, Hamilton.

[2] Trafalgar Pit, the first in England. *V.C.H. Gloucester*, II. 235.

[3] Geipel, *op. cit.* p. 103. [4] Jeans, *op. cit.* p. 212.

[5] Geipel, *op. cit.* p. 78.

[6] Very important work on electric transmission, in connection with light companies, was however being done in London by Ferranti in 1886. See his obituary notice in *The Times*, Jan. 1, 1930.

It was enforced by the ease with which the lighter British industries could install, and in fact already had installed, the new low power internal combustion engines. You could get gas anywhere in a British industrial area, and these were gas engines. Scientific experiments with internal combustion were nothing new; but the first gas engine to go into industry was Lenoir's of 1860, a very wasteful type judged by later standards[1]. It was followed quickly by Hugon's of 1865 and by Otto's first, so-called 'atmospheric,' engine of 1866. Ten years later this rather "noisy and spasmodic" affair was superseded by the 'silent' Otto, an efficient machine with a four-stroke cycle. None of these names is British; nor were the engines which preceded the silent Otto of 1876 much used in this country. But when an English firm took over the manufacture of the improved Otto, it came into use rather fast, fastest where it was most needed, in the light metal industries. By 1882 its introduction had already had "a marked effect in increasing the number of factories" in the Birmingham area[2]. About that time Clerk's two-stroke cycle engine came as a not very formidable competitor with the now established Otto. Experiments were being made with other fuels than coal gas. Compared with coal it was expensive, but the engine was generally small like the steam engines of sixty years earlier[3]. The convenience and economy in supervision of the little apparatus which could be hitched on to the ubiquitous gas-pipes fully justified its use for all sorts of odd and end industrial purposes in every kind of 'factory.'

A whole generation had run since Thackeray sang in his May Day Ode of the toiling engines, "England's arms of conquest." There was discomfort in the body economic, a tang of doubt in the air. Enemies of "the snorting steam and piston stroke" there had always been. The author of that contemptuous phrase[4] was just turning from a Democratic Federation to a Socialist League, which should rid the world of piston-dom and piston-lords, if not of pistons. But that is not for discussion in this place. Nor are those forces, political, geographic, commercial, monetary, demographic, which had changed the position of Britain among the nations. The question which is

[1] Ewing, Sir J. A., *The Steam Engine and other Heat Engines* (4th ed.), p. 585 *sqq*. Clerk, Sir D., *The Gas, Petrol and Oil Engines* (1909).

[2] Survey of Birmingham industry, 1871–82, by a retiring factory inspector: *Inspector's Report* for 1883 (1884, XVIII. 181), p. 52. Also quoted in Allen, *op. cit.* p. 229.

[3] Vol. I. p. 443.

[4] From the prologue to William Morris' *Earthly Paradise*.

relevant here is that of the engines themselves and of all the economic power for which they stood in the minds of those who used or valued them. Was there the old justification for pride in England's arms of conquest? Was any other nation so well equipped; or perhaps better; at any points; or at all? Not at all: that was certain. But even in 1851 the United States had been better equipped for some purposes—such as stitching, reaping, revolver-making, wool-spinning; and ever since, the adoption, though very likely with improvement, of American machinery for one thing or another had been curiously frequent; so frequent that the historian is tempted to adopt from it some general formula of technical progress in late revolutionised industries, which shall simplify his narrative and his causal explanations. This is not permissible. But it would be even less permissible, in any general summary, to minimise the contribution of the nimble American 'engine' to the industrial life of that generation[1].

Continental nations had enjoyed industrial superiorities over Britain in 1851, but they were not 'engine' superiorities. Even in 1840, it had been reported to Lord Palmerston that the states of the German Commercial Union were "in some respects" ahead of Britain in their "means of manufacture." The "means" suggested were "the arts of design"; metal working; and, as might have been expected among a definitely better educated people, "chemical knowledge in its various branches."[2] In what senses, if any, Germany had really been superior to Britain in metallurgy at that time need not be determined. She was at least ready to take her full share in the metallurgical and mechanical progress of the next forty years, as she had opportunity. Krupp's name was known in Britain before 1851. It was very well known indeed, and not only in connection with guns, by 1886. Her superiority in "chemical knowledge" Germany retained into the era in which the alliance between exact science and 'the engines' became of greater moment every year. Some of it she exported to Britain in human form—Siemens was born in Hanover; some in actual engines, as Otto's; some in processes, as Poetsch's system of sinking mines in ground artificially frozen[3].

[1] Above, pp. 12–14, 77, 89, 94–5, 97, 99. Another instance is the Hoe printing-press, first made by Whitworth from American designs, and from 1869 at the firm's London factory. Burn, D. L., in *E.J.* (*Ec. Hist.*), Jan. 1931, p. 302.

[2] Bowring, J., *Report on the Prussian Commercial Union*, p. 55.

[3] Above, p. 90.

Belgium, earliest industrialised of all continental nations, was making returns to Britain for what she had borrowed when the Englishman Cockerill introduced the new metal-working methods and powers at Seraing in 1798–1813, and when British capital and engineers helped to build her railways and her gas industry, from the 'thirties onwards. Solvay paid Britain the compliment of borrowing to undersell; the ventilation of her mines owed more to Guibal of Mons than to any other single inventor; those methods of utilising the by-products of her coke ovens which she was so very slow to adopt had been worked out for her mainly by two Belgian mining engineers, Coppée and Carvès[1].

To France the direct mechanical or industrial debt, in this generation, was perhaps somewhat less—though admirers of the Heilmann comb might dispute this. Certainly it was less than it might have been had France not been so busy with revolution and *coup d'état*, with war for prestige and war for life, between 1848 and 1873. The approximate completion of her railway network came late, later than in Germany, and this held industrialism back[2]. She continued to excel most in the least mechanical crafts, and she was not as yet able to compete with England in any one of the industries specially characteristic of the age, except in certain branches of wool-preparing and spinning. In spite of all this, French names and French processes recur in even a summary account of inventions affecting British industry[3]. In a story of thought and its final significance for economic life there would be more.

Indisputably, Britain still led the world's industrial motion. Still the only true 'industry state,' she had her immense accumulations of mechanical productive power; her cotton industry; her coal industry; with a dozen others supreme in mechanism; and she had large exports of every sort of machine—though there was some dispute whether this last was an asset or a risky liability, and whether some of her mechanical accumulations might not with advantage be scrapped because obsolescent. The basic engineering inventions had been nearly all British, the great steel inventions all. Single-handed, Britain had created modern shipbuilding. As it happens, shipbuilding is greatly

[1] Bone, W. A., *op. cit.*, p. 307. Above, p. 51.

[2] Clapham, J. H., *The Economic Development of France and Germany*, 1815–1914, pp. 146–7, 150.

[3] Above, p. 14 n. 1, 59, 109.

depressed in 1885, but the secretary of the trade union of the men who made the iron and steel ships says "so far as competition with England is concerned there is practically none." Asked, "Have we got it all our own way?" he answers, "Quite so."[1] But it will not be "quite so" very many years longer. The mechanical and industrial movement has become once for all international, and there is very little echelon in the advance. British mechanical deputations to the United States; continentals besieging Gilchrist Thomas before breakfast for licences to work his invention; Rathenau founding his *Edisongesellschaft*; or the careers of the brothers Siemens, planted in two countries yet working together, are symbolic of the new age. Engines are toiling indifferently for all. Mechanical or scientific industrial monopolies are short lived. Some people, and they not poets, are thinking that the world has too many engines, too many in certain uses at least, and that in spite of John Stuart Mill general over-production, or something which might with reasonable accuracy be so described, may after all exist if only in what economists call 'the short period.'

[1] *R.C. on Depression of Trade*, Q. 14,760–1, Robert Knight.

CHAPTER IV

THE DEVELOPMENT OF INDUSTRIAL ORGANISATION

THE era of metal and machinery had brought with it bigger industrial units all along the line. In the early 'twenties the largest and most famous of the old Thames shipyards, that of Wigram and Green, had employed perhaps 600 men "when...in full run."[1] In 1870 the average iron shipbuilding yard on the North-East coast employed rather more, and the average Scottish yard employed 800[2]. This is an industry in which the revolution had been carried through from start to finish during that half century, and in which the actual thing turned out, the ship, had grown hugely. Exactly how much the industrial unit in general grew, over any given period preceding the 'eighties, it is only possible to say for those textile industries about which returns of employment and machinery were made at fairly frequent, if irregular, intervals. It is known, for instance, that the average cotton factory in which spinning was done increased the number of its spindles by 30 per cent., and that the average worsted factory had a corresponding increase of 81 per cent., between 1850 and 1875[3]. What the representative, as opposed to the average, unit was at different dates there is no means of ascertaining with certainty. To the historian's great loss, the attempt made at the census of 1851 to collect and tabulate employment statistics for all industries was not repeated in succeeding censal years. A single return, of 1870–1, does however throw light on the average size of industrial establishments in all, or nearly all, the manufacturing industries, revealing those in which the factory had become normal and those in which the units were a mixture of factories and workshops. There are also some relevant special statistics, besides those for textiles. The return of 1871 was issued by the Home Office after two years' grappling with the Factory Acts

[1] Vol. I. p. 69.

[2] *Return of Factories and Workshops*, 1871 (LXII. 105). Figures collected in Nov.-Dec. 1870.

[3] *Fact. Ins. Rep.* 1875 (XVI. 251), p. 9. The figures may refer to whole factories (spinning mills) or to the spinning departments of what in Germany are called conveniently 'spin-weaveries.'

Extension Act and the Workshops Act of 1867 (30 and 31 Vict. c. 103 and c. 146). These were the Acts which brought nearly all the power-using metal industries, and also paper, glass, tobacco, printing and some others, under the Factory Inspectors, together with all places in which fifty or more persons were employed in manufacturing. They also put workshops under the inspection of the local authority, provided they contained women, children or young persons[1].

Though this return does not apply precisely to the conditions of the early 'eighties, it must do so very nearly. There is no reason to think that there was any important change in the scale of industrial operations in the interval. In 1870–1 the average British cotton factory employed 180 workpeople; in 1885, 191. Even in the hosiery industry, which the factory was just conquering and in which it was therefore likely to be specially expansive, the corresponding increase is only from 71 to 86[2]. The external conditions of most manufacturing industries, especially of the 'heavy' industries in which the units were the largest, were not encouraging between the crisis of 1873 and the early 'eighties[3]. This was not the sort of era in which businesses grow fast. Moreover, social averages of any sort seldom change much in ten years. It may be taken, therefore, that the 1871 returns give reasonably exact measurements of the statistical skeleton of British industrial organisation as it remained in the 'eighties; with the provisos, first, that the size of the localised industrial unit in the average industry may have grown by from 5 to 10 per cent. in the interval; and, second, that in some few industries, such as hosiery and bootmaking, the rapid progress of factory conditions may have increased that percentage to 20 or rather more.

The returns have a special interest of their own. They fall very near three culminating points in modern economic history —those of the age of steam; of the age of non-joint-stock industrial organisation; and of the age of undisputed British international supremacy in the old commerce and the new industry. Water power, so important in the earliest factory days and still of some significance in the 'forties, was now really of none; it furnished only 4·5 per cent. of all the h.p. (991,000)

[1] For the Acts see below, p. 416. The *Return* is that quoted above, 1871, LXII. 105.

[2] The 1885 figures from the *Return* in 1884–5, LXXXI. 1087.

[3] Below, p. 385.

which came under the view of the inspectors. Gas engine power had not begun to tell and electrical power was unknown. Joint-stock manufacturing companies existed in 1871, but they were rare and unimportant, except the public utility companies with which these returns do not deal. They grew rapidly in numbers during the next fourteen or fifteen years, but not in ways which markedly affected the scale of industrial operations[1]. That British economic superiority was near its nineteenth-century culminating point in or about the decade 1870–80 has been suggested in the narrative of industrial change and will be illustrated in other narratives. Here it is assumed.

The inspectors reported in 1871 on 2,417,000 employed persons of ten years old and upwards, and on 127,000 separate working places, 'works' they called them, in Great Britain. They claimed, and it would seem with reason, that for every place which came under the Factory Acts these returns might "be considered as nearly as possible accurate." Comparison with the census figures of the same year confirms this claim for the completely 'factorised' industries. For a few trades, the returns of workshops, which the inspectors procured from local authorities "in many cases disinclined to move,"[2] are remarkably full and seem certainly representative. But from some counties, and unfortunately from London, the workshop returns are lacking or quite inadequate. Even so, the sample of industrial organisation provided is of high value. It ignores all mining; all agriculture; a great part of the food and drink, clothing and building trades; and such scattered country trades as those of the miller, blacksmith and wheelwright. The inspectors had no oversight of outworkers, a fact which explains the inadequacy of their returns for the clothing trades, in which outwork is general.

The largest average unit recorded is in iron ship-building: 78 firms employed an average of 570·5 workpeople each: among these the 30 Scottish firms averaged 800. Primary iron-making 'works'—blast-furnaces, puddling-furnaces and rolling mills, separate or in combination—averaged 209 workpeople; but in Glamorgan and Monmouth 26 'works' of this class averaged 650. The general figure was brought down by Staffordshire, where the single blast-furnace firm and the small iron-mill were common. Contrasts within the metallurgical industries are illustrated in the table below. Industries printed in italics are

[1] Below, p. 138 *sqq*. [2] *Return*, p. 105. For the local authorities, below, p. 416.

those returned by the inspectors as being carried on partly in factories, as defined by the Acts, partly in workshops. The term 'works' covers both.

Metal-working industries of Great Britain, 1870–1

	No. of 'works'	No. of workpeople	Average
All metal manufactures . .	*18,000*	*622,000*	*34·5*
Iron making . . .	761	166,700	219
Iron ship-building . .	78	44,500	570·5
Manufacture of machinery .	1,933	163,600	85
Nails and rivets . . .	*1,604*	*13,200*	*8*
Cutlery, files, saws, tools .	*1,143*	*24,600*	*21·5*
Miscellaneous articles of metal	*7,900*	*75,400*	*9·5*

The last three groups illustrate the Sheffield, Birmingham, and Black Country trades, with a rare factory to swell the average and a host of workshops, or factories by definition only—*i.e.* small power-using, probably power-hiring, businesses—to keep it down. The figures must exaggerate the size of the average unit somewhat, because inspectors who seldom missed a factory no doubt failed to learn about many workshops. A relatively low figure for engineering proper, the ruling industry of the age, suggests, at first sight, that the little country machine shops are cancelling out the great firms of the industrial areas. This is no doubt a partial explanation. But as the Lancashire average (80) is below the national average, the main cause is evidently the existence of many small specialised shops in the industrial areas themselves.

The textile figures had not changed much since 1851, and not very much since the early days of factory inspection[1], though in all the industries the unit was growing.

Chief Textile Industries of Great Britain, 1870–1

	No. of factories	No. of workpeople	Average
Cotton	2,469	436,000	177
Woollen	1,768	124,000	70
Worsted	627	109,500	175
Flax	346	70,000	202
Jute	58	16,900	291
[Silk	692	47,000	68]
[Lace	223	8,300	37]
[Hosiery	126	9,000	71]

[1] In 1838 the average (mean) number of persons employed per factory was: cotton, 137; woollen, 46; worsted, 76. For elaborate statistical analyses of the inspectors' figures of this period, including calculations of the median as well as the mean, see Fong, *Triumph of Factory System in England*, p. 18 and *passim*. The medians in 1838 were: cotton, 92; woollen, 19; worsted, 57.

Three of the industries are bracketed because they are not in the same category as the rest. The silk 'factories' include 334 weaving businesses in Warwickshire averaging only ten workpeople each. But for these little Coventry ribbon shops—nearly half the 'factories' of the trade, with but one-fifteenth of its workpeople—the picture would be quite different. Lace and hosiery were still largely outwork, or factory-cum-outwork, industries, and the figures in this table refer to factories only. There was an outwork element of hand-loom weavers in every textile industry, but hardly great enough now, even in woollen, flax or silk, to affect the general factory character of the occupations. The low factory figures for woollen—much lower than for silk, if the Coventry figures are omitted—are such as had marked the industry throughout the century. It was not merely that tiny carding and spinning mills survived in Wales and Scotland. Yorkshire's average business was very little above the British average, because Yorkshire still contained a few of the old company mills and a great many small concerns near the borderline of the woollen and shoddy industries[1].

One textile entry in the inspectors' returns rouses a curiosity which it does not fully satisfy. They tabulated 12,800 'works,' and 44,000 workers, under hand-loom weaving unspecified. Of these 43, with 4700 workers, were called factories because of their size; the rest, workshops. The hand-loom factories were mainly in East Anglia—10 in Suffolk alone—and ranged, as is known from other evidence, from delicate silk to various other very rough fabrics. As the definition of a person 'employed' in a workshop under the Act was 'occupied with or without wages,' the remaining 'works,' in which the average employment figure is barely 3, are probably for the most part home-working families of weavers in all the industries, with a sprinkling of small employers' loom shops. Nearly 13,000 in 3800 'works' were in Yorkshire; 4300 in 2300 'works' in Lancashire; 3300 in 800 'works' in Ayr; 4700 in 1100 'works' in Lanark; and more than 1000 in each of Stirling, Renfrew, Forfar, Cheshire, Warwick and Suffolk. It is unfortunate that the workshop figures from Middlesex (Spitalfields silk) and some other counties are defective. The sustained importance of the

[1] For the company mills see vol. I. p. 194–6; for the shoddy mills, which the inspectors did not distinguish, above, p. 39. The Yorkshire average in 1870–1 was 74. It was only 80 in 1899: Clapham, J. H., *The Woollen and Worsted Industries*, p. 131.

hand-loom in Scotland, which contained 20,000 out of the reported total of 44,000 hand-loom workers, is notable. There it turned out mainly linens, with some woollens. In England there was not much linen, a good deal of woollen, and a great deal of silk.

Some selected miscellaneous industries give the following results. Italics as before denote an industry in which factories and workshops existed side by side.

Miscellaneous Industries of Great Britain, 1871

	No. of 'works'	No. of workpeople	Average
Boot and shoe	*9,500*	*62,000*	*6·5*
(Factories in ditto	145	18,200	125·5)
Tailoring and clothing	*8,000*	*43,000*	*5·4*
(Factories in ditto	58	77,000	132·8)
Millinery, etc.	*11,300*	*52,400*	*4·6*
Pottery	537	45,000	83·8
Bricks	1,770	22,500	12·7
Letterpress printing	3,550	48,300	13·6
Tanning and currying	*670*	*12,200*	*18·2*
Baking	*6,316*	*20,800*	*3·3*
Rubber and gutta percha	39	5,700	146·1
Manufactures connected with building (builder, carpenter, cabinet-maker, etc.)	*19,800*	*152,800*	*7·7*

For factory industries, such as pottery and rubber, these figures are no doubt almost complete. Judging by the census returns of the same year, they furnish a good sample for tanning and currying and for printing, and a fair sample for baking. They are sure to include all large urban tanyards and the larger bakehouses, so that the employment figures yield maximum averages[1]. Of the clothing trades outside the factories they do not tell much, partly because the samples are small, partly because there are such complications of outwork in all these trades. The figures of 'manufactures connected with building' tell still less; for they mix up builders with cabinet makers and apparently exclude all craftsmen who work for a builder outside his yard.

[1] Some returns of the Typographical Association in 1860 (*Trades Societies and Strikes: R. of the Assoc. for Social Science*, p. 91–2) give an average employment figure of only 7: they do not include London but do include Manchester, Liverpool and Leeds. About 1890 it was estimated that the average staff of a London bakery was 5 (*R.C. on Labour*, 1893–4, XXXIV. Group C, Q. 29,572). In 1891 the figure for baking and confectionery was 6. Booth, C., *Life and Labour of the People in London*, IX. 55.

Unfortunately no other figures or records help much to determine the sizes of the various types of representative firms in the building trades, either in 1871 or later. The trade-group grew fast, easily holding its old position as the group which contained more men than any other except agriculture. The builders and their associated craftsmen—bricklayer, mason, plasterer, carpenter, plumber and so on—increased in numbers from 634,000 in 1871 to 761,000 in 1881. To these must be added probably not less than 250,000 labourers. (Compare the 531,000 males in all textile industries whatsoever; the 735,000 in conveyance of every kind; or the round 520,000 working in and about the coal-mines, in 1881.) The scale of operations in building varied extraordinarily and no statistical picture of an average building business could be true. But the fact that, when the census began to differentiate between employers and employed, in 1891, there were in London itself only thirty-six members of all the building crafts to each person who described himself as an employing builder is at least a reminder of the recurrent emergence, and the continued if precarious vitality, of the small building 'undertaker.' This great group of trades still offered a career to talent. "Are not most of the master-builders men who have been workmen originally?" a competent witness was asked about this time. "Nearly all of them," he replied[1].

In the basic industry of coal-mining, the growth of the physical unit of operations, the colliery or pit, had been accompanied by an expansion of the average colliery firm or company. What might be called the feudal colliery enterprises—the Earl of Durham's or Lord Londonderry's; the Earl of Dudley's; Earl Granville's in North Staffordshire, or those of the Duke of Bridgewater's trustees in South Lancashire—had expanded by deepenings and fresh sinkings and were now among the greatest business concerns of the country[2]. In 1886 the Bridgewater trustees controlled 15 collieries; the Earl of Durham, 13; Earl

[1] *R.C. on Labour*, Group C, Q. 32,095. Cp. Booth, C., *Life and Labour*, v. 30 *sqq*. The census officials of 1891, it should be noted, regarded their new returns of employer and employed as "excessively untrustworthy" (*Census*, 1893–4, CVI. 36). They express surprise that under the heading 'Builder' there appeared more masters than men. If this was a reason for distrusting these particular results, it is a poor one; 'men' in the building trades do not call themselves builders as a rule.

[2] *Mineral and Mining Statistics for* 1886 (1887, LXXIX).

Granville, 8; Lord Londonderry, 5 very large ones. Comparable with these, or sometimes on a still larger scale, were such firms as James Joicey and Co. with 11 important collieries, and Bowes and Partners with 14, on Tyneside; Pease and Partners with 14 in South Durham; Andrew Knowles and Son with 11 on the edge of Manchester; the Wigan Coal and Iron Co. with no less than 29—many small; or the great new steam coal companies of South Wales, such as the Powell Duffryn with its 13 separate collieries. At the other end of the scale, curious but quite unrepresentative, were such enterprises as that of a certain John Lewis, "the owner of a small colliery at Thurgoland, and on the 5th of March [1885] he lost his life in it. He and two others were the only persons in the pit."[1]

Between these extremes came the normal coal mine of the 'eighties, of considerable size but owned by a firm which owned no other. In North and East Lancashire, a highly developed area which contained, besides the 26 Bridgewater and Knowles mines, 12 belonging to Colonel Hargreaves' executors, there was an average of only 2 "mines or collieries" to each of the 151 owners or companies, including the Hargreaves, Knowles and Bridgewater group. In North Staffordshire there were only 1·6 "mines or collieries" to each owner or company. In the West Midland coal areas, in Yorkshire and in Scotland the ratio was still lower; and even in Durham, North and South combined, it was only 2·2 separate collieries or mines per firm.

The representative mine varied with the character of the mining, being smallest where the seams were shallowest. Fairly representative of average conditions, in a well-developed district of moderately deep workings, would be those of West Lancashire, the country of the Wigan Coal and Iron Co. There, in 1885, the average number of persons employed "in and about" each of 151 separate mines was 213. Not many miles away, on the North Welsh fields of Flint and Denbigh, the figure was not much more than half this[2].

The growth of the average colliery enterprise, in a district which had been technically rather backward down to the 'seventies, is shown by some Scottish returns for the decade 1875 to 1885. They cover the Eastern inspecting district of Scotland, which stretched from Lanark through the Lothians to Fife, Clackmannan and Kinross. In 1875 the inspector had

[1] *Report of Inspectors of Mines for* 1885 (1886, XVI. 1), p. 165.
[2] *Ibid.* p. 255.

to deal with 218 firms, 144 of which each raised less than 40,000 tons a year, and 23 of which each raised more than 150,000 tons. Ten years later the number of firms had fallen to 171 and the number raising less than 40,000 tons a year to 80. Meanwhile the number raising more than 150,000 tons a year had risen to 31, the four largest of them raising more coal than all the 80 at the bottom put together. Besides illustrating the growing concentration of the industry, the figures bring out the wide diversity of its business units[1]. Some of the 80 small pits may have resembled John Lewis's "colliery" at Thurgoland.

The metalliferous mines, among which those of Cornwall had been outstanding examples of large-scale production fifty, and even thirty, years earlier, were no longer representative of the extractive industries. Dolcoath was still raising over 2000 tons of "black tin" in 1886[2]. Just over the Cornish border, the Devon Great Consols Mine, Tavistock, yielded 6000 tons of dressed copper ore. Foxdale lead mine in Man had an output of 4000 tons; and a few of the iron mines, such as Hodbarrow by Millom, were really big. But the total output of 53,000 tons of lead ore came from well over 200 separate mines; while to furnish 14,000 tons of "black tin," 78 mines, 4 open works, and a number of foreshore and river washeries were pottering away in Cornwall. All the metalliferous mines put together only employed 41,000 workers against 520,000 "in and about" the coal mines. No concentration of ownership or growth of the productive unit is perceptible.

In brewing, concentration can be traced very clearly over a period of years by the average brewer's growing consumption of malt, the accompanying slight decline in the number of brewers, and the marked decline in those brewing victuallers and beersellers who have been called the handicraft brewers[3]. The figures for England and Wales are as follows:

	1853	1864	1886
Brewers	2,470	2,295	2,242
Bushels of malt used . . .	21 millions	28 millions	39 millions
Brewing victuallers and beersellers	31,000	34,000	12,000
Bushels of malt used . . .	11 millions	11 millions	5 millions

The concluding twenty years are the critical age: the handicraft brewer declines everywhere except in remote areas such as

[1] *R. of Inspectors for* 1885, p. 102.

[2] *Mineral Returns*, as above: "black tin" is dressed tin ore.

[3] Vol. I. p. 170–1; and above, p. 37.

Carmarthenshire. Down to 1853, and even to 1864, he had dominated many parts of the country, though he had long been squeezed out of London and Norwich. The Birmingham district, for example, true to its character as the home of small industries, got nearly all its locally brewed beer from 1700 brewing victuallers and beersellers in 1864. They used fifteen times as much malt as the brewers. By 1886 this was all changed. There were still nearly a thousand of the small men; but six-sevenths of the malt now went into the vats of twenty-six Birmingham district brewers[1].

Fifty years earlier brewing had been in places what baking still was over wide areas, a household industry in which producer and consumer are one. Curious search might well find some domestic brewing, if only by Colleges of ancient Universities, in the Britain of the 'eighties; but if found it would be a survival without much meaning. Domestic baking as a habit of the people was far from meaningless in the North: it was perhaps declining, but not yet rapidly. In 1831 there had been, according to the census, only one adult baker to every 2200 of the population in Cumberland, against one to every 295 in Berkshire[2]. In 1881 there was a baker of some sort to every 600 in Cumberland; to every 83 in Berkshire; to every 263 in London, where the average bakehouse, it is to be presumed, was bigger than either in Berkshire or in the North[3].

Though an age of easy communications works inevitably against the endurance of 'household' industry, the system in which the household makes for its own use, it is not certain that a machine age always does. The sewing-machine probably gave the system fresh life between 1855 and 1885. But though the search for vigorous remnants, or revivals, of household industry about the latter year might not prove merely an insignificant bit of antiquarianism, like the search for beer-consumers' brew-houses, it is one upon which the historian need not enter—partly because the facts are very elusive, partly because, although they are elusive, it is certain that over the whole field of domestic consumption, and especially among the urban wage-earners, the use of factory-made and shop-handled goods was increasing.

[1] *Excise Returns A. and P.* 1854, LXV. 325; 1865, L. 701; 1887, LXXV. 79.

[2] Vol. I. p. 158.

[3] *Census of* 1881 (1883, LXXX), occupation summaries by county.

It is possible, but much less certain, that the working up of the consumers' raw material or half-finished goods by the craftsman, either on the consumers' premises or on his own, had declined in the sixty years since 'customer-weavers' of homespun linen and wool had been still fairly common in many parts of Britain[1]. There is an element of 'customer-work' in the endless jobbing repairs which the craftsman or craftswoman may carry out in other people's houses. Almost beyond question, the amount of such work had grown, not only absolutely but relatively, with the growing complexity of the Victorian home. There were hardly any plumbers in Sir Walter's Scotland: there was a plumber to every 508 of the population in the London of 1881[2]. Many of these were employed by builders, but many were small masters working on the customer's premises. A new and considerable industry in which, even in the 'eighties, "most of the masters had been workmen themselves,"[3] had been created by the consumer's necessity, in the full day of industrial concentration and Victorian capitalism.

The plumber type of jobbing workman was not exactly the 'customer-worker' of definition[4], because he supplied some at least of the material— if a plumber, lead piping and washers. Much closer to the definition were the scores of thousands of dressmakers and sewing women, whose work on the customer's premises, and often on the customer's materials and with her implement, the sewing-machine had certainly facilitated. What their exact number was in 1881 there is no means of determining; but even forty years later there were still 73,000 dress and blouse makers and milliners "working on their own account," that is, working either at home or on the customer's premises, and with no employer over them[5]. It is considerations such as these which would permit an argument, though not a proof, that customer-work as a whole had actually gained ground since 1850.

At all stages of economic evolution customer-work shades away into true handicraft—the system in which the working

[1] Vol. I. p. 159–62.

[2] *Ibid.* p. 164: *Census of* 1881, as above.

[3] Anderton, T., Sec. of the Operative Plumbers, before *R.C. on Labour* (1892, XXXVI. part 3, p. 43).

[4] The definition is German (*Kundenarbeiter*) and the system is commonest in fairly simple economic societies in which the craftsman owns little besides his skill and his tools.

[5] From the 1921 census: see *Eighteenth Abstract of Labour Statistics*, p. 11.

master owns tools and raw material, and sells finished goods or expert service or both, like the country blacksmith or the saddler. Horses still ruled the fields and the roads in the 'eighties, and London bus-horses had to be shod. The blacksmiths—men and sturdy lads—had not changed their functions much since 1851, or for that matter since 1551, although the census group included an uncertain number of men, perhaps a third of the whole, who were not shoeing and jobbing blacksmiths but just smiths associated with a variety of trades[1]. The total was no less than 132,000 in 1881. Even in London "little masters" still retained the bulk of the trade[2]. Down to 1871 the blacksmiths had grown almost as fast as the population. Between 1871 and 1881 they hardly grew at all. The ebb was soon to come.

The ancient handicrafts of the coach-builder, wheelwright and saddler were still almost intact. Twelve men to one employer in coach-building, and seven to one in saddlery, were the London figures in 1891[3]. The national averages in the 'eighties would be very much less. But these were threatened handicrafts, and already they had been linked up with industries of another sort. Saddlers had long drawn on the localised saddlery industry of Walsall, and country wheelwrights were forgetting how to make a new wooden axle for an old dung-cart. They had already forgotten how to make a wooden harrow, at least in Surrey[4]. The iron had entered deep into their trade.

Wheelwright, saddler, blacksmith, plumber; small carpenter, dressmaker or baker—the list might be lengthened—are typical survivals, or re-creations, of the producer who deals direct with the consumer either as customer-worker, repairing workman, or selling handicraftsman. Behind them was now usually some factory or other large-scale industry to supply their half-finished goods—iron axles; saddlers' ironmongery; iron bar; lead piping; sawn plank; sewing thread; flour—but they had the satisfactions, such as they are, and the risks, of economic independence and access to the ultimate consumer. Their journeymen and their lads had some fair prospect of succeeding

[1] "We do not cultivate having shoeing-smiths," the Sec. of the Assoc. Blacksmiths of Glasgow said to the *R.C. on Labour* (1893, XXXII. Group A, Q. 23,534).

[2] Booth, *Life and Labour*, V. 328.

[3] Booth, *op. cit.* IX. 55. Booth and his collaborators trusted the master and men statistics of 1891 about which the census officials were sceptical (above, p. 120, n. 1). That is why they are used here.

[4] Sturt, *The Wheelwright's Shop*, p. 20. Sturt went into business in 1884.

to these inheritances. Together they formed an important, though not an exactly measurable, part of the industrial population.

But most of the small masters who had survived, or come into existence, had some middleman or middlemen between them and the consumer; inevitably when the consumer was overseas and usually when he was not. In Birmingham the remains of the divided and sub-divided trade of gun-making, now that military demand had gone to the factories, worked for gun shops and those export merchants who kept half-savage tribes supplied. (They were suffering much from the suppression of slave-raiding and the checking of tribal war in Africa[1].) The declining watch-makers of Clerkenwell and their fellows in Coventry and other places, specialists who made not a watch but a main-spring, a hair-spring or a fusee chain, were hardly more than outworkers for the 'watchmaker' whose name stood on the dial[2]. Small masters in all the Birmingham, Black Country and Sheffield trades—they were still many—normally had their factor or merchant; or they might do jobs for a factory the doors of which had already closed on some of their fellows[3]. Above all in the cheap tailoring, furniture-making, and other London East-End industries, which were reproduced on a smaller scale in other great towns, there was every grade of small master and independent worker, in all sorts of different relationships with factories or with middlemen. In the East-End furniture trade the "typical producer" was a "man of small means, working with from three to six under him, and with little capital and no machinery."[4] This sort of man was on the increase in the late 'seventies and the 'eighties. Sometimes he would get material from "some superior employing firm or some intermediary."[5] There were also non-employing home workers, who supplied their own material and so might by courtesy be classed as independent handicraftsmen; though they were dangerously near common piece-paid outworkers. Below these were home workers using an employer's material, outworkers pure and simple.

In that unstable economic world men were always moving

[1] Allen, *The Industrial Development of Birmingham and the Black Country*, p. 265.

[2] Cp. vol. I. p. 177 n. 3. Booth, *op. cit.* VI. 26.

[3] *Birmingham and the Midland Hardware District* (1866), p. 454 n. Allen, *op. cit.* p. 327.

[4] Booth, *op. cit.* IV 164. [5] *Ibid.* IX. 204: for the increase 1875–90, IV. 163.

from class to class. They start as wage-earners. They try as independent workers. Perhaps when out of work they make the thing they know how to make, and sell it cheap to the dealer, so beating down the market. They may or may not succeed in getting enough business to become masters of men. If things go wrong, they try again as wage-earners. The simpler and cheaper the trade, the easier it is to experiment in independence. "The cabinet-maker...can start operations, albeit inadequately, and insecurely, with only £2 or £3 in hand, and with fish curers, makers of cheap magic lanterns and toys, of sweet-stuffs, gingerbeer and many other things, an even smaller capital is required."[1] It is to be remembered that in those clubs of queer trades which were East London, East Leeds, and North Manchester, new members from the Polish ghettos had brought with them a knowledge of simple economic conditions and a terrible passionless grasp of how such conditions can be handled for gain.

While Jewish immigrants were giving an unwholesome stimulus to all varieties of domestic industry in the slums, the last of the half-rural domestic clothiers of the North had gone. There were still a fair number of them in the 'fifties, especially in the smaller places. "Pudsey had never so many small manufacturers of woollens" as about 1860[2]; but even then, machinery had taken over at least half the business of cloth-making, machinery in the company-mills which the clothiers had clubbed together to build, or in the cloth-finishing mills run by, or for, the merchants to whom they sold. For a long time only jenny-spinning and weaving had been done at home. As the jenny finally gave way before the mule, prosperous domestic men got control of, or shared, little mills and had the weaving done 'out.' Prospering more, they built a weaving-shed and installed power-looms. Others went where the unprosperous go. For some years the domestic survivors, with those who had become small manufacturers, sold their pieces in the cloth-halls at Leeds in the old way. When in 1868 the North Eastern Railway wished to invade the site of the White Cloth Hall, it was forced to compensate the owners and frequenters by building another. But business in the new one was always

[1] Booth, *op. cit.* IX. 207.

[2] Lawson, J., *Progress in Pudsey* (1887), p. 86. The statement, introduced by a "perhaps," refers to "twenty to thirty years" before 1887. For 1858 see vol. I. p. 193.

slack. During the 'eighties it ceased. It was in the 'eighties also that an Act was passed authorising the trustees of the Coloured, or Mixed, Cloth Hall to sell their building to the Corporation. It was no longer wanted for trade and was an obstacle to traffic. The Corporation pulled it down: widened streets and a Post Office occupy its site. Thus the commercial shell of domestic clothing was broken. It had for some time been empty[1].

If domestic clothiers passed into the mills, as overlookers or ordinary wage-earners, the fact is not on record, though presumably a few did[2]. As the factory system gained ground in the Birmingham area, however, a parallel transition was quite common. "I was a little master locksmith for 22 years.... We nearly all work in large shops now," a man working for Chubbs said in 1863[3]. The small masters, Joseph Chamberlain wrote in 1866, were becoming "overlookers or foremen in large establishments."[4] The Birmingham, Black Country, and Sheffield trades showed more traces in their organisation of the absorption of 'masters,' or of methods natural in a field where small enterprise had been the rule and many masters had been absorbed, than any other trades in the country, except the building trades. Such methods were not at all new. The coal-mine 'butties,' pilloried by Disraeli in *Sybil*, were a class of sub-contracting small master-miners hardly known outside the Midlands[5]. Sub-contract was very general in the old-established Midland ironworks. "The puddlers employed their own underhands; the shinglers, the rollers, the mill-rollers, the saw-men, all employed their own assistants, varying in number from one to four. The sheet-mill was under a sub-contractor employing half a dozen subordinates; the hammerman had three; the iron-moulders, thirteen in number, were under a

[1] Heaton, H., *The Leeds White Cloth Hall* (*Thoresby Soc.* vol. XXII. 1913); *The Yorkshire Woollen and Worsted Industries* (1920), p. 391–2.

[2] Early in the century Benjamin Gott had five "manufacturers" in his great mill at Bean Ing, Leeds, with weavers under them. They made cloth to his order and paid him a commission to cover their overhead charges. *The Leeds Woollen Industry*, 1750–1820 (*Thoresby Soc.* ed. W. B. Crump, 1931), p. 34, 307. Whether anything like this happened later is not yet known. The clothiers vanished so slowly that there was no crisis: their places were simply not filled up.

[3] *Third Report on Children's Employment* (1864, XXII), p. 25.

[4] *Birmingham and the Hardware District*, p. 605. Cp. Allen, *op. cit.* p. 159 *sqq.*, where the system is fully illustrated.

[5] The system extended into Derbyshire. See *R.C. on Labour* (1892, XXXIV), Group A, Q. 7190 *sqq.*, 7463 *sqq.*

sub-contractor. The coal was brought in and the ashes removed by sub-contractors."[1]

In the Birmingham light metal trades, factory charges for "standings and light," though perhaps sometimes introduced as a way to make profit, suggest the master who came into a factory for convenience and had perhaps previously been in the habit of hiring power[2]. "Brass overhands" and "head brass-casters" were in much the same position as shinglers and rollers in the iron-mills, either sub-contractors out and out, or what have been called piece-wage foremen, who are their first cousins. The same conditions were found at Sheffield, where middlemen employing "cheap labour" often took on jobs "in the employer's factory."[3]

In iron ship-building, sub-contract, the master under the master, was no doubt a development from the old master-shipwrights' practice of taking on jobs in small groups, at a bargain price, and hiring what extra help they might need at a wage[4]. It was strongly approved of by pioneers of the new ship-building, like William Denny of Dumbarton, who described in 1876 the "bands of workmen in a ship-yard, engaged in the larger operations of plating or framing an entire ship and paid by one or more superior trades men."[5] As practised in Welsh slate-quarries, where the sub-contractors supplied tools and gunpowder but not expensive plant, it had stirred the enthusiasm of the economist Cairnes, and was to lead a much later apologist to compare the contracting quarryman to a "tenant-farmer under a kind of metayer system."[6] It was endemic—here the metaphor from disease is certainly warranted—in the cheap clothing trades. In railway building and other works of construction it had always been very widely used. But its spread was widest and its national importance greatest in the building trade.

The separate building crafts had never blended into one body of wage-earning artisans under an employing builder, though

[1] Schloss, D. F., *Methods of Industrial Remuneration* (1892), p. 118.

[2] Allen, G. C., "Methods of Industrial Organisation in the West Midlands," *E.J.* (*Ec. Hist.*), 1929, p. 543.

[3] *R.C. on Labour* (1892, XXXVI. part 2), Group A, Q. 19,020. And see above, p. 117. In the decade 1920–30 the tenacious Sheffield "little mesters working in tenement factories" were actually gaining ground. *Factory Report for* 1927 (Cmd. 3144, 1928), p. 45.

[4] Vol. I. p. 177.

[5] Denny, W., *The Worth of Wages*, p. 18, quoted in Schloss, *op. cit.*

[6] Cairnes, J. E., "Cooperation in the Slate Quarries of North Wales," *Macmillan's Magazine*, 1865; *R.C. on Labour* (1892, XXXVI. part 1), Group A, Q. 9040.

the tendency was in that direction. A large number of important building firms were "competent to do everything necessary in connection with their work from beginning to end,"[1] directing the various groups of wage-earning craftsmen through wage-earning foremen, generally recruited from among the joiners. This arrangement was commonest in London. But even in London sub-contracts, particularly with master-plumbers, master-painters, and master-plasterers—themselves employers —were common enough. In the North they were very much commoner. The ordinary Lancashire practice was for a building to be 'taken' by a master-joiner. He let out mason's, brick-layer's, plumber's, painter's work to other masters, who were in fact sub-contractors. The same arrangement is reported from the Yorkshire and South Welsh industrial areas. No doubt it was common elsewhere. But it was an unstable arrangement, for the more successful of these contracting master-carpenters were always turning into 'builders,' direct employers of all, or nearly all, the crafts[2].

In the late 'eighties and early 'nineties there was much discussion of sub-contract in its relation to the rather elusive industrial vice of 'sweating.' From the men's side, in the building trades, objection was very seldom, if ever, raised to genuine sub-contract under a small capitalist master. They regarded the finding of material, *i.e.* a measure of capitalism, as the test of the genuine master, whose acceptance of sub-contracts was 'legitimate.' What they all disliked was "sub-letting to the men," to mere "piece-masters," in which the sub-contractor's gain came from speeding up the work or breaking down the standard wage[3]. Obviously a 'legitimate' sub-contractor might also do these things: the things might or might not be abuses from the standpoint of national economy: the fact of interest here is the instinctive loyalty of the men to that small master system which was traditional, and still strong, in the building crafts. In spite of the great contractors, for the whole

[1] See evidence of Dew, G., Sec. of London Building Trades Committee, before *R.C. on Labour* (1892, XXXVI. part 2), Group C, Q. 17,380 *sqq.*

[2] The question of sub-contract was specially investigated by the *R.C. on Labour*, Group C. See especially 1892, XXXVI. part 2, Q. 18,463; 1893–4, XXXIV. Q. 32,061 and the Précis of evidence on the building trades in 1892, XXXVI. part 3, p. 34–48. See also Booth, *op. cit.* V. 40 *sqq.*, 151 *sqq.*

[3] *R.C. on Labour*, evidence of Dew, G., as above; of Otley, A., of the Operative Plasterers, especially Q. 17,295—objection to piece-masters "who do not find their material, but simply take work for labour only"; and the Précis, as above.

of those crafts, the crude ratio of masters of all kinds to men in London was only 1:13, at the census of 1891. For England and Wales, including London, it was 1:12 and for Scotland 1:10[1].

Some industries in which the small master flourished were also full of piece-paid outworkers. They were trades of the East London type, light and lightly skilled, in which as has been seen the two classes ran together. But the two most expansive trade groups in the country, during the generation which ended in 1885–6, building and coal-mining, had no place for the outworker; and in others there had been a continuous encroachment of factory work on outwork. Hand-loom weaving, woolcombing, frame-work knitting, lace-making, wholesale clothing, and boot and shoe making are the obvious instances. Little need be added to what has been said of these industries in the narrative of industrial change. The true outworker was still common in the bespoke boot-making and tailoring trades. There was a great deal of outwork on the fringes of factory tailoring, dress-making, boot-making, hosiery, and lace-making. A 'little mester' in Sheffield, and the man who corresponded to him in Birmingham, like the watch-maker of Clerkenwell or the home-working cabinet-maker in a street off the Curtain Road, was often no better than an outworker for some factory, or for some Birmingham factor turning manufacturer. These, however, were not growing cells in the body economic. More people were wearing factory boots, factory watches, factory clothes, every year. "There are now [1887] even in the good class bespoke trade [of London], but few masters who get their tops cut out and closed in the primitive manner by men working in their homes. More and more it is becoming the custom to make use of uppers made up in a factory."[2] Soon Goodyear's 'sew-round' machine, already known, would imitate the hand-sewn welted boot and annex another process from the pure hand-worker, so again diminishing the possible field of outwork. In factory centres, boot-making and hosiery trade unions were beginning to insist on factory work, because of the difficulty of enrolling and supervising the outworker[3]. Outwork tailoring for the bespoke trade had a longer expectation of life than outwork boot-making; outwork sewing and milliners' work an

[1] *Census of* 1891 (1893–4, CVI), p. xvi; Booth, *op. cit.* v. 153. The figures exclude builders' labourers.

[2] Schloss, D. F., in Booth, *op. cit.* IV. 71.

[3] *R.C. on Labour*, Group C; Leeds bootmakers, Q. 11,984–5; Midland Hosiery Federation, Q. 12,774 *sqq.* in 1892, XXXVI. part 2.

expectation longer still. But none of these groups except the last was numerically strong. And for the last long life was not greatly to be desired.

In some of the rural outwork industries there was still considerable vitality. Buckinghamshire chair-making, with its centre at High Wycombe, was in the main a mixed industry of small factories and workshops. It had grown remarkably since the 'thirties. As an export industry it was at its height about 1870. There were some fifty chair-making employers at Wycombe in 1885; but for miles around, in the cottages, tiny capitalists who had lathes, just as stockingers had once had frames, were supplying the simple beechen 'turned stuff' for front-legs and cross-bars. Backs, hind-legs, and seats were now always made in the factory[1]. North-East of the chair-country, along the Chilterns, lay the straw-hat country. The shadow of imported plait—first Italian and then Chinese—had already fallen across it. Cottage plaiting had declined conspicuously before 1880, in outlying districts where once it had flourished, such as the South-West corner of Suffolk and Western Essex. Even about Luton, which had won the headship of the industry from Dunstable by its earlier possession of a railway, there was less teaching by old women in plaiting schools and less frequenting of the Luton Plait Halls, in the early 'eighties, than there had been in the early 'seventies; yet outwork plaiting was still an important affair. As it contracted, other outworking jobs connected with the hat trade took its place, so that the villages of the Bedford-Buckingham-Hertford angle continued to be full of work[2]. There was also an important domestic or outwork pillow-lace industry in Bedfordshire, which still gave employment to nearly 5000 people at the census of 1881, after which date decline set in[3].

No important change had occurred in the industrial organisation of glove-making in the West, which still relied on outworking villages grouped round cutting-out shops and warehouses in Worcester, Woodstock, Yeovil, and Sherborne. The Sherborne industry had always been small. That of Yeovil had

[1] *Fact. Ins. Rep.* 1885 (1886, XIV. 797), p. 19 *sq.*; *V.C.H. Bucks*, II. 110–11. Cp. vol. I. p. 47, n. 2.

[2] County occupation figures in the *Census of* 1881 (1883, LXXX); *V.C.H. Suffolk*, II. 260; *V.C.H. Bedford*, II. 119 *sqq.*; statement of the Luton Chamber of Commerce in *R.C. on Depression of Trade* (1886), I. 96; for the earlier period vol. I. p. 47.

[3] *V.C.H. Bedford*, II. 123.

employed many thousands of women outworkers in the late 'fifties. There had been vicissitudes since, but no transformation. The Worcester trade, which had been in rather low water in the early 'fifties, had made a good recovery and sent out its parcels of gloves to be stitched in the cottages over a wide area. What proportion of the 13,000 women who returned themselves as connected with glove-making in 1881 were outworkers it is impossible to say; but probably the proportion was high. To them must be added some unknown figure for women who did a little 'gloving' but did not call themselves glovers, and for girls who helped their mothers yet might be returned as simply children without special occupation. Glovers' outworkers were not the most capable fillers up of a census schedule[1].

Southward over the downs from Yeovil, the rope, twine and net trade of Bridport—based originally on the fine Dorset hemp which was no longer grown—had been invaded by the machine and the competition of other districts, but not conquered. Sail-cloth had gone and rope was going; but netting flourished as an outwork cottage industry, because no machine could yet make square mesh or nets of irregular shape. Villages were specialised, not to the service of some master, but in the making of some particular size of mesh. It was all women's work. The men of the net-making families were mostly agricultural labourers, with a sprinkling of fishermen and miscellaneous coast workers[2].

These rural outworking industries are interesting but their aggregate demand for labour was small[3]. It is possible, but not very likely, that there were so many as 20,000 outworkers in straw-plait and hat-making, the greatest of them; certain that there were not 2000 in net-making, the least. One second-rate Lancashire cotton town could out-employ them all.

For over a century, the family business firm or small common-law partnership, with unlimited liability for all partners and unlimited freedom for dominating personalities, had cleared the way for industrial change. Some forms of enterprise required companies, but manufacturing had generally done without them. There were whole tracts of industry of which this was still true

[1] *V.C.H. Oxford*, II. 225; *V.C.H. Worcester*, II. 304; *V.C.H. Somerset*, II. 427–8; *V.C.H. Dorset*, II. 329; *Census of* 1881, as above.

[2] *V.C.H. Dorset*, II. 351 *sqq*.

[3] There were many others as interesting but smaller; cp. FitzRandolph and Hay, *Rural Industries in England and Wales* (1927).

in the 'eighties. "We have none in our district. I cannot remember one," a Bradford witness said of limited liability companies in 1885[1]. He was thinking, not of railways, gasworks or banks, but of ordinary manufactures. Until very recently there had been a curious, and no doubt largely irrational, reluctance in the manufacturing world to adopt modifications in the traditional type of business organisation, a reluctance which the tardiness of the state to permit any general system of limited liability had encouraged[2]. There had been experiments in manufacturing on a joint stock ever since one of the very earliest English joint-stock companies, the Elizabethan Mineral and Battery Works, first made wire at Tintern and 'battery' ware, that is to say hammered hollow ware of copper or brass, in London[3]. Jacobean patentees and many later patentees, especially since the repeal of the Bubble Act in 1825, had sought charters of incorporation to exploit their inventions with a joint stock. Companies of various kinds had always been common in the extractive industries, though most of them in the eyes of the law were only extended partnerships. Informal and legally irregular companies had been formed by the domestic clothiers of Yorkshire, to help them in their struggle against the dominating personalities furnished with capital[4]. But when nineteenth-century legal reformers first began to facilitate and regulate the creation of companies, and to make guarded general provision for limited liability, the response from British industry was uncommonly slow, though there were many industrial bubble promotions, as might have been foreseen.

Take for example the working of the Act of 1837 (1 Vict. c. 73), usually called the Letters Patent Act because it empowered the crown to give to companies by Letters Patent certain of the privileges which hitherto had only been attainable by Charter of Incorporation or Act of Parliament. Under it, in the next sixteen years, applications were made by such varied organisations as the Royal Mail and the Peninsular and Oriental Steamship Companies; St Augustine's Missionary College, Canterbury; the Chemical Society and the College of Preceptors;

[1] *R.C. on Depression of Trade*, Q. 6791 (Sir Jacob Behrens).

[2] For this tardiness see Shannon, H. A., "The Coming of General Limited Liability," *E.J.* (*Ec. Hist.*), 1931.

[3] Scott, W. R., *Early History of Joint Stock Companies*, II. 413 *sqq.*; Hamilton, H., *The English Brass and Copper Industries to* 1800, ch. 1–3.

[4] For coal-pit ownership in eighths, and down to sixty-fourths, see vol. I. p. 434; for the company mills, vol. I. p. 194–6.

the Canterbury Association which colonised New Zealand, Lord Ashley's Model Dwellings Society, several of the early Submarine Telegraph Companies, the East India Iron Company, and the Chartered Bank of India. The solitary home manufacturing Company whose application succeeded was the British Plate Glass of 1841, though applications were received from Shott's Iron Company, the Norwich Yarn Company—a scheme of 1838 to save the East Anglian worsted industry—and the Royal Conical Flour Mill, unsuccessfully promoted by the Earl of Essex and other gentlemen of rank in 1853[1]. In this latter year, which may serve to illustrate the position in the early 'fifties, out of 339 applications for provisional registration on behalf of projected companies of every kind except banking, 80 were railway projects; 54 gas projects; 35 were for insurance; 33 for all other public works; 32 for mining; and only 30 were proposals for "conducting manufactures, working patents, etc." Of these last, much the greater part never ripened[2]. In that year Henry Scrivenor was revising his *History of the Iron Trade*. He allowed to stand in it a passage from the first edition of 1840 in which he had asked the question, "Are Joint Stock Companies incompatible with success in iron making?" The lamentable results of those which had been projected or tried had seemed to suggest an answer in the affirmative. They ought not to be incompatible, Scrivenor went on to argue, given enough concentration of effort and enough working capital. These, he noted, were just the things which had generally been lacking[3]. To the serious industrialist, even when discussing iron-making, closely linked as it was with the extractive industries in which association of capital had long played a part, the words joint stock company still connoted irresponsible management, defective finance—actual fraud. He thought perhaps of that Northampton mining company of the late 'thirties which sank a pit three hundred yards deep and brought out coal which it had first put in, or of that Northern Coal Mining Company whose shareholders lost the whole capital of £500,000, and as much more, because of unlimited liability[4].

[1] "Return of all Applications for Charters with Limited Liability under 1 Vict. c. 73," *A. and P.* 1854, LXV. 611.

[2] "Registrations for 1853," *ibid.* p. 597. Registration had been provided for under 7 and 8 Vict. c. 110 of 1844. Legislation at that date had mainly railways in view. The printed lists are however incomplete. See Shannon, H. A., "The First Five Thousand Limited Companies and their Duration," *E.J.* (*Ec. Hist.*), 1932.

[3] Scrivenor, *op. cit.* p. 282.

[4] Vol. I. p. 434.

The government tradition of the early nineteenth century had been that, in order to establish a claim to a charter with limited liability, an enterprise must have one or more of certain 'notes' not found in the average manufacturing concern of the day—special risks, like that of a mining venture overseas; great size, like a canal or railway; need for a widely extended responsibility, as in insurance; or inability to exist at all without a large membership, like the College of Preceptors or the Chemical Society[1].

With a view to combining the maximum freedom of investment with reasonable security for careful management, in businesses which lacked these 'notes,' Benthamite legal reformers had tried to acclimatise the continental partnership *en commandite*, with unlimited liability for managing partners and limited liability for dormant partners. John Austin was praising it in 1825 and John Mill always praised it. But average British opinion was against them. In the year of Victoria's accession another legal reformer, Bellenden Ker, in a report to the Board of Trade which became classical, had summed up on the side of average opinion. His summing up was given wider publicity, at least in parliamentary and legal circles, when it was reprinted by a Select Committee on Joint Stock Companies in 1844[2].

Meanwhile companies were promoted recklessly or fraudulently whatever the law might say; for since the repeal of the Bubble Act mere promotion was not illegal[3]. Fortunes could be made and families ruined without any official having been asked to decide whether a project deserved Letters Patent or Parliament asked to adjudicate on a private Bill. So some cried for regulation. Others, whose voices were dominant after 1850, spoke of the desirability of relaxing "any restraints...on the free action of individuals or application of capital."[4] "All parties have advocated unrestricted competition. Why limit it in

[1] See Levi, L., *History of British Commerce* (1872), p. 289.

[2] *S.C. on Joint Stock Companies*, 1844 (VII. 1), App. I. For Austin's advocacy, *ibid.* p. 261. For Mill's, *Principles*, Bk V. ch. 9, § 7. Ker's report of 1837 was the basis for 1 Vict. c. 73. Cp. Holdsworth, W. S., *History of English Law*, VII. 195–7 on *commenda* and *commandite*. The system only came definitely into English law in 1907 by 7 Ed. VII, c. 24. The 1844 report led to the requirement for provisional and final registration of all joint-stock companies under 7 and 8 Vict. c. 110. The Act had in view unlimited companies.

[3] Decisions quoted in Holdsworth, *op. cit.* VIII. 221. Cp. a solicitor's evidence before the *S.C. on Companies Acts*, 1877 (VIII. 419), Q. 794 *sqq.*

[4] *S.C. on Law of Partnership*, 1851 (XVIII. 1), p. ix.

partnership?"[1] Why should not any company "as a matter of right, that is without a charter, engage in business without risking the fortune of each of its members?"[2] In the long debates, and the longer series of Acts, by which company creation was steadily made easier during the 'fifties, regulation and *commandite* were alike forgotten. Individualists wrote about "the unwarranted supposition that Parliament must make regulations for trade"[3]—any regulations at all, even that registration of companies which had been provided for in 1844. The upshot was the decisive Companies Act of 1862 (25 and 26 Vict. c. 89) under which any seven or more associates, provided their object was lawful, might constitute themselves a company, either with limited or unlimited liability, by simply subscribing a memorandum of association. Registration went on, but the Registrar had smaller powers than under the Act of 1844, and his register was soon cumbered with dead, still-born, or abortive companies[4]. In 1867 (30 and 31 Vict. c. 131) the legislators authorised a type of company in which directors might have unlimited, the rank and file of shareholders limited, liability. But such companies were never founded. The perfect liberty of the Act of 1862 was more attractive than this essay in *commandite*. As the wisest of Victorian fools sang:

> Some seven men form an Association
> (If possible, all Peers and Baronets)
> They start off with a public declaration
> To what extent they mean to pay their debts.
> That's called their Capital[5].

Perhaps it is not surprising that the average sober manufacturer remained suspicious or indifferent far into the 'seventies and 'eighties. If he was sober he could always get aid from a bank. The British banks "collected every particle of capital"[6] and meant to use it. By permitting overdrafts to men whom

[1] *Economist*, July 1, 1854.

[2] *S.C. on Companies Acts*, 1877, p. i.

[3] *Economist*, August 25, 1855. For the acts and debates of 1850–61 see Levi, *op. cit.* p. 337, and Shannon in *E.J.* (*Ec. Hist.*) 1931, as above; also articles "Commandite," "Joint Stock Company," "Partnership" in *Dic. Pol. Econ.*

[4] *S.C. on the Limited Liability Acts*, 1867 (x. 303), Q. 373. Under the 1844 Act the Registrar could not give final registration until he was satisfied with the deed of settlement for the government of the company. The 1862 procedure was more summary. In 1867 the Registrar (Hon. E. C. Curzon) wished to return to the 1844 practice. His successor was complaining in 1877 (*S.C. on Companies Acts*, Q. 5) that companies were often dead for years before he knew about it.

[5] Gilbert, W. S., *Limited Liability*.

[6] *Economist*, July 1, 1854.

they trusted, they were very like shareholders in many business concerns in the industrial areas. That was why the country did not need *commandite*, and why limited liability, as shrewd critics had foreseen[1], made no quick revolution and did most of its good work at first in fields for which companies had always been either essential, customary, or defensible. Its bad work was done where bad company work invariably had been done, among the blind and greedy.

Some great industrial firms operating in the appropriate fields made early use of the new Acts. Some new firms of the same class were created as limited companies. The Thames Ironworks was founded in 1857 under the older laws[2]. Before 1867, Ebbw Vale was a limited coal and iron company with a capital of £4,000,000; Palmer's Shipbuilding Company had a capital of £2,000,000 "held all over the country"; Bolckow Vaughan had £2,500,000 "held to a large extent in Manchester."[3] John Brown and Co. and Cammell and Co. of Sheffield, the Staffordshire Wheel and Axle Company, the Staveley Coal and Iron Company, and the Fairbairn Engineering Company of Leeds, are other illustrations of the spread of company organisation during the first five years after the Act of 1862 in those heavy trades among which Scrivenor had supposed, twenty years earlier, that companies ought to flourish, but did not[4]. He was thinking of businesses created as companies; and though, with the new facilities, there were successful creations in the years 1857–67, such as the Thames Ironworks, most of these big companies were private firms converted.

Gradually the many conveniences of the joint-stock with limited liability attracted the Victorian industrial leaders, especially when they wished to expand their businesses with lessened risk, and when they grew old. Men with large interests in some business, a prominent investing agent explained in 1877, "express a desire to limit that interest, and the only mode to do it is by forming a joint-stock company."[5] Perhaps they wanted to

[1] *E.g.* the *Economist*, as above.

[2] "Return of all J.S. Companies formed...since 18 and 19 Vict. c. 133," *A. and P.* 1864, LVIII. 289.

[3] *S.C. on the Limited Liability Acts*, 1867, Q. 857, 2342.

[4] For these companies and their dates see the "Return" of 1864, the *S.C. of* 1867, and the App. to the *S.C. of* 1877.

[5] Evidence of David Chadwick before the *S.C. on the Companies Acts*, 1877, Q. 2074 and *sqq.*; Chadwick gave similar evidence before the *S.C. on the Limited Liability Acts*, 1867, Q. 835 *sqq.* See the discussion of the work of the investing agents, below, p. 360.

divide the business among their family, or to "make it go on for ever." They would consult an investing agent, and with him they would find the seven men for the association. They themselves would be among the seven, with some friends of the agent's who would engage to put up capital. Sometimes all the capital would be found in the family and the company would be a private one. In this way Lowthian Bell's firm was 'limited' in 1873[1]. Next year Joseph Whitworth's great pioneering business followed[2]. The movement gathered way, especially in metallurgy and engineering. Even Birmingham witnesses, in 1885, while testifying to the persistent vitality of the small and the private firm, were able to give "a long...list of trades that have developed under the Limited Liabilities Act on a very large scale"; but they added that "almost without exception" these were private firms converted—Nettlefold, Tangye, Muntz, Perry—not new creations[3]. A process which was becoming familiar may be illustrated from a famous case outside industry. The Cunard Line became a limited company in 1878: shares were first offered to the public in 1880: three-fifths of the nominal capital remained in the hands of three families[4]. In the five years preceding October 1885, about 560 private firms were converted into companies, of which about 400 were still carrying on business at the latter date. A great many, probably a considerable majority, of these were not industrial. There had, for example, been numerous transformations among the textile warehouses in the neighbourhood of St Paul's Churchyard. But the proportion of 'industrials' must have been appreciable[5].

All experimental enterprises of the types which before 1862 might have tried for a charter, or risked their shareholders' fortunes without one, naturally registered under the Companies Acts. But, up to 1880, the transformation of old businesses, though steady, was certainly slow. Many, even in the industries specially affected by the movement, clung to their traditional organisation. Robert Stephenson and Co. remained a private firm down to 1886[6]. Samuel Cunliffe Lister only made Manningham Mills into a company in 1889, when he was about

[1] Macrosty, H. W., *The Trust Movement in British Industry* (1907), p. 26.
[2] *D.N.B.*
[3] *R.C. on Depression of Trade*, Q. 1520, 1525, 1591.
[4] Kennedy, J., *History of Steam Navigation*, p. 229.
[5] *R.C. on Depression of Trade*, Q. 668, 407. Cp. below, p. 311–12.
[6] Warren, *A Century of Locomotive Building*, p. 417.

to become a Lord[1]. In 1885–6 private firms did the "bulk" of the Birmingham business. There was nothing but private firms in the complex of Bradford trades. There were very few limited companies in Leeds, "and very few in the woollen trade generally." There were none in the jute industry of Dundee; none in the silk industry; few in the Nottingham trades; few in the cutlery trades, though a handful of strong ones in Sheffield steel and armament. There was a group of very large ones in shipbuilding; but a majority of that business, it was thought, was still in private hands. In the northern section of the cotton area, out of about 110 firms with 870,000 spindles and 40,000 looms in the town of Burnley, there were five public companies "whose shares are bought and sold in the open market," and one or two others "really private partnerships conducted under the form and law of limited liability." In Blackburn and Preston there were "hardly any." It was Oldham and the 'Oldham Limiteds' which provided most of the raw material for discussion of the relations between manufacturing and the free British limited liability law during the decade 1875–85[2].

Here, by 1880, was a really large group of spinning firms started on the joint-stock basis and containing one-seventh of all the spindles in the country. The thing was new. You could already take the temperature of the cotton industry with reasonable accuracy by averaging out the Oldham dividends or the discount on the Oldham shares. For example, the shares of 75 out of 94 mills in and about Oldham stood at a discount in 1885: in 1885–6 only 22 declared any dividend at all and only 6 more than 5 per cent.[3]

There had been many experiments with limited liability in the cotton trade since the 'fifties. The American Civil War and the cotton famine had checked the movement[4]. Only after 1872 did the company system get firmly rooted. "In 1874, owing to the few already in existence paying well, there was quite a mania for new companies, no less than 30 being registered in

[1] Above, p. 88.

[2] *R.C. on Depression of Trade*, Q. 1581 (Birmingham), Q. 6791 (Bradford), Q. 6331 (Leeds), Q. 5380 (Galashiels and the woollen trade generally), Q. 6207 (Dundee), Q. 7231 (silk), Q. 6601 (Nottingham), Q. 1205, 3438 (Sheffield), Q. 11,911 (shipbuilding), Q. 5595, 5752, 5798, 5810 (the cotton towns).

[3] *Ibid. Third Report*. App. A, VIII. 310–1. Cp. the discussions in Ellison's *Cotton Trade of Great Britain* (1886), ch. xi; Jones, B., *Cooperative Production* (1894), ch. xii.

[4] Watts, J., *The Facts of the Cotton Famine* (1866), p. 341, gives a list of 44 companies, or projected companies, "all or nearly all" projected since 1859.

two months, all of which, with the exception of two, were formed for building new large mills. The...two...were floated for the purpose of purchasing concerns already in existence.... The formation of these companies was done without the aid of professional floaters. In many cases the shares were subscribed for without even a prospectus being issued, all that was wanted being an application form."[1] "Within a radius of 4 miles from the Oldham Town Hall...are about 32 new cotton mills," the factory inspector reported in 1875[2]. The way in which the Lancashire textile machinists would design and equip a whole mill, an almost standardised unit of production, had been a great help, perhaps a temptation, to the promoters. Hostile critics suggested that promotion was promoted by the machinists, to whom no doubt the equipment of a score of large standardised mills was an attractive proposition. Critics also alleged that the shareholders were "recruited from all over England and even from the continent."[3] There was presumably some truth in this; but there is no doubt that much the greater part of the share capital and practically the whole of the loan capital was raised locally, which does not of necessity mean wisely. The directors, as a class, were certainly not persons from outside. "They are a persevering body of men," said the Oldham apologist of 1885–6, "and a glance at their avocation shows that nine-tenths of them have practically been brought up in the business of cotton-spinning, and not a few [an interesting touch] are to-day engaged as private spinners."[4]

The main interest of the 'Oldham Limiteds' in the history of industrial organisation lies in the extended use which they made of those borrowing powers on which the Companies Acts of the 'sixties had put no restriction, and in the class of people from whom they borrowed. Already in 1866 it was said that most of the early ones had "gone upon the borrowing principle."[5] In 1885–6 their capital of nearly £7,000,000 was divided almost exactly between shares and loans (£3,456,000 shares and £3,435,000 loans). Something like half of it was furnished by the "working classes in the immediate vicinity," mainly by

[1] Kidger, J., of Oldham, in *R.C. on Depression of Trade*, App. A, VIII. 308.

[2] *Report* (1876, XVI. 61).

[3] *R.C. on Depression of Trade*, Q. 5553 (a witness from Preston); and see Q. 5508.

[4] Kidger, J., as above. For the capital see evidence of co-operators before the *R.C. on Labour* (1893–4, XXXIX. part 1), Q. 1109 *sqq.*

[5] Watts, *op. cit.* p. 341.

way of loan[1]. This loan capital was subscribed in very small amounts at rates of interest which varied with the market conditions, not at a long period guaranteed rate like the later debentures. In 1874–5 the rate had been 5 per cent.: in 1877–9 it was as much as 6 per cent.: in 1885–6 it was down to 4 per cent.[2] It was a convenient form of deposit interest. Some trifling part of the share capital, possibly 5 per cent., came from the cotton operatives themselves[3]. Most of the loan holders in 1885, according to James Mawdsley, the Spinners' Secretary, were "small shop-keepers, publicans, and what I may call the odd hands about the mill—lodge-keepers, over-lookers, mechanics, and the people who work in the large machine shops of Oldham."[4] These people also held shares, but a much smaller proportion of the shares than of the loans. The circle of credit is curious. The textile machinist equips the mills, giving credit to the companies. The companies, when share capital runs short, raise money to pay him from the men who made the machines or from shop-keepers and publicans whose business depends on their successful working—an interesting if risky experiment in industrial democracy. (The money, it may be added, had been accumulated largely in the co-operative stores and was rendered available when they paid their 'divis.'[5]) But let the Oldham apologist of 1885–6 again be heard and his grammar and metaphors pardoned. "Private firms had not kept pace with the times, and the formation of Oldham Companies stepped into the breach and took the lead, and up to now have not been displaced.... Out of the whole of the companies formed in Oldham for the purpose of spinning cotton, only three have been in chancery, two of them were taken out by arrangement with the creditors, and the other one proceedings are now pending"[6]—a creditable record after six years of slack trade.

Hitherto the representative industrial joint-stock company had been in a double sense aristocratic. A relatively small number of dominant firms in dominant industrial groups had adopted limited liability. Aristocratic motives had usually influenced the adoption—motives of safety, of permanence, of

[1] *R.C. on Labour*, as above, Q. 1138 and figures in *R.C. on Depression*, App. A, VIII.

[2] Oldham evidence of 1885–6, *R.C. on Depression of Trade*, Q. 4334.

[3] *Ibid.* Q. 1141, 1180; where the cotton operatives' share is estimated at 7½ per cent.

[4] *R.C. on Depression of Trade*, Q. 5134.

[5] *R.C. on Labour*, Q. 1138.

[6] Kidger, J., as above.

family. In the Oldham area alone limited liability had prevailed in rank and file businesses and had attracted a democratic investing public. It will not be forgotten that in cotton-spinning rank and file businesses had long ceased to be small.

The Oldham investing public was democratic; but limited liability had as yet done very little to justify one hope of the 'fifties—that it would help to develop a type of large-scale industrial organisation in which worker and capitalist should be one, pure co-operative industry as then conceived[1]. It might even be maintained that the Oldham of 1885–6 had justified a cynical forecast of the individualists, made nearly a generation earlier. Arguing for limited liability and discussing the prospects of a very free law, the *Economist* had written in 1854: "Co-operative societies may be formed; attempts will be made to set up workmen against employers; some philanthropists will advance their £100 or their £1000, certain that more they cannot lose....But these will be momentary delusions, soon dispelled....At present numerous bodies of workmen believe that they will gain much by the change: only by putting their plans into execution can they be undeceived, and to give them the benefit of experience is the one reason why the law should be altered."[2] Workmen with this faith were specially numerous about Oldham. Rochdale of the Pioneers lies within what came to be the territory of the Oldham Limiteds, and the Oldham Industrial Co-operative Society was one of the earliest founded. When limited liability became easy to get, the workmen of Oldham had their experience. Some were disappointed, as the individualists had anticipated. Many were well satisfied with the various, if rather unexpected, results of the experiment.

So early as 1858, the Oldham Building and Manufacturing Society, promoted by co-operators, was registered as a joint-stock company under the old law, with calls on shares of 3*d*., and directors' fees of 6*d*. a week[3]. It tried weaving and did not do well. Re-organised as the Sun Mill Company for spinning and

[1] The hope, among others, of John Mill. Cp. *Principles*, Bk IV. ch. V, § 5. In 1860 "the working-class imagination was a little dazzled by the prospect of starting Joint Stock Companies under the Limited Liability Law." Redfern, P., *The Story of the Co-operative Wholesale Society* (1913), p. 17.

[2] *Economist*, July 1, 1854.

[3] It was not the first co-operative cotton mill. That was at Bacup, founded in 1850. From the start only a minority of the workers in the Bacup mill were shareholders; in 1851 thirteen or fourteen out of fifty-three. Ludlow, J. M., *Christian Socialist*, II. 277 *sq*. in Jones, B., *Co-operative Production*, I. 253.

weaving in 1862–3, it did much better but ceased to be in the full sense co-operative. Shareholders might still be wage-earners, but in 1867 only four of them were wage-earners of the company. There were experiments in profit-sharing, but these never included the regular operatives, only the managers and over-lookers. By about 1870 the company had settled down into something very like the 'limiteds' for which it had paved the way[1]. A few of these grew out of similar workmen's experiments in industrial organisation; but the promoting and organising functions passed a good deal out of true working-class hands. Perhaps an organising 'proletarian' became a 'capitalist,' a transformation very familiar in Lancashire at all times. Even lending to the Limiteds became rare among those who worked in them, as has been seen, and shareholding by a company's employees still rarer. The thrifty cotton operatives, and there were many, put their savings into banks and building societies, cottage property and co-operative stores, rather than into the mill companies which paid their wages. Like the sensible small capitalists that they were, they spread their risks. Yet if the Oldham Limiteds had not been got by small capitalism out of co-operation, they might never have had their unique popular features, nor perhaps some of their common popular failings. They helped to forge that double-edged economic tool, the industrial share of small denomination[2].

Of experiments in pure co-operative industry, between the 'fifties and the 'eighties, all that need be said here is this—however deep the interest which they stirred in men of good will unwarped by dogmatic individualism, however moving their ambitions and failures and their tiny successes, however great their possible value for a future not even yet revealed; in a map of industrial Britain drawn on the very largest scale they would hardly be visible at any date; as contributors to the

[1] Marcroft, W., *The Sun Mill Company Limited; its Commercial and Social History* (1877). Jones, B., *op. cit.* I. 282 *sqq.* Webb, Beatrice, *The Co-operative Movement* (1891), p. 129. Article "Cooperation (Partial, Oldham Limited Companies)" in *Dic. Pol. Econ.* (1894).

[2] The very small share appeared before 1858. In the *Companies Return of* 1864 covering the period since 1855 the £10 share is perhaps the commonest. The £1 share is fairly common. An unsuccessful mining project of 1856 has 5*s.* shares. A few newspaper projects have 10*s.* shares. The Plumstead and Woolwich Co-op. Provisions of 1861 has 5*s.* shares. Of about 2000 companies registered before 1862 there were 11 which proposed shares under £1. The Oldham Building and Manufacturing Company of 1858 had £5 shares but, as has been seen, 3*d.* calls.

aggregate welfare of the Britain of 1885–6 they were negligible. Even six years later, a keen co-operator could enumerate only eight manufacturing societies in the whole country which were co-operative in what he reckoned the true sense, that is, societies of "working men employing themselves in their own industries"; and of these some were quite new[1].

As with the hand-workers so with the directors of industry. They often came together to fight, not infrequently to sell; but there was not yet among them much co-operation for the actual business of production. Chambers of Commerce and trade Associations had multiplied, especially since 1860; but the Chambers, true to their title, were always more concerned with dealing than with making. Mixed bodies, often ineffective, they seldom discussed industrial policies and never executed them. In a number of industries and districts, the growth of trade unionism had turned Adam Smith's "tacit, but constant and uniform, combination [of masters] not to raise the wages of labour"[2] into something more vocal and organic, the trade Association. Besides handling questions of wages and hours, these Associations might collect statistics, discuss forms of contract, or direct parliamentary business when the trade's interests clashed, perhaps with railway interests, or perhaps with national policy. There was also a little overt price-fixing by Associations; and informal price-fixing was on the increase inside and outside them. But the imperfect evidence as yet available suggests that, at any rate during the generally prosperous and dynamic third quarter of the nineteenth century, there was rather less co-operation among 'capitalist' producers than there had been in the more difficult first and second quarters. Having secured from the state that free and open competition which theory and interest recommended, they wished, in the slang of the 'sixties, to 'paddle their own canoes.' Organised combinations of employers, a Royal Commission reported in 1869, were "comparatively very few in number," and, so far as the

[1] *R.C. on Labour* (1892, XXXIX. part I). Evidence before the Whole Commission. Greenwood, J. of the Hebden Bridge Fustian Society, Q. 959, and see App. XXVIII. For the successes of consumers' co-operation in distribution and its relations to industrial organisation see below, p. 308 *sqq*. It need hardly be said that Greenwood's definition of 'true' co-operation was disputed by other co-operators, *e.g.* by Benjamin Jones, *op. cit.* II. 775.

[2] *Wealth of Nations* (ed. Cannan), I. 68.

Commission had learnt, absolutely voluntary in character[1]. The Commission was not perfectly informed, but there was certainly no great love of association among the employers. Many of their spokesmen asserted with apparent sincerity, like the spokesman of the Clyde Shipbuilders and Engineers' Association, that their organisations were "entirely defensive" and "would cease if the workmen's unions were to cease."[2] Among themselves they were ready for a perpetual 'fighting trade.' Similarly the Midland Flint Glass Manufacturers had formed an Association "with reluctance" in 1858, to deal with a strike. Ten years later only half even of the local firms belonged to it[3].

Adam Smith's "tacit but constant...combinations" were naturally most widespread and efficient in old industries, nowhere more so than in agriculture. Some ceased to be tacit long before 1850. The London Master Printers, whose compositors had a union running back at least to 1801, had possessed a society from 1836 to 1849. It emerged as a regular Association in 1854–5 *vis-à-vis* the very strong and well-organised London Compositors' Society[4]. "All the large builders"[5] had been organised into the very respectable London Master Builders' Association since 1839. It may be supposed that Superior Dosset Forsyte was a member. It had benevolent funds and other disinterested activities. In 1867 it accepted through its Secretary the description of "a club of gentlemen belonging to your profession."[6] Probably like the National Association of Master Builders of 1877–8 it had the rule "no speculative builders...admitted."[7] Certainly its membership was small. It claimed that as an Association it never touched strikes, not wishing to interfere with the free action of its members; but

[1] *R.C. on Trade Unions and other Associations*, *Final Report* (1865–9, XXXI. 235), p. xvi. There is some contradiction in the Report which says further on (p. li) "that employers...in many departments of industry have entered into very powerful...associations"; and admits (p. xlix) that "a few great employers ...could in fact always make arrangements among themselves...without forming any definite association."

[2] *Ibid.* Q. 17,446.

[3] *Ibid.* Q. 18,305. Cp. the evidence of Sir Hugh Bell before the *R.C. on Labour* (1892, XXXIV.), Q. 1530.

[4] *R.C. on Trade Unions*, as above, Q. 19,481 *sqq.* (the Masters' Sec.). For the Compositors' early history Webb, S. and B., *History of Trade Unionism* (ed. 1902), p. 20 n., 24 n.

[5] *R.C. on Trade Unions*, Q. 340.

[6] *Ibid.* Q. 2754; the phrase was Tom Hughes'.

[7] See account in *R.C. on Labour* (1892, XXXVI. part 3), Digest of Evidence, p. 48.

working men said "they are organised to try to keep down wages"; and "they" admitted that in wage-crises the Association convened a trade meeting[1].

Long before 1880, probably long before 1850, and at various points all over the country, groups of master builders, speculative or not, had made arrangements with the men—more or less formal: more or less well observed—about wages and conditions of work. These were usually embodied in signed 'working rules.' Of the Associations and agreements there can often be no memorial, but they certainly existed. The General Builders' Association of 1865, not the first of its kind, was based on some eighty local associations, mainly in the North and West with a few in Scotland. It was interested in the terms of building contracts, the relations of builder and architect, and the settlement of trade disputes by working rules and arbitration. The Londoners, whose respectable Association would not at that time sign any treaty with the men, never joined it, and it had not a very long life. But its cells, the "tacit" or plain-speaking masters' combinations, had; or if they died, they rose again. In the labour discussions of the 'eighties a local masters' association is assumed[2].

There was no doubt a great deal of tacit price-fixing by masters in certain trades. The prices of bread and beer were almost as uniform locally in Victorian times as they had been in the years when the Assizes of Bread and Ale were still 'set'; but the processes of formal or informal setting by brewers and bakers are nowhere recorded. Now and again, in some industry or other, a price arrangement among producers is accidentally but clearly indicated in the full day of free and open competition. It is probably fair to assume that there were several hidden for each one disclosed. The salt industry furnishes one such accidental disclosure. There had been price-fixing associations in the first quarter of the century in this industry based on a local monopoly[3]. Many years later comes the evidence that its subsequent history, as might have been expected, witnessed

[1] *R.C. on Labour*, Q. 338 *sqq.* (George Potter for the men); Q. 2583, 2606 (the Association's admissions). And for the relations of the two sides, "The Strike and Lockout of 1859–60" in *Trades Societies and Strikes Report* (1860). Cp. Postgate, R. W., *The Builders' Story*, p. 171–2.

[2] For the Assoc. of 1865, *R.C. on Trade Unions*, Q. 2951 *sqq.*; for local agreements, *ibid.* Q. 190 (Applegarth, of the Amalgamated Carpenters and Joiners). And see Webb, *op. cit.* p. 209; Postgate, *op. cit.* p. 214.

[3] See vol. I. p. 200.

alternations of gentlemen's agreements and 'fighting trade.' "Implacable competition," said the *Salt Circular* for 1887, "has brought prices below all record,...the principle of association has been violated again and again, and with more disastrous results than ever yet known."[1] The polite phrase "the principle of association" needs no comment. The upshot of this last and worst spell of fighting trade was that Salt Union which is reckoned among the earliest of the late nineteenth-century industrial combinations. It was only a new device, made easier by limited liability, for handling an old problem.

Railway officials called upon to justify their rate agreements in the 'seventies and 'eighties used to argue that "really almost all traders make similar arrangements about prices." One of them in 1872 quoted ironmasters, coal-owners, "the china men," and the steam packet companies. Another, in 1882, said it was "perfectly notorious" that this was "the practice of nearly all the main trades of the country." To those quoted ten years earlier he added copper-smelters and screw-makers. A third mentioned tinplates, files, glass, nails and "others," and spoke of "a universal practice of endeavouring (how far it succeeds or not is another matter) to agree upon prices." He was defending the principle: as he was a man of wide business experience his reservation is significant[2].

The fixing of prices, or at least the determining of what was "to be deemed the current price," was recognised in a draft report of the Royal Commission of 1867–9 as one of the purposes of associations "among certain classes of employers, the iron and coal producers especially."[3] Price-fixing was no new thing in the iron trade. The witnesses of the 'sixties explained vaguely, but well within the truth, that the quarterly meetings of South Staffordshire ironmasters to fix the prices of marked bars "dated back forty or fifty years." The Association had no rules, however, until 1864[4]. Besides price-fixing, it did statistical and parliamentary work like other associations. The North

[1] Quoted from *The Times*, September 24, 1888, in Macrosty, *The Trust Movement in British Industry*, p. 181.

[2] *S.C. on Railway Amalgamations*, 1872 (XIII), Q. 148. W. Cawkwell of the L.N.W.R. *S.C. on Railway Rates and Fares*, 1882 (XIII), Q. 3892. Jas. Grierson of the G.W.R., Q. 3893, a question, in the form of a statement, by the experienced Sir Ed. Watkin. Cp. Cleveland-Stephens, *English Railways* (1915), p. 264.

[3] *R.C. on Trade Unions*, p. xcix.

[4] *Ibid.* Q. 9829. See vol. I. p. 204, based on Ashton, *Iron and Steel and the Industrial Revolution*, ch. 7, "Combinations of Capitalists."

Staffordshire masters had an Association modelled on it, but less effective as a price-fixer. They merely "endeavoured to get as near as possible to the South Staffordshire price," which itself, as one of them explained in 1867, was "really the price of a few firms in South Staffordshire, all the others, in reality, selling much under that price."[1] Like the South Staffordshire Association, the Cleveland Ironmasters' Association and the North of England Iron Manufacturers' Association took definite form in the early 'sixties. The former dealt with pig iron, the latter with manufactured iron. In 1867 they had a common secretary, who had previously served the South Staffordshire Association; and the same firm would often belong to both[2]. Although the secretary stated that they were formed for "regulating prices and the terms for selling iron," he was emphatic that there was "no such machinery for fixing prices in the North"[3] as in South Staffordshire. The action of the two Associations, so far as prices were concerned, was in fact very accurately described in the draft report of the Royal Commission as determining what are to be "deemed the current prices." Such current prices were announced at the close of the meetings, but producers were not bound by them. The Steam Coal Association of Tyneside did much the same sort of thing[4]. So far, but no further, had formal price-fixing co-operation progressed in the 'heavy' trades during the third quarter of the century.

Yet there was memory of more radical policies both in Staffordshire and on the Northern Coalfield. The 'limitation of the vend' of North Country coal, the most conspicuous output and price-controlling combination of the early nineteenth century, had only broken down in 1845. Its breakdown was due to internal difficulties over rationing. There was a rumour of renewal in 1850, but nothing came of it; for as G. R. Porter noted in that year, "the facilities for competition on the part of owners of inland coal-fields are far greater now than they were in 1845, while through the extension of railways these facilities are being continually augmented."[5] Similar forces were at work

[1] *R.C. on Trade Unions*, Q. 10,532. For the relative inefficiency of price control in S. Staffs see also *R.C. on Labour* (1892, XXXVI. part 2), Group A, Q. 15,486: "at one time it exercised a controlling influence on selling prices."

[2] *R.C. on Trade Unions*, Q. 9391 *sqq.*, his evidence; Q. 9414, a memorandum which he put in.

[3] *Ibid.* Q. 9551.

[4] *Ibid.* Q. 17,777 *sqq.*, evidence of Palmer, C. M.

[5] *Progress of the Nation*, p. 283–4. And see vol. I. p. 202.

in the iron trade. Regulation of the output of iron had been discussed a good deal and practised a little before 1830. In 1839 the Staffordshire masters—masters of the trade, as they supposed, in every sense—had agreed to reduce the make by 20 per cent. for six months, to maintain prices. But their restriction was accompanied by increases in other districts, particularly in Scotland, which drove the aggregate British make up instead of down[1]. Railway building at home soon rectified the price position. After 1850, for five-and-twenty years, with the markets of the world at their feet and prices generally good, Britain's primary producers had little need even to consider such extreme defensive policies. Limitation of output to keep up price was a charge brought against bricklayers and some other trade unionists. As a policy for manufacturers it became, in the 'sixties and 'seventies, a curious and, to the individualist philosopher, almost an indecent memory.

But the abrupt price fall of the late 'seventies led to the revival of this old policy—and again its fallibility was illustrated. When the 1880 recovery from the disastrously low pig iron prices of 1878–9 proved only temporary, negotiations began between the Cleveland and the Scottish masters. In the autumn of 1881 a 12½ per cent. reduction of output was agreed on for six months. It was continued for a second six months, and then broke down, because the strongest Scottish firm found that it could sell more iron than it was making. Cleveland continued its experiments. Early in 1884, with prices lower than ever, eighteen blast furnaces were shut down by agreement, the owners being compensated by the Association—a new device for spreading losses. Two years later, prices having fallen yet further, Scotland was ready to co-operate again and there was talk of a national reduction of output. But before agreement had been reached, a trade revival took off accumulated stocks and then sent prices slowly upward. A general 'limitation of the vend' of iron was not again discussed for many years[2].

Between 1871 and 1884 Britain's share of the world's known iron output fell from 53·2 to 38·5 per cent. The fall was most

[1] Vol. I. p. 205, based on Scrivenor, *History of the Iron Trade*, p. 290.

[2] Macrosty, *op. cit.* p. 57–60. No. 3 Cleveland pig iron averaged for the fourth quarter of 1879, 36*s.* 8*d.*; of 1880, 40*s.* 5*d.*; of 1881, 38*s.* 3*d.*; of 1882, 43*s.* 6*d.*; of 1883, 38*s.* 3*d.*; of 1884, 36*s.*; of 1885, 32*s.* 3*d.*; of 1886, 30*s.* 4*d.* Then the rise began to 44*s.* 11*d.* in 1889. *Stat. of Iron and Steel* (*Nat. Fed. of Iron and Steel Man.*), 1926, p. 15. Cp. Lowthian Bell's Memorandum for the *R.C. on Depression of Trade*, II. 323.

rapid after 1877, with the development of the open-hearth and basic processes and the extension of steel-making in America, Germany, France and Belgium. While rails had been of iron, that is till the late 'seventies, Britain had almost a monopoly of the export trade in them. Now Belgium and Germany had steel rails to sell[1]. The low prices of the early 'eighties led to an international 'fighting trade'; that in its turn to a thing unprecedented in British industrial history, indeed unprecedented in the industrial history of the modern world—an international market-sharing agreement. With the experience gained in their various Associations to help them, all the British makers of steel rails except one came together at the end of 1883. "It was decided to endeavour to associate the Belgians and the Germans with us as being the only two countries that exported rails."[2] All the Belgians came in and all the Germans but two. The upshot was an assignment of 66 per cent. of the export trade to Britain—a percentage slightly reduced later—27 per cent. to Germany and 7 per cent. to Belgium. The price was fixed from England "at very much what we considered the cost price would be at the least favoured works"—in economists' jargon, at the marginal price—and the different works were given quota according to their "assessed capabilities."[3] The thing did not work well either nationally or internationally and in April of 1886 it was dissolved; but the age of free and unrestricted competition had closed with this novel experiment in treaty-making by associated manufacturers, and this rationing of producers. It was less than forty years since the coal 'vend' had broken down.

Formal, if always voluntary, associations of producers had certainly made most progress before the 'eighties in the heavy basic industries. Besides those already mentioned, there was now a British Iron Trade Association which attempted to watch, without directing, the course of the whole industry. Parallel to it in the coal trade of the 'eighties was the Mining Association of Great Britain, with its six or eight local Associations on the principal coalfields. These also had no real directing power. Higher up the metallurgical scale were the Association of Tinplate Manufacturers and the Wire Trade Association, among others. Papermakers, English and Scottish;

[1] Belgian iron had appeared on the British market before this. Below, p. 248.
[2] Smith, J. T. of Barrow, *R.C. on Depression of Trade*, Q. 2271
[3] *Ibid.* Q. 2284.

Sugar-refiners; Alkali Manufacturers; Leather Manufacturers in Leeds and Bermondsey; and the powerful Master Cotton Spinners' Association of Oldham, which spoke for the owners of more than a quarter of the British cotton spindles, were among the other important organisations which were active enough to reply to a circular from the Royal Commission on the Depression of Trade and Industry in 1885–6 asking for their views on the economic health of the country[1].

Many of these Associations had little more to do with concrete industrial policies than the Chambers of Commerce, though all might serve as rallying-points for employers in times of trade dispute. In many places, especially in those dominated by a single trade, like Bradford, the Chamber did the statistical, parliamentary, and other work natural to a trade Association. No doubt meetings of either type of organisation gave opportunities for unofficial discussion of prices and labour, and perhaps even output. But the strongest Associations had no coercive power, and the weaker little value. The Secretary of the Alkali Manufacturers' Association informed the Commission of 1885 that he could tell them nothing because his members only met once a year; except, he added, "on occasions of urgency."[2] A request from a Royal Commission was evidently not such, and he did not explain what kind of urgency would have been held to justify a special meeting. Perhaps a strike or a new Alkali Act. The President of the Tinplate Manufacturers made a double confession of industrial impotence on behalf of his Association—"our wages are controlled not by supply and demand but by a trades union": "the great cause of depression in our trade is over-production, for which we are ourselves to blame."[3]

Several Associations spoke of over-production, actual or potential, national or international. It was not the business of the few of them which had tried to deal with the problem by policies of their own to explain those policies. The cure ordinarily suggested or implied was not associated action, except perhaps external action against the railways, or the rates, or the

[1] The total number of Associations replying was only 26, if the Mining Assoc. be taken as one. This includes such commercial organisations as the Linen Merchants' Assoc., the Flax Supply Assoc., the Nottingham Merchants' Assoc. and the Rye District Commercial Assoc., also two Builders' Assoc. and the General Shipowners' Society. *R.C. on Depression of Trade*, I. 114 *sqq.*, II. 409 *sqq.*

[2] Muspratt, E. K., to the Commission, September 17, 1885; *Report*, I. 115.

[3] *Report*, I. 119. And see below, p. 169.

income tax, or internal action against the trade unions, but individual reduction of costs, as put clearly, if with an interjected economic fallacy, by the Oldham Spinners—"there can be no doubt that our trade is suffering very greatly from over-production, but it is not that we are producing more than the world really requires, but that we are producing more than the world can really afford to pay for, and this points to the importance of lessening the cost of production to the last possible degree."[1] Here spoke the organ of a highly competitive individualist industrial group. So individualist and so competitive were many other such groups, that they had not recognised even the need for regular collection and dissemination of industrial facts, or for any standing organisation to handle labour questions. They had no Associations at all.

This indifference is to be explained in some measure by the still partial and local development of trade unionism. After the extension of the franchise in 1867 and the Trade Union Commission of 1867–9, legislation, at first haltingly and then decidedly in favour of the unions, had culminated in the replacement of the old unequal law of Master and Servant by the Employers and Workmen Act of 1875 (38 and 39 Vict. c. 90) and in Mundella's Trade Union Act Amendment Act of 1876 (39 and 40 Vict. c. 22). It was held in official quarters during the 'eighties that "every legal grievance of which the union complained" had been removed[2]. Most trade union leaders of the day would have agreed. They were now "liberated from the last vestiges of the criminal laws specially appertaining to labour," as George Howell said[3]. Some trade union critics maintained later that the unions had not only been given a free field, but had been privileged. However, more than ten years of free opportunity, and possibly some privilege were needed before the open land could be occupied. Besides, those had been years of shocking bad trade. The Unions' statistics of unemployment benefit, whose value as industrial barometers was just beginning to be recognised outside trade union circles, showed it. The Amalgamated Society of Engineers had an

[1] *Report*, II. 427.

[2] *Stat. Tables and Report on Trade Unions*, 1887 (LXXXIX. 715), p. 9. By Giffen and Burnett; the first of the annual Trade Union Reports of the Chief Labour Correspondent of the Board of Trade (Burnett).

[3] At the T.U. Congress of 1875; Webb, *op. cit.* p. 276

unemployment figure of 13·3 in 1879; the London Compositors one of 14·3; the Boilermakers and Iron Shipbuilders of 20·4; and the Ironfounders of 22·3. From 1884 to 1886 the Boilermakers' figure was continuously above 20·0, reaching 22·3 in 1885[1]. It was no time for expansion or difficult experiments. Some of the strongest societies were barely holding their own; others, once strong, had lost members and money wholesale.

It is probable that in the early 'forties, when the hopes of 1832–4 had died and missionary spirits had turned from the cause of the Union to the cause of the Charter, not more than 100,000 wage-earners were full members of trade societies, in spite of the strong union tradition in the old crafts and the resolute attempts to transplant it into new or revolutionised industries[2]. Law was unequal. Employers were hostile. Wage-earners were poor. Unions were born and died in dreary cycle. A Staffordshire employer had known "three sets of unions" in the iron industry before 1867[3]. There had been "scores of unions" in the Ayrshire coal-mines before 1886, Keir Hardie once said[4]. All had failed. How many trade unionists there were in 1867–9 the Commissioners of Inquiry of those years did not venture to calculate. But when drawing conclusions from the evidence, they unfortunately quoted a guess made by an ardent official of the London Operative Tailors, who had said that "there might be more but not less" than 860,000[5]. They would have done better to trust another contemporary trade union estimate that "there were never at any time more than a quarter of a million."[6] With more stable conditions, better organising methods, and reduced risks of legal embarrassment or death from a planned attack by employers, the unions of the 'seventies and 'eighties had more continuous lives than their predecessors; though there was still mortality among them. There is no doubt that aggregate membership moved up very rapidly during the good trade of the early 'seventies; and it seems probable that the formation of new unions may have balanced loss of membership in some old ones between 1876

[1] The figures which started modern statistical study of unemployment, first made public in the *Report* of 1887.

[2] Vol. I. p. 593–4.

[3] *R.C. on Trade Unions*, Q. 9839.

[4] *R.C. on Labour*, Group A, Q. 12,951.

[5] Druitt, G., Q. 18,222.

[6] Macdonald, W., *The True Story of Trades Unions contrasted with the caricatures and fallacies of the pretended economists* (1867), quoted in Postgate, R. W., *The Builders' History*, p. 205 n.

and 1886. But in 1886 no one knew to a quarter of a million how many trade unionists there were in Britain. When one government official suggested a probable figure of "over 600,000," another, better informed, countered with 1,000,000 as "not...an exaggerated estimate." The higher figure was certainly the more nearly correct; it may perhaps not have been quite high enough[1].

The big battalions of the movement, some of them thinned by the casualties of trade depression, were to be found in a limited group of industries—building, engineering and certain allied trades, coal-mining, the cotton manufacture. But some of the best bits of organisation and most complete triumphs of trade unionism were outside this group; such as the ancient society of the London Compositors with its 6600 members and virtual monopoly in important sections of the trade; the London Bookbinders and Goldbeaters with proved pedigrees of over a century; the Journeymen Hatters on whose behalf a more august claim has been put forward[2]; or the small exclusive and masterful unions, new on old foundations, in certain Sheffield trades, with their obvious 'gild' merits and defects. It was from Sheffield that these unions reported frankly in 1867–9, some that they had stopped taking apprentices because trade was bad; some that only members' sons were ever admitted apprentice; all that limitation of apprentices was a matter of course[3]. The Commissioners, who disliked limitation of apprentices, made no comment—probably because they were obsessed with the greater societies, not because they recognised the truth that these Sickle and Hook Forgers, Pen- and Pocket-Knife Blade-Forgers, Steel Fork Forgers, and members of the Work Board Branch of the Scissor Trade were on the border-line between the old fashioned independent craftsman and the wage earner. They could regulate apprenticeship because the apprentices

[1] The 600,000 was Giffen's figure (*Report* of 1887) based on the reputed 630,000 represented at the previous Trade Union Congress. The Chief Registrar of Friendly Societies (*Report*, 1887, LXXVI) pointed out that these figures were "far from including even all the largest" societies, and guessed 1,000,000. After the great Trade Union revival of 1886–91 Mr and Mrs Webb estimated the figure at 1,471,000 for 1892; *op. cit.* p. 415.

[2] See Unwin, G., *Industrial Organisation in the 16th and 17th Centuries* (1904), p. 215, where a continuous history from the seventeenth century is, with great probability, suggested. The facts about the other societies are in the *Report* of 1887.

[3] *R.C. on Trade Unions, Final Report* (1868–9, XXXI. 235), *App.* of T.U.'s which replied to a circular from the Commission.

really were theirs, not 'factory apprentices' of some great firm. They and their lads took jobs by the piece, in the factory or out of it[1].

The trade-unionist employer was well known in other industries, for sub-contract in one or other of its innumerable forms was common[2]; but he was slowly becoming rarer.

Down to about 1850, the masons, at that time the most powerful group in the building trades, of which they were the conscious aristocracy, still permitted 'operative masters' in their lodges. But the arrangement had become unnatural and it died out[3]. In all England, and even in the large stone-built towns of Scotland, masons were typical, if high-grade, wage earners. In England a mason rarely became a 'builder.'[4] In districts where he might do so, such as the West Riding or Wales, either he would avoid the lodge or there would probably be no lodge. Out of a loose federation of lodges had already been built up the Operative Stonemasons' Union, whose membership passed 9000 in 1854 and 18,000 in 1868 and 1872; touched its maximum, 27,188, in 1877; but fell away to below 13,000 in 1880, never to recover. The Scottish Masons' Society was still more unfortunate. It had raised its membership to nearly 14,000 by 1877. Next year it lost nearly all its funds in the failure of the Glasgow Bank. By the middle 'eighties its numbers were down to 3000 and less[5].

Trade depression, strikes on a falling market, the relative decline in the importance of masons' work, and defects of leadership were the proximate causes of decay. But defects of organisation had a full share. Even throughout the long fighting secretaryship of Richard Harnott (1847–72) the English masons had a shifting seat of government and no proper central organisation. They only agreed to a London office in 1883. Meanwhile, for lack of any central policy, "provincial lodges fought uselessly on their own funds or accepted defeat as they chose"[6]; and their membership fell away.

[1] For the term 'factory apprentice' see vol. I. p. 177. And see above, p. 129, for the persistence of this semi-independence.

[2] The "practically ubiquitous" of Schloss, D. F., *Methods of Industrial Remuneration* (1892), p. 120, suggests, however, rather more than there was. See above, p. 128.

[3] Postgate, *The Builders' History*, p. 150. Cp. vol. I. p. 595.

[4] Foremen, and so embryo builders, usually came from among the carpenters; above, p. 130.

[5] Figures from Postgate and the *Report of* 1887.

[6] Postgate, *op. cit.* p. 304.

The younger but far better organised Amalgamated Society of Carpenters and Joiners actually increased its membership in the early 'eighties—but partly at the expense of a rival and older carpenters' society. Founded in 1861, and built up by Robert Applegarth, secretary 1862–71, on an effective central organisation, substantial contributions from members, high Friendly Society benefits, no Owenite nonsense, and the policy of "doing all we can to extend"[1] friendly agreement between employers and employed, the A.S.C.J. had been, with a few reservations, the model union of the Commissioners of 1867–9. Applegarth left it with a membership of 11,000, which rose to 16,000 in 1876, and to a temporary maximum of nearly 29,000 in 1885. Although its rival, the General Union of Carpenters, fell from 11,000 in 1876 to under 2000 in 1883–5, there remained a net increase of trade union carpenters in those difficult years[2].

Conflict of unions inside the same craft was a common and enervating weakness of building trade unionism. Like the strong local and lodge feeling, the strong craft feeling, and the jealousy between the crafts—all equally common—it was natural enough in trades which had always existed everywhere, usually with some local society, and had each begun its modern inter-lodge organisation from several different geographical points. The bricklayers had two central English Societies from an early date, the London Order and the Manchester Unity[3]. Many local societies were not affiliated to either. There were several more or less competitive general societies among painters and plumbers: there were at least a dozen distinct painters' societies in London alone[4]. Where societies were primarily local, efficiency was impaired. The painters could not even get an arranged scale of pay for London. Where societies originally local aspired to national character, they were likely to gain it, if at all, only over the bodies of fellow societies. Jungle

[1] Applegarth to the *R.C. on Trade Unions* in 1867, Q. 191. For his life, Webb, *History of Trade Unionism*, p. 219 n. and *passim*, and Postgate, p. 456. He died only a few years ago.

[2] Figures from Postgate and the *Report of* 1887.

[3] Postgate, *op. cit.* p. 140, 222, 225. These are the early names: there were changes later, but the two main head-quarters remained.

[4] "I think there are about 12 or 14": there "may be eighteen." Painters' witness before the *R.C. on Labour*, Group C, Q. 19,144; for plumbers, among whom there was only one really strong English society and one Scottish, Q. 19,178.

law broke out among brethren—Amalgamated against General, Order against Unity. "We used Prussian methods on them" an old official of the Amalgamated Carpenters once said to an inquirer[1].

Craft pride led to inter-craft jealousy and, at its worst, to interminable disputes about 'overlap.' The old unchanged technique of the trades led each to regard certain jobs as its inalienable right. At the height of their power, the Operative Masons had been resolute to keep 'brickeys' in their place[2], just as barristers meant to keep solicitors. Later, Manchester bricklayers often struck to keep labourers and, by a turn of the wheel, masons off bricklayers' work. They had a ten years Trojan War with the plasterers to retain the monopoly of terra-cotta work—and lost it[3]. As the wooden shipwrights' trade declined, the Amalgamated Carpenters tried to stop the shipwrights' "endeavours to travel along the vessel" to their work[4]. Meanwhile the Amalgamated Engineers resented the growing activity of plumbers on iron and steel ships, as the liners acquired the sanitary conveniences of a house[5]. The extreme case is an 1877 strike of plumbers in the Potteries, which failed because a rival plumbers' society took on the jobs[6]. These enervating squabbles led to a scheme for a national federation of building trades unions drafted by Edwin Coulson, the strong man of the London Bricklayers, in 1880. Nothing came of it; and the building unions went on into the 'eighties still strong in numbers, as trade union strength then went, but striking against employers and bickering among themselves on the falling market. Their aggregate membership in 1885–6 was something like 100,000, out of a body of perhaps 775,000 building craftsmen in Great Britain[7].

It is to be noted that the associated master-builders of the

[1] To Mr Postgate, *op. cit.* p. 308 n.

[2] Postgate, p. 300.

[3] Postgate, *op. cit. passim*; the first full study of any group of associated unions.

[4] *R.C. on Labour*, F. Chandler of the A.S.C.J., Group A, Q. 22,011. Cp. A. Wilkie of the Associated Shipwrights, Q. 21,389 *sqq.*: the shipwrights had only just lost their old organisation; "till recently...the bulk of our apprentices used to be indentured," Q. 21,462.

[5] *Ibid.*, Group A, Q. 26,056 (Evidence from the Wear).

[6] Postgate, p. 300.

[7] The estimate for 1885–6 is based on Postgate and the *Report of* 1887. Mr and Mrs Webb estimated the membership of the same group of unions in 1892 at 120,000. Their table, *op. cit.* p. 420, deals also with the furniture trades, here excluded. The estimate for the whole body of craftsmen is based on the census of 1881 when the figure was 761,000: above, p. 120.

late 'eighties were of opinion that the amount of building work, particularly of bricklaying, done in an hour had been approximately halved during thirty years of fairly effective trade unionism[1]. Their opinion is not a proof; for they gave no statistics and had the cumulated bias of the employer, often of the self-made employer who has risen by abnormally hard work, and of the *laudator temporis acti*. The unions would have admitted some decline and been proud of it, for they had always set their faces against "chasing," "bell-horsing," piecework, and other speeding-up devices. They maintained that work was better done and that workers were not worked out[2]. They could easily have illustrated the scamping and ill-health that had often gone with speed. No balance can be set between this unmeasured slackening of the average pace of production and its technical and social counter-weights.

When Applegarth was working at the organisation of the Amalgamated Carpenters he took as his model the greatest piece of amalgamation which the trade union movement had then known, the Amalgamated Society of Engineers. "I lent him our books" said William Allan, the Engineers' Secretary[3]. The Engineers had proved their strength, and won the grateful admiration of the building trades and the whole world of labour, by subscribing £3000 when the London builders were locked out in 1859–60 because they would not sign a document, or give a verbal promise, renouncing trade unionism[4]. The A.S.E. had been created, appropriately enough, in the year of the Great Exhibition and its victorious engines, out of 121 distinct societies or branches of unions connected with the risen engineering industry. Naturally such an amalgamation was not complete. Two strong old unions, the Steam-Engine Makers founded in 1824 and the United Machine Workers of 1844, never came in. The Pattern Makers formed their own union in 1872 because they thought no general society could safeguard their special interests. There were several Smiths' societies, and a few others. But the A.S.E. gathered in most of the trade. Starting with nearly 12,000 members and surviving a great lock-out early in 1852—a reply to attacks on employment of 'illegal' men, piecework, and overtime—it grew fast,

[1] *R.C. on Labour*, Group C, Q. 32,216: Bird, S. G. of the Central Assoc. of Master Builders.

[2] Evidence on these points was specially abundant in 1867–9.

[3] *R.C. on Trade Unions*, 1867–9, Q. 1023.

[4] *Trades Soc. and Strikes* (1860), Article on the lock-out; Webb, *op. cit.* p. 210–12.

without further serious fighting, until it had over 33,000 members in its 312 branches in 1868[1]. It came through the depression of the 'seventies with a surprisingly low maximum unemployment figure, a hardly perceptible drop in standard wages, and only a small drop in membership. This was soon recovered, and the membership had reached 52,000 in 1886. Nothing illustrates more clearly the relatively easy task of a recruiter for the A.S.E. Engineering as a whole was so buoyant, in this age of the engineer, that it rode easily over the waves of trade cycles and price vicissitudes.

Under William Allan (secretary 1851–74) the society was built up on the principles which Applegarth borrowed—substantial and regular contributions of a shilling a week or more; generous superannuation, funeral, and other allowances; as few strikes as possible that these funds should not be dissipated; and, as a natural consequence, a high level of skill and earning power among the members. His successor, John Burnett (secretary 1875–86) carried on this safe policy, although he had come to the front as leader of a notable strike on the North-East coast which won the nine hours day in 1872. It was he who, having resigned his office to become the first Labour Correspondent to the Board of Trade, reported of trade unions generally in 1886 that "although strikes have of course not yet been entirely superseded" yet "there is a gradual tendency in that direction."[2]

Reluctance to strike and lack of interest in Utopia had not implied acceptance of an employers' standpoint on work and wages. Like their predecessors the millwrights, the Amalgamated Engineers aimed at high time-rates and none of that payment by results, that 'engineers economy,' whose partial introduction about the years 1815–25 had been intended both to break the millwrights and help scientific management[3]. We have "a very decided objection to piecework," Allan said in 1867, because it leads to "sweating."[4] He meant speeding up, followed, as it had often been, by a reduction in the piece-rate when the maximum working speed had been ascertained. Like

[1] Statistics in 1867–9 *Final Report*, p. 283; *Report of* 1887, p. 30 *sqq*. For the other unions, see also *R.C. on Labour*, Group A, Q. 22,353 *sqq*. (Pattern Makers); *Report on Trade Unions for* 1901, p. 18. For the lock-out, Thomas Hughes in *Trades Societies and Strikes*, p. 169 *sqq*.; Nasmyth, *Autobiography*, p. 298, an employer's point of view; Webb, *op. cit*. p. 195 sqq.

[2] *Report of* 1887, p. 9. For Allan and Burnett, Webb, *op. cit*. p. 216 n., 300

[3] Vol. I. p. 207.

[4] *R.C. on Trade Unions*, Q. 638, 672.

the millwrights again, the Engineers wanted to control admission to their trade. Allan was very plain. "What is your object in limiting...apprentices?" "To keep the wages up: no question about it."[1] They had taken their part in agitations and occasional strikes for a shorter working day. As in some districts the standard week was already down to 57 hours in 1851, the question was not urgent everywhere. By 1872 the 54-hour week had been secured generally, and with that the leaders, who had not been very active in securing it, were content[2]. Whether a more combative policy, on this and other issues, might have won more for the men between 1851 and 1874 is uncertain: the avoidance of too much combat in the decade following 1874 was undoubtedly wise.

The Engineers' nearest industrial neighbours, the Boiler-makers, more specialised and so hit much harder by trade depression, were struggling with unemployment and loss of numbers in the 'eighties, but remained a strong force and included nearly all the trade. Their recent rise had been easy and quick. Founded in Lancashire under William IV, this union of the men who made things out of iron plates had expanded until the ship-building element in it had swamped the true boiler-makers. The decade 1872–82 was its great era of expansion: the law was becoming friendly and the wooden ship was dying. From a membership of 7000 in 1870, it had reached 28,000 in 1883. Seeing that 20·0 per cent. of the members were unemployed in 1884 and 22·3 in 1885, it is creditable both to the leaders and to the loyalty of the rank and file that the membership had not fallen below 26,800 in 1886. Probably there were a good many nominal members and heavy arrears of contributions. The society was national, of the amalgamated type, with 212 branches and good benefits. Like the Engineers, its members had enjoyed the 54-hour week since 1872. Its leaders were now nursing their financial wounds and steering a judicious unprovocative course. Robert Knight, their secretary, was one of the state's most trusted consulting industrial experts[3].

[1] Q. 927.

[2] There is a summary of hours' history in the *Report of* 1887, p. 30: in 1851–61 hours varied locally from 57 to 63. From 1872–9 Scotland had a 51-hour week, which it lost later. See below, p. 449.

[3] *Report of* 1887, p. 10, 22, 30. Knight's evidence before *R.C. on Depression of Trade*, Q. 14,733 *sqq.*; before *R.C. on Labour*, Group A, Q. 20,680 *sqq.* He 'supposed' that the Union included 95 per cent. of the men, Q. 20,725.

Among the iron-workers who were not engineers or boiler-makers, the unions, with the exception of the Friendly Society of Ironfounders, had hitherto been either local or rather short-lived or both. The experience of the employer of the 'sixties who had known three sets of unions remained typical. At the close of the century no important society except the Iron-founders was credited with a continuous history which went earlier than 1880; although the Associated Iron and Steel Workers, never very large, carried on the functions of a similar society which started in 1862, and the Cleveland Blastfurnace-men established in 1881–2 a small association which later became national[1]. Constant technical revolutions; transferences of the industrial centre of gravity; the isolation of some of the greatest iron works and the resultant survival of so-called patriarchal relations; sharp alternations of prosperity and adversity; and, perhaps most important of all, the widespread existence of sub-employment, by puddlers, rollers, steel-makers and the rest, all tended to hamper local trade union activity and to make national activity almost impossible. Here the trade unionist employer had been very much at home. "Every puddler is a contractor; and they would like to pay their under-hands by the ton, but the under-hands will not have it." That concise summary comes from a district where unionism was fairly strong and from the year 1891[2]. The "under-hands" had only recently become assertive. It illustrates the divisions so adverse to anything like what came to be called later 'industrial' as opposed to 'craft' unionism, and so hampering to unionism of any sort.

The Ironfounders, belonging to an old section of the industry which existed everywhere and whose essentials had not changed for a century, were in a totally different position. Their Friendly Society dated from a year (1809) in which every wise trade union had underlined its 'friendly' character. Its principal work had always been on the friendly rather than on the industrial side. It had over 70 branches and over 7000 members in the late 'fifties; over 100 branches and nearly 10,000 members in 1868; 12,300 members in 1875 and 12,400 in 1885. The unemployment of the 'seventies had nearly ruined it with out-of-work pay. By 1880 its splendid reserve of over £60,000 was

[1] *Report on Trade Unions*, 1901, p. 18; *R.C. on Labour*, Group A, Q. 13,960 (Nat. Assoc. of Blastfurnacemen), Q. 15,301 (Assoc. Iron and Steel Workers).

[2] It was made by Ed. Trow before the *R.C. on Labour*, Group A, Q. 15,329, and refers to the N.E. Coast.

gone, and in the early 'eighties it was hardly in a position to perform the traditional friendly functions. The corresponding Scottish society, however, the Associated Iron Moulders of Scotland, was growing while the English society was stationary. It added 1000 to its membership between 1880 and 1885, when the total stood at 5600[1].

There were other effective metal-working unions, as the Sheffield trades show, but not one of them was large or of national importance.

No industry had registered more clearly than coal-mining the ebb and flow of the tides of trade unionism, or the difficulty with which the union was becoming part of the recognised industrial organisation of the country. On every coalfield at least a second and third, if not Keir Hardie's nineteenth and twentieth, attempt was needed to give unionism vitality and permanence. With the flow and ebb of local life goes the rise and fall of the national union ideal. Sometimes a measure of continuity can be traced behind a series of apparent new beginnings. Sometimes a local federation, important for a time in the life of a whole coalfield, disappears, leaving at most some pit clubs of little general significance, yet continuous. But such continuity of mere existence often only underlines the discontinuity of effective power[2]. The era begins at a time of dead water.

"At the close of 1855, it might be said that union among the miners in the whole country had almost died out."[3] Then came local revivals connected, among other things, with a Yorkshire fight for the introduction of miners' 'checkweighmen' to prevent abuses in the system of paying earnings by weight. Then also came Alexander Macdonald and his great scheme, itself a revival, for a National Miners' Union. It has been suggested that by the end of the 'sixties there were actually two hundred thousand miners 'in union.'[4] Through their political friends,

[1] Statistics in *R.C. on Trade Unions*, 1867–9, *Final Report*, p. 306, and in *Report* of 1887. For this and many other unions see the membership statistics 1850–90 in Webb, *op. cit.* p. 491–5. The Ironfounders have the most exact records of any society.

[2] Webb's *History* and Welbourne's *Miners' Unions of Northumberland and Durham* give the general story. And see vol. I. p. 217–18, 597.

[3] Alexander Macdonald, quoted in Webb, *op. cit.* p. 285.

[4] Webb, *op. cit.* p. 292. No authority given. The figure seems most improbable. The census of 1871 gives a maximum of about 350,000 coal-miners in Britain, a figure which includes most of the 'miners undefined' and all the boys and lads: 1873, LXXI. part 2 (England and Wales), LXXIII. (Scotland).

they were already a force in Parliament and had influenced legislation in 1860 and 1872[1]. The two hundred thousand level, if ever attained, was soon lost when prices broke and trade collapsed after 1873. The national ideal as an effective force was lost with it. By 1880 "the Lancashire and Midland...organisations...had either collapsed altogether, or had dissolved into isolated clubs, incapable of combined action."[2] In the single year 1878 the Durham men had paid away £54,000 in unemployment benefit[3]. In the years from 1875 to 1880, the Northumberland and Durham unions, the two strongest and the only two with continuous numerical histories, had fallen from an aggregate membership of nearly 56,000 to not quite 41,000. Both recovered a little during the next five years, so that the aggregate stood at 48,000 in 1885[4]. Probably this represented about half the enrolled coal-miners of Great Britain at that date, and the Durham union alone, with its 35,000 members, a full third. Lancashire was reorganising its Federation in 1882–5, but rapid recruitment only began in the final year. The Yorkshire Federation had at this time only about 8000 members. None of the Scottish, Welsh, or Midland areas had organisations which were numerically strong, though in nearly all of them during 1885, and still more during 1886, there was great activity in propaganda and enrolment[5].

In spite of the fall in numbers since 1875, the coal-miners' unions of the middle 'eighties contained about a quarter of the available men in the whole trade[6]. Where they were strongest, in Northumberland and Durham, the proportion was far higher. Built up rapidly on older foundations, during the politically and economically prosperous decade which followed the Reform Bill of 1867 and witnessed the freeing of trade unionism from the shackles of the old law, the Northumberland union had stood effectively in the way of any reintroduction by employers of that ancient fetter of the North-Country pitman, the yearly

[1] The Mines Acts, 23 and 24 Vict. c. 151 and 35 and 36 Vict. c. 76. See below, p. 420.

[2] Webb, *op. cit.* p. 372.

[3] Welbourne, *op. cit.* p. 194.

[4] *R. of Chief Registrar of Friendly Societies*, 1887, p. 63.

[5] The annual *Reports* and evidence before *R.C. on Labour*, Group A (given in 1891) are the main sources. The evidence of 1891, given by district officials, is particularly valuable.

[6] The *Survey of Industrial Relations* (1926) accepts the figures 434,000 (1881) and 595,000 (1891) for 'coal and shale' miners in Britain. The shale miners were only a few thousands but there were many lads.

bond. The Durham union had prepared a last fight against the bond in 1872, only to find that it was forcing an open door. Coal was at impossible prices. Miners were coming in from Lancashire and the Forest of Dean. The coal-owners were very ready to pay for willing work in cash and concessions. "The most pleasant and amicable feeling prevailed on both sides at the meetings of 1872"; and the men got fortnightly agreements and 20 per cent. on wages[1].

Their strength and moderation and the national position acquired by their leaders carried these two unions through the bad years that followed, when for a decade (1878–87) the average export price of British coal was all but 30 per cent. lower than it had been in the decade of prosperity. They did not get through without strikes, nor without the frank and uncompelled acceptance by their leaders of the principle of a sliding scale: 'that wages should be based on the selling price of coal.'[2] This acceptance was condemned at the time, and has been condemned since, as a compromise with the commercial doctrines of the coal-owners and a potential abandonment of the miners' standard of life; but there can be very little doubt that, like the engineers' no-strike policy, it helped to give the North-Country miners' unions complete uncriticised recognition, and an accepted place in the industrial organisation of the country. The sliding-scale in fact yielded a 'living' wage. Policy could be changed to meet fresh conditions. The local and national status of the unions were things established[3].

Where unionism was strong among the coal-miners, as on the North-East Coast, it was usually strong among the much smaller trade of the iron-miners. It was strong, too, among the quarrymen, especially the slate quarrymen of Wales. But among the tin, lead, and copper-miners it was—so far as can be ascertained—"absolutely unknown."[4]

[1] Welbourne, *op. cit.* p. 71, 114, 151 and *passim*. For the bond see vol. I. p. 217. Abandoned in 1844, it had been revived in Durham. An attempt to revive it in Northumberland in 1862 was fought successfully. In Durham it survived to 1872, as above.

[2] From an 1879 circular of the Northumberland Miners' Executive, quoted in Webb, *op. cit.* p. 325.

[3] The points are touched on, not without some confusion of thought, in Webb, *op. cit.* p. 324–5.

[4] Webb, *op. cit.* p. 421. For its complete absence from Cornwall see Price, L. L., "West Barbary or Notes on the System of Work and Wages in the Cornish Mines," *S.J.* 1888, p. 494.

In public estimation, and in the national position won by their leaders, the Cotton Spinners ranked with the miners and engineers, although their union had less than 17,000 members in 1885[1]. But then they were 17,000 out of a possible 20,000 at most. They were one of the dominant male groups in an industry full of women and children. Like the puddlers, they were wage-earning employers who hired their own piecers, 'big' and 'little,' from whom their successors were recruited. But piecers could not all succeed to spinners' work, because they outnumbered the spinners by more than two to one. A federation of local societies, each with its own rules and funds, the Association dated officially from 1853. It had enlisted a great majority of the trade by the 'sixties. Although in some places spinners maintained that, so late as 1881, mill-owners "would not listen to reason,"[2] in most there had been a growing friendliness ever since the common sufferings of the cotton famine. Up to the famine, "a majority" of masters would not even deal with a trade union[3]. In the democratic air of the Oldham 'province' the mill-owner was melting away into anonymity, and the spinner was as good a man as the machinist who put up money to help him to spin. Even in aristocratic Preston, employers were realising that the union committee was "a committee of conciliation and not...a paid body of agitators."[4] Within a very few years, the Spinners' Secretary would be explaining that over the whole area with which his Association dealt, there was not "the slightest trouble or friction" with employers[5]. More completely perhaps than any other union, the cotton spinners were a regularly working part of the industrial machinery of the country.

There were many more cotton unions, and their aggregate membership was far greater than that of the spinners, but they were still in the unfederated stage, or only just passing out of it. Except among certain specialists, and in places where the

[1] There were no spinners in Parliament, with Thomas Burt and the other early miner M.P.'s, but James Mawdsley, the Spinners' Secretary, had a national position.

[2] Cowell, J., spinner, of Preston, before the *R.C. on Labour*, Group C, Q. 4750.

[3] Evidence of Henderson, Jas., Factory Inspector, given in Nov. 1891 and referring to "thirty years ago." *R.C. on Labour*, Group C, Q. 7309. He added, "all this is now changed."

[4] Cowell, J., Q. 4751.

[5] *R.C. on Labour* (evidence taken in 1891), Q. 721. Spinners' history is in Webb, *op. cit.*; the fullest discussion of spinners' function in Webb, *Industrial Democracy* (1897), *passim.*

trade union spirit was particularly strong, they had, as yet, nothing like the spinners' control of the situation. A dozen or more local associations of power-loom overlookers, each with a few score or a few hundred members, safeguarded the interests of this aristocratic group. There were some efficient societies among bleachers, dyers, and calico-printers, with an aggregate membership which perhaps approached 10,000. Much more important were the local societies of weavers, cardroom operatives, and 'beamers' and 'twisters'; for all these, whose total membership may have been 80,000, admitted women—indeed contained a considerable majority of women. And these women, not less than 50,000, formed the only important group of women trade unionists in the kingdom[1].

Many of the strongest power-loom weavers' societies dated from the 'fifties, from the time of the final victory of the machine whose name they bore, and the established predominance of the woman weaver. Padiham and District, 1850; Blackburn and District, 1854; Chorley and District, 1855; Accrington and District, 1856; and so on. Some had taken over half-official agreements which were in existence before there was any permanent union. The Burnley and District Society, for example, which dated nominally only from 1870, worked on a 'local list' of weaving prices which was never revised in essentials during the forty years 1843–83, though percentages might be added or subtracted[2]. All the societies had admitted women from an early date, and the number of women members had grown with the decline of male weaving. There had just been formed (in 1884) the Northern Counties Amalgamated Association of Weavers; but the active life of the movement was in the twenty-five districts, with their local specialities and lists[3].

So too with the Card and Blowing Room societies. They were, as a group, a good deal younger than the weavers' societies and very much weaker. Two only, those of Bolton and Stockport, dated from the 'fifties: three more from the 'sixties. Although most of them allowed the women who span at the throstles and ring-frames to join—James Mawdsley's spinners

[1] Figures from *Report of* 1887 and subsequent *Reports* (that of 1901 has been used). Cp. estimates in Webb, *History*, p. 413, 423, 492 *sqq*.

[2] *R.C. on Labour*, Group C, Q. 1084–6.

[3] Association was in the air in 1884–6 (Webb, *History*, p. 422) but its importance is for a later period.

all tended mules—they had not as yet succeeded in enlisting an important proportion of the workers anywhere, except at Oldham, and even there the large numbers were a new thing. As for the unions among the 'beamers' and 'twisters'—people who prepare the weavers' beams for the loom and 'twist in' the ends of the new warp threads—they could not be large because their trades are small, and though they admitted women they only contained a handful. The cardroom people were just working out an amalgamation of their district societies. It was completed in 1886. The others had not arrived at this stage, and it was not likely that they ever would[1].

Throughout all the other textile trades, unionism was extraordinarily weak. There were a few old-established friendly societies of overlookers and other managing people; a few discouraged organisations among hand-workers—Midland knitters, Macclesfield silk-weavers, or the tiny remnant of cotton hand-loom weavers at Bolton[2]; some isolated local societies among general factory workers; and a few ambitious, but still weakly, beginnings, like the West Riding General Union of Weavers and Textile Workers of 1881. Scattered, sectional, poor in funds, their membership all told can hardly have exceeded that of the cotton cardroom workers. Great industrial diversity even inside particular industries, as in wool; late and incomplete revolutionising of technique, as in silk; geographical division; predominance of women and child workers; low pay for nearly all—these seem the main causes. To them add the stubborn local feeling of the West Riding: Guiseley did not work with Pudsey, and Birstall followed not Ossett.

Among the clothing trades of all kinds unionism was weaker still. Only a few of the tailors were in the Amalgamated or the Scottish Societies. A union which was to become very strong had been formed among the machine boot-makers in 1874; but in 1886 its membership had not passed 14,000. This, with a few old craft societies among shoe-makers, hatters, glovers and the like completes the scanty list.

The potters' unions were specialised, small, and independent[3]. The miscellaneous metal, leather, and wood-working

[1] *Reports* on Trade Unions and Webb, *op. cit.* as above.

[2] The Bolton Hand-loom Weavers still had 24 members in 1898, but were dissolved about the end of 1899: *Report of* 1901, p. 47. Cp. above, p. 81.

[3] Warburton, W. H., *Trade Union Organisation in the North Staffordshire Potteries* (1931), p. 168 *sqq*.

trades contained hundreds of unions, a few strong locally, like some of those at Sheffield, but mostly weak; though their aggregate membership was considerable. They were seldom representative of their trades, though most trades in the groups were represented by unions. There were at least a score of small societies in the brass and copper trades, besides the five thousand or so of the Amalgamated Brass Workers. Struggling little societies of tin-plate workers, braziers, and workers in precious metals were scattered about the country[1]. Twenty distinct unions catered for the needs of a few thousand coopers. A hundred or more of the very old shipwrights' societies had recently (1882) come together as the Associated Shipwrights; but a number were still standing out. Most shipwrights were in union locally; they always had been[2].

So were very many, if not most, printers. Besides the powerful London Compositors, the Typographical Association, founded in Sheffield in 1849 but with headquarters at Manchester since 1865, together with some smaller kindred societies, covered a great part of the trade. Yet the Lithographic Printers of 1879, strong in the 'provinces,' were weak in London: "so many shops...are up mysterious back places and courts and such-like that we cannot get at them," an official of the union once said[3]. The explanation deserves to be borne in mind; for it was true of many London trades, and it helps to account for the weakness and provincialism of many London trade societies.

Outside the skilled trades and the manufactures, unionism was still almost unknown. There were a handful of weak societies of builders' and general labourers. London stevedores and watermen, with a few other riverside groups, had local organisations. But the Amalgamated Society of Railway Ser-

[1] Up to 1887 tin-plate unionism was intermittent, in spite of the power which employers attributed to it (above, p. 152). Jones, J. H., *The Tin-plate Industry* (1914), p. 178.

[2] Evidence of Wilkie, A., of the shipwrights, *R.C. on Labour*, Group A, Q. 21,389 *sqq*. Cp. vol. I. p. 201, 212–13.

[3] Kelley, G. D. before *R.C. on Labour*, Group C, Q. 22,693. The evidence for the Typographical Assoc., London Compositors and Scottish Typographical Assoc. is also full and very valuable, both for history and function. In spite of the strength of the London Compositors, more than half the government-contract printing shops in 1891 were non-unionist; Bowerman, C. W., Q. 23,031. For the small printing shop, see above, p. 119, n. 1. Jones, Benjamin, in 1894 (*Co-operative Production*, II. 572) explained the absence of co-operation in printing by "the comparative ease with which a pushing man can become a small master."

vants, which had started with over 17,000 members in 1871–2, had fallen to 6300 by 1882 and was only slowly recovering, though its funds were better than its numbers. The first reasonably durable society ever formed among road transport workers was the Edinburgh and Leith Cabdrivers' Union of 1885. It was neither very large nor at all rich[1].

The case of the cotton spinners shows how slowly the most inclusive and best managed of unions were winning a fully recognised position, although the situation of the late 'fifties, when a majority of the employers in the cotton industry would not deal with a union at all, was a thing of the past. That ill-managed and not representative societies should win a recognised place was not to be expected. Yet, whether representative or not, ill managed or well, their importance at crises was often out of proportion to their numerical strength or their degree of formal recognition. For John Burnett's claim that they contained "the flower of their respective trades," if possibly biased, was probably true[2]; and their aims were the natural aims of every wage-earner.

That policy of persuasion and restraint which their most prominent leaders had pursued for over twenty years, combined with the old traditions of trade club and gild, had given prominence to their friendly society functions. Funeral benefit was the most universal of all: £10 to £12 was an ordinary figure for a member's funeral, and half as much for that of a member's wife. All strong unions gave sick pay, compensation for injury when the trade was risky, and superannuation pay. A few helped widows and orphans. The more strictly industrial strike pay, unemployment pay, and travel pay were less universal than funeral benefit, though they were the main items of expenditure in the greater societies. Strike pay might be as high as £1 a week. The more usual 10*s.* to 15*s.* might be supplemented by special levies or sympathetic contributions. Unemployment pay was never more than 10*s.* a week: so strong a union as the Boilermakers offered only 8*s.* It was never guaranteed indefinitely. Small as it was, small as the aggregate outlay from all trade union funds in a bad year can have been if

[1] Alcock, G. W., *Fifty Years of Railway Trade Unionism* (1922), p. 625. Evidence on transport and waterside unions before *R.C. on Labour*, Group B (1892, xxxv), *passim.* For the Edinburgh cabmen, *Report on Trade Unions of* 1901, p. 65. There had been ephemeral unions among London cabmen before 1886; see *e.g.* Webb, *History*, p. 355.

[2] *Report of* 1887, p. 14.

set beside the figures of the poor-rate, the friends of the unions did well to call public attention to the national utility of this growing system of co-operative insurance against the most grievous risk of the wage-earner's active life. It was not so long since respectable Scottish masons had been obliged to meet seasonal unemployment, 'when every other resource had failed them,' by public begging[1].

The local and national organisations in which many trade unionists now came together, Trades Councils and Trade Union Congresses, were not as yet fully representative and had no regular functions in national industry. Permanent Councils had not existed before the late 'fifties[2]. But there had often been inter-union committees in times of crisis, and it was usually a crisis which led to permanent organisation—to be ready for the next. Such organisations, being new and voluntary, were never inclusive. A quarrel in the printing trade, for example, threw up the Association of Organised Trades of Sheffield in 1858. Two years later, twenty-two out of the no less than fifty-five unions of the Sheffield area were affiliated[3]. The troubles in the building trades in 1859–60 led to the creation of the London Trades Council, from which in its early days most of the greater societies stood aloof. At that time there were only five permanent councils. Their numbers and strength grew slowly during the next twenty years, but at least they existed in most important centres during the early 'eighties. Yet they were often weak, and only some quite small proportion of the trade unionists in the country was even nominally represented in them[4].

The first Congress was called together, in 1868, by the Manchester and Salford Council as a publicity organisation in the anticipated fight over trade union law; and publicity remained the principal function of these necessarily short annual gatherings. In order to enlighten the "profound ignorance which prevails in the public mind" they were to "assume the character of the Annual Meetings of the Social Science

[1] Vol. I. p. 585–6 (referring to the 'forties). The 'friends of the unions' referred to are George Howell in his *Conflicts of Capital and Labour* (1878), p. 154–5 and *passim*, and John Burnett, in the *Report of* 1887. The illustrative figures in the text are taken from these two sources.

[2] See the full note in Webb, *History*, p. 225–6.

[3] *Report on Trades Societies and Strikes* (1860), p. 565–6.

[4] For their relative insignificance even in the early 'nineties see Webb, *History*, p. 466.

Association."[1] So the original summons said; and so they did. A trade union historian has written that Congress met "to talk about every subject under the sun except Trade Union Policy"[2]: a recent president has spoken with respect of how in those early days it "gave more attention than it does to-day to the consideration of fundamental principles of economic organisation and industrial development."[3] Most Congresses of all kinds have futile aspects, but may nevertheless have educational value. This Congress did not seek to direct trade union policy, and need not be blamed for failure to do so.

From time to time during nearly three generations, the state, conscious of friction in industrial affairs, had tried to furnish legal facilities for the settlement of industrial differences. There was the Act of 1800 'for settling disputes that may arise between masters and workmen engaged in the cotton manufacture in that part of Great Britain called England' (39 and 40 Geo. III, c. 90). There was the general Act of 1825 (5 Geo. IV, c. 96), a pendant to the Combination Law controversy of 1824–5. Under it the Justices of the Peace, on appeal from the contending parties, might appoint mixed panels of masters and men, from which the parties would choose referees. If no settlement were reached, the Justices might give a final award. No master manufacturer was to sit on the bench when such an award was given. Nothing could be fairer or more well-meaning. Nor was anything ever much less effective, though very occasionally, in the 'forties and 'fifties, a puzzled London police magistrate had to decide whether or not a piece of Spitalfields velvet was well made[4]. The law was still there, with its working parts intact, in the 'eighties. "It is, I presume, but seldom appealed to," Stanley Jevons wrote in 1882[5]. He was right.

Revived interest in industrial questions during the 'sixties had produced other ineffective laws. That known as Lord St

[1] Printed in Webb, *op. cit.* App. III.

[2] Milne-Bailey, W., *Trade Union Documents* (1929), p. 25.

[3] *Ibid.* p. 75. The President's Address for 1926.

[4] Hamill, J., Police Magistrate, before the *S.C. on Masters and Operatives*, 1856 (XIII. 1), Q. 2318 *sqq.*

[5] *The State in Relation to Labour*, p. 156. There is a comprehensive summary of legal history, and of arbitration history generally, in a memorandum of the *R.C. on Labour* (1892, XXXVI. part 5); and cp. Lord Amulree, *Industrial Arbitration in Great Britain* (1929).

Leonard's Act of 1867 (30 and 31 Vict. c. 105) was intended to promote "equitable councils of conciliation," with a half-memory of the French *conseils des prud'hommes*. It was an enabling act and a dead letter. Its successor of 1872 (35 and 36 Vict. c. 46), known as Mr Mundella's, "to make further provision for arbitration between masters and workmen," was never once used[1].

Goodwill had not spent itself entirely on vain laws "with the taint of the Justice of the Peace about them."[2] Though no trade of importance had ever gone regularly to the courts, there had been a number of private experiments in arbitration which had, in fact, inspired those who framed the later ineffective laws. The laws were meant to help on a movement which already had a history. The notion of a 'Board of Trade,' to fix wages, had been dear to the suffering hand-loomers and their friends in the 'thirties and 'forties[3]. In the 'thirties there was a short-lived committee of conciliation in the Potteries, and from 1851 it was customary to insert an arbitration-clause in the yearly contract of service between the potter and his employer[4]. Up and down the country, disputes had occasionally been referred to trusted local men as arbitrators. Between 1845 and the early 'sixties, the wage-earners' National Association of United Trades did valuable conciliatory work in many places, London especially[5]. In 1849 a silk trade arbitration board had been set up at Macclesfield, in imitation of the *conseils des prud'hommes*; but it broke up in four years, being said to have driven trade out of the town, as perhaps, with its strict insistence on standard weaving rates, it had[6]. In the printing trade there appear to have been small local committees very much earlier; but an attempt to create a regular court of arbitration, with a barrister as umpire, failed about the time that the Macclesfield board broke down[7]. It was in 1860 and at Nottingham, after a period

[1] Mundella, A. J. and Howell, G., "Industrial Association," in *Reign of Queen Victoria* (ed. Humphry Ward, 1887), vol. II.

[2] Jevons, *op. cit.* p. 167.

[3] Vol. I. p. 552.

[4] Owen, H., *The Staffordshire Potter* (1901), p. 114. Evidence of M. D. Hollins, employer, and W. Maitland, potter, before *S.C. on Masters and Operatives*, 1856, Q. 2386 *sqq.*, 2557 *sqq.* Warburton, *op. cit.* p. 67, 142.

[5] For its general history see Webb, *History of Trade Unionism*, p. 168–9; for its special conciliatory work evidence of T. Winters, Sec. and E. Humphries, of the Committee, in 1856, Q. 1 *sqq.*, 512 *sqq.*

[6] Evidence of S. Higginbotham, its promoter, in 1856; Q. 1890 *sqq.*

[7] Evidence of J. Avent, compositor, Q. 2715 *sqq.* Cp. Crompton, H. C., *Industrial Conciliation* (1876), p. 130–1.

of wearing industrial friction, strikes, lock-outs and bitterness, that Mundella, a manufacturer, managed to establish the Board of Arbitration and Conciliation for the Hosiery and Glove Trade, an elective body of twenty-one with secretaries for employers and employed. Disputes of all kinds were to be tackled first by the secretaries; next by a committee; only in the last resort by the whole board[1]. For some twenty years the system worked fairly well. In the 'seventies it controlled the knitting piece-rates for some 6000 separate articles[2]. The Board was much discussed and a good deal imitated. But in the 'eighties it was breaking down. The industry had changed greatly. Some employers had shown themselves hostile: naturally workpeople had not always been satisfied. In 1884, a strike which the Board failed to avert left bitter memories, and the machinery fell into disuse[3]. Unionism was weak in the hosiery trade and the system was thereby handicapped. But the method of settlement through the officials of associations of wage earners and employers had been taken over meanwhile by some better organised industries, and was bearing fruit in the 'eighties, especially in Lancashire[4].

Four years after Mundella's board started, Rupert Kettle, the County Court Judge of Worcestershire, attended a meeting called by the Mayor of Wolverhampton to settle a building strike[5]. He suggested permanent arbitration arrangements, and drafted a scheme for settling disputes by a joint board with an umpire or referee. The acceptance of arbitration became part of the wage contract. Master builders and carpenters agreed. Next year a conciliation clause was added which, as Kettle said later, was more useful than the arbitration clause. Soon the plasterers and bricklayers came in. The masons, relying on their strength to get what they wanted, stood out[6]. The system was imitated elsewhere, in the building trade and in other trades. Kettle was called on to arbitrate both by those who did,

[1] Mundella, *op. cit.* Price, L. L., *Industrial Peace* (1887), p. 43. Cp. Wright, C. D., *Industrial Conciliation and Arbitration* (1881: Boston); Weeks, J. D., *Labor Differences and their Settlement* (1886: New York).

[2] Compton, *op. cit.* p. 39.

[3] The memorandum for the *R.C. on Labour*, as above.

[4] See *e.g.* the account of how minor difficulties were settled by the "practical committee" of the Card and Blowing Room Operatives, *R.C. on Labour*, Group C, Q. 115.

[5] Kettle, *Strikes and Arbitration* (1866) and his evidence (Q. 6985 *sqq.*) before *R.C. on Trade Unions*, 1867–9.

[6] Crompton, *op. cit.* p. 112 *sqq.*

and those who did not, adopt his particular system. In 1880 this "prince of arbitrators" was knighted. Although, some years before, the bricklayers of his home area had rejected an award and withdrawn, there were important centres in the late 'eighties where arbitration was the rule in all branches of the building trade. At Liverpool the court—equal numbers of masters and men, with an umpire if required—had functioned from 1874 almost without a hitch[1].

While Kettle was showing what his method could achieve, boards more or less on Mundella's lines were set up, in 1868, in the Leicester and Derby hosiery and in the Nottingham lace trades, and in the Potteries. The last merely developed existing arrangements. "Long before we had our board," an employer wrote in 1876, "we settled our disputes on the same principle, by fixing on two workmen and two masters, and I never remember a single failure."[2] Failures came later. In the 'eighties the Leicester board went the way of Mundella's hosiery board; and stresses were developing in the Potteries board which led to its disintegration in 1891–2[3].

Early in 1869, iron-workers from the Middlesbrough district had appeared at Nottingham to study Mundella's methods. Within a few weeks (on March 22, 1869) the most famous and successful of the boards of conciliation and arbitration had come into existence—the North of England Iron and Steel, under the chairmanship of David Dale[4]. Its creation was something of a feat. The industry was young, without traditions, and without regular unionism. Men had come in from all quarters. They were sturdy, illiterate and well paid. They proved, however, "at least as ready" for the experiment as their employers[5]. Perhaps, without much book learning or very long experience, they had grasped the essentially fluctuating character of an industry which turns out 'production goods,' whose members are therefore well-advised not to fight as they ride those waves of the trade cycle which are always steepest in such industries. True, the Board had the good fortune to start with a rise of 6*d*.

[1] *R.C. on Labour*, Group C, Q. 18,473 *sqq*.

[2] A correspondent of Crompton, *op. cit.* p. 121. Cp. Warburton, *op. cit.* p. 150.

[3] The memorandum of the *R.C. on Labour*; Warburton, *op. cit.* p. 159 *sqq*.

[4] See evidence of W. Whitwell, employer, and Ed. Trow, ironworker, before *R.C. on Labour*, Group A, Q. 14,997 *sqq*., 15,159 *sqq*., on its working; Samuelson, B., paper before *British Iron Trade Assoc.* 1876, for its early history; Price, *op. cit.*, for the 'eighties.

[5] Whitwell, as above.

a ton in puddlers' wages. Within four years, in the boom of the early 'seventies, another 4*s.* 9*d.* was added. This was easy arbitration. But in 1891, leaders from both sides could report with justifiable satisfaction that only a few short stoppages of work owing to disputes had ever occurred, and then only "under circumstances of special irritation or excitement"[1]; although puddlers' wages had moved from the 8*s.* a ton of 1868, through the 13*s.* 3*d.* of 1873, to a nadir of 6*s.* 3*d.* in the later dark years. The conciliation of all sorts of minor and local disputes was done throughout by a standing joint committee. Great wage decisions went to arbitrators with an umpire behind them—Rupert Kettle or Tom Hughes from outside, Joseph Pease or Spence Watson from nearer home.

"Arbitration in the coal trade," Henry Crompton wrote in 1876, "is an accomplished fact, as far as England and Wales are concerned. As yet, however...no permanent board...has been adopted."[2] In Durham and Northumberland joint committees of owners and miners with an outside chairman were set up in 1872–3. These committees were soon dealing with some hundreds of particular and local issues yearly. Their decisions were "scarcely ever disputed" throughout the period[3]. For the settlement of general wage questions, however, *ad hoc* arbitration tribunals were created from time to time. The chief dangers of this system were already apparent by 1876. It tended to stimulate a "refined advocacy,"[4] with bad psychological effects on both sides; and the frequent recurrence of full-dress arbitrations—one was concluded in Durham during November 1874: another begun in April 1875—was unsettling to the industrial atmosphere. Why all this trouble for a five months' agreement? Why reverence the majesty of a law so little durable? Agreements could scarcely hope to be durable in the fierce price fluctuation of the 'seventies; but, as a result of such questionings, there was no general arbitration in Durham after 1882[5].

Gradually, during the late 'seventies, with or without formal arbitration, but of necessity through the preliminary work of some joint committee, in Durham and Northumberland and on many other English and Welsh coalfields sliding scales were

[1] Whitwell, as above.
[2] *Op. cit.* p. 68.
[3] Memo. for *R.C. on Labour* and evidence before Group A, Q. 1 *sqq.*
[4] Crompton, *op. cit.* p. 71.
[5] *R.C. on Labour*, Group A, Q. 1716 and cp. Price, *op. cit.*

adopted, under which wages shifted with prices; but the mere sliding-scale committees, such for example as that of South Wales and Monmouthshire, had not the organic character of the general-purposes joint committee of Durham and Northumberland. In itself the principle of the sliding scale was hardly a bond of union. Miners' leaders in Yorkshire and Lancashire never accepted it, though there was a short-lived West Yorkshire sliding-scale agreement in 1880. Several of the other agreements were terminated before 1885–6, and a campaign against the principle, based on the view that some 'living wage' minimum should be a first charge on industry, was carried on by the Miners' Federation in the years that followed[1].

In the South Staffordshire iron industry a conciliation board was started in 1872, and re-started in 1876 with Joseph Chamberlain as chairman. It failed the first time because, on the men's side, it represented only those who were in union, and the union was not strong. Employers who accepted its decisions found that not all their men did. The second time it did better, trying to get on to North of England lines. "We struggled on," the men's secretary said long afterwards, "but it was not growing strong enough."[2] In the 'eighties it was still struggling, but not to the satisfaction of either side. The standing committee arranged "hundreds of cases"[3]; but now it was the men who were complaining of non-observance of decisions by firms outside the forty-two who subscribed to the board[4]. In 1886 it was just changing its name from the South Staffordshire to the Midland Iron and Steel Board. In fact it had little to do with steel and never thoroughly controlled even the puddled iron.

It is not surprising that the success of the North of England board should have led to its imitation in the small associated industries of the Cleveland ironstone miners (1873) and the Cleveland and Cumberland blastfurnacemen (1879–80). Of these the miners' board had worked best. Its problems were relatively simple, for iron-mining has not the shattering variety

[1] The sliding scale is discussed fully, from the 'living-wage' point of view, in Webb, *History*, p. 323–7; a list of all known sliding-scale agreements is in App. II. p. 484–6. See also Munro, J. E. C., "Sliding Scales in the Coal Industry" (1885: a Brit. Assoc. paper); "Sliding Scales in...Coal and Iron... 1885 to 1889" (*Manchester Stat. Soc.* 1889).

[2] *R.C. on Labour*, Group A, Q. 15,615 (Wm. Ancott). Compare the contemporary account in Crompton, *op. cit.* p. 64.

[3] *R.C. on Labour*, Group A, Q. 15,486. [4] *Ibid.* Q. 15,617.

of coal-mining. More interesting was the attempt, begun in 1875, to adapt the machinery of conciliation and arbitration to the young and changing factory boot and shoe industry of Leicester. It was natural that the attempt should be made in that area; perhaps equally natural that it should not be an entire success in that trade at that time. The board was not continuously active nor always able to avert strikes. At the end of the 'eighties, though still in existence, it was reported to be only "on the whole" successful[1].

Behind the standard thought of the third quarter of the nineteenth century lay mechanical conceptions of the industrial world. It was a concourse of competing and clashing atoms. The law ought to equalise opportunity for atoms; no more. All atoms of capital should have equal access to the conveniences of limited liability. The more complex and heavier atoms of business organisation, the firms, were to have all markets opened to them—so far as might be—and were to be exposed to clashes from all. Atoms of labour were to be free to come together unhindered. It was hardly anticipated, as it had been by sanguine atomists of the first quarter of the century, that, if set quite free, they would perceive that it would be inexpedient to come together[2]. The full atomic chaos had never existed as pictured, nor had standard thought been universal. There were always protestants and co-operators. But it was to some such conception that those average minds tended whose workings mostly determine social activity. The best of them had thought about reducing friction between the sorts of atoms; hence the arbitration and conciliation. Prophets and poets had taught righteousness and honest workmanship, or had dreamed of a new world, of lands East of the sun and West of the moon. They had not thought hard and clear about the day after to-morrow. Those among them who had the spirit of the Old Testament, from Thomas Carlyle to Karl Marx, had feared, or looked to, the coming of some terrible or some glorious catastrophe, a Day of the Lord when the elements should melt with fervent heat into a great new thing.

It was among the atoms of labour that the phrase to be 'in union' had first gained a half-sacred meaning: indeed it had

[1] In the memorandum for the *R.C. on Labour*.

[2] The well-known view of Francis Place, among others.

religious associations[1]. The honesty of those business-man atoms who had protested that union for them was only a tiresome necessity need not be disputed[2]. Very slowly, and first from the other side, their union also came to be viewed, not indeed as sacred, but at least as a thing highly convenient socially, rather than as a mere fighting device. "Is the tendency of the employers to become organised?" a trade union leader was asked in 1891. "Yes." "And you thoroughly approve of it?" "Just so."[3] Such approval was recent and perhaps not usual, but very genuine. The atoms were grouping themselves, and small new things were coming, without catastrophe so far.

How the entire freedom of capital to flow and combine, while limiting its risks, might affect industrial organisation was very imperfectly pictured in the 'eighties, either by savers, capital handlers, or thinkers. The weakness of the joint-stock in industry had been debated far more than its future. In 1877 the Master of the Rolls, no doubt a conservative critic, had pronounced it unsuitable for manufactures and had advocated the partnership *en commandite* as an alternative[4]. Before the Depression Commissioners of 1885–6 it was definitely on its trial. In what ways the newly 'limited' family businesses might evolve was not much considered. Businesses had expanded, absorbed one another, run together, in the simple partnership age. Karl Marx had made of their inevitable expansion an historic dogma and a forecast. The facilities for expansions and absorptions were now greatly increased, as was being demonstrated in America. But when a general running together began in Britain, under limited liability law, about a dozen years later, it came unexpected by standard British opinion. If the economists had foreseen it, they had not distinctly foretold it.

[1] *E.g.* "Thus may we abide in union with each other, in the Lord" from John Newton's benediction hymn. Evangelical hymnology is never irrelevant to nineteenth-century labour history.

[2] Above, p. 146.

[3] *R.C. on Labour*, Group C, Q. 634–5 (Geo. Silk of the Card and Blowing Room Operatives).

[4] *S.C. on the Operation of the Companies Acts of* 1862 *and* 1867; 1877 (VIII. 419), evidence of Sir G. Jessel, Q. 2225 *sqq*. He allowed that it might be appropriate for 'limiting' a family business.

CHAPTER V

COMMUNICATIONS

HAVING conquered Britain by the early 'fifties, the railway consolidated and extended its conquest during the next generation, without any thorough-going change in weapons or tactics. Though the iron road had turned to steel, the engine which dragged Gladstone to face Parnell in 1886 was nearer in type to those which had dragged him, a Peelite unattached, forty years earlier than to the high-bellied bull-necked monsters of forty years later[1]. So good were the best early engines, and so permanent the way, that maximum journey-speeds went up very little between the 'forties and the 'eighties, though far more trains touched the maximum at the end. In 1845 the best expresses on the London and North-Western averaged 37 miles an hour[2]. In 1854, on the young North-Eastern, 37 to 41 is said to have been express speed[3]. In 1865–6 expresses in general were credited with "about 40"; but a more exact measurement of the quickest runs on various lines yielded only 36½[4]. In 1871 a still more exact measurement of 250 distinct expresses gave 37⅗. By 1883 as many as 407 trains averaged 41⅗[5]. The best practice of the 'forties had been slightly improved on and much extended. The improved service had been put within everyone's reach on most lines since the Midland Railway announced on May 19, 1872, that in future third-class passengers would be carried on all its trains[6]. But there was no technical revolution at all.

So also with amenities. The open 'thirds' of the early days died out. Seats were softened. But when in 1874 the Midland, always spirited, imported from Detroit an experimental 'American train' whose coaches were not cut up into compartments, its reception was mixed. English travellers, especially

[1] Above, p. 76. But there were experiments with compound engines from 1881.

[2] *R.C. on Railways*, 1867 (XXXVIII. part 1), p. liii.

[3] Tomlinson, W. W., *The North-Eastern Railway* (1914), p. 545.

[4] *R.C. on Railways*, p. lviii.

[5] Willock, H. B., "English Express Trains in 1871 and...1883," *S.J.* 1884, p. 259.

[6] Stretton, C. E., *The History of the Midland Railway* (1901), p. 201. The Great Western did not put 'thirds' on all expresses till 1890. Sekon, G. A., *A History of the Great Western Railway* (1895), p. 278.

Manchester travellers, "expressed a preference for the ordinary compartment vehicle"[1]: no revolution for them. The train was taken off and used in bits. The Midland persevered cautiously. It was accustoming first-class passengers to dining cars in the early 'eighties. First-class sleeping cars, which formed part of the experiment of 1874 and had been started on the East Coast route to Scotland a year earlier, seem to have been accepted from the start.

In 1848, although there was still plenty of railway work in hand, railway promotion was stagnant—not unnaturally, after the fever of the past three years. Nearly 1200 miles of line were opened and only 330 were authorised. Altogether 4646 miles were open for traffic in Britain at the end of the year[2]. The network seemed dense and complete, and the recently appointed Commissioners of Railways were pointing out that probably a great part of the 7000 odd miles of line, authorised but not yet made, never would be made. Why should it be, some people asked[3]. Since February 14, 1848, when the Caledonian was opened, there were even alternative railway routes to Scotland. There had already been racing on them. John Russell's Budget speech of 1848 had been put through to Glasgow at a journey-speed of nearly 46 miles an hour[4].

The 12,000 mile long railway system, which would have existed had all the lines authorised by 1848 been built, was not in fact reached for nearly twenty years, with the aid of a number of new trunk lines in England, railway systems for Wales and the Highlands, and a great number of branch lines, link lines, and short competitive stretches everywhere except in Wales and the Highlands. The total open mileage of British railways was:

1848 (Dec. 31)	4,646	1870	13,562
1858	8,354	1886	16,700

For the whole United Kingdom—British figures are not to be had—the number of passengers carried on the growing mileage,

[1] Stretton, *op. cit.* p. 206.

[2] Lardner, D., *Railway Economy* (1850), p. 54–5.

[3] An Act of 1850 (13 and 14 Vict. c. 83) was expressly designed to authorise the abandonment of Railways and the Dissolution of Railway Companies. Some 2000 miles were abandoned without authorisation. Cleveland-Stevens, E., *English Railways, their Development and their Relation to the State* (1915), p. 179.

[4] Tomlinson, *op. cit.* p. 486.

exclusive of season-ticket holders, increased nearly tenfold between 1850 and 1885, and the weight of goods and minerals nearly threefold between 1860—there are no figures for 1850—and 1885. No doubt the British ratios were much the same[1].

Of new trunk lines, the Great Northern was ready for its trial trip by August, 1850, in time to take part in the Great Exhibition rate war of 1851, when return fares, Yorkshire to London, fell to 5*s*.[2] It never got to York as had originally been planned. Its main line ended, as a standing jest said, "in a ploughed field four miles North of Doncaster,"[3] the point at which the ownership of the permanent way passed into other hands. The South-Western, which grew out of the London and Southampton, was putting together its long western trunk line by construction and purchase in the 'fifties. The London-Salisbury direct line was opened in 1857. In 1860 Exeter was reached and connection established with some far western lines already built or controlled[4]. All this had been contemplated before 1850. The chief additions to the English trunk line system as then conceived were made by the Midland, always striking out from its North Midland headquarters[5]. In 1867 it first brought goods into St Pancras and passengers through Peak Forest into Manchester. In 1875 goods, and in 1876 passengers, were carried along its second mountain line, the Settle and Carlisle through the High Craven and the Pennines[6]. Except the Settle and Carlisle, no important long lines were put in hand after 1870. The new mileage of 1870–86 was almost all branch, link, or local. Great enterprises of construction were of a different kind: in 1886 the Severn Tunnel was opened and the Forth Bridge was building.

The last years of the early railway age had been years of amalgamation and of George Hudson the Railway King. The Midland and the London and North-Western were created by

[1] From the Railway Returns summarised in the *Statistical Abstracts for the U.K.*

[2] See vol. I. p. 392 and the map facing p. 184 below; Grinling, C. H., *The Great Northern Railway* (1898), p. 103, for the rate war.

[3] Acworth, W. M., *The Railways of England* (1889), p. 207. Denison, the first chairman, is said to have made the remark to a shareholder.

[4] Sherrington, C. E. R., *Economics of Rail Transport in Gt. Britain* (1928), I. 42–3.

[5] See vol. I. p. 392–4.

[6] Stretton, *op. cit.* p. 168, 186.

amalgamations in 1843–6. Hudson made the Midland, Carr Glyn and Captain Mark Huish the North-Western. In 1847–8 amalgamation made the Lancashire and Yorkshire, the Manchester Sheffield and Lincolnshire, and that York Newcastle and Berwick from which, within a few years, the North-Eastern was born[1]. This was Hudson's home system; in York he had once been a linen draper. But it was at one of its meetings in 1849 that the question was asked which would make him homeless. Why had certain shares been sold to the company, by Hudson, at a price never touched on the Stock Exchange? His reply started the hunt. Once on the scent they found it rank. He had bought iron at £6. 10*s*. and sold it to his companies at £12. He had kept for himself shares 'placed at the disposal of the directors,' really to be used for palm-greasing. He had inflated traffic returns and treated capital as revenue; and so forth. For four more years, no longer a Railway King but still an M.P., he remained something of a Dock King, and did good work for Sunderland and the Hartlepools. By 1854 he was with Thackeray's gentleman exiles at Boulogne[2].

The year before, the directors of the York, Newcastle and Berwick, the Yorkshire and North Midland—another Hudson system, which served the triangle Leeds, Hull, Whitby—and the Leeds Northern[3], which skirted the gates of the Yorkshire Dales, having failed to carry an amalgamation bill, had strengthened existing working agreements. On July 31, 1854, their revived amalgamation bill received the royal assent. It established that North-Eastern Company which became, within little more than a decade, a standing British instance of the system of territorial monopoly, which in France had been adopted by the state as the basis of its railway system. After the absorption of the Newcastle and Carlisle (1862), the Stockton and Darlington (1863) and some lesser companies (1857–65), there was not a bit of permanent way between Berwick, the Pennine foot hills, the sea and the Humber which the North-Eastern directors did not control. Hull men did not like the North Eastern in the 'sixties, or subsequently: they said that it cramped them in the interest of more favoured ports farther North. In 1880 they projected a competing line into the York-

[1] See vol. I. p. 390–5.

[2] Tomlinson, *op. cit.* p. 493, 507, 548. The *D.N.B.* He returned to England later and died in 1871.

[3] Until 1851, the Leeds and Thirsk.

shire coalfields. It was opened as the Hull, Barnsley and West Riding in 1885[1].

Another and greater territorial monopoly had been discussed in 1848, when the companies, suffering from trade depression, were trying to reduce their working and fighting costs. A series of conferences was held between representatives of the North-Western, the Great-Western and the South-Western. Complete amalgamation, which would have put nearly all the western side of the country under a single control, was discussed, but no bill was promoted. When special meetings of the shareholders of all three companies had already been summoned to discuss the representatives' proposals, those proposals were abandoned because Carr Glyn and his board stood out for a North-Western predominance in the new company, which the two other parties to the negotiation would not accept[2].

In the years during which the North-Eastern was coming together there was talk of other great amalgamations. One of the plans might have produced, seventy years in advance of the fact, something very like the existing London Midland and Scottish, by an amalgamation of the North-Western, the Midland, and the North Staffordshire, which would have controlled a sixth of the mileage then existing in the United Kingdom. Another would have absorbed the Brighton line into the South-Western, a step towards the existing Southern[3]. Neither plan was carried through, although "the most experienced and the most able of the gentlemen connected with the management of the railways," in the early 'fifties, were decidedly favourable to amalgamation, and the notion of "perhaps seven" regulated monopoly areas for Great Britain was already familiar[4]. Railway opinion, however, was not clear about this notion and parliamentary opinion was definitely hostile. "No such engagement can in reason be asked for from Parliament," the Committee of 1853 reported, "nor would it be of any enduring value if it were given."[5] Next year, under the odd working of the Private Bill system, something very like an unregulated

[1] For the North-Eastern, Tomlinson, *passim*; for the Hull and Barnsley, Sherrington, *op. cit.* I. 124; for Hull and the N.E.R. at an earlier date, the evidence of H. J. Atkinson, Mayor of Hull, before the *R.C. on Railways*, 1867, Q. 881 *sqq*.

[2] MacDermott, E. T., *History of the Great Western Railway* (1927), I. 307; a fuller account than that in Cleveland-Stevens, *op. cit.* p. 171.

[3] *S.C. on Railway and Canal Bills*, 1852–3 (XXXVIII), App. VIII; *S.C. on Railway Companies' Amalgamations*, 1872 (XIII. parts I and 2), App. A; Cleveland-Stevens, p. 179–80.

[4] *S.C. of* 1852–3. *Fifth Report*, p. 3, 5.

[5] *Ibid.* p. 6.

monopoly area was given to the North-Eastern, which was never taken from it.

This Act, of July, 1854, sanctioned the only large-scale amalgamation of the 'fifties. In four out of the ten years there was not even a single small amalgamation. With the early 'sixties the movement was resumed. While the North-Eastern was absorbing the Newcastle and Carlisle, and fighting before absorbing the Stockton and Darlington, another almost complete monopoly area came into being in East Anglia by the establishment of the Great Eastern (1862; 25 and 26 Vict. c. 223). Its trunk, the old Eastern Counties, had been for years an ugly duckling of the railway world and a butt for public humour. No one had objected to the attempt made, in 1854, towards greater efficiency of service in a rural area, when the Eastern Counties was allowed to manage two adjacent lines, the Norfolk and the Eastern Union. It was merely a further stage in the end to end combination by which these small railways had themselves been made; the Norfolk, for example, by union of the Yarmouth and Norwich with the Norwich and Brandon. Indeed the bill of 1854 foreshadowed the complete arrangement of 1862 quite distinctly, reference being made in it to ultimate absorption of the two other constituent lines of the future Great Eastern, the East Anglian and the Newmarket. So the consummation of the union stirred no interest except among the shareholders of five unprosperous concerns. The outside world wished them and East Anglia better luck[1].

Large-scale amalgamation, or leasing of the lines of one company to another, went on steadily down to 1866. In 1863 the Great Western added nearly 400 miles to its system by taking over the West Midland and the South Wales; and the North-Eastern, as has been seen, annexed the Stockton and Darlington. Nothing striking happened in 1864; but 1865–6 were great amalgamation years in Scotland, the Caledonian and the North British absorbing many hundred miles of other companies' lines. The financial crisis of 1866 checked this form of enterprise. By 1870 the railway system was all but stabilised. The London and North-Western, in length of line and relations with its neighbours, had become very much what it remained when welded into the London Midland and Scottish of 1923[2].

[1] Cleveland-Stevens, *op. cit.* ch. ix, especially p. 221, 225; Tomlinson, *op. cit.* ch. xiv; Acworth, *op, cit.* ch. x; Sherrington, *op. cit.* I. 130–1.

[2] Cleveland-Stevens, *op. cit.* p. 227 (table of amalgamations in the 'sixties), 236–7; Sherrington, *op. cit.* I. 91 (the L.N.W.R.).

Stabilisation was not planned by the railway strategists. In part it just happened; in great part it was imposed on them. In 1867 the Midland, not yet at Carlisle, was dreaming of an amalgamation with the Glasgow and South-Western, which would be useful when it got there. Its dream was only dissipated in the Lords. After that it courted the Great Northern and the Manchester, Sheffield and Lincolnshire. There was always prospect of a revived Scottish alliance, when it should reach Carlisle. So the North-Western manœuvred for position and announced, late in 1871, that it would unite with the Lancashire and Yorkshire. The alliance was most natural. East and West the two companies might be needlessly competitive. North and South they were obviously complementary. For years their relations had been of necessity close, and as a rule amicable. There had been a series of ten-year traffic treaties between them, one of which was just running out. Natural as the alliance might be, it alarmed all adjacent or competitive lines. The fighting chairmen and the general managers who dominated their chairmen began to stir—Edward Watkin, of the Manchester, Sheffield and Lincolnshire and other lines, who spent a restless life in extending and amalgamating companies which rarely paid much to the ordinary shareholder; James Allport, who managed the Midland with patent success from 1853 to 1857, and again from 1860 to 1880[1].

Parliament and the public became uneasy about monopoly. Chambers of Commerce petitioned. A Select Committee of both Houses inquired into the whole matter in 1872. In the marginal analysis of its conclusions occurs the heading—'Amalgamation inevitable; and perhaps desirable.' The attitude thus disclosed raised the hopes of the North-Western projectors, who had withdrawn their bill for the time. But the opinions of nineteenth-century committees and commissions of inquiry were always singularly bad indications of what was likely to happen to particular railway bills. This one was thrown out in 1873. The evidence of opponents was never even called: the preamble, it was said, was not proved. With it was rejected a new bill for the amalgamation of the Midland and the Glasgow and South-Western. This blocked the amalgamation movement finally. Minor absorptions went on. Edward

[1] Watkin's evidence before the *S.C. on Railway Amalgamations*, 1872, Q. 4542*sqq*. Cleveland-Stevens, *op. cit.* p. 233, 239, 241, 296, 309; Jackman, W. T., *Transportation in Modern England*, II. 601; Stretton, *op. cit.* p. 280.

Watkin schemed and negotiated. There were fights and alliances, leases of lines and traffic agreements, but no important change in the railway map before the 'nineties[1].

Since very early days the lease, the alliance, and the traffic agreement had prepared the way for complete amalgamation, or had secured for non-amalgamated companies many of its benefits—for the public, as some argued, all its disadvantages. Even in 1852, the five rail and water routes between Liverpool and Manchester had "more or less a common understanding ...no rivalry exists bearing any analogy to the...competition of private individuals contending in the same trade."[2] At that date the London and North-Western and the Great Northern had a regular agreement about the division of traffic at certain competing points, with an arbitration clause in case of difference. Further East, the Great Northern and the Eastern Counties had an agreement "putting an end to any real competition." These compacts, which the Committee of 1852–3 reported, perhaps slightly exaggerating their real efficiency, were "only examples...of the general tendency"[3]; and of the generality of the tendency throughout the period there can be no doubt. When some change in the railway balance of power was threatened, such as a Midland line to London or to Carlisle, there was sure to be a fight, at least in the parliamentary committee, and perhaps for a time on the permanent ways. But co-operation soon reasserted itself, if never completely. Rate wars were a proved waste and were always dropped. There remained competition for access to bits of territory still unoccupied, and much competition in facilities; for the rest, local and general agreements of all grades up to those hardly distinguishable from amalgamations, like the ten-year treaties between the North-Western and the Lancashire and Yorkshire.

Co-operation had been much encouraged by the early establishment and quick development of the Railway Clearing House. Started in 1842 by "a few of the narrow gauge companies,"[4] in imitation of the Bankers' Clearing House, its

[1] See *Report of* 1872; and for the bills of 1873, Cleveland-Stephens, p. 241–2. For (Sir Edward) Watkin and Allport, the *D.N.B.*

[2] *S.C. of* 1853, p. 4. And see vol. I. p. 415, 418. [3] *Ibid.* p. 4, 5.

[4] *R.C. on Railways*, 1867, p. xviii, with the wrong date 1847 (copied in the *S.C. of* 1872, p. x, and naturally by Cohn, *Englische Eisenbahnpolitik*, I. 262). See Morrison, K., *The Origin and Results of the Clearing System* (1846); the chapter on the Clearing House in Lardner, D., *Railway Economy* (1850); and especially the discussion in Cleveland-Stevens, *op. cit.* p. 173 *sqq.* The early years of the Clearing House are obscure.

business was to facilitate through traffic and adjust the debts arising from through booking. By 1849 it included "all the railways of the kingdom, except the Great Western, the South-Western, the London, Brighton and South Coast, the South-Eastern and their branches and collateral lines"[1]; that is the broad gauge lines and the lines for which at that time long distance through traffic was impracticable. Within the 'cleared' area, through booking and through movement of waggons were universal. Carr Glyn and Denison, Watkin and Allport, might brief their gladiators for the committee room; but all the time Clearing House clerks in Euston Square and Clearing House agents up and down the country were balancing accounts, tracking consignments and taking the numbers of migrant waggons or tarpaulins, working the railways as an inevitably co-operative group. The system seemed so promising and efficient to Dionysius Lardner, in 1850, that he contemplated the possibility of the Clearing House growing into "an establishment for the maintenance of a general locomotive and carrying stock for the use of all the railways,"[2] a most rational ambition which was never realised.

At that time, as has been seen, a few people, possibly inspired from France, were toying with the notion not of a common rolling stock, but of regulated monopoly areas—"perhaps seven."[3] This was before the North-Eastern had created such an area. The notion revives from time to time in the railway discussions of the next thirty years. Before the Committee of 1872, both Allport and Watkin spoke in favour of what the Report called "districting," how far in the interests of the nation, and how far in those of the Midland or the Manchester, Sheffield and Lincolnshire, is not at this date worth determining. The committee observed curtly that it could not recommend any "attempt to make a new railway map,"[4] and left it at that.

As old as the notion of monopoly areas, though less vigorous, and like it a product of the reaction following the fever of 1845–7, was a suggested "union of all railway property...in one stock."[5] Its main object was to improve the security of shareholders. Neither its detailed working-out nor its implications were ever fully discussed. It remained purely notional.

So for that matter did railway nationalisation proper; but it has a more vivid history. Praised by a handful of experts in

[1] Lardner, p. 153. [2] *Ibid.* p. 164. [3] *S.C. Report of* 1852–3, p. 5.
[4] *Report*, p. xli. [5] *Report of* 1853, p. 6.

the 'forties, it had been embalmed in the Act of 1844. After twenty-one years, the state might buy up any railway built since the Act[1]. For twenty years, as was natural, there was little talk about the mummy. But Edwin Chadwick, that uncompromising innovator and centraliser, had praised state control of railways before the Statistical Society in 1859; and there were other critics of railway management and monopoly in the early 'sixties. Most remarkable among them was Walter Bagehot, who had taken over the editorship of the *Economist* in 1860[2]. In December, 1864, an article on *The forgotten Act of* 1844 revived memory of the repurchase clause[3]. It might be utilised as from October, 1865. Let it be considered, Bagehot argued. "No one would...suggest a wholesale purchase of the English railways. But if it was proved to be desirable it might begin...." He talked of railway monopoly and of the penny post. On January 7, 1865, he resumed under the title *The Advantages that would accrue from an ownership of the railways by the State.* His tentative notion was state ownership and co-ordination of the lines, with terminable leases to commercial working companies. "The present mode of railway management may be described as that in which trading management is at its worst": railway Boards have "many of the defects of Government Boards." Their members are peers and M.P.'s and merchants, everything but practical railway men. "Granting that a State purchase would be exceedingly beneficial, it becomes the plain duty of the Executive Government to *inquire* whether that transfer cannot be effected." Those were his closing words.

Whether the Royal Commission of 1865–7 would have inquired with more sympathy had its sittings not been cut across by a commercial crisis cannot be ascertained; but the probability is that it would not. The policies of repurchase, state control, and leasing were fully laid before it. It heard Chadwick, possibly with some impatience, for that ageing and

[1] Vol. I. p. 418-19.

[2] Chadwick's paper is in *S.J.* XXII. 381. It has the characteristic title "Results of Different Principles of Legislation and Administration in Europe: of Competition for the Field, as compared with Competition within the Field, of Service"; it deals with regulated monopoly areas for public services. See other critics quoted in Cohn, *op. cit.* I. 348. They are less important than Bagehot, whom Cohn does not quote.

[3] *Economist*, December 10, 1844. The present editor of the *Economist* agrees that these leading articles must be Bagehot's. They are not signed but the style suggests him. Even if they were not his composition, their policy would be his; but there is no precise record in the office.

omniscient Benthamite was dogmatic and tiresome[1]. It received an able memorandum from Rowland Hill, a commissioner, who finally put in a separate report in favour of the leasing system[2]. George Bidder, the 'calculating boy' become a railway engineer and director, having advocated the amalgamation of all the Irish lines, admitted that his argument applied "in some respects" to England. The state, he thought, might perhaps secure financial control by guaranteeing the prior charges of the railway companies and leaving the management and the common stock free[3]. All this the Commission heard, but its decision was simply "that it is inexpedient at present to subvert the policy which has hitherto been adopted."[4]

Once again, in 1872, advocates of systems approaching nationalisation were given an opportunity. Rowland Hill, now a very old man, was not called, but Captain Tyler, inspector of railways under the Board of Trade, was examined on an important memorandum which he had submitted. He was all for rigid control, though he did not "wish to appear here to advocate state purchase." He finished his evidence, in words much quoted at the time, "and then the question arises at last, whether the State shall manage the railways, or whether the railways shall manage the State."[5] Various business men, especially a Liverpool group, gave evidence in favour of nationalisation, or at least thorough state control. The *Economist* had been writing about "the expediency of inserting new conditions providing for compulsory purchase in the railway amalgamation bills." In discussing a quarrel between traders and the North-Eastern Railway, it had argued that the possession of that monopoly area by the state "would clearly be more advantageous to the public than its possession by a joint-stock company."[6] But in its final report this very strong and most representative joint committee of the Lords and Commons said that there was no "present necessity" to discuss state purchase[7]. The historian may agree with them.

"It is an admitted principle of political economy," Bagehot had written in 1864, "that all monopolies granted by the State ought to be under the superintendence or correction of the

[1] *R.C. on Railways*, 1867, Q. 17,179 *sqq*. [2] *Ibid*. p. cvii.

[3] His evidence is Q. 4213 *sqq*.: the quotation is from Q. 4301.

[4] *Report*, p. xxxvii.

[5] *S.C. on Railway Companies Amalgamation*, Q. 7020.

[6] Title of an article of Feb. 10, 1872, and quotation from one of Oct. 5, 1872

[7] *S.C. on Railway Companies Amalgamation*, p. xxxi.

State."[1] The state, which for good reasons was not willing to buy out the railway monopoly, blundered along into the 'eighties, sometimes assuming that there was no monopoly, at others that all things considered there was rather an efficient one. In this it was probably right. Meanwhile it had exercised a minimum of "superintendence and correction." Ever since Peel threw over Dalhousie in 1845[2], there had been no considered attempt to guide the territorial development of the railway system. Each project was a special case for the investor, the railway barrister, and the private bill committee. There had been no serious attempt to guide technical development, even on the vital question of the gauge. Talk of guidance there had been; but as the committee of 1853 had written, in pathetic helplessness, "what Parliament had...undertaken to settle by general legislation, Parliament, in compliance with the findings of Private Committees....forthwith proceeded to unsettle."[3]

To one matter at least Parliament had given real if limited attention—safety of travel. Since 1842 (5 and 6 Vict. c. 55) the obligation to inspect new lines and forbid their opening for traffic if they proved unsatisfactory had rested with the Board of Trade[4]. Its inspectors were the first and only permanent link between the railways and the state. They had to report on accidents also; but for nearly thirty years they had no compulsory powers. Until the passing of the Regulation of Railways Act of 1871 (34 and 35 Vict. c. 78) they must beg their information from the companies. Still, their reports kept before the public mind and before the companies the need for safety devices of all sorts. How far they influenced railway policy is hard to say; but at least their statistics of accidents, especially the accidents to railway men in the shunting yards, were there for all to read. Not many read, and in the matter of shunting fewer acted. Meanwhile, for the traveller, the British railways became remarkably safe, as compared with those of most other countries, or with most other forms of transport; so the companies always had a case, even when criticising the introduction of a safety device of such obvious merit as the block system.

Long known and advocated, this system was resisted by most of the great railwaymen of the 'sixties. About a fifth of the British mileage was under it in 1870, but that mileage was

[1] *Economist*, December 10, 1864. [2] Vol. I. p. 423. [3] *Report*, p. 13.

[4] See Cohn, *op. cit.* II. 219*sqq.* Cleveland-Stevens, *op. cit.* p. 76–7. There was an earlier Act dealing with safety, of 1840 (3 and 4 Vict. c. 97).

mainly of the second rank[1]. The North-Eastern, for example, had only 48 miles of line under the 'absolute' block system[2]. However, in 1871 steps were taken by the North-Eastern towards its general introduction. During the 'seventies it made rapid progress almost everywhere. More than a quarter of the North-Western was 'blocked' by 1872, and another fifth was in hand for 'blocking.'[3] So when Lord Buckhurst brought a Bill into the Lords in 1873 to make the system compulsory, critics could argue fairly that he was wasting effort. The Bill never became law. Compulsion was not applied to the outstanding minority of the railway mileage until 1889 (52 and 53 Vict. c. 57). The same Act imposed at length on all passenger trains the fitting of continuous brakes. By that time it was again only a case of whipping in the laggards. At least two well-tested types of continuous brake had been available twelve or fifteen years earlier[4]. Since 1877, Captain Tyler and the Board of Trade had been pressing their use on the companies, after an accident in that year at Morpeth in which their presence would have saved life. They were soon fitted on expresses, and by the mid 'eighties only inferior 'parliamentary' trains, or the small backward lines, were without them. At length the law compelled every one to do what nearly everyone was already doing.

The reluctance of the state, that is to say the statesmen, to prescribe in these technical matters is more explicable than some other of their reluctances. There was always the risk that prescription on the technical side might mean petrification; and it was only the railways, not the state, which could experiment. Among less explicable reluctances is the sustained one to touch railway rates and charges. Quite indefensible at first sight, closer inspection reveals two important lines of defence. First: the economics and ethics of railway charges, nowhere simple, are for geographical reasons especially complex in Britain, as committees and commissions soon found out. Second: since no British railway ever made very large profits, it was never possible to prove a general abuse of monopoly, however loudly particular abuses might be alleged. The initial action of the state, determined by inevitable ignorance married to lack of imagination, had been so primitive and casual that such alle-

[1] *E.g.* the London and Brighton, Cohn, *op. cit.* II. 210.
[2] Tomlinson, *op. cit.* p. 649.
[3] Cawkwell's evidence before the *S.C. of* 1872, Q. 1256 *sqq.*
[4] Sherrington, *op. cit.* I. 239.

gations began very early. In this matter of their charges, the railway companies, it will be recalled, were treated like the canal companies[1]. Short schedules of maximum tolls, to be levied on goods classified in a few rough categories, were inserted in the bills to which they owed their existence. These maxima were so high that they soon became futile, and there was no law against the greatest variety of charges within them. In 1845 the average charge of twenty-two companies for actually moving coal was 1·83*d.* per ton-mile[2]. Many of these companies were entitled by their schedules to charge a toll of 1·5*d.* for letting other people move it—which no one ever did. The 'parliamentary' 1*d.* a mile in a third-class stopping train, fixed in 1844, was below the then existing maxima but was nevertheless fairly high, as was shown in later years when the companies found that they could profitably move people faster and with infinitely greater conveniences at the same price.

No one ever complained of cheap excursion rates far below the penny, to attract those who otherwise might not have travelled at all; but when the companies applied this principle of 'charging what the traffic will bear' to goods, offering, for example, very low rates to consignments which otherwise might have gone by water, there was likely to be complaint from the waterless places, who attributed to railway vice what should have been attributed to Britain's good fortune in being an island with a much indented coastline. It was reckoned that goods charges from three-fifths of the stations in the country were affected by the competition of transport by sea[3]. Must the railways lower all their rates because they were forced unwillingly to keep three-fifths of them competitive with those of the cargo boats?

Supervision and revision of charges, and a public facing of such problems, might have been very suitable functions for the Commissioners of Railways created in August 1846 by 9 and 10 Vict. c. 105, when Parliament was feeling uneasily that the new railway jungle ought to be policed somehow[4]. But although these Commissioners issued some very valuable reports, they were given no executive powers at the start, and had never been given any when they were abolished without discussion in 1851 (by 14 and 15 Vict. c. 64), mainly for economy's sake. Their reporting and statistical functions reverted to the Board

[1] Vol. I. p. 414–15.
[2] Graham, W. A., in *S.J.* VIII. 222.
[3] *Report of* 1872, p. xix.
[4] Vol. I. p. 424.

of Trade, whose President, Labouchere, was both their chairman and their executioner. The Commissioners having been abolished just when they were learning their way about the jungle, it was easy and correct to argue, when railway regulation was again being discussed in 1853, that there was "no public department sufficiently educated to take the command."[1] Interest still centred in the problems of amalgamation, of the grant of 'running powers' to one company over the lines of another, and of the control of canals by the railways; but the Committee of 1853 also referred, with a touch of censure, to the "special favour" often shown by the companies "to particular classes of traffic," and suggested that the ordinary courts of law were not well qualified to settle the resulting disputes[2]. Much of the work of the Committee was wasted, but this reference bore fruit in the Act of 1854 (17 and 18 Vict. c. 31) which forbade railway companies "to make or give any undue or unreasonable preference or advantage to or in favour of any particular person or company, or any particular description of traffic." Here were many words to be interpreted by the Court of Common Pleas, to which the jurisdiction was assigned. But the Act was not much used, and the Court was neither very ardent nor very competent to interpret it. It did, however, decide, in the case of Ransome *v.* the Eastern Counties Railway, that preference given to the traffic of a place—to meet water competition, perhaps—was not "undue or unreasonable," though preference given to a person would have been[3]. And it is probable that the mere existence of the law acted as a deterrent to railway managers, when tempted to favour "particular persons or companies." Little is heard of personal favour after 1854[4].

The railways' toll-schedules, as has been seen, were crude and useless. They said nothing about haulage charges and nothing about charges for loading, unloading, and other terminal services. To meet the crudities of the toll-schedules, the Clearing House worked out an elaborate classification of goods for the use of all the lines—so great a convenience that the Commission of 1865–7 wished the state to adopt it bodily[5].

[1] *S.C. on Railway and Canal Bills*: evidence of Baxter, "an eminent railway solicitor," Q. 3496.

[2] *Ibid. Report*, p. 12.

[3] Case quoted in the report of the *R.C. on Railways*, 1867, p. xlviii.

[4] Hadley, A. T., *Railroad Transportation, its History and its Laws* (1885), p. 183. Cleveland-Stevens, *op. cit.* p. 195.

[5] *Report*, p. lxvii.

Like most of the wishes of that Commission, this was neglected. Twice during the 'sixties, in 1861 and 1866, the companies tried to secure Parliament's approval for the system of 'terminals.'[1] They were prepared to accept classified maxima in return for a statutory recognition of the principle. Twice they failed, and terminals remained an unregulated cause of friction and sometimes of complaint. Though perfectly defensible, provided they are not excessive, they continued to surprise parliamentary committees down to the 'eighties by their mere existence. Charges "alleged to be in excess of the maximum," said a Select Committee of 1882 naively, are defended by reference to "what is called 'terminals.'"[2]

The Committee of 1872, which considered amalgamation "inevitable and perhaps desirable," yet saw no "present necessity" to discuss state purchase or to "make a new railway map," was worried by the question of rates. A new classification on the Clearing House basis, it said, would be good. Equal mileage rates, which had been suggested, would be impracticable and bad. Terminals were hard to regulate: they might cover such varied services. "Undue preference" was a difficult conception; and so on. The one thing that they were quite clear about was that an expert tribunal, not an ordinary court of law, was needed to deal with disputes arising out of railway legislation. Parliament agreed, or half agreed. It passed the Act of 1873, "to make better provision for carrying into effect the Railway and Canal Traffic Act, 1854, and for other purposes connected therewith" (36 and 37 Vict. c. 48), the Act which set up the Railway and Canal Commission of three[3].

The Committee had thought of a strong permanent body with full powers, what Denison of the Great Northern called in the House "a sort of Railway Star Chamber."[4] They only got a five-year Commission, which was prolonged thereafter from year to year until 1888. It did something to prevent "undue preference" and encourage "reasonable facilities." But its life was uncertain. Its powers were limited. In its early years companies could defy it. Its injunctions could only affect the particular case tried, and the future. It could be appealed against, and could be called upon by the higher courts to "state

[1] *Report*, p. xxii. [2] *S.C. on Railways* (*Rates and Fares*), 1882, XIII. 1, p. iii.

[3] The fullest account of the Act is in Cohn, *op. cit.* III. 131 *sqq.* The Commissioners issued annual reports from 1875, *e.g.* 1876, XXI. 275.

[4] Hansard n.s. CCXV. 367, quoted in Cleveland-Stevens, *op. cit.* p. 274.

a case" as to whether a given matter was or was not within its jurisdiction. All this opened doors wide to the trained and well-paid legal forces of the companies. Few cared to fight them—not even the War Office[1].

The British railways of the early 'eighties, if conservative and rather arrogant[2], were neither generally inefficient nor corrupt. Manufacturers and traders criticised them and invested in them impartially. It may be doubted whether there was a comfortable family in the country which did not hold railway shares. So the companies were very strong in face of criticism. However, general prices had been falling for years. Looking about in its *malaise*, the trading community saw some real abuses on the railways; a great many things which it did not understand that looked like abuses; and a government mechanism for checking abuse—real or potential—which was unmistakably inadequate. At all costs traders wanted lower rates or better facilities, or a combination of the two, to meet the needs of the time. They alleged that they got neither, or that the wrong people—importers of foreign goods in bulk, perhaps—got both. Interest was now concentrated on prices; and it is significant that the first important parliamentary committee on railways in the 'eighties, that of 1881–2, was appointed simply to discuss Rates and Fares.

It dealt with most of the old questions—the need for a uniform classification of goods; the supposed evils of railway control of canals; the mystery of the terminals. It suggested that terminals should be recognised but published—what the railways had asked for twenty-one years earlier—and that they should be challengeable before the Commission. It even had the boldness to propose that the select committees which dealt with railway bills should take up this complex question of rates and fares. But its main wish was to see the Commission strengthened, made permanent, and made a Court of Record. Its scope ought to be widened. The right of appeal from its decisions ought to be curtailed[3]. To balance the weight of the

[1] *S.C. on Railway Rates and Fares*, 1882, Q. 5965. For the general history of the Commission, 1874–86, see Hadley, *op. cit.* p. 173 *sqq.* Cleveland-Stevens, *op. cit.* p. 270 *sqq.*

[2] Their arrogance, especially towards the Commission, greatly impressed the American observer, Hadley.

[3] In fact, in the first nine years of its existence (1874–82) the Commission decided 110 cases: there were only 17 appeals: only 6 successful appeals. Hadley, *op. cit.* p. 177.

companies, collective bodies such as Chambers of Commerce, not merely individual traders with a grievance, ought to have the right to appear before it by counsel. The Chambers, it should be noted, had been, and continued to be, active exponents of the traders' grievances. They now had an Association which, although it did not yet include London or Manchester or Liverpool or Edinburgh or Glasgow, could speak for forty-nine industrial communities, headed by Birmingham, Sheffield and Leeds[1]. Nothing was done in 1882. The business world remained uncomfortable and unappeased—prices were still falling—and Birmingham, in the formidable person of Joseph Chamberlain, Birmingham which had no sea facilities and no reverence for vested interests, was at the Board of Trade.

There was a pause; and then, in 1884, Chamberlain tabled a bill to extend the powers of the Commissioners[2]. It was not passed or even discussed; but it seemed so terrible to the boards of directors that a Railway Companies' Association was created to fight it[3]. As a counter-move to this bill, the great companies, acting together, prepared bills of their own for 1885, which interpreted the wishes of the Committee of 1881–2 about railway charges as the railways understood them. The traders rose in opposition: it was said that the object was to raise goods rates all round and legalise preferential treatment of foreign imports. Though this may not have been true, the object certainly was not to lower goods rates, which was what the traders would have wished. Once more railway business was crowded out in Parliament—Gladstone fell in June. The spring of 1886 saw him back with his Home Rule plans, and saw the companies beating up opposition to another Board of Trade bill, Chamberlain's modified and become Mundella's; for Chamberlain had just parted with Gladstone over Home Rule. Two years of political turmoil were to go by before a very different government found time to see a bill through[4]. It was at least evident in 1885–6 that a bill was coming, and that goods rates would not much longer be regulated only by antiquated maximum tolls and a few score of specific decisions in the courts or by the Commission. Railwaymen said that when Government did touch those millions of distinct, empirically determined, rates

[1] See its memorandum in the *Report of* 1882: App. 20, p. 395.

[2] "To amend the Regulation of Railways Acts and for other Purposes," 1884, VI. 333.

[3] See Grinling, *The Great Northern Railway*, p. 369.

[4] The Railway and Canal Traffic Act, 1888 (51 and 52 Vict. c. 25).

—manure from Cavendish to Long Melford; matches from London to Aberdeen—Government would burn its fingers[1]. They were not entirely wrong.

From 1846 to 1882, no Committee or Commission on the railways ever failed to discuss the fortunes of the canals[2]. And all the time the fortunes of the canals declined. After 1852 there was very little change in the mileage of railway-owned or railway-controlled canal, so that the map prepared for the Committee of 1872 represents with substantial accuracy the geographical position as it was throughout the period[3]. In view of all that was said at the time, and has been said since, about the destruction of water transport by railway control, the most remarkable feature of the map is the great network of canals and navigations which never was controlled. It was always possible to go by railway-free canal from London to Gloucester, Birmingham, Leicester, Newark and the Humber basin. The link canals between Trent, Severn and Mersey were in railway hands; but the chief of them, the Trent and Mersey (Grand Trunk), had not been captured by the North Staffordshire Railway but had made it[4], and remained in alliance with it. The canals across the Pennines had also fallen under railway control[5]; but it was never likely that much trade would pass from Yorkshire to Lancashire up 45 locks and down 54, and those not all of a size, once it became possible to send it in two hours by rail, and by railway siding into the works or up to the coal pit. Eastward from the West Riding manufacturing area, the Aire and Calder Navigation was never beaten. It was apparently the only canal which was "still spending large sums on improvements" in 1872[6]. The reason is simple. Its head

[1] See the opinions quoted in Grinling, *op. cit.* p. 374, where these years are discussed from the railway side. Cp. Acworth, W. M., *The Railways and the Traders*, 1891, a discussion, also sympathetic to the railways, by the best railway economist in England.

[2] *I.e.* from the *S.C. on Amalgamations of Railways and Canals*, 1846, XIII. 85 to the *S.C. on Railway Rates and Fares* of 1882. There was also a special *S.C. on Canals* in 1883 (XIII. 1). For the early period cp. vol. I. p. 398–9.

[3] See the map facing this page. The Kennet and Avon Canal was taken over by the Great Western Railway in 1852.

[4] Vol. I. p. 399.

[5] Between 1872 and 1883, however, the Leeds and Liverpool Canal and the Rochdale Canal came out of railway control, by expiry of leases. *S.C. on Canals*, p. 4, and below, p. 200.

[6] *S.C. on Amalgamations*, p. xxi.

offices in Leeds are about a hundred feet above sea-level: coal goes down it, timber and other bulky cargoes come up it, in quantities to this day[1]. On the other side of the Pennines, below most of the locks, the Bridgewater canals, though narrow and antiquated, did continuously good business until absorbed by the Manchester Ship Canal Company in 1887. The Weaver Navigation has always carried coal, salt and chemicals across the Cheshire flats. South of Birmingham, the Stourbridge and some other independent canals did well for years: "dividends of 16 and 12 per cent." are even heard of in the boom of 1872[2].

Prosperous canals were exceptional, not because of illicit railway devices, though there were such, but because of the sheer superiority of the railway as a means of transport. Of this there is no better illustration than the Fen Country. No railway ever controlled a furlong of its innumerable waterways, except the Witham Navigation from Boston to Lincoln. Locks were few. The whole of the country was waterish. For centuries, timber, coal and wine had been handled at Lynn and Wisbech, and there was a well-organised distributing trade from the heads of navigation. "By these Navigable Rivers," Defoe had written, "the Merchants of Lynn supply about six Counties wholly, and three Counties in part."[3] The railways came slowly into this 'marishy ground' and they were wide spaced. Yet they won with ease. The coal trade at Cambridge, Peterborough and Ely was soon based on the new railway stations. Cellars at Wisbech were still well stocked, but not now with wine which had come up the Lynn Deeps; and the Cambridge bargee, without whom there could have been no University, was dying out.

Committees and Commissions reiterated the need to keep canals independent of the railways. Almost as often their reports, or the evidence of some thoroughly competent witness, registered the technical inferiority of the average canal. "The railway can always carry cheaper," Donatus O'Brien of the Board of Trade said in 1846[4]. Canals had blackmailed projected railways for fear of their competition, the Committee of

[1] Its Secretary, however, complained bitterly of the railways in 1867 (*R.C. on Railways*, Q. 9899 *sqq.*) but then he was also Sec. of the Canal Association and so was bound to complain in any case.

[2] *S.C. on Amalgamations*, as above. The Manchester Ship Canal, which got its first Act in 1885 (48 and 49 Vict. c. 188) falls outside the scope of this volume.

[3] *Tour* (ed. Cole, G. D. H.), I. 73: perhaps a Defoeish exaggeration, but based on fact.

[4] *S.C. on Amalgamations*, Q. 154.

1853 reported[1]. The powerful Committee of 1872 underlined all occasional canal successes. But its report allowed that canals could not compete for the long haul, or for valuable cargoes, though they were efficient carriers of things like London dung. It was most desirable that they should be kept alive, said the report. But one could hardly hope to get Parliament "to vote money (as is done in France) not for the purpose of developing a profitable traffic, but for the purpose of maintaining a losing competition with railways."[2] Here the reporters touched the core. It had never been necessary to ask Parliament to endow railways. In no country of Europe since the railway was invented had, or have, canals been built by private enterprise[3]. There may be reasons, strategic or commercial-strategic, for building or remodelling them with public funds; but those reasons will always be at their weakest in Britain. They were infinitely weak in Victorian Britain. When the forty-nine associated Chambers of Commerce memorialised the Committee of 1882 in favour of the canals, they were thinking vaguely of maintaining that competition with the railways which had proved so ineffective, and were hoping, it may fairly be argued, for a cheapness of water transport which only direct subsidy could create. The Committee merely recommended that there should be no further control of canals by railways, an ancient and superfluous piece of advice. Next year yet another Committee, appointed to discuss canals only, had its attention called by a Board of Trade witness to that network of rather unprosperous ones which the railways never had controlled, and to the fact that since 1872 one long and one short trans-Pennine canal, the Leeds and Liverpool of 144 miles and the Rochdale of 35, had escaped from the railway grip[4]. Another witness mentioned that the Leeds and Liverpool, since its freeing in 1874, had reduced its tolls and paid very good dividends[5]. It crosses the Wigan coalfield between Liverpool and the hills, so that its plains section is in the same category as the Aire and Calder and the Bridgewater; and it can do local short haul traffic along its entire length. Its recent

[1] *S.C. on Railway...Bills*, p. 11. [2] *S.C. on Amalgamations*, p. xxiii.

[3] The late Sir William Acworth, in his last letter to the author, challenged him to find a single instance. Private enterprise started the Manchester Ship Canal but public support was required for its completion.

[4] *S.C. on Canals*, evidence of H. G. Calcraft.

[5] *Ibid.* Q. 827. Compare Jackman, *Transportation in Modern England*, II. 661 n. 2.

success was a strong reason for keeping it alive and a proof that, under favourable conditions, inland water transport in Britain still had its uses. It was no proof that public endowment of canals was in the general economic interests of the country.

Technically, the canals retained nearly all their old defects. With very few exceptions, such as the Aire and Calder Navigation, they had merely kept up the original works—with their different widths, their different depths, their locks of all sizes and occasional narrow tunnels[1]. The canal boat, the 'flat,' of one-horse power the wags said, was as standardised and unvarying as the state coach. On the coalfields it still had plenty of short haul work to do. To the quiet basin at Paddington it brought in Middlesex hay for the mews, and it took out London dung; but the term 'Paddington coal' had long since gone out of use[2]. Most of the landward coal rumbled into London by rail east of the Edgeware Road.

Parliamentary committees usually thought it as desirable that canals should unite as that railways should not; but though there were a few amalgamations[3], there was not vitality enough for an amalgamation movement. Apart from a few local groups of business men, investors were no longer interested in canals, and it would have been hard to raise capital for them. In 1855 *Fenn on the Funds* still tabulated in an Appendix twenty-six canals about which the general investor might be supposed to care. They ranged from the Stourbridge with its 12 per cent. dividend, through the Derby with 6½, the Grand Junction and the Birmingham each with 4 (the latter guaranteed by the London and North-Western Railway) to the 10*s*. of the Wiltshire and Berkshire and the 6*s*. of the Kennet and Avon. In 1883 the thirteenth edition of *Fenn on the Funds* did not think it necessary to mention any canal except that of Suez.

By the 'eighties, the small impersonal group of the railway companies rivalled the large and varied personal group of the makers of machines as direct employers of labour, though railway work could not compare with agriculture, building, coal-mining or the textile industries. From 65,000 in 1851, the male railway workers of all sorts had grown to 174,000 at the

[1] Vol. I. p. 82. [2] Vol. I. p. 283.

[3] *E.g.* the Leeds and Liverpool Canal and the Aire and Calder Navigation jointly acquired the short Bradford Canal in 1878. See the summaries of canal history in *R.C. on Canals and Waterways*, 1908, vol. IV. (Returns for all canals).

census of 1881, a growth in almost exact proportion to that of the railway mileage. The machine makers, employed and employers, were returned as 193,000. Though the railwayman dominated the transport business of the country, they formed only a fraction of the steadily growing mass of what the census officials called labour engaged in conveyance. This mass was quite comparable in size with that of the building trades. It contained 750,000 men and boys against their 761,000. Only agriculture was greater. Almost exactly one working man or lad in every twenty was now a conveyancer of some sort; for road conveyance is by nature extravagant of human effort.

A great part of the road users were always attached to special manufactures and trades, including the railways, as collectors and distributors for them. With the decline of the stage waggon and stage coach, general conveyance by road was localised, left to a few large carrying firms, like Pickfords, to many short distance country carriers, and to the cabmen and 'busmen and the new tramwaymen. Down to 1830, the number of 'hackney carriages' which could be licensed in London had been fixed by statute. A law of that year (1 and 2 Wm. IV, c. 22) had removed all restrictions and their numbers had grown fast. In 1881 there may have been 15,000 London 'cabbies.' The trade was always individualistic, its typical figures the owner-driver and the very small cab-proprietor. In 1892, out of about 3600 London proprietors, 3125 owned less than 5 cabs and only 4 more than 100[1]. Three years later, the single really large firm, a new one, giving evidence before a Home Office Committee, had "close upon 300"; but the other witnesses had 40, 34, and 24 respectively, and employer witnesses are always the big men of their trades[2]. London conditions had been reproduced in other towns with the growth, often long delayed, of demand for the cab that plies for hire, as opposed to the 'fly' hired by arrangement from the local liveryman or publican.

While the cab remained a small man's venture, the omnibus came under associated impersonal capital, international capital even. Omnibus owners had been more substantial men than cab proprietors from the first. After twenty years of experiment following George Shillibeer's first London omnibus venture of 1829[3], various lines of some size had grown up under in-

[1] Booth, C., *Life and Labour of the People in London*, VII. 287.
[2] *H.O. Committee on Cabs*, 1895 (XXXV. 1), Q. 992, 6007, 6251, 7239.
[3] Vol. I. p. 385.

dividual proprietors and private companies—Eagles, Favourites, and the like. The year of Corn Law repeal had seen the first twopenny fare and the first advertisements on the 'buses[1]. About that time the lines were co-operating a little; adjusting their runnings to fit one another; agreeing not to cut fares; jointly approaching the Metropolitan Roads Commission to ask for more granite macadam roads instead of the traditional London flint gravel "which destroyed their horses."[2] In 1855 there appeared from Paris the *Compagnie générale des omnibus de Londres*, a *société en commandite*. It was a product of that flamboyant era of Parisian company promotion which is connected with the names of the brothers Pereire, and which ended in the commercial catastrophes of 1857[3]. Perhaps it was appropriate that the London omnibus business should be organised from Paris, for Shillibeer, though he started life as a British midshipman, had been a Parisian coachbuilder, and had brought both the thing and its name with him to London[4]. Within a year of its foundation the company of 1855 had bought up "perhaps a little over half the carriages [omnibuses] in London; and the other proprietors" were "working in connection with them in associations."[5] In 1858 it became a British Limited Liability Company, with Edwin Chadwick as one of its directors. But it retained its Paris office and many French shareholders. It never lost the position gained at the outset. Indeed it improved on it. By 1877 it owned nearly 8000 horses and handled three-quarters of the metropolitan omnibus traffic[6]. There were smaller companies, and intermittent competition from 'pirate' 'buses; but the first serious rival, the London Road Car Company, only came in 1880–1. Within a few years there would be war between them. As yet the General was supreme, and had merely registered the challenge[7].

If the 'bus and the 'bus company were French, the tram and the tramway company, oddly enough, were American. The

[1] Morse, H. C., *Omnibuses and Cabs* (1902), p. 62.

[2] *S.C. on Metropolitan Turnpike Roads*, 1856 (XIV. 79), Q. 1592. Cp. vol. I. p. 92.

[3] See below, p. 364 *sqq.*

[4] Morse, *op. cit.* p. 11 and the *D.N.B.*

[5] *S.C. on... Turnpike Roads*, Q. 1447.

[6] *S.C. on Tramways (Use of Mechanical Power)*, 1877 (XVI. 445), iii and Q. 2407 *sqq.*

[7] Morse, *op. cit.* p. 100–1. Tramway evidence before *R.C. on Labour*, Group B, 1892 (XXXVI. part 2), Q. 15,746 *sqq.*

cars themselves for a time were American built[1]. It was odd because British railways were still using horse traction here and there, at the time of the first experiments with 'street cars.'[2] But British railways had been kept out of the streets and American railways had not. So the horse-drawn 'street car' came as a new notion, when an American tried one at Birkenhead, late in the 'fifties. By 1861 experiment had begun in London[3]. But the lines started without any regular authorisation in Bayswater, Westminster, and Kennington used a type of rail objectionable to the general traffic, and were pulled up. There was a halt, and then, in 1868, trams were started under a private Act in Liverpool. They succeeded. Next year London was tried again, but not Bayswater. The new lines, also built under private Acts, were the Mile End and Bow Road, the Kennington and Clapham, and the Vauxhall and Greenwich. The police reported favourably on them: so far from obstructing traffic, they were said to have the effect of shepherding the more wayward traffic towards its right side of the road[4]. This all helped the general encouraging and regulating Tramways Act (33 and 34 Vict. c. 78) which went through Parliament in 1870. It worked slowly. For the next sixteen years the average annual addition to British tramways was forty-five miles[5].

There were only 237 miles all told in 1878, when the tramways of Britain had just about as many horses as the London General Omnibus Company. After that they went ahead rather faster. The figures for 1886 are 779 miles and 23,000 horses. Besides, there were 439 steam tram locomotives, a new thing since 1877, when apparently the only line which really used steam traction was one which can still be seen in the grass by the roadside between Wantage Road Station and Wantage[6]. In the 'eighties, steam trams were mainly used on the steep gradients of the industrial North, where they were made.

Meanwhile the main roads of Britain, very little altered in their lay-out or gradients since Telford died in 1834 and

[1] Booth, *Life and Labour*, VII. 310.

[2] There was occasional horse-traction on the North-Eastern until 1864. Tomlinson, *op. cit.* p. 529.

[3] See the Report of Capt. H. W. Tyler, R.E., in App. to *Return of the Board of Trade under the Tramways Act*, 1870; 1871 (LX. 539).

[4] *Return*, as above, p. 14.

[5] *Tramway Returns*, 1895 (LXV. 1017).

[6] It used steam under a Tramway Order of 1876, *S.C. on Tramways*, 1877, Q. 147. The line may have been pulled up of late: it was there a few years ago.

McAdam in 1836, had been slowly brought up to something approaching McAdam's standard of surface, under a varied and halting administration. The slowness must be stressed. Even the Metropolitan Commission, one of the model authorities of the Early Railway Age, which managed all the chief Middlesex roads out of London, though served by three generations of McAdams, had not half its mileage macadamised with broken granite in 1856[1]. Pressure from omnibus owners had been needed to get it even so far. Its gravel roads had "destroyed their horses."[2] It kept its main toll-gates in the 'fifties and 'sixties, though it had moved some of them farther out of town. Each acted as an automatic terminus for the 'bus line[3]. Other Commissions and Consolidated Turnpike Trusts had done similar work; but the breakdown of the country Trusts before railway competition threatened its continuance[4]. Through two generations, after the opening of the Liverpool and Manchester Railway, the state had no considered policy for their fortification or replacement. So the roads waited on the road authority.

Boroughs, reformed by the Whigs, had full power within their bounds. Each at its own pace macadamised; or left muddy side roads mended with cinders; or paved its streets with local stone, or with the new small squared granite 'sets' from Charnwood Forest, Cornwall or Aberdeen. Sets stood the heavy traffic of the industrial towns, and their use was stimulated by tramway enterprise, since nothing holds rails so well. Just as that enterprise got under weigh, at the close of the 'sixties, the first trials of Val de Travers asphalt, "somewhat after the Paris model," were made in the City[5]. Ten years later came the wood block pavements; but neither system was of general application.

Even in the best days of the Turnpikes most British roads, and all the minor roads, had been kept up or neglected by the parishes, under the general supervision of Quarter Sessions. As Trusts decayed and collapsed, these old resistant cells of the national life revived, with that rating power which they had first used centuries back to maintain their parish churches. The Highways Act of 1835 (5 and 6 Wm. IV, c. 50) had

[1] See vol. I. p. 93; and for the position in 1856, *S.C. on Met. Turnpike Roads*, Q. 1593–4.

[2] *Ibid.* Q. 1592.

[3] *Ibid.* Q. 82–9.

[4] Vol. I. p. 94; and Webb, S. and B., *The Story of the King's Highway*, p. 192.

[5] Capt. Tyler's report of 1871, as above.

strengthened them: they might pay surveyors and road-workers from the rates: the old obligation on parishioners to survey the roads in turn gratis was abolished, together with the unpaid Statute Labour[1]. The Act, being a Whig Act, weakened rather than stiffened the county control of Quarter Sessions[2], and did nothing to make the parish a fit custodian for roads of national importance; but then the railways were already beginning to make men think that roads were not of national importance, only for local use. By the 'sixties, this would be the official view[3]. Where traffic was really heavy, you had the borough, except in Greater London. There the Metropolitan Commission is found in 1856 defending its toll-gates as the only practical alternative to "the parishes" and the rates[4]. But at that very time, under the Public Health Act of 1848, the first Boards of Health were being created in urban areas other than boroughs[5]. One of their functions, sanitary in origin, was the care of the highways. Such a Board, in Chelsea, had just taken its roads back from the Metropolitan Commission in 1856[6]. A few years later, an attempt was made under an Act of 1862 (25 and 26 Vict. c. 61) to encourage the creation of Highway Districts out of parishes grouped by the Justices in Quarter Sessions. Some grouping was done, but a number of parishes resisted, especially small urban parishes in the North. As a means of resistance, they 'adopted' the Local Government Act of 1858 (21 and 22 Vict. c. 98), which had reinforced the principles of the Public Health Act of 1848, so becoming 'sanitary authorities' with control of their own highways. The sanitary legislation of the 'seventies based rural sanitation on the Poor Law Union which, as a Rural Sanitary District, was to acquire control of the roads; but the creation of Sanitary Districts went on so slowly that more than 5000 parishes, rural and urban, remained supreme highway authorities until 1894.

Meanwhile the broken Turnpike Trusts were disappearing, not because any minister decreed their abolition, but because

[1] Cp. vol. I. p. 401–2.

[2] Webb, *op. cit.* p. 202.

[3] See *S.C. on Turnpike Trusts*, 1864 (IX. 331), p. iii, where the essentially local character of all roads is used to defend the policy of charging their upkeep on the local rates. A witness had explained that the Great North Road was now as local as "an ordinary parish highway."

[4] Before the *S.C. on Met. Turnpike Roads.*

[5] For what follows see the expert discussion of the local government problems involved in Webb, *op. cit.* (forming vol. V of *English Local Government*), ch. IX, on which it is mainly based.

[6] *S.C. on Met. Turnpike Roads*, Q. 825, 1593.

their gates annoyed a travelling people. The annoyance is very perceptible in 1856. It is clamorous by 1864[1]. The Highway Districts which might have removed its cause were not a success. These failing, a Committee of the Commons, regularly reappointed from 1871, took upon itself to kill the Trusts in turn as their leases of life came up for renewal, trusting to the Boroughs and Sanitary Boards to take care of the roads[2]. Tolls ceased in London in 1871; but there were still 854 Trusts in Britain. Ten years later there were 184; by 1887 only 15. The last was snuffed out in 1895 in Anglesey[3].

At the time of the Great Exhibition the electric telegraph was very little more than a railway convenience[4]. There were even important railways which had not made use of it. This was soon remedied. Three years later, eight out of the seventeen London telegraph offices were at the railway stations. This blending of railway and general telegraphy continued down to 1870. By 1854, business was developing and telegraph competition had begun. To the pioneer company, the Electric and International of 1846, had been added the British and Irish Magnetic. Others had been sanctioned or were in prospect[5]. Abroad, except in America, the state had everywhere taken control of the telegraph. In Belgium and Switzerland it was being worked satisfactorily by the Post Office. So obvious a solution attracted not only the more ambitious Post Office officials, flushed with the success of the penny post, but also leading inventors and promoters. Thomas Allan, an electrician who in 1851 had secured an Act authorising a company which was to levy "a uniform rate of charge irrespective of distance,"[6] published his *Reasons for the Government annexing an Electric Telegraph System to the General Post Office* in 1854. His company was still in abeyance: it only got started, as the United Kingdom Telegraph Company, in 1861. In 1856 a Post Office official[7] submitted to the Treasury a detailed plan for a nationalised telegraph system. In 1861 no less a man than J. L. Ricardo, M.P. for Stoke, Chairman of the North

[1] *S.C. on Turnpike Trusts*, 1864; evidence, *passim*.
[2] Such a policy was adumbrated by the S.C. of 1864; *Report*, p. iv.
[3] Webb, *op. cit.* p. 222.
[4] Vol. I. p. 395–6.
[5] *Return of all...Telegraph Companies*, 1860 (LXII. 189).
[6] *Ibid.* p. 14.
[7] Mr Baines. In the *Reports by Mr Scudamore on the proposed transfer to the Post Office...of the Electric Telegraphs throughout the United Kingdom*, 1867–8 (XLI. 555), App. B.

Staffordshire Railway and founder and Chairman of the Electric and International Telegraph Company itself, memorialised My Lords in the same sense[1]. Perhaps if he had not died next year action might have been quicker. His successor in the Electric chair took a different view.

Conceivably Ricardo was influenced by the growing troubles of competition. His company had felt bound to oppose Allan's United Kingdom project, but had been beaten. Besides, there was now the London District Company of 1859 catering for metropolitan business. The natural tendency was for competing offices to grow up thickly where business was dense, and far too sparsely elsewhere. The United Kingdom made its bid for patronage by applying Allan's principle of a uniform charge, as against minimum charges varying from 1*s*. to 5*s*. for distance, with all sorts of extras. Though it paid no dividend in its first four years, the United Kingdom posed, not unjustly, as a public benefactor on that account[2]. As for the commercial world, it wanted more uniform and cheaper facilities, and thought that the state, on the analogy of the penny post, should be able to furnish them. A final campaign was started by the Edinburgh Chamber of Commerce in the autumn of 1865.

The then Postmaster-General, Lord Stanley of Alderley, had long believed that his department ought to take over the telegraph[3]. He was glad to have his hand forced, and he set his officials to report. Edwin Chadwick, need it be said, was demonstrating, in memorials to the Treasury and papers for the Royal Society of Arts, that the state, and the state only, could maximise telegraph utility[4]. This time public opinion was unmistakably on his side. Although the Treasury, for very good reasons, did not act in 1866–7[5]; and although the Electric Telegraph Company, under its new chairman Robert Grimston, went down fighting in perhaps less sportsmanlike style than might have been expected[6], the telegraph system was finally

[1] Scudamore's *Reports*, App. C.

[2] *Ibid.* p. 87.

[3] See his covering letter to Scudamore's *Reports*. Scudamore was his Assistant Secretary.

[4] For the memorial Scudamore's *Reports*, p. 8; for a paper of Chadwick's, p. 159. For an earlier paper, Wood, H. T., *The History of the Royal Society of Arts*, p. 477.

[5] See below, p. 375, for the commercial crisis of 1866.

[6] Grimston was a noted boxer, swimmer, rider and cricketer. His life was written in 1885 by F. Gale, author of *Echoes from old Cricket Fields*. He produced a pamphlet—*A review of the leading principles involved in the proposed transfer of Electric Telegraphs...from Trading Companies to the State, etc.*, not mentioned by his biographer.

bought for the Post Office at a very high price under 32 and 33 Vict. c. 73 of 1869, and taken over as from January 31, 1870.

The Office had promised the Postmaster great things, not only cheap, uniform, extended facilities but also an efficient personnel and a large profit[1]. When taunted by Grimston with the supposed incapacity of local postmasters to handle the telegraph, it had replied that there were "even institutions at which girls are trained to use it."[2] For about two years all hopes seemed to be fulfilled. The girls learnt their job. The public secured a uniform 1*s.* rate for twenty words, addresses free; complete separation of railway from general telegraphy, with resulting convenience in the location of telegraph offices; and above all the abolition of what had perhaps done more than anything else to set opinion against the companies, their intelligence department. This had made the supply of news to the provincial press "a thorough monopoly,"[3] and had thrown that press on to Chadwick's side. Newspapers had been forced to take what the intelligence department gave, rarely receiving separate messages because the rates for them were too high. They wanted special rates for their own news-collecting association; and they got them.

The extension of facilities soon absorbed the promised profit —rightly, it may well be argued. Then came compensation for displaced servants of the companies; levellings up of stipends to the old Post Office scale; and, quite unexpectedly, the price and wage rise of the early 'seventies[4]. The ratio of working expenses to receipts, which had been $78\frac{3}{4}$ in 1871–2, stood at $96\frac{2}{3}$ in 1874–5, leaving no proper margin for interest and sinking fund on the telegraph debt. This produced inquiry, reorganisation, and revision of charges. Helped by these, and by the price fall after 1873, the ratio improved slowly. In 1875 the Treasury had urged the Post Office to aim at a ratio of from

[1] Scudamore's *Report*, p. 37–8.

[2] Scudamore's supplementary *Report*, a reply to Grimston's pamphlet, p. 133.

[3] *Report on the reorganisation of the Telegraph System of the U.K.*, by Scudamore, 1871 (XXXVII. 703), quoting Q. 1255 of the evidence before the *S.C. on the Telegraph Bill* of 1868.

[4] *Report of the Treasury Committee on the increased cost of telegraph service since the acquisition by the State*, 1875 (XX. 643). And see *S.C. on the Telegraph Department of the Post Office*, 1876 (XIII. 1). The price paid for the telegraphs was too high. Henry Fawcett once said that it ought to have been £7,000,000 instead of £10,500,000 (Buxton, *Finance and Politics, an Historical Study*, II. 50 n.), but this does not explain the deteriorating ratio of working expenses to receipts.

70 to 75. By 1881 the Post Office had achieved 80. Two years later it was only able to show 89·5. For 1884–5 there was no margin. All the same, it introduced the 6*d.* telegram in 1885, hoping to attract custom by a popular price. Figures showed that it was perfectly solvent, but its telegraph department was not. The letters paid interest and sinking fund for the wires[1].

Fundamental problems in the relations of the state to communications and transport were taking shape. On what principles shall railway rates be controlled? It is the same problem whether the lines are publicly or privately owned, and as yet it was unsolved. Is the public as traveller, or sender of goods and messages, to be served at the expense of the same public as taxpayer? This had been decided in the negative for the time being by the Railway Committee of 1872, without open discussion: the public as taxpayer could not be expected to subsidise the public as canal user, after the French style[2]. Shall one form of transport in the hands of the state subsidise another? This was being solved empirically in the matter of the letter and the telegram. After all there was only one Postmaster General, and he ran his whole concern at a profit. But Treasuries and business critics of departmental methods were uneasy, and rightly so. In the absence of the vulgar bookkeeping test of a profit, how shall the utility and efficiency of particular government enterprises be decided? With a government so little given to economic enterprise as that of late Victorian Britain the question was not very insistent. But, in view of the trend of thought and activity throughout the civilised world in the 'eighties, it deserved diligent consideration.

[1] See the *Report* and *Review* in 1886 (XXXVIII. 493 and 499). Buxton, *op. cit.* II. 52 (1888) spoke of the "wretched result" of the whole transaction and of the "appalling deficiency" on the telegraph account.

[2] Above, p. 200.

CHAPTER VI

OVERSEAS TRADE AND COMMERCIAL POLICY

RAILWAY building in and outside Britain, hunger in Ireland, growing population and free trade had given an extraordinary impetus to overseas traffic in the late 'forties. The tonnage of shipping entered and cleared from United Kingdom ports in 1844 was 10,300,000, exclusive of the coasting trade and of that between Britain and Ireland. Ten years earlier it had been 6,300,000. Three years later it was 14,300,000. When the worst of the famine and the commercial crisis of 1847 were over, there was a natural set-back; but the upward movement was resumed in the 'fifties—to 24,700,000 in 1860; to 36,600,000 in 1870; to 58,700,000 in 1880. Then came a slackening. Instead of a decade rise of from 50 to 60 per cent. as before, there was one of only 26 per cent., to 74,300,000 in 1890. The acceleration which registered the passage into a new era in the economic history of the world was over.

But the growth in Britain's strength at sea, and in her share of her own and other people's carrying trade, was not over yet, though there had been vicissitudes. In 1847–9, 69 per cent. of the tonnage using United Kingdom ports was British, and in 1850, so far as is known, something not very far below 60 per cent. of the world's 'civilised' ocean-going tonnage[1] was also British. The next decade saw a relative decline. The United States were at the summit of their naval strength. Their whalers were out from Nantucket; their supply ships were beating round the Horn to make the Golden Gate; their clippers were in the Canton river, the Mersey and the Thames. In 1860, United States shipping employed in the foreign trade and the whale fisheries alone[2] was more than half that of the United Kingdom, and nearly half that of the whole British Empire. The proportion of British tonnage in United Kingdom ports

[1] *Tables showing the Progress of Merchant Shipping in the United Kingdom and the Principal Maritime Countries*, 1912 (Ed. 6180). These tables are defective for 1850. For a number of countries no figures are available; but several of these, *e.g.* Italy and Greece, had not at that time many 'ocean going' ships.

[2] Excluding coasting, river, and lake shipping.

had fallen from 69 to 56. Some people wondered whether the repeal of the Navigation Laws had not been over hasty[1]. Next year the armies were loose in America. In July, 1862, the *Alabama* was away to raid Northern shipping from Birkenhead. When all was over, in 1865, Americans were thinking more of the prairies than of the seas: by 1870 the ratio of British ships using British ports was back at 68. It increased as steam tonnage grew, to reach its absolute maximum of 73 in 1895. It had been over 70 then for fifteen years, years during which, in spite of much slack trade, Britain had a greater share of the traffic of the high seas than at any time in her history.

In continent after continent that traffic had been fed continuously by new railways; those railways made more often than not by British capital. When Europe broke into Revolution in 1848, only Belgium had a complete skeleton through railway system, though Prussia had 1500 miles of line open, and there was activity in other German states[2]. France had a number of detached lines and a great unfinished scheme of construction on hand. In the United States by 1850 there were 9000 miles of line working, but it was not yet possible to go westward by rail without break from the Atlantic coast beyond Buffalo[3]. The twenty years from 1850 to 1870 saw Western Europe supplied with a fairly complete railway system, partly by private enterprise, partly by state enterprise, partly by some combination of the two. Spain, to take an illustration from a slow-moving country, which had not 20 miles of railway in 1850, had 3500 miles by 1870. In Eastern Europe, Russia got to work seriously after 1860, but in 1880 she had not as much railway on her huge surface as there was then in the British Isles. The Turk lagged, yet even he had his 1000 miles of railway before 1890[4].

The people of the United States, interrupted in the conquest of their continent by civil war, returned to it with insatiable energy after 1865. The railway map of 1870 shows a relatively dense network east of the Mississippi and the lower course of

[1] Clapham, J. H., "The last years of the Navigation Laws," *E.H.R.*, July, 1910.

[2] Clapham, J. H., *The Economic Development of France and Germany*, p. 142, 153.

[3] Johnson, E. R., *American Railway Transportation* (1904), p. 24–5, with a map for 1850.

[4] The best summary of construction, mileage, and policies is in the various articles under *Eisenbahnen*, by Cohn and others, in Conrad and Elster, *HWB. der Staatswissenschaften* (Ed. 1909), III. 805–926.

the Missouri; west of that hardly anything, except the single brand-new line reaching out over twenty-five degrees of longitude from Omaha through Utah to the Pacific. There was rather more railway in the United States that year than in all continental Europe—53,000 against 50,000 miles. During the next twenty years 110,000 miles were added, 70,000 of them between 1880 and 1890, mainly in the early years of the decade. If a single national contribution towards the making of the new era had to be selected for its world-wide economic importance, it would probably be this[1].

In Canada there was a similar, but later and as yet much less significant, development: the Canadian mileage in 1890 was still below that of the United Kingdom in 1870. The Argentine Republic and South America generally were later still. The Argentine had only 450 miles of line in 1870, 1400 in 1880, and even in 1890 not yet as much as there had been in Great Britain forty years before; though in the Argentine, as in all new countries, a few pioneering lines driven over virgin soil might have an influence upon world trade out of all proportion to their length.

So, for that matter, might pioneering lines in very old countries, as the Indian railways were showing. These were built on a far-sighted plan. Lord Dalhousie, who would have controlled the geographical development of British railways in the 'forties, had he not been baulked by his chief[2], was able by his minute of 1853 to determine absolutely both the geographical and the administrative development of the railways of India for the next twenty years, and to influence all future development[3]. The Mutiny first delayed and then hastened the completion of his grand design. Nearly 4000 miles were open by 1870; over 9000 by 1880, when there were only 800 miles in all the rest of Asia and they mainly in Ceylon and the Dutch Indies; nearly 17,000 by 1890. Perhaps, in the history of the human spirit, these Indian lines may prove to have been of greater moment than all the mileage of America.

The first Australian railways were opened before 1857 but progress was slow down to 1870, when the whole continent had

[1] Figures and maps in Johnson, *op. cit.* p. 26 *sqq.*

[2] Vol. I. p. 421–3.

[3] Hunter, Sir W. W., *The Indian Empire* (1892), p. 648. "The elaborate minute, drawn up by Lord Dalhousie...substantially represents the railway map of India at the present day."

only a little over 1000 miles of line, in sections running inland from its sea-coast capitals. There were more than 3500 miles in 1880, and more than 9000 in 1890. New Zealand, beginning ten years later than Australia and needing railways less, had shown relatively greater enterprise: she had 1250 miles open in 1880 and nearly 2000 in 1890. In Africa there had been a little building at both ends—Egypt, Algiers, the Cape—during the 'sixties and even the 'fifties; but, except for the cotton lines of the Egyptian delta, the African railways of the 'eighties had not great international importance. Their total length was not quite one half that of the Australian lines in 1890.

It has been reckoned that the whole earth, which had not 5000 miles of railway in 1840, had 24,000 miles in 1850; 239,000 miles in 1880; and 386,000 miles in 1890. Of the 386,000 miles, more than two-fifths were in the United States of America[1].

More important for Britain than the opening of many railways was the opening of the Suez Canal in 1869. Dreamed of by Frenchmen for centuries; planned and executed by a Frenchman and with French capital; opposed by old English statesmen who remembered Napoleon's Egyptian campaign, and by younger ones who fancied that it would benefit principally Levantines and other Mediterranean people, it soon verified the forecast of a more prescient Englishman made in 1867. France, Charles Dilke wrote, "will only find it has spent millions in digging a canal for England's use."[2] Many people had doubted the use; but English naval and military experts sent to report early in 1870 said that it was "undeniably a navigable canal for vessels of considerable draught"; that its success had "probably far exceeded the most sanguine expectations of its warmest supporters"; that, contrary to pessimistic expectations, its Mediterranean entrances need not silt up, nor its maintenance costs be prohibitive; but that as the "grand highway" between East and West it was too narrow[3].

Narrow or not, 2,263,300 tons of shipping passed it in 1879.

[1] Conrad and Elster, as above, *s.v. Eisenbahnstatistik*.

[2] *Greater Britain*, p. 569. For early plans see Conrad and Elster, VII. 1048, *s.v. Suezcanal*. For British opposition see *Cambridge Modern History*, XI. 637; Clapham, *The Economic Development of France and Germany*, p. 356. French investors took 52 per cent. of the first capital issue, the Khedive nearly all the rest. Hobson, C. K., *The Export of British Capital*, p. 129.

[3] *Report on the Suez Canal*, by Capt. Richards, R.N. and Lt.-Col. Clarke, R.E., *A. and P.* 1870, LXIV. 807.

Of this total 1,752,400 tons were British and only 181,700 French. Dilke could hardly have expected such a sweeping majority. It was France's misfortune that in this decisive decade she was both recovering from a lost war and ill-equipped for iron and steel shipbuilding. For the crowding of the canal with British tonnage owed much to the advent of the iron or steel screw steamer as a general cargo carrier, an advent which the existence of an interoceanic canal debouching in the not too navigable Gulf of Suez had, in its turn, helped to precipitate.

One pessimistic forecast which Dilke shared with most Englishmen miscarried: "it is hard to believe that it can pay."[1] In fact, helped by the screw steamer, it began to pay real dividends in 1875. When Disraeli bought the Khedive's shares in that year he bought them above par[2]. In 1879 the 500 franc share was never quoted below 600. By 1886–7 the original shareholder had received an average dividend of 7½ per cent. for the whole period, and his share was worth a round 2000 francs[3]. Prosperity had permitted that widening and deepening necessary to make the canal the grand highway of commerce. The work was begun systematically in 1884. Early in 1887, arrangements were made to render the passage by night possible. The passing tonnage rose accordingly to 6,783,200 in 1889. Dilke was still right. The British share of the whole was 5,352,900; the French 361,800.

On June 23, 1870, Lord Mayo from his bedroom at Simla had telegraphed in a few minutes to President Grant at Washington, by way of an evening party in Arlington Street, W. Grant had replied in "American idiom."[4] The party was given by the Chairman of the British Indian Telegraph Company to celebrate the successful laying of the last stretch—Gibraltar to Falmouth—of the direct and independent cable from England to Bombay. Very appropriately, de Lesseps of the Suez Canal was at the party. In the five preceding years the problem of the deep sea cable had been solved, after two decades of

[1] Dilke, Sir C. W., *loc. cit.*

[2] The best account even of the finance is in Monypenny and Buckle, *Disraeli*, v. 339*sqq*. Cp. Jenks, L. H., *The Migration of British Capital to* 1875 (1927), p. 321, 324; Conrad and Elster, as above.

[3] For the very complicated story of Suez Canal finance see Robino, J., "The statistical story of the Suez Canal," *S.J.* 1887, p. 495–541.

[4] The *Annual Register's Chronicle* for June 23, 1870.

experiment and disappointment. The early 'fifties had been the era of the shallow sea and narrow sea lines—Dublin-Holyhead; Dover-Calais, a cable which gave no trouble for nine years; Genoa-Corsica, and the like[1]. The late 'fifties were the era of heroic, if often careless, experiment in deep water—Cyrus Field and his Atlantic Telegraph Company; the cable that snapped; the cable that worked feebly from August 5 to September 1, 1858, and was then silent; discoveries about the awkward conformation of the ocean floor and about the behaviour of insulated and protected copper wire lying at two to three thousand fathoms in the globigerina ooze[2]. They were also the era of a feverish effort made by Lord Derby's government to link India to England after the Mutiny, as a result of which the Red Sea and Indian Telegraph Company of 1858 received a generous subsidy, and the Treasury itself ordered a cable for the Falmouth-Gibraltar route, a cable which was never laid there because the Atlantic had proved "the extreme risk of failure" in deep waters[3].

The Red Sea and Indian Company—Alexandria, Suez, Suakim, Aden and so to Karachi—reported that its cable line was "complete through its entire length" on March 14, 1860[4]. It did not remain complete long; and as the company had made no systematic arrangements for repair, it became derelict. The situation in 1860–1 was most discouraging. Although lines stretched "from Norway to the shores of Africa, from Nova Scotia to the Gulf of Mexico," and "from Great Britain... eastwards to Constantinople"[5]; out of 11,364 miles of submarine cable laid to date not much more than 3000 were working[6]. To the Atlantic and Indian failures were to be added, among others, the English Malta and Corfu and the Dutch Singapore and Batavia. Soon the blockade runner would supersede the cable ship off the coast of the United States. American

[1] Cp. Clapham, *The Economic Development of France and Germany*, p. 157.

[2] See the *Report of the Joint Committee of the Board of Trade and the Atlantic Telegraph Company...Submarine Telegraph Cables*, of April, 1861 (*A. and P.* 1860, LXII. 591): an excellent historical survey with full technical evidence. The conclusion (p. xxxvi) was that, with sufficient care and forethought, all the failures might have been avoided.

[3] *Papers on the Falmouth and Gibraltar Cable*, 1860 (LXII), p. 2. Treasury Minute of November 14, 1859. Cp. *Return of all...Telegraph Cables* and *Return of Correspondence with the Electric Telegraph Companies* in the same volume.

[4] *Return of Correspondence*, p. 17.

[5] Wilson, G., *The Progress of the Telegraph* (1859), p. 25.

[6] *Report of* 1861, p. v.

enthusiasm and enterprise were diverted for four years, and joint Anglo-American action became impossible.

But the cable ships were out as soon as civil war was over. This time it was the *Great Eastern*, employed by a new company[1]. After a failure in 1865, came the success of July, 1866. Then the broken cable of 1865 was recovered and completed[2]. Thereafter lines were laid rapidly about the earth by land and sea. The longest, carried overland in the late 'sixties, was not American but that of the Northern Telegraph Company of Copenhagen, across the full breadth of the Russian Empire to Vladivostock. Soon after the last link between England and Bombay was completed in 1870, the Northern laid short sea lines from Vladivostock into China and Japan[3].

These were met there by the cables of the Eastern Extension Company, coming from India south about Asia, and branching from Singapore through the Java Sea for Australia. South America was given direct communication with Europe by the Brazilian Company—Lisbon, Madeira, Cape Verde Islands, Pernambuco—in 1874. By the early 'eighties the best of the work was done. The North Atlantic was full of cables. They even crossed one another near Faraday Hill, a telegraphic eminence on the ocean floor. Africa, like Asia, was hung about with them. Mixed land and sea lines threaded the Turkish Empire and the Persian Gulf[4]. Only the Pacific remained virgin, from New Zealand and Japan to the looping inshore cables off the western coasts of South America and Mexico. It was not yet possible to telegraph to Honolulu, Iceland, New Guinea, or Tierra del Fuego. Nearly every other place of real importance not in the heart of China could be reached overland or under sea. The world, on the economist's projection, had shrunk into a single market. The final process of shrinkage had only taken about fifteen years and the greater part of it had been done in less than ten[5].

In the middle of this shrunken world, whispering along its copper wire news about the goods that slid along its lines of iron and steel to the seas, Britain lay now once for all an

[1] Above, p. 70.

[2] *Annual Register*, 1865 and 1866.

[3] Conrad and Elster, *op. cit.* VII. 1150, *s.v. Telegraphie*.

[4] In 1860 the Turks had been offered "une ligne sous-marine de Bagdad à Bassorah," *i.e.* up the Tigris (*Return of Correspondence*, No. 425), but that came to nothing.

[5] In 1866–75: see any cable maps of the 'sixties, 'seventies and 'eighties.

'industry state,' and a trade state, a state that lived by the export of its manufactures and could by no possibility feed itself for long in the way to which it was accustomed, nor find appropriate and sufficient raw materials for all its industries at home[1]. Rapidly as the imports of food of every kind had grown since Peel broke down the last serious barriers, the mere mass of the home-raised food supplies still outweighed that of the imports many times. The United Kingdom had, for example, in 1884–6 on an average 10,700,000 head of cattle[2]. She imported in those years an average of 372,000 head, together with 53,000 tons of beef. Beef imports even on this scale were a new thing. In 1872–4 they were only 12,500 tons. But for the most vital import of all, the bread corn, dependence on trade was now absolute. Even in 1850–2 it is possible that something like 25 per cent. of the consumption was imported[3]. During the eight years 1852–9 this proportion did not grow rapidly. Russia was at that time the leading source of supply and the Crimean War cut her off; but for the whole period the proportion imported was not less than 25 per cent. and may have been as much as 30 per cent. For 1860–7 it mounted towards 40 per cent., for 1868–75 towards 50 per cent. By the end of the 'seventies (1876–8) it was certainly over 50 per cent., the best available calculation suggesting more nearly 60 per cent.[4] No doubt the 60 per cent. line was passed in the early 'eighties, though the growth in imports of wheat and flour was not abnormally rapid after 1880. At the very end of the era, the picture of an island population getting from overseas two loaves of bread out of every three that it ate would not be appreciably out of drawing, though it might conceal the fact that few loaves were now made from home-grown wheat unmixed.

The loaves from overseas were mostly American by 1886. Wheat or flour, whenever allowed to come at all, had always

[1] Cp. above, p. 22.

[2] The figures were: Britain, 6,500,000; Ireland, 4,200,000. They are put together in the text because the only import figures are those for the United Kingdom and because Irish 'stores,' like Irish butter, were an important element in British consumption. The import of bacon and ham was very great: 372,000 tons in 1884–6.

[3] Above, p. 3.

[4] Lawes and Gilbert, "On the Home Production, Imports, Consumption and Price of Wheat, 1852–3—1879–80," *S.J.* 1880, p. 313 and *J.R.A.S.* 1880, p. 357. The figures are for the United Kingdom, but as Ireland no longer sent wheat to Britain they serve approximately for Britain alone. For Britain the higher alternative should always be taken because Ireland more nearly fed herself.

come in considerable quantities from the northern states of the Union[1]. Sometimes the American proportion had been high. In 1860 it was a full quarter of the wheat and more than two-fifths of the wheaten flour. But the main supplies at that time were European: Russian, North German, Danish, French, with a little from the Turkish Empire—Moldavia, Wallachia, and Egypt. The civil war postponed an American conquest of the British market. When it was over, the old position was not re-established at once. Russia was the most important supplier of wheat, and France of wheaten flour, during the four years 1866–9. But in the single year 1869 the United States sent more wheat than Russia and more flour than France. In the vicissitudes of harvests, Russia was once again the principal purveyor of wheat in 1872. France had fallen out. After that the dominance of the United States was unquestioned. From 1874 onwards, they sent again and again more than half the requirements of the United Kingdom in wheat and flour, whether measured by quantity or by value; and in one year, 1881, very nearly two-thirds. India first appeared as a really important contributor in 1877. She sent no flour, and in her most successful season, that of 1885, only one-sixth of the wheat, or one-seventh of the wheat plus the flour reckoned as grain. Russia made her contribution throughout, as did British North America, Australia, Germany, and many other countries; but this hardly affected the American dominance during the decade which ended in 1886[2].

British policy had however now restored to Europe the right to supply the United Kingdom with the greater part of her bulkiest and most widely used raw material, the one for which—tropical and sub-tropical materials apart—she had longest been dependent on imports: timber[3]. As a result of the huge discriminating duties on foreign timber imposed during the Napoleonic wars, the natural trade with Scandinavia and the Baltic had been crippled in favour of that with British America. The discrimination, though much reduced by Peel and again in 1851, survived until 1860[4]. Before Peel's reduction had taken

[1] Above, p. 3.

[2] Based on the annual trade returns which, for wheat, are very full and satisfactory.

[3] Above, pp. 5, 6, and Vol. I. p. 237–8, etc.

[4] *Customs Tariffs of the U.K.*, 1800–1897; 1897 (C. 8706), p. 290; Buxton, S., *Finance and Politics, an Historical Study* (1855), I. 344–5. Cp. Vol. I. p. 500.

full effect, in 1848, five-eighths of the timber imported was still British. In spite of the reduction of 1851, the American war helped to keep it British. For the four years 1856–9 the British and foreign imports of the timber which was measured by bulk almost precisely balanced[1]. In 1860 the duties were equalised at the nominal figure of 1*s.* a load on hewn wood and 2*s.* on sawn. In 1866 this odd irrational survival, without economic or imperial utility, was abolished. Geographical conditions had free play. By 1886 four-fifths of the imports which were measured by bulk were foreign. They were not all European. Besides the tropical woods, there was now a heavy shipping of pitch pine from the gulf ports of the United States, as mid-Victorian ecclesiastical and domestic architecture witness. But the major part of the imports came by the short sea passages from Northern Europe, and still nearly all in sailing ships. There was also now a great trade in pit-props from the lower Biscay coast. The grand total of measured imports stood in 1886 at no less than 5,100,000 loads (approximately tons). A generation earlier (1845–50) a yearly average of 1,870,000 loads had sufficed[2]. In the Britain of the 'eighties, economic life could not have gone on for six months without imported timber, and at certain seasons of the year not for three[3].

Lancashire's dependence on an imported raw material was primitive and inevitable. It helps to explain Lancastrian pacifism. Between 1820 and 1850 it had ceased to be a general dependence upon the world's cotton areas and become a special dependence upon the United States. In 1820 the United States had for the first time sent more than half the British import. In 1820–30 she sent three-quarters. From that time forward no other country had shown capacity to increase the crop in proportion to the growth of the world's demand. For the whole decade 1851–60 the American percentage of the cotton bales landed at British ports was 72; and as the American bale was heavier than others, and the American cotton more valuable than most, the absolute dependence figure was higher. For the year 1860, in which America sent nearly 500,000 more bales than she had ever sent before, and more than she sent again

[1] See a note in *S.J.* 1860, p. 85.

[2] Porter, *Progress of the Nation*, p. 579.

[3] Owing to the closing of the Baltic and White Sea by ice, Britain carries heavy stocks over winter. The spring timber contracts are for 'first open water' delivery.

until 1880, a Lancashire statistician put it as high as 85 per cent.[1]

There was already anxiety among the far-sighted. They had formed in 1857 the Cotton Supply Association, believing "that some dire calamity must inevitably, sooner or later, overtake the cotton manufacture of Lancashire; whose vast superstructure has so long rested on the treacherous foundation of restricted slave labour."[2] Some feared a servile war in America. Probably few anticipated a war of secession. They were being warned by Americans in 1860 that in any event there was little prospect of the American crop continuing to grow at the same rate as the world's demand, "and that as a consequence, the price of cotton would rise to a yet higher standard."[3] The reference was to a rise in prices which, in the case of average 'upland' cotton, was from just over 5¾*d.* a lb. for the decade 1848–57 to just under 6¾*d.* for 1858–60. In 1864 the small quantity of that cotton available was worth 27½*d.* a lb.[4]

Before the civil war, whose coming "the great mass of traders refused to credit"[5] until it came, the Association, aided by the Foreign Office and the Consular Service, had been collecting information and surveying cotton areas, actual and potential. When war began and the Association's fears were justified, inquiries, cotton seed, judicious advice, and commissioners were sent out broadcast: 500 tons of seed, 1200 gins, and "millions" of pamphlets are recorded by 1866[6]. Naturally India was the chief field of activity. She stood second to America as a source of supply for Lancashire in the 'fifties, and a belief was current that she had a crop equivalent to five or six million American bales[7]. (The European import from all sources whatsoever in 1860 was not the equivalent of five millions; the British not three and a half.) Inquiry showed that the equivalent of two and a half million bales was probably the outside figure for India, including all the cotton worked up

[1] Ellison, T., *The Cotton Trade of Great Britain* (1886), p. 91 and tables in App. Cp. *S.J.* 1862, p. 527 *sqq.* "The great crisis in the history of the Cotton Trade," and *S.J.* 1869, p. 428 *sqq.* "The Cotton Trade, 1862–8, as compared with 1855–61," by Elijah Helm of the Manchester Chamber of Commerce.

[2] Quoted in Watts, J., *The Facts of the Cotton Famine* (1866), p. 402.

[3] *The U.S. Economist* quoted in the 1860 Report of the C.S.A. in Watts, p. 403.

[4] Figures from Ellison. Those given by Neild, in *S.J.* 1861, p. 491, "Prices of Printing Cloth and Upland Cotton, 1812–60," are rather lower but show a similar rise to 1860. Upland cotton had averaged less than 6*d.* from 1838 to 1858.

[5] Watts, *op. cit.* p. 112. [6] *Ibid.* p. 404–5. [7] Ellison, p. 91.

in the country. Though prices doubled and trebled, and though in 1864 two-thirds of the much reduced quantity of cotton used in Britain was Indian, it was never possible to draw anything like the amount required from the East. Nearly 19 per cent. of the British imports had been already Indian in the years 1855–61; in spite of all efforts barely 28 per cent. of a reduced total were Indian in 1862–8[1]. Egypt and Brazil, whose cotton-growing industries were younger and more adaptable, showed greater elasticity of supply; but their total contribution was much less. Altogether, during the four war years 1862–5, the United Kingdom managed to secure a yearly average weight of cotton rather more than half that of 1860 and 1861, two seasons of abnormally heavy imports. The achievement was creditable and significant of the creative power of high prices, for the first of the four years was much the leanest; but the preponderance of rough short-stapled Indian cotton was unwelcome. Lancashire cherished the story of the Methodist spinner who interrupted extempore prayers for cotton with an anguished cry of "but not Surat, O Lord!"

For a few years after the 'famine' and the peace, the Indian supply kept up, while the American recovered and the Egyptian grew slowly. In spite of social revolution with its disturbing economic consequences in the Southern states of the forcibly re-united Union, America was able to send more cotton to Europe in 1871 than she had sent in 1861, although the peak figure of 1860 was not passed until 1879[2]. By 1870 more than half the British consumption was again American. A decade later India had fallen to a very subordinate place and America had re-established her old position, no longer on the "treacherous foundation...of slave labour."[3] During the five years 1880–4 she supplied 74 per cent. of the cotton consumed in Britain. Thanks to American enterprise and railways, to steamers and a fall in general world prices, the standard cotton which had averaged just under 6¾*d.* a pound in 1858–60 could be grown by freemen and delivered in England in 1880–4 for a minute fraction under 6*d.* But the problem of the Cotton Growing Association, how to relieve Lancashire, and indeed

[1] Helm in *S.J.* 1869, as above.

[2] Ellison, *op. cit.* p. 91 and tables.

[3] Indian cotton had not ceased to be exported, however, nor did the export fall off appreciably, except during the years 1877–9: it went elsewhere. Indian exports to Europe in 1882 were higher than in any previous year except 1866 and in 1883 higher than in any years except 1866, 1882, 1869 and 1872.

Europe, from undue dependence on a single source of supply, remained unsolved. American cotton being again so plentiful and cheap, the majority had again lost interest in the solution. What with the cotton and the wheat, the United States sent a larger share of the imports of the United Kingdom in 1880–4 than at any earlier date. It came to nearly a quarter of the whole, 23·7 per cent.[1]

The check to the cotton industry in the 'sixties had been registered in the prosperity of the other textiles and their heavy imports of material. For the quinquennium 1860–4, the imports of raw wool leapt up 41 per cent. above the level of 1855–9: 1865–9 was again 41 per cent. above 1855–9. Besides that there were more sheep in Britain in 1868 than in any earlier, or later, year. British flax-growing was almost extinct and not even the lack of cotton could revive it; but the imports of flax, hemp, and jute moved up with those of wool, and the acreage under flax in Ireland, which had averaged 115,000 in 1855–61, stood at 234,000 for 1862–8[2]. Even when the abnormal stimulus was withdrawn, the imports of these textile fibres continued to grow fast, though not so fast. The wool import of 1881–4 was more than double that of 1865–9, and although the flocks of sheep were at their minimum in 1882, they were recovering by 1886. The decline had coincided with a set of the fashions against fabrics made of the long wools which can be grown nowhere better than in England[3], and with the beginnings of the import of frozen mutton[4].

From 95·2 millions of lbs. in 1850–4, the imports of wool had grown to an average of 485·0 millions for 1880–4, of which more than half (264·2 millions) was re-exported. The home supply, including Ireland, may have been as much as 160 millions at the latter date. About a fifth of this was exported, but the balance, together with the skin-wool from slaughter-houses and the home-made shoddy, estimated together at 143 million lbs., met more than half the needs of the industry. Dependence on foreign supplies had almost ceased. Cheap, rough, 'carpet' wools were imported from all kinds of places.

[1] There are useful summaries and analyses of imports 1854–84 in *R.C. on Depression of Trade*, 1886, I. 127 *sqq*. The figure quoted is from Supplementary Table 6, p. 193.

[2] Helm in *S.J.* 1869, p. 420, and cp. Watts, *op. cit.* ch. XX.

[3] Lincoln and Leicester wools especially; cp. below, p. 281.

[4] Above, p. 90.

Some alpaca came from South America and mohair from the Levant and the Cape; but since 1850–60 the fine Saxon and Silesian merino wools had been finally replaced by those of Australia, New Zealand, and South Africa. So abundant had the Dominion supplies become that British buyers made hardly any use of the B.A. (Buenos Aires) wool from the river Plate, which now formed an important element of the continental consumption[1].

For technical reasons, it is not easy to compare specific wool prices of the 'eighties with those of earlier years[2]; but it is noticeable that whereas the average price of all cotton imported, as well as the price of a particular standard cotton, was slightly higher in 1880–4 than it had been thirty years before, the average price of wool was definitely lower. Transport from Australasia had greatly improved, and the carcase value of sheep had gone up, allowing that of the 'joint product,' wool, to fall a little, in spite of the world's ravenous demand[3].

No change of importance had occurred in the import of the other chief textile materials, apart from the gross increase in quantity set out below, and the way in which jute had, as it were, taken the pressure off flax and hemp. It is unlikely that supplies of those fibres could have been increased in proportion to the increased demand for sacking. Except in time of war, most of the hemp was Russian; most of the flax Russian and Belgian; all the jute was at all times Indian. Of the wool more than half was re-exported in 1880–4, as has been seen. About a seventh of the cotton; a quarter of the jute—for which Dundee was the depot; and varying proportions of the other fibres were also re-exported[4].

[1] The estimates are based on those adopted by the *Bradford Observer* and by the Sec. of the Bradford Chamber of Commerce. Cp. Clapham, J. H., *The Woollen and Worsted Industries*, p. 10, and Senkel, W., "Wollproduktion und Wollhandel im 19ten Jahrhundert," *Zeitschrift für die Gesammte Staatswissenschaft*, 1901; and above, p. 7.

[2] In early years little if any imported wool was 'scoured.' The yield of clean wool from greasy varies; and so on. Hence a lb. of imported wool means different things at different times.

[3] The growing import of scoured wool tells in favour of the argument, as it is more valuable than greasy wool.

[4] For jute, see above, p. 84, and for wool, pp. 7, 223. Silk is omitted from the table of quantities of textile raw materials imported, on p. 225, because of statistical difficulties connected with the returns. It is included in the second table of values. The average annual import of silk—'knubs and waste,' 'raw' and 'thrown'—was under £4,000,000.

United Kingdom imports in million lbs. annual average

	Cotton	Wool	Flax	Hemp	Jute
1850–4	825·6	95·2	175·5	107·6	48·4*
1860–4	946·4	167·2	176·2	102·9	132·9
1870–4	1524·3	307·0	265·0	132·8	420·3
1880–4	1714·7	485·0	215·7	150·6	616·3

* Three years only.

Reckoned by value, cotton was by far the most important of the incoming raw materials of all sorts. Its value varied between a third and a quarter of the whole. The timber, though it filled so much tonnage and was so essential, was worth less than the wool. The grouping of the raw material imports by value stood thus:

Principal Raw Material groups, annual average value of imports

1880–4	£
Total of raw material	141,000,000
Textile raw material	84,000,000 (Cotton 44,500,000)
Timber, all kinds	16,000,000
Metallic ores and unworked metals	15,000,000
Hides	4,000,000
Rubber and gutta-percha	3,000,000
Paper-making materials	2,000,000

Of the gross £141,000,000 worth of raw material imported, £36,000,000 was re-exported. Of this £36,000,000 no less than £15,000,000 represented the re-export of wool.

Since the first cargo of Spanish hematite was delivered at Hartlepool in 1861[1], the import, which fluctuated greatly, had risen to a maximum of over 3,000,000 tons in 1882–3. There were also occasional, but small, imports of pig iron. The days when England was on the balance an exporter of copper and a great exporter of tin and lead were over[2]. She still exported unwrought copper, but it was mostly smelted from imported ore; and there was besides an import of unwrought copper which averaged 40,000 tons a year. She exported her own lead, but imported nearly three times as much. She exported her own tin, but five times as much came in from the tin isles of

[1] Above, p. 50 n. 2. There were earlier deliveries in S. Wales.

[2] Vol. I. p. 240–1.

the East. Cornwall must suffer that the metallurgical industries might live and compete. In no case could the Duchy have supplied copper enough for the world's cables, which were mostly made in Britain, nor tin enough for the world's tin-cans, made there also[1].

The loss of the ancient British export trade in tin and copper had been much more than outweighed by the growth of the export of coal. That, too, was an old trade which, when it passed 1,000,000 tons in the year of Queen Victoria's accession, had seemed a very great trade. In the early 'fifties it stood at 3–4,000,000 tons. After 1855, although there were some annual fluctuations, there was a smooth steady rise from quinquennium to quinquennium, varying between 22 and 34 per cent., which brought the figure to 20,120,000 for 1880–4 and to 23,500,000 for 1884–6. The value of the exported coal was relatively small, not more than 4 to 5 per cent. of the total of United Kingdom produce exported, but it had a use disproportionate to its money value. By providing bulk cargoes outwards to balance the incoming timber, ores, grains and other bulky raw materials and foodstuffs, it often saved British ships from having to sail half-filled or in ballast, and so kept down transport costs both out and back. There was profit to be made on both voyages and the coal went all over the world, though mainly to Europe and the Mediterranean[2]. Made by coal, launched near coal, loaded with coal, the iron and steel tramps from the North-East coast were keeping British shipping in its high position.

Weighty bulk cargoes of iron and steel in their rougher forms supplemented the coal cargoes. There was nothing smooth in the course of this trade. Being a trade in production goods, it moved by jerks in the years of rapid railway construction and general industrial activity overseas. Also it was liable to interruption from the growth of primary metallurgical industries of the English type abroad, and from the tariffs which usually accompanied that growth.

[1] See above, p. 104, and p. 91. Strictly speaking it was only the tin-plates not the tin-cans which were made there: above, p. 91. The export of tin-plates grew from 116,000 tons in 1870–4 to 257,000 tons in 1880–4, in spite of trade depression.

[2] In 1886, 18,400,000 out of 23,200,000 tons of coal exported went to Europe and the Mediterranean. See Thomas, D. A. (Lord Rhondda), "The Growth and Direction of our Foreign Coal Trade during the last Half-Century," a classical article, in *S.J.* 1903, p. 439–522.

After a period of what then seemed extraordinary expansion, down to 1853[1], came stagnation during the Crimean War; a jerk to a higher level, and stagnation again after the commercial crisis of 1857; and so forward. The greatest jerk occurs after the American Civil War, when railways were being built at speed in many countries, in America itself above all. There

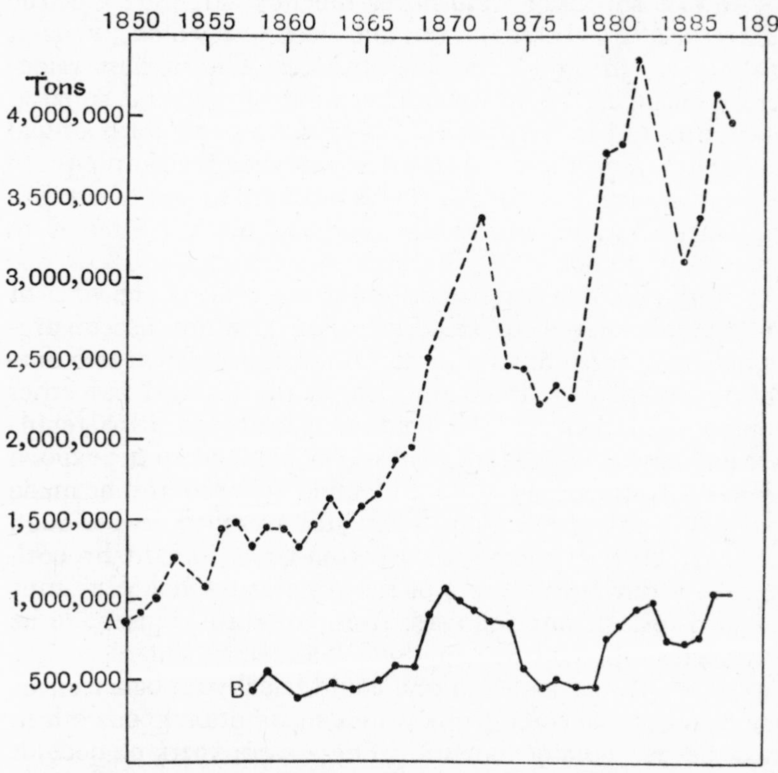

A. Exports of iron and steel, excluding machines, cutlery and hardware.
B. Exports of railway iron and steel.

followed the greatest check of the century, after the world-wide commercial collapse of 1873–4[2]. With 1880 came recovery. American purchases of British railway material revived, for the last time[3]; and although conditions of sale were so difficult that rail-makers were constrained to experiment in market-sharing with their continental rivals[4], the expansion of new markets,

[1] Cp. vol. I. p. 483, and above, p. 8. [2] See below, p. 381–3.
[3] In 1881 the United States took 294,000 tons: in 1884, 18,000 tons.
[4] Above, p. 151.

particularly within the Empire, raised the aggregate export for 1882 nearly a million tons above the great iron year 1872. And then another check, with a momentary fall below the level of the great year.

If the quantities of the iron and steel exports moved feverishly, their values moved more feverishly still. In values the great year and its successor were never touched. In 1872 pig iron had averaged £5. 1*s.* 10*d.* a ton and bars £12. 5*s.* 0*d.*; in 1873 pig £5. 17*s.* 3*d.* and bars £13. 10*s.* 0*d.* The highest yearly average for pig in the 'fifties had been only £3. 19*s.* 9*d.* in 1854, a war year, and in the 'sixties £3. 0*s.* 6*d.* in 1866, a post-war year. After 1875 the average price was always below £3. In the great exporting year 1882 it was only £2. 9*s.* 4*d.*: there was abundance of trade, but, as the saying is, not much fat on it. Hence the rail pool.

As producers of export values, the textile industries held their own, though they were steadily losing that numerical predominance in the industrial life of the country which they had achieved by 1850[1]. At no time could the mineral industries compare with them in the field of export. In 1850 textile yarns and fabrics of all kinds made up 60 per cent. of the exports of United Kingdom produce by value; in 1860 and again in 1870 they were 55 per cent. They still averaged 46 per cent. in 1880–4. Of textile exports the cotton goods formed throughout, except during the years of the American Civil War, fully two-thirds or, in round figures, from 30 to 40 per cent. of all the exports of the United Kingdom. Lancashire's markets were so widespread that losses in one could usually be balanced by gains in others; and its goods were consumption goods which had to be perpetually renewed. There were years of decline, but, with the great exception of 1861–5, they were due primarily to general price movements, which also affected the raw material. Even so, the percentage decline from one year to the next was never so much as six. When middling uplands cotton dropped from $10\frac{9}{16}$*d.* a lb. in 1872 to $6\frac{1}{4}$*d.* in 1876, the value of the exports fell only from £80,163,000 to £67,633,000; for, in spite of the depression after 1873, the quantities both of yarns and of manufactures exported had gone up somewhat in the interval.

Other textiles were rather less trustworthy as creators of

[1] Above, p. 29. Cp. Bowley, A. L., *England's Foreign Trade in the Nineteenth Century* (1893).

export values. Fashions and tariffs affected them more. Varied as their markets were, they had none to compare in size and permanence with the markets of India and China for cotton. The cotton trade, having come through its "dire calamity" of the 'sixties, showed itself again the backbone of the export trade of Britain, giving to it that cohesion and stability for which backbones exist.

The distribution of the greater or more significant export values in the quinquennium 1880–4 stood thus:

Annual average values, 1880–4

Of all British and Irish produce exported	£234,000,000
Of all yarns and textile fabrics	£108,000,000
(Of which cotton	£76,000,000)
Of coal, iron and steel	£38,000,000
Of hardware, cutlery and machinery	£15,000,000
Of articles of clothing	£10,500,000
Of foodstuffs	£10,000,000
Of chemicals and salt	£6,200,000

Those exports which were classified as going to British Possessions remained an oddly constant proportion of the whole, in spite of the growth of the Indian market and the economic expansion of the Dominions[1]. British Possessions had taken 35·1 per cent. of the exports in 1854; they took 34·5 per cent. in 1880–4. In the interval they had never, for any series of five years, taken more than 33·2 (1860–4) or less than 25·6 (1870–4). It is curious that in the five years of most furious trade and swollen prices the imperial percentage was least. It is not however very significant, because the chief trade fury was American and continental. Imperial trade was throughout valuable and expansive. From coal to the finest manufactures, the Empire absorbed the whole range of British produce. Tariffs checked the absorption very little, though the Dominions had gained complete control of them[2]. But foreign trade proper grew on the whole just as fast as imperial trade, sometimes a little faster, sometimes a little slower.

The United States had lost little of their importance as a market. Between 1830 and 1849 they took 15·7 per cent. of the

[1] The matter was investigated by the *R.C. on Depression of Trade*, from the Appendices to whose reports the figures are taken. Cp. Farrer, T. H., *Free Trade and Fair Trade* (3rd ed. 1886), p. 38.

[2] It is no part of the plan of this book to tell the political story of the emancipation of the Dominions: see *Camb. Hist. of the British Empire*, vol. VI (1930), *Canada*; Shann, E., *An Economic History of Australia* (1930).

British exports[1]. From 1850 to 1884 they took 12·6 per cent. But for the Civil War and the collapse in their purchasing power after 1873, there might have been little reduction. Some reduction could hardly have been avoided, because of their growing industrialism and protectionism. But the tariff was not high enough even at the close to divert British trade into indirect channels: the percentage was still 12·2 in 1880–4. British steel rails, though taxed, were going in freely: there was still a good market for fine cottons, linens, woollens and miscellaneous manufactures; for worsted dress-goods and coatings from Bradford an excellent market. America as yet did not make nearly enough of these to satisfy her needs[2].

France was never very accessible to British produce[3]. In every quinquennium, except 1870–4, when she was stocking up after war, she was definitely inferior to Australasia as a market. She took less absolutely; and what she took was cruder—more coal, less manufactures. But the combined market of Belgium, Holland, and the states which became Germany—it is necessary to combine them because so much of the trade of Rotterdam and Antwerp is transit trade for the Rhine—was from 1855 always more important than that of the United States. It never took less than 14·9 of the exports (in 1880–4): in the years of continental trade fury, 1870–4, it almost touched 20·0 per cent. The Belgian and German tariffs were most moderate at that time; the Dutch at all times.

Though never a really important buyer of British produce, France was a leading sharer in the English depot trade, the re-export of foreign and colonial produce, mainly raw materials and 'colonial wares.' This trade had always been valuable. It was most valuable in the 'sixties, when 17·5 per cent. of the imports of the United Kingdom were re-exported. In the late 'fifties, 1855–9, the percentage had been 13·6. Subsequently, on the five or ten years' average, it was always under 16·0. The rise in the 'sixties was connected with the addition to the old depot trade of the heavy new trade in colonial wool. For many years after that trade was established, little or no wool went from Australia to the continent direct[4]. All came under the hammer at the wool exchange in Coleman Street. Indeed it

[1] Cp. vol. I. p. 483.
[2] Cp. Cole, A. H., *The American Wool Manufacture* (1926), vol. II. ch. 28.
[3] For the Commercial Treaty of 1860 see below, p. 244–6.
[4] Cp. above, p. 7, 223.

was only at the very end of the period under review that direct shipment began. For 1880–4 the re-export was worth £15,300,000 a year out of a total re-export trade of £64,000,000. It was much the greatest single item in the total. Cotton, which came second, averaged only £5,500,000 and coffee, which came third, not £4,000,000. Rubber had already passed £1,000,000. The importance of the re-exports, not only in Anglo-French commercial relations, but in the whole Channel and North Sea trade, is shown by the proportions of British and Irish produce and of foreign and colonial produce absorbed by the French market and by the Belgian-Dutch-German market in 1880–4. In neither case was this proportion new: it had been much the same since the 'fifties.

Annual average imports from the United Kingdom, 1880–4

	British and Irish Produce	Foreign and Colonial Produce
By France	£16,500,000	£11,900,000
By Belgium-Holland-Germany	£34,000,000	£25,600,000

Most of this re-export trade went up the Thames to London and down it again for the narrow seas.

The early railway age had closed during one of the great swellings of the export trade in men—men mostly self-exported to places where, as they hoped, nature and society would add vastly to their productive value, besides offering them other and higher values. All Europe was affected; for if Europe had less famine it had more revolution than the British Isles. The Californian gold drew all impartially, and it was followed by the gold of Australia. But at that time, and for many years later, the British Isles were the chief source of supply of human export values. In the year of the forty-niners, 300,000 people left United Kingdom ports, 220,000 of them for the United States. For the next five years, 1850–4 inclusive, the average was over 325,000, the United States continuing to take more than 230,000 each year. This flood of emigration was mainly Irish. In 1852, the first complete year for which precise figures exist, 190,000 Irishmen emigrated from the Irish ports alone, and no doubt many thousands more from British ports. The movement into the United States was overwhelmingly Irish; that to Australasia was overwhelmingly British; and 1852, with its 89,000 travellers, still remains the peak year of emigration to Australasia. Judging by the figures of the next eight years, during which 365,000 emigrants went there, nearly three-quarters of whom were British, Britain's share of the emigration in the peak year can hardly have been less than 65,000[1].

Between 1853 and 1880 the aggregate outflow of British subjects from Britain was returned at 2,466,000. The permanent outflow was less. Down to 1876 the returns gave either no figures, or no satisfactory figures, of emigrants who came back. In early years such people were probably few. Most emigrants were very poor. Memories of the outward voyage, which in those days had points in common with the old slavers' 'middle passage,' would be deterrent[2]. But as travelling facilities improved, decent steamers replacing the detestable emigrant ships with advantages which it was "scarcely possible to exaggerate,"[3] there was coming as well as going. It became difficult to distinguish the emigrant proper from the long or short period experimenter in a new country. When the analysis of the immigrants by nationality had been made fairly complete[4], between 1876 and 1880, the difference between gross and net emigration of British subjects had become noticeably great. For the five years 1881–5, a period of renewed heavy outflow but also of quick inflow, more than a quarter must be subtracted from the gross figures. Even so the net emigration from Britain in that short period cannot have been much less than 675,000: the gross figure was 893,000[5].

An important transit business in European emigrants had developed, mainly along the line Hull to Liverpool. Even in the 'fifties Britain passed on Westwards some 35,000 foreign emigrants a year, and 55,000 in the 'seventies. In 1881–5 the annual average had reached 95,000. A new era of migration had begun for all Europe, with the opening up of the world and the social discomfort of those difficult years.

Not that emigration can be treated always, or even usually, as a mere product of distress. It was that in 1846–7, when there was famine in Europe and worse famine in Ireland and the

[1] The fullest statistical material is in *Papers relating to Emigration*, 1899 (CVII. 1). Cp. Johnson, S. C., *A Hist. of Emigration from the U.K. to North America* (1913); Carrothers, W. A., *Emigration from the British Isles* (1929).

[2] See Walpole, K. A., "The...movement...to remedy abuses on emigrant vessels...," *T.R.H.S.* 1932; *Gen. Rep. of the Colonial Land and Emigration Commission*, 1842 (XXV. 55).

[3] *R. of Emigration Commission*, 1870 (XVII. 111), p. 3.

[4] In order to distinguish emigrants of British and Irish origin from the continental emigrants who passed through England.

[5] The net emigration from the United Kingdom was 934,000.

Western Isles. It was not, when gold drew eager men to Bendigo and Ballarat. It was, in some degree, in 1869, a year of heavy emigration and dull trade. It certainly was not in 1872–3, years of still heavier emigration. Trade and agriculture were active enough in Britain; but being still more active in America and Australia they drew the capable, ambitious, and reasonably successful, besides some normal percentage of the distressful. Indeed there was some tendency for emigration to fluctuate with the export of capital, and so to coincide with industrial activity, since much capital was exported in the form of British capital goods. In the years 1876–8 there was a very low net emigration. At that time export of capital was stagnant. It is even probable that on the balance there was a net import[1].

The mass of the emigration was individual and unorganised, although official and officious organisations to promote it were always at work, especially in times of gloom. Philanthropic people might help out-of-work ribbon weavers from Coventry, or hand-loom weavers from Ayrshire, to get away from the country. Trade unions often kept emigration funds; but there is no reason to think that they financed very much emigration. The London Female Emigration Society of 1850, the Female Middle Class Emigration Society of 1861, and similar private organisations later, did work of mixed value in a limited field. Poor Law Authorities were empowered to help the destitute to emigrate. They did; but the number helped dwindled to 36 in 1864–5 and, after rising to some hundreds in 1871–5, was down again to 23 in 1878[2]. The only large scale and really important official operations were those carried on by the Colonial Land and Emigration Commissioners between 1847 and 1872. When the Commissioners handed over their remaining functions to the Board of Trade in the latter year, they explained that since 1847 they had selected and assisted 340,000 "government emigrants," of whom perhaps 240,000 would be British[3].

[1] See the discussion in Hobson, C. K., *The Export of Capital* (1914), p. 204. Hobson argues in favour of the view that there was an average net yearly import of £6,666,000 for the three years, more money being brought home from foreign investments sold than was freshly invested abroad. See below, p. 235.

[2] Johnson, *op. cit.* p. 59, 72, 81, 89–90, 255, 257.

[3] *Report*, 1873 (XVIII. 295): the last of an annual series. The British proportion is uncertain. It is based on the average proportion of British to Irish emigrants from the United Kingdom throughout the period: *Papers relating to Emigration*, 1899; as above.

For fourteen years before the Commission was wound up it had been running at low pressure. Three-quarters of its work had been done between November, 1847 and the end of 1858. This work was almost entirely Australian, with a little for the Cape and the Falkland Islands. In its most active year, 1854, the Commission had chartered 127 ships and sent 41,000 men women and children to Australia[1]. Its funds came, on Gibbon Wakefield principles, from the sale of Australian land. Of £4,864,000 spent between 1847 and 1870, all but £523,000, which the emigrants themselves found, was drawn from this source. As the colonies became more completely self-governing and more self-conscious, in the later 'sixties, they ceased to vote money from their land revenue, or even, as in the case of South Australia, used money intended to finance emigration for other purposes. That is all matter of Commonwealth history[2]. The historian of Britain has to record that by 1870 assisted emigration was out of fashion. The Commissioners themselves were reflecting most sensibly that, had government funds been available, emigrants and their friends would never have raised the £15,000,000 or so spent up to date on transatlantic migration[3]. The Commissioners were ripening for abolition; but they had done good work in their time, and had believed in it[4].

The export of men had always been connected, but in intricate and varying ways, with the export of British capital. The export of capital in its turn was linked with the export of capital goods; but was far from identical with it. Some capital emigrants took with them, usually not in the form of goods. Small as individual takings normally were, the aggregate must have been considerable. When British manufacturers were spreading the new industrialism in Europe, during the early years of the century, they had often taken their skilled men and their money too. Railway building on the continent in the great days of Thomas Brassey and Morton Peto (1840–70) involved heavy exports of capital and migrations of labour and directing

[1] *Report*, 1854–5 (XVII. 1), *Report*, 1873, p. 81 and Johnson, *op. cit.* p. 234.

[2] See Shann, E., *The Economic History of Australia*, esp. ch. IX, "Free Colonies and Assisted Migration." Cp. the criticism of colonial policies in *Report*, 1870 (XVII. 111), p. 3.

[3] *Report*, 1870, p. 3.

[4] So had John Stuart Mill. In all the editions of his *Principles of Political Economy* the passage in praise of Wakefield and of colonisation as a "national undertaking" stood; book V. ch. 11. § 14.

personnel, large at first though soon dwindling; but very little permanent emigration[1]. Railway building in India also involved migration of skilled men and a little permanent emigration. There were those who served the East Indian Railway from father to son[2]; but India was a land already full of men who understood clerical work and of others who could learn machines. It was principally in America and the Dominions that capital export brought men, accompanied men, and followed men—though distress emigration might have a very scanty accompaniment of capital. The export of capital, so far as is known, was at its peak in 1872. The estimate for that year is £83,500,000. Emigration was at its peak, for that decade, in 1872 and 1873, having begun to move up in the slack trade years 1867–9 when capital exports were low. The net emigration was very low in 1876–8; and in those years the estimated export of capital account shows a small adverse balance, as has been seen. Britain, the estimate suggests, had rather less than nothing for foreign investment when the necessary steps had been taken to adjust a trade balance upset by the disastrous harvests of the late 'seventies and by the blocking of export channels by war, the growth of foreign industries, tariffs and the depreciation of silver[3]. In effect, she had to sell a trifle of her foreign investments to pay her way. Something similar had happened, though the facts are more obscure, in 1847–8, when famine called for abnormal imports and revolution shut European markets. It was not to happen again until after 1914. In 1879 and 1880 the heavy flow of men was resumed. It might be called a distress flow, though it was not of the old tragic sort. They were building 10,000 miles of railway a year in the United States and wanted men. Meanwhile the capital position was being readjusted. From 1881, the country was at least able to keep the greater part of the earnings of its foreign investments abroad for fresh investment[4]. More it was not in a position to do at

[1] Brassey's enterprises are tabulated (after Sir A. Helps, *Life of Thomas Brassey*) in Jenks, L. H., *The Migration of British Capital to* 1875 (1927), App. p. 419.

[2] Cp. Kipling, Rudyard, *Among the Railway Folk*.

[3] The estimates are those of Hobson, *op. cit.* Cp. throughout Jenks, *op. cit.*, where it is argued that the adverse balance continued to 1880 (p. 414). For tariffs and silver see below, p. 249, 339.

[4] A mere statistical statement of the position: from 1881 to 1911 the fresh investment abroad is estimated not quite to have equalled the yield of existing foreign investments. Actually much of that yield was of course brought home by individuals, and new investments, slightly less in amount than the annual yield of the old ones, were made by other individuals.

this time. Emigration meanwhile reached another peak in 1883, to slide down again with the American crash of May 1884.

The link between the export of capital and the export of capital goods was not always strong or direct. No doubt the £163,000,000 worth of railroad iron of all sorts and the many locomotives exported in the thirty years 1856–85 were mostly associated with railway investment overseas. In one case, that of the Indian railways, it is known that a third of all the capital raised for them down to the 'eighties was spent on British rails and their carriage to the East[1]. But in the triangular workings of foreign trade, rails and other capital goods might go to countries in which the British investor was not interested. And such goods go largely to all countries in the ordinary way of trade, together with consumption goods like textiles, to pay for food and raw materials, even when no fresh investment is being made.

At least half the foreign investments were always in government securities. If these went directly in British goods at all—and the trade triangle might easily so work that a loan in America would show in the returns as an extra export of cotton piece goods to the East—they might go in Armstrong's guns, saddlery, uniform cloth, or luxuries for foreign potentates: consumption goods and destruction goods. Some part of the Egyptian debt was no doubt represented by a gilded locomotive, decorated to the design of the Slade Professor of Fine Art at Cambridge, which Robert Stephenson & Co. built for Said Pasha in 1862. A more workmanlike engine which they built for the Danish State Railways in 1868 may well have reflected British investment in the Danish 5 per cents. of 1864[2]; for governments sometimes buy genuine capital goods with their borrowed money. All that can be stated with perfect accuracy are the economic commonplaces that British foreign investment was covered, over a period of years, by British exports of goods and miscellaneous shipping and commercial services; that the goods were sometimes connected directly with the investment, but much more often not; and that, as many of the services were rendered overseas by ships, banks, and domiciled trading Britons, payment for them might be reinvested there and would not affect British trade returns, unless and until profits from it began to come back in the form of imports.

[1] Worked out by Jenks, *op. cit.* p. 227.

[2] For these locomotives see Warren, J. G. H., *A century of locomotive building* (1923), p. 411, 413.

The net addition to the stock of British capital invested overseas between the early 'fifties and the middle 'eighties was round about £1,000,000,000. By the latter date, with the growth of statistical material and method, estimation was not liable to very serious error, when in skilled hands. Sir Robert Giffen, in 1885, reckoned the total of United Kingdom capital invested abroad at £1,302,000,000. (For comparison, it may be noted that he estimated the capital invested at home to be seven times as much.) What the amount was in the early 'fifties is not known. Estimates have varied between £200,000,000 and more than £400,000,000. As the tendency of inquiry has been to reduce them, it may be wise to adopt a speculative maximum of £300,000,000. Whatever figure is accepted stands for the value of the investments immediately before tolerably accurate trade statistics begin, with the abandonment of the old 'official' values of imports in 1854[1].

By that time the pause in the outflow of capital which had occurred at the end of the early railway age was over. The Californian and the Australian gold were coming in. Europe was calm. In England the sharp upward movement of wholesale prices was under weigh which would set the average level of 1856–70 25 per cent. above that of 1849–51[2]. In 1852 Thomas Brassey had taken contracts for 264 miles of French railway. A little later there was at least one English director on the board of nineteen different French companies[3]. Contractors, the great contractors, were ceasing to be called in by companies. They were devising railway schemes for Europe and arranging for companies to be born to finance them. Into the American railways however investors put their money direct. Brassey did not work in the United States, though with Peto and Betts he was engaged in the disastrous business of the Canadian Grand Trunk; but it was believed in 1857 that £80,000,000 of American railroad stock was held in England[4].

[1] Facts and discussions in Seyd, E., *Journal of the Society of Arts*, XXIV. 309 (1875); Nash, R. L., *A short inquiry into the profitable nature of our investments* (1880); Giffen, Sir R., *The Growth of Capital* (1885); *The Excess of Imports* (*Essays in Finance, First Series*); Bowley, A. L., *England's Foreign Trade*; Stamp, Sir J. C., *British Incomes and Property* (with criticism of Giffen); Hobson, *op. cit.*; Jenks, *op. cit.* All the calculations depend on the accuracy of the trade statistics. After the abandonment of official values of imports in 1854, values computed according to a plan introduced by James Wilson were employed until 1870. From 1870 import values are those declared by merchants, as export values had long been. (See Bourne, *S.J.* 1871; Giffen, *S.J.* 1882.) So estimates which aim at a high degree of accuracy do not go back beyond 1870.

[2] See the price diagram, p. 378, below. [3] Jenks, p. 165. [4] Hobson, p. 128.

Early misadventures in America had been forgotten. Besides railways and the federal securities of the United States, those of a dozen of the constituent states were regularly quoted in London, together with issues of Brazil, Buenos Ayres, Cuba, Chili, Granada, Ecuador, Mexico, Peru, Venezuela and Guatemala[1]. All the while investment went on within the Empire and in European securities, particularly French and Spanish. Between 1855 and 1865 came such enterprises for the spread of industrial civilisation as the various continental gas companies and the water-works of Amsterdam and Berlin[2]. And there were mines of all sorts everywhere.

The world-wide commercial crisis of 1857[3] was specially destructive in the United States. Before investors had completely recovered confidence, the outbreak of the War of Secession led to a scramble to get rid of American securities. Investing England distrusted the North; with the help of investing France it found £3,000,000 for the South—and lost every penny. Its savings had been diverted more and more towards India, especially towards Dalhousie's Indian railways, since 1857. The railways were being built with a government guarantee of interest to the companies, and the security was attractive from every point of view; it was imperial, trade-making, and secure. Apart from the railways, the government of India was a constant and heavy borrower. By 1870 the colonial stocks proper ordinarily listed came to upwards of £45,000,000[4], nearly all of which was held in the United Kingdom. Ten years later, the colonial government securities mainly held in the United Kingdom were put at £98,000,000; the Indian government and railway securities similarly held at £196,000,000[5].

Confidence in the United States soon came back after 1865. Securities of the states were no longer in favour[6], but those of the Union and the new railway network more than replaced

[1] The securities quoted in the *Economist* are taken as those in which dealings were really current. The years are 1853–7. Guatemala appears in January, 1857.

[2] The enterprises which Herbert Spencer cited in controversy with Matthew Arnold to prove that England was not poor in ideas. Cp. Sombart, W., *Händler und Helden* (1915), p. 10, where the case is quoted as an illustration of England's *Krämergeist*.

[3] Below, p. 368 sqq.

[4] *Economist*, January 8, 1870.

[5] Nash, *op. cit.* chs. 2 and 3.

[6] Those of Pennsylvania, Virginia and Massachusetts were however still regularly listed in 1870.

them. By 1869 foreigners, and for this purpose most foreigners were British, were believed to have nearly £300,000,000 invested in the country[1]: 300,000 tons of railway iron were shipped there that year.

During the decade which ended in the second world-wide crisis, of 1873, borrowing by governments and borrowing for railways, to quote only the pre-eminent groups of borrowers, were constant and furious. There was greedy blind capital to spare for everyone. France had become a great lender under the Second Empire. Perhaps she had £500,000,000 abroad to Britain's £800,000,000 by 1870[2]. Paris rivalled London as a place of emission. The less reputable borrowing nations could play one off against the other and float their loans simultaneously in both. The Ottoman debt and the Egyptian debt, heavy with misgovernment and the future, took their modern form in these years. Brassey signed a contract for the Central Argentine Railway in 1864, and one for the Callao Docks in 1870. In 1868, the Association of Foreign Bondholders came into existence to watch doubtful foreign governments and keep the home government sensitive to bondholding opinion[3].

Climax came after the Prussian War. Helped by London, Amsterdam, and the sale of some of her £500,000,000 invested abroad, France easily paid Bismarck. Britain took a good deal of what she had to sell. American railways were being built faster than ever. The new Germany, victorious and enriched, was full of ordered, with some disordered, activity. The canal was open. The cables were being laid. India and the colonies were borrowing handsomely. As a Dominion, Canada was taking far more than she had taken when disunited[4]. Most of the borrowers were sound and honourable. Britain came through the financial bad weather of 1873 better than any of her neigh-

[1] Wells, D. A., *Report of the Special Commissioner of Revenue*, 1869, p. xxvii, quoted in Hobson, *op. cit.* p. 133.

[2] For France see Say, J. B. L., *Rapport...sur le paiement de l'indemnité de guerre* (reprinted in his *Finances de la France*, vol. I); Giffen, *The Cost of the Franco-German War* (*Essays in Finance, First Series*); O'Farrell, H. H., *The Franco-German War Indemnity* (1913). The rough estimate for Britain is based on Giffen, *The Growth of Capital*.

[3] See in general the *S.C. on Loans to Foreign States*, 1875, XI. For the Association of Foreign Bondholders and its Council see the evidence of Hyde Clarke its secretary, Q. 607 *sqq*. Cp. Feis, H., *Europe the World's Banker* (1930), p. 113–14.

[4] For her comparatively small borrowings before 1867 see Jenks, *op. cit.* p. 205–6.

bours: she had experience of that kind of thing. But when she was going over the broken spars and split sails in 1874–5, it was said that there were £76,000,000 of foreign loans in default, besides £165,000,000 of doubtful Spanish debt, of which a third was held "in this country."[1] The worst was a series of loans of the nominal value of £10,000,000 floated down devious and muddy channels by Honduras, Santo Domingo, Costa Rica, and Paraguay; on the whole of which, "with one unimportant exception," no interest had been paid except out of the original capital[2].

For ten years after 1875 the export of capital was slack, as has been seen. Investments overseas increased steadily, except in 1876–8; but it is probable that the investment of 1876–86 was not so great as that of 1872–3; and it is certain that this investment of 1876–86 was very much less than the total income from capital overseas during that period[3].

The ordinary Englishman was worrying about the balance of trade in the late 'seventies as he had not done for many generations. He was alarmed at the steadily growing 'adverse' balance, the arithmetical excess of imports over exports; and there was much wild abuse of statistics. Few men were so simple as the politician from the antipodes of twenty years later who supposed that this balance was paid in "golden sovereigns"[4]; but many fancied that it must be met by heavy sales of securities. Statistical science, in the person of Sir Robert Giffen, a little bewildered to find its "special study so little advanced," asserted roundly in 1882 that there was "no question at all of the nation bringing home capital in recent years,"[5] and proceeded to give such statistical precision as is possible to the facts of the trade balance; to show how—arithmetical misconceptions apart—the excess imports represent mainly earnings of investments and earnings of shipping, with earnings of banking, insurance and commercial service generally[6]. Giffen

[1] *S.C. on Loans to Foreign States*, Q. 5950.

[2] *Ibid.* p. xlv. Jenks makes far too much of the scabrous and picturesque story of these loans. They were not really representative of the foreign investment of the period and were trifling in amount: see below, p. 323 n. 4.

[3] Hobson, *op. cit.* p. 204, makes it not much more than a quarter.

[4] R. J. Seddon, Prime Minister of New Zealand, in 1903.

[5] "The Use of Import and Export Statistics," *S.J.* 1882, reprinted in *Essays in Finance* (*Second Series*) in which the quotations occur on p. 135, 195.

[6] Giffen only gave precision to the argument of the *Economist* of 1851, quoted above, p. 10. He was criticising semi-popular discussions, *e.g.* in *The*

did not point out that there had in fact been a sudden and quite abnormal excess of imports in 1876–8. Such an excess was not approached again until 1891–3[1]. If his "recent years" went back to the former triennium, as presumably they did, though there was indeed no question of bringing home large amounts of capital annually, there was probably a little bringing home as has been shown; and his estimate of the amount invested abroad "in recent years," if intended as a net estimate, was almost certainly too sanguine. Clumsily, ignorantly, and with much misunderstanding, the balance of trade controversialists were pointing to a real change in Britain's international position. "The export of a capital surplus was over. Her further investments were to come for a generation from the accruing profits of those which had already been made."[2]

John Stuart Mill, the economist of the age, died in 1873. Through seven editions in his lifetime and others after his death, his *Principles of Political Economy* reiterated his satisfaction that it was now hardly necessary, "at least in our own country," to do more than state without much argument the falsity of the "doctrine of Protection to Native Industry."[3] "The importation of foreign commodities, in the common course of traffic, never takes place except when it is, economically speaking, a national good." Even speaking politically, and considering war risks, the conclusion is the same: the more sources of food a nation draws on the safer it is. "It is ridiculous to found a general system of policy on so improbable a danger as that of being at war with all the nations of the world at once; or to suppose that, even if inferior at sea, a whole country could be blockaded like a town." (It will be noted that "a country" is an island, cosmopolitan as Mill conceived himself to be.) One exception he made, which became notorious as the case of the infant industry, the industry which government, "especially in a young and rising nation," may with reason protect "temporarily," provided that the industry is "in itself perfectly

Quarterly Review, July, 1881 and the *Nineteenth Century*, August, 1881 (Sir E. Sullivan). For more serious discussion see Bourne, S., "The growing preponderance of imports," *S.J.* 1877; Newmarch, "On the Progress of the Foreign Trade of the United Kingdom," *S.J.* 1878; Seyd, E., *The Decline of Prosperity* (1879).

[1] The average annual excess in 1876–8 was £128,000,000: in 1874–5 it had been £81,000,000: for 1879–88 it was £101,000,000.

[2] Jenks, *op. cit.* p. 333. Cp. n. 3 to p. 235, above.

[3] Book v. ch. 10, § 1.

suitable to the circumstances of the country." List and his national political economy of productive forces, as opposed to exchange values, Mill always ignored. It is not apparent that he realised how large a concession he had made to national economics, false and less false. Many nations feel young at times and claim the privileges of youth.

No one supposed, however, that Great Britain was "young and rising" in 1850–86. She was old, risen, yet still rising. The exception did not apply. It was only a matter for debate in the schools. Successive chancellors of the exchequer—Gladstone and again Gladstone and shadows of Gladstone like Northcote —had the rather simple task of pulling down surviving tolls on the entry of foreign commodities, when our expanding revenue or economies in the spending departments made the abandonment of receipts from them easy. As a great number of the tolls surviving in 1850–2 brought in no revenue, they could be abandoned with a superb gesture of freedom. In this way the home producers of "bandstring twist," blacking, "catlings,"[1] and many other things, were exposed to a not very shrewd blast of competition by Gladstone in 1853.

The only raw materials of importance on which duties remained in 1852 were timber, copper, lead and tin. The duties on all four were by this time trifling[2]. The timber duties worked out at 2 per cent. *ad valorem* and upwards. They alone survived the budget of 1853, low but very intricate. Teak, shovel hilts, and most tree-nails were free, and there was a preference for British timber throughout the schedules. The preference went in 1860 and the duties in 1866, as has been seen[3]. No doubt they would have gone earlier had not the vast import of timber made even 1*s.* or 2*s.* a load yield a revenue which chancellors could not lightly abandon.

After the controversies and suspensions of the famine years, the corn duty had settled down, as from February 1, 1849, at 1*s.* a quarter; that on flour at $4\frac{1}{2}$*d.* a cwt.[4] These so-called registration duties Gladstone did not touch, either in 1853 or in 1860: they were a legacy from his great chief. But after twenty years, he allowed Robert Lowe, then serving under him at the exchequer, to abandon them by 32 and 33 Vict. c. 14,

[1] *I.e.* catgut strings, as for violins.

[2] *Customs Tariff of the United Kingdom from* 1800 *to* 1897, Section 1845–6 to 1852–3.

[3] Above, p. 220.

[4] See vol. I. p. 498.

the budget Act of 1869[1]. With the corn duties proper went duties on rice, sago, tapioca and vermicelli. The imports of all were growing yearly: revenue lost an expanding source of easily raised money, the immediate loss being £900,000. Lowe was giving taxes away right and left that year, and the economic impropriety of this sole surviving tax on "raw material in its very rawest state" annoyed him. But abolition did not increase the English depot trade in corn, as he had hoped; and a political thinker who had not the least hankering after protection wrote in 1888—"it is pretty certain that if the duty were still in existence, it would now be retained."[2]

A few food duties besides that on corn escaped Gladstone's axe in 1853. He cut away those taxes on foreign imported fish which recalled an ancient rivalry with the Dutch in the fisheries; also duties on cider, because when made at home it paid no excise, and on honey. But he left small duties on raw fruit and eggs, with those on the agricultural manufactures butter and cheese, biscuit, and bread[3]. The complex preferential duties on sugar he did not touch. They had been fixed for six years in the interest of the West Indies, after a fight between Lord George Bentinck and the Whigs in 1848[4]. Next year, however, when financing the Crimean War, he carried through the equalisation of duties on foreign and colonial sugar which the Whigs had planned; but wanting revenue, he equalised rather by raising the colonial duty than by lowering the foreign[5]. For the next twenty years, while nearly all the surviving odds and ends of food duties were abolished, mainly in 1860, those on sugar and all sugary things remained an important source of revenue. They were reduced as opportunity offered, in the interests of the consumer, but they were never made very simple. There was much advocacy of their abolition. Finally Stafford Northcote abolished them in 1874, immediately after his chief, Disraeli, had expressed the opinion that the number of distinct sources of revenue was unwisely small[6]. For over

[1] In 1864 (by 27 and 28 Vict. c. 18) the *1s.* a quarter had been changed into the nearly equivalent *3d.* a cwt.

[2] Buxton, S., *Finance and Politics, an Historical Study*, II. 93.

[3] He also left the duty on hops, as there was a, not quite equivalent, excise on home-grown hops.

[4] Vol. I. p. 499.

[5] The duties were intricate: see *Customs Tariff of the U.K.* p. 219–20 and Buxton, *op. cit.* I. 152.

[6] Speech at Newport Pagnell, February 4, 1874, quoted in Buxton, II. 187 n.

a quarter of a century the United Kingdom consumed untaxed sugar.

The duties on manufactures which survived 1853 had for the most part no perceptible protective quality. Foreign china, earthenware, flint glass, or manufactures of bronze cannot have been excluded by a levy of 10*s*. on the hundredweight; nor cotton gloves by one of 3*d*. a dozen pairs; not even grand pianos by £3 each; nor "accordions, commonly called Chinese" by 1*s*. on "the hundred notes."[1] Ordinary cottons and woollens and all 'half-manufactures' such as yarns were free. Machinery, cutlery, and iron and steel manufactures paid 2*s*. 6*d*. a hundredweight. Such obstacles to trade may occasionally have diverted an order into home channels, but not often. More serious were the duties on luxuries like lace, cambric handkerchiefs, carpets (6*d*. a square yard) and shawls. That on paper, at 2½*d*. a lb., was no doubt definitely protective for all the common sorts. So were, and were meant to be, the long untouched series of silk duties—turbans 3*s*. each; dresses 30*s*. each; plain silk ribbons 6*d*. a lb.; with many more specific rates; and on all silks, not otherwise specified, 15 per cent. *ad valorem*.

As the world's trade lines lay in the 'fifties, the protective or possibly protective British duties interfered almost exclusively with that section which ran from Paris to London. Hence the importance of the Anglo-French treaty of 1860, the 'Cobden' treaty, combined with the budget policy of that year. How far the treaty made the policy or the policy the treaty, or to which side or to which persons the greater credit is to be assigned for the agreement, need not be discussed here[2]. Treaty and policy together, when the policy had been rounded off by the budget of 1861[3], put the United Kingdom into a position which no kingdom had occupied before since kings first took presents from visiting merchants or blackmailed the caravans. From October 1, 1861, when the paper duties ran out, no foreign manufacture whatever appeared in the British tariff except flour, alcoholic drinks, manufactured tobacco and sugar, gold and

[1] *Customs Tariff of the U.K.* p. 826.

[2] The points are fully discussed in Dunham, A. L., *The Anglo-French Treaty of Commerce of* 1860 (*University of Michigan*, 1830). Cp. the older accounts in Morley, J., *Life of Richard Cobden*, ch. XI–XIV and *Life of Gladstone*, II. 18 *sqq*.

[3] Which abolished the paper duties (24 Vict. c. 20). The great budget Act of 1860 was 23 and 24 Vict. c. 110. For the paper duties, custom and excise, see Buxton, *op. cit.* I. 259–68. In the political cant of the day they were the "taxes on knowledge." At most, they were only lightly protective.

silver plate, playing cards and dice. It is true that "ships with all their tackle...built of wood" paid 1*s.* a ton for admission to the British register; but that really was a fee and was levied on colonial as well as on foreign ships. Flour was no longer taxed after 1869, nor sugar after 1874. The ship registration fee had gone in 1866. Gold and silver plate were not free until 1890. Except for these, all the classic luxuries of the ages could come in freely, purple and fine linen, carpets of Ispahan, silk and cloth of gold, "and broideries of intricate design and printed hangings in enormous bales." The dice, those wicked dice, had paid a guinea a pair. They were freed, as it happened, when a Derby was prime minister and in the year of the second Reform Bill which gave the artisan his vote, by 30 and 31 Vict. c. 82. Remained the playing cards.

An Anglo-French commercial treaty meant reductions and reorganisations of the duties on wines and spirits. So it had been in 1786, and so it was again. This was what Britain really gave, revenue; and with it a promise not to prohibit or tax the export of coal. Had there been no negotiations, she would probably not have modified her wine-duties at that time, or exactly in the way she did; nor would she have made promises about coal. Also she might perhaps have retained some of the duties on luxury manufactures; but their abolition was in the direct line of a policy to which she was already committed. So was the unhindered export of the coal[1]. The pledge not to interfere with the export however had a political, rather than an economic implication, an implication which, in the year after the volunteer movement, some parties disliked[2].

France gave in return a great deal more than her protectionists approved. She abandoned the antiquated policy of prohibition, which had affected many of the finer British manufactures, and pledged herself not to levy on any of them—fine or coarse—more than 30 per cent. *ad valorem.* In the tariff

[1] Sir T. H. Farrer (later Lord Farrer), who was Assistant Secretary to the Board of Trade in 1860 and Secretary from 1865 to 1886, always maintained that "what we did was, with one doubtful exception, what we should have done, and ought to have done, had France made no relaxation in her duties" (*Free Trade versus Fair Trade*, p. 278). The exception was the wine duties, which gave "some advantage to French wines over the wines of other countries"; led to retaliation by Spain; and were eventually modified so as to admit the heavier peninsular wines at the same rates as the French—but not till 1886, by 49 and 50 Vict. c. 41.

[2] Among them the Prince Consort, who thought that we were 'giving the Emperor our coals and iron,' *Life*, v. 13, 23.

finally adopted the average was a good deal less; but it was at least as high as those protective silk duties which Britain had abandoned completely. As industrialism had made great progress in France since 1848, and as in many fine manufactures she equalled or excelled Britain, the result of the treaty was less remarkable than some had hoped and others have suggested[1]. There was a satisfactory expansion of trade, but part of it—it is impossible to say how much—would have come in any case. A large prompt increase in the export of British woollens balanced a corresponding increase in the import of French silks and Paris wares. In time, a substantial export of the finer British cottons grew up; but in 1868–9 cotton exports to France were worth little more than those to Holland, and less than those to Syria and Palestine. Though more French wines and brandies came in, the English did not become heavy claret drinkers. Whiskey, for years a favourite navvies' drink, was now coming into fashion, like the Highlands. France hardly increased her consumption of British iron and steel. In short, the direct trade between the two countries was not revolutionised. Exports of British produce averaged £6,000,000 in 1855–9. In 1860 they were £5,000,000. For 1861–4 they averaged £8,700,000 and for 1866–70, £11,000,000. To this must be added the re-export trade to France, which in the late 'sixties was actually greater than the direct trade, because of France's huge takings of colonial wool. The wool and the coal paid for an important part of Britain's very heavy French imports[2].

The 'Cobden' treaty was denounced in 1872, when France, fallen into that post-bellum mood in which the non-economic arguments for protection always have most power[3], was turning back towards an inherited and only half-interrupted system of full tariffs. It had been the first of a famous series of commercial treaties negotiated in a free trade spirit, which usually contained the most favoured nation clause. Britain alone con-

[1] *E.g.* Buxton, *op. cit.* I. 236.

[2] United Kingdom imports from France, 1866–70, averaged £35,000,000 a year; exports of British produce to France £11,000,000; and exports of foreign and colonial produce (mainly wool) £12,000,000. The imports contain freight charges, the exports do not. But freight would not nearly account for the difference. In the trade triangle, Britain was paying France by exporting to some third country.

[3] The mood of nationalism at war, convinced "dass alle internationalen Wirtschaftsbeziehungen ein notwendiges Übel sind, das wir so klein wie möglich machen sollen." Sombart, *Händler und Helden* (1915), p. 133.

cluded eight major treaties of this type in the 'sixties[1]. There were many more among the European powers, a whole network of them. The clause so worked as to extend any negotiated tariff concession to the whole group of 'most favoured' nations[2]. Side by side with treaty-made concessions, there was much autonomous lowering of duties as in Britain, though nowhere with such complete free-trading logic. War made France pause. In 1879 falling prices, gathering agrarian competition from overseas, and a need for revenue made Bismarck pause. Everywhere the economic protectionism of the natural man, and the political protectionism of the statesman thinking in terms of war-risk, asserted themselves: surely Bismarck knew! Even if started for agrarian reasons, as a war food-insurance fee perhaps, an upward tariff movement never missed manufactures. Russia, whose trade had not got very free, began such an upward movement in 1881; France in 1882. Italy, Austria-Hungary, and others were also moving. Yet the work done in Europe during this short era of falling tariffs and commercial treaties had not been completely undone by 1885–6. Prohibition as a habit was dead. Duties, a cautious commentator wrote, were "on the whole lower than before 1860."[3]

That was in Europe. The United States came out of their Civil War with a war tariff, high and unsystematic. During the free trade years, the directors of their policy had no sympathy with a creed which in America had been professed principally by slave-owning agrarian Southerners—'rebels.' Through fluctuating policies, which fluctuated little on the main issue, they had built up, by the 'eighties, a tariff wall such as Europe did not know[4]. The European mind had not yet conceived of a system under which cotton yarn paid 5*d*. a lb. and 20 per cent. *ad valorem*, or bituminous coal 3*s*. 1½*d*. a ton. That some fantastic impositions on fine manufactures accompanied these fiscal extravagances lower down the scale need not be said. Duties as a whole ranged from 35 to 100 per cent. *ad valorem*. Yet many manufactures, fine and coarse, still got over the wall.

In America and other continents, the British dominions,

[1] See the list in Levi, *History of British Commerce*, p. 511. The most-favoured nation clause has a heavy literature of its own, *e.g.* Schraut, *System der Handelsverträge und der Meistbegünstigung* (1886); Glier, *Die Meistbegünstigungsklausel* (1905).

[2] See the eloquent passage in Morley's *Cobden*, II. 342–5.

[3] Farrer, *op. cit.* (ed. of 1886), p. 61.

[4] See Taussig, F. W., *The tariff history of the United States*.

those "young and rising nations," were doing what Mill had almost encouraged them to do, taking care of their infants. Across that undefended line, Canada had the example of her southern neighbour. The Canadian tariff of 1879 was decidedly higher than the French or Italian, much higher than the German, very much higher than the Belgian or Dutch. Like the United States, Canada taxed bituminous coal heavily. Unlike the United States, she taxed anthracite coal rather more heavily. On typical British products, such as steel rails cottons and woollens, she levied duties which worked out at from 15 to 30 per cent. Australasian tariffs, with the sole exception of that of New South Wales, were also moving upwards in the 'seventies and early 'eighties[1].

Meanwhile the growing industrialism of the whole civilised world, with the absence of any obstacle to the entry of foreign produce into the British market, was producing its natural result. British imports contained a somewhat increased percentage of manufactured and part-manufactured goods. In the circumstances, the percentage increase over a quarter of a century was remarkably slow. It was[2]:

	Percentage of imports fully manufactured	Value million £	Percentage fully manufactured and part manufactured	Value million £
1855–9	6	10	14	24
1865–9	9	27	17	48
1875–9	13	48	20	75
1880–4	13	55	20	83

There is an upward jerk in the 'sixties. At the same time the finished manufactures become more than half of the total. The duties on the fine old luxury goods from abroad, which could always compete in an open field[3], have gone. A little later, competition begins to be felt in the home market for straightforward products of modern metallurgy. Even in the 'fifties, rail contracts in Spain had been lost to Belgium[4]. By 1867 an ironmaster is lamenting that the Belgians have "superseded us everywhere." They have sent iron to America and have even

[1] All the tariffs of the period are conveniently summarised in Farrer, *op. cit.*

[2] Based on the value figures compiled for the *R.C. on Depression of Trade*, I. 130.

[3] Above, p. 16–17.

[4] Jenks, *Migration of British Capital*, p. 192.

secured an order from St Thomas' Hospital "for what are called girders."[1] It was the fault of a trade union, he said: but that is as it may be. Next year the import returns included for the first time a distinct heading for 'iron and steel wrought or manufactured.' In 1868–9 the amount averaged £400,000. In 1875–9 it averaged £1,700,000 and in 1880–4, £2,600,000. Throughout the whole period, the silk and fine wool fabrics, mainly French, varied between about a third and about two-fifths of all the imported manufactures, by value. France also sent a varied selection of unspecified luxuries, and from £1,000,000 to £2,000,000 worth of gloves. Towards the close there was growing import of a most miscellaneous kind from Germany—some of the silk; much of the steel; masses of toys of every kind, including nearly all the lead soldiers of the nurseries; all the best chemicals and appliances of the laboratories; all the lead pencils worth using; with cheap and sometimes nasty imitations of British cutlery and other wares, which gave weight to the half-informed sneer of the middle 'eighties about things 'made in Germany.'[2]

It was most natural that after the trade collapse of the early 'seventies, and during the continued puzzling commercial and industrial difficulties which followed, plain men should begin to put the question—is it 'fair' to keep open market for nations who are closing theirs? Some of the plain men made much of the less desirable element in the imports, which in fact was trifling. Others put further questions, of varying relevance to the problems of commercial policy. Was it proper to call free imports 'free trade'? Had Cobden and Peel proved good prophets? Had it been sound politics so to arrange our tariffs as to exclude imperial preference? Did not various nations flourish under varied forms of protection? Was Bismarck a fool? Were we alone wise? Questions all well suited to the pamphlet, the platform, and the evening press; and many of them well worth the asking. They were mixed up with those doubts about the balance of trade which were disturbing the public mind in the

[1] *R.C. on Trade Unions* (1868–9, XXXIX), Q. 10,696: a witness from N. Staffordshire.

[2] The consular reports and those prepared for the *R.C. on Depression of Trade* are summarised in Farrer, *op. cit.* p. 161–6. The most important is Strachey's *Report on the effect of the German Tariff* (c. 4530) of 1885. By the Merchandise Marks Act of 1887 (50 and 51 Vict. c. 28) things 'made in Germany,' or anywhere else, had to be so labelled. The label was made the title of a popular book (by E. E. Williams) in 1896.

late 'seventies[1]. The 'fair trade' controversy and the balance of trade controversy "ran very much into each other."[2]

The questioners came together into a Fair Trade League in 1881[3]. Their scheme was not fully worked out at first and they never had to apply it. It did not at this time deflect British policy. For 'fairness,' it demanded at the outset a moderate import duty on foreign manufactures, to be removed from the goods of any country so soon as that country agreed to admit British manufactures free. For the Empire's sake, it demanded a lowering or abolition of duties on empire tea, coffee, fruit, tobacco and wine; and, though less decidedly, a light general tax on all foodstuffs coming from foreign countries. How dominion tariffs on British manufactures were to be dealt with was not declared. Nor were the implications of the proposed crude form of retaliation investigated. Yet, according to a recognised political tradition, for several years the country was represented by convinced Fair Traders and by politicians speculating in Fair Trade as dying for lack of what, in due course, if called in, they would prescribe. "Your iron industry is dead, dead as mutton; your coal industries...are languishing. Your silk industry is dead, assassinated by the foreigner. Your woollen industry is in *articulo mortis*, gasping, struggling. Your cotton industry is seriously sick." So Randolph Churchill in 1884[4]. He pressed for a Commission of inquiry into the very real trade depression thus garishly delineated. The Minority Report of that Commission gave the later form of the Fair Trade proposals—a 10 to 15 per cent. tariff "upon all manufactures imported from foreign countries," and similar duties "upon those articles of food which India and the Colonies are able to produce," when sent from foreign countries. The duties on manufactures were now treated as at least semi-permanent, because we might "be unable to alter the protectionist policy of other nations."[5]

[1] Above, p. 240.

[2] Giffen, *The Use of Import and Export Statistics* (*Essays in Finance, Second Series*), p. 132.

[3] The movement is generally dated from the issue in 1879 of *The Policy of Self-Help. Suggestions towards the Consolidation of the Empire and the Defence of its Industries and Commerce. Two letters by*...(W. Farrer Eckroyd).

[4] Churchill, W. S., *Lord Randolph Churchill* (1906), I. 291: speech at Blackpool, January 24, 1884.

[5] *R.C. on Depression of Trade. Final Report*, p. lxv *sqq*. Minority Report signed by Farrer Eckroyd, P. A. Muntz, Nevile Lubbock. Lord Dunraven also signed but with the reservation that he 'objected to protection.'

When the Minority and Majority Reports had been weighed, Randolph Churchill stopped speculating in Fair Trade. The movement seemed to die. Joseph Chamberlain, munitioned by the Board of Trade, had shot at it dangerously. The League and the name he helped to snuff out: years afterwards the spirit entered into him. For its strength lay less in its economics, though they were not negligible[1], than in its sense of a changing world and in its nationalism. Sampson Lloyd, its parliamentary leader, knew this when he translated and published, for the first time in English, Friedrich List's *National System of Political Economy*. That was in 1885[2].

[1] The Minority Report of 1886 deals scientifically, for example, with the creation of surplus productive power in protected countries and resulting competition and 'dumping' in neutral and open markets.

[2] For the Fair Trade movement generally see the Publications of the Fair Trade League. Farrer, *Free Trade versus Fair Trade*, though controversial, quotes Fair Trade writers verbatim. There is no good narrative in English. See Fuchs, C. J., *Die Handelspolitik Englands und seine Kolonien* (1893), p. 157 *sqq.* and Halévy, E., *Histoire du peuple anglais. Epilogue* (1926), p. 272–5.

CHAPTER VII

AGRICULTURE

DURING the first decade of the reformed Poor Law, anxious publicists had believed that men were redundant in rural Britain. They were probably right, as things then were. Forty years later the spectre was rural depopulation, not redundance. But careful inquiry in the 'eighties, applied to the fifteen most agricultural English counties, showed that between 1851 and 1881 there had been a decline of only 1 per cent., on one definition of the word rural, and of 2·1 per cent. on another. In an absolutely rural county such as Huntingdon, with no town of even 5000 inhabitants, there had, it is true, been a decline of 11·8 per cent.; but even in Huntingdon the population of 1881 was almost precisely what it had been in the year after the Poor Law was reformed. The new conditions of freedom, mobility, and a partly mechanised and less arable agriculture had done no more than lop off an intervening growth. Much the same was true of the other counties of maximum rusticity. One way and another, by agriculture and the occupations immediately dependent on it, the land was still carrying approximately the head of men that had once been too big, and carrying them in much greater comfort. They only seemed fewer when set against the multitudes of the streets. But the streets and the new worlds had apparently got hold of the best stocks. How else, the inquirer wrote, could you explain the now certain fact that there was more idiocy on the land[1]?

While the rural population proper remained about stationary, it was arguable, and was in fact being argued in the 'eighties, that the number of landowners was still "progressively dwindling"[2]; through the automatic working of the tradition of purchase by great proprietors, of family settlements which hindered sales, and of the law of primogeniture in cases of intestacy[3]. Down to 1870 no one knew with precision how the land of

[1] Ogle, Dr W., "The alleged depopulation of the rural districts of England," *S.J.* LII (1889), 205.

[2] Brodrick, Hon. G. C., *English Land and English Landlords* (1881), p. 111.

[3] The direct effect of the Law of Primogeniture was small, as nearly all landed estates descended under settlements and wills. See Kenny, C. S., *An Essay on...Primogeniture* (1878); Williams, J., *Real Property*; Pollock, Sir F., *The Land Laws* (1883), esp. p. 179–80. It was generally held that "a much larger

Britain was owned. An attempt made to ascertain the facts, in 1871–3, led to the issue of what contemporaries called "The New Domesday Book[1]." Those who compiled it only claimed that it was "proximately accurate": those who used it doubted even that. It was at best, they said, not "a perfect record of owners" but "an imperfect record of estates."[2] In it, *exempli gratia*, the Duke of Buccleuch counted as fourteen landowners because he owned in fourteen counties. But even the Book yielded the remarkable conclusion that about a quarter of the land of the United Kingdom was owned by 1200 persons, and about a half by 7400. One critic felt certain that, when allowance had been made for its errors, it showed that in England and Wales not more than 4000 proprietors owned about four-sevenths of the area reported on, which was the area assessed to rates[3]. It was pointed out further that the apparent dispersion of ownership in the remaining three-sevenths, or one-half, or whatever it might be, was connected as much with suburban freehold plots as with the properties of lesser gentlemen and 'yeomen.' The experiment of a New Domesday Book was not repeated, so the question whether or not the number of landowners was "progressively dwindling" down to the 'eighties cannot be answered. That the concentration of rural ownership was at least unweakened, and was excessive, is sure.

Various attempts had been made by the good sense of conveyancers and their clients, and by the law, to reduce the restrictive pressure of the older sort of family settlement and facilitate transference of family property. At law, down to 1856, the tenant for life under a settlement could not give a lease to run beyond his own lifetime, unless definitely empowered to do so by his settlement. Often he was empowered; and when he was not, relief might be secured by private Act of Parliament. In 1856 this relief was generalised (19 and 20 Vict. c. 120). Later, the Settled Estates Act of 1877 (40 and 41 Vict. c. 18) reversed the old presumption of law—leases might be granted unless forbidden in the settlement. To overcome the difficulties

area" was "under settlement than at the free disposal of individual landlords"; Brodrick, *op. cit.* p. 100. Under a strict settlement, of course, the 'owner' was properly only a life tenant who could not sell.

[1] *Return of Owners of Land*, 1874 (LXXII. parts 1, 2, 3) and the summary *Return* of 1876 (LXXX). It was made at the request of the House of Lords to disprove the popular view that there were not very many thousand landowners in Britain. It was hardly successful.

[2] Brodrick, *op. cit.* p. 163.

[3] *Ibid.* p. 165.

of sale by the tenant for life, the average settlement had long included clauses authorising the trustees to sell at his request and use the proceeds for discharging mortgages, or in other ways; though landed opinion always frowned on such impairings of the estate. For Scotland, the heir of entail had been given power to disentail in 1848. Finally, but only in 1882, Lord Cairns' Settled Land Act (45 and 46 Vict. c. 38) gave English tenants for life "as large and effectual powers of using the land to the best advantage as are compatible with settlements existing at all."[1]

Changes in custom had usually preceded changes in law. But neither had yet transformed the essentials. Tenants for life got free power to lease; but yearly tenancy remained the normal arrangement, though Scotland kept her nineteen-year leases[2]. In England, possibly through inertia, both owner and farmer usually preferred the short tenure. It was compatible with either a patriarchal or a commercial relationship. In Wales "hereditary succession [of farmers] prevailed on most large estates."[3] In what the eighteenth century would have called the improved parts of England, farming families moved about a good deal as profit directed. Thanks to the easing of settlements and to the ordinary ruins or extinctions of families, great and small, land came rather freely into the market. Estates were always being acquired or built up by new men, even by the newest, like Sir Roger Scatcherd of Boxall Hall, "whilom a drunken stone mason," now (1858) a great contractor[4]. A French observer in the early 'fifties, wishing to correct his countrymen's "erroneous impression...that landed property in England does not change hands," had pointed out that "properties of fifty to five hundred acres...in fact are sold every day."[5] He quoted typical advertisements for the guidance of the French. Yet in spite of the advertisements and of Sir Roger Scatcherd, Buccleuch still counted as fourteen landlords and the land was not effectively mobilised. If Sir Roger's estate were big enough, and he had sons, there would probably be a conveyancer and a settlement to 'make an eldest son.' Twenty-five years later, however, the law was preparing for a time when, given sufficient provocation, the land might begin

[1] Pollock, *op. cit.* p. 192. The Scottish Act is 11 and 12 Vict. c. 36.

[2] See vol. I. p. 109.

[3] *R.C. on Land in Wales and Monmouth*, 1896 (XXXIV), p. 291.

[4] Trollope, Anthony, *Doctor Thorne*, ch. 9.

[5] Lavergne, L. G. de, *The Rural Economy of England, Scotland and Ireland* (Eng. trans. 1855), p. 94–5.

to move faster. There was a foretaste of the provocation so early as 1853. Gladstone, stopping a gap in the fiscal system left unwillingly by Pitt, placed beside Pitt's legacy duty on personal property a small 'succession' duty on real property—the first new tax levied since Waterloo. Pitt had only proposed to tax collateral, not direct, succession to land; but Fox had fought even this on the ground that the principle would "enable the state to seize upon the whole property of the country."[1] There certainly was some such possibility latent in 'death duties.'

Custom again showed the way to law in regulation of the dealings between landlord and farmer. At common law, an outgoing tenant had no right to any particular notice, and could claim nothing attached to the land but the *emblements*, the growing crops or their value. When the typical farmer was a small open-field husbandman, not given to sinking capital in the land, this may not have been unjust. It was long since even small farmers in England had sunk capital in building their own houses; though in out-of-the-way districts they might have had very little capital assistance from their landlord. In eighteenth-century, and to some extent in nineteenth-century, Scotland and Wales they had built houses, such as they were. Tenant-built 'black houses' in the Hebrides long survived 1850 and 1885. The original Scottish leases had been designed to encourage tenants who sank capital in gathering up the stones, doing rough drainage, or running up a dry-stone house: the improvement was given nineteen years in which to exhaust itself. The strong nineteenth-century farmer, in Scotland Wales or England, always had a house provided, and so had no claim under that head; but he too had sometimes done all the draining, and had generally done part of it. He might also have stubbed wastes, or marled, or limed, or fenced, or used expensive and unexhausted 'artificials.'[2]

From these different sources—the primitive conviction of old-fashioned cultivators that they had done something for which they might claim compensation on quittance; and the calculated wish of intelligent landlords to attract farmers who would do something to deserve it—there had grown up 'tenant

[1] See Buxton, S., *Finance and Politics*, I. 114, 117; II. 292 for the parliamentary history. Fox's speech was May 26, 1796.

[2] On the law see Clifford, F., "The Agricultural Holdings Act," *J.R.A.S.* 1876, p. 129. For Wales, *R.C. on Land in Wales*, p. 576 *sqq.*, 690 *sqq.* For the Hebrides, below, p. 506. On drainage, etc., by the farmer see vol. I. p. 460–1, and Squarey, E. P., "Farm Capital," *J.R.A.S.* 1878, p. 167.

right' customs of different kinds in various parts of England and Wales, long before 1850. Caird found them "fully recognised" in that year amid backward conditions in Surrey, Sussex, the Weald of Kent and part of the West Riding, and among progressive conditions in North Nottingham and Lincolnshire[1]. Had he been into Wales, he might have added the moderately progressive Glamorgan and the rather primitive Brecon[2]. During the great transformation of Lincolnshire agriculture, enlightened owners like the Yarboroughs and the Chaplins, by guaranteeing compensation for unexhausted improvements, had secured what Scottish landlords had secured by the long lease[3]. As a Scot, Caird preferred the lease. He could not deny the merit of the Lincolnshire system; but he made much of the bad farming, stupidity and chicane connected with tenant right in Surrey and the Weald. Farmers "worked up to a quitting" and tried to get a good valuation on bad manure[4]. But a rogue can spoil any system. He can let a farm down in the later years of a long lease; and Caird himself was to argue in 1878 that the Scottish system needed, among other things, "some equitable rules to secure continuance of the tenant's interest in good farming to the close of the lease."[5]

By that time England had put the Lincolnshire custom tentatively into the law. The Agricultural Holdings Act of 1875 (38 and 39 Vict. c. 92) reversed "a presumption of law in existence for centuries past,"[6] by legalising compensation for tenants' improvements and fixtures and regulating the notice to quit. But it was a permissive Act. Farmers could contract out of the whole or any part of it, or they could contract for more than it gave, if local custom sanctioned more. The Act was adopted "in whole or in part on many estates."[7] Where not adopted formally it was not without influence as a model. Eight years later, when depression had come, tenants, or those who spoke for them, decided that this was not enough. The Agricultural Holdings Act (England) of 1883 (46 and 47 Vict. c. 61), a contemporary grumbled, showed that Parliament no longer trusted farmers to take care of themselves, and made com-

[1] Caird, J., *English Agriculture in* 1850 *and* 1851, p. 505 and *passim.*

[2] *R.C. on Agriculture,* 1882 (XIV; also 1881, XV–XVII); Doyle's report on Wales based on Q. 32,260; 65,808; 65,873. Cp. Little, W., "The Agriculture of Glamorgan," *J.R.A.S.* 1885, p. 165.

[3] For the Lincolnshire custom see Caird, p. 194. [4] *Ibid.* p. 119.

[5] *The Landed Interest*, p. 71. [6] Clifford, *op. cit.* p. 129.

[7] Clifford, F., "The Agricultural Holdings Act, 1883," *J.R.A.S.* 1884, p. 2.

pensation compulsory[1]. It was a cumbrous Act and was to require much interpretation and amendment. But it marked an important turning point in the history of the Land Laws.

Very soon political events would shake the social economic system of which those laws had been an expression. The country labourer would get his vote. The County Council would take over local government. Wise and popular resident landowners would continue to work for their county through its Council, but where landlords were not popular their power in local government would dwindle or cease. In South Wales, to take the extreme case, the County Council Act of 1887 "smote the whole class beyond recovery."[2]

From one vexation of his father and grandfather the mid-Victorian cultivator in England and Wales had been freed completely by the Reform Bill Whigs—payment of tithe in kind, or bargainings about the *modus* in money or corn, when that had replaced the actual taking of the tenth sheaf or tenth pail of milk, as in fact it generally had[3]. After 1850 there could be only family traditions of that "horrid greediness" in exacting tithe which according to Arthur Young was "the disgrace of England"[4] in 1792, and which, it is to be feared, had not become much less disgraceful in Cobbett's time. The Whig Law of 1836 (6 and 7 Wm. IV, c. 71) had been in good working order since 1840, and the tithe barn was becoming a matter for antiquarians instead of a centre of rather indecent clerical activity. The law had created a nationalised *modus*, a general commutation, whose history and economics are a complex thing apart. Caird believed that the removal of the liability to hand over part of the produce to tithe-owners had done good by encouraging farmers to break up sheep-walk for corn[5]. Perhaps

[1] Clifford, F., *op. cit.* p. 1. Cp. Pollock, *The Land Laws*, p. 154.

[2] Vaughan, H. M., *The South Wales Squires* (1926), p. 3.

[3] The Scottish *teinds* were quite different. Since the Reformation and the tithe-commutation of 1627–33 the clergy had no direct interest in levying them. They were in effect a levy on the rentals of the heritors (landowners). Scottish agrarian economists attributed a good part of the agricultural progress of Scotland in the eighteenth century to the absence of the vexatious tithe system of England and France. Anderson, J., *Essays relating to Agriculture* (1796), III. 157. For the general history see Cormack, A. A., *Teinds and Agriculture, an Historical Survey* (1930). For English tithe see Venn, J. A., *Foundations of Agricultural Economics* (1923), ch. 5, on which this section is based.

[4] *Travels in France* (ed. Maxwell), p. 332.

[5] *English Agriculture in* 1850 *and* 1851, p. 80. Venn's endorsement of this view (*op. cit.* p. 118) is open to question.

he was right; but after all plenty of the breaking up was done before 1836, and done at least as quickly as was wholesome. Moreover down-fed lambs and wool were tithable. Whether correct or not, his belief appears to have not much importance in the general economic history of the country. Nor has the tithe rent-charge itself, in the period from 1836 to 1886. Based on a seven-year average of the prices of the three principal grains, it fluctuated very little about par, that is the value of tithe as estimated in the 'thirties. Its lowest and highest were just over 10 per cent. below par in 1854, and nearly 13 per cent. above in 1874. In 1886 it fell to nearly 13 per cent. below[1]. After that a continuous fall created a new situation. Throughout the fifty years, £4,000,000 was about the figure of total tithe-rent charge at par. It was probably near to a tenth of the rental of lands in England and Wales in 1836–40. When it came back to par in 1883, after the rise of the 'seventies, it was only about one-twelfth of a rental also falling[2]. How it was divided between the Church, the Colleges, and the lay impropriator, is a matter for specialised histories. Always to economists a tax on rent, whatever it might seem to farmers, it had now assumed that character definitely, although by agreement the tenant very often paid it[3]. Neither its existence nor its apportionment affected the tenant's daily life as the tithe in kind had, though he might have politico-religious grievances about the way in which it was spent, especially if he were a Welshman.

Not much vexed by tithe, the mid-Victorian farmer was very little vexed by problems of open field and common, or by those of their enclosure. There was no county of England or Wales except Leicestershire in which enclosing was not done by Act of Parliament after 1850; but apart from some big enclosures of hill-common in Wales and the North-West, like the 16,036 acres at Llandewi-Brefi in Cardigan in 1863 or the 7637 acres of Ennerdale in 1864, it was a clearing up of scraps, with an

[1] The tithe-table is reproduced in the *Dict. Pol. Econ.* s.v.

[2] Cp. Caird, *The Landed Interest*, p. 132–3. Caird's contention that the land rental of England had risen 50 per cent. in the period 1836–78 is not borne out by the figures in Stamp, Sir J. C., *British Incomes and Property* (1927 ed.), p. 36 and *passim*. Probably 30 per cent. would be nearer the mark. Stamp's figures, based on the Income Tax, begin in 1842–3.

[3] It was only by the Tithe Act of 1891 (54 and 55 Vict. c. 8) that the liability to pay tithe rent charge was finally put on the owner, any contract to the contrary between owner and tenant notwithstanding. Cp. Venn, *Foundations of Agricultural Economics*, p. 121.

occasional and rare parish[1]. A writer on Hertfordshire in the *Journal of the Royal Agricultural Society* for 1864 was puzzled and shocked to find that all the fields of Baldock and Clothall still lay open[2]. The Enclosure Commissioners reported in 1878 that nearly 600,000 acres, the equivalent of a fair-sized county, had been dealt with since the General Enclosure Act of 1845; but of this nearly a quarter was done before the end of 1850[3], and the rest was mostly in the Ennerdale group. There were over 30,000 acres in Cardiganshire alone, and over 22,000 in Westmorland. It is worth noting that towards the very end of the age of enclosure there were still proved abuses on the unstinted hill-commons. In Westmorland, in 1868, Sunday was "often the favourite day for a quiet dogging of the neighbours' sheep," to make more room for your own. Monmouthshire hill farmers in 1870 were selecting shepherds and sheep for their fighting qualities. Some combative little breeds were as good as dogs in pushing weaker sorts off the best ground[4].

The decade 1865–75 marked the end of the enclosure age because there was not much left to enclose and because a crowded urbanised society, well fed from overseas, had come—naturally and rightly—to think of common, not as cattle ground, still less as potential corn-field, but as 'open-space.' The organised movement for preservation began in London. For ten years the Commons Preservation Society worked. In 1876 Parliament legislated for the first time about commons in general on the assumption that their destiny was not enclosure. With that common-land passed out of agricultural into social history[5].

Enclosure being done, what had been the ultimate fate of the cultivating owner, the 'yeoman,' who moves in close company with commons and open fields through history, in closer through

[1] *Return of Inclosure Acts*, 1914 (Cd. 399).

[2] *J.R.A.S.* 1864, p. 301. These were the fields which helped Frederick Seebohm to recreate the English Village Community. The last 'commonable fields,' of a different sort, to be enclosed in Wales were 50 acres at Llyswere in 1856 and 105 acres at Bronllys in 1860. Both places are in Brecknock. Bowen, Ivor, *The Great Enclosure of Common Lands in Wales* (1914), App.

[3] Between 130,000 and 140,000 acres. The *Return* of 1914 gives the acreages and years. Cp. vol. I. p. 454.

[4] *J.R.A.S.* 1868, p. 14, Westmorland; 1870, p. 289, Monmouth. Cp. Vol. I. p. 107.

[5] The Metropolitan Commons Act of 1866 (29 and 30 Vict. c. 122) had stopped enclosure within the London police area. The Act of 1876 is 39 and 40 Vict. c. 56.

legend? The probability is that his numbers and the area under his control did not change much, on the balance, between Victoria's accession and her jubilee. If there was any change, it was slightly downwards. Every one knew that he could be found rather easily in Cumberland, Westmorland, the Yorkshire Dales, the Isle of Axholme and the Fens, and with a little search in most places[1]. He was often bought out; but small men also bought land to work it, and farmers of all sorts bought occasionally. In the early 'nineties, about 4 per cent. of landholders owned part of the land which they worked, besides those who owned it all[2]. Wales with its "leech-craving" for land, as the drafter of an official document once put it in non-official style[3], shows both buying and selling at work. The occupying freeholders of the 'nineties turned out to be of "very recent origin."[4] Some had bought crown land on enclosure: there were many such in Cardigan, where so much had been recently enclosed. Others had acquired a sort of freehold in the good old way by squatting on crown land before enclosure, cribbing little crofts from it, and turning out a few sheep. Sitting tenants had bought and mortgaged to get security, in a society where news of occasional evictions ran angrily across the hills[5]. Welshmen challenged the statement of a Saxon assistant-commissioner who said in 1881 that "the half-starved proprietor of 10 or 20 acres" was "perpetually trying to persuade the larger owner to buy his bit of land"[6]; but such things happened. Lord Penrhyn told how he had himself bought out from 25 to 30 small men at their request[7]. When exact inquiry was at length made, in 1887 and subsequent years, it was found that from 10 to 12 per cent. of the cultivated land of Wales was occupied by its owner, nearly always a small man[8].

For Great Britain the same inquiries gave between 14 and 15 per cent.; for England between 15 and 16; for Scotland just

[1] The reports on the *Employment of Children* of 1867–9 noted that the numerous 'statesmen' in Cumberland and Westmorland were a bar to education: they kept their children at home to work (1868–9, XIII. 142).

[2] Curtler, W. H. R., *The Enclosure and Redistribution of our Land* (1920), p. 240.

[3] *R.C. on Land in Wales*, p. 313.

[4] *Ibid.* p. 291.

[5] *Ibid.* p. 549 *sqq.*, 576 *sqq.*

[6] *R.C. on Agriculture*; Doyle, A., Q. 32,050.

[7] *Ibid.* Lord Penrhyn's evidence, Q. 7350–8.

[8] The figures are from the annual agricultural statistics: *e.g.* in 1891 the Welsh figure was 11·6. The statistics deal with cultivated land "owned and occupied" by the same person.

over 12. In England certainly not all of this was yeoman land. A squire who cultivated a home farm, or who was forced by agricultural depression to cultivate an outlying farm through a bailiff, "owned and occupied" the land as much as any fenman or dalesman. The high proportion of occupying owners returned in 1887–8 in some counties not known to have been abnormally rich in yeomen, and known to have been hard hit by depression, suggests a good deal of this kind of owner-occupancy. Essex is in that group. It has always had its yeomen[1]. There may well have been 12 or even 15 per cent. of the cultivated area in their hands. But it is hard to believe that there was over 21 per cent. which is the figure for "land owned and occupied" in Essex in 1887. There were a good many farms without farmers on the Essex clays just then. As Cumberland and Lincolnshire, counties certainly rich in yeomen, had only 15 and 16 per cent. respectively of owner-occupied land, and as Lincolnshire like Essex would have a good many farms in hand, Cumberland few or none, it is unlikely that any county figure above 15 can represent nothing but working owner-occupiers. The aggregate English figure for their land must be somewhat lower, probably not above 12[2].

The nests of small owners in the Lincoln flats deserve particular notice. Everyone interested in such things had heard of the Isle of Axholme in the North-West, where, favoured by a soil good for all kinds of specialised crops, small men in the 'eighties still owned and tilled the strips of some surviving open fields[3]. Others were less widely known, such as Hogsthorpe in the marsh below Tennyson's wolds, where half the occupiers of twenty acres or less were owners, or Wrangle between the East Fen and the Wash, where the proportion was two-thirds[4]. At Cowbit, where the skating is, South of Spalding, almost everyone was a freeholder in the 'sixties[5]. None of these facts prove that Lincolnshire was a county, or Britain a country, of small owners; only that such people in fair numbers had survived, or

[1] Cp. vol. I. p. 101, 104.

[2] In 1913, when agricultural prices were fairly good and few farms would be in hand, the figure was 10·7. So 10–12 cannot be far out for the twenty-five years from 1887.

[3] Axholme is described and pictured in Slater, G., *The English Peasantry and the Enclosure of Common Fields* (1907) and in Venn, *op. cit*.

[4] See Major P. G. Craigie's classical paper "Agricultural Holdings in England and Abroad," *S.J.* 1887, p. 86 *sqq*.

[5] *R. on Children in Agriculture*, 1867–8, XVII. 74.

come into existence, side by side with Buccleuch and Sir Aylmer Aylmer[1]. They formed a much larger proportion of the landowners than their acres did of the land, because their holdings were so small. It will be observed that they were most numerous in districts where the hunting was not good, where air and water were rather bad, and where Sir Aylmer could not have inherited nor Sir Roger Scatcherd laid out a properly undulating park. It must be added that their situation in Lincolnshire, as in Wales, during the gloomy 'eighties was said to be "deplorable."[2]

Until those years of trouble, it was the universal opinion that the tendency still was for the average British holding, normally of course a tenant-farmer's holding, to grow. In the 'sixties farms were said to be getting bigger with the more extended use of machinery in Oxford and Berkshire; and the tendency, it was reported, "has been and is toward consolidation" in Westmorland[3]. A commissioner who had conducted inquiries in various districts from Cornwall to Cambridge, during the early 'nineties, reported that in all of them, from the 'forties to "within ten years...the tendency to amalgamate farms was universal."[4] In Wales there was a good deal of consolidation between 1865 and 1875. It was mostly on "arable lowland farms where machinery could be used," as in the Vale of Clwyd; but land-agents sometimes allowed the mean dwellings on little upland holdings to fall into decay, because in no way could the holding be made to yield a decent living[5]. At that time they saw in consolidation the only hope of progress, just as Scottish agents had when they cleared estates over-crowded with crofters and cottars. "Every Welsh farmer and every Welsh labourer" called down on them the curse reserved for him who lays field to field[6]. But even after "the most reprehensible...evictions" —the reference is to political evictions, but would apply to economic ones—the farms always let easily, to Welshmen[7]. So land-hungry were the Welsh. The English and the Scots were just as ready to risk the curse. They had longer experience of the business; and cursing, if it came, came fainter across the wider gap between farmer and labourer.

[1] See Tennyson, *Aylmer's Field*.

[2] *R.C. on Agricultural Depression*, 1882, p. 10.

[3] Oxon and Berks, *R. on Children in Agriculture*, 1867–8, XVII. 10; Westmorland, *J.R.A.S.* 1868, p. 8.

[4] *R.C. on Labour*, 1893–4, XXXV. 13.

[5] *R.C. on Land in Wales*, p. 347.

[6] *Ibid.* p. 357.

[7] *Ibid.* p. 314.

No doubt consolidation was going on more or less everywhere from 1850 to 1880. But the statistical evidence shows odd features and suggests the coexistence of consolidation and subdivision. The first oddity is that the number of people who returned themselves at census time as 'farmers and graziers' in England and Wales did not decline at all. There were 249,431 in 1851. In 1881 there were 233,943. In the former year the figure included retired farmers and graziers: in the latter it did not. An expert estimate for the retired of 1881 brought the two figures within 350 of one another[1]. Some land had been brought under cultivation in the interval, but not enough to add much to the average holding of nearly a quarter of a million farmers. Moreover a good deal had been lost to the towns and railways. So far as these figures go, there might have been no increase in the size of farms and no consolidation at all.

At the census of 1851 'farmers and graziers' were asked to make returns of the acreage which they farmed. They did so almost universally[2]. The returns covered 24,700,000 acres of cultivated land in England and Wales and gave an average farm of 111 acres. Only 7656 farms of under 5 acres were returned. Nearly 50 per cent. more of these small holdings were returned in Scotland, even though large numbers of crofters and cottars are known to have been omitted. For Scotland it is expressly stated that many of the small farmers had other occupations. It is evident that innumerable holders of small plots in England—butchers, carters, cowkeepers, market-gardeners, miscellaneous persons with a paddock or a hay-field—did not make returns because they did not picture themselves as farmers. When holdings not farmers came to be enumerated, in 1885, it appeared that there were 136,000 holdings under 5 acres in England and Wales against the reputed 7656 of 1851. The Scottish figure meanwhile had barely doubled, a change which a full return of crofters and some increase in the butcher-carter group would amply explain. Owing to the omission of these people in the English return of 1851, the 'average farm' of 111 acres in that year was much less of a statistical abstraction than the 'average English holding' of 60 acres in 1885. What looks at first sight like a huge increase of very small cultivators in the interval was mainly, there can be no sort of doubt, an increase in returns relating to miscellaneous holders of pad-

[1] Dr Ogle's paper on rural depopulation, as above, *S.J.* 1889, p. 219.

[2] *Occupations*, etc. I. 450 *sqq.* (England and Wales); II. 1025 *sqq.* (Scotland).

docks and accommodation-land. And the holdings of these people were by-products of urbanisation.

The upshot of the 1851 figures for England and Wales, omitting those referring to less than 5 acres, was:

Size	No. of farms	Acreage of group	Percentage of total acreage reported on
(i) 5– 49 acres	90,100	2,122,800	8·6
(ii) 50– 99 acres	44,600	3,206,500	13·0
(iii) 100–299 acres	64,200	11,015,800	44·6
(iv) 300–499 acres	11,600	4,360,900	17·6
(v) 500–999 acres	4,300	2,841,000	11·5
(vi) 1000 acres and upwards	771	1,112,300	4·5

The holdings figures of 1885 were not classified in precisely the same way. Instead of 5–49 acres the group is 'above 5 but not exceeding 50 acres,' and so on; the farm or holding of exactly 50 or 100 acres falls into a lower group in 1885 than in 1851, so slightly swelling the lower groups. This, among other things, prevents very exact comparisons. But the figures for 1885 are important, even apart from comparison[1]. They cover 27,700,000 acres in England and Wales against the 24,700,000 of 1851.

Size	No. of holdings	Acreage of group	Percentage of total acreage reported on
(i) Above 5-50 acres	200,100	3,888,700	14·0
(ii) 51–100 acres	54,900	4,021,000	14·5
(iii) 101–300 acres	67,000	11,519,400	41·6
(iv) 301–500 acres	11,800	4,472,300	16·1
(v) 501–1000 acres	4,200	2,737,600	9·9
(vi) Above 1000 acres	573	745,500	2·7

Evidently a great number of holdings between 5 and 20 acres were returned by persons whose predecessors or equivalents in 1851 would not have called themselves farmers. There is room for this, for there were over 126,000 holdings in that group[2]. From 50 acres upwards the tables are curiously similar. The extra 3,000,000 acres reported on in 1885 are mostly absorbed in the lowest groups, up to 20 acres. The excluded group, below 5 acres, accounts for 331,000 of them, whereas in 1851 it was almost empty. For true farming, the areas are nearly identical, and the figures show little trace of concentration;

[1] Used in Craigie's article, as above.

[2] The returns go into greater detail than the table given above, so the holdings of 5–20 acres can be separated out.

though 600,000 more acres are now in holdings from 100 to 500. The apparent decline in the highest groups and the unexpected increase between 50 and 100, *i.e.* in the farms which a family can work, are explicable in part by a simple hypothesis. Farmers are not confined to one holding. This fact was conspicuous in the 'eighties, when competent men in depressed arable areas who could keep their heads above water were taking over holdings from those who could not[1].

In 1851 such men would presumably return all the land they occupied, as they were asked to do. It would appear as a very large farm. Their more numerous successors would be split up, like Buccleuch, into several holders; for the basis was the holding not the man. A second partial explanation of the increase between 50 and 100 is that concentration in a district of small holdings—Wales, for instance—would show its results low down the scale: little hill farms under 50 acres had been thrown together. When these things are taken into account, the figures become compatible with a certain amount of concentration, if not with so much as the general descriptions would suggest. But all conclusions from statistical series with different bases are somewhat uncertain[2].

Figures continued to be collected on the 1851 base, but they were not again published in full. The census officials of 1861 did not think it necessary "to abstract all the information."[3] They did, however, abstract the number and sizes of farms in ten thoroughly representative counties, East and West, arable and pastoral[4]. The lower parts of their table are unsatisfactory, the upper instructive. The latter are as follows:

Farms in Ten Representative Counties

	Number	
Size	1851	1861
100–299 acres	15,900	14,700
300–499 acres	3,200	3,400
500–999 acres	1,529	1,582
1000 acres and upwards	323	308

[1] Cp. Hall, A. D., *A Pilgrimage of British Farming* (1913), p. 42–3.

[2] There are also the uncertainties of statistical collection and compilation which cannot be discussed here.

[3] On the ground that "there is now some prospect that England as well as Ireland will enjoy...agricultural statistics." *Census of* 1861: *General Report* (1863, LIII, part I), p. 29.

[4] Bucks, Cambs, Cheshire, Cumberland, Lincoln, Norfolk, Shropshire, Sussex, Wilts, the North Riding. The absence of Wales is the only defect, but this does not affect the comparison with 1851.

Here is evidence of definite but limited concentration. The reputed decline in giant farms is curious; but in so small a group it may be due to some accident of times or personalities. Not every one can farm a thousand acres, and those who can do not always get the chance.

In the census of 1871 appeared the figures for a different group of counties, seventeen this time, with about a third of the cultivated acreage of England and Wales. They were the big farm counties, for their average farm in 1851 had been of 143 acres against 111 for the country as a whole. By 1871 this figure had grown only to 152, a bare 6 per cent. in twenty years. This is decisive as to the slowness and limited nature of the concentration[1].

In the 'eighties, Dr Ogle consulted the unpublished census books of a single, small, purely agricultural and primarily arable county, Huntingdon, for the whole period 1851–81. He found the same consolidation of moderate-sized into large farms as the 1861 figures suggest for a wider area. The decline in Huntingdon was almost entirely in the groups 50–99 and 100–299 acres. There had been concurrently some breaking up of land into parcels. Huntingdon in 1851 had 296 'farms' of 5–49 acres: in 1881 she had 334. Ogle argued that some of these might "very probably be held in connection with other businesses,"[2] others by market gardeners who returned themselves as farmers, in spite of census instructions to the contrary. (They were to appear among the multitudinous small holdings of the agricultural returns.) Concentration there had been; but the number of census 'farmers' was kept near to the old figure by this growing class, although in Huntingdon, with its low urbanisation, there was a fall in these census 'farmers' from 1066 to 967 in the thirty years, even after allowance had been made for the change of census practice about farmers who had retired.

Through the minor uncertainties of all the figures, some certain facts show clear. Concentration had been going on far more slowly during this generation of maximum non-interference with the natural working of economic forces than almost any of the general references would suggest. And it had been accompanied by an incipient disintegration.

[1] *Census of* 1871 (1873, LXXI. part 2). The list includes no county S.W. of Hampshire and no county in the Western tier except Cumberland and Westmorland. It also excludes Yorkshire.

[2] *S.J.* as above, 1889, p. 220. He was no doubt right. We are dealing with what was called above 'the butcher-carter group.'

"In running my eye over the account which I wrote of... agriculture in 1850," James Caird said in 1878, "I find descriptions of good farming in nearly every part of the country, the details of which differ very little from the practice of the present day....The change has been not in any considerable progress beyond what was then the best, but in a general upheaval of the middling and the worst."[1] Neither the inconsiderable progress beyond the best of 1850, nor the generality of the upheaval, nor its height, are easy to estimate. It is evident that the ground had not been cleared for improvement, cleared in the literal sense, to anything like the extent which the best farmers of the early 'fifties would have wished. Common, it is true, had been cut to a minimum, but not hedgerows. To make room for more mechanical agriculture; to preserve the powers of the soil for the crops instead of spending them on thorn and hedgerow elm; and to let in light and air both for crops and cattle, the best farmers had been great grubbers of hedges. The work had often accompanied consolidation of farms. "All practical men," in Berkshire in 1860, were "agreed...that hedgerows are a great bar to agricultural improvement."[2] By 1861 in Yorkshire they were said only to survive in their ancient "wild luxuriance" on the land of a few non-improving owners; but the "woodland" farmers of North Hampshire who won reformers' praise by grubbing them sound like a minority; and the reformers of 1866 were complaining of the fourteen foot "ox-fences" of the Leicestershire grazing country, with their superfluous timber[3]. These fences had been prized for their shelter, but good farmers no longer exposed the beasts to weather bad enough to require them. Arable farming was at its best in districts newly enclosed from open field, sheep-run, and fen—the Lothians, the East Riding, Lincoln and Cambridge. There fields were big, hedgerows few and small; but in all old-enclosed districts there can be little doubt that hedgerows remained—as they still remain—very much more numerous and bigger than maximum agricultural efficiency would require. After Caird's report of 1878 came bad years in which the hedges were apt to stay and grow: grubbing and plashing cost money.

The leading hedge-grubbers were usually advocates of the brand-new system of steam cultivation. Agricultural literature

[1] *The Landed Interest*, p. 28.

[2] *J.R.A.S.* 1860, p. 3, Spearing, J. B., "On the Agriculture of Berkshire."

[3] *Ibid.* 1861, p. 92 (Yorks), p. 266 (Hants); 1866, p. 300 (Leicester).

during the 'sixties is full of it—the various methods; the costs; the soils and surfaces fitted for it; the size of farm which could carry its own steam tackle; the difficulties of hiring tackle. Actual progress was slow. There were only five sets of tackle even in East Lothian in 1865. Two years later, when committees of the Royal Agricultural Society made a full inquiry, they estimated that there might be 200,000 acres of steam-tilled land in the Kingdom. They maintained that its extension required, apart from mechanical improvements in the tackle and less folly in handling it, the introduction of a normal 30–40 acre field, greater freedom of cropping, the establishment of tenant-right, and more co-operation between tenant and landlord in getting rid of the hedgerows[1]. There is no estimate of progress for the next decade. Progress there was, but not so rapid as it might have been; for the committees' conditions were very imperfectly fulfilled. Soil and surface limit steam cultivation in Britain, but the human limitations were more decisive.

Yet there had been a great increase in the use of agricultural machinery. It was needed. There were still in the early 'fifties whole districts with the most antiquated implements and completely unmechanised[2]. In the Sussex Weald, ox-tillage, cumbrous ploughs, unchallenged flails, and cows which were bad milkers because they sprang from a "working race," recalled to a Frenchman one of his own "second-rate provinces"—at a time when some methods in a first-rate French province suggested to another Frenchman those of the thirteenth century[3]. In 1861 it was said that the Isle of Wight was "a century behindhand in practical agriculture"[4]: if this was true, the Island also was dangerously near to the Middle Ages.

In the next twenty years, however, the locomotive steam threshing machine penetrated almost everywhere[5]: its victory over the flail and the flail's successor, the rude hand or horse-driven thresher, was probably the most important change of the period. The victory was not yet complete. The flail was common enough on Welsh upland farms into the 'nineties. Indeed

[1] *J.R.A.S.* 1865, p. 102 (East Lothian); 1867 (reports of committees); 1868, p. 274 (Huntingdon).

[2] Vol. I. p. 461.

[3] Lavergne, *op. cit.* for Sussex; for the French province and the thirteenth century Delisle, L., *La classe agricole...en Normandie au moyen âge* (1851), p. xl.

[4] *J.R.A.S.* 1861, p. 359.

[5] Caird, *The Landed Interest*, p. 27.

at that time the plough was the only Welsh implement quite universally improved. The majority of Welsh farmers sowed broadcast, except for turnips, which not all of them grew. These were drilled[1]. In England, the leisurely adoption of new machines and implements can be traced in the series of prize essays on county agriculture issued by the Royal Agricultural Society. Neither the reaping nor the mowing machine was used "to that extent which it deserves" in Berkshire in 1860. Machines for cutting fodder and pulping roots were recent and "only partially adopted" by Nottingham farmers in 1861. By that year the scythe, which had driven out the sickle on the East Riding wolds before 1850, was "giving way to the reaping machine"; but in 1864 the sickle was still much used in Hertfordshire, the reaping machine apparently very little. From the Lothians, on whose big farms a fixed steam-engine for threshing and other work had long been "all but universal," it was reported in 1865 that the English type of peripatetic steam threshing machine was now "often found convenient." The most patriotic Scottish farmers had abandoned Bell's reaper: it was left to "rot in corners" now that varieties of more or less American ancestry were available[2].

The scythe was still usual for mowing hay in Leicestershire in 1866, though threshing was generally done by the hired machine. Worcestershire in 1867 was backward: there was much of the old high ridging of arable land on which reaping machinery was out of place. Mowers and reapers were known and the drill was almost universal; but in general the implements were old-fashioned, as were the buildings. In the fens of Huntingdon the scythe had driven out the sickle and the hook by 1868; but the fen arable was said to be mostly too soft to carry reaping machines. Middlesex, two-thirds of which was meadow land, was as backward as it had been in the 'forties. Then, the first man to use a rude threshing machine had been abused for robbing labourers of work: now, in 1869, there was not so much machine mowing "as you might expect," because the casual mowers who came in for the Middlesex hay-making were jealous of it[3]. It is true that Caird in 1878 spoke of the "general"

[1] *R.C. on Land in Wales*, p. 726–7.

[2] *J.R.A.S.* 1860, p. 22 (Berks); 1861, p. 165 (Notts), p. 103 (Yorks); 1864, p. 299 (Herts); 1865, p. 102 (East Lothian). For Bell's reaper, above, p. 13.

[3] *Ibid.* 1866, p. 296, 300 (Leicester); 1867, p. 450 *sqq.* (Worcester); 1868, p. 270 (Huntingdon); 1869, p. 9 *sqq.* (Middlesex). For Middlesex, cp. vol. I. p. 462.

introduction of reaping machinery as "the most striking feature" of the previous twenty years[1]; but general must not be read universal. Nor had Caird been on another comprehensive tour.

It was mainly of the Eastern corn-lands that men thought when they tried to gauge progress. Kentish fruit and hop-growing, in which machines had no place, seem to have been resting more than was wise on an old and merited reputation. There was, at any rate, still far too much grazing and mowing of the orchards in 1877[2]. Among the little milk and pasture farms of the North-West, the South-West, and the Welsh marches could be found plenty of bad casual farming, with an uninstructed reliance on the Western rain, which kept the pastures green, and on uncritical towns which took the milk, meat and cheese as they were. And so to Wales, with its primitive survivals and short stock of machinery. In Scotland there was a still wider gap—between the mechanical farm of the Lothians and the Skye croft with its *caschrom*, the foot-plough of primitive agriculture. But even in a westward shire like Stafford, in which the small and rather old-fashioned grazing farm was common, solid work had been accomplished since 1850 where it was most needed, in land drainage. Not a possible maximum amount, but nearly all that was absolutely essential, had been done by 1870[3]. This was probably true of most counties, though there was still too much old undrained pasture[4]. On the strong arable lands of Huntingdon, drainage was said to have doubled the yield in the twenty years before 1868. It had "worked wonders for the clay in Sheppey."[5] Similar evidence could be collected from most clay districts. It is true that an expert told a Committee of the Lords in 1873 that out of twenty million acres which needed drainage in England and Wales only three were yet drained. But 'need' is not an exact word; the expert was engineer to a drainage company; and both his figures were disputed by James Caird. Caird put the first at ten millions or rather more, not for England and Wales but for Britain; and allowed that four or five might not be too high for the second. He noted that in "scarcely any case...more than half of any

[1] *The Landed Interest*, p. 16.

[2] *J.R.A.S.* 1877, p. 97.

[3] *Ibid.* 1869, p. 263 *sqq.* There was good farming in Stafford in 1850. Vol. I. p. 460. For western farming, generally about 1850, see vol. I. p. 460–5. It changed slowly.

[4] *J.R.A.S.* 1868, p. 266 (Hunts).

[5] The *R.A.S. Report* of 1878, p. 316.

estate required" drainage, and that great stretches of chalk did not require it at all. He might have added some other soils[1]. His evidence is weighty. In 1850–1 he had reported an almost universal backwardness in the business. Since then, as an Enclosure Commissioner, he had supervised it. For, by what seemed a great anomaly to the Lords' Committee of 1873, "private transactions" in drainage and the financing of improvements had been "committed to the control of a Government officer."[2] The control originated with Peel's Act of 1846 (9 and 10 Vict. c. 101) and its £2,000,000 of government money to be advanced in drainage loans to landlords shaken by Free Trade[3]. The Whigs had added another £2,000,000 in 1850[4]. In the interval two important drainage and improvement companies had secured Acts, so that the work might be carried on when the Treasury grants were exhausted. Two others followed, in 1853 and 1856[5]. Interest and sinking fund on improvement loans, whether payable to the exchequer or to a company, could be so charged on estates as to take priority of existing mortgages. Supervision of some kind was therefore necessary, and it had been entrusted to the Enclosure Commissioners. "On the whole the drainage under Government inspection has been very well done," a grudging agricultural writer felt bound to admit in 1869[6].

There was a great deal done in which neither the government nor the companies had any hand. Farmers and landlords had begun the work before 1846 without external assistance, and they continued to help themselves, dividing the burden in various ways. At least the farmer carted the pipes: he might do much more[7]. Whether more had been spent in drainage without Government inspection than with it before 1873 Caird doubted: five years later, he had no doubt that in improvements generally landowners in Britain had spent "a much larger sum...from

[1] *S.C. of H. of L. on Improvement of Land*, 1873 (VI. 1), p. iii and Q. 830 for the expert (Bailey Denton); p. iii and Q. 4125–6 for Caird. Cp. his *Landed Interest*, p. 82–3.

[2] *S.C. of H. of L.* p. vii.

[3] Vol. I. p. 460 n. 3.

[4] By 13 and 14 Vict. c. 31.

[5] There was another in 1860. The companies were: The West of England and S. Wales (1848), The General Land D. and I. Coy. (1849), The Lands Improvement Coy. (1853), The Scottish D. and I. Coy. (1856) and the Land Loan and Enfranchisement Coy. (1860). *S.C. of H. of L.* 1873, App. A.

[6] Evershed, H., in *J.R.A.S.* 1869, p. 306, referring to Stafford.

[7] Cp. vol. I. p. 460; Lavergne, *op. cit.* p. 263; *J.R.A.S.* 1868, p. 25 (Lord Lonsdale deep drains 10,000 acres).

their own resources" than had been advanced to them by the state and the companies[1]. The advances had amounted to £12,000,000 in thirty years, of which upwards of £9,000,000 had gone in drainage. Advances made by the state (£4,000,000) had been largely repaid; many of those made by the companies had still long periods to run[2]. After 1878, though the work of drainage did not stop, the saddling of estates with heavy liabilities for it did; and the whole movement slackened as prices and rents fell away. But plenty of dry land with healthier crops and cattle testified to the good work done.

Much experience had been gained, and the technique of drainage had changed a good deal, since machines for making drain-pipes had first come into general use in the 'forties[3]. The early pipes, as advocated by Josiah Parkes, had been only 1 inch or 1½ inches bore. By the 'seventies none were under 2 inches and some were 5 or 6 inches. Many of the old drains had been remade deeper and with these bigger pipes[4]. It had been shown that there was such a thing as overdrainage on gravel or sand—a discovery which should not have been necessary—and that the proper amount of drainage for pasture land on various soils was not easy to determine[5]. Landlords had often felt that there was too much speculation in the system by which they paid a normal 7 per cent. for 25 years to a company, as interest and sinking fund, and got 5 per cent. on the outlay as extra rent, ostensibly for ever[6]. They felt it more sharply when rents fell before liabilities were cleared off. This experience also they bought.

Scientific manuring had hardly kept pace with scientific drainage. Léonce de Lavergne in 1854 said that most English farmers were "already familiar with the technical terms. They talk of ammonia and phosphates like professed chemists."[7] Perhaps he had not talked with very many, nor studied average practice closely. Phosphates and ammonia were known: all kinds of manures had been tried; and there was just then a rage among the progressive for guano. It came in at the rate of about

[1] *The Landed Interest*, p. 87.

[2] *Ibid.* p. 83. The General Land D. and I. Coy. (Bailey Denton's company) advanced £2,000,000 between 1857 and 1871. *S.C. of H. of L.* 1873, App. F.

[3] Vol. I. p. 458–61.

[4] *S.C. of H. of L.* Q. 4186 (Caird); *J.R.A.S.* 1868, p. 266.

[5] *Ibid.* p. iv; Lavergne, *op. cit.* p. 183 n.

[6] *S.C. of H. of L.* p. v. These were the normal rates.

[7] *Op. cit.* p. 220.

300,000 tons a year—enough to give a good average dressing to 2,000,000 acres[1]. But that left a great deal of land undressed. The 'antiquated farmer' whom Caird had found everywhere in 1850–1, who did not even make intelligent use of his farmyard muck, had still to be taught 'artificials.' He was a stubborn suspicious pupil. Even up-to-date men had their suspicions of chemistry. Caird was still preaching to them in 1878 that a cwt. of nitrate of soda was worth "fifty times its weight in farmyard manure" and could be applied "at one-fifth of the labour." Lawes' Rothamsted demonstration of this had "been before the country for more than thirty years," and yet it was "only beginning to be generally recognised."[2] While the use of nitrates was growing slowly, there had been a recent heavy fall in that of guano. Imports for 1874–8 were barely half what they had been in 1854–8. This was not surprising, for the average price at the ports in 1874–8 was £11 a ton, as against just over £9 ten years earlier[3]. Imported nitrate was coming down; but whatever its merits, it seemed dear to the ordinary farmer at £14 or even at £12. 10*s*. a ton, plus cost of carriage from the ports[4]. He figured out his farmyard manure at much less than 5*s*.; and as times got harder after 1876, he was tempted to economise on manures which meant cash outlay. Guano imports dropped abruptly—by 100,000 tons—in 1879 and never recovered. By 1887 they were negligible.

What the course of consumption of the home-made phosphates was there is no means of determining. Superphosphate of lime had become "the most largely used artificial manure" by the late 'seventies[5]. It had to a great extent superseded the phosphatic manures made from bones; and apparently it was replacing guano. It was relatively cheap and wise men used it freely. How freely it, or any of the artificials, was used below the levels of 'high-class' farm management is not known. Everyone had heard of superphosphate and probably most had tried it. But how often and how much?

[1] The average import in 1854–8 was 298,000 tons. Guano dressings ran from 2 to 4 cwts. an acre. Clarke, J. A., *R.A.S. Report* of 1878, p. 357. For the early days of guano, see vol. I. p. 456.

[2] *The Landed Interest*, p. 22.

[3] 'Computed real values' from the Trade Returns: similar computations for 1854–8 are not available.

[4] The price at the ports averaged £14 in 1867–76 and £12. 10*s*. in 1877–86.

[5] Clarke, *Practical Farming* in *R.A.S. Report*, p. 357. Clarke is speaking of 'high class' farming.

The cropping of the soil of Britain was in no essential way changed between 1850 and 1886. Even during the last struggle for self-sufficiency in bread-corn, between 1830 and 1846, the land of England and Wales appears to have been divided not very unevenly between arable and permanent pasture, a situation which seemed remarkable to the European visitor: "nearly half the cultivated soil has been maintained in permanent grass," Lavergne wrote with surprise but apparent admiration[1]. He was following, for lack of statistics, Caird's estimate made three years earlier[2]. Caird may have somewhat overestimated the permanent pasture; for when the first statistics were compiled in the late 'sixties, it appeared that it was then only about 43 per cent. of the whole cultivated area[3]. From 1870 the proportion rose, but slowly. It did not reach Caird's 1851 estimate until 1882, and the pasture exceeded the arable for the first time in 1883. In 1886, although the wheat area had been heavily reduced, pasture was still only 52·0 per cent. of the whole as against Caird's assumed 49·2 for 1851[4].

Even before 1850 crop rotations had become generally elastic. They became more elastic in the next generation. Strict 'Norfolk' four-course husbandry was maintained in many districts, especially in the East, with little change, except that to avoid 'clover sickness' red clover was now never grown oftener than one year in eight. There were various standard five-course shifts. But land in Britain varies so greatly, even on single farms, and heavy land in particular needs such different treatment in different localities and years, that much is heard of farming "as the seasons direct," of farming on "no regular system," or of farmers "having systems of their own."[5] Individual practice varied about varying local standards. Clayland men in Stafford, with an eye to cattle and dairying, used a five- or six-course shift with two or three successive years of seeds in the middle[6]. Cornwall had something similar but cruder with a trace of ancient 'outfield' agriculture in it[7].

[1] Lavergne, *op. cit.* p. 51.

[2] In *English Agriculture in* 1850 *and* 1851, p. 522. The basis is the rough assumption that the cultivated land is two-thirds pasture in the West, and one-third in the East.

[3] Venn, J. A., *Foundations of Agricultural Economics*, p. 381.

[4] These figures, taken from Venn, apply like Caird's to England and Wales, not to Britain.

[5] *J.R.A.S.* 1860, p. 15 (Berks); 1861, p. 274 (Hants); 1867, p. 450 (Worcester).

[6] *Ibid.* 1869, p. 272.

[7] Clarke, *Practical Farming*, as above, p. 329. Cp. vol. I. p. 24.

On heavy Hampshire land a "sort of double three-field system was sometimes found."[1] The standard Lothian shift was a very different six-course—seeds; oats; potatoes or beans; wheat; turnips; barley[2]. When applied to England, as it often was, a second wheat would be inserted somewhere[3]. The usual course in Aberdeen, which lived mainly by cattle feeding, was—seeds; seeds; oats; roots; barley[4]. Wheat was rare in these Scottish rotations. This helps to explain why, when crop statistics began to be collected (1866–7), 90 per cent. of the wheat of the United Kingdom was found to be English[5]. It explains also Scotland's greater resisting power for the crisis to come, which would be predominantly, though not entirely, a crisis of wheat.

Careful landlords always inserted some cropping conditions in the agreements with their farmers, and this was sometimes a farmers' grievance. But there is so much variety of cropping recorded[6] that interference with a good cultivator's liberty of action cannot often have been serious. Bad cultivators needed interference and hardly got enough. The system was certainly good on the average for agriculture and the land, the more so as breaches of the agreement were usually winked at, if within reason, especially in bad times[7]. In very bad times even unreasonable breaches had to be tolerated. In the 'eighties some discouraged farmers on the clays were falling back, just to save money, into that primitive three-course agriculture, with its recurring fallow, from which it had been a main object of agrarian reform and landlords' restriction to extricate them during a hundred years and more[8].

With its 40–50 per cent. of permanent pasture and its established connection between arable farming and the rearing of flocks and herds, the Britain of the 'fifties probably carried a bigger head of livestock in proportion to its area than any part

[1] *J.R.A.S.* 1861, p. 273.

[2] *Ibid.* 1871, p. 168.

[3] *Ibid.* 1860, p. 264 (Tuckett, P. D., "On the modifications of the four-course rotation"); Clarke, *op. cit.* p. 339 (Warwick); p. 350 (North Riding).

[4] *J.R.A.S.* 1871, p. 192.

[5] *S.J.* XXXI (1868), 140. Caird, "On the Agricultural Statistics of the U.K." Ireland by this time was important only as a producer of oats, potatoes, cattle and dairy produce. Her wheat export of the early nineteenth century (vol. I. p. 134) had ceased.

[6] Besides the cases quoted see Clarke, *op. cit.* ch. 6, a summary of cropping county by county based on the agricultural statistics of the previous decade.

[7] *R.C. on Labour*, 1893–4 (XXXV), p. 55, 75; evidence from Beds, Sussex, Hants.

[8] *Ibid.* p. 103 (Notts). An occasional fallow on clay may still be good farming.

of Europe. The number and quality of the sheep was what most impressed Lavergne in 1851–2. He believed that the United Kingdom kept as many sheep as France, and far better, on three-fifths of France's area[1]. This was the more remarkable, because there were few in Ireland and, in proportion to area, not very many in Scotland. He supposed that there were 30,000,000 in England and Wales and about 4,000,000 in Scotland. His figure was certainly a few millions too high; for the agricultural returns of 1867–79 showed that the total for Britain fluctuated between 28,000,000 and 30,000,000. In the early 'eighties, the range was between 24,300,000 and 26,500,000. Anything above 28,000,000 was exceptional; and that figure, which was returned in 1867 after a spell of unusually high wool prices, may be taken as a full normal head for the country[2].

It was sometimes argued during the 'seventies and 'eighties that the extension of Highland deer forests since 1850 had seriously curtailed the British flocks: once the sheep had eaten up the crofters, now the unthrifty deer had driven out the sheep. They had; but very careful calculations made in 1873 and again in 1884 showed that the maximum of evicted sheep could not exceed 400,000 and that the real figure was probably very much less, as these calculations required every forest, if cleared of deer, to carry its full potential stock of sheep[3]. In fact, important as the mountain flocks were in Scotland, England and Wales, they were far less important than those of the arable districts. There were always over 1,000,000 sheep in Northumberland, many of them on the Cheviots and the backside of the Pennines, but there were also over 1,000,000 in Lincolnshire, where the plough had been run through nearly every acre of wold sheep-walk before 1850; and there were 1,000,000 more in Kent. Sussex with its downs had not half as many. In no country at any time has the combination of arable farming and sheep-farming been so successfully carried out as in nineteenth-century Britain. The difficulties of the years after 1878 did not impair it.

Lavergne held that Britain excelled France less in cattle than in sheep, but that there was still "a sensible difference"[4] in

[1] Lavergne, *op. cit.* p. 14.

[2] The estimate for 1809 had been 19,000,000. *Lord's Report on the Wool Trade* (1828), p. 74.

[3] *Inquiry into the condition of the Crofters and Cottars in the Highlands and Islands*, 1884 (XXXII), p. 86 *sqq.*

[4] *Op. cit.* p. 31.

her favour both in quality and in numbers related to area. The figure of about 6,000,000 head of cattle which he accepted was probably correct; for it was the figure about which the recorded number fluctuated from 1867 to 1883, when a slow and intermittent rise began. "The consumption of milk under every form" by the English seemed to him "enormous." He thought that "their habits in this respect were those of past ages," and he quoted from Julius Caesar a sentence familiar to English schoolboys. "The quantities of butter and cheese manufactured," he added, "exceed all belief." He reckoned that the English farmers sold twice as much milk as the French and got twice the French price for it. "Not content" with all this, the English imported yet more butter and cheese[1]. He did not note that while the English had not milked their sheep for a very long time, and "lilting at the yow milking" had gone out in Scotland, sheep's milk was still regularly used in Wales. Twenty years later that use was declining: forty years later it would be extinct[2]. Unlike Lavergne's compatriots of Roquefort, these cheese-eating English had forgotten how to make ewe's milk cheese[3].

British superiority in cattle had been the result of concentration on milk and meat and deliberate neglect of ox-power. Even in 1878 ox-teams were still "employed to a small extent in Wiltshire, Devonshire, Cornwall, Sussex, and some other counties." A writer on practical agriculture had a few words to say about their feeding and management; but he added that "the exigencies of the meat supply and the ability of modern feeding processes to mature cattle of refined breeds into two-year-old beef" left no place for the draft ox[4]. It had been an anachronism since 1800 at least. All modern types of cattle: the short-horn now spread over the whole country[5], the Hereford, the Devon, the 'Alderney,' the Aberdeen-Angus and the rest were beef or milk makers, or both. Every year increased the

[1] Lavergne, *op. cit.* p. 34–5.

[2] *R.C. on Land in Wales*, p. 606, Q. 259, 359. The decline from 1875 is noted. By 1895 the practice was extinct.

[3] For the history and economics of Roquefort cheese, see Brunhes, *Géog. humaine de la France*, II. 501 *sqq.* The Roquefort caves which are held responsible for the quality may have no equivalent in Britain, although the island has its fair share of limestone caverns.

[4] Clarke, *op. cit.* p. 362–3.

[5] By the 'seventies the long-horn was "confined to a few amateur farmers in the midland counties"—*Ibid.* p. 277. Bakewell's long-horns had almost disappeared from Leicestershire by 1866, *J.R.A.S.* 1866, p. 328.

importance of meat and dairy produce as against grain crops, and that long before the great fall in grain prices. Caird thought that meat and dairy produce had "risen 50 per cent." in price between 1850 and 1867[1]. For wholesale prices 40 per cent. is probably nearer the mark[2]; but even 40 per cent. in seventeen years was encouraging to the farmer and his landlord. If the herds did not increase much in number, their care and management improved. Though at the end of the 'seventies there was still too much tying of cows and bullocks by the neck in "semi-open sheds or hovels,"[3] and too much herding of bullocks for the winter in open yards, the decently arranged milking stalls and the covered or part-covered yards which for years had been recommended[4] were to be found on an increasing number of well-managed estates.

Yard building, like cottage building and most drainage, was landlord's business. What proportion of the increasing rent-roll of the years between 1851–2 and 1878–9 was really interest on such new capital expenditure cannot be ascertained; but the proportion on many estates, perhaps on most, must have been very great. The cash increase in rents between these dates was impressive. For all Britain the income from Lands under Schedule A of the Income Tax[5] rose by nearly 28 per cent.—from £47,000,000 to £60,000,000. For Scotland the rise was 41 per cent.; for England and Wales 25. It was greater in the more pastoral West than in the ploughed East, greatest of all in green and land-hungry Wales. In the second half of the period alone (1864–5 to 1878–9) the rise for the six westernmost Welsh counties was 21·1 per cent.[6] For England and Wales, including those counties, it was 11·4 per cent. There must have been wide areas in the English arable East where the rise over the whole period 1851–2 to 1878–9 was well under 20 per cent.[7]; and it was on these arable lands, especially the clays, that most

[1] In *S.J.* XXXI. 141.

[2] Based on the price-currents of the *Economist* which there is not space to analyse here.

[3] Clarke, *op. cit.* p. 232.

[4] The *J.R.A.S. passim, e.g.* 1865, p. 88; 1866, p. 326.

[5] For the complex details of tithe and rent-charges see Stamp, *British Incomes and Property*, p. 41 *sqq.*, and books there quoted. The figure never quite touched £60,000,000 but was above £59,500,000 from 1876–7 to 1879–80.

[6] See the very interesting calculations in *R.C. on Land in Wales*, p. 469.

[7] In the five English counties whose climatic and agrarian conditions most nearly resembled those of West Wales—Cumberland, Westmorland, Cheshire, Devon, Cornwall—the rise from 1864–5 to 1878–9 was 17·2 per cent. *Ibid.*

landlord's capital had been expended. The increase there in pure rent, that is in the purchasing power of the payments for fertility and site value, may quite well have been negative, for prices were rising; but as it is not easy to set out a mid-Victorian clay soil landlord's cost of living index, the point must remain obscure. There is no doubt that landlords as a class felt comfortable, or that rents and land values continued to rise, until the end of the 'seventies. The figure for Schedule A, Lands, was indeed a trifle higher in 1879–80 than in 1878–9. After that it fell yearly until the end of the century—and beyond it.

"Times have been," a witness told the Royal Commission on Agriculture in 1881, "when there has been a very bad crop of wheat that prices have risen."[1] But it was not so in those disastrous wet years of the late 'seventies which lead in the great agricultural depression. Farmers had lost much working capital and the land was "four years to the bad, suffering from weeds and reduced manure."[2] James Caird put the price point to the Commissioners statistically. He took five bad harvest years between 1852 and 1862. With these he compared the five crescendo years of bad harvests in the 'seventies—1873, 1875, 1876, 1877 and 1879. For the early group he reckoned that wheat yielded on an average 24 bushels to the acre and fetched 61*s*. 1*d*. a quarter. For the late group the yield was 19 bushels and the price 49*s*. 10*d*.[3] If he had left out 1873, when wheat averaged 58*s*. 8*d*. and 1877, when the Russo-Turkish War drove it for a few months above 60*s*., he could have shown a still more disastrous price figure. For 1879, the year of the worst harvest of the century, the average was 43*s*. 10*d*. and it was 44*s*. 4*d*. for 1880. For a couple of years it held and then broke away again. It was 31*s*. in 1886 and 32*s*. 6*d*. in 1887. The other grains fell with wheat, but not quite so fast. The average price of wheat in the four years 1884–7 was 35 per cent. lower than it had been in 1874–7; that of oats was 31 per cent. lower and that of barley 28 per cent. lower.

Down to 1877 the index number of grain prices had remained very steady for successive groups of years, though there were steep monthly and yearly fluctuations. For 1867–77 it was

[1] *R.C. on Agriculture*, 1882 (XIV *sqq*.), Q. 34,682.

[2] Lord Randolph Churchill to his Mother, March 21, 1880; Churchill, W. S., *Lord Randolph Churchill* (1906), I. 117.

[3] *R.C. on Agriculture*, Q. 62,647.

only a trifle over 2 per cent. lower than it had been in the so-called hungry 'forties (1838–47)[1]. The lowest intervening figure for a group of years of any length had been in 1858–66, and that was only 9 per cent. below 1867–77. Each decade had seen some international dislocation which favoured the British farmer—a Crimean War, an American Civil War, a Russo-Turkish War—and until the late 'seventies these dislocations, helped by the quick growth of population and the relatively backward state of transport, allowed increasing dependence on foreign grain supplies to accompany a reasonably well-sustained level of prices and of the acreage under corn. Only about a fifth of the barley and less than a sixth of the oats available for consumption were imported in the late 'seventies; but for wheat the proportion had risen from 26·5 per cent. for the years 1852–9 to just over 48 per cent. for 1868–75[2]. The bad harvests of the late 'seventies drove it up first to nearly 60 and then to nearly 70 per cent. It never came down permanently; and the price of British wheat was slipping towards thirty shillings. American railways and British cargo steamers had done their work well for the consumer.

Caird reckoned in 1878 that there was no foreign competition at all with nearly one-fifth, by value, of the staple products of British agriculture. No effective competition with that fifth developed during the next seven or eight years. Taken together these products—milk, hay, and straw sold for town consumption—were twice as important as barley, and their importance, compared with wheat, was as 3 to 4. There had long been foreign competition in the beef market, and active foreign competition in the markets for 'hog-products,' butter, and cheese. But even in 1885, the imported beef was only about 9 per cent. of the total consumption by weight: no doubt less by value; and the imported mutton was between 7 and 8 per cent.[3] The movement of the index number for meat and butter reflects the situation. In the late 'sixties it had varied between 30 and 45 per cent. above the level of 1850–1[4]. It ran up to 60 per

[1] It is to be borne in mind however that general prices had risen so that grain had not retained its comparative position. See the diagram on p. 378, below, and cp. Layton, Sir W. T., *Prices in the Nineteenth Century*.

[2] Caird, *The Landed Interest*, p. 14; Lawes, J. B. and Gilbert, J. H., "On the Home Produce, Importation, Consumption and Price of Wheat, 1852–3 to 1879–80," *J.R.A.S.* 1880, p. 337: also in *S.J.* XLIII (1880), 313.

[3] Sauerbeck, A., in *S.J.* XLIX (1886), 606.

[4] *Ibid.* and also *S.J.* LVI (1893), 220.

cent. above 1850–1 in 1873, an abnormal year in every way; but the subsequent fall never took it, in that generation, below the level of the late 'sixties; and it only got down to that level in 1885. Taking decade averages, the index number for 1878–87 is only 5 per cent. below that of 1868–77. For milk, hay, and straw there are no trustworthy index numbers, but it is likely that they would show no serious fall[1].

Wool prices had a peculiarly disastrous history. Driven over-high by the cotton famine[2], and again by the trade boom of the early 'seventies, more was expected of them than they could maintain. By 1885–6 they were about half what they had been in 1873–4. Everything was against them—the gold position, slack consumption, cheapening transport, changing fashions. The last dragged down abnormally the prices of the long Lincoln and Leicester wools. One standard Lincoln grade, a staple raw material for Bradford, which could be had for 10*d*. a lb. in 1883–6 had fetched 22¾*d*. in 1873–4. For the whole period 1850–80 its price had averaged 18¾*d*. Farmers were left bewildered: there seemed to be neither precedent nor reason for these things. They meant black ruin on many of the great corn and wool farms of the Lincoln wolds[3].

The Commissioners of 1881–2 were misled by the belief that depression was primarily a matter of weather, of a quite abnormal cycle of lean dripping years. European experts "all agreed," they said, "in ascribing it mainly to...unfavourable seasons." English counties' fortunes had varied with their weather. Yorkshire had got off better than many because "the rainfall having been less than in the Midland counties, the crops did not suffer so much." Foreign competition the Commissioners allowed to be a true cause for Caird's dilemma of the

[1] Milk fell hardly at all. There are no comprehensive figures for the three years 1868–70, but on the assumption that they were not higher than those of 1871 the index number for 1868–77 would be 135·4: for 1878–87 it was 131·6. (The base year, 100, is 1900.) For the seven years 1871–7 it was 141·7. Probably the price was rather lower in 1868–70 than in 1871. *B. of T. Return on Wholesale and Retail Prices of* 1903 (Cmd. 321). These returns start with 1871; but some milk prices from the books of London hospitals given on p. 137 make it certain that prices in 1868–70 were at least not above those of 1871.

[2] Above, p. 223.

[3] Sauerbeck, in *S.J.* 1886, and the *Return of Wholesale and Retail Prices*, as above. The *Return* unfortunately exaggerates the wool situation because it is based almost entirely on Lincoln prices, and Lincoln wools had suffered most owing to changes of fashion. There is no means of correcting it, short of an elaborate inquiry.

reduced crop and the unrisen price; but they tended to overlook its importance. Whilst noting that the only part of the continent which had suffered little was the dairy country of Denmark, and that Cheshire had not suffered "to anything like the same extent as many counties,"[1] they did not underline what was already clear, that beyond the weather, and apart from that shift in the purchasing power of gold which they neither apprehended nor discussed, lay the question of corn transport; behind that, for the future, the new methods of transporting meat and wool[2]. So recently as 1878, Caird had thought that the British farmer might "rest content" with the "natural protection" of distance[3]; but distance had ceased to protect corn and would soon cease to protect meat. The age, as it was fond of saying, was engaged in annihilating distance.

Assistant Commissioners' reports in 1881–2[4] show that whereever wheat and arable were subordinate, or towns near and large, there no evidence of really serious distress was to be found; none in Cheshire, Lancashire, Cumberland, Westmorland, Northumberland or Durham; little in Kent, West Somerset, Devon or Cornwall; little among the Welsh hill farmers, though cold rains had brought some "disastrous" losses of sheep. While landlords in Eastern England were abating rents and losing tenants, Lord Penrhyn explained that on his Carnarvon estates there were no arrears and no farms unlet[5]. Indeed it became almost a Welsh national grievance subsequently that, in the six westernmost counties, rents, measured by Schedule A of the Income Tax, fell very little after 1878–9, remaining in 1893–4 no less than 18·5 per cent. above the level of 1864–5, though 2·1 per cent. below that of 1878–9. In the seven easterly counties there was a fall after 1878–9 very nearly to the level of 1864–5. English rents on the same basis, after a rise and fall, showed a net reduction of 15·2 per cent. over the twenty-nine years 1864–5 to 1893–4[6].

The actual fall, in England and Wales together, from 1878–9 to 1893–4 was 22·6 per cent.[7] In Scotland it was 18·5 per cent.

[1] *Report*, p. 12 (Europe and Denmark), 9 (Yorks and Cheshire).

[2] Above, p. 91, 224.

[3] *The Landed Interest*, p. 5, 7.

[4] They are summarised in the general *Report*, p. 9–10.

[5] *R.C. on Agriculture*, Q. 7467.

[6] *R.C. on Land in Wales*, p. 469.

[7] The *R.C. on Land in Wales* gives the English fall, 1878–9 to 1893–4, without Wales, as 23·7. In the five English counties least affected by the depression—Cumberland, Westmorland, Cheshire, Devon and Cornwall—the fall was only 10·5 per cent. *Ibid.* The other figures used here are from Stamp, *op. cit.* p. 49.

Scotland had a greater area of westerly conditions and much less wheat. In the English counties most affected, the fall was far more than 22·6 per cent.; for some landlords of the West got off easily as has been seen. An English corporation which at that time held land in thirteen counties, nearly all of which had to meet the full shock of falling prices, may serve as an illustration. Its net receipts from its estates fell by 38·9 per cent. between 1878–9 and 1893–4[1]. The fall of rents was greatest precisely in those areas where the rise since 1851–2 had been least, and where, as on the clays, there was a maximum interest element in it. A certain bitterness was natural among landowners who were criticised for taking an 'unearned increment,' or an excessive price, for the economists' 'natural and indestructible properties of the soil.' Such criticism there had always been; but never such a volume of it as in the 'eighties[2].

How desperate the position seemed to farmers, before there had been time for adjustment of rents, was shown by the inquiries of 1881–2. Rents, it is to be borne in mind, had been rising all through the lean years from 1875 to 1879. An increased rent at least on every change of tenancy had come to be assumed. A good deal of land had been bought by those who cultivated it, at the inflated prices which such rents implied. In Wales land had risen to an "absurd value."[3] Wales, as has been seen, was a relatively fortunate area. So were the English North-West and South-West. But in the counties of the Welsh marches and the West Midlands the situation was worse by the end of 1881 than at any time "within the memory of this generation."[4] In the East Midlands and East Anglia it was worse still, worst of all, it was said, in Huntingdon, which is all clay with an edging of fen; in Cambridge with its fen, gault, and chalk; and in Essex, where a little hilly chalk in the North-West soon leads down to long stretches of the London clay[5]. North and South, no county had escaped.

By 1880 the years of rising rents were over. There were arrears, abatements, remissions. As tenants died or threw up their land, a new scale began to establish itself. Some land

[1] These are the figures for King's College, Cambridge, as given in its 'Mundum' Books.

[2] The age of Chamberlain radicalism and of Henry George's *Progress and Poverty*. See below, p. 483 *sqq*.

[3] Colonel Hughes before the *R.C. on Land in Wales*, p. 468.

[4] Assistant Commissioner Doyle to *R.C. on Agriculture*, p. 9.

[5] *Ibid*. p. 10.

went right out of cultivation, 'tumbled down' to grass, or even to thistles and thorns. Of this there was not a great deal; off the clays very little. The cultivated area of Britain did not decline. But there was enough to be talked about; and for the years 1879–85 there were on the average 133,000 more acres of 'bare-fallow or uncropped arable' than there had been in 1874–8. Expensive drainage operations slackened off. A census of farmsteads and cottages rebuilt would not contain many entries for the decade 1878–88. From 1879, the *Journal of the Royal Agricultural Society* began to fill with papers on Dutch or Danish dairy practice and on the best and most economical methods of laying land down to grass. Whether laid down or 'tumbled down,' a million and a half acres, 10·5 per cent., were added to the permanent pasture of Britain between 1879 and 1887. Arable farmers were tempted to economise on 'artificials'; on the trimming and plashing of hedges; on the cleaning of ditches and water-courses; on hoeing and thistle-spudding; on deep expensive ploughing or on those repeated workings of the land which make the perfect seed-bed. Those who came best through the troubles had a sense of the market and knew how to farm light, to skim the land without too much risk to its 'indestructible' qualities. A few such men came through very well indeed, sometimes taking on farm after farm from less adaptable men who were going to the wall[1].

Farmer and land-agent witnesses, setting out their troubles before the Commissioners and Assistant Commissioners of 1881–2, had much to tell about a reputed decline in the quality of agricultural labour[2]. There was less willingness, less persistence, and so less skill, they said. Education and the Act of 1870 were blamed for this, and for its alleged cause, the growing social and political self-consciousness of a class not supposed liable to distracting discontents. Farmers had learnt no historical generalisations about the coming of discontent and revolution, not when circumstances are worsening, but when they are on the mend, though too slowly; so all this seemed to them most unreasonable. For every one agreed in 1881–2 that the labourer, whether his skill were declining or not, was "never in

[1] There were such episodes in the hardest-hit parts of Lincolnshire, for example (private information).

[2] *E.g.* Q. 34,066; 34,523. For the other side of the picture see W. C. Little's Report to the *R.C. on Labour* (1893–4, XXVII. part 2), p. 44.

a better position."[1] Ten years later, when depression had done all its work, the evidence was still more general and emphatic. The labourer's condition had "greatly improved...he dresses better, eats more butchers' meat, he travels more, he reads more, he drinks less."[2] Between the inquiries of 1867 and those of the years 1891–2 "a quiet economic revolution...with little aid from legislation" had "transferred to the labourer from one-fourth to one-third of that profit which the landowners and farmers then received."[3] The calculation must not be pressed; but it pointed towards a real transfer and dated it with fair accuracy. A foreign student of British economic conditions had just published a table of the estimated purchasing power of agricultural day-wages in terms of wheat. He suggested that whereas an average day's work in the 'forties yielded 16 lbs. of wheat, and in the 'fifties 17, it was worth 23 lbs. in the 'seventies and 30 in the 'eighties[4]. Men do not chew wheat. Millers' and bakers' pay had not fallen. A bread calculation is therefore not quite so favourable to the labourer, and it cannot be made so precise. But it suggests that, on the average, in the 'eighties he could get three four-pound loaves for every two that his father had in the 'fifties. In so far as he lived on bread, he was 50 per cent. better off[5].

The general course of his cash earnings, weekly, harvest and miscellaneous, together with the estimated money value of his allowances in kind—a small item—had been as set out below[6]. The curve shows these earnings for the year as percentages of those of 1892. It masks the varying movements of the counties

[1] *R.C. on Agriculture*, 1882, p. 22 and Q. 4791.

[2] C. M. Chapman, Assistant Commissioner, 1893–4, XXXV. 44.

[3] Little's *Report*, p. 2.

[4] Steffen, G., in the *Nineteenth Century*, quoted in Little, p. 161. Steffen's fuller discussion is in his *Studien zur Geschichte der Englischen Lohnarbeiter*, vol. III (1905).

[5] Bread prices for the whole country are not available. In London the average price fell nearly 24 per cent. between the decades 1850–9 and 1880–9. See below, p. 460. Earnings averaged over all the years of the two decades in the same way rose also by nearly 24 per cent. The statement in the text is a fair rough result.

[6] In the diagram on p. 286, based on Bowley, A. L., in *S.J.* 1898 and 1899. The figures for many of the years are statistical interpolations. It will be seen that a curve drawn through those years for which information is fullest would have the same general character. So would a curve based simply on weekly money wages, as in Bowley's *Wages in the United Kingdom* (1900). For "there is no reason to think that the ratio of wages to earnings changed to any great extent on the average since Arthur Young's time," *S.J.* 1899, p. 556.

to give a generalised national picture. But this masking of county differences is not important; for since labour had become more mobile the counties moved more nearly in step. Their wage levels differed, often widely; but there was no great risk of wage stagnation or fall in one coinciding with wage rise or stagnation in another. Movements at any one time tended to be in one direction.

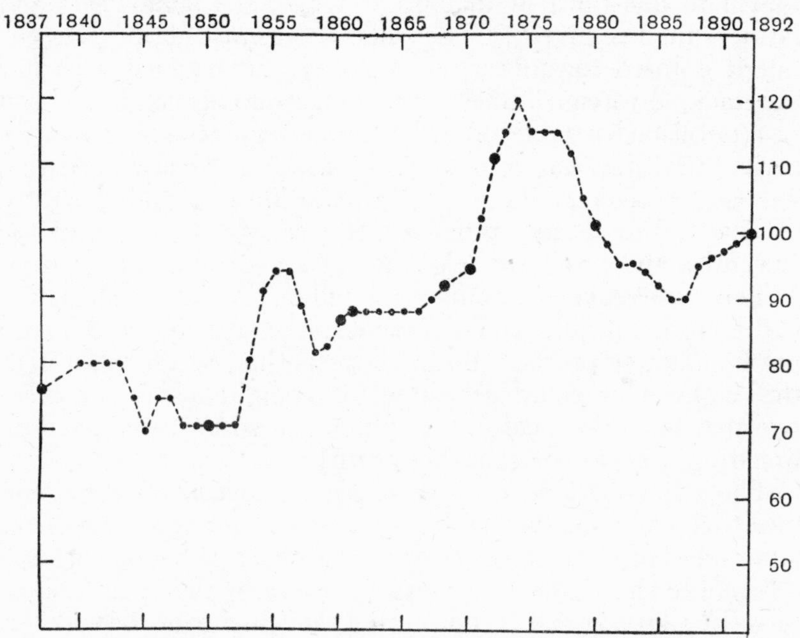

Agricultural earnings in England and Wales, expressed as percentages of the earnings of 1892. (After Bowley.)

The larger mark ● denotes years for which information is most complete.

The long depression, it is seen, brought a sharp fall in money earnings, just as the short depression which followed the repeal of the corn laws had brought a fall, though a slight one. To the labourer, whose peak wage of the 'seventies had been nothing magnificent, this fall might well seem unmerited and monstrous, although prices fell further. Perhaps he did sometimes work grudgingly, as the farmers said. In the areas from which evidence mostly comes, he had just been beaten in a wage-fight and he was looking to redress through his new vote and what people were telling him it would bring. Yet when earnings touched bottom, in 1886–7, they were still as high as they had been in the late 'sixties and nearly 27 per cent. higher than in the years about 1850. From 1887 recovery began. It was odd that its start coincided with the labourer's early use of his vote and with Victoria's jubilee: they were only coincidences.

In Scotland, the course of earnings, which is less well known than that for England and Wales, was similar but more favourable to the labourer. Comprehensive Scottish figures for the years about 1850, comparable with those which Caird collected in England, are lacking. But all the evidence suggests that the claim made in 1892 that Scottish earnings had risen 50 per cent. in the previous forty years was approximately correct—perhaps an understatement if the exact years 1852 and 1892 are taken[1]. (English wages, as the curve indicates, had risen 41 per cent. in the same period.) Nor had Scottish earnings during the 'eighties fallen quite so far as English from their summit of the 'seventies. Scotland's small wheat area helped both farmer and labourer when the crisis came.

The provision of adequate cottage gardens, allotments, potato patches and the like had become more general since 1850; but how much more general it is hard to say. The gardenless cottage was far from extinct in 1867. Sometimes whole villages, 'open villages,' like Docking in Norfolk and similar places in arable and late enclosed districts, were made up of very little else[2]. Sometimes a whole county was said to show an unusual number of them: Devon was such a county[3]. But the impression left by the inquiries of that year is reasonably satisfactory; and though there is not evidence of marked improvement in those areas where the garden position had been worst a generation earlier[4], there are many counties where it is said to be definitely good, counties so far apart as Hampshire, Hereford, North Lancashire and Yorkshire. In Yorkshire the garden was almost universal and was often accompanied—as it sometimes was in

[1] The claim is in the Report on Scotland of R. Hunter-Pringle and E. Wilkinson to the *R.C. on Labour*, 1893–4, XXXVI. 33. Scottish figures are "not so discursive nor so complete" as the English; Bowley, *S.J.* 1899, p. 140. The interpolated figure which Bowley accepts for 1852 is 60 against the basic 100 of 1892, or a rise of 66·6. In the depression of the 'eighties his lowest Scottish figure is 93 against the English 90.

[2] *R. on Employment of Children...in Agriculture*, 1867–8 (XVII), p. 35 (Docking) and *passim*.

[3] *Ibid.* vol. II (1868–9, XIII): Report of E. Portman on Hants, Devon and Cornwall.

[4] Cp. vol. I. p. 467–8.

Cheshire and Shropshire—by a 'cow-gate,' the right of grazing your cow in the lanes and by-places[1].

The allotment or potato patch had been adopted experimentally between 1820 and 1850 by landlords, farmers and parsons as a social palliative, especially in those districts where gardens were most scarce and the old poor law had been most abused. Parliament in the early 'forties had left the work in the hands of the men who had begun it, after playing with the idea of bringing it under government supervision[2]. Progress was intermittent and slow. A Berkshire report of 1860 speaks of retrogression except in the neighbourhood of towns[3]. The Commissioners of 1867–8 were convinced that there had been a considerable general advance since 1843; but though they could quote instances they could not gauge the movement. They noted with regret that the only public method of providing allotments, by the setting aside of land newly enclosed under the General Enclosure Act of 1845, had yielded no more than 2119 acres in twenty-two years[4]. The Commissioners of 1881 listened to discouraging evidence. One witness spoke of the disappearance of allotments in many counties, and Joseph Arch, the labourers' leader, offered an explanation when he complained of the exorbitant rents often asked for them by farmers and others[5]. Of this there is much good evidence[6]. It was Arch's ambition to see the labourer pass from allotment-holder into peasant-proprietor. Next year his parliamentary sympathiser, Jesse Collings, tried to help the cause by his Extension of Allotments Act (45 and 46 Vict. c. 80).

That Act did not work well and yet, when allotments and cottage gardens of fair size were first counted in 1886, the confessedly imperfect results were most encouraging[7]. The tide

[1] *Report*, as above, vol. I. p. 105 (Yorks); vol. II. 27 (Cheshire and Salop), 30 (Hants), 60 (Hereford), 154 (N. Lancs). The *R.C. on Labour* (1893–4, XXVII. part 2, p. 128) summarises the garden position for six sample districts, in Lincs, Cambs, Wilts, Worcester, Somerset, Essex. Nearly 20 per cent. of the cottages had only tiny gardens and 11·5 per cent. had none. But the cottager with no, or an inadequate, garden might have an allotment.

[2] Vol. I. p. 473–4. [3] *J.R.A.S.* 1860, p. 44.

[4] *Report of* 1867–8, as above, vol. I. p. xli–li.

[5] *R.C. on Agriculture*, Q. 59,303; 54,463–4 (Arch). These replies are quoted in Curtler, W. H. R., *The Enclosure and Redistribution of our Land* (1920), p. 280–2.

[6] Arch, Joseph. *The Story of the Life of Joseph Arch* (1898), p. 343; Heath, F. G., *Peasant Life in the West of England* (1872), p. 149; Stubbs, C. W., *The Land and the Labourers* (1891), p. 45.

[7] See the discussion by Major Craigie, "Agricultural Holdings in England and Abroad," *S.J.* 1887, p. 86 *sqq.* and Curtler, *op. cit.* p. 283.

had been flooding quietly while good men in a hurry were crying that there was no motion and some observers were unable to detect any. It appeared that there were in England and Wales 389,000 detached allotments, mostly within half a mile of the homes of those who worked them; 257,000 gardens of an eighth of an acre and upwards attached to cottages (those below an eighth of an acre were not reported); 93,000 field potato plots; and 9400 'cow-gates.' These figures excluded the gardens and allotments provided by railway companies for railway workers; but no doubt some considerable proportion of those included would be held by men who were no more agriculturalists than they. Yet even with a generous allowance for such men, it is evident that there were allotments, fair-sized gardens, and potato patches enough to serve most of the 580–600,000 agricultural labourers of twenty years old and upwards in England and Wales. Gardens and allotments might have been bigger and better and cheaper; they could not with advantage have been much more numerous. This was confirmed a few years later when it appeared that in most English rural Poor Law Unions the allotment supply approximately met the demand; that in none of the sample Unions reported on were there more than 14·6 inhabitants per allotment; and that in the most favoured Union there were only 5·3. The figures include small country towns and exclude gardens[1].

In Wales the allotment was not popular; but the field potato patch was, and it was found everywhere[2].

The Scottish figures for 1886 suggest at first sight a rather less satisfactory situation. There were only 46,500 allotments, good gardens, potato patches or cow-gates among some 70,000 labourers and shepherds of twenty years old and upwards. But living-in on small farms, or boarding with married men on large ones, were commoner practices in Scotland than in England, and the bothy system was not yet extinct; so there was less demand for allotments and gardens. The Scottish married labourer normally had his kale-yard or potato patch, though sometimes he preferred an allowance of potatoes to the toil of growing them[3].

Boarding unmarried labourers with a foreman or other leading hand was known also in England, being commonest in Notting-

[1] Little's Report to the *R.C. on Labour*, p. 134.

[2] Report on Wales (1893–4, XXXVI), p. 25.

[3] Report on Scotland (1893–4, XXXVI), p. 14, 27–8. For the bothy system, below, p. 511.

ham and Lincoln, where to a great degree it had replaced living-in[1]. Big modern cottages had been provided for foremen to facilitate the arrangement. Only the largest farmer could require them, so the system can nowhere be described as general. Perhaps it accentuated the gap between farmer and labourer, but it did not create it; and it saved many a young labourer the long tramp to his work which had been common before housing was adjusted to the various types of nineteenth-century farm. Side by side with it might be found, if not always any living-in, at least the meal shared by a small farmer with his man. Such habits never died out altogether even in the East: living-in was by no means extinct in Kent in 1867[2]. In the North-West they remained common[3]. But they were declining everywhere, even in Wales. At the census of 1861 there were Welsh counties in which more labourers lived in than out. By 1870 the decline of living-in is registered for Monmouth. By 1881 it was only possible to say of Wales that living-in was "much more general...than in England." That it might easily be[4].

Sharing meals is a good democratic habit; but the historian who has personal knowledge of living-in as practised at a later date in the English North-West and in Wales, or in France or in Switzerland, will not waste much sentiment over its decline.

Living-in, boarding, and the bothy system had been Scotland's solution of the labour problem where population was thin and farms big. In England, the Fens and the districts round about them, having the proletariat of small country towns and open villages to draw on, had supplemented boarding by the gang system[5]. As steam drainage made the fenland safe and firm, in the 'forties and 'fifties[6], those "immense bowling greens separated by ditches" which had delighted Cobbett were turned up black and put under wheat and potatoes. There were farms among them but no cottages, except a few bad ones used by horse and cattle men. The Norfolk sands above the Fen, Lincoln Heath, and the Lincoln Wolds had also been won for cropping

[1] *J.R.A.S.* 1861, p. 162 (Notts); *R. on Children in Agriculture*, 1867, p. 75 (Lincs).

[2] *R. on Children in Agriculture*, 1868–9 (XIII), E. Stanhope's Report, p. 26.

[3] Personal knowledge, for Lincolnshire; *R.C. on Labour*, A. W. Fox's Report, p. 6 for Cumberland and N. Lancs.

[4] *R.C. on Land in Wales*, p. 149 for 1861; *J.R.A.S.* 1870, p. 294 for Monmouth; *R.C. on Agriculture*, Q. 65,697 for 1881.

[5] Vol. I. p. 468–9.

[6] Vol. I. p. 445.

in the nineteenth century. The working of the close and open village system had delayed their appropriate equipment with cottages. And so from Castle Acre among the heaths and warrens of West Norfolk, from Chatteris, the Deepings and Spalding in the Fens; as from Louth, Caistor and Ludford, under the Wolds, the gang-master led out draggled troops of women and children to weed and pick stones and hoe. In Louth there was a little Irish colony which fed the gangs: elsewhere they were English[1].

The system hardly existed outside these newly won districts; and in them it often declined when the winning was finished; when "twitch had been almost eradicated and other weeds reduced to a minimum."[2] In the greater part of the country it was completely unknown. Because of the transition to arable in the fens, where the system was at its worst, it appears to have grown between 1850 and 1865; although at the same time provision of more cottages by such good landlords as Lord Yarborough, coincident with the final cleaning of the land, was cutting at its roots on the Lincoln Wolds[3]. Besides what came to be known as the public gangs, which included 6–7000 people in the 'sixties, private gangs organised by large farmers and put under their nominees were common in these same areas. The Commissioners of the 'sixties believed that they contained many more people than the public gangs; but the point was controverted and never decided. Even if they did, the gang population at its height was only a fraction of the rural population of a few counties. It was recruited very far down the social scale. The public gang-master was normally the type of man whom no respectable farmer would take on to his permanent staff[4]. Members of the permanent staff did not wish their wives and children to work under such people, and were not forced by need to let them do so. The wife of the regular labourer does not go to work, the Commissioners say, and the children "are

[1] *Sixth Report on Children's Employment* (*Agricultural Gangs*), 1867, XVI. 67, p. v, vi, vii, 6 (the Louth Irish), etc. See also Hasbach, W., *A History of the English Agricultural Labourer* (Eng. trans. 1908), ch. IV.

[2] *Report*, p. vi. Besides the districts referred to, *i.e.* Lincoln, Hunts, Cambs, and Norfolk, there were gangs, public or private, in Suffolk and Notts and a few in Northants, Beds, Bucks, Leicester and Rutland, generally also on newly won ground. *Ibid.* p. v and 1870, XIII (Index vol. to the *Children's Employment Commission*). The list of counties in the Report is not quite complete.

[3] *Ibid.* p. vi.

[4] *Ibid.* p. xi.

kept longer at school."[1] That is in Lincolnshire, where nearly a quarter of the gang population was enumerated.

Legislative control of this cheap, dangerous, and slavish system was a by-product of the factory and education movements of the 'sixties. The Gangs Act of 1868 (30 and 31 Vict. c. 130) forbade the employment of children under eight, regulated the working relations of men and women, and established licences for gang-masters. As it affected public gangs only, its first effect was to encourage private ones[2]. These, in so far as they relied on the work of very young children, were crippled in their turn by the successive education acts of the 'seventies. They had always been less liable to abuse than the public gangs. Meanwhile the housing position was improving a little; no more land was being cleared for the plough and cleaned after it; demand for gang work slackened. By the end of the 'eighties gangs were said to be "gradually dying out" in the Fens, though there were several about Swaffham, and no doubt at other points[3]. A few sad droves of women stone-pickers could be found on the Lincoln Wolds[4]; and some sort of temporary gang organisation was necessary for potato lifting, fruit picking, and hop-picking, as it still is. But these shrunken and regulated survivals from a harder unregulated time themselves showed that life on the soil was becoming more tolerable for those nearest to it, if more difficult for some others.

It is not easy to show any direct link between the improved position of the agricultural labourer of the middle 'eighties and the Labourers' Unions of the previous decade. The working of impersonal forces would account for all, or nearly all, of that improvement. True, without the Unions the wage peak of the 'seventies might not everywhere have been won; but then it was lost again. Certainly the Unions helped to educate labourers, politicians, and the public. This education bore fruit later. They also educated farmers—in the use of machinery; which proved good for labour in the end, though not for particular labourers at the time. Possibly they hastened the Reform Bill of 1884;

[1] *Report*, p. vi.

[2] As shown by the later inquiries of the same series as that of 1867. See 1870, XIII, *s.v.* Gangs.

[3] *R.C. on Labour*, 1893–4, XXXV. Chapman's Report, p. 22; Fox's Report, p. 9.

[4] And probably elsewhere: it is on the Lincoln Wolds that the author has seen them.

but even if they did, in economic fields reform bills work like delayed-action mines, and do not always blow up what they should.

There were strikes before the Unions. When food prices were running up in the summer of 1867[1], the strike of twenty-eight labourers at Gawcott, Bucks, a strike for 12*s.* a week in place of 10*s.*, caught the attention of the London press and of a sympathising public, now reasonably well-informed about rural wages, cottages and gangs[2]. Money flowed into Gawcott: Karl Marx in London read about it: the strike found its way into *Das Kapital*[3]. Next year the Rev. Edward Girdlestone told the British Association that, to his mind, the only way of bettering the labourers' condition was the formation of a national Union. Girdlestone was working in a particularly stagnant North Devon parish, where wages were low, cottages bad, and farmers savagely hard-fisted[4]. He was trying to speed up the mills of God, grinding slowly just then in the labourers' interest, by organised migration and emigration. Soon, news of the Trade Union inquiry of 1867–9 and of the Trade Union legislation of 1870–1 got through to the villages, where 1830 and 1834 were not forgotten and the Union Workhouse stood gaunt, the reminder of what society had to offer. Food was cheap in 1869–70, but from the harvest of 1870 prices moved up again, and not food prices only. For three years British wheat stood above 55*s.* and in the fourth, 1873–4, above 60*s.* Bread in London was dearer on the average in 1872 than it had been in any year since the Crimean War except 1867.

Quite early in 1871 a labourers' union was started at Leintwardine in Hereford, "and it was backed up by the rector." "It spread over six counties in a very short time." "No sooner had this Union caught on than wages in Hereford rose on an average two shillings a week, and all over the six counties there was improvement."[5] Like Canon Girdlestone, these men of the

[1] Wheat was above 60*s.* throughout the year, except for a couple of weeks in February, and reached 73*s.* 8*d.* early in 1868. Potatoes were also very dear.

[2] See *e.g.* the *Economist*, July 27, 1867.

[3] Hasbach, *op. cit.* p. 276 n., learnt of it from Marx.

[4] Heath, F. G., *The English Peasantry* (1874), p. 189. Girdlestone had come from a Lancashire parish where the labourers were "well paid, well housed... well cared for."

[5] Arch, *op. cit.* p. 110–11. See also his evidence before the *R.C. on Agriculture*, 1881, Q. 58,371 *sqq.* Cp. Clayden, A., *The Revolt of the Field* (1874); Heath, F. G., *Peasant Life in the West of England* (1872); Clifford, F., *The Agricultural Lock-out of* 1874 (1875); Hasbach, *op. cit.* p. 276–7; Webb, S. and B., *History of Trade Unionism*, p. 314–19.

South-West believed in betterment by increased mobility. "Emigration, migration, but not strikes" was their motto[1]. They helped their members to move into high-wage areas like Stafford, Lancashire and Yorkshire; and they organised a little emigration to America. Their Union was already full-grown when, in February, 1872, some men of Wellesbourne, on the Avon above Stratford, tramped North to Barford to ask Joseph Arch, a Methodist lay-preacher, ditcher and hedger, who had been an organiser of piece-work jobs for farmers while still in his teens[2], to come and address a meeting and start a Union. Warwickshire men dated the whole movement from the wet night of February 7, "when Arch beneath the Wellesbourne tree" so wrought on them that they "enrolled between two and three hundred members that night."[3]

They were on strike at Wellesbourne in March. Helped by bourgeois sympathy, including that of John Stuart Mill, and some bourgeois money, unionism spread fast[4]. Arch claimed "nearly fifty thousand enrolled members" by May. There were strikes or talk of strikes from Dorset to Norfolk. The demand for labour was brisk and wages in every trade were rising, so that the men very often got at least some part of what they asked. Arch believed in migration. Back in the 'forties, while wandering at his trade, he had compared the cottages and gardens of Eastern Wales to their advantage with those of Warwickshire[5]. But he was a fighter of Cobbett's breed, though, unlike Cobbett, he fought with biting Old Testament weapons, prophesying to valleys of dry bones and wielding the sword of the Lord and of Gideon. He never relied on migration alone; and when Girdlestone urged compromise, pointing out that Warwick was already much better off than Devon, Arch's only conclusion was that Devon needed a good fighting Union. So he and his followers sang:

> The farm labourers of South Warwickshire
> Have not had a rise for many a year,
> Although bread has often been dear,
> But now they've found a Union[6].

[1] Arch, *op. cit.* p. 110.

[2] With "men working under me," *op. cit.* p. 40.

[3] Arch, *op. cit.* p. 73. The line "When Arch beneath the Wellesbourne tree" comes from a Union song.

[4] Heath, *The English Peasantry*, p. 197 *sqq*. There was active support from the *Daily News* and other Liberal journals.

[5] Arch, *op. cit.* p. 43.

[6] Arch, *op. cit.* p. 87.

In 1873–4, when at the height of its strength, Arch's Union, the National, claimed a membership of 100,000 and branches in every English county except Cumberland, Westmorland, Yorkshire, Lancashire, Cheshire and Cornwall. The other chief organisation, the Federal, was something of a competitor. Even if Unionism could show a few cells in the North, it had not really touched the high-wage territory across the Trent, though the Federal had a strong footing in Lincolnshire[1]. In the East it had called out counter-organisation among farmers, beginning with the Association for Cambridgeshire and West Suffolk started at Newmarket in October-November, 1872. In April of 1873 the associated farmers of the Sudbury district locked out their Union men, and won[2]. There was friction, striking, farmers' stupid attacks on 'agitators,' labourers' crude abuse of farmers, and some persecution of non-unionists, up and down the Eastern counties all that year. In March of 1874 the Newmarket farmers followed the lead of Sudbury, and replied to a demand for a 14*s*. wage and a 54-hour week by a lock-out of Union men[3]. Before the end of the month the lock-out had affected nine counties and some thousands of men[4]. By July, for it was a long fight, the National Union had made grants to locked-out members in a dozen counties, but had spent four-fifths of its money in three, Cambridge, Suffolk and Essex. At the end of July it gave in, withdrew the grants, and resolved "to place migration and emigration at the disposal of the labourers, or the alternative of depending wholly on their own resources."[5] The Federal Union did much the same.

What with volunteer labour, surplus non-agricultural or non-union labour which was available almost everywhere, Irish labour, and machinery, the East Anglian farmers had come through well and were facing the harvest with confidence. "In-

[1] Clifford, *op. cit.* p. 17, 20. The Lincolnshire League, like some other County Unions, was affiliated to the Federal.

[2] *Ibid.* p. 9–11.

[3] *The Agricultural Lock-out of* 1874, of which Clifford wrote the story in letters to the *Times*. And see Bishop Fraser's letter to the *Times*, April 2, 1874.

[4] The total number thrown out before the struggle was over is uncertain. It seems to have been from 6000 to 10,000. The National Union claimed 3100 members locked out and the Federal 2500, and there were others. But the rival Union leaders accused one another of exaggeration. Clifford, *op. cit.* p. 21–2 and Hasbach, *op. cit.* p. 285.

[5] Quoted in Clifford, p. 146. Money had been received from industrial Unions, *e.g.* the A.S.E., as well as from bourgeois sympathisers; but the supply could not be maintained.

stead of employing twenty-six men," a representative Suffolk farmer said just before harvest, "I am doing with seventeen and my work was never more forward."[1] Observers noted that "the machine makers are not without hopes of perfecting a machine for tying up the corn in the wake of the reapers, which would indeed be a valuable ally to the farmer."[2] There was discouragement and dissension in the Unions, and their numbers fell off; but Arch still claimed 60,000 in his at the end of 1875. Then came the black years, and the most that he could claim in May 1879 was "some twenty-three thousand."[3] Farmers had begun to cut wages and turn off men, and would continue to do both. The Unions almost vanished away[4].

Arch threw himself into the franchise fight and, when the franchise had been won, into the new democratic politics of the country-side. At the election of 1885, in *A Word of Council to the New Electors*, he spoke of "men turned out to starve while the land by millions of acres is lying starving under your eyes for want of labour." Men had been turned out. By 1885–6 wages had fallen back to somewhere about the level at which they had stood when he went to "the Wellesbourne tree." But if some land was "starving...for want of labour" that was hardly the farmers' fault, or the landlords', with wheat at 32*s*. a quarter or less; and wheat at 32*s*. or less meant bread about 25 per cent. cheaper than it had been in 1871–5 when the Unions were most active. Bread prices still ruled country budgets, so this was no small matter. Cheese also was cheaper; tea and sugar much cheaper; bacon at least no dearer. And so the labourer of the late 'eighties 'dressed better, ate more butchers' meat, travelled more, read more.'[5] There was a little surplus now for these things; but it cannot be said that the Unions had done much to make it. Perhaps by instilling hope and strengthening self-respect, they were in part responsible for that other generalisation about the village labourer—"he drinks less." If so, they share responsibility with the chapel, the school, the allotment, the friendly society, the new cottage, the cricket club, with each and every thing that eased the cramped tedium of village life or revealed what lies beyond.

[1] Clifford, p. 179. A sample statement out of many.

[2] *Ibid.* p. 65.

[3] Arch, *op. cit.* p. 254, 333.

[4] At the end of the 'eighties they were very weak and existed only in 6 out of 38 districts inquired into by the *R.C. on Labour* (Little's Report, p.146).

[5] Quoted above, p. 285.

CHAPTER VIII

THE ORGANISATION OF COMMERCE

THE main features of the commercial organisation of Britain, as it existed in the later nineteenth century, were hewn in the rough even before the railway age. Few institutions of new type, few entirely novel practices, grew up in the three decades after 1850. Important modifications there were, no doubt. Writing in 1905, George Joachim Goschen could even refer to the "fundamental change wrought by the transfer of an enormous proportion of our industry and commerce from private individuals to public companies" between 1850 and 1885[1]. But this was only a change of balance, not to be over-rated. Well informed and cautious as Goschen was, there is more than a spice of exaggeration in his "fundamental" and his "enormous." As to changes of method—it is probable that after at most a morning's talk with Goschen in 1885, David Ricardo or Nathan Rothschild would have been able to operate in the City or at Liverpool with ease, though some of their slower witted contemporaries might have been bewildered by the pace, and by certain unfamiliar customs or instruments.

In the country, institutions and methods already moribund in the 'twenties had gone a step or two nearer the grave[2]. The travelling tinker or pedlar had been driven North and West and had lost ground every decade. The fairs, except the horse and cattle fairs, were fast dropping the remnants of their economic importance[3]. On corn or cattle market day in a country town farmers sold to dealers and dealers to the public; but only in outlying districts would there be much of the old-style direct trade in foodstuffs between country producers and town consumers[4]. Market selling was passing more and more into the hands of professionals, resident or migratory. In the

[1] *Essays and Addresses*, p. 7, referring to an address given in 1885. Cp. p. 138, above, and p. 311, below.

[2] Cp. vol. I. p. 220–5.

[3] Though there are men living in Cambridgeshire who can remember the farmers waiting for Sturbridge Fair to replace things lost or damaged.

[4] It survived most vigorously in Wales, *e.g.* Cardigan market day, even after 1900.

towns of the industrial North, the great market halls[1] were just shopping places for the multitude; though some of the stalls would be held by producers. All industrial or agricultural villages of any size had their shops of various kinds. The railway, the penny post and the telegraph had brought them within easy reach of urban influences, and had helped to assimilate their business methods to those of the towns.

Quick communications had extinguished a few trades and traders. Long-distance cattle-droving, to take an obvious instance, was extinct; though so late as 1847 some cattle had still been driven "120 miles or more" to market[2]. Bullocks or dead meat could go from Aberdeen to London by rail or steamer. But if the long trading chains of personal links, by which the country had once been attached to the metropolis and the greater towns[3], had often been shortened, by elimination of middlemen of one sort and another, the greater dependence of the island on imported foodstuffs had added to the weight of central markets and metropolitan dealers, and required fresh middlemen's work in distribution. At the same time, the growing size and intricacy of commercial operations of all kinds had called for additional specialisation, and so perhaps for new links in the commercial chains.

The readjustment of the internal grain trade after the repeal of the Corn Laws, and of the London coal trade after the making of the railways, illustrate these various tendencies. During the last years of the Corn Laws, when the complete cessation of export had simplified a trade now become strictly insular, most of the British wheat had been sold direct to the miller. Small millers would buy only locally, but some of the larger ones employed factors to buy over wide areas, and might resell as merchants what they did not themselves grind. Good quality barley went for the most part straight to local maltsters; the rest, with the farmers' surplus of oats and beans, came into dealers' hands, for local or distant distribution. Great quantities of these and a fair, but smaller, quantity of wheat were handled in Mark Lane. The factors sometimes sold 'growers corn' from the home counties, as the growers' agents; more often the

[1] Vol. I. p. 226. The older halls were of course continuously enlarged or remodelled between 1830 and 1880.

[2] *S.C. to inquire into the Necessity of the removal of Smithfield Market as a nuisance in the centre of the British Metropolis*, 1847 (VIII. 275), Q. 969.

[3] Vol. I. p. 219.

corn sold had been bought from the grower outright by London and country dealers. Millers and secondary dealers were the chief purchasers. In Mark Lane were to be found also a small group of jobbers, who bought to resell and "take advantage of momentary changes of the market"—market operators in later commercial speech. The various groups might overlap at almost any point. Meanwhile merchants, many of whom were outside the domestic corn trade, carried on intermittent and necessarily speculative dealings in foreign grain, which could be warehoused in London at times when it might not be sold there, or could be resold in cargoes and parcels for overseas consumption while still on shipboard. Some of these merchants were connected with the Baltic Coffee House, where a business club of the usual English sort had taken shape in 1823, to introduce order into the rather disorderly Russian trade, particularly the trade in tallow[1].

When the world was being searched for grain at the time of the Irish famine, the general merchants—Russian, East Indian, American, whatever it might be—necessarily did most of the work, because no group of specialised foreign corn merchants existed. When the collapse came, in a list of 460 failures which occurred between August, 1847, and August, 1848, only twenty-six of the bankrupts were definitely described as corn merchants, although corn dealing had helped to bring down far more than that[2].

The general merchant did not cease handling grain when the import trade became a regular and fast growing thing. But the growth gave scope for more specialists—merchants, brokers, jobbers—who took part in the London dealings and, from London, in the direction of cargoes to other ports according to their needs. Throughout the period London remained the chief consumer and distributor of foreign grain; though with the increased importance of American supplies, from 1867–70 onwards, Liverpool grew into a serious rival, particularly in the wheat trade; and Hull was always powerful. The Baltic became the headquarters of the larger and more speculative transactions, purchases of cargoes afloat and sales and resales of grain for

[1] Vol. I. p. 231, 232–3, 303–5 (the old corn trade). Torrens, R., *Essay on the External Corn Trade* (1815), says nothing of value about organisation. For the history of the Baltic, Findlay, J. A., *The Baltic Exchange* (1927). Thomas Tooke, the historian of prices, was on the first committee. The rules are of April 22, 1823; p. 14.

[2] The list is in Evans, D. M., *The Commercial Crisis of* 1847–8, App. p. lxix *sqq.*

future shipment. Its Russian and North German connections had attracted merchants from abroad, especially Greeks familiar with the South Russian, Danubian, and Mediterranean grain trades. Among the Tookes and Thorntons and Todds of the old Baltic firms moved Rallis, Rodocanachis and Schroeders[1]. The cutting of the Suez Canal and the laying of the world's cables gave scope for master minds at the Baltic, whose committee in 1857 had not inappropriately taken quarters in the South Sea House. Hitherto the trade had all been done in sailing ships. The set of the wind in the Channel was a regular item of the market reports down to the 'seventies: it affected all dealings on the Baltic. Now a change was in sight.

The Corn Exchanges in Mark Lane provided the link between the insular and the international corn trades[2]. Unlike the Baltic they had, and still have, their stands and samples like any provincial exchange. There had never been auctions: it was the quiet private dealing of factors, some farmers, merchants and millers about the stands. It had always been a 'spot' trade, and a 'spot' trade it remained when the foreign corn got regularly into it. As the personnel of the Baltic and the Exchanges overlapped, and as duty-paid foreign corn had been sold in Mark Lane under the Corn Laws, this easily happened. The bulk of the buying to resell and the professional operating tended to concentrate at the Baltic. Cargoes first handled on the Baltic might be resold on, or near, arrival at the Corn Exchange; but the chief business there was in parcels of grain actually arrived. As the import trade grew, all the foreign grains could be sampled side by side with Essex wheat and Norfolk barley. Through the dealers on the Exchange they passed out into the country, to local dealers and millers, as the use of foreign grain spread from the greater to the smaller centres of population.

The whole story might have furnished Herbert Spencer, the philosopher of the age, with apt instances of his favourite 'differentiation and integration' of social organisms and functions, had he concerned himself with the contemporary evolution of

[1] Findlay, *op. cit.* p. 17–21. For the growing importance of America, see *e.g. Economist*, March 12, 1870 (Commercial Review of 1869).

[2] Vol. I. p. 303–5. Dowling, S. W., *The Exchanges of London* (1929), p. 180. The second exchange in Mark Lane was started in 1828: it was the headquarters of the seed trade. The old exchange was rebuilt in 1881.

the corn trade as much as with those primitive Lepchas and Todas whom he had never seen[1].

Changes in the coal trade of London and the South were determined mainly by the simple facts that whereas in 1850 only 55,000 tons of coal came into London by rail, in 1860 the figure was 1,500,000; in 1870, 3,500,000; 6,200,000 in 1880; and 7,250,000 in 1886. The sea-borne supply, which was 3,500,000 tons in 1850 and 3,600,000 in 1860, fell to a minimum of 2,500,000 in 1872, rising again to 4,740,000 in 1886[2]. The early nineteenth century coal code, which stereotyped antiquated differences of commercial function, both on the Tyne and the Thames, had been abandoned in 1831[3]. In the mid-'forties, the North-East Coast 'committee of the vend,' which had regulated prices by the regulation of output, had broken down. Thereafter it was "practically an open fighting trade"[4]—free and unrestricted competition. If local associations of owners gave price rulings, as they sometimes did, they "had no means of enforcing the rules at all," so that they were not "in fact carried out...at least...not entirely."[5]

Since the elimination of superfluous intermediaries on Tyneside, and the inauguration of a permanent "fighting trade," the bulk of the coal had been shipped by, or on behalf of, the coalowners[6]. But it was not shipped to the order of London merchants. They bought on the London Coal Exchange through factors acting for the owners. (The Exchange had provided itself with a new building opened by the Prince Consort in 1849[7].) The greater merchants in the 'sixties and 'seventies sold for the most part directly to the consumer, manufacturing or domestic, not as at an earlier time mainly to 'second merchants.'[8] There was, however, a class of 'second merchants,' now generally called coal-dealers, who bought from the principals at the wharf or in the railway yard, "took the coals home to their own place and sold...as little as 14 lbs. sometimes," as a principal put it[9].

[1] Spencer, *Principles of Sociology*, *passim*.

[2] The figures are summarised down to 1870 in *S.C. on the Causes of the Present Dearness and Scarcity of Coal*, 1873 (x. 1), App. 1. There are annual returns.

[3] Vol. I. p. 233–6.

[4] George Elliot before the *S.C. of* 1873, Q. 7518. Cp. above, p. 149.

[5] *Ibid.* R. Tennant, speaking for the West Riding, Q. 2657.

[6] *Ibid.* Evidence of Sydney Cockerell, London coal merchant, Q. 7190.

[7] Dowling, *op. cit.* p. 129. [8] Vol. I. p. 235. [9] R. Cory, Q. 7136.

Such dealers frequented the yards more than the wharves; for the poor now consumed chiefly the 'inland coal' from Derbyshire and Yorkshire, not the 'best Wallsend,' with its old reputation and higher price[1].

Apart from points of quality, the inland coal was more economical to handle. There were no lighterage charges and less loss on the small coal through breakage in loadings and unloadings. When first it came, in the 'fifties, the inland coal had been consigned for sale like that sent by sea, but the selling of it was less formal and regular. It "is not sold in the London market in the same way as the sea-borne coal; therefore it is more difficult to get at the price."[2] Consignment for sale continued into the 'seventies and later, but purchase direct from the pit was increasing all the time. "We buy all we can direct": it is "loaded into our trucks at the pits' mouth," witnesses connected with this trade said in the early 'seventies[3]. Whether carried on in this way far from London, or by the small man in the station-yards, the dealings in 'inland coal' were particularly competitive. They helped to give the whole trade its fighting character. Though the air was full of rumours about an unscrupulous group of inland coal-dealers, described as the Forty Thieves, neither on the coalfields nor among the Londoners could a naturally suspicious Committee of Inquiry find any evidence of rings or combinations during the price inflation of 1873[4]. The Forty Thieves if they existed were individualistic bandits. And although the declaring of current prices, or nominal fixings of price, by coal-owners' associations made some little progress during the next decade, there was no change in essentials[5].

The farther it was removed from London towards the coalfields, the simpler the trade had always been, until on the fields themselves even domestic consumers able to buy in cart-loads could do so direct from the pit[6].

In the other primary metropolitan supply trades, milk, meat, and fish, there had again been both shortenings and lengthenings of the chain between ultimate producer and consumer, but mainly shortenings. On the eve of the railway age all the milk used in London came from an area with a twenty mile radius,

[1] Cory, Q. 7150. [2] Cory, Q. 7151. [3] Cockerell, Q. 7245, 7178.
[4] *S.C. of* 1873: *Report*, p. x. [5] Above, p. 149.
[6] Memories of the 'eighties of a home four miles from the pits where coal was delivered at 12*s*. 6*d*. a ton.

and very little of it from points on the outer fifteen miles. The bulk was provided by urban and suburban cowkeepers, mostly small, many of whom delivered their own milk, others selling to milk-dealers and dairymen[1]. By 1878 the "market for milk in London" affected "farms a hundred and fifty miles away"[2]; but the change from a local to a semi-national market had been slow, and in 1878 was by no means complete. The railways had not transformed the trade so quickly as had been anticipated[3]. At first they took no interest in it. Milk transport and milk cooling were not understood. Rail-borne milk was supposed to be inferior, and probably it was[4]. Like rail-borne coal, it went chiefly to the poor. But disease began to ravage the London cow-houses. Foot and mouth disease had been recurrent since 1839. The arrival of *Rinderpest* in 1865 led to the death or slaughter within a few months of four-fifths of the cows in London[5]. Milk-dealers were driven farther afield. Railway handling improved. Milk transport was mastered. The normal unit in the dairying business grew; "and by 1870 the trade was fairly started" on the lines upon which it was running in the late 'eighties[6]. Considerable companies were building up large scale buying and delivery organisations. This did not, however, carry with it the quick extinction of small-scale cowkeeping and dairying. After 1870 these trades fell into the hands of immigrant Welshmen who knew a good deal about cattle, little about anything else, and lived hard. In the 'eighties, their small businesses were numerous in poor neighbourhoods, particularly in Whitechapel. At the close of the decade, when the new County Council took over control, there were still nearly 700 licensed cow-houses in London proper; and at the census of 1891, in the whole metropolitan milk selling business, the employed were to the employers only as five to one[7].

The meat trade had been but little simplified, although long-distance cattle-droving had been cut out. Farmers and graziers

[1] Vol. I. p. 227–8. Cp. Pinchbeck, J., *Women Workers and the Industrial Revolution* (1930), p. 299.

[2] *R.A.S. Reports, Dairy Farming*, p. 670.

[3] Cp. the anticipations referred to in vol. I. p. 228.

[4] See the historical notes in Booth, C., *Life and Labour of the People in London*, VII. 173.

[5] *R. on the Origin and Nature...of the Cattle Plague*, 1866 (XXII). For the first observation of 'mouth and foot disease,' Q. 378.

[6] Booth, *op. cit.* VII. 177.

[7] Booth, as above. Note the scepticism of the census-takers of 1891 about the statistics of employers and employed discussed above, p. 120 n. 1.

might send their beasts to London for sale, or might sell outright to cattle jobbers[1]. Arrived in London, the beasts no longer made the City "almost impassable"[2] on a Monday on their way to Smithfield: bulls no longer got into City china shops: "that sink of cruelty, drunkenness and filth, the cattle market—where every other building was either a slaughter-house, a gin-palace, or a pawn-broker's shop,"[3] had been cleaned out since the opening of the Metropolitan Market at Islington in 1855, and of the Foreign Cattle Market at Deptford in 1872[4]. But this had not simplified the trade. The specialist commission salesman grew in importance with the growth of business. By the early 'sixties, men with foreign names were selling beasts for graziers in Schleswig-Holstein or for jobbers in Berlin[5]. About the new markets were grouped licensed slaughterers and carcass butchers, just as they had formerly been about Smithfield, the former killing for the latter or for retail butchers who did not themselves slaughter. Some carcass butchers had their own shops in Smithfield, but usually they sold through yet another group of specialists, the commission meat salesman[6]. More and more dead meat came up from the country[7]. The average retail butcher was no longer a killer but a purveyor of meat killed inside or outside London. In the 'forties and 'fifties he had very commonly killed at least the calves at the back of his shop; and there were private or commission slaughter-houses all over London. Since that date their number had declined greatly. There were still more than 1500 in the metropolitan area in 1873. When the County Council began to deal with them, fifteen years later, they had fallen to about 700[8]. Control, country killing, and frozen meat would carry forward the reduction and the concentration.

[1] For jobbers; evidence before the *Smithfield C. of* 1847, Q. 1244; for a bullock in a linen-draper's shop in High Holborn, Q. 1496.

[2] Vol. I. p. 226.

[3] Dumaurier, G., *Peter Ibbetson*, p. 65—obviously from personal reminiscence of London in 1851–6. Fully confirmed by the *Smithfield C. of* 1847—"a scene of great confusion and unnecessary cruelty": Q. 26—and by a second of 1849 (XIX. 247).

[4] Booth, *op. cit.* VII. 190–1.

[5] *E.g.* H. Gebhardt, who sold for the graziers referred to and for jobbers in Magdeburg and Berlin. *R. on Cattle Plague*, Q. 2031 *sqq.*

[6] The witnesses before the committees of 1847 and 1849 describe an organisation of trade almost identical with that described by Charles Booth's workers forty years later.

[7] The amount was called "astonishing" by a witness even in 1847: Q. 2075.

[8] Booth, *op. cit.* VII. 202.

Fish dealing was not greatly changed, but all its processes had been speeded up. Billingsgate, a wretched place of wooden sheds until the late 'forties[1], had been cleansed, twice rebuilt, and once enlarged before 1875. Fish brought to London by water was usually handled and sold at auction by the fish-carrying companies which had replaced the cutter-owners of the early nineteenth century. Their steam carriers collected from the fleets at sea. Fish brought by rail, the amount of which in the 'eighties was about twice that of the fish brought by water, was consigned by collecting companies and dealers in the fishing ports to Billingsgate commission salesmen, who sold mainly by private contract. Speed had provided work for a new, or newly grown, type of Billingsgate middleman, called in the slang of the day a 'bummaree.' The ice-filled 'trunks,' hurriedly despatched, contained fish of all sizes and sometimes of various sorts. The retailer usually did not want it like that, nor did he always want a trunk full. The bummaree therefore bought, sorted, and resold to the retailers, so becoming an operator and risk-bearer in a market which was already a by-word among economists for its hour-to-hour uncertainties and fluctuations. Thence to the fishmonger, still normally a man with a handful of employees, not yet a limited company[2].

In the general domestic trade of the country, there were forces obviously at work tending to the elimination of intermediaries between producer and consumer; but their working was much delayed and in various ways diverted or even counteracted. The clothing trades show them in operation effectively, though not uniformly. With the disappearance of the true domestic clothier in the woollen industry, for example, the old-fashioned type of Yorkshire home-trade woollen merchant, who came between the producer and the big wholesale metropolitan distributing or exporting houses, certainly declined. The metropolitan wholesaler, or his equivalent in other towns of the first rank, could not deal with a multitude of small clothiers in the heavy woollen district: a limited group of mill-owners was accessible to him. The rise of ready-made clothing factories led

[1] Cp. vol. I. p. 226.

[2] Booth, *op. cit.* VII. 207 *sqq.*, on which this paragraph is based, for the situation in the 'eighties. For fishing-boats and carriers, above, p. 72 *sqq.* The ratio of employers to employed in London fish-dealing was given as 1 : 4. The word bummaree is not in the Ministry of Labour's 1927 *Dictionary of Occupational Terms*.

to still more drastic elimination. They might buy in bulk from the mills and cut out the merchant entirely. Towards the close of the period, they were beginning to practise elimination on the other side—by opening their own retail shops; but as yet this was rare. Quite apart from the fall of the Yorkshire domestic clothier and the rise of the clothing factories, the forces of elimination were at work. A principal from St Paul's Churchyard indicated some of their lines of operation in evidence given in 1885. His firm dealt in everything except boots—silks, linens, cottons, woollens, knitted goods, ribbons, gloves. Twenty-five years ago, he said, "everybody, that is to say all retailers and shippers, had to obtain their goods" through them. Now, both retailers and shippers often went direct to the manufacturer or the manufacturer to them[1].

Why this had happened, particularly since the price-fall of the 'seventies, was explained concisely by a manufacturing witness from Preston: "our business was so exceedingly bare that we had to leave the merchant out and go beyond him."[2] The merchant whom they had left out was a shipping, not a home merchant, but the principle was the same. The witness added, however, that his firm's action was exceptional.

The tendency for the manufacturer to get more often into touch with the retailer was not confined to the clothing trades. One way in which it manifested itself was indeed uncommon, if not unknown, in those trades, that of the agency. Just when the agency system began is not yet clear; but the normal arrangements down to the 'fifties at least did not include it. This system, in which large manufacturers of goods in universal and regular demand kept agencies in all important towns and populous districts, was said in 1878 to have sprung up in "comparatively recent times." Its effect had been to curtail, but not abolish, the operations of the local wholesale dealers and factors, and to reduce the number of bagmen on the road[3].

The hardware and light metal industries of the West Mid-

[1] *R.C. on Depression of Trade*, Q. 4070. For the clothiers and the clothing factories, above, p. 118 and p. 92. At the end of the period the makers of clothing began to call themselves clothiers, the clothier proper having died out. There are no exact records of the decline of the Yorkshire home-trade merchants. They were numerous early in the century, rare towards its close; and the reasons are obvious. Cp. Clapham, J. H., *The Woollen and Worsted Industries* (1907), p. 162 *sqq*. based on personal knowledge and information.

[2] *Ibid*. Q. 5673.

[3] More information is needed on this question. The quotation is from Moffat, *The Economy of Consumption* (1878), p. 137. Allen, G. C., "Methods of Indus-

lands became homes of the agency system because of their standardised products; but not until they had reached the factory stage. A few, such as the manufacture of steel pens and of screws, had reached it in or before the 'sixties. Agencies for known brands of these things appeared early. A large number of Midland industries however, especially those which turned out light brassware and fittings, remained into the 'eighties at that stage of development in which a factor dominated and directed, with varying degrees of completeness, a group of small producers, through his control of capital and his knowledge of markets[1]. He would sell, as his predecessors since the eighteenth century had sold, to wholesalers or shipping merchants, sometimes to retailers. In the later 'eighties, owing to growth in the size and strength of the producing firms and to the progress of factory conditions, the factors of this type were in danger of "being reduced to the position of mere wholesale merchants."[2] In those light-metal trades which were now dominated by a few great manufacturing concerns, even the wholesale merchant was finding his sphere contracted in the home market, by extensions of the agency system or by manufacturers sending out their own travellers. This was a natural development, because the large manufacturers had frequently started as factors and so were familiar with distributive business. On the average of the West Midland trades, it would appear, the chain between producer and consumer had been shortened a little; in some of them a good deal. There might only be one shopkeeper between the factory and the user. There had seldom, if ever, been more than that in the steel-pen industry, since Joseph Gillott himself first made pens of steel and sold them to a local stationer for a shilling each[3]. His successors and competitors—he died in 1873—merely sold to more and more distant stationers, 'agents for so-and-so's steel pens.' But this was an exceptional trade, so young and personal that the factor or merchant, having never existed in it, had not to be eliminated. However it seems

trial Organisation in the West Midlands 1860–1927," *E.J.* (*Hist.*), 1929, p. 551, states that, in this area, the factor had "lost his dominating position"..."by the end of the century," owing to the development of the agency system.

[1] For the factor, vol. I. p. 255–6, and above, p. 126.

[2] Allen, *E.J.* (*Hist.*) as above, p. 551.

[3] See the *D.N.B.* Gillott was not the first to make them. They are heard of in 1809–10. There were twelve makers in Birmingham in 1849. See *Birmingham and the Midland Hardware District* (1866), p. 633 *sqq.* For the later history, Allen, *The Industrial Development of Birmingham and the Black Country*, 1860–1927 (1929).

not unlikely that it may have furnished an object lesson in elimination to other Birmingham factory industries.

General elimination of intermediaries between producer and consumer, or even between producer and retailer, was excluded by the growing variety of both production and consumption at home, even if the exotic sources of so much food and raw material are overlooked. As one door was shut in the middleman's face another often opened on his left hand. Producers of coal and iron, of some kinds of food, or of other primary goods, might establish direct relations with the larger, more corporate type of consumer—the gas company, the shipyard, the hospital—or even with the domestic consumer at their doors. Producers of standardised, and of what were coming to be called proprietary manufactured articles, like the pens, might supply retailers direct. But most of the consumers were domestic yet remote from the producers' doors: retailers seldom dealt in nothing but standardised or proprietary articles. In a thoroughly urbanised society, only a shrinking minority of families could get coal from the pit or milk from the farm. So for some of his requirements every retailer, and some retailers for all, must rely on the wholesaler, whoever he might be—warehouseman of St Paul's Churchyard; wholesale grocer, stationer, draper, chemist; iron merchant; cheese factor; carcass butcher; bummaree at Billingsgate.

Within sharply defined limits of occupation and geography, the co-operative movement, since the 'forties, had not so much shortened the chain between ultimate producer and consumer as put the control of an important section of it into the consumer's hands. By the close of the 'eighties, after two decades of conspicuous co-operative expansion, there were parts of Lancashire, the West Riding and Durham in which each man, woman and child spent on the average £5 a year at Co-operative Stores[1]. The figure for the whole country was 15*s*. 8*d*., weakness of co-operation in London, the South, and the rural districts being a principal explanation of the difference. For the years 1876–82, the figure had been 10*s*. 4*d*. and the average sales of British Co-operative Societies about £15,000,000. In 1863, the year of the foundation of the North of England Co-operative

[1] See the maps in the second (1892) edition of Potter, B. (Mrs Sidney Webb), *The Co-operative Movement in Great Britain*, giving expenditure at the Stores in £ per 100 of the population of the parliamentary constituencies.

Wholesale Society, an event which marks the opening of the second era of the movement[1], the sales had reached what co-operators rightly considered the fine level of £2,500,000[2]. That was less than 2*s*. per head of the population. In the middle of the 'eighties, statisticians believed that the total income of the wage-earners of Great Britain was about £480,000,000[3]. The average annual sales of the Co-operative Stores for 1883–7 were £20,000,000[4]. They did not sell houses[5], beer, or some other goods of less importance in the workman's budget. But they did handle things of which the aggregate wage-earners' purchases may have been so much as £350,000,000, and can hardly have been less than £300,000,000. In short, they had still to occupy some 94 per cent. of those fields of wage-earners' consumption which were their promised land; although here and there, in their native industrial territory, they had already occupied perhaps 50 per cent. of it.

From the beginning their trade had been based on provisions, and their first enemy had been the private grocer. With bakers there had been less friction: the wife did the baking in old co-operative territory, and the stores sold her flour. When the Wholesale Society began operations, it also was mainly a provision merchant, as was its colleague, the Scottish Wholesale of 1868. "During its first ten years" (1864–74) the Wholesale "grew fat on butter."[6] Irish butter, with a very little French and Danish butter, made up a third of its trade. When it decided to manufacture for itself, it began with biscuits and sweets. From provisions, the Stores and the Wholesale had passed to drapery, soap, boots and other articles of standard domestic consumption. Some goods regularly sold by Stores, of which coal was perhaps the most important, did not pass through the Wholesales[7]. For those things which the Whole-

[1] Or third era, taking the Owenite movement as the first: vol. I. p. 315, 599.

[2] Redfern, P., *The Story of the Co-operative Wholesale Society* (1913), p. 73.

[3] Giffen, *Essays in Finance, Second Series*, p. 463, with a deduction for Ireland.

[4] These are the sales as given by Mrs Webb, p. 251, on which the maps quoted above are based. The share of the Stores in wage-earners' expenditure is discussed by Mrs Webb on p. 234–5.

[5] Societies did help members to buy their own houses, but houses do not appear in the sales figures used here.

[6] Redfern, *op. cit.* p. 95.

[7] Co-operative coal-mining enterprises were without exception disastrous. The Wholesale lost money in them in the 'seventies. See the chapter (XXI) on "Colliery Failures" in Jones, B., *Co-operative Production*. Cp. Redfern, *op. cit.* p. 108. The Wholesale did not start a regular coal trade until 1891. *Ibid.* p. 138.

sales neither handled nor produced, and for things which they did handle but which the local co-operators did not appreciate, or preferred to procure locally, Store buyers went into the open market. Although all the capital of the Wholesales was held by the Stores, at the start there were many Stores not affiliated to them, and there were always some. These bought everything in open market like private retailers. There might at any time be local committee-men in affiliated societies who had no intention of buying only what the Wholesales chose to stock. In early Wholesale days (1869) there had even been a secession of such open-market men from the Rochdale Pioneers[1]. But when, at the close of the period, retail sales averaged £20,000,000, those of the two Wholesales were £7,500,000. As they sold only to the Stores, and as the Stores' sales figure includes profit and working expenses, it would appear that by this time the Wholesales supplied about half the Stores' needs.

The co-operating consumer had long ceased to sell his provisions across the counter to himself, as the Rochdale Pioneers did in the 'forties. But his committee controlled buying and selling policy, and superintended the managers and whatever assistants or buyers the size of the Store might require. The Wholesale necessarily employed experts at both ends from an early date—its sales were £1,153,000 by 1872—but, as it was made at Manchester by the federated Stores of the cotton towns and was governed by federal representatives, selling needed little 'salesmanship,' that dubious exercise of competitive commerce. For buying, on the other hand, all appropriate commercial qualities were required. There is no reason to suppose that they were lacking in the buyers from Lancashire and Yorkshire, or in the committee men who directed them. Yet an honourable dislike of the higgling of the market, and all the anti-social activities which sometimes go with it, was part of the co-operative faith inherited from Robert Owen. It drove the two Wholesales to reach out towards the ultimate producer—in 1882 they co-operated for the first time in shipping tea direct from China[2]—and to make all they could in their own factories. There had to be some higgling at the last, whether over goods which Stores bought on the open market, over raw materials bought for Wholesale factories, or over tea bought in China. But right along the co-operative chain, up to the jarring higgle

[1] Redfern, *op. cit.* p. 34.
[2] *Ibid.* p. 121.

of the open market purchase, buyers were salaried agents of the associated consumers.

Familiar marks distinguished the developed and legalised industrial co-operative society from the joint-stock company[1]—the limitation (to £200) of the shares in it which any one person might hold; the fixed and moderate return on them which kept their value stable; the equality of all shareholders in control, whatever the size of their holding; the share list always open to new members, and the small denomination of the shares, which made membership very easy; the 'divi,' proportioned not to shares held, but to purchases made; and reliance on the unpaid directing work of members whose co-operation was a lively faith. Many of these marks were lacking in the 'bourgeois' supply associations of the 'sixties which were registered under the Joint Stock Companies Act of 1862. But there was enough similarity in methods and aims between them and the working-class organisations to rouse a common enemy. A new trade journal, the *Grocer*, which tried to start a boycott of wholesale firms who supplied industrial co-operative stores, addressed the promoters of the Civil Service Supply as "two and sixpenny shareholders" and "Post Office and Piccadilly puppies."[2] The expanding population and trade of the country happily found employment for stores of both kinds, and also for grocers, some of whose trade methods, it is generally believed, were quickened and cleansed by the provocative competition of consumers' associations[3].

In spite of such competition, the adoption of a joint-stock or limited liability in the distributing trades, wholesale or retail, had been slow and rare. Before the 'sixties, companies for such things as coal or fish dealing had been projected but had never succeeded. There had been colonising and manufacturing companies which proposed to do wholesale trading, and sometimes did it[4]. Of the old imperial trading companies, the Hudson's

[1] See *e.g. Dictionary of Political Economy*, *s.v.* Co-operation.

[2] Quoted in Redfern, *op. cit.* p. 42–3.

[3] The evidence for adulteration and other undesirable practices in the grocery trade of the early nineteenth century is overwhelming (see *e.g. S.C. on the Adulteration of Food and Drugs*, 1856, VIII). How general it was is hard to determine. So is the extent to which improvement was due to co-operative competition.

[4] For projects and failures see the lists in English, H., *A Complete View of the Joint-Stock Companies formed during the years* 1824 *and* 1825 (1827): *S.C. on Joint-Stock Companies*, 1844 (VII. 1), App. IV, the promotions of 1834–6: the *J.S.C. Returns* of 1853 (1856, LXV. 597 and 611).

Bay remained in active business, but it was in a special category. It was no more the habit of East India merchants or City warehousemen than of West End shopkeepers to make use of the developing law of limited liability. Among the mercantile firms proper which went down in the crisis of 1857–8 there was not a single joint-stock company[1]. But after the Act of 1862, the slow change began whose effects impressed Goschen so much twenty years later that he even exaggerated them[2]. Most progress was made amongst the warehouses, least among the specialised merchants and shippers and the whole body of retailers. For a number of years after its establishment in 1864, the Fore Street Warehouse, the earliest successful public joint-stock distributive concern[3], was also the only such concern whose shares were regularly quoted in the Stock Exchange list of miscellaneous securities. During the 'seventies, the forces which were at work to bring about the transformation of private firms into limited companies gathered power in the field of distribution. In 1885 it was said that "a great many" of the City warehouses had adopted limited liability. But few had done so before 1880, and there was rarely full publicity or the quotation of shares[4]. Similar transformations of ordinary partnerships into private companies had occurred sporadically all over the field of distribution; but the company was not dominant, or even at all conspicuous, in any other part of it. The typical merchants' firm of the 'eighties was a pure family concern or private partnership, and so was the typical shop, from Bond Street to the Old Kent Road and from John o' Groats to Lands End. True, the Master of the Rolls told a parliamentary committee in 1877 that he had actually known a case "where a chandler's shop was turned into a limited company"; but his surprise shows what an oddity it seemed[5].

The shrinkage of the commercial world into a single market under pressure of steam and electricity necessarily altered the working of overseas trade, but can hardly be said to have shifted the bases of its organisation. The middleman's functions were

[1] Lists in Evans, D. M., *The History of the Commercial Crisis*, 1857–8, p. 52 *sqq*.

[2] Above, p. 297.

[3] See the *Return of all J.S.C. formed or registered since* 18 *and* 19 *Vict. c.* 133 of 1864 (LVIII. 291).

[4] *R.C. on Depression of Trade*, Q. 668, 4100.

[5] *S.C. on the Operation of the Companies Acts*, 1877 (VIII. 419), Q. 2225.

more often modified than abolished; though particular middlemen, too rigid to conform, together with some redundant types, no doubt disappeared. In the old commercial practice, heavy stocks were carried because they could only be renewed slowly and at long intervals[1]. The merchant was generally thinking of markets both distant and future. His methods could be leisurely. Under the new conditions of lighter, faster renewed, stocks and swift decisions, "the old-fashioned merchants...suffer or are extinguished" as an exceptionally well-informed contemporary put it in 1880[2]. But the mercantile function survived. As much skill was needed, probably more, to operate in markets which, though distant, were all telegraphically present, as in those both distant and future; and because the world market of to-day lay all before your eye, as it had never been before your father's, you were not free to neglect its probable position next month or even next season.

In the export trade, fresh facilities for quick intercourse and the spread of British firms and agencies over all the world had greatly reduced the practice of 'adventuring' by merchants—the term was quite extinct—and still more the practice of consignment for sale by manufacturers. Both had been decaying on the shorter trade routes even in the 'thirties[3]. The old-fashioned adventuring merchant had sent cargoes of suitable goods to markets where he hoped to find outlets. It is the method of all primitive trade, and it survived in branches of trade where conditions among the consumers were primitive. Much grey cotton cloth, to take an outstanding instance, was bought by merchants and consigned, 'adventured,' to the tropics[4]. In consignment by the manufacturer, the shipping merchant had taken goods from their maker or from some factor; made a percentage advance against them; and shipped them against orders or as an adventure, settling accounts only when they were sold. The method had never been liked or much practised by strong manufacturers in the nineteenth

[1] On the reduced need to carry stocks see evidence of G. Lord before *R.C. on Depression of Trade*, Q. 5278: he thought the effects of the Suez Canal, electricity and steam, were so to speak worked off by 1885. The new equilibrium was established.

[2] Farrer, *Free Trade and Fair Trade*, p. 191.

[3] Vol. I. p. 255–6.

[4] Consignment still "prevailed to an important extent for certain markets" down to 1914. *Economic Advisory Council: Report on the Cotton Industry*, 1930 (Cmd. 3615), p. 14.

century: they preferred working to the merchants' order[1]. Now, working to order dominated the export trade. The merchant consigning goods to remote or primitive markets gave orders to the manufacturer, carrying all risks himself. For many markets, he himself would receive orders from overseas, from a branch or agent or correspondent. There might be an element of adventure in the orders which he received: his Bombay house when ordering would not be certain of sales in Afghanistan. But it was not the old, pure, adventuring procedure.

Strong manufacturers might take orders from overseas direct. This was not a new thing. Wedgwood had done it and so had Boulton and Watt. It was a natural thing in trades where the manufacturer had a world-wide repute and made goods of high unit value and more or less specialised use—a table service for Catherine the Great or a steam engine for the Creusot works. The overseas consumer of such things knew what he wanted before manufacture began. Consumption of this class had much increased since 1850; although it did not form a very large part of the aggregate overseas consumption of British goods. Locomotives, liners, warships, large stationary steam-engines and teams of textile machinery fall into it. Outside manufacturing, the coal trade furnishes parallels. Coal consumers overseas included railways, gas-works and governments, who knew their exact requirements in advance and bought in bulk direct. Intermediaries of various kinds there might be in some of these trades, but there was not much room for the merchant proper.

Even in the textile trades, as has been seen, easy intercourse and hard times had provoked a few manufacturers to "leave the merchant out"; but this was admittedly exceptional[2]. Instances could no doubt be found in other trades than those in goods of high unit value and specialised use; but they too would be exceptional. The mass of the textiles, clothing, light metal goods and miscellaneous manufactures of every kind, from "bags, empty" to "stationery, other than paper"—to cull two entries from early and late in the official list—went through the hands of the export merchant, the shipper, as Lancashire called him to distinguish him from the home merchant[3]. As textiles and

[1] See vol. I. p. 256.

[2] Above, p. 306.

[3] This remained true many years later. "It would be incorrect to say that the whole of the export business in cotton yarns and goods was in the hands of 'shippers'; there are some houses which manage their own marketing abroad, but these are exceptions." Chapman, *The Lancashire Cotton Industry* (1904), p. 138.

clothing alone were worth more than all the rest of the exports put together, and as light metal goods and the miscellaneous manufactures were steadily increasing in importance, there was no general prospect of the shipper being left out. No doubt he handled a smaller share of the British exports in 1885–7 than in 1850–3, but probably not very much smaller.

In the import trades there had been a decline, and in some cases a complete disappearance, of the system of consignment so characteristic of the early nineteenth century—the system by which "merchants and planters in all parts of the world" consigned produce for sale in this country and "drew [bills] in anticipation of the value immediately,"[1] the British merchant or broker, as consignee, making advances to them in anticipation of sale by accepting their bills up to two-thirds or three-quarters of the probable value of the consignment. In the old, slow, pre-railway and pre-steamship age, he "frequently kept the goods for months or even years."[2] The system was most prevalent in the longest trades, East and West Indian and Australasian, but was at that time quite common on the comparatively short North Atlantic route. Down to the laying of the cables, the imports of cotton into Liverpool "were chiefly received on consignment by merchants"[3] from American merchants or planters, in the old way, the Liverpool merchant taking only a small commission which he shared with the broker who sold for him. He might buy in America, either through his own house or a correspondent; but consignment predominated.

The cables soon changed the whole position. "Firm offers of cotton were cabled from the other side, either by branch houses or agents of Liverpool firms, or by independent sellers."[4] The selling of consigned cotton on commission had ceased altogether some time before 1886, when this account was written. Incidentally, there had been a little shedding of superfluous middlemen from the cotton trade, though from the point of view of changes in legal ownership the disappearance of consigned planters' cotton from the Liverpool market meant a lengthening of the commercial chain. The middlemen shed were commission merchants and brokers. The former either became importing merchants or disappeared; and so did some

[1] Quoted in vol. I. p. 256 from the 1823 *Report on the Law of Agents and Factors*, p. 11.

[2] *Ibid.* p. 7.

[3] Ellison, *The Cotton Trade*, p. 279.

[4] *Ibid.* p. 280.

of the brokers. For at least twenty years before the War of Secession and the cables, all cotton handled by the merchant—whether as owner or consignee—was sold through his selling broker to a buying broker who acted for the spinner; and the few powerful spinners who imported cotton themselves employed brokers[1]. The cables facilitated this spinner-importing. They did more than that, by producing a fusion of the broker and merchant classes and the appearance of a hybrid type known for a time as a broker-merchant, a man who both imported and sold. Many of the strongest importing merchants continued to employ brokers, finding the brokers' expert knowledge valuable in a specialising market, and being in a position to pay for it because of their large transactions. But by 1886 not "any important portion"[2] of the cotton paid a double brokerage. Handling costs had been considerably reduced since about 1870[3], when the new era effectively began, apart from reductions in the cost of ocean carriage.

Though the course of events is not so well known in the grain trade, there is no doubt that the telegraph, first between England and the Continent and then between England and America, helped to kill the consignment system there also. That system had been extensively used, especially in the Anglo-Irish grain trade[4], during the 'twenties, at a time when the foreign grain trade was intermittent and necessarily rather speculative. As the foreign trade for home consumption settled down into a permanency after 1846, out-and-out purchase in the grain shipping ports appears to have increased rapidly. The dealings in cargoes afloat, which were in regular operation by 1851–3, presuppose it[5]. It was easy for importing firms to keep branches or agents in the grain-shipping ports of Northern Europe, such as Rotterdam and the Baltic towns, where there was an old and well-developed tradition of corn-dealing. Linkage by cable with London came during the 'fifties. The Irish trade declined

[1] The arrangements here described were typical of the period 1840–60. Ellison, *op. cit.* p. 181.

[2] *Ibid.* p. 280.

[3] Since "a dozen or fifteen years ago"; Ellison in 1886.

[4] Vol. I. p. 259–60.

[5] In the market reports of the *Economist* during the 'forties references to cargo dealings are rare. They remain rare in 1850. By 1853 they are regular. Their omission does not prove their non-existence. They certainly existed earlier but they could only become regular when the regular import was thoroughly established.

both relatively and absolutely after the famine and, with the telegraph, became less international in character. Consignment no doubt lingered in the more remote branches of the trade, such as those of the Barbary coast and the Black Sea; but by the time that American dominance set in, towards the close of the 'sixties, the course of European business was already quick, free, and modern. The market had changed gradually, instead of being abruptly transformed by the Atlantic cables like the cotton market. Those cables merely linked to it a fresh, powerful, and ultimately dominant, reservoir of supply.

In the tropical, sub-tropical, and Australasian trades old methods of business naturally persisted; longest of all in the wool trade. Here the nature of the commodity was a conservative force. Wool is never sold till it has been sampled. Cargo dealings would have been too risky and were never tried. In the early days of Australian wool growing the consignment system had been the only possible one: McArthur and his imitators shipped their wool in hope. It remained the natural one after the establishment of regular colonial wool auctions in 1835. The whole ritual of the wool exchange was based on it. Dealings were not just in wool of a recognised sort, like middling uplands American cotton, but in so-and-so's wool known by its brand. When strong commercial and banking firms with London connections grew up in Australia, the squatters entrusted to them all the technical work of wool-shipping and insurance, securing from them, at a price, heavy advances against the shipments. But the wool remained the producer's property until it came under the hammer in Coleman Street, to be bought through buying brokers by wool merchants and the larger manufacturers. It was consigned to members of the small group of London selling brokers[1].

Down to the 'seventies, very little was handled in any other way, and to the end of the period not very much. There had been some local selling from an early date. This increased with the establishment of regular auctions in Australia. The buyers were scourers, speculators, mercantile houses, or, as communications improved, representatives of English wool merchants[2]. But as the scourers, speculators, and Australian mer-

[1] See Clapham, *The Woollen and Worsted Industries* (1907), p. 90–3. For the origin of financing by the banks in the 'sixties, Shann, *Economic History of Australia*, p. 299–300. For the wool trade generally, above, p. 6.

[2] Senkel, *Wollproduktion und Wollhandel im 19ten Jahrhundert*, p. 74.

chants eventually consigned their purchases to London in the ordinary way, it was only the buying on English account which altered the course of trade and side-tracked the London auctions. From about 1870, Continental and American buyers had become important at the auctions in Australia, at which however only 32 per cent. of the clip was sold even in 1885–6[1]. It is evident, therefore, that when the foreign purchases, and those of wool subsequently consigned to London by an Australian buyer, have been deducted, the proportion of the wool shipped to England which did not go through Coleman Street remained inconsiderable.

Writing in 1840 about the commercial speculations of 1825, Thomas Tooke referred to one feature "which, although of not uncommon manifestation in the stock and share markets, has been of very rare occurrence in the markets for produce. There were some few articles, almost exclusively spices, which were the subject of successive purchases at advancing prices, without any intermediate delivery of the article."[2] This mania, he noted, did not at that time affect "in the slightest degree"[3] either the corn or the provision markets. It probably brought about the state of things which worried critics of the organised markets in futures of the late nineteenth century—the aggregate selling of much larger amounts of spices than could possibly be delivered to consumers[4]. Apparently these speculators had bought and sold spices in the abstract so to speak, not particular cargoes or parcels after the fashion already known in Mark Lane and Mincing Lane. Successive purchases of the wheat on board the good ship *Arethusa* bound from Odessa to Falmouth for orders were a different matter. "In Mincing Lane when cargoes of sugar were sold one cargo would change hands four or five times."[5] No one concerned in such transactions could be left 'short' at the finish, as a stock jobber might who had sold more stock 'for time' than he could easily lay his hands on. It would

[1] Senkel, *op. cit.* p. 75.

[2] *History of Prices*, III. 159: quoted also in Emery, H. C., *Speculation on the Stock and Produce Exchanges of the United States* (*Columbia Studies*, 1896, II), p. 34 n.

[3] III. 167 n.

[4] Cp. *British Association Committee, Report on Future Dealings in Raw Produce*, 1900, p. 6–7.

[5] Goschen, *Essays and Addresses*, p. 201, referring to the middle of the century, but descriptive of the practice, which was older.

appear that successive sales without delivery of the goods had occurred to Tooke's knowledge, even though very rarely, in other produce markets before 1840. His suggestion that they were outside any reasonable course of trading was perhaps overdone. In the 'arrivals' business, there was certainly plenty of sale without delivery of goods or of documents, during the 'forties, and probably earlier. "It is well known to be a common practice of the first merchants," John Francis wrote in 1849 when defending Stock Exchange methods, "to buy goods for arrival without the slightest intention of receiving them, and directly a profit can be gained or too great loss averted, they are resold without even the bill of lading having been visible to the buyer."[1] The reference to bills of lading suggests transactions in particular cargoes and parcels; but the description does not exclude more speculative dealings.

By 1849–50 dealings in 'arrivals' were common on both sides of the Atlantic. New York dealt in grain to arrive from the West and in cotton to arrive from the South[2]. The markets were there before either the European sea-cables or the oceanic cables were laid, though New York was kept sensitive by English demand news, brought by steamer to Halifax and telegraphed on. But the international cables were needed for market perfection. Before they were laid, we are told, Liverpool was slow to imitate New York 'arrival' methods[3]. She was not very familiar with them; but "the first merchants" of London had nothing to learn. There was however an outburst of pure speculation in East Indian cotton arrivals at Liverpool in 1857, stimulated—among other things—by the partial establishment of telegraphic communication with the East. During the War of Secession everyone who touched cotton was bound to be a gambler. Men bought and sold it not only 'to arrive,' but for shipment months ahead. In peace, the Atlantic cables gave regularity and permanence to such transactions. Sales began to be made in agreed grades. Future prices lost their purely speculative wartime character, and acquired a calculable relation to spot prices. By 1869–71, the Liverpool Cotton Brokers' Association, when regulating arrivals business, dealt with a type of general contract for delivery of "American, basis of middling, from any

[1] *Chronicles and Characters of the Stock Exchange*, p. 82.

[2] Emery, *op. cit.* p. 35: Dumbell, S., "The Origin of Cotton Futures," *E.J.* (*Hist.*), 1927, p. 259 *sqq*.

[3] Dumbell, *op. cit.*

port, Oct.-Nov. shipment." Here is the pure future transaction in cotton in the abstract, divorced from specific consignments, or even from "ship named," a phrase which occurs in other contract types of the same date[1].

These general contracts gave openings for the outside speculator, and were much disliked by conservative merchants for that reason. But regular dealers who bought by telegraph were selling futures as a hedge against price fluctuations; and spinners were already discovering that by buying for remote delivery they too could safeguard themselves. New York had the whole business in futures at work by 1870, with options and margins, but still had to defend it as an innovation[2]. After that it grew swiftly on both sides. Futures passed from hand to hand, and far more cotton was bought and sold than America and India ever grew. There were bulls and bears and shorts. Liverpool brokers started a Clearing House in 1876, "to unravel the tangles of purchases and sales which arrivals frequently found awaiting them,"[3] and straighten out differences. Merchants followed with a rival Exchange. The two came together into a Cotton Association, from which sprang in 1882 a Settlement Association, "to promote a system of periodical cash settlements in the Liverpool cotton market."[4] Although the fixed-date settlements were not at first used by all dealers[5], their establishment was the last important step towards the creation of an organised futures market in standard grades of cotton, precisely comparable in its working with the Stock Exchange markets for standard securities.

The evolution of future dealings in the New York cotton market had been affected by parallel developments in the wheat market at Chicago. Chicago might have influenced Liverpool and London direct. But there is no definite evidence that it did. The Liverpool Corn Trade Association has always maintained that it was not any tenderness for the pure speculator,

[1] As in "Charleston, ship named, not below good ordinary." An Indian cotton contract might be for "Dhollerah, fair new merchants, Cape or Canal, May-June shipment": Dumbell, p. 264 n., from the *Liverpool Mercury* of 1870. The possibility of 'Canal' within a year of its opening is significant.

[2] Dumbell (p. 266–7) quotes a New York broker's circular of June 1870, which explains the uses of futures, and argues that "the system has been denounced by superficial observers only because it is new": future contracts are made daily "by parties of the highest respectability."

[3] Chapman, *op. cit.* p. 124.

[4] Rule 4. The rules are given in Ellison, *op. cit.* p. 294.

[5] *Ibid.* p. 296.

or any wish to rival Chicago, which led to the institution of an organised futures market in wheat at Liverpool in November, 1883[1]. The wheat which was selected as the basis for future delivery contracts was in fact not a Chicago sort but Californian, at that time in large and constant supply[2]. Imports were always growing. It was desirable that stocks should be carried and the price curve be kept as smooth as circumstances would permit. The value of future dealings for smoothing cotton price curves and giving security to the serious merchant, who used futures for hedging, was becoming generally recognised. These were the utilities which the Association proposed to confer on the Liverpool wheat market. It was imitated by the London Produce Exchange, which started organised future dealings in wheat and maize in 1888[3]. So the period closes with the system on its trial.

It was only by careful grading and classifications that cotton or grain could be given something approaching to the absolute uniformity, the capacity of every parcel sold to meet the needs of any buyer who desires that amount of the article, which stocks and shares have by nature. Close definition of the goods to be delivered in future contracts, and provision for arbitration and adjustments when it came to actual delivery, were essentials for successful working of future markets with which Capel Court had never been troubled. One £100 of 3 per cents. had always been just like any other, and no buyer had ever challenged it on delivery. But few commodities besides stocks and shares and grain are even approximately uniform, as the organisation of the wool trade shows; and there was certainly no bias in the British mercantile community towards the application of uniform treatment to things of doubtful uniformity: very much the reverse. These new, exact, speculative and suspected practices in certain Liverpool and London produce markets were in no way representative of the British commerce of the 'eighties. Much more typical was the state of things in the oldest, bulkiest, and most varied of the great import trades, timber. Some timber was bought by the ton; some by the load; much by

[1] See *Liverpool Grain Futures: Operator's Guide* (1929), p. 7. Information has also been supplied by the present Secretary of the Association, Mr F. W. G. Urquhart.

[2] Broomhall, G. J. S. and Hubback, J. H., *Corn Trade Memories* (1930), p. 34.

[3] Sonndorfer, R., *Die Technik des Welthandels* (ed. 1905), II. 30. The futures market in London never became very important: Dowling, S. W., *The Exchanges of London*, p. 183.

the Petersburg 'standard'; some by other 'standards.' When partially worked, it might be bought by 'feet run,' by fathom, bundle, or square foot; by the thousand (barrel staves) or by the piece (spars). It was contracted for by importers, f.o.b. at the world's timber ports, or c.i.f. delivered in Britain. Though sometimes sold 'to arrive,' it was oftener sold 'ex ship.' These were the larger dealers' sales. It went to inland dealers, or into consumption, partly by auction at London and Liverpool, mainly by private sale after a spell in the importer's timber-yard in the old obvious way. There were no novelties and no speculative refinements[1].

The nature of stocks and shares and the fact that, early in the eighteenth century, the Bank of England closed its government stock books for six weeks every quarter, during which no transfer of stock could take place, had produced time bargains in Change Alley, in the teeth of public opinion and the law, before there was an organised Stock Exchange[2]. Men sold stock which they had not yet got "for the opening" of the Bank's books, trusting to get it in the meantime. This they did quite naturally. As naturally, periodic settlements of business in stock grew up. Operators might, and when it suited them did, accept and deliver not stock but price differences, in defiance of the clauses in Sir John Barnard's Act[3] against time bargains in consols and against "all wagers, puts and refusals." "One hundred and sixteen years have passed, the act is still in force, and speculative bargains have not only increased, but form the chief business of the Stock Exchange," John Francis wrote in 1849[4]. The Act was repealed, as long obsolete, in 1868 (by 30 and 31 Vict. c. 59), but Stock Exchange men looked back with complacency on their habit of defying the law, and persisted in it. "We disregarded for years and years Sir John Barnard's Act," the Chairman of the Committee said in 1875, "and we are now disregarding Mr Leeman's Act,"[5] an Act of 1867 which had tried

[1] The methods of dealing are summarised, with a continental dismay at this insular chaos, in Sonndorfer, *op. cit.* II. 252. Some information comes direct from a firm of timber importers.

[2] Francis, J., *Chronicles and Characters of the Stock Exchange* (1849), p. 80–1. Cp. vol. I. p. 301–3.

[3] 7 Geo. II, c. 8.

[4] *Op. cit.* p. 81. Cp. Duguid, C., *The Story of the Stock Exchange* (1901), p. 188–9.

[5] *S.C. on Foreign Loans*, Q. 477.

to regulate dealings in bank shares by prescribing that in every sale the serial numbers of the shares sold should be specified. All that the law could do was to say that contracts of certain kinds would not be upheld in the courts. The Stock Exchange had its own methods for insuring that members should honour all types of contract of which the society as a whole approved. Time contracts for government stock had gone on in spite of Sir John Barnard, and dealings in bank shares, the numbers of which were not given, went on in spite of Mr Leeman, because they suited the habits of the society.

All essentials of Stock Exchange organisation existed before 1850. The next generation saw a vast extension of dealings, but only secondary changes in the structure and methods of the dealing groups. The Committee, started in 1802 as a "domestic tribunal for the regulation of business entirely limited to English stocks,"[1] by the 'fifties had become a public, even an international, body in consequence of the growth of foreign investment after Waterloo. Its strength lay in its power to authorise official quotation of, and grant or refuse settlements in, new stocks and classes of stock. Without quotation no real market; without settlements no organised or speculative dealings. Our power has brought us "into touch with Ambassadors," the Chairman said in 1875[2], as it obviously would. They had allowed quotation of £15,000,000 of Peruvian loans because there were laws to sanction it. They had refused quotation of another £22,000,000 because they questioned the validity of a Peruvian Presidential Decree[3]. That some very doubtful but relatively insignificant South American issues had secured quotation since 1867, the outcome of which was the inquiry at which these facts were put in evidence[4], is only a further illustration of the Committee's international power and responsibility.

Broking and jobbing had been distinct businesses from the first. In 1850 the distinction was old and clear, and the groups of brokers and jobbers were sharply differentiated, not however

[1] *S.C. on Foreign Loans*, Q. 468. Evidence of the Chairman, Samuel Herman de Zoete, a name admirably symbolic of the Stock Exchange with its blend of England, Holland, Germany and Judaea.

[2] *Ibid.* In Q. 468 de Zoete gave a history of the Committee.

[3] *Ibid.* Q. 5476 (de Zoete again).

[4] See the *Report* of 1875 which sets out the whole story of these loans (cp. above, p. 240). The total sum involved was £10,000,000 nominal in eight years, only part of which was taken by the general public. During that period nearly £400,000,000 of new foreign loans had secured quotation. Q. 5527–8.

by rule but by function[1]. The broker bought or sold anything for his clients. The jobber was a specialist dealer in certain stocks or groups of stocks, always ready to make a price in any one of them, *i.e.* to quote his buying and selling figures to a broker. He might solicit business from the brokers. "I look upon a broker and a jobber as totally distinct," the experienced government broker told a Royal Commission in 1877[2]. When cross-examined, he admitted that though normally the distinction was one of persons it might on occasion be only one of function: a broker with special knowledge of some group of securities might himself deal in them and so become a "jobbing broker." But this was very rare and, by 1877 at any rate, no broker was "allowed to stand in the market and make prices as a dealer."[3] Since all the members of both groups were members of the Exchange on precisely the same footing, it was technically legitimate to pass from one group to the other, but such transfers were rare. Public opinion on the Exchange was against them and they were not easy to make[4]. Occasionally a broker who found his business unprofitable would drop it and take to jobbing. The reverse process was however unknown—at least to the government broker of the 'sixties and 'seventies[5]. For everyday purposes the groups were, as he said, "totally distinct."

Some experts in the 'seventies drew a distinction between the jobber proper and the dealer. The former was never a holder of stock if he could help it. He was "pretty well always even,"[6] that is he had agreed to sell as much as he had undertaken to buy, and looked to the price difference, the jobber's 'turn,' for his living. The dealer was more of a merchant and took bigger risks. He would buy large blocks of some security and job them off piecemeal, for he was necessarily a jobber. Through him the Stock Exchange was linked to that promotion of companies and flotation of loans upon which it depended for the expansion of its activities, but which was not properly stock-brokers' business.

[1] Francis, *op. cit. passim* and esp. p. 325.

[2] *R.C. on the London Stock Exchange*, 1878 (XIX. 265), Q. 467. Although this Commission had no compulsory powers the evidence given before it gives a full account of Stock Exchange organisation and practice.

[3] Evidence of the Secretary, Q. 347.

[4] *Ibid.* Q. 345.

[5] Evidence of J. H. Daniell, Government Broker, Q. 492, 709, etc.

[6] Evidence of L. L. Cohen, Q. 2817. He elaborated the distinction between jobber and dealer.

How that business had expanded the growing membership of the Exchange suggests without in any way measuring. When it started in Capel Court in 1802, there had been already upwards of 500 members[1]. Foreign loans, railways, and joint-stock enterprise generally had found work for more than another 300 by 1850–1, when the membership stood at 864. More loans, more railways, and the joint-stock companies legislation of 1855–62 raised it to 1100 by 1864. Yet more foreign loans, of which over £400,000,000 worth were listed between 1865 and 1875, and the slow introduction of the public joint-stock company into most fields of economic activity, lifted it once more, to above 2000 by 1877[2]; and the growth did not stop there. Meanwhile provincial exchanges had come into being, at Glasgow, Liverpool and Manchester. Some business was done on them in local securities, not handled in London; but as these new exchanges contained no jobbers[3], the general investment or speculative business was passed on to the jobbers of Capel Court, so further swelling their work and numbers.

The growth of limited liability companies after 1855 threatened to bring about one somewhat important change in Stock Exchange practice, but the threat came to nothing. Dealing in the shares of a projected public company before allotment to the whole subscribing public was a practice as liable to abuse as it was difficult to avoid[4]. Certain sections of the new legislation tended to encourage it. Before the Acts of 1860 and 1862, and especially in the Railway Mania, 'stags' had secured allotments of shares without making any deposit and had proceeded to trade in them. Under the new law, the investing applicant for shares had to make a substantial deposit. To attract him, nothing was more useful than some well-advertised dealings in the embryo shares at a premium. A series of unsavoury episodes connected with such dealings led the Committee of the Stock Exchange, in 1864, to refuse to recognise them as valid. But within a short time the decision was reversed[5]. The dealings had continued because company promoters and certain sections of the public liked them. They had merely been withdrawn from Stock

[1] Vol. I. p. 301.

[2] The later figures are from the *Report of the R.C.* p. 5, the earlier from Duguid, *op. cit.* p. 94, 159.

[3] The Secretary of the Stock Exchange said in 1877 that they had no "dealers or middlemen"; Q. 285.

[4] See Duguid, *op. cit.* p. 128, 149, 192–4.

[5] Duguid, *op. cit.* p. 193.

Exchange control. Fear of losing business, combined with the defensible conviction that if the thing was to be done it had better be done on the open Exchange, led the Committee to go back on its ruling in 1865. Thirteen years later a rather unusually ineffective Royal Commission suggested that these dealings should again be stopped[1]; but neither Parliament nor the Committee paid any attention. Though the new era in company history did not modify Stock Exchange practice in any important way, the flood of business which came with it led to the development of a fresh organ of which the 1878 Commissioners decidedly approved, the Clearing House of 1873. A proposal to clear stocks, much as bankers cleared cheques, and so to avoid the passing of tickets from hand to hand, had been made so early as 1851, but nothing had come of it. It was very characteristic of British business methods that the Clearing House of 1873, called after its founder Humphrey's House, was a private organisation within a private organisation. People joined or not as they liked, though the thing was so convenient that membership grew fast. It was not until 1880 that the organisation was taken over by a Settlement Department under the central Committee of the Exchange[2].

One of the suggestions of the Commission of 1878 was that the Stock Exchange should increase its standing, and the binding power of its by-laws, by securing incorporation from Parliament. There was a recent precedent in the Act of 1871 (34 Vict. c. 21) by which an even older private commercial organisation, Lloyd's, had become a body corporate, mainly in order to give full authority to its rules[3]. Lloyd's, and marine insurance generally, had lost something of their former importance during the Great Peace and the stagnation of shipping down to the 'forties. In 1843 Lloyd's had not half as many subscribers as in 1815. Among a crop of new marine insurance companies which sprang up in the 'forties, "only one had so long a life as three years."[4] But wars and revolutions in shipping made risks after 1850. With risks the business revived. Lloyd's became a more specialised society each decade, more exclusively a society of

[1] *Report*, p. 19. No one of the seven principal suggestions made by the Commission was ever put into a law or a by-law.

[2] Duguid, *op. cit.* p. 255–6 and references in the 1878 *Report*.

[3] Cp. vol. I. p. 288–91 and Wright, C. and Fayle, C. E., *A History of Lloyd's* (1928), one of the few first-rate specialised commercial histories in existence.

[4] Wright and Fayle, *op. cit.* p. 364.

underwriters; and with specialisation and incorporation its efficiency grew[1]. Its network of agencies spread over the whole earth. From 1869 it was developing its system of signal stations. It was always interested in life-boats. Yet in spite of all this, for the prime business of marine underwriting it was "scarcely more than a supplementary market" during the 'seventies and 'eighties[2]. To a small group of old joint-stock marine insurance companies in London and Liverpool, which had survived into the second half of the century[3], had been added a number of well-managed new ones since 1860. There was already a certain amount of mutual insurance among shipowners; and internal insurance by the stronger shipping lines would follow. But the reformed Lloyd's of the 'eighties contained 'Gentlemen Underwriters'[4] who, besides showing fresh enterprise in marine work, were experimenting or preparing to experiment with ancient risks hitherto regarded as beyond insurance—burglary, earthquake, hurricane—and with fresh risks created by fresh circumstance, such as reinsurance for fire companies, or insurance against the newly devised employers' liability[5]. Lloyd's became a sort of laboratory in which the limits—they proved hard to find—and the very clear benefits of the principle of insurance could be tried out, so that there might be greater security in an economic world whose chances and risks might be increased by man's ingenuity, unless counteracted by more ingenuity. The speculative insurer at Lloyd's smoothed out the risk curves of life like the speculative dealer in cotton futures at Liverpool, only with more certainty and with deliberate intent. And this he did not for Britain only, but for the world.

Meanwhile the ancient risks of property at sea, the first with which civilised man had dealt by way of insurance, had been almost completely covered by private underwriting, company underwriting, and the subsidiary methods. The uninsured hull or the uninsured cargo, exceedingly common in the eighteenth century and by no means rare during the first half of the nine-

[1] Originally it contained a number of members with shipping interests who were not professional underwriters or had ceased to underwrite. Apparently the proportion grew between 1815 and 1847, when there were only 185 underwriting to 621 non-underwriting members: by 1870 the ratio was 401 to 216. Wright and Fayle, *op. cit.*

[2] *Ibid.* p. 429.

[3] Vol. I. p. 288–91.

[4] The title adopted at the foundation of the Club.

[5] Wright and Fayle, *op. cit.* p. 431–2.

teenth, was now a discreditable exception among small obscure coasters or on the by-roads of the seas. 'A I at Lloyd's' had become part of the English language. Fraud in the insurance, or over-insurance, of a ship deliberately cast away[1] was probably more common than neglect of the obvious precaution of taking out a policy; though there might be cheese-paring under-insurance by impecunious owners. It was assumed as a matter of course that every shipwreck would have its repercussions at Lloyd's, or somewhere in the underwriting world.

Probably, by the 'eighties, commercial insurance against fire had become no less general than commercial insurance against the risks of the sea. But there were always some uninsured private dwellings and uninsured farming stock; though even by 1850 the insurance of houses was in a totally different position from what it had been when Adam Smith guessed that "nineteen houses in twenty or rather, perhaps, ninety-nine in a hundred were not insured against fire."[2] A record taken of the fires in London during a whole year in the early 'fifties showed that less than 18 per cent. of the buildings damaged or destroyed, but 40 per cent. of the contents of those buildings, were uninsured[3]. How far insurance policies, where they had been taken out, covered the risks, the record did not show; but it is known that insurance up to two-thirds of the value was a common practice[4]. London was the original home of fire insurance and the headquarters of the strongest companies, and so had a high proportion of insured property. But there were many strong country, and some strong Scottish, offices. Moreover the London offices, especially the oldest and most famous—the Sun, the Phoenix, and the Royal Exchange—did a great deal of country and Scottish business[5]. Even allowing for a crowd of uninsured cottages, and for the fact that in 1862 nearly all those people whose destructible property was worth less

[1] For which see Kipling, Rudyard, *Bread upon the Waters*.

[2] Quoted and discussed in vol. I. p. 284–5.

[3] *The Assurance Magazine*, 1854, quoted in Walford, C., *The Insurance Cyclopaedia*, v. 501.

[4] *Report* (revised) *on Fire Insurance Duties*, by George Coode, *A. and P.* 1863 (XXVI. 27), p. 25. The original report (of 1856) contained errors which were pointed out by Brown, S., "On the Progress of Fire Insurance in Great Britain as compared with other Countries," *S.J.* 1857, p. 135 *sqq*.

[5] Vol. I. p. 284. Cp. Walford, *op. cit.* III. 424. This fact makes the figures for England and Wales as against Scotland, given in Coode's *Report*, p. 36, of no value as a basis for the comparative amounts of insurance in North and South Britain.

than £300 were believed to be still uninsured, it is likely that, instead of Adam Smith's hypothetical nineteen in twenty or ninety-nine in a hundred houses not insured, ten in twenty would be a considerable overstatement. For in 1857 it was estimated that nearly half the total value of buildings and their contents was covered by insurance[1]. It has been seen that buildings were much more regularly insured than their contents; and the uninsured people with destructible property worth less than £300 were not normally owners of houses.

It was maintained, during the 'fifties and 'sixties, that the survival of a percentage tax on fire insurance policies, an ancient duty which had been doubled during the French wars and never lowered since, was a formidable handicap on the growth of a precaution socially necessary, and on a business of much public utility. 'The tax on prudence' was its nickname. As a result of it, so the companies and their friends argued[2], many large estates and great quantities of merchandise were left uncovered, and policies were taken out for sums much less in proportion to the value of the insured properties than was 'natural.' As the tax was 3*s.* for every £100 insured, a crushing percentage addition to an ordinary house-insurance premium, the argument cannot be disregarded[3]. It was enforced in practical politics by the domestic or commercial insurers' grievance that policies on farming stock had been exempt from duty since 1853. But the history of fire insurance under the tax suggests that the ill effects of this handicap on prudence and enterprise were less than the companies wished Parliament to believe.

By the end of the 'sixties, the tax, much criticised in and out of Parliament, was ripe for repeal. In 1863 it had produced £1,630,000, excluding the small sum collected in Ireland. Next year Gladstone halved the duty on insurances of stock in trade. The duty on houses was halved in 1866. Yet the halved duty produced more than £1,000,000 in 1868, the year before Robert Lowe decided to abandon altogether this "sort of penalty on providence."[4] With it went a series of official figures, by which

[1] Brown in *S.J.* as above.

[2] *E.g. The Assurance Magazine* as above. For the parliamentary assaults on the duty see Buxton, *Finance and Politics*, I. 333.

[3] The companies would insure first-class London house property at 1*s.* 6*d.* per £100, apart from the tax. The minimum for agricultural insurance was 5*s.*; on good warehouse sheds, 12*s.*; on theatres, "when insurable at all," £5. So on big risks the duty was no great burden. Coode's *Report*, p. 16.

[4] Buxton, *op. cit.* I. 333; II. 91.

the growth of fire insurance and the relative importance of the various companies can be gauged conveniently, if not with perfect accuracy[1]. The amount of duty paid in Britain in 1805 had corresponded to an insured value of about £260,000,000; in 1831 to one of about £500,000,000; in 1851 to about £800,000,000, to which must be added nearly £60,000,000 of agricultural insurance now exempt from duty. By the end of 1862 the two figures had risen to over £1100,000,000 and £75,000,000. In 1868 the agricultural figure had not increased, but the general figure had risen to upwards of £1500,000,000. The course of the two series does not suggest that freedom from duty, or liability to duty, had much to do with the growth of the insurance habit; though the elasticity of the yield when the duty was halved may imply a certain response to lower taxation, not merely a contemporary growth in the amount of property requiring insurance. In any case, considering the immense figure, the official adviser of the government, who had asserted in 1863 that "the limits of possible insurance have been nearly reached,"[2] cannot have been seriously in error; though his "possible" has to be interpreted by the insurance and building habits of the time, according to which many theatres were not "insurable at all," and insurances for sums under £300 were not encouraged by the companies. (Premiums of a few shillings were as tiresome to them as cheques for a few shillings were to the bankers of the period.) An estimate made in 1872[3] suggests that the growth of fire insurance immediately after 1869 may have been somewhat faster than the growth of insurable property, but certainly not much faster. When insurance against new types of risk began to develop in the 'eighties, insurance against fire was probably as complete as the standing reluctance of the insurer to take on doubtful propositions and of the owner of insurable property to appreciate his risks will ever permit, except perhaps in agriculture.

There had been a constant rise and fall of companies; but there was no serious change in the total after 1831–2[4]. Some

[1] They are used in Coode's *Report*; by Brown in *S.J.* 1857; and repeatedly by Walford. Returns were made of agricultural insurance down to 1868, though it was exempt from duty.

[2] Coode's *Report*, p. 33.

[3] Quoted in Walford, *op. cit.* III. 512. Lacking the basis of official figures, it is somewhat speculative.

[4] The date at which the position is summarised in vol. I. p. 287. Down to the 'seventies there are regular annals of the companies in Walford *s.v. Fire Insurance, History of.*

old ones dropped out or were absorbed; but, with few exceptions, they were from among those which did least business. The four companies which had been strongest early in the century, the Sun, the Phoenix, the Royal Exchange and the Norwich Union, still paid two-fifths of the percentage duty in 1851, and three-tenths in 1868. When this measure of the home business of the companies ceased[1], the Sun, which had done a third of that business in 1805 and a sixth in 1832, was still doing an eighth. The Norwich Union, however, was no longer the leading country office, having been passed both by the Liverpool London and Globe and by the Royal. The Phoenix remained the second town office; but it too had been passed by the Liverpool company, the most progressive society of the period, which grew with the cotton trade and the Lancashire towns, and took business from older institutions[2].

Of all commercial activities, insurance had probably altered least in principles and organisation. Incorporation had made no essential change in Lloyd's. There had been some spread of actuarial knowledge and exact method from the insurance of lives, where calculations of probability had been first applied, to the other fields of insurance; but this was a normal and slow process. The new developments of company law had little to say to fire and life insurance, which had always been exclusively company-businesses, or to marine insurance, which had been so in part for more than a hundred and fifty years. Some of the greater companies had done more than one of the older types of insurance—fire, marine, and life—before 1850[3]. There had been an increase in this composite class, as was natural. Towards the end of the period, established companies were experimenting with the newer types of insurance, particularly with that insurance against accidents which began—outside the Friendly Societies and Trade Unions—with the Railway Passengers' Company of 1848, and had been developed by a long line of small, experimental, and usually short-lived companies during the next twenty years[4]. But the great expansion of accident insurance, either by new or old companies, came later.

[1] The companies also did foreign business of which no measure exists.

[2] As the Liverpool it was only the tenth country society in 1841. As the Liverpool and London it was the sixth in 1851 and the second in 1861. As the Liverpool London and Globe it was the first in the country and the second in the Kingdom in 1868.

[3] Vol. I. p. 291.

[4] Walford *s.v. Accident Insurance*, I. 6 *sqq.*

One change of some importance there had been, characteristic of a time in which a certain amount of quiet combination was going on in the economic world, to the accompaniment of a distracting chorus in praise of free and open competition. In 1858, after several preliminary attempts, what came to be known as the Tariff Association of Fire Insurance Offices was formed, to introduce a uniform system of rating risks, and so allow the companies to present a united front to the public. It was the greatest success. "Several of the offices now in association" Walford, a frank partisan, wrote in 1874[1], "were formed with the express intention of operating independently; but found it so impossible to meet the unreasonable demands of their clients, that they were driven into association." "At the present moment," he went on to say, "there are very few offices...outside the Association. From time to time 'independent' offices are established; but in a few years they usually join the Association—or die." The offices continued to fight for business, but with swords of a standard length. The public and the press sometimes grumbled about monopoly. The insurance interest replied that the system "while kept within rational limits" was "for the common good of all concerned."[2] No doubt they were right; and there is no reason to think that at this time the limits set were irrational.

[1] Walford, *op. cit.* III. 530–1. Walford was personally connected with this movement and is a first-rate authority: see the *D.N.B.*

[2] Walford, *op. cit.* III. 530.

CHAPTER IX

MONEY, PRICES, BANKING AND INVESTMENT

WHEN, in the year 1865, the four principal franc-using countries formed what came to be known as the Latin currency union, it occurred to a few British reformers that, by an easy alteration of the alloy in the sovereign and a slight reduction of the gold in the American dollar, a uniform international gold currency might be created on the basis of £1 = 25 francs = 5 dollars. The "Teutonic nations," it was thought, would be too intelligent to stand out; and "a bag of the new sovereigns, or internationals, as they should be called, would go everywhere."[1] But the dollar was buried under greenbacks in 1865–6: within a few years the franc was shaken by war and indemnities: no British statesman, it may be assumed, ever gave the proposal ten minutes serious thought; and when intelligent Teutonic statesmen placed the currency of new Germany on a gold basis, economic nationalism decided that 20 marks gold should just not be the equivalent of the pound sterling. So Lord Liverpool's sovereign, with its subordinate silver and bronze, remained unaltered and unchallenged—the chief coin of the world.

When Peel had finished his bank-note legislation of 1844–5[2], it is probable that the circulation of gold coin in the United Kingdom, or in Britain, had not much exceeded that of the notes. The notes in the United Kingdom were nearly £40,000,000. The coin may have been £46,000,000. Twelve years later, with the arrival of the new gold and the rigid limitation of note issue, the notes had fallen somewhat; the gold had increased by over 50 per cent.[3] It was demonstrable that recent price fluctuations had had little or nothing to do with the trifling changes in the circulation of notes. William Newmarch, who had helped to demonstrate this, was in a position to speak of

[1] *Economist*, October 27, 1866, commenting on an article in the *Edinburgh Review* of October, 1866, on "International Coinage," which reviewed among other books Soetbeer, G. A., *Produktion der edlen Metalle*.

[2] Vol. I. p. 521 *sqq*.

[3] Newmarch estimated the gold in 1844 at £46,000,000 and in 1856 at £75,000,000. Palgrave, R. H. J., *Notes on Banking* (1873), p. 49, quotes Newmarch as saying £36,000,000 for 1844. But Newmarch corrected this, *History of Prices*, VI. 702.

bank-notes as "the mere small change of the ledger."[1] They became in time still smaller change. During the next twenty-five years they seldom exceeded by more than a few millions the figure of Peel's day; and in 1887 they were below it. Meanwhile the gold coin of the United Kingdom had increased to between two and three times the figure of the notes in circulation, that is to say to over £100,000,000[2]. With this position, after forty years working of his Acts, Peel, there can be no doubt, would have been content.

The note held its ground better in Scotland than in England because wages could be paid in £1 notes. A revival of the £1 note in England was sometimes discussed. By 1875 there were bankers in favour of it. But Walter Bagehot, the ablest of them, hesitated. "At first I own I should have a doubt about it," he said, though he admitted that it "might be rather advantageous than otherwise."[3] He still feared money panics and runs of small note-holders on the gold. In 1886, when possibilities of economy in the use of gold had come to the front with falling prices, a Scottish banker was advocating the £1 note as a gold economiser before the Bankers' Institute of London[4]. But his argument was not conclusive and politicians were nervous of touching the currency. The £1 note, and note policy generally, remained subjects of only academic discussion until 1914. This was natural. There was never any lack of cash for wages or retail trade, and all large transactions had been settled by bill of exchange or cheque for a long time.

Down to 1853, the London Clearing Bankers[5] had still

[1] *Presidential Address, Economic Section, British Association*, at Manchester, 1861. Compare the full discussion and figures in Tooke and Newmarch, *History of Prices*, VI. 583 *sqq*., 701 *sqq*. and the triumphant conclusion in V. 344, against those who had held that bank-note-issue was a determining cause in price fluctuations. Cp. also vol. I. p. 534.

[2] Ireland had a disproportionate note circulation, £5,726,000 out of £39,166,000 for the United Kingdom in June, 1886. She also probably had a disproportionate gold circulation. In 1875 R. H. I. Palgrave estimated that of £100,000,000 of gold coinage existing in the United Kingdom only £67,000,000 was in England. (*S.C. on Banks of Issue*, 1875, IX. Q. 5915 *sqq*.) Cp. Palgrave's *Notes on Banking*, p. 49. Palgrave's 1875 estimate was high. The estimates for the 'eighties (Palgrave, 1883: the Mint, 1888) put the gold at 257 or 260 per cent. of the notes. *U.S.A. Monetary Commission*, 1910. *Statistics for Great Britain, etc.*, p. 75.

[3] *S.C. on Banks of Issue*, Q. 8015.

[4] Kerr, A. W., *Scottish Banking*...1865–96 (1898), p. 96.

[5] Cp. vol. I. p. 283. Lists of the London clearing bankers at various dates are given in Martin, J. B., *The Grasshopper in Lombard Street* (1892), p. 169 *sqq*.

adjusted their accounts with Bank of England notes, and the Custom House required payment in notes[1]. In Scotland it had not been "the general practice for a customer to draw cheques ...for his individual payments. If he has to make twenty payments in the course of a day he will go to the bank in the morning and draw out in one sum a sufficient amount of notes to make all these payments."[2] By 1855 all London Clearing and Custom House business was done by cheque. "By far the larger amount of transactions"[3] were so conducted, the Governor of the Bank of England explained in 1857. A private banker from Ipswich said that the banking habit had increased fourfold of late among farmers and shopkeepers: "almost every farmer, even those paying only £50 per annum rent, now keep deposits with bankers." London cheques for quite small sums, "very frequently under £2," came down from poulterers, greengrocers and pork-butchers; though farmers did not yet send cheques to London[4]. As time went on the deposit produced the cheque, and there was a tendency for the cheque to supersede the inland bill as a means of payment. In 1841 an expert had placed good trade bills "with the security of the drawer, acceptor, and perhaps twenty endorsements on the back, in the first class of our currency." There was "no purpose of money except wages" to which bills were "not applicable in the provinces...though not seen in London in making payments."[5] The endorsements show how freely they circulated. In 1851 farmers commonly bought on the basis of a "good bill at three months," which bankers procured for them[6]. By 1873 the freely circulating bill of 1841 was unfamiliar to an experienced country banker, though the bill discounted once and sometimes rediscounted was familiar enough. The proportion of bills discounted to deposits had fallen considerably, so far as could be ascertained, since 1851[7]. Instead of discounting a bill, the

[1] *S.C. on the Bank Acts*, 1857 (x), Q. 97 (T. M. Wegeulin, Governor of the Bank of England).

[2] Gilbart, J. W., *The Principles and Practice of Banking* (ed. of 1873, describing the practice of the 'forties and 'fifties), p. 495.

[3] *S.C. on the Bank Acts*, Q. 671.

[4] *S.C. on the Bank Acts and the recent Commercial Distress*, 1857–8 (v). Evidence of W. Rodwell, Q. 1331 *sqq*.

[5] Leatham, W., *Second Series of Letters*, p. 37–8, quoted in Palgrave, *Notes*, p. 36–7.

[6] Newmarch, "An Attempt to ascertain the Magnitude and Fluctuations of the Amount of Bills of Exchange...in Circulation," *S.J.* 1851, p. 164.

[7] Palgrave's *Notes*, as above.

banker would make an advance on security taken, or on personal credit, against which cheques could be drawn. In Scotland the practice of carrying away notes for the day's payments was "very much modified—the English system of cheques being more common."[1] The forecast made in 1873, that in the circulation of the whole country cheques would "tend to supersede"[2] bills still further, proved correct. A decided decline in inland bills was registered again in 1885[3]. It was connected with the growth of cash payment, which meant cheques and the newer telegraphic transfers. As for coin, that formed not 1 per cent. of the payments into the banks in London and only about 6 per cent. in Manchester, in the early 'eighties[4]. The late Victorian British currency system and habits were established.

Rare as the use of coin was, the whole currency rested on its thin plate of gold. A most important part of British trade was with countries where the plate was thicker, but of silver. Now there had been vicissitudes in the supply and relations of the precious metals such as had not been known since the sixteenth century. After a long spell of low gold output in the known world, that of the Ural mines had greatly increased during the 'forties, reaching the then remarkable figure of £3,400,000 in 1846[5]. The effects of the Californian gold began to be felt in Europe in 1850. On September 3, 1851, the finding of gold in New South Wales was reported in London. The mere announcement influenced trade, freights, and prices; for California had shown what would follow. Together with older sources of supply, California and Australia raised the world output of gold during the decade 1851–60 to not far short of four times what it had been in 1841–50, and to nearly ten times the output of 1831–40. There was a slight fall from the high level of the 'fifties during the decade 1861–70, and a further fall in 1871–80; but the world output for 1871–80 was still more

[1] Note to the passage in the 1873 edition of Gilbart quoted above.

[2] Palgrave, *Notes*, p. 37.

[3] *R.C. on Depression of Trade*, Q. 582. Evidence of the Chief Receiver in Bankruptcy. For the general decline in inland bills see Jackson, F. Huth, "The Draft on London and Tariff Reform," *E.J.* 1904: "a great deal of business ...that used to be financed by inland bills is now financed by banker's overdraft."

[4] Pownall, G. H., in 1881 quoted in Nicholson, J. S., *Money and Monetary Problems* (ed. 1897), p. 143.

[5] Tooke and Newmarch (quoting a Consular Return of 1847), v. 531.

than eight times that of 1831–40[1]. Yet even this great output added only a very small percentage annually to the existing stock. So durable is gold.

At first the new gold went mainly into coinage. During the eight years from 1848 to 1856, England, France, and the United States together coined no less than £207,000,000[2]. It has been estimated that not more than 14 per cent. of the output of the 'fifties was absorbed in industry and the arts[3]. Twice, in 1854 and in 1856, France alone coined over £20,000,000 worth in a year. The new Empire was made glorious with gold. Afterwards industrial uses absorbed much of the annual increment, mounting to about 60 per cent. in the 'eighties. By that time, also, there was a steady drain to India. Experts thought that it might amount to £8,000,000 a year[4]. It was a new thing, dating from about 1870. Formerly the East had been content to take and sterilise silver in jewellery and hoards. Now she was sterilising gold also.

Throughout the era of the Second Empire, the currency of France, and to a lesser degree that of the other members of the Latin Union, had been effectively bimetallic. Gold had been coined in such quantities, not because it alone was standard money as in Britain, but because it was for the time being the more abundant metal. The French mint took the surplus gold and the French people, great coin users, were glad of it. But at an international monetary conference held at Paris in 1867, all the nations represented, except Holland, were in favour of the gold standard[5]. After 1871, the new German Empire, composed of states all of which had hitherto employed a silver standard, turned to gold. The United States were working out of the greenback period which had followed the Civil War into a period of gold and silver. In 1873 they declared the gold dollar the sole 'unit of value.' France, driven on to paper in 1870–1, like all nations unhappy in war, resumed specie pay-

[1] The accepted figures, based on the calculations of Soetbeer and others, and given in the *Dict. of Pol. Econ.* II. 220.

[2] Tooke and Newmarch, VI. 154.

[3] *Dict. of Pol. Econ.* as above, article by S. M. Leathes.

[4] Evidence of S. Pixley before the *R.C. on Gold and Silver, First Report*, 1887 (XXII), Q. 175, 180.

[5] Cp. Pierson, N. G., *Principles of Economics* (1902), I. 403–49; from the Dutch standpoint, but containing the best short account of the monetary history of the later nineteenth century, written by a man who had taken part in it both as economist and statesman. Pierson was prime minister of Holland. Cp. the historical section of the *Final Report* of the *R.C. on Gold and Silver*, 1888 (XLV).

ments in November, 1874. By an agreement of January 1 of that year, she and the other states of the Latin Union had restricted the coinage of large silver, the five-franc pieces. This first step towards the abandonment of genuine bimetallism, which implies a mint open for whichever metal is more abundant, foreshadowed a growing currency demand for gold. Britain, although she had cut her use of coin to a minimum, required an increased stock year by year for her increasing population and trade. Most other nations, whether they were or were not in a position to adopt gold as their standard, were anxious to add to their stores of it. Thus, in the later 'seventies, the currency, industrial, and hoarding demands for gold were all insistent.

By that time (1876–80) the United States alone were producing in a year considerably more silver than the whole known world had produced yearly in 1851–60; and Mexico alone not very much less[1]. In the 'eighties their output went far higher. It was the fast growing silver production of the early 'seventies which had made the Latin Union decide to restrict its free coinage, for fear lest the currency should become all silver, at a time when Germany's change over to a gold basis was throwing yet more silver on to the market. In 1878 the Union stopped coining large silver altogether.

The gold price of silver in London had remained extraordinarily steady from 1800 to 1870. It was rarely more than 1*d.* and a small fraction above, or a fraction of a penny below, 5*s.* the standard ounce. The fall, slow at first and then rapid, to 4*s.* 4¼*d.* in 1880, and to 3*s.* 5$\frac{11}{16}$*d.* in 1889, was a movement without a precedent in history, either in speed or in amount. Legislation in the United States compelling the Federal Government to coin unnecessary silver dollars, or issue superfluous notes against silver bullion, had failed to check the fall[2], which acted to some degree as an export bounty for the silver-using countries of the East, whose silver costs of production rose more slowly than the gold price of rupees, dollars, or taels fell[3].

There can be very little doubt that the marked upward heave of general prices between the triennium 1849–51 (a time of free trade and of quiet after storm) and the triennium 1868–

[1] Cp. *Dict. of Pol. Econ. s.v.* Silver, III. 395 and authorities there quoted; *R.C. on Gold and Silver*, *Report*, as above.

[2] The literature of the subject is vast: see the summary and references in Taussig, F. W., *The Silver Situation in the U.S.* (1893) and Conrad and Elster, *H.WB. s.v. Silber und Silberwährung.*

[3] "A fall in the Indian exchange will give a bounty to exporters from India if it is caused by a fall in the value of silver...which is felt in other countries

70 (also a time of free but quiet trade, with no war until August, 1870[1]) was closely connected with the great addition to the world's stock of coined and circulating gold, which was accompanied by a growing use of paper money in its various forms. Whether the general fall after 1873 was mainly, or to an important degree, due to causes connected with the precious metals was much debated at the time and remains perhaps more doubtful. Special causes for any particular fall could easily be assigned—virgin soil for wheat; metallurgical inventions for steel; the revolution in the transport system of the world for most things[2]. It could be argued that there was a fast growing use of bank money everywhere, which relieved pressure on gold; that the output of gold was still great, and that any slight contraction of it hardly affected the world's golden stock. Why then should gold prices fall? But those who pointed to the insistence of the new currency demands for gold; to the depletion of the stock available for circulating currency by the demand from industry and the hoarder, whether Hindu ryot or rajah, or Western State hoarding for financial security or for war[3]; to the way in which silver had been discarded and gold required to do its work; to the effect of the silver situation on the low gold prices which, for a time, might be accepted for Eastern produce—those who pointed to these things as the most important, though not the sole, causes of the unquestionably increased purchasing power of currencies based on gold, had the better of the argument, even if they could offer no precise measure of that importance for which they argued. So a strong Commission, set to inquire into the matter in 1886, was subsequently to report[4].

before it is felt in India: this will happen if more silver is raised in the West or less silver is wanted there; or if" etc. Alfred Marshall, 1888, *Memorandum for the Gold and Silver Commission: Official Papers* by A. M. p. 195. These hypotheses fit the facts of the period. Cp. the price diagram, p. 378 below.

[1] War was responsible for the rather higher level touched in 1861–6.

[2] As argued at the time by Wells, D. A., *Recent Economic Changes* (1889).

[3] "War Ministers, Indian peasants, and American negroes began to hoard gold." Alfred Marshall, *Memorandum*, as above, p. 21.

[4] *R.C. on Gold and Silver*, *Report*, as above. The report lays stress on the relative unimportance of increased supplies of silver and decreased supplies of gold (§ 22, 44 of Part I) and tends—though there were great differences of opinion among the Commissioners—to assign most importance to the abandonment of bimetallism. Economists, it is hoped, will pardon this summary of a controversy which in its day strained the acutest minds. Keynes, J. M., *A Treatise on Money* (1930) II, 164, argues that "for the decade ending about 1886 this explanation [i.e. the explanation suggested above, but stated by Keynes more briefly and more absolutely] is probably accurate."

In some important external aspects the banking organisation, through which Britain economised cash and accumulated capital, altered curiously little in the forty years after Peel's Acts. No doubt the Acts themselves stiffened it somewhat against change. When Peel came into power in 1841 there had been 321 private banks and 115 joint-stock banks in England and Wales. In 1875 there were still 252 private banks, and about 120 joint-stock banks whose business was strictly English. The corresponding figures for 1886 were 251 private and 117 joint-stock. The private banks to which Peel had left issuing rights in 1844 numbered 207; in 1875 there survived 114; in 1880, 104. There were still 74 in 1890. The general types of Peel's day had not changed, though their relative importance had. They had been, and they remained, very varied in function and size. There was the group of the old London 'general purposes' private banks. There was the large and important group of London firms, classed as private banks, which did specialised business mainly connected with foreign trade and investment—merchant bankers, and houses like Rothschilds, Barings, Morgans or Lazards[1]. There were country private banks, some of which now had many branches; and there were the joint-stock banks, both London and country, with branches or without. Above all stood The Bank, both its written and its unwritten constitution unchanged—although Tooke in 1856 had thought it "hardly possible to suppose" that the written part, Peel's Act, could be "maintained much longer"; although Mill had explained in 1857 that this Act's whole theory was wrong; and although Walter Bagehot, in 1873, had put forward a considered plan for a change in the unwritten constitution, with its short-term Governorship and its exclusion of true bankers from the Board[2].

Even the development of branch-banking between 1844 and 1886 seems less remarkable in retrospect than it did to some contemporaries. The policy was nearly as old as the joint-stock

[1] For 1841, vol. I. p. 512. A few of the joint-stock banks of that date were the young chartered colonial banks (for which see Baster, A. S. J., *The Imperial Banks*, 1929). The figures for 1875 are in App. XVIII of the *S.C. on Banks of Issue*: they do not distinguish this class, of which there were at that time 17. The figure for 1875 includes 60, and that for 1886, 77, London 'private banks.' A large number of these at both dates were of the Rothschild and Baring type. These can be picked out from the detailed lists of the *Bankers' Almanac*. Lists of Banks of Issue were published officially. For 1890 see the *Dict. of Pol. Econ.* I. 94. For Peel's Acts, English, Scottish and Irish, vol. I. pp. 522–6.

[2] Tooke and Newmarch, V. 612; Mill before *S.C. on the Bank Acts*, 1857, Q. 2284; Bagehot, *Lombard Street*, ch. 8.

bank itself. Its pioneer in England, the Manchester and Liverpool District Bank, had sixteen branches in the year after the Reform Bill[1]. Among the older joint-stock banks to which Peel had left rights of issue, the National Provincial of London, and among those without issuing rights, the London and County, were the most active in spreading their offices during the 'forties and 'fifties. By 1864 the former had no less than 119 branches and the latter 127. The Manchester and Liverpool District came third, with 34 branches. Deducting these, the remaining 114 averaged only just over four branches each. All told, there were 744 joint-stock bank branches and 272 private bank branches in 1864; for many private banks had one or two sub-offices, though only three of them had so many as ten. Twenty-two years later, again deducting the three joint-stock banks with most branches, the remaining 112 averaged ten branches each. The leading three were the London and County with 165, the National Provincial with 158, and the Capital and Counties with 99 branches. Six others now had more than 50, and some few private banks, like the firm then known as Lloyds Barnetts and Bosanquets, were spreading branches fast. These were important changes, but there was no radical transformation[2].

In Scotland the change was less because the banking system in the middle of the century had been more mature. Peel had regulated the issues of nineteen Scottish banks; all joint-stock; all furnished with branches. There were five more of the same type which did not issue. Failure and absorption had reduced the total to thirteen by 1864, all banks of issue; and to ten by 1886. Branches had been planted out freely—it was the old Scottish policy[3]—so freely that in 1858 a Select Committee of the Commons supposed there were as many bank offices, head and branch, in Scotland as in all England[4]. Probably there were not nearly so many[5]; though in proportion to population there were very many more. This Scottish excess of banking facilities

[1] Vol. I. p. 279.

[2] For 1864, *Return of all Banks...in England and Wales*, 1865 (xxx), the last full return. For 1886, the *Economist*, *Banking Supplement*, and the *Bankers' Almanac* for 1887.

[3] See vol. I. p. 267.

[4] *Report*, § 76.

[5] There are no returns for 1858; but the 1864 returns show 550 private and 861 joint-stock banking offices, head and branch, in England and Wales: 607 of all sorts in Scotland. Compared with population, the Scottish figure is astonishing.

continued. The ten banks of 1886 had 949 branches. England and Wales, with seven times the population of Scotland, had only about 2500 bank offices including the smallest agencies[1].

The small number of the Scottish banks and the concentration of the principal head offices in Edinburgh made joint action easy. There had been a clearing system in operation, at first for notes alone, since the eighteenth century. It was older than the Clearing House in London[2]. When the Western Bank with 101 branches failed in 1857, the others stilled the panic by agreeing, after a slight hesitation it is true, to accept its notes in the ordinary course of business[3]. In 1863 they all at once instructed their branches to follow promptly changes in the Bank of England discount rate[4]. By 1865, the last of them had abandoned old-fashioned banking secrecy, and all published annual reports with abstract balance sheets and statements of profit. In contrast with English diversity, "a uniformity of practice in the conduct...of business had been obtained throughout the whole of Scotland," before the 'seventies[5]; so that it was easy to make concerted changes, as when in 1885, feeling the pinch of hard times, all the banks together withdrew the old clients' privilege of interest on their daily balances[6]. Many years later, the smooth uniformity of Scottish banking practice still seemed "almost incredible from the English point of view."[7]

The Scottish banks had always had correspondence with London. Early in the century, they had settled their clearing balances with drafts at ten days on the Bank of England[8]. Peel's Act, by which they were permitted to increase note issues beyond a fixed minimum only against coin held in their head offices, made their relations with the Bank more intimate. They

[1] I make the number in the *Bankers' Almanac* for 1887, 2533.

[2] Kerr, A. W., *History of Banking in Scotland*, p. 81, 221. For the advantages of the concentration in Edinburgh, cp. Palgrave, *Notes on Banking*, p. 11 and the quotation from the *Bankers' Magazine* of 1876 in Powell, E. T., *The Evolution of the London Money Market* (1915), p. 510.

[3] Kerr, *History*, p. 262. Two recent books, Munro, N., *The History of the Royal Bank of Scotland* (1928) and Rait, R. S., *The History of the Union Bank of Scotland* (1930), do not add much of general interest to Kerr's narrative.

[4] Kerr, *History*, p. 270.

[5] Palgrave, *Notes*, p. 11 and Kerr, *Scottish Banking during the Period of Published Accounts*, 1865–96.

[6] Kerr, *Scottish Banking*, p. 10.

[7] Withers, H., *The English Banking System*, *U.S. Monetary Commission*, 1910, p. 49.

[8] Kerr, *History*, p. 221.

acquired the habit of drawing the extra coin necessary at harvest and other times of expanding note issue from its Newcastle branch[1]. Meanwhile the increased prosperity of Scotland was linking them closer to the London Money Market. They sent much "superfluous money" for use there by the bill-brokers in the early 'fifties[2]. At that time Scottish merchants seldom kept accounts in London or accepted bills payable in London, so far as is known[3]. By 1873 the situation was reversed. It was "quite an exception with large mercantile houses" in Scotland "to accept a bill payable there." They accepted those bills on London which the whole world wanted; for bills not payable in London were "simply unmarketable."[4] And the Scottish banks had "all their spare money...in London... invested as all other London money"[5] was.

Down to the 'sixties, the Scots worked their London business through agencies. In 1855 however the Clydesdale Bank had taken Roundell Palmer's opinion as to whether it could legally open in London without sacrificing its issuing rights in Scotland. Palmer said it could, but it did not[6]. In 1864 the National Bank of Scotland did; and in 1868 the Bank of Scotland[7]. The Royal Bank followed in 1874[8]. By 1883 all the important Scottish banks had their London offices. They had survived a Parliamentary attack in 1875, consequent on the 'invasion' of Cumberland by the Clydesdale Bank, which led to the inquiry of that year[9]. The law, it appeared, was on their side; but equity would seem to endorse a Bill drafted by Goschen, that never became an Act, under which a Scottish joint-stock bank, like every English joint-stock bank, must choose between a London office and its right of note issue[10]. The Scots retained both,

[1] *S.C. on the Bank Acts*, 1857–8, Q. 3186 (Sir George Clark).

[2] *Ibid.* 1857, Q. 5151 (D. B. Chapman of Overend and Gurney).

[3] *S.C. on Banks of Issue*, 1875, Q. 28 (a Scottish witness referring to "thirty years ago" with an "I daresay").

[4] Rae, G., *The Country Banker* (1885), p. 87.

[5] Bagehot, *Lombard Street*, p. 32.

[6] Macleod, H. D., *Theory and Practice of Banking*, II. 400.

[7] Kerr, *Scottish Banking*, p. 13. [8] Munro, *op. cit.* p. 267–8.

[9] *S.C. on Banks of Issue*: evidence was published but no report.

[10] In fact between an English domicile of any sort and its right of note issue, but London was in Goschen's mind. His Bill—*A Bill to amend the Bankers Acts*—suggested that "the power of any banker to...issue notes, whether in England or in Scotland, shall...be subject to the condition that such banker shall not...have any house of business...in the other of the said parts of Great Britain." Macleod (II. 397) was very truculent about this. The Scots' argument was that Irish and Colonial issuing banks had London offices, so why not theirs?

probably because the commercial and political worlds were no longer much interested in problems of issue. So the whole British army of bankers was concentrating on Lombard and Threadneedle Streets.

The Scottish contingent was much the most uniformly drilled and organised, its movements and resources the best known to those whom it served. England had her metropolitan and country, her North country and South country, customs and practices. Her private banks still preserved the old secrecy[1]. Not quite all the joint-stock banks issued reports and balance sheets even in the 'eighties. Only one provincial bank had yet imitated the Scottish raid on London. This was that active and "octopus-like establishment" the National Provincial, which had sacrificed its issuing rights to establish its position at the heart of the banking world[2]. When it announced its intention, in 1864, the *Economist* rightly thought that it was "long since so great an event had happened in English country banking."[3] The normal English bank, however, like Scottish banks before the 'sixties, went on doing its London business through an agent from among the old metropolitan firms.

London itself was not a fully organised banking unit even at the end of the period. In the early 'fifties, jealousy between the private and the joint-stock banks hindered co-operation. The joint-stock banks had started new policies. They "entered more and more into competition with the private banks, and by their practice of allowing interest on deposits [which the private banks did not do] began to accumulate vast amounts."[4] In June, 1854, however, a sort of treaty was concluded, when the private banks admitted the new-comers—some of them nearly thirty years old—to the conveniences of the Clearing House. After ten more years, in April, 1864, the Bank of England itself condescended, and was allowed, to take a hand in the clearings, besides acting as banker to all other clearers. In the interval, in 1858, Sir John Lubbock had started the 'country clearing,' by which country banks could write off claims against one

[1] The first agreement of some of them to publish accounts came only in 1891.

[2] See the account in *S.C. on Banks of Issue*, 1875, Q. 1815 *sqq*. The octopus metaphor is in Phillips, M., *A History of Banks...in Northumberland, Durham and North Yorkshire* (1894), p. 117. The National Provincial had opened at Newcastle in 1865.

[3] June 4, 1864.

[4] *Report of* 1858, § 7, and evidence of D. Salomons, of the London and Westminster, Q. 1130.

another, through their London agents. By 1871 all of them were doing so[1].

But cohesion among the English banks was still very imperfect, and arrangements for joint action in emergency did not exist. In a sort of song of triumph over the rapid and unexpected success of the joint-stock banks, Walter Bagehot, in 1873, noted as a dubious point their lack of care for ultimate reserves[2]. They left that to the Bank of England. The Governor of the Bank had noted the risk in 1857, when it was much smaller. But at no time in the 'seventies or early 'eighties, so far as is known, did the Bank negotiate with the banks about it, nor the banks with one another. Indeed the Bank itself had been slow to recognise fully its own position as a central bank, in the sense in which that term is used to-day, a position which no charter or Act had assigned to it. It was still halting somewhat between the interests of its shareholders and those of the nation, when Walter Bagehot "finally established with unanswerable brilliance and cogency"[3] the functions and duties of a central bank, in 1873. In 1876, an English expert was complaining that the "homogeneity" which made it easy for the Scots to "decide on a common course of action" was "difficult, if not impossible, with English bankers."[4] In 1879 a financial writer noted that although "the lenders of money in Lombard Street are all within a stone's throw of one another...the Channel might run between them, instead of a dark, narrow little street, for all the interchange of information or assistance that goes on...in times of panic neither would fortify his neighbour with ready money or help him with information."[5] Perhaps he exaggerated a little. Perhaps the Lombard Street men would have replied that Scotland had just had a great banking catastrophe and England had not[6]. Yet certainly there was not much conscious organisation, beyond that for clearing accounts; so little that George Rae in 1885 was explaining to banking readers that a certain desirable reform would require "a greater degree of concert and a livelier sense of a common danger, on the part of English banks, than exists at present."[7]

[1] *Report of* 1858, § 7, for 1854; Gilbart, *The Principles and Practice of Banking* (ed. of 1873), p. 452–3; Macleod, *op. cit.* II. 192, and Martin, *The Grasshopper in Lombard Street*, for the later events.

[2] *Lombard Street*, p. 254–5.

[3] *Report of the Committee on Finance and Industry*, 1931 (Cmd. 3897), p. 15.

[4] Croft, C. W., in the *Bankers' Magazine*, quoted in Powell, *op. cit.* p. 510.

[5] Ellis, A., *The Rationale of Market Fluctuations*, p. 36.

[6] See below, p. 383.

[7] *The Country Banker*, p. 40.

The chances of a strain at the centre had been increased by the arrival in the city of other people besides the Scots. Before 1850 there were a few well-established Americo-English merchant banking houses, such as Peabody's of London, or the firm which was to become Brown, Shipley & Co. of Liverpool, later also of London[1]. They were already so strong in the early 'fifties that it was usual for "the shipper of goods here for America" to draw bills "upon a great American house in this country for them."[2] But in 1857 Peabody's came on the Bank for help[3]. Firms, most of which were bankers, at least by continental definition, and whose names were seldom British, were rising in London or arriving there from Europe and America on the track of the Barings and the Rothschilds. Some had come to London, or risen in London, as exchange dealers and acceptors of foreign bills long before 1850. Such were Huths', Doxats', and Raphaels'[4]. But like the Rothschilds and Barings before them, they were turning more and more to the issuing of loans for foreign governments and foreign railways. They were joined by others to whom, whatever their original character, issuing, perhaps linked with concession seeking, was the main chance.

The Hambros came from Copenhagen about 1848. They were taking up Danish loans in 1849–50, Sardinian and Peruvian in 1851–2[5]. Bischoffsheim and Goldschmidt, of Paris, Frankfurt and elsewhere, had an office in London from about 1850, and were prominent in the issuing world between 1866 and 1875. Frühling and Göschen, originally dealers in exchange, acquired special interests in Egypt. J. S. Morgan & Co. succeeded to the Peabody business during the American Civil War; in 1871 they were competing with the Rothschilds over the finance of the French indemnity loan. Speyers of New York came to London in 1862, and were issuing American railway bonds ten years later. There were Oppenheims, Schroeders, and Erlangers; there was Baron Hirsch, son-in-law to a Bischoffsheim; and there were others, European or American and generally

[1] Jenks, L. H., *The Migration of English Capital to* 1875, p. 94; Cole, A. H., "Evolution of the Foreign Exchange Market of the U.S.," *J.E.B.H.* May, 1929, p. 391.

[2] *S.C. on the Bank Acts*, 1857, Q. 5134 (D. B. Chapman of Overend and Gurney).

[3] Evans, D. M., *The History of the Commercial Crisis*, 1857–8, p. 49 n.

[4] Powell, *op. cit.* p. 386.

[5] *Fenn on the Funds*, 5th ed. 1855, p. 151, 200, 241.

Jewish, some of whom went down in the troubles of the 'seventies[1].

"Since the Franco-German war," Bagehot wrote in 1873, "we have become to a much larger extent than before the Bankers of Europe."[2] "The German Government, as is well known, keeps its account, and a very valuable one it must be, at the London Joint Stock Bank."[3] What other governments, crowned heads, and personages kept valuable accounts in the secret places of the private banks could be a matter only of conjecture, not of common knowledge. No doubt the accounts were there. During the next twelve years most of the continental public banks, as distinguished from the private international issuing houses, opened offices in London. The Crédit Lyonnais and the Deutsche Bank are cases in point. Not one of these institutions or individuals but was in a position to draw, directly or indirectly, on the reserves of the Bank of England. There was foreign money on deposit and foreign money at call or short notice. The whole scale and range of operations had widened since the 'forties; and cables had shortened notices since the 'sixties. The mobile deposits in the British joint-stock banks had enormously increased. These were the considerations which made Bagehot insist, not that there was grave danger—"I am by no means an alarmist," he said—but that there was a delicate problem presented which had been imperfectly studied. "Money will not manage itself, and Lombard Street has a great deal of money to manage."[4] Happily there was never a risk of Britain's becoming involved in anything but little wars, between 1873 and 1886, and her economic complaints during those years were of the wasting kind, not of the feverish kind which makes panic. Also she had learnt by trial and error, if not by profound speculative study, some useful rules of thumb for the maintenance of her financial health. Her leaders might fairly have argued, after watching Europe and America in 1873, that at least they knew more about these things than their neighbours[5].

Following very often a Scottish lead, the joint-stock banks of England had been extending their functions. The "vast amounts"[6] which they had accumulated by allowing interest on deposits had been employed very largely in the purchase of bills.

[1] See the account of these firms in Jenks, *op. cit.* p. 267–8, also p. 171.
[2] *Lombard Street*, p. 17. [3] *Ibid.* p. 312. [4] *Ibid.* p. 20.
[5] Below, p. 381 *sqq.* [6] Above, p. 344.

They have "decidedly run into our business," the managing partner of Overend and Gurney said in 1857[1]. Overend's, the bill merchants, 'the bankers' bankers' of the early nineteenth century, liked to have as much bank money as possible lying at short notice with themselves. The joint-stock people were doing more of their own bill-dealing than the private firms had done.

Subsequently, but with more hesitation, the joint-stock banks encroached on another field, that of the 'accepting houses,' mercantile firms who employed knowledge and capital in accepting—and so making more marketable—foreign bills on London. Again Scots led the hunt for new business. One of the charges of the more staid English bankers against the raiders from the North in 1875 was their 'undesirable' practice of accepting. The London and Westminster made a virtue of having refused "many accounts of great value, simply on the ground that they would involve foreign acceptances."[2] In fact it did very little accepting, either foreign or domestic. In 1870 it had among its liabilities only £759,000 of acceptances, against £19,600,000 of deposits. The acceptances were presumably not foreign. But the Union of London, which at the same time had £4,100,000 of acceptances and £10,000,000 of deposits, must surely have dabbled deep in the undesirable practice to do so large a business[3]. Even in 1883, all the Scottish banks together had only £4,800,000 of acceptances and drafts—not all foreign—against £83,000,000 of deposits. The acceptance figure, however, had increased by 85 per cent. since the totals were first made available in 1865[4]. The business was growing, but the evidence does not allow of its exact study.

Experts believed in the 'eighties that this growth was "due mainly to that exceptionally good department of acceptance business supplied by the Colonial banks drawing on London, and not so much to mercantile acceptances."[5] The Scottish bank office in London was helping the colonial bank to remit,

[1] *S.C. on the Bank Acts*, Q. 5210 (D. B. Chapman).

[2] *S.C. on Banks of Issue*, Q. 7318. W. H. Crake, the director giving evidence, was himself in a mercantile house and had a clear, old-fashioned, view of the line between his two activities.

[3] Half-yearly reports quoted in the *Economist*, August 6, 1870.

[4] Kerr, *Scottish Banking*, p. 119, and *History*, App. B.

[5] Kerr, *History*, p. 315; originally written in 1883. The statement is introduced with "it would seem that...." Kerr was a working banker. It was suggested in 1875 that the Union Bank's big accepting business was due to connections with a large Indian bank. *S.C. on Banks of Issue*, Q. 6944.

a most unobjectionable practice. Like all accepting of 'finance bills'—which was not a new thing[1]—it might involve some divorce of the balance of indebtedness from those movements of goods which lie behind the mercantile acceptance proper. There were obvious risks in this divorce, but also the great conveniences which had first brought it about. Finance bills could be created abroad to assist remittance at times of the year when trade bills, representing actual goods shipped to England, were scarce—between clips in Australia, or between cotton and wheat crops in America. And the British banks were as good judges of foreign and colonial bankers' credit as the accepting houses could be of merchants' credit. No doubt their activities and those of their overseas banking correspondents—many of whom had themselves come to London—were curtailing the field of the private acceptor. A wool grower need not comprehend bills, nor a merchant in Sydney establish his credit with a London accepting house, when everything to do with wool finance has been taken over by the Sydney and London offices of the Bank of New South Wales[2].

Among the new minor activities of the banks was the business, "begun of late" Bagehot said in 1873, of collecting "people's...incomes for them." Not only were coupons on bonds and debentures "handed in for the bank to collect"; but "often enough" the banker was expected to keep the bond and cut off the coupon himself. "And the detail of all this is incredible, and it needs a special machinery to cope with it."[3] The joint-stock banks had first set up that machinery, as Bagehot pointed out, and the private banks often lacked it[4].

[1] See below, p. 371. The acceptor of such a bill undertakes to put money at the disposal of the drawer just as if he had bought goods from him. He of course trusts the drawer to repay at a convenient time.

[2] By 1886 there were 28 Colonial Joint-Stock Banks with London offices: the Bank of N.S.W., which had 171 branches, was the biggest: *Economist, Banking Supplement*, 1887. Cp. Baster, A. S. J., *The Imperial Banks*.

[3] *Lombard Street*, p. 279.

[4] Existing English bank histories usually say nothing at all about such internal functions and their modern development. The histories are antiquarian, personal, and external. See *e.g.* Grindon, L. H., *Manchester Banks and Bankers* (1877); Martin, J. B., *The Grasshopper in Lombard Street* (1892); Phillips, M., *A History of Banks, Bankers and Banking in Northumberland, Durham and North Yorkshire* (1894); Cave, C. H., *A History of Banking in Bristol* (1899); Bidwell, W. H., *Annals of an East Anglian Banking House* (1900); Easton, H. T., *The History of a Banking House* (Smith, Payne and Smiths) (1903); Lloyd, S., *The Lloyds of Birmingham* (1907); Matthews, P. W. and Tuke, A. W., *A History of Barclay's Bank* (1926); Saunders, P. T., *Stuckey's Bank* (1928).

While new banking activities developed, some old ones decayed. Of these, perhaps the most important was the Scottish system of cash credits or cash accounts, by which promising young men even "from low situations" could get credit from the banks, provided they could find a couple of bondsmen, that is, sureties[1]. It had been the habit of English writers on banking ever since the 'twenties to praise the system freely. They were still doing so in the early 'seventies[2]. But it was already in decay. Certainly it was moribund within a few years; for by 1896 "the day of the cash account was practically done,"[3] and such customs die hard and slow.

Not that an able Scot from a 'low situation' had fewer opportunities of getting help from banks than before. The cash credit system had grown up when such a man had no banking account. It had helped him to get one. Already in the 'fifties Scottish operatives kept accounts, and the Glasgow banks had savings departments open at night to assist them[4]. By 1875 there was about one banking account to every two Scotsmen of twenty years old and upwards, in all 418,000 accounts[5]. Any serious and promising young man would have one. There were branches everywhere: the agents knew their men. Bank funds accumulated and in the 'eighties were seeking employment at low rates. The cash account, which had involved a formal bond[6], gave way to less formal and cheaper methods of attaining the same end.

The state left the more important banking functions completely free. Legal relaxation of the usury laws, begun in 1833, had been carried so far by 1839, and their evasion was so well understood, that their complete abolition in 1854 (by 17 and 18 Vict. c. 90) did little more than recognise an established freedom[7]. The function which the state did regulate, that of

[1] See vol. I. p. 269. [2] *E.g.* Palgrave's *Notes on Banking*, p. 13.

[3] Kerr, *Scottish Banking*, p. 121. The system, Kerr adds, was "at its best during the period of free issues," *i.e.* before 1845.

[4] *Report* of 1858, § 33.

[5] *S.C. on Banks of Issue*, App. 7. There was no doubt some duplication of accounts. [6] Cp. Kerr, *Scottish Banking*, p. 121.

[7] Vol. I. p. 347–9, 509. For the abolition see Levi, L., *History of British Commerce*, p. 355. The Act of 1833 referred to in vol. I. p. 509 did not affect the Bank of England only: all three months' bills were put outside the usury laws. Longer dated bills soon followed. By 1839 (2 and 3 Vict. c. 37) usury had vanished from the law of personal contracts; but a man could commit usury over land!

issue, was becoming less important every decade. But the state had tried for many years to give stability to joint-stock banking by making rules about the constitution of the banks, or by denying them constitutional privileges reputed dangerous. Their growing stability owed little to these rules or these denials. For ten years after the first modern joint-stock bank was opened in London, in 1834, such banks had not even enjoyed the elementary right of suing and being sued in the names of their officers. They had got on quite well without it. They used trustees[1]. When Peel initiated the registration of joint-stock companies in 1844 he framed a special Act for banks (7 and 8 Vict. c. 113)[2]. They could only register if their capital was at least £100,000 and their shares of no lower denomination than £100. When in 1855 parliament began to feel its way towards a general law of limited liability, banks were at first excluded (from 18 and 19 Vict. c. 133). In 1857 Peel's bank registration Act was repealed and replaced (by 20 and 21 Vict. c. 49), yet the exclusion was not raised[3]. But after the catastrophes of 1857[4], and some shocking cases of bank failures with unlimited liability, parliament changed its mind, and by 21 and 22 Vict. c. 91 allowed new banks to be formed with limited liability, and old banks to register as limited[5]. Liability for notes however was in no case to be limited. Finally, the generalised limited liability Act of 1862 (25 and 26 Vict. c. 89) covered banks together with all other associations of seven men. But by that time effective bank creation was nearly over. The old and strong banks looked down on the 'limiteds' and thought that registration might impair their own credit. Sixteen years later, none of the Scottish banks was limited under recent legislation, and there were 69 unlimited banks in England and Wales, including nearly all the most important joint-stock concerns—the London and Westminster, the Capital and Counties,

[1] Vol. I. p. 510.

[2] *An Act to regulate Joint-Stock Banking in England*; this is the Act referred to in vol. I. p. 511 n. 2. See Shannon, H. S., "The Coming of General Limited Liability," *E.J.* (*Hist.*), 1931, and the very good short account of Joint-Stock and Limited Liability in Levi, *op. cit.* p. 333 *sqq*.

[3] This was a special *Act to amend the Law relating to Banking Companies*: the general Act of the year dealing with Limited Liability is 20 and 21 Vict. c. 78, concerned mainly with the winding up of companies.

[4] Below, p. 368 *sqq*.

[5] By 1864 there were 33 new banks registered under the Acts of 1857 and 1858, and 12 which existed before 1857 and had also registered. *Return of all J.S.C. formed or registered since* 18 *and* 19 *Vict. c.* 133: 1864, LVIII. 291.

the Manchester and Liverpool, the York City and County, and Stuckeys, to name only a few well-known firms in various districts[1]. But the failure of the criminally mismanaged City of Glasgow bank in October, 1878, killed unlimited joint-stock banking, as it were in a night[2]. Frightened shareholders, shuddering at the object-lesson of losses six times the amount of the losers' holdings[3], put pressure on directorates. "Many responsible holders of shares" in banks with unlimited liability "showed a desire to sell out."[4] Parliament (by 42 and 43 Vict. c. 76 of 1879) facilitated a change over to limitation, bringing into existence the principle of reserve liability, by which companies might increase the nominal amount of their shares, but might call up the difference between the amount actually paid on each share and its nominal amount only in the event of the company's being wound up. Within five years all banks of importance had taken action under the new law. They did so, however, in such sweeping fashion that, what with capital authorised but not called up before the Act and the new reserve liability created under it, to every pound share in a British joint-stock bank the average shareholder of 1885–6 was liable to add four more pounds, in the event of its failure. This was not an unlimited liability, but it would have seemed singularly like one had there been much banking in Britain so unsound as that of the City of Glasgow[5]. Security lay not in the law but in the management.

By the time that Bagehot published his *Lombard Street*, Palgrave his *Notes on Banking*, and the Committee on Banks of Issue the results of its inquiry (1873–5), the organisation by which all free British capital was sucked into the London money market was functioning almost perfectly. Compared with other

[1] See the *Return of Unlimited and Limited Companies*, 1878–9, LXV. 479, and cp. Macleod, *op. cit.* II. 400; Rae, G., *The Country Banker*, p. 260. Some of the older Scottish banks were limited by charter, Kerr, *History*, p. 306.

[2] Below, p. 383.

[3] This is not an exact statement of the final position: it refers to the call of 500 per cent. on the capital stock made at the end of November, 1878, to meet losses. The announcement of the bank's suspension of payment had appeared on October 2. Kerr, *History*, p. 294–8.

[4] Sir Felix Schuster: *Banking Interviews, U.S. Monetary Commission*, 1910, p. 34.

[5] The banks "so broadened the basis on which their credit stood, as to leave their liability practically unlimited"—Rae, *The Country Banker*, p. 261 (written in 1885).

national organisations, or lacks of organisation, it had been highly efficient even twenty years earlier. In the interval, Scottish and provincial branch banking had drawn in almost the last of those rustic hoards which country folk had kept "in their desks and cupboards"[1]; and a smooth open channel had been cut down which the aggregated northern surpluses flowed South. The channels from East Anglia, the South-West, and rural England generally, had been cut long before. Wealth slipped along them easily and without sound, very often from some placid Quaker pond in the country to a more or less Quaker reservoir in Town. Agriculture prospered. Country ponds overflowed. From Town, what was not used there ran out into the industrial districts, by way of the discount or rediscount of manufacturers' and merchants' bills. These were the greatest days of the London bill-brokers, the Lombard Street Houses[2].

In the 'fifties and subsequently, their business, except in moments of aberration, was to advance money on fine trade bills which fell due for payment in regular sequence day by day; although advances on dock warrants were one of their subordinate 'lines.'[3] The leading group were no longer bill-brokers in fact. In the 'fifties Overends repudiated the title, though everyone applied it to them. "We are not bill-brokers," they said: we are "money dealers."[4] Brokers in the strict sense, men who merely found bills for money and money for bills, always existed: they got a commission like any other broker, and were a distinct and inferior, though relatively numerous, group[5]. Distinct also was the tiny and interesting group of the money-brokers, "the great go-betweens in the banking and discount community and the Stock Exchange,"[6] men who moved

[1] A Scottish banker, W. B. Gordon, to the *S.C. on Banks of Issue*, Q. 4028.

[2] Chapman, of Overend and Gurney, had explained to the *S.C. on the Bank Acts* of 1857 how they discounted for Lancashire and Yorkshire with the aid of the rural surpluses put at their disposal by the bankers: Q. 5100. Cp. Jenks, *The Migraticns of English Capital to* 1875, p. 246, who perhaps overrates somewhat the subsequent decline of the bill-brokers. For their importance in 1910 see Sir Felix Schuster, as above, p. 43.

[3] Chapman, as above, Q. 5104–6, 5198–9, 5203.

[4] *Ibid.* Q. 4931, 5098. "We then acted as brokers" he said (Q. 4881), referring to the usury-law days.

[5] Powell, *The Evolution of the London Money Market*, p. 378; *The English Banking System, U.S. Monetary Commission*, p. 62. By 1931 these 'running brokers' were reduced to 8. *R. of the Committee on Finance and Industry*, p. 43.

[6] Evans, D. M., *Speculative Notes and Notes on Speculation* (1864), p. 88–9.

about daily to ascertain what floating surpluses were available, and what were likely to be the demands upon them from bill-brokers and stock-brokers, insurance companies, financial houses and sometimes banks. In the heads of these men the supply and demand curves for 'short money' crossed. They earned their living by arranging transactions for a commission at the day's equilibrium price. Even in the 'sixties their numbers were contracting[1]: not until the telephone reached the city did their function become superfluous.

The money-dealing bill-brokers stood at the centre of the short-money market. They bought bills to hold until maturity, and bills to sell to bankers and others who wanted them. The bills which they sold they guaranteed. Overends, in their great days, held no Consols or other securities whose price might fluctuate, only the bills and allied documents recording obligations of definite amount due for payment at precise dates[2]. This was the foundation of their practice of trading on borrowed money payable at call or short notice. Trust in the leading houses was so implicit that bankers were by no means the only depositors with them. Their position was always delicate, though in quiet times safe. But with the smallest breath of distrust among their depositors, the least fear that the parcels of bills falling due on any given date might not be met, strain almost intolerable set in. On one bad day in 1857 "a single discounting house paid...£700,000 to depositors and £100,000 to discounters."[3] It had to discount for its name's sake, although its working capital was so horribly fluid. Which house it was is easily guessed.

Until the limited liability legislation of the mid 'fifties, the business was all in private hands. Two discount companies had been established before 1858, one of which, the National, was successful from the first and by 1866 was in a strong position[4]. Others—they were never very numerous—rose and fell, among them Overend and Gurney Limited, which under its new designation found a public eager to subscribe in 1865, and crashed to ruin in 1866. Three only, including the National, were of importance in the early 'seventies; and of these two amalgamated

[1] Evans, as above: "not so numerous as they were"; mostly elderly men.

[2] Chapman, Q. 5104, 5216.

[3] Sir G. C. Lewis discussing the crisis of 1857, December 4, 1857. *Hansard, Third Series*, CXLVIII. 155.

[4] For its position in 1866 see *Fenn on the Funds*, 9th ed. 1867.

to form the Union with a capital of £1,000,000, 50 per cent. paid, in 1885[1]. The Union, the National, and about a score of private firms made up the 'discount houses' of the mid 'eighties[2]. The business had changed little in character and lost nothing in absolute, though perhaps something in relative, importance since the 'fifties. The lesser firms, other than the pure brokers, bought bills mainly to sell again. The greater both sold and held. The delicacy of the business had not decreased. It was a banker with late nineteenth century experience who said, early in the twentieth, that "the liability of the bill-broker is one which can only be met in ordinary times...in troubled times he is at the mercy of the banks and of circumstances."[3]

In its relation to the ordinary workings of British industry and commerce, the London short-money market was important mainly as a furnisher and economiser of circulating capital. Except when it was very feverish, it did not interest the investor who was neither manufacturer nor merchant. It was of more immediate importance to the merchant than to the manufacturer, because the circulating element dominates commerce. The mechanism of the discountable bill helped the creation of fixed capital—the textile engineer, it might be, drawing on the mill-owner—but fixed capital as such was never the concern of Lombard Street. The provincial banker gave every assistance to men whom he trusted, allowing them ample overdrafts at all times; but even he regarded plant, machinery "or works of any description"[4] as ideally bad security for loans. Almost all the fixed capital of manufacturing industry, as it existed in 1850, and the overwhelmingly greater part of the additions and renewals made during the next thirty-six years, came from what the economists of the age called—with more reason than

[1] The *Economist* (July 14, 1866) spoke of "a great many" new companies, but there were not really many. By February 12, 1870, it is taking interest only in the "three principal" companies—the National, the General and the United —and the six or seven "eminent" private firms. For the amalgamation, *Banking Interviews*, as above, p. 104 (the manager of the Union).

[2] In 1931 there were 3 public companies, 4 private companies, and 17 private firms. *R. of the Committee on Finance and Industry*, p. 43.

[3] *Banking Interviews*, p. 42 (Sir Felix Schuster).

[4] Rae, *op. cit.* The overdraft in the economic life of the industrial districts deserves a special study—if the facts are available. The sort of provincial banker who was dying out at the end of the nineteenth century used to speak of the men he had 'made' and wonder whether the modern type of banking would do the work so well.

their critics have sometimes allowed—the abstinence of those steady manufacturers whom the provincial bankers trusted[1]. Creation of fixed capital through the husbanded reserves of industrial companies was known but not yet important[2]. When he was doing well, when, in later economic jargon, he was drawing 'quasi-rents,' sort-of-rents; either rent of special ability, or rent of mere good-luck, or rent from the ownership of capital-goods of which the world's stock was for the time being inadequate[3]; then the manufacturer improved or extended his mill or his works. Britain, until the 'eighties, was so often an owner of capital-goods of which the world was short that—acting through her more fortunate and able manufacturers—she could for a time make some of those goods yield these rents, not mere fine-cut competitive profits; and with the rents she could build more works and more mills. From the standpoint of economic theory she was the world's great quasi-rentier. If, however, from some doubt of the near future, she hesitated to 'fix' her rents and her profits in plant to the normal extent, and her manufacturers left money on deposit with their bankers, Lombard Street got an abnormal supply and it was 'cheap.' This was perhaps the main link between the Street and the course of domestic fixed-capital investment[4].

But if, even in the 'eighties, most of the additions to industrial capital were still made directly by those who owned and managed industrial establishments, the early railway age had familiarised a great part of the nation with the attractions, methods, and risks of centralised investment and speculation. Railways had been promoted locally and London capital had at first been shy of them. That phase was nearly over before 1848 when, as Tooke wrote, "in every street of every town persons were to be found who were holders of railway shares."[5] Dealings were concentrating in the Stock Exchange. Whole grades of society to whom Lombard Street remained mysterious, even after Bagehot revealed it, had acquired some crude knowledge of Capel Court. Railway Gambling, pilloried by Tooke in capital

[1] Cp. *R. of Committee on Industry and Finance*, p. 162.

[2] For the importance to-day see *e.g.* Pigou, A. C., *A Study in Public Finance* (1928), p. 78 n.

[3] See Marshall, Alfred, *Principles of Economics*, Index, *s.v.* Quasi-rent.

[4] Cp. below, p. 379, and p. 385.

[5] *History of Prices*, v. 234. Cp. throughout Jenks, *op. cit.* p. 131–2 and *passim*. All discussions of investment, here and elsewhere in the text, are much indebted to Jenks.

letters, had turned into the soberest investment. By the 'eighties railway stock was, after Consols, the banker's ideal security[1]. Down to about 1850, well-managed banks had doubted the propriety of advances on it: they had left much of that work to an ephemeral type of concern called an exchange company. When the exchange companies had bought experience and died, the joint-stock banks took the business over[2].

With railway stock as a universal family investment, for all families which had anything to invest, went the other public utility stocks—of gas, water, dock and telegraph companies—and those of the joint-stock banks themselves. (Cemetery, pier, and market companies might become family investments locally; but they were in a lower grade[3].) City articles in the daily papers and the growth of a financial press spread information of varying quality. Continental railways, North and South American railways, colonial railways and loans, and the funds of all the more reputable governments became in turn investment, as opposed to speculative, securities—the kind of thing which a country lawyer might not question if found among the inherited capital of a maiden lady. All this paved the way for the entry of new classes of companies, and eased the work of those promoters who had to induce, first, narrow financial circles, and then the ordinary public of investors, to take an interest in them.

The list of companies provisionally registered in 1853[4], though a large proportion of them never got to work, shows where the main interests of promoters and investors lay just before the legislation of 1855–62 finally cleared the ground for the joint-stock age. Out of a total of 339, there were 80 railway schemes; 54 gas schemes; 35 insurance schemes; various mining, shipping and trading schemes; but only 30 for "conducting manufactures, working patents, etc." The total amount of capital even nominally involved was, by later standards, insignificant. Numbers and nominal capital remained low until 1862. For the five years ending in 1861, the annual average was 381 companies with a total nominal capital of £21,000,000. In 1864 there were registered 975 companies with a nominal capital of

[1] Rae, *op. cit.* p. 101–2.

[2] The definite evidence for these statements is Scottish (Kerr, *History*, p. 248), but they are no doubt generally true of England.

[3] There are a number of these in the 1853 returns of *All Applications for Charters with Limited Liability under* 1 *Vict. c.* 73 (1854, LXV. 611), including the London Necropolis Company. For piers, see below, p. 518.

[4] *A. and P.* 1854, LXV. 597.

£235,000,000[1]; and the figures for 1865 were 1014 and £203,000,000. After 1866 came a precipitate fall to a level not much above that of 1857–61. The nominal capital figure of 1864–5—a figure more important in the psychological than in the economic history of joint-stock enterprise, though in the psychological history very important—was not again reached until 1881–2; but even in the least active years of the 'seventies the annual crop of registrations was almost what it had been in 1864–5, and by 1887 it was twice as great[2].

The registrations of 1863–5 contain all the types of ten years earlier, though in different proportions[3]. Naturally there are fewer home railway companies, though it was a period of vigorous railway building. A few durable industrial registrations—the Shotley Bridge Iron Company; Chatwood's Safes; John Brown; Charles Cammell—stand out of a crowd of seven-man projects, industrial and commercial, which never came to anything. The railway waggon building business was developing in the hands of companies, as might perhaps have been expected[4]. There was a fresh spawning of joint-stock banks, British and overseas. A novelty which caught the public eye was the hotel company: the Randolph at Oxford was registered in April, 1863, and 46 others were registered that year[5]. There was also a crop of Indian tea-planting and similar enterprises. Of considerable importance in the general history of investment was a group of finance companies, or investment trusts, modelled on the Franco-Jewish *Crédit mobilier* of ten years earlier[6]. Their directorates were "a combination of the mercantile and banking elements"[7]: the International Financial Society of 1863 included Morgans, Heaths, Göschens, Huths, Sterns and Dobrees. Their objects were miscellaneous—com-

[1] The amount paid up was barely a tenth of this however—£24,229,633.

[2] The figures are in the annual returns, summarised in the *Statistical Abstracts* and in the *Economist*. The earlier ones are discussed by Leone Levi in an article on Joint-Stock Companies in *S.J.* 1870, p. 1–41 and by Max Wirth, *Geschichte der Handelskrisen* (2nd ed. 1874). And cp. Jenks, *op. cit.* p. 238 *sqq.*, the latest discussion.

[3] See the detailed *Return of all J.S.C.* of 1864.

[4] Cp. above, p. 98.

[5] For the public eye see Evans, *Speculative Notes*, p. 166–7.

[6] Perhaps the best contemporary account of the *Crédit mobilier* is that of Max Wirth, *op. cit.* (the first edition was 1858), p. 268 *sqq.* Cp. Art. *Finanzierungsgesellschaften* (by R. Liefmann) in Conrad and Elster, *H.WB.* IV. 261. See below, p. 364.

[7] *Economist*, August 22, 1863. See too the *Economist's Review* of 1863, February 20, 1864.

pany and loan flotation, concession negotiation, the assistance of other enterprises of all kinds, "in a word...all such operations as an intelligent and experienced capitalist might effect on his own account with a capital of millions."[1] In particular they gave British-promoted railways overseas, in their early stages, the help which British banking had hesitated to give to home railways when still a little speculative. The nature of the work which they set out to do can best be illustrated by a list of the chief enterprises in which one of them, the rather absurdly named Crédit Foncier of England, was interested after four years of life. They were the City of Milan Improvement Company, the Varna and Rustchuk Railway, the Belgian Public Works Company, the Irrigation Company of France, the Imperial Land Company of Marseilles, and the Millwall Docks[2].

By that time, August, 1867, "small dividends, if any,"[3] were being paid by the finance companies, and their shares were all below par. Several had died and the type had lost vitality. A variant and less adventurous type appeared with the Foreign and Colonial Government Trust of 1868. Its intention was "to give the investor of moderate means the same advantage as the large capitalist"[4], by spreading for him the risks of investment in government bonds over a wide range of countries, from Austria and Australia to Turkey and the United States. It was followed by the Submarine Cables Trust of 1871 and by others; but the type was not very important down to 1886[5]. Its object was security; that of the finance company had been enterprise. Mistakes were made by the directors of both types, but naturally fewer by those who looked to security.

The company uprush of the 'sixties was so swift and dramatic that its immediate importance in the economic life of the nation may easily be overrated. Exact measurement is impossible, but

[1] Prospectus of the General Credit and Finance Society quoted in Jenks, *op. cit.* p. 249. There is a very severe contemporary judgment of the companies in Levi's *History of British Commerce*, p. 429–30.

[2] *Economist*, August 24, 1867, "The Crédit Foncier of England."

[3] *Ibid.*

[4] Quoted in Powell, E. T., *The Evolution of the London Money Market*, p. 469. Jenks overrates these companies. They handled a very small part of the business of investment at this time. The accounts in Grayson, T. J., *Investment Trusts, their Origin, Development and Operation* (New York, 1928) and Glasgow, G., *The English Investment Trust Companies* (1930), are slight.

[5] Only 12 were quoted on the Stock Exchange list in 1886. The oldest then surviving (2) dated from 1871; 3 from 1873; 4 from 1879; 1 from each of the years 1881, 1883, 1884—*Economist*, October 7, 1886.

a contemporary estimate suggested that not 10 per cent. of the authorised capital of new companies registered was paid in prompt cash. The figure for 1863–6 is £35,600,000 out of a nominal capital of £373,000,000. This was only a small fraction of the national savings[1].

Far more important than many of the conspicuous flotations of new companies and new kinds of company was the process, gathering momentum gradually during the 'sixties, and 'seventies, by which old businesses were 'limited' and the flow of outside capital was directed into them. For this work there specialised out, in the best known instances from among accountants, a small group of men who came to be known as financial agents or investing agents. To them, as they acquired reputation, propositions were submitted by prospective vendors, representatives perhaps of an engineer who had died "leaving his business to his sons, who had been educated at college, and had paid no attention to business."[2] Thirty-nine such propositions out of forty, a leading financial agent told a Select Committee in 1877, had been refused by his firm because they came from firms on the down-grade trying to save themselves by 'limitation.'[3] Yet that single firm had averaged some £2,000,000 of flotations a year in 1867–77[4], and in sixteen years had found employment for the capital surpluses of 5000 rich men. Most of the companies floated by them had been large, but there were also "many private companies of small capital."[5] Latterly, trained valuers had always been employed at an early stage to assist the agents in their decisions, because in some of the first 'limitations' the company had been formed with a nominal capital which proved to be excessive, and as the Act of 1862 had not provided for reduction of capital, there had

[1] The estimate was that of the *Economist*, discussed by Leone Levi in "Joint-Stock Companies," *S.J.* 1870. Jenks' statement (*op. cit.* p. 238–9) that "during the early 'sixties" there was a "transformation of a considerable part of British trade and industry into companies with limited liability" is too strong. In industry the transformation was insignificant, in trade not considerable. Cp. above, p. 138 and p. 311.

[2] David Chadwick before the *S.C. on...the Companies Acts*, 1877 (VIII. 419), Q. 2008. His evidence in 1877 and before the *S.C. on Limited Liability Acts*, 1867 (X. 393) is the source of information. He had practised as an accountant since 1842; from 1860, with the new legislation, he became mainly an investing agent. *S.C.* of 1867, Q. 835 *sqq.* There were other firms of the same type—Q. 2157.

[3] Chadwick, Q. 2092.

[4] Q. 1993–5, 2081.

[5] Q. 1999.

been a burden of uncalled liability[1]. When the agents had received the valuers' report they offered the proposition "by private circular or prospectus to their friends." The statutory seven men to sign the memorandum of association were taken from these friends and those of the vendors. In a typical arrangement for a capital of £100,000, the vendors would take some £30,000; the agents' friends the same; "and we should feel certain before we registered...that the whole of the remainder would be subscribed." The agents in question always pressed for the appointment of a well-paid manager. "The nearer you can approach to the management of a private concern the better." This was how the work was done, or was said to have been done, by a firm who boasted that they had no connection with the Stock Exchange; that there was no jobbing "and very seldom any advertising"; and that nine-tenths of their flotations since 1860 were still not only afloat in 1877 but "eminently successful."[2] There were no doubt less thorough, less scrupulous, and less successful firms who may not have charged so much as the 1 per cent. on the capital floated which was Messrs Chadwick's substantial fee[3]; but it was in some such fashion, business-like and well considered, that the more important 'limitations' of the 'sixties and 'seventies and the increasing number of the 'eighties were carried out. Usually the capital remained in few hands and the company private or semi-private; but at the close there was a group, though a small group, of industrial securities regularly quoted on the London Stock Exchange[4].

[1] The legal provision for reductions of capital was one of the main points discussed before the committee of 1877.

[2] The quotations are from Q. 2041, 2075, 2007, 2045, 1991. Chadwick gave much the same evidence in 1867—Q. 835 *sqq*. The success of his flotations, if stated accurately, was in marked contrast with the fate of new joint-stock companies generally. Cp. Macgregor, D. H., "Joint-Stock Companies and the Risk Factor," *E.J.* December, 1929. Prof. Macgregor's statement that "conversion of family businesses into companies was a later development [later than 1880] facilitated especially by the Act of 1900, though referred to as a growing practice by the Committee of 1895," needs qualification.

[3] Q. 2114.

[4] The group classed as 'Commercial, Industrial, etc.,' given in *The Times* in June, 1886, is extraordinarily small. From 14 to 18 is the number usually quoted and of these by no means all are industrial. Bryant and May, Price's candles, and Spratt's dog biscuits are quoted fairly regularly. In most of the not very many 'industrials' dealings were decidedly intermittent. *The Times* list is of course far from exhaustive but it contains those 'industrials' which interested the general investor.

It would be unwise to reduce the economic history of Britain to a running commentary on the health or fever charts of the London money market. But, given the appropriate text, they provide decidedly the best approach to a greater and more complex story, the story of the contacts between the British economy—with its fully-used capital, its short-money market, and the growing 'anonymity' of its commerce and industry—and that world economy with which it was involved, and without which it could not even endure, still less prosper.

'Money' in London had never been so cheap for so long as it was between the middle of 1848 and the end of 1852. Nor had bread, since back in the eighteenth century. The island was tolerably active throughout those years, and very active in 1852; but at least until 1851 much of the world was neither. Europe was slowly getting back to work after famine, revolution, and war. France was being turned again by plebiscite into an Empire. Meanwhile her railway building was held up. America, however, was in high activity. Men poured into her much faster than ever before—three hundred and seventy-nine thousand of them in 1851[1]—and the forty-niners had set out to get the gold, singing "Oh California! that's the land for me." American prosperity always told in Britain; but at that time there might well be more than a year's lag. It took four months in 1848 for the first gold news to reach Washington, by way of Panama. In fact it was about the turn of 1850–51 that British exports "began to exhibit the influence of the large consumption in California."[2] Nine months later came the Australian news, which worked much more quickly. Meanwhile, shipment to California from all quarters had been for the time overdone, so that in the middle of 1851 "all new supplies of goods were wholly unsaleable"[3] there. Cotton and colonial produce were abundant, and the year closed with prices low and the Bank of England rate of discount about to fall from 3 per cent. to 2½ per cent.

In the course of 1852, while prices were rising steadily and freights to Australia precipitately, for nearly nine months the Bank rate stood at 2 per cent. Yet employment was very good

[1] The U.S.A. received 114,000 foreign immigrants in 1845. There was a steady rise to 1851: a halt for two years: a rise to 428,000 in 1854: then a fall to a minimum of 89,000 in 1863. *Final Report of the Industrial Commission*, 1902, p. 958.

[2] Tooke and Newmarch, v. 258.

[3] *Ibid.* v. 261.

and wages began to follow prices—first, most naturally, among the shipwrights. The rate of discount was low in spite of trade activity because America, once more an avid purchaser of all kinds of goods, was paying in gold, and the Australian gold was beginning to arrive, so that the Bank in July, 1852, held £22,000,000 of bullion; more than it had ever held before. It held only a few hundred thousand pounds less in December.

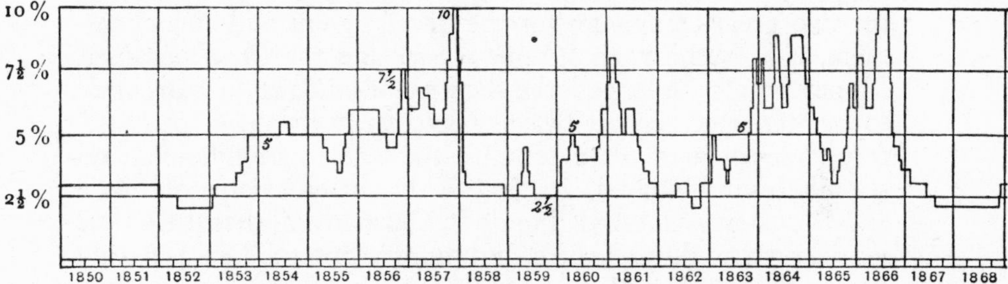

Bank of England minimum Rate of Discount, 1850-68.

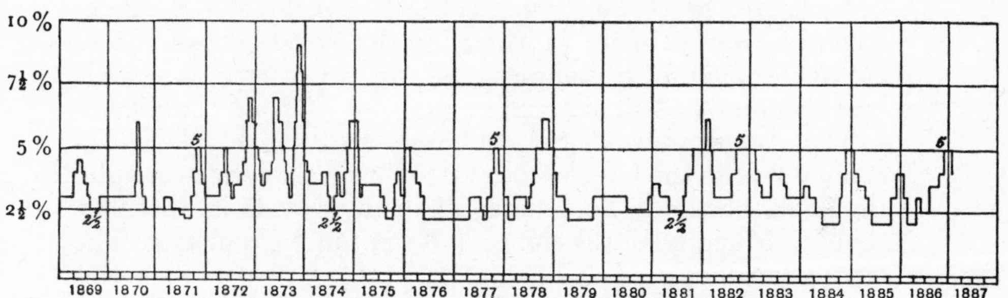

Bank of England minimum Rate of Discount, 1869-86.

"Many political economists even talked of a future time when ...the ordinary ornaments and utensils would be of the most massive auriferous manufacture"[1]; and less foolish people supposed that the rate of interest was permanently down. Old loan contracts were revised and new ones made on very easy terms. The banking world reflected with satisfaction that at least there would never be another gold panic[2].

It is easy to develop the earth with capital at 2 per cent. The men of the early 'fifties set about it. In 1852 Thomas

[1] Evans, D. M., *The History of the Commercial Crisis*, 1857–8, p. 9: the political economists are not specified.

[2] Evans, *op. cit.* p. 9 n.

Brassey, who had only averaged one small foreign railway contract a year since 1847, had taken five, including 113 miles of the Nantes and Caen and 539 miles of the Grand Trunk of Canada. In 1853–4 he took seven more, though not so large[1]. In France the Saint Simonians had made a religion of earth development, a religion of which the new Emperor approved. They were dreaming of the Suez Canal; making the P.L.M.; founding the Lyons gas and water works[2]. In 1852 appeared the two great companies for the development and encouragement of everything, the *Crédit foncier* and the *Crédit mobilier*. Money was to be lent on the security of land; state loans were to be underwritten; railways financed; ports developed; gas companies created; Paris rebuilt—the whole nation helped and stimulated and inflated. In 1853 the Darmstadt Bank for Trade and Industry was founded to do in Germany all that the *Crédit mobilier* was to do in France, and more[3]. Soon there was hardly a state, however small, in the old German patchwork which had not its credit bank. Nations borrowed. Railways were a-making everywhere. Brassey's contracts of 1852–3 included the Dutch-Rhenish, the Turin and Novara, and the Royal Danish. These are only a handful of samples of European enterprise. In the background was America, full of men and gold and confidence.

The American gold and the Australian which followed it could not keep the Bank's stock up to the level of 1852—nor did the Bank, a business house after all, in any way desire that they should. Much gold was coined and went into circulation. The circulation increased at least 50 per cent. between 1844 and 1856, mainly after 1850[4]. British exports contained a large proportion of capital goods, and another large proportion of goods —for the Australian markets and the like—which, although not capital goods, were necessarily sold at such long usance that the returns for them were hardly in sight. For the time being they were lent without return, like the railway metal and the locomotives for lines whose capital was held in Britain. There were also cash calls in London on foreign railway and government securities, much as in 1846[5]. Moreover, throughout 1852, while the Bank of England rate was at 2 per cent., that of the

[1] See the table of his contracts in Jenks, *op. cit.* App. A, quoted above, p. 237.

[2] Cp. Levasseur, E., *Histoire des classes ouvrières et d'industrie en France de 1789 à 1870*, II. 48c and Clapham, J. H., *The Economic Development of France and Germany*, p. 383 *sqq.*

[3] Wirth, *op. cit.* p. 285 *sqq.*

[4] Tooke and Newmarch, VI. 699, 701.

[5] Vol. I. p. 529.

Bank of France, which had gone back to cash payments only in August, 1850, was 3 per cent. Possibly some fluid international capital left London for Paris, and some which might have gone to London may have gone to Paris direct[1]. French historians have claimed that London gave way to Paris as a capital market at this time[2]. English historians would recognise at least a period of dual control.

Working together, these forces tugged at the gold in the Bank from December, 1852. The Bank put its rate up twice in January, 1853—prematurely, as its critics and the public thought[3]—again in June and once again on September 1, when it was known that the harvest had failed. Wheat prices were running up, to touch 80*s*. at Christmas. A winter of abnormal food imports threatened. So at the end of September the rate was raised once more. Even then it was only 5 per cent. As £2,600,000 of gold came from Australia in October and November, it stayed there[4]; although Turkey and Russia went to war and corn trade with the Black Sea stopped. If corn buying in America were to reverse the Atlantic flow of gold, as it might, there was now always the flow coming up from the far South. True the Bank had only £15,000,000 worth at the end of 1853; but down to 1851 it had never had more.

In March, 1854, war with Russia began. In the money market there was scarcely any disturbance. It was local war, not high seas war, like the old wars with the French. The gold flowed up easily from the South[5]. War reduced supplies of some important raw materials; helped to keep corn dear for two years; required remittances of treasure to the Near East and stimulated war industries at the expense of others. These things apart, what economic discomfort coincided with it was due mainly to other causes, such as the overbuilding of ships, a bad harvest in 1855, and temporary checks to the course of American prosperity; although heavy war remittances, coinciding with the failed harvest of 1855, kept the Bank rate particularly high

[1] This is uncertain. A difference of as little as 1 per cent. was not at that time sufficient to move capital in the form of bills. The argument which demonstrates this is probably best known from Goschen's *Theory of the Foreign Exchanges* (1865); but it is clearly set out, like so much else, in Tooke and Newmarch, v. 313. It is there argued that though even a difference of 2 per cent. would not move bills, it would "pretty certainly" divert investment.

[2] *E.g.* Levasseur, *op. cit.* II. 483.

[3] Tooke blamed it for keeping so long at 2 per cent. and then moving so fast (v. 280); but then he generally blamed it.

[4] Tooke and Newmarch, v. 299.

[5] Much of it *via* Egypt.

during the last months of the war (October, 1855–May, 1856). Even then, however, it was argued, and probably with truth[1], that the main cause of the stringency was not pressure of military necessity but the blunder of the Bank in reducing its rate to 3½ per cent. in the previous June, when its vaults happened to be full, instead of keeping them full to meet the emergencies of an unfinished war.

Economically speaking, the country slipped out of war in 1856 as easily and smoothly as it had slipped into it in 1854. "In the import markets," Newmarch wrote about the end of the year, "there has been a quiet and steady business; in the Manufacturing Districts, a fair share of prosperity, but entirely free from excitement or speculation."[2] He and his aged partner Tooke, "already turned of fourscore,"[3] were satisfied that the high rate of discount which had ruled since 1853—the Bank rate, after a drop in the summer, jerked up to 6 and 7½ per cent. in October–November, 1856—was "to be traced, in its origin and continuance, to extended demands for capital for the purpose of new, distant, and costly enterprises."[4] Resolute critics of the Bank Act, they registered with satisfaction that for nine years prices had either changed abruptly while the note circulation had been constant, or had gone down when notes went up and up when notes went down. They were convinced that, but for the new gold, the Act of 1844 could not have remained unbroken through the war; and that even the Act of 1819 might have been in danger[5].

From the heart of the money market the directing partner of Overend and Gurney supported them. "We have had an extraordinary amount of bullion arriving from Australia," he said in 1857, "and even from America, entirely beyond all

[1] Tooke and Newmarch, v. 318: compare the bullion figures in VI. 557, £18,360,000 in June, 1855, and £10,430,000 in January, 1856.

[2] v. 337.

[3] v. p. ix in the Preface dated February, 1857. From this time forward the historian loses Tooke's sound sense, economic insight, and exact knowledge of monetary and commercial affairs. Very little has been written in any language about those aspects of economic history on which he and Newmarch were specialists which does not come, directly or indirectly, from them. The preceding pages are no exception.

[4] v. 345.

[5] See Newmarch's evidence before the *S.C. on the Bank Acts*, 1857, Q. 1423 *sqq.* and the relevant passages in the *History*. Cp. an able letter from 'A Banker' in the *Economist* of February 21, 1857, who argued that loans and discounts might go down when circulation went up because the main users of bank notes had no bank accounts.

calculation, coming from the bowels of the earth, which has kept us alive during this extraordinary demand upon us for bullion for war and other purposes. We have looked to the arrival of these steamers from Australia as much almost as to anything else, to know whether we were safe in going on with our business."[1]

This was said in evidence before a Committee on the Bank Acts in June, 1857. Mill and Newmarch condemned them. Lord Overstone and G. W. Norman defended them. An aged representative of the Birmingham School, who recalled 1797 perfectly, attended to advocate plenty of money and a currency divorced from gold and silver[2]. The Governor of the Bank explained the working of the Bank rate and within what limits it could influence market rates and the exchanges. He also reported that since January 1, 1851, £109,500,000 of gold and £25,800,000 of silver had been brought into the country from the places of origin, and that £139,900,000 worth of treasure had been exported, taken into circulation, or consumed in industry[3]. He noted the result, that whereas the Bank's metallic reserve had averaged £15,000,000 in 1851 it had latterly been about £10,500,000, but he did not stress the associated risks in relation to a much expanded trade. Yet he and his colleagues were aware of them. All the year they were guarding their reserves with high rates—5½, 6 and 6½ per cent.—and were refusing to discount long-dated bills[4]. India had been on fire since March. Delhi was not taken until September 20; but the British harvest was good and there was no reason whatever, at the beginning of September, to anticipate acute financial distress. At that time the Bank was negotiating with the East India Company for the shipment of £1,000,000 in silver to the East[5]. It did not carry silver to that amount, and for years had been in the habit of buying it for Eastern remittance with gold. Paris was the best market; for the bimetallic currencies had been filling up with gold and ejecting silver so freely that in the eight years from 1850 to 1857 Europe sent East some £57,000,000 of silver,

[1] Chapman, before the same Committee, Q. 5310.

[2] John Twells, of Spooner, Attwoods and Co., Q. 4366 *sqq*. Let merchants find gold and silver when foreigners want them, he said. We did very well without metal for twenty years and he supposed we could again. Cp. vol. I. p. 311, 535, and Keynes, J. M., *A Tract on Monetary Reform* (1923).

[3] Evidence of T. M. Wegeulin, Q. 15 and *passim*.

[4] And were warmly commended for so doing by the *Economist*, April 4, 1857.

[5] Evans, *The History of the Commercial Crisis*, p. 63.

nearly twice as much as she received from the producing countries[1]. This particular contract was only a small item in the great account.

It had barely been made when bad news began to come from America, on September 15. In the year 1856 more than a fifth of the British exports had gone to the United States. Of foreign government securities ordinarily listed one-third were American. "Some persons estimated" the British holdings of American stocks and bonds at £80,000,000[2]. Liverpool and Glasgow were especially sensitive to any slight tremor from the other side. Now there came a jarring shock. American railway securities began to fall. A big Trust Company in Ohio collapsed. Banks first suspended payment in Philadelphia and Baltimore. Soon 62 out of 63 in New York followed. Railways pushing out into the West, which was Illinois in those days, went bankrupt; "and discounts ranged from 18 to 24 per cent."[3] For a time business all but stopped in the three Eastern gateways of the United States.

By October 27 the Borough Bank of Liverpool and two or three large Scottish mercantile houses were down. On November 7 Dennistoun & Co. of Liverpool, Glasgow, New York, and New Orleans, "American bankers and exchange brokers," failed for over £2,000,000. A few days later a London bill-broking house failed for more than £5,000,000. The Western Bank of Scotland broke on the 9th. The City of Glasgow Bank suspended payment on the 11th[4]. Next day, when, as the Governor said, discounts "had almost entirely ceased in London except at the Bank of England,"[5] the Chancellor of the Exchequer, following the precedent of ten years earlier, authorised the Bank to break Peel's Act if necessary. This was to enable it to discount freely, to support anxious banks or bill-brokers, and to carry out its bullion contract with the East India Company, which had begun to ship the silver about October 31. So long as it issued more notes than the Act allowed, the Bank was not to discount below 10 per cent.

In the week before the letter was sent the Bank had poured

[1] The figures, as known at the time, are in the *Report* of 1858, § 2.

[2] *Report*, § 15.

[3] Dewey, E. R., *Financial History of the United States* (1903), p. 263.

[4] The story of failures here given comes from Evans, *op. cit.*, a contemporary account written from Birchin Lane, Lombard Street, in 1859. Dennistoun's eventually paid in full: the City of Glasgow Bank resumed payment.

[5] Quoted in the *Report* of 1858, § 17.

more than £1,000,000 of gold coin into Scotland, where conditions were panicky; and £250,000 into Ireland[1]. The small savings-account depositors of the Glasgow banks wanted gold, not the famous Scottish notes. "These people who came for money would not take the notes of any bank," a Scottish director said[2]. Although the Bank had been moving up its discount rate steadily, and with great judgment as capable critics allowed[3], and had already pushed it to 10 per cent. by November 9, the paralysis of private discounting and this gold drain from the uneasy North forced it to use its extra-legal powers. (The stolid English shires, whose harvests had been good, were actually sending gold to London[4].) But for the drain to Scotland on November 9–11, the Directors thought, they might have got through legally. As it was, at night on the 12th, though there was still over £5,000,000 of gold in the issue department, their banking reserve was only £581,000. Their next return showed that they had fed it in the interval with £2,000,000 of extra-legal notes[5]. But "these steamers from Australia," and the high rate of discount which kept capital in London, soon helped the bill-brokers to resume their interrupted business. "It is expected," the *Economist* reported on November 21, "that by far the larger proportion of the £525,000 brought by the steamer *Australasian* from Alexandria will be sent into the Bank in a day or two." Gold also came back from Scotland. On Christmas Eve the Bank reported a stock of over £10,000,000 in the Issue Department; dropped its discount rate from 10 to 8 per cent.; thereby automatically cancelled its extra-legal powers of issue, and registered the end of the gold crisis. That crisis had been essentially internal. "With a foreign drain we have learnt by experience efficiently to cope," as Disraeli said in the House[6]. The Bank had been coping with it, or with the risk of it, in the approved way when the clamour of Glasgow spoiled its operation.

[1] *Report*, § 27.
[2] Quoted in *Report*, § 33.
[3] *Economist*, November 14, 1857.
[4] Evidence of W. Rodwell of Ipswich before the *S.C. of* 1857–8, Q. 1604. 'All' country banks were sending, or were ready to send, gold to London. He knew of no case of the reverse process.
[5] Of which less than £1,000,000 went into circulation. As the banking reserve of notes and coin stood at £1,553,000 on November 18 it could be argued that the "actual infringement was less than half-a-million" (*Economist*, November 21), *i.e.* much less than the gold sent to Scotland.
[6] December 4, 1857. *Hansard, Third Series*, CXLVIII. 159.

The business crisis was less easily passed, though its acute phase was short. There had been two important bank failures outside Liverpool and Glasgow—iron-country failures, at Newcastle and Wolverhampton. Apart from the merchants, the iron industry with its American connections showed most wreckage. Industry as a whole escaped lightly. Among the broken merchants, very many were described as in the German or North European trades[1]. The catastrophe had been world-wide, and Britain was among the least sufferers. Hamburg, which linked Northern Europe to America and England, and made heavy use of the bill on London, was among the greatest. "All transactions," in that community of merchants, "abruptly stopped and a complete dissolution of society threatened."[2] Every Northern and Central European business centre was affected, even so far East as Austria and Poland. The troubles had come, as Disraeli put it with his customary incision, "not from the mismanagement of the currency of this country, but from the mismanagement of the capital of Europe."[3] All the bubbles, blunders and dishonesties of five years' European exuberance and experiments in credit were tested or revealed.

In Britain, inquiry uncovered rather more than the usual proportion of common fraud, and the usual high proportion of stupidity—fictitious bills, "false reports and manufactured dividends,"[4] mixed up with credulous advances by banks to firms of doubtful stability, and the naïve belief of the self-making man that rising prices and expanding trade will put everything right on the day. It was noticed that, as compared with 1847, there were fewer failures of houses of good repute[5]. Almost everywhere the immediate cause of trouble was some stoppage in anticipated remittances from America. These remittances might be due for goods actually shipped, or they might be due under the system of open credits, by which British 'foreign banking' firms allowed themselves to be drawn upon to specified amounts by American, and other, correspondents, trusting that they would be put in funds by the correspondent before the liability incurred on his behalf matured. With banks shut all down the Atlantic coast, the most honourable American cor-

[1] There are complete lists in Evans, p. 180 *sqq*.

[2] Wirth, *op. cit.* p. 390.

[3] In his speech of December 4 quoted above.

[4] Evans, p. 47 n.: applies to the Western Bank of Scotland, the Liverpool Borough Bank, and the Northumberland and Durham District Bank.

[5] *Report*, § 35.

respondent might fail to remit. The use of these open credits, this international accommodation paper, not based like the old trade bill on actual mercantile transactions, was harshly criticised. Some people called it a novelty; but the Governor of the Bank of England rightly said that it was "not a new thing at all."[1] Presumably there has been some 'accommodation paper' ever since there has been 'paper.' Its use by solid and honourable firms who know one another's position is unexceptionable, and it oils the wheels of trade. It is also the familiar instrument of fraudulent 'kite-flyers.' There is evidence for a considerable extension of its use, especially in the North European trade, just before 1857. That was natural in those years of quickened communication and experiments with credit. It was also natural that the experimenters should not always be the solid folk, and would contain a full share of the rogues. Into which class should be placed a Newcastle firm that, starting with £2–3000 in 1854, failed for £100,000 of foreign credits in 1857 is uncertain[2]. At least its career illustrates the defects of the system. The old experienced merchant bankers of London who thoroughly understood the business, as the Governor knew, came through without disaster, if not untouched.

The trouble in Britain was due mainly, apart from fraud and crude incompetence, to the general reluctance to keep even small tanks of capital stagnant. Everybody wanted it to circulate and fructify the ground. They trusted to their regular or emergency feed-pipes—bankers to depositors and the Bank; bill-brokers to bankers, depositors and the Bank; acceptors on open credit to those sanguine and prosperous Americans, or to someone in Northern Europe. Blocks in the feed-pipes had produced a brief unpleasant drought. The Bank at once tried to force the brokers to keep fuller tanks by stopping discount for them altogether[3]. It would make quarterly advances to them, at the regularly recurring times when tax and government dividend money was off the market and in the Bank; but for the rest they must take care of themselves.

The sanguine Americans were justified in 1857–8[4]. All their

[1] *S.C. of* 1857–8, Q. 1690 (T. M. Wegeulin). In spite of his evidence, the *Report*, § 40, states boldly that "this practice appears to have grown up of late and to be principally connected with...the North of Europe." The evidence as a whole bears out the statements in the text—*e.g.* John Ball's, Q. 1663 *sqq.*; and Wegeulin's.

[2] Described in the *Report*, § 40.

[3] *S.C. of* 1857–8, Q. 616–18, 688.

[4] See *Economist*, January 2 and 30, 1858.

banks except those of Pennsylvania had resumed payment by the new year. The most important British firms in the American trade which had stopped were able ultimately to pay in full. Early in January, Paris and Hamburg were discounting at 5 per cent.; London at 4 per cent. before the end of the month. On January 27 the Bank had £15,000,000 of bullion; "half a million was overdue from Australia"; and America was again shipping gold. "There was never a more severe crisis nor a more rapid recovery."[1] The deep permanent springs of the world's wealth were intact. The gold which fascinated men into widening their outlets and clearing their channels remained abundant; and Britain's sustained exports of capital were increasing her claims on them yearly.

Yet the complete recovery of trade and industry, as opposed to the recovery from the acute phase of the crisis, was slow. For two years, except for a month in 1859 when there was a scare on the Stock Exchange[2], Bank rate was at 3 per cent. or less. Only at the very end of 1860, when South Carolina had already seceded from the Union, did it rise above 5 per cent. for the first time since 1857. In leading articles with titles such as *When will trade revive?* expert journalists had explained in 1858 that the business world could not be expected to recover its tone all at once[3]. Europe had been very badly shaken. British exports to America in 1858 were lower than they had been in any of the previous four years. As partial compensation, exports to India in 1858 were more than twice what they had been in 1853. The construction of the Indian railways, pressed forward for reasons of high policy after 1857, was absorbing capital goods and would open new territory to trade. On the other hand, Europe, though shaken, was now following hard after Britain on the tracks of industry and economic enterprise. She could do more of her own railway promotion and contracting, and was less dependent on the island for capital goods.

There was war in Europe in 1859. The rise in the Bank rate at the close of 1860 was due not to trade activity, nor to a failed harvest—harvests since 1857 had been good or fair—but to fear of war in America. When Mississippi, Florida, Alabama, Georgia, Louisiana and Texas—all cotton states—seceded in

[1] *Economist*, January 30.

[2] Described in Evans, *op. cit.* p. 148 *sqq.*; and see the *Economist*, April-May, 1859.

[3] *Economist*, January 5, 1858.

January, 1861, it rose for a time to 8 per cent. Gold was being taken out to buy silver for India; and India's claim on silver was said to be due to "wild orders"[1] for cotton, from men who in imagination saw the American supply cut off. It was not in fact cut off until much later. Anglo-American trade in 1861 showed a large increase in the American export of goods, sold eagerly by Americans while there was still time, and such a fall of British exports to America that gold moved West instead of East[2]. But as home trade was slack, Europe restless, and the Indian and other trades not active enough to counteract these deadening forces, the gold movement was easily arranged and the Bank rate was dropping during all the latter part of the year. It remained very low all through 1862. Mainly because of the check to Anglo-American intercourse, the years 1861–2 yielded the only horizontal section of the mounting curve of the aggregate import and export trades of the United Kingdom between 1850 and 1884[3]. The low Bank rate registers the same fact on a different scale. Between 1862 and the surrender of Lee at Appomattox on April 9, 1865, although Anglo-American trade as a whole did not improve, England was finding elsewhere outlets and sources of supply sufficient to enable her trade curve to resume its steep upward course—the French treaty of 1860 and its successors helping[4].

Apart from the cotton industry, with its principal source of supply closed, and silk, at last obliged to face French competition naked, 1863 was a very good year for British manufacturers and an excellent one for merchants, financiers, and company promoters[5]. In industry, much of what Lancashire and Glasgow lost, Yorkshire and Dundee gained. The heavy trades were particularly active. There had been good harvests and bread was cheap. A money market flurry at the close of the year only illustrated the growing efficiency and speed of control in London and Paris. There had been heavy cotton buying in India, Egypt and Brazil. Bullion was wanted for all three. The Bank of England pushed up its rate far and fast, once before and once after Christmas. The Bank of France did the

[1] *Economist*, February 9, 1861.

[2] Cp. Chapman, S. J., *The History of Trade between the United Kingdom and the United States* (1899), ch. 4.

[3] The curve referred to is not the crude curve, but the curve reduced by index-numbers to the values of 1889, given in Bowley, A. L., *England's Foreign Trade in the Nineteenth Century*.

[4] See above, p. 244, 247.

[5] See the *Economist's* Review of the Year.

same. "The scarcity rates of 7 and 8 per cent. had the effect of drawing to these cities in a very short time large amounts of capital from Germany, Holland and other places where the cotton pressure was not felt,"[1] so that the rates could be reduced as promptly as they had been raised.

Of really low rates in 1864 there was no question. Although America was now sending much treasure—from the Golden Gate to England direct, as more convenient in war time[2]—and Australia always sent it, the various demands easily carried off the supply. Wholesale prices for the year were a little higher even than they had been in 1857; and early in the year they were much higher, in spite of ample harvests in 1863. Bankers had to support a very vigorous home and foreign trade. Bills were many and discounting active. The new finance companies were making a sometimes experimental use of British capital abroad[3]. Other new companies readily absorbed any surplus funds available. There was less money than usual left on deposit for bankers to handle. Every now and then some drain, or anticipated drain, of bullion to one of the war-time sources of cotton supply, or some market excitement with which cotton was sure to be connected, drove up the Bank rate from the year's base, of about 6, to 8 or 9 per cent.[4] During the last of these spells of dear money, in September and October, a downward trend in prices and business was noticeable. The cotton market was beginning to discount the impending defeat of the South[5] and activity was slackening in other fields.

After so exhausting a war, and before the Atlantic cable was laid, peace in the United States could not at once restore Anglo-American trade. British exports to America were indeed nearly five millions less in the first eight months of 1865 than in the corresponding period of 1864. Europe was politically restless. Bismarck was sparring for position with Austria. There was an election due in England about midsummer. The slackening of business which began in the autumn of 1864

[1] *Economist's* Review of the Year, p. 2.

[2] £5,700,000 came that way in 1863 and £6,900,000 in 1864. *Economist*, April 26, 1865.

[3] Above, p. 358.

[4] According to the *Economist* (May 19, 1866) "but for admirable management" the international bullion drains would have caused a panic in 1864. The steady inflow of treasure must have greatly aided free and confident management by the Bank.

[5] Cp. *Economist*, April 22, 1865, on the fall of Richmond (Va).

continued. The Bank rate dropped steadily in nine months from 9 to 3 per cent. Then suddenly, in September, British exports leapt up by what was at that date the very remarkable figure of over £3,000,000 in a month. The delayed United States demand was beginning to tell; and there were others. The rise continued through the winter, and Bank rate went with it. During the first four months of 1866, the United Kingdom actually exported 30 per cent. more in value than during the corresponding months of 1865, though the price level was much the same. At the end of April, the period of rather dear money naturally resulting from this expansion of business, gave way to actual stringency. "The best informed people" felt no doubt that treasure was being withdrawn from London by "the foreign governments now preparing for war."[1] Stringency was followed by panic; by 10 per cent., the classical panic rate; and by a Chancellor's letter authorising a breach of the Bank Act. Overend and Gurney Limited had failed on Friday, May 11th, for over five millions. Exactly a month later the "foreign governments" began their war.

There was little that was international about the crisis, except some of its consequences. In spite of the preoccupation of the continental capitals with war risks, the rate of discount on May 10th was only 4 per cent. in Paris, 5 per cent. in Vienna, 6 per cent. in Turin, and 7 per cent. in Berlin[2]. There was no fresh gold drain of importance; nothing revolutionary in the course of trade; no abnormal locking up of capital in distant enterprises. It was a panic in every sense, and it was purely British. Those in the City who knew had long ceased to believe in Overends. Walter Bagehot had thought their failure possible "any time these three months."[3] When they became a limited company, in 1865, he had welcomed the change sardonically because now it would be "essential to publish an account of the nature of their business."[4] Everyone knew that its nature had changed since 1857. In 1860 the firm had been strong enough to try a fall with the Bank of England; but it had been beaten. It had withdrawn a huge deposit at an inconvenient

[1] *Economist*, May 5, 1866.

[2] Wirth, *op. cit.* p. 424. Those who recall August, 1914, and know the diplomatic history of 1866, may find these rates significant—highest in the capital where war was being most consciously planned.

[3] *Economist*, May 12, 1866 (assuming, as one safely may, that Bagehot wrote the article). Cp. Charles Oppenheim's letter to the *Economist* of December 22, 1866.

[4] *Economist*, July 15, 1865.

time as a fighting protest against the Bank's policy of not discounting for the bill-brokers—and it had put the deposit back again. "The Bank of England could not afford to be frightened"[1]; and it was not. The Overends of the 'sixties handled many things besides fine trade bills—finance paper of the more doubtful kinds, and what were known as the 'finance securities' of railway promoters and great contractors. These were bonds, debentures, and what not, issued by the directors-to-be to the contractor before the public had subscribed, and turned by him into cash, often on very onerous terms[2]. The inner city knew or suspected all this. To the outer city, and the country, the name of Overends was still a symbol of credit, and when it was blown upon you could trust nobody. Besides Overends the Bank of London went down and, fitly enough, Sir Samuel Peto's great contracting firm, known all over Europe and much of America for its daring promotions[3]. There was a winnowing out of light stock-joint enterprises of all sorts. Up to August 4th the wind had carried away a hundred and eighty of them[4].

At no stage had the Bank been seriously short of bullion. The trouble had been with the banking reserve of notes and coin: though the Governors managed to see the crisis through without feeding the reserve with extra-legal notes. Yet, in the general collapse of credit, Bank notes were in great demand. Even in July the number in circulation was nearly £6,000,000 above normal. Foreigners, supposing the catastrophe worse than it was, withdrew some capital from London. There was war on the continent. Early in July the banking reserve ran low a second time. As a result of all this, Bank rate remained at 10 per cent. for no less than three months—in fact, until peace between Prussia and Austria was certain[5].

[1] *Economist*, May 21, 1860. The *Economist* of the 'sixties and 'seventies, under Bagehot (1860–77) was so well informed and well written that it will always remain a chief authority for these years. A better cannot be found; and there was no Select Committee and Report in 1866 as in 1857–8.

[2] See the full account of this class of 'security,' which had become common "in the last few years" in the *Economist* of April 28, 1866 (before the crisis) in connection with failures of well-known contractors and the revelation of their methods.

[3] Cp. vol. I. p. 408–12 and the *D.N.B.*

[4] Wirth, *op. cit.* p. 431–2, a good account on the whole, based mainly on the *Economist*.

[5] The gold in the Issue Department never got really low, *i.e.* there was no serious foreign drain. It had been £12,000,000 on January 10. It was £11,300,000 on May 23, its lowest point. It touched £14,200,000 on June 27; was at £12,700,000 on August 8; and then rose again.

Given the circumstances, there would have been a panic under any banking law. Peel's Act and the doubts about its suspension increased the panic at home. Suspension, when it came, gave an exaggerated importance to the panic abroad. "The French fancy we have suspended cash payments," Bagehot wrote on the 19th of May[1]. Their fancies had probably not been calmed by the diplomatic circular of May 12, in which Lord Clarendon explained to all our representatives at foreign courts that the ordinary business of Britain was really quite sound[2]. Much trouble would unquestionably have been saved had Peel's Act contained what Bagehot called an "expansive clause," that is a clause providing for, and safeguarding, excess emergency issues without the terrifying incursion of a Chancellor's letter. If such a clause is not inserted, Bagehot wrote, "the Act will be repealed soon."[3] He was wrong. There was not even an official inquiry into the crisis[4]. As for the Act it survived, without any expansive clause, to be suspended in August, 1914.

It survived so long partly because there was never 'ten per cent.' again until 1914. Once the rate began falling, in August, 1866, it did not stop until it reached 2 per cent. in the following July. There it remained for fifteen months. Commerce recovered slowly from the shock of 1866. Owing to a run of bad harvests, bread in London in 1867 was almost 50 per cent. dearer than it had been in 1864, and it did not begin to fall until the middle of 1868[5]. Dear bread meant a sluggish home trade in 1867–8. In spite of high corn prices, the general course of wholesale prices, including the corn, was downward from 1866 to 1870, which suggests an inactive overseas trade[6]. In fact, although overseas trade grew absolutely, per head of the population it was stationary. By 1869, corn and bread were again cheap, and the start of a spell of furious railway building in America suggested that trade activity in Britain might come in again, as so often before, on an Atlantic wind. The raised basic level of the rate of discount in 1869–70, as compared with

[1] In the *Economist*.

[2] It was printed in all the papers and is translated in Wirth, *op. cit.* p. 434–5. The diplomatic mind naturally assumed that our business was unsound and that we were trying to conceal the fact.

[3] *Economist*, May 19.

[4] Though there was a motion for a Royal Commission on July 31 (*Hansard, Third Series*, CLXXXIV. 1706) moved by Mr Watkin. The Ministry had changed since May. Both Northcote and Gladstone, the in and the out, argued that inquiry would do no good.

[5] See the diagram, p. 460.

[6] See the diagram, p. 378.

1867–8, registers a growing activity. The omens had suggested quick growth in 1870. Lancashire was busy in January. By May trade revival was "general and marked."[1] But Bismarck and Napoleon, France and what would soon be Germany, willed that the later months of 1870 should be anxious and unprofitable; the early months of 1871 more anxious still.

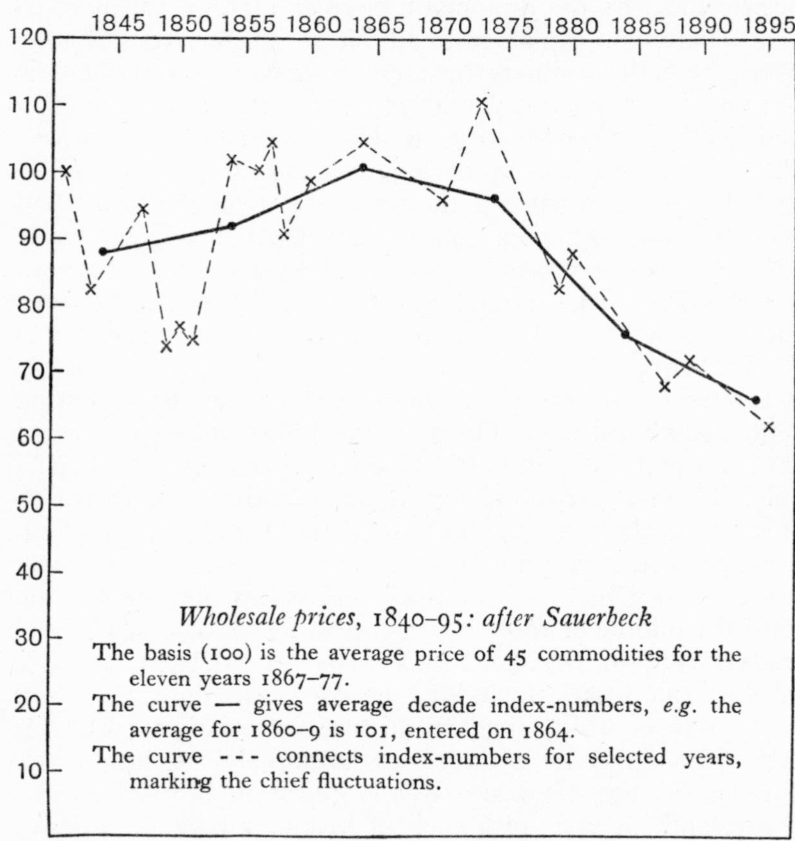

Wholesale prices, 1840–95*: after Sauerbeck*

The basis (100) is the average price of 45 commodities for the eleven years 1867–77.

The curve — gives average decade index-numbers, *e.g.* the average for 1860–9 is 101, entered on 1864.

The curve - - - connects index-numbers for selected years, marking the chief fluctuations.

How strong the economic and financial position of Britain was, and—as some might say—how sluggish her imagination, is suggested by the stability of the Bank rate while war was in the making and British neutrality, as it appeared for a time, in the balance[2]. 'Six per cent.' came only after the armies had clashed on the frontiers. It did not stay long. With Sedan the

[1] *Economist*, February 5, and May 14, 1870.

[2] Over the question of Belgium, it will be recalled. Cp. Morley's *Gladstone*, book VI, ch. 5. Gladstone was facing the possibility of having to send "12,000 or 20,000" men to Antwerp.

end seemed already in sight. The British people were doing what one of their ablest diplomatists had hoped they might do to the last in 1791—looking "at the French story like spectators in a theatre."[1] The play grew pitiful, tragic, ominous, with the terrors of the siege and the Commune. When every value seemed uncertain in the smoke hanging over Paris, the spectators held their breath. Their money did not stir. 'Two and a half per cent.'[2] Then effective peace; for the Communards, New Caledonia; for their countrymen at home, the toil and achievement of an unbelievable recovery; for Germany, the spending of France's milliards and confidence without limits, a confidence which spread among, and beyond, her German-speaking neighbours. Unlimited confidence and immense achievement in America also. Between Europe and America, Britain; cooler than any and more experienced in the treatment of economic fevers—in controlled excitement; making; lending; banking and carrying for the world; profiting by the free trade which she had taught, and which so many nations now seemed to have at least half learnt. Her wholesale prices rose some 20 per cent. between the middle of 1871 and the middle of 1873; the prices of many of her capital goods vastly more. Her overseas trade curve climbed precipitately. Her wages were very high and her bread reasonably cheap.

Excitement, control, and the pressure of trade on liquid capital resources are all to be read in the Bank rate chart for 1871–3, with its mounting basic level and its succession of steep-sided summits overtopping each other[3]. That the last summit is 9 and not 10 per cent. means that, by the experience which she had bought, by good management and perhaps some good fortune, Britain escaped the extreme phases of crisis and panic through which most trading and industrial nations had to pass in 1873. (But she was left with a deferred liability to be met in 1878[4].) No wonder that men who understood the forces

[1] *Cambridge History of British Foreign Policy*, I. 206. (Lord Auckland to his brother.)

[2] The rate was 2½ per cent. when Paris surrendered. It rose to 3 per cent. in March when the financing of an indemnity was anticipated, but fell again to 2½ per cent. during the Commune. "From the long suspense which has prevailed, and which has checked new undertakings of every kind, there has perhaps never been a greater accumulation of money in Lombard Street." *Economist*, April 15, 1871. As peace was not signed until May 18, and arrangements for the indemnity loan were finished in July, the accumulation remained: Bank rate was 2 per cent. in July. By October 11 it was 5 per cent.

[3] Above, p. 363. [4] Below, p. 383–4.

playing on Lombard Street from all the world, in these turbulent years, were oppressed with the responsibilities of those in charge of its ultimate reserves.

In the German lands and their neighbours 1872 was the great year of company promotion[1]—for railways, banks, building societies, credit institutions, public utilities, and all sorts of industry, especially blast-furnaces, iron works, and engineering works. There was furious land speculation in Berlin, growing like a Chicago and for a time the dearest town in Europe. Vienna too was developing, and completing her education in modern business methods and practices: there were thirteen Princes, one Landgraf, and sixty-four Counts on the boards of the Austro-Hungarian railways by 1873[2]. Paris had rebuilding to do, but the French were in sober mood. They had little capital to spare for that imaginative enterprise in which they had led Europe twenty years earlier. In 1872, although they raised more money for public loans and joint-stock business than any people in the world, they appear to have put less into joint-stock business alone even than the Italians[3]. France had claimed their money and French enterprises must wait. This saved them from the worst of the trouble when it came.

America was in a position from which it was not easy to escape without damage and discredit. She had a post-war depreciated currency; she was opening up half a continent, with furious energy; in spite of her disordered currency, she was becoming the world's greatest producer both of gold and silver; and she was also the world's greatest debtor nation, having borrowed both to develop and to fight. In 1868, when 100 dollars currency were worth only 71·5 dollars gold[4], the Treasury was in the habit of selling by auction the gold it got from import duties, which were payable in coin only, under a war-time law. New York's Black Friday, September 23, 1869, was the destructive local crisis resulting from the attempt of Jay Gould

[1] The best contemporary account of all the antecedents of the crisis of 1873 is in Wirth, *op. cit.* p. 450–614. Modern accounts for Germany are in Sartorius von Waltershausen, *Deutsche Wirtschaftsgeschichte*, 1815–1914 (1920), p. 261–81, and the books there referred to. A general sketch in Juglar, C., *Des crises commerciales* (1889), p. 390 *sqq.*

[2] Wirth, *op. cit.* p. 491.

[3] Tables published in the *Moniteur des Intérêts matériels* quoted in Wirth, *op. cit.* p. 469.

[4] Dewey, *Financial History of the U.S.A.* p. 376; Dewey also gives a good general sketch of the American situation.

and James Fisk to take advantage of this interesting arrangement by cornering the free gold and inducing the Treasury to limit sales. After 1869 the currency position improved; by 1872, 100 dollars currency were worth 89·4 dollars gold, and resumption seemed near. But if America got into financial trouble, there were sure to be voices raised—of greenbackers, cousins to the Birmingham school—who would look to plenty of paper money for a cure.

The construction of 6167 miles of railway in the United States during 1872 brought the figure for four years up to 25,000 miles[1]. Naturally the iron industry was inflated, with many others. Yet America had never bought foreign manufactures so heavily; and she bought mainly in Britain. She had now to find large sums to pay for carrying services which before the war she had performed for herself; and there was already a great deal of American money being spent by travellers and residents in Europe. She had paid her adverse balance of indebtedness partly with gold, but very largely with promises—bonds, national, state, and railway. The position was delicate and for her European creditors and clients dangerous. She might easily be forced to curtail her imports. Bankruptcy, if only of a few railways, would help to adjust her balance of indebtedness. It might come without being designed by anyone[2].

It was hard that Austria, turned out of Germany by Prussia in 1866, should have been the first to suffer when what might justly, if vulgarly, be called the Prussian boom of 1871–3 collapsed. But it was so. Austria's '*Krach*' came early in May. "For the first time," an Austrian who went through it recorded with a certain sombre pride, she suffered from this "aristocratic complaint of civilised states...and therewith in some sort paid her entry fee" into their circle[3]. Her sufferings, which did not very nearly concern Britain, but had repercussions through all Germany, have left their mark on the Bank rate chart in the first summit of 7 per cent., in June, 1873.

Through the summer months, collapse, liquidation and the resulting slack trade spread from one business centre in Europe

[1] See Adams, C. F., *Railroads: Their Origin and Problems*, 1878; Johnson, E. R., *American Railway Transportation*, ch. 3.

[2] The delicate position of a young country which has overborrowed was illustrated painfully in 1930–1.

[3] Wirth, *op. cit.* p. 461.

to another, without much more actual panic[1]. Stock Exchange values fell, and then commodity prices, except unfortunately that of corn, which was rising. France began to suffer, not for mistakes of her own, but through the shrinkage of demand for such things as her silks and wines. In London, discount had slipped down to 3 per cent. in August, and nothing worse than a period of slack trade seemed impending for "John Bull... throned untouched on his money bags," as a touched continental pictured him[2]. Then, on September 20, came cabled news of a crash in New York—some banks down; others closing their doors to avoid a run; a moratorium demanded for savings banks; a temporary closing of exchanges. Railway speculation, with all that accompanied it, and the locking up of capital in lines for the time unprofitable, had combined with the uncertainties and the opportunities for doubtful business provided by a depreciated paper currency in a gold producing country to bring things to a head. European capital had for some time fought shy of new American railway bonds. All kinds of expensive financial devices had been adopted to keep construction, and the companies, going. With the crisis, these devices became difficult or impossible to maintain. As a palliative, government undertook to provide more circulating medium by buying United States bonds with greenbacks recently withdrawn from circulation; but President Grant resisted the pressure put upon him to adopt a thoroughgoing policy of inflation[3]. When the liabilities of bankrupts came to be reckoned for 1873, they amounted to 93,000,000 dollars in New York alone, as against 21,000,000 dollars in 1872[4].

The American crisis completed the discomfiture of Europe. Speculation on margins had been common during the boom. The collapse of American securities started or hastened the general collapse. German financial centres, headed by Berlin, which had got through the summer, could not stand these autumn gales. Railways, banks and building societies went down. There was heavy mortality in industry, with capital reductions and combinations of over-capitalised firms. Whether

[1] There was something described as a panic at Bologna in July. Wirth, *op. cit.* p. 588.

[2] Wirth, *op. cit.* p. 594.

[3] Dewey, *op. cit.* p. 372.

[4] For all the United States the rise was from $121,000,000 in 1872 to $228,000,000 in 1873. The figures illustrate the concentration of the hurricane on New York.

there was more than the normal amount of dishonesty accompanying so widespread a madness of greed is hard to say; but it was natural to think so, when such people as the cashier of the Prussian Mortgage Bank, the Director of the People's Bank at Essen, a French ex-minister, and even business men from careful respectable Switzerland, became convicts[1].

In England the situation was worst, as might have been expected, on the Stock Exchange. There November 6 and 7 were days of panic—but Consols moved only a point or two. America, France and Germany had all been drawing on the London gold. British bankers had been drawing on their deposits at the Bank. Both reserves were low at the end of October, and the rate had been moved up steadily since mid-September from 3 to 7 per cent. It was moved again twice in November, just stopping short of the true panic rate of 10 per cent., but getting high enough to tell the continent that John Bull was touched at last. There was nothing in London to compare with the catastrophes of New York, Vienna and Berlin; although for a moment suspension of the Bank Act was feared. But as the reserve in the Banking Department was never reported below £8,000,000, nor the gold in the Issue Department below £18,600,000, the fear was unreasonable. Nine per cent. worked perfectly and very fast. By the middle of December there was a banking reserve of more than £12,000,000, and a rate of 4½ per cent. There had been losses and failures but, as yet, nothing extraordinary or discreditable.

By contemporaries the after effects of the crisis of 1873 were naturally confused with the early stages of the great price fall of the late nineteenth century, which began among them but was not in any true sense their consequence. A fall from the level of 1872–3 was inevitable and was anticipated; but a ten year fall, which was to draw out into a twenty year fall, was outside the experience of the generation which had to bear it. Five years of slow trade after so general an upheaval might perhaps have been anticipated: there had been four between the Overend crisis and the revival of 1870. But it is unlikely that any one could have guessed that, after a short and delusive recovery in 1879–80, the fall would be resumed at the old rate[2].

This resumed fall was the more discouraging because it might well have been thought that with the failure of the City of Glasgow bank on October 1, 1878, the full penalty of 1873 had been

[1] Wirth, *op. cit.* p. 569–70. [2] See the diagram above, p. 378.

paid. Though active and pushful, with many branches and a deposit business of over £8,000,000, the City of Glasgow had for years been of ill-fame in the inner banking world[1]. It had suspended payment in 1857 but had reopened after a month[2]. Whether it had ever been genuinely solvent since was doubtful; certainly it had been insolvent for years before 1878. Some of its bad debts ran back to the cotton famine[3]. Latterly, as appeared after the crash, it had systematically treated these debts as assets. Four debtors only, from the class which in America and Germany had been sifted out in 1873, owed and would never pay £5,793,000[4]. Gaol for its directors and its manager brought Britain into line with Europe, but did not help the firms which were dragged down with it, the shareholders with unlimited liability, or the army of small depositors. There is no more miserable episode in the economic history of the age. To it, and the resultant depression, has been attributed the ruin of the great majority of the Scottish trade unions[5].

Desperate as it was in Scotland, the City of Glasgow crisis was easily handled by the Bank of England with a short spell of 6 per cent. The Bank had only to go so high once again in the next decade, at the beginning of February, 1882, when the *Union génèrale* stopped payment in Paris. The Union, whose foundation in 1878 marked the return of France to large-scale imaginative enterprise, was among the most fantastic and ambitious creations of the time[6]. With a clerical and aristocratic clientele, it was a promoting, finance and holding company of the widest kind, whose special interests—as became the clientele—were in the Hapsburg lands. Its failure was the outstanding event in a Parisian crisis, against the repercussion of which on gold and the exchanges, the Bank of England defended itself again by the precautionary 6 per cent.

This was only an episode, and from the British standpoint an unimportant one, in a long stretch of fourteen years (1873–87) for the whole of which the average Bank rate was barely

[1] Kerr, *History*, ch. 25.

[2] Above, p. 368.

[3] Giffen, *Essays in Finance, Second Series*, p. 152. From the Essay "On the use of Import and Export Statistics" (1882): "the rottenness disclosed... having been largely due to the excessive investment of capital in the Eastern trade in the times of the cotton famine."

[4] The *Scotsman*, October 19, quoted in Kerr, p. 297.

[5] Webb, S. and B., *History of Trade Unionism*, p. 334.

[6] See Juglar, C., *Des crises commerciales* (1889), p. 447; Wirth, *op. cit.* p. 621–643.

3 per cent. There was no war in Western Europe. European harvest fluctuations were losing their power to hurt, since corn was coming to England more uniformly all round the year. For Britain the era of bank failures was over. America was more cut off by tariffs and more self-sufficient in capital goods than she had formerly been; Britain rather less confiding in her American and general overseas investment. Even the making of 35,000 miles of American railway in 1880–83, and the reaction which followed, did not leave such deep marks on British industry and the London money market as corresponding events had left ten years earlier. That quiet era in Lombard Street which helped a bad Bank Act to work without further inquiry was due partly to the removal of old dangers and fears; partly to accumulated experience in the Bank parlour, and to the way in which other parties in the Street had learned how to tackle old or new dangers. But things would not have been so quiet but for that numbness in the industrial and commercial life of the country which marked the years of falling prices and quickened international competition. When producers and dealers had surplus funds, there was hesitation about turning them into new machinery and plant or developing the business: money lay longer on deposit, and there was more of it to handle than Lombard Street could manage profitably[1]. Removal of dangers and increased wisdom may well explain the saving of Lombard Street from 10 and 8 per cent. The rare appearances of 4 and 5 per cent. require a less gratifying explanation. Reviewing the evidence given before that inquiry into Trade Depression with which the period closed, Alfred Marshall could find no proof that the general economic welfare of the country was abnormally depressed; but he admitted a severe "depression of prices, a depression of interest, and a depression of profits."[2] His admissions sufficiently explain the chill and heavy air of Lombard Street.

[1] Cp. above, p. 356. The statement that "money lay longer on deposit" is an inference from the other facts of the situation. I know of no precise authority for it.

[2] Before the *R.C. on Gold and Silver*, Q. 9824.

CHAPTER X

THE ECONOMIC ACTIVITIES OF THE STATE

JEREMY BENTHAM, it may be recalled, had once advocated the handing over of all Poor Law work to a National Charity Company[1]. As a rationalist son of the eighteenth century, he assumed that particular governments are likely to be both incompetent and corrupt. As a liberty loving philosopher, it was his axiom that "all government is in itself one vast evil."[2] But he held that whatever limited amount of this evil thing might remain should be rationally organised, very well served, very well informed, careful to put its information at the disposal of the public, consistently hostile to all kinds of monopoly, and watchful over the nation's health. His scheme of ministries was so exactly thought out that a twentieth century committee faced with the same problem arrived independently at a closely similar result[3]. (The scheme of course contained a Minister of Health, not to provide for disease but to anticipate it.) Inspectors reporting to Secretaries of State, recording registrars whose statistical results are widely published, and expert central civil servants are all typical Benthamite officials. When Edwin Chadwick and Walter Bagehot inclined towards different forms of railway nationalisation in the 'sixties[4], because railways were of the nature of monopolies, neither was outside the Benthamite tradition.

From the victory of 1832, which he just did not live to see, until the usury laws were abolished in 1854 and examinations initiated for those entering the civil service in 1855[5], there had been a bit of Bentham in every great reform, destructive or

[1] See vol. I. p. 312. The notion was not original. It had been discussed, in various forms, a century earlier. See Charles Davenant's *Essay upon the Probable Methods of making a People Gainers in the Balance of Trade*, Section 3.

[2] Quoted in Leslie Stephen, *The English Utilitarians* (1900), I. 287.

[3] *Report of the Machinery of Government Committee* (1918), Cd. 9230; and see Webb, S. and B., *English Poor Law History: The Last Hundred Years* (1929), p. 816–17.

[4] Above, p. 189.

[5] The first Civil Service examinations were qualifying, not competitive. Effective competition only began in 1870. See Morley, *Life of Gladstone*, I. 509–12; II. 314.

creative. No doubt he would have criticised each new thing. The examining of civil servants, for example, was not linked with the economical device which he had suggested of inviting them to tender against one another, so that the state might know which of them would do the work cheapest[1]. But he would have recognised, and probably overrated, his own touch; just as he had been glad to treat "Master Peel" as a "model good boy" when that associate of his prime enemy Eldon reformed the criminal law, made the new constabulary, or behaved in some other way like a pupil[2]. Indeed nothing could have been more to his taste than the 'Peelers,' since to him security was the primary condition of happiness, equality only a secondary.

Some old regulations and functions the state had abandoned, or was in course of abandoning. But it had been reformed in head and members—parliament, civil service, municipalities, guardians of the poor. It was stronger for the reforms. Without overstepping Bentham's circle, it had become stronger still by extending its activities, sometimes against the wishes of those who were readiest to invoke Bentham's principles, and by creating new instruments *ad hoc*. Success with the Penny Post had certainly increased its prestige[3]. It was at length publishing accurate statistics of trade and shipping, and of the output of minerals. Though it had no trustworthy agricultural statistics, and had made no attempt to gauge the production of manufactured goods, it had completed in the census of 1851 a remarkably ambitious statistical account of the whole kingdom—so ambitious that in later census years a number of the most valuable economic chapters were not continued. It had registrars of births, deaths and marriages, of friendly societies, and of joint-stock companies. It had poor law inspectors, textile factory inspectors, inspectors of railways, of weights and measures and of mines. In Scotland it had fishery inspectors, who branded herrings for market and linked the inspectorates of the nineteenth century with those of the eighteenth. For the sake of decency, safety or health it forbade women to work in mines; it even interfered a little with the labour contracts of male miners[4]; it laid down rules for the construction and working of steamships; and it had begun to build up a sanitary code to be

[1] Leslie Stephen, *op. cit.* I. 286.

[2] *Ibid.* I. 226–7; and cp. J. S. Mill, *Autobiography*, p. 99.

[3] And success with the Post Office Savings Banks after 1861 increased it further.

[4] See vol. I. p. 576: wages not to be paid in taverns, etc.

enforced with the aid of medical officers of health and various inspectors. It had just brutally interfered with liberty in the interest of security by ordering that every child born in England should be not only registered but vaccinated (16 and 17 Vict. c. 100)[1]. It had revived and strengthened the ancient laws which forbade the payment of wages—but not of all wages—in truck. It was working out a code which treated the seaman "as if he were a mere child,"[2] a code under which anyone might be punished who boarded a ship within twenty-four hours of her arrival in port and asked a sailor to lodge with him[3]. It had regulated the price of 'parliamentary' railway travel, though it had abandoned the Assize of Bread. Within a few years it would regulate in great detail the sale, if not the price, of gas.

The world of industry was become very intricate and in some ways increasingly dangerous. Men's minds and consciences were more sensitive than their grandfathers' had been. They asked for themselves and, when they had influence with government, for the people, a wide and specialised security that the grandfathers had not thought about. The state, purged and trained fine, better informed and better equipped, could supervise the carrying out of its decisions with a certainty which would have been nearly unthinkable two generations earlier. Whatever the conscious or sub-conscious doctrines about the proper sphere of its action by which legislators were influenced, it was probable, perhaps inevitable, that the organism of state, more sinewy and efficient, would also become more active. Among the legislators, whose often inconsequent and party-blinded votes determined its activities, were some not yet convinced that it ought to leave foreign trade and navigation alone; others certain that it had not gone nearly far enough in promoting health, safety, and the good life; some few who held with Bentham that there was one strongly fortified monopoly yet to be stormed—that of the land with its land laws[4]. Such groups were ready to use the machine of government at

[1] *An Act to extend and make compulsory the practice of vaccination*: 1853. The Acts for Scotland and Ireland only came ten years later, following a second English Act, rendered necessary by the comparative failure of the first.

[2] Jevons, W. S., *The State in Relation to Labour* (1882), p. 69. Jevons quotes most of the 'interferences' mentioned in the text. References are to the fourth edition, ed. F. W. Hirst, of 1910, in which the paging differs from the first.

[3] See below, p. 410.

[4] Cp. Walpole, Sir Spencer, *The History of Twenty-Five Years* (1904), I. 39 *sqq.*

opportune moments to gain their ends. There were those waiting outside parliament and outside the electorate who, when their time came, would be readier.

The average legislator, a man of property, reasonably content with the growth of wealth under a system of modified freedom, and proud of the economic leadership of his country, was averse from radical measures either of reaction or reform. Not until the difficult times of the late 'seventies would he be likely to listen to advocates of either, and not with any eagerness then. His leaders were not radicals of the left or of the right. Of the two dominating parliamentary gladiators whom he cheered[1], one had grown into economic liberalism empirically and by inheritance from his master Peel: there was no scrap of Bentham in Gladstone's intellectual and moral makeup. The other, who with the detachment of an alien genius could step outside his age and watch it, had done no more than acquiesce in certain economic liberalisms as appropriate to that age and useful to his party. They were expedients not principles, and it is of the nature of an expedient to be short-lived. But for the present they served.

In the year after Disraeli died, the most observant and acute economist of that generation put into words what in fact had been the normal attitude of government towards economic affairs, if one is to judge by the statute book. "We must rid our minds," Stanley Jevons wrote[2], "of the idea that there are any such things in social matters as abstract rights, absolute principles, indefeasible laws, or anything whatever of an eternal and inflexible nature." And again—"We must neither maximise the functions of government at the beck of quasi-military officials, nor minimise them according to the theories of the very best philosophers. We must learn to judge each case upon its merits."[3] Herbert Spencer, who may well have been the very best philosopher whom Jevons had in mind, broke out in 1884 into a last grumbling cry for *The Man versus the State*. Conscious of the state's growing power, and familiar by profession with the views of those thinkers who welcomed it, he made his protest against, among other things, the Public

[1] "Yonder and close to Mr Speaker's chair,
Enfolding all things in a net of words,
Stands our first gymnast." Wilfrid Blunt,
The Idler's Calendar.

[2] *The State in Relation to Labour* (1882), p. 6.

[3] *Ibid.* p. 171.

Libraries Act, "by which a majority can tax a minority for their books."[1] He was late, even belated. It was doubtful, too, whether the challenge came fitly from an evolutionary philosopher. Should one grumble at the amalgamation of the three hind toes of *eohippus* into the single hoof of *equus*, even if *equus* kicks one with it? In any case, statesmen and legislators were not regular readers of Spencer.

Mill they were at least supposed to have read: he stood for political economy. When a man set out between 1848 and 1886 to invoke, to attack or to defend, political economy, he generally meant Mill, if he meant anything[2]. Professed students as a rule still built on Mill or adjusted their thought to his[3]. Now in his theory of the state Mill had given cautious empirical innovators like Jevons all the justification they required, and plenty of encouragement to more radical reformers. In particular, his book had, from the first, been Bible and Fathers to those few who wished to reform the land law or the practices of land-holding.

Land being "the original inheritance of the whole species," its appropriation was in his opinion "wholly a question of general expediency."[4] Whatever "sacredness" property might have did not "belong in the same degree to landed property." The legislature might "if it pleased convert the whole body of landlords into fundholders or pensioners." And more dogmatically—"whenever, in any country, the proprietor, generally speaking, ceases to be the improver, political economy has nothing to say in defence of landed property as there established. In no sound theory of private property was it ever contemplated that the proprietor of land should be merely a sinecurist quartered on it." The conditions justificatory of the existing

[1] *The Man versus the State*, p. 10.

[2] See, for example, Ruskin's criticism of Mill in *Unto this Last* (1860); noble and perverse, sometimes even stupid.

[3] As in the Introduction to Henry Sidgwick's *Principles of Political Economy* (1883). And compare a passage in the *Economist* of May 17, 1873, obviously written by Walter Bagehot: "the writer of these lines has long been in the habit of calling himself the last man of the ante-Mill period....All students since begin with Mill....They see the whole subject with Mill's eyes." Alfred Marshall was working out his principles; the *Economics of Industry*, written in conjunction with Mrs Marshall in 1879, was beginning to tell; his thought was influencing pupils and scholars; but it was hardly yet a force in public affairs during the early 'eighties. See J. M. Keynes' *In Memoriam. Memorials of Alfred Marshall* (1925).

[4] Book II, ch. II, § 6.

form of landed property were "insufficiently realized even in England." In Ireland, with some "very honourable" individual exceptions, they were "not complied with at all." This plain speech about Ireland, and the report of Peel's Commission[1] on Irish land which lay behind it, were the intellectual legacies of the 'forties to the next decades. When in 1870, after many proposals and experiments by others, Gladstone brought in the regulative, but far from revolutionary, Bill which opened the late nineteenth century era in Irish land legislation[2], Mill was with John Bright among the small group of public men who wrote and spoke in favour of buying out the landlords—'converting them into fundholders'—and setting up peasant proprietorship out of hand[3]. As the Abbé Sieyès, also a logical individualist, had said long before, he did not want to abolish property but only to change the proprietors.

In another matter of state which cuts deep into the problems of property and its distribution, the law and taxation of inheritance and bequest, Mill remained to his death in 1873 only the philosopher who raises a standard—a standard to which few men had rallied even a dozen years after he died. For drastic reforms he certainly thought the times were not ripe; nor would be soon. (There had been no killing to ripen them as in Ireland, a cynic might have said.) The right of bequest he held to be a necessary corollary to any right of private property: the state must protect it. But inheritance was another matter. Through all his editions, his standard flew with the legend—"were I framing a code of laws according to what seems to me best in itself, without regard to existing opinion and sentiment, I should prefer to restrict, not what any one might bequeath, but what any one should be permitted to acquire, by bequest or inheritance."[4] He was generous. He was no envious egalitarian. He would permit a man to inherit "the means of a comfortable independence." In all this, whether he realised it or not, he was working tacitly for the

[1] The so-called Devon Commission: *Report of H.M. Commissioners of inquiry into the State and Practice in respect to the occupation of Land in Ireland*: 1845 (XIX–XXII).

[2] It merely confirmed Irish tenant-right customs; asserted that tenants' improvements were tenants' property; and arranged for damages in cases of unfair eviction. See Locker-Lampson, G., *A consideration of the state of Ireland in the Nineteenth Century* (1907), p. 339.

[3] See his *Speeches and Chapters on the Irish Land Question*, 1870.

[4] Book II, ch. II, § 4.

state. What power and knowledge would be required for the efficient administration of such a system? Impossibly great powers, he held, "unless the popular sentiment went energetically along with" the law. Still very great, it might be added, even if popular sentiment did.

Not contemplating a law of this kind as a near possibility, Mill applied the thought underlying his advocacy of it in his theory of taxation. Here he laid down very plainly the route along which the state would in fact travel within twenty-five years of his death. "I conceive that inheritances and legacies, exceeding a certain amount, are highly proper subjects for taxation: and that the revenue from them should be as great as it can be made without giving rise to evasions...such as it would be impossible adequately to check. The principle of graduation (as it is called)...seems to me both just and expedient as applied to legacy and inheritance duties."[1]

Mill never favoured the principle of graduation as applied to property or income taxes, even with a view to "mitigating the inequalities of wealth."[2] Not because he had the least dislike for mitigation of inequality by the state, but because he was always anxious in no way to discourage earning and saving. Therefore, in the state of his dreams, he would concentrate the differential taxation, with its mitigating effects, on inherited wealth. He discussed, very hypothetically and with many reserves, an income-tax not graduated but differentiated—"with one uniform rate for all incomes of inheritance, and another [lower] uniform rate for all those which necessarily terminate with the life of the individual."[3]

In his first edition, he had regarded the impossibility of finding out what people's incomes really were, "in the present low state of public morality," as an "insuperable" objection to any income tax at all. The word "insuperable" vanished from the later editions; yet after his death his authority could still be quoted for the view that "the fairness which belongs to the principle of an income-tax cannot be made to attach to it in practice," and that therefore the tax "should be reserved as an extraordinary resource for great national emergencies, in which the necessity of a large additional revenue overrides all objections"[4]—for war-time in short. Strong and well-informed as the state was growing, he did not anticipate the

[1] Book v, ch. II, § 3.
[2] The same section.
[3] Book v, ch. II, § 4.
[4] Book v, ch. III, § 5.

further growth, nor that parallel growth of wealth held in joint-stock and so taxable at the source, which would make these objections sound oddly antiquated to men of the next generation.

Another fiscal policy which Mill stamped with an economist's approval would also have called for much government activity—the taxation or absorption of future additions to incomes derived from the ownership of land. "This would not properly be taking anything from anybody; it would merely be applying an accession of wealth, created by circumstances, to the benefit of society, instead of allowing it to become an unearned appendage to the riches of a particular class."[1] He broadcast this explosive seed in 1848, and left it to the chances of political weather and soil, thorns and stony ground.

Mill's doctrine of the land, a rigidly Benthamite and Ricardian development, formed the intellectual bridge between the radicalism of the early nineteenth century and the socialisms of the late. He was deeply interested in socialisms[2]. His discussion of some of those of his own day, which after his first edition became more sympathetic while remaining faithfully critical, did not apply to developed doctrines of what came later to be called state socialism; but in his condensed handling of communism he touched on many of the valid general arguments bearing on systems in which "the land and the instruments of production" are to be the property "of communities or associations or of the government." Of these systems he had little economic fear. For the reasons which made men welcome them he had a great sympathy. "If...the choice were to be made between communism with all its chances and the present state of society with all its sufferings and injustices...all the difficulties, great or small, of communism would be but as dust in the balance." But he had humane fear lest "the absolute

[1] Book v, ch. II, § 5.

[2] He has sometimes been criticised for neglect of those early English socialists whose writings have been so much discussed since the publication (in 1899) of Prof. Foxwell's classical Introduction to Menger's *Right to the Whole Produce of Labour*. No doubt there was some neglect; but he only professed to discuss "the most prevailing forms of the doctrine" of socialism. He knew William Thompson, author of *The Distribution of Wealth*, well (*Autobiography*, p. 125), but evidently thought that his doctrine was not "prevailing." Foxwell overlooked this passage in the *Autobiography* when he wrote (*op. cit.* p. lxxviii) that "he [Mill] must have heard of Hodgskin from his father, and of Thompson, with whom he had much in common, from Bentham."

dependence of each on all, and surveillance of each by all," should "grind all down into a tame uniformity of thoughts, feelings, and action," and so intensify a prime and "glaring evil" of existing society, "in which eccentricity is a matter of reproach."[1]

Seeing that the laws of private property had "never yet conformed to the principles on which the justification of private property rests,"[2] there remained much destructive and creative work for the state to do before the ultimate place of property could be determined. From the first, Mill had approached the matter with scientific reserve and complete personal disinterestedness. He felt that an age of experiment lay ahead. "We are too ignorant either of what individual agency in its best form, or socialism in its best form, can accomplish, to be qualified to decide which of the two will be the ultimate form of human society."[3] Had he inserted the words "or what combination of the two," he would have anticipated the essence of all that advocates of the one or the other, when converted by experience to scientific reserve, are saying to this day.

Among the most urgent creative work which, in Mill's opinion, the state still had to do was law-making to encourage the diffusion of property. Hence his support of peasant proprietorship, limited liability, co-operation in all its shapes, more flexible laws of partnership, any and every movement of legal reform which might help to multiply small capitalists. It was when discussing partnership that he stretched out a hand to the industrial socialists and reaffirmed his "conviction, that the industrial economy which divides society absolutely into two portions, the payers of wages and the receivers of them, the first counted by thousands and the last by millions, is neither fit for, nor capable of, indefinite duration."[4] He had not in mind communal or state ownership of the means of production, but a diffusion of property with co-operative ownership. Yet although he had no great faith in the state, and had a horror of the spiritual tyrannies of communism, his influence tended to increase the strength and activity of government in his own generation, and still more in that which followed him. It was vain for Herbert Spencer to decry as inimical to *The Man* that

[1] Book II, ch. I, § 3: the paragraph on communism. The passage "If the choice were to be made" etc. is not in the first edition.

[2] The same section. This passage is in the first edition.

[3] The same section.

[4] Book V, ch. IX, § 5.

institution through whose decisions and legislative experiments alone "the ultimate form of human society" could be determined.

In spite of Mill's many editions, his recognised authority, and his influence on thinkers, there remained down to the 'seventies—and indeed later, as Jevons' forcible repudiation of any absolute political economy shows—a widespread opinion that the science prescribed, as from some pulpit of Mammon, eternal laws of state inaction. While Mill was arguing that the Irish land bill of 1870 was not nearly thorough enough, persons of importance were attacking it as contrary to the laws of political economy; and a disciple of Mill felt himself called to explain at length in an inaugural professorial lecture how "there is no security that the economic phenomena of society, as at present constituted, will always arrange themselves spontaneously in the way which is most for the common good."[1] Emphasis lay on the "as at present constituted." Cairnes was no socialist or paternalist. When in doubt leave things alone, was his maxim. But, like Mill, he was very sure that on a great number of questions there was no doubt. He had made a masterly study of the economics of American slavery[2], and he had taught political economy both in Dublin and in Galway. So anxious was he to dissociate his science from the stupid and interested *laissez-faire* of those in possession, that he claimed for it a complete detachment from particular systems, whether individualist or communist, which many of its early masters would have repudiated: "it stands apart from all...and is absolutely neutral as between them."[3]

Meanwhile another Irishman had started an attack on the whole method of Mill's master Ricardo, and had advertised the discredit into which it was falling among many German scholars[4], while Jevons, in a brilliantly written but conspicuously one-sided book, had suggested a revision of the fundamental economic analysis of value[5]. By the 'eighties, "disputes as to

[1] Cairnes, J. E., "Political Economy and Laissez-faire" (1870), in *Essays in Political Economy* (1873), p. 250–1. Cairnes added "What did we hear during the discussions on the Irish Land Bill? Political Economy again and again appealed to as having pronounced against that measure."

[2] *The Slave Power* (1862).

[3] *Essays*, as above, p. 251.

[4] T. E. Cliffe Leslie, *Essays in Political and Moral Philosophy* (1879). The Essays cover the years 1870–9.

[5] *The Theory of Political Economy* (1871 and 1879): cp. the criticism of Jevons in Keynes, J. M., *Memorials of Alfred Marshall*, p. 23.

particular doctrines" seemed to be broadening into "more fundamental controversy as to the general method of dealing with economic questions."[1] These were controversies of experts. The outer half-informed world, which was slowly learning that economists did not always teach strict *laissez-faire* from a pulpit, was in some danger of beginning to think that they did not know what they taught. When one of them reverted to the strict doctrine, in criticism of Gladstone's Irish Land Bill of 1881, Gladstone, in a phrase that stuck, said that he argued "exactly as if he had been proposing to legislate for the inhabitants of Saturn or Jupiter."[2] The banishment of political economy to Saturn became a catchword. In 1883, another economist set down his impression that the hostility of "influential artisans to the traditional Political Economy" had not diminished; it had "only changed somewhat from sullen distrust to confident contempt."[3] It was in this unfriendly atmosphere that Jevons underlined the scientific and 'each-case-on-its-merits' method of approach to problems of state action—a good method, but one which risks falling behind the act.

As yet the sphere of the state had not been greatly widened. Railway nationalisation had been talked about by a few people and dropped[4]. Land tenure reform in Britain had not got beyond the very modest inroad on the Common Law made by the Act of 1883[5]. Extension of factory and safety laws went on; but no fresh principles were applied. The Poor Law, untouched in all essentials, was being administered during the early 'eighties in as strict and individualistic a spirit as was compatible with its essence of Tudor paternalism. But, whether through indifference or contempt for "the traditional Political Economy," or through perfectly consequent use of the explosive material put into it by Mill, the inhibitions which had surrounded proposals for further state action were breaking down in many active governing minds. "The pet idea" of "the liberalism of to-day," Peel's aged and mighty disciple wrote to his political confessor in 1885, "is what they call

[1] Sidgwick, *Principles*, p. 6. And see Keynes, J. N., *The Scope and Method of Political Economy* (1891).

[2] Hansard, Third Series, CCLX. 895. Debate of April 7: the economist was Professor Bonamy Price.

[3] Sidgwick, *Principles*, p. 6.

[4] Above, p. 189–90.

[5] Above, p. 256.

construction,—that is to say, taking into the hands of the state the business of the individual man."[1] This was when Joseph Chamberlain was advocating peasant proprietorship, the large-scale acquisition of land by local authorities, a graduated income tax, and the break up of great estates; and when Randolph Churchill, from the other side, had already spoken favourably of radical housing reform, "the public wash-houses of Mr Jesse Collings," and the "idea of compulsory national insurance."[2] Mill would have given patient consideration to all these ideas, and resolute support to most of them.

A liberal-minded historian of finance was writing in 1887–8 that "the most striking and most disheartening feature of the last few years" had been "the disastrous expansion of the national expenditure."[3] He was thinking of budgets which dealt with figures in excess of £90,000,000, and of a revenue from taxes in the United Kingdom which had risen sharply from £69,800,000 in 1880–1 to £76,600,000 in 1885–6. There had been little wars in those years; and the warship costing more than £750,000, and now no longer an ironclad, had arrived. Modest as the figures of 1885–6 seem to a later age, the period of a rather rapidly accelerating growth in taxation and expenditure had in fact begun; but only just. The annual average tax revenue of the United Kingdom had grown since the 'forties as follows[4]:

1841–6	£52,100,000	1871–6	£65,300,000
1851–6	£54,400,000	1881–6	£72,900,000
1861–6	£62,900,000		

Compared with the growth between the 'forties and the 'sixties, or with that between the 'sixties and the 'seventies, that in the last decade of the period might well seem disheartening to an economist-politician bred in the school of Gladstone. Gladstone was in power, yet circumstances had been too strong for the man who had never seen the least glint of romance in public expediture.

[1] Gladstone to Lord Acton. Morley: *Gladstone*, III. 173.

[2] Churchill, W. S., *Lord Randolph Churchill*, I. 251. For insurance see below, p. 434.

[3] Buxton, Sydney (Lord Buxton), *Finance and Politics*, II. 319.

[4] These are not the ordinary figures of revenue, but the tax-revenue proper, *i.e.* they omit Post Office receipts, Crown Lands, and certain Miscellaneous receipts. As usually quoted, the figure for 1851–6, for example, would be £56,900,000.

Financially speaking, Gladstone had generally been in power. Of the thirty-six effective budgets following that of 1850 he had himself introduced thirteen; lieutenants in his ministries had introduced eight; and Stafford Northcote, an ex-lieutenant enlisted on the other side but full of respect for the strategy of the old warrior, another seven. Behind the power of Gladstone stood the shadow of the great name of his master Peel. In 1884, Gladstone, aged seventy-five, was combating a financial heresy with memories of the days when he himself, "a Parliamentary youngster," had been "extremely captivated" by it; but Peel "put an extinguisher upon me in half a minute and declared that he would not entertain for an instant a proposition such as this."[1] Argument followed, but first the great name was invoked; and it is hard not to believe that to Gladstone's loyal and reverent mind the invocation was the essential thing. To him the age of Peel was as the age of Homer when heroes fought and ruled. He looked back to it during his last years "with immeasurable yearning."[2]

The heresy concerned the doctrine of the Income Tax. About the history of that tax the financial narrative of the Gladstonian era may most fitly be grouped. For a whole generation after the victory of free trade in 1842–52 customs policy almost ceased to be a matter for discussion. Chancellors showed their skill in the choice of occasions for remission of duties; or by that mastery of their detail, still bewildering down to 1860, of which Gladstone had the secret; or by the economy which made abandonment of lucrative duties possible. When Gladstone's work was complete, the customs schedule was almost as short as the authors of the *Report* of 1840 could have wished[3]. About many forms of internal taxation there was even less difference of opinion than about the customs. Surviving excise and licence duties disappeared with universal approval whenever the chancellors could afford to do without them. Tories and Whigs had cut at the excise between 1823 and 1840. Peel, with the income tax in hand, dropped the glass duty in 1845. The duty on bricks went in 1850; those on soap, dice, and advertisements in 1853; the newspaper tax in 1855; the paper duties, after

[1] See Hubbard, Rt. Hon. J. G., *Gladstone on the Income Tax. Discussion...in the House of Commons on* 25 *April*, 1884, *with preface and historical sketch* (1885).

[2] *The Personal Papers of Lord Rendel* (1931), p. 132.

[3] For the detail of customs reduction see above, p. 219–20, 242 *sqq*. For the *Report* of 1840, vol. I. p. 496.

a famous fight between Gladstone and the Lords, in 1861. By the 'eighties, apart from the liquor excise, only the excise duties on patent medicines, playing cards, and plate remained[1].

So with the licences. The complex licences for 'the trade' necessarily survived. With them survived the licences for makers and sellers of tobacco, because it was taxed, and for dealers in plate and patent medicines, also taxed; for makers of the taxed playing-cards; for various responsible professions, such as solicitors and auctioneers; for game dealers, hawkers, pedlars and pawnbrokers. In a different class were the gun, game, and dog licences. But the licensing of those who sold tea, coffee, cocoa or pepper had been dropped in 1869; of soap-makers, paper-makers, still makers, makers of watch-cases and sellers of playing-cards in 1870; of horse-dealers, with the horse duty, in 1874[2].

On all this there was substantial agreement. Agreement about remission of taxes is easy. But as time went on, continuous remission told in favour of the retention of the debatable income tax. Gladstone was tied throughout to a personal and, as it must seem, somewhat perverse view by his loyalty to Peel, his own early opinions, and the triumphant success of the arguments with which in his first great budget speech of 1853 he had "marked it effectually as a temporary tax."[3] The view, so far as a Gladstonian view can be summarised in few words, was that the tax was unpopular, necessarily unequal in its incidence, very apt to encourage immorality among taxpayers, very useful for raising money in great emergencies, and to be borne by the nation as a sort of penance so long as it went to war or tolerated extravagance. He once told Bright that the income tax even promoted extravagance, because money was so easily raised by it[4]. That was just before he fought the election of 1874 on its abolition[5]. He lost. Ten years later he was

[1] Buxton, *op. cit.* I. 95, 123, 266–8. For the commutation of the malt-tax into a beer-duty in 1880 and the intricate history of the tax, see Buxton, *op. cit.* II. 276 *sqq.*

[2] Buxton, *op. cit.* I. 92, 104, 188; II. 375.

[3] He had criticised Peel's original proposal to revive it: W. E. G. to R. P. November 4, 1841; Parker, *Sir Robert Peel*, II. 502. For the sweeping success of his arguments in 1853 see Northcote, Sir Stafford, *Twenty Years of Financial Policy* (1862), p. 185. The speech was issued as a pamphlet, in which the phrase quoted comes on p. 34.

[4] *The Diaries of John Bright* (1930), p. 269.

[5] He was thinking of abolition so early as August, 1873: Morley's *Gladstone*, II. 478.

'promising a right honourable friend' that 'a sufficient number of years would pass over the heads of Englishmen before they had another opportunity of abolishing it.'[1] They have passed. Had anyone interrupted, 'why did you not get rid of it when they restored you to power in 1880?' who can doubt that he would have countered in stately confidence with some reference to extravagant Disraelian imperialism, and the cost of peace with honour—"peace with honour on tick," as his unstately lieutenant Harcourt put it?

When a revived income tax was discussed in the reign of George IV, no advocate had spoken of it as temporary, though that may have been in some minds[2]. But when Peel begged the gentlemen of England to give him 7*d.* in the £ of all incomes over £150, to help him to wipe out Whig deficits and reform the tariff, he asked for only three years certain, with two more if his work were not done in the three. He got what he asked, in spite of the opposition of John Russell and Richard Cobden[3]. When 1845 came, he had no difficulty in turning the two years into three, in order to make certain of finishing his work. By 1848 his party was broken up; there had been famine in Ireland, panic in London, and revolution abroad. Revenue was coming in so badly that the Whigs asked not for repeal but for 1*s.* in the £ for five years. They got 7*d.* for three. In 1851 and 1852 the tax was renewed for a year only, still on the old basis, and its prospects seemed uncertain[4].

J. R. McCulloch had declared against it in his *Treatise on Taxation* of 1845. Mill's new book had said that the objections to it were "insuperable," because of the low state of public morality. A strong committee, appointed at the instigation of Joseph Hume in 1851 to inquire into *The Present Mode of Assessing and Collecting the Income Tax*, had made no report. It had served only to give limited publicity to a very complex scheme, suggested to Hume by William Farr the statistician, for taxing not income but property, at varying rates according to its value, the nature of its tenure, and the age of its owner[5]. It was the contemplation of such intricacies which made Glad-

[1] In the debate of April, 1884, quoted above.

[2] Vol. I. p. 329 *sqq.*

[3] Parker's *Peel*, II. 524; Morley's *Cobden*, I. 240–3.

[4] Buxton, *op. cit.* I. 91, and see Moneypenny and Buckle's *Disraeli*, III. 361.

[5] The evidence is in *Reports, Committees*, 1852 (IX). Farr's scheme is in App. X and Q. 4853 *sqq.*

stone cling later to a hint from Samuel Gurney—"whatever your plan is, let it be simple."[1] An official who came before the committee had said that evasion would "go on increasing with the existence of the tax";[2] but he had not given very much evidence of fraud. Mill in his evidence had been less gloomy about public morality than in his book, but, in company with other witnesses, had stressed the great defect of the tax—its failure to discriminate between what came eventually to be called earned and unearned incomes[3].

The opinion of the commercial and professional classes was naturally with Mill. They were the more anxious for reform because income tax payers in general were becoming accustomed to think of the tax as a permanent thing—and no wonder, after ten years. There was a section of the middle class, organised in the Liverpool Financial Reform Association, which wished to see the treasury filled entirely through this and other direct channels of taxation. Pamphleteers were saying that Mill's "insuperable" was based on a needlessly gloomy reading of public morality; or that they could not "for a moment conceive that any large proportion of the community" would "consent to annul" a tax which was now bringing in more than a ninth of the public revenue[4]. A representative of the propertied middle class so solid as J. G. Hubbard, the Deputy Governor of the Bank of England, in his *How should Income Tax be levied?* of 1852, had shown no objection to the tax on principle—provided always that there was differentiation between what he called industrial and spontaneous incomes[5]. Hubbard was pertinacious. He was the 'honourable friend' whose case—the same case—Gladstone was overwhelming with precedent and oratory in a thin House thirty-two years later.

Hubbard's pamphlet was supposed by some contemporaries

[1] Morley's *Gladstone*, I. 460–1.

[2] Q. 292: Pressly of the Inland Revenue.

[3] Q. 5222 *sqq.* (Mill); Q. 5448 *sqq.* (Ch. Babbage).

[4] Symons, J., *A scheme for direct taxation for* 1853; Coleman, J., *Some observations on Direct Taxation in reference to Commercial Reform.* For an attack on the Liverpool Association, see Maitland, J. G., F.R.S., *Property and Income Taxes: the Present State of the Question.* Among the other pamphlets of the time are Hemming, G. W., *A just Income Tax how possible*; Major, M. H. C., *A review of the Income Tax...with suggestions for Removal of its Present Inequalities*; *Derecourt on Taxes and Duties*; and cp. Seligman, E. R. A., *The Income Tax* (1911), p. 136 *sqq.*

[5] He also wrote in 1853 *Objections to a Reform of the Income Tax considered, in two letters to...The Times.*

to have inspired the proposal in Disraeli's strangled Budget of December 1852 that business, professional, and farming incomes should pay only three-quarters of the rate to be levied on incomes from realised property[1]. As Disraeli sat on the Committee of 1851–2, there is no need to assume this; though no doubt the support of a conservative Deputy-Governor of the Bank was welcome. Nor need one endorse Gladstone's view that Disraeli's proposal was "flagrantly vicious."[2] Possibly, as Gladstone used to say, it was made "without any communication with the Revenue departments";[3] but Disraeli had before him their official evidence, so that is immaterial. Differentiation would no doubt have been hard to arrange, with the administrative experience then available; but if incomes could be differentiated according to their size—and Gladstone himself in the next year taxed those above £150 at one rate and those between £100 and £150 at another—it should not have been impossible to differentiate according to source, had it been thought desirable.

Gladstone's Budget speech of 1853, which "changed the convictions of a large part of the nation on the income tax,"[4] diverted liberal opinion from the policy of differentiation, and determined the form of the tax for the next half century, seems less convincing to-day than it did to contemporaries. He set himself to prove that landed incomes did in fact, as things worked out, pay the equivalent of a higher rate than many other incomes, because they were taxed gross and were encumbered with mortgages, annuities, and jointures. He made play with the fact that traders 'assessed themselves.' He objected strongly to any differential taxation of incomes from the funds, on the curious ground that, because much of the national debt had been raised with promises that its income yield should not be taxed, it would be a breach of public faith to tax that yield differentially; though it was no breach merely to tax it, provided you taxed all other incomes just the same[5]. He used the old 'inquisitorial' argument, which had carried so much weight with Adam Smith, against the inquiries which differentiation

[1] The *Economist*, December 18, 1852. See Buckle's *Disraeli*, III. 425, 431.

[2] Morley's *Gladstone*, I. 436. From one of W. E. G.'s fragmentary notes.

[3] From the speech of 1884.

[4] Northcote, *Twenty Years of Financial Policy*, p. 185. "When I became Chancellor...an immense majority would have voted for the plan of differentiating the income tax," Gladstone in 1884.

[5] The same point is made more fully in the speech of 1884.

would involve. He had no difficulty in showing how insensibly one type of income merges in another, and what varying combinations of interest on fixed capital, akin to land, with earnings of management were to be found in Hubbard's 'industrial' incomes[1]. He used Gurney's excellent practical plea for simplicity. He begged the House not to 'break up' a tax which was a working engine for emergencies. To avoid all uncertainty, he asked it to vote this bad useful tax for seven years at dwindling rates, while commercial reform went forward. At a known and anticipated time, the nation might, if it chose, see the last of it.

War came next year to spoil his plan. He doubled the income tax. When he returned to the Exchequer to foot other men's bills, in 1859, he raised the tax automatically from the uniform 5*d.* to which it had fallen to 6½*d.* or 9*d.*, according to the size of the taxed income, getting about a seventh of his tax receipts from this source[2]. The income tax was degenerating into a chancellor's umbrella, to be put up or down according to the signs of the financial skies.

In 1861, over Gladstone's resolute opposition and by a majority of only four, Hubbard secured a Committee to inquire into its *Mode of Assessment and Collection*[3]. The Committee, if not packed, was heavily weighted with Hubbard's critics—Gladstone, Northcote, Lowe—and was given no assistance by the government[4]. The evidence of the Inland Revenue officials examined was hostile to reform, but hardly conclusive: they were "in terror of their master's wrath," Hubbard wrote long after[5]. There was naturally much business and professional evidence in favour of differentiation; and there was no decisive evidence against Hubbard's other main proposal, to tax net rather than gross income. Mill, warmer than in 1851, sparred cleverly with Lowe in support of Hubbard. Lowe sneered at "this income tax," and made lawyers' points about life tenants of settled property. Mill retorted that such people had no obligation to save like ordinary recipients of life incomes[6].

[1] He asked how profits from Barclay and Perkins' brewery, or the income of Miss Coutts from the bank, could claim to be not what Hubbard called 'spontaneous' incomes.

[2] Buxton, *op. cit.* I. 188.

[3] *Reports, Committees* 1861 (III. 1).

[4] Hubbard's pamphlet of 1885 (quoted p. 398 above), Preface, p. 6.

[5] *Ibid.* p. 7.

[6] Mill's evidence, Q. 3538 *sqq.*

Newmarch the statistician was on Mill's side, and Farr, while not abandoning his intricate programme for the taxation of property, "certainly" preferred Hubbard's plan to the existing system[1]. The plan, put into a draft report, was then voted down; and the Committee reported that it was "brought to the conclusion that the objections which are urged against it [the tax], are objections to its nature and essence rather than to the particular shape which has been given to it."[2] But the Chancellors and the future Chancellors who formed the majority went on using it. There was never another inquiry, official or unofficial[3].

Gladstone's proposed abolition in 1874 seems uncommonly inopportune in retrospect. The boom was just over. The great price-fall had begun. That empire had come into being which taught men the value of new and costly weapons. But these things were hidden in August, 1873, when he made his plan. It was not the shameless electoral bribe that his enemies said. In view of his record, failure to make it, in some season of fair weather, would have been greatly to his discredit. The weather seemed fair, and the other side had dallied with repeal. Northcote, when he reached the exchequer, gave the country two years of a twopenny income tax—keeping the machine mounted for emergencies but running it at an uneconomically low pressure. The emergencies soon came, and with Gladstone back in power the machine was driven harder than ever. By 1885–6 an eightpenny income tax was bringing in nearly a fifth of the tax revenue.

Gladstone never discussed the tax at length as part of a system planned with an eye to exact distributive justice. His view of taxation was simple—a necessary evil, to be reduced to the practicable minimum. In his old age he rejoiced that his strength had been spent in pulling things down, in "opening doors and windows," not in doubtful construction[4]. But, had he ever been able to get rid of the income tax, he would not have relieved property of that small contribution to the needs of the state which was all that he ever wished any 'interest,' or section of the community, to make. In 1853 he had explained

[1] Newmarch, Q. 326 *sqq.*; Farr, Q. 2713.

[2] *Report*, p. iv.

[3] "It is probable that, during his [Gladstone's] time, his influence on financial opinion will be sufficient to prevent any further examination into the merits of the case, or any attempt to establish the tax on a broader foundation and a juster basis." Buxton, *op. cit.* I. 113 (1887–8).

[4] *The Personal Papers of Lord Rendel*, p. 95.

that the alternative to an income tax was a combination of some tax on "visible property" with increased legacy duties and a licence duty for all traders, instead of only for some. If he had been successful in 1874, the death duties would have been "reconstructed and enlarged."[1] For this he himself had prepared the way when, in 1853, he added to the small old probate duty, and to Pitt's legacy duty on successions to personal property, that parallel duty on successions to real property which Pitt would also have imposed, had not Fox and the landed interest thwarted him[2]. It was the first new tax levied since Waterloo and it proved not very lucrative. The three 'death duties' together yielded about £3,000,000 a year in the 'fifties.

Thirty years later they were substantially unaltered, though improved in various details, especially by Gladstone himself in 1880 and 1881. By 1886, with the growth of national wealth, they produced all together upwards of £7,000,000. Of this sum £4,000,000 came from the probate duty, the most universal of the three. It was derived from £140,500,000 worth of property passing at death. So lightly did the state press on inheritance. It had not yet listened to Mill, though disciples of his would soon gain its ear.

Customs and excise had provided about two-thirds of the tax revenue in the 'fifties: concentrated on a handful of semi-luxuries, they still provided more than a half. 'Stamps'—which included the death-duties, paid by stamp—had then brought in not quite one-eighth: now they brought in rather more than an eighth. Those taxes on comfortable people's surpluses which the income tax had in part replaced—the house duty, the remnants of the old land tax, and the 'assessed' taxes on certain luxuries—had produced about a twentieth (some £3,000,000) in the 'fifties. House and land tax now produced just over a thirtieth[3]. An income tax at 8*d*., as levied in 1885 and 1886, ranked almost with the customs as a revenue yielder,

[1] Gladstone, in the *Nineteenth Century*, June, 1887; an article quoted in Buxton, *op. cit.* II. 167.

[2] Pitt's original proposal applied only to collateral successions. In 1805 he extended the legacy duty to bequests payable out of, or charged on, real estate; Buxton, *op. cit.* I. 118. And see Morley's *Gladstone*, I. 463.

[3] The Land Tax, fixed and made redeemable by Pitt in 1798, had been redeemed unequally in different districts. Where it survived it affected the selling value of land. It was of no importance in nineteenth century fiscal history, though in the 'eighties it still yielded over £1,000,000.

producing £15,600,000 to their £20,000,000, out of a tax revenue of rather more than £80,000,000.

That national debt should be reduced systematically was an axiom both of Gladstone's and of Mill's political economy. But they also agreed that it was better to remove bad taxes, so setting free productive powers, than to hurry forward the reduction of debt[1]. The debt as Gladstone found it was nearly all in 3 per cents., the loans of higher denomination having been converted by Robinson, Althorp and Goulburn between 1824 and 1844. There had been both capital reductions and capital additions since the 'twenties[2]; additions for freeing the slaves, feeding Ireland, and helping West Indian planters; reductions from tax surpluses and the falling-in of annuities. As a result, the total capital amount of the debt was not very much less than it had been when Sir Henry Parnell drew up his programme for liberal financial reform in 1828–30. Funded and unfunded debt together were put at £808,000,000 for the year 1828. For 1850, the corresponding figure was £787,000,000, and for 1852, £779,000,000. The 3 per cents. had risen to par in 1852; they had only touched it once before since 1755. They held about par until the middle of 1853, but never saw it again until the 'eighties.

Gladstone had tried to snatch the moment for another conversion. He was too late. His complex scheme for creating a fair sized block of 2½ per cents. was explained on April 8, 1853. The French Toulon fleet was then at Salamis, and Stratford Canning had reached Constantinople three days earlier to play his strong lone hand[3]. Only a tiny block of 2½ per cents. resulted. Those 3 per cent. stockholders who had declined the treasury offer, and were to be paid off at par, got their cash in January, 1854, when the 3 per cents. were dropping towards 90 and the money was wanted for a probable Russian war. War added to the debt some £36,000,000—the cash price of a squadron of twentieth century battleships—and no more conversions were attempted until 1888[4].

[1] Mill, *Principles*, Book v, ch. vii, § 3.

[2] See vol. I. p. 318–19. The debt figure given there (£780,000,000) is the funded debt only. It is a round figure because the exact calculation of the burden of the annuities is difficult. See Buxton, *op. cit.* II. 203.

[3] *Camb. Hist. of British Foreign Policy*, II. 364–5.

[4] The story of the conversion is in Buxton, *op. cit.* I. 127–9.

The 'sixties saw a brief debt panic. In 1865 Jevons had argued that British coal was giving out. Mill had concluded that therefore the existing generation and its immediate successors were "the only ones which will have the smallest chance of ever being able to pay off" the National Debt[1]. So Gladstone put aside an extra half-million a year, whereby the debt might be paid off in 250 years, if there were no more wars; and Disraeli also did a little. In 1875 Northcote did something more systematic, in the creation of the new sinking fund. The annual debt-charge was to be raised, and reduction of debt out of realised income to go on more regularly and faster. Wars and other emergencies came to derange the programme, but the principle was maintained. Payments to the debt-charge in 1885–6 were almost as great as they had been thirty years earlier, just after the Crimean War[2]. At the close of the financial year 1885–6 the total liability, comparable with the £779,000,000 of 1852 and the £808,000,000 of 1856, was £742,000,000, against which might now be set such tangible assets as the telegraph system, probably overvalued however[3], and Disraeli's appreciating Suez Canal shares. The achievement was not heroic in a richening country; but growing riches made the fallen liability very easy to bear; and there was a good deal of coal in hand, though Mill was not yet proved a false prophet.

Outside the sphere of taxation, the state of the 'fifties was still using some of its strength in that breaking down of barriers which gave Gladstone so much healthy pleasure. The last scrap of the navigation laws, the monopoly of the coasting trade, was cleared away in 1854 (by 17 and 18 Vict. c. 21). With it (by 17 and 18 Vict. c. 90) went the shrivelled body of the ancient usury law. Systematic evasion had long since robbed it of vigour. Even in Queen Anne's day it had not been allowed to interfere with "parliamentary securities."[4] In 1833 the Bank of England had been empowered to disregard the legal rate of 5 per cent. in the short money market, and had done so for the first time during the commercial difficulties of 1839[5]. The crisis

[1] Hansard, Third Series, CLXXXII, 1525. Mill's speech of 17th April, 1866, referring to Jevons.

[2] In 1885–6, £28,000,000: in 1858–9, £28,400,000.

[3] Above, p. 209 n. 4.

[4] See 12 Anne, St. 2, c. 16, *An Act to reduce the Rate of Interest* [*i.e.* the rate more than which it was usury to charge] *without any Prejudice to Parliamentary Securities.*

[5] Vol. I. p. 518; and see p. 347–9, 509.

of 1847 had finally proved the usefulness of a flexible bank-rate. So, by permission and evasion, the money market was freed. In practice, the usury laws served only to interfere with mortgage operations, when the mortgage could not be arranged on a 5 per cent. basis, and occasionally to make a railway company in difficulties issue 5 per cent. debentures below par, because it might not create $5\frac{1}{2}$ per cents.[1] The law had been "practically swept away in all cases except where real security was given,"[2] as Campbell said in the Lords; and even the sphere of real property had been invaded; for usury, *i.e.* interest beyond 5 per cent., was already sanctioned for the convenience of building societies.

The repealing bill was introduced, very appropriately, by Gladstone as Chancellor of the Exchequer and James Wilson, founder of the *Economist*, as Financial Secretary to the Treasury. There was really no debate in the Commons; though one member thought fit to make a bad point against Peel's Bank Act by arguing that if the law restricted the creation of bank money it ought also to restrict interest. In the Lords, the bill was managed by Lansdowne, who quoted John Calvin's critique of usury doctrine. It was blessed by three Lord Chancellors present, past, and future[3]. It repealed Acts, and parts of Acts, stretching back for England to Henry VIII; for Scotland to James VI; and for Ireland to Charles I.

By an odd accident, the state, again working through Gladstone, had revived in 1843 a quaint, exceptional bit of labour legislation which only expired in 1856—the law regulating working conditions among the coal-whippers of London Pool. 'Whipping' was the job of filling and hoisting baskets of coal from the hold and emptying them into barges. In 1831 the Thames coal-code of 1807 had been repealed[4]; and the statutory control of whippers' wages, which had led to notorious abuses, lapsed. But in 1843 joint action by the City Corporation and the coal-whippers had produced a private bill which Gladstone took over, for the registration and employment of the whippers under commissioners. Its excellent intention was, in modern terms, to decasualise the work and secure jobs for gangs of registered whippers in regular rotation. The men, some em-

[1] See Gladstone's speech in the Commons, Hansard, Third Series, CXXIV. 929.
[2] Hansard, Third Series, CXXV. 581.
[3] *Ibid.*
[4] The code described in vol. I. p. 234–5.

ployers, and the clerk of the Thames Police Court believed that it succeeded. Renewed several times, in 1851 after full inquiry, it was allowed to expire in 1856, on the ground that it had done its work in delivering the men from "a state of squalid poverty."[1] Shipowners had bargained for its expiry by promising to start an office of their own and never to hire men or pay wages in public-houses. With this the Board of Trade was content. The question was never reopened, because the old-style whippers were passing away.

The connection of the coal-whippers with London and tide-water helps to explain this long-lived regulation. Parliament never controlled the loading of colliers at Whitehaven or the unloading of railway trucks. But the Thames flows by Westminster, and seamen, in one way or another, had always been a concern of the state. Navigation laws were but recently repealed. With them had gone laws, and clauses, requiring shipowners to adjust the numbers of seamen and apprentices to tonnage: as a result, the 31,636 enrolled apprentices of 1850 had fallen to 13,826 by 1854[2]. But, while abandoning this type of regulation, the state had been acquiring a new solicitude for the welfare of the seaman and of the traveller by sea, shown in a series of Passenger Acts, Merchant Seamen's Acts and Steam Navigation Acts, and embodied in the great consolidating Merchant Shipping Act of 1854 (17 and 18 Vict. c. 18), a code of two hundred pages[3].

All seagoing ships must have an appropriate equipment of boats and life-buoys. Seagoing steamers must have safety-valves to their engines; they must carry fire-hoses; when built of iron they must have watertight compartments; they must provide shelter against the weather for deck-passengers. The right of inspecting steamers lay with the growing marine department of the Board of Trade. For the general supervision of maritime affairs, an Act of 1850 (13 and 14 Vict. c. 93)[4] had

[1] See George, M. D., "The London Coal Heavers," *E.J.* (*Ec. Hist.*), 1927, p. 244. This paragraph is based on Mrs George's article.

[2] From a return quoted in the House by Cardwell, May 18, 1854. Hansard, Third Series, CXXXIII. 571.

[3] The early Passenger Acts are 43 Geo. III, c. 56; 9 Geo. IV, c. 21; 5 and 6 Vict. c. 107 (see Walpole, K. A., in *T.R.H.S.*, 1932: cp. p. 232 n. 2, above). The early Merchant Seamen's Acts are 7 and 8 Vict. c. 112 and 8 and 9 Vict. c. 116. The Steam Navigation Acts are 9 and 10 Vict. c. 100; 11 and 12 Vict. c. 81 and 14 and 15 Vict. c. 79.

[4] The Mercantile Marine Act.

called into being elective Local Marine Boards in all active ports, to co-operate with the Board of Trade.

Beyond the safety clauses, the consolidating law, which repealed forty previous Acts, contained sections dealing with these marine boards; with shipowners' liability, wrecks, salvage, lighthouses, pilotage, registration and tonnage; with the keeping of logs; with boats, lights, crimes and deaths at sea; with marine store dealers, and with the rights, obligations and welfare of seamen. The marine store dealers' sections (§ 480 *sqq.*) are curiously out of keeping with the reputed spirit of the age. Among various burdens laid on those who dealt in "anchors, cables, sails, or old junk, old iron, or marine stores of any description," was an obligation not to "purchase marine stores from any person apparently under the age of sixteen years." No doubt the clause was aimed at pilfering by ships' boys; but that does not make it less paternal or, with its "apparently," more easy to administer.

From the seamen's acts of the 'forties the law of 1854 took over the 'lime-juice clauses' and, in general, the attempt to provide a minimum of medical comfort and enough breathing space in the fo'castle. It carefully regulated apprenticeship, now become voluntary. It contained a whole wage-paying code, but no wage regulation. And it made premature solicitation of seamen by lodging-house keepers illegal. While leaving carefully untouched the central economic problems of value and the balancing of the factors of production, capital in ships and seamen's labour, the law had finally added a whole new province to the territory of the state.

It was a province difficult to administer, because the necessary disciplinary powers of shipowners and shipmasters, and the loneliness of the high seas, could often cover offenders' tracks[1]. In 1867 the 'lime-juice' and seamen's accommodation clauses of the Act of 1854 were improved, and the seaman was given a claim—obviously not easy to enforce—for wages during any period in which he was sick owing to the master's or owners' neglect to supply him with proper food and medicine[2]. In the early 'seventies there was a Merchant Shipping Act every other

[1] See, *e.g.*, the evidence given before the *S.C. on the Merchant Seamen Bill*, 1878 (XVI. 77).

[2] The Act is 30 and 31 Vict. c. 124. Up to this time the 'lime-juice clauses' had not been successful: there was still much scurvy. Simon, Sir J., *English Sanitary Institutions*, 2nd ed. 1897, p. 301–2.

year[1]. The seaman's friends in parliament were fighting those who made profitable capital of coffin ships, or risked men's lives by overloading. The last of the series was the Act of 1876 (39 and 40 Vict. c. 80) which at last declared the sending of an unseaworthy ship to sea a misdemeanour; regulated the stowage of grain and deck cargoes; and introduced the load line named after Samuel Plimsoll, once secretary of the Great Exhibition and from 1868 to 1880 radical member for Derby, who more than any one was responsible for the shipping legislation of these years[2]. When Plimsoll left parliament there came a halt in protective lawmaking for seamen, though the principles of the existing law of wages, apprenticeship, and certification of masters were extended to the English fisheries in 1883[3]. The Scottish fisheries had their own law and their old-established Board. It was in their interest that an Act of parliament of 1884–5, not applicable to England, dealt in its ninth clause with the construction and hooping of herring barrels[4].

John Bright had called the Ten Hours Bill of 1847 "a delusion practised on the working classes," which at "no distant day" would have to be repealed, because wages would fall[5]. In 1855 Harriet Martineau was foretelling that, if employers had to fence machinery thoroughly and carry the burden of mill accidents, they would "retire from occupations so intolerably burdensome."[6] But Queen Victoria's acceptance of a gold medal from the operatives at the hands of Lord Ashley, when the Ten Hours Act came into force in 1848, symbolised the state's definite approval of the policy[7]. Flouting Bright and Miss Martineau, not only real wages but even cash wages rose[8],

[1] In 1871, 1873 and 1875; 34 and 35 Vict. c. 110; 36 and 37 Vict. c. 85; 38 and 39 Vict. c. 88.

[2] Plimsoll lived till 1898. See the *D.N.B.* and his retrospective evidence before the *Labour Commission, Sec. B* (1892, XXXVI. part 2), Q. 11,244 *sqq.*

[3] By 46 and 47 Vict. *An Act to amend the Merchant Shipping Acts*, 1854–80, *with respect to fishing vessels and apprenticeship to...fishing...and otherwise.*

[4] 48 and 49 Vict. c. 70.

[5] Speech of February 17, 1847. Hansard, Third Series, LXXXIX. 1136.

[6] *The Factory Controversy. A Warning*, p. 41. This was when the Factory Law Amendment Association was compaigning against the Law and against Horner the Inspector. Hutchins and Harrison, *A History of Factory Legislation*, p. 113–16.

[7] 'Alfred's' *History of the Factory Movement*, II. 285.

[8] As Bright argued, owing to Corn Law Repeal. Trevelyan, G. M., *The Life of John Bright*, p. 158.

and the cotton mills of the later 'fifties were thought to be in danger of outrunning the supplies of cotton. The Ten Hours Act had soon required amendment, but was never repealed[1]. It had been evaded by a system of relay working, until the supplementary and perhaps more important Act of 1850 (13 and 14 Vict. c. 54) ordered that women and young persons should work only between 6.0 a.m. and 6.0 p.m. or between 7.0 a.m. and 7.0 p.m., with an hour and a half for meals, and should cease work at 2.0 p.m. on Saturdays. By an odd anomaly, the Act did not apply to children, and so had to be supplemented in 1853. Yet it established *la semaine anglaise* by law[2], and gave the short time committees of the North the basis for that general limitation of hours which they had always desired; although J. M. Cobbett's attempt to clinch the matter for them with a Bill which required the factory engines to stop between 5.30 p.m. and 6.0 a.m. failed[3].

The textile manufacturers' old and not altogether unfair grievance, that they were pilloried beyond their deserts, and singled out among manufacturers to be dragooned by masterful Inspectors like Leonard Horner, remained unabated until 1860. In 1847 Mark Phillips of Manchester had asked, as many had asked before and since, why there should be this indirect limitation of adult labour in one field only; and John Bright, referring to what to-day would be called welfare work in his own mills, had suggested that the law, by treating the master as the natural enemy of the operatives, would embitter industrial relations and spoil such work[4]. The manufacturers in the 'fifties had their Factory Amendment Law Association, which achieved something against Leonard Horner, their chosen enemy among Factory Inspectors. But the delayed and partial answer of the state to Mark Phillips' question came in 1860 and 1861, not in the form which they desired, but in the form of Acts "to place the employment of Women, Young Persons, and Children in Bleaching and Dyeing Works," and "Women, Young Persons, Youths and Children in Lace Factories under the Regulations of the Factories Acts."[5]

It was not suggested by reformers that these industries were

[1] Or rather was only repealed to be strengthened, in 1874, by 37 and 38 Vict. c. 44.

[2] See below, p. 448.

[3] In 1853. Hutchins and Harrison, *op. cit.* p. 110.

[4] Hansard, Third Series, LXXXIX. 1083, 1136.

[5] The Acts are 23 and 24 Vict. c. 78 and 24 and 25 Vict. c. 117.

particularly harmful, though all had their abuses: they were simply those nearest to the textile industries proper, the territory easiest to occupy. By infection from their neighbours, they had often already acquired factory habits. Dewhurst's of Salford, dyers and finishers, a firm "among the largest in the trade," was working factory hours, and rarely overtime, in 1854–5[1]. The rush of the finishing business, when merchants were hurrying to ship, did however mean spells of overtime throughout the trade. But the works did not employ an abnormal proportion of women and children. They were manned by "a very respectable class of work-people,"[2] who made good money. Employers, especially the larger bleachers and dyers, were not as a body hostile to the prospect of regulation. They justified their occasional long hours by explaining the cause, and by pointing out that the pace of work was not set by machinery; that there was a good deal of "stand off" in the course of the day; and that the workpeople were unusually healthy, especially the bleachers. The facts were not disputed; but logic and geography were against one set of living rules for spinners and weavers and a different set for bleachers and dyers. Hence 23 and 24 Vict. c. 78 of the year 1860. It was in the debates on this Bill that Sir James Graham, an upright embodiment of the Peel tradition and the mid-Victorian state, announced his conversion to 'factory principles.'[3]

In 1860 lace had just ripened for the control which this standard statesman was now ready to apply. When the Children's Commission had inquired in the 'forties, more than half the lace machines were worked by hand and in private houses. Besides, there was the true hand-made lace. Factories were not dominant and so the industry was reckoned unfit for regulation. This obstacle, Tremenheere reported in 1861, "may now be said to have ceased." Machine-made lace had become a factory product. Of 3000–4000 machines, "not more than ninety," and they old-fashioned, were "worked by hand in private houses."[4] So, with some unimportant adjustments, the textile code for 'protected persons' might be applied to the trade; and it was.

[1] *Report of the Commissioner appointed to inquire how far it may be advisable to extend* [the Factory Acts] *to bleaching works* 1854–5 (XVIII. 1), p. xvii.

[2] *Ibid.* p. vii.

[3] On May 9, 1860. Hansard, Third Series, CLVIII. 984.

[4] *Report on the expediency of subjecting the Lace Manufacture to the...Factory Acts*, 1861 (XXII. 461), p. 6.

By this time many reformers were dominated less by the particular evils of child labour than by its general interference with education. The educational aspect is prominent in the series of reports on children in "trades and manufactures not already regulated by law" which the Commissioners of the 'sixties issued between 1863 and 1867[1]. Just as prominent is the continued use of even the youngest children, for labour "in private houses" in the most insanitary conditions, and in the fields, wherever they were good for it. The unregulated sections of the lace manufacture yielded ugly evidence. So did hosiery and straw plaiting and other light trades. The common age at which to begin the work of seaming knitted gloves was five: a witness had seen "many as young as" three and a half[2]. Four years old was a usual, three and a half or three a not uncommon, age for entering the straw plaiting 'schools.' Things were much the same in pillow lace 'schools,'[3] and not very different in the horribly overcrowded 'mistresses' rooms' in which machine-made lace was finished[4]. As jobs got heavier, the demand for very young children to do them slackened. In the Birmingham trades, although work sometimes began at seven years old, nine or ten was much more general[5].

The fact that a child started to earn relatively late was no safeguard against ignorance, overwork, degrading conditions or excessive hours. There were the wretched little mould runners of the Potteries, hurrying with their loads for twelve hours a day in and out of temperatures of 100 to 120 degrees—a fire and ice purgatory in winter time; the child nailers in their "private houses"; the savage children of the brick-fields; the chain-smiths' boys distorted by wielding hammers too heavy for their strength. It was among the Midland metal-workers and at Sheffield that the Commissioners, their minds running on education, put questions to which were given such answers as these—"a King is him that has all the money and gold";[6] "the devil is a good person; I don't know where he lives"; "all go in the pithole, when them be buried; they never get out or live again."[7]

State control in the Potteries, in the Birmingham area, in

[1] Usually quoted as the Children's Employment Commission. The Reports are in 1863, XVIII; 1864, XXII; 1865, XX; 1866, XXIV; 1867 (agriculture), XVI.

[2] *Second Report*, 1864, p. xxxvi.

[3] *Ibid.* p. xxxix.

[4] *First Report*, 1863, p. 184.

[5] *Third Report*, 1864, p. x.

[6] *Fourth Report*, 1865, p. xv.

[7] *Third Report*, p. xvii.

the metallurgical trades wherever found, except the more modern branches of engineering, and at many other points on the industrial field, was made difficult by the prevalence of child-hiring, not by the firm but by the workman[1]. Dish, saucer, and plate makers hired the mould runners. The masters said they could not "correct it—without incurring the risk of exciting tumult."[2] In the Birmingham trades, most of the children and many 'young persons' were hired "by the adult piece-worker."[3] In iron-works, puddlers, shinglers, and forgers took on the lads. In the chain and nail and lock and saddlers' ironmongery trades, boys were rarely hired by the firm; "never in small works."[4] "We employ the anchor-smiths and they employ a mob or gang"[5] is a typical bit of evidence. Boiler-rivetters did the same in Lancashire. And at Sheffield "the workers even in factories keep much of the old independence of their masters, in fact, are more in the position of small masters themselves."[6] So the Sheffield men always had been, and would remain.

Yet there was legislation while the Commissioners' reports were coming in. The first report made plain that the old laws protecting climbing boys were inoperative in most places, "the metropolis and some other towns excepted."[7] Many pitiful cases came to light of children killed while climbing. There was a slave-trade in boys. "In Liverpool," said a master sweep, "where there are lots of bad women you can get any quantity you want."[8] On that report Charles Kingsley wrote his *Water Babies*, and left Mr Grimes the sweep eternally stuck in a chimney. Parliament at once accepted a restraining Bill of Lord Shaftesbury's (27 and 28 Vict. c. 37); but two years later the fifth report showed that the restraint was ineffective. It estimated the sooty and sore army of the climbing boys at two thousand[9]. Even in 1875, after yet another law, a working sweep believed that "there is plenty of boys climbing in large towns."[10] By a second Act of 1864 (27 and 28 Vict. c. 48) the six trades first reported on, which included the deadly lucifer match making, had been put under factory law. As one of them, fustian cutting, was not a mill industry, the term factory was defined

[1] Cp. above, p. 128. [2] *First Report*, p. xxviii. [3] *Third Report*, p. xi.
[4] *Ibid.* p. 12. [5] *Ibid.* p. 19. [6] *Fourth Report*, p. 2.
[7] *First Report*, p. lxxxiii. See vol. I. p. 577–8.
[8] *Ibid.* p. lxxxviii. [9] *Fifth Report*, p. xxi.
[10] *R.C. on the Working of the Factory and Workshop Acts*, 1876, XXIX. App. D, p. 149.

in relation to the six trades as "any place in which persons work for hire."[1] No objection was made to this novel definition. The *Economist*, which in 1847 had compared the Factory Acts to the Corn Laws, was writing that no one who knew how they had "worked in Lancashire and Yorkshire had any doubt *now* of the wisdom of those measures." Its sole concession to former principles was that it called them "the Children's Factories Acts";[2] which they were not.

The way was clear for that general widening of the law which the Commissioners desired. It was made by the intricate Act of 1867 (30 and 31 Vict. c. 103) which put a very long list of named industries, together with any place in which fifty or more persons were employed in any manufacturing process, under the factory code and the Home Office Inspectors—with a large number of exceptions and reservations, and some special prohibitions of women's or children's labour in dangerous processes, such as glass-melting and metal-grinding[3].

With the Factory Act was associated a Workshop Act (30 and 31 Vict. c. 146) covering all children, young persons, and women engaged in handicraft, "with or without wages," in "any room or place whatever" in which the employer had "the right of access or control." Thus it covered an employer's family but not his outworkers. Hours were made more elastic than in the factories; control and inspection were entrusted to the local sanitary authorities. The Act was vague and only permissive. The local authorities were supine, in country districts generally, but also in many towns. The task laid on them was heavy, but often it was not even faced. Three years later, in the area of one chief factory inspector, out of 352 authorities reported on, 172 had taken no steps whatever to enforce the law and only 110 had arranged for frequent visitation of workshops[4]. To correct these omissions, the inspection, but not the sanitary control, of workshops was transferred in 1871 to the Home Office staff, who thus became the too busy overseers of some 110,000, instead of only 30,000, work-places of all sorts and sizes[5].

When they were grappling with this heavy duty, Forster's

[1] A discussion of this is in Hutchins and Harrison, *op. cit.* p. 155.

[2] *Economist*, May 21, 1864.

[3] It has been held that the exceptions and reservations "nullified half the good the regulation might have done." Hutchins and Harrison, *op. cit.* p. 169.

[4] *Workshops Act, return on the enforcement*, 1870, LIV. 555.

[5] Hutchins and Harrison, *op. cit.* p. 230–1.

Education Act of 1870, with the corresponding Scottish Act of 1872, was applying the only general cure for child labour, direct compulsion to attend school. Meanwhile the textile unions of the North were working behind the women's petticoats for a 54-hour week: they got 56½ hours in 1874. The last of the doctrinaires were arguing that the law should not touch the liberty of adults, even of adults in petticoats. Advocates of woman's right to compete with the uncontrolled adult male supported them. Like the *Economist* of the 'sixties, they thought in terms of Children's Factory Acts. But their parliamentary leader, Henry Fawcett, Professor of Political Economy in the University of Cambridge, was well beaten when he moved "to omit the word woman" from the textile factory bill of 1874. The law was barely deflected by their efforts from a course long since set[1].

This was important, because in 1878 factory law was consolidated into a single great Factories and Workshops Act (41 and 42 Vict. c. 17)[2]. The work had been prepared by a commission appointed in 1875. Its evidence and reports are full of administrative problems, and only touch here and there on such gross abuses as fill the pages of earlier inquiries. The worst of these had at least been scotched; and "direct compulsion" to schooling, "accepted...with surprisingly little opposition," had "already produced satisfactory results."[3] The slight deflection of the law concerned grown women, as Fawcett and his supporters wished. The amendment "to omit the word woman" was, it is true, beaten on clause after clause. But the commissioners had suggested that at one point existing law might be reversed: under it, all dwelling-houses where women and children followed handicrafts were liable to inspection. They thought that by including women at this point the law went too far. The reversal was effected by a clause in the Act exempting from inspection workshops "conducted on the system of not employing children and young persons"—to the benefit of woman-driving laundry-men and milliners.

The essentials of the law, which now covered nearly all the 'in-working' manufactures of the country, had not been greatly changed since they had been worked out for the textile mills

[1] This episode is fully described in Hutchins and Harrison, *op. cit.* ch. IX.

[2] It repealed nineteen Acts, or parts of Acts, back to Peel's *Health and Morals of Apprentices Act* of 1802.

[3] *Report*, p. lvi.

in the 'thirties. Brief general statements about sanitation and safety leave room for the improved level of both towards which the inspectorate had been working. The standard day contains 10 hours work; Saturday 6½ hours. In most industries this standard day must fall between 6.0 a.m. and 6.0 p.m., or between 7.0 a.m. and 7.0 p.m. A child is anyone under 14, a young person any one under 18. A child between 10 and 14 when at work must be a 'half-timer,' a type which a generation of lawmaking had defined[1]. But the employer's obligation to see that factory children receive half-time education is retained "as a privilege, not imposed as a burden."[2] (The country had set its heart on education for all: the privilege would be continuously challenged.) From a few occupations women and children remain excluded[3]; but the list is not increased. They are excluded also from nightwork, except some 'male young persons' in metallurgy. Besides the group of women put outside the law, women and children employed in their own homes are also excluded, if no power is used and no hired persons found there. Such people had not been excluded under the Act of 1867. Outworkers proper all remain outlaws.

After 1878 the state, thinking that its work was good, rested from this sort of law-making for five years. There had not been so long a pause since 1844. A law of 1883 which ended it belongs to the old series. A fresh series, the late Victorian, was only opened in 1886 with an Act 'to regulate the Labour of Children and Young Persons in Shops.'[4] The commissioners of 1875 had glanced at that class of labour, but had decided to pass by on the other side[5].

But, during the pause in factory legislation, parliament, urged on by those most concerned, had written a fresh page in the law of employment. At common law, an employer's liability to the public was very different from his liability to his servants. If his servant caused injury to a third party, the employer was liable, even if the servant was doing what he had been told not to do. But if the employer had taken reasonable safety precautions, he had no liability should one servant hurt another.

[1] Since the Act of 1844: see vol. I. p. 576.

[2] From the *Report* of 1876, p. lvi.

[3] They are, for all females, coal-mining and glass-making; for girls under sixteen, brick-making; for boys under twelve, glass-making; for children under eleven, fustian-cutting and metal-grinding. An odd arbitrary list.

[4] 49 and 50 Vict. c. 55.

[5] *Report*, p. xxiii.

The Employers' Liability Act of 1880 (43 and 44 Vict. c. 42) started the process of assimilating the position of servants to that of the public. In the extreme case of the railways, the assimilation was complete. A shunter and a passenger killed by a negligent driver were all one to the new law. For other employments it did not go so far. Seamen, domestic servants, and those not employed in manual labour it did not touch[1].

Actual wage rates, except those of government servants, the Gladstonian state had not thought of touching. Nor had it strengthened the existing law against wage filching by payment in truck. There was no general Truck Act between that of 1831 and that of 1887 which, like the Shops Act of the previous year, belongs to the late Victorian group of labour laws[2]. The only legislative sequel to a wide, if not exhaustive, inquiry made in 1871[3] into survivals of truck was an Act of 1874 intended to check, not truck proper, but old abuses connected with frame rents in the outwork knitting industry[4]. There was a remnant of truck in that industry among about 1200 workers on the borders of Nottingham and Derby; but this was left to time and the old law, together with a good deal of open or veiled truck at the company shops of Welsh iron works, the stores of Lanarkshire collieries, and other places[5]. The few surviving middlemen truckers, in scattered outwork trades like knitting and nailing, were often publicans at whose houses the goods were handed in[6]. They were hit hard when in 1883 the rule against wage paying at public houses, which had been a part of the law of coal mines ever since 1842, was extended to every occupation, even to agriculture: "no wages shall be paid to any workman at or within any public house, beershop, or place for the sale of any spirits, wine, cyder, or other spirituous or fermented liquor, or any office, garden, or place belonging thereto."[7]

Lord Ashley's Coalmines Act of 1842 was a labour law not concerned with the shafts and workings. Those of the 'fifties were safety laws concerned with little else, and of incalculable value. By 1855 there were general rules for all mines, and

[1] See *Dict. Pol. Econ.* s.v. "Employers' Liability."

[2] See vol. I. p. 410, 562 *sqq.*

[3] *Report of the R.C. on Truck*, 1871, XXXVI.

[4] See vol. I. p. 563–4.

[5] *Report* of 1871, p. xxx (hosiery) and *passim*, and see below, p. 456 *sqq.*

[6] *Report*, p. xxvii, xxx.

[7] Barmen naturally excluded. The Act is 46 and 47 Vict. c. 98.

provision for the making of special rules for each[1]. It was in preparing these last that the inspectors learnt what further securities all the mines required. By 1860 (by 23 and 24 Vict. c. 151) a timid step was being taken beyond Ashley's Act. It had not allowed boys under ten to go down the shafts. Now they might not go under twelve, unless furnished with a certificate that they could read and write. Winding engine men must be eighteen years old: under the Act of 1842, a lad of fifteen at the engine might hold men's lives in his hand. But the words most important for the future were in § 29, which empowered the colliers in every mine "to station a Person (being one of the Persons...employed in such...Mine...) at the Place appointed for...weighing...in order to take an account thereof," and see to it that when they were paid by weight they were paid fair. A fierce struggle in Yorkshire lay behind that clause[2]. For years after 1860 it was fought or evaded by the coalowners. An Act of 1872 strengthened the position of the checkweighman a little; but not until 1887 did the law become all that the miners desired[3]. Yet the first recognition in 1860 of the bare right of a representative of the men to put his finger somewhere near the pay-sheets is the decisive historical moment.

The state had waged unsystematic war on disease with whole regiments of ill-assorted Acts ever since the pioneering Public Health Act of 1848, passed in cholera and typhus time[4]. Strategy had been halting because the state at once distrusted and over-trusted its tactical agents, the local authorities. There was in parliament a Whiggish suspicion of corporations not so long ago reputed corrupt. At the administrative headquarters there was a Benthamite faith in the expert, propagated by the first chief of staff, Edwin Chadwick. The whole tradition of local government, however, as the eighteenth century had bequeathed it, favoured permissive rather than compulsory legislation and a great reliance on that municipal initiative which

[1] Cp. above, p. 100. The series begins with 13 and 14 Vict. c. 100: "Whereas it is expedient that Provision should be made for the Inspection of Coal Mines," etc.

[2] See Webb, S. and B., *History of Trade Unionism*, p. 289–92.

[3] Under the consolidating Act, 50 and 51 Vict. c. 58.

[4] The tangled history of sanitary legislation is given in full in the *Second Report of the Royal Sanitary Commission*, 1871 (xxxv), p. 7 *sqq*. For the Act of 1848 see vol. I. p. 545.

produced local Acts of Parliament. Whig distrust of borough finance had made the Municipal Corporations Act of 1835 severe; and it was rigidly interpreted in the light of the expanding legal principle of *ultra vires*. It may be assumed that the Common Law would not have hindered an old unreformed borough from spending borough money on a fountain, had it been moved to do so; but special Bath and Wash-house Acts had been thought necessary in the 'forties to enable "inhabitants of towns through the Town Council to supply themselves with the means of cleanliness."[1] Without an Act, general or local, such obvious expenditures might be held to be *ultra vires*[2].

The General Board of Health of 1848, Chadwick's and Ashley's Board, was a patent replica of the Poor Law Commission of three—"two Lords and a Barrister, to preserve the health of the living," as it was said, "and then, after a year or so of doubtful success...a Physician to bury the dead";[3] for Dr Southwood Smith was only added at the time of the Metropolitan Interments Act of 1850. The Barrister and the Physician were salaried. The Board in the first instance worked through the Guardians of the Poor[4]. It could only force a corporate borough to accept for its Council the functions of a Local Board of Health, or force such a Board to be elected elsewhere, when the area in question had an abnormally high mortality. The ordinary procedure was for a town to petition to have the Act applied. At the end of five years only about two millions of urban population had come under it[5]. For twenty years more it was hardly felt except in urban and urbanised areas. In

[1] *Second Report of the Royal Sanitary Commission*, p. 15.

[2] According to Brice, S., *A Treatise on ultra vires* (1893), Preface, the doctrine is "of modern growth" and is "first prominently mentioned...in equity...in 1846." It was mainly applied, in the first instance, to Railway Companies. Robson, W. A., *The Development of Local Government* (1931), p. 194–6, seems to hold that the Municipal Corporations Act of 1835 (5 and 6 Wm. IV, c. 76) left corporations free to spend money on, and levy rates for, any object which was "for the public Benefit of the inhabitants" (§ 92); and that the doctrine of *ultra vires* was applied to them by false analogy. To me § 92 of the Act appears more restrictive, though it seems to give great liberty of expenditure to any borough so rich in rents and profits that it has no need to levy rates. The decision is for lawyers.

[3] Dr H. W. Rumsey, *Essays on State Medicine*, quoted in Simon, *English Sanitary Institutions*, p. 214.

[4] See its *First Report*, 1849 (XXIV. 1). "The Legislature contemplates the Poor Law Union...as the chief local administrative body," p. 24.

[5] *Report* for 1854 (XXXV. 1), p. 14.

1868 Suffolk had only three Local Boards, all in towns; the Welsh counties, excluding Glamorgan, an average of less than three; Hereford only two; Northampton and Huntingdon each only one[1].

Down to 1854, when the first General Board lapsed and Chadwick's official career ended with it, he and Ashley and Southwood Smith worked incessantly, advising and circularising where they might not command, promoting Common Lodging House Bills, Burials Bills and a whole series of minor drainage and waterworks Bills to confirm the provisional orders of the Board. If Chadwick had won all his battles, the Board would have secured complete control of burial throughout the country, and London would have had a unified system not only of drainage but of water supply. But as the Board said in its last report, "extensive interests" were "unavoidably interfered with" by its plans—undertakers, cemetery companies, water companies and engineers[2]. Chadwick was an awkward subordinate and no handler of men. His later official chiefs attacked his policies. Parliament became restive about centralisation and swept the Board away. For four years a precarious one-man board without salaried members replaced it, to be succeeded in 1858 by a department of the Home Office[3], and in 1871 by the Local Government Board.

The pace slackened after Chadwick left. Instead of the autocratic, single-minded, and clumsy-penned sanitarian, who respected no one, the sociable Tom Taylor was promoted secretary. He found time amid his sanitary duties to write plays[4], and died editor of *Punch*. Chadwick's allies, although they knew all his weaknesses, felt that they had been watching "the failure and foundering of a life-boat"[5] when he fell; but a group of health Acts of 1855, including that which created for London the Metropolitan Board of Works (18 and 19 Vict. c. 120), was some consolation. Within the next few years, the

[1] *Return...of the Local Boards*, 1867–8 (LVIII. 789).

[2] *Report for* 1854, p. 48. The report is self-defensive, self-righteous, very Chadwickian.

[3] Medical work came under a Committee of the Privy Council in 1858. See the evidence of Tom Taylor, the Secretary, in *First Report of Royal Sanitary Commission*, 1868–9 (XXXII. 303).

[4] *Our American Cousin* appeared in 1858. In 1857 he read to the Social Science Congress a paper on *Central and Local Action in relation to Town Improvement*, criticising centralisation.

[5] Simon, *op. cit.* p. 236.

Metropolitan Board took in hand the arterial drainage of London and cut the great outfall sewers, North and South, to Barking and Plumstead Marshes.

Eleven years later, the state moved forward again, its memory for sanitary needs having been jogged by a return of the cholera. The Sanitary Act of 1866 (29 and 30 Vict. c. 90), which included London, made sanitary inspection obligatory on local authorities and overcrowding a nuisance; and for the first time empowered a Secretary of State, upon complaint received, to compel those authorities to remove nuisances and to provide sewers and water supplies. "The grammar of common sanitary legislation acquired the novel virtue of an imperative mood."[1] It was time.

Sanitary law in the late 'sixties was scattered about in local acts, factory acts, burial acts, lodging-house, vaccination, alkali, smoke and food adulteration acts, with its core in the Public Health Act of 1848 and the Local Government Act of 1858[2], which had altered the constitution and powers of the Local Boards. The administering authorities overlapped, yet did not cover the whole field. The sewer authority was normally the Vestry; the nuisances authority the Guardians of the Poor. Even the greatest local authorities might be apathetic. Liverpool, anticipating parliament, had appointed the first British Medical Officer of Health in 1847[3]: Manchester did not follow for twenty-one years. In industrial matters especially, as the history of workshop inspection shows, there was a clear reluctance to adopt sanitary law as such; although the early 'sixties had seen the discreditable spectacle of tiny insanitary urban and rural districts adopting the Local Government Act with its sanitary obligations, which they neglected, to escape a recent Highways Act and keep their roads in their own hands, also to be neglected[4]. The very capable Royal Sanitary Commission of 1869–71 recommended that "all powers requisite

[1] Simon, *op. cit.* p. 300. The bill, it should be added, was planned by Simon, as medical officer to the Committee of the Privy Council, and H. A. Bruce, later Lord Aberdare, then under-secretary at the Home Office, in 1864, before the cholera.

[2] This Act, 21 and 22 Vict. c. 98, was "to be construed with the Public Health Act of 1848 as one Act."

[3] Hope, E. W., *Health at the Gateway*, a sanitary history of Liverpool (1931), p. 43.

[4] Robson, *op. cit.* p. 43–4. See the *Return of Local Boards* of 1867–8, which contains twenty-nine districts with populations under 2000.

for the health of towns and country should in every place be possessed by one responsible local authority";[1] but that is an ideal not even yet fully attained.

The report of this Commission served as basis for the Act of 1871 (34 and 35 Vict. c. 70) which created the Local Government Board; for succeeding Acts which concentrated sanitary power in the Board's hands; and for the consolidating Public Health Act of 1875. Unhappily for the cause of health, the Local Government Board absorbed, and on its sanitary side was dominated by, the old Poor Law Board. Now the Poor Law Board had a bad sanitary record. Only four years back, it had just been wakened from its "long sleep" of sanitary neglect[2]. Its system was formal and bureaucratic. It subordinated the medical consultant at headquarters to the administrative official. The district inspectors on whom it relied lacked medical knowledge and had been well trained in economy[3]. Although the Local Government Board was now obliged to establish medical officers of health everywhere, it acquiesced in a system inherited from the Poor Law. Its officers were usually 'part-timers,' whose often exiguous salaries might be expected to measure the amount of attention which they would give to their duties. Preventive policies, whether of destitution or sickness, had not flowered in the old Poor Law atmosphere. Wide gaps in the nation's health defences, still to be found in the twentieth century, might have been stopped thirty years earlier, if the Local Government Board of the 'seventies had made full use of the powers which the legislation of 1871–5 gave it, and of the medical knowledge and facilities for inquiry then available. When cholera strode north-westward from Egypt in 1884, the Board ordered a hurried medical survey of its coastal defences, of whose condition it appears to have been quite needlessly ignorant, only to find that the inferior sort of local authorities had "since their constitution done no efficient work," and that some of them showed "no desire even to be properly instructed as to the sanitary requirements of their districts."[4] There had been twelve years in which to instruct and if necessary coerce them.

[1] *Report*, 1871 (xxxv), p. 3.

[2] Chance, Sir W., *The Better Administration of the Poor Law* (1895), p. vii. See Webb, S. and B., *The English Poor Law*, part II, p. 319, 622 and *passim*.

[3] Based on Simon, *op. cit.* p. 387 *sqq*. Simon witnessed what he regarded as a retreat from policies which he had himself initiated, and may have been over-hard on the L.G.B.; but his authority is high.

[4] Report of Dr Ballard, quoted in Simon, *op. cit.* p. 404.

The survey of 1884–6 was called off before it was finished, and the age closed—cholera at its end as at its beginning—with a country much healthier than it used to be, but not nearly so healthy as it might have become, had administration done all that the law now permitted.

The Poor Law Board, whose traditions dominated the early days of the Local Government Board, had lived a threatened life of twenty years (1847–67) and had only been made permanent four years before it was absorbed[1]. That desperately unpopular extra-parliamentary body, the executive Poor Law Commission of 1834—"the three bashaws of Somerset House," had handed over to the parliamentary President of a phantom board in December 1847, when, as a result of the Irish famine and the bad trade of a year of crisis, the figures of pauperism were abnormally high. The executive Commissioners, in the thirteen years since 1834, had mapped out most of the country into the new type of Poor Law Unions, and had seen a workhouse of some sort established in nearly all of them[2]. Contrary to the expressed opinion of the *Report* of 1834, they had acquiesced, as a matter of administrative convenience, in the establishment of general mixed workhouses of the type which, when found under the unreformed system, had supplied the reporting Commissioners with their most beastly illustrations of abuse. "We recommended [in 1834] that in every Union there should be a building for the children, and one for the able-bodied males, and another for the able-bodied females; and another for the old; we supposed the use of four buildings in every Union," Nassau Senior said indignantly, many years later, protesting against what had become the universal policy[3]. But a single building was easier for the Assistant Commissioners to get built—few existing country poor-houses proved fit for

[1] A general reference can here be made to Webb, S. and B., *English Poor Law History: the last Hundred Years*, 2 parts, 1929. For the next generation it will be the classic narrative. Its best predecessor is H. Preston-Thomas' translation of Aschrott, P. F., *Das Englische Armen-Wesen*, first published in 1888. References below are to the second English edition of 1902. At some points Aschrott is, in my opinion, more useful than Webb.

[2] See vol. I. p. 465–6, 581–2. On p. 582, l. 5 the figure of out-paupers in 1848 should be 1,571,000 not 1,877,000.

[3] Before the *Poor Relief Committee* of 1861 (1862, x, Q. 6905). In Webb, *op. cit.* p. 129, he is quoted as saying "and another for the sick" instead of "for the old": it comes to much the same, no doubt. The explicit advocacy of "separate buildings" by the Commissioners of 1834 is on p. 306–7 of the *Report*.

any of the uses suggested—and much easier for Guardians to manage. Besides, it was hoped that able-bodied people would seldom go into workhouses at all; so it seemed wasteful to provide two separate ones for them. Indeed, the scanty evidence suggests that the Assistant Commissioners who did the local work never seriously considered the policy of classification by houses, and that the central body made no attempt to press it. They relied on regulations to secure classification inside 'the house,' with disastrous results, especially for the children and the sick[1].

The policy of not relieving the able-bodied except in the workhouse had broken down against the facts of London life and the sullen resistance of the industrial North. The new Board of 1847 confirmed the breakdown, after five years trial. It was "not expedient," ran the circular of August 25, 1852, "absolutely to prohibit out-relief even to the able-bodied."[2] (The most extreme advocates of the principles of 1834 had never suggested its abolition for widows and other impotent poor, who could most conveniently be relieved at home.) In each succeeding decade, the number of Unions to which prohibitory orders applied contracted, and the population of those to which they did not apply grew[3]. What had been thought of as a national policy in the 'thirties had become, by the 'seventies, a policy applied only to men in overcrowded rural Unions—and even there with exceptions. No doubt it had helped the good work of turning agricultural labourers into navvies, urban carters, railway men, policemen and emigrants[4]. A later generation has learnt the risks of relief systems which give insufficient encouragement to mobility and occupational adjustment. But it was hard that these risks should have been averted for forty years at the sole cost of the bread-and-cheese fed labourers, with their 9*s.* to 11*s.* a week.

Throughout the 'fifties the statistical position of poor-relief improved steadily. Starting in 1850 with a mean figure of a million people, or 5·7 per cent. of the population of England and Wales, in receipt of relief at any one time, it closed in

[1] Historians had overlooked this decisive divergence from 'the principles of 1834' until its history was written by Lord Passfield and Mrs Sidney Webb.

[2] *Fifth Annual Report of the Poor Law Board*, p. 22, quoted in Webb, p. 151 n.

[3] The prohibitory order is that of December 21, 1844: the laxer order, used for the towns, is that of December 14, 1852. Cp. Aschrott, *op. cit.* p. 165.

[4] The direct encouragement of emigration by the Poor Law authorities was insignificant. Above, p. 233.

1860 with 845,000, or 4·3 per cent. Of these, the number relieved indoors remained extraordinarily constant, at from 110,000 to 125,000[1]. As there was no important change in law or policy, it may be concluded that the statistical improvement registered, in a rough negative way, the share of the least fortunate in that improved national well-being which marked the decade. The Guardians had settled down into their local policies of administration and relief—by no means uniform, in spite of orders from the Commission or the Board—and these policies were becoming routines. Wage-earners and their families, especially in the towns, had lost none of their horror of 'the house'; nor had there been any change in their willingness to accept outdoor relief in emergency. The elective Guardians acquiesced in the outdoor system, and the central authority was in no position to coerce them, even had it resolutely wished to do so. It never raised any objection to the very general practice of giving a shilling or two a week to aged destitute folk in their own homes. Consequently, the mean number of those relieved 'out' remained nearly seven times that of those relieved 'in,' after a quarter of a century of the new Poor Law.

Those relieved 'in' included growing numbers of a class whose very existence the *Report* and legislation of the 'thirties had barely recognised—the vagrants, professional or occasional[2]. The able-bodied vagrant, and the vagrant is normally active if not always fit, had been offered 'the house' like any other able-bodied man of no resources. If he was a work-seeker become destitute, he would accept reluctantly; if a professional, with his whole heart. From Union workhouse to Union workhouse was an easy day's walk; and at the end was accommodation which the professional found perfectly satisfactory. In the metropolitan area not even a short day's walk was necessary. Various attempts had been made, during the later years of the original Commission and the early years of the Board, to deal

[1] The figures are summarised for the whole period in Aschrott, App. II. Figures from before 1849 (*e.g.* those quoted in vol. I. p. 582) are not comparable, being on a different basis. (See Mackay, T., supplementary volume to Nicholls' *History of the English Poor Law*, App. p. 603.) The figures here used are based on the winter and summer returns, January 1 and July 1, for each year.

[2] Cp. Webb, p. 402 *sqq.*, and Nicholls-Mackay, III. 371 *sqq.* The *Report* of 1834 gives two pages (338–40) to vagrancy and simply recommends "that the Central Board be...directed to frame and enforce Regulations as to the Relief to be afforded to vagrants...."

with the situation by law or by administrative order; but very little had come of them. A few Unions had started what in later years were known as casual wards; but most simply put the vagrants for their night's rest on the men's side of 'the house.' Especially in London, the crowding of workhouses with undesirable vagrants was causing anxiety at the Board in the late 'fifties. Plans were drawn up in 1857–8 for the creation of special metropolitan "asylums for the homeless poor"; but they came to nothing at that time[1].

At the close of the year 1860, in which the figures of poor-relief had touched a minimum, the Thames froze and a great weight of snow fell. For a month (December 17, 1860 to January 19, 1861) outdoor work was held up as it seldom is in the British climate. It was reckoned later that there was an abnormal increase of some 40,000 in what contemporaries, in the undiscriminating language of Poor Law circles, called "metropolitan pauperism."[2] Charitable people got to work; a relief fund was opened at the Mansion House; the meanness, incompetence, corruption and bumbledom of many London Poor Law authorities were pilloried[3]; and there was talk of the Poor Law having broken down. An echo of the old, and still strong, dislike of centralised administration was heard in the suggestion, very seriously made in Parliament, that the Poor Law Board with its orders was the main source of evil. Remove it, so the argument ran, and enlarge the unit of Poor Law administration; then a sufficiency of able, public-spirited men will come forward to take over and reform the system[4]. The Board, it is to be remembered, was not yet on a permanent footing: it had been created for only five years, but had been periodically renewed as a reasonably successful experiment.

For three years a strong parliamentary committee, whose leading members were Charles Villiers, Robert Lowe and Lord Robert Cecil, examined the law and its working, with special reference to the problems of London. While it was sitting the

[1] Cp. Ed. Twisleton's criticism of the reformed Scottish Poor Law of the 'forties for its neglect of such provision: vol. I. p. 587.

[2] *S.C. on Poor Relief*, *Report* (1864, IX. 157), p. 3. There are preliminary *Reports* and evidence in 1861, IX.

[3] For the intricacies of London poor relief, and the local Acts, see Aschrott, p. 71; Nicholls-Mackay, III. 486; Webb, *passim*.

[4] See the Debates of February 1861 in Hansard, Third Series, CLXI. 237, speech of Mr Ayrton. Ayrton was arguing for the abolition of any parochial independence and for the concentration of power in the Union.

American Civil War created fresh problems in Lancashire; but with these, as matters of special emergency, the committee did not deal.

Early unemployment difficulties in the cotton area were met by that lax administration of out-relief, to retain which the North had fought the Commissioners[1]. Poor-rates had been low in Lancashire, so for a time there was a margin to draw upon. Yet single parishes soon began to complain of their burden—too soon, critics suggested; for, as Charles Kingsley wrote to the *Times*, the poor-rate was far heavier in Hampshire than in Lancashire[2]. But Lancashire could make its voice heard in parliament. So early as August 1862, under 25 and 26 Vict. c. 160, it had been decided that when the rate in any parish rose above 3*s.* in the pound of rateable value the other parishes of the Union must share in it. If the Union rate got above 5*s.* the Poor Law Board might order other Unions to share, but only cotton-area Unions, that is to say Unions in Lancashire, Cheshire or Derbyshire. Such rates in aid had been contemplated even in the Elizabethan law[3]. A new principle was, however, inserted in this Act of 1862, at the instance of Cobden and the Lancashire members. The burdened Unions were given emergency borrowing powers. Hitherto there had been no legal borrowing for poor-relief anywhere.

Then came the Public Works Act of 1863 (26 and 27 Vict. c. 70) under which the Treasury and the Public Works Loan Commissioners were empowered to lend to Unions and local authorities on the security of the rates, for drainage and other works of permanent utility, with a view to providing for the unemployed. Not many cotton operatives helped to make the new drains. There were not 2300 of them on all the subsidised public works in January 1864, and not 4000 in December[4].

[1] The fullest account from the side of administration is in Nicholls-Mackay, III, ch. 18. See also Arnold, R. A., *History of the Cotton Famine* (1864 and 1865) and especially Watts, J., *The Facts of the Cotton Famine* (1866).

[2] The columns of the *Times* for November 1862 contain much correspondence. Kingsley was rather violent and laid himself open to rejoinder. The *Times* itself in an article on "The Distress and the Resources of Lancashire" (Nov. 13) pointed out temperately that the seven South-Western counties had a poor-rate burden 120 per cent. above that of Lancashire.

[3] See 39 Eliz. c. 3 (1597). In § 2 it is provided that other parishes in the Hundred may be rated for the needs of a necessitous parish; or the County to relieve the Hundred. So far as is known, these powers had been very rarely used.

[4] Watts, *op. cit.* p. 320. Probably these were not the spinners, etc. to any great extent, but general labourers from the mills, stokers, porters, etc.

For many operatives, the Unions with the consent of the Poor Law Board adopted the famous device, of which Lancashire was very proud, of giving relief on condition not of hand-work but of head-work; so many hours of education per week. With the aid of much private charity, and a straining of all the principles of non-intervention at the request of its prophets, the crisis was passed—though with a national pauperism figure for 1863–4 higher by 200,000 than it had been in 1860. By 1866, however, it was back, not at the exact figure of 1860, but at the 1860 ratio to population of 4·3 per cent.

Meanwhile the Committee had reported cautiously, and cautious action was being taken on its recommendations. "The continuance of a central authority" it had declared to be "essential," and it wished to see the authority placed "upon a permanent footing."[1] Hence permanence for the Board in 1867, and for its successor the Local Government Board of 1871. The Committee was further of opinion that the law had not broken down in 1860–61; that there had been much abuse of the charitable attempts to supplement it; and that the London Unions could have handled the emergency, though not easily. It saw no reason to interfere with the existing system of medical relief, although Poor Law medical officers had complained loudly before it of the arrangement which gave them "a fixed amount of money for a very variable amount of work."[2] It thought that workhouse education was "on the whole satisfactory,"[3] but it advocated the provision of separate Poor Law schools wherever practicable. There were already some. It had much to say about the religious difficulties in the workhouses and the grievances of Roman Catholics. There was a recommendation that "the general question of extending the area of rating," *i.e.* the policy of rating by Unions, not by Parishes, should be "further considered by the House";[4] there was decided advocacy of more thorough classification of the mixed multitudes who came within the view of the law; and there was a proposal that the burden of metropolitan vagrancy should be shouldered by the whole metropolis[5].

The suggestion of the Committee about Union rating; the

[1] *Report* of 1864, p. 11.

[2] Evidence of J. Rodgers, M.D., Q. 13,334.

[3] *Report*, p. 36.

[4] *Report*, p. 44. In its particular context this recommendation only applies to London Unions.

[5] These are only the more important recommendations.

satisfactory experience of Union as opposed to Parish rates under the Lancashire emergency system; and the well-known fact that parochial parsimony was a main cause of the social evils of the close parish, in which liability for the poor was kept down by keeping down the cottages, led to the decisive Union Chargeability Act of 1865 (28 and 29 Vict. c. 79)[1]. There had been a common Union fund for certain general purposes from the first. Since 1834 the charges thrown upon it had increased. Now the Union became the financial unit for all purposes. No parish could evade its share of the burdens of poverty in its district by arranging that potential paupers should tramp to work in it from neighbouring higher-rated open parishes. The Act was a logical development of the Union policy of 1834.

A still prompter outcome of the *Report* of 1864 had been the Metropolitan Houseless Poor Act of that year (27 and 28 Vict. c. 116) which established a common metropolitan fund upon which Guardians might draw to make special and appropriate provision for casuals and vagrants. It was a success. Classification of 'paupers,' so long urged by the wise, was at last becoming a reality. The Metropolitan Poor Act of 1867 (30 Vict. c. 6) and later supplementary Acts helped it forward. The common fund was made available for expenditure on asylums, small-pox and fever hospitals, poor-law schools, training-ships, and other specialised relief institutions and policies. The Metropolitan Asylums Board was created and was soon doing work of the highest social value[2]. Disgusting conditions in workhouse sick-wards and infirmaries, where paupers suffering from disease of every kind were tended only by other paupers, had been exposed in the *Lancet*; and Gathorne Hardy, President of the Board, had declared in the House in 1867 that the sick were "not proper objects" for the traditional deterrent workhouse policies. "We must peremptorily insist," he said, "on the treatment of the sick...being conducted on an entirely separate system."[3] The last President of the Board, Goschen, in his last report, was even toying with the possibility of extending "gratuitous medical relief beyond the actual pauper

[1] Questions arising out of 'settlement' were those which most interested poor-law reformers of the years 1850–70. See, *e.g.*, Pashley, R., *Pauperism and the Poor Laws*, 1852.

[2] See Webb, *op. cit.* p. 321.

[3] Hansard, Third Series, CLXXXV. 163. Quoted in Webb, p. 319, but with "different system" for "separate system."

class."[1] There was thus official driving force behind the new movement. But, outside the metropolis, the Unions were hard to drive. Improvement in workhouse infirmaries was already noticeable in 1869; but even the largest towns and Unions had made very little progress with specialised institutions by 1886.

Slack trade in the late 'sixties brought with it a slight statistical increase of pauperism. For four years (1868–71) the mean number of persons relieved, 'in' and 'out,' stood at just over a million, or 4·6 per cent. of the population. The mean number of able-bodied adults relieved 'out,' excluding the vagrants, was still almost equal to the whole workhouse population[2]. (In the 'fifties it had usually been greater, and in the difficult early 'sixties much greater.) Its persistence was a standing challenge to the many individualist thinkers and public men who hoped that progress, economic, social and moral, might one day render a Poor Law superfluous, and who believed that it was their clear duty at least to get rid of outdoor relief to able-bodied adults, by some process of depauperisation, possibly drastic. In 1870 Henry Fawcett was teaching Cambridge, and in 1871 telling the country in his *Pauperism: its Causes and Remedies*, that "it would be far better altogether to abolish the Poor Law than that the present state of things should continue."[3] His own aim was not to see the law repealed but "by gradual steps to discourage and ultimately to abolish outdoor relief."[4] Herein he was in the strict tradition of 1834, an appeal to which carried weight; for the tradition of 1834 had been hallowed by thinkers and Poor Law administrators much more than it had been followed or understood. In this case at least, it was rightly interpreted.

The spirit which inspired Fawcett also inspired the Local Government Board of the 'seventies and its inspectorate. There began what has been called the crusade against outdoor relief[5]. A few Boards of Guardians joined early from conviction. Others gradually felt the pressure of official reforming opinion. Down

[1] Quoted in Webb, p. 322.

[2] The mean workhouse population was 137,000 in 1867 and 158,000 in 1869. The 'outdoor able-bodied adults, excluding vagrants,' rose to 150,000 in 1870. The figures and the totals are not terrifying to the modern mind.

[3] *Pauperism*, p. 41.

[4] *Ibid.* p. 24.

[5] Prof. William Smart's phrase in the historical survey of the Law prepared for the Royal Commission of 1908–9, Vol. XII (1910, LI). A full discussion with bibliographical references is in Webb, *op. cit.* p. 435 *sqq.*

to 1877, from trade-boom into trade-slump and with a growing population, the mean number of persons relieved declined year by year. The whole number of those relieved 'out' fell to less than four times the number of those relieved 'in'; the able-bodied adults relieved 'out' to less than half the workhouse population[1]. There was a trifling rise in 1879–83; but in 1884–6, when the country was worried about depression in trade and industry, the ratio to population of those relieved by the Poor Law was lower than it had ever been before (2·8 per cent.) and the mean number of able-bodied adults relieved 'out' was much smaller than it had been in the trade boom of 1871–3[2]. How far this result merely registered an administrative achievement, accompanied by increased reliance on private charity and on what Thomas Chalmers had called "the many indefinable shifts and capabilities of the pauper himself,"[3] and how far it marked a national advance in forethought and average well-being, cannot be determined with certainty. There was crushed misery in the social depths and grinding strain in strata above them. But though profits were depressed and there was much unemployment, there had been a rise in average well-being. The able-bodied rustic pauper was a type almost extinct; and as the Minority Report of the Commission of 1885–6 pointed out, in spite of "the stricter enforcement of tests in the administration of the Poor Law...the aid...so widely given by friendly and trade societies limited or deferred the pauperisation" of the industrial unemployed[4]. There were reserves to draw upon, if scanty reserves.

As for true vagrancy, it remained pretty intractable, although, with the aid of the central authority and a law of 1871[5], guardians outside London had been giving it special attention and organising casual wards ever since 1867–8. Unhappily no proper attempt was made to sift destitute work-seekers on tramp from professional vagrants. The casual ward, like the workhouse, was made deterrent for all. So, very often, were

[1] The figures for 1877 are: 'indoor paupers,' 150,000; able-bodied adults relieved 'out,' 73,000; ratio of all paupers to population, 2·9 per cent.

[2] Figures for 1886: total, 781,000; indoor, 186,000; able-bodied outdoor, 78,000.

[3] See vol. I. p. 367.

[4] *Minority Report*, p. xlix. Cp. above, p. 385 and below, p. 477. In Fawcett's discussion of pauperism unemployment was ignored.

[5] 34 and 35 Vict. c. 108. See Nicholls-Mackay, *op. cit.* III. 384 and Webb, *op. cit.* p. 411 *sqq*.

those labour yards which throughout the whole period Guardians opened up and down the country in times of bad trade, requiring a usually repellent and not too useful task to be done in exchange for a modicum of relief. With easy-going Guardians, on the other hand, the yard might, and did, become a mere pretext for relief—the kind of thing against which the inspectorate of the 'seventies crusaded.

It was to avoid if possible these equally anti-social extremes that Joseph Chamberlain, during the unemployment of 1886, issued a notable circular from the Local Government Board suggesting to Town Councils the initiation of really useful relief-works, like the sanitary undertakings of the Cotton Famine[1]. The circular had no prompt effect. Chamberlain was soon busy with other things. But it was a signal flown by that new Liberalism which was so little to Gladstone's taste.

At that very time a Committee was inquiring into what was called National Provident Insurance. Commissioners on Friendly Societies, reporting in 1874, had described as a National Friendly Society a scheme laid before them by a very distinguished group of people, which proposed to extend existing, but little used, facilities for buying annuities from government through the Post Office, so as to allow of similar voluntary purchases of insurance against sickness, old age, and burial. The plan was to provide complete state security for thrift, in place of the insecurity of most existing Friendly Societies. The Commissioners could not see their way to recommend it intact, and nothing important was done[2]. Then, in November 1878, an article appeared in the *Nineteenth Century* with the prophetic title "National Insurance." Its author, the Rev. W. L. Blackley, a Hampshire rector, later a canon, followed it up next year with "Compulsory Providence as a Cure for Pauperism" in the *Contemporary Review*. In 1882 he founded the National Insurance League for propaganda work. He was untirable. Within a few years, there was "hardly a platform in any important town on which he had not stood."[3]

[1] *Sixteenth Annual Report of the L.G.B.* p. 3. Circular of March 15, 1886. See Webb, *op. cit.* p. 367, 644–8.

[2] *Report of the R.C. on Friendly Societies*, 1874 (XXIII. part 1), p. cxcvi. The memorandum is in App. IX. It was signed by both Archbishops, six Bishops, seventeen lay peers, thirty-five M.P.'s, etc. For the Friendly Societies at this time see below, p. 471 *sqq*.

[3] Blackley, M. J. J., *Thrift and National Insurance* (1906), a memoir and reprint of the articles referred to. The National Friendly Society was a part

In the 'eighties therefore National Provident Insurance meant what was known as the Blackley scheme, a rather crude proposal by which £10 was to be compulsorily deducted, through employers, from the wages of all young people between seventeen and twenty-one, and handled by the state through the Post Office[1]. Both sexes and every class were to make a similar payment, as their contribution to a national need; but only the wage-earner was to be given 8*s*. a week in sickness, and 4*s*. a week on reaching the age of seventy. Actuaries said the scheme was unsound: they were probably right. Officials said it could not be worked: they were no doubt wrong[2]. Compulsion, and the suggested contribution by those who would not benefit, were offensive to the average opinion of the day. The whole scheme was unwelcome to the vested interest of the Friendly Societies in voluntary thrift. The Committee of 1885–7 thanked Canon Blackley but decided to wait for the "further development of public opinion."[3] That would come; but when it came, bringing national insurance and old age pensions, the pioneer canon and his League were already in danger of oblivion[4].

The Scottish Poor Law had only been revised, by very conservative hands, in 1845[5]. It had immediately been subjected to the strains of famine in the Highlands and the Western

of John Acland's *Plan for rendering the Poor independent on Public Contributions* of 1786. In 1787 Joseph Townsend, in his *Dissertation on the Poor Laws*, proposed to make Friendly Societies universal and compulsory. There were several similar schemes. Those of Tom Paine, for old age pensions, kept alive the idea of public provision for age. Then interest in the subject lapsed. In 1837 Lord Lansdowne spoke favourably of public superannuation schemes. In 1867 Major Corrance advocated state assistance to the Friendly Societies (see Lamond, R. P., *The Scottish Poor Law*, 1892—originally 1870—p. 282). Before 1878 John Walter, M.P , of *The Times*, was advocating compulsory insurance: *Economist*, November 6, 1877.

[1] The scheme varied from time to time. This was its shape in 1885–7. There is a short summary of it in H. Preston-Thomas' part III, "Old Age Pensions," of the 1902 edition of Aschrott, *op. cit.*

[2] Their view was restated by Sir Robert Giffen before the *R.C. on Labour* (*General Session*), 1893–4 (XXXIX), Q. 7015 *sqq.*

[3] *S.C. on National Provident Insurance Report*, 1887 (XI. 1), p. ix. The Committee began work in 1885 but was interfered with by Home Rule crises and General Elections.

[4] Oblivion may be hastened by his omission even from the footnotes of the short section on National Insurance in Webb, *op. cit.* p. 615–21. It is hardly fair to the English pioneers to credit so much "to the example of Prince Bismarck's legislation" (p. 615). Hence this note.

[5] See vol. I. p. 365–9, 585–8.

Isles and of bad trade in the industrial districts. The ancient distinction between the 'legal' or 'enrolled' poor and the 'occasional' poor had been retained. 'Occasional' poverty was conceived of as due to sickness, accident, or other temporary incapacity; but in the bad year 1848 the Scottish Board of Supervision had been legally advised that "able-bodied persons ...unavoidably thrown out of employment" might be treated as occasional poor, and given temporary relief[1]. Before any serious use had been made of this opinion, it was overruled by the courts. Test cases decided in 1852 that the able-bodied had no right to parochial relief "in any circumstances"; and that their children, inseparable from the parents, had no right either. So the Scottish law stood throughout the period, envied by those drastic English depauperisers who were aware of it[2].

While these test decisions were being made, the business of providing Scotland with poorhouses was going forward. Most of the work was done between 1848 and 1865; but remnants of the pre-poorhouse system survived 1870. Before the revision of the law, there had been only a handful of hospitals and workhouses in the greatest cities. The usual practice had been for the parish authorities to hire ordinary houses for the accommodation of the sick and impotent 'enrolled poor,' or to board out both them and the destitute children. There were still a number of these bad, overcrowded, ill-furnished, promiscuous parochial lodging-houses in 1861; though by 1870 they were "fast disappearing."[3] Boarding-out of the children, whether orphan or deserted or separated from vicious or impotent parents, had worked well, especially in rural districts. It was continued, though not universally, after the poorhouses were built. Crofters made excellent foster-parents; the literacy of the poorest Scottish homes led on to education; and so the lot of many Scottish poor law children was in every way preferable to that of the ordinary English workhouse child[4]. By 1870 England was inquiring into the matter, with a view to possible imitation. There had been some sporadic boarding-out by

[1] Vol. I. p. 588.

[2] The cases are M'William *v.* Adams, and Lindsay *v.* McTear. The original decisions were of 1848: the business of appeal was not completed till 1852. Macqueen, J. F., *Reports of Scotch Appeals*, I. 120, 155.

[3] *Report on the Boarding Out of Poor Children in Scotland*, by J. J. Henley, Poor Law Inspector, 1870 (LVIII. 73), p. 8.

[4] *Report of* 1870, p. 35. Cp. *S.C. on the Operation of the Poor Law in Scotland*, 1868–71, *Report*, 1871 (XI. 389), p. xi.

English Guardians before that time. The inquiries of 1869, and the philanthropic agitation which had preceded them, led to a rather grudging official encouragement of the practice in England; but not until 1889 was the old and excellent Scottish system "whole-heartedly and permanently adopted"[1] by the Local Government Board.

Poor Law Unions had not been imposed on Scotland. Her large parishes never united for any purpose except the erection of what came to be known as combination poorhouses. Owing to the late dates of erection, these houses, the visiting inspector from England reported in 1870, had not "the repulsive features of those English workhouses that were built immediately after the passing of the Poor Law."[2] In 1870 only twenty-six parishes in the whole country had their own poorhouses. They were nearly all in and about Edinburgh and Glasgow[3]. The total of Scottish poorhouses was sixty-three, most of them 'combinations' serving whole counties, or great parts of counties, and incredibly small, judged by English standards, for the populations which they served. Sutherland had a population of 24,000 in 1871. The county combination house at Portinleek had room for 50 people. At the other end of the country, Kirkcudbright combination house could take 250 out of a population of 36,000. And because of the innate distaste of the Scot, especially the countryman, Highland or Lowland, for the poorhouse and all that it implied, even the scanty accommodation was not fully used. This distaste had been utilised by the Poor Law authorities to cut down outdoor relief. Claimants were offered 'the house' as in England; shied at it; and lost their claim. "Oh, Sir, they winna bide," said the governor of the Dalkeith house, when asked why it was so empty. "Oh, plenty of them sent here, but they just come in at the tae door and they gang out at the tither."[4]

The result of this and of kindred policies was that, in a growing population, the number of enrolled or registered poor relieved at any one time remained remarkably constant at between 70,000 and 80,000 from 1850 to 1870; and declined there-

[1] Webb, *op. cit.* p. 275. For the literature of boarding-out, see notes to Webb, p. 271–2.

[2] *Report*, p. 7.

[3] Details are in the *Reports on...the Poor Law in Scotland*, 1868–9 (XI. 1), App. 16, and 1870 (XI. 1), App. 15.

[4] Evidence of Sir John M'Neill (1868–9, XI, Q. 1382), quoted in Lamond, *op. cit.* p. 114.

after to 59,000 in 1886[1]. Besides these, there was a group of their dependents, wives and children, which averaged rather more than half the number of the enrolled. And there was a handful of casual poor with their dependents, kept small by the rigid Scottish law, which before 1870 averaged at any one time about 7000, and after 1870 was worked down to less than 5000. Yet, in spite of the very different principles and application of the English and Scottish laws, the net results, when both had been stiffened after 1870, were curiously similar. In England, by 1886, the mean number of persons relieved at any one time had been reduced, according to official figures, to 2·8 per cent. of the population: in Scotland to 2·5 per cent.[2]

The Scottish reaction to that slight increase of poor-relief during the late 'sixties, which in England had produced Fawcett's *Pauperism* and the crusade of th inspectors, had been a movement which invoked the name of Chalmers and urged a return to the ancient voluntary parochial system of relief[3]. Benevolent men in Edinburgh founded an Association for Improving the Condition of the Poor, and endowed the Chalmers Lectures on Pauperism. They also procured a parliamentary inquiry into the operation of the Poor Law in Scotland, hoping that the law might be condemned. The Committee, reporting in 1871, blessed the law and most of its operations, though it found the Scottish system of medical relief casual, unsatisfactory, and inferior to the English[4]. But it advised a stricter application of the poorhouse test, and it was "not prepared to accede to the suggestions made from many quarters, that a discretion should be given to parochial boards to grant relief out of the poor-rates to able-bodied poor in cases of commercial distress."[5] So it provided an official basis for that stiffening of administration which in Scotland, as in England, marked the close of the age.

It was remarkable that the state, whose inroads on individual liberty Herbert Spencer resented and Stanley Jevons watched

[1] Figures in the first *Report on...the Poor Law in Scotland*, 1868–9, App. 3, and in the *Statistical Abstract for the United Kingdom*; criticism of them in Lamond, *op. cit.* p. 129 n. They are not very good statistically.

[2] Neither figure is very satisfactory. The English is an average of one summer and one winter day; the Scottish is the figure for May 14.

[3] Lamond's book was originally written to combat this movement.

[4] *Report*, 1871, p. x.

[5] *Ibid.* p. xi.

with critical impartiality during the early 'eighties[1], should have managed thus to restrict its most ancient 'socialistic' activity within the very narrowest bounds—less than 3 per cent. of the people 'paupers' at any one time. Severe administration had been needed to attain this position, as has been seen. Dogmatically harsh though reforming administrators might appear, they had a noble conception of their duties. But for a few score thousand unhappy incapable folk, for whom the workhouses could be reserved, they believed that growing wealth, growing personal thrift—both were in fact growing[2]—and tonic refusals of poor relief might finally make a Poor Law superfluous. They stood towards that law much as Gladstone had stood towards the income-tax in the 'seventies. A little more prosperity, a little more thrift, joined with the better organisation of private charity to which they were pledged[3], might, they thought, get rid of all that was worst in it; just as to Gladstone only a few more years of peace, and another touch of retrenchment, were needed to finish off the bad tax.

Thinking, as they did, in terms of 'pauperism' and 'the principles of 1834,' they were not very open-minded to new policies, which might perhaps get rid of the 'stigma of pauperism' in other ways than by pressure. The best of them were making conditions of relief more tolerable for the few—young, aged, or infirm—whom they recognised as legitimate wards of society; but only deterrent methods for the able-bodied were recognised in strict Poor Law and official circles, in spite of Chamberlain's recent unemployment circular. Prospects opened out by Canon Blackley did not attract them. They probably agreed with Herbert Spencer when he wrote—"habits of improvidence having for generations been cultivated by the Poor Law, and the improvident enabled to multiply, the evils produced by compulsory charity are now proposed to be met by compulsory insurance."[4] That was indeed a proposal, as Spencer noted with disgust, both of Bismarck the militarist and of some Englishmen who reckoned themselves peaceful reformers of the left. A new territory for the state to occupy was being opened up.

[1] Above, p. 389. [2] See below, p. 450, 477.

[3] The history of the Charity Organisation Society is told, without much sympathy, in Webb, *op. cit.* p. 455–68. For the other side see Loch, C. S., *Charity Organisation* (1892). The Society was founded in 1869.

[4] *The Man versus the State*, p. 28.

CHAPTER XI

LIFE AND LABOUR IN INDUSTRIAL BRITAIN

THE Britain of 1851 had seemed crowded. Yet the crowd thickened fast during the next thirty-five years. While Ireland was emptying, though still over-full for a rural country, the sweeping upward curve of British population steepened in the 'seventies, and flattened out the merest trifle in the 'eighties[1]. Medical knowledge and sanitary law had pushed death back. The crude death-rate in England and Wales, which had been 22·2 per thousand in the 'fifties, was 19·1 for the 'eighties. William Farr's modest ambition of 1854, an urban death-rate of 20 per thousand[2], had been almost reached. London got below 21 in 1883, though Clare Market and other black patches had still a rate nearly double that, ten years later[3]. These were figures better than France or Belgium or Prussia could show; but not so good as they might have been if administration had kept pace with knowledge and the law. And young children still died about as fast as they had died twenty years earlier[4].

This was partly because the flow of life had hardly slackened. The birth-rate reached its recorded maximum—35·5 for England and Wales and 34·9 for Scotland—in 1871–5; and although after that the fall began which perhaps is not yet over, its effects were hardly perceptible until the late 'eighties. In the years about 1880, no important town in the island had a birth-rate below 30, not even Brighton; and some of the industrial towns had rates approaching 40. The gap between birth-rate and death-rate was wide almost everywhere. In this country, of whose people something like two-thirds were real townsmen, the average natural increase, the simple excess of

[1] There is a convenient collection of facts here used in the *Statistical Memoranda and Charts...relating to Public Health and Social Conditions* of 1909 (Cd. 4671).

[2] *S.C. on Public Health Bill and Nuisances Removal Amendment Bill*, 1854–5 (XIII. 413): Farr's evidence, Q. 1554: he thinks 20 per thousand 'practicable.'

[3] A part of Clare Market in 1891–2 had a rate of 41·32 and 800 people to the acre. Jephson, H., *The Sanitary Evolution of London* (1907), p. 363–4.

[4] For continental and infantile death-rates see Charts 2 and 5 in the *Statistical Memoranda and Charts*.

births over deaths, was more than 14 per thousand yearly. Towns had at least become habitable. They were not devouring an immigrant population, killing more men than they bred, as in the eighteenth century.

Ireland had been emptied, first by famine and pestilence and afterwards by the emigrant ship; but emigration from Britain, even when it approached 200,000 a year, as it did in the slack trade of the early 'eighties, made room for less than half of the new lives. At that time, the births always exceeded the deaths by more than 400,000 a year. As the new population grew to working age, the automatic operation of the industry state, guided only by the unseen hand of self-interest, found jobs for them, on the whole with astonishing success. (The number of jobs on the land was stationary or declining.) Some were blind-alley jobs and some were sweated; but the expansion and perpetual diversification of manufacturing and distributing processes provided very many fresh ones which were neither. For the census of 1881 it was necessary to make a new and much enlarged dictionary of occupations, which contained between "eleven and twelve thousand...having each its name."[1] It began with the all-rounder, the bambler, the barker and the bat-printer. Towards the end came the western-man, the wheel-glutter, the whim-driver and the whitster[2].

As some slight offset to British emigration, the 'seventies and 'eighties saw an appreciable increase of foreign immigrants which produced, in a few narrow areas, fresh competition for some of the humblest jobs. Down to the 'sixties, immigrants, apart from the Irish, had been almost all selected men of business or skilled craftsmen, successors to the Ricardos, Angersteins, van Mierops and Rothschilds, the Vulliamys and Bartolozzis of the eighteenth century[3]. These Germans, Greeks, Swiss, Jews of all nationalities, occasional Frenchmen, and Americans like George Peabody, were an invaluable and quickly assimilated addition to the human capital of the

[1] *Census of* 1881: *General Report* (1883, LXXX), p. 26.

[2] *All-rounder*, a man who can perform any process in boot-making; *bambler* is neither in the *N.E.D.* nor in the 1927 *Dictionary of Occupational Terms*; *barker*, of trees or of leather; *bat-printer* is not in the 1927 *Dictionary*, probably connected with the making of 'bats' for pottery kilns; *western-man*, a boatman who takes out pilots; *wheel-glutter*, one who mortices hub and fixes spokes of wheels, also a smith who fills up small V-shaped spaces in metal wheels; *whim-driver*, or *whimseyer*, a rag-cleaner in a shoddy mill; *whitster*, a foreman bleacher.

[3] Cp. vol. I. p. 289. Justin Vulliamy was clock-maker to George III.

country. There had been a few humbler folk, especially in the foreign quarters of London; but from the national economic standpoint they were negligible. At the census of 1871 there were only 105,000 people of foreign birth returned in Great Britain. Of these, 34,000 were Germans, including German Jews, and 18,000 were French. By 1881 the total had not risen beyond 124,000, of whom 60,000 were in London. The Russian, that is the Polish, Jews were now bracketed second, at 15,000, with the French, who had declined. There was a sharp increase after 1881, following on anti-Semitic movements in central and eastern Europe[1]. The resources of the Jewish Board of Guardians in London were strained in dealing with the destitute[2]. Complaints of underselling, based on underliving, came from the Gentiles of the East End, at a time when such irresistible competition was specially painful. The pressure was chiefly felt by the bakers, cigar-makers, and tailors; above all by the tailors. London had to face a disquieting social problem. So, on a small scale, had the tailoring quarters of Manchester and Leeds; but there was no national problem. There were only a few thousand foreigners in all Scotland, of whom an important section were seafaring Scandinavians; it is not likely that the whole foreign-born population of the country in 1886 was equal to the British emigration of that single year; and although among the East End Jews the second generation, now springing, would tend to remain a race apart, it would be more nearly assimilated to its economic environment than the first had been.

The decline in the London death-rate by about three per thousand between 1851–3 and 1881–3 was one statistical measure of what Shaftesbury, giving evidence for the last time before a Royal Commission in 1884, the year of his eighty-third birthday, called the 'enormous'[3] improvement in housing and sanitation during those thirty years. His mind was still haunted by memories of his earlier discoveries—the room with a family in each of its four corners: the room with an open cesspool immediately below its boarded floor: the room in which man and wife took turns at night watching a hole in the floor which led direct to the drains, to save their baby from

[1] See the *Memorandum on the Immigration of Foreigners* (by H. G. Calcraft), c. 112 of 1887.

[2] *Ibid.* p. 11.

[3] *R.C. on the Housing of the Working Classes*, 1884–5 (xxx), p. 4.

rats[1]. He had seen such things during his days at the first Board of Health, in the early 'fifties, days when even "in the mansions of the West End the cesspools were regarded as equally sacred with the wine cellars,"[2] although cesspools had already been completely cleared out of the City; days when some of the London Water Companies had their intakes below Teddington Lock[3], although in a hot summer a few years later—that of 1858—"the pestilential smell from the Thames" became so intolerable that there was "a question of changing the seat of Parliament."[4] The Metropolitan Board of Works was at that time cutting the arterial drains which carried off the London sewage and solved the parliamentary difficulty[5]; but Hammersmith in 1860–1 was still laced with foul sewers and ditches. It contained also "a morass of several acres...having no outlet, which received the sewage from a large area, the noxious emanations from which must be regarded as highly detrimental to health," as the Medical Officer put it[6]. There was still a great deal of 'town spring water' drunk in London; the Shoreditch officer in 1860 said he had "hardly ever exposed a sample of it to the heat of a summer day for some hours without observing it to become putrid".[7] In 1856 there was plenty of pig-keeping in Westminster; and in Fulham were mountainous dustheaps of the kind which made the fortune of Mr Boffin. Sanitarians considered them "a most injurious and offensive nuisance."[8] All these nuisances were but gradually abated. There were two courts in Islington of which the Medical Officer reported in 1863 that "young children cannot live in them. All that are born there, or are brought to reside there, are doomed to die within two years."[9] The return of cholera in 1866 revealed the "criminal indifference to the public safety"[10] of the Southwark and Vauxhall Water Company.

[1] *R.C. on the Housing of the Working Classes*, 1884–5, Shaftesbury's evidence, Q. 36–38.

[2] Simon, Sir J., *English Sanitary Institutions* (2nd ed. 1897), p. 252.

[3] Jephson, *op. cit.* p. 71: they were instructed to arrange intakes above the lock by 15 and 16 Vict. c. 84.

[4] Malmesbury, Earl of, *Memoirs of an ex-Minister*, diary for June 23, 1858. Under June 27 comes the footnote, "Although Mme. Ristori...sniffed the air with delight, saying it reminded her of her dear Venice."

[5] Jephson, *op. cit.* p. 90; and above, p. 423.

[6] *Ibid.* p. 101. Jephson's book is based on the reports of the M.O. of Health, now in the library of the London County Council.

[7] *Ibid.* p. 105. [8] *Ibid.* p. 115–16. [9] *Ibid.* p. 177.

[10] Dr Simon's report of 1869; quoted in Jephson, p. 192.

Slaughterhouses, cowhouses, piggeries and private manure-mixing yards in closely settled areas were worrying the Health Officer of St Mary, Newington, in 1871.[1] New drains in the 'seventies were sometimes as bad as the old. Shoddy houses were being built on old dustheaps, as University College and Hyde Park Gardens had been built before them; even a 'small town' grew up in Wandsworth on six or seven feet of made ground, made of filth[2].

The chaos of London government left the capital a medley of well and ill-administered sanitary areas, with inadequate central control of internal or external dangers. The Metropolitan Board of Works supervised the main sewers, main streets, and other principal works of the London area, but had no inspecting or coercive powers over the vestries. Only in 1866 did the Thames Navigation Act (29 and 30 Vict. c. 89 § 63–9) authorise regulation of the drainage of up-stream towns in the interests of London. Not until 1878 (under 41 and 42 Vict. c. 32) was the Board empowered to issue general regulations about foundations and building materials, so as to get rid of shoddy houses. Yet there was motion. The first stone of the Embankment was laid near Whitehall Stairs on July 20, 1864. The Embankment did not only give the river a better scour and London a highway of dignity. It covered a great low-level sewer which intercepted the drainage of all the slopes above it. Under the legislation of the 'seventies, the Board began the clearance of insanitary areas; and an improved public opinion told on the administration of all but the very worst of the local authorities. The death-rate was falling towards William Farr's ideal. But the infants were dying as before, and the growth of London was always setting new sanitary problems. By the mid-'eighties, the Thames sewage trouble had recurred, about the outfalls made a generation earlier. When some Royal Commissioners embarked at Woolwich in 1884, the river "for its whole width was black, putrid sewage, looking as if unmixed and unalloyed. The stench was intolerable." They thought this "a disgrace to the metropolis and to civilisation."[3] So settling tanks and the transport of the sludge to sea in barges had to be provided.

[1] Jephson, p. 246–7.

[2] Jephson, p. 228, quoting the M.O. of Shoreditch: cp. vol. I. p. 539.

[3] *R.C. on the effects of the discharge of Metropolitan Sewage into the Thames*, 1884–5 (XXXI. 341), *Second Report*, p. ix.

Not until the passing of the London Public Health Act of 1891 were some sanitary rules, which had been applied long before in the country at large, made universally applicable in the territory of the new County Council. Towns which had always had a single central authority were in a position to make prompt use of the general health legislation, so much of which was permissive, or to promote local acts of their own. Birmingham under Joseph Chamberlain is a case in point[1]. Most of the great towns had handled their water supply with vigour. Liverpool had struggled resolutely with the exceedingly difficult problems of sanitation and health in a seaport, originally ill-built, and full of not too sanitary Irish immigrants[2]. But in most manufacturing towns industrial were apt to outweigh sanitary considerations. There was little interest in smoke abatement and, with slow means of transport, a strong desire to keep people near their places of work. None of these towns had such large, comfortable, and relatively healthy residential areas as London. Many had more difficult sites. Birmingham stands on high and open ground where wholesome drainage is not too difficult; the Tyne is tidal up to Newcastle and the Clyde to Glasgow; but the towns of the West Riding and the Lancashire Pennines, in their narrow, hard-sided valleys, had no light task when, and if, they wished to alter their lay-out, or decided no longer to drain into the small and obvious river—Calder, Aire, Don or Irwell. Above Manchester, the Irwell has already passed some half-dozen manufacturing townlets and towns. In hot weather in the 'eighties it stank there much, one supposes, as the Thames had stunk at Westminster in June 1858[3]. The Calder and the Aire stank also, though perhaps not so badly as in earlier hot summers[4]. But Parliament never sat by any of them, and their stench is recorded in no *Memoirs of an ex-Minister*.

So, in spite of municipal governments which had at least opportunities for sanitary efficiency, round about 1880 none of the greater towns, except Birmingham and Bristol, had death-rates below that composite rate of Eaton Square, Clare Market

[1] Cp. below, p. 492.

[2] See Hope, E. W., *Health at the Gateway* (1931), *passim*; and below, p. 493–4.

[3] Memories of a boy who sometimes played by it, at an exciting place where a little clear stream, which had cut a canyon eight feet deep in red sandstone, ran under trees into the foul current.

[4] An old Leeds resident, in 1903, spoke of the great improvement in the stench of the Aire during the previous half-century.

and the Old Kent Road which stood for London. Newcastle, Sheffield, Leeds and Leicester were within a few points of it; Manchester, Glasgow and Liverpool were decidedly worse. Yet the cities of Britain were among the healthiest in the world, and were certainly the healthiest of the Old World. The death-rate of New York was worse than that of Manchester; those of Paris and Berlin worse than that of Liverpool; and that of the whole city which the Victorians knew as St Petersburg nearly 25 per cent. worse than that of a small, selected, black London area such as Clare Market. The census of 1891 would show that more than 11 per cent. of the population of England and Wales, and nearly 20 per cent. of the Londoners, lived more than two to a room, 'under conditions of over-crowding' as then officially defined[1]. No comparable figures exist for the foreign capitals; but there is no great doubt that, had they been collected, they would have been worse, except possibly in New York. The English sanitarians were never content, rightly; but there was something to show for fifty years' work when Edwin Chadwick, who was born in 1800, died in 1890.

"Hitherto it is questionable if all the mechanical inventions yet made have lightened the day's toil of any human being." So Mill wrote in 1847, and so the text of the people's edition of his *Principles* stood in the 'eighties[2]. Only "just institutions and the deliberate guidance" of the increase of mankind, he thought, could resolve the question. There was not much trace of this guidance in 1883–6. Certainly institutions had been made somewhat more just. What lightening, if any, had there been of the day's toil? Whether appropriate or not when written, was the question as it stood in the people's edition of Mill misleading?

Some heavy, even murderous, jobs had been killed, or nearly killed, by machinery since he first wrote. There were few 'bottom-sawyers' left; few, if any, carpenters worked out in fifteen years by handling the great jack-plane[3]. The sewing machine

[1] Cp. below, p. 490 *sqq*.

[2] Book IV, ch. VI, § 2. This is one of the many famous phrases of his which have too often been quoted without being dated. The fact that he allowed it to stand until his death does not prove that he reconsidered it. He described the United States as a country "in which the doctrine of Protection is declining, but not yet wholly given up" (Book V, ch. X, § 1) in all his editions.

[3] For bottom-sawyers see vol. I. p. 445. The jack-plane was a favourite illustration of Alfred Marshall's.

must have lightened an incalculable number of days' toil. It was easier to mind a completely self-acting mule than to push about the carriage of the old hand-mule. The power-loom shed was noisy, and its looms had been speeded up; but work in it was certainly lighter, day for day, than the bowed, endless, insanitary monotony of that lower-grade hand-loom weaving of the 'thirties and 'forties which alone had been completely superseded. Scything is a noble art; but it cannot be argued that a full day's scything is lighter than a full day's management of a reaper; nor that a day in an un-mechanised copper or lead mine is lighter than one in a fully equipped colliery.

Yet if mechanical invention was killing off some heavy jobs, it had made and was making others—stoking and coal trimming in a gale, or in the Red Sea; puddling, and all the exacting work of blast furnace and steel furnace; the long day, heavy with responsibility, of the signalman or the engine-driver; and scores of laborious and often dangerous tasks in gas works, chemical works and engineering shops. An hour's work in the caissons, or on the cantilevers, of the Forth Bridge may well be called heavier than one put in under Rennie on Waterloo Bridge. So the enumeration might go on; but no balance could ever be struck. For it is not even quite certain that twelve and a half hours' work, paced by the "wheels of iron," in the early cotton mills was heavier for the child than twelve and a half hours of the many different drudgeries to which he might have been assigned before the inventions[1].

It is hard to say how common twelve hours' drudgery for children had been before the inventions. After them, it was certainly common in the mills; and that was the justification for those factory laws to which, although the Ten Hours' Act had passed when he wrote, Mill gave a single page, containing no information, and occupied almost entirely by a protest against the extension of the laws to women. One object of the early acts had been to bring the child mill-worker's day more nearly into line with the customary working day of average adult wage-earners[2]. Cam Hobhouse had told the House of Commons in 1825 that, from inquiries which he had made, it appeared that ten and a half hours, and in winter in some cases eight and a half, was an ordinary day's work for "machine-makers, the moulders of the machinery, house-carpenters,

[1] Cp. vol. I. p. 371, 565. Twelve and a half hours was the day in the "best regulated" mills of the 'twenties. Hansard, XIII. p. 643.

[2] Vol. I. p. 377.

cabinet-makers, stonemasons, bricklayers, blacksmiths, millwrights," and many other craftsmen[1]. There were trades with longer regular hours; outwork of all kinds in which inclination or necessity determined the working day; continuous processes with twelve-hour shifts; and all sorts of emergency arrangements. But something like ten and a half hours was normal for the man or woman working to an employer's direction, or on his premises. So it remained down to 1848, and later. Its persistence, combined with the increased strain of some tasks connected with machinery, was probably the cause of Mill's dreary questioning[2].

A rather long day's work was normal in all serious occupations during the early 'fifties, not merely for wage-earners. It was the otherwise unimportant Factory Act of 1850 (13 and 14 Vict. c. 54) which, besides introducing the legal 60-hour week for women, really started the *semaine anglaise*, by ordering the stoppage of work at 2 p.m. on Saturdays[3]. As the textile factory code was extended to other trades, a Saturday half-holiday became the rule. The building trades, never under factory law, were securing it by negotiation or strike during the 'sixties[4]. But until 1854 even so capitalistic an institution as Lloyd's was open on Saturday afternoon[5]. At that time carpenters and joiners were working from 52 to 64 hours a week, according to the season, much as in 1825. So were bricklayers, and presumably the rest of the building trades. The week of a compositor in London was 63 hours all the year round. That of the engineer and the iron-founder was the same. Textiles, building, metal-working were all more or less in line, with a tendency for the state-protected textiles, once so far in the rear, to get a trifle ahead of the rest, because of the law and their women and children[6].

[1] Hansard, XIII. p. 1008.

[2] There is no reason to think that Mill had really studied the problem: he just threw out his suggestion.

[3] Under the Act of 1844 (7 and 8 Vict. c. 15) work, for protected people, stopped at 4.30 on Saturdays.

[4] See the evidence given before the *R.C. on Trades Unions* of 1867–9; R. Applegarth, for the carpenters, Q. 192; E. Coulson, for the bricklayers, Q. 2295; J. Wilson, a builder, Q. 4396.

[5] Wright, C., and Fayle, C. E., *A History of Lloyd's*, p. 356.

[6] The history of the day's work in the various trades is summarised in the *Statistical Tables and Report on Trade Unions* of 1887; Burnett's Report (LXXXIX. p. 715). See also Wood, G. H., "Some Statistics relating to Working Class Progress since 1860," *S.J.* 1899, p. 640–2.

For twenty-four years the 60-hour textile week stood. Then, in 1874, it was cut to 56½ under 37 and 38 Vict. c. 44. In the interval, some of the trades, by negotiation, strikes and threats of strikes had, in their turn, got ahead of the textiles. The English building trades did not manage to force their summer hours below 61½ or 61, either before or after 1874; but they got their winter week down to 48 hours or under; their average to something near 55, or less when inevitable weather stoppages are taken into account. By judicious use of the brisk demand for labour of all kinds in 1872, they made it 54; where it stayed. Both the engineers and the iron-founders, and with them necessarily the mass of the shop-working metal-workers, had brought their normal hours down to 57 before 1861. There was a pause; and then, with the boiler-makers and like the compositors, they utilised the splendid opportunity of 1872, when the A.S.E. averaged only 0·9 per cent. of its members unemployed, and the little close society of steam-engine makers only 0·6 per cent., to extort from employers with books full of orders the 54-hour week which became standard throughout their group of trades[1]. In Scotland the engineers beat the week down to 51; but they could not hold it there. When the bad times came, in 1879, employers took back the half-hour a day by which Scotland had got ahead of England. With unemployment figures in the metal-working unions ranging from 11 to 22 per cent., the men were in no position to fight. The week's work of 54 or 54½ hours, to which these unions of representative trades settled down in the 'seventies, was not to be changed for many years. It was never universal, and it was of course extended by overtime when trade was brisk, or reduced by short-time working, especially in the textile industries, when it was slack. But it was as typical of the fourth quarter of the nineteenth century as the 63-hour week had been of the first and second quarters. To that extent, at least, the day's toil for human beings had been lightened. Guidance of the increase of mankind had nothing to do with it: that palliative Britain, in her strong international position, did not yet require. In the background, mechanical invention, by increasing the divisible national dividend, had a great deal to do with it. In the foreground, institutions and laws, become more just, were directly responsible for the example set in the textile factories, and

[1] Unemployment figures are also in the *Report* of 1887, and have often been reproduced.

were partially responsible for the greater ease with which a trade union or group of half-organised men could negotiate or fight for a shorter day. In this matter of the day's work, the law or the union is more important than in the matter of wages. Wages may rise 'of themselves', when the balance of supply and demand is definitely favourable to the wage-earner. Between 1850 and 1886, the wages of the almost completely unorganised women in the cotton industry rose, it has been reckoned, in the ratio of 59 to 98; those of the women in the woollen industry, still less organised, in that of 62 to 96; those of women agricultural labourers in Northumberland, not organised at all, in that of 67 to 100[1]. In wage bargains made between individuals, the worker may ask for more pay, or the employer may propose it to attract him. Individual demands or employer's proposals for a shorter working week, though not impossible or unknown, are much less practicable and less common.

The rise in women's wages which accompanied the shortening of hours, a rise which in the cotton industry has been estimated at 66 per cent., is only a special case of that general wage rise which marks the years 1850–86 from the years 1830–50, when wages in general were almost stationary[2]. There were interruptions and set-backs in the rise after 1850. In most trades there was a slight fall, in some a sharp and painful fall, between 1874 and 1886; but when the chief occupations of the country are taken together, and when allowance is made for the steady transfer of labour from worse to better-paid occupations, wage-rates in the mass, so to speak, are estimated to have fallen during the twelve years not more than in the ratio of 156 to 148[3]. This cut away only a fragment of the gain made between 1850

[1] Wood, G. H., "Factory Legislation considered with reference to the Wages of the Operatives," *S.J.* 1902, p. 284–320. The Northumberland figure is for the period 1850 to 1883: figures for 1886 were not available. There is of course a margin of error in all such calculations. Textile wages are especially difficult. But the margins of error are relatively narrow and there is a very close agreement among statisticians about the general course of wages in this period. This explains, and justifies, the concise treatment in the text.

[2] Vol. I. p. 548, 561.

[3] The calculation is that of Wood, G. H., "Real Wages and the Standard of Comfort since 1850," *S.J.* 1909, p. 91–103. The article summarises and carries on the work done by Mr Wood and Prof. Bowley in the *S.J.* during the previous ten years and in Prof. Bowley's *Wages in the United Kingdom* (1900). It is the basis of the diagram on p. 452 below. Prof. Bowley calculated the fall from 1874 to 1886 to be rather greater—in the ratio of 142 to 130.

and 1874; for the figure for 1850 which corresponds to the 156 of 1874 is 100, the base line of the calculation. Even the fall after 1874 was more than compensated—on the average; not for everyone—by a contemporary fall in the cost of living.

These figures are statisticians' weighted index numbers, based on all known representative and trustworthy series of wage-rates, including those in agriculture. From the standpoint of national welfare they are the true figures, or at least the truest available, because they take account of the differing numbers of people earning the different rates of wage at successive dates[1]. As there was a continuous movement from lower to higher-paid occupations, not so much by individual wage-earners as by their children, this is a vital consideration. The relatively ill-paid agricultural labourers, to take the outstanding case, were a much smaller fraction of the whole body of wage-earners in 1886 than in 1850; and so, in any exact discussion of national welfare, it would not be proper to give their low wage so much weight for the former year as for the latter. But the 'average wage-earner' whose receipts, given equal regularity of work, rose between 1850 and 1886 in the ratio of about 100 to 148, is not a man of flesh and blood. He is the result of dividing the estimated aggregate amount of wages paid by the estimated number of wage-earners in all the occupations dealt with; a most important figure, but not human.

A man who had worked at the same trade from the Great Exhibition to the eve of Victoria's Jubilee, without losing any of his efficiency, could not show a rise of 48 per cent. in his weekly wage like this 'average wage-earner'; though one who had left the land as a young man for some urban job might well show more. The man who had remained in the station of life in which he was born had, on the average, lived to see a rise in his weekly or hourly rate of pay of something like 30 per cent. About this figure different trades and jobs fluctuated.

The English agricultural labourer came rather above the general average for the wage-earners of unchanged grade. His rise was some 40 per cent. But for the sharp drop after 1877, it would have been over 48 per cent. Trades already fairly well paid in 1850, like printing and engineering, had made less

[1] Chart 4 in the *Statistical Memoranda and Charts* of 1909 gives the unweighted average of wages, not taking account of changes in the sizes of the wage-earning groups. Bowley's weighted average, calculated in 1900, in a rather different way and with rather different material from Wood's, was almost identical, but gave a slightly smaller rise, 1850–86 (*Wages in the U.K.* p. 132).

progress: the former is credited with a rise of only 16 and the latter of only 25 per cent.[1] All the heavy trades come out badly, because iron and coal were specially hard hit in 1886. One

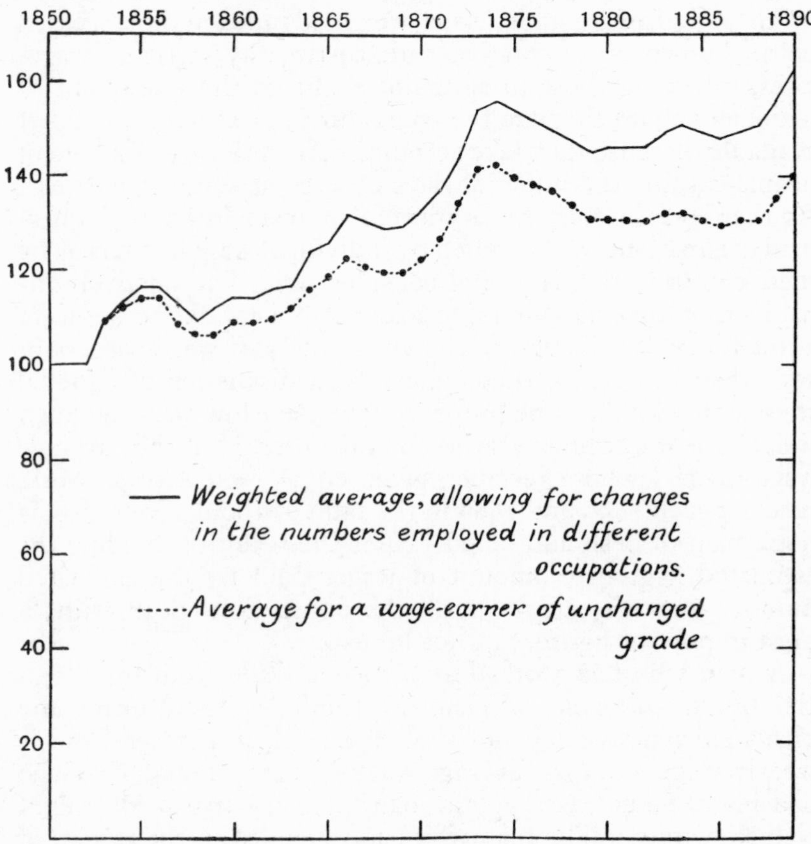

Course of Average Wages in Industry and Agriculture, as percentages of the average of 1850. Based on Wood, G. H., "Real Wages and the Standard of Comfort since 1850," *S.J.* 1909.

calculation gives the miners a rise of only 8 per cent.[2]; but it is agreed that in 1874 their wages had been from 60 to 70 per cent. above the level of 1850[3]. The building trades, untouched by

[1] These are Wood's figures. Those of Bowley show a rise of 21 per cent. for printers. But the results are very close.

[2] Wood. Here there is a more serious discrepancy in the statistical conclusions, as Bowley's figure is 20 per cent.

[3] There was a very rapid rise almost, if not quite, to the level of 1874 in 1886–91. This is one of the cases in which the 1886 figures are not representative.

machinery, working a shorter day and—by general consent—working slower, had at the same time managed to increase their standard pay by some 50 per cent.[1]

Cotton, with its difficult statistics and shifting mechanical practice, shows a rise, for men as well as women, well above the national average of 30 per cent., largely because jobs with the same name did not remain really the same. Only the mill mechanic, whose function did not change and whose wage rose from 27*s.* to 32*s.* (21 per cent.), comes below that level. The average wage of the various kinds of male jenny or mule spinners—a group of unequal units—rose in the Manchester district from about £1 to £1. 15*s.*, or 75 per cent. That of the carding over-lookers, whose job was fairly constant and not ill paid at the start, nevertheless rose from 27*s.* to 39*s.* 10*d.*, or 47·5 per cent. For the whole cotton industry, men women and children, the rise in average wages, taking into account the constant increase in size of the better-paid groups, has been estimated at 59 per cent.; and other methods of calculation have yielded an even higher figure[2]. It is certain, at least, that the great cotton industry as a whole—a complex of industrial grades, not a single job like bricklaying—had made not less than 48 per cent. improvement, which is the weighted figure for Britain.

It is possible that, in the particular year 1886, as compared with the particular year 1850, the position of wage-earners in the mass, and as individuals, was a little worse than the wage-rate arithmetic suggests. There was heavy unemployment in 1886. Except 1879, it was the worst year of that late period for which the growing supply of trade union unemployment pay figures begins to facilitate close discussion. In 1886, the Iron-founders had on the average 13·9 per cent.; the Associated Blacksmiths 14·4 per cent.; the Boilermakers and Iron Ship-builders 22·2 per cent. of their membership drawing out-of-work pay. Those are the extreme figures; but both the Amalgamated Engineers and the United Carpenters and Joiners had

[1] According to Wood. Bowley gives 42 per cent. which illustrates the close general agreement in these calculations. For the pace of building see above, p. 159.

[2] The 59 per cent. is Wood's figure (*S.J.* 1909) "based on an entirely new method, which discards...earnings in separate occupations, but takes into account the average earnings of all the operatives engaged in the industry as estimated by Ellison and others". Bowley, in *Wages in the United Kingdom*, made the rise 72 per cent.

over 7 per cent., a rather high proportion for these late nineteenth-century records[1].

By the standards of the time, 1850 was certainly a prosperous year. It has been suggested, on the evidence of the trade-union records[2], that a general unemployment figure of 4 per cent. might be assumed for it, as against one of 9·5 per cent. in 1886. But trade-union unemployment figures at their best, that is from 1875 onwards, are very incomplete. The farther back they go, the scantier and less typical do they become. For only a handful of unions do figures from the 'fifties exist at all. Even for the 'seventies and 'eighties, there are no series of importance from the textile trades; necessarily none from the outwork trades, whose members were seldom in unions; none from the miners; and none from the whole fields of agricultural, casual, unskilled, and women's labour. It is probable also that the ranks of the trade unions, especially in their early days, contained the picked and the fortunate men of their trades; and that the slack worker, who perhaps drank the money which might have gone in a union subscription, or the feeble worker of sub-normal capacity who took no interest in unionism, was likely to be the first to be discarded by an employer. From 1869 to 1886, and after, the Amalgamated Tailors never once showed an average unemployment figure so high as 0·6 per cent. Most creditable to the union and to its select membership of 12,000 to 15,000, in the 'seventies and 'eighties; but is it to be supposed that the grotesquely cheerful figure of 0·46 per cent. unemployed in 1879 can give any indication of the probable amount of unemployment and under-employment among the 170–180,000 tailors and tailoresses, mostly outworkers, in Britain in that bad year?[3]

During the fourth quarter of the century, textile mills and mines were apt to counter slack trade by short-time working or fewer shifts. Of this the available figures tell nothing. It was not a new practice; but in earlier years complete stoppages of

[1] For the thirty years 1860–90 the average unemployment figure of the A.S.E. (the modern A.E.U.) was 4·35 per cent.

[2] By Wood in the *S.J.* for 1909, as above, p. 102. The 4·0 for 1850 is given with a query; 3·9 is suggested without one for 1851. It is also the figure given in the *Statistical Memoranda and Charts* of 1909, p. 44. For prosperity in 1850 see the evidence in Tooke and Newmarch, *History of Prices*, VI. 249 *sqq*.

[3] The figures for 1881 were—tailors, in England and Wales, 108,000; in Scotland, 21,000: tailoresses, in England and Wales, 53,000; in Scotland, 3,000. *Census of* 1881 (1883, LXXX and LXXXI).

work were commoner. During the very bad trade of 1847–8 both methods are found in use. In June, 1847, of 40,000 mill hands in Manchester, the mills of 12,000 were stopped. How many more were working short time we do not know. Horner, the great factory inspector of the North, reported in June, 1848, that "as many mills have already closed and a large proportion have shortened their time of working,"[1] the ten-hour law was being applied quite easily.

In the 'fifties, the textiles were relatively more important than in the 'eighties. There was still a great deal of outwork in them; in the clothing trades far more. In important sections of the metal trades the outworker and the small master were typical[2]. For outworkers and small masters, under-employment, a bit of work here and a bit there, all at inadequate pay, is often widespread even in those good times when complete unemployment is rare. Agricultural labourers in 1850 formed a much larger part of the community than in 1886, and there can be no doubt that their chances of unemployment were also larger; though there are no statistics of unemployment among them for either date. It is probable, therefore, that good years in the 'fifties, such as 1850 and 1851, were far nearer in the aggregate of unemployment and under-employment to later bad years, such as 1886, than any calculation based on the handful of existing early trade-union figures would suggest.

A bad year in the 'fifties could be very bad indeed. Even on the basis of the trade-union figures, 1858, the year after the great commercial crisis, was worse than 1879 or 1886; and the average of the eight years 1851–8 was only a fraction better than the average of 1881–8, years in which the air was full of talk about unemployment and depression. So, even if the particular year 1886 was worse than the particular year 1850, as it may well have been, there is no reason to discount the wage rise which occurred between the 'fifties and the 'eighties by assuming any parallel increase in the average amount of unemployment in groups of years. Alfred Marshall astonished a Royal Commission in 1888 by telling them that in his belief there had not been "a larger number of people unemployed during the last ten years than during any other consecutive ten years";[3] and

[1] Quoted by Wood in *S.J.* 1902, p. 314; where the Manchester mill figures are also quoted.

[2] See above, p. 126, 131.

[3] *R.C. on Gold and Silver*: Marshall's evidence, Q. 9828. Presumably when he said a larger number he meant a larger proportionate number.

even though his decade included 1879 as well as 1886, it is more than likely that he was right. Statistical certainty was, and remains, impossible.

In some trades and places, during the 'forties, payment of wages in truck, in spite of the Truck Act of William IV and its many predecessors, had meant an effective reduction of the nominal wage[1]. The system, even when not seriously abused, was generally disliked by wage-earners as an infringement of liberty, and more bitterly by their wives. It died slowly. In 1863 miners are protesting against it with a vehemence which suggests widespread survival[2]. But though, in the 'seventies and 'eighties, there was still both corrupt and economically, if not legally, defensible trucking, there was hardly enough of either to affect any general conclusions which may be drawn from the course of money wages. Only in one district, and that very remote, was truck "in an oppressive form...general"[3] by 1871—the Shetland Islands, where the peasant knitters and fishermen, ignorant both of money and of prices, were at the mercy of dealers who paid them in bad 'goods,' precisely as English foggers and bagmen had paid nailers and knitters[4], and sometimes still paid them. It was reckoned in 1871 that 14,000 Midland nailers were 'trucked' by the foggers. The Truck Act "was simply disregarded";[5] and the truck was in every way corrupt. The trucking fogger, often a publican, paid in bad dear goods, and undersold the honest master. His subject nailers dared not invoke the law. In hosiery, however, at the same date, the system was almost extinct. The few middlemen's shops, in northern Nottinghamshire and the edge of Derbyshire, were said to serve not more than 1100 or 1200 knitters. The new hosiery factories had a clean record[6]. Truck of a corrupt sort was still practised by some of the mining 'butties' and 'doggies' of the Midlands and the South-West[7]. It was found occasionally, as might have been expected, in such outwork

[1] See vol. I. p. 409–10, 562–5.

[2] *Transactions of the National Association of Miners of Great Britain*, 1863, p. xi, quoted in Webb, S. and B., *Industrial Democracy*, p. 317, n. 2.

[3] *R.C. on Truck*, 1871 (XXXVI), p. xliv: a whole volume of the R.C.'s *Report* (1871, XXXVII) was given to evidence from Shetland.

[4] Vol. I. p. 564.

[5] *R.C. on Truck*, p. xxv.

[6] *Ibid.* p. xxx.

[7] *Ibid.* p. xxv. A complaint of 'butties' paying miners in liquor is in the *Transactions of the National Association* of 1863, quoted above.

industries as gloving and lace-making, where conditions nearly resembled those of nail-making or knitting. In remote places, works of almost any kind might occasionally start a shop, a 'tommy' shop, as a matter of convenience; and the working of the shop might become corrupt[1]. But the only large-scale survivals in 1871 were those in coal and iron areas where the system had been common twenty years before.

Once upon a time, in the steep remote valleys of South Wales and Monmouthshire, the company shop had been a blessing, a mine inspector said in that year[2]. Many employers held that it was so still. It did not now pay out wages in goods, for that was illegal. But as cash wages were only paid at long intervals—monthly at Ebbw Vale; sometimes only every twelve weeks at Rhymney—men might be given advances on account, to cover their shop purchases. Careful men avoided both the advances and the shop, which is its chief condemnation. The companies ran some shops direct; some were farmed. The stuff supplied in the bigger ones was generally good but dear. Dearness was defended on the ground that the shops gave credit, while outside tradesmen asked for cash. Had paydays not been so far apart, and had all the men been provident, credit would not have been necessary. The men, provident or not, naturally wanted short pays.

The shop was common also at the Lanarkshire and Ayrshire coal and iron works; and so were fortnightly or monthly pays. Perhaps 25,000 workers in that area were affected in 1871[3]. Sometimes there was actual compulsion to frequent the shop; but as a rule the long pays provided it with customers, as in Wales. Prices were habitually high, and goods, at least sometimes, inferior. All the best men and their wives hated the business. They did not go to law about it because the Truck Act was not properly adjusted to Scottish legal procedure. The aggrieved party would have had to prosecute. So the Act was "in abeyance altogether."[4]

How far this iron and coal truck, or semi-truck, was corrupt, wage-encroaching as well as unpopular, it is hard to say. There

[1] *R.C. on Truck*, p. lxxix. At Stephen's shipbuilding yard on the Clyde a store started by the men with the help of their employers had degenerated into a sort of truck-shop, the firm having allowed the store-keepers to make deductions from wages to cover accounts due. It was closed early in 1871.

[2] *Ibid.* p. v.

[3] *Ibid.* Q. 8575. Evidence of Alexander Macdonald. The Scottish evidence is discussed in the *Report*, p. xv *sqq*.

[4] *Ibid.* p. xx.

were certainly corrupt patches; there were also large healthy areas. Evidence of deliberate use of the shop to secure labour cheap, as among the nailers, is scanty. The Commissioners of 1871 were no doubt right when they argued that weekly pays would dispose of nearly all the attendant evils, if the shops were maintained. No law in that sense was passed, or even suggested, and there was no revision of the Truck Acts until 1887 (50 and 51 Vict. c. 46). But short pays became commoner. Company shops declined. By 1886–7 truck proper had sunk into insignificance, though there were still a few 'tommy' shops in lonely places, such as the chair-making villages of the Chiltern Hills. Some grievances akin to that of truck proper survived to be dealt with in the late Victorian Truck Acts—excessive charges by the employers for materials, or power, or powder, or candles used by workpeople; and those fines for irregularities and blunders which, in bad hands, might amount to systematic deductions from wages. But these were occasional and limited evils[1].

Part of the under-employment and unemployment in outwork industries, throughout the period, was connected with the technical innovations which were changing them in turn into factory industries; but how serious this 'technological' unemployment was in any given trade, or at any given date, is most difficult to determine. It had been very serious among hand-loom weavers of cotton, flax and worsted, from the 'twenties to the 'forties. There was no doubt a good deal of it among them in the 'fifties, and some later. But after the year 1860 it was unimportant, because the hand-loom was now only used for specialities or oddities; and for these it was discarded gradually. In woollen and silk-weaving, the transition from hand to power was so long drawn out that large-scale unemployment was avoided: death and the transfer of the younger generation did most of the work[2]. There may have been some technological unemployment among nail and chain-makers, handmade-lace workers and frame-work knitters, as machinery slowly conquered their trades[3]; and there must have been a little at every other particular industrial revolution. But at the most con-

[1] For the survivals at the end of the period see the article "Truck" in *Dic. Pol. Econ.* Very little was heard of it before the *R.C. on Labour* of the 'nineties.

[2] See above, p. 28 and p. 83.

[3] For the growth of factories in chain-making see *R.C. on Labour*, 1892 (xxxvi. Pt. 2), Q. 16,890 *sqq.* There is no suggestion of unemployment.

spicuous revolutions of these years there is no evidence that the amount was important; and when revolution was slow the final turn to machinery might well prove a godsend to those affected. Clothing became a factory industry so gradually and so partially, and the clothing factory was such a blessing to sewing women and sewing girls, that the certain and grave evils in the trade were never connected by any responsible person with the coming of the factories; rather with its delay. Though hand shoe-makers, in some places, struck against machinery at first, and probably suffered in consequence, on the whole it did very little harm to these 'seat men' as they were called. "The most competent machine workers" were "continuously recruited" from among them[1]. There were all kinds of half machine jobs to which the less adaptable of them could turn. And as easy processes passed into girls' hands, the male shoe-makers, following sound advice given them by well-wishers, deliberately kept their own numbers down[2]. The industry of the country as a whole was expansive enough to absorb those who, if they had not been so excluded, might have become stickit shoe-makers. And the bespoke trade was always there for the best craftsmen, just as in tailoring. The wages of hand shoe-makers certainly went up during the years when the machine was coming in, which they would not have done had machinery made any considerable number of them redundant. As factories spread in the Midland metal trades, small masters passed into them without, it would seem, any general gap of unemployment. There, as in the clothing trades, it was among late surviving outworkers that under-employment, sweating, foul working conditions, and all evil things were commonest at the close of the period. They were a handful of outworking locksmiths who in 1892, "in bedrooms...and in wash-houses and all about", worked, when work was to be had, from "six in the morning to ten at night and all night on Friday,"[3] so that their employers might undersell properly equipped factories. For these locksmiths a final industrial revolution was much to be desired, even if it should bring any added risk of formal unemployment, which was unlikely.

[1] Leno, J. B., *The Art of Boot and Shoe Making* (1885), pp. vii, 210.

[2] *Ibid.* p. 210: "The rank and file, acting under the advice...tendered thro' the pages of *St Crispin*, set sternly to work to reduce their numbers." Leno had been editor of *St Crispin* and also of *The Boot and Shoe Maker*.

[3] *R.C. on Labour* (1892, XXXVI. Pt. 2): evidence of E. Day, Q. 18,128, 18,229.

Although no complete or scientifically accurate cost-of-living index for industrial wage-earners from the 'fifties to the 'eighties has yet been constructed, the broad facts are not in doubt. That the money cost of living, on any given scale, including rent, had not gone up perceptibly is certain. The available evidence suggests that it may have fallen a trifle. Bread prices had fallen sharply[1]. Londoners, during the ten years 1850–9, had paid an average price of 8½*d.* for their four-pound loaf. For the seven years 1880–6 the figure was just above 6¾*d.*

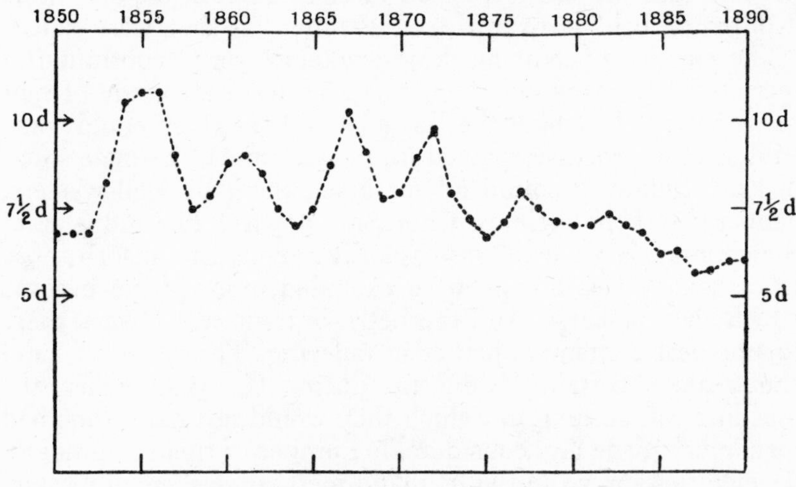

Average annual price of the 4-lb. loaf in London.

Even in the seven years of high prices and high wages, 1870–6, it had only been 8*d.* In 1887 it fell nearly to 5½*d.* (When Victoria came to the throne, a cheap year for the period, it had been 8½*d.*) Of other food prices important for the wage-earning consumer some, such as meat, had risen; but bacon had fallen and so had sugar and tea. Altogether they showed a definite fall. If the prices are taken of all those commodities of ordinary consumption, including bread, for which records are continuous, it appears that a miscellaneous collection of them which would have cost on the average 17*s.* 8½*d.* in the decade 1850–9 could have been bought for 16*s.* 2½*d.* in 1880–6. The difference would not have been so great but for the Crimean War and the price

[1] The general statistical discussion is in Wood, "Real Wages and the Standard of Comfort since 1850," *S.J.* 1909, quoted above, on which this account is based. The London bread prices used here are those given in the *Eighteenth Abstract of Labour Statistics* (1926), p. 143.

rise of the 'fifties. In 1851–2 the collection could have been bought for 15*s.* 6*d.* But even this low figure was above that of 1886 (14*s.* 7*d.*); and the figure of 1886 was never exceeded during the remainder of the nineteenth century. When Victoria's second jubilee came to be celebrated in 1897 the four-pound loaf in London stood at 5½*d.* and the cost of the same collection of commodities of ordinary consumption was down to 13*s.* 8½*d.* Trade-union unemployment was at 3·5 per cent. The people had votes: they cheered the Queen and a majority of them voted Conservative. It is not surprising. The mills of God, with a little supervision from man, had ground out, if not all that vision-seers had hoped, still some very sound nourishing stuff worth conserving.

How far the fall in retail commodity prices was offset by a rise in urban rents is much harder to estimate, for lack of figures[1]. Estimation is complicated by changes in housing. The normal wage-earning townsman of the 'eighties was rather better housed than his father had been. So far as is known, there had been a rise in average rent from about 4*s.* to about 5*s.* 6*d.* a week[2]. It has been suggested that perhaps half of this rise represented the price of better housing—more space, more conveniences; the other half, the increased rentable value of urban land and the increased costs of building, due mainly to higher pay and easier working conditions of men in the building trades. If this is approximately correct, the unavoidable rise in rent—that is, the extra cost of accommodation not better than the average accommodation of the 'fifties, estimated at about 9*d.* a week—would not quite absorb the net gain on bread and other articles of consumption[3]; and so the rise in money wages would be all available for improvement in the standard of living, including the rather better houses, unless unemployment had got worse, which is at least not demonstrable. It is unlikely

[1] This discussion of rent also follows Wood, *op. cit.* p. 95, and has no more authority than he claimed for it in view of its scanty foundations. I know no other treatment of the subject; though material for a fuller one should somewhere be procurable.

[2] The latter figure is of course much more certain than the former. The full inquiry made twenty years later (*Report on the Cost of Living of the Working Classes*, Cd. 3844 of 1908) showed *e.g.* that in Oldham, where 64 per cent. of the population lived in four-room houses, average rentals for such standard accommodation varied between 5*s.* and 6*s.* Outside London, the *maximum* rental for such a house only exceeded 6*s.* in eight out of the sixty-three towns reported on. There had been only a slight upward price movement since 1886.

[3] These estimates and hypotheses are again Wood's.

that more exact calculations, which could probably be made, would modify this conclusion much. In substance it was that of all observant contemporaries[1].

Among those conveniences for which the smaller householder paid increased rent, besides 'company's water' and gas-fittings and the like, were a whole range of public enterprises directly or indirectly beneficial to him, and all either new or improved since the Public Health, Public Baths, Common Lodging Houses and Public Library Acts of 1848–52. The trouble of collecting from small occupiers the Poor Rate, upon which other rates had been piled, had been recognised by law early in the century, and rating of the owner rather than the occupier had been permitted[2]. This compounding system was extended by the Small Tenements Act (13 and 14 Vict. c. 99) precisely in 1850, when the new municipal activities were just beginning[3]. If the annual rateable value of any tenement was below £6, the rating authority might deal with the owner. Local acts pushed up the figure. Finally, under an act of 1869 (32 and 33 Vict. c. 40), rendered necessary by the Second Reform Bill and the linking of rate-paying liability with the franchise, a uniform system of compounding was introduced for the whole of England and Wales. The rateable value below which compounding was permitted was raised to £20 a year for London, £13 for Liverpool, £10 for Manchester and Birmingham, and £8 for the rest of the country[4]. Rateable value being lower than renting value, this meant that the ordinary wage-earning householder everywhere paid nothing beyond his rent for all that the rates helped to provide—police and fire brigades; sanitation and vaccination; street maintenance and lighting; the growing provision of parks, open spaces, libraries and public baths; the whole business of poor relief, and the specialised hospitals which in a few of the greatest towns were growing out of it; and that new educational system which, although its cost to the rates had been casually estimated by Forster, when introducing the Bill of 1870, at much less than 3*d*. in the £ in the great majority of cases[5], was already, after fifteen years, drawing from the local exchequers what seemed the immense

[1] Cp. similar evidence about agricultural earnings, above, p. 284–7.

[2] By 59 Geo. III. c. 12, § 19.

[3] As the result of a recommendation from the *R.C. on the State of Large Towns and Populous Districts* of 1845: see vol. I. p. 544.

[4] Cp. Aschrott and Preston-Thomas, *The English Poor-Law System*, p. 80, 183

[5] Cannan, E., *History of Local Rates in England*, p. 137.

sums of £5,500,000 in England and Wales, and £1,360,000 in Scotland[1].

Reasonably efficient local government, a measure of cleanliness and order, some opportunities for rest and education, were the least that the towns owed their people. The debt was paid, if not in full, at least much more honestly than it had been a generation earlier. Peel Park by Manchester[2], the memorial to the lost leader of Free Trade, and Victoria Park in the London East End, both opened in the 'fifties, are perhaps not very radiant; but they, and their counterparts in other cities, must be judged before the background of the report of the Commission of 1845: "the great towns of Liverpool, Manchester, Birmingham and Leeds, and very many others, have at present no public walks."[3]

The central government, by the system of grants in aid of certain local services, contributed something towards their cost[4], besides providing the armour of political security and order for the body economic. The triumph of Peelite and Gladstonian finance was that this had been done with less and less pressure on the taxpayer, especially the wage-earning taxpayer, throughout forty years. It was estimated for 1882 that whereas the average amount of taxation per head in "the middle and upper classes" had increased by a bare 10 per cent. since 1842, in spite of the much greater increase of average wealth, in the "working classes" there had been a decline of 5 per cent.[5] In view of the rise in wages this meant, according to the estimate, that the average wage-earner with a family, who had paid out 16 per cent. of his income in taxes in 1842, paid only 7⅓ per cent. in 1882. Probably the position of the non-wage-earning family had been equally favourable when the income-tax stood at 2*d*. in the £ under Stafford Northcote; but in 1882 Gladstone's cabinet had ruthlessly pressed it up to 6½*d*., to pay for Disraelian imperialism and its own unanticipated military

[1] Compared with a total local expenditure of £62,000,000 for Britain and a national expenditure for the United Kingdom of under £90,000,000.

[2] Actually, in Salford.

[3] Quoted in vol. I. p. 545.

[4] Less than £5,000,000 in the mid-'eighties.

[5] By Prof. Leone Levi in *S.J.* March, 1884. The estimates are at best rough and must not be pressed; but they have been used, as reasonably trustworthy, by Prof. H. Clay in *E.J.* March, 1927.

obligations[1]. This was the year England went to Egypt and the year after Majuba Hill. Even so, the small actual increase of "middle and upper class" payment per head must have coincided with a decrease in the percentage of the family income paid out, though not so great as in "the working class."

Women's wages, poor as they still were if regarded as the livelihood of independent citizens, had risen in almost exactly the same fashion and ratio as those of men, where the woman was a regular whole-time wage-earner of industry or agriculture. Indeed, in the early 'eighties, the wage position for such women appears to have been relatively rather better than that of men. All wages had fallen since the slump of the 'seventies; but as women did not work in coal or iron or shipbuilding, they had escaped some of the most plunging falls[2]. The wages of domestic servants had also risen, perhaps in the same ratio; but in that great career which, in 1881 as in 1851, employed more than twice as many women and girls as all the textile industries put together, so much of the wage is paid in the most variable and unmeasurable kind that it has hitherto defied statisticians. Who knows whether the maidservant's food and housing and treatment by her mistress had improved at just the same rate as her money wage?[3]

What the improvement had been in the endless varieties of whole-time and part-time outwork—stitching trades of every kind, and a score of others such as box-making, brush-making,

[1] Imperialism and imperialistic obligations which, according to Lord Passfield, helped greatly to make socialists out of radicals: Webb, S., *Socialism in England*, p. 16.

[2] See the full study of *The Course of Women's Wages during the Nineteenth Century* by G. H. Wood, with a bibliography, published as Appendix A to Hutchins and Harrison, *A History of Factory Legislation* (1903). Wood's diagrammatic treatment shows that women's wages "on the whole...have not been so fluctuating" as those of men. He adds: "This is probably due to the rapidity with which wages change in the coal and iron and steel industries, where women are not employed" (p. 283). He also shows that women's wages, so far as known, were a little higher (about 5 per cent.) in 1883 than in 1886. Part of this small loss was recovered by 1888.

[3] An attempt was made to collect some statistics in 1886. Only 567 returns from large households were secured. Thirteen years later a fuller inquiry yielded an average wage for indoor domestic servants of £17. 16*s*. 0*d*. a year in London; £17. 6*s*. 0*d*. in the three chief Scottish towns, and £15. 10*s*. 0*d*. in England and Wales outside London. No attempt was made to value the board and lodging, because so "extremely difficult." *Report on the Money Wages of Domestic Servants* (by Miss Collet), 1899 (XCII. 1), p. iii.

or artificial flower-making—it is also quite impossible to calculate. These trades were the resort, among others, of the perfectly helpless, who perhaps lived partly on poor relief, and of wives who wanted to add to the family income. The finisher of shirts "is generally elderly, infirm, penniless, and a widow... she is nervous and timid and takes work at whatever price it may be offered to her....The young wife of the clerk with regular employment takes sealskin capes home from the warehouse where she worked as a girl."[1] It is very likely that the competition of such people had prevented the pay, for any given number of hours' work, in these trades from rising so much as the pay for corresponding work at the spinning-frame had risen. But young, quick and strong whole-time workers in them could make what was about the normal woman's pay in the poorer London artisan class of the 'eighties—10*s*. or 12*s*. a week. The Government paid 12*s*. to the charwomen of Whitehall, though 14*s*. was a common wage in the City and even 15*s*. is heard of[2].

About 20*s*. a week was the maximum for any ordinary woman worker, in a factory or at home. It was sometimes exceeded by a weaver minding four looms in Lancashire. At Oldham such a weaver could make up to 22*s*. 8*d*.; but the average earnings in that district were from 13*s*. to 19*s*.; in the Manchester district from 13*s*. to 15*s*. a week[3]. From nowhere in the Yorkshire woollen and worsted towns is a wage higher than 18*s*. reported: representative wages are the 10*s*. 9*d*. of 'preparers' and the 14*s*. or 15*s*. of weavers at Bradford. A pound a week was the top figure for 'clippers' and 'scollopers' in the Nottingham lace trade, and for circular-frame knitters in that neighbourhood. In the Staffordshire potteries, 3*s*. a day on piecework is given as the maximum: the normal pay for day-work was only 1*s*. 4*d*.[4] In the factories of East London, which were thoroughly representative of the miscellaneous

[1] Collet, Miss C. E., in Booth, *Life and Labour of the People in London*, IV. 259, 295. The inquiry was made in 1888 and all figures here quoted from Booth apply to that year. There had, however, been little change since 1886; and the object here is not precise statistical accuracy for a particular year, but illustration of the general position of the 'eighties.

[2] *Ibid*. IV. 260; VIII. 270.

[3] These are rates for 1882 and 1886 quoted in Bowley, *Wages in the Nineteenth Century*, p. 119.

[4] From the *Returns of Wages published between* 1830 *and* 1886 (1887, LXXXIX. 273). The wool, lace, knitting and pottery wages quoted all refer to 1883.

factory industries of the country, ranging as they did from book-binding, through confectionery, to corsets, matches, rope and umbrellas, the maximum of 20*s*. was never exceeded[1]. It was not touched in book-binding, confectionery or matches; not nearly touched in rope, where 11*s*. was the limit. Nowhere was it at all common. Except in fur-sewing, the most degraded of East End trades, ordinary full-work pay varied between 8*s*. and 16*s*., or between 10*s*. and 18*s*. for such people as the umbrella-makers or the better-class tailor's machinists, working in. Among outworkers, although a full heavy week would yield an elderly seamstress only a few shillings, there were those who could make their 20*s*. during the season (Easter to August) on good 'order work.'[2]

Between London and the typical manufacturing towns there was thus no marked gap. Everywhere the mass of full-time women workers made from 10*s*. to 14*s*. a week[3]. Only from the smaller towns of outlying manufacturing districts are definitely lower ranges reported—from 6*s*. to 15*s*. in the woollen mills of Stroud, or from 6*s*. 6*d*. to 11*s*. 6*d*. in those of Kendal. At Stroud probably, and at Kendal certainly, the earnings of the largest group would be below 10*s*. There would no doubt be corresponding ranges for outworkers in small towns, and for the surviving industrial outworkers in country districts; but the wages of these classes have been little recorded or inquired into.

The mass of wage-earning women in 1881 were still in the same great groups as in 1851—domestic service; the textile industries; the stitching industries; the washing industries[4]. The country having grown richer, there was a higher proportion of domestic servants. Including those on the farms, 11 per cent. of the whole female population as against 10 per cent. were in service. Neither the textile workers nor the stitching women had increased nearly so fast as the population; the women tailors had increased much faster. Machines accounted for these things. New industrial occupations for women were

[1] Booth, *op. cit.* IV. 318, a tabular summary.

[2] *Ibid.* IV. 258.

[3] The *Wage Census* taken by the Board of Trade in 1886, published in 1889 and later, which is the basis for all wage statistics of that year, gives an average wage for women of 12*s*. 8*d*. and for women and girls combined of 11*s*. 3*d*. The figures collected nearly all came from the textile trades, but evidently serve as a good sample for women's wages generally. Cp. the discussion in Wood, *The Course of Women's Wages*, as above, p. 260–1, 280.

[4] Above, p. 23–5.

developing slowly, though domestic and outwork jobs were passing into factories, both in the staple and the miscellaneous industries. But girls, it may be recalled, had proved competent to act as telegraph operators; and by the end of the decade there would be nearly 23,000 female clerks as compared with the 19 of 1851[1].

Factory Acts and Education Acts had kept the very youngest children from work, and so had subtracted something from family incomes. The subtraction, however, can seldom have been great. Under the Elementary Education Act of 1880 (43 and 44 Vict. c. 23) a certificated child of ten, and any child of thirteen, could begin earning. The early Factory Acts had put the normal age at nine, reduced in 1844 to eight for half-timers. In other industries, during the 'forties, regular work had usually begun between seven and eight. If there were babes making lace, straw-plait and hosiery, then and later, there were also boys of twelve to fourteen not yet at regular work in some trades and places. In the Birmingham trades of the 'sixties, nine or ten was the most usual working age; and the great engineering works of Lancashire employed only a handful of boys under thirteen, though no doubt some of the boys who came to them as improvers had run errands first[2]. London had never found much regular work for children under ten or twelve[3]. The obligation to keep them at school would hardly affect the economy of the average Londoner's household. It was among agricultural labourers that the curtailment of the child's earning years was most felt. And, of all classes, farmers had been the most critical of the new compulsory schooling. The clause of the Act of 1876 (39 and 40 Vict. c. 79), which allowed its relaxation during six weeks a year for children employed in agriculture, had probably been acceptable to all parties concerned.

For family earnings in the 'eighties there are not even 'misery' statistics, like those which gave the maxima for whole families of hand-loom weavers earlier in the century. But from the end

[1] *Census of* 1891: Occupations, 1893–4 (CVI, England and Wales; CVIII, Scotland). It appears from the figures that the woman clerk was commoner in Scotland than in England. For telegraph operators, above, p. 209.

[2] *Children's Employment Commission: Second Report*, p. xxxvi (lace and hosiery), p. xxxix (straw-plait); *Third Report*, p. x (Birmingham trades), p. 186 (Lancashire engineering).

[3] Cp. vol. I. p. 567.

of the decade onwards calculations and house-to-house inquiries began to be made which throw light back upon it: since these things do not change rapidly in a few years. Only the house-to-house inquiry can supply perfect data. In the 'eighties, many married women were in whole-time work everywhere, especially in textile districts; but common statistics do not tell how many of these were childless, or the wives of sick men, or of ne'er-do-wells. Nor can they tell of part-time work done at home, nor of receipts from washing and charing done out. Opportunities of work for children over school age varied: they were the best in the textile towns; worst, for girls, in the mining villages. In no rank of life do full-earning children normally stay for many years in the home, a fact which the inquiries from the end of the decade confirm. By far the largest wage-earning group of all, the girls who go into service, take their wages with them. "The match-girl and the jam-girl and the rope-girl...generally live at home";[1] but for all the trades of London, the regular wage-earners additional to the head of the house ranged from a minimum of 0·55 per household to a maximum of only 2·15, in the early 'nineties. Calculations made for a selected group of these trades, substantial trades like engineering, printing, railway service and the police force, suggested that on the average additional family earnings might amount to between 25 and 30 per cent. of those of the male head of the household[2]. When, in 1899, house-to-house inquiry for a population of 46,754 was first made at York, in a very different industrial atmosphere, it appeared that the additional earnings of every kind, excluding payments made by lodgers, came within a small fraction of 30 per cent. of the father's income[3]. The proportion is not likely to have been less in textile and light-metal-working districts. In colliery districts, one working lad living at home would supply as much. London and York between them represented most of the miscellaneous occupations of the country, and the York inquiry went to the very bottom of society. The close agreement between it and that of London, conducted in a totally different and much less personal fashion, suggests that for urban England an addition of from 25 to 35 per cent. of the earnings of the male head

[1] Booth, *Life and Labour*, IX. 380–1. The volume only appeared in 1897, but its basis was inquiry made in 1888–91.

[2] *Ibid*. The actual average arrived at was 26·9.

[3] Rowntree, B. S., *Poverty, a Study of Town Life* (1901), p. 83. The facts were collected in the autumn of 1899 (Preface, p. ix).

of a working-class household by the other members may have been about normal. Perhaps it was the same in the country; but that is much less certain.

The entry of a boy or girl into the serious business of earning was often casual, usually informal. Since the Children's Employment Commissioners of 1842–3 had been so much impressed by the vitality and the abuses of apprenticeship[1], abuses had certainly declined, and so had apprenticeship. But in modified forms, almost entirely without legal or official sanction, it had persisted, or grown up, in a number of those callings for which some formal spell of preparation was specially desirable. And the social problem of 'overstocking with apprentices,' which had vexed municipal authorities of the Middle Ages and Elizabethan legislators, still troubled Victoria's later years.

Throughout the textile trades, and in many others, especially the rougher factory trades, formal apprenticeship was all but extinct[2]. The child doffer picked up his simple job, became a piecer, and with luck a spinner. Luck was needed, because the spinner usually employed, and paid, two piecers. The sister of the girl who was about to leave the mill learnt standing by her loom, and then took it over. Lads were hired by the men who ran sub-contract gangs in the heavy-metal industries, or went into them under their fathers. On the other hand, the outworking journeymen of the older Sheffield trades, masters of a sort, had some rigid rules of admission, which generally favoured their own sons; and so had a number of other small unchanged crafts, coach-builders, basket-makers, coopers and the like[3]. The conservative shipwrights had not even abandoned the formal indenture, though it was dying[4]. Among patternmakers in engineering shops apprenticeship was universal, and five years was the minimum: often it extended to the age of

[1] Vol. I. p. 571.

[2] There were, however, survivals among specialists connected with the textile trades, such as beamers, stuff-pressers, overlookers. See Webb, S. and B., *Industrial Democracy* (1897), p. 460 n., 463, 478. The section on apprenticeship, p. 454–81, deals with the trade union aspect of the subject thoroughly.

[3] For Sheffield, *R.C. on Labour* (1892, XXXVI. Pt. 2), Q. 19,772; Webb, *op. cit.* p. 458; vol. I. p. 571. For the other crafts, Webb, *op. cit.* p. 462 n., referring, however, primarily to limitation of numbers by regulation of admissions, not to regulation of apprenticeship conditions.

[4] "Till recently...the bulk of our apprentices used to be indentured": A. Wilkie before the *R.C. on Labour* (1893, XXXII), Q. 21,462.

twenty-one[1]. The Admiralty still insisted on a full seven years' apprenticeship for all naval engineers[2]; but among engineers and boiler-makers generally, a rather informal spell, usually of two years, as a factory apprentice, plus a similar spell as an improver, was the rule[3]. There were standing controversies with employers over the ratio between the number of learners and of finished tradesmen. In Scotland, lads were so keen to get into the shops that some employers tended to overstock, by adopting what the men properly regarded as the outrageous ratio of one to two[4].

Machinery, always changing and always more easily minded, had broken down the engineers' attempt to retain an apprenticeship like that of their forerunners the millwrights; though the A.S.E. still kept up an ineffective struggle for the rights of apprenticed, as against 'illegal,' men[5]. It was the same wherever the machine had touched an old handicraft. The best cabinet-makers were still apprenticed; but in London, with the coming of machine-made furniture, apprenticeship was dying. Finished craftsmen, if wanted, were brought up from the country. But only a few were wanted, in London or anywhere else[6].

The building and printing trades, as might have been expected, retained apprenticeship in form and, to some extent, in fact. Young stonemasons were apprenticed to employers, but were nearly all masons' sons whom their fathers pushed on quickly. The apprenticeship described in masons' trade union rules was something far more formal; but then it applied only to the rest. In the other building crafts, the position was somewhat similar, but even less rigid. There was a theory in the unions, and some practice, of five to seven years' training; but unapprenticed men, who had picked up their trade somehow, had no great difficulty in practising it, especially if they practised where they had not picked[7].

[1] *R.C. on Labour* (1893, XXXII), W. Mosses, Q. 22,449.

[2] *Ibid.* Q. 24,548. This was abandoned in 1890.

[3] *Ibid.* Evidence of R. Knight of the boiler-makers, Q. 20,683.

[4] *Ibid.* J. Lindsay of Glasgow: Q. 23,288–9. These disputes were regulated by the treaty of 1893: Webb, *op. cit.* p. 457.

[5] The struggle was kept up "on the whole down to 1885." Webb, *op. cit.* p. 472.

[6] Evidence for the Alliance Cabinet Makers before *R.C. on Labour* (1892, XXXVI. Pt. 2), Q. 19,178*sqq*. By that time apprenticeship in London was said to be extinct: Q. 1973–5.

[7] Compare the evidence of rather ideal policy given before the *R.C. on Labour* (as above), Q. 18,512–13 (an employer), with the account of the working of the system in Webb, *op. cit.* p. 460–1, on which this paragraph is based.

In printing the thing was much more formal and regular. Compositors claimed that it was universal. Certainly the unions required it[1]. The best employers endorsed the requirement. But there were plenty of compositors outside the unions, and innumerable small master-printers who would take on men who could work up to their rather low standard. The unions had failed completely to control entry to the trade: men who had merely picked it up could get, not only into the little shops, but even into the unions themselves.

Except for a remnant of reputedly 'overstocked' and under-trained apprentices to the Thames lightermen[2], and the gentlemen apprentices of the greater shipping companies, the system was extinct in all the industries of transport. The lad came on as he could, say from engine-cleaner to fireman, and so to the driver's foot-plate, if he had it in him to drive and was chosen from above. In the coal-mines there was no kind of apprenticeship, and the miners' unions took no more interest in it than did those of the cotton spinners. Probably a majority of trade unionists shared this indifference, making not even a nominal effort to control access to their trades[3]. There were skilled and apprenticed men outside the unions; but a system for which only a minority even of unionists were ready to fight had lost all national significance. Of course boys and girls still had to learn; but just how the vast majority of them learnt, or what the relations of learners to practisers should be, was neither the affair of the state nor of any lesser social organisation.

Even in the harsh 'forties, great numbers of wage-earners, in agriculture as well as in industry, managed to find contributions to some village club or town burial society or, if more fortunate, to one of the friendly and provident Orders which were springing up and splitting off, and spreading with extraordinary speed from town to country[4]. The Lancashire cotton area was the forcing ground of burial clubs, the birthplace of the collecting friendly society[5], and the headquarters of that representative Order, the Manchester Unity of Odd Fellows,

[1] *R.C. on Labour* (1893–4, XXXIV), Q. 22,624–5, G. D. Kelly of the A.S. of Lithographic Printers; Q. 22,799 *sqq.*, H. Slatter of the Typographical Association, who mentions the existence of much informal 'apprenticeship' in London. For union weakness in London, see above, p. 169.

[2] For whom see *R.C. on Labour* (1892, XXXV and XXXVI. Pt. 2), Q. 7469 *sqq.* and Q. 14,081 *sqq.*

[3] Cp. Webb, *op. cit.* p. 473–4.

[4] See vol. I. p. 588–9.

[5] *R.C. on Friendly Societies*, 1874 (XXIII. Pts. 1 and 2), p. xci.

in the 'forties still an unregistered organisation, because its structure did not comply with existing friendly society law. After examining the Odd Fellows' Grand Master, whose name was Smith, a Committee of the House of Lords in 1848 had been almost terrified at its strength. "The Order," they reported, "has reached such gigantic Proportions, and attained such extraordinary Popularity, that it seems to possess the greatest Attractions for the younger Portion of the Labouring Class, and threatens to supplant all minor Institutions of the Kind."[1] They had been told of a membership of 260,000[2] and an income of £340,000. They had no present reason to doubt the loyalty of the Odd Fellows; but it was the year of Revolutions, and they felt bound to remark that such "an affiliated Body with such resources...must become highly dangerous, if it should ever be turned from its legitimate objects." It is not easy to picture those whom Lancashire has always known as the Oddféllers in the rôle of Jacobins or Carbonari, even in 1848; but the Lords were taking a distant view. They went on to pillory certain 'objectionable' customs of the Order—"the Employment of secret Signs, the Circulation of Lectures, and the Introduction of Funeral Orations after the Burial Service." The Grand Master had been quite unable to comprehend their anxieties about these things.

This inquiry bore on proposals for legislation, which in the end, by 13 and 14 Vict. c. 115, enabled the Orders to come within the scope of the law[3]. The Manchester Unity entirely approved: it had of late lost £4000 to an embezzling secretary, because it had no legal status[4]. If its lodges now 'turned from their legitimate objects,' John Tidd Pratt, the Registrar of Friendly Societies from 1846 to 1870, might hope to know[5]. But in fact the Orders were, and remained, singularly innocent

[1] *S.C. of the H. of L. on the Provident Associations Fraud Prevention Bill*, 1847–8 (XVI. 249), p. 4.

[2] According to later statistical work, this should have been 249,000: Neison, F. G. P., "Some Statistics of the Affiliated Orders of Friendly Societies," *S.J.* March, 1877, p. 45–6.

[3] The earlier friendly society law had only made provision for, and offered registration to, unitary societies, not for what were classed after 1850 as 'societies with branches.' The Odd Fellows were registered in 1851: see vol. I. p. 590 n.

[4] Evidence of W. B. Smith before the *S.C. of the H. of L.* as above, Q. 87.

[5] The Registrar's unforgettable name was a power for good in the societies: 'if you do so-and-so you will have Tidd Pratt upon you,' it was said (Brabrook, E. W., *Provident Societies and Industrial Welfare*, 1898, p. 12). He was a voluminous writer, an F.S.A., and a founder of the Reform Club.

of revolution. Even in 1848, from 15 to 20 per cent. of the Odd Fellows were "in a station of life to forego their claims" on the funds[1], subscribers who were not a liability, tradesmen, some medical men, and in the country many of the clergy. As patrons and friends, these mingled with the artisans and operatives, the upper-grade wage-earners, who formed the rank and file. It is fairly certain that the lodges, with their ceremonial, "their jewellery and haberdashery," encouraged what modern Moscow calls a bourgeois ideology[2].

Burial clubs were widespread in the 'fifties, but outside the cotton country they were not very important[3]. Inside it their hold was extraordinary. Of 80,000 inhabitants in the Poor Law Union of Stockport, more than 49,000 were insured for burial in 1853–4. There were at least 46 district societies in Wigan. A witness before a parliamentary committee spoke for societies with a membership of 90,000 in Liverpool[4]. The Blackburn Philanthropic Burial Society, founded in 1839, in 1850 had over 45,000, and by the early 'seventies 130,000 members—the child could be entered at 16 weeks old—out of a total burial society membership of perhaps 750,000 in all England at the latter date[5]. From time to time public opinion was alarmed by horrible cases of the murder of insured children, and the law was called in to impose preventives; but it was never shown that murder was common, or that it was a special product of child insurance[6]. People have been murdered at all ages for the sake of the money which their deaths will bring to the murderer.

Closely associated with the burial clubs, because they too insured against death, were the general collecting societies, so called because they lacked the personal intimacy of a village social club or Odd Fellows' lodge. Liverpool was their place of origin, the Royal Liver of 1850 their representative institution. Above them again, linking the wage-earners' provident to the ordinary insurance society, were profit-making companies like the Prudential, which began industrial insurance

[1] *S.C. of the H. of L.* p. 5.

[2] The rather superior reference to jewellery is in the *R.C. of* 1874, p. xxxiv. Most of those who signed it had decorations or court dress.

[3] Lists for 1850, compiled from the returns of the Registrar, are in Walford, C., *The Insurance Cyclopaedia*, IV. 565.

[4] *S.C. on the Friendly Societies Bill*, 1854 (VII. 127), Q. 1395 (Stockport), Q. 1080 (Wigan), Q. 1321 (Liverpool).

[5] *R.C. of* 1874, p. xciii, c; and for 1850, Walford, as above.

[6] *S.C. of* 1854, p. iv, v; *R.C. of* 1874, p. cxxxiii.

in 1854 and was the first company to take infant lives. Its membership, drawn from many classes, had passed 1,000,000 by 1872[1].

Down to that time, village clubs, dividing societies—vulgarly, share-outs—and public house 'free-and-easies' had made small pretence to actuarial knowledge. Good-fellowship was the foundation, calculated providence only a light upper storey. The village labourer of the 'seventies, it was said, could not tolerate a club with "no beer, no feast, no fire."[2] Nor were the finance and management of the collecting societies generally satisfactory. Their finance depended too much on 'lapses'; it was to their interest to evade obligations by declaring that subscribers had lapsed[3]. Even the great Orders, between 1850 and 1875, still lay wide open to the actuarial criticism which had been directed against them in the 'forties, when they had not quite emerged from the good-fellowship phase[4]. The Manchester Unity began regular valuations before 1870, to find that few either of its lodges or its districts were technically solvent[5]. The Foresters, next to the Unity in size, had never even ascertained their deficiencies down to 1875. The cure, often heroically applied, was to meet threatened insolvency by levies or curtailment of benefits. The defence of such action was that benevolence, self-denial, and mutual help were of the essence of a friendly society.

But the relative insecurity of the best societies, the competition, chicane, and actual fraud of the worst, kept government uneasy. The state had long dabbled in insurance, by offering annuities suited to the needs of the people through savings banks and associations. Few had been taken. Gladstone, inspired by William Farr the statistician, had planned in 1864 a whole system of annuities and life insurances, to be worked through the Post Office. For once, a financial plan of Gladstone's miscarried. It was curtailed in parliament and little used in the country[6]. But the somewhat exaggerated criticism of

[1] *R.C. of* 1874, p. cxxviii *sqq*.

[2] *Ibid.* p. xxi, from the report of Sir George Young, one of the Assistant Commissioners.

[3] *Ibid.* p. cix.

[4] See vol. I. p. 591.

[5] *R.C. of* 1874, p. xxxvii. Cp. Baernreither, J. M., *English Associations of Working Men* (Eng. trans. 1889), p. 273, 383. There was great improvement by 1886. See *S.C. on National Provident Insurance*, 1887 (XI. 1), p. vii.

[6] Walford, *op. cit.* v. 478–9, 483. Walford prints Farr's Memorandum. Baernreither, *op. cit.* p. 340; Hansard, Third Series, CLXIII, debates of March 4 and 7.

friendly societies which Gladstone had allowed himself stimulated reform in the Orders. Penetrating inquiry by a Royal Commission, which sat from 1871 to 1874, "rather frightened"[1] the worst of the collecting societies and led to some setting in order of houses. From the Commission's work emerged the consolidating Friendly Societies Act of 1875 (38 and 39 Vict. c. 60). It recognised more completely than any earlier law had the federal nature of the Orders. It brought down many rotten societies of every type, which could not comply with its rules, and led to improvements in the finance and management of the survivors[2].

The federal Orders gained ground everywhere at the expense of the purely local type of society in public house, schoolroom, dissenting chapel, or place of business, which early legislation had favoured. Even before the Act, the local clubs were fulfilling the prophecy of the Lords' Committee of 1848: "we cannot stand up against" the Orders, they were saying[3]. In the decade after the Act, 9283 registered societies were turned into registered branches of Orders[4]. The Foresters had been the chief gainers. They had absorbed thousands of country clubs. By 1886 they had over 5000 'courts' and over 667,000 members[5]. The Manchester Unity of Odd Fellows at that time was not quite so large, but its membership was above 600,000. Even in Scotland, for every local club of the old type registered in 1886, there were eight branches of the general Orders of English origin—Foresters, Odd Fellows, Rechabites, Shepherds. Scottish invasion of England was only indicated in a list of public houses, filling several folio pages of an official publication, in which met branches of the Grand Independent Order of Loyal Caledonian Corks. It is to be supposed that this Order resembled the Royal Antediluvian Order of Buffaloes, of which the Commission of 1871 had reported—"it is said to be wholly convivial." Working men's clubs, convivial and political, were also registered as friendly societies in the early

[1] *R.C. of* 1874, p. cxxv.

[2] *Report of the Registrar of Friendly Societies* (J. M. Ludlow) *for* 1885 (1886, LXI); *S.C. on Friendly Societies* 1888 (XII. 119), Ludlow's evidence, esp. Q. 9; Brabrook, *op. cit.* p. 60.

[3] *R.C. of* 1874, p. xxiv.

[4] *Report for* 1885, p. 3.

[5] The Foresters had 84,000 members in 1848, 135,000 in 1858, 349,000 in 1868, and 491,000 in 1876; Neison in *S.J.* 1877, p. 60. The figures for 1886 are in Baernreither, *op. cit.* p. 372–3.

'eighties. How far potation in all these was checked by the Order of Total Abstinent Daughters of the Phœnix the reports do not say[1].

The serious Orders, and friendly societies generally, spent far more money on sick benefit and accident than on funeral allowances; the Manchester Unity, for example, about three times as much[2]. Only in the 'eighties did they begin to study superannuation allowance at all carefully[3]. In constitution they were self-governing; in spirit, as in name, friendly. Collecting societies, on the other hand, specialised in death. To the Registrar of the 'seventies and 'eighties, J. M. Ludlow, they were "necessary evils"; evil, because they lacked self-government, had a "vast official network," and were too much mixed up with child insurance; necessary, because they met a want in those lower social grades where there are seldom reserves enough to provide for the emergency of the grave[4]. Many of the crude old burial clubs had vanished; but the term survived at Blackburn, whose Philanthropic Burial Club shared with the Royal Liver, the Liverpool Victoria, and the Royal London the distinction of having more, far more, than 100,000 members. It will be noticed that three of the four were domiciled in Lancashire[5].

Altogether, the collecting societies of 1885–7 had upwards of 3,000,000 'members'; the single club societies of the old-fashioned type certainly more than 2,000,000; and the federal Orders about 1,750,000. The figures are for Britain. In addition, there was an overflow of the Orders into the dominions, colonies, and even foreign countries[6]. There is some overlap in

[1] These details are from the *Report for* 1885 and the *R.C. of* 1874, p. xxxi.

[2] Expenditure is analysed by Neison; *S.J.* 1877. It is interesting to notice that in 1848–52 the Odd Fellows (Manchester Unity) issued 4721 'travelling cards'; in 1868–72 only 2204. This overlap of functions with the trade unions has not, I think, been studied.

[3] "Still in its infancy," Baernreither, *op. cit.* p. 423.

[4] Ludlow's evidence in 1888, as above, Q. 8, 75.

[5] The special success of the burial societies in Liverpool and Lancashire generally, and the frequency of Irish names among witnesses at all inquiries into them, suggest that they owed a good deal to the poor Irishman's desire for a corpse-wake.

[6] *Report of the Chief Registrar for* 1886 (1887, LXXVI), *Report for*...1887 (1889, LXXI. Pts. 1 and 2): *Dic. of Pol. Econ.* s.v. "Friendly Societies," for the statistical position, which is not perfectly clear owing to the neglect or intermittence of returns to the Registrar by the societies. No attempt has been made to give a picture of such associated movements as those of the building societies and the savings banks; partly for reasons of mere space and partly for

the figures, and the friendly society movement overlapped other movements. A Forester might insure members of his family in the Royal Liver. An Odd Fellow might well be also a co-operator and a trade unionist. The minimum certainty is that nearly 4,000,000 adults, mostly wage-earners, were active participants in the life of the societies; and that many, possibly millions, more were in a position to make some formal provision for themselves or their children by way of insurance. In addition were the large sums which these people, or people like them, had put into savings banks, building societies, and trade union benefit funds. Foreign visitors, who studied the Britain of the 'eighties against Friedrich Engels' background of the Britain of the 'forties, were writing of "the complete revolution...in the lives of a large number of English workmen" and of "an improvement...beyond the boldest hopes of even those who, a generation ago, devoted all their energies to the work."[1] Of this revolution and this improvement the friendly societies were at once a witness and a cause.

It is not easy even to guess what a representative wage-earner during this generation of progress, self-help, and Gladstonian finance was thinking—or should one say feeling?—about the economic order of society and his place in it. "A thousand times in a thousand shapes," when moving among "the distressed operatives" of the previous generation—the average men of the Chartist age—a friendly inquirer heard one and another of them say "that he had a right to a better condition, inasmuch as he had taken a part in raising society to the conditions which established a higher average of comfort than that to which he could attain."[2] This was the plain, sound, raw material of average working-class opinion or instinct out of which, with the tools of Ricardian economics and the measuring rod of Patrick Colquhoun's estimate that the wage-earners received a bare quarter of the national income, scattered thinkers of that generation had constructed those theories of value, doctrines of the right to the whole produce of labour, which

reasons suggested in the remarks on savings banks in vol. I. p. 592. Co-operation and trade unionism, which have points of contact with the friendly society movement, have been discussed elsewhere.

[1] Baernreither, *op. cit.* p. 5.

[2] Taylor, W. C., *Notes on a Tour in the Manufacturing Districts of Lancashire* (1842), p. 155.

Karl Marx was subsequently to put into crabbed dialectical shape[1]. Very often, no doubt, among the enemies of the new Poor Law who had supplied so many recruits for Chartism[2], the claim to a better condition had meant little more than a claim to poor relief as a right. Tom Paine and Cobbett had taught this. The people, they said, were owed compensation for land filched from them. The compensation was already payable in part through the rates. These ought to be supplemented, so Paine had argued, by unconditional payments to enable the poor man to set up in life and to provide for his old age, which should come from death duties on landed property[3]. How far, or how well, the sound had carried of the more refined arguments used by that group of writers whom modern scholars have called the Ricardian socialists is uncertain[4]. The scarcity of their books and pamphlets suggests a rather short radius and an indistinct hearing. But, either directly or relaid, Paine and Cobbett had certainly 'come through' well, and were easy to 'get' at long range.

So in all probability was 'Bronterre' O'Brien, the thinker of Chartism, for he had written in half-a-dozen popular journals and could hold a public meeting "for four and even five hours"; though a mere "three hours was about the usual time he occupied."[5] O'Brien had said that property was theft, long before Proudhon coined that glittering phrase which later he alloyed with qualification. O'Brien had called capital accumulated labour. He had maintained that the French Revolution had been a failure because rent was still payable to individuals and not to the state. He had argued that the nation alone should decide how much land any person or family ought to hold; and had asked why individuals, and not the public, should secure

[1] See generally Foxwell, H. S., Preface to Menger, *Right to the Whole Produce of Labour*; Beer, M., *History of British Socialism*; Dolléans, E., *Le Chartisme* (1913); Hovell, M., *The Chartist Movement* (1918), esp. ch. 3, "The rise of anti-capitalist economics."

[2] See vol. I. p. 583.

[3] Paine's *Agrarian Justice*.

[4] Those of Hodgskin, author of *Labour Defended...or the Unproductiveness of Capital Proved* (published anonymously in 1825), were spread fairly well by his lectures at the London Mechanics Institution. See Halévy, E., *Thomas Hodgskin* (Paris: 1903).

[5] Gammage, R. G., *History of the Chartist Movement* (first published in 1854), p. 77. O'Brien wrote in *The Poor Man's Guardian*, *The Northern Star*, *The National Reformer*, *The British Statesman*, *Reynolds' Newspaper*, and probably in other journals.

the increment of value that results from the opening of a new mine or the building of a town[1]. Like all Irishmen, he cared most for agrarian socialism, about which he was still writing in *Reynolds' Newspaper*, long after the political collapse of Chartism, down to his death in poverty in 1864[2]. But he had defended with almost equal zeal Owen's notion of a currency to be based on units of labour, the precious metals to be retained only as a matter of international convenience, until such time as labour should be equally productive and equally rewarded everywhere[3].

The little Owenite church, to which alone into the 'forties it was customary to apply the epithet socialist, had kept its faith in community distinct from other reformers' faiths, though it was often sympathetic towards them. In its Halls of Science, in grimy streets, the faithful had sung hymn Number 129[4]:

Community, the joyful sound
That cheers the social band,
And spreads a holy zeal around
To dwell upon the land.

In *The Book of the New Moral World*, Part v (1844) the old prophet, never disheartened, had preached the old faith, adding to it the pregnant suggestion that the state should buy up the new railways and broad strips of land on either side of them, to be so laid out that there, on the land, joyful communities might bring in the New World without any harsh breach with the Old. But the church was then weakening. Men had passed through it into other communions. Their interest in its distinctive teaching decayed; though their love and respect for the prophet never. By 1846, the Social Institution in John Street, one of its early homes, had become the Literary and Scientific Institution[5]. The *Reasoner*, edited from that year to 1861 by G. J. Holyoake, reasoned more about utilitarian morals, re-

[1] His opinions on these questions are fully illustrated in Dolléans, *op. cit.* I. 84, 98, 99. He had not preached confiscation of the land, merely state purchase as it came into the market. His moderation resembles that of Thomas Ogilvie's *Essay on the Right of Property in Land* (1781).

[2] Beer, *op. cit.* II. 240; Dolléans, *op. cit.* II. 486, and for his agrarian socialism, Niehuus, H., *Gesch. der englischen Bodenreformtheorien* (1910), p. 99 *sqq.*

[3] See the article in the *Northern Star* for 29 March, 1845, quoted in Dolléans, *op. cit.* I. 104.

[4] Podmore, F., *Life of Robert Owen*, II. 472; the hymn is from the hymn-book of 1840. Cp. *A Bibliography of Robert Owen*, Welsh Bibliographical Society; 1914.

[5] Podmore, *op. cit.* II. 581.

publicanism, and secularism than about community. Even the co-operative workshops of 1848–54, into which had been poured the enthusiasm—and the money—of men who had learnt under Owen, and of that other band of prophets who had taken the name of Christian Socialists, and had preached "production...by the Trade Unions"[1] to the Amalgamated Engineers in 1852—even these workshops, imperfect embodiments of the complex community as Owen had conceived it, yet seemingly for that reason more likely to endure, had shown a discouraging instability[2]. But the simple two-storey structures of the co-operative stores were rising and standing. Here the tools of social faith were put to definite limited uses, instead of being strained and broken in attempts to construct an ideal city out of refractory material at once. As soon as the small job was done, bigger ones were to be put in hand. About, and from, the stores should spread the whole Co-operative Commonwealth. But the immediate business was to get them built[3].

When Owen died in 1858 there can have been few people left to call themselves socialists, though the growing body of co-operators all looked to him as the preparer of the way. The leaders of Chartism were scattered or dead. Many had emigrated. Some were lecturers, journalists, doctors, lawyers—democrats all, but of no uniform type. Those who had ever had it, had lost the hope of quick success for any doctrine or social reformation. William Lovett, the noblest of them, in early life "half an Owenite, half a Hodgskinite, a thorough believer that accumulation of property in the hands of individuals was the cause of all the evils that existed,"[4] lived on till 1877. As he had always known that a new moral world was unlikely to arise among an uneducated people, it was probably with no regret that he gave the best of his later years to the cause of popular education. Meanwhile old Chartists of the rank and file acted with left-wing liberals and radicals, and thought more of the democratic conquests yet to be won than of any changed social order which might perhaps follow them. After all, the Charter was a political programme, and there had never been any agree-

[1] Ludlow, J. M., in the *Economic Review*, April, 1892, quoted in Raven, C. E. *Christian Socialism*, 1848–54 (1920), p. 299.

[2] See Raven, *op. cit.* and above, p. 144–5.

[3] Above, p. 308 *sqq.*

[4] Francis Place's description of him, from the Place MSS. quoted in Hovell, *op. cit.* p. 56. And see his own *Life and Struggles of William Lovett* (1876; new edition, ed. R. H. Tawney, 1920).

ment on social doctrine. In the Gladstonian age, the political objectives were being reached one by one; through the rhythm of good and bad times economic progress was obvious. There were still bad laws to be broken down; abuses to be cleared away; all that work of demolition and 'opening of windows' in which Gladstone delighted and was glad to co-operate[1]. Nearly all the best minds among wage-earners and their friends were as fully occupied with the task as he. Like him they were working with confidence and in hope; for though the ageing Chartist might look back to brave days of drillings, imprisonments, and 'sacred months' of general strike, with the regrets of an old fighting man, it was fairly evident that, however bad to-day might be, the former days were not better than these. There was motion, and with that, as all the signs suggest, the average industrial wage-earner, down to the trade collapse of the 'seventies, and perhaps after, was reasonably content. A natural revolutionary he had never been. Chartists had always found London politically apathetic—because too well paid, they thought[2]. Radical reformers of all sorts, during the thirty years after 1848, must often have noticed the same apathy in the whole country. There is little doubt that Karl Marx did, whatever his opinion of the pay.

London was his headquarters for nearly twenty-five years[3]. In the British Museum, among the blue-books and the economic literature of the centuries, *Das Kapital* took shape. But the first part only appeared in 1867 in German, and in 1873 in French[4]. Engels' preface to the first English edition is dated November 5, 1886. He can hardly have meant the dating as a grim joke. Neither he nor Marx had humour; and he prefaced it by repeating Marx's opinions that "England is the only country where the inevitable social revolution might be effected entirely by peaceful and legal means." However, as he noted that "Marx never forgot to add that he had hardly expected the English ruling classes to submit without a 'pro-slavery rebellion' to this peaceful and legal revolution,"[5] it is just possible

[1] See above, p. 404. [2] See vol. I. p. 584. [3] He died in 1883.

[4] The French edition was "entièrement revisée par l'auteur," and in it some Englishmen read their Marx during the next twelve years. The rest of the book only began to appear in German in 1885. I doubt if one professed English economist, or socialist scholar, in five has studied the latter parts closely to this day. They have had no influence whatever on English socialism, and were first translated, at Chicago, in 1909.

[5] Preface, p. xiv.

that he thought of the English edition as an explosive. He had anticipated revolution in England within three years in the 'forties: in 1886 he was sure that "the sighed for period of prosperity would not come."[1] If he did suppose that he was touching off the powder, he was wrong. Marx, even at second hand, has had little influence on English thought; on English action, almost none. The untranslated Marx of the 'seventies and early 'eighties was read by a mere handful of students and people curious in continental economics. No one added an appendix on Marx to Mill's discussion of socialism. When younger economists wrote volumes of Principles they ignored him, like Sidgwick, or later noted his blunders in stray magisterial asides, like Marshall[2].

During the whole of Marx's residence in England, no contribution of any importance to technical socialist thought was made by an Englishman[3]. The instinctive socialism common among men well below the half-way line of society was dulled by better times. Trade union leaders were busy breaking down fences and promoting their group interests in society as it was. They had not much time for society as it might become. But meanwhile Mill's influence, far more effective in keeping men's minds open to possibilities of social change than any socialist dogmatics, was spreading among all those who thought. With it spread generous and confused criticism of industrial society from the prophets of the age—Carlyle, Kingsley, Ruskin. None was more critical than Mill himself, in the restrained passion of those ordered paragraphs available latterly in cheap editions for the people. His care for individuality—"the importance, to man and society...of giving full freedom to human nature to expand itself in innumerable and conflicting directions"[4]—kept him hostile to all precise and authoritarian forms of socialism, with their 'over-government'; but, as the later editions of his *Principles* had shown, and as his *Autobiography* of 1873 and his posthumous *Chapters on Socialism*

[1] Preface, as above; cp. vol. I. p. 580.

[2] Sidgwick's *Principles* (1883) has no index; I do not think there is a reference to Marx in the text. There are three concise references, showing characteristically thorough consideration of Marx's arguments before their rejection, in Marshall's *Principles* (1890).

[3] Beer, *op. cit.* II. 189, has claimed Richard Jones' recognition, in his *Text-Book of Lectures* (1852), of capitalism as "but a stage in the economic development of mankind" as a contribution of considerable interest; but it is hardly technical socialist thought.

[4] *Autobiography*, p. 253.

of 1879[1] showed more evidently, he had been making throughout his life a "greater approximation, so far as regards the ultimate prospects of humanity, to a qualified Socialism."[2]

His doctrines of the land and of inheritance were themselves revolutionary, judged by the common standards of the day; while his tenacious belief in the social value of a diffusion of property, his co-operative enthusiasm, and his dislike of the prospect of eternal wage-paying and wage-earning, had kept him in sympathy with the three strongest currents of action among wage-earners—those represented by the friendly and building societies, the co-operators, and the trade unions. But in thinking of the future he was haunted by the ghost of Malthus; and, almost to the time of his death, he had taught a wage doctrine not only unspeakably distasteful to wage-earners but also, as with his usual candour he had himself admitted, wrong[3]. Both the teaching and the recantation helped to produce among them that "confident contempt" for "the traditional political economy" of which economists wrote ten years later[4]. This contempt had been embittered by the fashion in which economic thinkers, not excluding Mill himself, had often written about the relation of Malthus' teaching to wage problems[5]. So, great as was Mill's indirect influence on thinkers in all social ranks, there were obstacles to his direct influence on the world of labour. It was natural there to assume that political economy, and he, taught just what the stupider members of the propertied classes had implied that they taught[6].

In 1879–80 there appeared to that world, indeed to all British worlds, a new prophet with a gospel. First published at New York in 1879, and republished there twice in 1880, Henry George's *Progress and Poverty* went through ten London editions between 1881 and 1884. The prophet followed his book, and proved not less moving with the spoken than with the written word. There was every sign of a religious revival. *Progress*, an unsympathetic contemporary wrote, was circulated "like the testament of a new dispensation. Societies were

[1] Published in the *Fortnightly Review*.

[2] *Autobiography*, p. 191. There is a more decided profession of qualified socialist faith on p. 231–2. But the *Chapters* harmonise with the phrase quoted.

[3] The old wages-fund doctrine, which appeared to set rigid limits to the efficacy of movements for the increase of wages: see *Dic. Pol. Econ.* s.v. *Wages Fund.*

[4] Sidgwick, *Principles*, p. 6.

[5] It was easy, if incorrect, to infer from Mill that in a growing population wages could not rise.

[6] As sketched above, p. 395–6.

formed, journals were devised to propagate its saving doctrines, and little companies of the faithful held stated meetings for its reading and exposition."[1] Not Mill before him, nor Marx after, ever had such honour in Britain. Though five minutes' simple arithmetic with the income-tax returns would have displaced the keystone from the arch of Henry George's doctrine, his wage-earner's record, magnificent ardour, honest care for the poor and the disinherited, apocalyptic American eloquence and short way with Malthus, combined with the smooth soaring curve of the doctrinal arch, made disciples everywhere, even if the discipleship of many was short. "The limit to the population of the globe can only be the limit of space":[2] so much for Malthus. "What I, therefore, propose as the simple yet sovereign remedy, which will raise wages, increase the earnings of capital, extirpate pauperism, abolish poverty, give remunerative employment to whoever wishes it, afford free scope to human powers, lessen crime, elevate morals, and taste, and intelligence, purify government and carry civilisation to yet nobler heights, is—*to appropriate rent by taxation*."[3] That is the arch. And the keystone is—"*to abolish all taxation save that upon land values*."[4] Whether or not land values should be specially taxed is a reasonably simple problem in applied economics. Mill always had a clear view of it. The suggestion that a European state could live by such taxation alone is of course absurd. But George had watched the magical growth and gamblers' distribution of the land values of California. He had seen poverty beside the home of the speculator in real estate. These things obsessed him. And indeed the land values socially created in nineteenth-century America would have gone some way towards maintaining even a Federation of States, could it have got control of them wisely and in time.

George's function in Britain was that of a ferment. The single-taxers were never more than a sect, like the pure Owenites before them. But the crusade set men thinking about inequality, and stirred old memories among many who were never professed disciples. Thomas Spence[5] and Tom Paine, Cobbett and the early socialists, the Chartists, the radicals of every shade, Mill himself, Joseph Arch and Joseph Chamber-

[1] Rae, J., *Contemporary Socialism* (2nd ed. 1891), p. 441.

[2] *Progress and Poverty* (an ed. of 1884), p. 94.

[3] *Ibid.* p. 288: italics in the original.

[4] *Ibid. loc. cit.*: italics in the original.

[5] See vol. I. p. 313.

lain, all had been land reformers of one kind or another. Feargus O'Connor had collected the pence of hard-pressed industrial wage-earners—who themselves perhaps, or whose fathers, had come into industry from the countryside—for that National Land Company which was the last, and rather unhappy, product of Chartism. A few small holdings "on a high plateau exposed to all the winds,"[1] at Minster Lovell in Oxfordshire, still survived as its memorial. Mill had founded the Land Tenure Reform Association in 1870–1, and had put on record in its programme that "an active and influential portion of the working classes had adopted the opinion that private property in land was a mistake."[2] (He thought not; but was sure that it had been abused.) He had always been as willing as George himself to annex unearned increment for society by taxation; but he had no delusions as to its amount. In the year when George first toured the country (1882) Alfred Russell Wallace had published his little book on land nationalisation, dedicated to the working men of England[3], and with a few friends, most of whom had much less experience than George of the wage-earner's life, he had founded the Land Nationalisation Society. Also in the year of the first tour, and again quite independently of it, H. M. Hyndman, who had studied Marx and sought his friendship, republished Spence's lecture on *The Real Rights of Man*. A year later, in September, 1883, the Democratic Federation which Hyndman had helped to found in 1881, and which had put land nationalisation into its programme[4], turned itself into the Social Democratic Federation and became, within a short time, a powerful organisation of socialist propaganda.

Its leaders thought meanly, not of George, but of his system, as semi-Marxists and builders on the socialist element in Mill's teaching well might. During the second tour (1884) Hyndman disputed publicly with George in St James's Hall on socialism *versus* the single tax. Without the prophet from California, the socialist could hardly have secured so large and respectable a sounding-board. And the ferment which George set up was equally useful to William Morris's Socialist League, to the newly founded Fabian Society, and to other more obscure

[1] Jebb, L., *The Small Holdings of England* (1907), p. 121. The holdings were still there in 1907.

[2] Quoted in Beer, *op. cit.* II. 241.

[3] It had three editions in 1882; the third, with about 250 pp., sold for 8*d*.

[4] But not a prominent part of it.

organisations. Adherents of Henry George's views in their "little propagandist societies...gradually developed in many cases, into complete Socialists."[1]

The foreigner could note; the statistician could prove; and old wage-earners might remember, that there had been "a complete revolution...in the lives of a large number of English workmen"[2] since Peel's day. But there was squalid poverty and misery enough still in the depths. The sharp crisis of unemployment in 1878–9 had opened the possibility of a fall into the depths to skilled men who as a rule moved above them. When George first visited England, unemployment among the trade unionists, as it happened, was abnormally low; but from the year of his second visit to that of Victoria's jubilee it was persistently and abnormally high. Engels, convinced that it was merely a disease of capitalism, was prophesying with a gloomy satisfaction that "the sighed-for period of prosperity would not come"[3]; and even those people who looked with most complacency on the improvement in the wage-earner's position could say no more than that "the aid...so widely given by friendly and trade societies limited or deferred the pauperisation"[4] of their members, when unemployed. (There are no statistics of the unemployment in those depths from which membership of a trade or friendly society was all but unattainable.) Though there was no good reason to suppose that, in the familiar jingle of pessimism, the rich were getting richer and the poor poorer; and although statisticians were engaged in estimating that more than five-twelfths of the whole national income of Britain went to the manual labour classes in 1883, as compared with considerably less than a third fifty years earlier[5],

[1] Webb, Sidney, *Socialism in England* (1890), p. 21. According to Beer, *op. cit.* II. 245, "Some four-fifths of the socialist leaders of Great Britain in the 'eighties had passed through the school of Henry George." I am not in a position to check this fraction, but the impression which it is meant to give is certainly correct.

[2] Above, p. 477.

[3] In fact, trade union unemployment was at a minimum, just over 2 per cent., in 1889–90.

[4] Above, p. 433.

[5] Giffen, Sir R., "Further Notes on the Progress of the Working Classes," *S.J.* 1886, reprinted in *Essays in Finance: Second Series.* Giffen estimated a national income for Great Britain in 1883 of £1,198,000,000 and a 'manual-labour class' income of £515,000,000. (In *Socialism Made Plain* (1883), which had a circulation of about 100,000, the Democratic Federation was saying that the workers'

this estimated share—had they agreed about it—might very well seem entirely inadequate to the sons, now educated and voting, of those men of the Chartist age, who had held that their contribution to the progress of the country gave them "a right to a better condition."[1] The sons did not need either to read or to believe Marx's dialectics of value, nor to be in any sense revolutionary, in order to come to this opinion. It might, and usually did, serve merely to stiffen their backs in some wage fight or in some wage negotiation diplomatically conducted by their leaders.

The world was still full of inequality. Democrats of all shades chuckled over Joseph Chamberlain's gibe at those of the old governing class who "toiled not neither did they spin," and welcomed his advocacy of a graduated income-tax. Whatever Henry George may have failed to do, he had proved to demonstration, though not for the first time, how in one great field at any rate inequality was a result, not of over-riding economic forces, but of an alterable human law of property. And meanwhile Gladstone was making solemn fun in the House of Commons of an elderly, conservative, director of the Bank of England, who for a generation had urged the differentiation of the income-tax on the ground that all incomes were not equally 'earned';[2] while Gladstone's political opponents, and some of his recent allies, were denouncing him for his very restrained, if perhaps not very wise, handling of property rights in the Irish Land Act of 1881[3].

The representative wage-earner had not begun to call himself a socialist by 1886; far from it. But many politically active wage-earners, especially in London, had. From the stock-in-trade of radicalism, some of the more socialist pieces were being brought down from the upper shelves of the mind. Disraelian conservatism and Tory democracy could repudiate *laissez-faire* without denying their past. It was probable that the new electors in town and country, while conservative in many things, would not use their votes to maintain permanently

share was £300,000,000 out of £1,300,000,000.) His corresponding estimates for the period just before 1843 were £432,000,000 and £122,000,000. Colquhoun for 1812–15 had estimated a bare quarter.

[1] Above, p. 477.

[2] Above, p. 401.

[3] See *e.g.* Locker-Lampson, G., *A Consideration of the State of Ireland in the Nineteenth Century* (1907), ch. xv. It was over this Act that the Dukes of Argyle and Bedford parted from Gladstone.

both the rights of private property, as understood by the average middle class mind of the 'seventies, and that slender taxation of the greater, and the 'unearned,' private incomes with which Gladstone was content. The minds of electors, to whatever social class they belonged, were not all clear or far-sighted or likely to remain consistent. Though there were close independent thinkers, and would be disinterested voters, in all classes, the view which majorities would take of the economic order and of the voter's place in it, and of the changes immediately necessary, would depend on the political programmes put before them, and on the pressures which economic forces in the whole world—for these all played on Britain—might exert on individual voters. It was now certain that, as time went on, more and more drastic proposals for change would find their way into the political programmes, even though at the time of the Irish Home Rule controversy British economic issues had fallen for a time into the background. The pressures of the outer world on Britain were exceptionally severe; and the relaxation which was to come shortly could not, in 1886–7, be foreseen. Engels might prove to be right this time. Prosperity might not return. If so, it was not unlikely that the average wage-earner's thought about society would move, as fast as thought ever moves in Britain, from right to left.

CHAPTER XII

THE FACE OF THE COUNTRY, 1886–7

WHEN Victoria's jubilee was approaching, most people in Britain were within earshot of the crash or mutter of a town by day. Many of those who were not, unless they lived North of the Highland Line, could yet catch the clank of trains in a still night. Few railway lines had been built of late, so the clank had not often come as a new sound of the night. Here and there it had, preceded by some fresh gash in a hillside or some raw embankment abutting on a viaduct of unweathered brick—common sights forty, and thirty, years back. But in most places the railway had sunk into the landscape, like the road and the canal before it. All that it brought in sight and sound had become established, and familiar as the uninterrupted spreading of the mutter of the towns. Towns had become the birthplaces not merely of "a large part of the British race," as William Farr had anticipated in 1851, but of the major part[1]. Its critics called the race street-bred. If the streets were not really England, they seemed so to most Englishmen; and London streets were England to nearly one Englishman in seven. So the streets should be looked at before the fields, or the hills, or even the sea-coasts.

Whilst giving evidence before the Royal Commission on the Housing of the Working Classes in 1884, Lord Shaftesbury said there had always been "the greatest desire in London and other large towns that every man should have his own house... It would be a great blessing. But in such a vast city as this it is next to impossible."[2] He had in mind principally the congested core of London across which his name would soon be written, such districts as that of which another witness reported that five families to six rooms was about the average[3]. Yet, even in London, Shaftesbury's ideal was much more nearly realised than his words suggest, more nearly perhaps than he knew;

[1] Vol. I. p. 537.

[2] *R.C. on the Housing of the Working Classes*, 1884–5 (xxx), Q. 40.

[3] *Ibid.* Q. 1948. There was a good deal of evidence to suggest that, in such areas, there had been an actual increase of overcrowding in the early 'eighties.

for he had lived to face the worst, and all that was terrible was reported to him[1]. It is true that when he spoke more than a fifth of the people of London were living under what would later be defined as conditions of overcrowding, that is more than two to a room;[2] but as soon as you got away from the central and other specially congested quarters, with their big old houses gone to decay, there began those long unlovely streets which still were urban England—'two parallel walls of brick pierced with holes.'[3] In them a man with a family might have a house, such as it was. Since in all London there were less than eight people to each inhabited house, and since both the tenement houses and those of the rich and the fairly well-to-do with their servants would often contain more, the house with five or six people in it was obviously the commonest of all[4].

It might be a wretched thing, jammed against its neighbours and overcrowded like any tenement house in Clerkenwell or Whitechapel: it was likely to be that in inner London. In inner East London, mixed up with the older bigger houses, were the "houses of three rooms, houses of two rooms, houses of one room—houses set back against a wall or back to back, fronting it may be on to a narrow footway, with posts at each end and a gutter down the middle."[5] In Bermondsey there were plenty of two-room houses, the rooms one above the other. The people preferred them to tenements; and though all were old, "very few were built back to back."[6] In newly built districts on the Middlesex side, there was "only a small demand for houses which are subdivided into separate tenements."[7] The artisan demand, as opposed to that of the unskilled, the floating and the semi-criminal population of the true slums, was for three, four and five-room houses, especially four-room. A company

[1] Cp. p. 442 above.

[2] All references below to overcrowding refer to 1891, when statistics were first collected (*Census of* 1891, 1893–4, CVI). The conditions in 1886–7 would be nearly identical. The census definition of 'more than two' to a room is used, because no other is available for most towns, not Charles Booth's definition of 'two or more' to a room, which is retained for purposes of comparison with Booth's *Life and Labour* in the *New Survey of London Life and Labour*, I (1930), p. 150, 169, etc.

[3] Pasquet, D., *Londres et les ouvriers de Londres* (1914), p. 45.

[4] The census 'house' was "all the space between the external and party walls of a building"; its 'tenement', each separate occupation (cp. vol. I. p. 547). For all London the population per house was 7·82 in 1881 and 7·72 in 1891.

[5] Booth, *Life and Labour*, I. 30.

[6] *R.C. of* 1884–5, Q. 4622.

[7] *Ibid.* Q. 12,203.

which was trying to provide for the artisan what he wanted, and what he could afford, found nothing so popular as "our little four-room cottages." They found too that their larger houses, including some of the four-room, were "almost invariably let partly to lodgers."[1]

What kind of a London was growing up of itself, and how Londoners lived when they had room, is best shown in some such place as West Ham, although West Ham was not technically London. As an urban area it had only come into being since 1850. Its statistics have never been much complicated by the homes of the well-to-do. It was too new to have many houses either of the old Middlesex sort, once prosperous now broken into tenements, or of the old room-above-room Bermondsey sort. It had not attracted the philanthropist or the building company with a conscience. It was a 'builder's' town, for wage-earners and lesser city workers—'clerks on thirty bob.' Here not more than about 10 per cent. of the population lived 'under conditions of overcrowding,' and the representative inhabited house contained almost exactly six people and a half. This house was at least four-room, or there would have been a great deal of overcrowding, and is perhaps best pictured as holding a family and a lodger or lodgers. 'Our lodger' was almost as normal in Cockney life as he is familiar in Cockney rhyme. If the house had six or seven rooms, it was likely to contain two families[2].

The impossibility of every man having his own house, in London's central area, had produced the model dwelling movement connected with the names of George Peabody and Sydney Waterlow. About the same time (1861–2) they had begun the erection of what to the eye of to-day are their "large and dreary block tenements."[3] Peabody's trustees carried on the work after his death in 1869. Since 1863, Waterlow had been working through the Improved Industrial Dwellings Company to show that sanitary housing could be made to pay. He succeeded, on an average weekly rental of 2*s.* 1¼*d.* a room. By 1884 his company had built, or had in hand, tenements for 25,000

[1] *R.C. of* 1884–5, Q. 12,062, 12,124.

[2] A common arrangement in the Canning Town dock area was two families to a house, with three rooms per family, plus a common kitchen, etc. *S.C. on Artisans and Labourers Dwellings*, 1882 (VII. 249), Q. 1430. Statistics of housing, when not otherwise stated, are from the Census of 1891.

[3] Wood, E. E., *Housing Progress in Western Europe* (New York, 1923), p. 13.

people[1]. The Peabody Trust, at a rental of 1*s.* 11½*d.* was in course of providing for about 20,000[2]. Waterlow's success was drawing out imitators, as he had hoped it would. Up and down inner working-class London, above the huddled 'gardens' and 'rents,' the blocks of 'models' were rising. But they housed only a tiny proportion of the Londoners. Their erection, Charles Booth wrote, "an effort to make crowding harmless, is a vast improvement, but it only substitutes one sort of crowding for another. Nor have all blocks...a good character, either from a sanitary or a moral point of view."[3]

Outside London, the more completely an English town had taken shape under the pressure of nineteenth century conditions, the more likely was it to be a place of numberless little houses, and to conform to Shaftesbury's ideal of a house for a man. But if the pressure had been mainly applied rather early in the century, there was considerable risk of there not being enough room in the houses, judged by the standards of the 'eighties, for the men, their families, and the occasional lodgers; unless an active municipality had been recently at work. Very early in the century "every workman had a home of his own," in Birmingham[4]. There was "never any serious overcrowding," Joseph Chamberlain said with justified pride in 1884: "we have no flats and no cellars." "Nor do working class families often take in lodgers," he added. It was under his guidance, in 1875–6, that the city had utilised current legislation to carry out one of the earliest schemes of slum clearance: it had also acquired, and greatly improved, its water supply, completed a sewerage system, and brought in a new and strict set of building by-laws[5]. It averaged only five people to each house, and so had very little technical overcrowding.

At Liverpool the municipality had a far worse inheritance. It had taken action early. Even in 1860 it had begun "some large blocks of dwellings out of our own corporate estate."[6] Latterly, under local acts and national legislation, it had been closing bad tenements as nuisances, scheduling insanitary areas, and acquiring house property to demolish it. But in the 'forties,

[1] Waterlow's evidence before the *R.C. of* 1884–5, Q. 11,905 *sqq.*

[2] *Ibid.* Q. 5063, 11,570–1. Cp. *S.C. of* 1882, Q. 1897, 2589.

[3] *Life and Labour*, I. 30. There is a full study of the 'models' in vol. III.

[4] Vol. I. p. 37.

[5] Chamberlain's evidence to the *R.C. of* 1884–5, Q. 12,359 *sqq.*

[6] *R.C. of* 1884–5, Q. 13,421 (evidence of an ex-mayor of Liverpool).

just before effective sanitary legislation began and before the city had adopted proper building by-laws, builders had endowed it with 14,500 houses in 2500 blind courts—the houses facing one another at 10 or 12 feet range, and backing on to similar houses[1]. They usually had an attic, two rooms, and a cellar which down to 1871 had too often been a tenement, and was sometimes "secretly occupied" still[2]. Fourteen hundred of the worst of these court houses had been swept away by the authorities, mostly since 1882. In spite of the many surviving, the city, young and vigorous, could show a house population of under six and an overcrowding percentage of probably not more than twelve[3].

The textile towns of the North—Manchester, Salford, Blackburn, Bolton, Oldham, Preston, Bradford, Halifax, Huddersfield—with other representative industrial towns such as Leeds, Sheffield, Nottingham and Leicester, all had an average house population within a few points above or below five. Yet, so inadequate was the accommodation of the cottages in the originally stone-built and not easily remodelled towns of the Yorkshire valleys, that they were among the most overcrowded places in England—Bradford, Halifax and Huddersfield having a slightly larger proportion of their population living more than two to a room even than London[4]. The number of two and three-room 'inhabited houses' in these places was evidently still very great. The overcrowding was less in Leeds, much less in Sheffield, and very much less in the cotton towns. Preston had remarkably little, and even Manchester-Salford, where there were many architectural survivals from the bad days described by Friedrich Engels, had less than West Ham[5]. The grimed and slated little red-brick houses of the Lancashire side, under their low grey sky, held a population in the main comfortable and well satisfied with them, itself, and its county.

[1] *R.C. of* 1884–5, Q. 13,336 *sqq.* See Hope, E. W., *Health at the Gateway*, Ch. IX, where on p. 158 a photograph of one of the old courts is reproduced. And cp. vol. I. p. 16, 546.

[2] *R.C. of* 1884–5, Q. 13,467 (another witness).

[3] The proportion of the population 'overcrowded' in 1891 was 10·9. The number of people per house was 5·99 in 1881 and 5·68 in 1891. This comparatively rapid motion suggests that overcrowding may have been perceptibly worse in 1886 than in 1891.

[4] London, in 1891, 19·7; Huddersfield, 19·9; Bradford, 20·1; Halifax, 21·3.

[5] Manchester, 8·2; West Ham, 9·3. For Engels' Manchester, see vol. I. p. 538; for some survivals Marr, T. R., *Housing Conditions in Manchester and Salford* (1904).

Most comfortable of all, judged by the tests of average house population and overcrowding, were towns which had been comparatively little affected by the first uncontrolled movements of population and the attempts to house it, such as Derby, Nottingham and Leicester. These three had average house populations below five and overcrowding percentages of only from two to four. In view of the decisive and degrading influence of the early nineteenth century Irish immigration on housing habits and housing conditions[1], it may be noted that whereas 9 per cent. of the Lancashire population in 1851 had been actually Irish born, the corresponding figure for Derbyshire was 1·5, for Nottinghamshire 0·9, and only 0·7 for Leicestershire[2]. Leicester had been spared a social disease, and had made good use of its immunity: in Liverpool "most of the inhabitants" of those insanitary courts were Irish in 1884. If a reforming municipality began to flush the courts in the morning, they were foul again at noon[3].

Bristol and Newcastle had inherited awkward sites and some of the ancient houses of historic seaports, split, like those of London, into tenements. Away from its centre, parts of which were "worse than Whitechapel,"[4] Bristol had also inherited quantities of small two-roomed cottages; for the housing standard of the West had been low both in town and country. Like London, it had made a beginning with model dwellings—two blocks of them with 131 'lettings' in 1884. This did not greatly help; and the two-room cottages drove up both of its test figures[5].

North of the Tees, not only in Newcastle but in Gateshead and Sunderland and throughout Northumberland and Durham, those figures were exceedingly bad; but the reality was rather better than the figures. The inherited town house of the North-East coast was either the large house fallen to tenements, or a smaller house of two storeys built for tenements—"each storey being a complete small house of itself"[6]—or some variant of

[1] Cp. vol. I. p. 62. [2] *Census of* 1851. *Occupations*, etc. I. ccxcv.

[3] *R.C. of* 1884–5. Evidence of H. Farris, Q. 13,463 *sqq.* The quotation is from Q. 13,626.

[4] *Ibid.* Q. 7018. Whitechapel was the synonym for bad housing conditions in the 'eighties.

[5] *Ibid.* Q. 6947, 7018; and cp. vol. I. p. 547. For country housing in the South-West, below, p. 510.

[6] *Ibid.* Q. 7452. And cp. vol. I. p. 27–32, on Scottish and North Country housing. For the larger North Country, or Scottish, rooms see Q. 19,396 and vol. I. p. 29, n. 6.

the one-roomed or two-roomed Northumbrian miners' and agricultural labourers' cottage. There had been in fact, and there remained, an approach to housing conditions typically Scottish. Population per house in the towns was nearly as high as in London, and the habit of living more than two to a room was far more widespread. The rooms may have been larger on the average, as they probably were in the Scottish towns, and certainly were in the Northumbrian, as compared with the South Country, agricultural districts. It was just as well; for in Sunderland over 32 per cent., in Newcastle over 35 per cent., and in Gateshead over 40 per cent. of the whole population lived 'under conditions of overcrowding.' The census officials who first reported on the matter, not fully apprehending the local peculiarities, were puzzled to find that their figures showed more overcrowding—more cases of three people in one room or five in two—in Northumberland and Durham when all the towns were excluded than when they were included[1]. But it was natural that the old Northumbrian one or two-room way of living should survive least altered among the pits or in the dales.

The old Scottish urban way was little touched, whether in the towering many storied houses of Edinburgh and Stirling; in the three and four-storied ones among which burrowed the Glasgow wynds; in their fellows of grey granite at Aberdeen; in the two-storied, often of two flats as at Newcastle, common in the smaller burghs; or in the one-storied, 'single end' or 'but and ben,' which linked town to country and collected about the coal mines and iron works[2]. The Scottish way of living had been got by ancient country habit out of ancient town necessity, and it was a one or two-room way, very tough and indestructible, as were the eighteen inch or two foot stone walls of the houses which encased it. "The single-room system," the Commissioners of 1885 reported in a not quite lucid phrase, "appears to be an institution co-existent with urban life among the working classes of Scotland."[3] In Edinburgh the house of a skilled man—Scottish witnesses called it a house, though English Commissioners said tene-

[1] *Census of* 1891: *Final Report*, p. 22. This would of course have been a surprising result south of the Tees. The officials noticed that the 'percentage of over-crowding' dropped plumb from 34 in Durham to 16·5 in the West Riding.

[2] See the *Report on Housing in Scotland* of 1917, p. 41–2, 47, 49.

[3] *R.C. of* 1884–5: *Scotland* (XXXI of 1884–5), p. 4.

ment—was "generally a room and a kitchen";[1] sometimes two rooms and a kitchen. The unskilled man had just a room. There were 14,000 'single-room houses' in the city, and 19,000 'houses' which had only one room with a window to it, though 5000 of them had two rooms of a sort[2]. About a quarter of the whole population of Glasgow lived in one-room 'houses.' The Bridgeton division was the masterpiece. In 1881 it contained 8946 families of all sizes, from the widow living alone upwards. Of these only 882 had more than two rooms fitted with windows[3]. The municipality of Glasgow, under its own Acts of Parliament, had done some admirable slum clearances and street making since 1866; but it could not change the system[4]. For the whole of urban Lanarkshire, out of 176,000 families, 42,000, or not 24 per cent., had 'houses' with more than two rooms fitted with windows. The granite streets of Aberdeen were less congested: nearly 40 per cent. of its families were in that favoured position. Dundee was more congested: the percentage of favoured families there was under 24. All this is for 1881; but, in the nature of the case, the position was changing very slowly[5]. It is not surprising that the Scottish census of 1891 did not imitate the English by applying a persons-per-room standard of overcrowding. The arithmetical results would have been disastrous. More than half the urban population would have appeared overcrowded; although a Glasgow official in 1884, taking a cubic-foot-of-air-space standard, had maintained that not more than 5 per cent. of the Glasgow houses could be so described[6].

Experts of the Peabody Trust knew that their models "would not fill if erected in the outskirts";[7] and it was noticeable, towards the end of the decade, that working class tenement blocks filled much better in Westminster than in Deptford[8]. Pressure was so great West of the City that blocks of flats were being built for the use of the more comfortable classes. "Dined with Willie and his wife," John Bright noted in his diary, on April 10, 1883: "their rooms or *flat* in Victoria Street not so

[1] *R.C. of* 1884–5, Q. 18,594.
[2] From the *Census of* 1881: in App. to the *R.C. Report of* 1884–5.
[3] *Ibid.*
[4] *S.C. of* 1882, as above, Q. 736.
[5] It had changed comparatively little by 1917.
[6] *R.C. of* 1884–5, Q. 19,508.
[7] *R.C. of* 1884–5 (xxx), Q. 11,701.
[8] Booth, *op. cit.* III. 5.

inviting as a *house* would be."[1] Before 1880 such buildings had been rare; though inner London had always provided lodgings for every social grade, and had specialised in chambers and apartments for single gentlemen. Her comfortable, normal, family men had standardised continuous houses like the wage-earners of the outskirts, not in low, but in high unlovely streets and squares and gardens—basement; portico; stucco or brick front; four stories, and attics for the maidservants; with mews, and sometimes a scrap of slum round the corner. The type was reproduced with variations in the inner residential belt of many English towns, becoming rarer as you went North, partly because the inner parts of industrial towns were less fit and less prized for comfortable residence, partly because more spacious ways of living could be got relatively near.

In London they could only be got with any ease in the true suburbs, with some of which communications were defective, judged by a rising standard of mobility, although it was communication—the radial railways—that had made them. The suburb was much the same all over the country. It had real gardens, if ever so little, and shrubs and hedges of holly or privet. When, as a suburb, it was old, there would be imbedded in it houses restrained, balanced, usually rectangular in mass and fenestration, of red brick or stuccoed, inconspicuously roofed, dating from before the railways and the publication of *The Stones of Venice* (1851–3). But whether old or new, the suburb was dominated by what average builder-architect opinion had made out of the Gothic Revival and John Ruskin. Slated roof and gable were assertive. There might be patterns on the slates. There was likely to be a wooden or iron finial on the gable end, and perhaps machine-made open work on its crest. Latterly, the half-timbered gable had become prominent. Turrets were possible; curved bays or some deliberate avoidance of the rectangular almost certain. True Gothic windows were awkward and scarce, but some of the windows could be given round heads; others small panes. Worked stone, for beauty and diversity, would be mixed with the normal brick in various ways, if only in the single bow window of the smallest semi-detached villa residence, or in the diminishing perspective of bow windows along the stretches of continuous house between the true suburb and the town. Attention had

[1] *The Diaries of John Bright* (1930), p. 498.

been called to the Venetian decoration of wall veils with inset marble slabs;[1] so there could be patterns of red brick on white, and of blue on red. Porches gave great scope for Gothic detail, because they need not be comfortable[2]. It was on a porch, but of a public-house in Ealing, that Ruskin had seen in 1873 brickwork "which would have been in no discord with the tomb of Can Grande, had it been set beside it at Verona."[3] Discord with the best Italian Gothic had not, however, been universally avoided.

The suburbs had no bounds. They shaded away into the country; and even villages remote from London had often been suburbanised, judged by the standards of the country squire. "The enormous rise in the value of all sites within easy reach of great towns or railway stations," wrote the Hon. George C. Brodrick in 1881, "sometimes offers to great landowners an inducement to sell which they cannot resist. In this way... detached portions of great estates...are bought up by land-jobbers and sold in petty blocks to retired tradesmen. The villa-residences of such immigrants from towns, fronting the road in unsightly rows, with an acre or two of freehold land at the back of each, are a characteristic feature of many country villages, and have been too much overlooked in popular descriptions of rural England."[4] The village as popularly described was not extinct. It had hall and parsonage and perhaps another house or two whose inhabitants, unlike the "immigrants from towns," took "an active part in county interests."[5] But one had to go into the depths of the country to find it. When found, its houses might be quite untouched by the Gothic Revival, unless the parsonage had been rebuilt lately, or a hall of no pretensions had been replaced by something gabled and arched, possibly with stained glass in it and a pitch-pine staircase[6].

Apart from the definite encroachment of towns, suburbs,

[1] See Ruskin's Preface to *The Stones of Venice*.

[2] An architect who has been consulted writes of the average designs of this period—"all houses had as many gables as could be crowded on to them, and as great a variety of building materials as the designer could assemble."

[3] Ruskin, Preface to the 1873 edition of *The Stones of Venice*, p. vi.

[4] Brodrick, *English Land and English Landlords*, p. 154. "But this class," he adds, "though of great importance to election agents, fills a very small place in the agricultural economy, or even in the social life of an English county."

[5] *Loc. cit.*

[6] Cp. Cobbett on the earliest Gothic revival houses quoted in vol. I. p. 36.

pits and factories, and of the railways with their brood, the country itself, if thought of as a series of landscapes, had not changed so very much since Cobbett rode about baying at tax-eaters and Scotchmen and pitying the fortunes of the poor. It had become increasingly difficult, even during Cobbett's lifetime, to find landscapes with "those very ugly things, common fields" in them[1]. In a few places, bits of the patchwork of the "ugly things" had survived until a main railway line was driven across its shots, headlands and gore acres[2]. You could see it from no main line now. Only well-informed people knew where to look for accidentally preserved specimens. Naturally there were rather more remnants of the Scottish equivalent, the runrig field, in the untouched Hebrides; there was some runrig too in Ireland; perhaps a few fields cut up into 'quillets' in Wales. In England there were men "still living who had held and worked farms under" the "inconvenient rules" of the open-field system, and who knew the "meaning of its terms and eccentric details";[3] but even the memory was perishing. The thing itself had gone out of the English scene for ever.

At a time when it seemed not unlikely that they would follow it, the surviving commons and wastes had been maintained by acts of deliberate policy, in that dwindled and regimented state into which they had fallen by the 'seventies. In the really fertile parts of the country, few of any consequence had escaped enclosure by the end of the first quarter of the century. The survivors were most numerous and extensive on the sandy soils. Few had yet been turned into golf links. Fewer had kept much of their former economic character. There was not a great deal of firing gathered or turf cut, not many goats and swine fed, on your average English common. Often the suburbs had got all about it, as they had got about some of the almost unrecognisable 'moors' of the industrial North[4]. Among them it served its purpose, yet not the old purpose. Well beyond the suburbs, gypsies might still find camping ground on it; but vagrant life had been much confined and policed. Peter Bell

[1] Vol. I. p. 20.

[2] As can be seen in some of the early plans for the Eastern Counties Railway, the present L.N.E.R. line from Liverpool Street to Cambridge.

[3] From F. Seebohm's Introduction to his *English Village Community* (1883), p. xiv.

[4] There was still a little heather on Kersal Moor (Manchester); not any, I think, on Woodhouse Moor (Leeds).

no longer lay out beside his asses. By the time that George Borrow died in 1881, there was little left of that society of the open sky among which the Flaming Tinman had travelled and fought[1]. There were the county constabulary and the Commons Preservation Society.

The hill commons of the West and the North had been regulated or portioned out, but not otherwise greatly changed. A wire fence now divided the Wasdale fells from the fells of Ennerdale; but the intakes had gained no ground on the lower slopes—if anything they had lost since the dales became more accessible. Not even as a romantic possibility was the carrying of cultivation, "rich as that of a flower garden...to the very tops of Ben Nevis and Helvellyn,"[2] any longer anticipated. Whether wanderers from the towns below or the grouse deserved more consideration on Kinder Scout; whether the sheep with their shepherds or the deer and their gillies had the best title to the use of the Cairngorms—about these things there was discussion; and there would be more. But in the true Highlands, except at the prescribed times, there were fewer men than ever amid the loneliness of "the seven bens and the seven glens and the seven mountain moors."[3] In the Pennines, solitude could be found without much seeking, all the way from Kinder Scout to Cross Fell; although the railways pierced the hills, and the smoke of Cheshire and Lancashire broke against their southern ranges, blown on the South-West wind.

For over two centuries there had been little forest in Britain. The English landscape was full of trees but astonishingly empty even of woodland. Not five per cent. of the surface of the country was wooded, in spite of the hedgerow and roadside timber, the parks and gardens and spinneys. In Scotland the percentage was less than four. The work of clothing Scotland with trees, undertaken in the eighteenth century[4], had been checked after the decade 1820–30. When the railway age came, a line was driven through the best wooded districts, Athole, Badenoch and Strathspey, and much of the standing timber went in sleepers. It was said that by 1872 Scotland had 200,000 acres less forest than she had just before Waterloo. There had been

[1] There was most of it in Scotland, where the vagrant 'tinkler' survived.

[2] Macaulay's *Essay on Southey's Colloquies on Society*, *ad finem*.

[3] A favourite refrain of Catriona MacGregor, later the wife of David Balfour of Shaws.

[4] See vol. I. p. 13–14.

some replanting since. Interest in forestry was reviving. The woods of Scone, Blair-Atholl and Strathspey were considerable, and much of the timber was magnificent. But the ground lost to forest had not been regained; there was little management, as a trained forester understands it; and to a visiting continental expert, Scotland, with its great spaces and forest climate, seemed a land of infinite lost opportunity[1].

In England opportunity was far less, but what there was had not been seized. The state took little interest in oak, for oak had no longer its immediate fighting value. The state was not yet wise enough to interest itself vigorously in any timber with a view to the long future. Schemes for replanting in the New Forest, after what was called the Deer Removal Act of 1851, were stultified by the opposition of the commoners and the public. The commoners were no doubt shortsighted but wise in their generation. Very possibly the public was wise for future generations. England was so full that she had to balance forest against 'open space.' But a little more modern forest might have been made there in Hampshire. As it was, some 40,000 acres of William's hunting ground lay "bare and unproductive," if beautiful[2]. "Before long it will *not be here*," M. Boppé, the Forest Inspector from Nancy wrote in 1885, "that a professor of Sylviculture...will choose to pitch his tent." Only in the Forest of Dean did he find a little workmanlike management on Crown land[3].

Where the town and suburban railway crawled round the trees, as at Epping, the transition to open space was inevitable. The other fragment of the old forest of Essex, Hainault, was disafforested in 1851 and its deer removed or destroyed, like those of the New Forest. It had melted into common agricultural land, all but a remnant, which still retained some of the ancient woodland peace and survived to become an open space in the twentieth century. Much of Epping had been nibbled away by unlawful enclosure. In the 'seventies, when the Corporation of London began to take interest in its future, barely 3000 acres of open waste remained. In 1878 came the *Act for the disafforestation of Epping Forest and the preservation and management of the unenclosed parts thereof as an Open Space* (41 and 42 Vict. c. 213), as a result of which, after long

[1] *S.C. on Forestry*, 1884–5 (VIII. 779), Q. 319 *sqq.* (Scottish evidence): p. 45 *sqq.*, Report of M. Boppé of Nancy on the British forests.

[2] *V.C.H. Hants*, II. 454. [3] His *Report*, as above.

arbitration, Queen Victoria proclaimed it free to her people, from High Beech, on May 6, 1882. The securing of it had cost the City more than a quarter of a million pounds[1].

For the rest, plantation had gained ground here and lost it there, but was nearly all of one uneconomic kind. In Nottinghamshire, since the dissipation of Sherwood, woodland had increased and was increasing. But as was said later, in words which would have been approximately true of the whole country, the increase was "almost entirely due to...the luxurious value of forest trees and coverts,"[2] as beautifiers of a landscape and shelters for game. There were a few remnants of ancient woodland, in Sussex parks, or the New Forest, or Savernake; there was some planting of native forest trees; but most nineteenth-century planting had been of conifers, those upstarts of the English woods[3]. These had won their way into good society and become part of England. Soon poets would think of the Sussex pines much as they thought of the Long Man of Wilmington, forgetting that the upstarts were little older in the county than the Brighton Pavilion.

Among the plantations and the hedgerow elms which made England seem so green and heavily wooded, when viewed from ground level, on that level itself green had been spreading in slowly from the West—from the "land not of farmers but of graziers"[4]—since the repeal of the Corn Laws. But as yet the amount of land newly laid down, or tumbled down, to grass was not great enough to affect the colour scheme of the island much. If a man could have flown high over it at the time of the first Reform Bill, again at the time of the Crimean War, and again at the time of the third Reform Bill, his broad visual impressions would have been much the same. Over the fens, unless he were there when the corn was young, he might even have noted less verdure on his third flight than on his first: many of Cobbett's "bowling greens,"[5] now safely drained by steam and the suction pump, had gone under the plough. On his second flight, he would have missed the glint from the thousand acres of water in Whittlesea Mere. It had just been turned into arable, after a great struggle and one failure: the

[1] *V.C.H. Essex*, II. 623–4. Hainault Forest was an attractive place as described in the 'seventies and 'eighties.

[2] *V.C.H. Notts*, I. 380; and vol. I. p. 9–10.

[3] See vol. I. p. 9 *sqq.*

[4] Cobbett's description of the Yorkshire dales and other parts of the north-west, quoted in vol. I. p. 50.

[5] See vol. I. p. 8.

young wheat was on it already in 1853, and still recurred in its proper rotation, a generation later[1].

And the pattern of the island surface had not changed very much, either in design or in size, since the last open fields had been cut out of it. The big, rational, more or less rectangular 'several' fields of the final era of enclosure required no fundamental alteration, and had received none. The campaign of the agricultural reformers against unnecessary hedgerows, in districts enclosed earlier or anciently, had been vigorous and effective in places since the 'forties[2]. It had enlarged bits of the pattern, and made it a trifle more uniform. But there were whole counties and regions in which very few hedges had been grubbed up. There was not one in which a field system previously irrational, judged by the standards of the strict agricultural economist and agricultural mechanician, had been thoroughly rationalised. Just a little squarer; just a little larger; just a little less 'nook-shotten'[3]—there had been no more change in the pattern than that.

One change there was appropriate to the age in which England, as Ruskin said, had become "the man in the Iron Mask," the outbreak of wire in the fences which made the pattern. When John Leech and Robert Smith Surtees died in 1864, it was still almost unknown. Leech's Mr Briggs did not come to grief over it: the cry of 'ware wire' is not heard in Surtees' hunting stories; although there is a reference to a farmer who mended a broken fence with a bit of wire rope in the last of them. In the 'seventies, so the memories of old riders to hounds tell them, the wire began to be a nuisance. With the 'eighties, it became common; occasionally it was barbed[4]. A country already fenced had less use for it than countries of prairie and sheep-run; but you could not possibly go far without meeting it, either as primary or secondary fencing. Where the business of fencing was new, as on the Cumberland fells, its meagre economical lines might run for miles.

[1] Wells, W., "The Drainage of Whittlesea Mere," *J.R.A.S.* 1860–1. For the amount of change in the country at large from arable to pasture by 1886, see above, p. 284, below, p. 504.

[2] Above, p. 267.

[3] Full of nooks and corners—"will sell my dukedom
To buy a slobbery and a dirty farm
In that nook-shotten isle of Albion." *Henry V*, Act III, Sc. 5.

[4] Both the hunting information and the Surtees information come from Mr W. H. Macaulay of King's College, Cambridge.

The crops that filled in the pattern of Britain had changed even less than the pattern itself, except that wheat had shrunk by about 900,000 acres, between 1874–7 and 1884–7, and the whole acreage under corn by rather more. A little rye was still grown, because saddlers and packers of pots wanted rye straw; but rye had long ceased to be a British crop. There were the three standard grain crops; the three principal root crops; the clover, rotation grasses, vetches and lucerne; very little else. Flax had dwindled to a mere 2000 or 3000 acres; and there were no other industrial crops of any significance. The potato acreage had grown steadily, though not so fast as population. It was still well under 2 per cent. of the cultivated area, much less relatively than in neighbouring European countries. There was a small, almost fixed, acreage under hops; some scores of thousands of acres in cabbages and other miscellaneous crops; and the same in orchards. In many districts there had been no orchard extension, and a backward and negligent orchard practice, as in most of the apple orchards of the South-West. But in the whole country the area under fruit was growing slowly[1]. Gladstone's advice to depressed agriculturalists that they should get a living by making jam may have had something to do with it, though growth began before depression.

In its broad features cropping was uncommonly simple. Everything but the staples had been subordinated to the point of neglect. The system had grown up when the staples were in no danger. The danger to some of them, which had threatened since 1875–9, had not yet led to any important adjustment, beyond the obvious one of an addition of some 2,000,000 acres to the permanent pasture. This was merely an acceleration of an existing process which, working slowly at first, had turned into additional grazing land perhaps 5 per cent. of the area of Britain, and 9 per cent. of the cultivated area, between 1850 and 1886. By that amount the face of the country had become permanently greener.

Although in some counties the suburb had spread far into the villages, the great houses of England—Tudor, Jacobean, but predominantly Hanoverian and Whiggish[2]—stood secure in their parks, little changed and seldom deserted since Whigs

[1] A verbal summary of the agricultural statistics of the period.

[2] See vol. I. p. 35–6.

began the work of Reform. The fanciful mind may picture them listening, with no fear but some high-bred bewilderment, to the noises of a populous, steely, and democratic time. "Our land laws were framed by the landed interest, for the advantage of the landed interest," a man bred in one of them was heard saying a few years later: "we are now come, or are coming fast, to a time when Labour laws will be made by the Labour interest for the advantage of Labour."[1] That need not mean the near fall of Blenheim, or even the change of Stowe into a school. Randolph Churchill was impulsive. He might be mistiming events, or he might be quite wrong. Still change really seemed to be coming. Was even decay possible?

In sixty years few great houses had been built, and not many of the second rank. New Balmoral had grown out of the "little castle," itself new, "with numerous small turrets, and white-washed," which Prince Albert had found there in 1848[2]. A few more noblemen's castles had been built or rebuilt in one or other of the Gothic styles. Rather lower in the scale came such places as Peel's Drayton Manor, where a house "neither Italian nor Elizabethan, but relieved in its outline by towers and turrets," had succeeded the plain rows of window and short square chimney stacks of old Drayton Hall[3]. Other manors and halls had felt the hand of the time spirit; but they were a minority. Only on the villa level had he found a field reasonably clear.

Of farmhouse and farmstead building there had been a great deal, so long as agriculture had prospered. There were not many of the "rickety and shapeless"[4] houses now left in the home counties, nor in any county of vigorous agriculture, whether it was mainly pastoral like Cheshire or mainly arable like Norfolk and Lincoln. When an important farmhouse was old, it was generally a manor house, become the headquarters of a modern farm with modern buildings attached. Except for these, there were not anywhere on the larger farms many houses older than the last era of enclosure; and old farm buildings were rarer than old houses. Even on the smaller and smallest farms, houses had nearly all been rebuilt, or in

[1] Lord Randolph Churchill in 1892; *Life*, by Winston Spencer Churchill, II. 459.

[2] *Life of the Prince Consort*, II. 109. It was built by Sir Robert Gordon, brother of the then Lord Aberdeen.

[3] There are pictures of both in Parker's *Peel*, vols. II and III. The quotation is from Murray's *Guide to Staffordshire* (1874).

[4] Vol. I. p. 34.

some way modernised, although this was not so true of the Western side of the country as of the East. It was least true of Wales, where there was no sharp line between farmhouse and cottage. Everywhere, it was on the border line between farm and cottage, or among the cottages below it, that the oldest dwellings and types of dwelling were to be found. And these were most numerous all along what it would soon become the fashion to call the Celtic fringe[1].

On its furthest edge were the 'black houses' of the Lewis: "the cattle occupy one end...the walls range in thickness from 3 to 6 feet, and are built of two tiers of stones with a wall of turf between. The roof is of somewhat loose thatch...the floor is of clay in most instances. The human portion of the dwelling is usually divided into a 'but' and a 'ben.' In the living room the fire is in the centre of the floor, and the smoke finds its way out as best it can, there being usually no chimney. ...In the cattle end the manure is allowed to lie all the year until it is required....The houses are often end to end and back to back."[2]

That is a good black house. In the worst, cattle and people lived "in the same undivided space."[3] Variants of the type were to be found scattered in many parts of the Highlands and Islands; but on the mainland they were said "to be disappearing" in 1884[4]. Even in South-Eastern Scotland there had been still a few "of the old turf houses" in 1870;[5] Dumfries had been full of the one-room Scottish stone houses with their box beds; and Ayrshire full of what were described as hovels[6]. Twenty years later, although the turf houses seem to have disappeared from the Lowlands, "in some of the older and inferior dwellings, both in the north and south...there was actually only one large room."[7] (So there was in very many of the Scottish miners' houses at the same date[8].) But taking rural

[1] The phrase is credited to A. J. Balfour in 1892: see the *Times*, March 24, 1930.

[2] This is 'the black house' as it remained in the twentieth century: *R.C. on the Housing...of Scotland*, 1917 (Cd. 8731), p. 211. There is a similar account in the *R. on the Crofters and Cottars in the Highlands and Islands* of 1884 (XXXII), p. 48.

[3] *R.C. on the Housing of the Working Classes: Scotland* (1884–5, XXXI), p. 9.

[4] *Loc. cit.*

[5] *Fourth Report on Children and Women in Agriculture* (1870, XIII. 177), p. 19. Cp. vol. I. p. 29.

[6] *Ibid.* p. 20 and vol. I. p. 29–30.

[7] *R.C. on Labour*, 1893–4, XXXVI. 9.

[8] See Keir Hardie's indignant evidence before the *R.C. on Labour* (1892,

Scotland as a whole, it was supposed that there might be more three-room than one-room dwellings. The standard labourer's house everywhere was still the one-storey, two-room, 'but' and 'ben,' like those of the Lewis, except that it was, in Hebridean language, 'white'—that is to say mason built—not 'black.' Scottish rooms as compared with English were big, and these houses were probably better than the worst in England, better for example than a one-storied mud-walled Somerset hovel, with "two compartments each being about three yards square," described by an angry reformer in 1872[1], and possibly still standing in the 'eighties. The Scot used his space in the ancient way. "The practice of putting one or more beds in the living room is inveterate, and to insist on a departure from it is much resented."[2] Of some other things he had not always learnt the use: the constant abuse of privies when provided had greatly hindered their provision. Yet of the better Scottish cottages it was said that "comfort was written both inside and outside them."[3]

The Welsh equivalents of the worst Scottish hovels were the so-called ink-bottle houses of squatters in the Mid-Welsh hills, rough one-room affairs with a central chimney from which they got their name. These had become rare; but there were still one-roomed mud-walled cottages, with chimneys of wattle and daub, in the South-West, and one-room "square box" stone cottages in Anglesey, all furnished with cupboard beds of the old sort. In general the Welsh cottages were inferior to the English and, it would seem, less roomy than the Scottish. Their users still had something to learn. Even when the cottage was fairly good, its chimney might be blocked up by the occupant, and its slops might be thrown out of the door[4].

In England the one-room cottage hardly existed South of the Tees, though the two-room was still common. Northumberland and Durham had a few with a single big room, 24 feet by 16, and a small loft above. Cottages of this type were being built down to about 1848; and there were said to be still far too

XXXVI. Pt. 2), Q. 12,482 *sqq.*, and the evidence of a colliery official that when his firm built two-room houses the tenants sublet one of the rooms, Q. 13,458.

[1] Heath, F. G., *The English Peasantry* (1874), with a picture of the hovel.

[2] *R.C. on Labour*, 1893–4, as above, p. 24.

[3] *Ibid.* p. 24, 33.

[4] *Ibid.* p. 22–3. Cp. Doyle's Report on Wales in *R.C. on Agricultural Depression*, 1882: cottages generally worse in Wales than elsewhere: sometimes mere hovels.

many of them twenty years later. At that time (1867–9) the situation was changing fast owing to active cottage building by landlords, the most popular type of house among the North Country labourers being the so-called 'two-ends,' with a couple of big divisible rooms on the level, like the Scottish 'but' and 'ben.'[1] It was a house with no 'upstairs,' such as had worried Cobbett greatly in the 'twenties[2]. This type, and South Country 'upstairs' types with more rooms, had become general North of the Tees by the 'eighties[3].

Similar rapid improvement had been made in the Lothians. So early as 1870, a Scottish expert maintained that in no county of England was the "average so good as in Berwickshire."[4] There is no reason to reject his evidence; for the really ancient type of Scottish hovel was so primitive that it could hardly survive in a vigorous neighbourhood, whereas in England types slightly better in their day survived nearly everywhere to be denounced in the 'eighties. The typical lowest grade English cottage could be found in nearly every rural district, though by no means in every village, from Lincolnshire and East Anglia to Cornwall. It was "of mud, clay lump, or lath and plaster."[5] The living room was some 9 feet square. There was a single bedroom, or perhaps a room and a bed-closet. In the worst of all—there were happily few of these—the ceiling was only 6 feet high, or even less, and access to the bed-loft was by ladder. Now and again there was no privy; there was never a good one[6].

Such places were mostly found on land which had once been waste, as in Cornwall or Hereford, or in that class of village which was still described as 'open.' Down to 1865, the working of the Poor Law had perpetuated the distinction between the close and the open parish—the former controlled entirely, or almost entirely, by a single landlord; the latter in many hands[7]. It had been to the interest of the landlord of

[1] *R. on Employment of Children...and Women in Agriculture* (1867–8, XVII), p. 65. Report of J. J. Henley on Northumberland and Durham.

[2] See vol. I. p. 31.

[3] In the Northumberland Union of Glendale, in 1890–2, 67 per cent. of the population living in small tenements (*i.e.* tenements of less than five rooms) lived in tenements of one or two rooms. *R.C. on* [Agricultural] *Labour*, 1893–4 (XXVII. Pt. 2), p. 100.

[4] *Fourth R. on Children and Women in Agriculture* (1870, XIII. 177), p. 19.

[5] *R.C. on* [Agricultural] *Labour*, 1893–4 (XXXV), p. 33. C. M. Chapman's description of the C grade English cottage.

[6] *Loc. cit.*

[7] Cp. p. 431 above, and vol. I. p. 467–8.

the close parish to have relatively few cottages, occupied by families in good regular work, and so to limit the liability of his parish for poor rate. Casual workers and undesirable families were left to the open parish—from which their surplus might tramp to work, when wanted in the close. The Union Chargeability Act of 1865 (28 and 29 Vict. c. 79), by spreading the rate burden evenly over the whole union, had removed the main incentive to keep down the parish stock of cottages, and had combined with good prices and rents to make the quarter of a century from 1854 to 1879 one of very active building of 'estate cottages.' The example had been set well before 1850, by such landlords as the Duke of Bedford[1], and it had been extensively followed, as in Northumberland and Durham. But, even with good will and some economic incentive, the business of transformation had been slow and remained incomplete. For at no time had the building of good cottages paid.

A Commissioner who, during 1868, had visited 300 parishes in Norfolk, Suffolk, Essex, Sussex and Gloucester had been entirely satisfied with only two[2]. He had found places in which the lowest grade one-bedroom house actually prevailed. The worst, he reported, belonged to squatters, speculators, or the parish—these last old poor law cottages, which poor law reform had superseded but not destroyed. Elsewhere, ancient freehold or copyhold cottages in the hands of what literary people called the peasantry, or cottages owned by small squires with nothing but their land to live by[3]—the cottages of Old England in short—were among the worst. A more fortunate Commissioner of 1867–9 reported much good building in Lincoln, Nottingham and Leicester; but also that the lowest cottage type survived there in most open villages[4]. In Northamptonshire's many close villages—it is an attractive county for the resident landowner—cottages were usually new and excellent, the three-bedroom type predominating. In open villages they were of all sorts, some vile. Much the same was true of Cambridge, Bedford,

[1] Vol. I. p. 472.

[2] Fraser, the Rev. J. (later Bishop of Manchester) reporting to the *C. on Children and Women in Agriculture*, 1867–8 (XVII), p. 11 *sqq*.

[3] For the first class, see Boyle, R. F., in *C. on Children and Women in Agriculture*, 1868–9 (XIII), p. 128; for the second, Joseph Arch's *Life*, p. 127.

[4] Stanhope, E., in 1867–8, XVII. 91 *sqq*. His eight worst villages contained 24 three-bedroom cottages; 193 two-bedroom; and 178 one-bedroom. The average number of dwellers in the one-bedroom cottages was 3½.

Buckingham and indeed of most counties South of the Trent; except that the Fens, unsuitable for gentlemen's places or easy sanitation, had a high proportion of vile cottages, and that the South-West, especially Somerset, had also a high proportion[1]. From Somerset in 1868 there came the gloomy news, which might perhaps have been anticipated, that "the worst...are generally the small freeholds, inhabited by the person who owns them."[2]

The general situation for Southern England in 1867–9 was summed up thus by a Commissioner who had conducted inquiries in Surrey, Wiltshire, Warwick, Worcester and Hereford: the cottages that landlords built, "and they are building a great many, are almost universally good."[3] There was even reasonable complaint that the greatest landlords, with their urban-rural rent rolls and their policies *de grand seigneur*, had set impossible standards of excellence, so that the small squire was being indicted for his poverty, like the indwelling freeholder of Somerset.

North of the Trent, Derbyshire had many new cottages and a standard above the English average. Yorkshire was said to be "vastly superior to the South." In most parts of the county there was "much comfort in the cottages,"[4] not to mention the gardens and cowgates. In North Lancashire it was the same; in Cumberland and Westmorland worse; but as these were small-holding regions, where living-in was usual, the housing of the handful of manual labourers was a subordinate matter[5].

One tendency these inquiries, made just before 1870, had registered in counties so different and far apart as Lancashire and Somerset—that a three-bedroom cottage was apt to have a lodger in its third room, unless this was prohibited by the owner. However, the building of three-bedroom and other types of cottage went steadily on so long as agriculture prospered, and did not quite stop when distress began. There was a touch of the Gothic revival in some of these mid-nineteenth century estate cottages, perhaps an arched window head or a slightly ornate chimney; but most new cottages, whether estate or not, were plain brick boxes or pairs; tiled in some districts; more often slated; very seldom thatched. Thatch recalled old

[1] From the various assistant-commissioners' reports in 1867–8, XVII and 1868–9, XIII.

[2] Boyle, in 1868–9, XIII. 128.

[3] Norman, F. H., in 1868–9, XIII. 69.

[4] Portman, E. B., in 1867–8, XVII. 105.

[5] Tremenheere, J. H., in 1868–9, XIII. 142–55.

bad memories. Slate, distributed easily from Wales or Westmorland by rail, had become the symbol of progress. When Joseph Arch's father died in 1862, leaving a freehold cottage to his son, Joseph not only put in windows—practicable windows presumably—but he "took off the old thatched roof ...and made it as smart and comfortable as it is to-day."[1] In every way Joseph was a man of his age.

Scotland still kept its bothies for unmarried farm labourers, but they were declining. They had never been much used in the West, where farms were small. The Lothians, Perth, Fife, Forfar and Kincardine had been their headquarters; and in the far North the arable country on the shores of the Moray Firth. Originally comfortless enough, some at least were reputed very comfortable by 1870, especially those which had a married woman in charge as cook and caretaker[2]. By the end of the 'eighties, the system was said to be "unknown in the Lothians" and decadent in Fife[3]. The bothy for unmarried women, which had been familiar in Haddington and Edinburgh so late as 1870, and was found occasionally elsewhere, seems to have disappeared. While it existed, its occupants had often been recruited from among the Edinburgh Irish. In spite of the general decline of the bothy system, many of the worst sort of bothies for men survived into the 'nineties, to be labelled "dens of dirt and confusion" and "a disgrace to Scotland."[4]

For England and Wales, some statistical material collected in 1891–3 pictures in arithmetic outline the state of the rural cottages, when the work of the 'seventies and 'eighties was done. At the census of 1891 tenements were enumerated, and the small tenements were defined and distinguished from the large. The definition of a small tenement was one of four rooms or less. On the land, tenement and cottage were almost synonymous: there was no regular tenement dwelling in the urban sense. The sample figures collected rather later[5] showed that a respectable percentage of the population did not live in 'small tenements' at all, but in five-room, or even six-room, cottages. These figures came from six widely scattered and representative districts so far apart as Lincolnshire and Somerset; but as

[1] Arch's *Life*, p. 57.
[2] *Fourth R. on Children and Women in Agriculture*, p. 21 *sqq*. Cp. vol. I. p. 31.
[3] *R.C. on* [Agricultural] *Labour*, 1893–4, XXXVI. 28.
[4] *Loc. cit.*
[5] For the *R.C. on Labour; General Report on Ag. Lab. in England and Wales*, by W. C. Little (1893–4, XXVII. Pt. 2), p. 99 *sqq*.

they excluded Wales and the 'two ends' cottages beyond the Tees, no doubt they exaggerate somewhat the proportion of 'large tenements,' as defined by the census, among the cottages. They make it over 19 per cent. Possibly 15 or 16 per cent. would be near the mark for the whole country South of the Tweed. The census statistics of small tenements in rural districts showed that just over 14 per cent. of the 'small tenement population' lived in one or two-room tenements. Owing to the five or six-room cottages, the small tenement rural population was less than the agricultural labouring population, perhaps 20 per cent. less, because the bigger cottages would generally house the biggest families. Further, the two-room tenements of England and Wales included the roomy and popular 'two ends' dwellings of the North. It is probable, therefore, that not more than some 11 or 12 per cent. of the rural labouring population was left in the bad, cramped, two-room, and very scarce one-room, cottages of central and southern England, or of Wales. That was far too much, even though such a house, if in fair condition, might be tolerable for a young married couple, an old man and wife, or some similar little family group. But unquestionably the percentage would have been higher had it been reckoned at any earlier census, and very much higher at that of 1851. The Somerset hovel which stirred the reformer of 1872 to indignation contained one old man: the occupants in the 'forties had been a man and wife and six children[1].

Since Augustus Petermann mapped the results of the census of 1851[2], there had been few important changes in the geographical distribution of industries in Britain, and hardly any of first-rate magnitude, judged merely by their effect upon employment. Most industries had expanded; but as a rule they had expanded in and from their old headquarters. The cotton areas; the coal areas; the wool and worsted areas; the endlessly varied industrial areas of the Birmingham country and of London, were bigger and denser. There had been important changes in their internal organisation and structure. Some few urban industries had declined, locally or even generally; but none of them were great, and their decline had not affected the life of the areas, or the look of the country.

[1] Heath, F. G., *The English Peasantry*, p. 48.

[2] See the map at the end of the volume.

Some rural industries had been dissipated, or had condensed into towns and manufacturing villages, with the spread of machine production; or had been part dissipated and part condensed; but the dissipations and condensations were relatively small. Yet the more important of them had national significance.

Hosiery showed a still incomplete condensation into industrial villages and towns, but no other change of importance. Its headquarters were fixed before 1851; and the number of people engaged in it in 1891 was very nearly what it had been forty years earlier. (The output was of course enormously increased.) The rural, domestic, and by-industries of straw plait and lace showed both condensation and dissipation. Down to 1870–80, rural straw plaiting had held its own fairly well in the belt of country from Buckingham to Suffolk, where Petermann registered it. So late as 1874, a hall was built at Hitchin to which country workers might bring in their plait[1]. It recalls the central cloth and linen halls of earlier rural industries. Numerically, the combined plait and straw-hat industry seems to have shrunk between 1851 and 1881; but the available figures are not perfectly comparable[2]. Strictly comparable figures for 1881 and 1891 register the marked shrinkage of the 'eighties, when the rural industry was going down before imports of Italian and Japanese plait, and the urban industry was assuming more of a factory character, as at Luton. In the 'nineties, the plait hall at Hitchin became a Mission Church.

Country lace-making had vanished almost completely from Buckingham, Devon, Northampton and the other counties in which it had been something of an industry in 1851. The number of people engaged in making lace, either by hand or machine, fell by nearly a half between 1851 and 1891. In the latter year, more than two-thirds of the 35,000 engaged in the manufacture were in the town of Nottingham, and most of the small remainder in other North-Midland towns; though fair quantities of home-made lace still came from Devon. Of other

[1] Hine, R. L., *The History of Hitchin* (1929), II. 431. The hall was sold in 1898. In 1867 in S. Beds and N. Bucks 'all females,' and many males, plaited straw. *Children and Women in Agriculture*, 1867–8 (XVII), p. 134. Plaiting was very important in Herts in the 'sixties: Evershed, H., "The Agriculture of Hertford," *J.R.A.S.* 1864. There were still over 2000 women and girls employed on it in South-West Suffolk in 1871: in 1881, only 781: in 1891, none. *V.C.H. Suffolk*, II. 248.

[2] The census classifications of the two years are not on the same basis.

industries which showed numerical decline, linen and silk were the chief. Linen had long been drawing out of England into Ulster. By 1891 it had become completely insignificant; and it had ceased to be a great industry even in Scotland[1]. The transfer had been so continuous as to be almost imperceptible: it had left no important gap, few decaying mills, no districts once industrial quickening back into agriculture. Hand-loom weaving was nearly dead, and most of the mills had been put to other uses or rebuilt for them. The decay of hand-loom weaving in silk, though less thorough-going, partly explains the numerical contraction of the industry; but there had been also what might be called absolute decline of manufacturing power in certain branches and localities. Yet there was still a little silk-working in every county, if not in every place, where Petermann had found it[2]. The two most considerable changes in the geographical distribution of the industry, its slow and now nearly complete disappearance out of London, and its recent growth in the West Riding[3], were after all but tiny and indistinct features in the industrial map, obscured by the smoke and growth of the towns.

Indistinct and tiny also were the traces left by the extinction of hand-loom weaving, and the concentration on a few Gloucestershire Cotswold valleys, in the old woollen industry of the West. Forty years were needed to reduce the whole working staff from about 24,000 to about 10,000, in all the counties westward from Wiltshire and Gloucester. The slow ebb had left behind it some weavers' cottages available for other people, and a number of mills in green West-country valleys, most of which had been diverted to fresh, often odd, uses—they made umbrellas, or hairpins, or sporting goods; few having slipped into a decay which in such surroundings might have been pleasing enough. Wales still had her diminutive rural spinning mills, and something which could be called a cloth or flannel industry in every county, though her whole wool-working population—mill people and the surviving cottage weavers—could have been fitted easily into a dozen fair-sized Yorkshire mills[4]. Scotland also retained a scattered domestic and semi-domestic industry, with important factory

[1] Above, p. 85.

[2] The reference is to the Census of 1891, as indicating the situation at the close of the period.

[3] Above, p. 87–8.

[4] The distribution in 1901, when there were still a few wool-workers in every Welsh county, is shown on the map in Clapham, J. H., *The Woollen and Worsted Industries.*

concentrations much where they had been in 1851: there was no radical change in the industrial map[1].

The greatest change in the whole island was of a type which can only occur rarely in an old industrial country—the shifting of the primary metallurgical industries to fresh sources of ironstone and to the sea. Neither Middlesbrough nor Barrow, still less Frodingham, is marked on Petermann's map; though Middlesbrough might have been called a town in 1851. Nor does the map show an important iron industry at Cardiff or at Newport. By the late 'eighties, more than a quarter of the British ironstone miners were working in the Cleveland hills, and a third of the British pig iron was made in and about Middlesbrough. A community, perhaps more highly specialised than any which earlier industrial change created, had risen around its blast furnaces[2]. Quite recently another mineral industry had appeared. So early as 1859 salt had been struck by boring at 1200 feet, South of the Tees, and in 1874 at 1127 feet, North of it. By 1882 the engineering difficulties had been mastered: brine was being pumped: salt was being made. Ten years later the annual output would be well over 200,000 tons[3].

The growth of Barrow-in-Furness had been more remarkable than that of Middlesbrough because more varied. Only in 1844–6 had the railway line which made the place been laid out. Cumberland hematite was being mined at that time for shipment to Staffordshire and South Wales;[4] and a few charcoal iron furnaces lingered on in the Furness fells. When the Barrow docks were opened in 1867, the Barrow and Workington districts were smelting an important part of the local ore; by 1875 the whole of it. In 1880 the largest iron steamer yet laid down, except the *Great Eastern*, was building at Barrow. By 1885 Cumberland and Furness were producing more than a sixth of the total 'make' of pig iron; and Barrow was busy with her iron and steel-making, with ship-building, and with marine engineering[5].

[1] But all Scotland only had 44,000 wool-workers in 1891, against 203,000 in Yorkshire.

[2] See Ch. III above, *passim*; and Lady Bell, *At the Works*, for the community.

[3] Grigg, R., "On the Middlesbrough Salt Industry," *Trans. Inst. Mech. Eng.* 1893; *V.C.H. Durham*, II. 293.

[4] Above, p. 49 and vol. I. p. 50, 189.

[5] Cp. the table on p. 49 above: Stileman, F. C., "On the Docks and Railway Approaches at Barrow-in-Furness," *Trans. Inst. Mech. Eng.* 1880: the historical account of Barrow given before the *R.C. on Depression of Trade and Industry*, 1886, Q. 2183 *sqq*.

The tracking southwards of those ironstone beds in the lias formation which had made the fortune of Cleveland had led, first to mining—or rather open working—of ore in an agricultural district of North Lincolnshire, and later to the erection of modern blast furnaces there, in the fields of Scunthorpe and Frodingham. The process had been repeated further south in Leicester, Rutland, Northampton and even Oxford; but only in Northampton had the furnaces followed the ore workings, and marked a rural area about Kettering and Wellingborough with the signs of the iron age. By the mid-'eighties its output was not far behind that of Lincolnshire. The other counties sent their ore North and West into districts marked for the iron age long before, districts most of which were now declining as iron makers and dismantling antiquated blast furnaces, without thereby losing an industrial and metallurgical character, or causing any deep change in the face of Britain[1]. A few fresh derelict patches, with their "scum of dross, old plash of rains and refuse patched with moss," stood out in landscapes which, at best, had shown only a grim plutonic beauty. Such patches were familiar in counties where the smoke hung low. No one as yet had taken in hand their salvage; though often some new smoke-making use was found for parts of them in course of time.

Away in South Wales and Monmouth, where iron-making and the steel-making which now went with it were well maintained, any derelict patches were back in the hills: iron-making did not die, it moved to tide water. The raising of native ore had nearly stopped, and it was easier for the coal to slide down the Glamorgan and Monmouthshire valleys than for the sea-borne ore, first Cumbrian then mainly Spanish, to be dragged up them. Some of the up-valley iron works were still smelting in 1885; but most of the smelting was done along the coast, from Swansea by Cardiff to Newport. The valley works of Ebbw Vale, Rhymney and Blaenafon all now smelted at Newport. While in Glamorgan more than four furnaces in every five were cold, together with all those in the upper valleys of Monmouth, at Newport twenty-one out of the thirty-eight large modern ones were in blast[2].

The ironstone mines of Britain reached their maximum output in 1882. The decline which followed was to prove not a fluctuation but a permanent shift to a somewhat lower level.

[1] See the *Mineral Returns* for the underlying facts.

[2] *Mineral Returns* for 1886.

It had not, however, affected the new geography of the industry. None of the areas now at work was in danger of going derelict. The position in 'half precious' metal-mining was greatly different: the stagnation of tin-mining since 1870, a sharp contraction in lead-mining since 1877, and the almost complete collapse of copper-mining, had scarred the face of the country. Scars left by declining or derelict lead workings were mostly hidden in the folds of Welsh or Pennine hills. Nor were the derelicts as yet very many; for the decline of output from its maximum was not yet 40 per cent., and to this decline most mines had contributed. But in the year of Victoria's Jubilee the whole output of fine copper from British ores was 889 tons: it had been 13,540 tons in 1860[1]. Old and famous Cornish districts were gaunt with abandoned mines and impoverished villages. The mines still working had a weak hold on life. Tin-mining held its own fairly well, but did not grow. There was gloom in Cornwall and her miners were taking their skill beyond the seas[2].

For lost copper-mining the Duchy had some compensations on her long double coast-line. Fishing was still reasonably vigorous, fresh mackerel and mullet sent to London having replaced losses in the export of barrelled pilchard to the Mediterranean[3]. China clay, quarried within easy reach of the sea and whitening the country-side, was taken in increasing quantities both coastwise and abroad, in vessels which could make even the smallest Cornish ports[4]. Potato-growing and market-gardening were now old-established at selected points on the southern coast. Flower-growing for the market had just reached the mainland from its original headquarters in the Scilly Islands, where it first became remunerative about 1880[5]. Perhaps more important still was Cornwall's share—not yet very great but to her valuable—in those large-scale migrations to the sea for recreation and residence which had flooded Brighton and Margate before the railway age[6] and, helped by increased earnings and savings in all ranks of society, had been carried by the railways to make or remake, after the pattern of the day, small hamlets and ports all round the island.

[1] The 1887 output was an absolute minimum: it was 1472 tons in 1886 and 1456 in 1888. In 1856 Cornwall alone had produced 13,274 tons: that was its maximum.

[2] Above, p. 104: Jenkins, *The Cornish Mines* (1927): *V.C.H. Cornwall*, I. 570.

[3] *V.C.H. Cornwall*, II. 582–6.

[4] *Ibid.* II. 577–8.

[5] *Ibid.* II. 578.

[6] Cp. vol. I. pp. 8, 9.

The second, the railway, stage in the resultant shiftings and fresh permanent accumulations of people had been indicated distinctly even in the census of 1851. Among the towns which had grown fastest during the previous decade were two pure seaside residence and recreation towns, Southport and Torquay[1]. Since 1851 each successive census had registered the arrival of fresh places in this class. Their rise had usually been marked, among other things, by the establishment of a pier company. Brighton had been equipped with her chain pier since the time of George IV and no ambitious 'resort' was perfect without some such accessory. Southport got its company, with 117 foundation shareholders, in 1859. Three years later a company was founded to provide, by means of a pier, "an extensive and agreeable promenade at Blackpool, Lancashire, over the sea, at high water." A year later again—the thing was infectious—a pier company was promoted for Lytham[2]. Lancashire had capitalised some of her prosperity into promenades just when the War of Secession was interrupting it. Recovering, she had built a second pier at Blackpool, with other facilities. And now, East, West, and South about Britain, where the seas were not too abruptly deep or too stormy, the new-style piers straddled into them on their iron legs. At its extremity the standard "iron promenade pier not made for trade"[3] swelled out to carry a pavilion. Brighton had a pavilion, though on land. Margate's second pier, of 1856, lacked the swelling[4]. This was added after 1871, "to meet the requirements of visitors,"[5] and on it the appropriate pavilion was built. The piers were as symbolic of what archaeologists call a culture as are axe-heads and beakers and other durable products of man's handiwork. This is not the place to speculate on their duration and uses, or to interpret their symbolism. There they stood. No visitor to the island could miss them. From them the least seafaring of the islanders could watch his ships go by with the joy of vicarious ownership.

[1] Weber, A. F., *The Growth of Cities in the Nineteenth Century* (New York, 1899), p. 55, groups Southport and Torquay with Birkenhead, Cardiff and Grimsby—all growing fast—as seaports; but that is not the explanation.

[2] *Return of all Joint Stock Companies Formed or Registered since* 18 *and* 19 *Vict. c.* 133. 1864 (LVIII. 291): under 1859, 1862, 1863.

[3] *Harbour Authorities: Return of Works executed within the last Twenty Years*, 1883 (LXII. 433). The harbours are in alphabetical order. The quotation refers to Skegness.

[4] For the first, see vol. I. p. 8.

[5] *Return of Works*, as above, under Margate.

The maritime resources and maritime dominion of Britain had never been more apparent, even to ignorant watchers. Her shallow seas were thronged. The sailing tonnage of the United Kingdom, though sinking, was as great in 1885 as it had been in 1850; the steam tonnage was nearly 4,000,000 greater. The steam tonnage alone had all but twice the capacity, and many times the carrying power, of the whole merchant navy of sixty years earlier. Perhaps a third of the world's sea-going ships were on the British register; of the world's steamships nearly five-eighths[1]. The last and finest of the clippers were on it also.

For their help, the Trinity House of Deptford Strond, as it was still called in official language, and the Commissioners of the Northern Lighthouses were perfecting their lights and buoys. There was now left undone very little building or placing that could possibly be of use. In Northern waters, the Skerryvore lighthouse had been finished by 1843. At the gates of the Channel, the Bishop's Rock was lighted in 1858 and the Wolf Rocks in 1869. The new Eddystone, stronger and safer than the old, came into use in 1882. The Thames estuary triangle, between the North Foreland lighthouse and the floating lights of the Gunfleet and the Nore, had long been studded thick with buoys, lights, and beacons[2]. The lights there fell on clouds of sail and small shipping; for against every steamer which made the port of London there were still between two and three sailing ships, mostly small coasters; so that the average size of all the ships entering the Thames with cargo was still only about 230 tons. At Liverpool the situation was very different and was becoming more different yearly. In 1873, the steam ships and sailing ships using the port had been equal in mere numbers. In 1884 the ratio was two to one: by 1889 it would be three to one. The average ship entering with cargo was of well over 500 tons. At Cardiff it was of about 400 tons. In fact the trade of the Thames retained traits of an earlier time, which that of Cardiff or of Liverpool had lost[3].

[1] *Tables showing the Progress of Merchant Shipping*, 1902 (Cd. 329), p. 48–51.

[2] Cp. vol. I. p. 7–8, and see the series of *Reports...by Trinity House of Deptford Strond and the Commissioners of Northern Lighthouses*, *e.g.* for the new Eddystone, 1883, LXII. 211.

[3] For harbours, docks and port facts and statistics in the 'eighties, see Harcourt, L. F. V., *Harbours and Docks* (1885), and Dorn, A., *Die Seehäfen des Weltverkehrs* (1891), 2 vols.: very thorough. Detailed figures of trade at the various ports are in the annual *Trade Returns*, and summary figures for all the more important ports in the *Statistical Abstracts for the U.K.*

Though it was no longer usual to speak of London and the 'out ports,' as if these last were of little account, London remained the greatest port of Britain and of the world—judged by all tests but one. The tonnage entered and cleared was between 50 and 60 per cent. greater than that of the Mersey; the aggregate trade was more valuable, but as an exporter of British produce London was now far behind Liverpool; for cotton manufactures still made up more than a quarter of the British exports, and they were not the only goods shipped principally from the Mersey. Yet London's great and various import and re-export trade, together with the growing size of ships, had called for a long series of additions to the dock system of the Thames. After more than twenty years during which no works of importance had been undertaken[1], early in the free-trade era the Victoria Dock below the mouth of the Lea was begun, to be opened in 1855. In 1864 the Commercial Docks in Rotherhithe were extended and their control amalgamated with that of the adjacent Surrey Docks. The Millwall Docks in the Isle of Dogs had been made, and an existing cut just North of them had been turned into the South West-India Dock, by 1870. After a halt, the Albert Dock between the Victoria and Gallions Reach was opened in 1880. Its opening led to the transfer of the Peninsular and Oriental sailings from Southampton to the Thames. Lastly, miles along the Essex shore, the Tilbury Docks were dug out of the Chadwell Marshes, and opened in 1886. In spite of amalgamation, there were still four distinct dock companies: these movements down stream were steps in a race for the sea, and for the patronage of the big ships, between the London and St Katharine's Company, which owned the Victoria and the Albert, and the East and West India Company, which replied to the Albert with the Tilbury[2].

Under the competent monopoly of the Mersey Docks and the Harbour Board, a trust which did not work for profit, the long chain of Liverpool Docks had reached the mouth of the estuary with the opening of the Langton and Alexandra basins

[1] Since the opening of St Katharine's Docks in 1828 (vol. I. p. 5). Dates of later docks are in Harcourt, *op. cit.*; Dorn, *op. cit.*

[2] The other companies were the Surrey and Commercial and the Millwall. There is remarkably little official information about the port of London in the Free Trade era. Parliamentary Papers are abundant for 1795–1801: there is a Report on Docks of 1823; and one on the State of the Port of London of 1836. The next Report is of 1902.

at the northern end in 1881. The construction of independent docks on the Cheshire side had begun in the 'forties; but this incipient Birkenhead system had been incorporated with the main system in 1855, since which date management had been unified and construction continuous. Between 1846 and 1881 nearly 250 acres of docks had been added on the Lancashire shore alone; and eventually for more than seven miles "the monumental granite, quarried from the Board's own quarries in Scotland" fronted the river, "in a vast sea wall as solid and enduring as the Pyramids, the most stupendous work of its kind that the will and power of man has ever created." So a Liverpool historian has described it, not without justification[1]. By this "vast sea wall," not yet at its full length, a quarter of the imports—by value—and more than a third of the exports of the whole United Kingdom moved with the tides.

In 1886 Liverpool was, as it were, pausing at her "stupendous work" to see what would come of a rival undertaking, long discussed, sharply fought over, and that year begun—the construction of the Manchester Ship Canal[2]. It was aimed explicitly at her dock traffic. Its completion, so many people supposed, might mark the end of her great era of economic and geographical expansion.

Glasgow, who like Liverpool had drawn life from the Atlantic trade, had no such anxieties. Unlike Liverpool, with her suburbs and daughter towns she was her own industrial *hinterland*. She had made for herself Port Glasgow at a time when it was not certain that engineering skill would be able to bring modern ships to the Broomielaw. But Port Glasgow was no longer needed. By judicious utilisation of the scour of the current and heavy labour in dredging, widening and embanking, the engineers in a whole century of work had turned the river Clyde up to Glasgow Bridge into something which gave foreign visitors "the impression of a magnificent canal,"[3] 150 yards wide and 24 feet deep at high water. A couple of docks led out of it; but the river itself, with its quays, was Glasgow harbour. What competition she had to fear came from below,

[1] Ramsay Muir, *A History of Liverpool* (1907), p. 301.

[2] Its history belongs to the next generation.

[3] Dorn, *op. cit.* II. 1015. A concise history of the Port, by Sir W. H. Raeburn, Chairman of the Clyde Navigation Trust, appeared in *Brassey's Naval and Shipping Annual*, 1928. See also Macgregor, G., *A History of Glasgow* (1881). Some information has also been supplied by the General Manager of the Clyde Trust.

where the Clyde needs no deepening and the recent completion of the James Watt Dock at Greenock invited ships to turn in. But Greenock, though well placed and active, was hardly to be counted a rival of the city which with her suburbs had ten times Greenock's population.

From Greenock to the Glasgow quays on the South bank, and about Dumbarton on the North, lay the Clyde shipyards, many, efficient, and as the pioneering work done in them merited, dominant—Napier's, Elder's, Denny's, and the rest. They had been offered every opportunity and had neglected none, opportunities in coal, in iron, in skilful and tenacious labour, in an engineering tradition which reached back to James Watt, and a tradition of shipwright's work soundly based in wood. Two-thirds of the steam tonnage of the United Kingdom was either built or engined on the Clyde. So were a great number of the steamers, particularly of the mail steamers, used by foreign countries. One-sixth of the tonnage built in the United Kingdom in 1881–6 was for foreign account; and the Clyde did the greater part of this trade.

At Hull, the gate of Yorkshire and the third port of Britain—Glasgow judged by the value of her trade being only fourth—dock-building was as essential to trade as at Liverpool. Without it, loading and unloading in the Humber could only be by lighter. The half circle of small inland docks about the old town was complete before 1830. The additions of the 'forties and 'fifties along the waterside—a railway dock and others—had raised the dock acreage to 48 by 1863. Between that year and the completion of the Alexandra Dock, east of the town, in 1885 the acreage was almost tripled[1].

These four great ports—the Metropolitan; the Northern industrial, West; the Northern industrial, East; and the Scottish industrial—had sucked in an inordinate share of the expanding trade of the country. The coming of the railway and the great ship had meant stagnation or decadence to many harbours all round the coast, some of which fifty years earlier had served areas really important, others areas important to them. There had still been some 1300 tons of shipping a week, exclusive of the fishing boats, making use of the port of Whitby in 1863: there were barely 500 in 1882[2]. The fenland ports, Boston and Lynn, if not actually decadent, had lost greatly in national

[1] Dorn, *op. cit.* II. 988; Harcourt, *op. cit.*; *Return of Works*, Hull.

[2] *Return of Works*, 1883, as above; Whitby.

importance since the invasion of the fens by the railway[1]. It was reported in 1883 that no sum worth mentioning had been spent on harbour works at Boston for over twenty years. There came into it weekly from 500 to 600 tons of "sloops, schooners, brigs, barques and screw steamers."[2] A coast railway had cut the lines of supply and distribution to and from the sandy little ports of North Norfolk. On the Suffolk coast, nearly two ships every week had still made Southwold in 1863: there was not one a fortnight in 1882. The rail from Hailsworth and improvements at Lowestoft were indicted as the causes, though nature had collaborated in destruction[3]. To some of the Cinque Ports she had long been unfriendly: Winchelsea and Hythe had been stranded for generations,—

"and near and far across the bar
the ploughman whistles at the plough."[4]

Now the big ship and the railway were finishing what nature began. Sizable vessels were no longer built at Rye. Its tonnage of trade was not half that to which Whitby had fallen[5]. Like Whitby and other harbours in reduced circumstances, Rye was learning to eke out a living by the entertainment of paying guests.

On the Bristol Channel, the trade of Minehead and the other small ports of West Somersetshire had "very much decreased"[6] since the railway from Taunton was finished in 1874. Trade up the Gloucester and Berkeley Canal had sunk very low by 1875; but the opening of the Sharpness Docks at the canal mouth in that year was restoring it. Bristol's trade had never declined, had in fact grown steadily since the railways came, but the city had to struggle with her awkward situation upstream in a part of England relatively unpopulous and non-industrial. Considerable improvements had been made since 1860 in the river harbour works. A company had finished the Avonmouth Docks in 1877—at almost twice the estimated cost. Later, the Corporation had interested itself in the docks at Portishead. But the aggregate tonnage frequenting the port in the 'eighties was only about half that of Hull; the tonnage engaged in

[1] Cp. above, p. 199. In the sixty years 1831–91 the tonnage using the port of Lynn increased by less than 40 per cent., that of Boston by barely 30 per cent.

[2] *Return of Works*, Boston.

[3] *Return of Works*, Southwold.

[4] John Davidson, *A Cinque Port*.

[5] Above, p. 67, and *Return of Works*, Rye.

[6] *Return of Works*, Minehead.

international trade was not a quarter; and, to those familiar with the ports now dominant, it was "difficult to realise" that Bristol "was once the second port of Great Britain."[1] Though neither decadent nor stagnant, as she had been when Dupin visited her in the 'twenties[2], she had been outpaced, not, however, since the railway age but before it.

The tale of little ports choked by coastal railways and the ease of distribution from bigger neighbours could be told all up the West coast of Wales, England and Scotland—Carmarthen, Aberystwyth, Carnarvon, Lancaster, Ayr, Troon. The trade of Aberystwyth in the 'eighties was only a quarter of what it had been twenty years earlier: the digging of Glasson Docks at the mouth of the Lune had not saved Lancaster from a similar, if less abrupt, decline[3]. Like the stranded ports of the East coast, those of the West had often started new careers as watering places; but Lancaster had powerful neighbours carrying on this business, for the profitable pursuit of which she stood in any event too far up the river. So the capital to which Liverpool owed allegiance, though not without an industrial life of its own, had a population little greater than that of King's Lynn, the half-discarded seaport of the Fens.

The railway had made far more trade than it had choked, but not so many ports. Some of its comparatively few creations had been out of nothing, like Fleetwood and Barrow. Others had been made out of nearly nothing like Grimsby, whose population increased fourteenfold between the census of 1831 and that of 1891[4], or Cardiff where the increase was thirteenfold. Of those not made but remade, Southampton was the chief. Left far behind the ports of the West and North in the seventeenth and eighteenth centuries, it grew very slowly until the coming of steam. Through railway communication with London had been completed in May, 1840. Two years later the Royal Mail Steam Packet and the Peninsular and Oriental Companies made Southampton their headquarters[5]. At that time serious work on docks and quays and channels had hardly begun. It had continued ever since, the railway and dock companies

[1] Harcourt, *op. cit.* I. 530. Cp. Dorn, *op. cit.* II. 1062 and *Return of Works*, Avonmouth.

[2] See vol. I. p. 6.

[3] *Return of Works*, Aberystwyth, Lancaster.

[4] Population in 1831, 4200, in 1891, 59,000.

[5] Sherrington, C. E. R., *Economics of Rail Transport in Great Britain* (1928), I. 24, 42.

working hand in hand[1]. The tonnage which cleared from the port in 1851–2 had been 213,000; in 1882 it was 909,000, although expansion had been checked temporarily by the transference of the Peninsular and Oriental sailings to Tilbury. But all through this later period, Southampton was far ahead of Bristol in aggregate tonnage, and very far ahead of her in ocean-going tonnage.

Cardiff had sprung above Newcastle into the position of the world's greatest coal exporter and, for mere tonnage cleared with cargo in the foreign trade, into that of the third port of Britain; for coal is bulky. "At Cardiff one sees nothing but coal, coal dust or coal-blackened faces, and talks of nothing but coal," the foreign visitor said[2]. The Bute family, who owned it, had begun the docks which bear their name in 1839; but the main dock and harbour development had been in the 'fifties and 'sixties; and the great growth of the coal export trade had come with the victory of steam at sea during the 'seventies and 'eighties. It had now outrun the port facilities of Cardiff, those of Penarth across the bay, and the much inferior facilities of the other South Welsh harbours. In November, 1884, work had been begun nine miles to the South-West on one of the greatest harbour-making enterprises of the century, the construction of Barry Docks by the Barry Dock and Railway Company, to handle the overflowing coal[3]. Barry would be more easily accessible for ships than Cardiff, but was not yet ready to compete with her.

Railways had not made Tyneside; it was Tyneside that made them. Nor had they undermined the coal trade from the North-East into London; though they had set limits to its expansion. The Tyne still shipped some 4,000,000 tons of coal a year coastwise, principally to the Thames; and the Thames took in from the Tyne and elsewhere 4,750,000 tons. In coastwise and overseas coal trades combined, the Tyne was very near to Cardiff. Its general trade was much more important; its aggregate trade very much more valuable. Under its Improvement Commission, constituted by Acts of 1850 and 1861, it had been dredged and quayed, provided with docks on its lower

[1] *Return of Works*, Southampton Docks.

[2] Dorn, *op. cit.* I. 1048.

[3] Contemporary admiration is in Harcourt, *op. cit.* I. 525; Dorn, *op. cit.* II. 1050. The general character of the trade of Swansea and Newport resembled that of Cardiff, bulk cargoes of coal and iron out, of ore timber and provisions in, dominating all three.

course, and with a swing bridge in place of the old low bridge of Newcastle—fitted to carry whatever Armstrong, Palmer, or Wigham and Richardson might put into it. At its mouth, the two great breakwaters begun in 1856 were still unfinished. There had been damage by storm, changes of plan, shortage of funds; but the work was going forward[1].

Such deliberation in coastal works had been more the habit of the state than of a local commission; though the Tees southern breakwater, built of Middlesbrough slag and concrete, and started by local enterprise in 1863, took more than twenty years to finish[2]. Towards the close of the early railway age, when the navy was still under sail and the *entente cordiale* with France had just broken down, the state had begun to build the 'national harbours of refuge and defence' at Dover, Portland and Holyhead. Convicts worked at Portland from 1849 to 1871 on the long breakwaters of rubble stone which had never been much used either for defence or refuge. At Holyhead, the rubble mound, also begun in 1849, was left to consolidate before it was given a worked stone superstructure. That was finished in 1873. It enclosed the New Harbour which had a limited value in the age of steam. Dover Pier was the first large breakwater designed as an upright wall of masonry. It too was begun in the 'forties, and finished, with an extension of the original plan, in 1871. But the complete design for the harbour, "the most important of all the harbours started by the Government," had not been carried out when that description of it was written in 1885. It remained in the "most unfinished state" of them all[3]. There had been a long peace in the Channel, with the retrenchment which accompanied it in the Gladstonian age; there had been revolutions in both the

[1] *Return of Works*; Tyne Improvement Commission: Harcourt, *op. cit.* I. 318. With the Tyne harbours must be classed Sunderland and Hartlepool, whose joint trade was about a third of that of Newcastle and North and South Shields in the 'eighties, in tonnage; and in general character similar.

[2] Harcourt, *op. cit.* I. 200. The South breakwater, "approaching completion" in 1883, was finished before 1886. The North was only begun in 1882.

[3] Harcourt, *op. cit.* I. 333. The official literature extends from the *R. on the alleged deficiency of Protection for Ships on the North-East Coast of England and the North-West Coast of Wales*, 1836 (XVII) and the *R. on the most Eligible Situations for Harbours of Refuge in the Channel*, 1845 (XVI); through the *Quarterly Reports of the Engineers on the Harbours at Dover*, etc. 1850–75; to the *R. on Harbour Accommodation*, 1883 (XIV), with some discussion of convict labour and the *Return of Works*, quoted above. The works themselves are described and discussed by Harcourt, *op. cit.*, *passim.*

merchant service and the royal navy; and the Admiralty Pier served cross-channel traffic adequately.

These old-planned state enterprises had been carried out with little use of the new structural material—concrete. They need not have neglected it, for its value in harbour work was known even when they were originally designed. Italians, it is said, had been the first to repair masonry under water with concrete applied in bags. Poirel had used it for the port of Algiers in the 'thirties, both in mass to set under water and in artificial blocks to replace stone in rubble-mound breakwaters. He had given his methods to the world in a stately quarto in 1841[1]. England was rather slow to follow him, in spite of the reduction of risks due to improvements in cement[2]. By the 'sixties, concrete was being extensively used for dock walls; but in the mid-'eighties, all that could be said of breakwaters was that few were "constructed entirely without it."[3] One, however, was nearing completion in 1883 which was made of nothing else—that of Newhaven, designed to protect a system of modern harbour works, the start of which went back to an Act of 1862, from the south-westerly swell driving into Seaford Bay[4].

Concrete had first been used in Britain, on a large scale and under difficult conditions, in the construction of the new South breakwater at Aberdeen in 1870–3:[5] the concrete wall protecting the seaward slope of the slag-mound breakwater slowly pushed out on the South side of the Tees came rather later. Aberdeen and the other East Scottish ports had not enjoyed the commercial opportunities of Glasgow or Hull. As shipbuilders and shipowners they had declined with the decline of wood. But trade had increased and equipment with it. There had been most increase in the Forth. Leith had extended its two piers, each now more than half a mile long. It had a dock system which, like nearly every British dock system, contained both a Victoria and an Albert. Its trade was comparable in value with that of Southampton, but in character more metropolitan, with a dominance of imports and re-exports, as in the port of

[1] Poirel, M., *Mémoire sur les travaux à la mer*.

[2] Cp. above, p. 44.

[3] Harcourt, *op. cit.* I. 141; for its use at Millwall Docks in the 'sixties, I. 416.

[4] *Return of Works*, Newhaven: Harcourt, *op. cit.* I. 134, 345. The works were only started effectively after a second Act, of 1878. The old wooden jetties mentioned in vol. I. p. 3, had served until the 'sixties.

[5] *Trans. Inst. Civ. Eng.* XXXIX. 127, and Harcourt, *op. cit.* I. 131.

London[1]. Grangemouth, controlling the eastern end of the Forth and Clyde canal, had become the leading timber port of Scotland: she could pass Baltic supplies across to Glasgow by water and save the Scandinavians the navigation of the Pentland Firth. There was coal-handling also for her and for the other harbours on both sides of the Forth.

Dundee had kept her quays and docks along the Tay well in line with the needs of her very active industries—"right well and practically arranged" the foreigner called them, adding, however, that "other things of note beside harbours and factories Dundee cannot display."[2] Aberdeen had her old and new breakwaters, and a spacious Victoria Dock, as the chief elements in a first-rate equipment; but her foreign trade was hardly commensurate. Judged by the standards of the day, she had too poor and empty a *hinterland* for an international port of the first, or indeed of a much lower, rank[3]. But she was busy with a coasting trade—mainly in granite and cattle—which occupied seven-eighths of the still considerable tonnage that frequented her harbour.

The coasting trade, so important at Aberdeen, Bristol, Newcastle, London, and in all ports from the lower ranks not here set out, must not be thought of as a mean or secondary thing because it was so little discussed at the time and has been so very seldom described. It has always been a principal source of Britain's wealth, since few important places are far from tide-water. For the entire United Kingdom—which, in this connection, cannot be divided into Britain and Ireland, for statistical reasons—the coasting trade was somewhat greater in cargo tonnage than the whole of the overseas trade proper. That was largely because of the coastwise trade in coal, and of that Anglo-Irish trade which from a British standpoint might almost be regarded as foreign. But besides these, there was a huge miscellaneous coasting business, carried on in small and not well known 'liners,' in second-rate steam 'tramps,' which would fit a little home-seas carrying into their world-wide wanderings in search of profitable cargo, or in the Thames barges, or in those "sloops, schooners, brigs and barques"[4] which poked into all the third-rate harbours where big ships

[1] Cp. Dorn, *op. cit.* II. 1006, 1067.
[2] *Ibid.* II. 1009.
[3] She appears only among 'other ports' in the *Statistical Abstracts*.
[4] Above, p. 523.

could not go. By a last gesture of confidence and faith in freedom, the coasting-trade had been thrown open to the ships of all nations: the foreigner had not secured one-half of one per cent. of it. The trade still bred seamen, as it had once bred Captain Cook.

In the true overseas trade, of vessels entering United Kingdom ports with cargo, just a third—by tonnage—had been foreign in 1875–7. By 1885–7 the proportion was barely a quarter. The rest, with the coastwise shipping, was British. Clippers that brought wool round the Horn; square-topsail schooners doing the odd jobs of the narrow seas; steam tramps with wheat or cotton or pitch-pine from American ports; liners from all the great harbours of the world—the pageant of sea-power had at no time been so varied or so stately. And now at length had become fully true of the men of Britain and their ships what was said in the seventeenth century of the Dutchmen and theirs—"the which except they stir, the people starve."[1]

[1] Above, p. 22.

INDEX

BOOKS BY R. TURNER WILCOX

The Dictionary of Costume
Folk and Festival Costume of the World
Five Centuries of American Costume
The Mode in Furs
The Mode in Footwear
The Mode in Hats and Headdress
The Mode in Costume

THE DICTIONARY OF COSTUME

THE DICTIONARY OF COSTUME

R. Turner Wilcox

CHARLES SCRIBNER'S SONS New York

to RAY WILCOX
and RUTH WILCOX

3 5 7 9 11 13 15 17 19 M/C 20 18 16 14 12 10 8 6 4

PRINTED IN THE UNITED STATES OF AMERICA
SBN: 684-10660-4 (cloth)
Library of Congress Catalog Card Number 68-12503

PREFACE

A dictionary, according to one definition given by Webster, is "a reference book listing alphabetically terms or names important to a particular subject . . . along with discussion of their meanings and applications." In the present case, the subject pertains to historic costume and its many branches. No longer will it suffice to recount only the Ancient, Medieval, Renaissance and Western periods to provide the researcher of today with the foundation upon which to build. For build he must, as our world grows ever smaller while peoples increase in undreamed-of numbers and distances decrease as airtravel carries men to the farthest corners of the earth.

In costume, such words as aba, agal, amout, bürka, caften, chadar, chogā, dhoti, djellaba, kaffiyeh and hundreds more, are becoming everyday words in the language of the mode. And at the same time, the aborigines are intrigued into adopting and wearing clothes of Western make. In this day and age, we, the Westerners, have learned to manufacture textiles not from the age-old staples such as cotton, linen, silk, wool and fur but to produce beautiful fabrics from air, gasses, chemicals and what not! All of which creates words and more words to be recorded in the language of costume and fashion.

To dig in and record this vast subject, I found to be a task of unusual proportions. In fact, I discovered that it was almost impossible for a lone individual to both write and illustrate such a work in a given length of time and without assistance. I am deeply indebted to my editor, Miss Elinor Parker, for her checking and rechecking of the many, many items in the manuscript and for her long hours of work that went into alphabetical arrangement.

R. T. W.

THE DICTIONARY OF COSTUME

A

aal Hindustani name of the East Indian morinda bush of the madder family which yields a red dye.

aba, abba, abayeh a primitive Moslem garment of Africa, Turkey and Persia which serves as cloak and blanket, a square of cloth with openings for head and arms. Usually of wool, plain or striped; camel's or goat's hair for travelers, or silk for upper classes. The woolen cloth itself is called aba.

abaca Filipino name for manila hemp from the banana stalk native to the Philippine Islands, and the most important of cordages. Used for fabrics and straw hats.

abalone a shellfish lined with mother-of-pearl, which is used for inlaying ornaments, buttons, beads, etc.

abaya the silk scarf of fallahs, or peasant women, in Egypt, Syria and other Arabic countries.

abbé's cape the three-tiered shoulder cape of the abbé's cloak.

abbés Cape

abbot cloth a canvaslike, coarse cotton fabric in basket-weave similar to monk's cloth.

abnet a long scarf or sash worn by a Jewish high priest or officer. Of fine linen or wool with embroidery.

abolla a Roman military cloak similar to the Greek chlamys, fastened at the neck. Worn by ancient soldiers on parade. see *birrus; byrrus; pænula; Oxford gown.*

abolla

academic gown a full-length black gown with long flowing sleeves. Accompanied by a cap or mortarboard and perhaps a hood, which is draped over the shoulders. Worn by faculty, students and graduates of colleges and universities and by honored celebrities upon official academic occasions. Slight variations in design indicate the rank of undergraduate, bachelor, master and doctor.

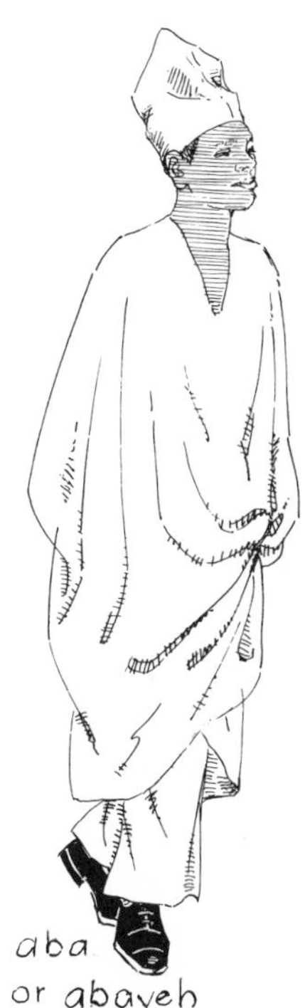
aba or abayeh

academic Gown

accessories a term which covers all items that complete a costume and if not carefully chosen, such hat, shoes, gloves, handbag or whatever, can mar a costume.

accordion pleating see *pleating.*

acetate one of the first man-made fibers produced in America, by the Celanese Corporation of America in 1925.

acorn an ornamental knob attached to men's hat cords. Also, a small military motif on the cap or collar of a uniform, representing the rank and corps of the wearer.

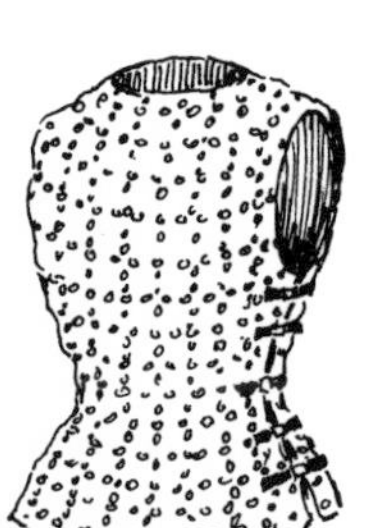

acrilan trademark of a liquid derivative of natural gas and air. It is used alone in lightweight fabrics such as challis and is combined with other fibers for children's clothes, blouses, skirts, uniforms and work clothes and pillows.

acton see *gambeson, pourpoint, doublet.*

acus an ancient Roman hairpin or bodkin of copper, bone or silver. The Saxons, who also used such a pin, called it a hair-needle and fastened their mantles with it.

adati a fine light cotton fabric imported from Bengal, India.

Adolpho see *couture, haute*

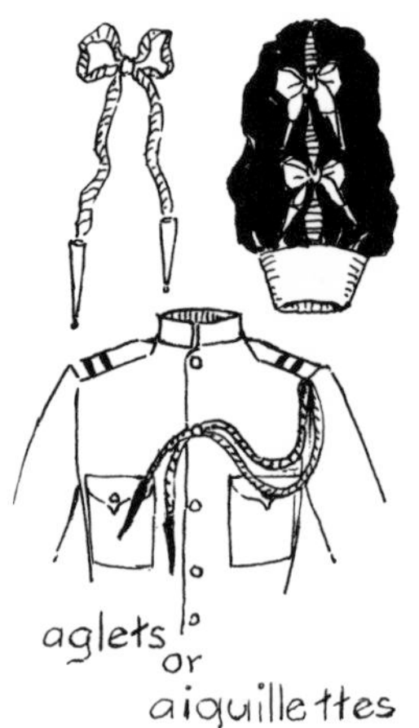

Adonis wig see *wig, Adonis.*

African capes see *lamb shearlings.*

agabanee a Syrian-made cotton fabric embroidered in silk.

agal the hoop or fillet of thick cords of wool or goat's hair which holds the

kaffiyeh or cloth of the African headdress in place. The agal is often wound around with gold and silver threads. see *kaffiyeh.*

agate a stone, chalcedony of variegated colors, cloudy and striped, used in ornaments and costume jewelry. Moss agate is white or gray, with black or green flecks.

agbada the Nigerian man's cape, worn over pajama-like breeches, both of cotton. Of brilliant, dazzling colors with printed motifs. see *iro.*

agilon the trademark for stretch nylon yarn, the original yarn used for stretch seamless stockings. Also used in sweaters, other sportswear and carpets.

aglet, aiglet, aiguillette a metal point or tag attached to a ribbon, cord or lacing for tying dress accessories in the fifteenth, sixteenth and seventeenth centuries. Sleeves were so tied to the armholes. Also called points. Aglets were replaced by buttons and hooks in the mid-seventeenth century. Aiguillettes survive today in an ornamental festoon worn with military officers' full dress uniforms.

Agnès, Mme. see *couture, haute.*

agraffe, agrafe a fastening for clothing originally devised for armor in the form of a hook, clasp or buckle, which lasted into the eighteenth century.

aiglet see *aglet.*

aigrette plume or tuft of plumes, used for woman's hairdress, etc.; the feather aigrettes of commerce were formed of the plumes of various egrets. see *egret; Audubon plumage law.*

aigrettes

aiguillette see *aglet.*

airplane cloth a plainweave pima-yarn cloth, water-repellent, with a mercerized, highly lustered finish which was used for covering lightweight airplanes and gliders. Later, much in use for sports and work shirts.

aketon see *acton.*

akwaba doll young women of Ghana wear a doll tied around the waist as part of their draped toga-like cotton clothes, which are in brilliant designs and colors. The akwaba doll is a sign that the wearer is unmarried.

alabaster as a color, resembling alabaster, a mineral of fine texture, usually white and translucent and carved into small works of art.

à la mode a surah type of silk, a popular fabric from Surat, India. Soft, lightweight, twilled cloth. The lustrous quality was called surah and the heavier grade, silk serge. Used for dresses and blouses. Nineteenth and early twentieth centuries.

Alaska or **American sable** see *skunk* or *raccoon.*

Alaska sealskin see *seal.*

alb, alba a Latin secular garment worn up to the ninth century. It was white and embroidered, a long-sleeved full-length vestment put on over the cassock and girdle. Now worn by priests at mass.

albatross a soft, fuzzy and loosely woven material used principally for warm nightgowns, negligées and infants' wear, and for nuns' habits. Usually woolen, but can be cotton.

Albert cloth an overcoating of double cloth construction, all wool and reversible, each side a different color and requiring no lining.

Alençon lace made in Alençon, France, and has been called "the queen" of French handmade needlepoint laces. It dates from the early seventeenth century. On a fine net ground, the design, usually floral, is worked and outlined by a heavy thread or cordonnet. The early pieces were copies of Italian lace, the art having been taught by Italian lacemakers, since the wearing of lace not made in France was prohibited by royal edict. It was used for altar hangings, ecclesiastical garments, gentlemen's cravats and for adornment of court ladies' dresses. Often used today in bridal dresses and veils.

alépine a silk and wool cloth used for

akwaba doll of Ghana

alb or alba

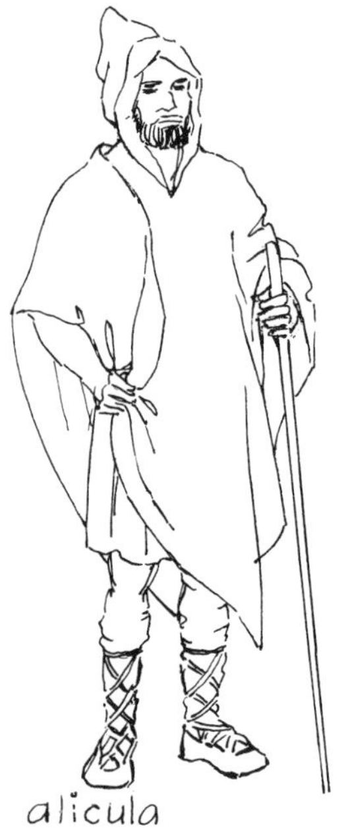
alicula

men's apparel in the early eighteenth century.

Algerian stripe an imitation of Moorish cloth woven in rough, knotted cotton and silk in alternating colored stripes on a cream ground.

alicula a Roman traveling and hunting cloak with sleeves and cowl, worn over the tunica. Greek for red, because it was usually red. see *byrrus; birrus.*

A-line, trapeze silhouette dress or coat style, flaring slightly from shoulders to hemline without a break. Launched by the youthful Yves Saint Laurent in his first collection shown at Dior's, 1958, after the sudden death of the maestro. It brought him great acclaim. see *trapeze line.*

alizarin, alizarine a purplish-red dye, formerly obtained from madder root, first discovered in 1831. In 1869, a method of manufacturing the dye from coal tar was produced. The first synthetic or artificial dye.

alligator the tanned hide of a water reptile from the United States and India, with square boxlike markings. Belly and shanks only, of baby alligators, are used for shoes, handbags, luggage, etc. Imitation alligator leather is stamped with hot rollers to produce the square alligator markings. see *leather.*

"all-in-one made possible by stretch nylon and the slide fastener—1940's

all-in-one a corselet, or combination brassière and corset for the heavy figure, which first appeared in the 1920's, with steel replacing whalebone. In the 1930's an all-in-one which obliterated the "debutante slouch" was introduced. It was made of lastex, a two-way stretch fabric in a one-piece body garment, which held the body firm without the aid of gores and stays.

alloutienne a French silk which has a slight slub in the weave and is sturdy enough not to pull at the seams. Used principally for formal evening gowns.

allover a term applied to a pattern or design which is repeated or covers the whole surface of the material.

amuce • aumusse

almuce, aumuce a cloth hood lined with fur or a fur hood with cloth lining worn by the clergy in the thirteenth, fourteenth and fifteenth centuries, in cold weather. Attached to the cowl, it could be dropped in back and was called a monk's hood.

alnage an ell, or forty-five inches, the former English measurement of cloth, now little used. Of varying measure in different countries.

aloe hemp or fiber any species of Agave, an important genus of plants which give a hemplike fiber used for lace, cloth, embroidery, musical instruments, etc.

aloe lace a fragile lace made of aloe fibers.

aloha shirt a brilliantly colored printed silk shirt, a copy of the Hawaiian man's garment, generally worn outside the trousers. Its breezy comfort made it

a fad, beginning in the 1930's and continuing to the present.

alpaca long hair of the Peruvian alpaca, a species of llama. Used principally for women's suits and sportswear, the cloth woven of hair alone or combined with wool. see *vicuña; llama.*

alpargata sandal of woven hemp or rope in shaped sole with attached straps. Worn by Spanish, Italian and French. see *espadrilla.*

aluta laxor heavy leather boots of ancient Rome made of aluta leather softened and made pliable by alum.

amazon a woolen dress goods in a satin or twill weave with the nap raised and shorn for softness. Amazon, from the Greek signifying a female warrior. The word passed into the European languages to designate a horsewoman, later a tall, strong woman. In French, it is applied either to a horsewoman or her long riding skirt.

amber a brittle fossil resin similar to vegetable resins ranging in color from pale yellow or light brown. Found by the ancients, as it still is, on the coasts of the Baltic sea. It may be cloudy, opaque or transparent. Sicilian amber is reddish brown. Baltic amber is yellow and Burmese amber honey-toned, and occasionally black. Often used for jewelry and smokers' articles and in blending certain perfumes.

amber, black see *jet.*

American cloth the name given by the British to American oilcloth, used occasionally for waterproofing caps, jackets and traveling cases.

American Indian costume When the explorers first came, Indian dress consisted of skins and furs beautifully dyed, feathers, and the soft bark of trees and grasses. New England Indian women wore a short wraparound skirt of skin, and men a breechclout of skin. If needed, men and women might wear a short, sleeveless type of skin poncho. In New England and Virginia, an Indian woman's dress was sometimes made of two elkskins fringed, beaded and tied with thongs at the sides and over the arms, belted by a thong. *Footwear,* from Virginia northward moccasins were worn, but southern Indians, as a rule, went barefoot. Along with moccasins, in New England and the upper Mississippi valley, leggings of tanned deerskin were worn by both sexes. They were decorated with red, yellow and blue motifs. *Headband,* worn by both sexes, of dyed black cloth sewn with porcupine quills, beads, wampum, feathers and small stones. *Headdress,* masculine, a natural cut or artificial roach of deer hair was worn by Indian men of New York and New England. Southern Indians wore a topknot and Indians of the Great Lakes braided long hair. Indian women wore long, braided hair and, occasionally, cut a fringe over the forehead. *Mantle,* when needed, a robe or cloak was worn by both sexes; it was made of moose, deer, elkskin, fox or squirrel. Indians fashioned beautiful cloaks of iridescent turkey feathers woven with self-made twine.

American sable see *skunk.*

American shoulders known in France as *épaules Américaines,* because most male American tourists wore broad, straight, padded shoulders from the late

amice

Mennonite woman in two tones of gray homespun wool or cotton—black neckerchief, shoes and stockings

amout

nineteenth and early twentieth centuries up to World War II.

American tiger see *jaguar* under cat.

amethyst a crystallized quartz of violet to purple, the finest specimens from India, Ceylon and Brazil. Used in jewelry as a semiprecious stone; the deeper the hue, the more valuable.

amice a liturgical hood of fine white linen, a rectangular piece folded diagonally with strings tying over the chest. Up to the thirteenth century, a priest covered his face with a hood upon mounting the altar.

amictus the general term for apparel in ancient Rome.

Amish

Amish dress the plain black costume of the Christian Mennonites, or "Plain People." Both sexes wear black or a muted, dark color in public. Garments are fastened by hooks and eyes, and have no buttons or ornamentation, for which reason in earlier days the Amish were called hookers.

amout see *parka.*

amulet a piece of jewelry worn around the neck to ward off enchantments, accident or any ill luck.

anadem a poetic term for a chaplet or wreath of flowers worn upon the head.

anadem or Chaplet

anamite string color or the color of unbleached twine.

androsmane, Kevenhüller, continental a Swiss military hat, popular to both civilian and military men. To the French it was *androsmane,* and to English and Americans, the *Kevenhüller,* named after the famous Austrian field marshal. Really a bicorne, it was built high in front and back with a spoutlike crease in the center front. Worn by General Washington, it was also called the *continental hat.* see *hat, cocked.*

Androsmane-Kevenhüller-Continental

angel skin or **peau d'ange** a modern finish—waxy, smooth and dull—applied to satin. Popular in the early twentieth century.

angel sleeve see *sleeve, angel.*

Angelus cap see *cap, Angelus.*

anglesea early twentieth century trade name for the slightly curling curve in men's hat brims.

Angleterre, English edging small needlepoint loops of cord or braid, worked to an edge.

Anglo-Saxon embroidery an ancient embroidery, the design outlined with long stitches and couched with silk or metal thread.

angora an overcoating of twill-woven cloth, soft and woolly, made of angora cat, rabbit or goat hair. The cloth originated in Turkey.

Angora cat

angora goat, mohair the wiry, lustrous and strong hair or wool of the angora goat of central Asia Minor, usually pure white and four to seven inches long. Formerly used as fur for the large nineteenth-century muffs, now imported for weaving with other fibers and called mohair.

Angora Goat

angora rabbit hair originally from the Madeira Islands, the animal was successfully raised in England and as a sideline by American farmers, rapidly becoming one of the important small industries in the United States. The fur is spun into yarn for sweaters, gloves and scarfs and sometimes mixed with wool. The hair is clipped or plucked, the plucked bringing a higher price.

Angora rabbit

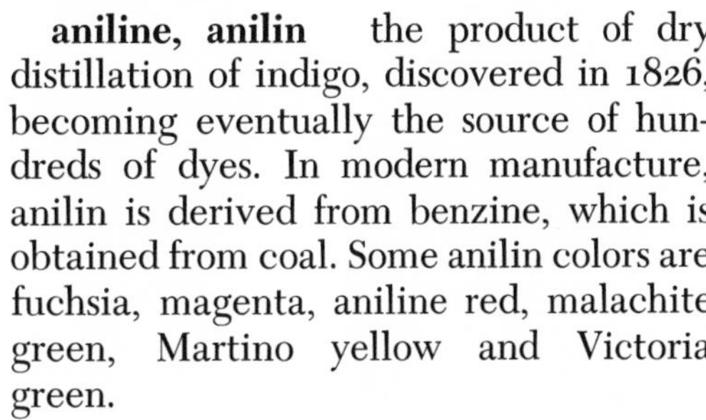

aniline, anilin the product of dry distillation of indigo, discovered in 1826, becoming eventually the source of hundreds of dyes. In modern manufacture, anilin is derived from benzine, which is obtained from coal. Some anilin colors are fuchsia, magenta, aniline red, malachite green, Martino yellow and Victoria green.

animal fiber fibers taken from animals such as sheep, goats, camels, vicuña, etc. for the purpose of weaving, felting or knitting into fabric.

animal skins or **peltries** *Furs* are from fur bearers of both wild and domestic animals. *Pelts* are from sheep and lamb families. *Skins* are from goat and kid families. *Hides* are from cattle and horse families.

anklet a short sock, generally with a cuff, worn by children or for sports. An ankle bracelet, sometimes adorned with tiny nameplate or with jewels.

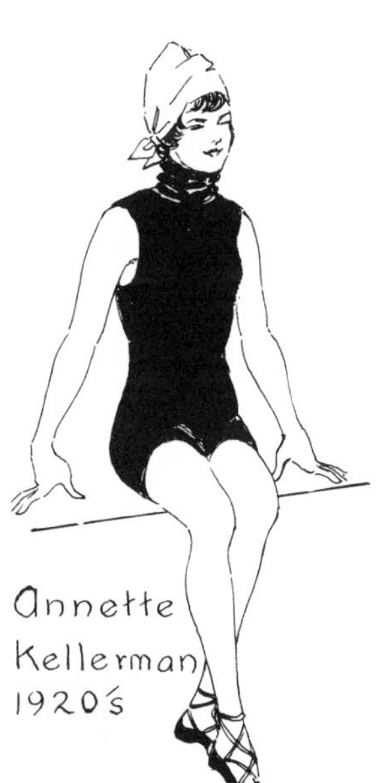

Anne Boleyn costume named for one of Henry VIII's queens (1533–1536). A tight bodice with square décolletage and wide flaring sleeves; a bell-shaped canvas underskirt, forerunner of the hoop or farthingale.

Annette Kellerman a swimsuit which was practically sleeveless and which ended a good two inches above the knee, named for a famous swimmer who wore such a shocking garment as early as 1909. The first rib-knit, elasticized wool swimsuit, a one piece tank suit was made by Jantzen in 1920 for American women, and from then on it became more abbreviated.

anorak see *parka.*

antelope soft, velvety, light leather dressed with suede finish on the flesh side. The antelope gazelle, the best-known species from Africa, Arabia and Persia. A small graceful animal, usually brownish or silver-tan.

anteri a short white undervest quite generally worn by both sexes in the Balkans.

anti-crease a process whereby cotton, linen, rayon fabrics are rendered crease-resistant by synthetic resin.

antique finish a "weathered" or satin finish of wax and oil applied to shoes and leather goods.

antique satin see *satin, antique.*

Antwerp lace a rare bobbin lace, the original design representing the angel's Annunciation to the Virgin Mary. The surviving motif is a basket or pot of flowers.

apodesme, stethodesme bosom band of wool, linen or chamoised leather which was either tied with tape or pinned with fibulae. With it was worn a wide stomach band called the *zona.* see *bosom band.*

apparel clothing or garments. Also, the embroideries on the liturgical alb, amice or almuce.

Appenzell embroidery point d'Alençon embroidery which originated in the Swiss Canton of Appenzell. It is very fine drawnwork embroidery on very sheer white linen or lawn; used for kerchiefs, handkerchiefs and aprons.

appliqué embroidery French, meaning "applied to." A style of embroidery used on fabrics, lace, net, leather, etc., in which cutout motifs are sewn on by hand.

apron a shield or protection for the wearer's dress, and most often secured by strings or ties. The earliest European apron was worn by the blacksmith, gardener and stone mason, and was of leather. Farm women and housekeepers wore the long apron of homespun or white linen. In the sixteenth and seventeenth centuries fashionable ladies adapted the apron. It was then made of fine sheer linen or lawn, embroidered, lace-trimmed, beruffled and finished with colored ribbons and bowknots. This dainty piece in the nineteenth century became the small "tea apron," pinned on and therefore called a pinner. see *Hoover apron.*

aquamarine a beryl or semiprecious stone of clear light blue or blue-green.

arabesque a type of ornamentation used in textile design, employing flower, foliage and fruit. The intricate, interlaced pattern of lines is founded basically on the acanthus and palmetto designs of the early Roman Empire.

aralac a fiber resembling wool but of casein base, used for clothing and sometimes as a substitute for wool and some other fabrics in the millinery trade.

Aran sweater see *fisherman sweater.*

araneous lace thin, delicate, cobweb-like lace using the long, straight lines of the spider's web as the pattern. The term in the Middle Ages was used for embroidery in general.

Arctic fox see *fox, Arctic.*

Arctic half-boot see *mukluk.*

Arctic hare heavy, long-haired animal from Russia and Siberia processed to simulate white fox. Blue fur fiber with white, tan or bluish-gray guard hair, the white peltries most desirable to the fur trade. Also some from Arctic North America but not in demand.

arctics, galoshes waterproofed, heavy black cloth overshoes with rubber soles, fastened by buckles. Worn by men, women and children. see *galoshes.*

argentan lace also called point de France, an edging, insertion or banding. A needlepoint originally of Alençon, later made with a bolder floral pattern and a more open mesh.

Argyle, Argyll a multicolored diamond pattern in woolen socks, sweaters and scarfs. Formerly hand-knitted in Great Britain, now mostly machine-made in England and America. Also, a sock having this pattern. Argyll is the name of the clan whose tartan is imitated in this kind of knitting.

arisard the mantle or plaid worn by Scottish women to the mid-eighteenth century. It was long enough to cover the head down to the ankles, being draped at the waist.

armband a band worn around the arm as identification or, when black, as a sign of mourning. *see mourning band, brassard.*

Armenian cloak a fashionable gentleman's cloak of the 1850's and 1860's. With the exception of the deep velvet collar, the cloth was all in one piece with no inserted sleeves, but with side seams forming very loose arm coverings.

Armenian lace a handmade narrow edging in tiny pointed scallops, used for infants' wear, handkerchiefs, lingerie, collars and cuffs.

Armenian rat the Greek term for ermine because imported from Armenia. see *ermine.*

armet a helmet of the fifteenth and sixteenth centuries.

Arctic Hare

arisard-Scottish plaid wrap-around cloak to mid 18th C.

Armenian cloak

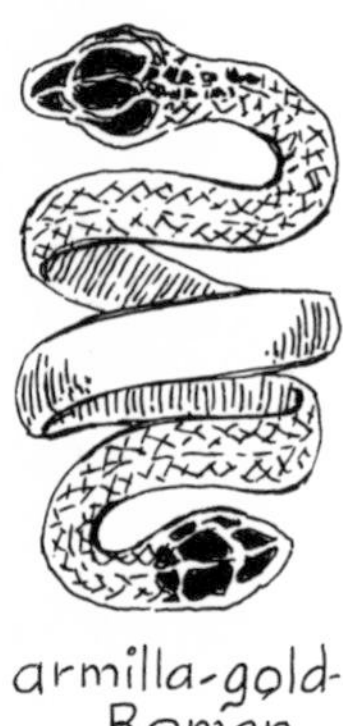

armilla-gold-Roman

armhole the opening left in the garment for attaching the sleeves. see *armscye.*

armilausa a short cloak or cape of cloth or silk, worn over armor in the medieval period.

armilla, armil, armlet bracelets of antiquity in bronze, silver and gold. Worn by Greek ladies and by Roman men, conferred upon the latter for heroic deeds. A pair of armillas is part of the English regalia used at the Coronation.

armlet a very short, plain sleeve sewn into the armhole or armscye.

armlets see *armilla.*

armor, armour as protective body covering in battle, has been in use from ancient times to the Renaissance. It was made principally of metal and cuir-bouilli, or boiled and hardened leather. European armor dates from about the twelfth to the fourteenth century, in mixed mail and plate, and complete plate armor from the fifteenth to the seventeenth centuries. Decorative armor dates from after 1600, with partial plate lasting to 1700. The advent of the sturdy buffcoat and the cuirass of buff leather in the sixteenth and seventeenth centuries spelled the doom of heavy metal armor. see *buffcoat, cuirass.*

armozeen, armozine a heavy corded silk, usually black, formerly used for waistcoats but now for scholastic and clerical robes.

armscye a tailor's term for the armhole; also, the shape or outline of the armscye.

armure in medieval times a fabric woven with a small pattern resembling link-chain armor, hence its name. Still woven with small design in several colors on rep or twill ground in silk, wool, cotton and synthetics. Used for men's scarfs, waistcoats, formal costume and also drapery. see *barathea.*

Arnel trademark for synthetic fabric of cellulose triacetate.

arras the European tapestry which originated in the medieval Flemish town of northern France, Arras. The people also produced beautiful patterned leathers which rivaled those of Spain. They wove cloth from English and Scottish wools which was used by the other European countries and also sent to the East in exchange for Oriental luxuries.

arras lace bobbin lace made in Arras, France, and similar to that of Lille.

arrasene embroidery stitching worked with a chenille cord having wool or silk pile which produces a velvety effect.

arrowhead an embroidered triangle placed at the ends of seams of tailored garments, pleats or pocket joinings, as a stay.

artificial silk An eminent British scientist writing a book in 1664, foresaw the possibility of spinning out fiber-like silk. Commercial development delayed until 1910 when it was established by the American Viscose Company. Since the new fabric was not identical with pure silk, being produced from varied raw materials such as wood pulp, corn protein and chemical compounds, it was given the name of *rayon.* A fine synthetic fabric, it not only possesses the good qualities of the natural fiber but also is endowed with many advantageous features that pure silk can never have. Gabrielle Chanel first displayed a collection of models made of rayon at Deauville in 1915. In the United States, any metallic weighting in a silk fabric must be so labeled. Pure silk should be labeled "silk," "all silk," or "pure dye." see *rayon.*

artois a fashionable garment of the late eighteenth and early nineteenth centuries, worn by both sexes. It was a cloak named for the Count of Artois, brother of Louis XVI, and later Charles X of France. The style, a long cloth coat with three or four short capes ending at the waist, lasted a long time as the coachman's box-coat.

artois cloaks

asbestos a non-inflammable, non-metallic mineral fiber which is woven into fabrics used where flame-proof protection is required in such as a theater curtain. Cotton with asbestos is sometimes used in covers for ironing boards.

ascot a double-knot cravat with wide square ends folded over and held in place by a plain or jeweled scarfpin. Worn with a cutaway coat, especially to the fashionable English Ascot Heath horse races held early in June. The Ascot tie appeared first in the 1850's and was the origin of the Ascot puff of the 1870's. Its distinctive feature was its very wide puffed ends. Used periodically to the present by men and women as a wide kerchief or stock.

Asiatic cat see *caracal.*

ascot or puff-scarf

Assisi embroidery a form of cross-stitch where the design itself is left plain or perhaps outlined.

astrakhan formerly a general name for broadtail or karakul lambs from Astrakhan in Russia. A type of lambskin now called *caracul.* see *caracul,* under lamb.

astrakhan cloth a manufactured cloth made to resemble astrakhan fur.

atef crown of Egypt about 3000 B.C. When the victorious King Narmer united Upper and Lower Egypt, he added the red wicker crown of Lower Egypt to the white felt crown of Upper Egypt, placing it on top of the felt crown. Crowns were ornamented with the royal asp or uraeus.

atef-Egyptian crown

athletic underwear general name for the light, loose lisle underwear adopted by athletic men in the early twentieth century. Drawers were cut knee-length, shirts low-necked and sleeveless, with deep armholes. Undershirt and cotton briefs of today.

attar of roses an essential oil, fragrant and volatile, obtained by distillation from rose petals, especially the damask rose. Used pure or as a base for many other perfumes.

attifet bonnet and coiffure; a heart-shaped style with a point dipping over the forehead, the bonnet held in shape by wire frames. Worn by Catherine de' Medici in black, and Mary, Queen of Scots in white, mid-sixteenth century. The fashion survived as the widow's peak and cap to our times. see *barbette.*

attifet Coiffure

auburn usually pertains to hair color, a dark brown with reddish or copper-colored tinge.

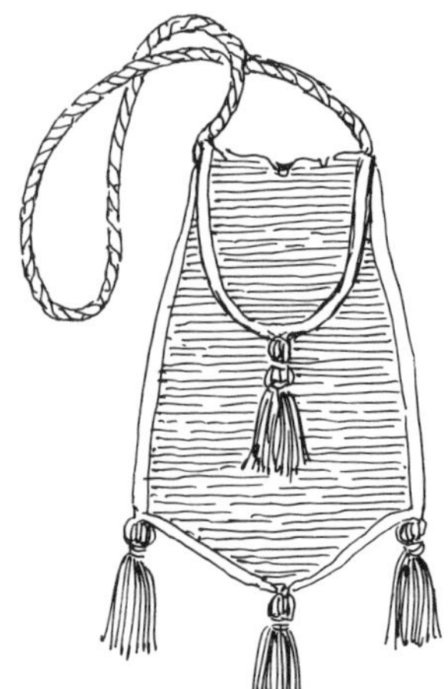
aumônière for carrying alms

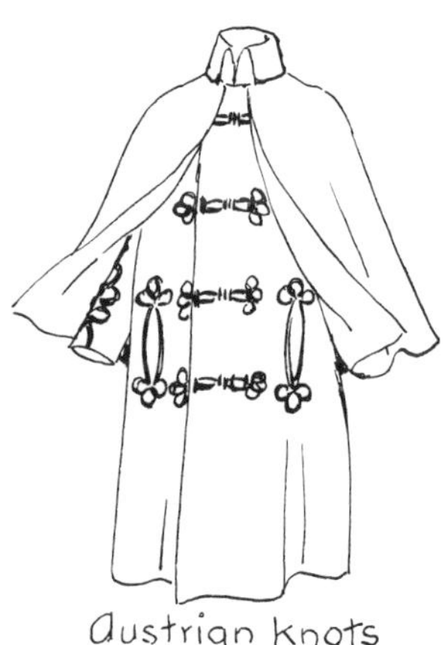
austrian knots

automobile togs

Aubusson a shade of red, rather like brick red.

Aubusson stitch a vertical canvas stitch founded upon that used in the wall tapestries made at Aubusson, France.

Audubon plumage law passed in 1905 to prevent the slaughter of native birds and the importation or merchandising of bird of paradise or egret feathers in the United States. In 1941, an agreement was reached between the Audubon Society and the Feathers Industries of America Inc. whereby the use of wild bird plumage for millinery and decorative purposes ended.

aumônière a small bag carried in the Middle Ages by men and women. Originally of fabric or leather with a drawstring, it hung from belt or girdle, and was called a hanging pocket. During the Renaissance as men acquired pockets in their dress, they gave up the bag. Women continued its use, making it of silk or velvet and covering it with handsome embroidery and beadwork. see *reticule; pockets.*

aumuse see *almuce.*

aune the old French fabric measure of forty-five inches, or one and a quarter yards.

Australian wool a fine type of wool raised in Australia from Spanish merino stock.

Austrian knots heavy, black silk braid ornamentation on military uniforms appliquéd in looped designs. It decorated Austrian military dress, was copied by the Napoleonic and European armies, and adopted by the American armies in the nineteenth century.

automobile togs necessary motoring attire in the early twentieth century. Cap and goggles were worn by men and women, with a long linen or silk coat or "duster"; women tied a long chiffon scarf over their hats, large and small, and, very often, over the face. see *veil, motoring.*

Ave Maria lace a type of Valenciennes bobbin lace made at Dieppe, France, in the sixteenth and seventeenth centuries.

aventurine a form of quartz, usually green but sometimes brown and yellow, containing a mass of tiny mica flakes which give the stone a speckled sheen. Used in jewelry.

avocado a light greenish yellow, fashionable in dress and house-furnishing fabrics, named for a West Indian fruit with flesh of this shade.

awning cloth or heavy, brightly striped canvas copied in narrower-striped cotton for summer sports clothes such as women's skirts and men's blazers.

Ayrshire embroidery a dainty, popular Scottish embroidery on linen and cotton. Small floral patterns worked in eyelets. Used on dresses and linens.

azür a Hungarian greatcoat made of black or white felt, or sheepskin with the fur to the inside in winter. The full-length broad lapels turn into a wide collar in back and the enormous sleeves are rarely used, being sewn closed to carry things. The coat is elaborately decorated on the skin side with variegated color appliqué of cut-out motifs accented with silk embroidery. It is a contemporary cloak.

azure a term covering many hues of blue ranging from sky-blue to lapis lazuli.

B

babiche an Algonquinian word meaning cord or thong of rawhide, sinew, etc.

babouche the ancient Moslem slipper made without heel or quarters, often of leather embroidered in gold and silver.

babushka; shale the Russian peasant head-scarf of wool, called the *shale*, is tied under the chin. The silk, summer scarf, *platok*, is tied at the nape. Because the older women refused to discard the head-kerchief it came to be called *babushka*, the Russian word for grandmother.

baby bunting a flannel swaddling bag, with gown, hood, and sleeves made all-in-one and ribbon-tied at the neck, wrists and lower end. see *barrow coat.*

baby lace usually Valenciennes, a very narrow lace made for baptismal dresses, layettes, etc.

baby pins tiny gold bar pins usually in pairs and sometimes joined by a fine chain, set with semiprecious stones or pearls.

baby ribbon a very narrow ribbon about a quarter of an inch wide, usually white, pink or blue. Much used in the late nineteenth and early twentieth centuries for threading and bowknots on fine hand-made lingerie of white nainsook, lawn and batiste; used also on infants' wear.

baby seal see *seal, baby.*

Baby Stuart cap see *cap, Baby Stuart.*

Babylonian work the name by which Babylonian embroideries were known. Linen was used but the principal fabric was wool elaborately embroidered with separate motifs founded upon the design of the rosette. Garments were always trimmed with fringe and tassels. The Babylonians were fond of brilliant colors, reds, blues, greens and purples. The purple kandys embroidered with gold was reserved for the king. see *kandys; kaunace.*

bachlik, bachelik a short cape with hood finished with a fat tassel. A return to an ancient garment, worn since the beginning of the present century in France and the Balkans.

backstitch a stitch used for strength in hand-sewing and embroidery, made by setting the needle back half the length of the last stitch on the under side, coming out on top, a half-stitch length ahead, making a continuous line of stitches on both sides, like machine-stitching.

badger a heavily furred mammal allied to the skunk and weasel family, with coarse, durable hair of black mixed with white, gray or tawny; American badger the best. Badger hairs are important for pointing long-haired furs. Used for collars, cuffs and trimming.

badger whiskers prescribed for the navy by the Honorable George E. Badger, Secretary of the United States Navy, 1841, "sailors' whiskers not to descend lower than one inch below the ear and on a line with the mouth."

bag see *aumonière; handbag; musette bag; pouch; purse; reticule; shoulder bag.*

bag sleeve see *sleeve, bag.*

babushka hood

Babylonian-assyrian-ancient

badger

badger whiskers-American-1860's

Baju-Malaysian jacket

bag wig see *wig, bag.*

bagheera see *velvet.*

baishan sleeveless coat worn by Chinese men as everyday costume.

baize a coarse woolen cloth used for servants' clothes. In the time of Queen Elizabeth I, it was made at Colchester, England, but first made in Baza, Spain.

baju a short, loose white cotton jacket with simple collar, breast pocket and short sleeves. Worn with short or long cotton breeches in Malaysian countries.

Bakelite trade name of a synthetic resin formed by the condensation of chemicals producing a high electrical and chemical resistance resembling hard rubber and celluloid. Used for costume accessories such as buttons, buckles, pendants, etc.

Balaclava

baku, bakou a fine straw of dull finish made from the unopened leaf stalks of the talipot palm of Malabar and Ceylon.

bal a convertible collar.

bal, bicycle see *bicycle bal.*

balaclava a heavy woolen helmet crocheted or knitted by British and American women for the soldiers in World Wars I and II. Of khaki-colored yarn, it had a cuff around the neck that could be drawn up over the chin. It was also a winter cap for younger boys. The name comes from Balaklava, a seaport village on the Crimean coast of Russia, the scene of the memorable Charge of the Light Brigade in 1854.

Balagnie cloak-17th C.

balagnie cloak an elegant garment of the seventeenth century in the reign of Louis XIII. A cape with deep collar draped over both or only one shoulder, and held in place by cords attached under the collar.

balandrana, over-all, supertotus a traveler's coat; a raincoat cloak of the sixteenth and seventeenth centuries which had a hood and enveloping sleeves and was worn by men and women.

balandrana or raincoat- 17th C.

balayeuse French for sweeper, or a dust ruffle which was sewn to the under side of the long, trailing skirts of fashionable women in the late nineteenth and early twentieth centuries, to protect the skirt fabric. see *dust ruffle.*

balbriggan first made in Balbriggan, Ireland, an unbleached cotton fabric with fleeced back manufactured in variations of tan and gray. It was used especially for men's winter underwear, which came to be known as balbriggans. Also used for hosiery, sweaters and such.

baldric a wide silk sash or leather belt, often richly decorated. Worn over

baldric of silk- English- Restoration- 1660's

the right shoulder and fastened on the left hip to carry sword, bugle, powder horn, etc. see *balteus.*

Balenciaga, Cristobal see *couture, haute.*

baline a coarse woolen or cotton fabric used for packing. Also, a hemp or jute fabric used for stiffening in handbags or upholstery.

Balkan blouse a long-waisted blouse shirred into a wide hip-band with long, full sleeves gathered into tight wrist cuffs. Made of fine linen, lawn or voile and colorfully embroidered in combinations of red, blue, or black cotton thread in cross-stitch. A Western fashion during the Balkan War in 1913 and after, for several decades.

ball gown a formal, full-length gown, usually with décolleté corsage.

ballerina the toe-dancer's traditional dress of tight bodice and the tutu, a very short full skirt of layers of tulle or gauze that stand away from the body. Worn over tights. see *tutu.*

ballerina dress the short dinner or evening dress was an origination of Valentina, an American couturière of Russian extraction. The length proved a happy solution in the postwar years, filling a woman's need of an informal but dressy look when her escort was in business suit. see *Valentina,* under *couture, haute.*

ballet or **chorus shirt** a garment worn by members of the corps de ballet for rehearsals; a plain white cotton shirt with turned-down collar.

ballet slippers soft, low, flat slippers with a well-boxed toe to support toe-dancing, laced with ribbons. The style copied in comfortable bedroom slippers, 1940's.

ballibuntl, balibuntal a hat of light-weight woven straw manufactured in Luzon, Philippine Islands.

ballibuntl, baliluk, ballybuntals, bally-wags all are straws from the unopened palm leaf stems.

balloon sleeve see *sleeve, balloon.*

balmacaan a loose, flaring coat of Scottish origin, with flaring sleeves, usually of tweed, gabardine or raincoat fabric with military standing collar and slashed pockets.

ballet tutu-19th & 20th C.

Balkan blouse

balmacaan overcoat similar to the raglan- 1850's

Balmoral petticoat

Balmain, Pierre see *couture, haute.*

balmoral a laced-up shoe or half-boot with closed throat, introduced by Prince Albert about 1853. Everything new and smart at that time was named Balmoral, after the royal castle in Aberdeenshire, Scotland, built by the Prince and Queen Victoria. Also, a tennis shoe, 1890's. see *tennis dress.*

Balmoral-man's patent leather

Balmoral-feminine

balmoral cap see *bluebonnet.*

bambino hat of the 1930's

balmoral cloth British fabric of a twill weave, striped in red, gray, blue or black.

balmoral petticoat a red woolen underskirt striped in black and worn under a long dress looped up for walking, popular in the 1860's and 1870's.

balteus a form of the baldric worn in ancient Rome. Also, a leather girdle worn by soldiers and ecclesiastics.

bambino hat a large-brimmed hat framing the face in halo fashion. Named after the famous round plaques of the Christ Child by the fifteenth century Florentine sculptor, Luca della Robbia.

bandeau concealed under bird

band in American colonial days, the neckband which finished that part of the white linen chemise next to the face. The simple collar of the Puritans was a plain band. The wider collar edged with lace which lay upon the shoulders was a falling band, as were the linen strips or tabs of the clerical and academical collars, still worn by clergymen.

band strings used in the sixteenth and seventeenth centuries to tie bands, collars and ruffs. Band strings ended in tassels or crochet-covered balls and often jewels.

bandanna, bandana from the Hindu bāndhnū, the East Indian word for tie-dyeing. A large silk or cotton headkerchief dyed in brilliant colored spots on a dark ground.

bandbox small, round, lightweight boxes originally for holding bands or collars. Charmingly decorated or covered with pretty wallpaper, they held various accessories, including hats.

bandeau a narrow brassière, formerly worn to support the breasts. A narrow buckram band covered with silk or velvet to tilt a hat on the head. Also, a narrow fillet of jewelry, ribbon or wreath of flowers encircling the head.

banditti a small panache of feathers on a feminine bonnet in the early 1800's.

band or falling band with band strings

band and strings-Pilgrim

band-plain-Puritan

bandle in Scottish and English dialect, a word meaning two feet wide. Also Irish linen, coarse, homemade and two feet wide.

bandoleer, bandolier see *baldric;* also, coarse, woven fabric belting for military and sportwear use.

bandore the widow's black-veiled headdress of the eighteenth century.

Bangkok a fine lightweight straw woven into a hood from fibers of a palm tree which grows in the vicinity of Bangkok. The finished hat is also known as a bangkok.

bangle bracelet a ring bracelet or anklet from which dangle tiny tinkling charms.

bangs fringe of hair covering forehead; has occurred as a coiffure fashion some time in every century for both men and women.

banian see *banyan.*

Ban-Lon the trademark of a crimped knit yarn, permanently set, of an attractive texture which is imparted to fabric and garments made from it.

Bannockburn a cloth made in Bannockburn, Scotland, a tweed center. A typical British tweed and one of the best used for suitings and topcoatings.

banyan, banian a luxurious negligée wrap worn by men and women in the seventeenth and eighteenth centuries, especially in the American South. Usually of bright color in silk, velvet or wool striped and lined to be worn either side out. see *Indian gown.*

bar pin a long, narrow brooch or breast pin, a design in jewelry much worn in the first half of the twentieth century. About 3 inches long, of platinum or gold, it was sometimes set with a row of gems, usually diamonds.

bar tacks stitches forming a bar to reinforce the edges of seams, tucks, pleats, buttonholes, pockets, etc.; commonly used in tailoring.

barathea a more general name for armure, so called because of the pebbly weave which resembles chain armor. Ribbed, plain or striped, woven in silk, cotton, combined with synthetics and often in two colors. Used for suits, dresses and scarfs. see *armure.*

barbette a mourning headdress of widows in the sixteenth century. Of white linen worn over or under the chin, it has survived to modern times in nuns' dress.

barbette

barbute a helmet of the fourteenth century, Italian origin, first with a high pointed crown and later round. The face was almost entirely covered with large cheek pieces. Also, a variety of the fifteenth century sallet.

barcelona the kerchief in Spanish dress worn around head or throat or carried in the hand. Of twilled black silk and also in solid colors, gay patterns and checks.

bare midriff a style first used in beachwear and briefly incorporated into

banditti plume-1800

banyan

bangs

evening dress in 1939, when the naked section between short bodice and belt was exposed. Modest females filled in the space with flesh-colored chiffon.

barège a gauze-like fabric originally made in Barègas, France. Of wool, silk and wool, or cotton and wool, and used for veils, dresses, etc.

Barentzen, Patrick de see *couture, haute.*

Bargello work see *Florentine* or *Flame stitch embroidery.*

barmcloth, barmskin From barm, the English word for both lap and the apron of leather. Worn by workmen.

Baronette trade name for rayon fabric with high luster in satin weave and cotton back.

barong tagalog the Filipino shirt or blouse worn in place of a dinner jacket. Often made of banana fiber cloth and embroidered.

barong tagalog

baroque period of extravagant ornamentation as from the fifteenth and sixteenth centuries to late nineteenth, equivalent to rococo. Of irregular form, as a baroque pearl.

barracan, barragan a camel's hair or goat's hair cloth for menswear. Also, a kind of moleskin cloth in England. Used for cloaks and mantles in Eastern countries.

barracan-draped red and white barracanos of the spani police corps-worn over the kamis

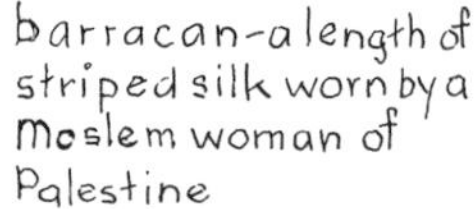

barracan-a length of striped silk worn by a Moslem woman of Palestine

barracano a Bedouin cloth blanket of coarse camlet carried by travelers or cavalry troops.

barré silk or cloth, barred or striped from selvedge to selvedge. Used in costume and interior decoration according to weight and quality.

barretino Italian for bonnet, a long stocking cap of knitted wool, or of felt in red or black. Worn in various shapes, folded or hanging, by Italian fishermen, Portuguese fishermen and farmers. It is used for carrying small possessions, even lunch.

barretino

barrette a bar-shaped clip of varied length for holding women's hair in place. Much used in the late nineteenth and twentieth centuries when the coiffure was dressed up off the nape. Made of metal or shell, later of plastic.

barrister's wig see *wig, full-bottomed, professional.*

barrister's Wig

barrow coat a baby-bunting or pinning blanket, a flannel or knitted wrap for an infant. Usually a baglike garment with cap attached, folded and pinned and ribbon-tied at neck, wrists and lower end. Today the zipper has replaced such fastenings.

Basque knitted shirt

bateau neck-line-1920's

Basquine

Lady's fishing costume-see Basque bodice 1870's

basil sheepskin tanned by various processes. Used for shoe linings, less often now than formerly.

basinet, bacinet a light helmet of a single piece of steel, the conical point was the special feature. A chain-mail hood worn over the camail in the thirteenth century.

basket weave a style of weave resembling a plaited basket, produced by the interweaving of double threads.

basque a short, skirt-like termination of an upper garment, formerly on a man's doublet, now on a woman's bodice. The same general effect was created by a woman's wearing a man's fishing jersey over the tightly corseted figure of the latter nineteenth century. The Princess of Wales, wearing such a jersey on an impromptu fishing expedition, created a vogue for the form-fitting Basque bodice in the 1870's.

basque belt, masculine corset a confining girdlelike garment to give the desired small waist and corseted look; worn by many men in the 1830's and '40's.

basque shirt originally the shirt of Basque fishermen of Spain and France. Of knitted wool and cotton with horizontal strips of contrasting colors, crew-neck, and half-sleeves.

basquine, vasquine a fitted, boned hip-length garment with petticoat. A bolster was tied around the waist over the petticoat to produce the drum-shaped silhouette seen in the Velázquez portraits. The masculine basquine was a fitted, padded doublet fastened down center front. Both sexes wore a heavy canvas corset shaped with steel busks and tightly laced.

bassanet see *basinet.*

bassarisk see *sable, mountain* or *rock sable.*

basting temporary stitching.

basting cotton thread used in long stitches to hold the fabric in place for final stitching. The thread is thin, soft and easily broken.

bateau neck a boat-shaped straight neckline reaching from shoulder to shoulder, equally high front and back.

bathing dress, feminine The custom of resort or surf bathing dates from the mid-nineteenth century when body-concealing suits were worn by both sexes. Women wore a real dress with short sleeves and a short skirt over pantalets or bloomers and black stockings. The fabric was flannel, alpaca or perhaps plaid

Basque Bodice

worsted, usually dark blue, brown or black with braid trim. After World War I the clinging one-piece, knitted maillot from France became fashionable and about 1935, again from France, the two-piece silk suit of top and shorts. In 1947 came the bikini comprising bosom-band and cache-sexe. see *bikini; Annette Kellerman; maillot.*

bathing dress, masculine The popularity of seashore bathing was linked up to railroad building, the trains enabling people to reach shore points on vacation trips. The earliest outfits were of flannel, alpaca and worsted in navy blue, brown, black or a mixed gray cloth which later in the period changed to a machine-knitted fabric called jersey. At first it was a one-piece garment, usually sleeveless and reaching to the ankles or just below the knees, eventually shaping into knee breeches and a sleeveless "jumper top." In the early twentieth century, young men especially, doffed the top and simply wore shorts. see *jersey.*

battle or Eisenhower jacket-W.W.II

bathrobe a full or knee length garment, often of Turkish toweling or terry cloth, worn by men and women before and after bathing. Also, a dressing gown.

batik an ancient method of resist-dye coloring which originated in Java. A design is planned, and some parts of the fabric are coated with wax, leaving only the uncoated parts to absorb the dye. The process is repeated for each new color.

batiste a sheer, finely woven cloth of linen, wool lighter than challis, silk or spun rayon. Named for the inventor Baptiste Chambrai, a French weaver of the thirteenth century. see *wool batiste.*

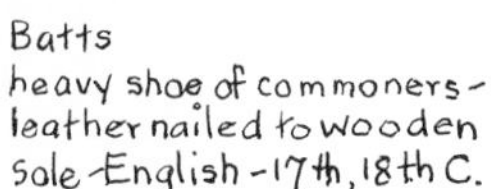

Batts
heavy shoe of commoners-leather nailed to wooden sole-English-17th, 18th C.

Battenberg lace a coarse form of Renaissance lace handmade or machine-made of linen thread, braid or tape and varied in design. The handmade is used for dress trimming and the machine-made for draperies.

batting felt, cotton or wool in sheets prepared for interlining or padding.

battlemented stitching see *castellated.*

battle jacket waist-length, single-breasted jacket used by the United States Army in World War II. Adapted to sportswear later. see *Eisenhower jacket.*

batts the popular women's shoe of the seventeenth century, resembling the heavy masculine shoe of black leather with medium heel and latchets tied over the tongue. Batts were shipped to the American colonies as early as 1636, and worn with home-knitted cotton or wool stockings.

batwing a popular name for a man's bow tie. Also a feminine sleeve, see *sleeve, batwing.*

bauble any trifling, cheap ornament.

baudequin a tissue of silk and gold thread originally from Baghdad and later from Cyprus and Palermo. Brought back by the Crusaders and used by European royalty for throne drapery and robes from the twelfth to the sixteenth centuries.

bautta an Italian cloak of black cloth with a hood which may be arranged to conceal the face.

Bavarian lace also known as peasant's or beggar's lace. Bobbin-made of heavy linen or cotton thread, the coarse lace is used in fancy work and the fine in clothing. see *torchon lace.*

bavolet a woman's headdress worn in the sixteenth century by European bourgeoisie and peasantry. The wearer was called a bavolette. Called a tovaglia, it is still worn in Italy. The bavolet was a towel-like piece of white linen, about two yards long and eighteen inches wide with fringed ends, folded and pinned to the cap. The deep back-ruffle on any bonnet was called a bavolet, a style revived in the nineteenth century.

bayadere fabrics and ribbons striped horizontally in brilliant colors. Also the name of a female dancer and singer of an East Indian temple.

Bayeux lace see *black lace.*

bazna sash the silk sash of an Algerian woman's dress.

beachwear garments designed for wear on the beach and while swimming.

bead embroidery tiny, sparkling, variegated glass or metal ornaments which are sewn to fabric by hand following a design. see *paillettes; sequins; spangles.*

beading; entre-deux a very narrow insertion resembling hemstitching, used in seam-joining of fine handmade lingerie in white batiste, lawn and nainsook. It is also made wide enough for threading narrow baby ribbon.

beads probably the oldest form of adornment, aside from berries. They have been found in the most ancient Egyptian tombs and have been made of bone, metal, wood, pottery, ivory, amber, coral and jet. Modern glass beads are accredited to the Venetians in the fourteenth century.

beanie, beany a twentieth century American name for the calotte.

beany or calotte-1930's

bear-white-black-Himalayan-Isabelline

bear, black a durable fur used for coat trimmings and, in Great Britain, for the tall cap of Guard Regiments. General in North America, best from Canada. The animals have fine, dark-brown under fur, guard hair long and bright black. Brown, whitish-brown and cinnamon are color phases of the bear shipped to European and Asiatic markets.

bear, Himalayan or **Isabelline** a heavier and more lustrous fur than that of the American black bear, from the large black bear of Eastern Asia. This fur was popular for the large muffs of the eighteenth century.

beard The masculine beard has been an object of attention in all ages and all lands. The manner of wearing it has changed with each epoch, and has even been banned. In some periods it has proven a costly vanity what with cuttings, trimmings, shavings and even perfumes. In the seventeenth century the gentleman wore a pasteboard box to protect his well-groomed beard while asleep. In the nineteenth century whiskers were very popular. Dundreary whiskers were those separated by a shaven chin. The cathedral beard was a broad square-cut beard, so named because it was worn principally by academics and churchmen. After the middle of the nineteenth century appeared the imperial, as worn by Napoleon III, a pointed tuft on the chin accompanied by a small mustache. Beards and whiskers disappeared in the 1880's but the mustache retained its popularity; in the twentieth century the clean-shaven face has generally been favored. see *side-whiskers, sideburns.*

bavolet-16th century

bavolet or fanchon bonnet-1857

beard-Roman

beard-Greek

beard after Napoléon III-Imperial

beard Dundrearies, sideburns or mutton-chops

Beards
Egyptian
Persian
Babylonian
Greek
Etruscan
Byzantine
16th C.
Roman
Moorish
Frankish
9th C.
Italian-
early
16th C.
Cavalier or
Van Dyck
1622
1831-
Polish
1643-
Swedish
English-
1536
Van Dyck or
or Cavalier
1630's
19th C.
moustache - imperial-
side whiskers or muttonchops
German
1519

bearskin the tall fur shako of black bearskin worn by the five foot regiments of the British Household Brigade of Guards.

bearskin pants characteristic white bearskin pants worn by the men of Thule at the most northern end of Greenland, the pants known as the "trademark" of the men of Thule.

bearskin pants, white, of the men of Thule, Greenland

bear's paw see *solleret.*

Beatles four young British entertainers in 1960's who grew longish coiffures and adopted Mod, or Edwardian clothes, styles quickly taken up by many young men. see *Mod.*

Beatle haircuts 1960's

Beau Brummell George Bryan Brummell (1778–1840), an English dandy and a friend of the Prince of Wales, later George IV. He was arbiter in the details of dress and famed for his skill in tying a cravat. It was he who first wore black or dark blue evening pantaloons instead of breeches, thereby making trousers popular.

beau-catcher, spit curl the coquettish curl in the middle of a woman's forehead, popular at the turn of the century.

Beau Feilding Robert Feilding, the first of the great English dandies who exercised an influence over fashion. He was known at the Court of Charles II as Handsome Feilding. He died in 1712.

Beau Nash Richard Nash (1674–1761), a dandy and leader of English society and fashion. The king appointed him master of ceremonies at the resort town of Bath, where he ruled in matters of deportment and dress.

beauty patches worn in ancient Rome not only by women but by men and we are reminded that the mole was considered a beauty mark. From Italy in the sixteenth century came the fashion of patches, or as the English said, "patching the face." Also worn in the seventeenth century, of black velvet, taffeta or court plaster, they were carried in tiny jeweled boxes. Patches were placed near the eyes, on the cheeks, the throat and breasts. And there were gallants who wore them too. see *mouches.*

beaver see *bevor.*

beaver *castor* in French. Found widely in North America and Canada, in the Rocky Mountain States to the Pacific and some protected colonies east of the Mississippi. The best comes from the Province of Quebec, and some from western Russia and eastern Siberia. The fur

black bearskin—Coldstream Guards

Beau-catcher or Spit-curl—1890s

beauty patches

beaver or castor

is soft, warm and durable; a rich brown, from light to dark with long, black or reddish-brown guard hair; used for coats, jackets and trimmings. Beaver imitations, all noted as beaver-dyed, are Australian opossum, coney (rabbit), mouton (lamb), raccoon and skunk. Beaver-dyed coney is an old English name for rabbit processed to simulate beaver. Sheared beaver is a fashion developed in the second half of the twentieth century in which the dehaired, thick underfur is trimmed short, making a less bulky fur and removing the tendency to curl when wet. Russian beaver is sometimes dyed and pointed to simulate sea otter.

beaver cloth fur imitation, thick-napped woolen cloth sheared to produce a close, dense surface like the fur; originally made in England. A wide range of finishes suitable for overcoats, uniforms, hats, etc.

beaver fustian a coarse, rough overcoating fabric made in and around Philadelphia since the early nineteenth century. It is dark blue and similar to kersey.

beaver Cavalier hat

beaver hat fur hat which was the fashionable headpiece of American men and women of the seventeenth century. A costly item, it was so valuable that it was often left as a bequest in a will. In the nineteenth and twentieth centuries, men and women wore hats of nappy felt for general wear.

bed jacket, bed sacque a short, flattering, feminine jacket of any favored material or weight, to wear over the nightgown when sitting up in bed.

bed socks ankle-high, knitted, warm socks for winter bed-wear.

Bedford cord first made in New Bedford, Massachusetts. A worsted fabric made with raised, rounded cords or ribs running lengthwise; may be in combination fibers, rayon, cotton, silk or wool. Favored for riding habits, livery wear, suits and children's coats.

beech martin see *marten, stone* or *beech.*

Bedouin sheik's costume—KIBR of plaided white cotton—white kaffiyeh with black agal—babouches, red or yellow

Bedouin—desert—mounted police force under French flag—Berber, Moorish and Tuareg—white cotton with black accessories

Beefeater's hat a black beaver hat with red, black and white ribbon cockards around the crown, of sixteenth century origin, worn by the British Yeomen of the Guard and the Warders of the Tower of London.

beehive bonnet see *bonnet, beehive.*

beehive coiffure hair worn piled very high over a back-combed base, 1950's.

Beene, Geoffrey see *couture, haute.*

Beer see *couture, haute.*

beer jacket a twentieth century college fashion. A simple straight jacket of flannel, cotton or linen which male students originally wore to beer parties in the twenties and thirties.

beetling a finish for cotton and linen fabrics achieved by hammering the fabric flat over rollers. The process produces an increased luster.

beggar's lace known as *torchon lace.*

beguin, biggon, biggin a headcovering for men, women and children from the twelfth century on. Worn in Byzantium and later by the Béguines, women of religious orders, hence its common name. A three-piece cap, it was of finest linen for elegant folk and of coarse weave for commoners. It was worn by the clergy, under nobles' crowns, and of leather or felt under the helmet. In the fifteenth century the white linen coif was replaced by felt or velvet, often red. In the eighteenth century it was worn under the wig and was retained in the nineteenth century under the wig of the British barrister.

Belgian laces see *Antwerp; Brussels; Mechlin; Valenciennes.*

Beguin, biggin or coif

bell skirt see *skirt, bell.*

bell-bottoms the flaring trousers worn by sailors for four centuries. A seaman's breeches had to be roomy enough to permit the acrobatic movement necessary aboard a sailing ship. Today's breeches have but slight flare to the bottoms.

bellboy's cap a small round hat of stiffened fabric and color matching the hotel bellboy's uniform. see *pillbox.*

bellows pocket see *pocket, bellows.*

bellows tongue a man's work or sports shoe with a broad folding tongue stitched to either side of the quarter to keep out water when laced.

bells, silver small tinkling bells in fashion in the fourteenth and early fifteenth centuries. They were suspended from leather belts, jeweled girdles, and around the neck of men and women. Particularly used for the jester's costume of particolored clothes, hood and short cape with castellated edges, all tinkling with bells.

belt a band to encircle waist or hips, male or female. It may be of leather, cloth, chain links or decorative cord, and plain or jeweled. It may serve to carry gun, sword, money bag or purse, and may be tied, hooked or buckled; according to the mode, it may tightly shape the waist or loosely hold the folds of robe or cloak.

belt, Basque see *Basque belt.*

belt, Sam Browne a wide leather belt supported by a narrow strap passing over the right shoulder, worn by army officers. A sword belt designed by the British General Sir Samuel Browne (1824–1901).

Bemberg trademark owned by American Bemberg Corp. for the rayon yarn

Beefeater's or Warder's hat-London

beer Jacket

Sam Browne belt-designed by British Gen. Sir Samuel Browne worn in World War I

béret

made by a process called cuprammonium composed principally of cotton linters.

bench-made a British term for "bespoke" or custom handmade shoes. So called because the workmen, before the days of machinery, sat on benches along the wall, each workman making a complete shoe.

two berets

Bengal stripes a cotton gingham cloth originally from Bengal, India, woven in colored stripes. This cloth was the origin of the multicolored striped silks popular in men's neckwear.

bengaline a general term applied to silk and wool fabrics with a corded or rep effect. The heavy, soft-spun woolen weft is covered closely in the weaving with silk or wool. Used for coats, dresses and draperies. Made first in Bengal, India.

plumed béret 1530's

béret a very simple form of headgear; a round piece of woolen cloth or felt drawn up at the edge with a thong to fit the head. The history of the béret goes back to ancient Greece and Rome, reaching the Basque country by way of the traders. The modern béret of dark blue felt is shrunk to shape and size in the dyeing. The tiny spike, or tontarra, is sewn on last to cover the "eye" of the weave. The béret is worn today by men and women of many lands.

Basque béret-1920's

beretta see *biretta.*

Berlin or **German wool** a fancy-work yarn made from wool of Merino sheep mostly of Saxony. Generally dyed very bright, strong colors.

béret of British General Montgomery-W W II

Berlin work embroidery done on "Berlin canvas" using various stitches, but principally cross-stitch, worked in Berlin wool. Popular handiwork in the nineteenth century.

Bermuda shorts feminine, knee-length for sports. see *pant lengths.*

Bersagliere a distinctive hat named for the Italian army corps of riflemen and sharpshooters whose uniform it is. Of black glazed felt with cock plumage.

Bersagliere-infantry corps of riflemen in the Italian army. Hat of black glazed felt with cock plume

Bertha of lace

bertha a capelike collar of varying length and generally made of lace, which recalled the Palatine capes. see *Palatine.*

Bertin, Rose see *couture, haute.*

beryl a stone of beryllium aluminum silicate, of great beauty and hardness when transparent. In colors, bluish-green, yellow, pink, and white. Emerald and aquamarine are varieties.

bespangled decorated with sparkling spangles, tiny disks of gold, silver, or steel, extensively used in the late nineteenth century for formal evening gowns.

bespoke tailoring the British term for custom-made clothes. The only ready-to-wear worn by the well-dressed Englishman is confined to certain overcoats and raincoats or utility sports coats of outstanding tailoring.

Bethlehem headdress an ancient Moslem headdress worn by women of Bethlehem, Jerusalem and Nazareth; a tarboosh, red or green, to which are sewn gold and silver coins representing the dowry. A chain is often attached to the cap, hanging below the chin, from which dangle more coins. The married woman wears a large white veil draped over the cap.

Bethlehem headdress

Betsie or **cherusse** a small ruff or collarette of several rows of fluted Brabant lace or mull. The fashion originated in England where it was named for Queen Elizabeth I; carried to Paris by the famous tailor Leroy and renamed cherusse. It became popular with the low-necked gowns of the First Empire. By 1807 the collarettes had acquired six or seven falls of lace.

bevor, beaver a movable piece of armor attached to the armet, a helmet of the fifteenth and sixteenth centuries. When lowered, it protected the lower part of the face.

biagga gallas see *Lapland bonnet.*

bias a line running diagonally across warp and woof threads. Bias-cut bindings are easier to apply to curved edges, and lingerie cut on the bias may have better fit and wear.

bib a small pad, plain or fancy, fastened around the neck of an infant to protect its clothing. Also, the upper part of an apron, above the waist. Decorative deep-front collars are sometimes called bibs.

bicorne, chapeau bras an evolution of the tricorne; supplanted the three-cornered hat in the 1790's. It folded flat for carrying under the arm, hence the name. It became the ceremonial dress hat worn to the present day in the American, British and French navies.

bicycle bal a leather or canvas ankle shoe with low heel and front lacing nearly to the toe. Worn for bicycling. Bal, short for balmoral, late nineteenth century.

Biedermeier a German style of furniture and furnishings, less ornate than the preceding French Empire, of the period from 1825 to 1860. The term includes the German version of dress similar to the Second Empire mode in France.

bietle a jacket of deerskin worn by Apache Indian women.

bietta meaning bright; a red cloth that American Indians coveted and made efforts to procure either by trade or war. The Spanish, who used it for uniforms, brought it to America first. The Indians used it sparingly and effectively on their deerskin garments.

Betsie or cherusse

bib

bicycle bal

Bikini

biggon, biggin see *beguin.*

bikini the most abbreviated form of feminine bathing dress, originally created by the House of Heim, Paris. It consists of two separate pieces: a band covering the breasts and the *cache-sexe.* Though it first appeared on French beaches in 1947–48, a late Roman mosaic of 406 A.D., recently uncovered in central Italy, reveals several ladies wearing the identical garb.

biliment an elaborate but delicate headdress of the sixteenth century, usually of a lace of gold threads worked with beads, jewels, ribbons, gauze, and even sometimes a single feather.

biliment headdress

billicock, billycock a Briticism for the hard felt hat with round crown; the derby, bowler or melon. "Billycock" was derived from William Coke, Earl of Norfolk, who made the hat popular. see *derby; bowler.*

Binche lace one of the earliest of Flemish laces, bobbin-made at Binche. It has floral scrolls spreading over the ground, sprinkled with spots like snowflakes.

Billycock or Melon-1862

binding tape cut on the bias used to bind edges. It is available in single or double fold, in several widths and many colors. Seam binding is a narrow ribbon-like tape, about a half inch wide, formerly of silk, now of rayon, in all colors.

bird of paradise any one of the beautiful birds of the Paradise family of New Guinea and adjacent islands. Noted for brilliant and elegant plumes, the importation of which was banned in the United States in 1905. see *Audubon plumage law.*

birdseye a small geometric pattern woven with a dot in the center resembling a bird's eye. Birdseye pattern is used in cotton, linen, silks and synthetic fabrics and there is also a diamond weave in piqué cotton for gentlemen's evening wear accessories, such as waistcoat and bow tie.

bird of paradise feathers

biretta a stiff square cap with three or four projections rising above the crown, radiating from the center and often finished with a pompon. Originally a choir skullcap, it became a headdress for the clergy about the fifteenth century, being worn by secular academicians as well as the clergy. Today the birettas worn by cardinals are red, bishops wear purple, priests black, and some canons and abbots, white.

biretta of universities and professions

biretta of a Venetian general

biretta of cardinal

birrus see *byrrus.*

bishop's or **Victoria lawn** a fine lawn made for clerical vestments, especially the bishop's full sleeves.

bishop's sleeve see *sleeve, bishop's.*

bison see *buffalo.*

bi-swing a sportswear jacket which, by an inverted pleat or gusset from shoulder to waistline in center back, gives a play of extra material when the wearer is in action.

black an absence of color.

black amber see *jet.*

black fox see *fox, silver.*

black lace made in the seventeenth century at Bayeux, France, and sometimes called Bayeux lace. The fashion for wearing it was brought to France by the Spanish Infanta who married Louis XIV in 1660.

black tie a popular term denoting men's semiformal evening wear consisting of a dinner jacket (tuxedo), a black waistcoat or cummerbund, and a black bow tie worn with a soft white shirt. The term is often used on invitations to indicate that semiformal dress will be worn, as opposed to formal dress or "white tie." see *dinner jacket, tuxedo.*

black tie-semi-formal, single-breasted dinner jacket cummerbund-contemporary

blackwork black counted thread embroidery on white fabric, principally linen and cotton. English sixteenth and seventeenth centuries. see *Spanish blackwork.*

blanket coat same as Hudson Bay coat, worn with a woolen sash. Copied from the cloth peasant coats of Normandy and introduced by the early French settlers of Canada.

Blass, Bill see *couture, haute.*

blazer a lightweight jacket, usually of flannel, in solid color or brilliant regimental or club stripes. Originally, the scarlet jacket of the English Cambridge University students for cricket or tennis. The jacket was taken up later for informal country wear by British army and navy men.

blazer

bleeding the running of color when a fabric is immersed in water. A characteristic of madras.

blends combinations of certain synthetic fibers. A blend can change a texture to smooth or coarse, make the weight heavy or light, soft or more wrinkle-proof.

bliaud, bliaus a medieval shirt which was the origin of the linen blouse or smock worn by European peasants of both sexes today. The bliaud was worn over the chainse, or chemise, and slit up the sides to allow freedom for the legs when riding horseback. Today's shirt, blouse or shirtwaist is simply a form of the original bliaus. Similar to the *gertrude.*

block printing a process where a design is carved on wooden blocks, coated

with coloring matter and then pressed onto fabric by hand; practiced in China and Japan for many centuries.

blond, blonde hair, flaxen or golden-hued.

blonde lace a very fine silk bobbin-lace, closely woven, originally in cream color but now bleached white or dyed black.

bloomer dress a style of play dress with matching bloomers for little girls.

bloomers in general, any knee-length leg garment worn by women and girls. Originally long, loose pantaloons gathered at the ankles, showing below full skirts. Designed by Mrs. Amelia Jenks Bloomer, an American social reformer who appeared publicly in the costume about 1850. Worn by schoolgirls in the 1910's and '20's with a middy blouse, for athletic uniform.

blouse a sleeved or sleeveless garment generally reaching below the waist, but of varying lengths. It evolved from the bliaud. see *Balkan blouse; middy blouse; over blouse; Russian blouse; sash blouse.*

blouse, middy see *middy blouse.*

blouse, Russian see *Russian blouse.*

blouse, step-in see *step-in blouse.*

Blücher a shoe or half-boot invented by Field Marshall von Blücher (1742–1819), commander of the Prussian forces at Waterloo. A laced shoe in which the quarters reached to the front over the instep and were laced together over the tongue.

blue one of the three primary colors blue, red, and yellow. Blue mixed with red gives the secondary color purple, and mixed with yellow, the secondary color green. Blue plus purple gives the tertiary color blue-purple; blue plus green, the tertiary color blue-green. The blue-purples include such names as periwinkle and hyacinth; the blue-greens include aqua, teal and peacock. The palest blues are sky blue and baby blue; the bright medium shades are cornflower and royal; with black added the tones deepen to navy and midnight. Grayed blues include powder, Wedgwood and horizon.

blue fox see *fox, blue.*

blue jeans see *levis.*

bluebonnet, balmoral the traditional cap worn by shepherd, soldier and gentleman in Scotland, woven in one piece without seam or binding, of dark blue wool with either a red or blue tuft on top. A ribbon cockade, a sprig of native evergreen and feather signified the wearer's rank in his clan. Three feathers were permitted the chief or head of the clan, two for the gentleman and one for the clansman. The cap was named after Balmoral Castle, Queen Victoria's summer home. see *cap, Glengarry.*

bluff edge a braid-bound hand-felled edge on a cloth coat.

boa a long, cylindrical neckpiece of

feathers, fur, tulle or lace, according to season; a graceful fashion of the late nineteenth century. The boa was very long, usually six to eight feet, so that a lady could wrap it around her neck with floating ends that hung below her knees. Revived in the 1930's and 1960's.

boarded calf see *calf, boarded.*

boater or **hard hat** a man's sennit straw sailor coated with shellac from India, popular in the late nineteenth century. The English wore it punting, hence the name. In America it was worn almost universally from June first to September first. The name "sennit" comes from the nautical term "seven-knit," a method of braiding rope.

boating wear functional sports clothes developed before World War II. Both men and women wear lightweight slacks, shorts and T-shirts or sweaters in mild weather and for poor weather lined waterproof nylon. Lined nylon trousers have elastic at waist and ankles and lined nylon anoraks are high-necked and have drainage vents in pockets in case of a ducking. The nylon used is available in several different colors, white being avoided because sea water turns it yellow.

bob wig see *wig, bob.*

bobbed hair Small boys were the first to wear bobbed hair following the Dutch style, cut straight around covering the back and straight-cut bangs over the forehead. In the second decade of the twentieth century some of Paul Poiret's mannequins adopted the coiffure as did some of the dancers of Isadora Duncan's troupe. First made fashionable in America by the ballroom dancer Irene Castle, bobbed hair did not become an established fashion until the 1920's when a mannish haircut was necessitated by the fashion of the head-hugging felt cloche of the same period. During the vogue of the bob, fruitless efforts to revive long tresses succeeded only in establishing a still shorter cut. The boyish bob or shingle was clipped very close in back and trimmed to a V at the nape. The windblown bob was a style with the hair cut short and tousled. The page boy bob was a style of the 1930's favored by young women. This coiffure was founded upon the medieval page-boy style, the hair cut shoulder-length with the ends rolled under. The same shape was given the bangs rolled under on the forehead. see *windblown bob.*

bobbin a spool-like device used on a lock-stitch sewing machine which feeds the thread for the under side of the stitching; also a small pin or cylinder which is used in the making of bobbin lace.

bobbin lace, bone lace, pillow lace lace made on a pillow with the design marked out by pins, and the bobbins or bones worked back and forth over the pins. The name distinguishes it from needle lace.

bobbinet a net made with a hexagonal mesh. Of twisted cotton or silk yarn, it was originally made by hand with bobbins. It is used for lace grounds and dresses.

bobby pin a style of clip hairpin which appeared with the fashion of bobbed hair in the nineteen-twenties and resembles the cotter pin of modern machinery.

bodice the part of a woman's dress above the waist. In medieval times it meant two "bodies" of boiled leather or canvas which were boned. Front and back were first hooked together to shape a small waist. Next, the bodies were whaleboned and laced tightly together, forming an underbodice or corset.

bodice, Basque surplice see *surplice bodice.*

bodkin a long, pointed pin of bone or bronze used as a hairpin by the ancient

boa of fur-1800

bobbed hair-1920

bobbed hair Dutch cut-early 20th C.

Greeks and Romans. It was called a hair-needle by the Saxons and was used for fastening the mantle, see *acus.* also, a large-eyed, blunt-ended needle used for drawing elastic, ribbon, etc., through a hem or row of eyelets.

body stocking-1960's

bodkin cloth of the seventeenth century, a rich cloth woven of silk and gold. The name is a corruption of Baghdad.

body garments those worn next to the body such as lingerie, sleeping apparel, underwear.

body paint see *tattooing.*

body stocking a finely knit body garment of stretch nylon backless to the waist and low-necked in front with the narrowest of shoulder straps; a step-in which eliminates brassiere and girdle. 1960's. see *leotard; tights.*

Bohan, Marc see *couture, haute.*

Bohemian lace a coarse net with a design worked in a braid effect.

boiled leather see *leather, boiled.*

boiled shirt a former inelegant colloquialism in the United States for a man's white shirt with stiffly starched bosom.

bolero hat-bolero jacket-bullfighter's frilled shirt-Spanish

bolero a tailored short Spanish jacket reaching to the waistline, ornamented with braid. Worn open over a fine white shirt and a wide crushed silk sash of brilliant color.

bolero hat see *hat, bolero.*

bolero, Scanderbeg see *Scanderbeg bolero.*

Bolivar hat see *hat, Bolivar.*

Bolivia a woolen cloth with a soft, plushlike surface, light to heavy quality, with pile tufts in either vertical or diagonal rows. Used for suits and coats.

bombachas long, full pantaloon breeches gathered at the ankles and held at the waist by a silver-studded leather belt. Worn by some gauchos of Uruguay.

bombachas-gaucho of Uruguay

bombast or peasecod-bellied fashion-Spanish-16th C.

bombast, bombace a type of cotton stuffing and padding, originally French. Used by the Spanish in the peasecod-bellied doublet shaped of buckram and busks, which influenced the fashions of the European courts. The period from 1545 to 1620 was known as Spanish bombast.

bombazine a plain, twilled English fabric, made of cotton in the Middle Ages, later of cotton and wool and later of silk and wool. Generally dyed black for mourning use. In the eighteenth century the name was given to a silk made in France and Milan.

Bonaparte helmet a gathered white silk bonnet with a forehead band of black velvet embroidered with gilt laurel leaves and mounted with a panache of white ostrich, early nineteenth century.

bonded fabrics laminated fabrics employed principally as interfacings. Fibers are pressed into thin sheets held together by plastic and adhesive. In the latest process, fabrics are bonded back to back, as for instance, a silk sheet applied to a woolen cloth, eliminating the need of a lining.

bone or **ivory** a warm, creamy white sometimes designated as parchment color or antique white. Most often used for feminine accessories.

bone lace of linen thread, lace made over bobbins of bone instead of wooden ones.

bonet, bonaid Scotch forms of the word *bonnet.*

bongrace a short headdress of silk, velvet or chiffon which hung free in back but dipped over the forehead in a peak, sometimes weighted with a pearl or other jewel. Also called an attifet headdress, sixteenth century.

bonnaz a type of embroidery made on a sewing machine supposedly invented by a Monsieur Bonnaz.

bonnet, bonet any soft head covering with strings tied under the chin. The same pattern as the medieval three-piece white cap but later made of coarse woolen green cloth called bonet. The cap was called bonnet to the sixteenth century.

bonnet in the nineteenth century became a frivolous feminine headpiece, the wearing of which was not permitted a young woman before her debut in society or her marriage. She wore a hat. The widow wore a black crêpe bonnet draped with a heavy veil.

bonnet, American Indian a headdress of upstanding feathers attached to a headband, with two feathered streamers hanging down the back. Imitated in a British colonial army fashion, early nineteenth century, with a shallow black velvet cap with upstanding ostrich plumes and bead earrings.

bonnet, beehive a lady's simple straw bonnet of the early nineteenth century made in the shape of a beehive and trimmed with a ribbon which tied under the chin.

bonnet, coal scuttle, poke bonnet, capote of straw with crown and a coal-scuttle-shaped brim. Worn over a lingerie cap and tied with ribbons. English late eighteenth century.

bonnet, conversation with turned-up brim of red-and-yellow-striped silk. French, early nineteenth century.

bonnet, cottage a fashion for summer wear. Of straw with squarish crown and a brim faced with silk or velvet, turned up in front and down in back; ornamented with moss roses and worn over a frilled lingerie cap, ribbon-tied under the chin.

bonnet, ducal see *corno.*

bonnet, Easter the feminine, usually brand new spring hat, flower-trimmed, that is worn to church on Easter Sunday. Late nineteenth and early twentieth centuries.

bonnet, Hardanger a four-piece square bonnet for children and young girls of Norway. Fashioned of scarlet velvet or woolen cloth, it is edged with black velvet and embroidered with motifs of fine beadwork.

bonnet, Lapland see *Lapland bonnet.*

bonnet, Pamela a yellow straw bon-

bongrace of black velvet- pearl earrings- French- late 16th C.

bongrace-white satin with pearls- and aigrettes- Italian- 16th C.

beehive or cottage bonnet

bonnet- American Indian-British Army captain- son of Joseph Brant-1812

ducal bonnet or Corno of the doge-Venetian-15th C.
"bonet" of green felt-Medieval
bonnet with bird-English-1880's
bonnet-black lace-French-1884
bonnet or mobcap-kate Greenaway 1883
bonnet-poke with ostrich plumes-1833
bonnet with frills-1797
cottage bonnet with cap-1804
Pamela bonnet-1865
Fanchon bonnet-1865
Bibi bonnet-with ostrich-French-1847
bonnet Thérèse spotted gauze-French-1780's
poke bonnet-straw-19th C.
calash-bonnet
bonnet-capote-poke or coal scuttle-English-1797
bonnet-cabriolet-French-1844
widow's bonnet of crepe-1880's

net, having a very tall crown, with daffodils and rose-colored ribbons which tied under the chin. French second decade, nineteenth century.

bonnet, Phrygian the ancient Greek cap or bonnet of felt or leather with chin strap. When the masters of Rome freed a slave, they placed the Phrygian bonnet upon his head. Later, Rome made it an emblem of liberty to be worn by manumitted slaves. In the eighteenth century it was again adopted as *le bonnet rouge* of the French Revolutionists. The female figure personifying Liberty wears such a cap.

bonnet, Quaker or **Friends** a version of the Directoire mode, in gray or brown cloth, felt or straw in cabriolet or wagon-top style. The fashion of the day was followed, but the bonnet was shorn of trimming except for the bavolet or ruffle in back which was usually of the fabric of the dress.

bonnet, Salvation Army Lassie the original bonnet of the Army's uniform lasted well into the twentieth century. Of black straw or felt according to season, it was lined with dark blue silk and tied with silk brides. The contemporary bonnet is smaller and jauntier, though still dark blue with the edge piped with red. The bonnet is secured by a chinstrap of dark blue silk finished with a large bowknot at the left side and the silk band lettered Salvation Army.

bonnet, slat bonnet or **sunbonnet** of cotton fabric, plain or figured and fashioned with a brim or poke held in shape by stitched slots holding thin wooden slats. In general, the sunbonnet was a peasant type of headdress with a bavolet. It had a wide brim of straw or stiffened, starched fabric and a gathered full crown with chin ties.

bonnet, sugar-loaf a man's high cap worn with bobbed hair; French mid-fifteenth century.

bonnet, Watteau see *Watteau bonnet.*

Bonnie and Clyde the name of a contemporary suit for young men and women inspired by a popular movie. Of dark gray or dark blue cloth pin-striped with white and with flaring trousers.

book linen a firm, sized linen used in men's wear to stiffen collars and belts.

boot, ankle a lumberman's ankle-high boot of thick leather for wear over heavy boots.

boot, carriage worn by women in the days of carriages, over dainty slippers to keep the feet warm. Made of cloth or velvet, they continued to be used in the automobile and for evening wear in winter.

boot, chukka see *jodhpur.*

boot, cavalier; boothose, French seventeenth century; leather boots with bucket or funnel tops wide enough to crush down, often worn over lace-edged boot hose which flared over the cuffs. Completed with wide quatrefoil spur leathers and jungling rowels.

boot, Courrèges a mid-twentieth century fashion, first designed for warmth, which developed from lined and often fur-topped galoshes. As skirts grew shorter the boot became longer and, by the sixties an almost indispensible part of winter dress. Principally white, of real or imitation leather.

boot, cowboy a type of boot worn by the western horseman, a calf-high boot with a high slanting Cuban heel to hold the foot in the stirrup. The tops are usually of fancy cut with appliquéd motifs.

Watteau hat-straw or felt-ostrich and ribbon-powdered hair in puffs and cadogan-French-1770's

bonnet-Quaker or Friend-19th C.

bonnet of the Salvation Army

Phrygian bonnet-red-French-1790's

bonnet-sunbonnet-stitched and slatted-mid-19th C.

Boots

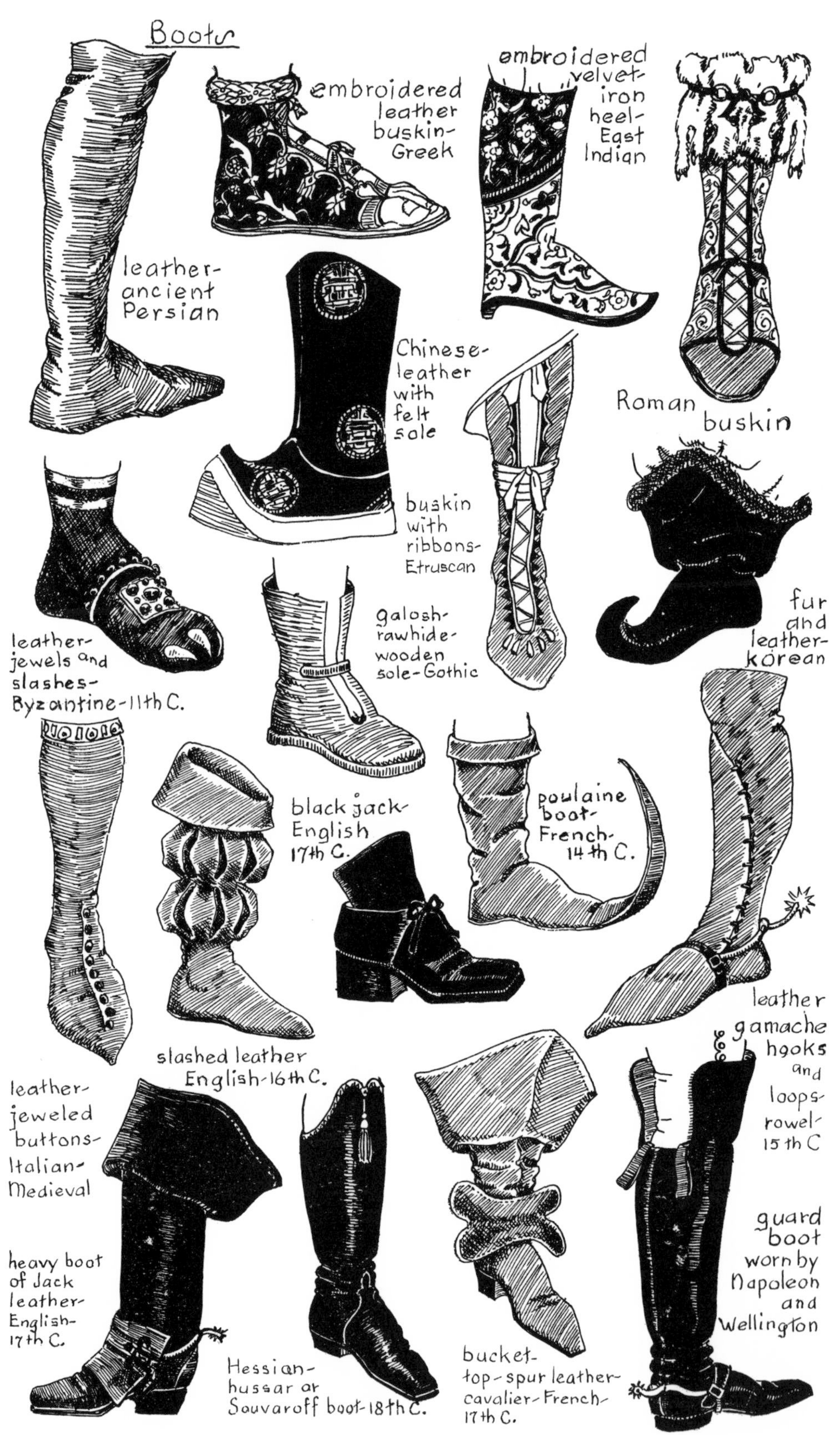

leather-
ancient
Persian
embroidered
leather
buskin-
Greek
embroidered
velvet-
iron
heel-
East
Indian
Chinese-
leather
with
felt
sole
Roman
buskin
buskin
with
ribbons-
Etruscan
leather-
jewels and
slashes-
Byzantine-11th C.
galosh-
rawhide-
wooden
sole-Gothic
fur
and
leather-
korean
black jack-
English
17th C.
poulaine
boot-
French-
14th C.
leather
gamache
hooks
and
loops-
rowel-
15th C
slashed leather
English-16th C.
leather-
jeweled
buttons-
Italian-
Medieval
guard
boot
worn by
Napoleon
and
Wellington
heavy boot
of Jack
leather-
English-
17th C.
Hessian-
hussar or
Souvaroff boot-18th C.
bucket-
top-spur leather-
cavalier-French-
17th C.

Boots

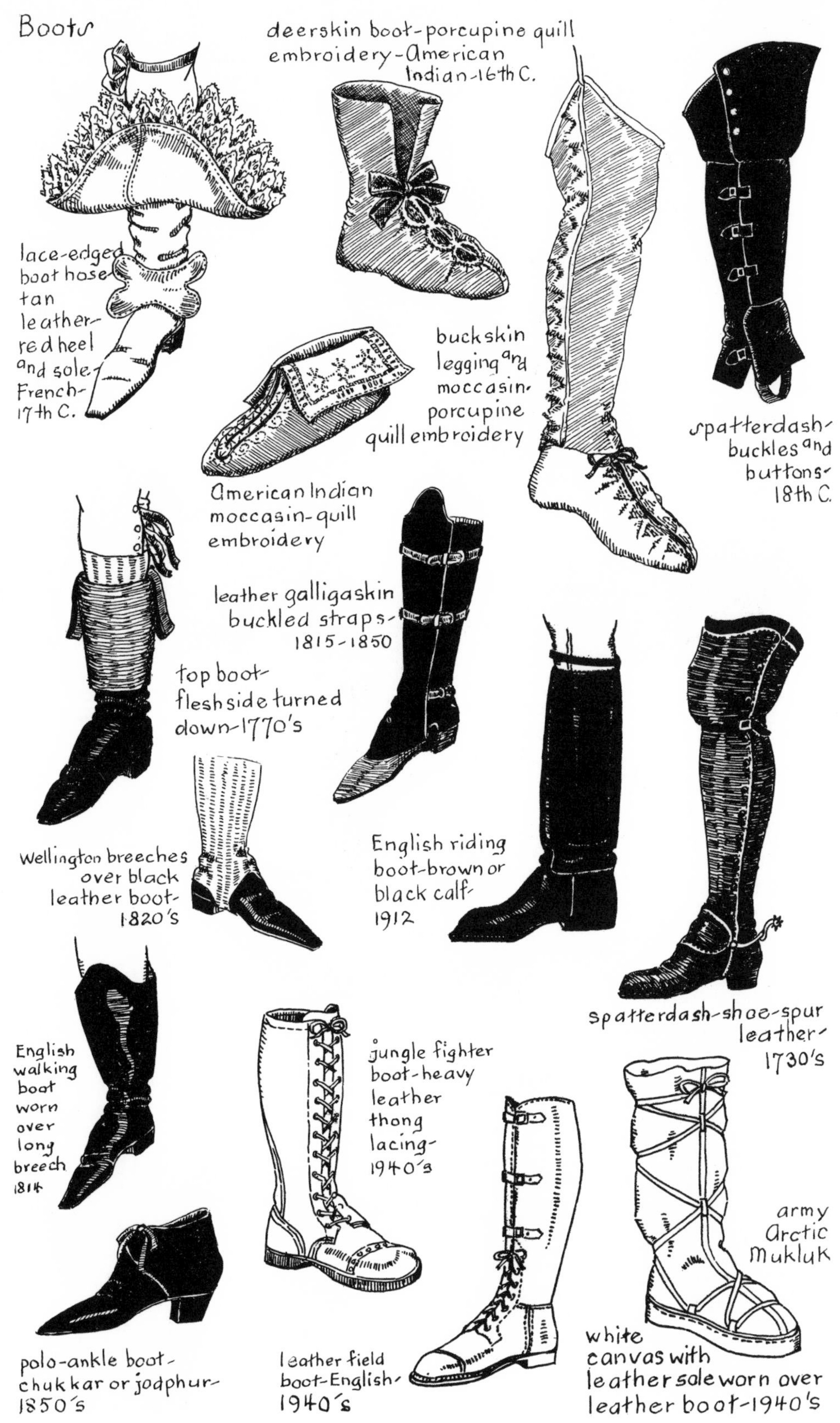

deerskin boot-porcupine quill embroidery-American Indian-16th C.
lace-edged boot hose-tan leather-red heel and sole-French-17th C.
buckskin legging and moccasin-porcupine quill embroidery
spatterdash-buckles and buttons-18th C.
American Indian moccasin-quill embroidery
leather galligaskin buckled straps-1815-1850
top boot-flesh side turned down-1770's
Wellington breeches over black leather boot-1820's
English riding boot-brown or black calf-1912
spatterdash-shoe-spur leather-1730's
English walking boot worn over long breech 1814
jungle fighter boot-heavy leather thong lacing-1940's
army Arctic Mukluk
polo-ankle boot-chukkar or jodphur-1850's
leather field boot-English-1940's
white canvas with leather sole worn over leather boot-1940's

Boots-feminine

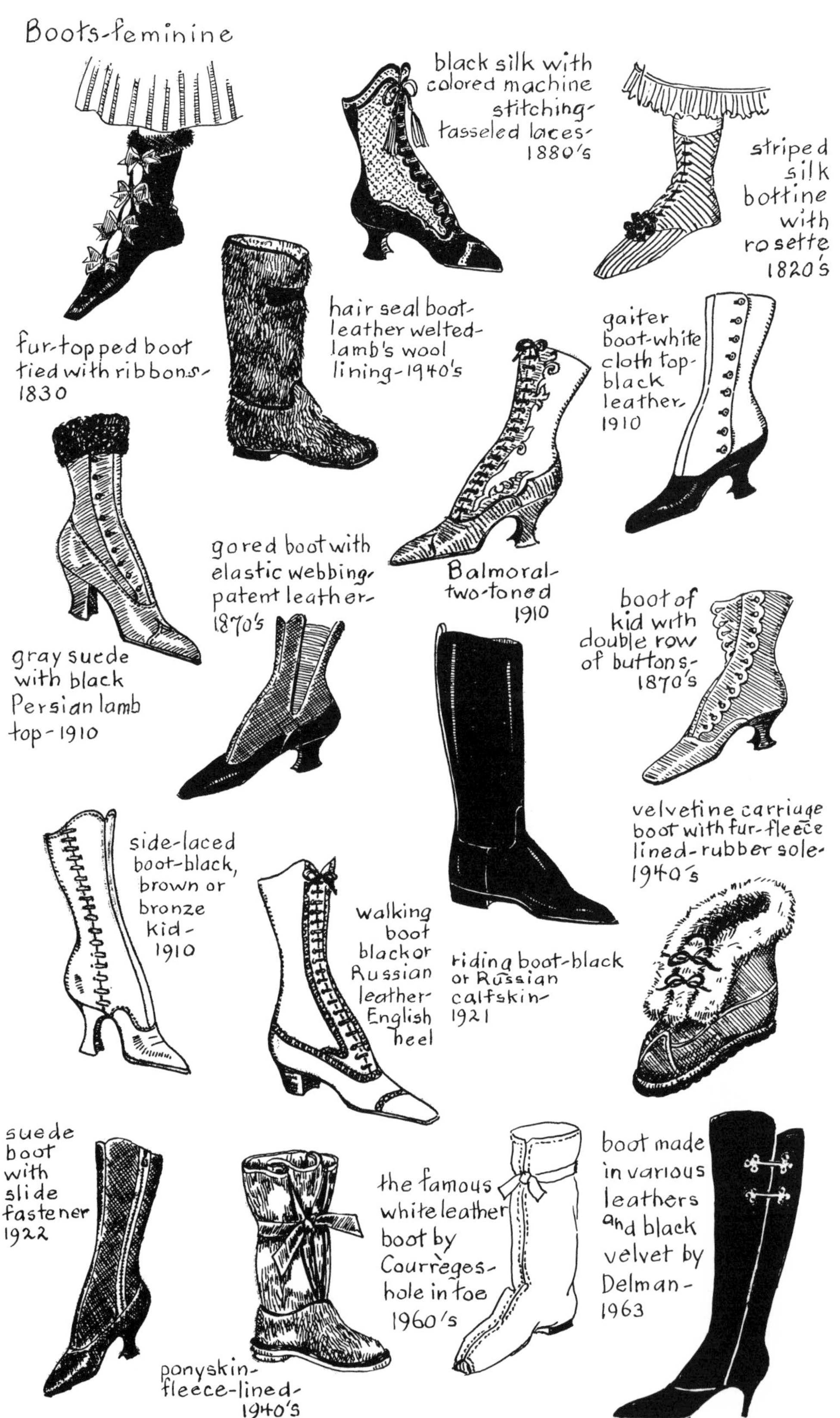

boot, flight a chukkar type of boot worn by the "plane pushers" of the big aircraft carriers in World War II. The former high boot with hooks was discarded as dangerous. Of natural color, the flight boot was made flesh-side-out with a nonskid traction sole. It became official equipment on all United States carriers.

boot, Hessian, Souvaroff, or Hussar boot worn by the Hessian mercenaries hired to fight the American colonists. To the Americans and English it was the Hessian boot, and to the French the Hussar boot. A tassel swung from a dip in the top just below the knee. The boot was adopted for civilian wear in the late 1790's.

boot, hip or **wading** of rubber, reaching to the hips and used for fishing.

boot hose were of sheer white linen with wide lace frills worn to protect the cavalier's costly silk hose worn underneath. The lace frill hung over the leather top of the boot. Especially smart in the mid-seventeenth century and worn even by some dressy Puritans in the Colonies.

boot, jack the generally-worn boot of the seventeenth and eighteenth centuries, large enough to wear a shoe or slipper inside it. It was lined with pockets enabling the wearer to carry papers and small objects. It was made of jack leather, a wax leather coated with tar or pitch, the same leather employed for the huge tankard which held beer and ale.

boot, jungle fighter or **paratrooper** a Blücher-style boot of oiled, stout brown leather, water-resistant and laced with leather thongs. In World War II, because of the dangerous hooks, it was replaced by the chukkar style of laced boot.

boot, Napoleon also worn by Wellington, a military guard or army officer's boot, of heavy black leather, chamois-lined and a square top cut out in back. Worn by the officers of the European armies.

boot, Oxford half-boot the first Oxford, a shoe of heavy jack leather. English, seventeenth century.

boot, paratrooper see *boot, jungle fighter.*

boot, pegged a boot having soles fastened on by wooden pegs.

boot, Souvaroff see *boot, Hessian.*

boot, top of the 1780's and 1790's. Of black grain leather with flesh side turned down and a strap around the knee. Used for such sports as riding, hunting, fishing.

boot, Wellington guard or officer's boot, also worn by Napoleon. Heavy black leather, chamois-lined with square top cut out in back.

boot, Wellington half- worn up to the 1860's under the trousers, which were fastened under the sole with strap or gaiter.

bootee any low boot made of leather, fabric, especially knitted yarn or fabric for infants.

bootjack a V-shaped device for pulling off boots.

Borgana trademark for a deep-furred pile fabric used exclusively for women's coats. A blend of Orlon, Darlan, and Dynel.

borsalino a hat of Italian make, supposedly the finest of men's felt hats. Of natural fur which has been aged for three years; the felted body is aged for another year. All detailing is done by hand. The hats have been made in Alessandria for over a century.

bosom band a band of wool, linen or chamoised leather worn by Greek women next to the body. It was tied with strings or pinned with fibulae, the Greek safety pins. see *apodesme.*

bosom or **breast knot** a scented bowknot or rosette of colored satin ribbon of the eighteenth century, a vogue from about 1730 on. Its particular name was "perfect contentment."

Botany trademark of fine wools, worsteds, yarns and fabrics manufactured by Botany Mills, Inc. and licensed for woven woolens in men's, women's and children's manufacture.

lady's black satin bottine–black net stocking over pink cashmere–1830's

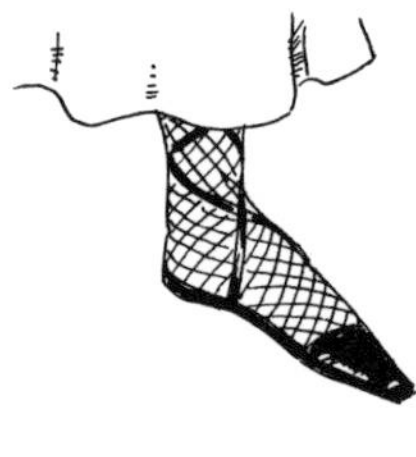

lady's bottine elastic webbing–fabric and leather tip

bottine or **jemima** a lady's gored boot of beige fabric with black leather tip and elastic inserts. It was first designed for Queen Victoria, in 1836. The first elastic cloth or webbing woven with rubber was invented by T. Hancock of Middlesex, England. The shoe was designed by J. Sparkes Hall, bootmaker to the queen. It had either cloth or leather uppers with elastic gussets at the sides and was a style worn by men and women. "Jemima" was the British term.

bottles as used in feminine dress of the late eighteenth century, a small slim bottle holding water and fresh flowers which was tucked into the bosom of the stomacher. Also, a small flat bottle holding water and fresh flowers tucked into the elaborate headdress.

bouclé, boucle French for looped or curled. A rugged-looking but soft fabric for sportswear woven or knitted with tiny loops. It may be of any knitted fiber but is executed principally in wool. Also, a wool knitting yarn with a silk thread that gives it an uneven texture. Used for sweaters and sports suits.

boudoir cap a flattering head covering worn to cover a lady's undressed hair. It was a dainty, softly shirred cap with a pretty lace ruffle. Today called a curler cap, its purpose being to cover a head done up in pincurls and rollers.

boudoir slipper see *mule.*

bouffant French for puffed, puffy. Generally applied to full, stiff skirts.

bouffant, bouffants from the French for puffing in costume. Bouffants appear in the mode from time to time, sometimes in panniers, sleeves or breeches and often in the coiffure. The eighteenth century was decidedly an era of bouffant dress.

Bourbon lace a net ground with design and edge worked with cording.

bourette, bourrette a yarn of silk, cotton or linen with a rough uneven appearance made by nubs and knots. Also, the fabric woven of it.

boutique French word for shop. The advantages of shopping in the boutique are many, the greatest of all being able to browse over the copies of ready-made clothes, including accessories and gadgets, which are much less expensive. Usually copied in the finest fabrics, they cost less because of no fittings. Priced $150. to $500, while a second degree boutique may be $50. to $150, at the same time, building a splendid clientelle.

boutonnière from the French for buttonhole. In France under Louis XV a gentleman wore a boutonnière of artificial flowers. The fashion returned in the early twentieth century, men wearing a single fresh flower or very small spray, a fad of about a half century.

bow tie a man's small tie in a bowknot having two loops and two short ends for daywear. Also a small tie in a bowknot for evening wear, white with tail coat and black with dinner jacket. see *neckwear, masculine.*

bowknot a flat, black ribbon which secured the looped-up cadogan of the eighteenth century coiffure. Also, a flat black bow which ornamented the black leather slippers or pumps.

bowler-American-1879

bowler a British name for the hard, dome-shaped felt hat which appeared in 1850, designed by the English hatter, William Bowler. The Americans called it a derby because the Earl of Derby always wore the bowler to the races at Epsom Downs. see *derby*.

box coat of tan covert cloth-1899

box coat a coachman's overcoat new in the 1830's, straight and loose-fitting, of heavy beige cloth with or without cape. Single or double breasted. Worn by the driver sitting on the box of the coach, hence its name.

box pleats see *pleats*.

boyish form-1920's

boyish form, debutante slouch a fashionable stance in the second decade of the twentieth century. A pose of hands on the hips, the pelvis thrown forward to produce the desired flattening of the bosom, By the 1920's the stance had developed into a pencil-straight, low-waisted figure aided by a Poiret-designed flattening brassière and an unboned knitted elastic girdle.

braccae All Asiatics, barbarians and the northern Europeans wore braccae in the form of a piece of fabric wrapped around the hips and legs as is worn today in many Eastern countries. When the Roman legionnaires invaded the country of the Franks, Gauls, and British Celts, they adopted the braccae of the "panted people" or "breeched people" as a protection against cold. Upon returning home, they divested themselves of the forbidden garment before entering Rome. Their own leg-covering was short, made of wool or coarse linen and cross-gartered with strips of cloth or leather. In time, the northerners copied the short woolen tunic of the Romans. see *drawers*.

bracelet an arm or wrist ornament which may be in ring or chain form, of gold, silver or other metals, plain or set with jewels. see *bangle bracelet; charm bracelet; slave bracelet.*

bracelet sleeve see *sleeve, bracelet.*

braces British for suspenders which hold up trousers. see *bretelles; gallowses; suspenders.*

braconnière a part of late fourteenth and fifteenth century armor; hip-length skirt formed of hoop-shaped steel plates overlapping one another, hinged on one side and fastened on the other side by leather straps and buckles. It gradually shortened, finally disappearing in the seventeenth century.

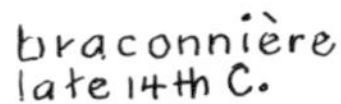

bragou-braz of the Breton peasant-leather belt

bragou-braz the very full knee breeches of the French Breton peasant worn with a wide sash or vest and short jacket. Of coarse dark blue linen shirred to self belt. Worn at the hips, ending with tight knee cuffs. Worn to modern times.

braguette French word for codpiece.

braid a narrow flat strip of woven, pleated or interlaced wool, cotton, silk, linen or metallic thread. Used for trimming, binding or appliqué work on apparel. *Coronation braid*, a round braid alternating thick and thin evenly, used to outline a design. *Military braid*, a flat, silk braid of diagonal basket weave. *Rickrack braid,* a flat woven braid in an even zigzag pattern. Made in cotton, silk and wool in many colors and used for trimming. *Soutache,* a very narrow, flat cord with uses such as finishing an edge, or a seam, or for decorative motifs. On men's clothes braid came into fashion about 1850 as edging or binding on jackets, coats and capes, or stitched down the side seams of trousers, a decoration which survives today on trousers worn with tailcoats.

braid verb or noun in *headdress.* to plait or "braid" strands of hair together, usually three in number, making a "braid."

braid, middy a narrow ribbed braid in various colors used especially for trimming navy middy blouses, hence its name.

braids, straw see *straw braids.*

Brandenburg decorative fasteners on outer garments in braided loops and buttons. They were termed *Brandenburgs* by the French after contact with the Brandenburg troops of Prussia in 1674 whose cassocks were so ornamented. The long loops and buttons or "frogs" which covered the whole front of the Hussar dolman date from 1812.

breeches-Roman drawers and tunic

brassard, brassart medieval armor for the arm; today, a badge worn on the arm such as a mourning band of black crêpe, or the fringed white satin ribbon tied on the arm of a young first communicant of the Roman Catholic Church. see *mourning band.*

brassière, bra, brasserole The brasserole of medieval days was a type of camisole worn by little girls, also by women in childbed. The brassière, which was shorter and without sleeves, was a night garment for both sexes from the fourteenth to the seventeenth centuries. Fur-lined, it was a winter piece. A short quilted jacket popular from 1600 to 1670 was called a brassière by Molière. From the Middle Ages to the twentieth century, the feminine bosom was firmly held by a high boned corset. Finally, Paul Poiret, in 1912, designed the modern brassière or bra to wear with a low-cut, soft girdle. see *uplift.*

Brazilian mink see *marmot.*

breacan-feile the older form of Scottish Highland dress, worn until 1746. The piece of cloth, some two yards wide and four to six yards long, was folded in half and pleated and fastened around the hips by a leather belt. The lower part formed the kilt, the upper half being fastened over the left shoulder by a brooch, with the end hanging in back forming the plaid. The right side, which was longest, was tucked into the belt and could also be drawn up over the head in inclement weather. The plaid or tartan of the wearer's family colors was a cloak by day and blanket by night. During the English Prohibition Act of 1746–1782 the breacan-feile hung from the shoulders in back to conceal the wearer's Scottish garb. see *Scottish Highland dress.*

breast knot see *bosom knot.*

breastpin former name for a jeweled brooch. see *pin; brooch.*

breechclout, breechcloth a cloth worn round the body.

breeches, Hussar very tight breeches of the French Directoire period. The favored colors for the breeches were canary yellow and bottle-green with the frock coat usually brown.

breeches, petticoat or **Rhinegrave** came to France on the person of Count Salm Rheingraf in the mid-seventeenth century. The garment was kiltlike or in divided skirt style and ornamented with ruffles, lace and ribbons. A small apron

breeches-canians with codpiece-English-16th C.

breeches-Venetians-with picadills-1572

breeches-Spanish Slops-1623

breeches-trunk hose and canions-English-1624

breeches-petticoat or Rhinegrave 1660

masculine "habit à la française" of coat, waistcoat and breeches-1770's and 1780's

breeches of buckskin-fob seals-Hessian boots-1797

of ribbon loops concealed the front closure. Canions were worn under the petticoat breeches in Louis XIV's day, the canions being tubes of white linen, lace and bowknots tied around the knees.

breeches, Spanish see *Spanish slops.*

breitschwantz from the German for broadtail.

breloque an ornament, charm or seal which formerly hung from a man's watch chain.

bretelles French term for suspenders which hold up trousers or a skirt.

Breton sailor a straw, felt or fabric hat with wide brim turned up evenly all around, originally worn by the peasants of Brittany. Also the name of the shape.

Bretonne lace a net ground worked with an embroidered design in heavy colored thread.

bridal dress In ancient Rome the pagan bride's dress for several centuries was of white wool, symbolizing virginity. The white wool cord girdle tied in a Hercules knot was to be untied only by the husband. The bride wore her hair long and flowing, covered with a flame-colored veil and with a chaplet of vervain or myrtle. The white dress of present-day custom dates to about 1800. see *wedding gown; orange blossoms; train.*

bridal or **carnival lace** see *reticella lace.*

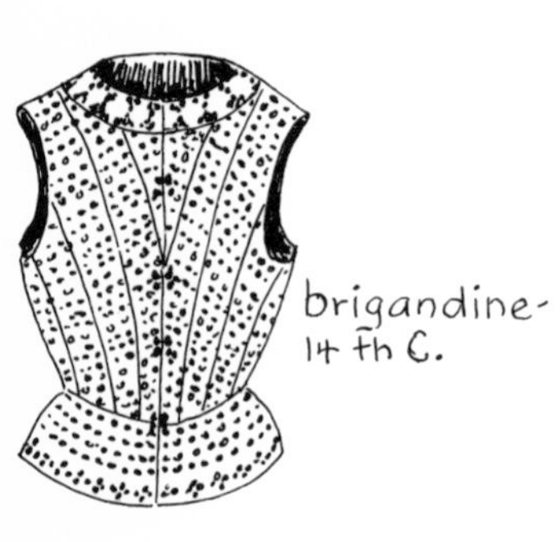

bridge trousers see *pantalons à pont.*

brigandine the first corset, fifteenth century; a piece of armor worn by a soldier knight, consisting of overlapping metal plates and scales sewn between layers of canvas, linen and leather. Such soldiers were called "brigands" and the companies, brigades.

brilliantine a plain or twill-woven fabric of cotton and mohair with a lustrous surface used for men's jacket lining. In toiletry, an oil for dressing the hair.

British warm the short warm, or car coat of suburban living. Also called duffer, duffel or tow coat, it came into use on the ski lift after World War II when surplus English Navy coats were made available to civilians. Worn by men, women and children, often of Tyrolean cloth with wooden toggles and hemp loops.

Brittany work the embroidery of Breton peasants, geometric and floral patterns worked in chainstitch.

broadcloth formerly, cloth made wider than twenty-nine inches. A high grade woolen cloth used especially for men's wear, a lighter fabric being made for women's wear. Woven of the finest felting wool, usually dyed in the raw, but always made in a wide width, thus its name. see *cotton broadcloth.*

broadsilk silk made wider than 18 inches.

broadtail see *karakul.*

broadtail, American South American lamb processed to simulate broadtail. Pelts of animals one day to nine months old, sheared very close.

broadtail, Persian pelts of very young or prematurely born Persian lamb. Lustrous, flat pelts with beautiful moiré design, delicate, costly and fragile.

brocade a luxurious fabric woven on a jacquard loom in an allover pattern of flowers and figures with contrasting colors and gold and silver on a background of satin or twill weave. Originally, a rich silk cloth embroidered in gold and silver; then silk embroidered in arabesques; and, finally, made without metal threads.

brocatelle, brocatel a brocade made in combination of yarns. The design is in high relief of silk or linen upon a plain or satin ground. Used for upholstery and draperies especially in the eighteenth century.

brodequin see *buskin.*

brogue, brogan a sturdy low shoe, of Irish-Scotch origin, for country wear. Originally hobnailed.

brolly a British colloquialism for a tightly furled umbrella.

brooch feminine and masculine, an ornamental piece of jewelry which is fastened to a garment or hat by means of a spiked pin hinged to the back. The brooch may be of simple design or set with jewels and of great beauty and value. see *Celtic brooch; pin.*

brooch masculine, a large, jeweled pin or clasp worn by gentlemen on their velvet or beaver hats in the sixteenth and seventeenth centuries.

Brooks, Donald see *couture, haute.*

brown a color in the red-yellow group; with white added, the shades vary from tan to beige. The darker shades, with black added, deepen to chocolate.

brown, Devonshire see *Devonshire brown.*

Bruges lace a coarse Belgian bobbin-made lace in a weave resembling guipure tape. Coarse weaves are used for table linen and the fine for dresses.

brummaggem old local name of Birmingham, England. The name applied to a counterfeit coin made there and later, to the cheap, tawdy jewelry manufactured there.

brushed wool a knit or woven cloth made of long fibers which have been brushed or teaseled. A fabric appropriate for sweaters, scarfs and trimmings.

Brussels lace any lace made in Brussels. A bobbin-made lace with the ground executed first, the threads following the curves of the pattern. A ground of hexagonal mesh is put in later.

buck see *buckskin.*

Buckinghamshire lace made in England since the sixteenth century. A fine bobbin-made lace with simple accented design.

buckle a fastening device in use since antiquity for leather belts and armor. In the medieval period, buckles held up the long hose and fastened all parts of dress including footwear. Pumps with buckles of brass, steel and silver, some set with pearls and diamonds, either real or false, appeared in the 1650's. Round and oval shapes came in the eighteenth century and by the nineteenth century buckles became fashionable accessories on women's shoes.

bucko, reversed calf see *calf, reversed.*

buckram a coarse open weave of linen or cotton sized with glue and used as far back as the sixteenth century for stiffening parts of dress. It was much used in the period of bombast. It was first made as a floor covering under fine rugs in Bukhara, from which derived the term *buckram.*

buckskin, buck formerly made of deer and elk, but calves and sheep now included. The skin of the buck, yellowish or grayish-white, made strong, soft and pliable. Genuine buckskin is made from small deer of Mexico and South American countries. In the nineteenth century, buckskin was the popular name for a tan-colored leather riding gaiter.

brogue-rawhide with single thong-British Celt

brogue or cuaran-waxed rawhide-Scotch-1632

modern calfskin version of the Highland rawhide cuaran or brogue-origin of the modern ghillie-Scotch

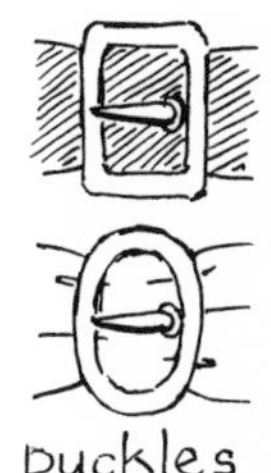
buckles

budge an old English term for lambskin dressed with its wool and used as lining and trimming edge.

buff, buffskin buffalo skin given oil tanning like chamois, turning it into a stout, velvety, brownish-yellow leather. Elk, deer and oxen are dressed the same way.

buffalo The American bison is the largest of American animals, has dark-brown, long shaggy hair over head, shoulders and forelegs. Both European and American species are now nearly extinct. Formerly used for buff leather or buffskin and buffalo robes.

buffalo or American bison

buffalo cloth a cloth with considerable nap which was popular in cold-winter territory. Now replaced by mackinac or mackinaw.

buffcoat the military coat of the sixteenth and seventeenth centuries made of buffalo hide and worn with buff gauntlets. The body was formed of four pieces with deep skirts, some thong-laced in front. Those of the officers were richly embroidered, the sleeves trimmed and edged with lace, buttons and loops, often in gold and silver.

buffonts a scarf of gauze worn with a low-necked gown and puffed over the bosom in "pouter-pigeon" effect. A fashion of the late eighteenth century, advertised in the New England papers of the 1770's.

buffskin see *buff.*

Bulgarian embroidery worked in strong, bright colors on coarse linen for peasant garments. Solidly stitched in silk, gold and silver in flat stitches.

buffcoat or or cassock—16th and 17th C.

bulgha slipper shoes of soft, yellow-colored leather worn by the village people of Egypt.

bull leather see *leather, bull* or *cow.*

bullion embroidery gold wire embroidery, originating with the Phrygians.

bullion lace a lace of gold or silver thread used in robes of state or church vestments. Also, a braid or heavy twisted fringe of gold or silver thread.

buntal a fine white fiber of the Philippine talipot palm, used in the making of straw hats.

bunting, baby see *baby bunting.*

bur'a' modern name for the Egyptian yashmak or face veil of crocheted silk yarn.

Burano lace Italian needlepoint lace with square mesh and cordonnet design made on the island of Burano, Venice. Most of it was a coarser version of Venetian point lace.

burberry cloth a mercerized, waterproofed cloth. Also, a staple cheviot, twill-woven overcoating, topcoating and suiting. A similar cloth of lighter weight is called roseberry cloth.

bure a loosely woven, heavy, brown woolen cloth worn by Roman slaves and the peasants of Gaul. It also served as a chest or table cover and eventually was called bureau, the name of the chest. Used until the seventeenth century.

burgonet, burganet, bourquinotte a bonnetlike helmet or casque similar to an armet with cheek pieces and sometimes a nosepiece. Its distinctive feature was the browpiece or umbril to shade the eyes. First worn by the Burgundians in the fifteenth century, and lasting to the end of the seventeenth century. One of the last types of helmet, which was in use to about 1670.

buriti, burity leaf fiber of the Brazilian palm, used in making straw hats.

burka, burkha, bourkha the traditional cover-all with which a Moslem woman drapes herself when she appears in public. It conceals her from head to foot except for a bit of lace over her eyes to see through. Many women now forego the burka.

burkä or Haik of the Moslem woman when in public

Burmese man-holiday dress-sarong-like skirt-white cotton jacket-plaid pillbox-

Burmese-sarong-like skirt-white cotton shift-two hats-straw and turban-

burl see *slubs.*

Burmese costume see *tamehn; longi.*

burnous, burnoose a long, circular mantle with hood and neck opening worn by Arabian men and women when traveling. With it the men sometimes wear straw hats and the women, veils. The caid or tribal magistrate of Algeria wears a burnous of vermilion cloth with a separate white hood topped by a varicolored wide straw hat. European, mid-nineteenth century, also a hooded cloak of cloth, the hood weighted with silk tassel.

burnous-red cloth with white hood-straw hat-worn by Algerian caid

burnous-traditional Moslem circular cloak for men and women

burnous-French-1850's

burnous-European version-1850's

bush safari jacket-wind and water-proof cotton-1950's

burnsides see *side whiskers.*

burunduki see *chipmunk, Siberian.*

busby a tall fur shako originally worn in the eighteenth century by the Hungarian hussars, artillerymen and engineers. A colored cloth bag hangs from the top on the right side, originally designed to be fastened to the shoulder to ward off sword thrusts. Also another name for the bearskin worn by the English Brigade of Guards.

bush jacket a traditional jacket for the African bush safari, or beach. Made of water-repellent corduroy, heavy linen or cotton, suede-finished and waterproofed. It is furnished with game and shell pockets, breast and hand-warming pockets.

bushel a tailor's thimble. Also, to alter or repair a garment.

bushelman a tailor who repairs or alters a garment.

buskin, brodequin, cothurnus, kothornos first worn in Greek drama, thus "tragic kothornos." Over the centuries, there followed many variations, the distinct feature of boot and sandal being a thick sole of three or four inches which added to the actor's height on the stage. The Roman cothurnus was strapped up the calf of the leg and decorated with an animal paw, tail and perhaps a snout swinging from the top. As the brodequin of the Middle Ages, it was fashioned of soft dyed leathers or costly fabrics brocaded and embroidered.

bust forms of foam rubber-20th C.

bust forms pads separately molded of foam rubber and worn inside the brassière to round out a flat bosom, 1930's. Popularly known as "falsies." Less popular in the 1950's and 1960's because replaced by the padded or contour brassière.

Buster Brown a small boy character of a New York City Sunday newspaper at the beginning of the present century. He was created by artist R. F. Outcault, who was also the originator of the "Yellow Kid." The serial ran for years and years, his dress and Dutch hairdo being copied by many of his admirers. His style of collar is still known as the Buster Brown collar.

Buster Brown and his collar-early 20th C.

Buster Brown collar see *collar, Buster Brown.*

bustle or **tournure,** (French) originally a crinoline, which it replaced in 1869, but with rows of whalebone placed

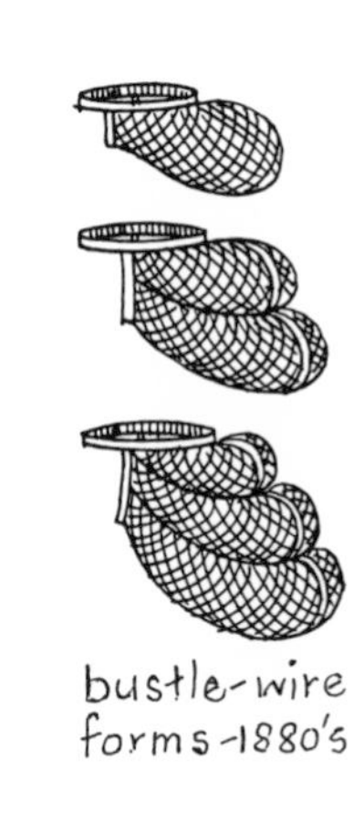
bustle-wire forms-1880's

bustle gown-1870's

only from the sides around the back. The wide flare of the hemline disappeared and a bunched-up tunic or polonaise in back created the bustle look of the 1870's, called "tied-back time." In the 1880's the bustle was fashioned of one, two or three rolls of braided wire or perhaps a stuffed cushion tied around the waist by tapes, all of which disappeared in the 1890's. see *crinoletta.*

butcher's linen a coarse homespun linen formerly used for butchers' jackets and aprons. Also, a white linen, strong and coarse, formerly used for backing men's shirt bosoms.

butterfly sleeves see *patadyong; terno.*

butternut homespun, strong, twilled cotton cloths, woven prior to and during the Civil War; called butternut because they were colored brown with a dye from the butternut tree.

button It is recorded that buttons were worn in the reign of Edward III, 1327–1377. They became very fashionable during the period of Charles I, 1625–1649. Jeweled and sewn to handkerchiefs, they were known as handkerchief buttons. From 1860 buttons were used lavishly on the vest, cuffs and pockets of the male costume. Made of wood, bone, metal or passementerie over a form, the shapes varied from flat, round, ball, olive, to tiny mirrors in the eighteenth century. Hand-painted miniatures on ivory framed with chip diamonds were not rare. Button-making began in the American colonies in 1706, and has been a prosperous manufacturing business ever since. Horn buttons appeared in the nineteenth century. By the middle of the century dyed vegetable ivory became most popular, continuing to the present. In Birmingham, England, 1807, B. Sanders invented the metal button of two discs locked together by turning the edges, and the shell button with metal shank. In the United States in 1827 Samuel Williston of East Hampton, Massachusetts, patented the invention of a machine to produce cloth-covered buttons. The vogue of buttons for fastening and trimming continues in varied shape and size. They are sewn on or attached to garments by shank or holes and are made in bone, plastic, glass, metal and other compositions. Cloth-covered buttons often match suit and coat. Hoop and knot are early words for the button. The Chinese and Japanese use knots of silk or cotton as buttons. see *mother-of-pearl; temple jewelry.*

buttoned-down collar see *collar, buttoned-down.*

buttonhole In a handmade buttonhole, the cut edges are first overcast with a plain stitch and then worked over with a close stitch and a firm looped or single purled edge. It is similar to a blanket stitch, which is much larger and broadly spaced.

buttonhole, bound a slit cut for button-entry, bound with braid or fabric instead of being finished with buttonhole stitchery.

buttonhook an implement for drawing buttons through buttonholes of shoes, spats and gloves, used in the late nineteenth and early twentieth centuries.

Byrd cloth cotton cloth made to the specifications of Admiral Richard E. Byrd for his Polar expeditions; a lightweight fabric, strong and water-repellent, wind-resistant and porous, designed to take the place of the fur parka.

byrnie a coat of chain or linked mail used as body armor by northern Europeans. see *hauberk.*

byrrus, birrus similar to the heavy woolen cloak with cowl of the ancient Romans. Worn all through the Middle Ages by commoners. see *alicula.*

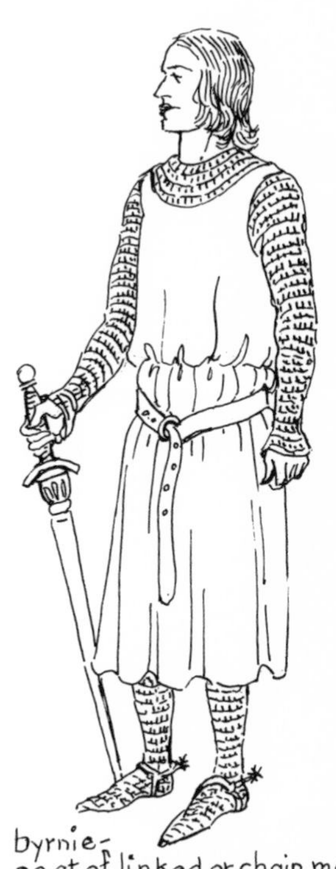

byrnie–
coat of linked or chain mail–
and linen tunic–13th C.–
Gothic and Celtic

Byzantine

cloth hose
with garters-
leather shoes-
9 th c.
cloth hose
with garters-
leather boots-
9 th c.
the white linen camisia-
cloth hose with garters-
leather boots-
4th and 5th c.
empress in
embroidered
silk stola over
long tunic-
6 th c.
emperor wearing
metal lorica
over long sleeve
tunic- white
braccae-
jewel sewn
leather boots-
11 th c.
woolen tunic
over linen camisia-
embroidered braccae-
footless hose-
leather shoes-
11 th c.
leather or wooden
soles with
linen or leather
bandelettes-
9 th c.

Byzantine
boy in camisia with colored bands-fabric or leather hose-4th c.
the linen camisia or undershirt-boots of soft leather(calcei)
soldier wearing braccae and linen camisia-woolen tunic-4th c.
empress wearing white linen or silk camisia under stola of heavy colored silk-4th c.
emperor in white camisia worn under woolen tunic and metal lorica-leather boots-4th c.
early Christian wearing linen camisia under embroidered woolen dalmatic-5th c.
emperor in white camisia under tunic of brocaded silk-4th c.

byssus a name applied to linen, cotton and silk. It is also thought to have meant, more properly, a yellowish flax from which linen was made for mummy cloths.

Byzantine embroidery motifs

Byzantine The Byzantine period runs from about 400 to 1100 A.D. when Byzantium, later called Constantinople and now Istanbul, was the capital of the Roman Empire, Rome itself having fallen to the barbarians. From Constantinople emanated the prevailing mode worn by the upper classes. The making of clothes became an intricate and very important craft for which exorbitant prices were charged. The Emperor Diocletian in 301 A.D. finally settled on a maximum selling price for every article. At the same time he divided the industry into two classes: the workmen who fashioned the outer draped garments, and the artisans who produced, cut and fitted pieces. Those who made the elaborately embroidered flowing robes and cloaks were dress-makers, while the group who made tunics and braccae and were called bracarü or breechmakers, were actually the tailors. The undertunic, the shirt or camisia, was long-sleeved, knee-or ankle-length for men and full-length for women. It was visible at neck, sleeves and hem and usually adorned with strips of embroidery similar to that on the priest's chasuble. For ordinary folk the garment was made of very coarse linen or canvas and worn under the outer woolen tunic. The wearing of two tunics now became common. The Christian Church advocated a covered body in contrast to the sinful exposure of the pagan. Therefore hose were worn, along with shirt and underdrawers. Fascia or tibiale, strips of leather or cloth were wound round the legs, or in winter, there were leggings of cloth, cut, and sewn. Knitting in the round was known then as is revealed by a tube-shaped sock which belonged to an abbé of the seventh century. Fine linen, silk and velvet went into the making of hose for the wealthy, while linen, canvas or a heavy blanket cloth was used for the hose of the commoners. Rich hose were enhanced with colored silk and gold thread embroidery. Breeches and hose were gartered with bandelettes of linen and leather. Beginning with the fourth century the Byzantine mode became more and more sumptuous, and its influence is evident throughout medieval and Renaissance Europe. It was the foundation of Russia's costume, lasting into the twentieth century in the vestments of the church. See illustrations on preceding pages.

Byzantine juppe or tunic-12th C.

C

cabasset an open-faced helmet shaped like a high-crowned hat with a narrow, straight brim, a small sized morion. see *morion.*

cable stitch an overlapping link stitch, by machine or hand, in a serpentine pattern alternating with straight lock stitch to form a raised design.

cabretta a species of Brazilian haired sheep which produces a fine-grained leather like kid which is used for gloves and shoe linings.

cabriolet a bonnet shaped like the cabriolet carriage top and tied under the chin. It was collapsible too; eighteenth century.

caddie, caddy Australian term for the slouch hat.

caddis a plain, thin woolen fabric made since medieval days. When woven of fine wool, the product is similar to flannel.

cadogan a club-shaped knot into which men and women dressed their hair at the nape in the late eighteenth century. A cadogan wig of the 1770's, named after the Earl of Cadogan of earlier date, was worn by the Macaronies. It was looped up and tied by string or the black solitaire and was sometimes held in place by a small comb or, like the ladies' hair, confined in a net.

café au lait a light, creamy brown color.

caffa, kaffa a rich silk made in the Arabic town of Al Kufa in the sixteenth to eighteenth centuries. Also the name of a painted cotton made in India during the sixteenth and seventeenth centuries.

caftan, kaftan a long, coatlike Oriental garment with long sleeves covering the hands, worn by both sexes throughout the Levant. Often worn under an outer cloak. Usually of handsome cloth in striped or brocaded silk, velvet or cotton, held by a cummerbund or hizaam wrapped around the waist. Worn by members of the Mohammedan priesthood, in Turkey, Arabia, Egypt, etc. see *djellaba; litham; gallibaya; jelab; haik; mandeel; djubbeh; yasmak, etc.*

cai-ao a long tunic of rich silk worn by both sexes in Vietnam, with standing collar and long sleeves, buttoned on the right side. The woman's tunic is slit from hip to hem.

caiquan Vietnamese trousers, men's of white linen, women's of black silk or velvet.

cairngorm a quartz crystal, grayish yellow to smoky brown, found especially in the Cairngorm Mountains of Scotland. Formerly considered the gem of Scotland.

calamanco, calimanco a European woolen cloth of satin weave in an imitation of camel's hair. Used for coats and popular until the late eighteenth century. Also a glazed, shiny woolen used for garments as well as quilts. Also the name of a cap made from the cloth.

calash, calèche, Thérèse a cage for the huge eighteenth century coiffures; of black silk sewn on reed or whalebone

cadogan held by comb in wig-1795

caftan worn by man of Uzbek, Russia-19th C.

caftan-traditional Oriental robe of the Levant

felt calotte and hat-cord with bead

Calotte or skullcap-ancient Greece

calpac of astrakhan-Cossack officer-1830

hoops which could be raised or like a carriage hood. A bonnet worn in the eighteenth and nineteenth centuries.

caleçons see *underdrawers.*

Caledonian silk having a small checked pattern of color on a white ground, new in 1817.

calendering a process of finishing cloth to produce a smooth, glazed or watered (moiré) surface.

calf, calfskin a fine-grained leather from cattle a few days to a few weeks old. It is finished in high polish, suede and patent leather, dyed all colors, and especially used for gloves and shoes.

calf, boarded or **box** a novelty leather of the late nineteenth century, calfskin tanned with chrome salts. Rolling it crosswise, then lengthwise, produced square markings on the grain, thus the term *box calf.*

calf, reverse finished heavyweight calfskin dressed on the flesh side. It has a napped surface. Also called bucko because of its resemblance to buckskin.

calf, veal upper leather from large-size or partly grown calf. A soft, heavy, durable, waterproofed leather used principally for ski and woodsmen's boots.

calfskin see *calf.*

calico a cotton textile printed on one side. Used for dresses, aprons etc. It came from Calicut, India, where printed cottons originated in the mid-nineteenth century. At the same time it filled a great need in clothing for families traveling and settling in the American West.

California embroidery the braiding and stitching on leather garments done by the California Indian women of the pre-Spanish period.

California sports shirt a fashion for men of cotton velours, in plain colors, light or dark or striped, with short sleeves, and round, crew or collared necks. The cloth is washable and requires no ironing.

caliga the shoe or sandal of the Roman soldier up to and including the centurion, varying in design according to rank. It was a heavy-soled leather sandal, often hobnailed with iron or bronze nails. Characteristic was the gartering, or ligulae, which involved an elaborate manner of tying above the ankle.

calimanco see *calamanco.*

Callot Soeurs see *couture, haute.*

calotte, calot, zucchetto headgear of ancient Greek origin commonly worn by all classes, the fabric varying according to the wearer's means and position. A small round skullcap covering the tonsure, it was often worn under the hood or crown and gradually acquired significance in color, especially among churchmen. The scarlet zucchetto was a skullcap worn by the clergy at all times to cover the tonsure; fifteenth century.

calpac, calpack, shapka, Cossack cap the Cossack officer's traditional cap of astrakhan.

camail a chain mail hood with buckled fastening worn over an iron skullcap with steel circlet; English, thirteenth century.

camblet see *camlet.*

Cambodian costume see *sampot.*

cambric of linen but also a fine white cotton; a fancy costume fabric glazed on one side, made in Cambrai, France, but originally made in Camerike, Flanders.

Cambridge mixture see *Oxford cloth.*

camel's hair, camel hair There are three types of camel hair, a down type next to the hide, short, soft and silky in beautiful beige shades which may be used natural or dyed; a shorter, moderately coarse fleece between the outer hair and the down; the outer hair, coarse, tough and wiry, reddish-brown to brownish-black. The camel is not shorn or plucked but sheds its hair in clumps which are gathered by the caravan end man. Camels are native to all the desert regions of Asia and Africa, but the finest fiber comes from Mongolia.

camel's hair coat, polo coat of natural-color camel's hair cloth, worn by both men and women. It appeared in the first decade of the twentieth century evolving from the British *wait coat* thrown over the shoulders between periods of play at polo matches.

camel suede a cotton fabric resembling camel's hair cloth.

cameo a gem carved in relief, usually of two colors with the design carved in one color and a second color serving as a background. Of Oriental origin, it may be of shell, onyx or sardonyx. During the reign of Augustus, first Roman emperor 27 B.C.–14 A.D., little cameo portraits became the rage.

camicia rossa see *Garibaldi shirt.*

camisa the Spanish word for the Philippine overbodice made of rengue, a native pineapple cloth. Wide-arched butterfly sleeves with fine embroidery.

camisia in ancient Greece, a short tunic or sleeping garment; the root of the word, in the Byzantine era, an undergarment to protect the robe from body wear. The robes were of heavy, sumptuous fabrics lavishly embroidered and bejeweled. Though two millennia have come and gone since the Ionian camisia was first worn, it still exists as the basic white linen shirt, smock or blouse. *Camisia* in Italian, *camisa* in Spanish, and *kami* to the Orientals.

camisole an underbodice and formerly a corset cover. *Camisole top,* the upper part of a slip, snug over the bosom and held by shoulder straps. *Camisole neckline,* an evening neckline cut straight across the bosom and held by shoulder straps.

camlet, chamlet a closely woven fabric originally made in Turkey of camel's hair and later imitated in Europe; made mostly of Angora wool with silk, linen or cotton. The name came from the place of manufacture in England on the River Camlet. Used in the seventeenth and eighteenth centuries by the American colonists for petticoats, cloaks and hoods. see *paragon.*

camoca, kamaka a rich, figured silk of the Middle Ages. Originally from China but later imported from Persia and elsewhere in Asia.

campaign wig see *wig, campaign.*

Canadian embroidery the name given the primitive and artistic work created by the Indians of Canada. A unique decoration of animal skins with cut and dyed porcupine quills combined with colorful beads.

candy stripe an imitation in fabric of striped candy. bright-colored stripes of varying widths on silks and ribbons.

candys, Persian a shaped and sewn garment of linen or wool with flowing sleeves which fell into set pleats in back of the arm. This was the first appearance of a set-in sleeve. There were carefully arranged pleats in the skirt.

cane, walking stick a costume accessory in vogue in various periods down the centuries, doubtless a follow-up of carrying a sword. In the eleventh century

camisa–traditional overbodice of embroidered gauze–of the Philippines

sticks of applewood are recorded as a French fashion. Dandies of the Italian Renaissance carried small canes like the modern swagger stick. Henry IV of France (1589–1610) is noted as the first owner of a specially designed walking stick. Spaniards in the sixteenth century wore sword, dagger and rapier attached to the belt. In the seventeenth and eighteenth centuries, tall sticks with ivory tops and tasseled cords were à la mode, and the cane often concealed a sword. The tall lady's stick of the last quarter of the eighteenth century was usually of scented wood, tortoise shell or ivory, with a gold or silver top which held powder and perfume. In the nineteenth century the man's stick was cut shorter, to measure from the hand of his slightly bent arm to the ground. The handsome gold-headed cane was carried all through the nineteenth century. During the Prohibition Period in America, a cane concealing a slim bottle was popular, but since the Depression the smart walking stick has virtually disappeared. In the 1920's there was a fad of swagger sticks for women.

canezou—shoulder cape with belted ends—1830's

canepin fine leather made of lambs', kids' and chamois' skins were used for gloves and hairpieces.

canezou a lady's short cape of the 1830's, of sheer muslin with embroidery, worn over the bodice. A false canezou was simply a deep ruffle or bretelle with long ends.

caniche from the French for poodle, a cloth with curly, tufted surface in imitation of the French poodle's coat. Used for baby caps and tiny jackets.

cap of shirred lace—Baby Stuart—English 1634

canions with codpiece canions or canons of the sixteenth century were shaped, short breeches. These were of silk and paned or slashed, the codpiece of silk with embroidery. see *codpiece.*

cannelé a style of weaving producing a channeled or fluted surface; a taffeta-type fabric resembling rep.

cannetille a very fine gold and silver thread twisted spirally, used in embroidery. Also a lace made of the same thread.

cannons, canions tubes of white linen and lace ruffles with bowknots tied around the knees, worn under French petticoat breeches; seventeenth century. see *canions with codpiece.*

canotier French for the straw sailor worn by a sailor of a *canot,* or small boat.

Canton crêpe originally from China and made of silk, today also of rayon. A durable fabric with pebbly surface. Used for dresses and linings.

Canton flannel see *flannel, canton.*

Cantrece the trademark of a kind of nylon yarn with the sheerness and resiliency necessary to the fit and look of a stocking.

canvas a coarse fabric with square mesh, plain-woven and strong, with soft finish or sized. Of linen, cotton, flax, tow or jute, bleached or unbleached. Used for tropical clothing, shoes, stiffening material and other items, such as embroidery canvas.

canvas, Java see *Java canvas.*

cap, Angelus the tied headkerchief peasant cap shown in *The Angelus,* a famous painting of the nineteenth century by the French artist, Jean François Millet.

cap, Balmoral see *bluebonnet.*

cap, Baby Stuart cap of shirred lace with baby lace edging. English, 1634; from the portrait of an infant Stuart prince painted by Van Dyck.

cap, bellboy's see *bellboy's cap.*

cap of
cloth for
country wear-
German-1830's
Jockey cap-
black velvet-
tasseled ribbon
bowknot-French-
1790
trembling cap of
gold cord-pearl
band-Italian-18th C.
cap-
tam-o'-shanter
riding cap of
velvet-French-
1836
cap or
képi of red
cloth-blue
leather-white
braid-silver
buttons-
Italian-1848
Windsor cap
of straw-
velvet ribbon
and ostrich-
French-1864
mobcap of sheer
white lawn and taffeta
ribbon-American-1780's
Glengarry cap with
crease for folding-
blue wool with
feathers, cockade
and evergreen-
Scotch-1805
sailor cap-
"Pie-Pan or
"Pie-Plate"
dark blue
cloth with
black ribbon band-U.S. Navy
Gob
or "white cap"
machine-stitched
cotton-U.S. Navy
cap-
tam-o'-shanter
for cycling-
plaid wool-
black quills-
American-1890's
Glengarry cap-
modern-blue wool-
red and white diced
band-black ribbon
cockade and lappets-
Scotch
cap-
boy's tam-o'-shanter-
plaid woolen cloth with
pompon-English-1890's
helmet-formal hunt cap-
black velvet
reinforced
crown-black
bowknot
denotes
gentleman
rider-
20th C.
overseas cap-
khaki woolen
cloth-officer
U.S. Army-1940's
blue cloth cap-earflaps-
black leather visor-
cockade-black cock
brush-Austrian Tyrolese
soldier-1940's
Gandhi cap of
white undyed
homespun-1940's
Jinnah cap
of karakul-
the tarboosh
worn by men
of Pakistan
boy's military
cloth cap-
leather visor and
chinstrap-French-1860's

cap, boudoir see *boudoir cap.*

cap, calotte see *calotte.*

cap, Cossack see *calpac.*

cap, curler see *boudoir cap.*

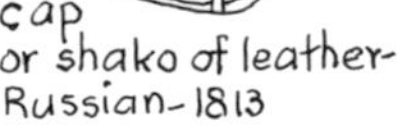

cap or shako of leather-Russian-1813

cap of black cloth-red and black diced band-British Rifle Corps

Deerstalker cap-visor front and back-earlaps and reversible scarlet crown

cap, deerstalker a cloth cap with visor back and front, usually having turn-under earflaps and a reversible crown of scarlet poplin. The style is popularly associated with the character of Sherlock Holmes.

cap of the frontiersman-American-19thC.

cap, duckbill or **jockey cap** an extreme style of cap of straw or felt with a very long peak or visor worn by the merveilleuse of the French Directoire period.

cap, flat English, after 1565; the hat of city folk, merchants, professional and elderly men, also apprentices and servants; the "city flatcap" or "status cap." Queen Elizabeth I passed a law compelling every person over seven years of age in the middle class to wear the cap on Sundays and holidays upon pain of fine. Made of wool, felt or black yarn, it was an important commercial item.

city flat-cap of black wool-English-16th C.

cap-escoffion of brocade-with wimple-Italian-14th C.

cap, forage, képi in the mid-nineteenth century the military shako was replaced by the cap. French troops in Algeria adopted the German kappi, or cap, which was copied in 1857 during the American Civil War and called a forage cap.

cap-"fore and aft"-earflaps-travel and sports-English-19th C.

cap, fore and aft for traveling and sports, of plaid woolen cloth with earflaps; English, 1870's.

cap, fur worn by the American frontiersman; made of fox, squirrel, coonskin or bear; eighteenth century.

fur cap-American frontiersman-18th C.

cap, Gandhi a cap of cotton or woolen cloth, named after the Indian

jeweled Juliet cap at back of head-Italian-15th C.

political leader, Mahatma Gandhi (1869–1948). A cap he wore constantly.

cap, Glengarry not as old as the bluebonnet, dating only from 1805. It was named for Glengarry, Invernessshire, Scotland, the members of the Glengarry Clan being the first wearers. A flat cap with center crease. It has a red checkered tartan band of the Stuarts finished with a black ribbon ending in lappets. The tuft or boss on top is either red or blue. The wearer's clan brooch is worn pinned on the left side.

cap or roundlet-black velvet-gilt embroidery-Italian-16th C.

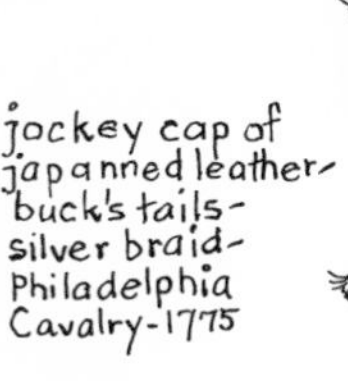

jockey cap of japanned leather-buck's tails-silver braid-Philadelphia Cavalry-1775

cap of red cloth-blue tassel and braid-U.S. Army-1860's

cap, gob worn by the enlisted men of the United States Navy. Of white cotton twill with four-pieced round crown and full-stitched brim. "Shall be worn squarely on the head and shall not be crushed or bent in the middle."

cap-hunting-of japanned leather-French-1833

cap, horned see *cornet.*

cap, jinnah the karakul tarboosh worn by men of Pakistan, named in honor of Mohammed Ali Jinnah, Pakistan's founder and first governor general.

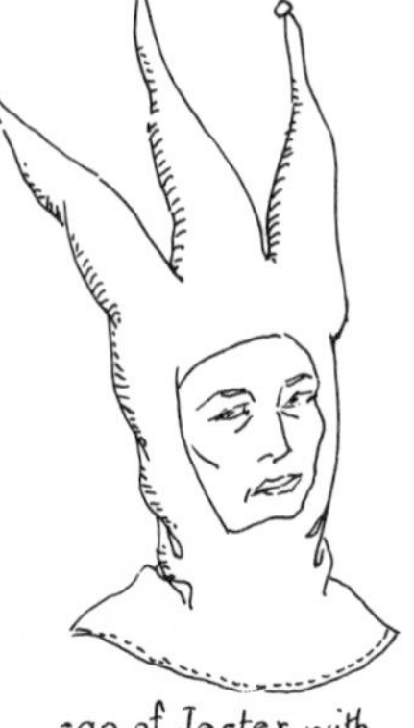

cap of Jester with bells-Medieval

cap like the képi-plaid woolen cloth-New York-1880's

cap, jockey a close-fitting cap with a rounded peak, worn by jockeys in horse races and displaying the owner's stable colors.

cap, Juliet an evening cap of wide, open mesh sewn with pearls and jewels. A tiny calotte usually worn by Juliet in Shakespeare's tragedy. Both renaissance and modern.

mortar-shaped cap of felt or velvet-gauze veil-frontlet-French-14th C.

cap, Liberty see *bonnet, Phrygian.*

cap, Monmouth originally made in the town of Monmouth, England, a knitted, close-fitting cap with turned-up band and hanging crown, a stocking cap, as it is known. It was used by sailors and workmen in the Colonies.

cap, montero a man's cap, popular in Europe and the American colonies for

cap under hat-worn by peasant-Medieval

cap, montero-cloth faced with fur-1858

cap-pillbox over chignon Venetian-1500

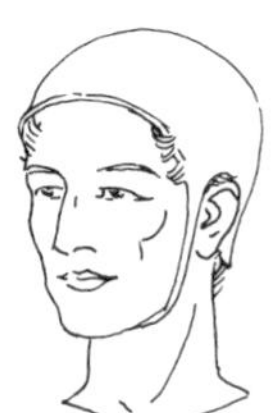
cap-pilos, Greek-pileus, Etruscan or Roman-athlete's cap

cap of red felt-wig or frizzed natural hair-Venetian-1510

cap with attached beaded béret-ostrich plume-English prince-16th C.

jeweled steeple hennin or cap over wimple-Italian-11th C.

sleeping cap-"dormeuse"-sheer lawn, lace and ribbon-English-1770's

cap of varnished leather-metal shield and ostrich-American rifleman-1770

satin negligée cap-shaved head-English-18th C

Queen Victoria's military cap-wide gold braid black visor-1840

cap-sports-red and green wool plaid-tiny feathers-French-1844

Princeton cap-orange and black-college cricket-1870's

Yale cap-blue felt-college cricket-1870's

polo cap-Piping Rock Club-1870's

Windsor cap-worn with the Beatty Tilt-1920's

cap pillbox-black velvet-jeweled buckle-black silk fringe-French-1940's

negligée, hunting and riding. Of cloth or felt with flaps usually of fur which could be turned down; seventeenth century. It is worn today by farmers and hunters. see *Eugénie's wigs.*

cap, negligée see *negligée cap*

cap, overseas World War I; fashioned along Glengarry-cap lines with center crease, of olive drab wool cloth.

cap, ski with flaps to let down and tie under the chin. Has a long, squarish peak or visor.

cap, stocking see *Monmouth cap.*

cap, swordfisherman's of water-repellent cotton with a very long visor of plastic or leather.

cap, toboggan the long, knitted, woolen, pointed stocking cap ending in a tassel or pompon and worn when tobogganing. The same cap was also worn as a nightcap.

cap, trembling see *trembling cap.*

cap, trencher see *mortarboard cap.*

cap, watch a knitted cap of dark blue yarn with turned-up cuff worn by the United States sailors in bad weather.

cap, Windsor of straw with ostrich tips and velvet ribbon; French, 1864.

cap and bells refers to the jester's costume. The jester originated in Byzantium to amuse royalty and reached European courts after the Crusades. His costume included a fool's cap with ass's ears and a petal-scalloped shoulder cape. His scepter was a rattle with miniature head, cap, cape and bells. The custom of having a court jester disappeared in the seventeenth century. see *motley; bells, silver.*

cape, cloak or **mantle** masculine or feminine, a sleeveless outer garment which may be of shoulder length or reach to the ankles. In shape, it may be circular and flaring, or cut and seamed to hang in straight silhouette. Capes became fashionable in men's dress in the eighteenth century when worn with or attached to loose cloth overcoats called wrap-rascals. Since then the cape has been worn by all classes of both sexes and by the military.

cape seal see *seal.*

cape sleeve see *sleeve, cape.*

capeline see *skimmer.*

capes see *lamb shearlings.*

capeskin a washable, glacé-finished, soft leather. Formerly from the Cape of Good Hope in Africa, it now comes from other countries as well.

capibara see *capybara.*

capishaw a hood on a child's winter coat. A Canadian corruption of the French *capuchin.*

capoc see *kapoc.*

capote a long, full military overcoat. In the Levant, a coat of shaggy cloth; also, a medieval cloak worn by women and also a bonnet of the mid-Victorian period with strings and a bavelot or deep ruffle at the back of the head. see *fanchon; coal scuttle bonnet.*

cappa, capa Spanish for cape or cloak. A long cape or cloak, ecclesiastic or academic. Also the scarlet cape of the Spanish toreador.

cappa magna the long, trailing, luxurious cape or cloak, a ceremonial vestment hooded in ermine or silk; red for bishops or cardinals, violet for some other prelates.

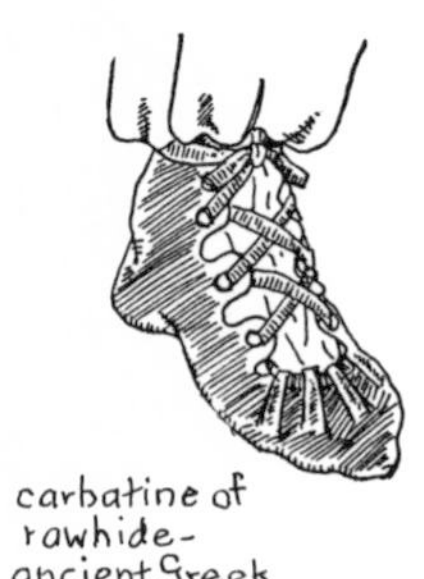
carbatine of rawhide-ancient Greek

capulet-worn by women of the Pyrenees-early 17th C.

caraco-long basque with peplum-French-1780's

cappadine silk floss or the waste obtained after the silk has been reeled off the cocoon.

capri pants same as pedal-pushers but loose and tapered and ending at mid-calf. see *pant lengths, feminine.*

capuchin see *hood, French; capuchine.*

capuchon in medieval times a hooded cape, short or long, worn by men, women and churchmen. The pointed hood developed into the chaperon, a hood with a long tail called a liripipe. see *chaperon.*

capucine French for nasturtium, a fashionable flower at the beginning of the nineteenth century. In hues known as capucine buff, lake, orange, red and yellow.

capulet a feminine short cape and hood with tasseled end worn in the Pyrenees and copied into the mode. Early nineteenth century.

capybara the fur or pelt of the largest living rodent, of South American origin and related to the guinea pig. The skin is similar to pigskin, elastic and soft; used for gloves and leather goods.

car coat see *British warm; cardigan.*

caracal local name for Asiatic cat; a Turkish word meaning black ear, a species of lynx from India, the warm sections of Asia and northern Africa. Reddish brown with black ears tipped with long black hairs, a poor fur, seldom imported. see *wildcat, lynx.*

caraco a gown of the 1780's; a long-waisted, long-sleeved, tight-fitting basque finished with a peplum. Sometimes called à la Créole. Also, a woman's short coat or jacket, usually about waist length; from Turkish alpaca coat called kerrake.

caracul see *karakul.*

carbatine, karbatine the shoe of the earliest Greeks and Romans and primitive Europeans. The British name was "es-cid," meaning protection from hurt, and "brogue" was the Scotch name. Made of one piece of rawhide drawn up by thongs through self-loops of the leather, quite like the modern gillies, the shoe was worn to recent times by the Scotch and Irish and was akin to that of the early American Indians.

carbuncle formerly any polished red stone; now, specifically, a garnet.

carcan French for the iron collar of a criminal, a punishment suppressed in 1832.

carcanet a high jeweled or pearl-beaded collar, often called a dog collar; a necklace or chain of precious stones, late nineteenth and early twentieth centuries. see *carcan.*

cardigan originally a short military jacket or dolman of knit worsted designed and worn by the Earl of Cardigan, a British general in the Crimean War. It was trimmed with fur, braid and buttons. As such, it was worn to World War I. Today, a sweater with or without sleeves and buttoned center front.

carcanet-evening necklace-pearls and jeweled bars 1890's

cardigan jacket was suggested by the Hussar jacket

Cardin, Pierre see *couture, haute.*

cardinal a feminine shoulder cape with hood resembling the bishop's mozetta of scarlet cloth. Seventeenth and eighteenth centuries. see *French hood.*

cardinal or French hood-silk, cloth or velvet, worn by all women of all nations-17th and 18th centuries

cardinal red the color of vestments worn by cardinals, a bright yellowish-red.

cardinal's red hat originated in the black-brimmed hat commonly worn by clergy and laity. Tied under the chin by a cord, it was slung in back when off the head. In 1245 Pope Innocent IV granted the red hat to cardinals. The rank of the wearer is designated by the number of tassels which terminate the cords.

cardinal's red calotte or zucchetto-1630's

caribou; reindeer caribou is the American Indian name. A wild and domestic animal found in northern Canada, United States, Europe and Asia. The animal, along with food and transportation, furnishes fur and leather for clothes and boots. Grayish-brown with white neck, under and hind quarters.

carmagnole a short vest or jacket worn by the French Revolutionists; originally worn by Piedmont workers who came from Carmagnole in Italy. The deputies of Marseilles took the garment to Paris in the 1790's where it was adopted by the Revolutionaries. It buttoned down the front, had pockets, revers and a turned-down collar.

carnelian an orange-red, brown and wax-yellow chalcedony quartz, uniform in texture, of a waxlike surface. Used for jewelry.

carnival, or **bridal lace** see *bridal lace; reticella.*

Caroline spencer a revival of the short jacket invented by Lord Spencer in the 1790's. It was named for Caroline, queen and wife of the British George IV (1820–1830). It was of white kerseymere or black velvet and lined with pale blue satin. see *spencer.*

carriage boot see *boot, carriage.*

cardinal's red biretta-Spanish-17th C.

cardinal's red hat with cords, beads and tassels-14th C.

Carmargnole jacket of the French revolutionists-1790's

Caroline spencer jacket of velvet-English-1820's

carrick-topcoat for driving-1830

carrick a gentleman's greatcoat for driving. Of heavy fawn-colored cloth, double-breasted and with deep collar. It had one, two or three shoulder capes. Of the 1850's and popular to the end of the century. The coach was called carrick, named for a Britisher, John Carrick.

Carrickmacross lace a lace which originated in Ireland. The design is cut from sheer fabric, the edges whipped and then applied to the net with buttonhole stitch. Also, *Carrickmacross guipure* made without net.

carroting a process used in preparing hat furs for felting. It consists of a treatment of nitric acid and quicksilver before the skin is defurred.

cartridge pleats in military dress, small round pleats to hold cartridges; simulated in civilian dress as ornamentation.

cartwheel ruff see *ruff, cartwheel.*

cassock-cloth, velvet or buffskin 18th C.

cartwheel ruff of lawn and lace-wire supportasse-Spanish-16th C.

Carven, Mme. Carmen Mollet see *couture, haute.*

casaque originally a sleeveless short jacket worn over armor and also worn by civilians. Today's term designates the short silk jacket of brilliant colors worn by jockeys in France.

casaquin a short negligée or dressing sacque with full flaring back worn with petticoats at home; eighteenth century.

cascade a fall, frill or ruffle of lace or soft fabric hanging vertically to cascade from neck, waist or skirt. see *jabot.*

Cashin, Bonnie see *couture, haute.*

cashmere the soft wool found under the hair of goats raised in Kashmir, Tibet and the Himalayas. Such goats are now raised in America. The fine, soft wool is mixed with sheeps' wool. Overcoatings, suitings, vestings and sweaters are of Indian commercial cashmere. The famous cashmere shawls are made of the undercoat hair of the cashmere goat.

cashmere work a beautiful, elaborate appliqué embroidery of patterned cashmere cutout motifs which practically covered the large fringed shawls of India, and became a Western fashion in the nineteenth century.

casque a helmet or defensive headpiece in ancient and medieval armor.

casquetel a light open helmet without beaver or visor.

cassimere, kerseymere a soft-textured cloth of medium weight, coarse and fine, plain and twill-woven, in checks, plaids and stripes. Usually made of wool, the name is a variant of cashmere.

Cassini, Oleg see *couture, haute.*

cassock originally the outer coat of the European foot soldiers and horsemen of the seventeenth century; a flaring, knee-length coat of cloth buttoned down the front; also of buff leather and worn by the mousquetaires. The cassock of the clergy is of cloth with a standing collar;

a straight, full-length garment buttoned from neck to hem, worn indoors and out, and sometimes with a sash. Worn under a surplice for church services. Also worn by acolytes and members of vested choirs under a cotta. see *soutane.*

castellated, battlemented the ornamental slashings of the edges of garments into square-cut edges like the crenellated parapets of castle towers; stitching in that style, a fashion of the Middle Ages. see *dagged.*

Castilian red a brilliant red with a yellowish hue, also called Dutch scarlet.

cat, civet see *civet.*

cat, house a tamed member of the Felidae family. The best fur from wild or semiwild animal. It has thicker fur than the domestic cat and is raised all over the globe. The best peltries come from Holland and Belgium, the American grade is poor. Colors are white, black and bluish-gray, used for trimming and children's fur sets.

cat, leopard from China, India and Africa. The best peltries are small and from Somaliland, with very short hair shading from white or pale yellow to tawny and orange with black rosette markings; a durable pelt used for coats, jackets and trimmings.

catercap see *mortarboard.*

Catherine wheel see *farthingale.*

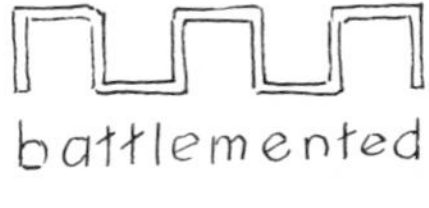

Catherine or St. Catherine's wheel-farthingale or hoop- English and French- 1530 to 1630

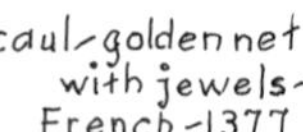

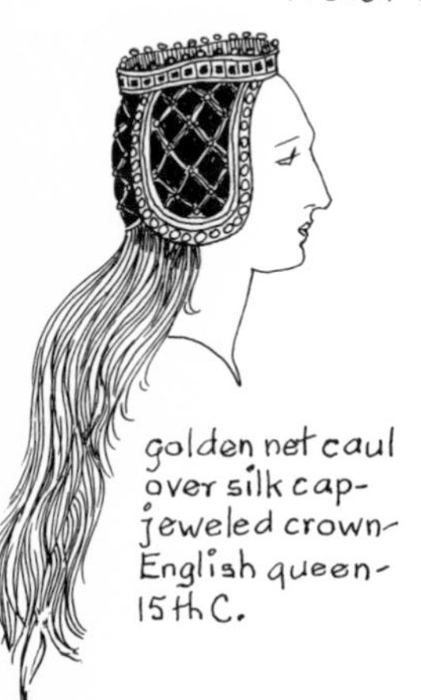

caul a medieval headdress known also as crepin, crestine, crespinette, tressure, tressour. The hair was concealed in silken cases and covered with a heavy net of reticulated gold or silver cord interspersed with pearls, beads or spangles.

caushets an early American and now obsolete word for corsets.

cavalier one of the party loyal to Charles I of England. Their elegant costume included handmade boots with spur leathers and falling tops showing boot hose of sheer white linen, lace-edged, worn to protect costly silk hose inside.

cavalry twill, tricotine a stout twill weave with a decided diagonal cord of wool, cotton or rayon. Used for sportswear and uniforms.

Celanese trademark owned by the Celanese Corporation of America, which produces fashion fibers of Celanese acetate and rayon. see *acetate.*

Celtic brooch Among the many fine pieces of pure gold jewelry unearthed in Ireland during the past few centuries were brooches which fastened an animal skin or a woolen shawl. The characteristic Celtic brooch was formed of a long pin hinged to an open circle; the pin was inserted through the fabric and the end snapped through the circle opening, which was generally finished with two decorative knobs.

cendal a fabric of the Middle Ages, possibly from China, often mentioned. It was still worn in the seventeenth century. It was made very sheer and also heavy and was used for the dress of nobles and ecclesiastics. It could be painted upon and was used for banners.

cepken a richly embroidered bolero-like jacket worn by Turkish men over a fine white shirt and with a sash.

cerevis a visorless type of pillbox cap worn by German university students.

cestus the magic girdle of Venus, a beautifully embroidered sash worn outside the chiton. It encircled the waist and hung down in front. In Greek and Roman mythology, the wearing of it made the lady irresistible to any man she set her heart upon having. Also, a boxer's glove of leather bands loaded with pieces of iron; ancient Rome.

Ceylon native dress see *comboy.*

chadar, chuddar an enveloping black mantle which Persian women always

wore in public. Banned in the 1920's in favor of Western dress, it is still worn by many women in winter. In summer it is now seen in light colors and gay flowered prints, often over Western dress.

chain mail the first form of protective armor, of flexible meshlike metal links and rings.

chainse the body garment of man and woman, noble and peasant, which later became the shirt or chemise. It was made of hemp, linen, sheer wool or even precious silk, the fabric varying in quality according to the wearer's station and means. see *chemise.*

chalcedony a translucent variety of quartz usually pale blue or gray tinge with waxlike luster. Varieties in other colors are known as carnelian, agate, onyx and chrysoprase. Used for jewelry.

chalk stripe cloth with stripes that appear to have been marked with white chalk.

challis, challie formerly a wool and silk fabric, lightweight, now made of fine wool, or wool with rayon or cotton. Usually printed with a delicate floral pattern and used for negligées, dresses, infant's wear and nightgowns. The Anglo-Indian name is *shalee.*

chalwar the very loose, baggy trousers with long drapery that all Persian women wore until the 1890's. The baggy pantaloons of the Turkish and Balkan women reach to the ankles. When spread out, the pantaloons resemble a pillow case open at either end. A blouse is worn with the chalwar and over the blouse the eték or jacket, and very often over that the beautifully embroidered caftan. Albanian pantaloons, when fully draped, require for either man or woman a piece of fabric measuring about ten yards or ninety square feet of material thirty-six inches wide. Persian women were ordered to change this dress to short skirts in 1890, following a trip of their ruler to Paris where he saw the short skirts worn by dancers in the ballet.

chambord a woolen mourning cloth with ribbed surface which may contain silk, rayon or cotton.

chambray a fine-quality gingham with colored warp and white filling with a linen finish. Named after Cambrai, France, where it originated and was first used, for sunbonnets.

chamma-toga-like piece about 4 yards long. The man's right arm left free-the woman's left arm free-Ethiopia

chamma the principal outer garment for Ethiopian men and women, a white cotton toga-like scarf about four yards long. A difference lies in the manner of draping, the man leaving the right arm free while the woman leaves the left arm free. The wearer's rank and position is indicated also by the manner of wearing. The women's chamma is often bordered with a wide band of brilliantly colored embroidery. The traditional Ethiopian robe, it continues to be worn.

chamois a very soft, strong and pliable leather from the skin of the chamois goat; or the skin of sheep or goat with the grain removed. Of a deep yellow color. Used for gloves, garment interlining, pockets.

chamois cloth a yellow-dyed thick cotton fabric napped and sheared to simulate the leather. Used for sportswear and gloves.

champagne color the pale golden color of the sparkling wine, a delicate amber hue.

chandelier earrings very long earrings, sometimes reaching to the shoulders, worn with evening dress. Of delicate design, articulated and set with sparkling gems; early 1960's.

Chaps or chaparajos of deerskin with hair left on sides and front-U.S. cowboy

Chanel, Gabrielle one of the most influential of French twentieth century couturieres. A pioneer in the use of fabrics which have later been universally adopted; in 1915 she introduced rayon or artificial silk into fashion and in the 1920's, wool jersey. Shortly after World War I she presented the elegant and casual tailleur, a skirt with hip-length boxy jacket which has been worn for decades and has become the "Chanel suit, an American classic."

chang-fu the long, plain Chinese robe with standing collar of the Ch'ing Dynasty (1644–1912), the basic dress for several centuries.

chang shan a long gown worn by Chinese men for formal dress, sometimes with a black outer jacket.

Chantilly lace a delicate silk or linen bobbin lace on a simple ground, mostly black but sometimes white. Made formerly at Chantilly but now chiefly at Bayeux.

chaparajos, chaps batwing cowhide overalls open in back and worn over riding trousers as a protection against brush and thorns. California leggings of deerskin with the hair left on the front and sides for warmth and protection.

chaparajos or chaps-batwing style-U.S. cowboy

chaps of angora goat hide-American cowboy-19th C.

chapeau bras see *bicorne.*

chapel de fer, helmet, iron hat worn over the camail or hood of chain mail; early thirteenth and fourteenth centuries. Reappeared as the montauban in the seventeenth century.

chaperon hood and shoulder cape in one, worn by churchmen, nobility and commoners from the twelfth to the sixteenth centuries. The hood acquired a

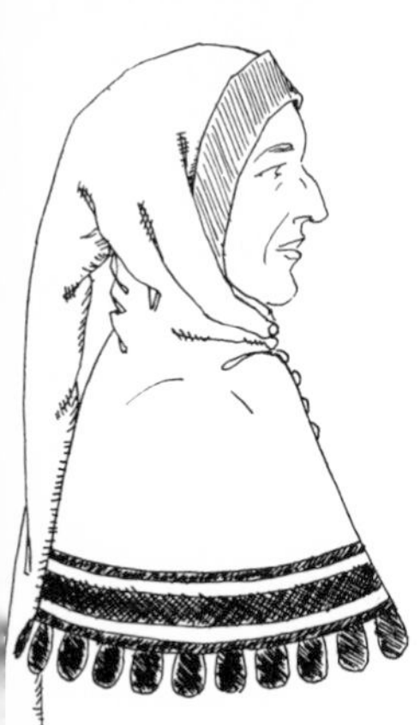

chaperon with liripipe-Medieval

chaperon or hood worn by all classes-men and women-13th C.

chaperon-black velvet with fur-jeweled silk caul-French-1330

chaperon-French-14th C.

chaperon turban-roundlet over coif-chaperon and liripipe pleated and draped-French-15th C.

chaperon-turban with liripipe-Flemish-15th C.

long tail, or liripipe, which was arranged in all manner of styles. see *liripipe.*

chaplet a wreath or garland of leaves or leaves and flowers worn upon the head, bestowed as a mark of honor or symbol of esteem. Also, a necklace of beads.

chaps see *chaparajos.*

chaqueta Spanish name of a heavy cloth or leather jacket worn by Texas cowboys.

charcoal gray a rich, grayed black produced by weaving together black and gray yarn or fiber.

charm bracelet a feminine bracelet usually of flexible links to which bangles or charms are attached, each charm supposedly a gift of remembrance. A contemporary fad.

charm string a necklace of the 1880's composed of small fashionable buttons strung together combining pearl, gilt, silver, cut steel, enameled and others.

charmeuse a formal dress satin new in the early twentieth century. A semilustrous surface with dull back and fine draping quality.

chartreuse a luminous yellowish-green, the color of the liqueur made by the Carthusian monks in France.

charvet elegant silks of irregular twill weaves formerly called Régence but better known as Charvet et Fils de Paris. Used for gentlemen's accessories such as neckwear, mufflers and waistcoats.

chasuble the outer garment of Roman Catholic, Greek and Anglican priests at Mass. Formerly a long, sleeveless cloak, with an opening for the head. *Planeta* in Latin and *pianeta* in modern Italian.

chatelaine, troussoire sixteenth and seventeenth centuries and later, a long gold or silver chain or chains fastened around the waist and pinned to the skirt. It carried keys, mirror, scent box, smelling salts, handkerchief and sewing things, including a pincushion.

chatelaine watch a ladies' watch, often with a hunting case, worn on a long chain and tucked into the waistband. 1890's and 1900's. see *watch, hunting case.*

chatta from Hindu *chata;* East Indian word for umbrella.

chausettes French for socks or anklets. Stockings are called *bas.*

chechia a name for the Berber tashashit or cap with tassel in the same

chechia, red with white scarf and tassel-French Zouave-1830's

chechia or Zouave cap-red cloth with blue tassel-French-1854

cheongsam or Hong Kong sheath of flowered silk

Chesterfield overcoat-black cloth-velvet collar-fly front-silk top hat-1890's

category as the fez and tarboosh. A deep-crowned, flat-topped cap of felt, it is the headgear of the Zouaves and Spahis of Africa, with tassels of varied colors for the different regimental companies.

checks small squares or plaids woven or printed on cloth. see *glen checks; gun club checks; hound's-tooth* and *shepherd's checks.*

cheesecloth unsized cotton of plain weave, thin, soft, bleached or unbleached. Used for garment interlining, covering of padding and in many other ways.

cheetah sometimes sold as leopard, which the fur resembles. It is not adaptable to costume use.

chemise the body garment of medieval times was a chainse which, by the thirteenth century became the sherte or chemise, made of soft wool or linen in a saffron color. A new fabric for the chemise appeared in the thirteenth century, closely woven and sheer, made of fine linen thread. By the nineteenth century the chemise had become a knee-length garment worn next to the body under the corset, the beginning of modern lingerie. Handmade, embroidered, lace-trimmed, it was of soft, white cotton or silk; today, mostly of fine nylon.

chemise, shift, sack, sheath a recurring classic one-piece silhouette in women's fashions dating from ancient Greece and Rome to the French Consulate and First Empire, 1799–1815. It returned in 1914 and was generally worn by 1925. The chemise hangs straight from the shoulders to the hem, with no tuck at the waist, though it may be loosely fitted or sashed. In 1950 *Vogue* magazine displayed a knitted T-shirt dress, forerunner of a revival in 1954. Paris designers presented their versions, and in 1958 Saint Laurent sponsored the Trapeze or A-line with a slight flare in the side seams. see *cheongsam; shift.*

chemise à la reine a popular style from 1781, worn by Marie Antoinette. A comparatively simple dress of sheer cotton or light silk but noteworthy as being the introduction of the lingerie frock into Europe. It was nevertheless a luxury, as cottons and prints were imported from India. Late eighteenth and early nineteenth centuries.

chemisette an underbodice of lawn and lace with short or long sleeves. Worn to supply sleeves and cover the cutaway neck of a jumper frock. A style for women and girls of the late nineteenth and early twentieth centuries. see *guimpe.*

chenille French for caterpillar. A yarn with protruding fibers like the caterpillar's tufts. It is used for embroideries and fringes and woven into luxurious carpets. Also used for knitted or crocheted accessories.

chenille embroidery originated in France; the design is worked with fine chenille yarn of various colors in flat stitches producing a velvety texture.

chenille lace a French needlepoint of the eighteenth century, a six-sided mesh ground net with the design outlined in white chenille.

cheongsam the modern Chinese sheath, popularly known as the Hong Kong sheath. It is straight, high-collared, short-sleeved, of silk or cotton with a slit on one side of the skirt. The length of the slit prescribed by Chinese stylists is eight to ten inches, and not extending more than four or five inches above the knee.

cherusse or **Betsie** see *Betsie.*

chesterfield a classic knee-length overcoat of the late nineteenth and early twentieth centuries, named after the Earl of Chesterfield. A single-chested fly-front coat of black cloth with velvet collar and plain back.

cheviot a woolen or worsted fabric used for suits and overcoats. Twill-woven from the coarse, shaggy wool of the sheep of the Cheviot Hills on the border between England and Scotland. Also the name of a shirting, a plain or twilled heavy cotton with soft finish.

chevron an inverted V device or motif used on heraldic shields. Also one or more V-shaped bars worn on the sleeve of noncommissioned officers to indicate rank. Chevron, broken twill, herringbone, zigzag fishbone pattern, all similar, of woven cloth. Used for top-coats, suits and sports.

chicken skin used formerly for fans and gloves. The gloves, worn overnight by both men and women as a beauty aid for the hands, proved effective, but in 1778, a perfumer wrote that these gloves were really made of a strong, thin leather dressed with almonds and spermaceti.

chiffon a lightweight transparent fabric, dyed or printed. Of silk, rayon or cotton, and durable despite its flimsiness.

chiffon velvet see *velvet, chiffon.*

chignon hair twisted into a knot at the nape or top of the head, a coif copied down the ages. see *Psyche knot.*

Chignon—the classic coiffure of Venus de Milo

chimere a sleeveless robe of black or red satin worn by Anglican or Episcopal bishops over the rochette.

chimneypot a name applied to the tall top hat when of black felt.

China mink see *mink, China.*

China silk originally a pure silk fabric made in China. Now a plain-woven, lightweight, lustrous fabric of silk or rayon, used for slips and dress linings.

chinchilla a very soft, beautiful fur of delicate bluish-gray with black markings; fragile, costly and scarce. A squirrel-like beautiful fur of delicate bluish-gray with black markings; fragile, costly, and scarce. The fashion craze of the late nineteenth century practically exterminated the chinchilla, a squirrel-like rodent native to the Andes of Peru and Bolivia. Now being bred in the United States and Canada, but still rare. Used by the Incas for mantles and also woven into cloth. The fur is used today for coats, jackets and trimming.

chinchilla cloth a heavy double-woven fabric with a napped surface of tufts and nubs, similar to petersham but softer and finer. Not an imitation of chinchilla fur. Used for children's coats, bonnets and trimming.

chinchilla rabbit or **coney** the result of a French experiment with a black-and-white hare now raised in California. A feathery salt-and-pepper fur, fairly durable and used for jackets. see *rabbit.*

chinchilla rat see *rat.*

chinchilla squirrel processed to simulate chinchilla.

chiné French for the Chinese technique of coloring the warp threads before weaving, thereby producing a silk of variegated or mottled effect. Also, a fabric with a chiné design.

Chinese damask see *damask, Chinese.*

Chinese dress see *balshan; cheongsam; koo; shan.*

chinchilla—length, 9"—tail, 5"

Chinese—blouse—pantaloons and apron

Chinese everyday dress—same for men and women—

Chinese woman's field-dress

Chinese embroidery originally, painted designs worked over in satin stitch with floss and metal threads. Embroidered on silk and velvet for garments, screens, hangings and many other objects.

Chinese sable see *marten, Himalayan.*

chin piece a piece of armor to protect the chin.

chin scarf or **medieval headdress** a stiff linen toque-shaped cap, often without top, the scarf or barbette passing under the cap and under the chin. From the twelfth century on. see *barbette.*

chin strap a leather strap to hold cap, hat or helmet on the head; a strap worn at night to prevent a sagging chin.

chino a twilled cotton fabric of stout texture for uniforms, riding togs, work clothes, sports, etc. In the nineteenth century the British in India dyed their white uniforms with coffee, curry powder, mulberry juice, etc., calling them by the Hindu name khaki or dust-color. The Americans in the Philippines followed suit and named the cloth chino.

chintz originally, in the twelfth century, a printed or stained calico from India. Now, cotton cloth printed with colorful bird motifs and flowers, and usually glazed. Used for both costume and interior decoration.

chipmunk a short-haired, silky fur popular for coat linings; from the North American ground squirrel, smaller than the gray species, reddish-brown and gray with black-and-white striped back and short-haired silky fur.

chipmunk, Siberian burunduki a striped ground squirrel with more stripes than the American rodent, usually four white and five black. A fragile skin used for lining, trimming and jackets. Also from China.

chirinka a former Russian feminine accessory, a square of silk or muslin embroidered in metallic threads and fringed with tassels. An elaborate kerchief, it was held in the hand when going to church, a party or any ceremony.

chiripa the South American gaucho's skirt worn over very full long pantaloons. It is formed of a large, square, colored woolen blanket with the center cut out for the waist and held up by a heavy silver belt of chains and buckle.

chiton the basic garment of ancient Greece worn by both sexes with or without belt. There were two distinct styles, the feminine version reaching to the ankles and the masculine to the knees. The rectangular piece of woolen or linen cloth was sewn partway up the sides and fastened on the shoulders by fibulae. Usually purple, red, blue or saffron. Roman and Athenian women wore a full-length chiton which could be girded up short for sports or let down for housewear. The fold above the belt was a rectangle of woolen cloth of variable size worn over the

chiton and himation
ancient Greece

chiton, unsewn and fastened on the shoulders. The bloused section was called the kolpos or deploidion and was carefully arranged in artistic folds and weighted with lead pellets.

chitterlings linen frills which appeared on the gentleman's shirt front in the late eighteenth century and were worn through the nineteenth.

chivarras a colloquialism for leggings in southwestern United States and Mexico.

chlamys in ancient Greece a light summer mantle worn chiefly by young people on horseback. Of woolen cloth, it was a rectangle about one by two yards with weights at the four corners to prevent its blowing. It also served as a protection against rain and as a blanket when sleeping. In ancient Rome the chlamys was a cape of woolen cloth semicircular in shape fastened on the right shoulder or in front by buckle or fibula. It passed into Byzantine dress and was worn for centuries more in Europe as a sports and traveling piece.

chogā Nehru tunic, a Mohammedan tailored coat slightly fitted, worn by East Indian men, principally in Kashmir and the Punjab. Presently in the Western mode. Brought out in London, 1967, and followed by the Paris-made suit for women. Usually of black silk crepe, a tunic-length jacket, most often buttoned down center front with a standing collar. Also called guru, Mao, oriental, meditation or mandarin. Of woolen cloth, cotton, heavy linen, velvet or handsome silk, it is knee-length, has side slits, a standing collar and is buttoned down the center front.

chogā-Moslem
outer coat of white
linen or brocade
for formal wear

choker a woman's high, snug collar in fabric, fur or jeweled form such as one or more rows of pearls. A fashion of the late nineteenth century continuing into the twentieth.

choker collar see *collar, choker.*

chola derby see *derby, chola.*

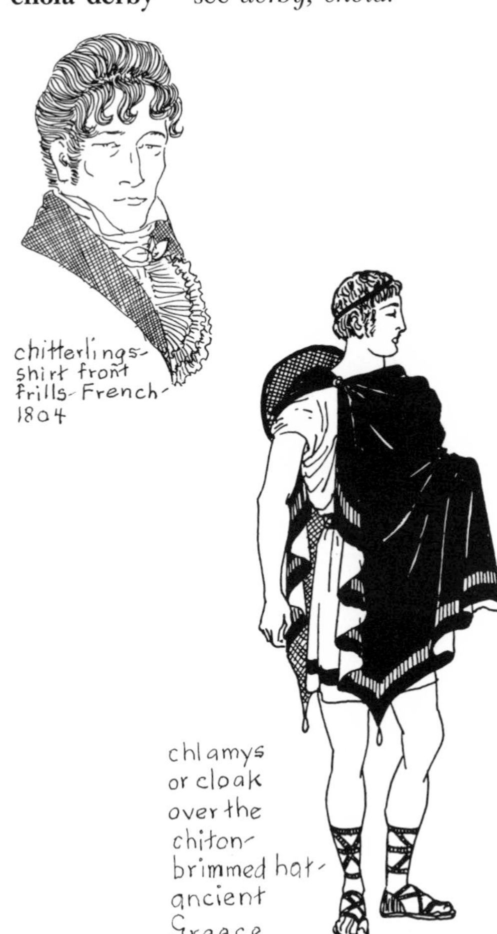

chitterlings-
shirt front
frills-French-
1804

chlamys
or cloak
over the
chiton-
brimmed hat-
ancient
Greece

cholee or choli-blouse worn under the sari-Hindu

choli, cholee the short-waisted cotton blouse with V-neck and short sleeves that the Hindu woman wears with the sari. In the north and central part of India a short, full skirt, the ihenga, is usually worn with the choli.

chopines originally from Turkey, reaching Europe by way of Venice in the sixteenth century. "Chapineys", the European name, were high wooden stilts designed for sand and mud and suited the Venetian ladies, who traveled by gondola. Chopines were popular in Italy and Spain, but seen only occasionally in northern Europe.

chopine of wood-jeweled strap-Turkish-16th C.

chorus shirt see *ballet* or *chorus shirt.*

chou French for cabbage; in fashion, a cabbage-shaped soft rosette of tulls, lace, velvet and ribbon used as a feminine dress ornament at the neck or on hats. Late nineteenth century.

chrisom a veil, robe or mantle signifying innocence, thrown over an infant at a christening ceremony.

chrome leather see *leather, chrome.*

chromo embroidery work in which the design to be embroidered is printed on a paper pattern laid on the fabric and worked over in satin stitches.

chukker or polo shirt-fine white cotton knit-20th C.

chrysoberyl a semiprecious stone; varieties are *chrysolite,* pale yellow to green yellow; *alexandrite,* green in daylight, red in artificial light; *cymophane,* a chrysoberyl cat's-eye.

chrysoprase a green form of chalcedony quartz, used for jewelry.

chuddar a form of the Hindu word *cadar,* the name for bright green, the color of billiard cloth; in Anglo-Indian usage, a square of fine wool worn as a shawl. see *chador.*

chukka-of East Indian origin for polo play-20th C.

chukka a two-eyelet, ankle-high boot of suede or smooth leather with rubber or leather soles. The low jodhpur boot fastens with a strap. The two names are of East Indian origin, chukka being a period of play in polo and jodhpurs the riding breeches with which the boot is worn. see *jodhpurs; riding breeches.*

chukker a man's pull-over sports shirt, round-necked, short-sleeved, of knitted soft white cotton. see *polo shirt.*

church or **laid embroidery** work in which the design in silk or metal threads is laid on the fabric and held in place by tiny couching stitches.

cidaris the tiara of ancient Persian kings and Jewish high priests.

cigar case a gentleman's pocket case of leather or metal, made to hold cigars.

cigarette case a small case to hold cigarettes, often of silver or gold and jeweled, carried by fashionable men and women in the first half of the twentieth century. Ladies also carried jeweled cigarette holders of amber or ivory.

cilice a haircloth shirt formerly worn by monks as a penance.

cimier an ornament forming the apex or crest atop the helmet worn in ancient times and down the centuries. Its forms have ranged from the floating lambrequin, plumage, horses' tails, carved birds and fantastic animals, most of which were movable when the wearer was in action. see *cointoise.*

circassienne a fabric of wool and cotton mixture with a diagonal weave.

circassienne gown a bell-shaped var-

iation of the polonaise, with three bouffant panniers drawn up on silk cords. Made of two different-colored silks, the underskirt of ankle length.

circingle see *surcingle.*

circular skirt see *skirt, circular.*

civet the popular name for the so-called North American civet cat, really little spotted skunk, a species of skunk but without the disagreeable odor. The underwool is short, thick and dark, with irregular markings. Used for coats, jackets and trimmings. Also bleached and dyed to simulate fitch and marten.

civetta a native cat of Africa and used more for its secretion than fur. It is two or three feet long and brownish-gray with black bands and spots on body and tail. It produces most of the commercial civet used as a perfume base.

clavi purple stripes or badges which told the wearer's rank and profession in ancient Rome. The stripes were either woven or sewn to the toga and tunic, a wide one for a senator and narrow ones for knights. Also, narrow decorated panels used vertically.

claw-hammer coat evening dress coat in the swallow-tail fashion of two long tapering skirts falling in back. see *tails.*

clay-worsted serges, diagonals and worsteds woven after the process of Clay, Huddersfield, England, and so named. Fabrics used for men's and women's suits.

clip, clip brooch a twentieth century decorative jeweled ornament that is fastened by a strong clip to an edge of a garment, such as collar, lapel or neckline.

cloak following the mantles of the ancient Greeks, Romans and Byzantines, a shorter, bell-shaped outer garment developed as a wrap or coat during the Middle Ages. The name is from cloke or cloche, French for bell, finally becoming cloak in English.

cloak, Armenian see *Armenian cloak.*

cloak, balagnie see *balagnie cloak.*

cloak, Inverness see *Inverness cloak.*

cloak, Kerry see *Kerry cloak*

cloak, opera see *opera cloak.*

cloche a small and tight hat with the narrowest of brims, became popular as the bobbed head of the 1920's evolved into the shingle. Of felt, both for summer and winter, it enveloped the head to the neck in back and came to the eyes in front. Reboux of Paris produced this hat with no decoration but the ornamental shaping of the felt. This was relieved occasionally by a grosgrain ribbon band or a jeweled pin. Frequently revived but popular into the mid-thirties.

clock a decorative line of colored silk embroidery which eliminated the former ankle-shaping machine work on stockings.

clogs see *pattens.*

cloisonné bracelets, necklaces, rings, buttons and bric-a-brac inlaid with enamel. Formerly applied to precious metal but today mostly on brass.

cloister cloth a drapery fabric in a rough, canvaslike weave similar to monk's cloth.

cloqué or **cloquet** French for blistered or swelling; thus, silk or other cloth in a blistered effect. The cloth is backed with a very thin lining and then machine- or hand-stitched in an allover pattern to give the blistered surface. An Americanism for the French word is "cloky."

cloth see specific terms of *cloth; airplane, Albert, American, Astrakan, bodkin, Balmoral, beaver, buffalo, burberry, chamois, chinchilla, coronation, convent, druids, forestry, Granada, grass, hair, honeycomb, moleskin, monk's, Moorish, mummy, Orleans, Palm Beach, parashute, peasant, pilot, pima, polo, Saxony, Shetland, Sicilian, suede, tapa, Tibet, tinsel, Venetian, waffle, west of England.*

clothes a general term for pieces of attire worn by men and women.

clothes horse a stand or frame of wood or iron, upon which to hang garments while the wearer lounged.

cloud a light, fluffy, three-cornered head scarf of lace, net or loosely knitted silk or yarn, worn in the evening, especially in winter. The seventeenth century spelling was clout. Other names in use to the end of the nineteenth century were opera hood and Molly hood.

clown costume a masquerade dress in cotton cloth with neck, wrist and ankle ruffs, and a peaked hat with a pompon which evolved from the traditional Pierrot costume of the Italian commedia dell'arte.

club bow tie a straight-cut bow tie for evening wear, white with tailcoat and black with dinner coat.

Cluny lace a lace of Cluny, France, of heavy colored linen or cotton thread. Originally a meshed net with a darned design of wheels, triangles, etc. A coarse, bobbin lace.

cnemis, greaves leggings of bronze, brass or hard leather worn with sandals by the Greek and Roman military man as a protection to the left from knee to ankle. Those of metal were leather-lined.

coal scuttle bonnet see *bonnet, coal scuttle.*

coal tar colors mauve was the first obtained, in the manufacture of coal gas, separated into fractions which upon further refining yielded many compounds. These yielded dyes such as aniline, phthaliens, indigo and alizarin for modern manufacture. The process was discovered by Sir W. H. Perkin, English chemist (1838–1907).

coat an outer garment for the upper part of the body, but lengths vary: floor length; full length to the hemline; three-quarter length; above or below the knee, depending on the fashion. see *cote.*

coat, all-purpose a coat for all kinds of weather and temperatures, made of water-repellent and stain resistant fabrics, often reversible.

coat, barrow see *barrow coat.*

coat, blanket see *blanket coat.*

coat, box see *carrick.*

coat, British lounge often worn instead of the cutaway or morning coat. Black cheviot with braid-bound or bluff edge and waistcoat to match, heavy silk four-in-hand scarf and gray striped trousers. Worn with a homburg or derby.

coat, camel's hair see *camel's hair coat.*

coatee a single-chested coat buttoned to the waist in front but with skirts in back, as in the West Point dress uniform.

coat, car see *British warm.*

coat, coolie see *coolie coat.*

coat, English or Prince Albert see *frockcoat.*

coat, guard's see *guard's coat.*

coat, polo see *polo coat.*

coat, raccoon see *raccoon coat.*

coat, Red River see *Red River coat.*

coat, sleep see *sleep coat.*

coat, swallowtail see *tails.*

coat, tow see *British warm.*

coat, toggle see *toggle coat.*

coat, trench see *veldt coat.*

coat, walking see *frock coat.*

coat of mail a hauberk or tunic of metal scales or chain mail worn by the medieval soldier.

coat-tails the skirts of a man's frock-coat, cutaway or swallowtail coat. see *cutaway coat.*

cobra any of several very venomous snakes of the genus naja (serpent of the hood). The largest length is five feet, variable in color. Used for women's shoes and handbags.

coburg a lightweight cloth, originally from Germany, worsted, silk or cotton; often used for mourning apparel.

cockade, French **cocarde** a rosette of pleated ribbon, originally a military insignia, of a different color for each nation. Eighteenth and early nineteenth centuries.

cocked hat see *hat, cocked.*

cockers, cokers, cocours old English for untanned leather half-boots and gaiters and for knitted woolen leggings without feet, worn by country men. The term was still used in the nineteenth century.

cocktail dress a fashion which originated in the late 1940's, a semiformal dress for late afternoon and evening.

codpiece a small bag or box that concealed the front opening of men's breeches. It was of fabric, usually of silk and often elaborately decorated. Codpiece and trunk hose were secured to the doublet by points and lacings. A fashion of the European courts, of Spanish origin. It was popular in the fifteenth and sixteenth centuries. Considered a sign of virility, the container really served to hold

British lounge coat often worn instead of cutaway—contemporary

coatee of the cadet—American

coif-Norman and English-9th C.

coif-French bob-circa 1468

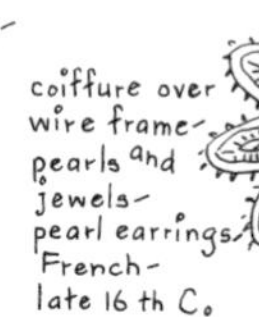

coif Zazzera-yellow silk wig-Italian-15th C.

coiffure over wire frame-pearls and jewels-pearl earrings-French-late 16 th C.

attifet coiffure-hair dressed over wire frame-bandeau of gold enamel and jewels-French-1585

coiffure with love lock-Swedish-1643

widow's coif-black silk with pearls-heartbreaker curls-French-1663

coiffure-wired ringlets tied with pearl-weighted bowknots-spotted breast feathers-Spanish-1650's

coiffure à la moutonne (lam chignon in back-Dutch-1632

coiffure fontange-bonnet à la Fontanges-framework, commode or palisade-1680's

coiffure "tête de chou"-cabbage head-French-1680's

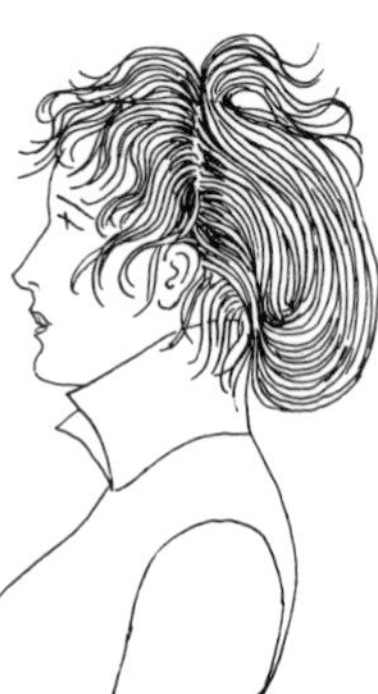

coiffure in cadogan style worn by Josephine-1798

coiffure-hedgehog with falls sides and back-1780's

coiffure Titus-velvet ribbon filet-French-1802

coiffure-Byronesque hairdo of the period-English-1820

coiffure-"waterfall"-tiny ribbon hat-1860's

money, handkerchief and sometimes, bonbons.

coiffure any style or method of dressing the hair. see *bob, curls;* illustrations, for specific types.

coin dots an all-over pattern of dots usually about five eighths of an inch in diameter.

cointise, quintise the scarf or favor either worn over a lady's headdress or presented to a knight who wore it floating from his jousting helmet in the tournament. The scarf was also called mantling or lambrequin in heraldry. see *cimier; heaume.*

cokers see *cockers.*

colberteen, colbertine a coarse French lace resembling net named for Jean-Baptiste Colbert, one of the ministers of Louis XIV.

cold wave see *permanent wave.*

collar originally and for centuries part of a linen shirt or chemise. It then became an extra fabric piece finishing the neck of the garment, growing to an extravagant addition of yards of sheer lawn and costly lace in falling bands and ruffs. The French Revolution did away with frills and laces, and in the nineteenth century the man's collar became a simple, starched, detached white linen. In the twentieth century it again was joined to the shirt. see *falling band; ruff; gallila.*

collar, Buster Brown the stiffly starched lay-down collar with soft bow popularized by the newspaper serial character, a small boy, in the 1900's.

collar, buttoned-down a style in which the two collar points are held in place by small buttons.

collar, choker the fashionable high collar of the 1890's which lasted into the

first decade of the twentieth century. A woman's collar of tucked or crushed fabric, often boned to the ear tips.

collar, clerical or **Roman** a stiff standing collar buttoned in back, with attached tabs. see *rabbi.*

collar, coat for various types, see illustrations.

collar, dog during the time when the very high dress or shirtwaist collar was in fashion, a tight necklace of several rows of pearls held in line by tiny bars studded with diamonds or other stones, was worn with evening dress.

collar, Dutch a simple, lay-down collar with round or pointed ends.

collar, Eton a starched white linen, folded, lay-down, rather wide collar with round corners worn with four-in-hand scarf. The Etonian uniform dates from 1820 when the boys were ordered to wear mourning clothes at the funeral of George III.

collar, fused a collar in which wilting and shrinking have been eliminated by the use of a specially prepared interlining which is laminated to the outer layers. circa 1920's.

collar, Gladstone a comfortable standing collar with flaring points worn with a silk scarf in a bowknot. Worn in the 1850's by William Ewart Gladstone, Prime Minister of Great Britain.

collar, mandarin, Nehru or Johnny a standing collar about one and one half inches high attached to a close-fitting neckline of coat, jacket, dress or blouse. Nehru was the name given the jaunty collar in 1967. see *Mao suit.*

collar, Medici shaped like the falling band but pleated and wired, rising from a low décolletage and standing high in back. Originating in Italy, it was worn by the Medici women, including Queen Marie of France, 1573–1642.

collar, moat an upstanding narrow collar, bateau neckline; English, thirteenth century.

collar, mourning of black velvet on a light-colored coat, worn by the refugee aristocrat on his return to France as a sign of mourning for Louis XVI. The Revolutionist wore a red collar on his coat, giving rise to many street quarrels between the Blacks and the Reds.

collar, mousquetaire turned-down collar or whisk of starched linen with points; the style revived in feminine fashion in the eighteenth, nineteenth and twentieth centuries. see *bertha; palatine.*

collar, Napoléon a high-standing, folded-down collar with wide revers and black satin cravat.

collar, Peter Pan a lay-down round collar about two or three inches wide, attached to a round neck, closing in front with rounded ends. Named for the hero of the play "Peter Pan" by Sir James Barrie, 1904.

collar, Piccadilly see *wing collar.*

collar, poet's from the Ossianic or Romantic period; the soft, unstarched collar of a shirt or blouse, preferred to a bulky cravat, especially among writers and artists. It was notably worn by three contemporary English poets; Lord Byron (1788–1824), Percy Bysshe Shelley (1792–1822), and John Keats (1795–1821).

collar, poke a stiff standing collar with slight front opening and points softly bent forward. Early twentieth century.

collar, Robespierre a high-standing coat collar with deep fold and broad pointed revers filled in with a softly falling lawn jabot.

collar, roll a long collar without peak or notch. Also called shawl collar.

collar, Roman see *collar, clerical.*

collar, sailor part of the sailor's uniform; two thicknesses of cloth, broad and square in back, narrowing to a V-pointed neckline in front.

collar, shawl see *roll collar.*

collar, slotted a man's soft shirt collar with slots on the under side to hold tiny plastic stays which keep the collar in shape.

collar, surplice see *surplice collar.*

collar, tuxedo on a woman's coat, a long straight fold forming the collar going around the neck and down the front edges to the ends of jacket or coat.

collar, Van Dyck see *falling band.*

collar, Windsor the early nineteen-thirties, widespread, cutaway collar adopted by the popular Prince of Wales, later the Duke of Windsor. Worn with a tie arrayed in a fairly large and intricately tied knot, called the Windsor knot.

high coat collar worn by Robespierre-French-1794

high collar-black satin cravat-habit, red with gold embroidery-Napoleon

collar-black velvet-mourning for Louis XVI of France-1805

collar worn by poets-Byron, Shelley, Keats-1830's

choker collar of the late 19th and early 20th C's

collar worn with Eton jacket and top hat by boys of Eton College

collar worn by Gladstone-Prime Minister of Britain-mid-19th C.

Collar-narrow and standing-20th C.

Collars

white linen and white scarf-French 1814

collar attached to shirt-English-1830

starched white linen and black silk-French-1808

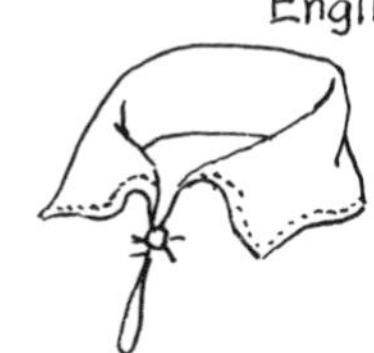

collar attached to shirt-long silk tie-English-1830's

collar attached to shirt-plaid silk tie-French-1840's

white linen collar-silk tie-French-1820's

collar attached to shirt-black silk tie-worn by Abraham Lincoln-1862

collar attached to shirt-silk scarf-New York-1868

separate, starched collar-narrow silk tie 1862

separate starched collar-silk cravat-1870's

starched collar-striped muslin-silk cravat-French-1870's

high collar and silk scarf-English-1890's

high starched collar-silk cravat-American-1890's

formal dress-wing collar with bow tie of fine white piqué-English-1890's

wing collar-bow tie-American-1890's

linen collar-round corners-silk cravat-1913

soft buttoned-down collar-attached to shirt-1930's

collar, wing, white wings, Piccadilly a standing collar with pointed turned-back tabs. Worn for formal day or evening dress, beginning in the 1880's.

collarette a high-ruched feminine collar of the sixteenth century worn inside any outer flaring collar.

colletin a piece of plate armor in combination standing collar and shoulder piece which protected neck and shoulders; Middle Ages.

cologne see *eau de cologne.*

color *Hue* is the name of a color or color family whether light or dark, dull or bright, such as the blue-greens; *value* refers to the darkness or lightness of a color, *intensity* to the dullness or brightness. Colors in fashion are constantly changing and different names, generally self-descriptive, appear each season. The relationship of colors can be easily determined by referring to a color wheel.

comb a toothed toilet article for cleaning and dressing the hair which dates back to antiquity. Made of ivory in Egypt and of boxwood by Greeks, Romans and Germans. Bone and horn combs have been found in Swiss lake-dwellings and have come to light in early Christian tombs. Modern machinery has added rubber, celluloid and plastic to the list of usable materials.

combination see *teddy.*

combing an advanced form of carding, separating the choice fibers from the poor, which is called noil. Combing removes all foreign matter from the fiber. Only the best grades of cotton, wool and other important fibers may be combed.

combing jacket see *rayle.*

comboy a skirtlike garment, part of Ceylon national dress, worn by both sexes. The man's is wrapped around the figure and gathered into the belt in front. Above the belt or sash he is naked or wears a short-sleeved bolero jacket. The woman often adds a sari, bringing it over her left shoulder and tucking it into the belt. The length and width of the comboy indicates the wearer's class. Those of the lowest may not wear one below the knee.

commode, palisade from about 1675 into the early eighteenth century, the hair was dressed high off the forehead in clusters of curls arranged over a silk-covered wire frame called a commode or palisade. Occasionally the hair was powdered. see *fontanges.*

compact, vanity case a small case of gold, silver, metal or plastic containing powder and puff, a mirror in the cover, and sometimes a lipstick.

conch a woman's enveloping, full-length cloak worn in most European countries from the sixteenth century on. Of black woolen cloth or crepe, it was boned

conch or huke mounted on a wooden frame-Flemish-16th C.

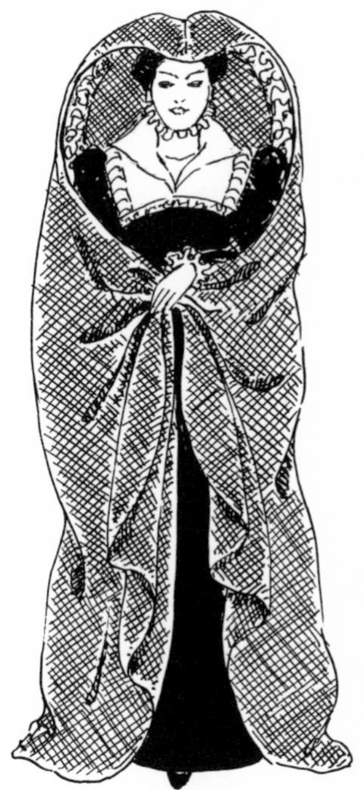

comboy-national Singalese dress wrap-around worn by man-woman and child

Comboy as worn by women, half draped with sari-Ceylon

comboy-worn by small Ceylon boy

or hooped into a conch-shell shape from the waist up, covering head and shoulders. Used especially as a mourning cloak.

coney, cony an old English word for rabbit dressed to simulate more expensive peltries. see *rabbit* for the many commercial names.

coney, beaver-dyed an old English name for rabbit, or rabbit processed to simulate beaver.

confetti dots an allover pattern in small dots and varied colors.

confidents curls tied with velvet bowknots. Also called heartbreakers. Also the name of a silk hood tied under the chin. French, second half seventeenth century.

Congo brown a dark brown with an orange cast.

congress shoe see *gaiter.*

Connolly, Sybil see *couture, haute.*

contact lens a tiny dome-shaped glass which adheres to the pupil of the eye, thus eliminating the need for spectacles.

continental see *androsmane.*

continental heel see *heel, continental, French.*

convent a lightweight crêpe-woven cloth used for female religious habits.

conversation bonnet see *bonnet, conversation.*

coolie coat see *shan.*

coolie hat see *hat, coolie.*

coonskin see *raccoon.*

cope a cape or cloak worn over the alb by priests and bishops. It is an exact semicircle of silk or brocade and embroidery, sometimes with hood but no sleeves. Open in front and fastened over the chest by a brooch called a morse or by a self-band. Originally an outdoor garment worn alike by laity and churchmen.

coq plumage the lustrous black and dark green feathers of the male barnyard fowl. Used especially on European military officers' hats and the dress hats of the Italian bersaglieri.

coquard French for "old cock," a toque or bonnet worn by Swiss and German knights in the sixteenth century. Satin and ostrich plumes attached to a linen coif or cap.

coquille French for shell, a shell-like edging or ruching used as trimming on neckwear and baby bonnets.

coral a branchlike formation of compound sea animals, the individual polyps of which arise by budding. Of varying shades of pink, red, oxblood and white, cut and polished and used as jewelry.

cordelière a heavy, ropelike cotton cord with knotted ends, used as a girdle by Franciscan friars. Fashionable in women's dress in the twentieth century, made of cord and fabrics with knotted or tasseled ends.

cordonnet a fine cord of cotton, linen or silk used to edge or outline lace. Also used for fringe, tassels and embroidery.

cordovan soft, fine-grained colored leather made of goatskin at Cordova, Spain, in the Middle Ages. Now made of split horsehide, goatskin, pigskin and other skins; nonporous, durable, expensive and usually a rich, dark brown. Cordwain and cordwainer are archaic words for cordovan leather and the cordovan shoemaker of medieval times.

corduroy originally *cord du Roi* or cloth of the king; a cotton velvet with narrow or wide wale. In medieval days used for the king's livery or outdoor servants. Today it enjoys wide usage in casual clothes.

corfam a trade name for a chemically-made leather substitute by Du Pont. It is the first man-made shoe upper leather that is soft, supple and porous.

cornercap three- or four-cornered velvet cap worn in Europe with ecclesiastic or academic robes—fourteenth and fifteenth centuries.

cornet or **horned cap** of muslin or lace and of varying style, was much worn in the fourteenth and fifteenth centuries. The starched nurse's cap of modern times is based upon that medieval headdress as is the chef's cap of stiffly starched linen which has survived to our day.

corno the ducal bonnet of the Venetian doge and dogaresse. Of brocaded satin or velvet ornamented with a band of gold galloon, pearls and jewels. Worn over a white linen coif with cap strings, late fifteenth and sixteenth centuries.

corona Latin for a crown bestowed by ancient Romans as an honor. Also, a fillet or circlet in religious vestments.

coronation braid see *braid.*

coronation cloth created in England and first seen at the coronation of Edward VII (1901–1910). A cloth used in coronation regalia, it is of wool and unfinished suitings in solid colors with gold or silver tinsel stripes about an inch apart.

coronet a lesser crown worn by nobility or persons of rank. Usually refers to the gilded circlets worn around a red velvet cap by British peers and peeresses when robed for state occasions such as coronations or the opening of Parliament. The design varies according to the rank of the wearer. The peeresses' coronets are smaller replicas of the peers' and are worn pinned to the hair, behind the tiara.

corsage a small bouquet of flowers worn on the shoulder or bosom, or carried in the hand. Also, the décolleté bodice of

corno with jeweled knob and gold circlet-Italian-15th C

corno-crimson satin and pearls-Venetian-16th C.

coronet of gold and pearls-Byzantine-6th C.

cornet or Dutch coif, a starched linen cap worn by Dutch Bourgeoisie, 16th to 18th century.

cornet-Dutch-1620

cornet over wire-edged cap-German-1630

cornet-wired and embroidered cap-Dutch 1630's

cornet of lingerie fabric with wired edge-French bourgeosie-1630's

cornet-sheer lawn-wired and embroidered-German-1630's

an evening gown. With the growth of the florist industry and refrigeration, which prolonged the life of cut flowers, the corsage became a dress accessory. Fresh Parma violets were very popular c. 1890–1910. Violets were succeeded by gardenias, orchids and camellias, formerly considered "fast." At a dance, flowers were generally worn at the waistband of a dress, the lapel of a coat, or pinned to a muff. In the 1920's, with dropped, loose waistlines, flowers were pinned on the shoulder. Corsages are occasionally worn on a wristband, or pinned to an evening bag, so as not to be crushed while dancing. see *boutonnière.*

corselet in ancient Crete, a short jacket open in front, displayed the bare bosom, but was laced tightly together under the breasts in corset fashion. After the decline of Cretan civilization about 1400 B.C., the corset does not appear again until the late European medieval period.

corset The history of the corset began with man's desire to shape a living torso, male or female, into the prevalent mode. Its forms have varied, rarely comfortable, yet it remains ever in demand. The Cretans of about 1500 B.C. exhibit the first idea of a corset, a wide leather belt or "cinch girdle" and the smallest waist in the history of costume for man and woman. The corset in the fourteenth and fifteenth centuries was a fitted underbodice of heavy canvas or boiled leather, for both men and women. Wooden stays were used as busks and the garment was tightly laced together. In the sixteenth century, men, women, girls, and even small boys wore the basquine, made of boiled leather and worn over a quilted underbodice. In the Renaissance the corset was reinforced with wire and pierced steel. The tapered form was known as the Spanish body. After 1600, steel and cane were replaced by whalebone; in England the garment was called stays instead of a corset. "Peasecod-bellied" was the description given the long-pointed doublet front with busk and small waist, the Spanish gift to the European mode of the courts. Ladies and courtiers dieted to acquire the Spanish figure.

By the late seventeenth century the feminine corset became slim and deeply pointed in front and laced in back. It rose high under the armpits and over the breasts, a "pair of bodies" of heavy linen or brocade reinforced with whalebone. It had piccadills around the waist to which the underskirt was secured by lacing. During the Directoire period, 1795–1799, the mode was no longer dictated by Versailles but was launched in Paris at summer gardens and public winter balls. Following a trend of ancient Greek and Roman style, a bandeau which held the breasts firm was worn under slip or chemise and the torturous corset was replaced by a muslin corsetwaist fitted to the normal figure and only slightly boned. After the French Revolution, English tailors seized the ascendancy in taste and design, and have held it ever since. In the first half of the nineteenth century, the masculine trend was toward a fitted waist acquired by wearing a corset or basque belt of boned canvas or leather. The nineteenth century meant the tightly fitted, boned and laced bodice of the 1830's and 1840's for women and was the return to the corset of steel stays. Reaching from bosom to hips, shaped to a small waist, it hooked in front and laced in back. The corset of the 1890's was of heavy cotton coutil, boned to produce the fashionable wasp waist. An eighteen-inch waist was the desired measurement of the day, and called the hourglass silhouette. Twentieth century—Paul Poiret was responsible for the demise of the armorlike corset with the creation of his Empire style in 1912. His mannequins wore the brassière, which he designed. A similar garment had been worn as a night garment in earlier periods and as a kind of corsetwaist for young girls. In the 1920's, the body-garment emerged as a natural form-fitting piece. It was built in many styles: an all-in-one, a foundation garment, a girdle long or short, and a panty girdle, all boneless satin or elastic, both fabrics stretchable. Two-way stretch Lastex does not ride up on the body, thus bones were no longer necessary. It was comfortable and improved the figure, and for the first time in the history of costume, the form-shaping piece was worn next to the body. see *body stocking; corselet; foundation garment.*

corset busks invented in 1829 by Jean-Julian Josselin; the first front busk closure in two pieces fastened by clamps. The corset was laced in back.

corset cover of the nineteenth century was a low-necked, sleeveless underbodice to cover the corset to the waist. Of linen or fine muslin, it might be embroidered, lace- and ribbon-trimmed.

corset, masculine see *basque belt.*

cosmetics In ancient Egypt cosmetics were used by men and women. The eyes were accented with two colors, black and green, the latter powdered malachite. The cheeks were colored with red clay ointment mixed with a touch of saffron. Carmine was applied to the lips, eyelashes were tipped with black pomade and the veins of the bosom accented with blue. Women used white lead to paint the face. Creams, oils and ointments were lavishly indulged in, men employing perfumed oils for shaving. In ancient Greece, breast toiletry was an additional feature. As the tints of the complexion were enhanced by cosmetics, so the whiteness of the bosom was heightened by the use of pastes in hyacinth purple and jasper green, which came from India and was applied with a fine brush. Face-powdering came into fashion in the Renaissance and was the result of hair-powdering with the discovery of the flattering mat texture produced by a dusting of powder on the face. In rouges, there were French red, Chinese red, Spanish red, carmine, and Bavarian red wine, the latter also taken internally. Spanish papers and Spanish wool were impregnated with rouge to rub on the

skin. There were many lotions and toilet waters, but plain water was carefully avoided. Venetian ladies sponged their faces with water but immediately coated them with paint. Venetian gentlemen also painted, powdered and patched.

In the sixteenth century Catherine de Medici brought the art of face-painting to the French Court. Pigments consisted of a base of white lead with vermilion paint for color. By the eighteenth century French face-painting was definitely the mark of the French upper class at court and at all fashionable assemblies. The cheeks were entirely rouged and some English ladies writing from Paris in 1733 said they were compelled to rouge because their natural color was conspicuous by contrast. Other countries did not carry the fashion to such excess, the English in fact disapproved of paint.

Cosmetics in the early days were made of crude and injurious ingredients. The bourgeoise, actresses and ladies of quality all rouged, but the coloring of the lady was a bit more subtle. When a complexion was too rosy, it was toned down with "Spanish white," or wool saturated with white lead and chalk. "Spanish papers," the first compacts, were tiny books of leaves covered with red-and-white pulverized paint. Made in the seventeenth century, they were still available in the twentieth century as a French product.

The use of cosmetics in the United States was frowned upon for centuries as only permissible as theater make-up. It took Hollywood to efface the prejudice, by the 1920's, every woman, rich or poor, could avail herself of the many beauty aids on the market. Too, they can be safely used because the contents of all preparations today are under the watchful eye of the law to insure their being harmless. In this period body paint was a passing fad for beautifying legs exposed to view by the short skirts and the sheerest of stockings. It also appeared in designs of flowers and stars painted on the face, knees and ankles. see *rachel; rice powder; rouge; fingernails; eye makeup; lipstick.*

Cossack cap see *calpac.*

Cossack officer of World War I wore a dark colored cloth coat, caftanlike with flaring sleeves and skirt. Rows of cartridge pockets on either side of chest, a black satin muffler and leather belt with sword and dirk. Leather boots and astrakhan cap.

costume jewelry designed in the 1920's for special gowns, furnishing a desired effect and color note. Jewelry with an intrinsic value so slight that silver or gold-plated metal with semi-precious or glass stones suffices. The clip, a jeweled ornament which simply clipped to a garment, was new and considered smarter than the brooch. see *temple jewelry.*

cote, cotte old English and French for the man's and woman's outer garment. The masculine cote was a tunic varying in length halfway between waist and knee. The feminine cotte was a complete dress fitted at the waist and reaching to the floor. The word has remained in English as coat.

cote-hardie an Italian medieval fashion worn by both sexes, full-length for women and tunic-length for men. It varied in style from the twelfth to the fourteenth centuries but generally, sleeves were long and the body closefitting.

cothurn, cothurnus, kothornos see *buskin.*

cotta a short white linen vestment with square yoke worn in Anglican and Roman Catholic churches from the twelfth to the fourteenth centuries, but generally, sleeves were long and the body close-fitting. Still worn by members of robed church choirs.

cottage bonnet see *bonnet, cottage.*

cotton the soft, fibrous substance covering the seeds of the plant; the most important of textile raw materials. Durable, with a wide range of uses, particularly in apparel. It is inexpensive and grown around the world in suitable climate. Its substance is pure cellulose. Cotton is first mentioned in the fifth century B.C. when the Greek historian Herodotus, returning from a trip to India, told of trees from whose fleece the natives made cloth. An English explorer visiting India in 1350 described tiny lambs growing on a tree. The conquests of Arabians and the Crusaders carried cotton to Europe. When the Conquistadores arrived in the New World, they found cotton fabric being manufactured in Peru, Mexico and southeast North America. Today the bulk of the world crop is from the United States.

cotton broadcloth a fine, durable, mercerized fabric put out in white, dyed or printed patterns. Used for men's and women's garments.

cotton crepes crepe yarn and crepe weave used in wide range of quality, texture, and finish; white, printed and dyed. The surface comes in crinkled, plain, granite or pebble effects.

cotton, Sea Island a cotton which has a fiber of uncommon length, silky luster, and fineness. Formerly grown on the islands off the coasts of Georgia, Florida, South Carolina and Texas. Because of the prevalence of the boll weevil in these states, it is now grown largely in the West Indies.

couching an effective raised embroidery done with fancy braids and round cords that outline a design and then are secured to the groundwork by fine stitches over the cord.

countenances French for the dainty small mirror, pin and needle cushion, small scissors, each one suspended by a ribbon attached to the lady's waist, sixteenth and seventeenth centuries.

Courrèges see *couture, haute.*

Courrèges boot see *boot, Courrèges.*

coutil drill or **ticking** a sturdy cotton of hard-twisted yarns used for corsets and girdles before the days of lastex.

couture from the French word for sewing; *couturier,* male dressmaker; *couturière,* feminine dressmaker: *Maison de Haute Couture,* a top dressmaking establishment. In American usage, all terms pertain to dressmaking in its highest form and creation, most fashionable and expensive.

couture, haute some well-known names:

Adolpho a successful native Cuban designer of millinery has established himself in New York where he is successfully creating all phases of feminine attire.

Agnès, Mme. well-known Parisian milliner famed for her small, snuggly-draped turban of tricot banding. 1920's.

Amies, Edwin Hardy of Savile Row, London. Born of an old Kentish family in 1909. He is dressmaker to the Queen, a title he shares with Norman Hartnell. As designer of expensive ready-made clothes and accessories for men and women, he opened his establishment and boutique in 1950. His has been a tremendous and international success founded upon designs that well-dressed people appreciate.

Balenciaga, Cristobal Spanish and in the opinion of experts, the world's greatest dressmaker. Maintains couture houses in Paris, Madrid, San Sebastian and Barcelona.

Balmain, Pierre a successful Parisian designer who first studied architecture at the École des Beaux Arts, opening his own house in Paris, 1945.

Barentzen, Patrick de couturier of

draped turban of knitted banding - Mme Agnès - 1920's

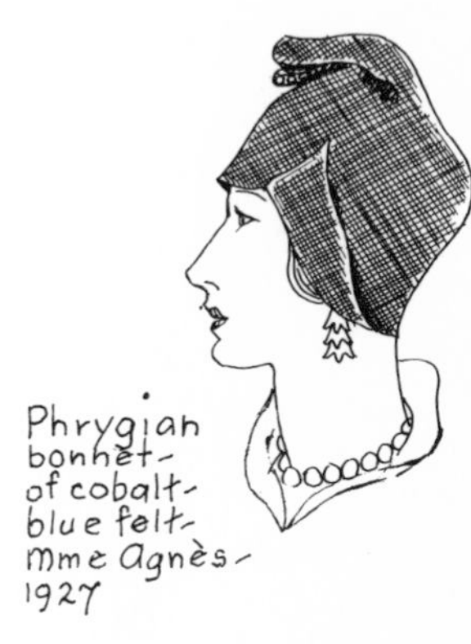
Phrygian bonnet - of cobalt-blue felt - Mme Agnès - 1927

large hat with black wings - hat and dress avocado green - black velvet coat - black astrakhan - Balenciaga - 1948

three-piece ensemble-black wool topcoat over camel hair coat, over sleeveless striped sheath-Bonnie Cashin-1950

Rome. A newcomer with many new ideas not only in feminine dress but in men's dress as well.

Beene, Geoffery an up-and-coming American designer from Hainesville, Louisiana, who changed his mind as to his career, dropping his medical studies and taking up instead, dressmaking design.

Beer a German by birth, he was the first couturier to open an establishment in a house on the Place Vendôme in Paris. He was famed for elegant dresses and beautiful lingerie and his success dated from around the turn of the century.

Bertin, Rose first of the French couture and dressmaker to Queen Marie Antoinette. She was renowned for her handsome gowns and had an establishment in London for her English clientele. Ambassadors' wives from various parts of the world ordered her creations. She was loyally devoted to the queen.

Blass, Bill a New York City Seventh Avenue designer and manufacturer who is vice-president of his successful, wholesale, ready-made business. He began his designing career in the 1940's. He served three years with the United States Army during World War II, a stint which took him to Paris. He has since become one of our top American designers.

"Chanel Look" revival-navy blue wool jersey blue bow tie-1954

Bohan, Marc a gifted, artistic designer who served apprenticeship in the 1940's with Piquet, Molyneux, de Rauch and Jean Patou. He also did free-lance designing in New York City for Originala. In 1958, at the age of thirty-two, he did work for Dior for the English market. Today his title is *Marc Bohan of Christian Dior.*

Brooks, Donald in 1962, Donald Brooks made his debut at Bendel's in New York by designing clothes for a Broadway musical, "No Strings."

Callot Soeurs three French sisters whose house, the Maison Callot, was the leader in fashion from 1895 until just after World War I. From Maison Callot came beautiful creations in lace, chiffon, georgette and organdy. During that period, the world of fashion was in their hands.

Cardin, Pierre made his start in the couture by first spending three years with Dior. In the 1950's he opened boutiques in London and Tokyo. In the 1960's, he added men's clothes to his list. In women's dress he added ornamental cutouts which caused some few of his creations to be labeled "kooky," but many of his designs hit the mark, causing them to be freely copied by his fellow designers.

Carven, Mme. Carmen Mollet as a young woman studied architecture, becoming a dressmaker just before the war and the Occupation. After the liberation of Paris, Carven again opened her couture house to a successful career. Her perfume, "Ma Griffe," is a great favorite.

Cashin, Bonnie known widely as "the great American individualist," a title bestowed upon the New York couturière when she was presented with the Coty Fashion Critics Award in 1950. In 1961, she was awarded a Coty Special Award and in 1964, received the New York Sunday Times International Fashion Special Award. She delves into every facet of costume design, at the same time giving her fashions an Oriental and Californian flare, the result of a youth spent in those parts of the world.

Cassini, Oleg Loiewski Russian, born in Paris 1913. He was raised in Florence. He studied art and law but deciding to be a designer, opened a dress salon in Rome, 1933. He came to New York in 1937, became an American citizen and an international celebrity.

Chanel, Gabrielle went to Paris as a young girl to be a milliner but became known for her skillful and remarkable use of jersey fabrics in dresses and suits, and world famous for her perfume "Chanel, Number Five." see *Chanel, Gabrielle.*

Connolly, Sybil of Dublin, Ireland, famed for her beautiful tweeds and knits and hand-loomed linen dresses with handmade laces and embroideries.

Courrèges a Basque, who first opened his small white Paris salon in 1961, creating a sensation with women's short pants-suits, architectural-looking coats and white boots. This he followed with men's fashions.

Creed, Charles an English family of fine tailors who settled in Paris, having been persuaded to make the move by French refugee customers returning home after the French Revolution. The firm still carries on in London and Paris with a reputation over two hundred years old. The house was originally a man's tailor but early in this century, women's tailoring was included.

Daché, Lilly born in Beigles, near Bordeaux, France. She came to New York as a young woman, set up shop and became a most successful and fashionable milliner. To own a "Lilly Daché hat" was the desire of every smartly-dressed woman.

Dessés, Jean born in Egypt in 1904. Though of Greek ancestry, he is typically French. He studied law before he entered the field of fashion, opening his own couture house in 1937. His clientele has included many members of royalty and he has been more or less official couturier to the Greek royal family.

Dior, Christian 1905–1957. A former Parisian picture dealer who turned couturier, meeting with instant success. In 1947, he created a sensational change in women's fashions which became known as the "New Look." see *New Look.*

Doucet of Paris, came to the fore in the late 1870's but his establishment was founded by his grandparents in 1824 and as a lingerie house. Doucet became known for his tailleur or tailor-made suit. He was the first couturier to make fur coats with the fur to the inside as lining.

Erté the famous French artist and designer originally worked with Paul Poiret in Paris in 1912. When Erté came to New York in 1968 at the age of seventy-six, he was fêted by the Metropolitan Museum of Art with an exhibition of his early stage and fashion drawings. He planned to return to designing costumes for the Paris boutique of Paraphernalia.

Creed-evening coat-brown velvet with black passementerie-1939

Fath, Jacques 1912–1954. His successful designing reached its apex in 1948, a remarkable success which was cut short by his untimely death. He was also a painter and especially enjoyed creating for Americans.

Galanos, James of Greek descent with a flare for designing, got his start by selling his sketches on Seventh Avenue, New York, and in Hollywood. He finally settled in Los Angeles in 1951, founding "Galanos Originals." His sumptuous evening gowns are, as he himself says, "elegant and sophisticated," and his prices are high. He commutes to New York several times a year to display his collection.

greatcoat of black wool-velvet cap-Dior-1949

Galitzine, Princess Irene of Rome, Russian-born. She specializes in lingerie and at-home gowns and it is claimed that her evening clothes are the most beautiful in Paris.

Gernreich, Rudi born in Vienna in a family that fled to the United States in 1938 when he was sixteen years of age. He studied art at the Los Angeles City Art College and became a designer in couture. His first efforts were concentrated upon knitted swimwear, followed by the topless swimsuit, and next, the soft, boneless brassière which really filled a need.

cream-colored faille with frieze of appliquéd crimson velvet-three-cornered shawl of crimson velvet-Lanvin-Castillo-1955

"after five" ensemble-black broadtail skirt-sleeveless beige knitted jumper-tailored beige jacket-Mainbocher-1954

Givenchy, Hubert de born 1927 in Beauvais, France, of an aristocratic family. Studied at the École des Beaux Arts, Paris. At seventeen, he worked with Jacques Fath. Like other couturiers in the 1900's, he is following today's trend in having recently opened a ready-to-wear boutique where his models are to be had at a price quite a bit lower than the creations displayed in the main salon of his house.

Grès, Alix At first widely known as Alix, she became Madame Grès to the admiring world. She always worked as an artist, draping and manipulating fabrics as if she were a sculptor. An original mark of her skill was her manner of cutting into silks and cloths on the bias. Another sign of the artist was her great talent in color combinations.

Griffe, Jacques Born in the village of Carcassonnne in southern France where his mother was a successful milliner. When twenty years old, he went to Paris to work for Vionnet, sending five years there. World War II intervened and he served in the Zouave Regiment until 1942. From then on, he became a most successful couturier. He came to America in 1952, his clientele consisting of royalty and many well-known English and American ladies.

Hartnell, Norman of London. Dressmaker to the Queen and other members of the Royal Family. He had his first success with crinoline *robes de style* made for the Queen Mother. He specializes in elaborately embroidered gowns for State occasions, of which the Queen's coronation dress is the outstanding example.

Khanh, Emmanuelle a young French designer who had modeled for Balenciaga and Givenchy. She made all her own clothes in an effort to create new designs for a "New Era," and displayed her first collection in 1961 when it at once took hold.

Lanvin, Jeanne great-aunt of Bernard, the present ruler of the haute-couture House of Lanvin founded in 1890. Madame Lanvin was famous for her *robes de style* and the beautiful embroideries with which she finished the gowns. Today, the women's division is handled by the well-known Paris designer, Jules-Francois Crahay, and Mrs. Bernard Lanvin. Mr. Lanvin is in charge of a ready-to-wear boutique, which opened in Paris in 1968.

Lelong, Lucien 1889–1958. An internationally-known Paris dress designer and perfume maker. He was the first couturier to launch perfumes as part of couture.

Lucile, Lady Duff Gordon a titled English woman with establishments in London, Paris, New York and Chicago. She was a designer of great talent and famous for her elegant, beautiful gowns, suits and coats. Died 1937.

Mainbocher (Main-Rousseau-Bocher) born in Chicago. In the U.S. Army and demobilized in France 1919. He was a fashion editor to Vogue and in 1930, he opened his own house of couture in Paris. After World War I, he returned to America, and established himself in New York City.

Molyneaux, Captain Edward an Irishman who first worked in London with Lucile (Lady Duff Gordon). He opened his own house in Paris after World War I, designing clothes for stars of the French and English stage and well known society women. He was also a painter.

Norell, Norman who launched his career in 1922, was originally a designer for such stars of the silent screen as Gloria Swanson and Mae Murray. He is considered an elegant designer.

Paquin House of Paquin, founded in Paris, 1892, famed for the elegance of its clothes and for exquisite lingerie. Paquin was the very first couturier to

skirt and cummerbund-
pewter gray linen-
white embroidery-
white bodice-
Sybil Connolly-
Dublin-
Ireland
leg-of-mutton
sleeves-black
astrakhan choker,
muff and pillbox
with ribbon ties-
Jacques Fath-
1953
gown of brown
chiffon-shirred
bodice-brown
velvet ribbon-
Jacques Fath-
1953
white taffeta with
black polka dots-
flamenco flounce
set low in front-
black faille toque-
de Givenchy-
1954
Edwardian
princess gown
of black slipper
satin with
boned bodice-
Galanos-
1953

Dior's New Look with full bosom and small waist-1947

make use of fur as trimming on suits and coats. The mannequins, all chosen by M. Paquin, were considered the most beautiful girls in Paris.

Pertegaz, Manuel is considered one of the most successful of Spain's designers. He opened his salon in Barcelona in the early 1940's and has been catering to Spanish and many American women since then.

Poiret, Paul 1840–1944. He was a great artist who died poor nevertheless. As a boy, he sold his costume sketches to Paquin, Redfern, Worth and many others. He designed the gowns of many of the great actresses of the day, Réjane, Sarah Bernhardt, Mary Garden and others. His friends were all the great artists of the time. In his wonderful fashions, he created the minaret skirt and the harem skirt.

Pucci, Marchese Emilo of Florence, known for his slinky gowns of uncrushable silk jersey signed "Emilio," his printed leotards and his "Capri pants" of the 1960's.

Pulitzer, Lilly originator of the American version of the shift under which one wears nothing. A socialite of Palm Beach, Florida, she designed, with the aid of her clever dressmaker, a one-piece cotton housedress which has been popular since the 1950's, known as the "Lilly."

Quant, Mary the English originator of "Mod Fashions" which appeared in London in the 1960's. Though they shocked the fashion world, they were adopted none-the-less by that same world. As a reward for the volume of business that grew out of the Mini-Skirt, Mary Quant was awarded the Order of the British Empire.

Reboux Maison Reboux, the Paris milliner who in the early 1920's created a revolution in women's headgear with her chic little cloche. Of chiffon or hand-

Dior's New Look with full bosom and small waist-1947

gown of pleated mauve-pink chiffon-jersey hem-length scarf of white tied over shoulder and breasts-Grès-1952

greatcoat of broadcloth-beaver or seal collar-leather belt-felt tricorne-Griffe-1951

evening gown by Poiret- chiffon with fur bands- metal and wool embroidery on cloth- cord girdle with tassel- 1910

empire-styled gown with train- gray moiré silk- jet flower corsage- Molyneux-1948

"dinner shirtwaist dress" of two layers of white organdie- black velvet belt and poppy- Norman Norell- 1945

chinoise coat-dress of soft gray wool with black braid and buttons- Pauline Trigère- 1948

kerchief felt, it was manipulated into a head-hugging hat with no trimming except perhaps a couple of tucks and as many stitches, a grosgrain ribbon band and perhaps a brooch. It suited the times after World War I and all women, and it accompanied all costumes though limited to the colors beige, brown or black.

Redfern the English house of Redfern, was established in the Rue de Rivoli, Paris in 1881 and later, branches in London and New York City. Designed gowns for Sarah Bernhardt and Mary Garden.

Renta, Oscar de la a Dominican who lived in Spain for fifteen years, went to Paris and then came to New York in 1965 at the age of thirty-one. He joined the house of Jane Derby as designer and part owner.

Ricci, Nina founded her Paris house with her son in 1939. She works in fabric rather like a sculptor, finishing with fine handwork. Her models are presented in French cities, European capitals and cities in North Africa, her orders usually outnumbering those of other Paris couturiers.

Rodriguez, Pedro a Spanish couturier with salons in Madrid, Barcelona and San Sebastian. Rodriguez opened his first house in Barcelona in 1918, the second establishment in 1939 and the Madrid house in 1941.

Saint Laurent, Yves came to Paris, 1954, from his native Algeria to receive a prize and an apprenticeship to Dior who was one of the judges. In 1957, upon Dior's sudden death, he became chief of Dior's vast empire. The "trapeze silhouette" in 1958 established his reputation and in 1962, he opened his own couture house.

Scaasi, Arnold a successful designer from Montreal where he studied design, worked in Paris at the House of Paquin, and in New York with Charles James, an American designer with a well-founded reputation. Scaasi went into wholesale designing and now makes beautiful and expensive clothes for his clientele.

Schiaparelli, Elsa was born in Italy. She settled in France in the early 1920's and designed for Mme. Lanvin. Being very fond of sports clothes, she designed and made sweaters which became the "rage," as did her favorite color of vibrant pink known as "shocking pink."

Schön, Mila a German who is one of the best known of new designers in dress and furnishings. She opened a shop in Milan and has acquired an important position in style and design, being patronized by all who appreciate her flair for the unusual but wearable.

Scott, Ken American from Indiana. He specializes in the beautifully printed silks and among designers, holds an enviable position in the art. He settled in Milan, where in 1967, he made his mark with a display of twenty-five Milanese university male students clothed in handsome pajamas. Each man escourted a mannequin in a printed flowered silk dress. His silk scarves are veritable works of art.

Sophie of Saks Fifth Avenue, New York, outstanding as a designer and American couturière. Her clothes are noted for the beauty of their shapes, fabrics and colors and are flattering to the wearer. She is the wife of Adam Gimbel, president of Saks.

Tiffeau, Jacques the designing partner of Tiffeau Busch of New York. A French farmer's son, who, having learned tailoring at school in France, turned to provincial tailoring. In 1951, at the age of twenty-three, he came to America where he joined the firm of Monte Sano, a Seventh Avenue house. He also took a course at the Art Students' League to learn to sketch. His designs drew notice especially when in 1964, he raised the skirt hems above the knees. He then went on to creating simple dresses with cardigan jackets which also accompanied pants. His name has become one of the outstanding of New York's couture.

Trigère, Pauline a French couturière who held forth on Seventh Avenue, New York, for a quarter century before she became all-American. She is the creator of beautiful clothes which have earned for her a high reputation, in fact, she is considered one of the best in her art.

Ungaro, Emmanuel a tailor who had worked with Balenciaga and also with Courrèges, went out on his own in Paris in 1961 when he was thirty-eight years old. He is very popular, and in 1967 following the growth of boutique craze, he opened his own ready-to-wear shop in the front of his made-to-order salon.

Valentina an American couturière who, in the early 1940's, created a short dinner dress to be worn when one's escort was attired in business clothes. Called ballerina, it was either dress or short-jacket suit, usually black in brocade or faille silk. see *ballerina.*

Valentino couturier of Rome, a contemporary newcomer with new and original ideas in the use of fabrics and colors.

Vionnet, Madeleine born in Aubervilliers, France. As a young woman, she went first to London, then returned to Paris, working for Doucet for five years. In 1912 she opened her own establishment on the rue de Rivoli and from 1918 to 1939, the Vionnet dress was every woman's desire, including royalty. She became a great success and had a definite influence upon the foremost couturiers of her period.

Weitz, John an American designer born in Berlin, educated in British public school, has been designing fashions since 1948. He claims to build fashionable clothes for functional men. He has been most successful in the United States and his clothes are carried in London and the important cities of western Europe.

Worth, Charles Frederick born in England, 1826. As a small boy he worked in London fabric shops. He left for Paris around 1846 when about twenty years old. He married his talented model and in the 1850's, the Worths opened their couture house on the rue de la Paix, which turned out to be a most successful venture. He was the first dressmaker to open a salon in Paris and to display his new creations on live mannequins. Also, he created the princess-line dress and sheath. He died in 1895.

coverall interchangeable with overalls; protective working garments of sturdy fabric. see *overalls.*

coverchief a head covering fashioned from a kerchief.

covert cloth a diagonal, twill-woven, stout woolen coating, hard- or soft-finished.

coverts short top coats worn by the British when fox-hunting. The cloth, like a gabardine, was water-repellent and tear-proof when going through coverts and thickets. Long coats, suits and raincoats were also made of the cloth which was sold in the United States in the mid-nineteenth century and called Orleans cloth.

cowboy boot see *boot, cowboy.*

cowboy dress see illustrations; *chaps.*

cowboy hat see *hat, Stetson; Ten-Gallon.*

cowhide heavy leather from cowhides are used for boots and soles. Today, however, almost any skin with natural beauty suitable for use can be transformed into a supple, durable leather. Cowhide

cowboy in Spanish-Mexican habit-California-20th C.

"cow girl" in feminine ranch dress-cotton velvet with embroidery American western

can be dressed to resemble pony or stenciled to simulate ocelot, leopard or giraffe. Such leathers, used for sportswear and trimmings, come from Denmark, Latvia, Estonia and northwest Russia.

cowichan sweater a sweater made by Indian women on Vancouver Island who card and spin the wool but never dye it; the dark areas of the designs are knit from the wool of black sheep. Used by Canadians for sportswear, twentieth century.

cowl the hood usually attached to a monk's robe. It has been imitated in feminine fashions, sometimes draped in back but also in front or just draped in a soft fold around the neck. All such forms with or without hood, are called "cowl neck."

Croatian-origin of the cravat-17th C.

coxcomb a narrow strip of notched red cloth which was worn on the caps of licensed jesters. An imitation of the cock's comb.

coyote see *wolf.*

coypu see *nutria.*

crackow see *poulaine.*

crape see *crepe.*

craquelé French for crackled, an effect given to silk, lace or net.

crash from the Latin *crassus,* meaning coarse; a coarse linen or a coarse woolen suiting in homespun effect obtained by weaving thick uneven cotton, linen or rayon yarns. Used for men's sportswear.

cravat-haircut-hoop earrings of the Incroyable-Directoire-1795

cravat a neckcloth or tie. An important fashionable accessory in the early nineteenth century. It could be folded and tied in a number of ways, some requiring considerable skill and patience. The earliest mention of the cravat dates from 1660 when a Croatian regiment visited Paris, fresh from a victory over the Turks. They wore colorful linen neckerchiefs knotted around their necks, the first neckties, called royal cravattes. The cravat became so important in the early nineteenth century that a little book was published in the 1820's describing thirty-two styles of tying the piece. By 1800 the soft, folded stock of white cambric was the popular form of men's neckwear. Europeans and Americans favored the wearing of two cravats at the same time, a white one twice around the neck and a black silk one tied over it. In the 1830's colors appeared. Collar points began to turn down and by 1850 the stiff white collar with scarf tied in varied knots began to take hold. see *focal; stock.*

cravenette from the tradename for an English rainproofing process on worsted and woolen cloths, a method discovered more than half a century ago. It is still used on covert, gabardine, elastique, tricotine, whipcord and other cloths for rainwear.

crea a linen or cotton fabric much used in Spain and Spanish America for common wear.

crease-resistant term applied to textiles of cotton, linen, or rayon chemically treated to virtually eliminate wrinkling.

Creed, Charles see *couture, haute.*

crenelated see *castellated.*

crepe the generic name for a thin, almost semi-transparent fabric with a crinkly surface produced by twisting in reverse the weft and warp of hard-twisted threads. The weaving of crepe in the Orient dates back to antiquity but was not taken up in the West until after the Crusades. The Italians were the first to make crepe, in the thirteenth century. It was produced at Lyons in France in the sixteenth century, and later in England. Dull black crepe was originally used principally for mourning dress. see *cotton crepes.*

crepe-back satin see *satin, crepe-back.*

crepe, Canton see *Canton crepe.*

crepe, cotton see *cotton crepe.*

crepe de chine a popular silk fabric of long standing. Plain or printed, it is washable and extensively used for dresses, blouses and lingerie. An imitation widely used is made with cotton warp and silk filling.

crepe georgette named for the designer, Mme. Georgette de la Plante of Paris. A highly creped, fine, sheer fabric of all silk, silk and cotton, or silk and rayon.

crepe marocain a silk or wool combination of yarns producing a heavy dress-weight fabric.

crepe meteor a silk or rayon face texture, lightweight and with the effect of crepe georgette. It is soft, launders and wears well. Often called satin-backed crepe because one side is satin. Used for blouses with the satin back as trim.

crepe plissé a lightweight cotton crepe with puckered stripes, similar to seersucker. Used for men's and children's undergarments, and for nightwear.

crepe rubber a crimped-surface natural or synthetic rubber used for soles and heels of semisports shoes.

crepe, woolen a mourning cloth with a crimped surface. Also, a strong, lightweight worsted material, much used in ecclesiastical attire.

crepida an ancient Roman sandal similar to the Greek krepis. The *crepida,* which was of various styles, was considered the shoe for traveler, young man and warrior.

crepine see *caul.*

crespinette see *caul.*

crestine see *caul.*

Cretan dress, ancient see illustrations.

Crete lace a lace made on the island of Crete, of colored flax with loose bobbin stitch in geometric figures.

cretonne gaily printed white cloth of hemp, linen or rayon, a decorator's fabric which gets its name from Creton in Normandy, France. Usually printed in floral patterns. Occasionally used for informal summer clothes, smocks and housecoats.

crew cut a haircut of the 1940's and '50's favored by young men. The hair was cropped very closely except on top where an inch or less stood up bristly. Though also known as the G.I. or Prussian haircut of World War II, it is really a collegiate style which originated among the varsity crews to differentiate them from other undergraduates and was called the varsity cut. When the top is slightly longer and casually tousled, it becomes a feather crew or Ivy League cut.

crew hat see *hat, crew.*

crew neck a flat, round neckline against the throat, from a sweater neckline worn by boat crews.

crewel a two-ply wool yarn with a slack twist used for fancy work, embroidery, laces and fringes.

crewel or **Jacobean embroidery** a combination of varied stitches in worsted yarn, silk and cotton. A decoration for bedspreads, draperies, wall hangings and furniture covers presently enjoying a revival in fancy work. Used occasionally as

white loincloth-
red belt-blue roll-
white apron-
Cretan-1300 B.C.

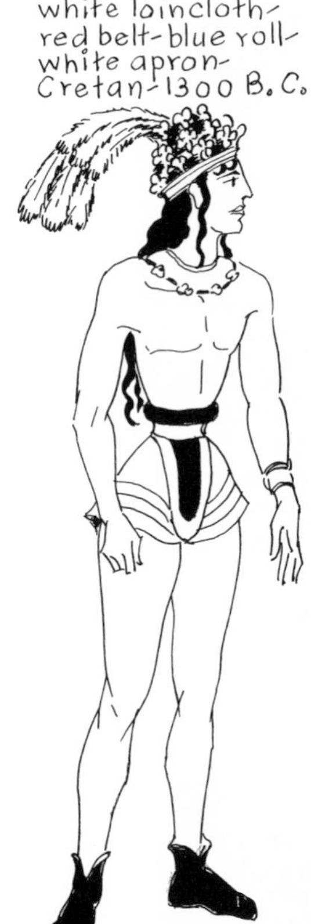

boned and laced corselet-
embroidered apron-
ruffled skirt-
Cretan-1700 B.C.

decorative motifs on women's clothes, particularly on cashmere sweaters. Popular in the seventeenth and eighteenth centuries for furnishings, clothing and accessories.

criades French for criers, screechers or brawlers; the name given to the early panniers worn by fashionable women in the seventeenth century. Hoops were encased in a petticoat of gummed canvas which "cried" and "squealed" at every move. see *panniers.*

crinoletta a form of bustle in the late nineteenth century, in cylindrical shape of steel or whalebone, sometimes covered with narrow ruffles.

crinoline, crin a braid for stiffening petticoats appeared early in the 1840's, made from *crin,* or horsehair, as in French. The crinoline was a petticoat corded and lined with horsehair and finished with a straw braid at the hem. Early in the 1850's, the crinoline was a quilted cotton petticoat reinforced with whalebone and worn with several starched white muslin petticoats with flounces tucked and embroidered. Eventually the many petticoats were replaced by a cagelike frame of flexible steel hoops still called a crinoline. It was invented by an Englishman and was known as Thomson's Crown Crinoline in which the skirt was cone-shaped. An improvement was the Cage Americaine with the upper half in skeleton form and only the lower half fabric-encased to reduce the weight of the garment. Victoria Cage was the trade name of a British hoop of steel patented in the late nineteenth century, giving the wearer the round hip and bustle shape which followed the crinoline. see *hoop.*

crinoline fashion-black velvet and lace-1842 French

crinoline revival in the twentieth century, the crinoline made its reappearance in full, stiff petticoats worn under the skirts of Dior's "New Look," 1947. see *New Look.*

crochet lace a handmade lace fashioned of a single thread manipulated by a crochet hook. Sometimes the motifs are worked separately and applied to net or fabric.

crocodile term wrongly used for alligator leather. Not legitimate in the trade, as crocodile skin has not yet been successfully tanned.

croquis French for a quick sketch in pencil or ink, especially a fashion drawing.

cross fox see *fox, cross.*

cross-stitch embroidery crossed stitches "x" executed on linen or square-meshed canvas, and used chiefly for pictorial sampler work but occasionally in decorative motifs on children's or informal wear. The basic, simplest and most popular of stitches.

crotch in sewing, the area where the two leg sections of pants, bloomers or drawers from back to front, are joined together.

crown of Oriental origin, coming to Europe by way of Byzantium, a royal or imperial headdress or cap of sovereignty. A coronet is a lesser crown worn by persons of rank. A tiara, in secular usage

Medieval crowns

Roman crown of laurel

crown of emperor- Byzantine 6th C.

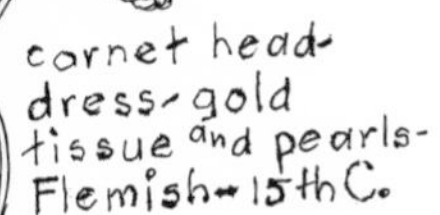

cornet head-dress- gold tissue and pearls- Flemish- 15th C.

royal crown over a wimple- precious metal and stones- French- 14th C.

English- small crown- pearls on wires and in coiffure- late 16th C.

Crown of England

Viscount coronet, silver gilt miniver- 16 silver gilt balls- red velvet cap

Earl coronet, with 8 tall rays each with a ball- red velvet cap-

coronet, marquess- red velvet cap- four gold strawberry leaves- four silver balls- jeweled band- miniver edge

jeweled gold crown over black velvet chaperon- pleated white frill with jewels- French queen- late 14th C.

queen's headdress- white velvet brim edged with gold- gold crown with jewels and pearls- gauze streamers in back- pearl earrings- French- late 16th C.

signifies no rank, but because it is usually jeweled its use is restricted to ladies of wealth and fashion when wearing full evening dress. see *coronet, miter, tiara.*

crow's-foot a three-pointed embroidered motif placed as a stay at the ends of seams or to reinforce a joining with strength and finish.

crystal see *rock crystal.*

cuaran or **rullion** a Scotch brogue of waxed rawhide. Perforations, pinked edges and thong laces were long a part of the design of the highlander's shoe. A writer of the seventeenth century remarks that "new good shoes are thus cut for the water to flow out when fording streams."

Cuban heel see *heel, Cuban.*

cucullus a hood joined to a cloak and having long ends which were wrapped around the neck. Worn in ancient Rome.

cue see *queue.*

cuff a turned-up fold on trouser leg or sleeve. *Barrel cuff,* a single cuff fastened by means of a button and buttonhole. *French cuff,* a double cuff of a man's shirt turned up and fastened with cuff links through buttonholes. *Mousquetaire cuffs,* ornamental wide turned-up cuffs worn by the mousquetaires, seventeenth and eighteenth centuries. The traditional open cuff on a man's jacket or coat sleeve was originated by Beau Brummell, (1778–1840), first a slit with linen frills showing and eventually the overlapping slit with buttons. *Single cuff,* a cuff without a turn-back and fastened with a button.

cuff links a pair of gold, silver or pearl buttons connected by several chain links or a shank or a bar which fastens the turned-up shirt cuff of a man's blouse by means of a couple of buttonholes. Stiffly starched cuffs were fastened with cuff links. Usually gold. Appeared about the 1840's. see *studs.*

cuirass originally, a piece of body armor of buff leather used in place of the earlier metal body protection. A close-fitting body garment of metal with breast-piece and back-piece reaching from neck to waistline and finished with a short hip-piece. Troopers of the sixteenth and seventeenth centuries wore metal helmet and cuirass. Still worn by some European calvary.

cuir-bouilli French for boiled, molded leather which was used especially

barrel cuff

for armor and corsetry in the medieval period. see *armor, armour.*

culottes In the sixteenth century when men's haut-de-chausses or waist-high stockings were joined, becoming real breeches, they were called culottes. Today the word is applied mostly to feminine informal dress, the culottes being long and full enough to look like a skirt. Culottes for women were first a style of divided skirt devised in the 1930's before shorts became generally acceptable for women; designed especially for bicycling in Bermuda, where strict regulations as to dress prevailed. When the wearer is standing, such culottes look like a skirt with inverted pleats at the front and back center seams. Bell bottoms as worn in the 1960's are pantaloons or pajamas and are worn by many fashionable women as lounge or informal evening costume. Such pajamas when of rich fabric appear less formal as evening dress than the décolleté gown, upon certain occasions. They were known in Italy as palazzo or party pants, and were approved wear for discothèque dancing.

cummerbund from the Persian Hindu word, *kamarband,* a wide, soft sash worn around the waist and originally a carryall for small possessions. In the hot summer of 1893, it was adopted by Europeans and tailored in pleated black silk for wear with black tie instead of the waistcoat for summer dinner dress. Still worn with men's dress clothes and sometimes adapted for women's outfits.

curch, curchef English and Scotch for a woman's plain cap or kerchief of white cotton or linen, as worn in the American Colonies.

curl papers see *papillotes.*

curls Among the ancient Romans the women wore beautiful, elaborately dressed wigs, in which the hair was braided, frizzed, curled and waved by curling irons. The hair was threaded with ribbons and strings of beads, and false hair was added if needed. The Roman lady of the first century wore a toupee of Cypriot curls, a solid mass of ringlets built up on a wire frame, reaching from ear to ear. A yellow wig was the sign of the courtesan. Many kinds of curls were popular in the seventeenth century: lover's curl at the nape of the neck hanging over the shoulder, the English ringlets, kiss curls, heartbreakers, and many others of pretty name. Masculine curls in the seventeenth century included à la comète, a long curl over one shoulder. There was also the cadenette or lovelock, a curl to one side, lower right. Favor, a curl tied with ribbon, center top. Spit curl, a slang expression of the 1890's for a single curl plastered to the forehead. Before the permanent wave era, *wire curlers* covered with leather, soft and thick, about 5 inches long, the wet hair twisted around and left to dry. *Curl papers* or *papillotes,* the wet hair twisted around curl papers, pinned and left to dry. *Curling irons* or *tongs,* a heated pair of tongs with wooden handles used to press the hair into the required shape. Pin curl, in twentieth century hairdressing, is set by winding dampened hair into a flat curl and fastening it with hairpins or clips to dry. Wire or plastic rollers became preferable by

the 1960's, sometimes in combination with pin curls. see *permanent wave.*

custom-made clothes made and fitted by a custom tailor who makes clothes to order only. In British parlance, bespoke tailoring.

cutaway, morning coat a man's single-breasted coat with skirts cut away in front and hanging to the bend of the knee in back, a waistline seam, flap pockets; made of black or oxford gray cheviot or unfinished worsted. Worn with striped or checked trousers and matching or contrasting waistcoat. Its use has declined since World War II, both in Europe and in America. see *frock coat.*

cutwork embroidery a needle-made lace also called reticella. The cut-out designs are edged with purl stitch and joined by embroidery-stitched bars. Such handiwork was the foundation of Italian lace-making in the twelfth century. see *reticella.*

cyclas a short, capelike cloak or tunic worn by men and women from ancient Greek and Roman times to thirteenth-century England; made of a rich silk cloth called cyclas because it was manufactured in the Cyclades. Greeks, Romans, Franks and Goths wore the garment. At the coronation of the English Henry III in the thirteenth century, the guest "citizens of London wore the cyclas over vestments of silk." In the same period, knights wore the cyclas over their armor as a surcoat.

cyprus a black crepe veiling made in Cyprus. Used as hatbands for mourning in the sixteenth and seventeenth centuries.

Czechoslovakian embroidery usually on linen, most often white or natural and worked with cotton, wool or silk threads in geometric folklore designs of brilliant coloring.

D

Dacca an untwisted skein silk used in embroidery, from Dacca, India.

Dacca muslin a very fine, sheer, cotton cloth.

Daché, Lilly see *couture, haute.*

dacron a trade name for polyester filaments and staple fibers, used in all types of apparel. Soft and wool-like, it shapes well in suits, shirts, ties, sweaters, socks, slacks and dresses.

dagged, petal-scalloped fantastic, ornamental edgings of garments from the fourteenth to the seventeenth centuries, a rage that existed in England and on the Continent. It was carried to such excess that sumptuary laws were passed to forbid it. see *castellated.*

Dalmatian sleeve see *angel sleeve.*

dalmatic a simple robe, long and straight with long flaring sleeves, robe or gown originally from Dalmatia. It influenced Roman costume, then Byzantine, royal and clerical dress, and over the centuries was worn for European state ceremonies. In modern times it is one of the robes worn by the English sovereign at the Coronation. The Armenian bride of today wears the traditional bridal dalmatic of beautiful fabric, and the dalmatian sleeve survives in modern Western mode. Eventually the robe was shortened and elaborated with embroidery and lace, becoming part of liturgical apparel. see *sakkos.*

damascene lace an imitation of Honiton without needlework filling, the sprigs and braces joined by corded bars.

damask a rich fabric, known in England in the thirteenth century and in use ever since. Woven of silk or linen and made originally in Damascus. The flat-woven pattern combines satiny and flat surfaces for light and shade effects. Sword blades and other articles of steel were "damascened" to resemble the cloth.

damask, Chinese a reversible figured fabric of linen, silk, wool or rayon. One side of satin on a twill-woven ground and the other a twill-woven motif on a satin ground.

damask, satin see *satin damask.*

dandy one who gives undue attention to dress and personal grooming; a fop, a beau.

dandyess, dandizette female dandy of the English Regency period, 1811–1820.

Danish embroidery see *hedebo embroidery.*

darned lace any square-meshed lace on net, the pattern filled in by needlework.

darnick see *dornick.*

dart a pointed tuck taken up in cloth to shape a garment to the body or to cause the garment to hang better.

debutante slouch see *boyish form.*

décolletage a low neckline front and back, as in formal evening dress.

décolleté adjective meaning with the

dagged edges on houppelande and chaperon—15th C.

dalmatic and tiara worn by Serbian monk

neckline cut low, front and back, usually with bare shoulders.

deerstalker cap see *cap, deerstalker.*

degrained leather see *leather, degrained.*

de Joinville a popular scarf of the nineteenth century, a variation of the Ascot puff of the 1870's. Named for Prince de Joinville, soldier and author.

Chola derby - the hard, black felt bowler worn by Chola Indian women - La Paz, Bolivia

delaine a sheer woolen and cotton dress fabric, no longer in use.

Delaine Merino an American variety of Merino sheep.

Delft blue, delf blue a grayish, purplish blue, the predominating color on pottery made in Delft, Holland.

Delhi embroidery East Indian stitchery worked on satin and various fabrics in chain and satin stitches with metal and silk threads.

Della Robbia colors colors used by the Florentine sculptor and potter, Luca Della Robbia, of the fifteenth century; noted for his plaques which were covered with a soft glaze in grayed hues. The figures were usually white, in relief against a lovely blue background and often framed with a wreath of fruits in natural colors.

dhoti - the draped white cotton loincloth of the Hindu man

demi-bosom a short bosom for semiformal or formal day wear. The bosom may be stiff or pleated.

demi-toilet subdued evening dress.

denier denotes the size of a fiber filament as applied to silk, rayon, acetate and synthetic fibers; based on a French measurement of a standard strand, the higher the number, the heavier the yarn. Denier in stockings refers to the thickness of the nylon yarn, the lower the denier number, the sheerer the stocking.

denim a firm, washable fabric of twill weave in colored warp threads and white weft which creates a powdery tinge. Formerly used only for overalls, and blue jeans, but today used also for dresses and suits. Its name is a contraction of "de Nîmes" a city in France.

Denmark satin a strong, coarse worsted fabric woven with a twill surface, formerly used for shoe uppers.

dentelle French for lace.

dentelle au fuseau bobbin lace.

dentelle de fille thread lace.

dentelle de la vierge a wide type of Dieppe point lace.

derby hat the American term for bowler. A derby hat of lighter weight and softer felt was introduced in 1959. see *bowler.*

derby, Chola a hat worn by Chola Indian women of La Paz, Bolivia, who must have seen, noted and acquired a man's derby in the first decade of the twentieth century. The Indians, who had always worn hard white felt hats of their own manufacture, have since worn the factory-made model in black, brown, or beige.

dernier cri French, meaning the very latest fashion.

deshabillé, dishabillé French for negligée or undress.

Dessés, Jean see *couture, haute.*

Devonshire brown a rich brown supposedly the color of the soil in Devonshire, England.

dhoti the loincloth of white cotton which the Hindu man wraps around his loins. The ends are passed to the back between the thighs and tucked in at the waist. The dhoti is especially favored by both men and women because it is cool and comfortable in the hot climate.

diadem A crown, emblem of regal power and sovereignty.

diagonal weave see *twill weave.*

diamanté French for "ornamented with diamonds"; such items as buttons, buckles and fabrics used for formal evening wear.

diamond a precious stone; before the Middle Ages the diamond was regarded as a monarch's jewel and was mounted in scepters, crowns and other royal pieces but seldom as an individual ornament. The idea of wearing the diamond as a personal trinket was fostered by Agnès Sorel, the mistress of Charles VII of France (1403–1461). It is the hardest substance known (pure carbon) and when not cut into gems it is used as an abrasive. Usually colorless or nearly so, some specimens being of pale colors, yellow to brown, rarely blue, green, red. When cut for jewelry a remarkable brilliance comes to life. India was the chief source of diamonds for centuries, then Brazil and, presently, South Africa. see *gem cuts.*

diaper soft, absorbent cloth used as infants' breechcloths, now generally replaced by disposable garments.

diapered fabrics cloth embroidered all over with small conventional and geometric designs in lozenges, crescents, stars and flowers, the unit of design being repeated and connected in a diamond framework and varied in color. Originally made of costly silk in Damascus and Baghdad, the fabric has been made in cotton and linen, especially white, since the Renaissance.

diaphragm that section of the body from the waist to the chest, more often termed the rib-cage in modern fashion writing.

dickey, dicky an English innovation about 1809; a stiff, standing collar, followed by a separate shirt front in the 1830's. It was tucked, pleated and embroidered and of finer linen than the body garment of which it was part. see *fill-in.*

Dieppe point lace of the seventeenth and eighteenth centuries, made at Dieppe, France; a bobbin lace of the Valenciennes type.

dimity a sheer fabric for summer use, generally made of combed cotton. The raised, corded or checked surfaces are obtained by weaving several threads together. It was made first in Damietta, Egypt; used from the eighteenth century to the present.

dinner jacket The dinner coat first appeared in England in the 1880's and was called the "cowes" or dress sack coat. It was described as a dress coat without tails and was used for dinners and dances in country homes. In the United States the jacket was named the "Tuxedo," because it was first worn at Tuxedo Park. In France, it is known as "the smoking," its design having originated in the smoking or lounge suits of the 1840's. It became more popular in America than in Europe, American men liking its informality. see *black tie; tuxedo.*

dinner or **theater suit** the feminine "covered-up" look for evening of the 1930's and '40's, consisting generally of a long black skirt, a delicate blouse, a cummerbund and short jacket, emulating the informal evening dress of a lady's escort.

Dior, Christian see *New Look; couture, haute.*

diploidion the extra upper length of a very long chiton folded and left to hang over a tight belt. The peplos was a separate square of fabric fastened on the shoulders and left to hang. see *peplos.*

Directoire 1795–1799, the period in French fashion when the designers of women's dress went back to the classic robes of ancient Greece and Rome for inspiration.

Directoire a cotton, semitransparent chemise gown which was worn over a taffeta slip. This fashion of wearing thin cottons in winter was believed to be the cause of an epidemic (probably of influenza) in Paris, 1803, which was called muslin disease.

dirndl skirt of Tyrolese origin; a full skirt gathered at the waist, in peasant style and coloring, worn with a shirtwaist. In fashion in the U.S.A. for several decades, 1940's, 1950's, and early 1960's. see *Tyrolean dress.*

ditty bag a sailor's small box or bag in which he carries threads, needles, tapes, and other small necessaries.

djellaba, litham a native Moroccan caftan-like robe open at the neck, of woolen cloth with long, loose sleeves and below knee-length or longer. An age-old hooded cloak of North Africa and the Near East worn by men and women. Women add a scarf, the litham, a sheer embroidered square folded diagonally to cover nose, mouth and neck. Men also use the litham when the sand is blowing, but it is a plain scarf or face cloth. see *gallibaya; haik; jelab; jellaba; litham; mandeel; yasmak.*

djubbeh see *jubbah.*

dobby, dobbie a small loom resembling a jacquard. The fabric is also called dobby, and includes simple woven motifs such as geometric and floral designs. The textiles, cottons, rayons and silk include shirtings, huck towels, diaper cloth and dress goods. The name of the loom comes from dobby, the boy who sat atop the loom drawing up the warp threads to form the design.

doeskin the buffed inner side of sheep, lamb or doe which is used for gloves and leather goods. Also a high-grade woolen suiting and trouser cloth, finely twilled, closely woven and in many finishes.

doeskin a fine quality satin weave woolen cloth with a dress finish; used for waistcoat, riding habit, broadcloth coating and trousers in men's and women's costume.

dog collar jeweled, see *collar, dog.*

dog fur from a species of Siberian dog similar to the Eskimo dog. Foxlike fur of poor quality, much used in the nineteenth century for caps, coats, lining and muffs.

dogaline an important, aristocratic fashion of the fourteenth century worn in Italy by both men and women. A robe of brocade or velvet, with the knee-length, flaring outer sleeves, which were often fur-lined and fur-bordered.

dogskin a fur also called Chinese dog imported from Manchuria and Mongolia. Its use as fur is recent. Good peltries have

dogaline costume with long fur-lined sleeves-Italian-14th C.

dogaline costume with long fur-lined sleeves-Italian-14th C.

good fur fiber and long guard hair which is bleached, dyed and left natural length. Used for trimming on popular-priced garments and for men's utility coats.

dogskin leather imported from Mongolia and China. It is soft and durable, resembling goatskin.

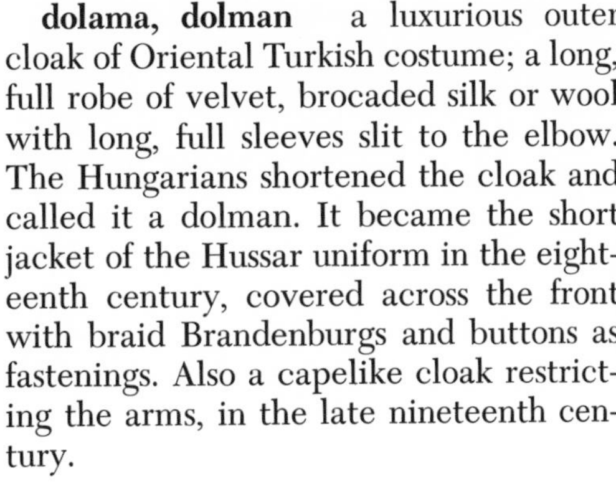

dolama, dolman a luxurious outer cloak of Oriental Turkish costume; a long, full robe of velvet, brocaded silk or wool with long, full sleeves slit to the elbow. The Hungarians shortened the cloak and called it a dolman. It became the short jacket of the Hussar uniform in the eighteenth century, covered across the front with braid Brandenburgs and buttons as fastenings. Also a capelike cloak restricting the arms, in the late nineteenth century.

dolama of blue velvet over a silk djubbeh-turban with fringe-Turkish

dolman or dolama-worn over striped caftan or djubbeh-silk sash or abnet-bonnet-Anatolian professor

dolman jacket of the hussar's uniform-usually worn slung over one shoulder-a feature was Brandenburgs and buttons-white wig with pigtail-18th C.

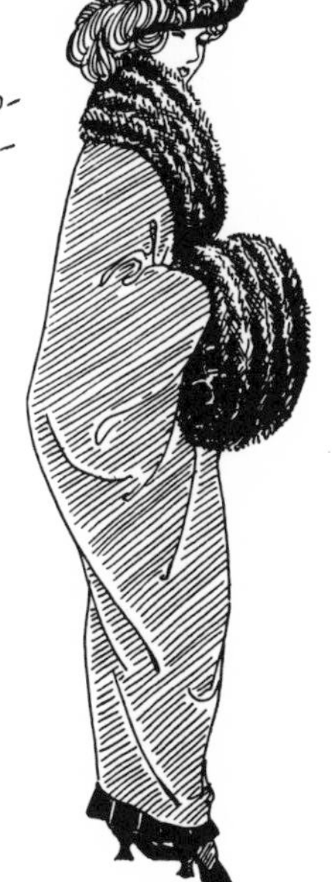

dolman wrap-fur-trimmed-1912

dolman-sleeved robe-black sheepskin bonnet-Russian farmer

domino and half mask—18th C.

doll hat see *hat, doll.*

dolls, fashion see *fashion babies.*

Dom Pedro a heavy leather brogue with one-buckle closure introduced as a work shoe by Dom Pedro, Emperor of Brazil, 1822–1834.

domet see *outing flannel.*

domino the hooded woolen cloak formerly worn by the clergy in winter. The wearing of the domino with a half mask originated in the eighteenth century in Venice, where it was worn to carnivals and masked balls. For such purposes, the robe was voluminous and usually of silk.

Donegal tweed originally made by Donegal Irish peasants on hand looms, a hand-scoured, homespun tweed. Also loosely woven tweeds of Yorkshire yarns dyed and finished in Donegal. Today they are mostly machine made with the slubs woven in. For suits, topcoats and sportswear.

dopatta—silk or cotton scarf with gold and silver thread worn by Mohammedan and Hindu men and women—

Dongola kid see *kid, Dongola.*

dopatta a scarf worn as a shawl or veil by Hindu and Mohammedan men and women in India. Of muslin or silk woven with gold and silver threads. see *uparnā.*

dorea, doria an East Indian muslin with stripes of varied widths and colors. Probably used for the doric, see *doric.*

doric of Oriental origin, a rectangle of sheer or fine Indian cotton, later of silk, caught together over the arms by fibulae or buttons, forming sleeves when buttoned.

dorina the enveloping cloak of the Bosnian woman in public, covering her from head to foot and secured by a string-tied belt around the waist. It is a length of checked cloth in light color accompanied by the sheer black yashmak curtaining the face. see *feredeza.*

dorina—the coverall of a Bosnian woman in public—thin checked cloth and black gauze yashmak—

doris see *dorea.*

dormeuse French for "sleeper"; an English sleeping bonnet of the 1770's, the cap was of sheer lawn, fine shirred lace and satin ribbon with frills, which hugged the cheeks.

dormouse a squirrel-like rodent native to Europe, some species in Asia and Africa; very fine soft fur, tawny red above, paler underneath and a white patch at the throat. Used for trimming.

d'Orsay, Count Guillaume Gabriel French society leader and dandy, Paris and London. Also a painter and sculptor, 1801–1852.

d'Orsay pump see *pump, d'Orsay.*

d'Orsay roll see *hat, top.*

dot patterns see *confetti dots; coin dots; polka dots.*

dotted Swiss, Swiss muslin a crisp, sheer cotton fabric ornamented with small dots of matching or contrasting color which are either clipped or swivel. The original cloth is still made in Switzerland and exported.

double-breasted coat or **jacket** overlapping fronts and a double row of buttons, one for closing or fastening.

doublet see *gambeson; jerkin.*

doublet, peasecod-bellied see *peasecod-bellied doublet.*

Doucet see *couture, haute.*

doupioni silk silk fibers joined at intervals making rough yarns such as those used in good quality shantung and pongee. The filament is the result of two silkworms having spun two or more cocoons together.

dowlas originally from Daoulas in Brittany. A coarse linen cloth for working blouses made in Scotland and England in the seventeenth and eighteenth centuries. Now replaced by a stout calico.

drabbet a coarse, drab-colored linen made in England and used for men's working smocks.

draper, draper's shop in the eighteenth and nineteenth centuries, a skilled tailor or dressmaker kept a shop where fabrics and trimmings could be purchased. He also made garments to order.

drawers an undergarment for the body and legs. They were worn by the Franks and Saxons from the ninth century, but in a contemporary Latin description of Charlemagne's dress, the garment is noted as "feminalia." In the sixteenth century, drawers and breeches were often confused, although drawers, being of fine linen and white, must have signified a body garment. In the seventeenth century, English gentlemen's "longe linnen" drawers are noted to wear under breeches. A type of drawers new in the seventeenth century was especially designed for Italian and French ladies who rode horseback. And Samuel Pepys in the seventeenth century, mentions lying in his cool "holland" drawers in hot weather. Until 1800 in feminine dress, only two or three known references to this piece of apparel exist, until the transparent Empire sheath gown made some leg covering necessary. From about 1805, French and English fashion journals occasionally referred to the new item. It was the first appearance of the garment in women's dress, and it remained uncommon in German countries and England. It was worn by little girls in the 1820's but was not adopted by women until the 1830's.

drawn-work a type of embroidery in which some threads are drawn out of the fabric and the remaining edges embroidered to complete the design.

drawstring a manner of securing loose fabric around neck, wrist, waist or ankle by drawing a tape or cord through a slot sewn at the edge of the garment.

Dresden à la Pompadour a fabric on which a dainty flower design is printed on the warp before weaving.

Dresden point lace eighteenth century, made in Dresden, Saxony; of fine linen made with a square mesh formed by drawing some threads and embroidering those left. The design was usually of small flowers on a net ground in a coarser imitation of Brussels bobbin lace.

dress form a life-size woman's torso or trunk, of papier mâché or wire, often adjustable, for the fitting and draping of garments.

dress improver a device of two small hoops to round out a woman's hips, which developed into the bustle of the eighteen-eighties and 'nineties.

dress patterns see *paper patterns.*

dress shield a crescent-shaped piece of rubberized silk or cotton, worn under the arms to protect clothing from perspiration.

dressing gown see *negligée* or *sacque.*

dressmaker formerly a woman skilled in cutting, fitting and dressmaking who went to her customer's home several times a year to make up clothes required for the coming season. Today, the customer buys ready-made, couturier-made, or makes her own.

dressmaker suit a more feminine version of the tailored suit of jacket, blouse and skirt. Made of softer, dressier fabrics, it permitted a wider choice of colors, some trimming, and special dressmaker details in sewing and finish.

drill, drilling a stout, twilled cotton or linen used for men's shirts, middy blouses, linings, summer trousers and uniforms.

du Barry fashion-taffeta with ruchings and bowknots-powdered hair-1762

drip-dry literal description of a fabric. One can wash out a garment made of drip-dry fabric, and when dry, it may be worn with little or no pressing, the garment having returned to its original form.

drugget a heavy woolen cloth formerly used for coats, usually gray or brown. Also a coarse cloth used to protect carpet and furniture. A rug of cotton and wool also called India carpet.

druid's cloth similar to monk's cloth; a canvaslike fabric in a rough basket weave.

du Barry costume of the period of Louis XV, 1715 to 1774, known as Rococo Period, elaborate ornamentation in dress and furnishings—panniers, shell motifs, flowers, feathers, and ribbon bowknots. Du Barry, the favorite of Louis XV, retired from the court upon his death in 1774.

ducal bonnet or cap-mortar shaped-red felt-Italian-15th C.

ducal bonnet see *corno.*

ducape a heavy corded silk of plain color, durable and popular; mentioned in inventories of the second half of the seventeenth century, and popular in the eighteenth. Used for hoods, cloaks and dresses in the American Colonies.

duchesse lace similar to Honiton but of fine thread and daintier. A bobbin-made lace having the effect of very fine tape with flowers and floral sprays made separately and joined by brides. A favorite for bridal gowns.

duchesse satin see *satin, duchesse.*

duck a fabric rather like canvas or tightly woven cotton or linen, with plain and rib weaves. Of various weights and possessing great washability, it is used for work clothes and sportswear.

duckbill cap see *cap, duckbill.*

dude a colloquialism in the United States of unknown origin; a name given the fastidious dresser, dandy or fop, or any Easterner by the Westerner.

duffel, duffer see *British warm.*

dulband see *turban.*

dummy a common term for a model or dress form.

dungarees workman's overalls; formerly made of an East Indian cloth dungaree but now made of denim.

dundrearies, Dundreary whiskers see *beards.*

dupioni silk see *doupioni silk.*

Durable Press trademark for a chemical treatment of fabric by baking the garment in ovens, thus making the creases permanent and eliminating the need for ironing. Sportswear, blouses and dresses, men's and children's wear are frequently durable pressed.

duster a long cover-all light coat of linen or tussore silk that men and women wore as a very necessary protection against dust, when traveling in the open motor car around the turn of the century. Today, a woman's dress-length housecoat, also an unlined summer coat. see *automobile togs.*

dust ruffle see *balayeuse.*

Dutch collar see *collar, Dutch.*

Dutchman's breeches full breeches gathered to a band above the ankles. Worn with traditional costume.

duvetyn, duvetyne, duvetine a smooth fabric resembling velvet, used for women's wear and millinery.

Dynel trademark for synthetic staple fiber of natural gas and salt. Soft and wool-like with good draping quality. Used for knitwear, underwear and sportswear.

E

earmuffs a pair of adjustable ear pads of velvet or plush attached to a metal headband used for winter protection. Worn formerly only by men and boys, especially for skiing, but now adopted by hatless young women as well. Twentieth century.

earrings favored ornaments from time immemorial. Pendant earrings were usually a symbol of rank in ancient Babylonia, Assyria and Egypt. Men and women wore rings in pierced ears, nose and lips. The European courtiers of the mid-seventeenth century delighted in the fashion of a single pearl hanging from one ear. Earrings virtually disappeared in the late nineteenth century, to be revived in the early twentieth by the appearance of a screw or clip device which permitted wearing the trinkets without piercing the ear lobes. The fashion for pierced ears was revived by young girls in the 1950's. see *chandelier earrings.*

Easter bonnet see *bonnet, Easter.*

eau de Cologne at the beginning of the eighteenth century, an Italian perfumer living in Cologne, Germany, concocted a toilet water, which became famous and is in use today as "eau de cologne." It was prepared from vegetable extracts, oils and rectified spirits but the inventor kept the formula a trade secret. see *perfume.*

"échelle," French for ladder of bowknots on stomacher with busk—1685

échelle French for ladder; a separate front bodice panel, a form of stomacher in the seventeenth and eighteenth centuries. It was reinforced with busk and whalebone and decorated with ribbon bowknots graduated in size from bosom to waist. A variation was the cross-lacing of narrow ribbons.

Edwardian the period of Edward VII, King of England (1901–1910), which coincides with the American Gibson girl fashions. The English period recalls the hourglass silhouette for women and the long, narrow fitted suits for men.

eggplant color a rich dark muted purple.

eggshell color a creamy white or beige-white in fabrics and leather.

egret the pure white plumage of various herons which was used as the egrets of commerce. see *aigrettes; Audubon plumage law.*

Egyptian costume, ancient see illustrations, pages 115 and 116.

Egyptian lace a handmade knotted lace beaded between the meshes and used for trimming.

eider yarn a soft knitting yarn made from fine wool.

eiderdown named after the down of an eider duck. A knitted or woven cloth with napped surface and fluffy feel to both sides. Used for negligées, bathrobes and infants' wear.

Eighteenth Century costume see pages 117–127.

Egyplian- schenti or loincloth- beaded collarette- schenti

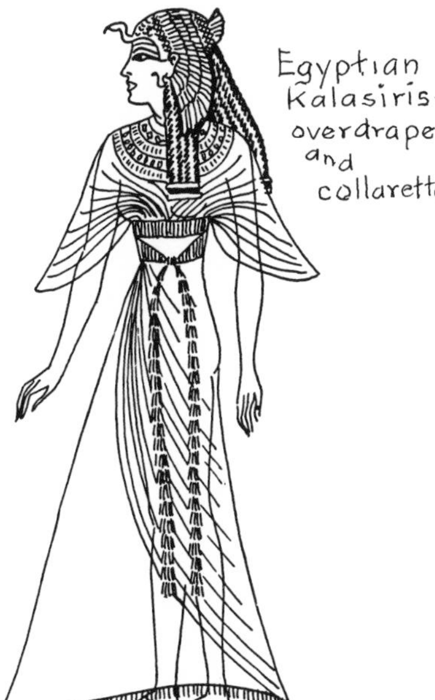

Egyptian kalasiris- overdrape and collarette

Egyptian embroidered kalasiris with shoulder straps

Egyptian king- striped linen headdress and beard or gold postiche

bulgha- traditional Moslem slipper- yellow or red morocco

Egyptian kalasiris over tunic- belt with jeweled apron

Egyptian libas- traditional pantaloons- bolero, waistcoat and fez

Egyptian queen- wig- gold circlet with jewels- 3rd C.-BC

Egyptian

1200 B.C.
king in schenti-
kalasiris-
royal apron
and cape
king
in schenti
and
kalasiris
1420 B.C.
woman worker
wearing
the schenti
1900 B.C.
king in
pleated
schenti-
jeweled belt-
1970 B.C.
an official
in schenti
and kalasiris
1500 B.C.
a servant
wearing
the schenti-
1420 B.C.

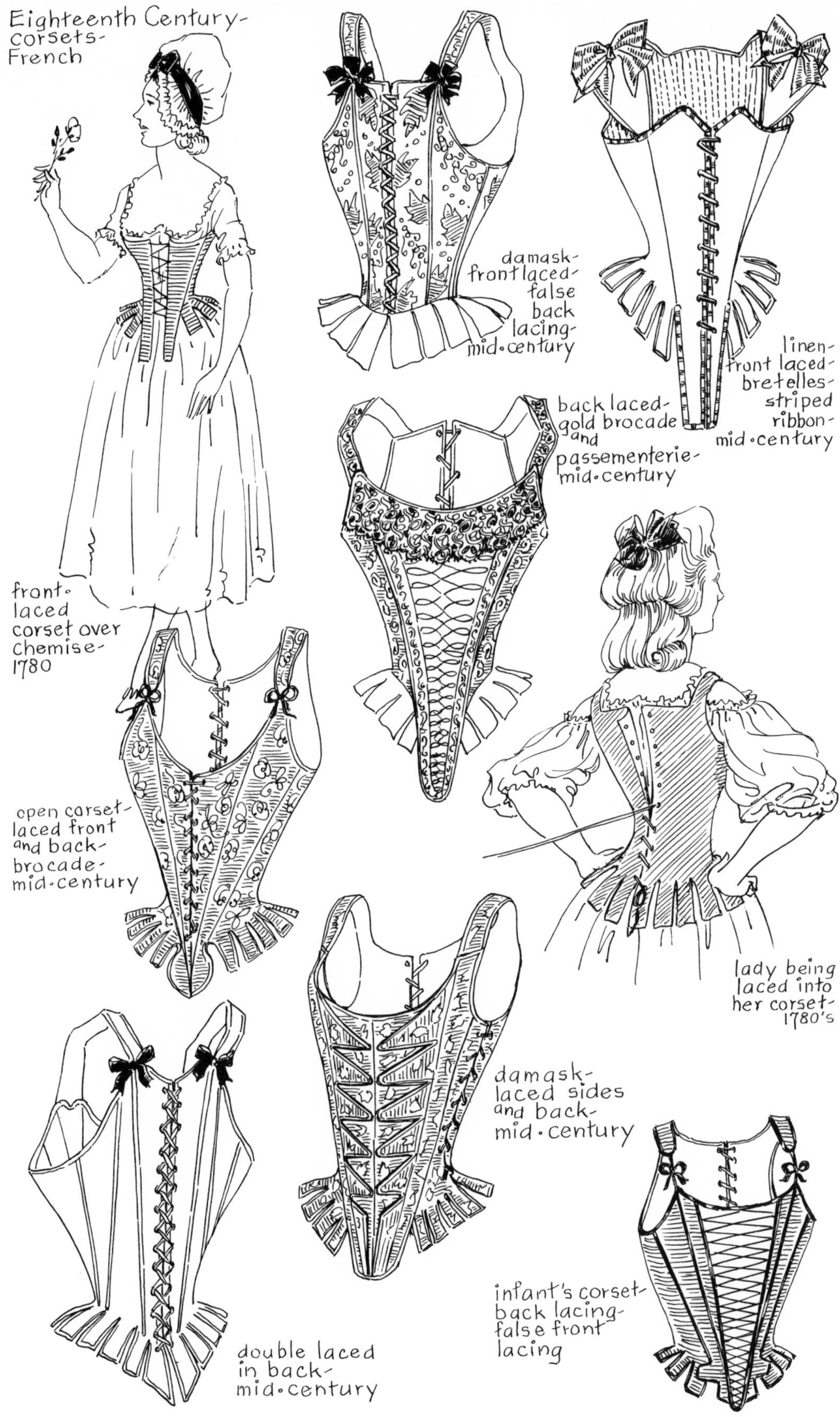
Eighteenth Century-
corsets-
French
damask-
front laced-
false
back
lacing-
mid•century
linen-
front laced-
bretelles-
striped
ribbon-
mid•century
back laced-
gold brocade
and
passementerie-
mid•century
front-
laced
corset over
chemise-
1780
open corset-
laced front
and back-
brocade-
mid•century
lady being
laced into
her corset-
1780's
damask-
laced sides
and back-
mid•century
infant's corset-
back lacing-
false front
lacing
double laced
in back-
mid•century

Eighteenth Century-
chemise-
underpetticoat-
corset
chemise and
petticoat-
linen, lace
and bowknots-
2nd decade-
French
linen chemise
and cap-
French-
mid-century
boned chemise
with stomacher
of bowknots-
French-1767
chemise and
corset laced
in back-
French-
1771
front-laced
corset over
chemise-
French-
1780
actress wearing
tights under
chemise-
English-
1798
cap and
chemise of the
Directoire
Period-
1798

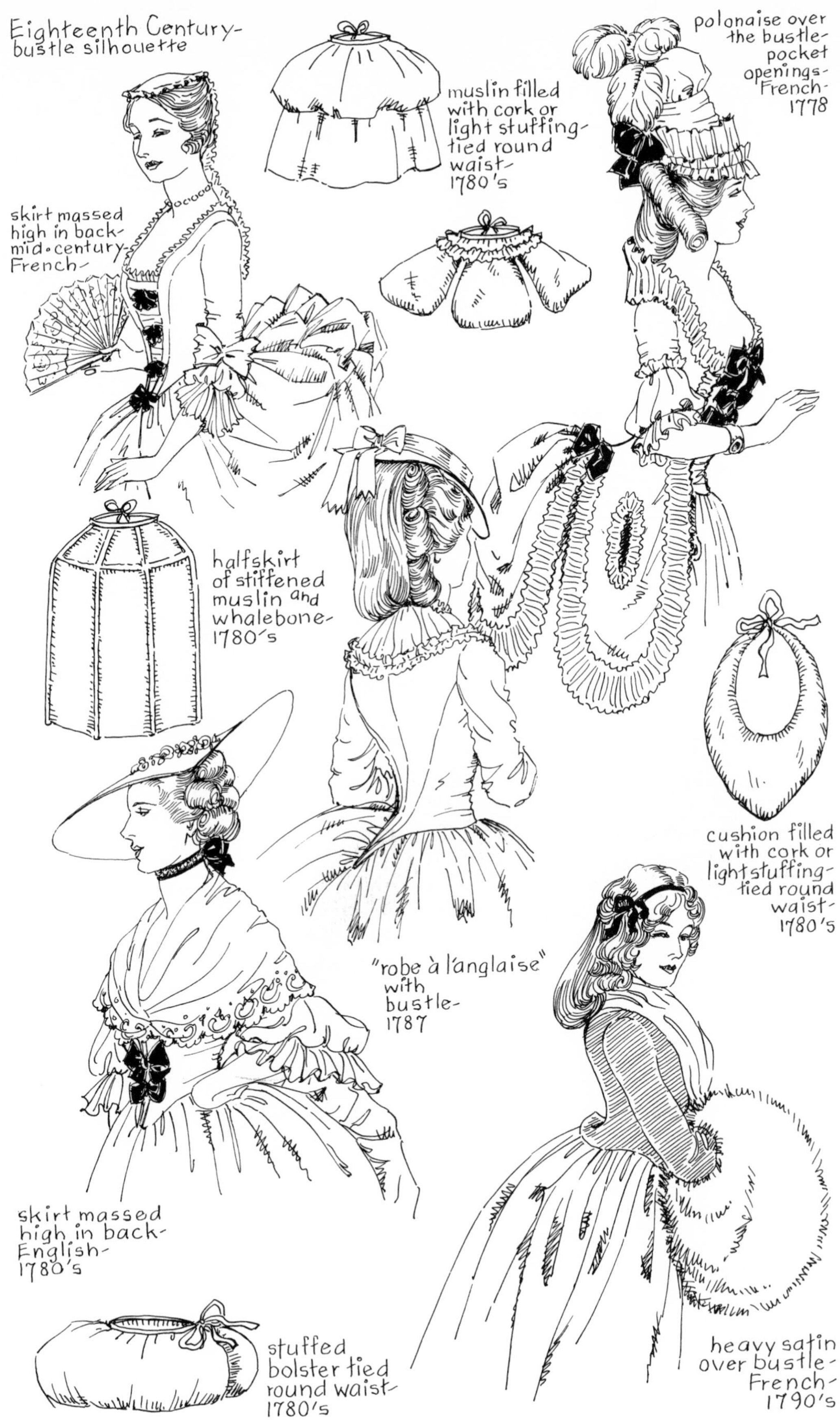
Eighteenth Century-
bustle silhouette
muslin filled
with cork or
light stuffing-
tied round
waist-
1780's
polonaise over
the bustle-
pocket
openings-
French-
1778
skirt massed
high in back-
mid-century-
French-
halfskirt
of stiffened
muslin and
whalebone-
1780's
cushion filled
with cork or
light stuffing-
tied round
waist-
1780's
"robe à l'anglaise"
with
bustle-
1787
skirt massed
high in back-
English-
1780's
stuffed
bolster tied
round waist-
1780's
heavy satin
over bustle-
French-
1790's

Eighteenth Century-
negligée
and sports
woolen cloth
house coat
with cap
to match-
French-
1760
footed
drawers of
stockinette-
legs separate
joined at belt-
drawstring
in back-
English-
1790's
garb of a
wrestler-
breeches,
stockings
and shoes-
English-
1788
silk
house
coat with
Brandenburgs-
English-
1740
house
coat of
brocaded
silk-
fan pleats
longer than
skirt-
French-
1770
powdering
mantle of
light silk
or cotton-
French-
1780's
drawers of
linen or flannel-
late period-English
white
linen
sports
costume-
English-
mid-century

Eighteenth Century-
vest and waistcoat
embroidered
silk vest
laced in
back-
French-
1720's
vest buttoned
to left-coat
to right-
English-
1730's
elaborately
embroidered
white faille
silk-
English-
1720
lace-edged
satin vest
with
stiffened
skirts-
French-
1745
embroidered waistcoat-
French-
1780's
shortening
of the
vest-
French-
1770's
striped waistcoat
of the Directoire-
French-
1795
striped waistcoat
of the
"incroyable"-
French-
1796

Eighteenth Century
panniers
and hoops
wire hoops
and metal
bands-
1711
starched, embroidered
circular petticoat-1736
Watteau
sack over
wide
panniers-
1730
criade
of gummed canvas
or oilcloth and
wire-1718
silk with
whalebone-
pocket openings
over hips-mid-century
gown over
"janseniste"
panniers-
1762
silk
or muslin
with
whalebone-1720 to 1750
wooden
oval hoops-
flat front
and back-
Venetian-
1750
pocket
panniers-
whalebone
hoops-
1750
"janseniste"
panniers with
pocket openings-
corset over chemise-
underpetticoat-
1740 to 1770
gondola or
double panniers-
muslin over
wooden frame-
1760
hinged metal
elbow panniers-
to fold under arms-
1770

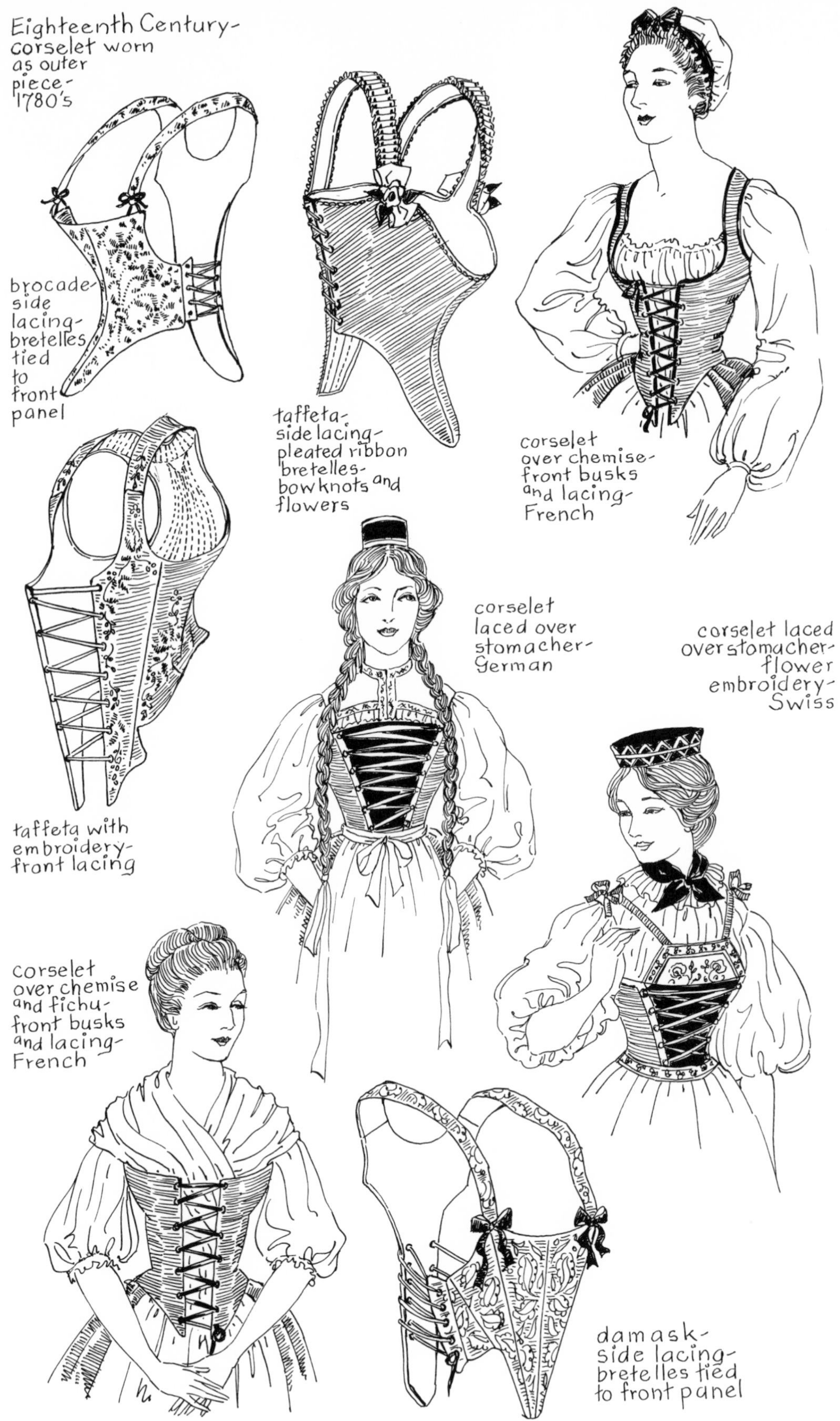
Eighteenth Century-
corselet worn
as outer
piece-
1780's
brocade-
side
lacing-
bretelles
tied
to
front
panel
taffeta-
side lacing-
pleated ribbon
bretelles-
bowknots and
flowers
corselet
over chemise-
front busks
and lacing-
French
corselet
laced over
stomacher-
German
corselet laced
over stomacher-
flower
embroidery-
Swiss
taffeta with
embroidery-
front lacing
corselet
over chemise
and fichu-
front busks
and lacing-
French
damask-
side lacing-
bretelles tied
to front panel

Eighteenth Century
shirt and
cravat
negligée-worn
without jabot
or cravat-
English
gentleman's
shirt of fine
muslin-jabot
and ruffles of
point d'Alençon-
turned-down
collar-buttons
and buttonholes-
French-
mid-century
black taffeta
solitaire-French-
1733
corset laced in
back-drawers of
linen or stockinette-
English-
1790's
workman's
muslin shirt-
French-
first half
of period
folded cravat-
American-
early period
collar points
over black
silk cravat-
American-
1775
black
ribbon
solitaire-
lace jabot-
English-
1730's
tied cravat-
embroidered
sheer lawn-
American-
1796
linen smock
of the farmer-
English
military cravat-
black silk
over white-
linen jabot-
English-
1780's

Eighteenth Century-
corset-bodice
and stomacher-
French
brocade corset•bodice
laced in back-front
open over stomacher-
basque of silk and kid-
mid•century
corset•bodice
laced under
stomacher
or in back-
2nd half
of period
stomacher
of bowknots-
in "échelle" or
ladder form-
2nd half
of period
corset•bodice
laced under
ruche-
1777
embroidered
linen
stomacher
with cord
lacing
corset•bodice
with laced
stomacher-
1785
stomacher
of
embroidered
frills-
1752
stomacher
appliqued
with
passementerie-
1750

Eighteenth Century-
negligée-
the rayle-
French
rayle or
combing jacket
of fine lawn-
embroidered
scalloped edge-
1740's
powdering
mantle in
light silk
or cotton-
1725
silk or cotton
rayle-corset over
chemise-"modesty
bit" tucked in
bosom-brocaded
petticoat-
1730's
negligée of white
muslin-rose
corset bodice-
"modesty bit" tucked
in bosom-
1743
silk
morning rayle
worn outdoors-
silk hood
over white
lawn hood-
velvet bow-
first half
of period
wadded silk
pelisse edged
with marabou-
white muslin
petticoat-
dormeuse bonnet
of sheer white
lawn-velvet
ribbon-
1778

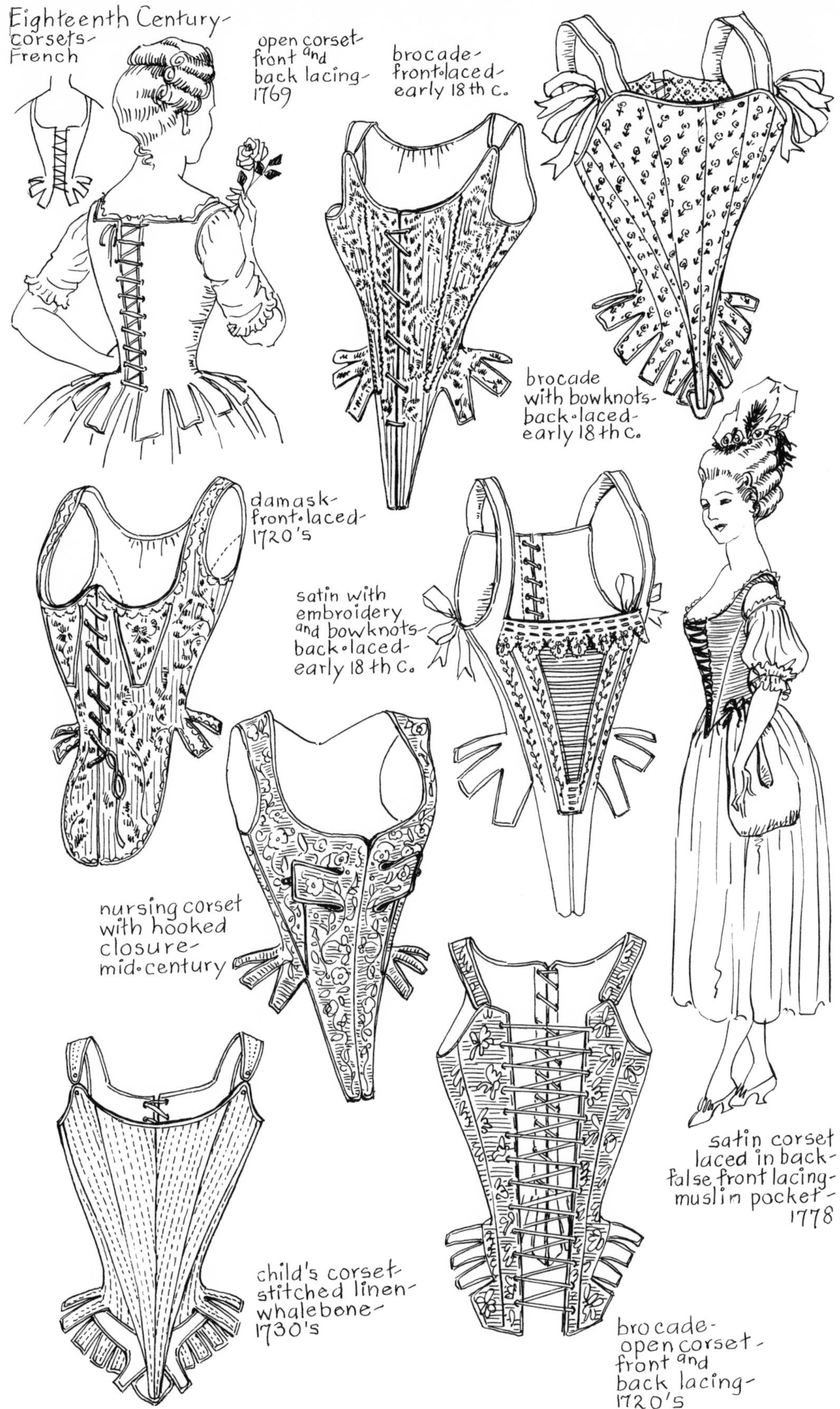
Eighteenth Century-
corsets-
French
open corset-
front and
back lacing-
1769
brocade-
front•laced-
early 18th c.
brocade
with bowknots-
back•laced-
early 18th c.
damask-
front•laced-
1720's
satin with
embroidery
and bowknots-
back•laced-
early 18th c.
nursing corset
with hooked
closure-
mid•century
satin corset
laced in back-
false front lacing-
muslin pocket-
1778
child's corset-
stitched linen-
whalebone-
1730's
brocade-
open corset-
front and
back lacing-
1720's

Eisenhower jacket a waist-length, belted jacket in olive-drab cloth with turned collar and buttoned-cuff sleeves. Worn with a drab cloth shirt, black silk scarf and garrison cap. Named for General Dwight D. Eisenhower. see *battle jacket.*

elasticized fabric with rubber invented by T. Hancock of Middlesex, England in 1820. It was called elastic cloth or webbing and replaced the ribbons and ribbon garters then in vogue. From 1836, when Charles Goodyear made his important discovery of a method of treating the surface of gum, the use of elastic in dress became more practical.

elastique a steep, double twill worsted cloth similar to cavalry twill. Made elastic by being interwoven with fine threads of India rubber which renders it stretchable. Used for riding breeches, slacks and army uniforms.

elbow panniers see *panniers, elbow.*

electric seal see *seal, imitations.*

elephant skin see *leather, elephant skin.*

Elizabethan costume the mode during the reign of Queen Elizabeth I, 1558–1603. The feature of women's dress was the wheel farthingale with a long, pointed, corseted bodice and stomacher, and high heeled shoes. The queen's gorgeous ankle-length gowns permitted a glimpse of her silk stockings. Men wore the peasecod-bellied doublet and adopted the pump. The starched wired ruff appeared and lace was much used. The fabrics of this late Renaissance Period were very handsome.

elk originally smoke-tanned hide of elk, but today of cowhide and calfskin dressed with smoke-tanned color and odor. Tanned elk is called buckskin and is a soft, pliable, oilless leather.

ell old European measurement of cloth, different in different countries. The English ell was 45 inches but today 36 inches or more is generally accepted.

embossed a raised pattern on velvet or plush created by shearing and pressing sections of the design flat; also a raised pattern that stands out in relief on fabrics, leather and jewelry.

embroidery a general term for any form of ornamental needlework. Embroidery is of ancient origin, the earliest surviving examples being fifth and fourth century B.C. work from the Altai Mountains in Siberia. This is appliqué worked with horsehair, using leather, felt and woolen cloth. The earliest piece using linen is a Greek fragment, fifth century B.C. Embroidery was important in the Mediterranean area from early times; Islamic examples from Egypt, Mesopotamia, southern Italy, Sicily and Spain use a large variety of stitches, indicating an active tradition in such work and the great superiority of the Mediterranean culture and the achievement of Saracenic textile art. During the Middle Ages embroideries or hangings were used to illustrate biblical themes, episodes in the lives of the saints and even to expound religious doctrines. By the fourteenth century secular themes appeared, hunting being a particular favorite. In northern Europe English embroidery was outstanding; the oldest known piece is a chasuble of 850 A.D. The Anglo-Saxon work, which survived the Norman Conquest, was known as opus anglicanum and reached its peak in the thirteenth and fourteenth centuries. The famous Bayeux Tapestry, c. 1070, which is embroidered, not woven, is an isolated example of non-Anglo-Saxon work at this time. Opus anglicanum vestments and hangings, primarily worked in silk but using some gold, were commissioned by prelates from all over Europe. Wars and plagues brought a decline of this work, and English embroidery next attains prominence in the sixteenth and seventeenth centuries, chiefly in secular work. Besides such furnishings as hangings and cushions, much time and effort was spent on costume—everything was embroidered: jackets, caps, coifs, gloves and later aprons. The gorgeous dresses of Elizabeth I, encrusted with jewels, can be studied in many portraits.

The late eighteenth century also offered opportunities for embroidery on men's coats and waistcoats and to some extent on ladies' dresses. In Germany the prevailing style was whitework, embroidery worked in white linen thread on white linen, called opus teutonicum. Some examples of this also appeared in Italy and Switzerland. Beautiful embroideries in colored silk, mostly on vestments and ceremonial robes, were done in the Netherlands and Spain, fourteenth to sixteenth centuries.

In the Far East, especially in China and Japan, embroidery has embellished ceremonial costume for centuries. Although beautifully executed and with an exquisite use of shaded colors, the stitches employed indicate a limited repertoire of techniques. So-called peasant embroidery, worked in bright cottons or wool, has had a continuing tradition of use, especially for festival dress, in the Balkan countries, the Near East, eastern Europe and Scandinavia.

embroidery see specific types of embroidery; Anglo-Saxon, Appenzell, appliqué, arrasene, Assisi, Ayrshire, bead, Beauvais, Berlin, Bulgarian, bullion, California, Canadian, chenille, Chinese, chromo, crewel, cross-stitch, cutwork, Czechoslovakian, Delhi, drawn-work, eyelet, flame stitch, Florentine, Genoese, Hardanger, Holbein, Jacobean, Madeira, Madras, net, opus anglicanum, Paris, Persian, Rococo, Romanian, shadow, Sicilian, Spanish blackwork, Swiss, tinsel, Turkish, Venetian, Wallachian, Yugoslavian.

emerald a precious stone of a variety of beryl in rich green color. Oriental emerald is a rare green variety of corundum. The finest specimens, from Colombia, are usually executed in step-cut and cabochon.

emery a sewing accessory for keeping needles polished. Usually a tiny bag of emery powder in the shape of a strawberry.

Empire fashions the mode of the First Empire, 1804–1814. As worn by the Empress Josephine it was one of the loveliest in fashion's history. The general silhouette was that of a chemise gown, of velvet, silk or lingerie fabric worn over a sheer slip. The dress with long or short sleeves, perhaps with low décolletage, was belted under the bosom. Shawls, tiny bosom jackets and the long, enveloping redingote were in vogue. Bonnets and turbans completed the picture.

empress cloth a cloth of the rep family much in demand in the Second French Empire, 1852–1870. It was a cloth of wool or wool and cotton, resembling merino but not twilled.

Empire fashion-formal dress-claw-hammer tails-powdered wig-1814

Empire fashion dark green velvet coat-felt bonnet with ostrich-1814

Empress Eugénie hat, see *hat, Empress Eugénie.*

enamel opaque or semi-opaque, applied to fingernails and bare toenails.

end on end a fine check formed by a weave of alternate warp yarns of white and color. Used in cotton broadcloth, chambray and Oxford cloth for shirts, pajamas and sportswear.

engageantes French for sleeve ruffles, usually three of graduated width from elbow to wrist. Of sheer muslin, lace or embroidery and fashionable from 1660 to about 1760.

English coat see *frock coat.*

English drape a short-lived masculine fashion which appeared late in the 1920's; a one-button jacket falling loosely in front and baggy trousers with pleats at the waist. By 1938 the style had been revised to the English paddock suit with a high two-button closing.

English edging see *Angleterre.*

English foot socks see *socks, English foot.*

English gown, robe Anglaise an important fashion of the 1780's, beloved by the portrait painters of the day, especially Gainsborough, who delighted in painting their sitters in the costume. It was of unusually simple design, heavy satin with a long, full skirt and fitted bodice, gauzy sleeves and neckerchief and worn with a huge velvet hat with sweeping ostrich plumes. see *robe Anglaise; robe à la Française; Velasquez; Watteau gown.*

ensemble, feminine The three-piece costume, supplanting the severely tailored suit and coat in the 1920's. It was made in soft, colorful wools, the most popular being wool jersey and the colors beige and brown. It consisted of dress and coat, or skirt, sweater or overblouse, and coat, and eclipsed all other styles for fashionable daytime wear.

ensign blue a dark navy blue or midnight blue.

en-tout-cas a small umbrella for sun or rain, mid-nineteenth century.

entre-deux see *beading.*

envelope bag see *handbags.*

envelope chemise a lingerie piece of the twentieth century, chemise and drawers in one, 1915.

eolienne a fabric similar to poplin but lighter in weight. Usually of silk and wool or silk and cotton with crosswise corded effect in the weaving.

epaulet military and shoulder decoration suggested by the steel épaulières of armor, worn to protect the shoulders. In the seventeenth century epaulets served to hold the shoulder belt in place and thus prevent the musket from slipping. Still later, epaulets became military decoration and insignia in various armies.

"English gown" favored by portrait painters- Gainsborough hat-1780's

They were handsome shoulder pads edged with heavy gold or silver fringe indicating the officer's rank.

epaulet sleeve see *sleeve, epaulet; epaulettes.*

ephod a hip-length vest of white linen with wide bretelles, worn by the Hebrew high priest. It was belted and handsomely embroidered in gold, silver, violet, purple and cerise threads. Worn in Biblical times.

ermiline see *rabbit.*

ermine the smallest of weasels, with cold weather coat of pure white fur, summer coat pale brown, and tip of tail always black; from Northern Asia, Europe and North America. The American species is designated weasel by the fur trade and is used for coats, jackets and trimmings. It has been used from medieval times for royal and legal robes and as heraldic insignia. It was also called miniver, which in modern British usage signifies ermine, and is geometrically spotted with black lamb pieces and worn in robes, crowns and coronets in British ceremonies. Russian ermine is the best, with Alaska weasel comparing favorably and becoming the more used in the twentieth century. The Chinese and Korean species are poor. Champagne Ermine is white ermine dyed a beige hue. see *armenian rat; weasel.*

ermine, Alaska or **Manchurian** a larger, coarser weasel, cream to white sides with pale yellow or orange back. It resembles, but is less durable than Russian ermine.

ermine, laitice, létice of the medieval and Renaissance periods. "A beast of whitish-gray color" resembling ermine and used for edging of neck, sleeves, tunic and ladies' trailing gowns. The width used designated the rank of the wearer.

ermine, summer stoat the British name for the natural brown weasel which changes its protective coat to white in winter. It is light or reddish-brown above and sulphur color below the black tail. A flat, not very durable fur, small in quantity and therefore high in price, used for coats, jackets and trimming.

ermine in winter when pure white-stoat in summer when light brown-tail always black-tipped

erminette see *rabbit.*

escarpin a lady's black satin slipper with ribbon ties.

esclavage French word for slavery; a slave bracelet or slave necklace made of multi-strands of gilt chains and beads.

escoffion an elaborate headdress of the fourteenth and fifteenth centuries which began as the golden net caul, crépine, reticulated cap of velvet or satin covered with a jeweled gilt net. It developed fantastic two-horned shapes and was finally supplanted by the tall hennin with long, flowing veil in the fifteenth century.

Eskimo dress see illustrations, next page; *kamiks; parka; timiak; kooletah.*

espadrille the braided cord or rope-soled canvas shoe worn by the Italians and French of the Midi, and Spaniards.

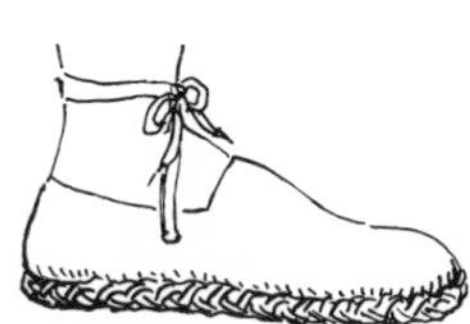

espadrille-canvas shoe with braided cord sole-worn by Italians and southern French

estamene, estamin a twilled woolen dress fabric resembling cheviot but with a rough, nappy surface.

Eton collar see *collar, Eton.*

Eton jacket as worn by the boys of Eton College, England. A slightly tapered coat reaching to the hips with wide lapels and open in front. It was adopted as a

Eton jacket and top hat worn by boys of Eton College, England

Eskimo woman of Alaska carrying baby in parka. Tunic, shirt, breeches of sealskin, fur to the inside

Eskimo woman in modern blue parka over fur parka and fur breeches

Eskimo woman of Greenland - costume of sealskin, fur to the inside - beadwork

Eskimo of Alaska - N.W. Territory - fox or wolf with leather fringe

Eskimo of Alaska - N.W. Territory - quilted cotton parka fur-lined - dark blue fur-lined breeches - white skin boots - fur to the inside

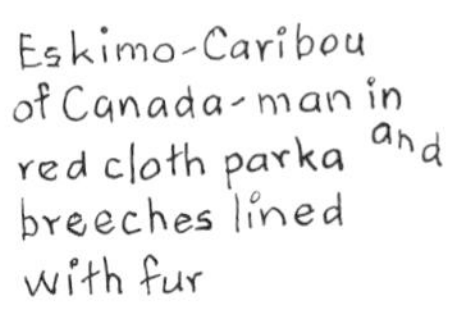

Eskimo-Caribou of Canada - man in red cloth parka and breeches lined with fur

feminine fashion in the 1860's and remains a constantly-recurring fashion with slight variation.

Etonian uniform morning coat and silk top hat; inaugurated and worn by the boys at Eton in 1820 at the funeral of George III, who was a great benefactor of the famous public school in Buckinghamshire, England. It is still worn.

Etruscan the costume of the farming people who lived in Etruria about 1000 B.C. reveals Greek influence, both Asiatic and European. Their few garments were covered with colorful patterns and the edges finished with characteristic decorative braids. The male tunic, a simple sheath and narrow, with the edges finished with handwork, was worn without an undergarment by the young men, but the older men wore a pleated, longer chiton underneath. The feminine short-sleeved tunic was long, snug-fitting and colorfully embroidered. The woman's cloak was a rectangle large enough to cover the whole figure. The man's cloak, called a tebenna, was a large rectangle or semicircle of woolen cloth. A favorite motif used in sculpture on tombs and smaller articles, was based upon the ancient Greek design known to us as the Greek key pattern.

étui French name of a small box or fancy bag of pretty fabric or leather usually attached to the edge of the bodice. It was used as the container for a woman's toilet and sewing articles from the seventeenth to the nineteenth centuries.

Eugénie's wigs the *Montero,* a huntsman's cap worn from 1600 by Spanish mountaineers, in Europe and the American colonies, and today. A round cap with a flap round back and sides which can be turned down to cover neck and cheeks in bad weather. Made of knitted yarn, woolen cloth or of fur. Named for the French Empress Eugénie who presented the fur caps to the Arctic Exploration group in 1875.

Etruscan headdress-
curls and felt cap
in tutulus shape

Etruscan headdress-
braided and curled
in tutulus shape-
jeweled tiara

"Eugénie's Wigs"-
knitted Montero
caps with fur.

evening bag see *handbag.*

evening gown in the time of Henry VIII, meant a night gown. see *night gown; gown.*

Evzone a soldier of a select corps in the Greek army who wears the fustanella, a very short flaring, pleated kilt. see *fustanella.*

eye make up generally consists of *eye shadow,* a thin coating of cream on the lids in violet, blue or green; *eye liner,* a pencil line at the base of the lashes; *mascara,* a thin cream to darken and thicken the lashes; *eyebrow pencil,* a soft crayon pencil to outline or emphasize the brows. *False eyelashes,* which became popular in the 1960's, are made of real mink, seal, hair or plastic. The lashes are provided with a liquid or cream adhesive and applied to the base of the real lashes for each wearing.

eyeglasses or **spectacles** Lenses for aiding impaired vision are commonly said to have been invented in the thirteenth century; by 1482, spectacle-makers had opened shops in Nuremberg. The first lenses were joined by a nosepiece which clung to the bridge of the nose. In the sixteenth century the joined lenses were attached to a vertical metal piece which could be suspended from under the front hair or hat. A great improvement in the eighteenth century were horizontal temples which hooked back of the ears. Frames were of heavy tortoise shell or horn until the nineteenth century, when lighter gold or silver frames were adopted. Notable today are improvements in plastics for frames, the harlequin shape of 1940 and the contact lenses which first appeared in the 1950's. see *contact lens; harlequin spectacles; lorgnette; pince-nez; monocle.*

eyelet embroidery floral patterns of openwork eyelets with solid stitchery used for foliage and bowknots. see *Madeira embroidery.*

eyeleteer a bodkin or small stiletto for punching eyelet holes for embroidery.

F

facing a false hem sewn to the underside of edges of collar, cuffs, or edge of skirt. It usually provides a better finish than the turned-up edge of self fabric alone.

fagoting, faggoting a kind of crisscrossed openwork stitch used in the space between two edges, as in an "open seam."

faille a glossy fabric, soft and lustrous, woven in silk, rayon or cotton with a flat, horizontal ribbing.

Fair Isle sweater a cardigan or pullover knit with colorful bands of geometrical designs; only the stockinette stitch is used. Supposed to have originated on Fair Isle, a small isolated island between the Orkneys and Shetlands, but actually a widespread type of knitting in the Scottish highlands and islands.

faja the wide, crushed, brilliantly colored sash of the Spaniard's costume consisting of white shirt with bolero or manta, breeches and hose in dark blue, green or black. Still worn in most provinces.

faja or wide sash of fiesta dress- all dark blue and embroidered-white blouse-Spanish

faldetta-a cloak worn by women of Malta-of Moorish origin

"falbalas" and "furbelows"-names for cut-out motifs applied as trimming-French-17th C.

falbala see *furbelow.*

falderal, falderol a piece of finery; a trifling ornament; a trinket.

faldetta a combination cloak and hood worn by women in Malta; more commonly known as a huke, a long, black cloth wrap of Moorish origin. see *huke; haik.*

fall a pendant ornament in costume as a cascade of lace, ruffles or ribbon. Over the top of the English hood of the sixteenth century hung a "fall" of black silk or velvet. Also a fashion new in 1966, a thick mane of hair worn pinned to the top of the head where it is usually dressed high, or cascaded into large rolls, or left

to hang slightly curled, or straight. Of European hair, usually in lengths of sixteen inches or more. Inexpensive falls are made of synthetic fiber.

falling band, Van Dyck a collar of fine white lawn edged with lace, also called a rabat. A wider version which lay on the shoulders, was called a rabatine, and was also known as a Van Dyck because it is shown in many portraits painted by the Flemish artist, Sir Anthony Van Dyck (1599–1641).

false hem see *facing.*

false sleeve see *sleeve, false.*

falsies see *bust forms.*

fan used in China, Japan and India since the eleventh century B.C. The folding fan originated in Japan, it is said, about 670 A.D., reaching China in the tenth century. The Egyptian fan, a symbol of rank and power, dates back to the thirteenth century B.C. The Egyptians, Assyrians and Persians were cooled by servants or slaves carrying long-staffed fans of grasses, leaves, and feathers. From Asia Minor and Egypt, the fan reached Europe by way of Italy, where hand fans were imported from the East in the twelfth century A.D. They were made of peacock, ostrich, parrot and Indian crow feathers with jeweled ivory handles. Small, dainty, square-shaped flag fans mounted on carved ivory sticks were carried by court ladies in the early sixteenth century. The folding fan was first used in Spain, passing to Italy and then to France, where it was introduced by Catherine de' Medici. The folded fan was made of leather, chicken skin, vellum or parchment, and decorated by the greatest artists of the day. The vogue continued into the eighteenth and nineteenth centuries, when the exquisite black lace folding fan of Spain was notable. In the early twentieth century, large ostrich feather fans were beautiful accessories with formal evening dress.

fanchon a bonnet of the Mid-Victorian period with a bavolet or deep ruffle at the back of the head. see *capote.*

farmer's satin an Italian imitation of real silk cloth, but the name now used for a lining fabric. see *satin, farmer's.*

"far-out" or fantastic, **"far in"** or conservative, two popular descriptive terms for such fashions of the 1960's.

farrajiyah a long cloak of the African desert worn by the Tuaregs. The sleeves are long and wide, resembling angel sleeves, in white or colored cotton.

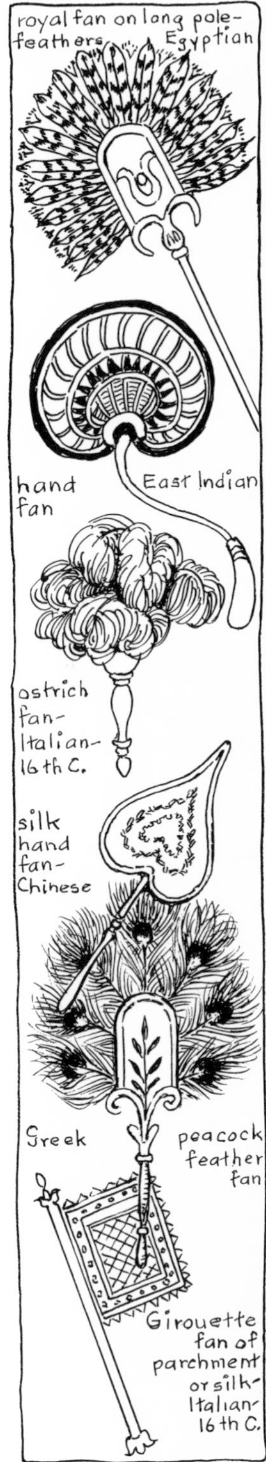

farthingale, verdingale, vertugadin, hoop, Catherine wheel Of Spanish origin, worn in France during the days of Louis XIII and in England under James I and Charles I. The flat farthingale was known in England as the Saint Catherine's wheel, a mode lasting from about 1530 to 1630. An ugly fashion, gowns were sometimes made with two hoops, the hoop actually being a stuffed roll that rested upon the hips. In France, the modish woman wore the hoop under several petticoats. The skirt or outer robe was "la modeste," the next under, "la friponne" or in English, "hussy," and the under one, "le secret." The foundation petticoat was of heavy canvas or linen with wicker hoops, the stuffed bolster being placed over or under that petticoat and tied around the hips.

farthingale breeches breeches with a small stuffed hoop resting on the hips as a protection against sword thrusts. Especially favored by the English Charles I (1625–1649).

fascia, tibiale rolls of woven cloth and leather which were wrapped around the legs. They were worn by the Roman legionnaires and copied by the farmers and peasants in Northern Italy and Etruria.

fashion is the current style of the moment. Fashion may be elegant, pleasing or even ugly, as long as it is the prevailing mode. *Style* is the mode of expression in any art; in costume it may be a manner of carriage, poise, line and color.

fashion babies, or **fashion dolls** served as the fashion journals of past centuries. The mannequin dolls, dressed in the newest styles, were sent out from Paris as early as the fourteenth century and, according to one record, one went to the Queen of England. By the eighteenth century many were sent to European capitals from Paris where Marie Antoinette and her modiste Mlle. Bertin were the dictators of the mode. In the eighteenth century fashion babies reached New York and Philadelphia by way of London. They were eagerly awaited, as they showed the latest changes in fashion.

fastener the mechanical slide fastener was perfected by the 1930's, manufactured in all colors and used to fasten girdles, foundation garments, dresses, coats, in fact wherever a trim, concealed closure is required; a zipper.

Fath, Jacques see *couture, haute.*

favors see *ribbons.*

feathers see *aigrette; Audubon plumage law.*

fedora a man's soft felt hat, known also as *Tyrolean hat, Alpine hat* and *Homburg,* the latter named for the place of its manufacture. The crown has a center crease from front to back. The name *Fédora* was after the heroine of Sardou's drama in Paris, 1883. A feminine fedora or alpine hat of brown felt with wings, ribbon band and spotted veil was worn for cycling in the 1890's. The masculine fedora is still the prevailing style of hat for men.

feile beag, fillebeg, filibeg, filabeg, philabeg, philibeg, kilt the lower part of the breacan-feile laid in pleats and worn as a skirt. see *Scottish Highland dress.*

felt cloth unwoven cloth. Wool, fur or combinations of matted fibers are felted by the use of moisture, heat, steam, pressure and hammering into a compact piece. Felt is used for hats, sportswear, house slippers, trim and many other items. Felt for hats is made of fur fibers by a process of manipulation and shrinkage that cannot be loosened without tearing. The fur of animals trapped in winter makes better felt. The principal pelts are those of beaver, muskrat, nutria, otter, and coney. Felt was used for cloaks and caps by the ancient Greeks. The matting together of wool and hair while moist was the means employed then, as today, in its manufacture.

feredeza a baglike ankle-length cover-all of black cotton which the Balkan woman wears in public. It has long, loose sleeves and is tied with a string belt and accompanied by the yashmak. Similar in shape to the dorina, which, however, is of checked fabric and light-colored. see *dorina.*

feridgé a luxurious cloak of woolen cloth of Turkish origin but rarely seen in Turkey today. A woman's wrap with large sleeves and cape. It reached to the floor and with it was worn the old-time headkerchief and djellaba.

ferris-waist trade name for a corset-waist worn by children, early 1900's. Made of strong cotton fabric reinforced with strong tape and buttoned in back, it had pendant garters for holding up stockings, and drawers were buttoned to it around the waist.

feridgé of red velvet with hanging sleeves caftan, blue satin-entari, white silk crepe chemise—red fez with blue tassels—all gilt embroidery—Turkish-Albanian

ferronière a fine chain or narrow ribbon tied around the head with a jewel suspended in the middle of the forehead. Of Oriental origin, it was a Renaissance fashion in Europe worn with the Madonna coiffure by Italian and French ladies. In the early nineteenth century, the ferronière was worn by French and English ladies.

ferronière of pearls and jewels—French—1500

festoon a garland of foliage, flowers or lace hung in scallops around a full skirt.

fez a brimless felt or wool cap shaped in a truncated cone, dark red or black with a silk tassel in dark blue or black. Also worn swathed with linen or silk in turban fashion. The fez was made part of Turkish official dress by the ordinance of Sultan Mahmud II (1808–1839) in the early nineteenth century. All Turks, including those not Moslems, were required to wear the cap. It remained the national headdress until outlawed in 1923 when Turkey became a republic, but it is still worn by other Easterners. The fez got its name from the sacred City of Islam in French Morocco, Fez. It was supposed that the dull crimson hue from the juice of a berry which grew in the vicinity could not be had elsewhere. Following the discovery of synthetic dyes in recent times, the cap has been successfully made in France and Turkey. Jews who live in Morocco wear a black fez. see *tarboosh.*

fez—dark blue or dark red—blue or red silk tassel

fiber the thread or filament used in weaving fabrics such as silk, wool, cotton, linen, asbestos and rayon. Fibers are classified as animal, vegetable, mineral and man-made.

fiber lace a trimming for sheer fabrics, the lace made of banana and aloe fibers, frail as well as expensive.

fibula the pin or brooch of ancient Greece and Rome, which the modern safety pin resembles. The ancient piece was simple and was basically the same

fibulae—ancient Greek safety pins

useful gadget, fashioned of one piece of metal wire.

fichu- white lawn puffed up over bosom-18th and 19th C.

fichu a neck cloth of the eighteenth and nineteenth centuries worn with different types of gowns. Of sheer white cotton or mousseline de soie, it was draped around the throat and shoulders and usually bunched above the small tight waist, giving a pouter-pigeon look to the figure.

filament the fiber or thread used in the weaving of a textile.

filasse raw fiber such as jute or ramie.

filature raw silk, the delicate untwisted silk threads reeled from the cocoons.

filet lace a handmade lace or net having a square mesh with a pattern formed by darning stitches; known also as darned filet lace.

filibeg see *feile beag.*

filigree fine metal openwork of gold, silver or copper wire in delicate design used in jewelry ornamentation.

fill-in a separate yoke with collar to be worn with dress or suit having a deep open neck. see *dicky.*

findings, notions all work accessories of couture, such as pins, needles, threads, buttons, hooks and eyes, fasteners and braids.

fitch- furrier's name for fur of the ferret

fingering yarn a finely twisted woolen yarn for knitting and crocheting.

fingernails, painted a custom centuries old in the Orient but comparatively new in Western grooming. The ancient Egyptians used henna to color the fingernails a dark red. Modern nail lacquers appeared in 1916, and in the 1950's false, long plastic shapes to apply over one's own by means of an adhesive. That was a short-lived fad. Toenails may be groomed as well, being manicured, creamed and painted.

finnesko a Lapland boot made of tanned reindeer skin with the fur outside.

fisherman's sweater traditional handknit sweaters of Ireland and the Hebrides, of heavy natural wool in which the lanolin has been retained to make the garment water-repellent as well as warm. A number of different stitches are used in each garment, cables, ribbing and lozenge patterns being combined in an almost infinite variety. According to legend, each sweater was different so that the families of fishermen, who frequently met death by drowning, could recognize the bodies when they were washed ashore. Also known as Aran sweaters, after the Irish islands of that name where the art of knitting has been predominant for centuries. Adopted for fashionable use as sportswear after World War II.

fisher-pekan French name of American Indian origin. Largest of the marten species, and one of the rarest and most valuable furs. Found in the densely wooded regions of northern Canada to as far south as the Allegheny Mountains. Darkly shaded blue-brown underwool with fine, strong, dark, glossy guard hair and a rich tail, almost black. A durable fur used for scarfs and jackets.

fitch called *polecat* or *perwitsky* in Europe. A fur from Europe and Asia, durable, creamy yellow and tawny underwool with long, shining black guard hair. The largest skins come from Denmark, Holland and Germany, smaller and silkier from Russia. Dyed, but used more often natural. When dyed sable color it is called sable-dyed fitch. Used for coats, jackets and scarfs.

flame stitch see *Florentine embroidery.*

flammeum, ricinium the saffron-colored veil of the pagan Roman bride and the Roman lady. It was fastened to the back of the head with the long ends left to float in back. It was of Coan gauze made by the women of Coa, an island of the Dodecanese. The color was orange-yellow, which had been the festive color of the Etruscans.

flandan see *pinner.*

flannel from 1796, a demand for English flannels for scarfs and shawls developed with the wearing of muslin dresses in all seasons. A soft woolen fabric of plain and twill weave in a wide range of textures and weights in solid colors, stripes and plaids. It was used for dresses, negligées, sleepwear and quilts. During the nineteenth century red flannel was in demand all over Europe for men's winter underwear, which came to be known as "red flannels."

flannel, Canton first made in China, a heavy, warm cotton cloth widely used.

flannel, kimono see *kimono flannel.*

flannel, outing a lightweight cotton cloth popular for children's wear.

flannel, shaker see *shaker flannel.*

flannel, vegetable see *vegetable flannel.*

flapper in the early 1900's a British term for the English girl who had not yet "come out." Her hair, whether braided or hanging, "flapped in the wind." The American flapper appeared in the 1920's with short hair, short skirt and overblouse or sweater. She wore Oxfords and rolled stockings and a beret or calotte. She was named "flapper" because in winter she wore galoshes which were always unbuckled and flapping.

flash a bunch of ribbon, the remains of the ribbon-tied queue of the soldier's wig of the eighteenth century.

flat cap see *cap, flat.*

flat point lace a Venetian type of lace without any raised stitches.

flax a plant of the genus *linum* commonly cultivated for its fiber. A long, silky bast fiber used in linen. see *linen.*

flea "puce" in French; a color brought to the mode by Marie-Antoinette. There were at least a half-dozen variances of the color, such as old flea, young flea, and so on. In general, it was a reddish-brown.

fleur-de-lis "flower of Louis," the conventionalized motif based upon the iris. It was used as the royal emblem of France since Louis VII in the twelfth century and has remained a popular motif for artistic decoration.

Fleur de lis-Louis XIV

flight boot see *boot, flight.*

floconné from the French for snow-flaked, small flakes in white on a colored ground. Machine-stitched on fabrics.

Florentine or **flame stitch embroidery** a type of canvas embroidery shaded up and down in a zigzag pattern of colors; used for draperies and covers but formerly

Florodora Sextette-famous American chorus-gown of white lawn and lace-black velvet hat with ostrich-fluffy parasol-1899

for bags, pockets and accessories. Also known as Bargello work and Hungarian point.

Florentine neckline a broad décolletage extending from shoulder to shoulder and cut lower across the front than the back.

Florodora Sextette a very popular number in the musical play "Florodora," 1899. The costumes were the epitome of contemporary fashion. see page 139.

flounces strips of cloth varied in width, cut straight or bias, shirred or pleated, applied to a garment with the lower edge left free to flare. see *ruffle.*

flowers, artificial generally of silk or velvet, used as trimming or accessories to feminine dress in the first half of the twentieth century. Some very beautiful flowers were produced, particularly in France and Italy.

fluting, goffering usually of fine muslin for neck and sleeves. Made by an iron implement with a turn handle and ribbed with grooves which, when heated, made small pleats in ruffles or ruches. It was known as a goffering iron.

fly fringe a silk fringe consisting of tufts or small tassels, a popular dress trimming of the nineteenth century.

fly-front a closure to conceal buttons and buttonholes or slide fasteners. Hidden underplackets used especially on men's coats, jackets and trousers.

focal, focalia a square of linen that the Roman legionnaire wore loosely tied around the neck and which served as handkerchief and towel. From this piece of neckwear developed the woolen cravat of the Croats, who were descendants of the peoples of a Roman-conquered province. The neckpiece eventually became the Western man's scarf. see *cravat.*

Fontanges In 1680 the Duchesse de Fontanges, mistress of Louis XIV, her hat blown off at a royal hunting party, tied her curls in place with her garter, arranging a bowknot in front. From the happening evolved a cap of tier upon tier of upstanding, pleated, wired ruffles of lawn, lace and ribbons. The hair dressed in that style became the coiffure à la Fontanges. The cap became the bonnet à la Fontanges, and the silk-covered framework, the commode. The cap often had lappets of ribbon and lace in back and over the whole arrangement was often a black silk hood. After 1710, and much ridicule, the headdress lost its fantastic tower and ended as just a little linen or lace cap. see *commode.*

foot mantle a woman's mantle worn in Colonial days on horseback. see *safeguard.*

footing a narrow edging of plain lace net.

footwear see *arctics; balmoral; batts; bicycle bal; Blücher; boots; bottine; bulgha; carbattine; culiga; chopines; chukka; cockers; escarpin; espadrille; gaiter; galoshes; geta; huaraches; jackboot; juliet; kamiks; krepis; larrigan; loafer; moccasin; mule; oxford; pattens; pedule; pegged boot; poulaines; pump; rubbers; sandals; scuffer; scuffs; shoes; slings; slippers; sneakers; solleret; tips; tsaruchia.*

forage cap see *cap, forage.*

fore and aft cap see *cap, fore and aft.*

forestry cloth an olive drab cloth of twill weave made of worsted, wool, cotton and blends. Used by the United States government as uniform cloth in the Forestry Service.

Fortuny gowns were designed by the Italian Mario Fortuny, son of the Spanish painter. The first Fortuny gown, worn in Paris in 1910, was created for the dancer, Isadora Duncan. It was a beautiful clinging gown of permanently pleated silk, dyed in artistic color. The style became a cult, now many decades old. Though originally intended as tea gowns, they were worn by the owners as evening dress. With long sleeves or sleeveless, the gown goes over the head and is tied around the neck by a drawstring. The gowns were canceled in 1949 upon the death of the artist but occasionally a "Fortuny" is found by a collector. The term is also applied to printed velvet gowns, examples of which are in museum collections.

foulard a twill-woven lightweight silk, plain or printed, with an allover pattern of small motifs on a solid color; also a rayon or mercerized fabric. Used especially for scarfs and dresses.

foundation garment a gored, fitted and boned combination of corset and brassière, introduced in the late 1920's. The bosom section, also boned, furnishing the desired "uplift look."

foundation net a stiffened, coarse net used in dressmaking and millinery.

fourchettes small forked pieces of fabric or leather set in between glove fingers. see *trank.*

four-in-hand a nineteenth-century scarf named after the sport of driving a four-in-hand. A long necktie, narrow around the neck with slightly widened ends; one end was placed shorter than the other and tied in front into a slip or sailor knot, then pulled tightly, straightening the knot and ends to hang vertically. It was a popular tie of the late nineteenth and early twentieth centuries.

fox of the canine family found in Europe, North America and Asia, not south of the equator. In order of value: silver, black, cross and red, this latter most common and most important to the fur trade. see *fox, red.*

fox, blue found in Alaska, Hudson Bay Territory, Archangel, Norway and Greenland. The finest from Archangel and Greenland; rich, smoky blue or dark brown with bluish tone. The dark color most desirable. Underwool thick and long with fine top hair. The summer coat also blue but not as rich and thick as the winter coat. Used for scarfs and jackets.

fox, common found in North America, Europe and Asia and a few in Australia, originally carried there for hunting. Varied in size with coloring from gray through red with long, soft, glossy fur. Better quality from North America and the Arctic Circle. Dyed and used mostly for scarfs and trimming on women's cloth coats.

fox, cross wild red fox, sometimes marked on the back with a cross of brownish black. Found in North America, Europe and Asia, the best from Hudson Bay to Labrador. Also found in ranch-bred red fox and used for scarfs.

fox, gray found in the United States, some in Mexico and Central America. Serviceable fur of stiffer hair with close, dark underwool and coarse, regular top hair of grizzly gray. Used natural or dyed for scarfs and trimming.

fox; kit; kitt or **swift** first two names for European species; third name American species. Small, slender fox found in the plains of the northern section of the United States and Canada, Europe, Russian steppes and Siberia. A durable fur with short, soft underfur and top hair, pale gray mixed with yellowish white. Used natural or dyed, principally for trimming.

fox, platina Norwegian trade name for silver fox mutation. see *fox, silver or black.*

four-in-hand scarf—popular in the late 19th and early 20th centuries.

Fox-Arctic-white from October to spring-northernmost America, Europe, Asia

fox, platinum United States name of silver fox mutation. see *fox, silver or black.*

fox, pointed the common red fox dyed black and pointed with silvery badger hairs to simulate silver fox; used for scarfs.

fox, red found in most countries north of the equator, the strongest, most durable and finest peltries from Alaska and Kamchatka. Long, silky guard hair and underwool thick, soft and long, varying in color from pale yellow to dark red. It is dyed black to imitate natural black fox or dyed and pointed to simulate silver fox. Used for garments, scarfs, muffs, and trimming.

fox, silver or black a mutation which appears in red fox litters. It is termed black when black the whole length of the back. The silvery quality is given by the black guard hairs which are topped with white, the underwool close and fine and the black tail tipped with white. Silver fox is the most valuable of fox furs and the most difficult to imitate. It is found in the far north, the finest coming from Labrador. Most silver fox today is scientifically ranch-bred. Used for capes, jackets and scarfs.

fox, silver pointed thickly furred peltries lacking sufficient silver hairs, augmented by gluing in silver guard hairs taken from damaged fox pelts.

fox, South American not a true fox, more canine than fox. Found from southern Brazil to the tip of the continent in the eastern part and in parts of Chili; the best peltries are from the southern part. Dark grayish-blue to pale, purplish blue; used natural or dyed, the guard hairs given silvery tips. Used for scarfs and trimming cloth and fur garments.

fox, white or **arctic** found in the most northerly regions of North America, Europe and Asia. The arctic fox becomes white from October to spring. The summer coat is a sooty-brown and yellowish white with the underwool usually gray but concealed by heavy guard hair. The imperfect peltries are dyed pale shades of gray and brown to imitate blue or black fox. Used for jackets, scarfs and trimming.

foyne the medieval name for marten.

frangipani perfumed gloves introduced to the European courts in the early seventeenth century by the Italian Count Frangipani. He discovered the process of making liquid perfume by treating solid scents with alcohol.

French hem see *hem, French.*

French hood see *hood, French.*

French seal see *seal, French.*

frieze, frise a stout woolen cloth with a shaggy or "friezed" pile used since the fourteenth century; first made in Wales, now in Ireland. A very warm fabric for jerkins and, "gowns," meaning overcoats.

frize, Holland a fine bleached Holland linen of superior quality, once in great demand for men's shirts.

fringe by the yard a narrow braid edged on one side with thread fringe, knots, or tassels as a trimming edge or decoration.

fringe, in **coiffure** meaning hair cut short over the forehead and hanging either straight or curled, also called bang or bangs. see *bangs.*

frock coat, English coat, Prince Albert single or double-breasted with skirts joined at the waistline and hanging in back to the bend of the knee. Pockets were sometimes placed in the back skirt pleats. Unlike the more formal cutaway,

frock coat-single-breasted-2nd half 19th C.

the skirts are not cut from the waistline center front rounding to the sides, but meet from waist to hem. Of black or Oxford gray cheviot, or unfinished worsted worn with trousers striped or checked in gray and black, and a matching or contrasting waistcoat. see *walking coat.*

frock coat, Orby a frock coat of the first decade of the twentieth century, single-breasted with the fore and aft sections out and made without waist seams. The back had a center seam which terminated in a vent at the waist.

frogs looped braid fastenings. see *Brandenburgs.*

frontlet worn by ladies in the fifteenth century when foreheads were exaggeratedly bare. It was a tiny pendant loop of velvet or silk, the loop being attached to the edge of a calotte worn under the hennin or escoffion. Ladies of rank wore a loop of black velvet or gold, the loop of gold indicating that the fair wearer had an income of at least ten pounds a year.

fuchsia a purplish red, the color of the flower.

full dress, military the prescribed uniform worn on state occasions at home and abroad. Civilian full dress, see *tails.*

full-bottomed wig see *wig, full-bottomed.*

fullers workers among the Romans who washed new cloth with fuller's earth, shrank it and finally pressed it. They also cleaned soiled garments.

fuller's earth an earthy substance of nonplastic clay resembling potter's clay, which has been used since ancient times to full cloth, i.e. remove the oil matter from cloth.

full-fashioned a process of flat knitting in which the seam edges are shaped by reducing or adding of stitches. Used for hose, sweaters and underwear.

fur coat the fashionable coat with "fur to the outside," was largely new in the late nineteenth century. It was originated by the Paris couturier, Doucet. Rarely until then had a fashionable coat been made with the fur to the outside.

frontlet, gold chain-black velvet hood-cap with frills-English-15th C.

fur, fake synthetic fur cloths; among the imitations are Persian lamb, broadtail, beaver, sealskin and other short-haired furs. First used in the 1950's.

fur, "fun" an expression coined in the 1960's for relatively inexpensive furs made up for young women. Moderately priced in Russian lynx, a South American skunk called zorina, and gray, cross and red foxes.

fur paws garments and trimming made of animal paws pieced together; among those used are karakul, leopard, mink, Persian lamb and silver fox.

fur peltries see *animal skins.*

fur, pieced trimmings and garments are made of remnants of peltries using tails, paws and the lighter underparts. The bits of lamb, karakul, fox, squirrel, etc., are matched and joined.

fur processing many operations including curing, tanning, dressing, dyeing, tipping, topping and feathering.

furbelows the Anglicized word for French *falbalas,* used in the late seventeenth and eighteenth centuries to describe the decorations on court costumes, flounces, tassels, fringe, lace, braid and heavy embroidery.

furs, summer between 1910 and 1915 fur bands ornamented gowns of chiffon and lace worn in summer, a short-lived use in trimming. By the 1940's, fur wraps in the form of capelets, stoles, boleros and sling jackets were in use for summer wear in the city and at resorts.

furs, tipped, topped, feathered terms meaning that only the tips of the long guard hairs have been dyed, with a fine brush.

furs, unprime furs taken from animals during molting season, when not in the best condition.

fused collar see *collar, fused.*

fustanella the short, very full and stiffly pleated kilt of the evzone, a Greek Highland soldier.

fustian a stout cotton or flax cloth used by the Normans, especially the clergy. Originally of Oriental origin, it had been woven since the Crusades. Made in solid color, usually gray or brown, tufted or striped and sometimes rich-looking. see *beaver fustian.*

G

Gabriel princess gown- gray silk over a crinoline- white collar- yellow gloves- 1867

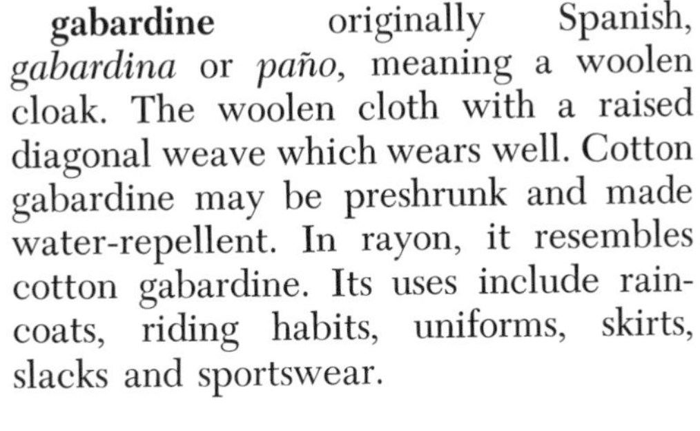

gabardine originally Spanish, *gabardina* or *paño,* meaning a woolen cloak. The woolen cloth with a raised diagonal weave which wears well. Cotton gabardine may be preshrunk and made water-repellent. In rayon, it resembles cotton gabardine. Its uses include raincoats, riding habits, uniforms, skirts, slacks and sportswear.

Gabardine-the outer cloak of Jews during the Middle Ages-hood with liripipe- 15th C.

gabardine name of the Jewish gown or mantle worn during the Middle Ages, usually of black cloth, silk or moiré. Ankle-length and buttoned in front to the waist.

gable headdress the English gable- or diamond-shaped headdress; though decorative in design, it was a severe form of the hood. It was worn by older women and entirely concealed the hair. Comprising gable, wimple and gorget, the fashion lasted from 1500 to 1550.

Gable hood with wimple and gorget of white linen-long veil in back-English- 1500

Gabriel princess gown a dress fitted and gored from neck and shoulder to hem, which appeared first in the 1860's and remaining popular into the first decade of the twentieth century. It was made of gray silk, fastened the length of the front with buttons or tiny bowknots and finished with a narrow white collar and a bit of black guipure braid.

gaiter trousers- or Wellington breeches with under strap- 1820's

gaiter or **congress shoe** man's boot of leather with uppers of brocaded silk and side gores of elastic webbing which eliminated the opening; 1850's. see *bottine; spats.*

gaiter shoe gored with elastic webbing- 1880's

gaiters or spats worn by the dude- white or tan cloth with black shoes- 1890's

gaiter trousers, gaiter bottoms breeches cut snugly at the ankle, extending out over the instep and held down by a strap passing under the boot. First half nineteenth century.

gaiters a cloth or leather covering for ankle or leg buttoned at the sides and a buckled-strap under foot.

gallibiya, kibr or caftan-silk with embroidered tasseled cord-kaffiyeh and agal-Saudi Arabia

Galanos, James see *couture, haute.*

galants see *ribbons.*

galatea a stout, white cotton twill, printed or striped, used in beach, sports and children's shoes.

galilla; whisk a small neat collar of sheer lawn mounted on pasteboard or held out fan-shaped by a wire edge, accredited to Philip IV of Spain, (1621–1665). Its Spanish name was galilla; to the English and American colonists, it was a whisk. It was a semi-circular and was often edged with lace.

Galitzine, Princess Irene see *couture, haute.*

gallibiya the traditional cotton robe, long-sleeved and collarless of the Arabic-speaking world.

galligaskin or gaskin-leather legging with straps and buckles-1815-1850

galligaskin, gaskin wide breeches or hose of the seventeenth century worn by seamen and sportsmen. In the early nineteenth century, they were leggings buckled and strapped under the foot.

galliochios, galoshes meaning Gaulish shoes. Wooden-soled shoes with leather straps which protected fine shoes from rough stone pavements. Worn from ancient Roman times, through European periods and American colonial days.

galoshes or wooden clogs to protect shoes on the street-lady's and gentlemens'-17th C.

galloon, galon a fancy finishing braid used both in costume and upholstery work. A narrow passementerie of cotton, silk, velvet, gold or silver cording.

gallowes, galluses, braces, brettelles see *suspenders.*

galoshes, modern a thick wooden clog with wide leather strap or uppers. Also of water-proofed canvas with heavy rubber sole and fastened with metal clips. Known as arctics.

galuchat French for polished sharkskin, first used by Galuchat of Paris in the eighteenth century. He introduced pebbled or grained leather. see *shagreen; sharkskin.*

galyak, galyac flat thin fur of lamb or kid born prematurely or dead, with or without moiré design. Of poor wearing quality and used for trimming.

gamashes in the seventeenth century, leggings of cotton cloth or velvet worn with shoes and riding boots to protect the fine leather. Linen leggings remained the distinguishing mark of peasant or farmer for centuries. see *spatterdashes.*

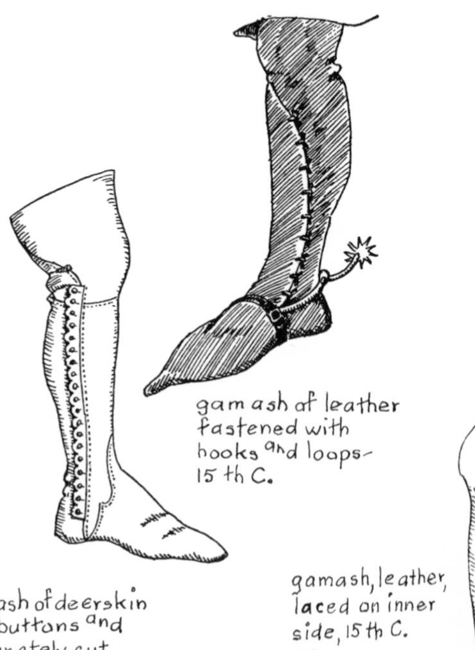

gamash of leather fastened with hooks and loops-15th C.

gamash of deerskin with buttons and separately cut vamp-English-mid 15th C.

gamash, leather, laced on inner side, 15th C. Often worn under boot during 15th and 16th C.

gambeson, pourpoint or jacket-stuffed with wool or cotton and quilted-worn by men, women and children

gambeson or **pourpoint** a doublet, often sleeveless, of leather or cloth, stuffed and quilted. It was worn as a pad under armor in the Middle Ages and in civil dress by men, women and children.

gambeto a thick woolen cloth short topcoat worn by the men of Catalonia in Spain instead of the mantua or plaid.

Gandhi cap see *cap, Gandhi.*

gandoura, gandourah, gondura a long-sleeved or sleeveless shirt or chemise of cotton or wool worn in North Africa by men and women.

gansey see *guernsey.*

Garibaldi shirt, camicia rossa a woman's shirtwaist popular in the 1860's. It was a copy of the tailored red cloth shirt worn by the Italian patriot Garibaldi and his soldiers. It had long sleeves gathered to a wristband, a small turned-down collar and a tailored bosom with four buttons.

Garibaldi-famed Italian hero whose red flannel shirt became the rage in the 1860's

garland a headband or fillet, usually of wool, worn by priests in Greek and Roman antiquity.

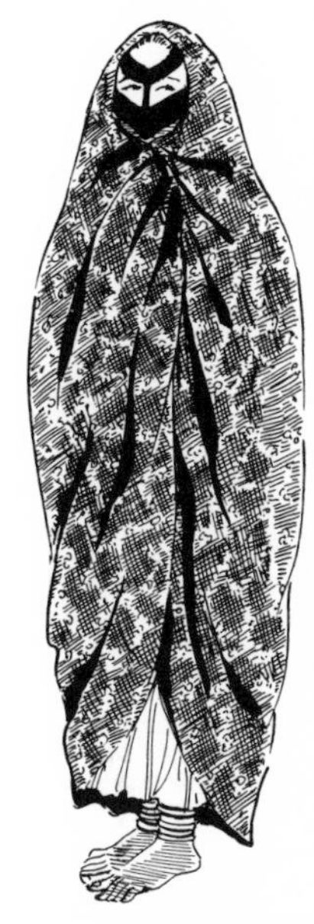

gandoura, white cotton undergarment-flowered huke-black yasmak-Arabia

garment, garmenture any piece of body wearing apparel.

garnet a popular stone in Victorian jewelry. The favored color of the garnet is deep crimson and transparent; the gem may be any color but blue—there are no blue garnets. They are found in Russia, Canada and Pennsylvania, and the Near East where they were highly prized in classical times.

garter any band or supporting strap to hold up a sock or stocking. Until the mid-nineteenth century, before the invention of elastic cloth or webbing, garters were ties of silk, cloth or leather often embroidered and sometimes adorned with rosettes. Norwich garters, as worn by the New England colonists in the early seventeenth century, were silk bands tied in large bowknots.

gartering of Anglo Saxon costume, little exists earlier than the tenth century. Contemporary writers mention *"brech* and *hose"* cross-gartered in cloth, woolen and leather bands. Linen bands distinguished the monks from the laity, who wore woolen gartering. Gilded straps marked the head of a clan. In the Middle Ages men's chausses (stockings) reached to the waist, where they were tied to a belt, and women's chausses reached above the knee, tied by bands or ribbons.

gaskin see *galligaskin.*

gatyák long, flaring white pantaloons of cloth resembling a divided riding skirt and worn as such by the Hungarian cow-

Gatyak-fringed white linen pantaloons and blouse-felt hat and bolero-Hungarian cowboy-contemporary

gazelle antelope of Africa

boy. The pantaloons are finished with a coarse white fringe or peasant-made crochet lace. Twentieth century.

gaucho, Argentina-chiripa worn over shoulders-white cotton shirt-long full pantaloons-contemporary

gaucho the cowboy of Argentina, who wears a distinctive costume: the shiripa, a skirt formed of a square woolen blanket wrapped around the hips and held by a heavy, elaborate silver belt; white cotton shirt; and pantaloons tucked into high boots. Over his arm, he carries a woolen poncho and an ornamental quirt. Twentieth century.

gauge in stockings, the number of stitches in each 1½ inches of the nylon fabric. The higher the gauge number, the stronger the stocking.

gauntlet a glove with a protective forearm cuff. see *glove; mousquetaire.*

gauze a sheer, transparent fabric first made in Gaza, Palestine. Of silk, cotton or rayon, its use depending upon the yarn of which it is made, whether veilings, dresses, curtains or surgical dressings.

gauze, silk a curtaining of thin silk in plain weave; also of cotton or rayon in leno weave.

gazelle hide or leather from a small member of the antelope family, the best known species from Africa, Arabia and Persia. Graceful and delicately formed, the gazelle is usually brownish with silver-tone or white stomach. The sheered pelt is used for casual coats.

gem a precious stone cut or polished. A jewel is a precious stone set and worn as an ornament.

gem cuts *baguette,* a flat table-cut in the form of a long, narrow rectangle. *Brilliant,* mid-seventeenth century; said to have been invented by Cardinal Mazarin to increase the diamond cutter's trade. The pyramid forms and facets are doubled, making for greater brilliancy. *Cabochon:* formerly an uncut and polished stone in convex form. Now cut in convex form or smooth-arched dome and highly polished but not faceted. *Emeraude* or *emerald,* a step cut in which the shape of the gem is square or rectangular. *Marquise,* a cut in which the gem is generally elliptical in shape but with pointed ends. *Old-Mine,* a diamond cut in a now obsolete nineteenth-century style, producing less sparkle than the modern brilliant. *Rose-Cut* or *Rosette,* developed by gem-cutters in Amsterdam, 1520. A rose-cut stone is like a squat pyramid with flat base and facets in mul-

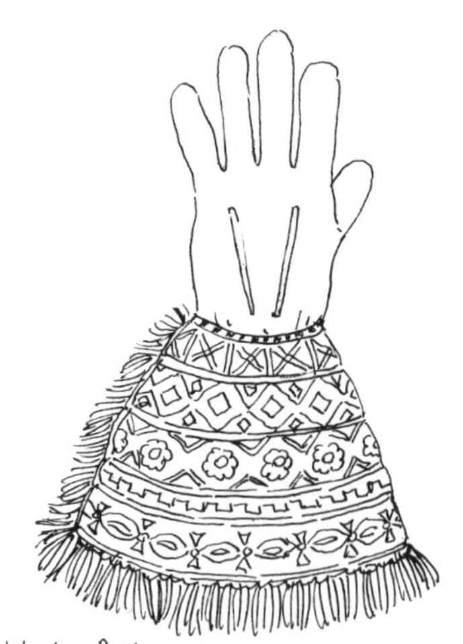

gauntlet of the mousquetaire-embroidered and fringed-17th C.

tiples of six. Small diamonds and fine garnets are often so cut. *Step* or *Trap Cut:* oblong in form with a heavy, broad table forming a series of straight facets which give the appearance of steps as they decrease in length. *Table-Cut:* evolved from the double, pyramidal shapes placed together, the points cut away. There are many variations today which may be square or oblong with four or more facets on the underside of the stone. Emeralds and sapphires are occasionally table-cut. The girdle of a gem is the edge which is grasped by the outer rim or setting.

gem weights the metric carat is recognized as standard weight for gems. For pearls, the weight is a grain, equal to a quarter of a carat.

genappe a smooth worsted yarn used in braid and fringes.

genet, spotted cat the pelt of a small European spotted cat allied to the civets, from southern France, Spain and Greece. The name also applies to the European black cat reared for its pelt, soft, well-furred and more generally used in Europe than America. Common genet is dark gray spotted with black and has been in use from the Middle Ages. Use for trimming on clothing dates back to the sixth century A.D. Very little used in America, but in demand in European markets.

Geneva gown and bands long, loose, clergyman's gown with large sleeves. Of black silk or woolen cloth buttoned down the front, a pair of white lawn bands at the neck.

Genoa lace Genoa, Italy, was a lace-making center in the seventeenth century. It was known for bobbin, tape, macramé, needlepoint and gold and silver laces.

Genoese embroidery done in buttonhole stitches worked over a cord of linen and the fabric cut away between the motifs. A trimming used for dress and lingerie.

georgette see *crepe georgette.*

Gernreich, Rudi see *couture, haute.*

gertrude the long tunic of earliest times, worn by both sexes from the Carolingian period to the thirteenth century, when it became a general garment for infants, a baby's flannel petticoat. It was named for Saint Gertrude, (1256–1311) who was born in Saxony. Some babies, especially in Europe, still wear flannel petticoats and the name "gertrude" is still used.

geta a Japanese clog for all kinds of weather, worn for centuries. It varies in height from two to six inches and varies widely in design.

gew-gaw a trinket, pretty and showy but worthless.

Gibson Girl or **Shirtwaist Girl** the type of woman immortalized by the American artist, Charles Dana Gibson (1867–1944). She wore a simple blouse of starched white linen and Ascot scarf with a habit-back tailored skirt, hair in a pompadour and sailor hat.

gibus see *hat, gibus.*

gilet a type of vest. The contemporary feminine gilet is a sleeveless blouse or bodice front worn under a suit jacket or to fill in the neckline of a dress.

gillie, ghillies a shoe of the Anglo-Saxons of rawhide without a tongue but laced through self-loops by thong or woolen gartering over linen or woolen leggings.

gilt a wash of gold or brass color applied to metal, especially jewelry, so as to make it resemble gold. Jewelry so treated is termed gilt or gold-plated. see *pinchbeck.*

gimp a flat, narrow, ornamental braid of silk, cotton or wool often interwoven

Japanese white percale tabi fastened in back-wooden gēta

Famous Shirtwaist Girl by Charles Dana Gibson, white linen shirtwaist with linen Ascot scarf

with coarse silk or metallic wire. An upholstery finish also used for costume. see *guipure.*

gingham a popular cotton fabric of pre-dyed yarn in a plain weave but of several colors in checks, plaids and stripes.

girandole in jewelry, an earring with several pendants or small stones framing a larger one.

girdle a short, light corset confining the body below the waistline. see *corset.*

Givenchy, Hubert de see *couture, haute.*

glacé kid glove leather, smooth, glossy, and highly polished. see *kid, glacé.*

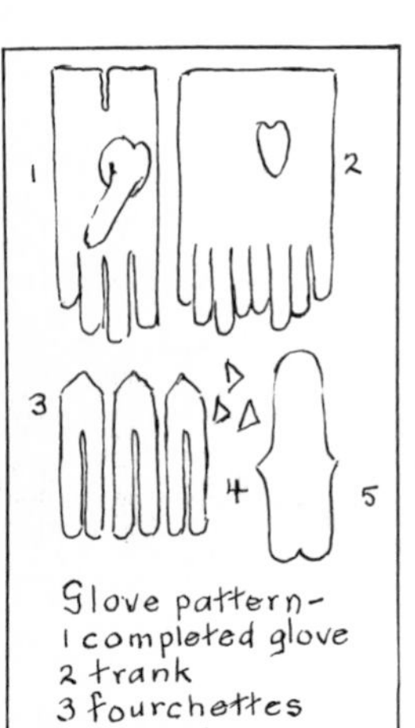

Gladstone collar see *collar, Gladstone.*

glass fibers produced by forcing out molten glass into a continuous thread form. Resistant to heat, moisture and chemicals.

glass suits worn for the first time in 1965 by most of the automobile drivers in the Indianapolis 500 race. The lightweight suits protect the wearer against heat and fire. Fiberglas, trademark for fine filament glass fiber owned by Corning Fiberglas Corp.

glasses, harlequin see *harlequin glasses.*

glasses, opera see *opera glasses.*

glazing a process of applying a smooth, glossy surface to a fabric, e.g., chintz or leather coated with paraffin, then calendered by being passed between heated rollers.

glen checks one of the Scottish Glen or District checks, each one a plaid unique to the particular district.

glen plaid a pattern of very narrow lines crossing at right angles; generally in subdued tones of brown, gray and black or navy, on a neutral background, sometimes crossed at intervals with a single thread of red or bright blue or other conspicuous color. Used for suitings.

Glen Urquhart a Scottish plaid of dark blue, dark green and black, overlaid with a fine scarlet line crossing at right angles in boxlike formation.

Glengarry cap see *cap, Glengarry.*

Glengarry cloth an English homespun tweed made of the waste stock of woolen yarns.

glove a shaped covering for the hand enclosing each finger separately in a sheath. Archaeologists claim that hand covers or gloves of leather were worn by cavemen as long ago as other leather garments, which could be hundreds of thousands of years. Such gloves were roughly dressed and sewn with a bone needle. Knitted gloves have been found in Egyptian tombs. Although gloves were worn by workmen to protect their hands, neither Persian, Greeks nor Romans wore gloves for warmth. Warriors wore gloves, as did hunters. Falconers wore gloves made of deerskin and dogskin. Gloves appeared in Europe on the hands of kings and bishops, becoming by the ninth century a symbol of power and part of official and religious dress. The medieval knight wore his lady's glove in his helmet at tournaments and battles. Most gloves were shaped like mittens, separate fingers not appearing in Europe until the eleventh century. French glovers under Louis XIV invented glacé kid gloves.

glove fastenings The pull-on or slip-on glove has always existed but in the late nineteenth century the wrist-length glove for ladies was closed by means of tiny pearl buttons and buttonholes. There was also a style with silk cord which laced alternating hooks from the wrist down. A recent style is the fastening on the back of the hand from the base of the fingers down, by a zipper or buttons and buttonholes.

glove, free-finger or **three dimensional** from the trade name of a glove designed (1938) with a strip making the side walls of all five fingers in one piece.

glove lengths wrist-length (shortie) one-button; mid-forearm, four- or five-button; elbow, eight-button; above elbow, twelve-button; shoulder, sixteen-button.

glove, shortie a short or wrist-length glove of the Victorian Age which was revived as a slip-on, especially in chamois, in the 1920's and later in cotton, nylon, and leathers.

glove stretcher a long, slim pair of wooden or ivory tweezers to stretch the glove fingers before putting on, often necessary in the days of tight-fitting gloves.

glover's stitch the seams are to the outside of the glove and alternately stitched on each side, the thread drawn through on one side and then on the other.

gloves, York tan see *York tan gloves.*

goat, angora see *angora goat.*

goat, gray fur of a half-grown goat which has turned gray; used for trimming.

goat, pulled or **mouflon** Mongolian goat with guard hair plucked, leaving long, silky, furlike hair resembling the wild sheep known as mouflon in gray, white or smoky-blue.

goatee, goatbeard a man's chin beard trimmed into a long, spiky tuft like the beard of the male goat.

goatskin a leather prepared in all finishes and colors and dressed to imitate antelope and deerskin. Nearly all of the goatskin in American-made shoes is imported from the Far East.

gob cap see *cap, gob.*

godet, gore, gusset a tapering or triangular piece of cloth inserted for extra width or flare. An umbrella is made of gore-shaped pieces, and skirts are often gored. With the appearance of elastic webbing in the nineteenth century, gored shoes came into vogue for both men and women.

Godey's Lady's Book the first American woman's magazine, a periodical dealing with women's fashions, needlework and etiquette. It was founded in Philadelphia in 1830 by Antoine Godey and published until 1898.

goffering see *fluting.*

gold cloth or **tissue** cloth with metal warp of gold color and silk weft. An evening fabric for wraps, gowns and trimming.

gold lace formerly made of gold wire; later a lace of braid with silk weft threads covered with gilt or gold leaf.

golf the feminine outfit for golfing in the 1890's called for a tailored linen shirtwaist with separate skirt, a Norfolk jacket or a short golf cape of tweed which matched the skirt, and a little felt fedora. The tailored shirtwaist or shirtwaist dress was replaced by a real sports frock in the 1920's. Worn over shorts, it buttoned down center front. It appeared in the 1930's and was suitable for both golf and tennis.

goatee beard

black silk top hat-French-1890's

gondolier net of black silk braid—with ribbon—French—1870's

golf hose heavy knitted woolen or worsted hose with a deep, decorative cuff which turns down below the knee. Worn with knickerbockers.

golf shoes Oxfords made with protruding buttons or nails on the soles to prevent slipping.

gondolier net fashion of the 1870's; a wide-meshed hairnet of narrow black braid or ribbon held by a cadogan bow in back and sometimes by one on top of the head.

gondoura see *gandoura.*

gore see *godet; gusset.*

gorget originally a collarlike piece of steel armor protecting the throat. By 1600 steel armor tended to disappear, the buff-coat taking its place. Only the steel or silver gorget, a small crescent-shaped piece suspended from a fine chain around the neck, remained, engraved with the officer's grade. It was worn with full uniform by both American and British officers in the Revolutionary War. The word *gorget* was also applied to some wimples and headkerchiefs when covering the feminine head and throat.

greatcoat, carrick or coachman's coat—heavy, warm coat—1814

gorro the traditional cap of the Catalonians in Spain. A knitted yarn stocking cap and very often two, a tasseled one hanging down in back and a second on top drooping over the forehead. In red, purple and brown.

gourgandine a corselet of silk or velvet with few stays, laced in front, of the late Louis XIV period. It was worn en negligée with a handsome petticoat until the hour of dressing and putting on a real corset.

gown from the Saxon word *gunna,* a long, loose garment worn by all Anglo-Saxon women for centuries. It was also called a cote, surcoat or robe. From the fourteenth to the seventeenth centuries, the word gown was applied to any long, loose robe, masculine or feminine. In the sixteenth century the fashionable man wore a gown over his doublet or jerkin. It was circular in cut, open in front, short or long, and capelike. Gown, today, is also used for the robe, academic or clerical, of either sex, and for evening dresses.

gown, academic see *academic gown.*

Goya, Francisco José de (1746–1828) Spanish court painter to Charles III and Charles IV. He followed Velásquez and like him, left many memorable portraits illustrating the court styles of his day.

grain leather see *leather, grain.*

Granada the Italian *granito* or grainy-surfaced cloth, a fine-finished fabric of worsted stock.

granite cloth a lightweight, durable fiber made of twisted yarns and sometimes linen; a figured weave in a pebbly, hard-finished surface. Used for men's and women's outer-wear.

grass cloth a fabric made in China, loosely woven of vegetable fibers. It comes in the natural brown color, bleached or dyed; used for sportswear.

gray a combination in varying degrees of white and black. Pearl gray is one of the lightest shades, charcoal gray one of the darkest.

gray, charcoal or carbon a very dark gray, almost black, fashionable for men's suits after World War II.

gray goods see *grège.*

greatcoat any heavy overcoat.

greaves see *cnemis.*

Ancient Greek

"Grecian bend" due to bustle- plum-colored and lilac velvet with fur- 1873

grebe plumage of the grebe, a water-bird of the loon family; silky, smooth and downlike in ivory flecked with brown. Formerly used for millinery, muffs and accessories.

Grecian bend a popular name for the fashionable lady's stance in the 1870's and 1880's when the wasp waist and bustle prevailed.

Greek costume, ancient see illustrations, page 153 and above.

Greek lace same as reticella in a heavy needlepoint lace.

green one of the three secondary colors which are green, purple and orange. Green is a combination of blue and yellow. The shades with a greater proportion of blue include jade and bottle green, those with more yellow include lime and olive.

Greenaway, Kate a style in children's clothes named for the English illustrator and author (1846–1901). The children in her pictures wore Empire style. Her work was charming and distinctive and had a lasting popularity. The style survives in the attire of child attendants in many wedding parties.

grège any fabric in untreated condition as it comes from the loom before bleaching, dyeing or finishing. Grège is also used as a fashion term for a grayish-beige color.

gremial veil an embroidered cloth or apron spread over the knees of a bishop when seated during high mass.

grenadine a silk popular in the late nineteenth century; much like marquisette and used for blouses, dresses and men's neckwear.

greys, or **petit gris** the fine white belly fur of the very small Siberian squirrel with gray black. Precious, and called "menu vair," it was used in the medieval period to line the mantles of kings, professors and court counselors.

grillage the grill work or bars across open spaces in lacework.

grisette a gay, free-mannered working girl in Louis XIV's day. So called because all Frenchwomen of humble condition wore dresses made of *grisette,* a coarse gray woolen fabric.

gros de londres lightweight silk or rayon dress goods with ribs of alternating width. It is piece-dyed and made changeable or warp print in effect. A glossy finish is given the cloth that is intended for the millinery trade and dresses.

grosgrain a stout, close-woven silk fabric or ribbon corded from selvedge to selvedge.

grosgram a fabric popular with country women of England and the American Colonies. It has a diagonal weave of silk and wool or all wool with a rough finish. Formerly manufactured in Scotland, where heavy travel cloaks were made of it.

gros point also known as Gros Point de Venise. A Venetian point lace with raised work and large motifs.

gros point any embroidery worked on canvas with less than sixteen meshes per inch. There is no special gros point stitch. Aubusson stitch or Gobelin stitch are sometimes used, tent or cross stitch being more common.

guanaco, guanaquito larger of the two wild species, guanaco and vicuña, of the South American family of which domesticated varieties are llama and alpaca. They are found high in the Peruvian Andes. Formerly, only guanacos less than twenty days old were used for fur. A soft, woolly, pale fur, reddish brown, similar to vicuña but coarser, used natural or dyed brown and dressed to simulate lynx.

guard's coat man's traveling coat, long and loose, of tweed or homespun with inverted pleat in center back, and deep side folds held in place by a half-belt. Early twentieth century.

guepière from the French for wasp. A small lightweight corset made to produce a tiny waist, trim above and slightly rounded below. It appeared in 1945, paving the way to the "New Look."

guernsey a sailor's knitted woolen shirtlike garment which originated in the Channel Islands. Guernseyed means "to be wearing a guernsey."

guimpe a short blouse of sheer white lawn or batiste with sleeves, collar and frilled neck, worn with a pinafore style of dress in the late nineteenth and early twentieth centuries. It had been a distinctive feature of the costume of the early sixteenth century, both sexes wearing the lingerie guimpe showing above the squared neckline of the period. In the twentieth century it was worn by little girls for several decades.

guipure a heavy lace, the patterns or motifs raised into relief by twisted cords, made without a ground, the design connected by bars.

gun club checks a pattern produced in worsted, flannel and tweed, in checks of different colors and alternating rows. Made for men's and women's wear in street dress and sportswear.

gusset originally a piece of chain mail or plate inserted in the joints of armor for reinforcement. see *godet.*

gypsy or **Romany stripes** of brilliant colors and varying widths, based upon designs of fabrics worn by Spanish gypsy dancers.

gypsy girl of Granada, Spain—red checked cotton dress—red satin bands—fringed, embroidered black shawl—white stockings—black slippers

H

haberdashery a retail shop selling men's furnishings. Both the shop and the wares are called haberdashery and the dealer is a haberdasher.

habergeon, haubergeon a high-necked, long-sleeved, hip-length tunic of chain or ring mail worn over a cloth smock by horsemen in the fifteenth century, with a leather belt to hold the sword.

habiliment dress; attire; vestment.

habit-back skirt a tailored sports skirt of the late Victorian period. It was usually of heavy cloth, well fitted over the hips with a reinforced, ankle-length flaring hem. An inverted pleat at center back stitched partway down accounts for the term "habit-back." see *Gibson girl.*

habutai, habutae, habutaye a lightweight silk originally woven on hand looms, now woven on power looms in the Orient. Heavier than China silk and in natural color, it is used for dresses, blouses, jackets, office coats and pajamas.

Haik of white wool or cotton-worn by the Algerian woman-white lawn yashmak

haik a long piece of cotton or woolen cloth, according to weather, which envelops the Algerian woman in public. It is draped over the tarboosh and the body, belted at the waist, covering the chalwar and pantaloons. Mostly of hand-woven wool, plain or striped, the haik has been and continues to be worn by both sexes of Arabs, Moors and Mohammedans for centuries. see *huke.*

hair, bobbed see *bobbed hair.*

hair cloth a resilient material woven of cotton or linen warp with the weft of horsehair from tail or mane. Used as a stiffening interlining in jackets or coats and in upholstery.

hair coloring a practice many centuries old which became widespread in the mid-twentieth century with the improvement of materials and techniques. The fad for platinum blonde hair can be traced to the popularity of Jean Harlow, a cinema star of the 1930's.

hair net an accessory centuries old, first made of silk by the Chinese. The caul or net of medieval times was made of silk or gold cord. In the 1850's the net was of braided silk, chenille or velvet ribbon fastened with small gilt buttons or buckles. Later came nets of human hair, and now they are made of nylon. see *caul.*

hair pieces the modern commercial term for any false part of a hairdo or for a man's toupee. Women still use the word wig for a complete false hair cover. There are wiglets, switches and falls of human hair and artificial dynel. see *fall.*

hair seal see *seal, hair.*

haircuts see illustrations on opposite page.

hairdresser one who designs and arranges coiffures, trims, curls or straightens, dyes, bleaches and shampoos hair.

hairlace a net or fillet over the coiffure; a decorative fashion of the Victorian era.

Haircuts
Egyptian king-wig of spiral curls-2nd C. B.C
frizzed hair-Persian-9th C.B.C.
spiral curls-wreath of olive leaves-military-Greek
feather cut-leather fillet-charioteer-Greek
frame of Cypriote curls-Greek
curls and tutulus of felt-Etruscan
natural hair or wig-ends rolled-Roman 4th c A.D.
emperor's crown of laurel-ribbon-Roman-4th C.
Norman and English-9th C.
bobbed hair-French-15th C.
center part moustache-mutton chops and monocle-English-1870s
hair parted up and down-French Empire-c.1809
page boy-curled ends-felt béret-French-15th C.
center part-monocle-English-1870's
football player's haircut-American-1890's
side part-1st decade-20th C.
cropped haircut-also called Crew, Varsity, Prussian or G.I. Bob-1940's

hairline stripe a light stripe of one-thread thickness woven into dark-colored worsted.

hairpins from antiquity until the 1920's hairpins were fashioned of twigs, wood, bone, ivory, shell, wire and celluloid in bodkin or forked shape. But modern short hair required something different. It was solved by the bobby pin which was suggested by the wire cotter pin of modern machinery. Another twentieth century invention was the invisible hairpin of fine wire, very short and crinkled. see *bobby pin.*

half-slip see *slip.*

haling hands heavy work gloves worn by seamen and miners, usually of wool with leather palms. Haling derives from the word "hauling."

halter a more or less triangular piece of sturdy material made to tie or fasten at the back of the neck and waist; for feminine wear as the only garment above the waist, leaving the arms and back bare for tanning.

halter neckline a neckline new in the 1930's, high of neck at center front, shoulders bare and entirely bared in back. First designed for beach wear; a version for daytime and another for evening followed. The style continues to be in fashion.

hamster, golden hamster small rodent found in parts of Europe and common in Russia and Germany. A lightweight and very flat fur, of pale yellowish brown marked with black. Used principally in Europe for men's coat linings.

handbag a development of the twentieth century. Any small satchel or bag which holds a lady's daily traveling necessities. During periods of bouffant skirts, farthingales and hoops, there was no need of ladies' bags because large pockets were concealed in skirt folds. As fashion changed to Directoire, a small pouch bag of handsome fabric embroidered and beaded came into vogue. This was the reticule or, humorously, "ridicule." During the style of the high-waisted, unlined Empire gowns, the soldier's leather cavalry bag or sabretache was copied in handsome fabric, embroidered, fringed and tasseled. Purses next became small and in the 1880's fabric bags had metal and jeweled mounts and steel beaded bags became favorites. In the 1890's, the new-styled pocketbook of leather was a flat, folding, book-shaped purse with compartments. In the first decade of 1900, small leather bags were popular until the saddle-bag returned. The large, flat envelope bag was of leather with many compartments and a large flap. In the 1920's and 1930's there were exquisite and costly small evening bags of fine bead embroidery and gold and silver linked mesh. The fittings of bags were now given as much thought as the exterior. Added to mirror, comb and change purse were the cigarette case and cigarette holder of beauty and value. In the present era of round-the-world travel, the large leather bag is a necessity for carrying passport, toiletries and such, as well as money. Bags for summer and sports are made in a wide variety of colorful materials and often may be simply baskets. see *shoulder bag.*

hand-blocked print fabrics upon which the design has been printed by hand with either linoleum or wooden blocks.

hand-glasses a nineteenth century New York name for spectacles and eyeglasses and lorgnettes.

handkerchief a small square of linen, cotton or disposable tissue to use for wiping the nose, eyes or face. A larger square may be used as a neckerchief. Handkerchiefs may be used solely for decoration, as when tucked into the breast pocket of a man's or woman's suit. In Rome of the second century A.D. the handkerchief, a white linen square and a costly luxury, was in use on the stage in comedies and satires. Handkerchiefs were plentiful in the early Christian Era and were waved by spectators at the games. They became expensive accessories embroidered with silver and gilt and edged with fringe, forming part of church and coronation rituals. In the Medieval period, English ladies presented their men with small squares which were worn in the hatband. During the Renaissance fine sheer handkerchiefs were a fashion at the courts of France, Spain and England. Of Venetian make, they were of cambric, lawn or linen edged with beautiful lace, one corner weighted with a tassel, button or acorn. In the sixteenth century the use of all shapes and sizes of the handkerchief became general in Europe. Finally, by royal decree under Louis XIV in 1685, it became a square. Round and oval-shaped handkerchiefs had a short-lived vogue in the time of Louis XV. Early in the nineteenth century, the gentleman's handkerchief settled into an accepted size of about eighteen inches, of white linen with a hemstitched edge and an initial in one corner. The average-sized woman's handkerchief is twelve inches square. The vogue of the lace handkerchief, it is said, dates from the tearful departure of Marie-Antoinette from her beloved Austria to France. She dried her tears with a piece of lace from her gown. The ecclesiastic handkerchief, called a maniple, was carried in the hand and survives in the narrow band worn pendant from the left wrist by the celebrant at mass.

hand-pricked edge used instead of machine-stitching on collar and lapel of a man's informal suit, a feature new in the 1930's.

hanging sleeve see *sleeve, hanging.*

hank a commercial length of yarn: as worsted yarn, 560 yards; silk, 120 yards; cotton, 840 yards; linen, 10 leas in England; 12 leas in Ireland and Scotland. A lea is a varying measure of yarn.

haori a Japanese black silk coat for street wear over the kimono for men and women. The feminine, either long or knee-length, the man's knee-length and plain, while hers may be elaborately embroidered. Instead of the surplice closing of the kimono, his coat fastens in center front, tied by tiny silk cords. As on the man's kimono, the wearer's crest decorates the haori; a very small motif is embroidered or stenciled on either side of the chest, in center back and at the tops of the sleeves.

hard hat see *boater.*

Hardanger bonnet see *bonnet, Hardanger.*

Hardanger embroidery and **cutwork** a Norwegian embroidery worked in squares or diamond shapes on linen or canvas. All embroidery is completed before the unwanted ground is cut away. Used for edging fancy work, especially for aprons, blouses and dresses.

Hardanger skaut traditional headgear of the Hardanger matron of Norway. A large square of stiffly starched white linen which is folded and fastened in back and worn in many different ways. The skaut is reminiscent of the headdress worn in the sixteenth century when folk dress began to take hold.

skaut—Hardanger, Norway—large square of starched linen draped and pinned in place

hare fur from a rodent of the same genus as the rabbit, or jack rabbit, this latter name commonly used in the United States for both animals. The hare, larger than the rabbit, is from Central Europe and Central Siberia and used principally in the hatters' and textile trades. The colors are white, tan and bluish-gray. The very best breed in the fur industry is Belgian hare, a rather small, slender rabbit. This hare and also the chinchilla-dyed French rabbit are

hare—"varying hare"—white, tan or bluish-gray-colored in summer—white in winter. Arctic hare.

remarkably similar to chinchilla. see *rabbit.*

hare, arctic the long-haired hare comes from Siberia and Russia, those of arctic North America being few and not used by the fur trade. The long-haired animals are those processed to simulate white fox. White peltries are most desirable to the fur and hat trades, despite being higher priced because small in quantity.

harem skirt see *skirt, harem.*

harem pants see *pants, harem; culottes.*

harlequin a character in British Pantomine derived from Arlecchino of the Italian Comedy Theatre. The traditional costume is a close-fitting one-piece garment of brightly colored diamond checks, long-sleeved and reaching to mid-calf; white stockings and black slippers; a shaven head usually simulated with a tight stocking cap; a mask with slanting eyeholes; and a lath sword. *Harlequin* used as an adjective has come to mean parti-colored.

harlequin glasses spectacles with an upward tilt at the outer corners of the plastic frame. Introduced in the U.S. in 1944. So-called because of the resemblance to the mask traditionally worn by the Harlequin character in pantomime.

Harris Tweed trade-mark of the Harris Tweed Association of London for a soft tweed woven on the islands of the Outer Hebrides, Harris, Lewis, etc., off the northwestern coast of Scotland. One fabric is woven from hand-spun yarn and another woven from machine-spun yarn. Used for men's and women's suits and topcoats.

Hartnell, Norman see *couture, haute.*

Harvard shirting a twilled cotton cloth shirting, plain or striped, and similar to oxford cloth.

hat, Alpine or Tyrolese a soft felt hat with a brim, generally dark green in color and banded with a dark green ribbon or a heavy cord. Usually ornamented with a feather of bristle brush.

hat, bambino see *bambino hat.*

hat, beefeater's see *beefeater's hat.*

hat, beaver see *beaver hat.*

hat, bolero a small hat with upturned boxlike brim, peaked crown, some pompons and a chin strap; worn by Spanish men when dancing the bolero.

hat, Bolivar 1783–1830, a style of felt hat worn by the great South American liberator when not in uniform.

hat, Breton sailor see *Breton sailor.*

hat, cardinal's see *cardinal's red hat.*

hat, cartwheel a feminine hat with a low flat crown and a wide straight brim of even width. Usually a summer hat of straw which has appeared occasionally, in the eighteenth, nineteenth and twentieth centuries.

hat, cocked see *Androsmane; bicorne.*

hat, continental see *Androsmane.*

hat, coolie a conical-shaped hat of straw, worn by men, women and children in China as protection against sun and rain.

hat, cowboy see *hat, Stetson* or *ten gallon.*

petasos-ancient Greek hat of straw or felt-from a Tanagra statuette
the "little" hennin-silk or velvet-velvet frontlet-French-15th C.
gray or fawn-colored cloth top hat-English-1840's
sugar-loaf felt bonnet-French-15th C.
Hunting hat over wimple-Italian-14th C.
postilion beaver riding hat-powdered hair in cadogan-1790's
black silk hat-ribbon band-American 1921
leghorn skimmer hat over lawn cap-English-1750's
slouch hat of felt-American-1850's
Mexican riding hat-gray felt-Black or gray ribbon
black silk topper-French-1840's
straw sombrero-chinstrap of colored beads-Mexican
the Ten-gallon hat of range and dude ranch-American
bolero hat worn over silk bandana-black felt-chinstrap and pompons-Spanish
Garibaldi's braided pillbox cap copied by women-1850's
Merry Widow straw sailor-New York-1904
doll's hat-black ostrich-pink cabbage rose-velvet ribbon-1930's
coolie hat of straw over headscarf-worn by women of Taiwan

Hats-

Albanian-
beaver
German-
1580
Spanish toqued
of velvet or
silk-jewel
band-
16th C.
Pilgrim's
hat with
buckle-
1620's
Ramillies cock-
black felt-
French-
1729
Quaker-
beaver-
silver
buckle
as worn in
Paris-1780's
bicorne of
Napoleon-black
felt-tricolor-1814
Style
Nivernois-American general-
1770's
beaver or
felt-silver
buckle-silk
band-
Puritan-1630's
Kevenhüller,
Androsmane
or Swiss hat-black
felt-cockade-
powdered hair-
in queue-
American general-
1780
black
bicorne-
hair tied in queue-
Spanish-circa 1800
black
japanned leather-
white edge-
powdered hair-
in queue-
American Marine
1775

Hats

mourning top hat-black silk with black faille band-worn by Abraham Lincoln
topee or topi-pith helmet-white cotton-green facing-1860's
Hungarian or pork pie hat with ribbons-1850's
Tyrolese felt hat with cord, tassel and feathers-1880's
Bersagliere-black glazed felt-cog plume-Italian-1850's
Homburg-gray felt and ribbon-worn by Prince of Wales-1890
straw boater-with silk band-monocle-English-1890's
black felt derby-1st decade-1900's
black silk topper-with d'Orsay roll-English-1880's
gray or tan felt with four dents-southern planter-American-late 19th C.
melon shape-felt or straw-worn in London, Paris and New York 1860's

1930 to 1940
gibus, opera or collapsible evening hat-black grosgrain or merino cloth-formal
black silk top hat-formal day or evening
black silk hunting hat with guard
polo cap-white cotton covered-reinforced
gray derby worn to the races-British
stitched tweed hat for country wear
felt riding hat-colored cord-Mexican
gray felt topper worn with cutaway coat-British
black Homburg-business or semi-formal evening
tweed grouse shooting hat
dark gray pork pie felt
black felt derby for day wear in town
snap brim-brown felt with feather
Montego hat-vegetable fiber-for resort wear
black hunting derby-reinforced
"ten-gallon hat" pale tan felt-ranch or range
tweed cap for sports
black velvet hunt cap-reinforced-worn with pink coat
straw with dark red cotton puggree band
two-tone straw-spotted silk puggree band
brown leghorn-white shantung puggree band
for duck shooting-tan gabardine-corduroy flaps
boater of sennit straw-silk club band
panama with black grosgrain band
ski cap-dark blue gabardine-flaps inside-black ribbon
pith helmet for tropics-tan gabardine
Basque béret-dark blue woolen woven in one piece
black felt Tyrolese hat-cord band-feathers
yachting cap-navy blue-gold insignia
deer shooting-bright red cloth-leather visor

hat, crew a sports hat of white cotton twill or natural-color linen, a four-pieced crown with button on top and ribbon band, and a stitched brim. Early 1900's. Currently a soft cotton hat with a small turned-down brim, worn to shield the eyes from glare while boating. Generally made of twill or denim and usually white; a gored crown topped with a small button, and a stitched brim.

hat, derby see *derby hat.*

hat, doll a small, coquettish shape with tiny ostrich plumes which was in vogue for a short period after the appearance in the 1930's of the Empress Eugénie hat. The fashion was followed by Schiaparelli's little doll hats, frivolous headpieces instead of hats, 1950's.

hat, Empress Eugénie a small, coquettish hat with tiny ostrich plumes. Its tremendous vogue in the 1930's was short.

hat, Gainsborough or **Marlborough** of black velvet or taffeta with mauve ostrich plumes and taffeta ribbons. Called Gainsborough by the British because it was often painted by Thomas Gainsborough (1727–1788). To the French, it was the Marlborough because it was worn by the Duchess of Marlborough and also because of a popular French song, "Chanson de Malbrouck." The black velvet hat was revived in the first decade of the twentieth century.

hat, gibus a collapsible opera hat of black silk faille invented and made by a Paris hatmaker named Gibus. Built over a strong spring, it closed to a flat shape for carrying under the arm. It first appeared in Paris in 1823 and was patented in 1837. Worn by gentlemen with full evening dress until the mid-twentieth century when it became smart to dispense altogether with a hat.

hat, gob's a hat of white cotton twill with four-pieced crown and stitched brim. "Gob" is slang for the U.S. sailor. 20th century. see *cap, gob.*

hat, hard see *boater.*

hat, Hungarian or **slouch** of black felt with a rolling brim and two ribbon ends floating in back. Dates from the visit of Lajes Kossuth, the great Hungarian patriot, to England and America in 1852–1853. see *pork pie.*

hat, iron see *helmet; chapel de fer.*

hat, Korean see *Korean hat.*

hat, Marlborough see *Gainsborough hat.*

hat, mushroom see *mushroom hat.*

hat, Neapolitan a woman's summer hat with wide floppy brim and conical crown. Sheer, it was made of lacy horsehair braid or woven fiber. Usually black or straw-colored, it was originally made in Naples. Early 1900's.

hat, opera see *hat, gibus.*

hat, Panama a hat made from finely hand-plaited straw from carefully selected young leaves of the jipijapa plant. The hat is made in Ecuador, Peru and Colombia, but not Panama. It had been made for nearly three centuries when discovered by American soldiers in 1895 and so was named for Panama where it was marketed. It had been worn for a long time by the British in the tropics and in

Hat-crew hat-white cotton twill or natural color linen

clerical felt hat uncocked-German-18 th C.

Hat-"gob's" hat of white cotton twill-four-pieced crown and stitched brim.

Gainsborough or Marlborough hat-black taffeta mauve plumes and ribbon-1870's

western scout hat of felt in light brown or gray-19 th C.

"Henry Higgin's hat" wool tweed worn by the character in the play "My Fair Lady"—1950's

Pennsylvania, Holland or Quaker hat—beaver, brown or gray, 2nd half 17th century

Robin Hood

Shovel-hat worn by Anglican and Roman clergy

the American South where it was known as the planter's hat.

hat, picture see *picture hat.*

hat, Pilgrims' usually a wide-brimmed black felt hat with ribbon and a small silver buckle. Most Puritans and Pilgrims preferred very plain dress, seldom changing the style. Seventeenth century.

hat, planter's see *hat, Panama.*

hat, pork pie a feminine hat of the Victorian Era, small and round, known in England as the pork pie hat. Two long ribbons floating in back were named "follow me, young man." There was also a masculine pork pie hat in the same period.

hat, postilion or **postillion** a beaver hat with high, flat-top crown and silver-buckled ribbon band. French, 1790's.

hat, Puritan see *hat, Pilgrims'*

hat, Quaker a "wide-awake" hat of felt or beaver with the brim rolling or cocked and commonly gray or brown. Second half of the seventeenth century.

hat, Robin Hood a style associated with the legendary twelfth century English outlaw. A soft felt with turned-up brim, pointed crown and a long pheasant feather.

hat, sailor's until the 1770's, a small leather tricorne which changed to a small round hard hat with a narrow brim, of varnished or japanned leather. Late in the eighteenth century the same shape appeared but of shellacked sennit, a straw. This hat was adopted by Eton College to honor Admiral Lord Nelson; it is still worn and known as a boater. see *boater; hard hat; cap, gob.*

hat, shovel a black felt hat with low, round crown and plain flat brim turned up on both sides, protruding back and front and looking like a shovel. Worn by Anglican and Roman clerics.

hat, slouch see *hat, Hungarian.*

hat, steeple see *hennin.*

hat, Stetson, or **ten-gallon** the sombrero of the American western cowboy which came to be known as the Stetson because John B. Stetson, a Philadelphia hatmaker in the 1870's, decided to produce a quality hat for cowboys.

hat, Tansui a hat resembling the Panama, made of plant leaves grown at Tansui in Taiwan.

hat, ten-gallon see *hat, Stetson.*

hat, top, high, silk According to one story the high silk hat was invented in Canton about 1775 by a Chinese hatter for a Frenchman, who carried his headpiece back to Paris. Another story is that the silk hat was invented in 1760 in Florence. The hat was seen in the early 1820's but did not reach perfection until the 1830's when it was generally adopted. It was first made of polished beaver, called silk beaver, but later fashioned of plush. The d'Orsay roll was the important feature of the man's top hat in the 1830's, as it was worn by Count Gabriel d'Orsay (1801–1852). Amateur of the fine arts and a society leader in Paris and London, he was the greatest swell of his day. A few Anglo-American names for the top hat were round hat; topper or silker; John Bull, 5 and 3/4 inches high; stovepipe, 7 inches high; chimney-pot, 7 1/2 inches high; kite-high dandy, 7 3/8 inches high.

hatpin a necessary accessory in the late Victorian and early twentieth century period. About eight inches long; often used in pairs, it secured the hat to the high-dressed coiffure. It was topped by an ornament, often gold and jeweled.

haubergeon same as hauberk but a shorter garment.

hauberk a hooded, long-sleeved, knee-length garment of chain or ring mail worn by nobles in the twelfth and thirteenth centuries. It was worn with a belt of leather, a steel helmet and leg and foot bands of mail.

haute couture see *couture, haute.*

havanese or **Havana embroidery** conventional or geometric designs buttonhole-stitched in colors on heavy fabrics.

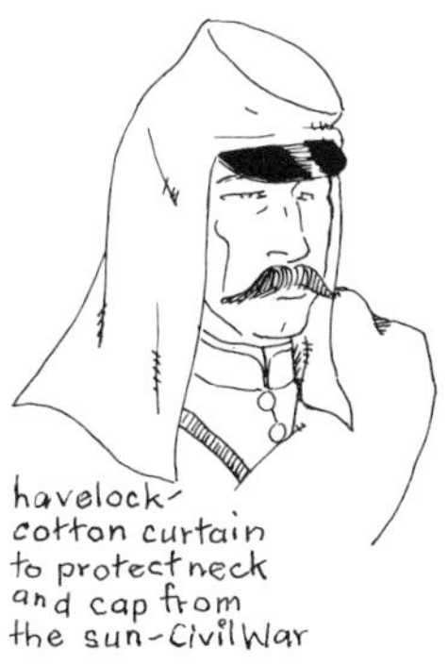

havelock a curtain of white washable cloth which covered and protected neck and cap, copied for the soldiers in the American Civil War. Though worn by ancient Persian soldiers, it bears the name of the British General in the Sepoy mutiny, 1857, Sir Henry Havelock.

headpiece see *fall.*

headrail the headdress of Anglo-Saxon women from the fifth to the eleventh centuries. Of linen or cotton, it was circular, square or oblong and was wrapped around the neck like the Persian or Roman chin cloth. It was held in place by a metal fillet or crown.

heartbreakers wired curls which trembled constantly, a fashion of the seventeenth century, worn at the nape and cheeks.

heather mixture trade name for a combination of varicolored interwoven fibers giving the effect of heather on a moor. Used principally in tweeds and some other woolen fabrics. Used for suits and coats in men's and women's wear.

heaume In medieval days the jousting heaume, a large helmet, was the general headdress in games and pageants, though various other styles of helmets were worn. The heaume was draped with a scarf of soft leather or silk with dagged edges and it was so attached to the heaume that it pivoted gaily in the wind. The drapery was known as the mantling or lambrequin. see *cointoise.*

hedebo embroidery cutwork and drawnwork embroidery usually white on white and originally used by Danish peasants to ornament all garments and household linens. Used today on sheer white for collars, handkerchiefs and table linen.

hedgehog wig see *wig, hedgehog.*

heel The heel has been in use in the Orient for centuries. The ancient Egyptian butcher wore heels when slaughtering cattle; the Persians used heels to raise the feet off the burning sand; and the East Indians and Mongolians kept the foot in the stirrup by means of a small heel. From the flat pattens and clogs came the idea of the modern heel, which was first worn at the Italian and Spanish courts, and supposedly was the idea of Leonardo da Vinci. In the eighteenth century the gracefully curved three-inch French heel became known as the Louis XV heel returning to fashion several times since. The red heel of nobility was of Venetian origin and appeared first in the sixteenth century on the black leather shoes of royal valets and slaves.

heel, baby Louis the low form of the Louis XV heel for women's shoes.

heel, Cuban of medium height and

usually built in layers or lifts of leather. Used for walking shoes.

heel, continental, French, Spanish similar in shape and very high, the difference being in the inside curve. Usually of wood covered with leather.

heel, platform see *wedge* or *platform sole.*

heel, spike or **stiletto** in vogue for the past several decades. Higher than the French heel, very slim and built with metal tips.

heel, sports low, flat, and broad, and usually of layers of leather. Used for men's, women's and children's shoes.

heel, stacked well-shaped, tapering wooden heel of varied height. Built of slim layers of wood, hence the term "stacked."

heel, wedge see *wedge* or *platform sole.*

helmet in general, any defensive covering for the head; specifically the headpiece in armor. The helmet of antiquity was made of boiled leather, the leather having been boiled in oil, wax or water and then steamed for hardness. The helmet of Europe following the fall of Rome was a hat fashioned of leather on a wooden frame reinforced with metal. It was a shell-like design with a serrated comb or crest of iron. About 1440 the Italians invented a small rounded shell of iron or steel with plating over the ears, neck and chin and a movable visor. Modern warfare has brought back some ancient pieces such as the padded helmet of steel or tin hat.

helmet, Bonaparte see *Bonaparte helmet.*

helmet, pith see *topee, topi.*

helmet, tilting a heavy, large helmet worn in medieval jousting tournaments, a contest in which a knight would tilt another knight off his horse.

hem the border of a garment made by folding back the edge and sewing it in place.

hem, false see *facing.*

hem, French a pinked edge reinforced with a line of machine stitching ⅛ of an inch from the edge, turned up to the wrong side and then carefully slipstitched to the fabric with silk thread which leaves no mark after pressing.

hem, hand-rolled for sheer fabrics and chiffon. The edge may be machine-stitched for firmness and trimmed, leaving one eighth of an inch of fabric, then folded or rolled and hand-stitched in alternating diagonal stitches, one to the fabric and one to the fold, with fine needle and thread.

hem, soft-roll done like the French hem with a pinked edge reinforced with machine stitching. But if the garment is to be interlined, the hem may be stitched to the lining. A soft rolled hem is not pressed.

hemlines the unstable hemline of the twentieth century began its rise in the second decade, reaching knee-length in 1925, and above, in the 1960's. Since the 1930's, there have been two distinct hemlines, full-length for formal and short for day. During the war years in the 1940's, came the short dinner dress created by Valentina, American couturière, which continues in fashion.

hemstitch embroidery a form of punchwork executed in backstitch with a large needle called a punchwork needle. A hemstitched effect is given by drawing the thread tightly.

hemstitching a decorative space at the top of a hem, usually on sheer fabric.

European Helmets

European Helmets

Made by drawing out a number of horizontal threads for the space desired. Then, with threaded needle, gathering equal numbers of threads and securing the groups first at the hemline, and then, at the top of the transparent space, working from the wrong side.

henna a tropical shrub native to Africa and Asia. A brownish, reddish-orange dye is obtained from the leaves of the plant; used for dyeing cloth and tinting the hair. A fashion of the early twentieth century.

hennin an Oriental headdress dating back to antiquity, no two authorities agreeing to its origin. It was brought to France by Isabella of Bavaria in the latter part of the fourteenth century, its vogue lasting a hundred years. It was commonly called a steeple headdress and was usually attached to a tiny skullcap from which was suspended the black velvet frontlet on the forehead. The wearing of the frontlet was a privilege only to those having an income of ten pounds a year or more. There were many styles, each invariably draped with a veil, floating or with wired edge. The hennin became so extravagant in size that the authorities found it necessary to regulate the height according to the wearer's social position. see *escoffion.*

henrietta a once popular cloth, little used today. A dress fabric that varied in finish, sometimes like cashmere or of the salt-and-pepper mixture type, used mostly for children's clothes. Named for Queen Henrietta Maria, wife of Charles I of England.

herringbone weave an irregular twill weave in zigzag repetition of short diagonal lines resembling a fishbone pattern. Similar to chevron weave, a cloth for suits, topcoats and sports.

Hessian boot, Souvaroff, Hussar see *boot, Hessian.*

hibernian embroidery Irish handwork in satin and purl stitches done on silk, velvet or coarse net for cushions, screens and garment trimming.

hickory cloth a coarse-twilled cotton fabric, resembling ticking but not as firm and of lighter weight, striped and checked. Used for work garments in institutions.

hides see *animal skins.*

Highland dress see *Scottish Highland dress.*

himation the cloak of men and women in ancient Greece. It comprised a piece of fabric, usually white, about 1½ by three yards in size, draped about the figure and over one shoulder. Young men and philosophers are pictured wearing it as the sole garment, in which case it appears to be securely belted at the waist. Women, too, wore it without the chiton.

hip boot see *boot, hip.*

hipster pants a term of the 1960's applied to snug, straight pants, replicas of the cowboy's blue jeans and cut only as high as the hipline, where they are secured by a narrow leather or self belt.

hizaam a word of varied spellings, a wide white silk sash wrapped in cummerbund fashion over the Arabian caftan, usually holding a silver dagger.

hobble skirt see *skirt, hobble.*

hobnails short, sharp-pointed nails with large heads used for studding heavy shoe soles and other leather accessories.

Holbein work or **Romanian embroidery** made in conventional and geometric patterns. Done in Holbein or double running stitch and used for samplers, fine linens and garments. Of the period of Hans Holbein, the younger (1497–1543), German court painter to Henry VIII.

French hood-black taffeta over white satin-velvet loops-1689

Holland linen a plain-woven stout linen cloth of many muslin types made in Holland, usually unbleached. It is also known as shade cloth. It has a smooth brilliant finish and is used in shirtings and suitings and for model dress forms.

hollie point lace a needlepoint lace made in England from the mid-sixteenth century, worked in a twisted buttonhole stitch. The name is a corruption of holy point, referring to church laces. Also called hollie-work.

Homburg soft felt hat of Tyrolese origin later called Homburg because manufactured there. A tapered crown with ribbon band and curled stiff brim in black or midnight blue for semi-formal and colors for day wear.

homespun a fabric loosely woven originally by hand in a plain weave in wool, linen or cotton. Now made by machine of wool, cotton or rayon with coarse yarns in a plain tweed pattern to simulate the early homemade look.

hood of silk over white lawn and lace cap-English-1670's

honeycomb a weave with a small allover pattern resembling honeycomb cells; also a reversible fabric of this weave used for clothing.

Honiton lace any of the laces made in Honiton, England. Specifically, bobbin-made floral motifs, the ground later filled in with bobbin or needle-made net of varied stitches. With applied motifs, it is termed Honiton Appliqué.

hood, academic a purely ornamental hood worn with academic or ecclesiastical dress, put on over the head and hanging down in back. The length of the hood depends on the academic degree, bachelors' being the shortest and doctors' the longest, with masters' between the two. Generally of black silk on the outside but faced with the colors of the college, university or seminary, which are displayed in the turnover of the cowl. The binding, generally of velvet, indicates the subject in which the degree has been given, such as blue for philosophy, red for divinity, purple for law, yellow for letters, green for science, white for arts.

widow's hood-black cloth over gorget of white linen-French-16th C.

hood, French of black velvet or silk tied under the chin; worn by English, French and American ladies for centuries with little change in style. When worn over a sheer white cap it was a flattering piece of headgear. Under Edward III (1327–1377), women of ill repute were forbidden to wear it. Madame de Maintenon, wife of Louis XIV (1643–1715), wore the hood constantly, which no doubt added to its dignity. It was worn by the Quakers and generally called the "Venerable hood." The contemporary hood follows the early model and is made of silk, wool or velvet.

hood, French of the eighteenth century worn by women of all nations including the American Colonies, was made of silk, velvet or sarsanet. It was attached to a long cape or a short shoulder cape and was then known as a capuchin after the cloak of the Capuchin monks. Quilted, fur-lined or fur-edged for winter wear, the hood of the early period was usually scarlet, cherry red or cardinal, and known as a cardinal or "red riding hood."

hood, gable, kennel, pedimental names for the English hood of the sixteenth century. A fall of black silk or black velvet hung over the top and in back. A white linen wimple and gorget were worn with it.

hood, widow's of dull black faced with white and worn over a coif and gorget, both of white linen; French, early sixteenth century.

hooded seal see *seal, hooded.*

hook and eye a device for fastening clothes; believed to have been first patented in 1808 by a Frenchman named Camus, for the production of hooks and eyes by machinery.

oop-vertugadin
the Velasquez
rtraits-velvet
d galon-head-
ess of curls,
athers, ribbon
d flowers-
anish-
58

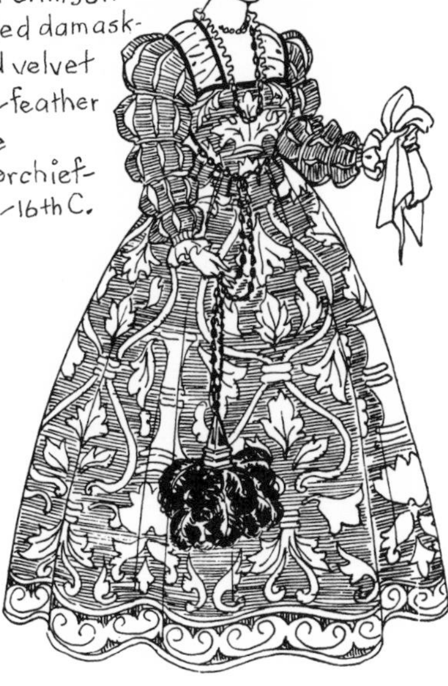

hoop-
roundlet and
gown of crimson
brocaded damask-
slashed velvet
sleeves-feather
fan-fine
handkerchief-
Italian-16th C.

hoop-
taffeta with lace
falling band-
fine lawn fichu-
beaver hat with
plumes-English-
1630's

oop-
ale blue cloth
silk-bodice
mbroidered-
ack velvet
im and hat-
strich plumes-
leated rose
ilk apron-
erman-
th C.

folding metal panniers
connected by tapes-1770's

double panniers-
Louis XV-1715-1754

hoop-robe à la
française-old blue
taffeta-stomacher
in échelle style-
pagoda lace
sleeves-ribbon
and flower trim-
French-1760's

hoop-hip-length-
whalebone and
tape

hoop-silk shirred
over whalebone

short hoop of
shirred silk over
whalebone

hoop-
corset and
whaleboned
petticoat in one

short
hoop-
of steel hoops
and tape-opening
in front-1857

hoop or bolster
used from
1570 to 1610

hoop-
crinoline petticoat
with steel hoops
opening in front
1857

houppelande with long sleeves-brocaded cloth-sugar-loaf hat-15th C.

hoop a circle or circles, of a stiff material, designed to spread the skirts of a woman's dress. see *Catherine wheel, crinoline; farthingale; panniers; verdingale.*

Hoover apron an apron with reversible front, first popular during World War I when Herbert Hoover was Food Administrator. Called a *wrap-around.*

hopsacking a coarse, woven sacking, of hemp and jute made into bags for gathering hops. Today, made of cotton, linen and rayon and used for coats, suits and dresses.

horned cap see *cornet.*

horsehair mane and tail hairs of a horse used to make horsehair fiber cloth. Used for hats and stiffening.

horsehide a tough, durable skin of lesser quality used for utility jackets, work gloves, shoe uppers, leather goods, and imitation Russian leather.

hosen see *paltock.*

huibil grande, festival headdress of Tehuantepec-Mexico

hostess gown an at-home costume, less formal than an evening gown, with long skirt or sometimes with flaring culottes. A style that has enjoyed varying degrees of popularity since 1930.

hound's tooth check a brilliant broken check, the design simulating canine teeth. The pattern may be woven in wool, worsted, cotton or rayon.

houppe, huppette a pompon or bongrace of swansdown attached to a black puff protruding from under the houppelande or shawl, high on the forehead. Worn in the sixteenth century by ladies of the Low Countries. see *huke; bongrace.*

houppelande a style which originated in the Low Countries, worn by both sexes from the mid-fourteenth to the early sixteenth centuries. A long, trailing and voluminous cloak with or without sleeves, wadded with cotton or fur-lined. In the fifteenth century it often had long, flaring Dalmatian sleeves and was belted.

hour-glass silhouette see *wasp waist.*

house coat a loose buttoned or zipped coat, long or short, for feminine at-home wear, often of a rich and elegant fabric but not necessarily so. see *hostess gown.*

housedress see *morning dress.*

huanaco see *guanaco.*

huaraches Mexican peasant sling-back sandals of wood with leather insole and braid edging, leather thongs laced through loops.

hug-me-tight a facetious name for a feminine shoulderpiece, crocheted, knitted or quilted, with or without sleeves, also called a bed-jacket, late nineteenth century.

Huguenot lace a simple lace fashioned of cutout motifs of mull applied to net.

huipil a headdress worn with festival costume by the women of Tehuantepec, Mexico. It is all white, of cotton and lace. According to legend, the headdress was copied from some finely made baby clothes washed ashore from a Spanish shipwreck in Colonial times; the Indian women admired the garments without knowing what they were for. The word has several spelling variations.

huke, Dutch a full-length black woolen mantle covering the figure and worn over a white linen coif with a bongrace; second half sixteenth century.

huke, huque, haik in Europe, a woman's wrap reminiscent of the period when the Saracens held sway in Spain. A square of black woolen cloth large enough to envelop the whole figure. Worn since the eleventh century, it survives in Spain and North Africa and in the Kerry cloak of Ireland. It is topped by a cloth-covered ornament. English 1590. see *houppe, huppette.*

hula skirt skirt of rich green ti-leaves, worn by a Hawaiian dancer in the classic native dance. With it is worn a bodice of embroidered silk and a flower lei.

humeral a shoulder veil or scarf of the same color as the vestments worn by a Catholic priest giving benediction with the Blessed Sacrament.

Hungarian folk dress see *Magyar folk dress.*

Hungarian hat see *hat, Hungarian.*

Hungarian point see *Florentine embroidery.*

hunt dress in contemporary fox hunting: the Master and hunt officials wear scarlet coats, white breeches, black boots with tan tops, and black velvet visored caps; members of the hunt in formal attire wear the same as the Master and hunt officials, but with a top hat instead of a hunt cap; black or Oxford-gray coats, fawn or mustard-yellow breeches, black boots and black top hats; others in less formal garb wear approximately the same, but a hunting derby instead of top hat. Everyone wears a white shirt with a white stock. Green is worn by the Master and hunt officials in many hunts during the cubbing season and in certain hunts which have specified green instead of scarlet; green is worn generally by beaglers and harriers. (The term *pink* for scarlet is no longer used.) Collars of the hunt color and hunt buttons are worn only with the permission of the Master. Ladies have a formal coat which may be single or double-breasted and may be black, Oxford gray or dark blue; the double-breasted swallowtail coat is known as a shadbelly.

hunter's green a rich hue of dark green, slightly yellowish, used for coats.

hunter's watch see *watch, hunting case.*

hunting sack or **shirt** a blouselike garment of suede, khaki or woolen, usually with turned-down collar and large patch pockets; used by trappers and huntsmen.

huppett see *houppe.*

huque see *huke.*

hurluberlu a madcap wind-blown bob which appeared in 1671; a lady's hair cut short and curled into tight ringlets forming a chou-fleur (cabbage flower) on either side of the face. In vogue to the end of the century.

Hussar boot see *Hessian boot.*

Hussar breeches see *breeches, Hussar.*

Hussar's uniform see *dolama, dolman.*

cloak called haik-
pleated tunic or
gandoura over
footed chalwar-
Arabian-Moor

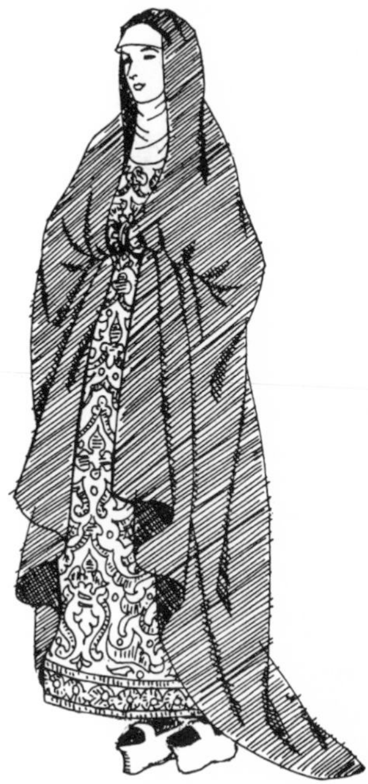

cloak called
huke or haik-
of Moorish origin-
chopines-
Spanish-
16th C.

Incroyable cravat-folded stock of white cambric-1800

imperial-a pointed tuft of hair on the chin and a moustache-Napoléon III

Incroyable-hair cut in "dog's ears"-bicorne-bulky cravat-Directoire-1795 to 1799

I

ichella the long, fringed shawl of woolen homespun cloth, woven by Auracanian Indian women of Chili. The wide border of geometric design is brilliant in color and fastened at the chest by a huge silver pin with a large disc of floral design.

idiot fringe an Americanism for the collegiate football player's haircut around the turn of the century. It was a Dutch cut with bangs.

ihenga a short full skirt, worn with the choli in northern and central India.

ihraam a form of dress expressing a religious state of self-denial, worn by the pilgrims to Mecca, the birthplace of Mohammed. Clothing consists of two lengths of white cotton without any stitching, one wrapped around the loins, the other thrown over the back, leaving shoulder and right arm free.

ikats silk fabrics of Sumatra, Java and Bali which are *chiné,* meaning that the warp threads have been printed, painted or dyed before weaving to produce a Chinese effect.

illusion a silk tulle used in veils, dresses and trimmings.

imperial a tiny beard worn by the French Emperor Napoleon III (1852–1873). It was a pointed tuft just under the lower lip.

Inca costume, traditional see illustration this page.

incroyable French for "unbelievable," of the Directoire Period, the dandy or fop of the times. He made a cult of the extreme in dress; he peered at people through his perspective or quizzing glass,

Incan Indians of Peru-costumes of hand-woven woolen cloth-black with vivid colors-note large silver flower pin

penciled his eyebrows and used quantities of amber perfume.

indestructible voile also called indestructible flat chiffon. From the trade name for a type of sturdy all-silk voile.

Indian see *American Indian costume; bonnet, American Indian.*

Indian gown a negligée or dressing gown imported from India in the seventeenth and eighteenth centuries by the Dutch who carried on a vast trade with

the Orient. The robe was so important that the English king and queen had their own appointed Indian gown maker. Also called banian. see *banyan.*

Indienne a painted or printed muslin from India which was introduced to France and England, becoming exceedingly fashionable during the seventeenth and eighteenth centuries. About the middle of the eighteenth century, shops were established in Europe for the hand-block printing of linen, cambric and cotton.

indigo a vegetable dye obtained from a tropical plant known from earliest times; a synthetic form is now available. The color is deep, dark blue, both brilliant and permanent.

infanta style see *robe de style; Velásquez.*

infula, infulae the lappets which hang from a bishop's mitre, which originated in the pendants of a pagan priest.

inlay a decoration or motif set into the surface of a piece of jewelry or other metals or wood.

inseam in glove manufacture, a glove with stitched seams turned to the inside of the glove. In tailoring, the length of measure from crotch to edge of trouser leg and the forearm seam of the sleeve.

inset an insert of fabric or lace into a garment for fit for ornamentation.

insignia any design or characteristic mark used as a distinguishing sign or badge of honor.

insole the inside sole of a boot or shoe whether felt or leather, attached or removable.

instep length the length of a garment three or four inches off the floor.

insurgeant fashion so named and worn by French women in sympathy with the American Revolutionists. It was a simplified style of the much-frilled gowns worn from 1775 to about 1782.

intaglio a carving in a hard substance such as a gem. The design is hollowed out in reverse and below the surface.

interlace to weave in or out, or braid together cord or ribbon, producing a symmetric design.

Inverness a sleeveless cloak with short cape of checked woolen cloth from Inverness, Scotland. Cloth belt and leather-covered buckle. Usually worn with cap of the same cloth. 1880's.

inverted pleats see *pleats, inverted.*

iridescent having a soft play of changing rainbow hues or shades in a fabric or piece of mother-of-pearl.

Irish crochet lace copied from Spanish and Venetian needlepoint. Durable and decorative with medallions of shamrock, rose or leaf design, set in chain stitched square meshes. It is made lacy-looking by picot edge and scallops.

Irish linen fine, plain-woven full-bleached linen cloth of Irish flax. Used for shirts, handkerchiefs, blouses, etc.

Irish poplin originally made in France; a ribbed fabric with fine silk warp and a heavy worsted filling. Used for dresses, coats, suits, raincoats and ski suits. Carried to England and Ireland by Protestant refugees, eighteenth century.

iro-the draped overskirt of the Nigerian woman-white linen blouse-cotton underskirt and bandana-contemporary

iro, ire a straight, uncut piece of brilliantly printed cotton worn by Nigerian women. It is draped and pinned in place forming an over tunic with kimono-like sleeves. see *agbada.*

iron, flatiron used in pressing and smoothing cloth and garments. The pressing iron has been heated by flame, steam, gas and electricity, the electric iron being the invention of the twentieth century.

iron hat see *helmet; chapel-de-fer.*

Isabelline a color named after Infanta Isabella of Austria (1566–1633), daughter of Spanish Philip II. During the siege of Ostend which lasted three years, she vowed she would not change her chemise until Ostend was taken. During that time her cream-tinted garment changed to a buff or tawny hue, a color which became fashionable and stayed in vogue for more than a century.

Isabelline see *bear, Himalayan.*

Italian cloth see *satin, farmers'.*

ivory a bony substance obtained from the tusks of the walrus, narwhal, elephant, hippopotamus, also from ivory-colored bone.

ivory nut the seed of a Venezuelan palm. When dry, it is very hard and resembles natural ivory in color. see *vegetable ivory.*

Ivy League look a manner of masculine dressing first observed among men of Yale, Harvard and Princeton universities and some smaller colleges. A cult of the twentieth century based upon the conservative elegance made traditional by Bond Street, London, and Madison Avenue, New York. All through the straight and broad-shouldered era, the suit with the Ivy League look kept to the slender trousers, natural shoulders and narrow lapels on a straight, unshaped and above all, unpadded jacket.

Izar the outer garment of the Moslem woman of the poorer class, a piece of white calico large enough to cover the whole person. *Izar* is the Hindu and Persian word for veil.

J

jabot ruffles which concealed the front closure of a gentleman's fine shirt. Of sheer batiste or fine lace, they were tied at the neck with a ribbon cravat string. The style originated in the Louis XIV period, surviving to the middle of the nineteenth century, reappearing from time to time in feminine dress. see *cascade.*

jabot-origin of frills to conceal shirt closure Louis XIV period

jabul a large cloth shawl worn as a mantle by the Moro women of the Philippine Islands.

jack a homemade coat of mail. A short jacket usually sleeveless. It was made of two layers of canvas or leather with small metal pieces in between held in place by stitching or quilting; sixteenth century.

jackboot a knee-high boot of heavy black leather with broad heel, worn by cavalrymen and fishermen. Popular in the seventeenth and eighteenth centuries.

jackets see specific types; *beer, bush, dinner, Eisenhower, Eton, lumberjack, mess, monkey, Norfolk, pea, pilot, shooting, smoking, Zouave.*

Jacobean embroidery see *crewel embroidery.*

jaconet a light, soft white cotton cloth rather like cambric but a little heavier. Used for dresses and infants' wear.

jacquard a knitting stitch in which the motif is raised in bas relief. Named for Joseph Marie Jacquard, son of a weaver who, in 1801, revolutionized the textile industry by inventing a mechanical loom to weave patterns or brocaded fabrics. The French Government bought his loom in 1806, granting him a royalty and a yearly pension. In 1837 he invented and patented another remarkable machine for making flowered net resembling handsome lace.

jade a semi-translucent gem capable of high polish, ranging in color from white to a deep green, also red, yellow and lavender. Ancient carved green is prized for its color. It has religious significance for the Chinese and is called the sacred stone of China. The choicest is semitransparent "Imperial jade." Used in carved forms and beads, also rings, pins and earrings. There are two kinds with different components: nephrite and jadeite.

jaguar or **American tiger** the largest member of the cat family in the Americas. It ranges from Texas and southern California over South America, except the southern end, and east of the Andes. The largest supply of peltries comes from Guiana. The fur is soft, rich, white to brownish-yellow and buff, with dark rosettes and spots larger than leopard markings. Used for coats, jackets and trimming.

jamb, jambeau a protective piece of leg armor of Medieval times.

jams flowered shorts, about knee-length, from the word pajamas, became a Nassau beach fashion when a surfer cut off the legs of his gaily-printed pajamas to make a more comfortable garment.

Japanese mink see *mink, Japanese.*

Japanese geisha-black satin haori over kimona-colorful silk obi-white cotton tabi-felt sandals

Japanese haori-coat over silk kimona

Japanese national costume see *kimono.*

Japanese sable see *sable, Japanese.*

jardinière French for an ornamental flowerpot. A multicolored design of flowers, leaves and ribbon bowknots on a multicolored ground. Also a narrow lace of the seventeenth and eighteenth centuries which was used as an edging for linen pieces.

jargoon see *zircon*

jaseran, jaserant an Algerian chemise of the thirteenth century of very fine chain mail worn as body protection. Also, a jacket made of linen and sewn with overlapping metal plates. In the sixteenth century, jaserant was the name of feminine collarettes made of rows of fine gold chains.

jasey a British colloquialism for a wig made of yarn, probably of Jersey yarn.

Java canvas a coarse, porous canvas used for embroidery.

javel water a bleaching agent and an antiseptic and disinfectant used to whiten clothes. French *eau de javel* is chlorine bleach.

jean a stout, twilled cotton cloth which originated in Genoa, Italy, and has been used for men's, women's and children's work and play clothes since the eighteenth century. It is available in solid colors and stripes but most commonly in blue. "Blue jeans" is the common name for breeches made of the cloth in that color. see *levis.*

jelab, jellaba a hooded woolen robe, centuries old, worn by natives of northern Africa; a three-quarter length garment for poor weather. see *djellaba, litham.*

jemima a British term for the shoe with elastic gussets. see *bottine.*

jerkin In the fourteenth century, the man's cote-hardie developed into a garment known as the doublet or pourpoint, both words meaning a wadded jerkin, jaque, jacket or gambeson. A similar garment for women was called jerkinet. The jerkin became a sort of waistcoat in the north of England, worn up to the early twentieth century.

jersey an elastic cloth in tricot or stockinette stitch. The hand-knitting of wool with needles has been going on for some 2,000 years but the first knitted shirts or tunics appeared in the fifteenth century on the islands of Jersey and Guernsey in the English Channel. Guernseys, ganseys or jerseys, were knitted by women for sailors and fishermen. The knitted tunic, though it absorbed sea spray, did not feel damp. In the 1890's, when sports became fashionable, the knitted woolen garment acquired great popularity. Today knitted cloth is made of wool, cotton, silk, rayon, nylon or any possible combination of fibers. Chanel, in 1918, introduced jersey to the mode in the chemise frock and her famous suit. see *knitting; Chanel, Gabrielle.*

jersey knits, synthetic knitted, flat or round, very popular for dress and suit fabrics in the 1960's. There are single, double and triple knits providing cloth of varied textures and weights. To be had in a variety of prints and hand-screened designs ranging from subdued to most sophisticated designs.

jester's costume see *motley; cap and bells.*

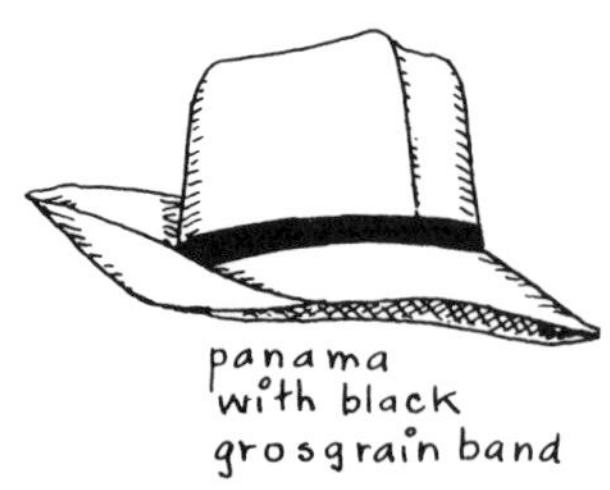

panama with black grosgrain band

the Hong Kong sheath - printed copper colored silk - self-colored underskirt - large folded hat - necklace of ropes of beads - Dior

jewel neck a high-cut, collarless neckline for day to permit the wearing of an ornamental chain, a collarette or for evening wear a necklace of beads.

jewelry, costume see *costume jewelry.*

jewelry, paste see *temple jewelry.*

jet, black amber a variety of black mineral coal capable of a brilliant polish in the making of mourning jewelry, ornaments or buttons. Black jet was a vogue throughout the second half of the nineteenth century. It came from England where it was found in layers of shale and had been in use for centuries. The supply diminished and an inferior quality was supplied from Spain. White jet came from Norway and black glass imitation jet from Germany.

jinnah cap see *cap, Jinnah.*

jipijapa a hat made from the fibers of a palmlike plant of Central and South America. see *hat, Panama.*

Job's tears seeds of an Asiatic grass, pearly white and capsule shape. Grown in India, strung and used as beads. Also the name of olive-green grains of chrysolite worn as gems.

jockey cap see *cap, jockey.*

jodhpur, chukka an ankle-high boot with two eyelets, of suede or smooth leather and rubber or leather soles. Known by the name of East Indian origin, chukka, signifying a period of play in polo.

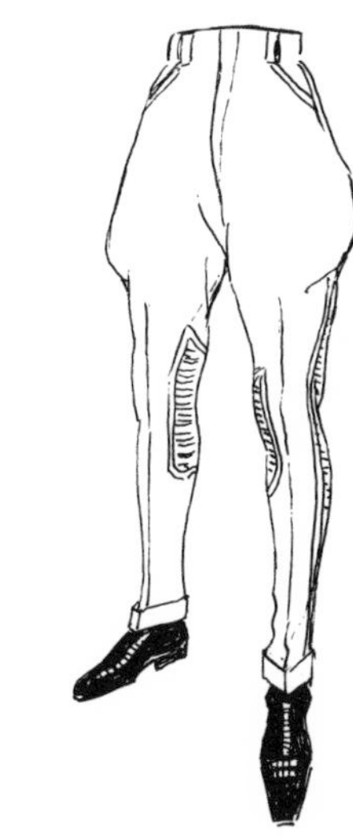

Jodhpurs-East Indian style of riding breeches adopted by men and women-1920's

jodhpurs a style of riding breeches from India, new to the Occidental world in the second decade of the twentieth century. Full to the knees, tight from the knee to the ankle, and held down by a strap passing under the boot. The low jodhpur shoe, not the riding boot, is worn with the breeches.

Johnny collar see *collar, mandarin.*

jonquil the bright yellow hue of the jonquil blossom.

Joseph or **Josie** of the eighteenth century; a lady's full-length redingote or riding coat buttoned full length down front. When unbottoned it was called a flying josie. It was made of josette, a heavy twill cotton resembling khaki.

Joseph, or "josie" when unbuttoned - riding coat or redingote - 18 th C.

jours motifs in lace-making, connected by bars and brides permitting daylight to shine through. *Jours,* French for daylight.

jouy prints modern reproductions of French prints of the eighteenth century printed on white or light-toned cotton or linen, the motif in monotone. see *toile de jouy.*

jubbah the Hindu name of a long, loose garment with long, loose sleeves worn by Parsees and Mohammedans in India and Arabia by both men and women. Made of cloth or camel's hair cloth, sometimes embroidered and sometimes fur-lined for winter wear.

jube a padded sheepskin greatcoat with the skin to the outside, the winter coat of most Balkan peoples. Heavily embroidered in silk and wool and appliquéd with brilliantly colored woolen cloth motifs. The overlong sleeves usually have sheepskin sewn-in mittens.

Jugoslavian embroidery stitchery worked in brightly colored yarns with various stitches, principally cross-stitch, double purl-stitch and slanting satin-stitch. Done on coarse linen.

sheepskin coat or jube-coat of most Balkan peoples-sewn-in sheepskin mittens-appliquéd red cloth motifs-white linen tunic and breeches-red woolen cummerbund-black sheepskin tarboosh-Bulgaria

Juliet cap see *cap, Juliet.*

juliet shoe a lady's house slipper of simple and graceful design with high front and quarter, and cutout U-shaped sides. Early twentieth century.

jump British term for a contemporary short outer coat or jacket, thigh-length and buttoned down center front.

jumper a nineteenth century playsuit for infants, top and bloomers in one piece, made of cotton cloth. see *rompers.*

jumper a loose blouse or pullover for women; a one-piece, sleeveless frock worn over a guimpe or blouse; a one-piece garment with low-cut bodice, having only shoulder straps and worn over a blouse or T-shirt. see *pinafore.*

jumper frock in the 1960's, a one-piece dress of tent or shift silhouette, sleeveless, and worn over blouse or knitted shirt with sleeves either short or long.

jumpsuit the twentieth century work or play overalls made for men and women in cotton, denim and synthetics and usually striped, dark blue, charcoal gray or brown. The top and pantaloons are joined by a self-belt and the garment fastened in front. see *siren suit.*

jungle fighter boot see *boot, jungle fighter.*

jusi a delicate fabric for dresses made in the Philippine Islands. Of pure silk or silk with hemp or piña fiber. Also woven in a lacy pattern.

justaucorps French for body coat; one of the styles of the seventeenth and eighteenth centuries, leading up to the modern man's suit jacket as a piece different from the outer cloak.

jute a glossy fiber of two East Indian plants used chiefly for sacking, burlap, cheap twine and wrapping paper. Sometimes combined with silk or wool and made into fabric.

K

kabaya the jacket, in Western style, of the Indonesian woman's costume, most often white but also of a gay print; worn with a sarong length of contrasting printed cotton draped in skirt fashion with a deep front fold, the skirt held by a silk scarf tied around the waist.

kaffa see *caffa.*

kaffiyeh, keffiyeh the Arabian and Bedouin headdress of cotton, linen or silk, plain or striped, and varied in name, pattern and color. Worn for thousands of years, it remains the favorite head covering of the Arab for all occasions. He wears it even with Western dress. Folded into a triangle and placed upon the head, two points fall over the shoulders providing a tie, if wanted, and one hangs in back to protect the neck. A skullcap is often worn underneath. The scarf is held to the head by the agal which is bound around the head several times.

kaftan see *caftan.*

kaitaka a mat worn as a cloak by the Maoris of New Zealand. It is made of the finest flax, giving it fine texture, and is sometimes finished with a decorative border.

kalasiris a long garment of tunic fashion worn by both men and women in ancient Egypt. It was a close-fitting sheath of woven or knitted cloth, but at the same time lightweight and transparent. It was held up by one or two shoulder straps or sometimes made with short sleeves cut in one with the body.

kalmack, kalmuk a cloth made of wool or shaggy cotton, resembling bearskin.

kamaka see *camoca.*

kambal a much-used, coarse woolen shawl or blanket in India.

kamelaukion an ancient cap of felt or fur, tall, cone-shaped and brimless, worn by religious fanatics of various Mohammedan sects in some of their ancient rites. see *taj.*

kamiks high boots of hairless skin into which Eskimos tuck their hairy skin trousers. Both sexes wear them, and inside the roomy boots they wear short socks of sealskin, the hair to the inside. The women of Greenland embroider their boots handsomely with intricate geometric motifs cut from dyed leather, and beaded lace patterns and feather trimming.

kamis an Arabian undergarment in general use, of white cotton reaching to the ankles and worn over loose, wide trousers. It is embroidered around the neck and across the front with red or white silk. When worn indoors, a wide colored sash and a white cotton skullcap complete the costume.

kandys a short skirt of goatskin or sheepskin, retaining the hair as decoration, which was the original ancient garment of the Sumerians, Babylonians, Assyrians, Persians and Hebrews. The upper part of the body was bare. see *candys, Persian.*

kangaroo, wallaby, wallaroo, wombat, koala native Australian marsupial ani-

kabaya (jacket) draped sarong skirt-draped linen headdress-Indonesian

kamelaukian of felt or fur-also worn draped round with yards of cloth or silk-Persian-16th C.

"kangaroo walk"-result of straight-front corset-early 1900

mals. Wallaby and wallaroo are smaller species of the kangaroo, the quantity of pelts limited, and not suitable to styling. Poor fur with no underwool, used only for sports coats and collars.

kangaroo a soft, supple, durable shoe leather exclusively from Australia, limited because the animal is not raised commercially.

kangaroo walk the name given by humorists to the resulting movement of a woman's figure encased in a straight-front corset at the turn of the century. see *wasp waist*.

kapa in Yugoslavia, a small round cap in pillbox style, of black velvet with red top denoting an unmarried female; the married woman wears an all-black one. Also a national headpiece for men.

kapok the mass of silky fibers from the seeds of the kapok or silk-cotton tree. Formerly used commercially for stuffing muffs, but now used for household needs such as pillows and mattresses.

kapta-a full-skirted tunic of Lapland costume-of fur in winter-cloth in summer-contemporary

kapta a full-skirted tunic worn by Lapland men with rather fitted breeches. The outfit is made of reindeer skin for winter and of cloth for summer use. The skins are dehaired as well as tanned; in winter two kaptor are worn, one with fur next to the body. The colorfully embroidered costume of cap, tunic, breeches and boots, is worn by men, women and children.

karakul a hardy breed of sheep originally from the Karakul Valley in Russia near the Caspian Sea, now native to Asia Minor.

kaross a square rug of animal skins worn by Hottentots, a South African race allied to the Bushmen and Bantus.

kasha a trademark for a type of soft, silky wool mixed with hair of cashmere goat in a twill weave. Used for dresses and for men's wear.

kata a "benediction" or ceremonial silk scarf. It is customary in Sikkim, Tibet and Bhutan, upon important occasions, to exchange scarfs between friends and guests. An ancient Tibetan rite.

Kate Greenaway frocks see *Greenaway, Kate*.

kaunace a skirt of dressed leather or felt, or later, woolen cloth, which was worn over a white linen tunic, high-necked and short-sleeved. It evolved from the ancient kandys worn for centuries. Both sexes wore the skirt, full-length for women and short for commoners and soldiers. The tunic of the king and high officials was fringed, tasseled and embroidered, the latter famed as "Babylonian work."

kelt a kind of rough woolen frieze cloth usually white and rough on one side. Made in Scotland and northern England. Used for skirts, suits and coats.

Kendal green The name of a cloth and its color. It is made by Flemish weavers working in Kendal, England. Used for skirts, suits and coats.

kepi see *cap, forage*.

kerchief a cloth worn as a head covering.

Kerry cloak a full-length cloak with a hood, of black cloth, traditional in Ireland. Essentially the same garment has been worn all over Central Europe for centuries, and originated in Spain during the Saracen occupation (c. 700–1500).

kersey a cloth which originated in Kersey, Suffolk, England. Manufactured as far back as the thirteenth century; a firm, pliable all-wool cloth, coarse and ribbed. Men's long stockings were made of it.

kaunace embroidered-worn over linen tunic-Mesopotamian

kaunace and shawl of wool with fringe-Mesopotamian

embroidered silk or wool-over linen tunic-a felt mitre-Mesopotamian

kerseymere see *cassimere.*

kēthoneth a three-quarter-length tunic of white linen, with sleeves, worn over a full-length undergarment by the Hebrew high priest.

kerry cloak or huke still worn in Ireland-of black cloth

Kevenhüller see *Androsmane.*

khaddar a cotton homespun cloth made in India in a movement to combat the use of foreign goods.

khaki, khakee from the Hindu word meaning dusty, dust-colored. As applied to cloth, originally a durable, brownish cotton cloth used for uniforms in the Anglo-Indian army, now widely used by armed forces throughout the world.

Khanh, Emmanuelle see *couture, haute.*

khirka a shawl or mantle originally made of patches and shreds of cloth and worn by Moslem dervishes.

khurkeh, Bethlehem dress a rich, colorful costume worn by women in the Near East and still worn. A straight, narrow gown, long enough to be bloused over a wide crushed sash of figured linen or silk and still reach to the ankles. Over it is worn a short, bolero style of jacket with

Bethlehem dress-see khurkeh

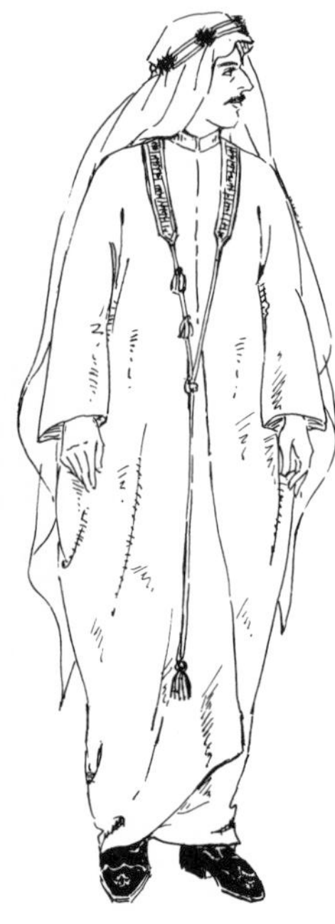

kibr of white silk worn over tobe-gold cord neckband-kaffeyeh and agal-Saudi Arabia

wrist-length flaring sleeves. The dress, usually dark blue or dull red linen, is trimmed with embroidery, braids and beads in varied muted hues. see *Bethlehem headdress.*

kibr a hooded robe with sleeves, of striped cotton or silk. An Arabian cloak which is worn over the ankle-length white cotton tobe, typical Arabian dress.

kick pleats see *pleats, kick.*

kid see *kidskin.*

kid, Dongola a leather resembling French kid; made of goatskin, calfskin and sheepskin by the Dongola process of tanning and finishing.

kid, glacé goatskin finished with a highly polished effect and smooth surface; used for gloves. *Glacé* is French for glazed.

kid, undressed leather finished on the flesh side by the sueding process.

kid, Vici the trade name for goatskin tanned and finished by a special method producing a bright glazed finish.

ainu girl in kimono

kidskin shoe leather; a tanned leather of mature goats usually $2\frac{1}{2}$ years old. It comes in all finishes and colors and is dressed to imitate antelope and deerskin. Also beautifully marked, fragile goatskins, mostly from China but also from Africa and India. In natural, gray, black and white, which may be dyed all colors, and used for shoes and bags of all styles, both masculine and feminine.

kidskin, Chinese thousands of skins are exported from China. Gray especially in demand but dyed all colors. Those with flat or semiflat moiré pattern are used for broadtail coats and jackets.

kidskin, Mongolian very soft under-wool, dying to any color. Often sold as mouflon when dressed and top hair removed. see *goat.*

Kiki skirt a knee-high skirt made its first appearance in New York in 1923, creating a sensation when actress Leonore Ulric wore it in Picard's play, "Kiki."

kilmarnock a broad-topped woolen cap in flat tam-o'-shanter style, of woven plaid with a pompon on top. Named for a town in Ayrshire, Scotland.

kilt in Scottish dress, formerly the pleated section of the belted plaid which hung from waist to knees. In modern times the kilt is a separate short skirt of clan tartan, hanging in pleats from waist to knees. Worn by men in parts of Scotland and by some Scottish, Irish and Canadian regiments. Also worn by smart women for casual wear. see *breacan-feile.*

kiltie, kilty tongue a leather tongue, usually fringed, covering the laces of a sports shoe.

kimono a loose gown tied with a sash, part of the Japanese national dress. Worn as a dressing gown by Western women. It remains Japan's national costume, despite the fact that Western dress is now more commonly worn for travel and business. The masculine kimono is dark in color and has shorter sleeves, but otherwise is similar to the feminine robe. All garments of men and women fasten from left to right. The man's robe is ankle-length and his family crest in a tiny motif is embroidered or stenciled on each side of the chest, in center back and at the top of the sleeves. For daily wear, a wide sash called the heko-obi goes around the waist two or three times and ties in a loose bow. The kaku-obi, a sash of heavy silk, is worn on formal occasions and is tied in back in a double knot. The feminine kimono may be floor-length or shorter, the longer being held by a cord tied around the waist. Men and women of the Ainus, the original inhabitants of Japan's Hokkaido Island and a remnant race which has lived on Hokkaido for at least 7,000 years, wear a kimono somewhat different from that of the mainland over regular trousers and boots. The women's robe is ankle-length; the masculine garment reaches halfway between knee and ankle. The cloth is woven of elm-bark fiber called attush, and varies in color from a powdery blue to very dark. It is appliquéd in small geometric patterns and embroidered over in chain stitch in white geometric scrollwork. Everyday work clothes are those of the Westerner, white cotton shirt, slacks and sweater.

kimono flannel flannelette; a soft cotton cloth printed with colorful motifs of Japanese design.

kimono sleeves see *sleeve, kimono.*

kincob, kinkab, kinkob, kinkhob a heavy brocaded silk with gold and silver flowers and large figures. Most often used by rich Hindus for turbans.

king klipper a Mod note of the 1960's from London. A four-in-hand, five inches wide, of polka dot or vivid Paisley silk tied in a bulky knot and long enough to reach the belt.

kips East Indian hides of yearling cattle, tight-grained from a breed of small oxen. Dressed to imitate box calf and cheaper leather. Kips is the commercial term for pelts fifteen to twenty-five pounds.

kirtle the kirtle was either tunic, chemise or long petticoat, mentioned from in the fourteenth century through the reign of Queen Elizabeth I, 1558–1603, when it was made of silk, velvet, taffeta and satin, varied in colors and with elaborate trimmings. The kirtle disappeared in the seventeenth century.

kit, kitt, or **swift** see *kit.*

kittle a white cotton robe worn on Jewish religious occasions; a gown in which Orthodox Jews are buried.

klompen see *shoes, wooden.*

knee breeches breeches fitted to the knee; knickerbockers which have some fullness. "Knickers" is a more general name.

knee buckles of plate or silver, used to fasten men's cloth knickers at the knee. Small boys' knickers were secured either by a buckled strap or an elastic band in a slot. First half twentieth century.

Kilmarnock, a flat-top tam-o'-shanter worn in Scotland—1820's

knickerbockers full, baggy breeches fastened at the knee with band and buckle instead of a cuff. The name derives from Dietrich Knickerbocker, the pretended author of the *History of New York* written in 1809 by Washington Irving.

knickers a woman's garment for winter wear worn over muslin underdrawers. Usually of wool or silk, rather full and held by knee bands.

knife pleats see *pleats.*

knitting a process of forming a piece of fabric by means of a single thread and

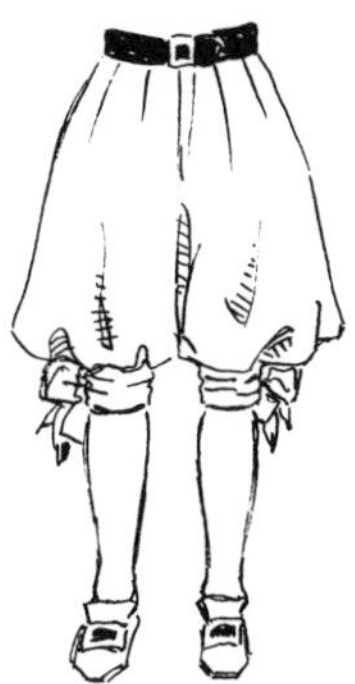
Knickerbockers Dutch Colonial—Ribbon ties

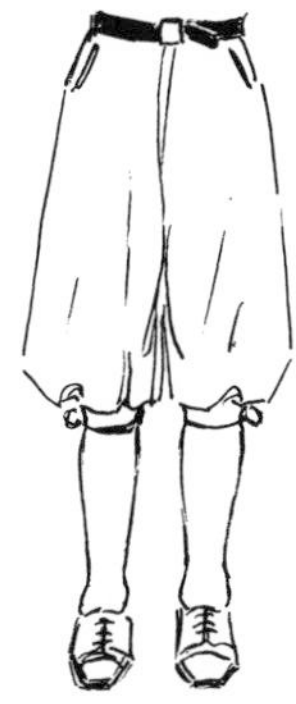
Knickers—19th C. buckled or buttoned bands

Plus Fours—1920's

kolah-traditional Persian hat-black felt or Persian lamb-or worn draped in turban fashion

a pair of needles. Knitted woolen socks found in an Egyptian Coptic tomb of a period between 400 and 500 A.D. are proof that the Egyptians knew not only how to knit, but how to shape the garment while knitting. Short socks were occasionally knitted in the ninth century and skullcaps in the thirteenth, fourteenth and fifteenth. Liturgical gloves knitted of silk were worn by churchmen. Hand-knitted silk stockings first appeared in Spain during the sixteenth century, a pair of which was presented to Henry VIII. Queen Elizabeth was the first English woman to wear silk stockings.

knob sandal see *sandal, knob.*

knop yarn a novelty weft yarn with variously colored knots or lumps throughout its length.

knot, Windsor see *Windsor knot.*

kooletah-coat of caribou skin with red leather fringe-Canadian Caribou Eskimo

knots have served as ornaments and buttons through the ages, used especially by the Chinese and Japanese for decoration, fastening of garments, embroidery and lace-making. *Button knot*—a knot in regular size to be used as a button. *Josephine knot*—a decorative braid knot composed of two loops with the ends free for fastening. *Lover's knot*—a ribbon knot, worn as a remembrance bit. *Macramé*—a decorative knot in macramé lace. *Shoulder knot*—a shoulder ornament of braid, ribbon and lace, sometimes jeweled, worn in the seventeenth and eighteenth centuries for military and special occasions. *Tailor's knot*—a knot used at the end of the thread in sewing, a small hard knot to prevent the thread slipping through the fabric.

knots, Austrian see *Austrian knots.*

knotted lace a lace in which the decoration or design is executed in knots on the fabric surface, the best example of which is macramé.

koala see *kangaroo.*

kolah the traditional hat of the Persians, a brimless hat of cloth or Persian lamb which, according to the wearer's status, may be wrapped turban-fashion with a strip of fine muslin of varied colors. Color and the winding of a ten-to-twenty yard strip indicates standing. Royalty adds a badge of aigrette plumage or a heron tuft. Worn upon special occasions today.

kolinsky mink see *mink, kolinsky.*

koo dark blue cotton sacks worn as everyday dress by Chinese men, women and children.

kooletah a coat made of caribou skin worn by the Eskimos of Greenland and Labrador origin.

Korean hat a tall-crowned, wide-brimmed hat of woven horsehair, bamboo and silk, painted black, tied under the chin with black silk ribbons. Traditionally worn by Korean men after marriage when the hair, worn in a queue by bachelors, is dressed into a tight bun on top of the head and confined by a strip of black horsehair covering the head like a skullcap. The hat is never removed, not even for sleeping. In wet weather it is covered with a conical hat of oiled paper or silk. This custom, although now passing, is still observed in some parts of Korea.

koteny the traditional Hungarian apron worn for festivals and holidays by both young men and young women. It is decorated with embroidery and appliqué and treasured as an heirloom.

kothornus, cothurnus see *cothurn.*

krepis a popular Greek and Roman sandal of the fourth century. The sole was a "finger's thickness" and was held to the foot by a decorative leather strap that laced over the instep and round the ankle.

krimmer lamb from the Crimea (Krim, the ancient Russian name). It is a curled fur of mixed, gray and black and

Korean-white silk coat and pantaloons-horsehair hat over

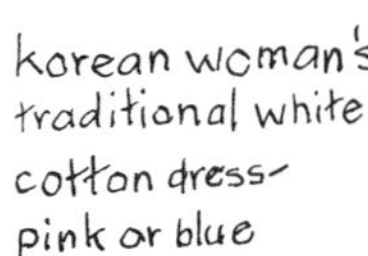
korean woman's traditional white cotton dress-pink or blue

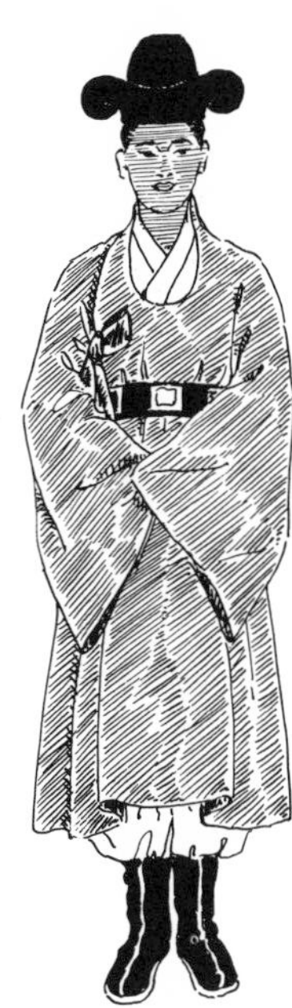
Korean wedding dress-scarlet over white-black velvet hat and boots

Korean bride in brilliant colored wedding dress with a tiny crown of beads

white hairs producing a bluish-gray color. A durable fur used for coats, jackets and trimming, especially in children's wear.

k'sa the outer cloak of the North African Moor which is skillfully draped into a wide-sleeved caped mantle. It is a straight piece of wool or cotton, indigo blue or white, about six yards long.

kulah a conical cap of felt or lambskin, the headgear of Middle Eastern monks and dervishes.

kumbi a silky fiber of the East Indian white silk cotton tree. The fiber resembles kapok, and probably, like kapok, is used for stuffing and padding.

kumya the body garment or shirt of the North African Moor. It fastens down the front with buttons and loops and is worn over full-length cotton pantaloons.

kūrtā Moslem blouse worn by men and women with trousers or pantaloons. The masculine blouse is a long white cotton shirt fastened to the left side with button and loop. The long sleeves are buttoned to the wrists. The feminine blouse is sleeveless and reaches only to the waist.

kusak a wide silk sash worn by Turkish men, many yards long, wrapped around the waist holding the full pantaloons, long or short, in place.

kusti a sacred girdle of woolen cord worn by the Parsis in India, a religious sect which fled Persia in the seventh and eighth centuries.

kūrtā, white linen shirt-rose silk pagri (turban) brown jodphurs-moroccan shoes-worn by Sikh of Ludhiana, India

L

la modiste in English, the "modesty bit" which was tucked into the bosom of the eighteenth century gown. It consisted of gauze or lace accented with ribbon bowknots. see *modesty bit or modesty piece.*

la robe The surcoat disappeared in the fifteenth century and a real dress called la robe, with a fitted bodice and long, tight sleeves, joined by a belt to a full skirt, came into fashion.

Labrador seal see *seal, hair.*

lace Before the creation of lace on a net ground, all laces were cords or threads of flax, cotton, mohair, aloe fiber, gold or silver. To work the braid into a pattern, the fingers were used as pegs in a sort of weaving process with braids. When looped, twisted or plaited together with a needle, it was called needlepoint. When worked with bobbins or pins on a cushion or pillow, it became pillow lace.

As a network formed of interlaced cords, lace has existed since antiquity. It had been made by slaves in Egypt, Persia, Byzance and Syria. Needle lace is mentioned by the ancient Greeks and Hebrews. It is said that Italy was the home of earliest European lace-making, but Spain claims the distinction of the art having been brought first to their country by the Saracenic invaders, the Moors. Lace is next noted in Flanders, north France and Belgium, reaching Holland, England and Ireland in the sixteenth and seventeenth centuries. The lace used for masculine linens was point de Venise, for women's lingerie point de rose, and for prelates point Colbert. During the French Revolution, because of royal patronage the lace factories in France were demolished, especially those of Chantilly. Some of the lace-makers were put to death and their patterns destroyed. "Real" lace is that made with a needle on net, bobbins on a pillow. The term can be applied to crochet or knitted lace, but never to machine-made.

See specific types of lace: *Alençon, aloe, araneus, argentan, Ave Maria, baby, Battenberg, Bavarian, Bayeux, bobbin, Bohemian, beggar's, Binche, black, blonde, Bourbon, bridal, Bruges, Brussels, Buckinghamshire, bullion, Burano, carnival, Carrickmacross, Chantilly, chenille, Crete, crochet, damascene, darned, Dieppe point, duchesse, Egyptian, fiber, filet, flat point, Genoa, gold, Greek, Irish crochet, knotted, Limerick, lisle, Maltese, margot, Mechlin, Medici, metal, mignonette, needlepoint, Northampton, Nottingham, opus araneum, orris, Paraguay, parchment, peasant, peniche, Plauen, point de gaz, point d'esprit, point de Paris, point plat, poussin, power, princess, Renaissance, reticella, Roman, rose point, Saint Gall, Saxony, Schleswig, shadow, Shetland, Spanish, Swedish, tambour, Teneriffe, thread, tondor, torchon, trolley, Turkish point, Valenciennes, Venetian, warp, yak.*

laced an adjective meaning the tying or securing garments with lace or cord. Pertaining to men's hats, coats or uniforms, it signifies the use of braids or cords as ornamentation, now usually of gold or silver braid or cord. Gold or silver lace today is made of silk or cotton thread that is silvered or gilded.

lacis a former name for the square net foundation or for lace marked on net.

lacquer red a color yellowish-red in hue, similar to the finish on furniture obtained by using Chinese or Japanese lacquer, a spirit varnish.

laid embroidery see *church embroidery.*

Lakoda trade name for a skin, a natural sheared Alaska fur seal which lends itself to fine tailoring.

lamb see *astrakan, broadtail, budge, galyak, karakul, krimmer, merino, moiré, mouflon, mouton, swakara.*

lamb, Persian a silky, tightly curled fur, the best of the lambs from Russia, Persia, and Afghanistan. Now raised in Africa. A regular curl varying in size which opens rapidly, usually after the lamb is five days old. Silky in texture and naturally rusty, black or brown but usually dyed jet black. Persian peltries are luxurious and heavy. Those of Afghanistan have smaller, finer curl and medium weight; African, fair curl, glossy and light weight.

lamb shearlings the sheared peltries of lambs that are about eight months old, are processed to resist curling when wet. Dyed to simulate beaver and called beaver-dyed lamb, mouton and mouton-processed lamb. From Canada, United States, Australia and Africa. The African shearlings are called capes.

lamba a square shawl or mantle worn by Madagascan women. Woven in brilliant colors and patterned with stripes, circles, squares, discs and plaids. Part of the native costume.

lambrequin a mantling or decorative scarf which hung from the medieval knight's helmet to protect it from heat and wet. It was also called cointoise. see *heaume; helmet; cointoise.*

lambskin shoe lining; also the skin tanned white and dressed with wool of fine-textured sheepskin.

lamé a silk brocaded fabric with flat threads of silver and gold. A sumptuous cloth for evening wear in gown or wrap.

laminated or **bonded fabric** two pieces of material, one thick and one thin, or one of wool and one of silk bonded together with resin acetate. The process gives the cloth more body and the silk acts as a lining. New in the 1960's and much used.

lampas an elaborate and decorative fabric similar to damask, woven in silk or wool and in many colors. Used in upholstery and also in simple sheath frocks.

lansdowne a dress fabric, sheer and wiry, of silk and wool in a plain weave. Used for women's dresses.

Lanvin, Jeanne see *couture, haute.*

Laotian costume, traditional see illustrations on this page.

lapel a part of the roll or "fold-back" of the front of a jacket or coat, combining collar, lapel and rever. see *collar and lapel; peaked or peak lapel.*

lapin French for rabbit. see *rabbit.*

lapin, blocked rabbit fur closely sheared, cut into small squares and sewn together for novelty use such as inexpensive fur coats for young people and children.

lapis lazuli a semi-precious stone of the feldspar group sometimes noted as the sapphire of the ancients. An opaque, deep blue with a tinge of green, often marked with iron pyrites or spangled with gold.

Lapland bonnet, Laplandic, biagga gallas a four-pointed bonnet known as the "hat of the four winds" or sorcerer's cap. Three points are stuffed with down to use as a pillow, the fourth serves as a

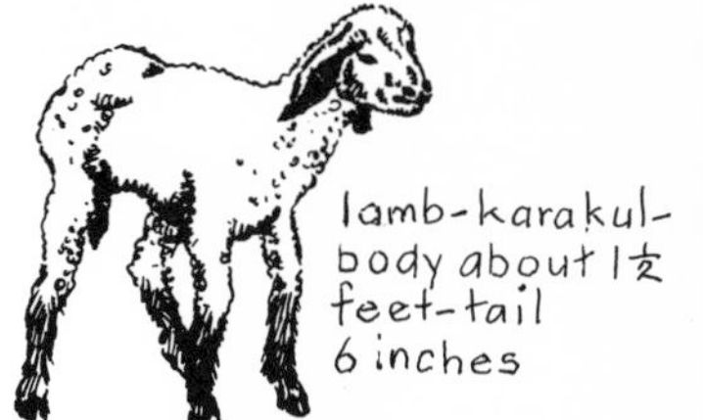

lamb-karakul-body about 1½ feet-tail 6 inches

Laos-chieftain's daughter-black velvet calpac and dress-red and yellow embroidery-silver hoop necklaces-contemporary

Laos-government secretary-black silk turban and coat over white shirt and trousers-ivory badge-sign of rank-contemporary

Lapland bonnet "the four winds"

Lapland bonnet of knitted wool with tassel of reindeer strips

pocket and purse. Though occasionally still worn by elderly Lapp men, the peaked cap has now taken its place.

lappets flat lace, ribbon or fabric pendants, usually a pair, attached to a cap, bonnet, crown or clerical headdress.

larrigan knee-high, oil-tanned leather moccasins used by Canadian and United States lumbermen and trappers.

Lavinia hat-satin with ribbon bride-French-1804

last a mold or wooden form made on standard-size measurements over which a shoe is built. The operation is called lasting.

lastex the rubber core around which any textile yarn may be wound. Lastex may become the warp or filling of any fabric, making that fabric stretchable in any direction. Used in all items of apparel which call for elasticity. First used successfully in the 1930's.

latchet the fastening of a shoe or sandal, usually in the form of a narrow strap, thong or lace.

laticlave one of two broad purple stripes down the front of the ancient Roman tunic. Two purple stripes were considered a badge of high rank.

Laton trade name for an elastic yarn wound with cotton, very fine and very soft, for lightweight elastic garments such as underwear, swimsuits and stockings.

lava-lava the printed calico kilt or loincloth worn by Polynesian peoples of the Pacific Islands.

lavaliere, lavalier, lavallière a small jeweled locket worn on a chain around the neck. Named for Louise de La Vallière, mistress of Louis XIV in the 1660's. Also a man's scarf worn during the Third French Republic in 1870. It was of wide, soft silk tied in a loose knot with long ends.

lavinia hat a large straw hat tied under the chin by a ribbon which went around brim and crown, popular early nineteenth century.

lawn a delicate, sheer white cloth of linen or cotton in use for centuries. Made in Laon, France, in the sixteenth century and used in Elizabethan England for wimples, ruffles, ruffs, gentlemen's shirts, handkerchiefs; still used for the sleeves of Anglican bishops' robes. It has always been popular for dresses, blouses and aprons. see *bishop's or Victoria lawn.*

layette a complete outfit for a new baby consisting of bassinet, bedding, clothing, etc.

leather the skin or hide tanned or preserved of any beast, reptile, bird or fish. Hides are the commercial term for pelts over twenty-five pounds, also the undressed skins of full-size animals such as cows, steers, and horses. Kips are the undressed skins of smaller animals. Skins are those of calves, sheep, goat and such.

leather, boiled or **cuir bouilli** French

for leather boiled in oil, wax or water and, while soft, molded into shape and then steamed for hardness. All parts of armor and corsets for men and women were made of it. Used from antiquity through medieval period.

leather, bull or **cow** heavy, fibrous leather used chiefly for heels and soles, principally sole leather for heavy boots. It is also skived and dressed on the flesh side in black and colored box, grained and patent leather.

leather, chrome tanned by the chrome method, a quick mineral process used mostly for shoes, also for glacé kid gloves.

leather, degrained leather which has been masked, giving a smooth finished skin.

leather, elephant skin is tanned and dressed before being shipped to the manufacturers. It requires about four years to bring it to a pliable state, and gray in color. England makes it into luggage and women's bags. Italy, Spain and Portugal make it into shoes and in the United States, it is used principally for belts and watchbands.

leather, grain any leather dressed on the grain side of the skin; often a split from a thick tanned skin like cowhide.

leather, jack wax leather coated with tar or pitch. Used for boots, tankards and a huge jug called a blackjack, seventeenth century.

leather, japanned or **enameled** the dressed flesh splits of white-hair seal which are japanned. Enameling is done on the grain of the leather.

leather, man-made see *Corfam.*

leather, patent a japanned or lacquered leather which appeared in the first quarter of the nineteenth century and was used for harness. Seth Boyden, a harness-maker of Newark, New Jersey, made the first patent leather in the United States in 1822. It was used for the soft, little slippers then in fashion and continues to be used for slippers and for other uses such as fine handbags.

leather, roan a low-grade sheepskin used for bookbinding, slippers, etc. It is tanned with sumac and colored to imitate ungrained morocco from which many styles of traveling cases are made.

leather, Russian originally from Russia; a lighter leather from the hide of young cattle dressed brownish-red and black. It is tanned in willow bark, dyed with cochineal and sandalwood, which makes it insect- and moisture-resistant, and birch bark which gives it a fragrant odor.

leather, saddle vegetable-tanned cowhide used for leather goods, including women's bags and belts and men's and women's sports shoes.

leather, Scotch grain usually of cowhide with a pebbled grain stamped on by plates and roller. A heavy, durable leather for men's shoes.

leather stockings Indian leggings reaching from ankle to mid-thigh, shaped to the leg and held by a thong tied to the belt. Embroidered and fringed like the moccasin. see *American Indian Costume.*

leather, synthetic made of coated fabric, fiberboard, pasteboard, composition rubber and cellulose, the finished article resembling leather but minus its scent.

leather, vegetable an imitation leather made of cotton waste. Put to the same uses as real leather.

leatherette, leatheroid trade names for imitations of leather made of paper and cloth, or paper and rubber.

lederhosen German for leather breeches or shorts held up by crossbar leather braces. Worn by men in the Tyrolean Alps, traditional Alpine dress.

leggings leg covers of leather or cloth worn by children, reaching from foot to waist with a strap passing under the shoe. see *gaiters, gamashes, spatterdashes, spats.*

leghorn a large picturesque hat made from finely plaited straw grown in Tuscany, Italy. It is cut green and bleached and is cultivated especially for hatmaking.

lei-Hawaiian wreath of leaves, flowers or feathers

leg-o-mutton sleeve see *sleeve, leg-o-mutton.*

lei a flower necklace worn by Hawaiians. A thick rope of fresh, colorful, fragrant tropical flowers.

Lelong, Lucien see *couture, haute.*

leno, leno weave a gauze weave for men's summer shirtings. An open weave for hot weather, made in a variety of pattern effects.

leopard a large cat, in ancient Egypt the symbol of royalty. A costly, fine fur. Due to modish demands, the fur is becoming rare, especially skins from Somaliland. The hair is short with rosettes well marked on a pale ground. The snow leopard, which is very rare, inhabits high altitudes of Tibet and Siberia. A pale yellow-gray color with long, silky hair and long fur fiber. The markings resemble spots more than rosettes. Both leopard and snow leopard coats are costly.

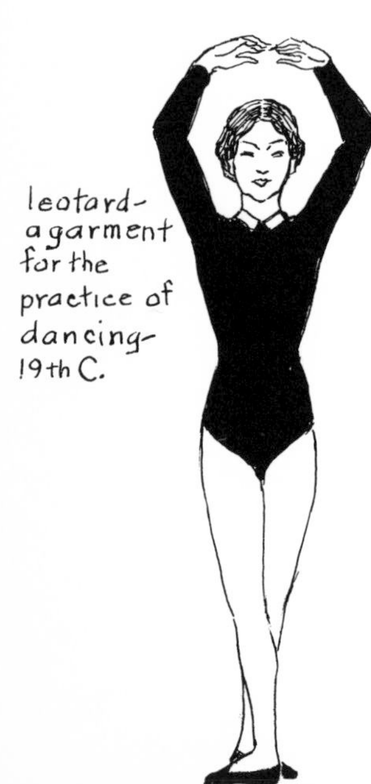
leotard-a garment for the practice of dancing-19th C.

leotard, or **tights** designed by a 19th century trapeze artist, Jules Leotard, the name later adopted for the garment by professional dancers. A practice costume of ballet dancers, acrobats and gymnasts. The long-sleeved garment reached from neck to crotch and was always black. In 1956 a leotard reaching from neck to toe of stretch nylon became available in red, green and blue to be worn with Bermuda shorts, kilts, ski and skating costumes. see *body stocking.*

létice, laitice see *ermine.*

Levantine a firm, twilled silk cloth first made in the Levant. It was the same finish on both sides but of different colors and was used principally for robes and sashes.

leviathan canvas a coarse, strong embroidery canvas which takes a large or double cross-stitch and a thick woolen yarn for the working of embroidery.

leviathan wool a thick woolen embroidery yarn made of many strands and used on leviathan canvas.

levis, blue jeans strong cotton pants of indigo blue denim reinforced with copper rivets at crucial points. The creation of Levi Strauss who went to California in 1850 seeking gold. They are worn by men, women and children for work or play.

levis or blue-jeans-plaid cotton shirt-black felt stetson or ten gallon hat

levis or blue-jeans-plaid cotton shirt-black felt hat-black leather boots

Levite gown-silk and satin-straw hat with ostrich-powdered hair-French-1780's

levite gown a type of redingote with a train, inspired by the Englishman's redingote of the 1770's. There was also a redingote gown with a short, double-breasted jacket with wide lapels, which were considered very extreme.

libas the traditional Egyptian cotton pantaloons, very full and draped, reaching to knee or ankle. Worn with a white or colored shirt or a gandoura or the gallibiya or even sometimes as a waistcoat. see *gandoura.*

Liberty a trade name used by Liberty of London for fine-textured fabrics in silks, cottons and woolens.

liberty cap see *bonnet, Phrygian.*

Liberty satin see *satin, Liberty.*

Lille lace of Lille, France. A fine bobbin lace, sometimes dotted with motifs outlined with a heavy flat cordonnet.

Lillian Russell costume the fashion of the times identified with the American actress (1861–1922). She had a handsome buxom figure and wore form-fitting gowns with a train. Her marcel-waved pompadour was topped by a large black velvet hat of Gainsborough style with ostrich plumes.

Lillian Russell-"figure of the day"-American 1861-1922

"Lilly" see *Pulitzer, Lilly* under *couture, haute.*

Lily Langtry wave a curled coiffure with crisped bangs and low chignon worn by the English actress (1852–1929), famed as the most beautiful woman in the world.

Limerick lace a pattern which originated in Limerick, Ireland, embroidered on net stretched in a tambour or embroidery frame, the stitches run through by means of a hook or a tambour needle. see *tambour lace.*

Lindbergh jacket worn by Charles A. Lindbergh, who made the first solo flight across the Atlantic from West to East, 1927; similar to the battle or Eisenhower jacket of World War II.

line a thread, string, cord or stripe; also, shape or contour.

line for line copy exact or nearly exact reproductions of Paris models made in the United States, especially on Seventh Avenue, New York.

linen the product of the flax plant, one of the five varieties of the bast family. It is thought to be older than cotton or silk of India and China, and is known to have been cultivated in Egypt for 5,000 years. A fibrous material in the stem of the flax plant produces smooth and strong fibers ranging from very coarse to very fine. Whether fine or coarse, it makes a durable fabric suitable for many items from sheerest handkerchiefs to wearing apparel of various types. In ancient Egypt linen fabrics were woven from the various bast fibers, but linen made from flax was the important and all-around Egyptian

Lily Langtry-"most beautiful woman in the world" wearing chinchilla-

textile. During the period of the Old Kingdom, linen was treasured and stored in the royal storehouse. It varied in texture from closely woven to a very fine gauze. Pieces of five thousand years ago have been found in tombs, of a sheerness surpassing modern manufacture. So finely woven and of such transparency were some cloths that the fabric was called Egyptian lace for many centuries.

linen, book see *book linen.*

linen, butcher's see *butcher's linen.*

linen cambric plain weave linen, sheer or coarse. Used for handkerchiefs and dress goods.

linen canvas an open-mesh canvas used for embroidery.

linen, Irish see *Irish linen.*

linen-textured rayon a wide range of rayon fabrics with various linen textures and weights.

linene trade name for a linen substitute, usually of cotton in a heavy, plain weave. Used for skirts, middies, aprons and such.

linge from the French for linen. Until the twentieth century white linen was the fabric used for underclothes, often called body linen, and religious vestments.

lingerie French for ladies' underwear, first used as an English word by *Godey's Lady's Book*, mid-nineteenth century. From about the thirteenth century until the nineteenth, underwear consisted of a shift or smock-like piece of apparel, of wool or linen and embroidered at neck and hem, called a shirte or camise. Nineteenth century underwear consisted of a chemise worn under a boned corset, a corset cover, drawers or pantalets and several petticoats, always white and made of soft cottons such as nainsook, batiste, longcloth, cambric and others, with lace and embroidery. In the twentieth century lingerie became greatly simplified, often with garments all-in-one. Synthetic materials requiring no ironing are now widely used as is lastex for girdles and nylon for other pieces; the range of colors including prints is unlimited. Some former names for a lady's underwear were underpinnings, under-things, unmentionables, indescribables.

lingerie and corsetry Lingerie and corsetry in the early twentieth century became practically one unit composed of bra, panties and slip. Next, an abbreviated form-fitting girdle of lastex with few or no bones was evolved which was worn with a soft, but controlling brassière. All pieces are made of sheer, yet firm, delicate synthetic silks and gauzes in pretty colors.

linsey-woolsey a coarse, woolen linen or cotton warp cloth very popular in the American Colonies; first made at Linsey, Suffolk, England.

lipstick a pomade for coloring the lips put up in stick form and enclosed in a tiny case, appeared in the first decade of the twentieth century. Colors ranged from white and flesh through pink to deep reds. The popular use of lipstick took hold in the 1920's, becoming scarlet-red in the 1930's. By mid-century, the blood-red mouth gave way to a pale or nude coloring which was succeeded by a more natural color. see *cosmetics.*

lipstick red a brilliant red in costume and accessories in the 1930's and 1940's, named after the popular shade of lipstick.

liripipe, liripipium the peak or tail of the chaperon hood. By the thirteenth century the liripipe had so lengthened that it almost touched the ground. The headpiece was worn by liveried servants in the fourteenth and fifteenth centuries. It could be folded on top of a stuffed roundlet or wrapped around the neck. It became the custom to fling the liripipe and roundlet over the left shoulder. From this custom evolved a miniature replica which is still worn on the left shoulder of the French magistrate and on the robe of the British Knights of the Garter and liveried servants. In the fifteenth century, only a noble was permitted to wear a hat with liripipe or, by its English name, tippet. see *tippet.*

lisle a fine, hard-twisted thread of staple cotton formerly used in the manufacture of fine hosiery, underwear, gloves and many other items. It was named for the Flemish town of its origin.

lisle lace a fine bobbin lace woven with a flowered design outlined by a cordonnet.

lisse a fine, smooth gauze used for ruching.

litham a sheer embroidered square folded diagonally to cover nose, mouth and neck, the ends tied, worn by Arab women. Men also use a plain litham when the sand is blowing. see *djellaba.*

little black dress introduced by Patou of Paris in 1921. In black jersey, silk or wool, the dress became standard for day wear after five o'clock. It was decidedly chic and has remained in vogue.

Little Lord Fauntleroy a small boy's best suit which became popular for one or two decades after the publication in 1886 of *Little Lord Fauntleroy* by the English-American novelist, Mrs. Frances Hodgson Burnett. Reginald Birch, the illustrator, chose the style of the Cavalier period for the costume of the young hero, a black velvet suit with deep lace collar, a red and black sash and a plumed hat. Sentimental mothers favored the ensemble but it was truly loathed by most of its young wearers.

liturgical headdress The miter and tiara are both of Persian origin and were worn by Christian and Jewish prelates alike, with no special religious significance before the eleventh century. A sign of rank was the sacred fillet of white wool with infulae or lappets. Early in the twelfth century the bishop's miter was enclosed in two pointed panels at the sides, then placed back and front where they have since remained. The white linen miter was also worn by the Levitical priest. The tall conical tiara of Asiatic origin became the papal crown, but popes wore the miter as late as the fifteenth century. The papal crown with one crown was worn by Nicholas I, (858–867 A.D.) In 1065 Alexander II added the second coronet and the third appeared with Urban V (1362–1370). In the sixteenth century a mound with a cross atop instead of a jewel completed the triple crown of the pope, and remains the symbol of his temporal power. A triple-crowned tiara was worn by the ancient Jewish high priest.

livrée, livery In the feudal era at a stated annual date the lord of the castle made gifts of cloth or costume to the noblemen of his estate. The gift was called livrée, origin of our word "livery," the uniform of a servitor. The law governed the amount of one's possessions in wearing apparel, the size of a cloak and the width of trimming. Nobles were permitted to wear hoods with long tippets, while the commoner had to be content with just a hood.

lizard a scaly, decorative and durable leather from Java and India, which does not crack. Used for shoes, belts, handbags, etc.

llama a South American animal of the camel family. The coarse, woolly fleece is dyed to simulate wolf and fox. see *alpaca; guanaco; vicuña.*

llautu a cord of fringed vicuña wool worn around the head by the ancient Peruvians as a badge of nobility.

loafer the heeless Norwegian slipper

litham or face veil worn by Moslem Tuareg of the desert against sun and sand

Little Lord Fauntleroy— hero of the popular novel, whose costume set a boy's fashion— 1886

Llama- S. A. animal of the camel family

moccasin loafer–elk tanned leather–20th C.

first introduced in the U.S. in the 1940's; it quickly developed into a tailored style because of its comfort and slip-on qualities. Worn by men, women and children. Sometimes tasseled.

longi or sarong-type of skirt worn by men and women–Burma

Lochlana a trade name for a modern cloth which "feels like cashmere, wears like wool" and is made in Scotland. It is used for men's fine shirts in America.

loden a waterproof cloth resembling Irish frieze, made by the Tyrolean peasants from the wool of their mountain sheep. It is woven and dyed in several colors but especially a bluish green known as loden green. see *toggle coat.*

loincloth, breechcloth, breechclout a brief garment worn round the loins by primitive peoples.

long cloth a closely woven, plain weave cotton cloth made of fine combed yarns, especially adapted to infants' wear. It was one of the first fabrics to be woven in a long piece, hence its name.

longi, lungyi a sarong-like skirt that both sexes of the Burmese wear with white cotton blouses or short jackets. The skirt is draped around the waist and hips with a deep pleat folded to the left and tucked into the belt, often giving the effect of trousers. The "acheik" longyi is a handloomed piece in a colorful broken pattern on silk or cotton. It is costly because it requires months to weave.

Loo mask of black velvet lined with white silk–French–16th C.

loo mask, loup riding half masks worn by men and women in winter or strong sun. They were made of black silk or velvet, green silk or linen, and were popular in the American Colonies during the eighteenth century. see *mask.*

loom a machine or frame of wood or metal upon which thread or yarn is woven into a textile. The threads running lengthwise form the warp, those running crosswise, the weft, woof or filling.

loongee a large square of cotton or silk folded and carried over the shoulder. This piece, worn in Afghanistan, is used as handkerchief, muffler or sash for holding one's possessions.

Lord Chumley a cape overcoat popular in Europe and America in the 1890's. A man's travel coat named for a play of the period.

lorgnette–eyeglasses mounted on a decorative folding handle–19th C.

lorgnette eyeglasses mounted on a handle into which the glasses fold when not in use. In the nineteenth century they were especially fashionable as a feminine accessory. see *quizzing* or *perspective glass; opera glass.*

losh a hide, generally elk, dressed only with oil.

lounge suit–blue serge–wing shirt collar–bow tie–English–1880's

lounge, sack coat, sakkos a jacket for informal wear, of British design, which appeared in the 1850's. It was a coat without a waist seam, at first considered eccentric. Single or double-breasted, it was worn generally by the 1870's and today is almost universally worn. see *sakkos.*

lounging robe a comfortable indoor robe for lounging or extra warmth. Of flannel, velvet, silk or brocade and often lined, the length is variable. Worn by men and women.

loup see *loo mask.*

lovat a heather-colored fabric produced by combining blue or green with gray or beige threads.

love-lock a single long curl over either ear, tied with a bowknot. The wearing of the love-lock prompted a celebrated French soldier, Count of Harcourt (1601–1666) to wear an earring in the exposed bare ear. This fashion was introduced into England by Charles I (1625–1649).

love-lock tied with ribbon favor-laced hat - English-17th C.

Lucile see *couture, haute.*

lumberjack an imitation of the coat worn by lumbermen. A straight, short jacket usually belted in back and closed in front by a slide fastener. It is made of water-repellent cotton, heavy cloth, plain or plaid, or leather and furnished with large pockets. Worn by men, women and children.

lumberjack shirt formerly worn by Canadian lumberjacks. Always made of plaid fabric in thick wool, cotton or rayon blend and worn for work or for winter sports.

lungi or **lungee** the long cotton cloth which the East Indian uses as turban, scarf or loincloth.

lutestring, lustring a fine corded silk popular for ladies' dresses, seventeenth to nineteenth centuries. A narrow silk ribbon used as an eyeglass cord.

lycra spandex trademark for a man-made fiber composed largely of "elastomer" or stretch fibers. It is used especially for feminine undergarments such as girdles, brassières, the body stocking and support stockings.

lynx, wildcat an animal with short tail and ears tipped with tufts. Found in Norway, Sweden and North America, as far south as California. A larger animal comes from Scandinavia and Russia; the best from Hudson Bay and Sweden. Pale gray fur with fine streaks and dark spots; underhair less thick than fox. A four-inch-long silvery top hair used natural or dyed, often a lustrous black. Used for scarfs and trimming and the busby of the British hussar. A smaller form of lynx with flat, reddish or gray fur and slightly spotted fur comes from western United States and British Columbia. Used for trimming. see *caracal.*

Lyons velvet see *velvet, Lyons.*

lumberjack-mackinaw-bush jacket or short warm-of plain or plaid wool or leather-fur collar and zipper

M

Macfarlane coat-
plaid breeches
over black boots-
black silk hat-
British-1850's

macaroni a term in England about 1760 applied to young fops who were exquisite in dress. They wore tiny hats as did their feminine counterparts, who were also called macaronies.

macclesfield, spitalfields fine silk scarfs manufactured and named for localities in England. Overall patterns of small design and subdued coloring. Names interchangeable. see *spitalfields.*

Macfarlane cloak a cloth topcoat with separate sleeve capes and side slits to permit hands reaching inner pockets. British, from 1850's to end of century.

Mackinaw, Mackinac a short, heavy, outdoor coat of woolen blanketing usually in bright plaids or wool fleece. Used by hunters and lumbermen.

Mackintosh, mac, mack a cloak of rubber-coated fabric, therefore waterproofed; named after Charles Mackintosh (1766–1843). He designed the raincoat and patented the first waterproofing process.

macramé lace of Arabian origin but made mostly in Genoa, Italy. A knotted lace woven in geometric patterns, often fringed with many of the ends tied together. Coarse pieces used for table covers and bedspreads; made in silk for scarfs and shawls and throws.

Madeira embroidery white embroidery on linens and garments in conventional and floral designs in overcast eyelets, such as is made by the nuns of Madeira.

Madonna coiffure a simple hairstyle of Renaissance Europe, the hair parted in the middle and looped in front of the ears and drawn back into a chignon. Seen in many paintings and statues of the Madonna.

madras a muslin or cotton fabric named after the city of Madras, India, of colorful gingham in plaids, checks or stripes sometimes intermingled. There is also an East Indian madras in colorful plaid or striped silk or cotton which bleeds when laundered, creating an unusual color scheme. Used for summer apparel of both sexes. see *punjum.*

Madras embroidery brightly printed silk and cotton handkerchiefs which are embroidered in a variety of stitches.

magenta a color discovered in 1856 by the British chemist Sir W. H. Perkin, and the first synthetic dye. The color was later named for the Battle of Majenta, 1859. It is a bluish red in hue varying from high to a raw brilliance.

Magyar or **Hungarian dress** notable for elaborate embroidery in brilliant colors. Applied to the feminine blouse and the man's shirt, both of white linen, an overskirt and, invariably, a long apron also for both sexes. The man's szür or greatcoat of black or white felt or leather is lavishly decorated. The costumes are often the work of a lifetime and are handed down from generation to generation.

maharmah, yashmak a muslin cloth formerly worn over the head and lower face by Turkish and Armenian women. see *mandeel.*

Magyar or Hungarian-
young man in Sunday
dress-basically black
with colorful embroidery-

mahoîtres high, standing, padded shoulder puffs of sleeves worn in the sixteenth century.

mail see *chain mail.*

maillot a knitted one-piece, tight-fitting swimsuit. Also French for swaddling clothes of a small baby. Also tights and leotard. see *bathing dress.*

Mainbocher see *couture, haute.*

maison de couture Parisian dressmaking establishment. see *couture.*

makeup, maquillage the collective noun for complexion cosmetics applied to the face, comprising foundation, rouge, powder, lipstick, eye mascara, etc. *Maquillage* is the French word.

Malabar an East Indian handkerchief of Hindu design printed in brilliant colors.

maline, malines a silk or cotton gauze net with a plain woven hexagonal mesh. Used in veilings, ruchings and millinery work.

malo the Hawaiian man's girdle or loincloth. Originally of tapa cloth which was made from tree bark, but now of cotton dyed in brilliant colors. Also, an ornamented royal girdle.

Maltese lace a guipure lace in which the Maltese cross, dots and simple geometric patterns are used; formerly a bobbin lace.

mameluke sleeve see *sleeve, mameluke.*

Manchu headdress a cap of black satin bands shaped by a fine gold wire. Only imperial princesses were permitted to wear the headdress and, because it was so fragile, its wearing was confined to the palace. Sewn, wired and glued to it were hundreds of tiny ornaments, among them the phoenix bird, butterflies, bats, kingfisher feathers, flowers and miniature pieces made of jade, rose quartz, pearls, etc. The Manchu princess headdress of the Chi'ing dynasty was worn 1644 to 1912.

mandarin collar see *collar, mandarin.*

mandarin robe formerly worn by Chinese mandarins and their wives prior to the establishment of the Republic in 1912. The robe had wide long sleeves and was long, loose, and richly embroidered. The motifs were indicative of the wearer's rank as were the jeweled button atop his cap and the long string of beads of amber, coral or jade. The large squares of embroidery, one in front and one in back, told what governmental office the mandarin held. Many of the robes became fashionable as handsome evening wraps or hostess gowns for Western women in the twentieth century.

mandayas a long outer garment resembling the cope worn during the Greek Orthodox Church services.

Mandeel—embroidered lawn or linen—worn by a Moroccan woman—other names are litham, maharmah, yashmak and veil

mandeel name for the feminine Moslem veil which may be white, figured colored muslin, lacy or black and hangs over the forehead and chest.

mandil an Oriental name for a Turkish or Persian turban.

mandilion or tabard—cloth jacket worn by commoners and as livery—16th and 17th C.

mandil—Oriental name for Persian or Turkish turban—16th and 17th C.

Mantee—a sheer coat to display stomacher and petticoat—Thérèse bonnet of gauze—French—1770's

mandilion, or **tabard** a kind of dalmatic worn by common folk in inclement weather, twelfth to sixteenth centuries. A hip-length garment with hanging, open sleeves, it was put on over the head, worn by heralds, soldiers and knights. In the sixteenth and seventeenth centuries it became a piece of livery and also a short, capelike cloak worn by the Puritans. see *tabard.*

manga a Mexican garment much like a poncho but with self-formed sleeves, formerly worn for riding.

Manila hemp the most important cordage fiber. see *abacá.*

maniple a narrow band worn hanging over the left forearm by the celebrant at mass; of the same material and color as the chasuble.

mannequin, manikin, mannikin a tailor's or dressmaker's lay figure; also a living model upon which a garment is designed, fitted or displayed.

manta from the Spanish for shawl, blanket or poncho, a large square of thick, black, coarse cotton fabric worn in the manner of the European haik. It is draped over the head, falls over the shoulder, and is pinned at the chest, and hangs to the ankles; it conceals most of the woman's form and perhaps a baby held in its folds. The short cape which a Spaniard wears over his bolero is a manta and so is the shawl, blanket, or poncho. Manta is also the name of the Spanish headdress, a square shawl, always black, of lace or silk for the aristocratic type of woman, or of thin cashmere or alpaca for the woman of lesser social standing.

man-tailored said of a woman's suit or coat made and finished by a tailor who duplicates the fine details of well-made masculine clothes.

mantee a feminine cloak of the eighteenth century, open in front to display stomacher and petticoat.

mantelletta a sleeveless, short robe of silk or wool worn by high prelates of the Roman Catholic Church.

mantes beruffled scarf-like capes of gold and silver tissue imported from Mantua in Italy in the eighteenth and nineteenth centuries. Such mantes were worn by ladies of the various European courts and society, a more conservative style being worn by commoners. There was a mante for mourning and for women of the Church, accompanied by a hood. The mante is still to be seen in various countries today.

mantilla the lace scarf or veil, black or the white lace known as blonde, that the Spanish lady drapes over a high tortoise shell or ivory comb in her coiffure. The white shawl is worn for dress, especially to bullfights and on

mantilla - scarf, veil or shawl of lace worn by Spanish women over a high comb

Easter Monday. The black Chantilly lace mantilla which later came to be associated particularly with Spanish women appeared late in the eighteenth century and was French-made.

mantilla, Watteau see *Watteau mantilla.*

mantle a loose garment, wrap or cape, usually without sleeves.

manton de Manilla of the nineteenth and twentieth centuries. Shawls of heavy silk crêpe with deep silk fringe covered with brilliantly embroidered flowers and birds. Worn by Spanish women but made by Chinese women living in the Philippines. Fashionable in the 1920's as evening wraps. see *Spanish shawl.*

mantua-maker a cloak-maker. Until the late seventeenth century only tailors fashioned women's clothes. From then on, they came to be distinguished as couturiers or dressmakers, mantua- or cloakmakers, and modistes or milliners.

Mao suit first brought out in London for men, followed by the Paris-made suit for women. The feminine version, smart in its simplicity and long, slim lines, was of black silk crepe, the tunic finished with a standing collar. 1967.

maquillage see *make-up.*

marabou the soft fluffy feathers covering the quills of the wings and tail of the African stork. Used for trimming since 1800. Available by the yard in dyed colors and used on dresses and negligées.

marabout a form of twisted, or thrown raw silk and the fabric made of it. Used principally for scarfs.

marcasite a glittering mineral made especially into buckles, buttons, jewelry and other ornaments.

marcel wave a fashion of curling the hair with irons into deep waves carefully

mantle of embroidered cashmere-velvet collar-felt hat-striped ribbon-French-1829

manton de Manilla-also known as Chinese and Spanish shawls-silk crêpe with flower and bird embroidery-19th and 20th C.

Marcel wave invented by Marcel of Paris becoming a vogue of the 20th C.

Mao Suit of black silk crepe-London and Paris-1967

Marie Antoinette costume-"queen's gown" of gauze with Medici collar-satin sash-straw hat-hair cut hedgehog-1783

arranged around the head; named for Marcel, the Parisian hairdresser who set the style. Late nineteenth century. see *permanent wave.*

margot lace a delicate modern lace used for ruffles, flounces and trimming. It is machine-embroidered in heavy cotton thread on fragile silk net.

Marie Antoinette costume a long-corseted bodice with low décolletage and tight sleeves with ruffles, the hooped skirt was festooned with ribbons, flowers and ruffles. The powdered coiffure was dressed with ribbons and flowers.

Marlborough hat see *hat, Gainsborough.*

marli a gauze much like tulle used as a ground for embroidering lace.

marlotte a dress cloak that many modish European women wore with only slight variation in the second half of the sixteenth century. A full-length robe of simple design, in handsome brocade with a small stand-up collar and short puffed sleeves. It fastened only at the neck, flaring open over the hooped skirt of the gown.

marlotte-an overdress with short puffed sleeves-fastened at neck-very fashionable-French-16th C.

marten-fur of the weasel and sable species-

marmot an inexpensive fur much used in Europe from a ground squirrel common in the Alps and the Pyrenees. Also, fur of the Russian and Chinese rodent dressed, dyed and striped to simulate mink, called Brazilian mink. A fur with poor durability, the best coming from Russia. It is used for coats, jackets and trimming. The American species, woodchuck or groundhog, is little used.

marquise a woman's three-cornered riding hat; French, 1735. Occasionally worn today and still a smart hat.

marquise a silk and lace carriage parasol of the nineteenth century; its special feature was the folding handle. see *umbrella.*

marquise in jewelry, a finger ring set with a long, narrow cut gem, either oblong or elliptical. see *gem cuts.*

marquisette a lightweight gauze made of cotton, rayon or silk; in white, solid colors, and novelty patterns; used for dresses.

marten animal of the weasel and the sable species, larger than a weasel and yielding a valuable fur. Found in the northern regions of America, Europe and Asia. Russian and Siberian are most precious, American next. The underfur very fine and soft with long, rich guard hair and the animal has a handsome long tail. Most marten is blended. Used for jackets, scarfs and trimming.

marten, American; Hudson Bay sable Found in the pine and spruce forests of North America, some in the Rocky Mountains and on the Pacific coast. A beautiful, durable fur, many of a dark color and almost as silky as Russian sable. The general color is medium- and yellowish-brown. Those of Alaska are poor. Used natural, blended or dyed if very pale and principally for scarfs and trimming.

marten, baum or **pine** found in the

mountainous regions of Siberia, Norway, Germany, Switzerland, Asia Minor and the Himalayan Mountains. The best from Russia, the color ranging from pale to dark bluish-brown with fluffy underfur and silky guard hair. Used natural, blended or dyed, if pale. Used for coats, jackets, scarves and trimming.

marten, Himalayan better known as Chinese sable, yellow to yellowish-brown. Blending and tipping increases the luster. Used for jackets, scarves and trimming.

marten, Japanese the same class as the European stone marten but less costly. An inferior woolly fur with coarse top hair. Canary or dull yellowish coloring dyed various shades of brown to resemble sable. Used for scarves and trimming.

marten, stone or **beech** from Russia and Asia. Underwool grayish white and bluish with very rich, dark top hairs. The best from Russia. Used natural for jackets, scarves and trimming.

martingale the leather strap fastened to a horse's girth, intended to hold his head down and prevent his rearing. In costume, a stay, strap or partial belt to hold folds in place. On a modern coat, a belt across the back and attached at the sides to hold the fullness in place.

mascara a cosmetic cream for darkening the eyelashes.

mashru an Arabic word meaning lawful, as applied to a fabric of mixed cotton and silk. Moslems were formerly forbidden to wear pure silk at prayer.

mask an important piece in the Greek and Roman theater, the actors' faces usually masked when on the stage. The mask appeared in the European mode in the sixteenth century as a protection in bad weather. It was also worn by women who wished to appear incognito in public. By the eighteenth century, the use of the little black velvet mask or half-mask was general and worn by women and children in the American Colonies. European men and women wore the mask for the theater and the street. The small Venetian mask, called loup, or in English, loo, meaning wolf, because it frightened children, was of black velvet lined with white silk. A later mask of black and green silk covered the whole face and was held in place by a glass or silver button placed between the teeth. The earliest masks were held by a wire that curved over the forehead and on top of the head. Later, strings were attached to the sides and tied in back.

mat finish a dull, unglazed, smooth surface of silk, cloth or leather.

mat texture the flattering look of powdered skin was discovered by the fashionable use of hair powder in the seventeenth century. see *cosmetics.*

matara fur seal, of a rich, dark brown. see *seal, Alaska.*

matchcoat a British name for the garment of coarse cloth or fur worn by Indians, especially the Algonquins, along the Eastern seaboard of the American Colonies.

matelassé, matelas French for mattress, a crêpy fabric of silk, wool or other material with a net back. Machine or hand-stitched and embossed with small motifs similar to quilting or blistering. Used for dresses and wraps, early twentieth century. see *cloqué, cloguet.*

maternity wear a development of the twentieth century, when it was no longer considered proper for pregnant women to remain in seclusion as soon as their condition became evident. Dresses are made full, often hanging straight from the shoulders or a yoke; smocks or tunics are worn over a skirt which has an expandable waistline or is cut out over the abdomen.

mauve, mauveine a delicate lilac

color produced by a violet dye, obtained in 1856 by the British chemist Sir W. H. Perkin by the oxidation of aniline.

Mechlin lace a bobbin lace made in Mechlin, Belgium; formerly any Flemish lace.

Medici collar see *collar, Medici.*

Medici lace French bobbin-lace similar to Cluny lace, but of finer thread. Woven closely and open in intricate pattern with one edge scalloped.

medieval, gothic, moyen-age Historians place the Middle Ages as the period between the Fall of Rome A.D. 476 and the Fall of Constantinople in 1453. Other scholars designate the period between the tenth and fifteenth centuries as the flowering of the Gothic period. With the close of the Dark Ages, men and women were still wearing the Greco-Roman costume with its Byzantine influence but which, due to the teachings of Christianity, tended more and more to conceal the figure. In fact, religious bans governed both style and color of all laymen's dress. see illustrations.

melon sleeve see *sleeve, melon.*

melton a heavy, felted woolen fabric finished with a close even nap without luster. First made in England; in many grades. Used for overcoats, windbreakers, uniforms, pea jackets and regal livery.

meltonette a lightweight women's wear cloth for suits.

Mennonite a Protestant sect of German origin, settlers of Pennsylvania in the late seventeenth century. Their clothing was very simple, following strict rules. see *Amish.*

men's dress, modern had its start in the 1660's when the justaucorps and the doublet changed to coat and vest. The idea came from France where Charles II of England had spent his exile. Pepys' *Diary* tells us that the change occurred in October, 1666, when Charles, giving his officials a month's notice, dressed them all in a new vest and coat after "ye Persian mode." And he adds, "it was all black and white." Today, the standard simplicity dates from the French Revolution in the 1790's. The principal change was the substitution of trousers for culottes or breeches.

mercerized, mercerizing a permanent finish given cottons to make the yarns softer, silkier and stronger. Named for the discoverer, an English calico printer and chemist, John Mercer (1791–1866). see *schreinerize.*

merino a breed of fine-wooled sheep originating in Spain and raised mostly for the wool. The original Spanish breed is nearly 2,000 years old. The woolly pelt is sheared and dyed to simulate more expensive furs and is also used for trimmings. The best in the world now comes from Australia. The fleeces are obtainable from Argentina, Austria, France, Germany, Ohio, U.S. and the Union of South Africa. Merino yarn is considered the best for weaving by the weaving trade, and the best for worsted and woolen knitting by the knit trade. The woven fabric resembles cashmere and is used for suits, coats and sportswear.

Merry Widow sailor a wide-brimmed cartwheel style of feminine straw hat which appeared in 1908 during the run of the popular operetta, *The Merry Widow* by Franz Lehar.

Merveilleuse, à la La Merveilleuse the feminine counterpart of the Incroyable during the Directoire Period in France, 1795–1799. She wore a diaphanous gown with short tight bodice and an extreme style of bonnet.

mesh bag a lady's small handbag of flexible link mesh in gold, silver or plated

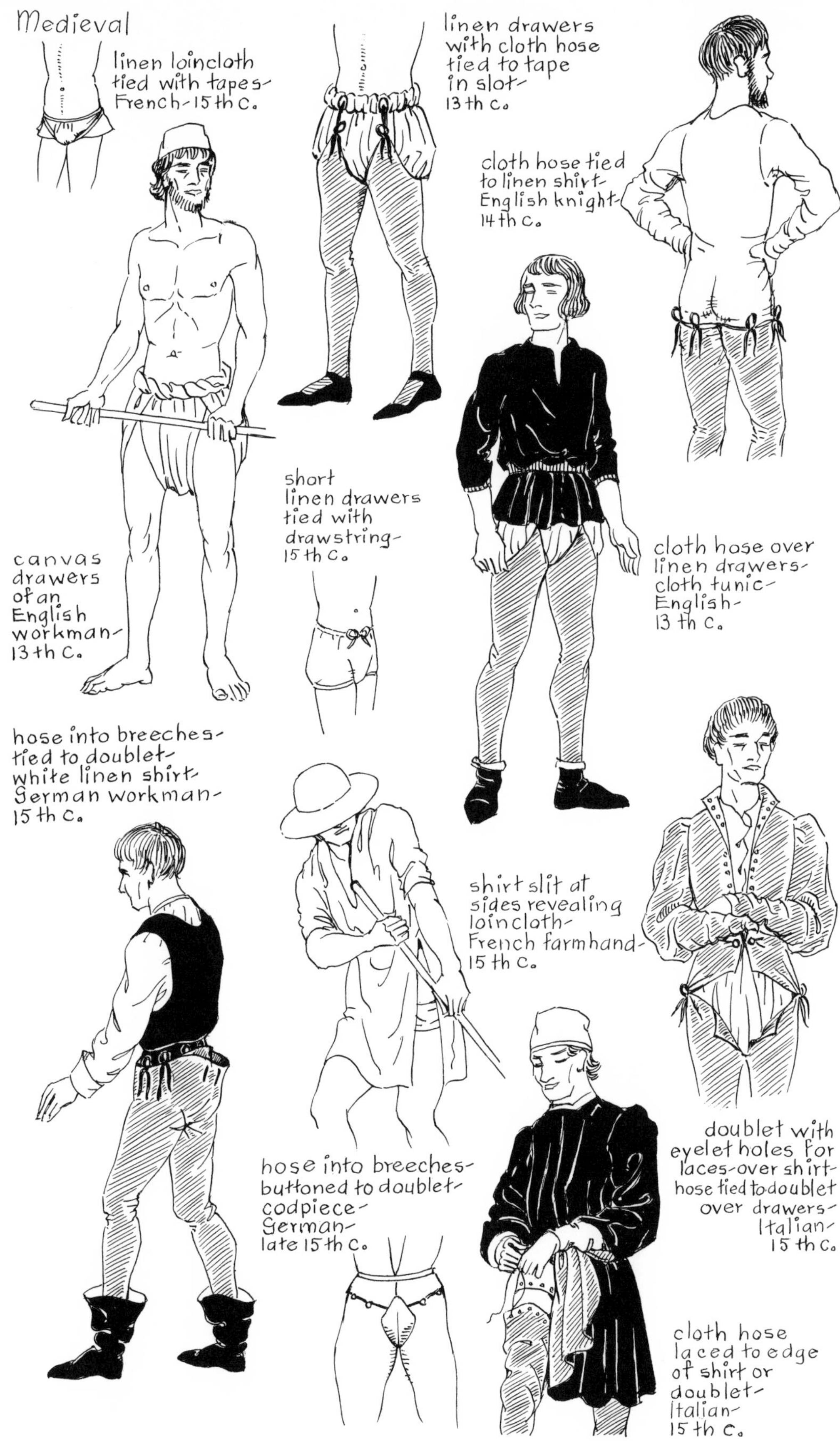
Medieval
linen loincloth
tied with tapes-
French-15th c.
linen drawers
with cloth hose
tied to tape
in slot-
13th c.
cloth hose tied
to linen shirt-
English knight-
14th c.
short
linen drawers
tied with
drawstring-
15th c.
canvas
drawers
of an
English
workman-
13th c.
cloth hose over
linen drawers-
cloth tunic-
English-
13th c.
hose into breeches-
tied to doublet-
white linen shirt-
German workman-
15th c.
shirt slit at
sides revealing
loincloth-
French farmhand-
15th c.
doublet with
eyelet holes for
laces-over shirt-
hose tied to doublet
over drawers-
Italian-
15th c.
hose into breeches-
buttoned to doublet-
codpiece-
German-
late 15th c.
cloth hose
laced to edge
of shirt or
doublet-
Italian-
15th c.

Medieval Corsets

Medieval
long-sleeved shirt worn under cuirass-braccae cross-gartered-Romanesque Italian-8th and 9th c.
tunic skirt tucked up over linen braies or drawers-leather boots cross-gartered-French peasant-8th to 10th c.
hair shirt worn as a penance by the Christian pilgrim-4th to 14th c.
surcoat worn over the tunic-French-13th c.
loose linen brech or drawers under woolen tunic-English woodsman-13th c.
brech or drawers ending in ties below the knees-drawstring belt-English worker-13th c.
brech or drawers fastened at the knees by drawstrings-English-13th c.

Medieval Shapes

metal. An evening bag popular in the first half of the twentieth century.

mesh fabrics open mesh texture cloths woven of cotton, linen, wool, nylon, rayon or in combinations; used especially for men's underwear and sportswear.

Mesopotamian costume, ancient see illustrations, pages 212, 213.

mess jacket a short, tailless uniform jacket worn on semiformal evening occasions by officers of the Armed Services; in dark blue or white, as prescribed.

messaline a lustrous, lightweight silk fabric of satin weave for general use in women's wear, including lingerie.

metal lace a net foundation with motifs of gold, silver and copper threads, woven either by hand or machine.

metallic cloth any fabric, such as lamé that has gold, silver or tinsel threaded through the design.

Mexican costume a combination of the characteristic features of colonial Spanish style and ancient Aztec. see *huipilli; mantilla; rebozo; serape; sombrero.*

middy blouse- U.S. naval midshipman's blouse- popular feminine fashion early 20th C.

middy blouse a copy of the United States Navy seaman's blouse, originally worn by midshipmen. Of heavy white twill or closely woven cotton with a dark-blue flannel sailor's collar bordered with white soutache. A black silk neckerchief, thirty-six inches square, is folded diagonally around the neck under the collar and tied in front. The blouse, a feminine fashion of the 1910's and 1920's, was popular with young girls and children, especially as a school uniform or for athletics. see *sailor suit.*

middy twill a twill-weave cotton cloth in white and colors. see *jean.*

midnight blue a color for men's formal or evening wear. It is claimed that midnight blue has a deep richness that looks blacker than black itself. It was introduced in the mid-1930's and is still smart.

midriff that section of the body from the waist to the chest; the diaphragm or rib-cage.

mignonette lace a narrow bobbin lace resembling tulle, with an open mesh.

Milan straw manufactured in Milan, Italy, and used for women's hats.

Milanese textile a silk or rayon warped knitted fabric which has a distinctive diagonal cross effect. Used for feminine underwear and gloves.

milaya the long, dark mantle of cotton that the Egyptian woman wears over her cotton print dress. With men present she may draw the milaya over the lower part of her face.

military braid see *braid.*

mess jacket- military and naval- worn semi-formal evenings. U.S.

milaya- same as haik or huke- black cloth cover worn in street- bur'u', a crocheted face veil- Egyptian

military-styled hat- peacock blue velvet and ostrich-velvet rosette- French- 1813

Mesopotamian

Mesopotamian
belt and short fringed skirt worn over the kandys or shirt- Assyrian soldier- 1200 B.C.
fringed skirt worn over the shirt-shawl of fringe- Assyrian king- 9th c. B.C.
kandys or shirt with rolled fabric belt- Assyrian woman- 7th c. B.C.
man in white linen kandys or shirt with embroidered corselet- Assyrian- 9th c. B.C.
fringed white linen shirt or kĕthŏneth worn under woolen caftan- Hebrew- 7th c. B.C.
short shirt or kandys-rolled fabric belt and leather strap- Assyro-Babylonian- 7th c. B.C.
fringed white linen shirt or kĕthŏneth- Hebrew- 7th c. B.C.
handmaiden to queen- woolen cloth kandys or shirt- Assyro-Babylonian- 7th c. B.C.

milium a trade name for satin lining coated on the mat side with an aluminum insulating material, or milium, with a foam back, making the garment thoroughly warm without adding weight.

mill run, or **run o' the mill** fabric not factory-inspected and often low grade.

millinery Fine felt, fabric and straw hats made in the Duchy of Milan in the fifteenth and sixteenth centuries were known as Millayne bonnets, hence, the English word "milainer" for the maker of feminine caps and bonnets. Felt hats were first made in England during the reign of Henry VIII.

minaret a knee-length tunic with wired flaring edge giving the effect of a lampshade, over a slim straight skirt; created by Paul Poiret in 1912, such frivolity ending with the start of World War I, 1914.

mineral fibers those, such as asbestos, that are procured from minerals in the earth. see *asbestos.*

mini-dress- worn by young and mature women of 1960's

minidress a feminine frock introduced in 1966 with its hem above the knees.

miniskirt, minijupe see *skirt.*

miniver from the French menu-vair; a valuable fur of the Middle Ages in gray and white squirrel. Today's British usage signifies ermine or the white winter coat of the stoat or weasel, officially the fur used for state robes of British peers. see *ermine.*

mink, maük, Swedish; vision, French the valuable fur of a semiaquatic animal of the weasel family found throughout North America, Russia, China and Japan, the very best from the Province of Quebec. Slatey or smokey dark brown, the valuable skins dark to the root. An even, close underwool, very strong, even guard hair and a fine, bushy tail, with size and color varying according to region. Much coarse, and therefore cheap mink, comes from Louisiana, of which the smaller and finer peltries of the female and young males are the most desirable.

mink, black see *mink, wild.*

mink, blended natural mink of a light color, darkened by a feather dipped in dye and brushed over the longer hairs.

mink, Brazilian see *marmot.*

mink, China of the mink family and similar to the American and European animal. The texture, length and color of the hair varies according to district, a pale yellow necessitates dyeing.

mink, European a natural dark, ranch mink and also, a white Aleutian mink imported from Denmark, Finland, Norway and Sweden. The skins are being fashioned into the modish coats of the day, with men favoring those of dark mink. Mink is supposedly the warmest of furs.

mink, Japanese or Jap a smaller animal but silkier than Asiatic mink. It has shorter, darker fur and a muddy yellow color which necessitates dyeing. Used for less expensive coats and trimming.

mink-a semiquatic animal of the weasel family-

mink, kolinsky also called red sable or tatar sable, the better quality of mink found in Siberia, China and Japan. It has short underwool, usually yellow, and long, brown, silky top hair. It is successfully dyed dark to simulate sable and is used for scarfs, coats and trimming.

mink, let-out a manner of manufacture, the skins reshaped by being slashed into narrow diagonal strips and then resewn into long, rather than wide sections, enhancing the richness of the fur.

mink, mutation ranch-bred or half blood, domesticated mink having nearly the same qualities as the wild animal, but the wild is stronger. Mink mutation has developed many new colors other than natural.

mink, wild the animal living in its natural state has a finer, silky, well-furred skin with thick underfur, sturdier and more dense than the ranch-bred. Labrador wild mink is considered the finest in the world.

mino a cape or overcoat of straw, rushes and such, worn by Japanese peasants.

mintan the Turk's traditional fine white linen shirt which is still worn. It buttons closely down the front and has an embroidered collar.

mirrors, countenances The making of glass mirrors on a commercial scale was first developed in Venice in the fourteenth century. From then to the middle of the seventeenth century, when large mirrors were made, fashionable men and women carried small pocket mirrors in little cases of silk or ivory. The tiny mirrors which women carried suspended on a ribbon from the waist, along with small sewing items, were called countenances.

miter or tiara words of Greek origin, signifying a crown, the name given alike to the varied headbands worn by the Babylonians, Assyrians, Medes and Persians. The modern miter or tiara is a section of a crown worn over the forehead. Fashionable in modern times as a woman's formal evening headdress. see *liturgical headdress.*

mitten a hand-covering usually of knitted or crocheted wool, thick cloth or leather and often lined with fur or wool. A mitten is fashioned to cover four fingers in one section with a separate stall for the thumb.

mitts Fingerless knitted gloves were worn by the ancients as protection at work or hunting. In the medieval and Renaissance periods, such gloves were of leather and chamois. In the American Colonies of the eighteenth century, mitts of knitted or crocheted cotton or silk thread became a feminine fashion. From Paris in 1842 came mention of ladies' mitts in black lace or black velvet which were worn at tea. Mitts were still to be seen in the early twentieth century and had a short revival c. 1930.

moat collar see *collar, moat.*

mob, mobcap the frilled lingerie bonnet of the eighteenth century, which originated in England. It was suggested by the cap worn by the women of

mino-cloak of straw or rushes worn over shoulders as a raincoat—Japanese

miter or tiara—papal—white with gold and jewels—head cloth—10th C.

miter or tiara—gold fillet with lappets tied in back—Jewish high priest

miter or tiara of bishop—gold embroidery on white—red lining—12th C.

mobcap of black taffeta, black gauze and white lawn with bowknots—English—1789

mobcap of sheer white lawn over wire frame—American—late 18th C.

mobcap worn by Charlotte Corday-spotted white muslin-flutted frill-taffeta ribbon-1793

Ranelagh Market in London. Eventually any cotton bonnet was called a mobcap, or just plain mob.

moccasin a soft leather shoe without a heel; the sole and sides are made of one piece whose edges are joined with a gathered seam to a U-shaped piece covering the instep. Moccasins worn by North American Indians were embroidered with beads and dyed porcupine quills and had a fold-over cuff tied in back. Moccasins are worn today by American woodsmen and are a favorite playshoe of American youngsters.

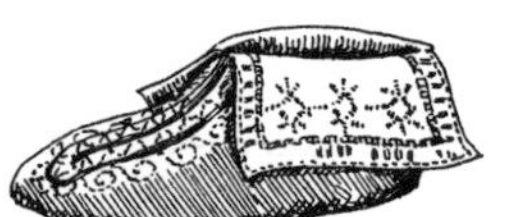

deerskin moccasin-bead embroidery-American Indian

mocha derived from sheepskin of hair sheep from Africa, Arabia and Persia. After the grain is removed by a severe liming process, the fibers below the grain are suèded. The color mocha is a dark, grayish brown named after an Arabian town on the Red Sea famous for its coffee.

mockado also called mock velvet—a deep-piled velvet with better grades made in silk; cheaper, in wool. Used in the sixteenth and seventeenth centuries.

mocmain a fiber, soft and silky, which is used for stuffing. It is from an East Indian cotton tree.

Mod in England, a young person who affects an ultramodern version of Edwardian dress, manners and haircut, 1960's.

mode a manner of living and dressing which depends largely upon taste and caprice of the period; fashion.

model in costume, an original design created as a pattern from which copies will be made. Also, the mannequin or living model upon whom the creation is fitted and displayed.

modesty bit, modesty piece a pouf of lace and ribbon worn across the top of the stays to conceal a low V or U décolletage of a gown. Eighteenth, nineteenth and early twentieth centuries.

modiste a dressmaker or milliner who makes and sells fashionable dresses and hats for women.

mogador, mogadore a corded tie silk with vividly colored stripes which resembles fine faille. Named for Mogadore, a seaport of Morocco.

moggan an old Scottish term for a tight knitted sleeve or a knitted stocking without foot, formerly worn by the Highlanders.

mohair the wiry, lustrous, strong wool of the Angora goat of Asia Minor used in mohair fabrics. see *Angora goat.*

moiré or **watered silk** a wavy or watered pattern pressed into silk or synthetic silk by passing it between rollers engraved with the design. Used for formal gowns.

moiré in fur, the watery design of broadtail and galyak classed as flower, lake or ribbed. Flower is like petals scattered over the ground. Lake, large, long ovals of moiré. Ribbed, when the design follows the spinal column and ribs of the animal.

mole a very small rodent, six to seven

inches long, from North America, Europe and Asia. Skins from Scotland, northern England, Holland, Belgium, Denmark, Germany, France and Italy. Dutch, Scotch and German, preferred. Fragile, beautiful, lightweight fur of a very dark bluish-gray, with guard hair and fur fiber practically the same length. It is dyed all colors and used in coats, jackets, sweaters, linings and trimming.

moleskin cloth a close-twilled cotton, heavy, strong and backed with a nap. Used for hunting and sports clothes.

moleskin fur the skins of moles sewn together and used as fur; fragile.

Molyneaux, Captain Edward see *couture, haute.*

monk bag a small purse worn by sailors' round the neck on a cord, containing their money and valuables.

monk's hood see *almuce.*

monk's robe a straight, full-length garment of cloth with standing collar, buttoned from neck to hem and usually sashed with a tasseled cord. The cassock of ecclesiastics. see *cassock; soutane.*

monk's shoe a low shoe of soft but heavy leather with heel and plain toe and a strap passing over the instep and buckled at the side.

monkey fur from monkeys of the Colobus genus of tropical Africa. Long, silky, lustrous hair either all black or black and white with no underfur. The black is dipped in dye to darken the skin. Used for capes, muffs and trimming since the Great Exhibition in London in 1851 when a few dressed peltries were first displayed by furriers. A revival of the fur occurred in the 1920's, but it has been rarely seen in the mode since.

monkey jacket a sailor's jacket for rough weather. Short, heavy and snugly fitted, of dark blue cloth.

monkey suit a colloquial term for a man's tuxedo.

Monmouth cock see illustration.

monocle a single unframed lens or glass of rock crystal used by men for one eye of impaired vision. It appeared in England in the 1820's and is still seen there today. The Englishman became adept in the handling of the lens which he might carry in a pocket or on a black silk cord worn round the neck.

monogram the initials of a person's name joined into a decorative motif for engraving jewelry, embroidering pieces of apparel, or stamping leather goods.

monotone weave a tweed of leather mixture in checks or plaids with the yarn pre-dyed in several toned-down colors.

montagnac trade name for a woolen fabric considered one of the highest quality overcoatings available. Genuine montagnacs have varying amounts of camel and vicuña hair in them. Imported from France.

montauban see *chapel de fer.*

montenegrin a semifitted, caftanlike sleeveless outer garment worn by Montenegran women (Yugoslavia). It is usually embroidered in brilliant colors.

montero cap see *cap, montero; Eugénie's wigs.*

moonstone one of the feldspar group of gem stones, with a milky-blue sheen.

Moorish cloth see *Turkish toweling.*

moreen a water-embossed finished fabric of wool and cotton, coarse and stout, with ribbed effect.

the mole is trapped for its rich, soft, black fur. Found in N. A. Europe and Asia.

Monmouth Cock-beaver hat with feather fringe and white ostrich-cocked at the sides-worn by Duke of Monmouth, British-1670

Monocle-fawn-colored felt hat-black ribbon band-English-1870

morion helmet which appeared in Europe about 1550, introduced by the Spaniards, who copied it from the Moors; worn by foot soldiers in the sixteenth and seventeenth centuries. The hatlike piece had crown, brim and eartabs. see *cabasset.*

morning coat see *frock coat.*

morning or **house dress** simple cotton frocks that women wore for "morning chores," before the days of sports clothes and pants of the twentieth century.

Morocco goatskin usually dyed red; originally produced by the Moors. The modern leather is of calfskin, sheepskin and other thin leathers with the pebble graining and finish imitated by printing and embossing. Used for ladies' bags, wallets, purses, men's and women's lounging slippers, etc.

morse a clasp or brooch that fastens the liturgical cope or cloak worn by priests and bishops.

mortarboard academic cap with flat, square top projecting beyond the round skullcap and long, silk tassel. see *catercap.*

mortier, medieval; a deep skullcap with a flat round table-top made of pleated velvet or silk with a gold braid or ermine band around the head. Worn by certain high functionaries of the law in France.

mosaic an inlaid design of small colored stones arranged in geometric forms; building a composition according to a prearranged pattern or picture. Used in buttons, jewelry, especially pendants and earrings.

"Mother Hubbard" or wrapper—of fabrics from cotton to silks and velvet—late 19th and 20th C.

Mother Hubbard also known as wrapper, dressing or tea gown according to its fabric and use. Made of materials ranging from calico to fine silk and velvet, lace and ribbon trimmed. A long, flowing gown gathered to a fitted square or round yoke and often tied with a self-belt. Worn in late nineteenth and early twentieth centuries. The American wrapper was the origin of the Hawaiian muu-muu. see *muu-muu.*

mother-of-pearl; nacre the iridescent lining of various sea shells; used for buckles, buttons and other items requiring hard, decorative material. The first and smallest mother-of-pearl buttons, used on a man's shirt, appeared in the early nineteenth century.

motif an ornamental design used singly or repeated, printed on fabric, embroidered, crocheted or appliquéd to a surface.

motley dress composed of various and sundry parts and colors. The jester or fool of the Middle Ages wore a motley costume, variegated in color. see *cap and bells.*

motoring veil see *veil.*

mouches the French word for "flies" was used to denote beauty patches. They were made of black silk court plaster, cut in diamond shape, round, crescent and star, but always very small. see *patches.*

mouflon a small wild sheep with an abundant mane found in regions of northern mountainous Russia and on the islands of Corsica and Sardinia. It has short, reddish-brown hair on the upper part of the body. see *goat.*

mountain sable see *sable, mountain.*

mountmellick embroidery used for household linens. An embroidery of coarse white cotton thread worked in large floral designs and finished with knitted fringe.

mourning band a broad band or brassard of black cloth worn on the left coat sleeve; originally of black crepe. It was customarily worn by all men after a death in the family, when not wearing a black coat; men servants also wore it with livery. This custom is still observed in parts of Europe. In the United States the practice of wearing any kind of mourning has largely been given up since World War II, but military officers still wear a band at state funeral ceremonies.

mourning black Among gentlefolk in the seventeenth century the wearing of mourning was carried even into negligée and nightclothes. Sheets and coverlets were black and, sometimes, the bed was painted black. Some families kept a mourning bed in reserve, to be loaned to friends when needed. There were toilet articles in black also. In the nineteenth century mourning was part of a widely accepted pattern in length of period and type of dress.

It was strictly observed by both sexes whose outer wear was black, the woman's gowns, coats and hats being trimmed with dull, heavy black crepe. One came out of mourning gradually, in purple, lavender and white for summer. With the changing way of living, mourning apparel is rarely seen in the twentieth century.

mourning colors black was the color of mourning in Europe, as it had been in ancient Greece and the Roman Empire. The Romans of the republic wore dark blue. Purple and violet were for cardinals and kings of France. Ladies of ancient Rome and Sparta wore white, also the color of mourning in China. Until 1498, it was the color of mourning in Spain. Violet was the custom in Turkey. White silk hatbands are still customary in several English provinces. Yellow for Egypt and Burma, and in Brittany some peasant widows wear yellow caps.

mourning, white the wearing of all white instead of all black. A royal custom probably originated by Mary, Queen of Scots, whose first husband, Francis II, King of France, left her a widow at the age of eighteen. The court was dominated by her mother-in-law, Catherine de Medici, who was already wearing mourning for the former king, Henri II, and the difference in costume afforded the younger queen some distinction.

mousquetaires, musketeers bodyguards of the kings of France, which originated in the sixteenth century. In the seventeenth century, under Louis XIV, there were two companies, known as the Blacks and the Grays, from the colors of their horse blankets. No uniforms were adopted until the eighteenth century which followed the mode of the cocked hat, deep cuffs, collar, vest, etc.

mousquetaire collar see *collar, mousquetaire.*

mousquetaire glove a heavy leather glove with a flaring wrist extension fringed and embroidered with colored silk thread; seventeenth century. The feminine mousquetaire is a long glove with forearm length, a short wrist-opening with several tiny pearl buttons, which was first worn by Sarah Bernhardt in the 1870's. Eventually for formal dress it became de rigueur made with the unopened armlength. So it has remained to date, worn crushed down casually. Made mostly in white, but black, fawn color and pale tints; in glacé kid or suède were also fashionable.

mousseline a fabric of cotton, wool or silk, very fine and soft. Also in heavier weights for use in linings and trial patterns.

mousseline de soie a muslin of silk or rayon rather like chiffon but crisp and firm. Used for linings in collars, yokes and cuffs.

moustache, mustache see *beards.*

mouton French for lamb. Sheared lamb of the Merino species dyed or bleached to imitate more expensive furs, principally beaver, nutria and seal, and called mouton pressed lamb. Used for all-purpose coats for men and women; heavy, warm and durable.

Moygashel, Inc. the trade-mark of an imported Irish linen of excellent quality. Used for dresses, blouses and suits.

moyle see *mule.*

Mozambique a loosely woven dress fabric with a warp of double cotton threads and a soft cotton filling.

mozetta a short linen shoulder cape worn over an alb. A bishop's vestment.

muff of fox-with ribbon bowknot-frockcoat with tassels-powdered hair-leather jockey boots-French-1779

muffs indispensibles, the English name, were soft bags open at each end for warming the hands. They were originated by the French in the seventeenth century. They were also used to carry the little pet dogs then so popular. For men, mostly of plush stuffed with cotton and wadding; of gold or silver tissue ornamented with ribbons and laces for the ladies. Muffs continued popular with both sexes in the eighteenth century but were used only by women in the nineteenth and early twentieth centuries. Women favored a small, fur muff in this later period.

muffetees a pair of small muffs which many Englishmen carried in the early seventeenth century. By 1663, the large, simple muff was modish. During the 1790's, many Englishmen in deference to the public interest in Charles James Fox, the statesman and orator (1749–1806), carried very large muffs of red fox fur. Muffs were equally popular in the American Colonies and also used by men and women. The muff was a mark of dignity among older men.

mule or boudoir slipper of velvet or satin and lace

muffler an ornamental scarf or neckerchief of wool or silk, worn by men and women, especially in winter as throat protection.

mufti a term derived from the British services in India; civilian dress worn when off-duty by naval or military officers.

mukluk Arctic half-boot of sealskin or walrus hide with flesh side out and fur inside. Canvas top and tanned leather sole and laced with thongs. An army Arctic boot worn over a leather boot with white canvas uppers and white leather sole, 1940's.

mule or **moyle** slippers without heels or heel counters, to the sixteenth and seventeenth centuries. They acquired heels in women's fashions in later centuries. Also called *boudoir slipper.* see *scuffs.*

mull an old-fashioned fabric in a plain-woven, very lightweight silk or cotton. Formerly popular for women's blouses and children's frocks. Late eighteenth and early nineteenth centuries.

mummy cloth a cloth, no doubt linen, in which Egyptian mummies were wrapped. The cloth was also used for embroidery.

mungo, mongo, mousée reclaimed wool made from milled, felted or hard-spun woolens.

muscadine a pastille scented with musk; the name was applied to effeminate young men of the French Revolutionary period who overdressed and used quantities of the scent.

musette bag a soldier's leather or canvas bag on a shoulder strap for carrying provisions.

mush a Briticism for an umbrella.

mushroom hat of felt or straw; a simple round crown with a downward-shaped round brim, banded with ribbon.

mushru an East Indian satin fabric, sturdy, cotton-backed and often striped or figured.

musketeers see *mousquetaires.*

muskrat or **musquash, mushquash** the latter name is of American Indian origin and still used in the London fur market. Muskrat is a durable fur of a prolific rodent found in the United States and Canada. The fur is dark, glossy brown or black with thick underfur and strong top hair; the three types known as northern, southern and black. The skins are worked for certain garments in let-out mink fashion and are dressed, dyed, bleached and sold under many fancy names.

muslin a staple, plain-woven cotton first made in Mosul, Mesopotamia. It comprises weaves from sheerest batiste and soft nainsook to heavyweight bedding.

muslin model a muslin sample of a garment design made for try-out or fitting. see *toile.*

moustache, moustachio see *beards.*

mustard yellow a rich brownish-yellow, the color of mustard sauce.

muted a term applied to colors, meaning subdued values.

mutton chops see *side whiskers.*

muu muu The dress of the Hawaiian woman began as a cotton wrapper or robe with which the early American missionaries clothed the "pagans." The natives added charm to the garment in flower motifs and color and in the 1930's some American college girls discovered the simple style. Led to the shift as a fashionable dress. see *Mother Hubbard.*

muskrat-durable fur dressed, dyed and bleached-sold under many names

ermine cape and muff edged with tails-white silk Brandenburg-velvet gown and hat-crown of plumage

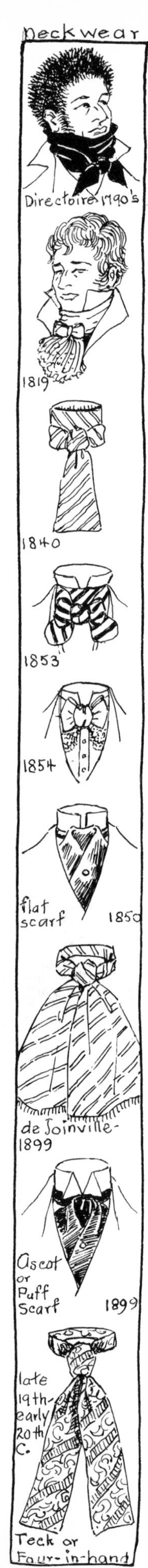

N

nacre mother-of-pearl.

nacre velvet see *velvet, nacre.*

nail a cloth measurement; one-sixteenth of a yard, or $2\frac{1}{2}$ inches.

nail cosmetics see *fingernails.*

nainsook a soft, fine cotton striped, barred or plain, originally woven in India. Used for men's underwear and pajamas.

nankeen, nankin a strong, buff-colored Chinese cotton woven of a fibrous tissue of a tree or shrub grown in the East Indies and China; named for Nanking where principally made. It was introduced into America in 1828 from Sicily and became especially popular for summer breeches and riding breeches. Also a fabric made with tussah silk or rayon in plain or twill weaves and in a natural or ecru color. Weight and texture vary with quality. see *shantung; tussah; pongee.*

nap hairy fibers of uniform length and texture on some fabrics, lying smoothly in one direction and forming a soft surface, not a pile.

napa a soft leather made in Napa, California, by tanning sheepskin or calfskin with a soap and oil mixture. Used the same as real leather.

Napoleon boot see boot, Napoleon.

Napoleon collar see *collar, Napoleon.*

napping a finishing process to produce a soft, fuzzy surface on some cloths, coatings and blankets. Used also on hat felts of poor quality, for the same purpose.

natural the off-white color of undyed fabrics or yarns.

Neapolitan hat see *hat, Neapolitan.*

near seal see *seal, imitations.*

neck ruff made of fur, cloth or silk held by a satin fold around the neck and finished with satin loops. 1890's. see *ruche; cartwheel.*

neckband shirt standard contemporary masculine shirt with a neckband having buttonholes back and front for separate collar.

neckcloth scarf, muffler, neckerchief or other neck dressing worn by men and women in the eighteenth century.

neckerchief a kerchief for the neck.

necklace an encircling ornament for the neck, usually in such pliable form as a string of beads or a chain of links in gold, silver, other metals or jewels. There are varied styles, see *lavalière; rivière.*

neckstock originally a black satin or white linen cravat wrapped twice around the neck over a standing starched collar. The ends were either tied in front or buckled in back. Eighteenth and early nineteenth centuries.

neckwear, masculine In the 1830's and 1840's the muffler tied in back, and the neckcloth in front filled in the space above the waistcoat to the chin. The white evening bow tie often sported embroidered ends. It was Beau Brummell, the famous English dandy, who discovered the use of starch to stiffen his cravat to the right consistency to preserve the proper folds of the neckpiece. From then on the stiff collar or "underproper" and cuffs became important accessories in their own right. In the 1840's, collar points turned down becoming, by the 1850's, a true folded-down collar. Also in the 1850's came the small, narrow bow tie. It was stiffened by an inner lining, the bow sewn on and the scarf fastened by a strap and buckle, the first ready-made tie. see *collar; cravat; focal; four-in-hand; muffler.*

needle, steel It is believed that the Chinese were the first to use steel needles, which were carried westward by the Moors. A needle-making industry was established in Nuremberg in 1370. The manufacture of needles was carried on in small shops during the reign of Queen Elizabeth I, eventually developing into important industries in England and Germany.

needle tapestry embroidery worked on canvas in a variety of stitches, giving the effect of woven tapestry.

needlepoint counted embroidery stitches worked with a needle over the threads of a canvas; the term generally refers to such work done in tent stitch.

needlepoint lace a lace made entirely with sewing needle instead of bobbins, and worked on a paper pattern with buttonhole and blanket stitches.

needlework see *stitch.*

negligée an informal and usually flattering robe that a woman wears for leisure at home. Formerly it was worn during the rest period after lunch which was indulged in without the steel-boned corset.

negligée cap of red velvet-shaved head-American 1767

negligée cap a man's cap of the wig-wearing period, worn at home and especially in the American South during hot weather. The cap, always of handsome fabric, was occasionally worn for a gentleman's portrait.

Nehru tunic see *chogā.*

net, netting openwork fabrics made with meshes of varied size in silk, cotton, linen, cord or twine, according to the requirements. Used for veils, dressmaking, curtains, fish nets, tennis nets, etc.

netcha an Eskimo word for a sealskin coat.

net embroidery various net stitches worked on a net ground, the completed piece often called lace, especially Breton.

New Look a dramatic change in fashion which occurred in 1947. At the end of World War II a new couturier, Christian Dior of Paris (1905–1957), a former art dealer, turned his creative talent to feminine dress. Under his guidance the slim, flat, rather masculine figure acquired bosom, hips, abdomen and derrière with small waist and clothed in a bouffant fashion. Women donned the guipière or waist-cincher, and costumes were boned, lined and padded. The long full skirt, extravagantly bias-cut, was a welcome reaction to the skimpy clothes of wartime when fabric was often government-rationed.

New Look created by Dior of Paris-corseted small waistline-long-waisted bodice-tiny suede tricorne-with jewel-1954

New York surtout—short black overcoat with seam at waist—silk braid edged rolled collar—carrying black bowler—1851

New York surtout a man's fashionable, short, black overcoat with skirts cut straight around. A wide collar to the waistline, finished with wide black silk braid; 1850's.

Newmarket surtout a British overcoat named for Newmarket, England, a town famed for its race meets. The coat, a long, skirted, double-breasted cloak in redingote style, worn for riding and driving in the nineteenth century. It was always finished with a velvet collar.

Newmarket surtout or overcoat in redingote style—chamois-colored cloth—always a velvet collar—black satin stock—black beaver hat—gaiter breeches—early 19th C.

nightcap a negligée or undress cap which came into vogue in the late sixteenth century. It was much worn by gentlemen in the seventeenth century as undress, especially when without a wig. Nightcaps were often luxurious headpieces of velvet with embroidery, gilt and lace. A gentleman often had his portrait painted in a plain velvet cap. Women also wore nightcaps, but of sheer cottons with frills, lace and embroidery.

nightdress old English; there were many names for the feminine sleeping garment which varied from century to century. Fifteenth and sixteenth centuries: nightdress, nightgown, night rail or rayle, night shift; seventeenth and eighteenth centuries: nightsmock, nightgown, nightdress; nineteenth to date: nightgown or nightdress.

nightgown, evening gown in the period of Henry VIII, a night gown was an evening gown, there being record of one worn by Anne Boleyn (1507–1536) of black satin. A diary of 1771 notes that the writer and her mother called on a bride who was "dressed in a white satin nightgown."

nightshirt a tailored garment reaching below the knees with side seams partway open. Worn by men and boys until the appearance of pajamas, late nineteenth century. Center front buttoned down to the waist; long sleeves and standing or turndown collar. Cuffs, collar and front were often decorated with red cross-stitch embroidery on white cotton or linen.

nightsmock Ladies and gentlemen of the seventeenth century slept in "night smocks," common folk in their "day smocks," or regular clothes. The smocks of the upper class were made of "Holland fine" with cambric sleeves and point-lace edging. Inventories tell us that such owners owned one to two dozen fine smocks.

ninon a stout silk voile with transparent surface. Used for dresses, neckwear and lingerie.

Nineteenth Century costume see illustrations, pages 225–247.

Nithsdale a hooded riding cloak of red cloth, often fur-lined, popular in the eighteenth century. Named for Lady Nithsdale, whose husband, a Jacobite rebel under sentence of death, escaped from the Tower of London wearing his wife's cloak, 1716.

Nineteenth Century-
Empire corset
elastic webbing
side inserts-
single front lace-
French-1803
damask zona
laced in back-
whaleboned-
French-1805
long, English
corset laced
in back-
1810
front bands of
elastic webbing-
French-1804
linen bandelette
after ancient
Greek design-
French-
1810
white
dimity
corset
laced in back-
French-1813
front-laced
colored
corselet over
embroidered
chemise-
French-1822
white ninon
corset-frilled
shoulder straps-
French-
1810

Nineteenth Century-
corset-
1830's
"instant"
unlacing by
pulling out
whalebone rod-
French-
1830
back-laced
corset with yoke
and whaleboned
foundation
cap sleeves-
French-c.1839
back-laced
corset hooked
in front-
embroidery-
French-
1837
gray satin
corset laced
in back-
French-
1835
corset with
dropped shoulder
straps-double
lacing through
tiny pulleys-
French-
c.1835
pregnancy
and nursing
corset-white
with rose ribbon
trimming-
French-
1830
single
back lacing-
French-
1839

Nineteenth Century-
corset-
1840's
back-laced
corset with
reinforced
front-
French
lacing through
pulleys-two
single strings
laced from
top and
bottom
to waist-
French-
1840
back-laced
corset-
French-1845
lacings
through pulleys-
embroidered
edging-
French-
1846
corset-cover
of fine
lingerie fabric-
lace-edged
sleeves-
English
single back
lacing-
embroidered
edging-
French-
1845

Nineteenth Century-
first half-
bustle-lingerie
accessories
"Swiss
petticoat"
with
fan pleats-
1820
corset over
chemise-
bustle tied
over corset-
English-
c.1828
chemisette
and brassière-
ruff called
"Betsy"-
English-
1810
pleated
crinoline
"wheel"
tied over
corset-
French-
1840's
pair of
wicker or
wire mesh
cushions
over the
corset-
1840's
sleeve cushion
tied round
arm-
1830's
chemisettes and undersleeves-
lawn with embroidery
lace and tucks-1840's
bustles of varied
shapes and sizes-
1830's

Nineteenth Century-
first half-
chemise
Empire chemise-
sheer cotton
or linen-
French-
first decade
lingerie nightcaps of
lawn, lace, tucks and
embroidery-
c.1830
batiste
chemise-
frills of
self fabric-
French-
1805
the "Swiss"
petticoat-
cambric slip
with corded
hem and
embroidered
ruffle-
1820
chemise (shirt)
into separate
lingerie
shirtwaist-
French-
1829
linen
nightgown
with frills-
lace cap-
1825
chemise with
flap to conceal
corset top-
1840's
chemise
with simple
embroidery-
1820's

Nineteenth Century-
first half-
waistcoat and
neckwear
pull-over
waistcoat-
muslin
cravat-
French-
1800
shawl-collared
waistcoat-
whaleboned
stock-
French-
1825
muslin stock-
striped
waistcoat-
French-
1809
velvet waistcoat-
muslin cravat-
Spanish-
1st decade
velvet waistcoat-
muslin stock-
French-
2nd decade
plush waistcoat-
piqué stock
and cravat-
French-
1828
cloth waistcoat-
Brandenburgs-
silk muffler-
pearl scarfpin-
French-
1829
piqué waistcoat-
black silk
cravat-
French-
c.1830
turned-down
collar-black satin
muffler-cashmere
waistcoat-
English-
1842
shawl-
collared
waistcoat-
black satin
muffler-
English-
1830's
bow-tied
stock-
striped silk
waistcoat-
English-
1834
striped cravat-
embroidered
waistcoat-
French-
1831
black velvet
waistcoat-
black satin
cravat-
French-
1840

Nineteenth Century-
first half-
shirt and
neckwear
frilled shirt-
collar points-
muslin cravat-
French-
1805
linen
smock-
English
collar points-
silk scarf-
French-
1823
collar points-
muslin stock-
English-
1810
2nd decade-
English
whaleboned
striped
silk stock-
French-
1827
collar points-
muslin stock-
French-
1820's
1820's
English
muslin
dress
stock-
French-
1829
turned-down
collar-silk cravat-
French-
1830's
black satin muffler
fastened with
solitaire gem-English-
1840's
1820's
English
collar points-
muslin stock-
two waistcoats,
muslin and
brocade-
French-
1834
collar points-
black silk
cravat-
English-
1840's

Nineteenth Century
first half-
negligée
organdy and
black lace-
French-
1830's
brocaded
velvet robe-
silk muffler-
French-
1839
taffeta with
pleated frilling-
French-
1839
the "amazon"
in masculine
robe and shirt-
French-1830's
cloth and
silk braid-
French-
1840's
robe of
brocaded silk-
French-
1840's

Nineteenth Century-
first half-
drawers-
pantalets
small girl
in pantalets-
English-
1810
corded
pantalets
and frock-
French-
1816
young lady
in embroidery-
edged
pantalets-
American-
1837
front and back
of opera (open)
drawers-laced
in back-
English-
2nd decade
drawers-
knitted silk-
drawstrings
tied at sides
and inside
legs-
English-
2nd decade
muslin frock
and
pantalets-
French-
1836
back view-
pantalets
with tucked
bottoms-
1830's
small boy
in pantalets
and frock-
American-
1820's

Nineteenth Century-
second half-
children's lingerie-
1880's
nightdress-
pink
batiste-
red wool
embroidery
bustle
petticoat tied in back-
white muslin-tucks
and embroidery
little girl's
initialed chemise-
batiste with
lace edge
bustle ruffles
buttoned on-white
muslin
and lace
boy's bodice
and drawers-
muslin with
lace edge
red flannel stays-
girl's 6 to 12-
laced in back-
whalebone
supports
long waisted
petticoat-
white muslin
with colored
embroidery
linen underdrawers-
boy's 10 to 12-
ties, back
and legs
muslin
knickerbockers-
girl's 6 to 8-
buttoned at
sides-pleated
cambric frill-
bobbin lace
insertion-
extra fulness
in back
day shirt-
boy's 12 to 14-
white muslin
with white
embroidery

Nineteenth Century-
second half-
feminine
smallclothes
girl's
linen drawers-
buttoned at sides-
tucks-embroidery-
1863
winter garment-
corset cover
and bloomers-
knitted fabric-
1890's
crocheted wool
under petticoat-
white and scarlet-
1863
white
cotton
corset
cover-
lace
edging
and
insertion-
1890's
winter under
petticoat-
quilted
calico-
back
view-
1870's
corset over
chemise, drawers
and under petticoat-
striped stockings-
1870's
black
corset
over chemise
and drawers-
crocheted
lace-black
lisle or silk
stockings-
1890's
white cotton combination
corset cover and drawers-
lace, tucks and embroidery-
1890's
white cotton
combination corset
cover and drawers-
buttoned in front-
lace insertion-
embroidery edging-
1878

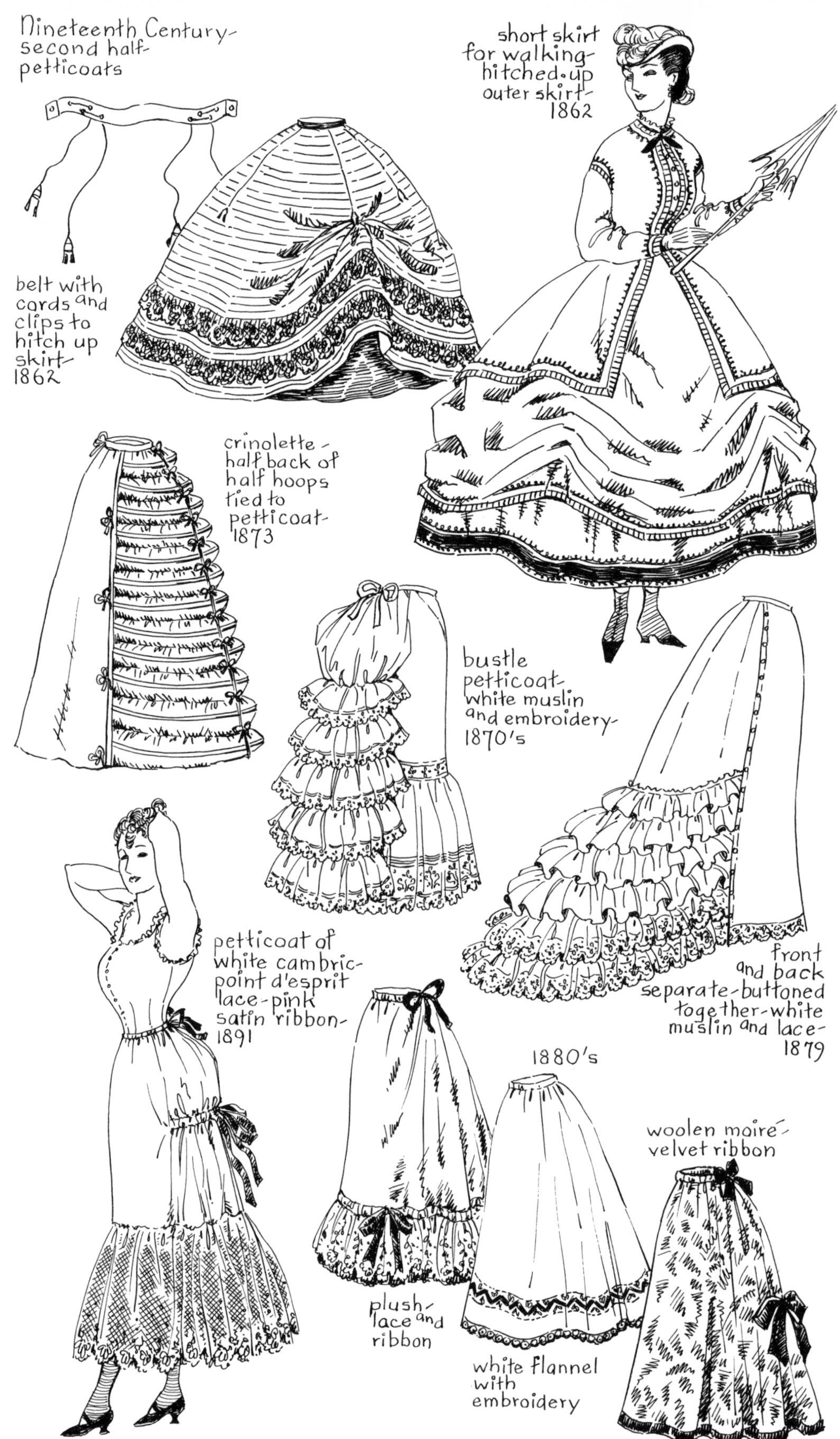
Nineteenth Century-
second half-
petticoats
belt with
cords and
clips to
hitch up
skirt-
1862
short skirt
for walking-
hitched-up
outer skirt-
1862
crinolette-
half back of
half hoops
tied to
petticoat-
1873
bustle
petticoat-
white muslin
and embroidery-
1870's
petticoat of
white cambric-
point d'esprit
lace-pink
satin ribbon-
1891
front
and back
separate-buttoned
together-white
muslin and lace-
1879
1880's
woolen moiré-
velvet ribbon
plush-
lace and
ribbon
white flannel
with
embroidery

Nineteenth Century-
second half-
crinoline
bloomer costume-
protest against
exaggerated
crinoline-
1857
muslin
interlined
with steel hoops-
front closing
panel-
1857
steel hoops-
embroidered
petticoat-
corset
cover-
1857
crinoline puff
with steel hoops-
ribbon ties-
worn over
petticoat-
1860
elliptical
steel hoops
held by tapes-
1867
scarlet flannel
crinoline -buckled
straps -steel
hoops-
1869
steel hoops held
by suspenders
front and back-1869
bustle
crinoline of
steel hoops-
1870
crinoline puff
with
steel hoops-
1863

Nineteenth Century-
second half-
bustle
steel hoops
with tape-
chemise,
corset and
petticoat-
c. 1870
hoop skirt
with bustle-
steel hoops
and crinoline-
1873
stretchable
spiral
wire
bustle-
1880's
the polonaise-
taffeta and
fluted velvet
ribbon-
1869
folding
bustle-
steel hoops
and muslin-
1880's
dress
improver-
horsehair
and
embroidered
dimity-
1872
bustle skirt
with steel
hoops-
1871
bustle over
corset-
rows
filled
with
down-
lace
edging-
1886
dress
improver-
horsehair
ruffles-
1872
bustles and
breast forms
of braided
wire-
1880's

Nineteenth Century-
second half-
chemise and
nightgown
nightgown of
linen or cotton-
tucks-fluted
frills-
1862
linen chemise-
fluted frills-
fine tucks-
1862
short linen
nightdress-red
cross-stitching-
1863
fine linen-white
hand-embroidery-
buttoned neck
to hem-embroidered
hem ruffle-
1880's
nightgown of
rose China silk-
eyelet embroidery-
point d'esprit lace-
rose satin ties-
1891
white cotton
nightgown with
embroidered
yoke, lace
and ribbon-
1894
chemise of
batiste or silk-
lace and
embroidery-
threaded
with baby
ribbon-
1890's
white cotton
nightgown-
tucks and
embroidery-
1894

Nineteenth Century-
second half-
negligée
negligée-white
jaconet-fitted
back-full front
held by belt-
scalloped
ruffles-
1852
negligée-French
blue cashmere
over white satin
petticoat-
appliquéd
Paisley
motifs-
1866
wrapper of old blue
cashmere-jabot and
frills of cream lace-
satin ribbon sash-
pleated hem ruffle-
1883
morning jacket-
pink Saxony
flannel with
pillow lace-
bowknots
on cuffs-
1886
tea gown of
cashmere-
Maline lace
and insertion-
shirred yoke
and cuffs-
balloon
sleeves-
1894
circularcombing
mantle-white
cambric-frill of
embroidery-
satin tie-
1887

Nineteenth Century-
second half-
corsetry
waistband laced
in front-pleats
in back-
1862
little girl's
corset laced
front and
sides-elastic
back panel-
1862
back-
laced through
pulleys-hooked in
front-1850
front
fastening-
laced in
back-
1862
plush
edging-
laced in
back-front
closure-
1867
crossed latchet
fastening back
and front-
1868
laced
sides and
lower back-front
closure-ribbon-
embroidery and
shirred panels-
1879
front
closure-back
lacing-hand
embroidered-
1878
known as
pear-shaped busk-
spoon busk-
swan-bill busk-
ribbon-threaded
embroidery-
back lacing-
1878
fitted corset-
cover of longcloth-
Valenciennes lace
and embroidered
insertion-
1878

Nineteenth Century-
second half-
corsetry
girl's
buttoned
corset waist
of twill-
1880's
reinforced
waistline-
elastic inserts-
embroidery-
1880's
dancer's corset-
low back
with
lacing-
1880's
close back
lacing-flower
motifs-
embroidered
edging-
1880's
buttoned,
whaleboned garment-
corset and corset
cover in one-
fancy
braid-
1890's
corset with
skirt
supporter-front closure-
side lacings-1880's
striped
coutil with
embroidery-
front closure-
back lacing-
1890's
buttoned
corset waist-
adjustable
shoulder
straps-long
knitted
drawers-
black cotton
stockings-
1880's
infant's
corset
waist-
buttons
to hold
stockings
and underclothes-1890's
satin corset-
back closure-
wide front busk-
eyelet embroidery-
1890's

Nineteenth Century-
second half-
the shirtwaist
chemisette or
habit shirt to
wear with vest-
lawn with tucks,
embroidery and
frilling-satin tie-
1852
linen camicia-
lace edging-
corselet with straps
to tie up sleeves-
Italian
peasant
camicia rosso
or Garibaldi red
shirt-silk with
black braid-black
velvet tie-1862
tailored shirtwaist
of striped percale-
pearl buttons-
silk tie-1896
vest of
fawn color
cashmere-
standing collar-
silk tie-
1863
shirtwaist of
the Gibson girl-
heavy white
linen or piqué
with Ascot tie-
1899
shirtwaist of
lawn with
embroidered
insertion-
black baby
ribbon-black
satin stock-
1899
lingerie
neckwear-
butterfly bow-
back of neck-
embroidered jabot-front-
late 1890's

Nineteenth Century-
second half-
shirt and sleepwear
Garibaldi red
shirt-"camicia
rosso"-smock
design-tied
silk scarf-
c.1860
false bosom-
dickey-linen
with tucks-
1850's
linen shirt
buttoned in back-
tucked front-
Napoleon or
Windsor scarf
of black satin-
woven elastic
braces-
1850's
dress shirt buttoned
in back-crossbar
dimity bosom
with frills-
1850's
flannel undershirt-
red or white-open underarm
seams-feather
stitching-1863
dress shirt
with stiff bosom-
tab for drawers'
button-1883
nightshirt of
cotton, cotton or
woolen flannel-
1890's
dress shirt with
fluted frills-
one-end tie of
pique or lawn-
1860's
pajamas
of cotton
or silk with
braid fastenings-
1890's
nightshirt of
cotton, cotton or
woolen flannel-
1880's
colored stripes on
white-white collar
and cuffs-four-n-
hand scarf-
late 1890's

Nineteenth Century-
second half-
knitwear
knit sports
shirt worn
at Oxford-
1863
knit
underdrawers-
late 1860's
knit striped
polo shirt-
1877
child's knit
bathing suit-
French-
1880's
underwaistcoat
over undershirt-
scarlet flannel-
ribbed cuffs-
lined with
chamois leather-
1880's
knit swim
suit-red and
white striped
shirt-gray
trunks-
1890's
knit swim suit-
navy blue and
red striped
shirt-blue
trunks-
1890's
knit "union
undergarment"-
wool, silk, cotton
or combinations-
1880's
cotton-Scotch
plaid-white
top-1870's
cotton-stripes
varicolored-
1860's
black silk-
flower
embroidery-
1890's

Nineteenth Century-
second half-
bathing suit
corset over
bloomers-
skirt and
tunic-blue
or black-
bag cap-
English-
1877
bustle style-
serge or flannel-
braid trim-
straw hat
over bag cap-
French-
1870's
blue flannel-
white braid-
white canvas
cape and
bag cap-
German-
1864
black or
brown
mohair-
white
braid-
French-
1880's
serge or flannel
in light color-
braid trim-
black cotton
stockings-
American-
1880's
suit and cap
turquoise blue
flannel-white
lace-ribbon
bow at neck-
English-
1880's
two-piece
knit suit-
pleated frill-
Belgian-
1890's
white flannel
metallic thread
embroidery-
flesh pink
tights with
knee-high
drawers-
French-
1890

Nineteenth Century-
second half-
haberdashery
dressing gown-
fawn colored
cloth-multi-
colored braid-
c.1860
waistcoat-
plain cloth
with braid-
1850's
waistcoat
over the
cambric
shirt-
1850's
double
breasted
waistcoat-
plaid cloth-
Oxford tie-
1870's
lounge
jacket-red
velvet-black
satin collar
and lining-
waistcoat
figured
cloth
with
braid-
1859
gray cloth
waistcoat
worn with
Prince Albert
wing collar
ascot
puff-
1890's
evening dress-
linen shirt-
stiff bosom-
poke collar-
Oxford tie of
lawn or piqué-
waistcoat
of linen or
piqué-
late 1890's
elastic webbing
and leather-
mid-century
embroidered
satin with
elastic and
leather-
1890
elastic
garter-
1883
sash vest for
summer evening
dress-buckled
in back-of
ribbed or
surah silk-
1892
hooded
bathrobe of
striped cloth-
cord girdle-
1880's

Nithsdale riding hood of red cloth often fur-lined—popular in the 18th C.

nivernois a diminutive tricorne worn by the English Macaronies with the cadogan wig in the 1770's. Named for the Duke of Nivernois, Louis-Jules Mancin Mazarani (1716–1798).

none-so-pretties fancy, decorative tapes used for trimming garments in the eighteenth century in the American Colonies.

Norell, Norman see *couture, haute.*

Norfolk jacket a sack or jacket with straight front, with or without a yoke, box pleats down front and back under which passes the self-belt. The style of yoke, pleats and pockets vary. The coat of the Duke of Norfolk's hunting suit, the first "Norfolk," appeared in the 1880's with knickerbockers, a revival of knee breeches for day wear.

Setesdal dress of Norway—worn for festivals—pinafore style over blouse—"pincushion hat" with ribbons—Norway

Norfolk jacket and knickerbockers—tan and yellow plaid woolen cloth—knitted woolen hose—linen gaiters—1880's

Northampton lace English bobbin lace of the sixteenth and seventeenth centuries imitating Flemish patterns.

Norwegian costume, traditional see illustration; *Hardanger skaut.*

nosegay a boutonnière or small bunch of fragrant flowers. see *boutonnière.*

notched lapel the V-shaped notch on the outer edge of jacket or coat where the collar is seamed to the body. A tailoring term of the early nineteenth century.

Nottingham laces many kinds of net made by machine in Nottingham, England, such as Cluny, torchon and Valenciennes, commonly called Val.

nub yarn a yarn with recurring twists or thick places used for weaving cloths such as chinchilla cloth, or ratiné lace.

nun's cotton an embroidery cotton of fine white thread.

nun's dress in 1965, after wearing the same style of habit for more than a century, the nuns of the Order of the Sisters of Mercy put on a new dress. It was designed by Sybil Connolly of Dublin who is famous for beautiful romantic ballgowns, very often made of Irish handkerchief linen and Irish crochet lace. Both the designer and nuns had hoped the habit would be changed to gray instead of black but because of teaching and nursing in many different climates, the final choice was black gabardine. In the change, some hair was permitted to show under the white cap, the dress was shorter, and pumps with Cuban heels are worn with gun-metal-colored stockings.

nun's veiling a lightweight, semi-transparent woolen fabric in black, white and colors. Used in black by nuns for veiling, dresses and cloaks.

nutria; coypu, coypou an aquatic rodent half the size of the beaver, native to South America, and now found in England. The best fur is from Argentina and is called Island Nutria. Argentine fur is heavier and more expensive than Brazilian and Chilean, durable with soft, dense underfur after being dehaired. It is a rich bluish-brown or occasionally black. Ranch-bred, deep-piled white and champagne color are used for coats, jackets and trimming. The fur is imitated in sheared and dyed raccoon.

nylon the strongest, finest, most elastic and all-purpose chemical fiber for clothing fabrics. As a filament, it can be blended with other man-made or natural fibers. Of weaves combined with nylon, the first and most widely used is tricot. There are silk weaves, such as taffeta, shantung, crepe, plissés, marquisettes and nets, and plain weaves in linen and cotton types. Nylon is also combined with silk and wool created by Du Pont chemists. Nylon was the first completely synthetic, commercial fiber made from air, water and coal and was created by the chemists at DuPont. see *acrilan; dacron; dynel; orlon.*

nutria or coypu-an aquatic rodent found only in S.A. Durable, soft fur, bluish brown-length to 3 feet with tail 1 foot long

O

obi Japanese, a wide sash of brocaded silk, lined with contrasting color and interlined with stiffening and worn over the kimono. The obi measures fifteen inches wide and four to six yards long. The back ends are tied in a large flat bow or a large butterfly bow, the latter for brides and maidens. Inside the butterfly knot is the obiage, or small cushion for padding.

obiage see *obi.*

ocelot; South American spotted cat a wildcat of the leopard family found from Texas to Patagonia. Abundant in Central and South America. A flat fur with short guard hair and practically no underfur. Variable markings in dots, rosettes and lines well marked. Used for coats, jackets and trimming.

off-the-rack a Briticism for ready-made garments. see *ready-made.*

off-white white with a faint tinge of another color; names include oyster, ivory, bone, eggshell, cream.

oil frock a waterproof slicker coat worn by fishermen, miners and others.

oilcloth cotton fabric which has been painted and varnished; a wide variety of uses includes cap visors, belt linings, jackets, capes and many household needs. Known in Great Britain as American cloth.

oiled silk a silk fabric, thin and plain-woven, made waterproof by being soaked in boiled oil and dried. Used in rainwear and in items of apparel where water-proofing is required, often as a lining, although gradually being replaced by more modern water-proofing.

oilskin a heavy cotton cloth made waterproof by being impregnated with oil and gum. Used for sailors' apparel and called oilskins or slickers. see *slicker.*

ombré French for shaded, an adjective and weaving term for stripes of variegated colors melting into each other. Also a cloth woven, or a surface painted, in graduated hues of a special color.

omophoriom a vestment of bishops of the Greek Church, an embroidered silk strip worn around the neck with the ends crossed on the left shoulder and falling to the knee.

onyx a form of quartz with black and white bands. Sardonyx has red and white bands. Used in the nineteenth century for men's cufflinks, watch fobs, seals. Also in women's jewelry such as rings, earrings and brooches combined with gold.

ooze usually calfskin with a suèded or velvety finish made by the use of a tanning liquor of oak, bark, catechu, etc.

opal a stone composed of silica with a variable amount of water which causes an iridescent play of colors. Opals may be white or black; fire opals are reddish-orange.

opera cloak a man's knee-length cape-like coat for evening dress wear. Of velvet or fine cloth, it had a standing collar fastened by tasseled silk cords and was worn about the 1850's. The feminine version for formal evening dress was of

opera cloak–with velvet collar–over evening habit–velvet waistcoat–Gibus, collapsible grosgrain opera hat (gibus) 1834

costly brocade, velvet, silk or fine fur, the costliest being Russian sable.

opera glasses a small binocular telescope was made for use at the opera or theater, carried by every elegant lady. Sometimes with a handle like a lorgnette, sometimes folding and carried in a leather case. It was generally mounted with mother-of-pearl, smoky or white. Still in use today.

opera hat see *gibus.*

opera pump see *pump, opera.*

opossum American derivative of the American Indian name, apasum, meaning "white beast." The only pouched mammal found in North and South America. A durable long-haired fur with close, silky and whitish underfur and long guard hair in brown and silver. Used natural or dyed to simulate fitch, marten and skunk, or sheared to resemble beaver and nutria. It is popular in silvery yellow and used for coats and trimming. South American opossum of the gray, dark gray or black type is inclined to be woolly.

opossum, Australian not a true opossum but of the phalanger family. A durable fur but unlike the American opossum, consisting of underhair and top hair; the effect is feathery, close and even. The color varies according to region from gray-blue to reddish yellow with dark and white markings, reddish most common, and gray-blue the most desirable. The fine pelts are used for coats and trimming and the lower grades for collars on sheep-lined jackets. The ringtailed opossum is found from South Queensland to South Australia. A deep bluish-gray, the underfur tinged with dull red which is used natural or dyed gray or brown. The quantity is small and used mostly for trimming.

opossum–from Indian name "Apasam" for white beast–durable, long-haired fur

opus anglicanum the embroidery of Anglo-Saxon England executed in split stitch, a long outline stitch held to the ground by a tiny stitch through the center.

opus araneum lace a handmade bobbin lace using the straight lines of the spider web (araneum) for the pattern. The term was used in the Middle Ages for embroidery in general.

orange one of the three secondary colors with purple and green, orange being a combination of red and yellow. The shades with a greater proportion of red include vermilion and coral; those with more yellow are amber and topaz.

orange blossoms in the nineteenth century language of flowers, orange blossoms denoted chastity. The flowers, generally artificial, were traditionally worn by brides as a chaplet holding the wedding veil in place. The custom lasted well into the twentieth century.

orby an American-designed, man's single-breasted walking frock coat eliminating the waistline seam. A seam down center back terminated at the waist. 1907.

Orby–cutaway, frock coat or morning coat–waistline seam omitted–braid-bound–American design–1907

organdie, organdy a fine muslin in plain weave, slightly stiffened, in white and colors. Used for dresses, blouses and collars, cuffs and apron sets.

organza a slightly stiffened sheer muslin, plain or figured, in white and colors. Used for picturesque diaphanous gowns for bride and bridesmaid apparel. Also used for *robes de style* created by Lanvin of Paris and popular in the 1920's and 1930's.

orle of rolled silk-two principal colors of the wearer's crest-Italian-1385

organzine a thread used for the warp in silk weaving. Also, the name of the fabric made of the thread.

orle a heraldic term for a wreath or torso of two colors of silk twisted together, representing the principal metal and color of the wearer's crest, worn around the knight's helmet or as a feminine headdress. Fourteenth and fifteenth centuries.

Orleans cloth see *covert cloth.*

orlon trade name for a fabric made of coal, air, water, petroleum and limestone. It is soft, wool-like and drapes well. Used for sweaters and other sportswear.

ornament that which is added to a costume for adornment, as a piece of jewelry.

orphreys the tissues and bands with gold work, fringe and lace applied to chasubles, copes and vestments. They were often made separate, permitting change from one garment to another, especially on royal dress. The jeweled work of the eleventh century called anglicanum was highly valued on the continent. The word *orphrey* originally signified both gold and Phrygia, the home of gold-embroidered tissues.

orrice a gimp or braid trimming woven with gold or silver thread, popular in the eighteenth century.

orris lace or braid, originally called Arras, after a town in France. Made of gold and silver thread and popular in the eighteenth century.

orris root the aromatic rootstock of a European species of iris. It is very fragrant and when powdered, is used for perfume and sachet.

osnabruk a coarse linen imported from Osnabruk, Prussia, used for men's jackets, shirts and breeches.

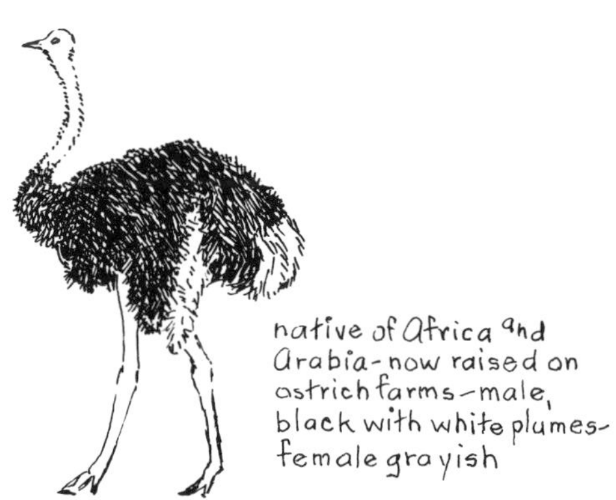

ostrich the largest of existing birds, native to Africa but commercially raised elsewhere. The soft, curling feathers of the small useless wings and of the tail have been used in headdress since the fourteenth century. Large ostrich-feather fans, dyed all colors, were fashionable

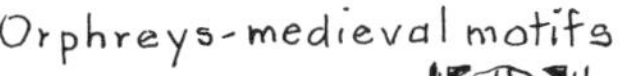

Orphreys-medieval motifs

from about 1910 to 1940. The quill-holed leather is used for handbags and other leather accessories. In the late 1960's there was a revival of ostrich fringe on evening gowns and dresses.

otter, American and Canadian found in the Northwest, the middle Atlantic region and the Pacific coast of the United States. A slender dark brown animal; the finest eastern peltry from Labrador and the finest Pacific peltry from Alaska.

otter, imitation sea from Russia, where beaver is sheared, dyed and pointed with white hairs to simulate sea otter.

otter, river an aquatic animal of the weasel family living on banks of rivers, streams, and along the coast of every continent but Australia. The best fur comes from the coldest regions. Varying in color according to locale, the color ranges from very dark or reddish brown to almost yellow, the most desirable being blue-black top hair with a slightly lighter-colored underfur. It is used as often unplucked as plucked, because of lustrous silky guard hair. It is not dyed unless poor in color. It was used on men's garments for centuries; today principally for feminine coats, jackets and trimming.

otter, sea a large, powerful species of the weasel family found in the North Pacific. A valuable fur; rich, dense, silky wool with soft, short guard hair requiring no dehairing process. It is gray-brown to rich black with occasional white or silver hairs. It is especially valued in Russia and China and was formerly used to trim Chinese mandarin robes. Threatened with extinction, sea otters are now legally protected.

ottoman a fabric ribbed cross-wise like faille silk but with larger, rounder ribs. The filling is of worsted, silk or cotton. Used for coats, dresses, men's waistcoats and trimmings.

outer wear a general term for all outside apparel for men and women.

outfit a noun comprising the complete ensemble for any specific occasion such as travel, sport, etc.

outing flannel a cotton flannel of many uses, especially for undergarments and nightwear. Plain-woven of soft yarns and well-napped on both sides and sometimes has a wool mixture. Also called tennis flannel, domet or domett.

over-all see *balandrana.*

overalls loose-fitting overtrousers with a front bib held by a strap around the neck. Made for working wear of dark blue or brown denim or duck. Designed for workmen originally but used also by women and children when practical. Late nineteenth and twentieth centuries.

overblouse any blouse that is worn outside the skirt.

overcheck a check pattern woven over another of different color.

overcoat a topcoat or greatcoat worn over the suit coat or jacket. see *greatcoat.*

overcoating special fabrics woven for overcoats such as covert, melton, montagnac, cheviot.

overplaid a finer line plaid laid over a basic ground plaid usually of neutral

overcoat-black broadcloth lined with nutria-otter collar-1918

overcoat of dark blue chinchilla cloth-chamois gloves-gray spats-1924

overcoat-Chesterfield-dark blue vicuña-black velvet collar-white silk muffler-gibus or opera hat-1941

overcoat in British Guard style-double breasted dark blue melton cloth-1942

tones, one check superimposed upon the other in the weaving.

oversack a large, loosely fitting overcoat of sack or box style; also, an ulster. Worn first decade, twentieth century.

overseas cap see *cap, overseas.*

man's Oxford-jack leather-English-17th C.

oxford a low shoe for men, women and children, laced or tied over the instep. The first oxford was a half-boot of heavy black jack leather, seventeenth century England. *Button oxfords* also appeared with a leather piece over the instep which buttoned to one side, on the outer side.

Oxford built on boot last-tan calfskin-contemporary

Oxford bags an English fashion in which trouser bottoms flared, sometimes to a width of 24 inches; 1920's.

Oxford cloth also called Cambridge mixture. A woolen cloth woven combining black and white or gray, producing a fabric of black or steel-colored ground lightly sprinkled with white.

oxford, gillie a low-cut sports shoe with open lacing over the instep and the laces tied around the ankles. Late nineteenth century.

Oxford gown see *academic gown.*

Oxford half-boot see *boot, Oxford half-boot.*

Oxford shirting first made in Oxford, England. A stout cotton fabric in plain or fancy basket weave or with narrow colored stripes.

oxford ties masculine, low, soft patent leather shoes for evening dress laced and tied over the instep.

oyster white an off-white, yellowish-gray in hue, resembling the inside of an oyster shell.

oyah see *Turkish point lace.*

P

pac, pack a heavy felt half-boot worn in winter by loggers; also, a moccasin of oil-tanned leather.

paddock suit see *English drape.*

paenula a poncho-like garment for bad weather, worn by the Romans and earlier by the Etruscans, with or without hood, open at the neck, where a buckle or fibula fastened the wrap. It became very popular with civil, military and legal classes in ancient Rome. Though condemned and banned, the paenula eventually replaced the elegant but difficult toga even for senatorial use in the second century A.D. The paenula lengthened to the feet, a long, sleeveless cloak retaining the opening for the head. After changes of design, it became in the seventeenth century the Gothic chasuble, a church vestment. see *abolla; byrrus.*

pafti the heavy silver buckle of the Hungarian woman's belt.

page boy coiffure a medieval style adopted by young women in the 1940's. Shoulder-length hair is worn with the ends turned under.

page boy uniform of cloth with braid and buttons, a fitted short jacket with johnny collar and pillbox cap with chin strap. Worn by hotel bellboys, twentieth century.

pagoda sleeve see *sleeve, pagoda.*

pagri, puggree the turban worn by Hindu men. A large self-draped strip of cotton five to twenty-five yards long, wound round the head in varied styles, often with an end hanging in back.

paillettes, spangles, sequins tiny, round, sparkling metal discs finished in gold, silver and other colors. Pierced in the center, they are sewn to evening dress, fancy costumes and costume accessories.

paint see *cosmetics.*

paisley see *shawl.*

pajamas, pyjamas The masculine lounge and sleep costume came to the Western world from India and Persia. East Indians wore cotton pajamas in the streets and British colonials copied the custom, bringing them back to England about 1870, originally for lounge wear and finally, by the turn of the century, adopting the Eastern jacket and trousers for sleepwear instead of the nightshirt. see *nightshirt.*

pajamas, feminine cotton or silk jacket and trousers, introduced as women's sleepwear in the early 1900's

pagri of the Hindu man—large self-draped turban of printed cotton—Malayan

pagri—Hindu meaning turban—fringed scarf wound round conical cap—British Indian officer

palatine or pelerine-shoulder cape of fur carried to France by a Palatine princess-1671

and first worn more by little girls than by women. Beach pajamas of gaily colored cotton and lounging pajamas in rich fabrics with very wide trousers had some vogue in the 1920's and 1930's before slacks or pants were accepted for round-the-clock wear. Palazzo pajamas 1960's, so called in Italy because intended for dress evenings at-home pajamas. The wearing of pajamas by Italian women, formerly taboo, was later approved when covered with a caftan-like robe or toga. see *culottes, feminine.*

palatine, pelerine a deep cape-like collar of lawn or lace which covered the shoulders, either cut high to the neck or in bateau line. The little cape, first made of fur and called a palatine or pelerine, was introduced into France by the Palatine Princess Charlotte Elizabeth of Bavaria, second wife of the Duc d'Orléans, brother of Louis XIV, 1671. see *pelerine.*

paletot, paddock a single-breasted man's frock overcoat with sewn-on skirts. The names appear to be interchangeable, but some authorities claim the paddock has a one-piece front and a skirted back, others claim the paletot is full-skirted. *Paletot* in the early seventeenth century was the French name for a silk overcoat worn over armor. It was revived in the nineteenth century for an overcoat of heavy cloth for winter use, or of light fabric for warm weather.

palisade see *commode.*

palla a rectangle of woolen cloth, a shawl-like wrap which was also used as bed covering. Wrapped or draped, it was worn by men, women and children in ancient Rome. see *himation; pallium.*

pallettes in the fifteenth century armor, a pair of decorative saucer-like steel plates, one placed on each side of the chest to protect the armpits.

pallium the Roman name for the himation, which had been the cloak of the Greeks of antiquity. Eventually it became an ecclesiastic vestment of the Roman Catholic Church. It was the characteristic

paletot or paddock-fitted overcoat with waist seam-pleats in back topped by two buttons-evolution of the redingote-1858

paletot-feminine traveling coat-beige and brown checked cloth-pleats and two buttons in back-1886

robe of the philosopher and scholar and very often his only garment. A large piece of woolen cloth, larger than the himation. see *himation.*

Palm Beach cloth a trademarked name for summer suiting for men and women. Originally woven of cotton and mohair, the name is now applied to other fiber-blended fabrics manufactured by the same firm.

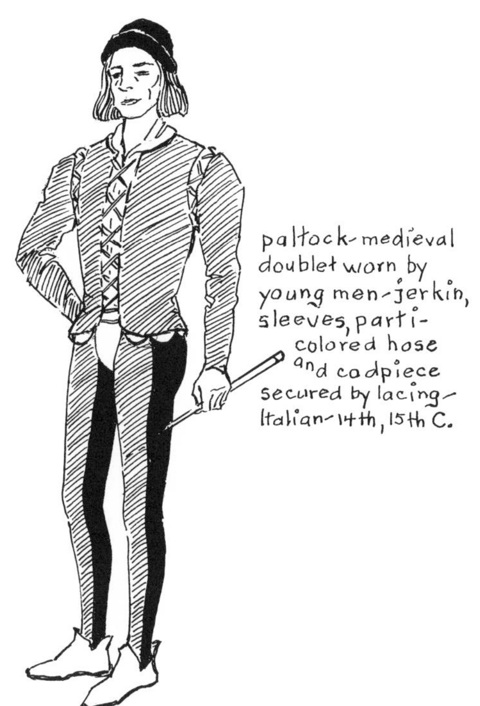

paltock-medieval doublet worn by young men-jerkin, sleeves, parti-colored hose and codpiece secured by lacing-Italian-14th, 15th C.

paltock a jacket worn by pages in the fourteenth and fifteenth centuries. A short, fitted doublet of cloth or silk buttoned or laced like a waistcoat to which hosen, or stockings and codpiece were fastened by lacings.

paludamentum, paludament the official royal and military cloak worn by a Roman general. A mantle of purple woolen cloth fastened on the right shoulder.

Pamela bonnet see *bonnet, Pamela.*

panache a plume on a helmet, hat or cap. It is sometimes called a brush when small.

Panama hat see *hat, Panama.*

Panamanian native dress see *pollera.*

panel in dressmaking, usually a featured rectangular shape and part of the design of the garment. It may be sewn close to the body or left to hang. It may also be attached to the shoulders as a train.

panes a feature of men's and women's dress during the Renaissance. The old decoration consisted of panes or squares and slits cut onto a costume, permitting a silk lining of contrasting color to show through. It was taken up all over Europe, a fashion lasting into the 1530's. see *slashings.*

panne velvet see *velvet, panne.*

panniers the démodé hoop of the seventeenth century returned to fashion in a new form. It followed the hoop worn under the Watteau flying gown. Already the fashion in England, it was called hooped skirt. Adopted in France about 1730 and made of reed or whalebone shaped like a wicker birdcage, the French called it a pannier, or basket. The framework being covered with taffeta or brocade, was accordingly a taffeta or brocade hoop. At first funnel-shaped, it grew very broad at the sides and flat front and back, reaching a circumference of eight feet. Mademoiselle Margot, a couturière, invented an inexpensive pannier, making the fashion accessible to all women. see *criades.*

panniers, elbow extremely wide panniers on which the elbows could be rested, were known as elbow panniers and the very small ones, called considérations, were for morning or negligée dress. The full skirt of the riding habit was worn over panniers. 1770's.

paludamentum-ancient military cloak of Roman general-purple woolen cloth

panes and slashes-peasecod-bellied pourpoint-trunk hose-cap with feather brush-English-16th C.

pocket panniers accessible through side openings - heavy silk gown - lingerie fichu and cap - French - 1775

pantaloons à pont or bridge trousers - square front panel - worn by French patriot - 1793

panniers, pocket In a popular style, pockets were formed by pulling the drapery through hip pocket holes. The dress, usually ankle length, had box pleats called Watteau pleats (1775) attached to the shoulders in back. It was a fashion that eventually spread to the bourgeoisie, becoming, finally, the habitual dress of servants. see *Watteau, Jean-Antoine.*

pant lengths, feminine ankle length for sports and home entertaining; *Bermuda shorts* knee length, for sports; *capri pants,* same as pedal pushers but tapered; *Jamaica shorts,* ending at mid-thigh; *pedal pushers,* loose and ending mid-calf; worn for bicycling and sailing; *regulation shorts,* two inches above the knee; *short shorts,* the very shortest.

pantalettes long ruffled drawers worn by little girls, c. 1800–1820, under the chemise.

pantalets The classic, sheer, slim Empire gown of early 1800 made some form of garment a necessity under the dainty chemise. The result was a two-legged lingerie piece called drawers. Though frequent reference to it occurs, until 1820 it was worn only by little girls. English and French fashion journals occasionally showed evening frocks of shoe-top length with frilled satin pantalets showing below. Drawers were often false ruffles held by tapes tied at the knees. Real drawers were not adopted by women until the 1830's.

pantaloons à pont, bridge trousers trousers which opened in front by means of a panel buttoned to the vest by three buttons, the panel operating like a drawbridge, a style worn by sailors until the past decade. The pantaloons were also known as broadfalls or frontfalls. Worn in World War II, but changed about mid-century.

panties; step-ins women's modern panties were a development of the twentieth century. Usually fitted over the hips, the legs flare skirtlike to a little above the knees. Originally fastened with tiny buttons on one side. An elastic waistband, eliminating a side placket, made the garment a step-in. Panties may be knee-length and close fitting, half-thigh length and flaring, called trunks, or quarter-thigh length and close-fitting, called briefs. Nylon is the preferred fabric, with a combination of nylon and wool or all wool for cold weather. Colors are generally white, pastels and black, but any color may be used in an ensemble with matching slip or petticoat. see *pantalets, pettipants, snuggies.*

pantihose or **panty stockings** a twentieth century luxury which has never before in any age been available to women. They reach from toe to waist in a suave fit. They are to be had in all textures from sheerest to firm silk nylon or lace and in all colors.

pantoffle the sixteenth century pantoffle was an overshoe without back quarter, leather covering only the front of the foot. It eventually became a house slipper, retaining its use and shape over the centuries to our day.

pants a colloquialism for trousers.

pants, bearskin see *bearskin pants.*

pants, harem slim bloomer shape, made of supple, handsome silk. The bloomers fall into soft folds covering the knees. The body section is either a sleeveless jumper or a jacket of hip length. Designed for home wear.

pants, hipster see *hipster pants.*

pants suit for feminine wear, trousers and jacket of regular suitings for city, suburban and country wear; man-tailored, accompanied by simple accessories. Velvet for evening dress, permitting a soft, lingerie blouse with lace-trimmed ruffles.

pañuelo the gauzy fichu of the traditional feminine costume of the Philippines. It is made of rengue, a starched gauze produced from native pineapple, and is beautifully embroidered in silk.

panung the traditional feminine dress of Thailand; printed silk or cotton one yard wide and three yards long, wrapped to form a gracefully draped skirt. Worn with blouse or jacket.

panung, masculine a straight length of cotton or silk drawn up between the legs to the back, thus forming pantaloons which reach down between knee and ankle. The traditional men's dress of Thailand.

paon a velvet resembling panne velvet but heavier, with the nap laid in one direction.

paper clothes introduced in the 1960's in men's undershirts and swim trunks, women's shifts and some children's clothes; inexpensive and disposable.

paper patterns designed by Ebenezer Butterick (1826–1903), a young tailor and shirtmaker of ability. He started in the 1860's by making a pattern of the shirt worn by Italy's hero, Garibaldi, and a pattern of a suit for little boys to be made by the home dressmaker.

papier-mâché a strong substance made of paper pulp, mixed size, and various other ingredients, especially glue, of which dress forms in particular are fashioned.

papillotes, curl papers small folded pieces of paper around which were wound wisps of wet hair. When dry and undone, the wisps became curls. Both men and women curled their hair in this way, especially in the eighteenth century.

Paquin see *couture, haute.*

parachute cloth a tightly woven fabric of nylon, dacron, silk or rayon, originally perfected for parachutes, World War II. After the war, many women bought leftover parachutes and made dresses and curtains of them.

paradise feathers elegant plumage, especially the long-tailed feathers of the adult male bird of paradise inhabiting New Guinea and adjacent islands.

paragon a popular cloth of the seventeenth and eighteenth centuries made in Turkey. Formerly of camel's hair, resembling camlet. Used for common wear and also for upholstery.

Paraguay lace combination hand and machine-made lace, the pattern worked in single thread spider web and wheel design. A fine weave is made for dresses and a heavier weave for other uses.

parasol see *sunshade.*

paratrooper boot see *boot, paratrooper.*

parchment, parchment color beige or deep ivory, the color of the skin of goat, sheep or other animal prepared as parchment for writing on.

parchment lace a lace formerly made of fine strips of cut-up old parchment, wound with gold, silver or silk thread and called cartisane and worked in a raised design. Mentioned in the time of Elizabeth I and similar to guipure.

pareu, pareo a Polynesian skirt or loincloth of standard size and colors, a rectangle printed with conventional flower designs; contemporary.

Paris embroidery a fine white cord embroidery appliquéd in satin stitch on piqué. Used in washable linens and garment accessories.

parka, anorak, amout a hip-length hooded outer garment of sealskin, worn universally by Arctic Eskimos. It is made alike for both sexes except that the

panung-Thailand wrapped breeches worn by men and women

anorak-Scandinavian

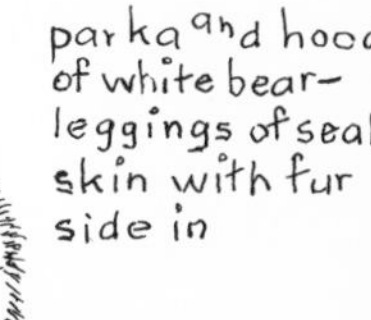

parka and hood of white bear-leggings of seal skin with fur side in

parka and breeches of sealskin with overdress of navy blue cotton-rick rack braid trim-modern Alaska

woman's garment has an extra hood for carrying a small child. The name *parka* comes from the Aleutian Islands; in Greenland the garment is called anorak (masculine) or amout (feminine). The modern anorak is a Scandinavian parka made of lightweight cotton or silk having wind resistance, water repellancy and allowance for ventilation, worn for sports such as skiing and sailing.

parta the Hungarian bride's tall tiara; a glittering, bespangled headdress worn only once, built up of artificial roses of white and in delicate tints, with silk ribbons floating in back.

parta-Hungarian bride's tiara of white roses and small tinted flowers-white lawn ribbons

parti-colored clothes worn by ladies and gentlemen of the European courts in the fourteenth and fifteenth centuries. The whole costume was divided into variegated colors and the family coat-of-arms, emblazoned upon the dress, stamped in gold and silver leaf and colored enamels. Such costumes were passed down the family and valued as historic dress. The jester in his parti-colored costume is a survival of the period. see *motley*.

parti-colored hose, masculine fitted and sewn tights reaching from waist to toe and being made of cloth or silk, the two legs of different colors, worn to the end of the fifteenth century.

partlet a neckerchief, chemisette, piccadilli-band or collar which was detachable from the garment. Usually of white linen for men and embroidered or jeweled for women.

parure a set of matching jeweled ornaments to be worn together, e.g., tiara, necklace, earrings, brooch and bracelets.

parvati an all-cotton cloth from India, named after an ancient Indian goddess. It is handwoven, heatherlike fabric with a mixed texture and color effects, used by women for sportswear.

parti-colored surcoat over gown-French-15th C.

parti-colored hose and shoes-brocaded jerkin-Dalmatian sleeves-cap with jewel-English-13th C.

parti-colored hose-satin "gown" with velvet collar and lining-slashed sleeves-velvet cap-Italian-15th C.

pashm, pashim, pashmina Persian word for wool; the underfleece of the Tibetan goat, used for scarfs, shawls and other items.

passementerie of cotton, silk, metal and galloon and appliquéd embroidery fashioned of beads, guimpe, fringe, tassels and cording. Used for costumes of theater, church and military.

paste jewelry A lead-glass compound with considerable brilliancy used for imitation jewelry, invented by Joseph Strasser, a German jeweler, and often called Strass. The Louis XV and XVI periods are designated by connoisseurs as "the golden age of paste," the French strass being unsurpassed in design, delicacy and finish. It was worn by the aristocracy and was considered more of a substitute for, than an imitation of valuable ornaments.

pastel color a term for soft, delicate hues.

patadyong the traditional costume of Philippine women, each tribe having its own distinctive dress.

patch pocket see *pocket, patch.*

patches, mouches in ancient Rome men and women made use of the beauty spot or patch of Oriental origin. The patches were of soft leather, the Romans being skilled in the preparation of fine leather. It is recorded that the Romans, when speaking from the Tribune, wore patches. The patch was intended to simulate the mole, which was considered a beauty mark. The fashion came from Italy in the sixteenth century, called by the English "patching the face." Also worn in the seventeenth century, of black velvet, taffeta or court plaster, and carried in tiny jeweled boxes. Patches were placed near the eyes, on the cheeks the throat and breasts. Black silk patches, gummed, became fashionable in the second half of the seventeenth century, and ladies carried them in exquisite little boxes. Mouches, as the French called them because they looked like flies, were cut in various shapes such as flowers, crescents, stars, even figures and animals. Patches were first worn in Venice in the mid-sixteenth century by the ladies of the court, hence the name "court plaster."

patchwork pieces of cloth, silk or leather of varying color and shape, sewn together to form a conventional design or, as in a quilt, a "crazy quilt" arrangement. Patchwork madras is used today in separate sports skirts and in men's sports shirts.

patent leather see *leather, patent.*

patola a wedding sari made in Gujarat, India, of a silk cloth woven in Chinese technique and known as chiné.

pattens; clogs footwear fashioned of wood, oak or poplar, raised off the ground very often by an iron ring and fastened to the foot by leather straps. They were most necessary in bad weather and when crossing the cobbled pavements. Clogs were also made of wood covered with silk to match the dainty slippers of the eighteenth century. Men, women and children wore clogs on cobbled pavements in European cities and in the American Colonies.

patadyong-Philippine traditional dress-wide-arched sleeves of rengue or pine-apple cloth

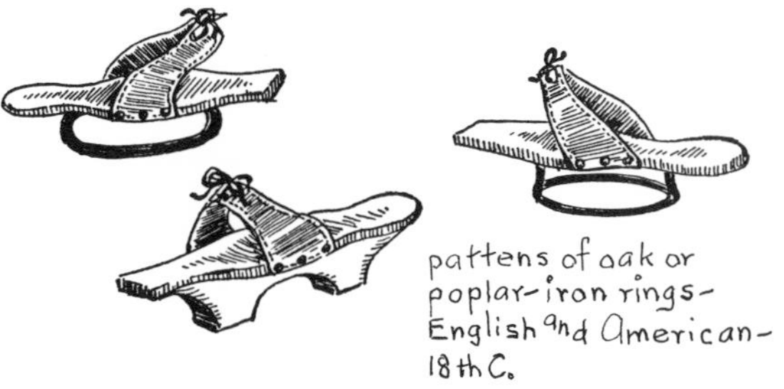

pattens of oak or poplar-iron rings-English and American-18th C.

pattern in British usage, a small sample or swatch.

patterns, dress see *paper patterns.*

pattu, patteo, pattoo an East Indian shawl woven in Punjab and Kashmir. Woven also as homespun woolen cloth and tweed yardage.

pavé from the French for pavement. A jeweled setting in which the stones are set together closely to cover a metal ground.

pea or **pilot jacket** a heavy, short coat worn by sailors from 1850 on. Of closely woven cloth in dark blue. Used as a model for small boys' coats in lighter weight.

peacock feathers The peacock was introduced into England, France and Germany in the fourteenth century. The long, gorgeously colored, gold-tipped tail feathers became the favored hat ornament for prelates and nobles. The vogue lasted several centuries until the feather was finally supplanted by ostrich plumes brought from Africa.

peacockery when said of a man, meaning vanity and ostentatious display of fine clothes.

peak or **peaked lapel** a lapel which rises to a sharp point, leaving a space between the peak and collar point.

pearl the result of a dense nacre concretion formed within the shell of some mollusks. The form is variable and there are many colors, the first having a silvery or satiny luster. The best specimens are from the pearl oyster and are very costly. The pearl was a favorite jewel in the sixteenth century, worn in the coiffure, sewn to women's gowns and a single drop pearl earring worn by gentlemen. A single string around a feminine throat became classic.

pearlies the British name for costermongers, a name for apple vendors in past times. Their dress worn yearly at Epsom Downs on Derby Day is covered with white pearl buttons. Sometimes a whole family, including children, will appear so attired. A custom still observed once a year.

pearls, baroque irregular in shape but lustrous and rich in coloring.

pearls, cultured or **Oriental** so called in the trade, first appeared about 1915. An irritant on which the pearl forms is placed in the shell and the oyster kept in a seed bed for a number of years. A process invented by the Japanese.

pearls, imitation or **simulated** a process perfected by Jaquin of Paris about 1680. Hollow blown glass is filled with essence composed of silvery particles left in the water in which whitebait has been washed.

pearls, natural the natural pearl forms when a small irritant such as a grain of sand accidently becomes lodged in an oyster's shell.

pearls, seed very small pearls, often irregular in shape. Used in embroidery of women's costume and accessories, especially small handbags. They were popular in Victorian jewelry when the pearls were strung on horsehair and mounted in elaborate patterns to form brooches, earrings, etc., a craft requiring painstaking skill and handwork. Still in vogue today for evening bags and some bridal attire.

peasant blouse of the Central European countries, a full blouse usually of soft white voile with a round smock-stitched neck and long full sleeves smock-stitched into wrist size with short ruffles, the smocking done in red or dark blue embroidery cotton. Popular and worn with the full dirndl skirts in the 1930's and 1940's.

peasant cloth a gaily dyed or printed stout muslin popular for dirndl and play clothes.

peasant costume the regional dress of people who have retained the original basic design and artistic qualities of their ancestors' clothes. Such garments reveal the influence of religion, superstition and historical events on earlier natives, and are often an inspiration to modern designers.

peasant lace a coarse, unimpressive bobbin lace like torchon, made by European peasants.

peasant sleeve see *sleeve, peasant.*

peasecod-bellied doublet an extreme fashion of Spanish origin of the fifteenth and sixteenth centuries. The stuffed doublet had a wooden busk in front for shape. Worn with trunk hose.

peau d'ange French for angel skin; a popular silk early in the twentieth century.

peau de soie a plain-colored, firm and soft silk fabric with the same dull finish on both sides. Used for evening dresses and trimmings.

pebble grain, pebble goat a leather, imitation leather or fabric given a grained surface by running it between rollers under pressure.

pebble weave a rough-surfaced fabric produced by weaving together shrunken, twisted yarns.

peccary, pecari, pecary a wild boar native to Mexico, Central and South America. The leather, limited in quantity, is fine-grained, lightweight pig leather.

pectoral a decorative, jeweled breastplate worn by Egyptian kings and Hebrew high priests. The breastplate of the Roman military was of leather and that of the Gauls was copper. A pectoral cross is a cross worn on the breast by bishops and abbots. The ancient Hebrew pectoral was composed of two large square plaques, one hanging in front and one in back joined by gold chains over the shoulders. The front plaque was set with twelve jewels on which were engraved the names of the twelve tribes.

pedal pushers see *pant lengths, feminine.*

pedule a rawhide boot of northern medieval Europe. Sometimes boots and breeches were made in one.

peek-a-boo blouse a shirtwaist of sheer lawn, voile or eyelet embroidery, a popular fashion of the 1890's and the first decade of the twentieth century. It was worn over a lacy, frilled corset cover.

peg-top skirt, tonneau or **barrel** silhouette of 1912 with bouffant fullness around the hips sloping in to the ankles. Introduced by Paquin.

peg-top trousers trousers which were cut wide and full around the hips, slim-

pelisse of gray cloth with mink collar and cuffs-fastened with brandenburgs French-1823

pelisse-brown cashmere lined with wadding and mauve silk-white fur-gray felt bonnet with feathers-1833

ming down sharply to the ankles; first decade of the twentieth century. Later, a widespread fashion in the 1950's.

pekin a handsome dress silk, originally from China, with warp-wise alternating stripes of velvet and satin in contrasting colors.

pegged boot or **shoe** leather shoes with the sole fastened to the uppers by wooden pegs.

peignoir a lingerie jacket or robe tied at the neck; literally a combing jacket or gown, the name founded upon the French word for comb, *peign.* Worn since the sixteenth century when it was fashioned of printed cottons, velvet or brocade. Today, the available modern synthetic fabrics present a wide choice of handsome materials for the garment.

pelerine literally, a pilgrim's cloak; in the nineteenth century a feminine short cape with long ends in front. It was made of light or heavy silk, velvet or fur, according to season. see *palatine.*

pelisse a cloak popular from the twelfth to the fifteenth centuries and worn by men and women. A full-length robe wadded with cotton or lined with fur, with long sleeves. Sometimes the lady's train was so long that a page was needed to carry it. In the early nineteenth century the feminine pelisse again acquired popularity, following the Empire mode, high-waisted, long-sleeved, fur-lined and fur-trimmed in all lengths and styles including the spencer, hussar and canezou jacket. Men also wore the pelisse, fur-lined and fur-trimmed.

pellon a trade name of a fabric made by a process patented in 1951, neither woven, knitted nor felted. Of several weights and thicknesses, in black and white, it is used as interlining and shape preserver.

peltries see *animal skins.*

penang a heavy cotton percale from Penang, Malaysia. Originally made in Calcutta and then made in England.

pencil stripe in weaving, stripes which are two or three warps wide, of contrasting color on a ground of solid color.

penelope British for a sleeveless, knitted jacket.

peniche lace a Portuguese bobbin or pillow lace made with a large mesh ground, either black or white. Can be made in two ways: executing the design first and then working the reseau around it; or working it in one piece, forming pattern and ground of the same thread.

penistone a coarse woolen cloth made from the sixteenth to the nineteenth centuries in Penistone, Yorkshire, England. It was used for cloaks and dresses. Also known as "forest white."

penitentials a colloquial English term for garments worn by "penitents" in black or "penitential stripes."

peplos the bloused section worn over the chiton in ancient Greece. A rectangle of woolen fabric, unsewn and fastened on the shoulders, it hung in arranged folds weighted with lead pellets. The Greek woman's gown which had various names and was costly.

peplum to the ancient peplos of Greece it was an outer tunic while the modern peplum is usually a short flounce or overskirt suspended from bodice or belt. A woman's garment.

péplum impératrice of the 1860's named after the French Empress, Eugénie. It was a basque bodice with a draped-up tunic or panniers.

pepper and salt mixture a combination of black and white yarns twisted together and woven into cloth, giving the effect of a dark or light ground sprinkled with dark or light specks.

percale similar to cambric; plain-woven cotton fabric with a firm, smooth finish. It is printed in shirting patterns and used for pajamas and sportswear.

perfumery The use of perfumes goes back to the ancients of Biblical times when sweet-smelling odors were concocted from the juices of herbs and flowers. They were used by men and women both for religious rites and to enhance their own persons, using a pomade which they made up. It is said that in ancient Rome the use of perfume may have surpassed that of all time. It was available in liquid, solid and powdered form and was applied not only to the body, but to all articles and possessions.

The making of perfume was revived in Renaissance Italy, founded upon the knowledge brought back from the Orient by the Crusaders. René, an Italian perfumer, opened the first perfume shop in Paris about 1500, and by the mid-sixteenth century perfume pervaded all Europe. Many scents were thought to possess miraculous powers of healing as well as beautifying. Perfumes and toilet water were used by men in the eighteenth century. Frenchmen used eau de cologne and Englishmen lavender water, but American men frowned upon the use of scents of any kind. However, such items do appear in the accounts of George Washington. A truly American after-shave lotion, "Florida Water," is still catalogued today and claims to have been a favorite since 1808.

Only the most delicate flower perfumes were used by American women until the twentieth century. In modern commercial usage cologne is a less concentrated form of perfume and toilet water is even weaker than cologne. see *toiletries.*

peridot a green gem stone of the olivine mineral family.

periwig wigs and false hair had been a periodic fashion through the centuries but the last revival and rage occurred about the middle of the seventeenth century. The French word perruque became peruke in English, then perwyke, periwig and finally just plain wig. A set of ringlets, a corner of hair, or a single curl was also a wig. It was predominantly a masculine fashion until the mid-twentieth century but the wig is still a wig in feminine parlance and the masculine item is a hairpiece. see *wig.*

permanent wave, permanent the vogue of the Marcel wave in the 1890's and the early twentieth century led to the invention of the permanent wave in 1906 by Charles Nestlé, a fashionable coiffeur in London. The permanent wave was first applied by an electric heat machine; a later method using lotions instead of heat was called a cold wave. This method has the advantage of making it possible to curl the hair right to the head, obviating the need of thick protective pads, and is much faster and safer than the machine method.

permanent press see *durable press.*

perpetuana or **petuna** a woolen cloth, glossy and durable, resembling parchment in texture. Worn by the Puritans in the American Colonies, in the seventeenth and eighteenth centuries. Made in England.

Persian a tiara or bonnet of wool or leather worn by the Persian and Arabic nobleman of ancient times, in Phrygian style, over his frizzed hair. see *tāj.*

Persian costume, ancient see illustrations on next page.

Persian embroidery Ancient garments were elaborately embroidered. Appliqué work originated with the Persians in place of all-over needlework. Their contemporary embroidery features types of drawnwork, darned work and appliqué,

péplum impératrice-gray cashmere over royal blue silk-blue velvet ribbon and buttons-French-1871

Persian

leather or felt
costume over
linen shirt
and loincloth-
Persian-
6th c. B.C.
silk kandys
over linen
shirt and
loincloth-
Median-
6th c. B.C.

silk and linen
costume worn over
white linen shirt
and loincloth-
Persian-
4th c. B.C.
embroidered or
dyed linen
loincloth-
Lycian-
1400 B.C.

the designs outlined in dark color and completely filled in by various filling stitches.

Persian lamb see *lamb, Persian.*

perspective glass see *quizzing glass.*

peruke the English form of *perruque* which became perwyke or periwig and finally wig. see *periwig.*

Peruvian costume, traditional see illustrations.

perwitsky European name for fitch or polecat. see *fitch.*

perwyke see *periwig.*

petal-scalloped see *dagged.*

petasos, petasus a hat worn by the ancient Greeks, wide-brimmed and low-crowned, of felt or straw. The two-winged cap of the Greek Hermes and Roman Mercury was a petasos, as was the pointed-crowned hat of the Boeotian woman.

Peter Pan the blouse or shirt of the costume worn by the young hero of Sir James Barrie's play, "Peter Pan." With a belted, Russian-styled tunic, he wore a round collar, bow tie and knee breeches, an ensemble which became popular for small boys. see *Peter Pan collar.*

Peter Thompson frock a girl's private school uniform worn early in the twentieth century, designed by a navy tailor, Peter Thompson. It was a belted one-piece dress of dark blue serge or white linen with sailor collar, long sleeves and a body pleated from yoke to hem.

petersham a heavy wool overcoating with a rough, knotty surface formerly called nigger-head. A finer, softer example is known as chinchilla.

petit gris see *grays.*

petit point any embroidery worked on canvas with sixteen or more mesh per inch. There is no special petit point stitch as such. see *gros point.*

petticoat an underskirt, in modern usage. In the fourteenth century the "petticote" was an undercoat worn by both sexes, shorter than the outer coat. The feminine version was worn under an open gown and developed into a handsomely decorated skirt which was retained as an underskirt after gowns were no longer designed with an open front. see *slip, pettipants, crinoline.*

petticoat breeches see *rhinegrave breeches, petticoat.*

pettipants, snuggies twentieth century feminine winter underpants of nylon, knitted wool or wool jersey in colors and black, knee-length and close-fitting.

petuna see *perpetuana.*

Philippine costume the formal gown has a fichu and elbow-length, wide-arched butterfly sleeves of stiffly starched gauze. The skirt is floor-length with a pointed train. For tribal dress, see *patadyong; barong; tagalog; saya.*

Philippine embroidery fine handwork in dainty floral motifs done by native women in the Philippine Islands.

phrygium the Phrygian cap of white woolen material worn by the popes of the Middle Ages at nonliturgical ceremonies. The cap later developed into the papal tiara. see *bonnet, Phrygian.*

phulkari Hindu word for embroidery; principally an embroidered flower pattern. Also the flower-embroidered cloth worn as shawl or mantle by the Anglo-Indian. see *chuddar.*

piccadil, pickadil, piccadilly scalloped or castellated edgings of collars or jackets in the seventeenth century. On a

Peruvian aristocrat of pure Spanish ancestry-embroidered shawl over tortoise shell comb

Peruvian caballero habit-black and red velvet-cordovan charaparos or chaps-black leather boots

Philippine traditional, formal dress—wide-arched sleeves and fichu of pineapple cloth—skirt called SAYA

fashionable street in London lived a tailor who specialized in piccadills or edgings for ruffs. He became known as the "piccadilly tailor" and in later years the road was named for them.

picot an edging formed of very tiny loops on cloth, ribbon, lace or braid.

picoté adjective meaning edged or finished with picot, either by machine or hand-done.

picture hat a wide-brimmed, richly trimmed hat, such as in Gainsborough's portraits of ladies. Banded with wide satin ribbon, weighted with gorgeous ostrich plumes and worn atop a stunning wig. see *hat, Gainsborough.*

pie-plate or **pie-tin cap** the name given the flat-top cap worn by the sailors of the United States Navy in the nineteenth century. Of Tam'o' Shanter shape, it was held in form by a metal hoop. White cotton for summer and navy; blue woolen cloth for winter wear.

piece-dyed fabrics, of wool, cotton or silk dyed in the piece or after weaving.

Pilgrim in brown cloak, hat and jerkin—sleeves red and yellow—yellow breeches with frills—white lawn collar and cuffs—spur leathers on boots

Pilgrim—underskirt and sleeve puff, violet cloth—cap, capes, sleeve and cuff of lawn—fur muff—felt hat.

pierrette costume the feminine counterpart of Pierrot wore a tight bodice of black or vivid-colored velvet with full white satin sleeves and skirt, muslin ruffs at neck and wrists and a peaked cap decorated with a pompon.

pierrot a character of Italian Commedia dell'Arte, seventeenth century. He wore a voluminous smock and long, wide breeches of white satin with white pompons. The costume also included soft white slippers and a black felt calotte. The face painted white with black-arched eyebrows, red lips.

pigeon's wings a feature of the man's powdered wig; loosely rolled puffs over the ears. First half of the eighteenth century. see *wig, bag.*

pigskin a stout, coarse-grained leather made of hog's hide. It has a decorative surface caused by bristle holes and is long-wearing and durable. Most pigskin comes from China.

pigtail in general, any tight braid of hair hanging down the back; specifically, the Chinese queue.

pigtail wig see *wig, pigtail.*

piked or **peaked shoes** see *poulaines.*

pile a thick surface of standing threads as in velvet, produced by an extra set of warp or filling yarns which are later cut and sheared. It is to be distinguished from a cloth in which a nap lies flat.

pileus The Greek pilos became the Etruscan and Roman pileus, a close-fitting cap with chinstrap. It was worn by soldiers and sailors and also by athletes at festivals and public games.

Pilgrims the earliest colonists of New England. They wore the contemporary dress of seventeenth century England. see illustrations.

pillbox a small round hat of stiffened fabric, originally of silk or velvet sewn with pearls and worn over the chignon in eighteenth century Italy, now usually worn by women on the back of the head. see *bellboy's cap.*

pillow lace see *bobbin lace.*

piloi a short, felt sock of sheep or goat's hair worn by farmers in northern Greece in winter.

pilot cloth a dark blue woolen cloth, coarse, strong and thick, twilled with a nap on one side. Used for sailors' jackets and overcoats.

pilot jacket see *pea jacket.*

pima a fine, strong cotton developed in Pima County, Arizona, a cross between Sea Island and Egyptian cotton. Used for tire fabrics, balloon and airplane cloths.

pin, common originally a shank of brass wire with one end bent into a head. In the thirteenth and fourteenth centuries pins were costly, hence the expression "pin money." Englishwomen of all classes saved their money to buy pins on the first two days of January, as Parliament permitted pin merchants but two days a year on which to sell their pins. A tax was levied on the common people to pay for the English queen's pins. An act of 1483 prohibited the further import of pins so that by 1626 most ordinary pins were English. As late as 1812 the ordinary pin of brass and wire-bound head of English make was still a luxury costing as much as a dollar for a small package. In 1831, in the United States, the first successful machine for making solid-headed pins was invented by John Ireland Howe of New York.

pin, safety developed from the ancient Greek fibula, at least 2000 years old; shaped with a loop at one end to furnish spring, with the point held by a protective hood. The modern version was invented by Walter Hunt, an American, in 1849.

piña cloth a cloth woven from leaf fibers of the pineapple plant, chiefly in the Philippine Islands. Transparent, crisp and delicate, it is used for handkerchiefs, scarfs, dainty shawls and lace grounds.

pinafore a sleeveless dress buttoned in back which can be worn over a blouse or chemisette, or by itself as an informal warm weather play dress; worn by women and little girls and generally made of cotton. It resembles the jumper dress but is distinguished from it by being buttoned instead of slip-on. Black sateen pinafores were once worn in school by both girls and boys to protect their other clothes, a custom which still survives in France.

pince-nez eyeglasses which are held to the eyes by a tiny spring which clips the nose. see *eyeglasses.*

pinchbeck an alloy of copper and zinc used for imitation jewelry. It was invented by a London watchmaker, Christopher Pinchbeck. see *gilt.*

pincheck minute squares of color produced by interweaving colored yarns, creating a confetti look.

pine marten see *marten, baum.*

pinking an ornamental jagged edge given to fabric by a small machine with a ribbed roller or by the use of pinking shears, which have blades with a sawtooth inner edge. Also used as a seam finish, to prevent raveling.

pinner a small dainty apron of exquisite workmanship which was pinned over the front of a gown in the seventeenth and eighteenth centuries; worn by ladies-in-waiting. In the nineteenth century, pinners were often the badge of the parlor

modern pillbox pinned to chignon-Dior-1951

maid. Children's aprons were also called pinners. see *apron.*

pinner or **flandan** of the eighteenth century; a lace-edged cap of white batiste with two floating lappets in back.

pins see *bar pin; breastpin; brooch; clip brooch; fibula.*

pin-striped in weaving on a solid ground, a stripe slightly thicker than a hairline stripe.

piping a very narrow bias fold or cord, usually of contrasting color, used as an edging or seam-finish in dressmaking.

piqué a stout, ribbed cotton fabric, sometimes of silk or rayon. Also woven in figured patterns and in a fine waffle piqué. Popular for women's dresses, blouses, separate collars and cuffs, men's shirts, waistcoats, scarfs and evening ties.

pirnie or **pirny** a Scottish nightcap of striped woolen cloth.

pistole pocket see *pocket, pistole.*

pith helmet see *topee, topi.*

placket a fold of fabric sewn to the underside of an opening in a dress to which buttons, hooks and eyes or snap fasteners were sewn. Every closure had a placket, very often secured by attached strings. The slide fastener or "zipper" eventually solved the problem with expertise.

plaid a tartan pattern of bars of varied colors crossing each other at right angles. Also, the name used by the Scots for a traveling shawl or rug or scarf in a plaid pattern. see *Scottish Highland dress.*

plain weave the simplest form of weave with the threads interlacing alternately at right angles. Also known as taffeta weave.

plait a flat fold or doubling back of cloth. see *pleat.*

plaited hair long hair braided by entwining three or more strands, one over the other, producing a ropelike contexture.

planter's hat see *hat, Panama.*

plastic a man-made substance capable of being molded into a form or textile.

plastron a metal breast plate in medieval armor; a protective padded breastplate worn by the fencer; an ornamental stomacher laced to a woman's bodice as in peasant dress. see *stomacher.*

platform sole a thick sole of cork or wood. see *wedge heel.*

platina fox see *fox, platina.*

platinum, platina a precious metallic element, noncorroding and grayish-white. Found as grains and nuggets in neutral gray, slightly bluish with brilliance. Made into fine jewelry and set with precious stones. Found in the Ural Mountains and Colombia.

platok see *babushka.*

Plauen lace of Plauen, Germany. A lace pattern embroidered on muslin, net and such and treated chemically to burn out the fabric ground.

pleated bosom a man's white shirt for formal or semiformal day wear or semiformal evening wear. Soft or starched pleats of identical or varying widths.

pleats or **plaits** a series of folds of cloth. In accordion pleating, the fabric is pressed so that creases of equal length alternate inward and outward; in sunburst pleating used especially in skirts, the folds gradually increase in depth. In knife pleating the folds are doubled over so that only one crease shows and these creases all point in the same direction; in box pleating the folds are in pairs, one crease pointing right and the other left.

pleats, inverted box pleats in reverse.

pleats, kick short, inverted pleat about four or five inches high, from the hem, placed in center back or sides of a narrow skirt for extra walking freedom.

pleats, sunburst a type of machine-pleating used especially in skirts; the pleats radiate from waist to hem, narrowest at the top and gradually widening to the bottom.

pleats, unpressed unstitched pleats, as in a skirt, left to flare for a soft effect.

pleats, Watteau loose box pleats or pleats falling in center back from neck to waist, then free from waist to skirt. Eighteenth century.

plumage since the passing of the Audubon Plumage Law only wings or plumes of goose or chicken feathers are permitted for trimming. United States. see *Audubon plumage law.*

plume three upstanding ostrich feathers with a veil are worn with English court dress, indicating that the wearer has been "presented" to the Sovereign. They are worn slightly to the left side of the head with the tulle veil not longer than forty-five inches. This is a survival of a fashion at the court of Marie Antoinette. The three ostrich feathers which are the crest of the Prince of Wales have their origin in the arms of Anne of Bohemia, consort of Richard II (1367–1400). The custom of court presentations has been discontinued by Queen Elizabeth II.

plumpers "beautifiers" which appeared in 1690; small, round, light balls of cork which elderly ladies carried in their cheeks to fill out the sunken spots, probably due to loss of teeth.

plus fours knickers for sportswear, voluminous in width and length, late 1920's. The term originated in the British Army when breeches were measured as reaching to the knees, plus four inches.

plush a fabric with pile higher than velvet. Can be made from most of the principal textile fibers; has a wide usage in imitation furs.

pocket, bellows an outside jacket or coat pocket especially adapted to hunting and shooting. Bellowed pleats on the outside give added space and a buttoned flap keeps the pocket closed. see *saddle bag pocket.*

pocket, panniers see *pannier pockets.*

pocket, patch a pocket made of the garment's fabric, matching weave and design in its application; sewn to the outside of the garment.

pocket, pistole formerly, the right hip trousers pocket, in which a gun could be carried.

pocket, saddle bag pockets of self fabric with pleats and buttoned-down flap applied to a man's sports jacket or coat. see *pocket, bellows.*

pocket, slashed a pocket on the inner side of the garment, reached by a finished slash on the outer side, with a flap over the opening.

pocketbook the reticule or dressmaker type of pouch bag with drawstring top, the bag of nearly two centuries, was finally replaced by the leather pocketbook in the 1890's, a flat, folding booklet-shaped purse with compartments closed by a silver or gold ornamental latch. It was very little larger than today's wallet.

plume-court headdress-three ostrich tips and floating veil-jeweled stars-English 1890's

The sabretache of fabric or leather of the Directoire Period returned in the early twentieth century and from then on, women's leather handbags became more functional, spacious and handsome. see *handbag.*

pockets, feminine originally made in pairs and sewn to a tape which was tied around the waist. With farthingale, overskirt or panniers the pocket could be worn under the skirt. This fashion was prevalent c. 1650–1850, when pockets began to be inserted in skirt seams. The old pockets were often embroidered and many beautiful examples of such work have survived.

pockets, masculine up to the Middle Ages there were no pockets in clothes. Money and necessary small articles were carried tied in a kerchief or a square of cloth. This evolved into small bags or sacs drawn closed at the top by cords, fastened to the belt and used by both sexes. Small articles like coins and keys were later carried in the codpiece, a small box or bag first designed to conceal the front opening of trunk hose of the fifteenth and sixteenth centuries. Pockets were inserted in the trunk hose of the sixteenth century. see *aumônière; codpiece.*

poet's collar see *collar, poet's.*

point d'Alençon embroidery see *Appenzell embroidery.*

point d'Angleterre a bobbin lace which originated in Brussels and was smuggled into England as English lace to avoid import duty. Later, it was actually made in England.

point de gaz lace fine needlepoint with a delicate net ground having looped meshes decorated with a realistic floral pattern. Made chiefly in Brussels, and also called Brussels rose-point lace.

point d'esprit a fine cotton or net with tiny dots, a Normandy lace with square or oval dots, or old guipure lace with a small figure.

point de Paris a narrow bobbin lace with flat design on a hexagonal mesh ground. Also, a machine-made lace resembling Val lace but with a heavier outline pattern.

point plat French for flat point lace or tulle, as opposed to raised or relief work with cordonnet.

pointed fox see *fox, pointed.*

points see *aglet.*

Poiret, Paul (1880–1944) one of the greatest of French designers. He was the first to place the belt just under the bosom in true Empire style and he was responsible for the open-necked kimono bodice eliminating the set-in sleeve and high collar. He admired Oriental colors, often using brilliant hues of green, cerise, vermilion, royal blue and purple. Best known for his tunics and the hobble skirt, 1910–1914.

Poiret twill a fine dress cloth named for the French couturier, Paul Poiret. A twill-woven fabric similar to gabardine but smoother and made also of rayon or wool blends.

poke bonnet see *bonnet, coal scuttle.*

poke collar see *collar, poke.*

polar seal see *seal, imitations.*

polecat see *fitch.*

Polish costume, traditional see illustrations.

polished silk called beaver, was invented in Florence, Italy, and not perfected until 1823.

Polish bridal costume of Lowicz-brilliant, deep colors-black velvet bodice, sheer white blouse-huge headdress of fresh flowers-leather boots

Polish peasant dress-red or blue jacket-white linen shirt-cap with panache of onion plant and ribbon

polka dot a printed pattern on silk, linen or cotton with alternating round dots, but evenly spaced. New in the first half of the nineteenth century and popular for generations. Polka dots still worn today for dresses, blouses and scarfs.

pollera the national feminine costume of Panama, based upon the colonial dress of Spanish ladies. Of soft white voile, it has a waist-deep flaring bertha, embroidered in red and black. There are yards and yards of hand embroidery on bodice and skirt and as many yards of fine lace. The lady wears a coiffure of quivering, sparkling flowers and pearls on tiny springs.

polo cloth a napped camel's hair and wool mixture for coating. In natural colors and dyed any color. Trademarked by the Worumbo Company.

polo coat the twentieth century all-around coat for man or woman of natural color camel's hair; evolved from the British wait coat thrown over the shoulders between periods of play of a sport. see *camel's hair coat.*

polo coat-natural color camel's hair-horn buttons-soft felt hat-1936

polo shirt a man's summer shirt, usually a pull-on of white knit cotton with round neck or Peter Pan collar.

pollera, national Panama dress hand-embroidered in deep color-yards and yards of fine lace

polonaise gown a feminine fashion from 1776 to 1787. Its special feature consisted of three panniers, one in back and two side sections which rounded away in front. The panniers of the polonaise were drawn up on cords and could also be let down to form a "flying gown." The cords were run through rings or tape loops, and were finished with tassels and rosettes, although later the panniers were sewn in position with the cords simply ornamental.

polyester a generic name as ruled by the Federal Trade Commission for the man-made fiber composed largely of dihydric alcohol and terephthalic acid.

Polonaise gown with three panniers-striped and plain silk-cords, tassels and ruches-French-1776

pompadour in marcel wave created by Marcel of Paris-1903

Used for wash-and-wear apparel when combined with cotton, rayon and other man-made filaments.

poncho-Mexican vaquero or cowboy-white with dark blue-felt sombrero

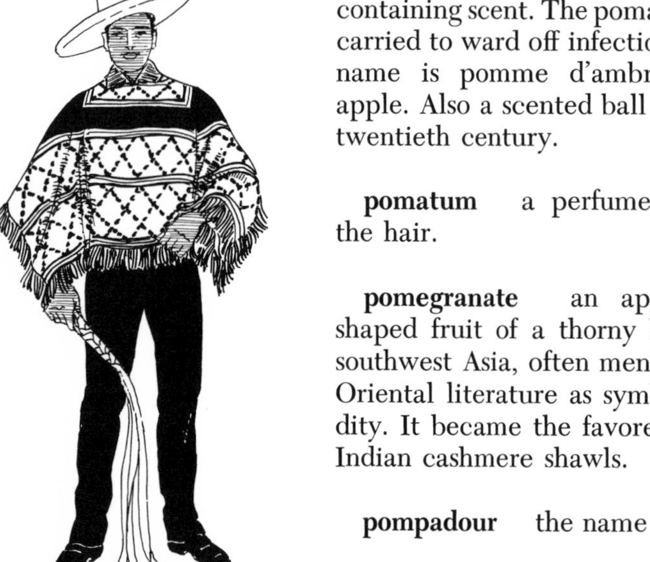

pomander sixteenth and seventeenth centuries; a small apple-shaped ball of gold or silver filigree which held a ball of musk, ambergris or other perfume. It was worn on a chain around the neck or suspended from a lady's girdle. Men, especially dandies, carried a pomander in the hand, often of hollowed-out oranges containing scent. The pomander was often carried to ward off infection. The French name is pomme d'ambre, or scented apple. Also a scented ball for wardrobes, twentieth century.

pomatum a perfumed unguent for the hair.

pomegranate an apple- or pear-shaped fruit of a thorny bush native to southwest Asia, often mentioned in early Oriental literature as symbolic of fecundity. It became the favored motif of the Indian cashmere shawls.

pompadour the name of various features of the period of the Marquise de Pompadour (1721–1764), mistress of Louis XV of France. Her simple and distinctive coiffure, the hair brushed up off her face and up in back, gave its name to the pompadour style which periodically returns to favor. Worn by the Gibson girl in the 1890's and at the turn of the century. Other Pompadour items are flowered taffeta, laces, velvet ribbons, small dainty aprons, etc.

pompons ornamental colored balls of wool, feathers, silk or felt, used mostly on caps.

poncho of the South American Indian; a square of rough woolen cloth hand loomed with broad stripes of brilliant color, worn largely by Spanish-Americans. It has a hole in the center for the head, reaches below the waist and is worn by men and women. It is both cloak and blanket. Also, a waterproof garment of similar shape worn in England and America as a raincoat.

pongee a summer fabric in natural color, rough woven in tussah, a thin silk. Used in men's and women's suits and sportswear. see *tussah; shantung; nankeen.*

poncho in bright colors-hand-woven and fringed-hole in center for the head-Peruvian Incan Indian

pony-skin a fashion new at the beginning of the twentieth century; durable, lustrous, flat fur from the young colt or foal, at times resembling moiré karakul. From Poland, Russian Europe, Baltic states, South America and China, the Chinese fur poor. Colors beige, gray or black; dyed, bleached or used natural for coats and jackets.

poodle cloth a fabric knitted or woven with a knotted or looped woolly surface resembling the coat of a French poodle dog.

poor boy sweater a fashion of the 1960's, beginning in France; a knitted, vertical ribbed wool usually black, a collarless pullover sweater which clings to the figure. Worn by young women.

poplin a lightweight ribbed fabric woven like grosgrain. Of linen or cotton warp with wool or nylon filling, usually plain-dyed; used for both masculine and feminine apparel.

poplin, Irish see *Irish poplin.*

porosity the porous quality of a summer fabric with meshlike spaces for coolness.

porpoise a good-quality leather for stout shoes; really the hide of white whale, dressed for hunting and fishing boots.

Portegaz, Mañuel see *couture, haute.*

portmonnaie French for the pocketbook or hand purse carried by women in the late nineteenth century. see *pocketbook.*

Portuguese costume, traditional see illustration.

possum see *opossum*

postiche literally, artificial. A hairpiece or wig. In ancient Egypt men wore no beard or moustache, but the pharaohs and high dignitaries wore the postiche or false beard, with which a woman, if queen, also adorned herself. The postiche was attached to a chinstrap, gold no doubt, which was part of a frame or cap worn under the bonnet or wig. Postiche today, a feminine hairpiece worn in addition to the wearer's own hair.

posy a nosegay, small bouquet or a single flower.

pouch a small handbag for carrying small articles.

pouf a stuffed cushion or cushions worn under panniers. Also a small, hair-stuffed cushion worn under the high puffs of the Louis XVI coiffures.

poulaines, crackowes or **piked shoes** the style for dandies, mid-fourteenth century to about 1480. The long, pointed toes grew to such lengths that it became necessary to hold up the stuffed points by gold chains attached to the ankles or knees.

Portuguese of Aveiro in traditional dress-red sash and jacket-black trousers-black and red hat-silver buttons with braid loops

"poor boy sweater" a phase of the "mod" trend in black-worn with straightened hair-1960's

poulaine or piked shoe of heavy leather-French-medieval-14th C.

poulaine-blue leather laced on inner side-wooden patten-French-15th C.

Noblemen were permitted toe lengths of two feet and gentlemen, one foot; the commoner could extend only six inches beyond his toes. The shoes originated in Cracow, Poland, and became fashionable at all European courts. The French called them poulaines after Poland and the English crackowes after Cracow.

pounce a powder in a pouncet box to rub over thin perforated paper, thus transferring a design to a fabric to be embroidered.

pourpoint see *gambeson; jerkin; action.*

poussin lace a type of Valenciennes bobbin lace made in Dieppe, France. Narrow and delicate, its net resembling the square of chicken wire; hence its name, French for a young chicken.

powder see *cosmetics.*

power lace or **net** made of thin rubber on a bobbinette machine, used mostly for girdles, corsets, brassières. The fabric stretches in all directions; new in 1966.

pre-shrunk a manufacturer's term for fabric processed to guard against shrinking over three per cent in a standard test.

prête-à-porter French for ready-made clothes.

pretintailles of the late seventeenth century and Louis XIV period; cut-out motifs of lace and embroidery appliquéd or gummed to the skirts of gowns, making an elaborate ornamentation.

Prince Albert frock coat see *frock coat.*

princess gown a gown made of fitted sections and worn over a crinoline. Appeared first in the 1860's, a favored fashion of the first decade of the twentieth century. see *gabrielle.*

Prince Albert frockcoat-satin-faced lapels-high collar-gray silk Ascot scarf-trousers-black with gray stripes-silk top hat-white spats-English-1906

princess lace a very fine imitation of Duchesse lace, with the motifs usually applied by hand.

princess silhouette the lines of a dress or coat, usually gored, close-fitting to the waist and flaring to the hem. A recurring fashion in the twentieth century.

prunella, prunelle a woolen cloth in smooth or twill weave of the eighteenth and nineteenth centuries; much used for academic and clerical robes, as well as a dress fabric.

psyche knot a hair style with a chignon at the back of the neck, copied from representations in Greek art of the mythological princess loved by Cupid. see *chignon.*

Pucci, Emilio see *couture, haute.*

puce or **flea color** a deep reddish-brown color of which there are many

princess gown-white batiste, Valenciennes lace, embroidery, fine tucks-black straw hat with aigrettes-1909

hues. Made fashionable by Marie Antoinette.

puffed sleeve see *sleeve, puffed.*

puffing a form of dress trimming in bands of gathered and puffed fabric. see *panes; slashings.*

puggree, pugaree the Hindu turban or hatband of many spellings. For the turban, a wide strip of cotton plain or striped, five to twenty-five yards long wrapped round the head in varied styles, often with a hanging end in back. Around a sun helmet or the crown of a straw hat, a wide, soft, pleated silk band, plain, figured or striped. It originated as a sun protection and is widely copied in western dress.

pull-on or **pull-over; slip-on** or **slip-over** pertaining to any garment without front, side or back opening, put on by slipping it on over the head. A glove, sweater or girdle without opening is a pull-on or slip-on.

Pulitzer, Lilly see *couture, haute.*

pump a low-cut shoe without lacing or strap with thin sole and low heel. First mentioned in the sixteenth century. Pumps were worn principally by footmen which gave rise to the English practice of calling such servants "pumps."

pump, d'Orsay 1830's; the gentleman's shoe originally with cutaway sides and low broad heel; introduced by Count d'Orsay, a society dandy and leader of London and Paris. The pump remains classic today for men and women. The masculine evening shoe worn with formal evening dress is of dull black calf or patent leather with tailored black grosgrain bow. see *oxford ties.*

pump, opera, feminine a woman's low-cut high-heeled slipper for evening wear is usually cut from a single piece of fabric of satin or velvet and untrimmed in the present mode. At times, handsome rhinestone buckles are worn and the French heel varies in height according to the mode.

punch work open work embroidery in the round instead of the squares of drawn-thread embroidery. The round holes are made by a stiletto, and edges reinforced by embroidered stitching. Used principally for household linens, or in costume, holes required for lacing together jacket edges as a closure, etc.

punjum madras piece goods of cotton cloth made in southern India.

pure-dye a commercial term which, when applied to silk, means that the fabric has not been weighted more than ten per cent and therefore is washable.

Puritan hat see *hat, Puritan.*

brown leghorn-white shantung puggree band

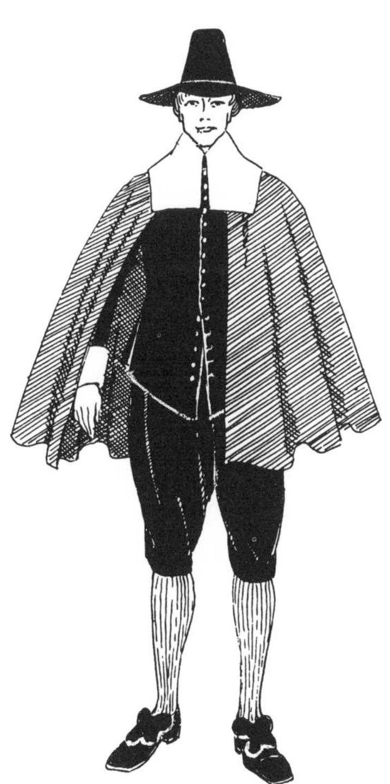

Puritan-habit black, brown or gray-white linen band and cuffs-black felt hat-gray or green stockings-spur leathers on shoes

Puritan-gown plum, gray or brown cloth-collar, cuffs and apron of white Holland linen-black felt hat

purl a looped stitch in gold or silver thread edging on collar, cuffs and caps. Also a basic stitch in knitting.

purple one of the three secondary colors, green, purple and orange, a combination of blue and red. The violet tones have a greater proportion of blue, the wines a greater proportion of red.

purple The origin of the word purple is the Latin *purpura,* the name of the shellfish which yielded the famous Tyrian dye. It was not violet but a deep crimson color.

purse see *aumônière; pocketbook; reticule.*

puttees a narrow strip of cloth wrapped spirally around the leg from ankle to knee. Or, a fitted leather legging secured by laces, strap or catch. The first puttees appeared in the Anglo-Indian Army late in the nineteenth century. They were worn by American and British Infantry through World War I. Puttees are of East Indian origin, from *patti,* a Hindu word which signifies a strip of cloth.

pyjamas see *pajamas.*

Q

Qiana a new man-made fiber presented in 1968 by E.I. du Pont de Nemours & Co., Inc., the producers of Nylon in the 1930's. Qiana is claimed to be the most luxurious of all silk fabrics, more silk-like than most other man-made fibers that are available on the market.

Quaker's hat see *wide-awake hat.*

Quaker fashion of many years-brown satin-white lawn kerchief fastened under belt-silk bonnet over frilled lingerie cap-1860

Quant, Mary see *couture, haute.*

quarter the part of a shoe which forms the side, from the vamp to the heel.

quartz general term for a group of stones with a silica base, used as gems. Rose quartz is pink. Other varieties include rock crystal, amethyst, jasper, aventurine, chalcedony, bloodstone, chrysoprase, carnelian, agate and onyx.

quatre-foil spur leathers worn by the seventeenth century cavalier to conceal the fastenings of his spurs. Quatre-foil signifies a conventional, ornamental design of leaf or flower with four leaves.

quatre-foil spur leathers to hide spur fastenings-bucket-top boots-red sole-red heel-French-17th C.

Queen Elizabeth wig see *wig, Queen Elizabeth.*

queue a long braid of hair hanging in back, a Chinese fashion of centuries. In 1644, as a sign of submission, the Manchu conquerors imposed the wearing of the queue. With the establishment of the Republic in 1912, the Occidental haircut replaced it.

queue, cue wig or the tail of a wig. In the eighteenth century with the fashion of wigs on the wane, men, especially army officers, adopted a ribbon-tied queue during the hair-growing process. If extra length was desired, more hair was added and the "whip" bound with black ribbon or leather. see *wig, periwig, cue.*

queue-natural hair in queue-large unlooped or uncocked hat recommended by Washington for the troops

quiff British slang for a man's hair oiled and dressed off the forehead, or for a forelock of hair.

quill a large stiff feather from a bird's wing or tail or a spine of the hedgehog or porcupine, sometimes used as an ornament for hats.

quilt noun or verb, a coverlet made by quilting.

quilting two pieces of cloth with a layer of cotton batting in between, the three pieces stitched or quilted together in fancy or geometrical patterns. Quite often used for suits and skirts.

quintin a very sheer lawn made formerly in Quintin, Brittany.

quintise see *cointise.*

quitasol a large fan covered with colored oil silk, which was carried for shade as well as breeze, before the invention of parasols. American, eighteenth century, but probably of Spanish origin.

quizzing or **perspective glass** a single round lens carried on a black silk cord or ribbon, or on a chain around the neck, or mounted on a short or long handle of tortoise shell, silver or gold. Early nineteenth century. Fashionable females often had the lens set in a fan, particularly in a jeweled or painted fan.

R

rabanna a textile imported from Madagascar. Used for hats and bags.

rabat see *falling band.*

rabatine see *falling band.*

rabato, rebato a starched or wired collar band standing up at the back of the neck. Also, a support for a ruff. Early seventeenth century.

rabbi the pair of square lawn or linen tabs attached to a starched collar band which is buttoned in back.

rabbit a rodent of the hare family, originally from southern Europe but native today in most parts of the world. It was introduced into Australia in 1859 and the largest American imports come from Australia, Tasmania and New Zealand. Varied in color, ranging from white through gray, brown to black with white varieties coming from France, Germany, Belgium and Austria. The winter coat is whitest though not a durable fur. It is dressed and dyed to simulate better furs. Extensively used for coats, jackets and trimming and in the manufacture of felt hats. Some commercial names: angora rabbit hair; beaver-dyed coney; chinchilla coney; ermiline; erminette; French beaver; French seal; lapin; leopard-stenciled lapin; marmotine; near seal; polar seal; sealiner; squirreline. see *hare.*

raccoon a North American mammal. A durable, long-haired fur, the best from northern United States. Also called coonskin. It is pale brown with deep underfur and long, dark and silvery-gray tophair. The poorly colored skins are dyed brown or black for the British military busby. The fur in its natural state was popular in the first quarter of the twentieth century, used for full-length coats and as trimming on cloth coats. It is now sheared to simulate beaver and nutria; sheared, dyed and sewn like let-out mink.

raccoon coat a craze for the huge, bulky raccoon coat in the 1920's was due to riding in open touring cars; it was particularly favored for attending football games.

rachel a flesh color or tawny-pink color face powder, previously mostly white, which appeared in the 1880's. Named after Madame Rachel, a famous London beauty specialist.

radium a lustrous, plain, smooth silk or rayon, which has crispness, yet supple, draping quality. Used for lingerie, linings and dresses.

raccoon coat-horn buttons-black derby-1928

wired rebato of lawn and lace-rolled gauze turban-English-1621

rabbit-rodent of the hare family-fur of many names

raccoon-a durable, long-haired fur-N. A. mammal

raglan overcoat—tan whipcord—similar to the balmacaan—1939

raffia a strong, silky smooth, straw from the leafstalk of the raffia palm of Madagascar. Used for hats, bags, baskets, and many other items.

raglan a loose topcoat with sleeves cut to join the garment from underarm to neck. Named for Lord Raglan, who devised the design for his soldiers during the Crimean War. 1850's.

raglan sleeve see *sleeve, raglan.*

raincoat a garment for wear in the rain, made of synthetic fabrics, water-repellent, stain-resistant, often reversible and occasionally fur-lined. There are also some cottons, silks and woolen cloths which are oil-processed for lighter weight. Such fabrics, impregnated with oils, provide satisfactory showerproof garments and permit the use of style and material necessary in an all-purpose coat. see *cravenette; mackintosh.*

rainy daisy see *skirt, rainy daisy.*

rajah see *nankeen.*

ramie, rami a perennial plant of East Asia commercially cultivated in China and Japan for its fiber. It can be spun and woven into fabrics, as is done in the United States and Europe. In Asia, it is woven into cloth and made into fishing lines, nets, laces, hats, etc. The fiber is strong and glossy.

ramillies, ramilies a cocked hat of the eighteenth century in which the back flap turned up sharply, rising higher than the two front flaps. The two front flaps protruded outward in a spoutlike crease.

ramillies a favorite army wig which got its name from the Battle of Ramillies in 1706, fought between the English and the French. It was an English victory under the Duke of Marlborough. The wig had a pigtail tied top and bottom with black ribbon. Sometimes the braid was looped under and tied.

raploch a coarse, rough homespun woolen cloth made principally in Scotland.

rason see *rhason.*

rat a small roll or pad of false hair worn under the natural hair to shape a required silhouette, as for the pompadour. Early twentieth century. Also, fur used as costume trimming by the French couturiers during World War I. The animal was hunted and killed in the rat-infested trenches by the French soldiers, and was presumably the wood or field rat which has a clean, soft brown, black or white velvety fur.

rat, Armenian see *ermine.*

rateen, ratinet several coarse woolen cloths of the seventeenth and eighteenth centuries. "Ratinet" was the name of those of lighter weight of the same weave. Used for dresses, coats and capes.

ratiné, retine cotton in a loose, plain woven cloth which can be bleached, dyed or printed and is given a high luster or other finishes. Used for dresses, suits and coats.

ratiné lace a trimming for heavy cotton dresses. A groundwork done in heavy loops similar to Turkish toweling.

ratinet see *rateen.*

raw silk see *silk, raw.*

rawhide untanned cattle hide that has undergone some preparatory processes; used for luggage, whips, laces, etc.

rayé French for striped. An obsolete term for pin-striped fabrics whether silk, cotton or wool.

rayle, rail a loose garment worn over the bodice, generally in cape form, for indoor or outdoor wear; another name for a combing jacket. French, eighteenth century.

rayon a generic name for a man-made glossy fiber made of a viscous solution of modified cellulose. Also, the textile woven from such a fiber. There are many types of rayon, each with its own trade name.

rayonne a hood much worn in the American Colonies in the second half of the seventeenth century, of black ducape, a popular heavy corded silk cloth. The hood was lined with a striped silk of contrasting color and the padded fold was turned back around the face and tied with ribbons.

razor Latin, rasare, meaning to scrape or rase. A steel blade attached to its case or holder which also acts as a cover when not in use. Safety-razor, the twentieth century model, a smaller, more compact implement with removable blade which is easily replaced by a new one.

ready-made, ready-to-wear, off-the-rack apparel in all sizes, of varied styles and fabrics for men, women and children, sold in shops and large stores. A twentieth century development. "Off-the-rack" is the British term.

Reboux see *couture, haute.*

rebozo, rebosa, reboso a piece of Mexican and South American costume centuries old. It may be either a thin, dark-colored linen scarf worn around the head and shoulders or a long, strong woolen shawl tied around the shoulders and hips as a carryall for the baby, marketing or almost anything.

red one of the three primary colors with blue and yellow; red mixed with blue gives the secondary color purple, and, mixed with yellow, the secondary color orange. Red plus purple gives the tertiary color red-purple, red plus orange the tertiary color red-orange. The palest reds are the pink tinges, the darkest include ruby and garnet. The purple-reds include rose and crimson, the yellow reds scarlet and flame.

red feather In medieval days, a red feather in a knight's helmet was a sign of an unusual act of chivalry performed by the wearer. According to legend, a robe of red feathers worn in the Orient meant that the wearer had donated outstanding service to the community. In Hawaii only chiefs and nobles were permitted to wear a red feather headdress.

red fox see *fox, red.*

red riding hood see *French hood.*

red river coat a hooded frock coat with brass buttons, worn in Canada.

red sable see *mink, kolinsky.*

Redfern see *couture, haute.*

redingote French for riding coat, originally a man's outer coat of the eighteenth century. A double-breasted coat with large collar and revers and some-

rebozo-a S.A. or Mexican scarf used as a carryall-centuries old

redingote-"Levite"-Pennsylvania or Holland hat-velvet breeches-lingerie cravat-French-1780's

times a short cape; it was adopted by women late in the century. As a woman's coat it reappeared in the 1890's, still double-breasted with tailored collar and revers, a fitted body with long flaring skirt and full puffed sleeves. Made especially of mastic-colored broadcloth, it was fastened with bone buttons. see *levite gown; witzchoura.*

reefer a jacket or short overcoat, double-breasted and of very heavy cloth, worn by cattlemen, seamen and other workmen. see *pea jacket.*

reeled silk see *silk, raw.*

regalia symbols and emblems of royalty such as crown, scepter, insignia and decorations of an order. Thus, special dress and finery.

regatta a stout English twilled cotton usually in blue and white striped material, especially British.

regency the period during which a regent governs. Specifically, the French Regency (1715–1723) when the Duc d'Orléans was regent for Louis XV, and the English (1811–1820) when George, Prince of Wales, afterward George IV, was regent for George III. These two regencies in particular, affected costume.

regimental stripes a general term for diagonal stripes on a man's necktie. In British usage, stripes in the colors of a particular regiment; such a tie may be worn with civilian dress only by officers of that regiment.

reindeer heavy, durable leather used for shoe uppers. see *caribou.*

Renaissance In Europe, the period originated in Italy, brought about by the decline of Greco-Roman influence and the undertakings of the Crusaders. It began in the thirteenth and fourteenth centuries, was fully under way at the beginning of the fifteenth, its height about the middle of the century and its climax about 1500. Costumes were ornate and made of rich materials. From the East came gems and rare stones, cloth of gold and silver tissue; from Russia and the north, came furs such as sable, vair, ermine, marten, lynx, fox (*continued on page 290*)

Renaissance
chemise tops
partlet or
guimpe of
the costume
of the
lansquenet-
German-
16th c.
laced and
sleeved doublet
over white shirt-
Italian-
16 th c.
the frilled shirt
décolletage
worn at court-
French-
1530's
doublet
with
embroidered
partlet or
guimpe-
Italian-
1521
gentleman's night
shirt-embroidered
and frilled-black
velvet coif-
French-1580
falling band
with
Spanish blackwork-
academic robe-
English-
1580
short doublet
with sleeves-
over white
shirt-fashion
called "braggard"-
English-16th c.
infant's
doublet with
partlet or guimpe-
French-
1st half
16th c.
shirt
embroidered
with
Spanish
blackwork-
English-
1540

Renaissance
shapes of the
early period
silhouette
of the
Italian
corsetto-
undoubtedly
of boiled
leather-
1470
high bosom and
slim body of
the "corps piqué"
(quilted linen
corset)-
French-
1520
Florentine
silhouette
of the
leather corset-
1485
chemise into
partlet or guimpe-
laced corselet-
German-
1st half
16th c.
gown
with partlet
or guimpe-
(simulated
chemise top)
Swiss-
1520
the slim
"Spanish body"
with
flat bosom-
shaped by
a leather
corset-
mid.15th c.
all.white
widow's dress-
with partlet
or guimpe-
leather
corset-
French-
mid.16th c.
gown and apron-
worn over a
linen corset-
German-
1516
laced corselet-
over a leather
or linen corset-
German-
1564

Renaissance
the Spanish body
and the farthingale
satin gown
over iron corset
and drum-shaped
farthingale-
French-
1581
boy's costume
over
corps piqué
and
farthingale-
Spanish-
1575
exaggerated
form of the
Spanish body-
dome-shaped
farthingale-
English-
1590
black velvet gown
with ribbon bowknots-
over iron corset-
cone-shaped
farthingale-
Spanish-
1551
brocaded and
embroidered
gown over
"busto" (iron
corset) and
"Venetians"
(bloomers)-
Venetian-
1590's
costume worn over
basquine and
French bolster
type of farthingale-
Dutch lady of the
1590's

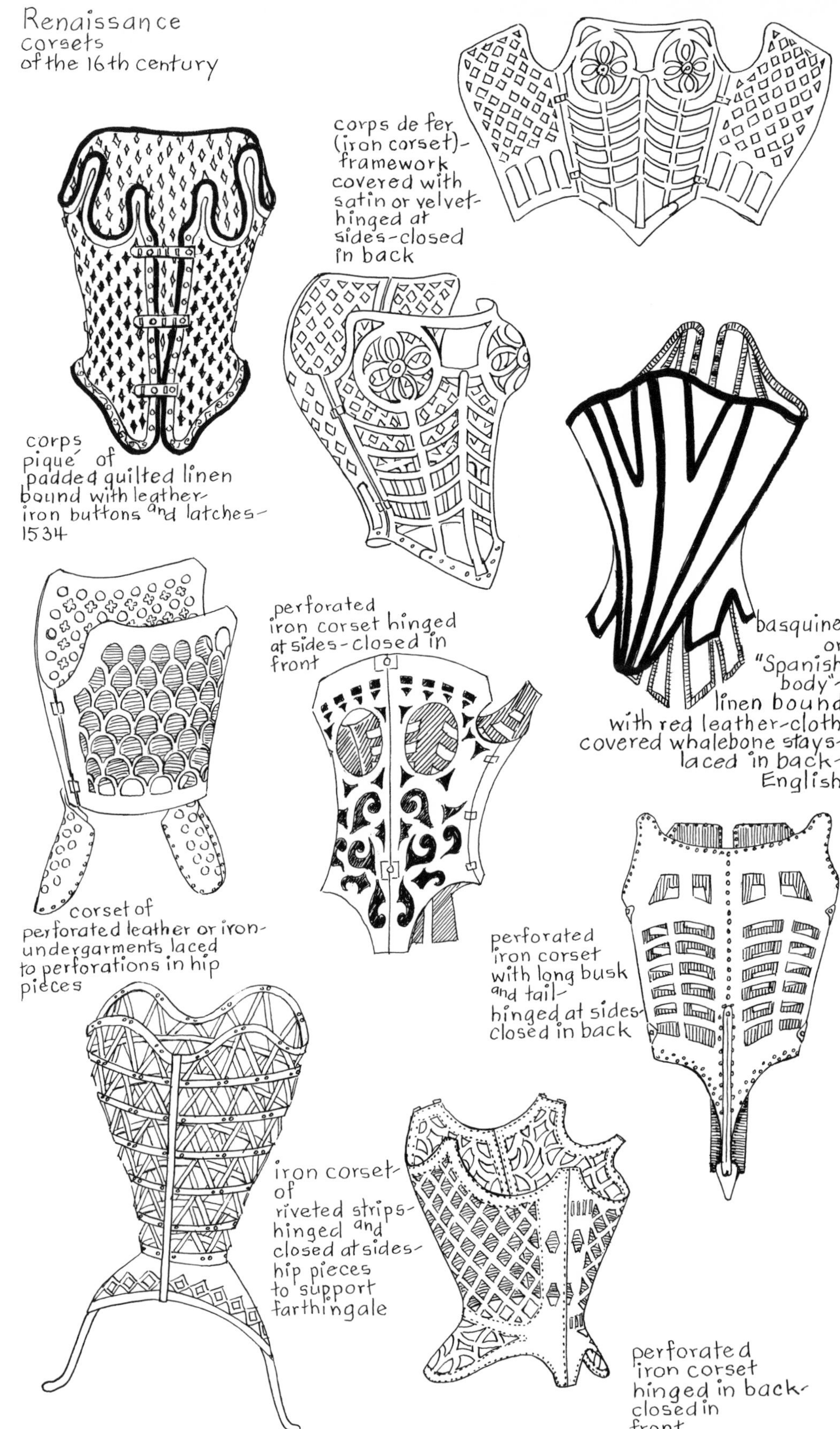
Renaissance
corsets
of the 16th century
corps de fer
(iron corset)-
framework
covered with
satin or velvet-
hinged at
sides-closed
in back
corps
piqué of
padded quilted linen
bound with leather-
iron buttons and latches-
1534
basquine
or
"Spanish
body"-
linen bound
with red leather-cloth
covered whalebone stays-
laced in back-
English
perforated
iron corset hinged
at sides-closed in
front
corset of
perforated leather or iron-
undergarments laced
to perforations in hip
pieces
perforated
iron corset
with long busk
and tail-
hinged at sides-
closed in back
iron corset-
of
riveted strips-
hinged and
closed at sides-
hip pieces
to support
farthingale
perforated
iron corset
hinged in back-
closed in
front

Renaissance masculine corseted shapes
brigandine-padded leather corselet with rivets-15th c.
peasecod-bellied corselet of steel with turn-buttons-French-1575
"corset"-boned and pleated jacket worn over high-collared and sleeved doublet-French-1415
soldier's quilted and fringed "jack"-(jacket)-linen or leather-Flemish-15th c.
sleeved and skirted doublet over armor-velvet and satin embroidered and jeweled-English-c.1590
brigandine-red velvet riveted with nail heads-Italian-1552
fitted doublet of small boy-English-1574
velvet jerkin worn over doublet with sleeves-Austrian-1567
peasecod-bellied doublet of slashed velvet-falling band of lace-English-1583

and lambskin. From Rheims came rich brocades, and from Venice, beautiful silks and velvets. The Renaissance in France reached full bloom in the reign of François I, (1515–1547). The French Court owed much of its brilliance to Italian influence. Parts of the costume were slashed and colors were lighter than those in Italy, sky-blue and white, lilac hues, rose, gold and silver being much used.

Renaissance lace a modern lace fashioned of tape motifs joined by lace stitches. A beautiful lace when made up over pale blue or pink satin of the trailing gowns worn to semi-formal parties worn by the Gibson girl and Lillian Russell types around the turn of the nineteenth century.

reinforcing in sewing, adding a piece of facing or binding to strengthen a spot exposed to extra wear.

remnant the end of a bolt of cloth or a left-over piece after completion of sewing.

rengue a Philippine fabric made from native pineapple; a delicate gauze stiffly starched. It is used for the traditional fichu and the wide-arched butterfly sleeves. see *camisa.*

Renta, Oscar de la see *couture, haute.*

rep, repp a cloth of silk or wool or both with a crosswise ribbed or corded surface. Also, any fabric with traverse line markings on the face. A firm material used for men's and boy's clothing and for women's suits.

repellent cloth a fabric that repels moisture but may not be waterproof.

reprocessed wool wool fibers woven and manufactured but never used, reduced again to fiber and spun and rewoven into fiber.

reptile in the leather trade, the skin of an animal that crawls on its belly or short legs such as snakes, the alligator, lizard, boa, cobra and frogs, etc.

reseau from the French for net or network of small regular meshes; the ground work or foundation of a lace pattern.

resist printing a fabric dyed after printing the pattern in dye-resistant chemical, leaving the design white. The resist chemical is removed after dipping.

resort wear appropriate clothes for the social life and sports activities of summer or winter resorts.

Restoration England: the period after the commonwealth when the Stuarts returned to the throne (1660–1685). Charles II had spent his exile at the court of Louis XIV and brought the French fashions of that period back with him.

Restoration France: 1815–1830, the return of the Bourbons after the defeat of Napoleon was marked in fashion by smaller waistlines for men and women and the return of the corset.

reticella or **Roman lace** the first form of needlepoint lace having drawn work and cut work with geometric designs connected by picot brides. Now used principally for table linens.

reticulated headdress the hair worn in a jewelled net. see *caul*

reticule, ridicule a small handbag of knitted silk, beading, brocade, plush or embroidery fashionable in the eighteenth century. The slim cotton gowns permitted no pockets and as a pleasantry, the inadequate little bag was called a ridicule. It held fan, handkerchief, card money and perfume bottle. see *aumôniére; handbag.*

rever, revers part of the turned-back or lay-over of the front of the jacket or coat, combining collar, lapels and revers.

revered a style of drawn work or stitching ornamenting linens, handkerchiefs, sheer dresses made of cotton, lawn, percale and batiste.

reverse calf see *calf, reverse.*

reversible coat an outer coat that can be worn either side out, made of a single reversible fabric or of two fabrics.

rhason, rason a cassock-like robe worn by prelates of the Greek Orthodox Church.

rhinegrave breeches see *breeches, petticoat.*

rhinestones small water-worn pebbles of rock crystal found mostly in the Rhine River in Germany. They are facet-cut to resemble diamonds.

ribcage the diaphragm, or that section of the body from waist to chest.

ribbed hose stockings knit with lengthwise deep ribs.

ribbon wire a narrow plastic tape with wired edges for use in millinery.

ribbons, galants, favors seventeenth century, clusters of variegated colored ribbon loops which ornamented feminine and masculine costume until the French minister Mazarin placed a ban against extravagant trimming. An elegant person often used as much as three hundred yards of ribbon on all parts of dress, including the hair.

Ricci, Nina see *couture, haute.*

rice braid a braid strung with cotton rice-shaped pellets.

rice net a coarse, cotton net stiff enough for crown and brim foundation in women's hats.

rice powder made with a base of pulverized rice. It was white and used—principally to avoid a shiny nose—until the late nineteenth century when tinted powder appeared in London.

ricinium see *flammeum.*

rick rack see *braid.*

ridicule a small handbag. see *reticule.*

riding habit a specific costume for horseback riding, formerly jacket and skirt for riding side saddle, now jacket and breeches, wide through thighs and tight-fitting calf-length legs. see illustrations, next page; *stock.*

riding petticoat see *safeguard.*

ring, dinner a handsomely wrought jeweled ring for late afternoon or evening occasions.

ring, engagement usually a gold or platinum ring set with a single gem, the solitaire diamond having become most favored. Worn on the third finger of the left hand.

ring, signet a ring made with a flat surface upon which is engraved a monogram or crest. Originally worn by nobility to authenticate and seal letters or documents with an imprint in sealing wax.

ring, wedding placed upon the third finger of the left hand of the bride during the ceremony. Usually a plain gold band or a jeweled circlet for the bride and, in some cases, a plain gold band for the groom. In some countries, such as Germany, worn on the third finger of the right hand.

rivière a diamond necklace fashioned in several strands, giving the effect of a river of diamonds.

roach see *American Indian headdress, costume.*

riding habit-
velvet brocade
and red cloth
skirt-black
hat with
red plumes-
Louis XIV-
1652

riding habit
with panniers-
and waistcoat-
tricorne hat-
powdered hair-
French-18th C.

riding habit-
"London smoke"
gray cloth-velvet
collar-black
satin stock-black
silk hat-gray veil-
white muslin strap
breeches-
French-1844

riding habit-
gray cloth-
jacket braid-
edged-black
satin stock-
gray felt hat-
gray veil-
white gloves
black patent
leather boots
1885

riding-
cross-saddle habit
of whipcord-brown
coat-beige breeches-
soft, beige felt hat-
1925

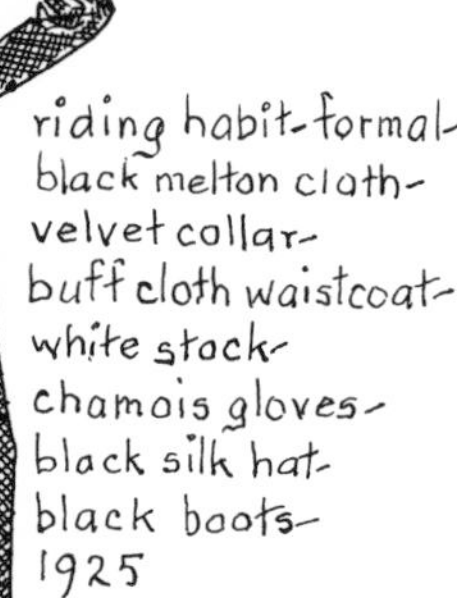

riding habit-formal-
black melton cloth-
velvet collar-
buff cloth waistcoat-
white stock-
chamois gloves-
black silk hat-
black boots-
1925

riding habit-gray
tweed coat-gray
whipcord breeches-
black and white
checked flannel
waistcoat-white
piqué scarf-black
bowler-tan leather
field boots-1930

robe à la française, Watteau gown designed by, and named after the painter, Watteau, 1730's. By 1770, it had become the formal dress for court functions. It had six box pleats stitched flat to the back and ending in a train.

robe à l'anglaise see *English gown*

robe de style the twentieth century infanta style, an evening fashion for which Lanvin of Paris became famous; its vogue was in the nineteen twenties and thirties. It had a tight bodice with a bouffant skirt, ankle or floor length. see *Velásquez.*

"robe de style" of heavy white satin with crystal beaded ribbons- beaded rose corsage- Lanvin 1923

robe, mandarin see *mandarin robe.*

Robespierre collar see *collar, Robespierre.*

Robin Hood hat see *hat, Robin Hood.*

robings an obsolete term for materials and trimmings for robes and gowns.

robozilla a flattering headdress of the young women of the Balearic Isles. A headkerchief of sheer silk or gauze that covers the back of the head and ties around under the chin.

rocket or roquet- vestment of lawn and lace worn by bishops

robozilla-embroidered lawn and pleated silk gorget- Balearic Islands

rochette, rochet a full-length garment of white lawn with full sleeves, worn over the cassock and under the chimere; part of an Anglican bishop's vestments.

rock crystal a colorless form of quartz, very effective in costume jewelry when facet-cut.

rock sable see *sable, mountain.*

rocket, roquet a short, full, smock-like, woolen garment worn from the Middle Ages to date. In the fifteenth century, it was worn by commoners and pages with hooded shoulder cape. It was worn to the eighteenth century by men and women in Europe and the American Colonies. In the nineteenth century, worn by ecclesiastics, of white linen with the lower half from waist down, of heavy lace.

rocket or roquet- Medieval blouse and hood-also worn by monks

rococo of the eighteenth century, a period of ornate extremes in Italy and Germany with the shell design predominating in jewelry, accessories, and decorative motifs.

rococo embroidery a design style carried to extreme in asymmetrically curved forms and shell motifs. Executed in a narrow one eighth inch wide ribbon known as China ribbon.

Roller Hat of felt or straw-boys and girls-early 20th century

Rodriguez, Pedro see *couture, haute.*

roll collar see *collar, roll*

rolled hem a very fine handkerchief hem made by rolling the edge and fastening it by minute slip stitches. Also used for scarves and sheer or chiffon dresses.

roller a small, round hat of felt or straw with rolled brim and a ribbon band, worn by boys and girls. Early twentieth century.

roquelaure or roquelo-cloak of cloth, velvet or silk-hooded, collared or buttoned-early 18th C.

romaine a sheer fabric in a basket weave that French ladies of the sixteenth century used for head scarfs.

Roman collar see *collar, clerical.*

Roman cut work see *cut work embroidery.*

Roman lace a needlepoint of geometric pattern, see reticella.

Roman stripes cloths striped with vivid colors in different widths running in the weft direction. The name is applied to all cloths so striped, regardless of fibers. Used in dress goods, trimming and many other ways.

Romanian costume, traditional see illustrations page 297.

Romanian embroidery see *Holbein work.*

white shirt or undertunic-Roman-early c. a.D.

Romany stripes see *gypsy stripes.*

rompers a one-piece garment combining waist and short, full bloomers worn by young children and formerly by young girls and women for gymnasium exercises. see *jumpers.*

rondelle, rondel a bead or gem cut into a slim disk with center hole to string between beads or gems of larger size for a necklace. Often of clear crystal to set off colored beads. A term also used for round decorative motifs, as in embroidery.

roquelaure, roquelo a cloak first worn in the eighteenth century by the Duke of Roquelaure, and named for him. Of heavy woolen cloth and camlet in bright colors; hooded, buttoned down the front, knee-length. It was popular in Europe and the American Colonies and worn by men and women into the early nineteenth century.

roquet, rocket a raincape of the early eighteenth century made of heavy cloth called rocket or gray russet. Worn with or without sleeves.

rose point lace an elaborate needlepoint lace with delicate flowers, foliage and scrolls accented with string cordonnet connected by brides and finished with buttonholed edges.

rose quartz a milky pink to rose mineral of little value, but attractive for jewelry, especially when carved.

roseberry cloth a lustrous cotton fabric, closely woven, mercerized, waterproofed and resembling fine reps; used for raincoats, hunting and fishing capes. A staple cheviot cloth known as Burberry cloth. see *Burberry.*

rosehube a hat of roses worn by women of Schwyz, a canton of Switzerland. Between the wings of the lace cap the hair is held in place by a rose hat pin.

rosette ribbon shirred or pleated into a round shape or formed of ribbon loops.

rouge French for red; any cosmetic of that color used for lips and cheeks. see *cosmetics.*

roughers woolen cloth as it comes from the loom before filling and perching on the horizontal bar for examination and perfecting.

Ancient Roman

rouleau French for a piping or roll of ribbon; used as hat trimming or apparel.

roundlet with draped liripipe-silk or cloth-French-15th C.

roundlet with liripipe a man's turban-like hat, the medieval chaperon made up over a stuffed roundlet. The noble was permitted a long tail, while that of the commoner was very short; fifteenth century. see *chaperon; liripipe.*

rubashka the Russian smock blouse of heavy white linen with full sleeves, narrow cuffs and a narrow standing collar. Collar, cuffs and hem are embroidered, as is the left-side opening in front from collar to waist. An important garment whether worn belted with leather belt or tucked inside the trousers.

narrow ruche, forerunner of the ruff-French-16th C.

rubber a substance obtained from the milky juice of certain tropical plants, which has been used commercially since Charles Goodyear discovered the process of vulcanization which he patented in 1844. Rubber boots and outer soles are made using this process. Rubber as a fiber for elasticized garments is composed of a core of natural or synthetic rubber around which other yarns are wrapped; this is used for garters, girdles, foundation garments, waistbands, etc.

rubber, crepe see *crepe rubber.*

ruff of starched lawn-beaver hat with embroidered lady's glove and ostrich-English-16th C.

rubberized describing waterproof fabrics such as silk impregnated with rubber or a rubber solution. The first patent for making rubberized cloth was taken out in 1801 in London by Rudolph Ackerman, but E. Mackintosh of England patented the first practical process for waterproofing in 1823. In 1820, T. Hancock of Middlesex, England, invented the first elastic fabric with rubber in it.

rubbers low overshoes of rubber worn to protect the shoes in wet weather.

ruby a variety of corundum crystallized and colored pale rose to deep red or "pigeon's blood." Red rubies are from Burma, light red from Ceylon, and dark brownish red from Thailand.

ruche a pleated or goffered strip of lace net or linen lawn, worn around the neck. Ruches appeared in Spain, in the first half of the sixteenth century, as tiny frills finishing neck and sleeves of the fine lawn masculine shirt. After the middle of the century the ruche became a fully developed ruff with lace edging. see *ruff.*

ruching an edging for collars and cuffs of finely pleated lace or other material.

ruff a kind of stiffly starched collar completely encircling the neck, wider than a ruche, late sixteenth and early seventeenth centuries. By the 1580's the ruff was a large cartwheel, starched and wired. The width of the fashionable ruff was about a quarter of a yard wide and the length eighteen to nineteen yards of fine linen lawn or Holland cambric. A frame of wire covered with silk thread was worn under it, the edge of the ruff also wired. Ruffs were starched in various colors, blue and green, with yellow a favorite and worn all over Europe.

ruffle a strip of cloth fulled, pleated or gathered to a straight edge as a frill.

rullian a Scottish brogue. see *brogue, brogan.*

rumal, remal a silk or cotton made in Bombay, India and worn by men as headdress or turban.

rumba, rhumba a Spanish dance costume of black satin, short black velvet jacket with cap sleeves, body bare from bolero to waistline. Long, tight black skirt with narrow, multi-colored ruffles flaring from thighs to floor.

russet a coarse peasant cloth of yellowish-red or grayish-brown used for everyday clothes in past centuries. Russet remains the name for such garments, also for the color.

Romanian sheepskin bolero with black lamb and embroidery-worn over linen smock

Romanian-szür-embroidered black felt-black sleeveless jacket (sarafan)-black felt hat

Russian-shuba of embroidered white felt with black braid edge and black Persian lamb collar-black felt hat

Russian woman in quilted cotton caftan-linen smock-white felt calpac with bride-contemporary

Russian festival costume-sarafan, (jacket) over rubashka (smock) black lamb fur-black embroidery-soft felt hat

Russian caftan of rich brocade-velvet skirt over satin skirt-headscarf of brocade-late 19th C.

Russian Youth dress U.S.S.R.-dark green with red and yellow braid over red breeches-red fox cap

Russian blouse of white or colored linen, hip-length or a little longer with long, slightly fulled sleeves gathered into cuffs, and a standing collar opening to the left side of the neck. Collar, opening, and cuffs usually embroidered in colorful stitchery. A leather belt or tie belt is worn. see *rubashka.*

Russian costume, traditional see illustrations.

Russian embroidery done mostly on linen in brilliantly colored geometric designs. Used on collars, cuffs and wide hem borders on skirts. Also, a colorful embroidery worked in outline motifs on holland, a canvas of plain weave, sized and glazed. The canvas is cut away upon completion.

rust a reddish-yellow hue, the color of iron rust.

S

saad, sad colors the grayed hues of any color, generally gray, dark brown and black. Favored by the Puritans, seventeenth century.

saba a variety of the genus of banana grown in the Philippine Islands. A fine textured fabric produced from the fiber of the plant.

sable, Alaska or **American** see *skunk* or *raccoon.*

sable a marten of the weasel family from northern Europe and northern Asia. The name is from *sabelum* of Slavic origin.

sable, Chinese also called Himalayan marten; yellow to yellowish-brown and dark golden brown. Blending and tipping is necessary to increase luster. see *marten.*

sable, Hudson Bay see *marten, American.*

sable, Japanese yellowish-brown peltries, coarse in texture. Lack of luster necessitates dyeing.

sable, mountain or **rock** commercial names; the small animal is a bassarisk or ringtail and related to the raccoon. Originally from Mexico and now found in Mexico, Central America, Southwest United States from Texas to California, Oregon and Nevada. Its hair is silky like the marten pale yellow hairs. Usually dyed dark brown and illegally called mountain or rock sable. Used for scarfs and trimming.

sable, red see *kolinsky.*

sable, Russian or **Siberian** the most highly esteemed of all furs, known as Russian crown sable under the Romanoffs. Underhair close, fine and very soft; top hair silky, fine and flowing; durable, lightweight and very warm. Lustrous color from gray to brown, almost black. Rarely used for coats because of time and cost required to match skins. Used for scarfs and trimming on fine cloth coats or fine broadtail coats.

sable, tatar see *mink, kolinsky.*

sabot see *wooden shoe; klompen.*

sabotine a shoe of rawhide with a wooden heel made as a makeshift by soldiers during World War I.

sabretache a military leather pouch for carrying orders and dispatches by a cavalryman. It hung from the belt on the left, or sabre, side. Copied in feminine fabrics during the Directoire period and again in the early twentieth century. see *handbags.*

sabrine work fancywork in flower appliqués applied by chain or purl stitch on jackets and borders of skirts.

sac see *sacque.*

sachet a small scent bag usually of silk padded with cotton, holding a powdered perfume substance called sachet powder. Used to scent garments and linens in chests and wardrobes.

sack coat a masculine coat, plain,

Ivy League

British

Continental

Spanish

Sack Coat•Masculine•Contemporary

short and without waist seam, single or double-breasted. The Norfolk is a type of sack coat. see *lounge coat.*

sackcloth or **sacking** coarse, heavy linen, cotton or muslin used for sports suits. Sackcloth in ancient times was worn as an act of mourning or penance because of its rough texture.

sacque, sac a feminine short, loose jacket with sleeves usually of silk or flannel, worn with petticoat or slip as a negligée. see *Watteau sacque; bed jacket; bed sacque.*

saddle bag pocket see *pocket, saddle bag.*

saddle oxford a low, broad-heeled sports shoe appeared about 1915, worn by men, women and children. Of white buckskin with a saddle of black or brown leather across the vamp and a three-eyelet lacing down the instep.

safari seal fur dyed a light brown. see *seal, Alaska.*

safeguard a wrap-around skirt worn when riding, to protect ladies' clothes from mud and dust. Used in England and the American Colonies in the seventeenth and eighteenth centuries, and especially by farmer's wives when going to market. It was usually made of red, gray or black homespun and known by the various names of *foot mantle, fote mantle, weather skirt, riding petticoat.*

safety razor an invention of the late nineteenth century which replaced the long blade used for centuries. A small fine precision blade of steel was protected by a guard to prevent cutting the skin, the blade easily removed for a new one, or for stropping.

saffian leather leather made of goatskin and sheepskins, tanned with sumac and dyed bright colors. It is frequently confused with moroccan leather, because named for the Moroccan seaport called Saffi.

saffron a species of crocus with bright yellow stamens which, when dried, are used to color and flavor food and were formerly used as a dye. The flower was known throughout the ancient Mediterranean world and the East. In medieval times it was used in Europe for dyeing linen and silk and also as a hair dye. Buddhist monks wear saffron-colored robes because the color is considered a peaceful one. The Hindu pundit wears a sacred spot of yellow on his forehead.

sagum of Gaulish origin, worn by ancient Rome and early Germans. A folded rectangle of woolen cloth fastened by a thorn instead of a fibula. Opened out, it became the military blanket of the army. "Putting on the sagum" came to mean a declaration of war.

sailcloth heavy duck or canvas used for sails, tents and such. It was once

Sailor Suit-white linen and navy blue cloth-collar edged white braid-rolled black silk neckerchief tied with white braid-black straw hat-black ribbon-1850

sailor suit-two-piece suit, navy, tan or white, of duck, serge, flannel or broadcloth-straw sailor hat, black and white shoes, black stockings-black braid trim-1870's

samarre-worn over vest and petticoat-velvet with padding and fur-worn in the colonies-17th and 18th C.

sampot worn by both sexes to form either pantaloons or skirt effect

popular among tailors for stiffening coat fronts. Sometimes used for casual skirts or jackets.

sailor, Breton see *Breton sailor.*

sailor collar see *sailor collar.*

sailor hat see *hat, sailor's; gob's cap.*

sailor, Merry Widow see *Merry Widow sailor.*

sailor suit a British and American outfit worn especially by young boys. In the 1850's, a custom tailor of Bond Street, London, designed a sailor suit for Queen Victoria's children: short jacket with long trousers; headgear consisted of small round caps and flat straw hats. The fashion was seized upon by American mothers who adopted the uniform of the American Navy enlisted man though not always with regulation as to detail. The suit was usually of dark blue cloth trimmed with white braid. For small boys, the suit consisted of a loose overblouse with the sailor collar, narrow in front and broad and square in back. The sailor suit of the small boy comprised blouse and knee-pants, and the middy suit had long trousers. see *middy blouse;* illustrations on preceding page.

Saint Gall lace a Swiss imitation of Venetian lace. A process of embroidering cotton or woolen fabric with silk or cotton thread, then dissolving the wool and retaining only the embroidery.

Saint Laurent, Yves see *couture, haute.*

sakkos or **sacco** from the Greek *sakkos,* meaning a bag or sac. see *lounge coat.*

sakkos; soccos an embroidered vestment worn by bishops of the Eastern Orthodox Church, corresponding to the dalmatic of the Western Church. It is made all in one piece and symbolizes the seamless robe of Christ.

sallet or **salade** a simple helmet with or without visor and made to extend over the back of the neck; fifteenth century.

salloo a twilled red cotton fabric similar to calico, made in England and which became popular in East India, hence its Hindu name, *sālū.* The pretty cotton substituted occasionally for the beautiful Indian silk cholee or blouse, and the sari or luxurious scarf.

salt sacking cotton and worsted in coarse, plain weaves and rough, homespun types in suitable summer weights which are used for sports and riding habits.

Salvation Army lassie bonnet see *bonnet, Salvation Army lassie.*

Sam Browne belt see *belt, Sam Browne.*

samarre; simar a Dutch jacket of the seventeenth and eighteenth centuries worn by women over a petticoat of heavy satin, en negligée. The jacket, worn over a waistcoat, was short, loose and flaring, of velvet, plush or silk and sometimes fur-edged. Dutch masters such as Vermeer delighted in painting this costume. The samarre was popular in the American Colonies.

samite a luxurious silk fabric of the Middle Ages interwoven with gold and silver threads was used for the robes of the nobles and ecclesiastics.

sampot part of the typical Cambodian costume; a length of cotton or silk wrapped around the waist and drawn up in front producing the effect of full pantaloons, worn by men and women. For ceremonial occasions, Cambodian women wear the sampot draped in skirt fashion. Of beautiful, heavy silk with pleats in center front and an extra handsome scarf draped over the left shoulder, leaving the right shoulder bare.

sanbenito a smock of sackcloth was

worn by those condemned to death by auto-da-fé during the Spanish Inquisition. The color was yellow or black, according to the degree of guilt. From 1480 through the sixteenth century.

sandals a sole held to the foot by leather straps or cut-out uppers tied and buckled.

sandals, knob the knob sandal or clog has been worn since ancient times in the Orient and is still worn there and by the Bedouins in the African desert. This sandal is broad and heelless with red moroccan leather straps over the instep. It is held to the foot by a large decorative knob, usually silver, between the large toe and the next.

Sanforized a patented process of compressive shrinkage which guarantees that the cotton or linen so treated will not shrink beyond a quarter inch to the yard in either direction.

sanitize a trade name process which renders textiles germ-proof, self-sterilizing and antiseptic, and prevents perspiration odors.

sans culottes a name for the French Revolutionists or Jacobins, to distinguish them from the aristocrats. Literally, without breeches; the term referred to the fact that men of the people wore trousers rather than the fashionable knee breeches of the nobility. see *trousers;* illustration on next page.

Santa Claus costume of bright red flannel or cotton velvet; coat and knickers. The coat is usually trimmed with something white and furry-looking such as plush for collar, cuffs and border. A buckled wide leather belt, boots and a fur-trimmed red cap complete the costume. The English Father Christmas wears the same costume.

sapphire a pure variety of corundum in transparent or translucent crystals used as gems. Blue is the most valuable; sap-

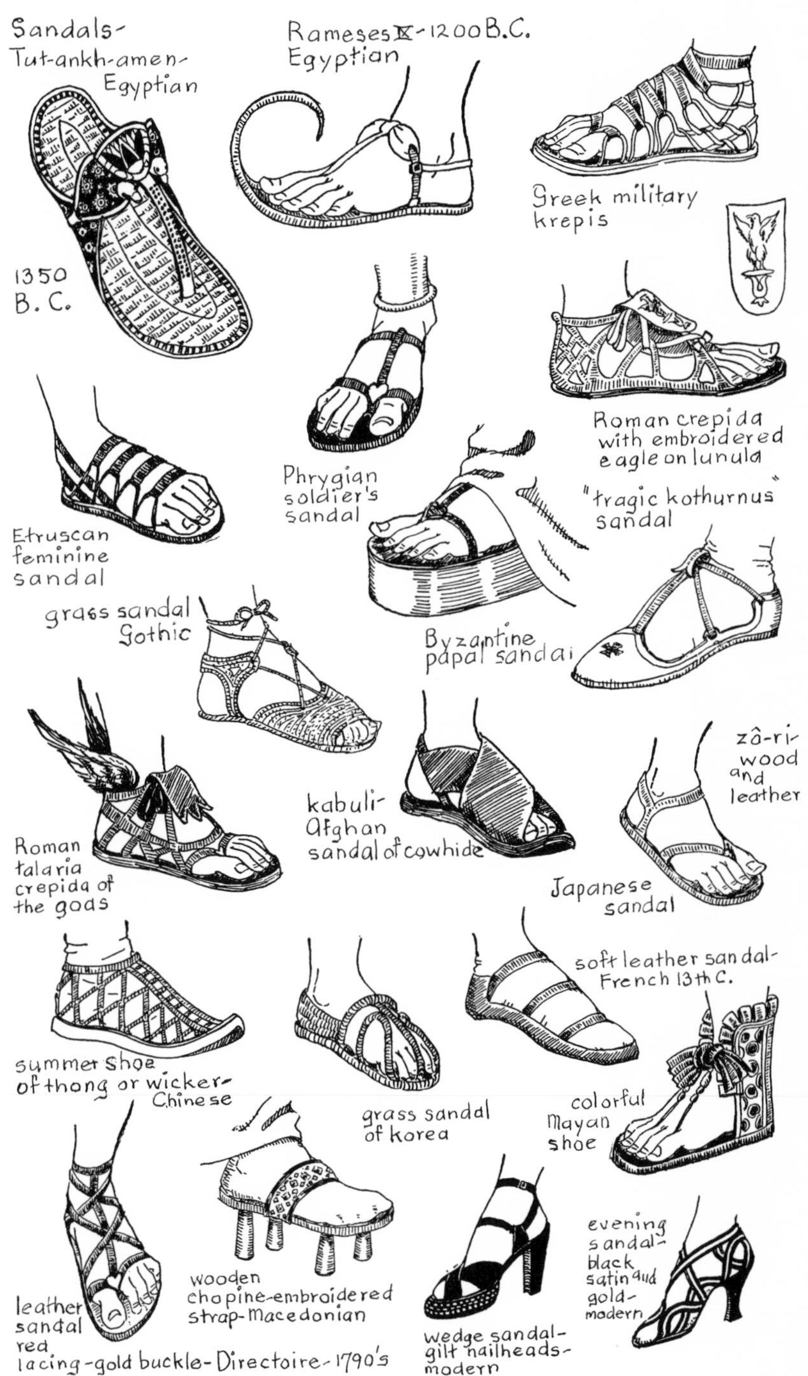

sans-culottes-blue jacket-tricolor • striped breeches-black felt hat-hair in queue-French-Revolution

phires occur in yellows, greens and colorless stones.

sarafan the traditional dress of old Russia and still worn by Russian peasants. A long full skirt of brocade or wool gathered to a sleeveless bodice with either square or round neckline. It is worn over a full, soft white blouse gathered at the wrists into ruffles or cuffs. An embroidered, sleeveless jacket or bolero is also often worn. Both overdress and jacket are called sarafans.

sarape, zarape a colorful, fringed shawl-like wrap worn by Mexicans and South American Indians. Unlike the poncho, which has a hole in the center for the head, the sarape opens down the center front. It is a larger square than the poncho and the woven motifs are more Aztec in design and color than those of the poncho. The cloak derives from the Aztecs.

sarafan (jacket) Venetian red velvet with white paillettes and ribbon-worn in the Youth Parade, Lenin stadium, Moscow

Saratoga trunk a huge and popular traveling trunk of the late nineteenth century. Used especially for summer resort vacations, it held a large wardrobe of clothes and was built with a top tray which held the fashionable large picture hats.

sari a piece of fabric about 40 inches wide and five to seven yards long. Of cotton, silk or both, brilliantly colored or embroidered, it is worn over the choli, a short blouse of white or solid color, and a petticoat tied around the waist by a drawstring. The sari, in folds, is tucked into the drawstring and wrapped around the waist to form a skirt, the end carried up in front over the left shoulder. The end is left to hang and may be draped over the head as a hood. The sari is the most important part of the Hindu woman's dress. Girls wear it from thirteen or fourteen years of age.

sarong a colorful piece of cotton or silk worn by both sexes of the Malay Archipelago, Ceylon and some parts of India. Four or five yards long, it is sewn at both ends, wrapped around the hips and tucked into a sash, forming a draped skirt varying in length from knee to ankle.

sarsanet a fine thin silk woven by the Saracens, dating from the thirteenth century, which was especially in favor from the fifteenth to the seventeenth centuries. It was used for dresses, veilings and trimmings and in more recent times, became popular in England for linings. Also spelled sarcenet, sarscenet.

sartorial pertaining to the tailor and his work on men's clothes.

sash a long, wide piece of fabric worn around waist, hips or over one shoulder. see *cummerbund; faja; obi.*

sash blouse a blouse with long ends crossed in front in surplice style and tied in back.

sari draped over left shoulder as worn by Moslem or Hindu women-over right shoulder by Parsi

Sari of sheer dark green cotton-beige silk border-dark blue choli-(blouse) Pakistan

Sassoon, Vidal at first a London "crimper," who became in the 1960's the fashionable hairdresser of London and New York. In his hands, the permanent wave of the past half century had straightened and lengthened into a "fall" which stood high over the forehead with the long ends lying on the shoulders. Often, he curtained the forehead with a deep fringe of straight hair.

satara a ribbed woolen cloth from Satara, India, highly dressed and lustered.

sateen an imitation of satin made of cotton warp and cotton or wool filling, with the face of the cloth, silk or rayon. This makes for a firmer, more durable fabric. Glycerine and repeated calenderings will produce a more satiny finish. Used for linings, pajamas, and the heavier qualities of corsets, shoe linings, and such.

satin a silk or rayon in many varieties. Of thick, close texture with smooth, glossy surface and dull back. The glossy surface is the result of finishing between hot rollers. Also made with cotton back.

satin, antique a fabric woven to resemble an old satin, as, for instance, white turned ivory or parchment color.

satin, crepe-back of silk, rayon or mixture; satin face and crepe back. Satin face and crepe back are often used to trim each other.

satin, damask a satin with a rich arabesque or flower pattern, sometimes in a velvet pile. For negligée robe or evening cloak.

satin de chine from the word *sztum*, satin being originally a Chinese creation called *zetin* and, lastly, *satin*. It was known in medieval Europe of the twelfth and thirteenth centuries and in England by the fourteenth century. Because of its exquisite texture, it became a court favorite. There are many different satin weaves in warp and filling and all costly, because silk is used to produce a lustrous and unbroken surface.

satin de lyon satin with a ribbed back. Used for masculine evening wear trim such as top hat, waistcoat, lapel or trouser stripes.

satin, Denmark see *Denmark satin.*

satin, duchesse a heavy, firm, highly lustrous, soft silk material. Used for evening coats and formal gowns.

satin, farmer's highly lustrous with cotton warp and worsted in cotton filling. Used for petticoats.

satin jean, satin turk a twilled-back silk fabric, soft-finished and smooth-faced, used for waistcoats, linings and shoetops in the eighteenth and nineteenth centuries.

satin, Liberty trade name for soft, closely woven fabric dyed with raw silk warp and spun silk filling. Used for turbans, blouses and linings.

satin, Skinner's an American silk of lustrous quality and popular in the late nineteenth and twentieth centuries. Used for dresses and linings.

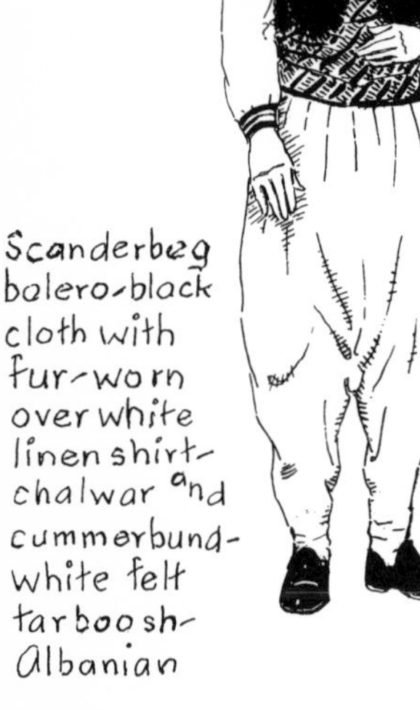
Scanderbeg bolero-black cloth with fur-worn over white linen shirt-chalwar and cummerbund-white felt tarboosh-Albanian

satin, slipper a closely woven, semi-glossy surface with dull back used as a fabric for evening slippers and gowns.

satin stripe a dull-surfaced fabric with a stripe of satin weave, usually used for underskirts.

saurians any lizard-like reptile skins used for footwear. Fashionable in the 1960's.

sautoir a long, fine gold or silver chain upon which women carried a watch, or a small gold or silver chain purse or, perhaps, a medallion, any one of which was tucked into the belt. Late nineteenth and early twentieth centuries.

Saxon embroidery see *Anglo-Saxon embroidery.*

Saxony cloth a suiting of Saxony wool rather like tweed or fine cheviot in solid colors and chalk stripes. Also, a long-napped, soft or velour-finished cloth like cashmere.

Saxony lace embroidered drawn work lace of the eighteenth century; an imitation of real lace in which the ground is chemically burned out, leaving the embroidery, an imitation Brussels lace with the design worked on a tambour drum.

Saxony yarn a fine, closely twisted knitting yarn from Saxony, Germany.

saya the long silk sarong skirt with train which is part of Philippine and Spanish-American formal dress. Gay Philippino evening dress is worn by both sexes. In walking or dancing, the train is carried over the left forearm in graceful manner. see *Philippino traditional formal dress.*

Scaasi, Arnold see *couture, haute.*

scabbard a leather or metal case for dagger, sword or bayonet; the silk case for a furled umbrella.

scalloped an edge cut into semicircular curves or projections as an ornamental design.

Scanderbeg bolero a fur-trimmed black cloth bolero named after the Albanian chief and national hero who resisted the Turks from 1443 to 1468.

scapular formerly a monk's working robe; now a monastic garment with front and back panels and hood but without sleeves, worn by Benedictine and Dominican friars.

scarf, artist and poet black silk cut on the bias and hemmed all around. Worn with an easy or soft collar and tied into a loose bowknot in front. It was the favored neckwear of poets, artists and youths. Nineteenth century.

scarf, chin see *chin scarf.*

scarf, masculine the flat scarf of the nineteenth century appeared in the 1850's, origin of the ascot puff of the 1870's. The ascot first worn at the Ascot Heath races, was responsible for the vogue of the ready-made cravat. Variations of the style were the de Joinville, named for the Prince de Joinville and the four-in-hand, or Teck, named after the Prince of Teck. Clubs were formed of drivers of four horses harnessed to a single carriage driven by one person who was identified by his scarf, which is the origin of the name. The four-in-hand replaced the made-up scarf by the end of the century. see *ascot; four-in-hand; de Joinville scarf; Teck.*

scarfpin, stickpin, tiepin an ornamental pin of gold, silver or other metal about two and one half inches long, usually mounted with a jewel. The pin was placed in the cravat below the knot, thus holding the scarf in place. It was especially worn with the ascot or the four-in-hand in the late nineteenth and early twentieth centuries. The use of the scarfpin lasted past the mid-twentieth century.

scarpetti shoes with hempen soles used for rock climbing by European peasants.

schenti loincloth of the ancient Egyptians, prototype of modern shorts. The masculine garment of all classes; king and slave alike wore it with the rest of the body bare.

Schiaparelli, Elsa see *couture, haute.*

schlappe a lace cap with pleated black and white gauze fan-shaped wings, one on each side; a flattering headpiece still worn by the women of Appenzell, Switzerland.

Schleswig lace fine Danish needlepoint lace executed in religious and other motifs; seventeenth century.

Schön, Mila see *couture, haute.*

schreinerize a process to schreiner or mercerize cotton, giving it a lustrous finish by pressing it when wet between two hot, heavy steel rollers, one engraved with lines and the other smooth.

scissors a two-bladed cutting instrument, each blade three to six inches long, each with a handle joined by a pin at the center upon which they work, move and cut. see *pinking shears.*

scogger, vamp a kind of sock worn in parts of northern England. Usually of worsted, and footless; used over the arms and over shoes. Much used in Colonial America, and called *vampay.* see *vamp.*

Scotch fingering yarn a medium weight, 3-ply finely twisted woolen yarn used for crocheting and knitting.

Scotch tweed see *tweed, Scotch.*

Scott, Ken see *couture, haute.*

Scottish Highland dress in contemporary use: the kilt; a hill jacket, generally of dark green tweed with staghorn buttons, and shoulder tabs; the sporran, knee-length stockings with a skean dhu in one; and a bonaid or Glengarry cap. For dress occasions men wear a kilt in dress tartan, if entitled to one; a black velvet jacket with silver buttons; a frilled jabot and the plaid fastened on the left shoulder with a large brooch; black pumps with silver buckles; ladies wear a simple white evening dress with the clan plaid fastened on the left shoulder. see *kilt; breacan feile; sporran; skean dhu; cap, Glengarry.*

screen printing a hand process of applying color to fabric through wire or bolting cloth screens to the motif to be colored. Each design color requires a different screen. It is costlier than roller printing, but unusual color effects can be obtained by the process.

scuffer a sandal-like, lightweight play shoe with a sturdy sole used by children for play and adults for sports.

scuffs light, soft slippers without quarters in which one "scuffs" or walks barely lifting the feet. see *mule.*

scye see *armscye.*

seal a furred or haired marine, aquatic, carnivorous mammal found off the coast of Alaska, Western Canada, Uruguay, South Africa, Japan and Siberia.

seal, Alaska, matara finest of the fur seals from the herd of the Pribilof Islands, Alaska. The quantity taken is limited by the United States and Canada. A durable, handsome fur, deep-pelted and of uniformly good quality with coarse, long

schlappe—Swiss bonnet of pleated black and white gauze—Appenzell

Scottish Highland dress worn during English Prohibition Act 1746—repealed 1783

guard hairs which must be hand-plucked. A dark coat naturally lustrous, but all pelts are dyed black; matara, a dark brown; or safari, a lighter brown.

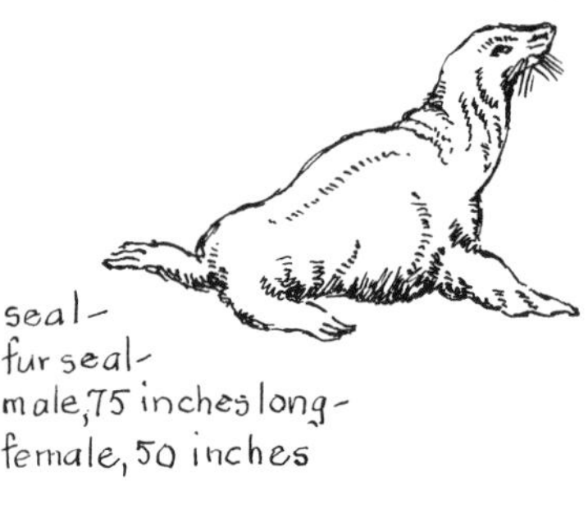

seal, baby, white coat or **wool** the coat of month-old harp seal. A creamy white woolly coat, used natural or dyed. The older harp seal, up to five years, has mottled white patches on a bluish-black ground.

seal, cape from the Cape of Good Hope, South Africa. It has a lighter, thinner skin and not as fine quality fur as Alaska seal.

seal, electric see *seal, imitations.*

seal, French see *seal, imitations.*

seal, hair found in all parts of the world and more numerous than fur seal; taken principally for oil and leather. There are many species, but only the harp and hooded seals are common in fur markets. Formerly used for leather, but now more for sports and casual wear, especially the Labrador seal.

seal, harp see *seal, baby.*

seal, hooded The coat of the young seal is bluish-black with cream or white belly, used natural or dyed.

seal, imitations electric or near seal, sheared hare; French seal, rabbit; Hudson seal, muskrat; polar seal, rabbit; seal-dyed coney, rabbit; sealing, Australian, rabbit.

seal, Labrador see *seal, hair.*

seal, pin fine pin-grain seal known as Levant morocco, a strong, durable leather of the white hair seal. It has an irregular grain, highly prized for bookbinding; also used for gloves and accessories.

seal, polar see *seal, imitations.*

seam the joining together by sewing of two pieces of fabric. The two unfinished edges are turned to the wrong side, and the smooth seam side is turned to the right side.

seam, French the edges of two pieces of cloth stitched together on the right side, trimmed off close to the seam, then turned to the wrong side and stitched again, making a neatly finished seam without raw edges. Used in sewing fine garments.

seam, piped a seam with a very narrow insert of fabric between the two joined pieces of fabric, either the same material or contrasting in color and texture, to show on the right side.

seam, welt a seam first stitched on the wrong side, one edge then cut narrower to about a quarter inch. The wider edge is then folded and basted under the narrow edge and finished by stitching on the right side. This raised or swelled seam is used as decoration in tailored work.

seamstress a woman who hand-sews and finishes as opposed to a dressmaker who cuts, fits and makes.

seed pearls see *pearls, seed.*

seersucker a wash-and-wear fabric of cotton, silk or rayon with or without a crinkled stripe made by varying the tensions of the warp yarns. Used for summer suits, dresses, pajamas, etc. Needs no ironing if hung very wet to dry.

selvage, selvedge the webbed edge of a woven fabric which prevents its raveling.

sendal, cendal a thin, silk fabric of the Middle Ages, possibly from China. It was still used in the seventeenth century. It was made both very sheer and heavy and was used for the dress of nobles and ecclesiastics. It could be painted and was used for banners.

sennit a braided straw of fiber used by the Japanese and Chinese in making hats. The hard straw sailor is fashioned of sennit straw, coated with shellac. Sennit is a contraction of seven-knit in nautical language, after a method of braiding rope.

separates parts of the feminine costume, coat, jacket, blouse, skirt, sweater or jumper—all of which are planned to coordinate in design and color, each part interchangeable; twentieth century.

sequins see *paillettes.*

serge a fabric of worsted yarn with a diagonal twill on both sides. Formerly, a popular fabric for men's and women's tailored suits and coats, especially in dark blue. Now made in wool, cotton and blends and forced to share the market with many new cloths.

serge, silk a twilled silk fabric of a heavy grade of surah especially used for lining men's coats.

serge, wide-wale a cloth with a definite diagonal weave, sometimes called cheviot serge.

sergedusoy, serge du soie woolen cloth used by common folk for men's coats and waistcoats in the eighteenth century.

serul an undergarment worn in Arabia and northern Africa; a long strip of white cotton, wrapped and tied to form short breeches and a pocket to hold the knife.

set-in sleeve see *sleeve, set-in.*

Seventeenth Century costume see illustrations, pages 308–315.

sewing machine A machine for stitching or sewing, was invented, perfected and manufactured in the mid-nineteenth century, thereby creating a new world of clothes for everybody in ready-mades.

shad belly see *hunt dress.*

shade cloth see *Holland linen.*

shadow embroidery, shadow stitch floral motifs worked on the wrong side of transparent fabrics.

shadow lace a filmy, machine-made lace with shadowy flower patterns.

shadow skirt, shadow-proof panel a panel or slim straight underskirt set into the petticoat or slip which masks the transparency of the outer skirt. A need that arose and became popular in the twentieth century when the custom of wearing several petticoats declined.

shag a heavy woolen or silk cloth with long nap popular for men's coats and women's coats and dresses; seventeenth century.

shagreen untanned leather prepared in Russia and the East. It is covered with seedlike granulations and dyed bright colors, chiefly green, to resemble sharkskin. Also, the name of an obsolete silk made to resemble shagreen or pebbled leather. Used for shoes, purses and bags. see *galuchat; sharkskin.*

shaker flannel a well-napped, plain-woven, fine grade of flannel with cotton warp and wool filling. Used especially for infants' wear. Originally made by the Shakers, a religious sect.

shaker goods a general term for plain, heavy woolen ribbed variety of socks; also fabrics and yarns manufactured by the Shaker communities in New York State and Ohio. The Shaker sect was a religious and communal group which originated in England 1747 and came to America in 1774. Their principal location was at New Lebanon, New York. Their dress was simple in design and reserved in color.

Shaker dress of alpaca with white lawn kerchief-cape of homespun-brown percale bonnet

Seventeenth Century
children in corsets
ruff, farthingale and corset-
French princess-
1613
baby-
corset doublet-
silk brocade-
linen and lace collar and apron-
Spanish-
1602
little girl in elaborate gown with corset bodice-
Flemish-1st half of century
paned and slashed costume over corset-
French prince-
1613
small boy-
corset doublet-
braid-trimmed costume-
Dutch-
1631
two-year-old girl in farthingale and corset-
English-
1606
corset doublet-
satin with linen undersleeves and collar-
boy's dress-
Dutch-
c.1650
corset-bodice-
silk frock with linen and lace-
French prince-
1643

Seventeenth Century neckwear
the golilla-
starched sheer
linen lawn-
Spanish-
1620's
falling band of
fine thread lace
with strings-
English-
c.1610
falling ruff-
three layers-
linen and
point lace-
Dutch-
1624
falling band with
tassels-camisole
or brassière with
slashed sleeves-
Dutch-
1665
falling band-
Richelieu collar-
1630's
falling band
of point lace-
half shirt tied
with drawstring-
English-
1630's
cravat of
Venetian lace-
taffeta bow-
German-1687
falling band-
linen and
point lace-
French-
c.1632
"playne"
or falling band
of the judiciary-
English-
1660's
the steinkirk-
linen and lace
held in buttonhole-
French-
1693

Seventeenth Century
masculine
corset shapes
doublet with
median busk-
lace whisk-
silver gorget-
brocaded and
embroidered
silk-
English-
1616
doublet with
median busk-
slashed silk-
lawn and lace
whisk-
Dutch-
1617
young man
in satin-
median busk-
falling ruff-
Dutch-
2nd decade
slashed doublet
with corselet and
bowknots-
falling ruff-
French-
1620's
buffskin doublet
with median busk-
"playne band"-
shirt shows in
sleeve openings-
Dutch-
1620's
snug fitting vest
with sleeves-
Brandenburgs-
steinkirk cravat-
English-
1690's
elaborately
embroidered doublet-
lawn and lace whisk-
English-
1613

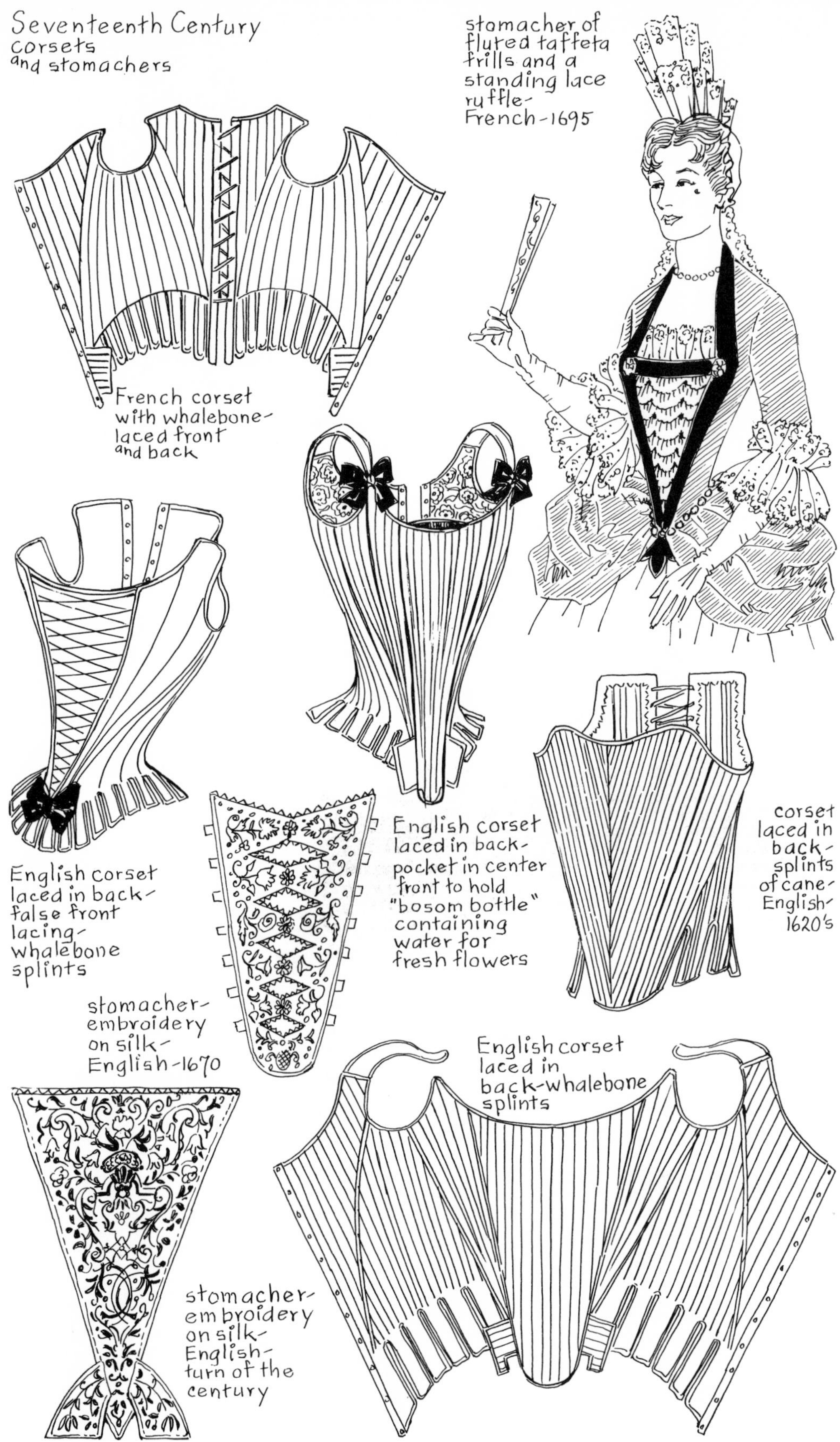
Seventeenth Century
corsets
and stomachers
stomacher of
fluted taffeta
frills and a
standing lace
ruffle-
French-1695
French corset
with whalebone-
laced front
and back
English corset
laced in back-
false front
lacing-
whalebone
splints
English corset
laced in back-
pocket in center
front to hold
"bosom bottle"
containing
water for
fresh flowers
corset
laced in
back-
splints
of cane-
English-
1620's
stomacher-
embroidery
on silk-
English-1670
English corset
laced in
back-whalebone
splints
stomacher-
embroidery
on silk-
English-
turn of the
century

Seventeenth Century-
the boned
"corset•bodice"
false lacing
and jeweled
buttons-
French-1630
elaborately
embroidered silk
doublet-separate
lace collar, yoke
and silk oversleeves-
English-1607
the "Spanish
body"-
1655
satin gown
with embroidery
and jeweled
buttons-
German-
1680
court gown
with corselet
embroidered
and jeweled-
French-
1694
boned satin
doublet with
fur collar-
Dutch-
1660

Seventeenth Century
shirts
and sundries
"half shirt"-
lace jabot-
drawstring
in edge-
English-
mid-century
brocaded silk
robe-velvet
lining-cap
to match-
French-
1690's
shirt of
fine linen
and thread
lace-rabat
and jabot
of lace
points-
English-
1632
simple linen
shirt with
"playne band"-
English-
mid-century
shirt with
lace jabot-
drawstring
puffed
sleeves-
French-
1660's
linen shirt-
ribbon loops or
"galants"-petticoat
breeches-
French-
1660's
linen under
drawers-
English-
1680's
shirt with
falling band,
embroidery,
lace and
hemstitching-
English-
mid-century
shirt with
embraidered frill-
button and bowknot-
Danish-1648

Seventeenth Century
waistcoat-
gourgandine
and vest
embroidered gourgandine-
laced in front-no bones-
French-
1690's
waistcoat
embroidered-
boned in front-
laced in back-
English-
c.1670
riding
habit-skirted, sleeveless
buffskin vest-linen shirt-
lace cravat-ribbon bowknots-
English-1664
negligée robe-
gourgandine
and
petticoat-
French-
1690's
quilted
waistcoat
laced in back-
hooked in front-
English-
c.1670
negligée robe-gourgandine
and petticoat- French-1690's
embroidered
gourgandine-laced
in front-no bones-
French-1690's

Seventeenth Century
feminine lingerie

shako a military headdress with a high stiff crown and plume. Of Hungarian origin, it was the same in European and American armies. The tall, black, polished felt with a feather pompon on the left side was prescribed by Congress in 1810. The flaring, bell-shaped polished felt shako or "tarbucket" adopted in 1913 is still worn by cadets at West Point.

shaksheer long, full pantaloons worn by Turkish women outdoors, especially for fieldwork.

shal see *babushka.*

shalloon a fabric of worsted or wool, light, fine and close-woven, twilled both sides and dyed plain colors. A lining first made in Chalons, France, hence its name.

shako-black cloth and leather-white pompon and cords-gilt insignia-scale chinstrap-U.S. Infantry-1813

shako-black polished felt-feather pompon-ribbon band-U.S. Army-1810

shako of felt or cloth-chenille pompon-powdered hair-leather queue with bowknot-English-1807-9

shalwar see *chalwar.*

shamiya the headkerchief of red, green or white silk worn by Bulgarian women. The young girl ties hers around the head, the ends floating in back; the married woman ties hers under the chin. The favored headdress when working in the fields.

shan the dark blue cotton jacket worn by Chinese men, women and children called "everyday workaday dress." The man's jacket buttons diagonally from the neck, over the chest and under the right arm.

Shanghai dress see *cheongsam.*

shank the narrow part of the shoe under the arch of the foot. Also, the shaped piece of steel or leather which keeps the shoe in shape.

shank-button a button with a metal loop or shank attached for sewing it on.

shantung a tussah silk or rayon fabric rather like pongee with a nubby texture, used in men's and women's sportswear and summer suits. see *nankeen; pongee; tussah.*

shapka see *calpac.*

sharkskin leather of certain sharks and rays covered with small, hard, round granulations. Also a fabric with small pebbly or grained surface woven to resemble the leather. A summer sports fabric woven of synthetic fibers. see *galuchat, shagreen.*

shatoosh a gossamer fabric, honey-beige in color, woven by East Indian women from hair of the beards of the Himalayan goats. The hairs are found on bramble bushes, where goats have nibbled leaves. The cloth is soft and costlier than vicuña. Used for hoods and scarfs.

shawl a square or oblong covering for the neck and shoulders, often finished with fringe. Varying in size; of wool, cotton, silk, chiffon and lace, they were originally handwoven and embroidered, and later woven on power looms.

shawl collar see *collar, shawl.*

shawls the fashion for the cashmere shawl, a luxurious accessory, took hold in the French Empire period and lasted nearly a century. It dates from the return of Napoleon's armies from Egypt. Beautiful ones were then made in France. From Paisley in Scotland came shawls woven on power looms in intricate pomegranate or Persian cone patterns. The design required four months of work, but the actual weaving on British power looms was accomplished in a week. Ladies took lessons in the art of wearing the shawl. see *Spanish shawl.*

shearlings see *lamb.*

sheath gown a tubelike gown, straight, narrow and close-fitting. A recurring silhouette in the history of fashion.

sheepskin the skin of sheep after removing the wool and finished to resemble other leathers and parchment. Sheep and lamb hair-covered peltries are important to the modern furrier due to the ever-lessening supply of wild-animal peltries. Some have wool or hair texture quite similar to that of wild animals and can be processed into imitations for coats, boots and gloves and many other fur uses.

shell a sleeveless overblouse, which is part of an ensemble with jacket and skirt. 1950's to date.

shell edging a scalloped edging in shell design executed in crochet work.

shepherd's check or **plaid** a twill-woven cloth with even checks in black and white or contrasting colors. Of wool, rayon, cotton or blends; chiefly used for sportswear.

sherryvallies from the Spanish *zaraguellas,* loose pantaloons buttoned or laced to the belt over fine leather breeches, about two yards around the seat. Formerly for masculine riding as a protection against mud and dust.

Shetland knitting yarn made from the wool of Shetland sheep, fine and thin with a slight twist.

Shetland cloth a shaggy cloth made from the wool of sheep raised in the Shetland Isles off Scotland. An informal suit and overcoat cloth, lightweight and warm.

Shetland lace an openwork needle-made lace of Shetland wool; used for infant's wear and covers, and for knitwear in lace stitches.

shields see *dress shields.*

shift originally, and for centuries, the chemise or shirt of white linen worn by men, women and children, basically a work or sleeping garment with long sleeves. It was smocked at the shoulders for extra fullness. In the 1950's it returned as a fashionable woman's dress worn very short. see *chemise; sheath gown.*

shingle a feminine haircut. In the 1920's the hair was cut very short and shaped to the back of the head, just covering the ears, with a sharp point at the nape, a style revived in the 1960's.

sheath gown - blue silk and black velvet - lace and embroidery - 1910

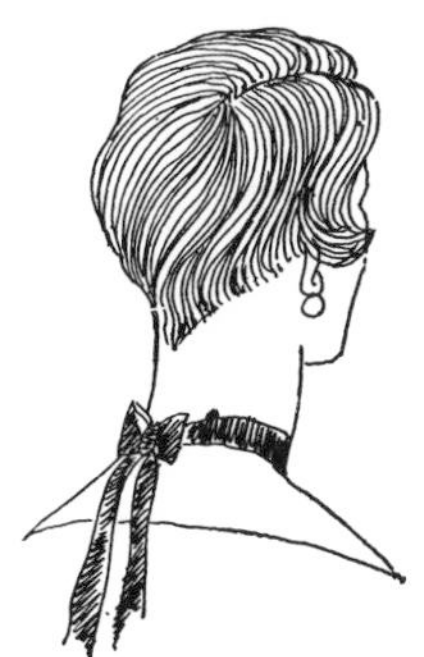

shingle haircut - 1923

shingle coiffure with false front curls - French - 1800

shintiyan Turkish name for wide, loose pantaloons still worn by Moslem women.

shirring in sewing, a series of close parallel lines of running stitches drawn up to make the material set in gathers.

shirt in general, any of certain garments for the upper part of the body; specifically, the loose garment for men and boys worn under a coat or vest, or a close-fitting undergarment. A man's business or everyday shirt is generally of fine white cotton broadcloth. Other fabrics used are airplane cloth, batiste, chambray, madras, Oxford, percale, summer piqué, poplin and a heavy voile. Also, there are figured silks or plain, plaid and striped cottons of varied colors. The shirt of deep or dark color in wine, navy, red, green or brown worn with light-toned jacket and trousers was introduced in the 1930's. The man's white shirt or nylon appeared in the late 1940's during the scarcity of white cotton and proved a sensation with its qualities of washability, quick drying and requiring very little, or no pressing. The man's dress shirt for formal evening wear with tailcoat has a starched bosom, wing collar and single or French cuffs. The man's shirt for semi-formal evening wear with dinner jacket has a plain or pleated bosom, fold collar and single or French cuffs. see specific types: *aloha; basque, boiled; chukker; Garibaldi; hunting; lumberjack; neckband; polo.*

shirt, riding habit worn under the waistcoat by lady and gentlemen riders of the eighteenth century. A shirt of fine cambric or lawn, usually with stiffened collar and lapels, the lapels edged with self fabric. The feminine was like the masculine, but had a tape attached at center back and tied around the waist.

shirts, shertes The shirt or chemise with sleeves has been worn for hundreds of years by men and women. The Norman shirt of the nobleman in the fourteenth century developed neckband and cuffs. In 1442–1483, the time of Edward IV, shirts were made of wool, linen and Holland, and an occasional silk garment for royalty. In the sixteenth century, bands and cuffs were edged with embroidery. Frills next became wide and were made separate from the garment. They were fashioned of fine cambric, Holland and lawn, silk embroidered and edged with lace. An English law was passed forbidding the wearing of a pleated or embroidered shirt by a man without social rank. In the seventeenth century, there were ruffles at the neck, down the front and showing below the short doublet or jacket. The jabot and Steinkerque cravat became important in the eighteenth century. In the late eighteenth and early nineteenth centuries, the voluminous neckcloth concealed the shirtfront until Beau Brummell made a rule of displaying the ruffled shirt for day and evening wear in 1806. With that ruling, dressy gentlemen took to wearing a collar like Brummell's with points projecting upwards.

shirtwaist the feminine adaptation of the masculine shirt at the turn of the century. Of heavy white linen or muslin, with stiff starched collar and a small bow tie or a four-in-hand. It was immortalized by the modern Charles Dana Gibson (1867–1944) in his Gibson Girl paintings.

shirtwaist dress essentially a shirtwaist extended to dress length, with straight, gored or full skirt according to fashion. Generally buttoned to the waist, hipline, or hem, often with a fly front. Round or convertible collar; sleeves of any length or sleeveless; belted or sashed or worn loose in shift style. Any color of almost any fabric, including such formal ones as taffeta and damask. Because of its adaptability the shirtwaist dress of the 1930's has become a twentieth century classic and is considered one of America's outstanding contributions to fashion.

shocking pink a fuchsia pink

launched by Elsa Schiaparelli, the Paris couturière, in the late 1920's.

shoddy fabric made of reclaimed wool spun from old woolen rags chopped into waste, then carded and spun into threads of varied thickness. It can be woven into cloth patterns which sell at very low price. A good-size yardage is used in less expensive men's wear. As an adjective, shoddy means cheap and of poor quality, as in fabrics, workmanship, etc.

shoe, congress see *gaiter.*

shoe, high or **high-buttoned** buttoned or laced shoes reaching well above the ankles, a fashion of the nineteenth and early twentieth centuries for winter wear.

shoe horn a shaped piece of metal or plastic used to ease the foot into a snug-fitting shoe. So named because formerly made of a polished piece of cow's horn.

shoe, juliet see *juliet shoe.*

shoe, monk a low-heeled shoe of brown calf, usually buckled at the side, a type worn by monks.

shoe, piked see *poulaines.*

shoe rose a rosette worn on the instep or vamp. Late in the sixteenth century, the new-style shoes with tongues and side pieces called for latchets or straps and colored shoestrings; the latter were tied with a lover's knot and eventually hidden by a shoe rose, a costly extravagance of the seventeenth century. Shoe roses are still part of the costume of the Warders of the Tower of London.

shoe, running an athlete's soft leather shoe with light-turned sole, with or without cleats.

shoe, saddle see *saddle Oxford.*

shoe, tennis or **sneaker** a low, laced oxford of canvas with rubber sole. Originally used largely for tennis, hence tennis shoe; *sneaker* is an Americanism.

shoe tree a form of metal or wood put inside shoes to preserve the shape when not worn.

shoe, wooden In Europe of the twentieth century, galoshes of leather with wooden soles in boot or low-shoe form continued to be the general footwear of country people, especially in winter. The work shoe or sabot of peasants in France and the Low Countries was shaped from a solid block of wood. The Dutch call theirs *klompen.* Sabots and klompen are still worn by farmers' children. Also to be seen occasionally in France worn with regional costume, are facsimiles of heeled leather slippers carved of wood, painted black and ornamented with ribbon bowknots or shoe roses.

shoe rose of fine lace-jewel in the center-17th C.

shoe rose of lace-white punched leather-red heel and sole-17th C.

shoemaking about 1812, the manufacture of shoe nails to replace wooden pegs; 1830, diagrams for cutting shoes; 1846, the first sewing machine patented by Howe; 1851, Singer Sewing Machine with foot treadle; 1858, the Blake machine for sewing uppers and soles together; 1860, McKay sole-sewing machine patented by Blake and McKay, making sewing possible instead of nails, then "straights" neither right nor left, finally replaced by rights and lefts, and worn by Civil War soldiers, and civilians.

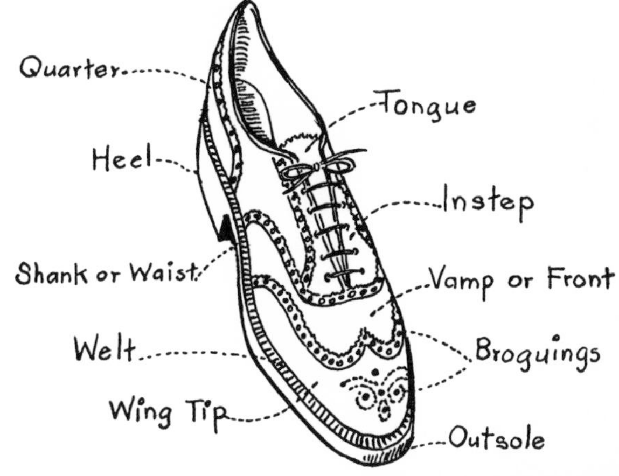

shuba—sheepskin coat-fur to the inside-black woolen shirt, "rubashka"-black sheepskin bonnet-Russian farmer of Caucasia

shoepack a heavy half-boot worn in the seventeenth century and still worn today by loggers in winter. The name is derivative of the Lenape Indian word *shipak.* It is made like the Indian moccasin without separate sole, ankle-high and of oil-tanned leather, usually white.

shooting jacket see *bush jacket.*

shopping bag see *tote bag.*

short warm or **car coat** a reversible coat of two different clothes, shell and lining. Usually of Loden cloth from the Tyrol with wooden toggles and hemp loops. A continental fashion worn by men, women and children after World War II. see *British warm.*

shorts short trousers worn by both sexes for casual or sports wear. Bermuda shorts reach the knee; Nassau shorts come to mid-thigh; Jamaica shorts are even shorter. see *pant lengths, feminine.*

shot silk see *silk, shot.*

shoulder bag a variation of the handbag with a long strap, to be worn either diagonally across the torso or with the bag hanging straight from one shoulder. Originating as part of the uniform of the women's services in World War II, it left the hands free and gave a trim appearance. Popular for all daytime wear during the 1940's and revived as a casual fashion in the 1960's.

shuba—snow leopard-gray or cream color marked with black rosettes-red fox cap-Russian Kazakh chief

shovel hat see *hat, shovel.*

shroud the burial garment or winding sheet used for many centuries and still in use.

shrug a feminine jacket, waist-length or shorter.

shuba a Russian sheepskin coat worn with the wool inside in winter. The skin side, which can be worn alone in milder seasons, is decorated with colorful embroidery and motifs of appliquéd dyed leather. Also worn in Rumania and Yugoslavia.

sibeline French for sable. see *zibelline.*

Siberian chipmunk see *chipmunk.*

Siberian dog or **fur** see *dogskin.*

Siberian sable see *sable, Russian.*

si-bonne trademark of a rayon lining, soft, thin and slithery.

Sicilian, Sicilienne cloth a kind of mohair, heavier and coarser than brilliantine. Used for men's and women's summer coats and suits.

Sicilian embroidery see *Spanish embroidery.*

sicyonia a shoe of reticulated design laced in front, of colored or gilt leather. Worn in ancient Rome by women and fops.

side whiskers, sideburns long in the 1840's and even longer in the next two decades. To the English they were mutton chops or Piccadilly weepers, and to the French, cutlets or tavoris. Americans called them *dundrearies* after Lord Dundreary, a character in a popular play, *Our American Cousin,* by Tom Taylor. *Sideburns* was an American colloquialism after the general and politicians, A. E. Burnside (1824–1881). Originally, the word was burnsides. With the twentieth century, the "clean-shaven look" took over, to last until the 1960's when young men again grew sideburns.

side whiskers-moustache and imperial-French-1857

silhouette a profile or shadow outline of an object, filled in with black; also, a profile, cut with a scissors from black paper. Of ancient origin although the name dates only from mid-18th century. Etienne de Silhouette, French Minister of Finance, was notoriously unpopular for his program of taxation and economies, and his name became a term for anything of plain or simple form. In time, the word *silhouette* was applied to the outline or shape of a fashion in dress.

silk a fiber derived from the cocoon of the silkworm and also from a species of spider. The cultivation of the mulberry tree, upon whose leaves the silkworm feeds, dates back to about 2640 B.C. in China; Chinese records of that period mention the use of silk in robes, sunshades, etc. Silk probably became known to the Mesopotamians, Egyptians and Greeks some time in the second century B.C., through Persian and Phoenician traders. Although it was worn by Cleopatra in the first century B.C. it was rarely used in Egyptian textiles until the fifth century A.D. Heliogabalus (204–222 A.D.) was the first Roman emperor to wear silk. In the Byzantine period, raw silk was imported from China and woven in the emperor's palace in Constantinople, its production being controlled by the emperor. This woven silk was valued at fabulous sums. In 360 the Persian king, victorious in a war against Constantinople, carried away the most skillful weavers. This was the foundation of the subsequent fame of Persian silks. It was in the sixth century during Justinian's reign (527–565) that Byzantine silk culture was again at its height, to last another three centuries. Under his patronage, eggs of the silkworm and seeds of the mulberry bush were brought from China by two Persian monks, concealed in their hollow bamboo staffs.

silk, artificial see *artificial silk.*

silk cotton a cotton-like substance enveloping the seeds of any of various trees, especially that of the balsa tree.

silk, doupioni see *doupioni silk.*

silk, raw, reeled silk filaments unwound from cocoons and joined onto a long thread such as is first reeled into skeins and hanks. These are the long fibers of all classes and the finest grade of silk.

silk, shot textile term for changeable colored silk, especially taffeta, produced by the use of warp threads of one color and weft threads of another.

silk, spun a trade term for floss, waste silk, damaged cocoons and yarns, carded and spun. Lacks some luster but makes a strong fabric.

silk, thrown two or more twisted "singles" which are threads twisted in the direction opposite to the natural twist.

silk, weighted silk made heavier by salts used in the dye and finish to give the cloth weight in draping, a richer look and more luster. Such treatment, however, is detrimental to the silk.

silk, wild made from the larvae of wild silkworms and commercially valuable.

silkaline a soft, thin cotton fabric with smooth finish resembling silk. Plain or figured and used principally for lining.

silks see *Caledonian; China; gauze; oiled; polished; pongee; serge; shantung; Thai; tie; tied and dyed; tussah; vegetable.*

silver cloth or **tissue** cloth made with metal warp of silver color and silk weft. Used for evening wraps, gowns and trimmings.

silver fox see *fox, silver.*

side whiskers and moustache—French—1842

side whiskers and moustache—English—1862

side whiskers and moustache—American—1870's

silhouette—usually in profile—outline filled in with black ink

simarre-Venetian robe worn by magistrates and professors- of rich brocade- mortarboard cap-16th C.

sinhs, traditional skirt of Laos-women- wrap-around of brocade-scarf called uparnā- worn by Indian men and women

simar a lady's short "at home" jacket of brocade, velvet or plush worn over a petticoat and stomacher. The long sleeves and the edge of the jacket were banded with fur. It was a popular negligée jacket in the American Colonies. Dutch, seventeenth and eighteenth centuries.

simarre (French), **simarra** (Italian) a long, sumptuous robe of handsome brocade which originated in Venice, sixteenth century. It flared to the floor with long, wide Dalmatian sleeves. Venetian ladies wore a simarra with a long train.

sinamay a coarse, open, stiff textile woven chiefly from the Philippine abaca.

single-breasted closure of jacket and waistcoat fastened by a single row of buttons and buttonholes which appeared with the lounge jacket or sack coat in the 1850's and 1860's. see *lounge coat; sack coat.*

sinhs The traditional wrap-around skirt of Laotian women, usually of ankle-length and of beautiful brocade. It is folded into a deep front pleat. Worn with a sari-wrapped scarf of striped silk over the left shoulder, the right shoulder bare. Contemporary.

siren suit British wartime name for a "jump suit," so called because it could be quickly donned when sirens sounded for a night raid.

sisal a species of straw grown mainly in the Philippines and shipped to China; an expensive straw, finely woven with a linen finish.

sizing a finishing process in which fabrics are endowed with smoothness, stiffness and strength by the use of starch.

skaut see *Hardanger skaut.*

skean dhu a short dirk or dagger worn in the knee-length stocking of Scottish Highland dress. see *Scottish Highland dress.*

skein a quantity of yarn, silk, thread, etc. which has been taken from the reel in a loose, twisted loop.

skein-dyed applied to fabrics made of yarns, wool, cotton or silk, which have been dyed in the skein before weaving.

skeleton vest a man's backless waistcoat for summer wear, particularly with evening dress. Early 1950's.

ski a strip of wood bound one on each foot and used for gliding over snow. see *snowshoe.*

ski clothes usually stretch pants and parka for both men and women, although changing fads of fashion appear almost every season. The nature of the sport requires garments that allow freedom of action and are lightweight but warm and waterproof.

skilts knee-length Dutch breeches worn by boys and farmhands during the Revolutionary period in the American Colonies. They were very full, fit snugly at the waist, and required no suspenders.

skimmer; capeline a wide, soft-brimmed leghorn hat faced with silk, worn over a white lawn cap and tied with velvet ribbons; English, 1750's. The flat-crowned, wide-brimmed straw sailor worn by Eton students was also called a skimmer. In the late nineteenth and early twentieth centuries, the style was revived by fashionable men and women for sportswear.

skimmer hat -leghorn with green silk facing-silk or velvet ribbons- frilled white lawn cap- English- 1750's

Skinner's satin trade name for a general line of satin and lining that enjoyed a long popularity in fabrics.

skins commercial term for pelts, weighing up to fifteen pounds of small animals such as goat, sheep, calf, etc. see *animal skins.*

skirt that part of a costume which hangs from or below the waist. Also, an underskirt or petticoat. The skirt cut separately and sewn to a bodice first appeared in Italian court dress of the fourteenth century.

skirt, bell a flared, gored skirt, fashionable in the 1890's, shaped by haircloth interlining from waist to hem.

skirt, circular of the 1890's, cut circular and held in shape by haircloth interlining from waist to hem. Revived with the New Look, late 1940's.

skirt, dirndl see *dirndl.*

skirt, habit-back see *skirt, rainy daisy.*

skirt, harem a divided or "trouser skirt" launched unsuccessfully in Paris about 1910. A very full skirt of soft silk, draped and gathered to the ankles to simulate Turkish pantaloons.

skirt, hobble a very narrow, tapered ankle-length skirt. It made walking difficult, inspired ridicule, reflected in its name, the "hobble." Sometimes it was only a yard around, making a deep slit at the side a necessity for walking.

skirt, hula the skirt of Hawaiian dancing girls, a grass skirt, knee-length or longer.

skirt, micro, miniskirt, maxiskirt see below.

skirt, 1960's the *micro* which just covers the hips; the *miniskirt* of a length between thigh and knee introduced by the London "Mod" designer, Mary Quant; the *maxiskirt* with hemline somewhere between knee and ankle.

skirt, peg-top see *peg-top skirt.*

skirt, rainy daisy, or **habit back** a sports skirt of the first decade of the twentieth century. An ankle-length, fitted cloth skirt, worn for walking, rainy days, golf and roller skating.

skirt, weather see *safeguard.*

skirt, wrap-around a one-piece skirt which can be made on the straight of the cloth with a few darts or tucks to shape the hips, the two straight ends overlapping in front. This has been a standard twentieth century style for some decades. Another wrap-around skirt, of the 1920's, was cut on the bias in one piece, the surplus material brought around to center front and draped into soft folds or box pleats at the waistline. In mid-century, a one-piece bias-cut skirt was introduced for casual wear, which crossed in the back and fastened with ties brought around to the front, allowing an adjustable waistline.

skirt—"Hobble" with taffeta sash—lace over old blue taffeta—French—1911

skiver the grain side of split sheepskin tanned in sumac and dyed. Cheap, soft leather used for lining men's hats, pocketbooks, book binding, etc.

skivvies U.S. Navy term for men's underwear.

skullcap a small, round cap fitting the top of the head, without brim or peak. see *calotte* under *cap.*

skunk from the Algonquin Indian name "Seganku." Also called black marten and Alaska sable, formerly dressed and sold as such. An American animal of the weasel family found from Hudson Bay to South America and coast to coast. Smaller numbers and poorer in quality in Mexico, Central America, Brazil and Argentina. The best skins from New York

striped skunk—American animal of weasel family

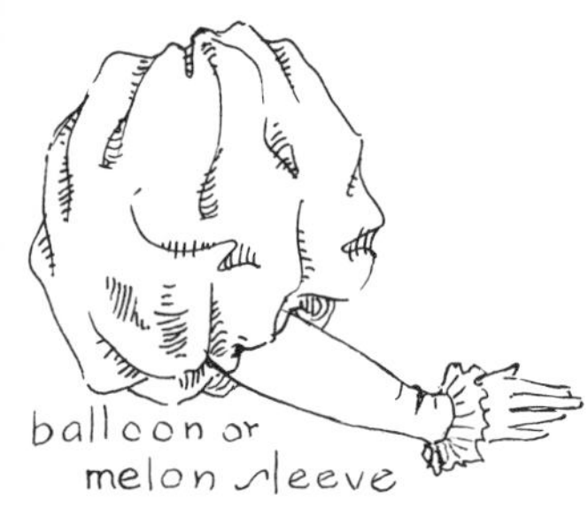

and Ohio, very durable, silky and natural fur with flowing top hair, all black or black with a white stripe. see *civet.*

slacks a general term for sports pants worn by either sex. Masculine sports ensembles were adopted by women in the 1920's for winter sports, and by the 1930's for other sports such as sailing. By the end of World War II slacks were accepted for feminine casual wear at any time. see *pants suit.*

slash pocket see *pocket, slash.*

slashings a Renaissance fashion in gentlemen's clothes. All articles of clothings were slashed, even gloves, shoes and stockings, revealing puffings of contrasting material and color. Slashings appeared in the fifteenth century and lasted to the mid-seventeenth. The decoration originated among the Swiss soldiers in 1477 when they won a battle against the Duke of Burgundy and mended their ragged uniforms with strips of tents, banners and furnishings left behind by the vanquished Burgundians. The fashion spread over Europe, reaching its height from 1520 to 1535.

slat bonnet see *sunbonnet.*

slave bracelet usually a link bracelet or a bracelet worn above the elbows. Also, a hoop band with loops to which the wearer adds small charms.

sleep coat a man's coat of cotton or rayon, knee-length with half or full-length sleeves and long lapels; usually tied with self belt. Sometimes worn instead of pajamas or nightshirt, twentieth century. Also worn by women, 1960's.

sleeve, angel the long, loose flowing sleeve of the robe or dalmatic worn in the Western church and upon English state occasions. Originally called Dalmatian sleeve.

sleeve, bag a Flemish medieval sleeve, long and very full and soft, gathered into a plain, tight wrist cuff, fifteenth century.

sleeve, balloon or **melon** popular in the 1890's. The forearm fitted to the elbow and a full, rounded puff from elbow to shoulder, the puff lined with muslin or buckram for stiffening. 1890's.

sleeve, batwing a sleeve cut to fit an armhole reaching from shoulder to waist and shaped into a small cuff or fitted wristband.

sleeve, bishop's a long, soft sleeve fitted over the upper arm and flaring at the bottom, or gathered into a band cuff. A woman's fashion of the first decade of 1900, modeled on the full linen sleeve of a prelate's rochet.

sleeve, bracelet a three-quarter-length sleeve leaving the forearm bare halfway to the wrist to display the wearing of bracelets. Contemporary.

sleeve, cape a sleeve cut circular and fitted to the armscye, usually elbow-length with a wide capelike flare.

sleeve, Dalmatian see *angel sleeve.*

sleeve, dolman attached to an armscye cut from shoulder to waistline, the sleeve itself shaping down to wrist-size.

sleeve, epaulet a set-in sleeve with an epaulet formed of self-fabric, trimming or a roll extending around the top of the sleeve. Called "wings" in the medieval period. Late sixteenth and early seventeenth centuries.

sleeve, false or **hanging** of Italian origin, the false or hanging sleeve was part of the outer jerkin. The sleeve which covered the arm was part of the doublet or under-jacket and often was just laced to the armscye. Medieval.

sleeve, kimono wide at the armscye, usually cut in one with the body; characteristic of Japanese dress.

sleeve, leg-of-mutton a fashionable sleeve of the 1890's, known as a *gigot* in French. It fitted the forearm but flared from the elbow into a balloon shape which was gathered or pleated into a fitted armscye.

sleeve, mameluke a fashion of the French First Empire (1799–1815), named for the soldiers of a squadron of Mamelukes created by Napoleon I. A woman's sleeve, long, with a series of puffs, large at the top and diminishing in size to the wrist, finishing with frills. see *sleeve, virago.*

sleeve, melon see *sleeve, balloon.*

sleeve, peasant a long, full sleeve gathered or shirred into a dropped shoulder and usually shirred at the wrist.

sleeve, puffed both masculine and feminine sleeves were elaborately puffed in varied shape and width in the sixteenth and seventeenth centuries. They were divided into sections.

sleeve, raglan a sleeve with the seam reaching from the underarm, back and front, to the neckline. see *raglan.*

sleeve, set-in a tailored long sleeve of dress, jacket, or coat, sewn to a fitted armscye.

sleeve, shoulder-puff a long, fitted sleeve topped by a puff from shoulder seam to underarm depth.

sleeve, three-quarter see *sleeve, bracelet.*

sleeve, virago a full sleeve evenly divided into many small puffs tied by ribbon bands, the ribbon band also called viragos. Worn by men and women in the sixteenth century. see *sleeve, mameluke.*

slendang a fine cotton scarf which the Javanese woman drapes over her shoulders.

slops—breeches called "full slops" laid in pleats—brocaded silk—English—17th C.

smock frock of homespun, flax or hemp—smock stitching—English farmer

slicker A coat for rainy weather or nautical wear in waterproofed fabrics, oilskin or rubber. see *oilskin.*

slide fastener A tape of varied length with a flexible closing device, either metal or plastic, now also in nylon, worked by a slide pull. Used first in galoshes by B. F. Goodrich Co., and named *zipper.* 1920's. see *zipper.*

slings, slingbacks slippers with vamp or front but simply a strap in back.

slip a feminine undergarment reaching from armpit to hemline. A full slip is a fitted slip with shaped bosom and narrow shoulder straps. Of cotton, silk or rayon, often lace-trimmed, it serves as undergarment to the dress. A half-slip is a petticoat without top, also of silk, nylon or lace-trimmed but only waist-high. Mini-slip is a very short slip. The modern slip cut on the bias became popular in the 1920's following the success of Chanel and Vionnet, about 1916, with their bias-cut gowns and dresses.

slip-on, slip-over see *pull-on.*

slippers for men and women, a light, low-cut shoe easily slipped on the foot for indoor use and ease, usually without the aid of fastening. Dressy, high-heeled slippers are worn by women for formal attire.

Sloppy Joe a knitted woolen, loose-fitting pull-on worn with round or pointed white blouse collar showing at the neck and, generally, a string of pearls. Fashionable with school and college girls, 1940's.

slops an old English term in the sixteenth and seventeenth centuries for many garments. From Spanish slops, a European fashion. see *Spanish slops.*

slotted collar see *collar, slotted.*

slouch hat see *hat, Hungarian; slouch; pork pie; caddie.*

slubs slightly twisted or thick places in wool, cotton or silk woven into the cloth, as compared with skein-dyed or piece-dyed fabric woven with smooth, clean fiber.

smallclothes, smalls eighteenth century name for close-fitting masculine breeches or underdrawers.

smock frock a yoked shirt or loose blouse of coarse linen worn by field laborers in Europe over regular clothes, originally smocked, now often not, despite its name. Many farmers in Colonial Virginia wore smock frocks. The smock is now much worn as a coverall by professional people at work, especially artists. An obsolete English term for a woman's smock was "smicket."

smocking stitchery which resembles a honeycomb pattern; stitches which divide and hold together tiny pleats allowing for fullness, yet at the same time giving ease to the garment.

smoked pearl dark gray to black smoky mother-of-pearl from various sea shells; used for studs, buttons and other ornaments.

smoking jacket a sack or lounge coat, formerly for smoking at home. Of brocade, velvet or cloth of a dark, rich color, braid bound and fastened with Brandenburgs. Worn late nineteenth and early twentieth centuries in Europe and America.

snakeskin leather of which modern shoes, handbags, wallets and many other items are made, procured principally from farm-raised reptiles. They include the cobra, of which there are six or seven species in Asia and Africa; the boa, principally from the Amazonian region; the python of tropical Asia, Africa and Australia; the watersnake of southern United States, Malaysian Archipelago and Africa.

snap fastener, snapper a fastener made in two metal pieces, a ball and a socket clasp, the ball fitted into the socket for closing.

sneakers an Americanism for canvas oxfords or gymnasium shoes with rubber soles. Worn especially for tennis. see *shoe, tennis.*

snood originally, a ribbon or fillet worn by unmarried Scottish maidens. Later, *snood* signified the coarse hairnet or fabric bag, sometimes attached to a hat, to hold a woman's hair loosely at the back of the neck, a Victorian fashion which had its origin in the medieval caul or hairnet of gold thread. The snood was a hair fashion of the 1930's, sometimes with a tiny hat attached.

snow cloth a heavily fleeced woolen cloth such as camel's hair, blanket cloth or the like, used for winter coats.

snowshoe an oval wooden frame with two crosspieces, strung with waterproofed thongs. It spreads the wearer's weight and allows him to walk on soft snow without sinking.

snowsuit an outer garment for children of heavy waterproof or wadded cloth made with coat, hood and leggings in one garment. Formerly tied and buckled but now equipped with zipper fastenings.

snuffbox a tiny box of silver, gold enamel or ivory which holds snuff, a mixture of tobacco leaf and stem, ground and perfumed. The sniffing of a pinch of snuff was a widespread habit of the eighteenth century, indulged in by men and women, especially in England. Purses to hold the snuffbox were of leather set in gold mounts or of knitted silk worked with steel beads and tasseled ends.

snuggies see *pettipants.*

socks, bed see *bed socks.*

socks, English foot a separately knit sole joined at both sides to eliminate the center seam on the sole of the foot. First made for military use and then for sportswear.

socks or hose, golf heavy knitted woolen socks worn with knickers for outdoor sports, especially golf; knee-length, often with a cuff in a decorative pattern. Shorter knitted woolen socks are worn with slacks.

solleret—escarpin or bear's paw—leather or velvet slashed over color—16th C.

solana a crownless straw hat worn in the sixteenth century when blond hair was in fashion. Italian ladies sat in the sun with their hair spread over the wide brim of the hat to bleach the hair.

sole the underside or bottom part of any piece of footwear.

snood of red chenille with velvet toque—1935

soleae of ancient Rome, similar in style for both sexes. They were sandals of boxwood or cowhide with leather straps for wear indoor with the tunica; those for street wear rose higher and were laced with straps. As the wearer's status rose, shoes were cut higher and enriched with gold and silver, these latter being the prerogative of magistrates.

solferino red a bluish red named after the Battle of Solferino in Italy, 1859.

snood of red velvet with bowknot—day or evening—1939

solitaire a single gemstone, set alone. Generally designates the single diamond of the conventional engagement ring.

solitaire a black silk ribbon which tied around a man's wig in back, and the bag which held the wig. The ribbon ends of wig and bag were brought around and tied in a bowknot in front. This was the origin of the gentleman's black silk tie, eighteenth century. see *bag wig, solitaire wig.*

solleret; bear's paw The Italian scarpino of the sixteenth century followed the long-toed poulaine. It was called solleret because it resembled the armor foot-

Spanish gypsy-red velvet jacket-velvet hat, cloth sash, breeches and leggings, all black

covering of thin, articulated steel plates. The point gradually disappeared, becoming a broad, square toe. In fact, with the use of moss stuffing, it became exaggeratedly broad. In France, Germany, England and the Low Countries, the toe grew square. In the mid-sixteenth century, the English Queen Mary was forced to limit the width to six inches. The style is generally associated with Henry VIII of England and in France with François I. The bear's paw was worn by the German mercenary foot soldiers, the lansquenet, from the fifteenth to the seventeenth centuries.

sombrero a broad-brimmed felt or straw hat, originally Spanish, worn by horsemen of Spain, Spanish America, Mexico and the United States Southwest. The Mexican brim is sometimes two feet wide and known in U.S. West as the ten-gallon hat. It is usually of tan, gray or white felt for the charro or gentleman horseman whose hat is banded and faced with silver lace, and of straw for the peon.

Sophie see *couture, haute.*

soutache see *braid.*

soutane see *cassock.*

South American fox see *fox, South American.*

southwester, sou'wester a seaman's bad-weather hat made of rubber or tarpaulin, a canvas covered with tar, paint or other waterproofing. A wide, slanting brim, longer in back than in front.

Spanish fiesta costume, all in black and white - man of Turégano

Spandex a man-made fiber that has the stretch properties of rubber but is lighter in weight; valuable in the world of corsetry and swimwear. Such fibers have changed these former rigid pieces of corsetry into comfortable lingerie. Trademark owned by Du Pont.

spangenhelm followed the shell-like helmet in Europe. It was also of boiled leather with pieces of iron rising to a point and topped by a knob of wood or colored glass. The feudal lord of the ninth and tenth centuries wore such a helmet, while his followers went into battle bareheaded or wearing a felt cap.

spangles see *paillettes.*

Spanish blackwork of ancient Persian origin; used in the sixteenth and seventeenth centuries. An elegant and distinctive embroidery, especially on men's lingerie or fine linen shirts. It was worked in small geometric designs in black silk accented with gold or red stitches.

Spanish comb a high comb thought to have been originally a metal head ornament to raise the kerchief or shawl off the forehead. Later made of silver and finally, in the nineteenth century, of a carved tortoise shell. When shaped like a large shell, it is called a *teja* (roof tile). Still worn today in Spain and Spanish American countries. The mantilla can be draped over it.

Spanish or **Sicilian embroidery** a design on muslin or cambric worked like embroidery by filling in with herringbone stitches. A lacier effect can be achieved by filling in with braid and buttonhole stitches.

Spanish hair see *wig, Spanish hair.*

Spanish heel see *heel, Spanish; continental; French.*

Spanish lace pure silk lace of different meshes with flat, heavy floral designs; called Spanish blonde whether white or black.

Spanish mode of the sixteenth century, a style distinctive and elegant which had an influence upon the European mode. The Spanish gave to Europe the ruche, the ruff, the short cape, the corset, the hoop, the bombast of the padded doublet and trunk hose, followed by unpadded breeches. Knit silk stockings were a Spanish innovation and for a long time surpassed those of other countries.

Spanish papers see *cosmetics.*

Spanish shawl of black silk crepe edged with deep silk fringe and covered with birds and flowers in brilliant colors. Worn by Spanish women with superb grace. Nineteenth and twentieth centuries. see *manton de Manilla.*

Spanish silk kerchief a distinct feature of Spanish dress, worn by men and women in a different manner in each province; as a head covering, over the shoulders or around the neck by women while men wear it around the brow tied like a turban.

Spanish slops or **breeches** breeches of the sixteenth and seventeenth centuries which are noted as being "very full," as were the Dutch slops or sloppes in the same period recorded also as very wide. Slop, or sloppes, was an old English name which was applied to various other garments that were loose-fitting, such as cassocks, nightgowns or shoes.

Spanish toque an evolution of the beret, the soft crown wired into shape, finished with a narrow brim and a jeweled necklace or "band." Fashionable in Spain, Italy, and France in the sixteenth century and worn by elegant ladies and gentlemen.

sparterie a straw fabric for hats and shoes made of esparto grass from Algeria and Spain. Also used for footwear.

spats a short form of cloth gaiters, after the Colonial word spatterdashes. Spats were considered very smart in the late nineteenth and early twentieth centuries, and were worn by men and women with oxfords or pumps. Of heavy

broadcloth in white, gray or tan and buttoned at the sides. Of linen for summer wear. see *gaiters.*

spatterdashes high leather leggins, about 1770. The joining of legging and shoe was covered by spur leathers. see *spur leathers; gamashes.*

spectacles see *eyeglasses.*

spectator sports clothes any simple costume appropriate for those watching a sport but not participating in it; any casual outfit. For men, usually a sports jacket and contrasting slacks; for women a tweed or cotton suit, or a shirtwaist dress and cardigan. Topcoats and headgear depend on the weather.

spencer jacket of velvet-white muslin gown-French Empire-1800

spencer a very shortwaisted jacket worn with the Empire dress of the 1790's. It was designed by Lord Spencer, who claimed fashion is so absurd that he, himself, could concoct a new style and make it a rage. And the following is his tale. He cut the tails off his own coat and went for a stroll. In two weeks all London was wearing the "spencer" and soon fashionable men and women of the Continent and the Colonies were also wearing the same little jacket. The masculine spencer has come down to the present in the mess jackets of military officers. Also worn by civilians for semiformal dinner dress in warm weather. see *Caroline spencer; canezou.*

spider web stitch an embroidery stitch in a spider's web design, used especially at corners.

spider work a heavy bobbin lace resembling opus araneum.

spike heel see *heel, spike.*

spinel a gem stone of magnesium oxide, red, brownish red, gray-blue, deep-greenish, indigo or violet. A variety from Ceylon is black. Some so-called rubies are actually spinel. The large red stone in the British Imperial State Crown known as the "Black Prince's Ruby" is a spinel and of less value than a real ruby.

spinning the process of drawing out fine fibers into a fibrous thread or filament by twisting, either by hand or machinery. Spun silk, spun rayon, spun linen and spun glass are some of the spun textiles.

spinning jenny an early machine for spinning wool and cotton by means of many spindles. It was invented c. 1767 by James Hargreaves, an Englishman.

spinning wheel a machine with a single spindle formerly used for spinning yarn or thread. Driven by a wheel operated by hand or foot.

spit curl see *beau-catcher.*

spitalfields fine silk scarfs manufactured in a section of London called Spitalfields, the name being a mark of quality of the basket-woven silks. see *macclesfield.*

spliced heel a trade term for hosiery made with a heel of double thickness.

sponging a term reserved for the last operation given woolens and worsteds, meaning treating with live steam to give the final shrinkage test and finish.

sporran a large pouch or purse worn in front of the kilt by Scottish Highlanders. It may be of leather, silver-mounted, or of animal skins with fur or hair. Evening sporrans are made of baby seal or other light-colored skins.

sports clothes a term applied to play clothes or apparel designed so as to make the enactment of the sport easier and more successful.

sports clothes, feminine In the late nineteenth century lawn tennis, bicycling, golf and yachting became popular, necessitating practical clothes. For golf the smart woman wore a shirtwaist and separate skirt, and a golf cape or Norfolk jacket; for bicycling, a short skirt or full bloomers with a short fitted jacket. The tailored walking skirt of shoe-top length was known as the rainy-day skirt.

sports footwear in the Victorian period the first sports model, a laced rubber-soled shoe with fabric uppers, later

Golf 1890's
Hunting 1849
Hunting 1887
Beach dress-1880's
Bicycling-1890's
Yachting-1886
Fishing-1857
Tennis-1895
Skiing-1950's
Beach-1930's
Beach-1939
Skiing-1928

called the "sneaker," was worn for croquet, archery and lawn tennis. The ankle-high, laced leather shoe having a sole shod with protruding nails and buttons to prevent slipping, was worn for golf.

sports heel see *heel, sports.*

sports jacket, or **coat** a man's loosely cut jacket of tweed or cotton, worn with contrasting slacks or shorts for informal wear.

sports shirt a man's or boy's shirt for informal wear, generally worn without a tie, open at the neck or with a harmonizing ascot tuck-in. Long or short sleeves. Made in a variety of materials, for year-round use, such as plain, checked or plaid flannel; madras and gingham; sheer nylon or mesh knit. see *aloha shirt; California sports shirt.*

spotted cat see *genet.*

spun gold or **silver** fiber threads which have been wound with thin metal strands.

spun rayon yarn short lengths of filament too short to reel, twisted together and used in the same kind of weaving as cotton, linen and silk.

spun silk see *silk, spun.*

spur a pointed metal implement attached above the heel of a rider's boot to urge the horse by pressure.

spur leathers large quatrefoil shapes worn especially in the seventeenth century over the instep of leather boots to conceal the fastenings of the spurs.

squirrel a land rodent found in all parts of the world except Australia and Africa. The largest quantities of fur come from Europe and Asia, the best from Russia and Siberia, well-furred and of silky texture. Squirrel is used natural or bleached and dyed to simulate many other furs, for coats, jackets and trimming. see *miniver; vair; chinchilla.*

stambouline-short-sleeves and fastened down front-over it, a dolman with hanging sleeves-white silk turban-worn by sultan of Turkey

stacked heel see *heel, stacked.*

stambouline a gorgeous robe worn by Turkish Sultans. Of velvet, brocaded fabric or white satin fastened down center front with jeweled gold buttons, long, and with short sleeves. Over it was worn the doliman, a sleeveless robe with hanging sleeves. A white silk turban draped around a tarboosh completed the costume; one feather worn indoors and two feathers when in public.

stamin, stammel a coarse woolen cloth usually dyed red; formerly used for underwear in shirt and drawers for men and as an underpetticoat for women.

stamped velvet see *velvet, stamped.*

starch an odorless, tasteless, powdery substance obtained from plants and diluted with water for application to garments. When dry, the starch stiffens the fabric. The starching of sheer fabrics used in caps, wimples, collars and ruffs originated in Flanders and was perfected in Holland. In 1564, a Dutch gentlewoman taught young English ladies of rank to starch. Blue, goose-green and creamy yellow were the principal colors used for ruffs and the starch employed was either English or Dutch. Starch is white today.

start-up, startop a peasant's boot consisting of a sturdy low shoe and a separate knee-high legging of leather, wool or linen, tied top and bottom; seventeenth century.

stayhook a small, ornamental silver hook with a pin to be fastened to the edge of the bodice for holding an étui, a fancy bag or case in which to carry toilet and sewing articles. Late nineteenth century.

stays see *corsetry.*

steeple hat see *hat, steeple.*

steeple headdress see *hennin.*

steinkerk, steenkerk a scarf of lawn,

lace or black silk loosely tied, with the ends tucked into shirt or vest or drawn through a buttonhole or ring. It became a fashion in 1692 after the Battle of Steinkerk in Belgium, when the victorious French charged the opposing cavalry with their dress in disorder and cravats untied and flying. Ladies also adopted the fine white neckerchief of batiste and lace, the fashion lasting a good half century.

stencil a cutout pattern or design to apply to another surface by painting, stippling or brushing through the openings.

step-in blouse a blouse and drawers made in one piece, to obviate bunching at the waist; 1920's.

step-ins see *panties.*

Stetson see *hat, Stetson.*

sticharion a robe or tunic of white linen, corresponding to the alb, worn by prelates of the Eastern Church.

stickpin see *scarf pin.*

stiletto a small instrument of bone, ivory or steel for puncturing holes to be embroidered. Used in eyelet embroidery.

stirrup-hose overhose of the seventeenth and eighteenth centuries for horseback riding. The tops, nearly two yards wide, were edged with eyelet holes and laced to the breeches or belt.

stitch, stitchwork, needlework employed in hand-sewing, embroidery and tapestry. Executed with an eye-needle passing through cloth, leaving a thread stitch in the fabric. All stitches, and there are more than two hundred made with needle and thread, are founded upon seven basic stitches: back stitch, blanket stitch, chain stitch, cross stitch, knot, overcast and running stitch.

stoat see *ermine, summer.*

stock a starched neckcloth wrapped twice around the neck and buckled in the back; successor to the cravat, eighteenth century. Still worn with riding habits by both men and women.

stockinette an elastic or tubular textile formerly made on a knitting frame, usually cotton with a fleeced back. It was used for undergarments and stockings. Also, a close-woven, heavy elastic material, mostly white, used for livery breeches.

stockings a close-fitting covering for the leg and foot, generally knit or woven. The word appeared first in the sixteenth century and derives from the Anglo Saxon "prican," to stick. Because hose were "stock" or "stuck" with sticking pins or needles, hose became stocken, then stocken of hose, and finally stockings. Knee-length hose were stocks. Leg coverings went through many forms before being joined together in one piece in the fourteenth century, when they reached the waist. They were secured to the short skirt of the jacket by laces with points. Women's stockings or chausses reached above the knee and were gartered. Chausses were seamed up the back and made of cloth, cotton, linen or silk. By this time in the fifteenth century, the tailor was cutting the cloth on the bias for a better fit. In the sixteenth century, chausses consisted of two sections, upper stocks and lower or netherstocks. In the mid-nineteenth century, vivid-colored silk petticoats came into fashion with stockings to match, even to horizontal stripes. Then, in the 1890's, the reaction was for black stockings worn with all shoes regardless of color. A shapely feminine leg sheathed in sheer black was considered the height of allure, the black stocking holding its own to the 1920's, with tan for sportswear. In the second decade of the twentieth century the tan silk stocking gave way to gray, taupe, beige and white for summer. Nude or blond was first worn in Paris. see *stockings, nylon; pantyhose; panty-stockings.*

stockings, leather Indian leggings of Colonial days. Reaching from ankle to mid-thigh, the side seams were fringed and embroidered and tied to the belt by thongs. Form-fitting, they were sewn to the leg and often worn to tatters.

stockings, lisle made of a fine Egyptian cotton made silky by a mercerizing process, the result known as mercerized cotton; the wealthy woman's stockings until silk became common in the late nineteenth century.

stockings, machine-knitted Until 1610, stockings were hand-knitted worsted, crewel, linen, jersey openwork and sewn cloth. Spanish hand-knitters excelled in their product from the sixteenth to the eighteenth centuries when France usurped the reputation. In the seventeenth century, red was for daily wear, and dress usually white.

stole and muff of ermine-white bowknot on muff-black silk gown-green velvet bonnet with green and gray ostrich-1844

stockings, nylon came on the American market in 1939, followed by World War II and the curtailment of nylon until 1945. With the war's end, nylons again became available to American women. Contemporary "nylons" are available in a wide range of textures and jewel-like tones.

stockings, silk It is noted that the first silk stockings, a Spanish invention, were worn in France by Henri II (1519–1559). Silk knits from Spain are also known to have been presented to Henry VIII. The first knit silk stockings worn by an Englishwoman were presented to Queen Elizabeth by her "silk woman," Mistress Montagne, who knitted them. The queen was so delighted with the stockings that she said that she would never wear cloth hose again. But silk stockings were not manufactured in England until the following century, though one of Elizabeth's subjects invented the first knitting and stocking frame.

stola a full-length straight robe with short, set-in sleeves, generally of linen or light wool, worn by women of ancient Rome.

stole or **scarf** a long, straight, shoulder scarf of fur or velvet cloth, or knitted, often with fringed ends. Originally the stola was the ancient Roman matron's long garment. Also, an ecclesiastical vestment, a long narrow scarf with embroidery.

stomacher a decorative and elaborate separate front panel ending in a deep point. The stomacher was essentially an evolution of the Spanish figure. Though worn over a tightly fitted bodice, it was rather like a breastplate, fashioned of steel and splints of ivory, mother-of-pearl or silver covered with satin or velvet. It was worn by men and women in the sixteenth century and by women into the seventeenth and eighteenth centuries. Laced to the figure, it was ornamented with lace, ribbons and often jewels. A favored feminine version had ribbon bowknots in graduated sizes and was called an échelle, from the French for ladder. see *échelle; plastron.*

stone marten see *marten.*

stove-pipe a very tall, high silk hat. see *hat, top.*

Strasbourg work see *Roman cut work.*

strass see *paste; jewelry.*

straw braids about one quarter to three inches wide, used in the manufacture of hats. Made of fine straws from Italy, Switzerland, and South America, and of less expensive straws from China and Japan.

straw hats hats made mostly of Belgian and Swiss straw in the past but now of straws grown in Japan and China.

stretch pants women's pants for

sports or lounging wear made from cloth woven of stretch yarn.

stretch yarn a fine natural or synthetic filament wrapped with silk, nylon, rayon or cotton yarn and used with such threads in weaving.

string tie a man's very narrow necktie or scarf.

strophium in ancient Greece, a bandelette worn outside the chiton under the bosom. It served the same purpose as the apodesme. A more elaborate piece, often ornamented with gold, pearls, and other stones. It was often worn as a filet around the head. The Roman version of the strophium was made of wool, linen or a fine, soft chamoised leather called "aluta" which was dyed purple.

studs jeweled shirt fasteners for formal or semiformal wear in plain gold, pearls, and cabochon-cut stones. Studs fastened collar and bosom, usually gold. Tethered studs, three on a fine chain to fasten bosom front. Appeared 1840's. see *cufflinks.*

stuff in costume, any material not made into garments.

style in costume, the display of distinctive elegance in design and color and the fitness to the occasion. However, a costume can also be in poor taste. see *fashion.*

subarmale a sleeveless tunic with short pleated skirt worn by ancient Roman legionnaires under the metal cuirass.

suclat Anglo-Indian name for scarlet; also European-made woolen broadcloth for army tunics.

suede from the French for Swedish, the velvety finish having originated in Sweden. Formerly made from kidskin only, much of the leather is now from baby lamb and calfskin.

suede, antelope-finished a leather sueded to resemble antelope. The leathers so used are calfskin, lambskin and goatskin.

suede, camel see *camel suede.*

suede cloth, suede finish a knitted or woven cloth with the surface napped and shorn to simulate the leather. Suede finish is also applied to some wool and cotton fabrics.

sugar-loaf bonnet see *bonnet, sugar-loaf.*

suit originally a livery, uniform or habit. Now, for men, a coat or jacket with matching trousers and sometimes a matching waistcoat. For women, a coat or jacket and matching skirt, worn with a blouse or pullover.

suit, dinner see *dinner suit.*

suit, man's The change in western man's dress occurred first at Louis XIV's court in 1666, which Charles II of England followed in the same year by dressing his courtiers in the new vest, coat and breeches of Spanish cut. This was the habit à la française. In the first half of the eighteenth century, the long, flaring buckram-lined skirts of coat and waistcoat were modified. By the time of the French Revolution, men's costume had settled upon fitted coat and waistcoat, and longer breeches. In the late eighteenth and early nineteenth centuries, one notes the modern style of dress in London, where the English tailors had settled upon breeches below knee-length, fitted waistcoat, a long outer coat and the top hat. In the 1860's the lounge suit appeared, prototype of today's habit or suit with trousers, waistcoat and short coat or jacket, the modern man's basic dress.

suit, paddock see *English drape.*

sultane—long skirt held up by hoops and buttons en négligé—popular in the Colonies—18th C.

sultane a feminine robe worn in Europe and the American Colonies in early 1700's, after the Turkish emperor's robe; open down center front and caught up by buttons and loops.

summer furs see *furs, summer.*

sun shods, Mexican a trade name for an Indian sports sandal fashioned of two wide leather straps crossed over the instep and attached to the leather sole by nail-heads.

sun suit a one-piece summer garment for little children.

sunbonnet, slat bonnet of cotton fabric, plain or figured and fashioned with a brim or poke held in shape by stitched slots holding thin wooden slats. In general, the sunbonnet was a peasant type of head covering with a bavolet. It had a wide brim of straw or stiffened, starched fabric, a gathered full crown, and chin ties.

sunburst a jeweled brooch designed with rays radiating from the center, the rays usually set with small diamonds. Late nineteenth and early twentieth centuries.

sundress a backless dress worn for sunbathing.

sunfast a term signifying that a dyed fabric has met a standard test for not fading by sunlight.

sunglasses spectacles with colored lenses to protect the eyes from strong sunlight.

sunshade, parasol from the middle of the sixteenth century both men and women used sunshades which were called "umbrellas." In the seventeenth century court sunshades were lined with gold and silver lace, becoming lighter in weight. By the eighteenth century umbrellas for rain closed but sunshades and parasols did not. Early in the nineteenth century, a tilting parasol with hinged or folding stick, named the Pompadour parasol, appeared. It was a pretty shadepiece of moiré with ruffles and fringe. see *umbrella.*

suntan era late in the 1920's the smart world took to lounging on the beach, and immediately many kinds of oils and lotions came on the market to hasten a sun-tan or to protect a delicate skin during the process. Brownish face powders for women became the vogue and if one's skin did not take on a fashionable tan, then one painted the flesh the desired color.

supertotus see *balandrana.*

Supp-hose trade name for firm-holding hose and stockings for men and women. Of man-made fibers, nylon, lycra and spandex. Owned by Du Pont. see *nylon; lycra; spandex.*

supportasse a wire frame which held up the great ruff in the sixteenth and seventeenth centuries. see *underproper.*

surah a soft-finished silk or wool fabric, the heavier cloth called silk serge and that with high luster called satin surah. Used for dresses, men's scarfs and mufflers.

surcingle the girdle or belt worn with a cassock.

surcoat, surcot, surcote a fashion of the Middle Ages for men and women which derived from the armor covering worn by the Crusader to eliminate the glare of the sun upon his armor when in the East. The original covering hung straight front and back, two rectangles caught at the sides and reaching to the knees. There was a hole for the head to pass through. The lady's surcoat was short and sleeveless with wide armholes and was worn over the bliaud or gown. It was fastened by shoulder buttons.

surplice a loose white vestment with flowing sleeves worn over a cassock by ecclesiastics during religious services in the seventeenth century, generally slipped over the head, but it sometimes was cut open in front to accommodate the wearer's wig. Still used in some denominations.

surplice bodice any bodice or waist the closure of which overlaps in front reaching from side to side at the waistline.

surplice collar a collar which follows the same line of closure as the surplice bodice.

surtout, Newmarket an overcoat made in the style of a frock coat, worn when riding or driving. It was named Newmarket after the town in England celebrated for its racing meets. Late nineteenth and early twentieth centuries. see *New York surtout; Newmarket.*

suspenders see *braces; bretelles; gallowses; galluses.*

swag festoons or draperies, especially as used in the late eighteenth century in interior decoration and on women's gowns.

swakara a breed of karakul lamb from southwest Africa; lightweight, slim and supple with lustrous markings. New on the market in the 1960's.

swallowtail coat see *tails.*

swansdown the soft feathers of the swan used as costume trimming; also for powder puffs. Also a thick, warm cotton cloth first made in China and called Canton flannel or swansdown.

swatch a small piece of fabric used as a sample of texture, color or design.

sweat shirt a pullover shirt worn by athletes. Usually of thick cotton, a fine-ribbed cloth with fleecy underside. A ribbed high or round neck, wrist and hip bands. Also called T-shirt. see *turtle neck.*

sweatband men's hats and caps are lined with a soft leather band which absorbs perspiration and prevents stain to the hat itself.

sweater any knit or crocheted jacket or blouse; an American term formerly considered inelegant but now in general use; until the mid-twentieth century knit garments opening in front were known in England exclusively as cardigans, and those without an opening as pullovers or jumpers. The two, in a matching set, are called twin sets, a fashion more prevalent in the British Isles than America, because of climatic differences. The knitted shirt first appeared on the islands of Jersey and Guernsey. Jerseys and ganseys, as they were called, were knitted for sailors and fishermen by their wives. Because the garment made of wool and retaining its natural oil, absorbs rain and salt water without feeling damp, its fame spread over Europe, especially among working men. In the 1890's, the jersey was taken up by American sportsmen and college athletes, who called the shirt a sweater, hence its name. In the 1920's, Lanvin, Chanel and Schiaparelli took note of the sweater and, in the 1940's, Mainbocher lined sweaters with chiffon and silk and added bead embroidery. see *Aran sweater; Cowichan sweater; Fair Isle sweater; jersey; fisherman's sweater; poor boy's sweater; sloppy Joe; turtle neck sweater.*

swag-silk gown with panniers and swags of silk on the skirt—called Circassian gown-French-17th C.

Swedish lace a pillow lace of the torchon type, Swedish-made.

swell, heavy swell a Briticism for an ultra-fashionable man of the 1870's and 1880's.

swift a box which holds a swift or reel, a turning instrument upon which is wound yarn, thread or silk.

swim suit a one-piece knitted woolen suit for active swimming. see *maillot; Annette Kellerman.*

swirl see *tie-about.*

Swiss embroidery see *Madeira* or *eyelet embroidery.*

Swiss muslin see *dotted Swiss.*

switch a tress or tresses in the form of a plait or curl to add to one's own locks. Separate tresses are bound at one end. Formerly called corners of hair, in the 1960's known as falls. Though usually made of natural hair, they are now more often made of manufactured strands of acetate or nylon, which are lustrous manufactured fibers in beautiful colors and hand washable.

sword a weapon with a long blade pointed and sharpened on both edges. Its history dates from the Bronze Age and the Iron Age. Many centuries passed before the blade became slim and lighter in weight, and further centuries before the clumsy hilt was simplified. It finally became a ceremonial ornament, a costume piece more than a weapon of defense. In modern times the sword retains its significance as a symbol of military, judicial or legal authority.

swordfisherman's cap see *cap, swordfisherman's.*

sykchos in ancient Greece, a soft, low leather boot of Oriental origin. Inside the boot, the Greeks wore a sock of white wool, felt or linen as protection against cold and dampness. Greek comedians wore it on the stage and from this comes the old English expression applied to actors as "gentlemen of the sock and buskin." Hence the origin of our word sock.

synthetic fabrics artificial fabrics were introduced with the invention of rayon in 1891 when Count Hilaire de Chardonnet established the first successful rayon production. In 1886 he had experimented upon the findings of many other scientists working to produce a commercial process for manufacturing artificial silk. Its name of rayon was created by Kenneth Lord Sr. of Galey and Lord. The first finished product was shown at the Paris Exposition in 1889 and from then on, it has been produced round the globe. It is generally considered a nineteenth century European invention and a twentieth century development. In fashion, Chanel was the first couturière to use rayon, 1915. Many synthetics have been perfected and are marketed under trade names such as nylon, orlon, dacron, arnel, etc.

syrma a long trailing robe worn by tragic actors of ancient Greece.

szür a Hungarian cloak, decorated with embroidery or appliqué.

szür—black or white felt or leather—with fur to inside—long sleeves closed as pockets embroidered and appliquéd motifs—Hungarian

szür or cloak—white felt or leather appliquéd yellow, orange, green, purple—white woolen breeches with crochet lace—turban of green foliage—Hungarian wedding guest

T

tab a small flap sewn to a garment to hold a section in place by a button, snap or hook.

tabard a sleeveless or short-sleeved jacket worn by soldiers over armor and by monks and commoners. It was put on over the head and open at the sides. When worn by a knight it was embroidered with his arms and called a coat-of-arms. Heralds also wore tabards displaying the arms of the lord they served. see *mandilion.*

tabby any of several silk fabrics of plain, watered or striped weave made in a quarter of Baghdad named Attāb.

tabi a white cotton Japanese foot-glove with a separate stall for the large toe, and a thick sole. It fastens up the back with hooks or snaps. The only footwear for indoor use, since shoes are not worn in the house.

tabinet, tabbinet an Irish-made poplin, often with a moiré pattern, much used in the eighteenth century.

tablion the Roman toga gradually evolved into the full-length semicircular mantle worn by the Church and Byzantine emperors. The tablions with which it was ornamented were twelve-inch squares solidly embroidered in gold and colored silk thread and accented with varicolored jewels and pearls. The squares were placed at the front corners of the semicircular cloak and at the edge in center back.

taces see *tass*

tack to baste or make temporary stitches. see *tailor's tacks.*

taenia a narrow girdle or cord worn around the hips by Greek maidens. Tied in an intricate knot, the Herculean knot was a symbol of virginity to be untied by the husband on the wedding night.

taffeta a rich, thin silk first noted in the seventeenth century, used for doublets and pages' dress. A luxurious fabric of plain weave and several finishes in the eighteenth century; later plain-dyed, brocaded and changeable in beautiful colors.

taffeta weave see *plain weave.*

tagal a straw braid made from Manila hemp which comes from Tagal, a province in Java. Used for hats.

tagalog see *barong tagalog.*

taglioni a short braid-bound overcoat, nineteenth century. It was named after the Italian dancer, Taglioni.

tailleur see *suit, feminine.*

tailored suit, feminine a simple suit of cloth comprising jacket, skirt and shirtwaist. By the first decade of the twentieth century, it had become the smart street costume, in navy serge or black broadcloth. For resort wear and sportswear, it followed the English fabrics, was very often white and worn with Norfolk jacket. The style was launched by Doucet, Paris couturier in the 1880's.

tailor's chalk talc or soapstone in small pieces for marking fabric before cutting.

Taglioni over-coat—braid trimmed and lined with plaid wool—

tailor's tacks basting stitches alternating with loop stitches sewn to two pieces of material. The pieces are then cut apart, leaving marks to follow in sewing. Also called mark-stitches.

"tails or white tie"-formal evening dress-black or midnight blue worsted-high silk hat or collapsible opera hat-contemporary

tails the colloquial name for the swallow-tailed coat. Another name is claw-hammer coat. Part of a man's formal evening dress; of black or midnight blue worsted with silk lapels and braided side seams on the trousers. "Tails" call for the stiff bosom shirt, wing collar, white tie and white waistcoat, and top hat. see *swallowtail; claw-hammer coat.*

tāj Persian or Arabic for crown; the tall, brimless cap to be seen in all Moslem countries, where it is a headdress of distinction. Its origin is the ancient tiara of the Mesopotamian valley. see *kamelaukion.*

talar Latin for ankles, hence *talaria,* winged slippers; *talaric,* ankle-length chiton or tunic. In mythology, winged shoes fastened at the ankles were worn by the Greek god Hermes and the Roman god Mercury.

talc, talcum powder an American commodity which was placed on the market about 1890. It is composed of perfumed talc and a mild antiseptic especially soothing to tender skin. Used by men, women and children, especially in hot weather.

talisman an amulet or charm, a piece of jewelry on a chain, worn around the neck to ward off evil. Nineteenth century.

tallith, taleth, tallit, tallis, talith, talit, talis the Jewish prayer shawl or tasseled white scarf bordered with blue and worn over head and shoulders.

talma a man's long cape or cloak sometimes hooded, named after the French tragedian, François Joseph Talma (1763–1826).

tam-o'-shanter a jaunty cap named after a poem by Robert Burns; of heavy brushed wool and of certain colors, the number used varying according to a man's status. Popular in the nineteenth century and still popular with women and girls in the twentieth.

tambour lace or **work** net or sheer cotton stretched on an embroidery hoop or tambour frame, formerly embroidered in the tambour stitch, now replaced by the chain stitch and worked with a crochet needle. see *Limerick lace.*

tamein the sari or sarong-like draped garment of Burmese men and women. see *lungi.*

tammy a cloth of wool or wool and cotton, often highly glazed. It has many uses and formerly was used for linings and curtains.

tanjib a fine muslin of East Indian make.

tank tops hip-length sweaters or jerseys with round neck and usually sleeveless, worn over tailored straight skirts and miniskirts. 1960's.

tanning the process of converting rawhide and skins into finished leather.

Tansui hat see *hat, Tansui.*

tapa cloth, Hawaiian a fabric made from the bark of a mulberry tree by steeping and beating. Used for many purposes including raiment on most South Pacific islands.

tapalo a coarse homespun scarf worn in Spanish-American countries.

tape firmly woven, narrow strips of cotton, linen, silk, rayon, etc., available in small rolls. Of varied widths and for varied sewing uses; such as seam tape, bias tape, mending tape, etc.

tape measure a narrow strip of firm but flexible cloth, marked into inches and subdivisions of inches, used in sewing. Usually sixty inches long and about a half-inch in width.

tapestry a heavy hand-woven fabric, usually figured, used as a wall hanging, furniture covering or carpet. The art of tapestry weaving originated in Flanders in the fourteenth century and spread throughout Europe. Modern tapestry can be made by machinery and is used in costume for accessories such as handbags and luggage.

tapis a square of black silk worn on the head by Philippine peasant women.

tarboosh, tarbouch the Arabic name of the truncated red felt cap, a cap of ancient Greek origin. Both men and women of the Mohammedan faith wear the tarboosh. The Egyptian wraps a scarf around his tarboosh and certain Indian races drape it around the kulah, a pointed skullcap. The tarboosh was introduced into India in the nineteenth century by the Indian-born educator and reformer, Sir Sayyad Ahmad. see *fez.*

tarbucket see *shako.*

tarlatan a thin, textured muslin with an open mesh, usually heavily sized and used as a stiffening in garments, such as the crinoline.

tarpaulin a cloth such as canvas covered with tar or other waterproofing. Used especially for a sailor's southwester. see *southwester.*

tartan originally the woolen cloth in plaid patterns worn in the Scottish Highlands where each clan had its distinctive tartan. Now a term for any plaid cloth resembling tartan. The patterns of a true tartan are foursquare, that is, the same color sequence is followed in each direction working out from the center square to the main cross line.

tartan velvet a woven or printed plaid on a short-napped velvet.

tartar sable see *mink, kolinsky.*

tartarine an ancient and costly silk cloth supposedly woven by the people of Tartary.

tashashit see *chechia.*

tash-tass an East Indian cloth woven of gold and silver thread used for robes worn on ceremonial occasions.

tass or **tasses; taces** a piece of armor which appeared in the fifteenth century. It was composed of steel bands or plates; four to eight over the hips, reaching from waist to mid-thigh, hinged on the left side and buckled on the right. It was worn until the late seventeenth century.

tassel originally a cloak fastening; now a pendant ornament of thread or cords headed by a decorative knob top to hold the fringe intact.

tattersall a general name for heavy woolen fancy vestings of small plaids and checks in gay colors. Named for the famous London saleroom for racing stock and thoroughbreds. Specifically, a check of narrow lines crossing at less than one-inch intervals on a neutral background.

tatting a knotted lace edging with wide usage for lingerie and linens. Made with a small shuttle and the fingers, a single thread forming tiny loops in varied designs.

tattooing a primitive form of body ornamentation which has been practiced since antiquity by the ancients, the North and South American Indians and still today particularly by some tribes in Africa, New Zealand and the Marquesas Islands. In more recent centuries the art rose to its highest form especially in Japan and many European aristocrats, both men and women, traveled to the Orient to have an exquisite picture tattooed on arms and chest. The old-time practice consisted of pricking the skin with sharp instruments and inserting pigments under the skin in the tiny holes. Usually powdered charcoal was used, which turned a deep blue and became indelible. Other pigments have been discovered. Slaves were often tattooed with their master's name, and sailors of all nations have delighted in being tattooed with pictures. "Body pictures" were back in fashion in the 1960's but the modern artwork was applied with ballpoint or felt-tip pens and was removable with soap and water.

taupe the color of a mole's coat, a dark brownish-gray; from the French word for mole.

tawing a form of mineral tanning in preparing skins with alum, salt and other agents.

tcharchaf a name for the casual kind of dress among Moslem women of the village, which has replaced the old dress since Turkey became a republic in 1925. Under a colorful wool or silk shawl, a lace cap is worn to the eyes and the shawl held over nose and mouth. A sleeveless chemise of below-knee length covers pantaloons or chalwar, both these garments of striped cotton.

tea gown an at-home gown of the late nineteenth and early twentieth centuries. A Victorian fashion of fitted yoke to which full sleeves and the dress body were joined. Usually of handsome fabric, lace-trimmed, and full length.

teal a color named after the blue-winged teal, a small wild duck; a bluish green hue with low brilliance.

tebenna the cloak of the ancient Etruscan man; a large rectangle or large semicircle of woolen cloth. see *Etruscan.*

teck band a popular scarf of the four-in-hand style, named for the Prince of Teck. It was an imitation of the original four-in-hand necktie. Late nineteenth and early twentieth centuries. see *four-in-hand.*

teddy also known as a combination; a feminine undergarment combining slip and panties in one piece. 1920's.

tegua a buckskin sandal or moccasin of the Keresan Pueblo Indians of New Mexico.

teja see *Spanish comb.*

temple jewelry artificial jewelry of the seventeenth century made on the rue du Temple, Paris. It was an acceptable and fashionable type of what would today be called costume jewelry, set with stones of brilliant colors. Extravagant jeweled buttons were a particular fad of this time. see *costume jewelry.*

Teneriffe lace a lace of circles and wheels similar to Paraguay lace, made chiefly in the Canary Islands.

ten-gallon hat see *hat, Stetson.*

tennis dress White is the conventional color for both men and women. For men, trousers or shorts and a short-sleeved shirt; for women, shorts or very short full skirt and a sleeveless blouse, or a very short one-piece dress; white ankle socks and sneakers. Like most sports attire for women, the tennis costume has become abbreviated and practical. The feminine tennis costume of the 1890's was a tailored white linen shirtwaist and separate skirt of ankle length. The skirt was of printed muslin or white linen worn with white canvas tennis shoes called balmorals or bals and black lisle stockings.

tennis flannel see *outing flannel.*

tennis shoe see *shoe, tennis.*

tensile strength the strength of a fiber or piece of cloth as recorded in pounds on an instrument built for the purpose.

tent silhouette first launched in 1951 by Balenciaga in a wonderfully simple, black woolen coat flaring widely from a low standing collar. It was followed in the 1960's by Yves Saint Laurent's A-line silhouette. And in 1967, Madame Grès used the tent silhouette in her lovely, flaring evening gowns.

terno the traditional long evening gown of Philippine ladies, its special and unique feature being the short puffed wired sleeves called butterfly wings. Contemporary.

terry cloth see *Turkish toweling.*

tewke see *tuke.*

textile woven from textile fabrics—cotton, linen, wool, silk, synthetic, etc., especially woven or knit cloth.

texture a quality of the surface of a cloth produced by the manner of weaving and the fibers employed.

Thai silk Oriental silk fabrics resembling nankeen, rajah, shantung and tussah made with silk or rayon in plain or twill weaves, in either natural or beautiful combinations of color. The weight and texture vary with the quality. The hand-woven silks of Thailand have become widely known. In a silk-weaving village, the natives raise their own silkworms, tie the silks in tie-and-dye manner, and weave them into interesting broken patterns of fine color.

theater or **dinner suit** see *dinner or theater suit.*

Thérèse a huge cage of fine gauze worn over a high-dressed coiffure. It was kept in shape by very fine wire. French, 1780's. see *calash.*

thickset a kind of cotton, fustian or velveteen used formerly for men's work clothes.

thimble a finger guard for the sewer. Open-ended bronze thimbles have been found among the ruins of Herculaneum, and bronze and brass thimbles have been dug up in Roman remains in the Thames. In Central Europe of the fourteenth century, leather thimbles called thummels were used. The modern thimble, a Dutch invention, reached England in the seventeenth century. First worn on the thumb, it was called a thum-bell. The tips were smooth but the sides were finely pitted.

tholia a feminine straw hat of ancient Greece. It had a round brim and a sharply pointed crown and was worn over the head veil. This is the hat often seen in contemporary terra-cotta Tanagra figurines.

thread a very thin filament or cord made by spinning the fibers of cotton, linen, nylon or silk, also yarns of wool hard-twisted and finished for use in sewing.

thread lace a hand-made lace of linen thread, other than cotton or fancy thread.

three-dimensional glove see *glove, free-finger.*

thrums a kind of cap, knitted from the ends, usually about nine inches long, of warp threads left on the loom and which could not be woven; these are called thrums.

thummel see *thimble.*

tiara of Oriental origin, reaching Europe by way of Byzantium. The tiara which was worn by the ancient Persians was adopted by Christian and Jewish prelates alike. Before the eleventh century, it carried no special religious meaning. In modern times, the jeweled tiara or frontlet became a handsome evening headpiece worn by fashionable ladies with formal evening dress. Nineteenth and twentieth centuries. see *crown; coronet; miter.*

tiara, papal jeweled triple coronets

tent coat-woolen cloth-kimona sleeve-narrow neckband-black suede pagoda cap-black fox muff-French-Balenciaga-1951

tholia-woman's hat of ancient Greece-worn over headcloth

of interwoven white folds and white lappets with gold embroidery. Worn by the Pope over a white linen coif.

Tibet cloth a cloth woven from Tibetan goat's hair and used for dresses and wraps.

tibiale see *fascia.*

ticking a closely woven, heavy cotton or linen fabric of which mattress, pillow and bolster covers are made. It is usually striped but may also be printed with floral designs. Used mid-twentieth century for feminine sports clothes and summer coats.

tie see *necktie.*

tie-about also known as a swirl. An apron-like house dress with overlapping backs having sash ends that cross in back and tie in front.

tie clip a piece of masculine jewelry, a clasp of gold or silver to hold the ends of a four-in-hand tie to the shirt front.

tie silks silks such as foulard used for men's scarfs because resilient, pliable and firm in tying and knotting. Varying in weave and texture, and small-patterned.

tie tack a small stud with a shank that pierces the necktie and shirt and screws or snaps into a little metal base.

tie wig see *wig, tie.*

tied and dyed silks a hand process of dyeing a silk such as surah by tying off sections to resist the dye, thereby creating interesting effects and designs. Used especially for expensive neckwear.

tied-back time the period of the 1870's, so called by the British because all interest centered in back of feminine costume.

tiepin see *scarfpin.*

tiffany a gauzy silk used for head scarf or fichu in the eighteenth century; today, a muslin or transparent lawn, used for blouses or lingerie.

Tiffeau, Jacques see *couture, haute.*

tiger markings reproduced in tiger skin patterns printed on cloth, silk or fake fur. The fur of a real tiger is not used in costume.

tiger, American see *jaguar.*

tights skin-tight garments, generally covering legs and hips, worn by theatrical performers, acrobats or gymnasts, fashionable with mini-skirts and girls' fashions, 1960's.

tikka the red spot which the Hindu woman, usually married, wears on the center of her forehead. It is a good-luck spot and may also be worn by unmarried women. It may be any color and has no caste significance.

tilter a bustle worn under the petticoat which tilted when the wearer walked.

tilting helmet see *helmet, tilting.*

timber wolf Canadian-Arctic. see *wolf.*

timiak the shirt of a Greenland Eskimo man, woman or child made of birdskins sewn together with the soft down worn next to the body. The long sleeves and neck are edged with dog fur.

tinsel cloth cloth woven with sparkling metallic threads. Used for decorating costumes for party and holiday wear, especially Christmas fetes.

tinsel embroidery embroidery done with tinsel threads.

tippet originally, a liripipium, medieval, the long pendant of a hood; a pendant streamer attached to the arm; a woman's separate neckpiece of fur with long front ends of the nineteenth century. A long black scarf, similar to a stole, worn by Anglican clergy at non-sacramental services such as Matins or Evensong; the ends may be embroidered with ecclesiastical symbols. see *liripipe.*

tips half-rubbers with a sling back, worn to protect the vamp and sole of a woman's shoe, but not the heel.

tissue a gauze or sheer fabric of open weave, of silk, gold or silver thread.

titian a reddish-brown color favored by the Italian painter, Tiziano Vecellio (1477–1576). A term usually descriptive of hair as Titian blond. An admired shade of hair.

tobe Arabian undergarment, an ankle-length, loose-sleeved shirt of cotton, usually white, which slips on over the head. Worn under an outer garment, the aba, a large square which is often of brilliant colored woolen cloth.

toboggan cap see *cap, toboggan.*

toe box a piece of leather stiffened with gum, placed between the outer leather and lining to preserve the shape of the shoe.

toenail cosmetics see *fingernail.*

toff British vernacular for a dude, especially in the 1890's.

toga During the first three centuries of our era, the Roman toga was the principal garment of both sexes but later was worn only by men. Its use was the same as the Greek himation but it was very different in shape. The Greek wrap was a rectangle and the Roman, when folded, a semi-circle. The wearing of the toga became an art with its hanging folds weighted by pellets and each fold named. The toga was the cloak of peace as the sagum was that of war. see *himation; pallium; sagum.*

toggle a peasant's button and loop. A small wooden block, the thickness of a finger and half as long, it is secured to the cloth by a cord around its middle. Pushed through a loop on the opposite edge for fastening.

toggle coat an Austrian peasant-style travel coat fastened by the wooden buttons and loops called toggles. A knee-length winter coat of coarse woolen cloth with plaid lining and a removable hood. see *British warm, similar coat.*

toile French for any cloth. A dressmaker's sample design made up in temporary fabric.

toile cirée French for oilcloth.

toile de jouy originally a linen or cotton printed fabric made in Jouy, France, from 1760. The design was usually a pictorial landscape or floral design and was printed in a single tone of red, blue, brown, purple or green on a natural ground. The name is now generally used for any printed fabric with similar designs. Used mainly for interior decoration but occasionally for women's summer suits or dresses.

toilet, toilette the grooming of an individual in coiffure and costume, especially as pertaining to fashion.

toilet water see *perfumery.*

toiletries, feminine see *cosmetics; perfumery.*

toiletries, masculine until the turn of the century, the use of toiletries by men was frowned upon in America but not in Europe. A change has occurred in the past half-century. To shaving cream, talcum powder and scented soap, deodorants, perfumes and toilet water have been added. There now exist many well-known toiletry

Tobe and breeches of white cotton-knitted skullcap with embroidery-Saudi Arabia merchant

tobe-worn under western jacket-over the jacket, an aba-on the head, kaffiyeh held by goat's hair agal-western cotton shirt and shoes-Arabian business man

manufacturers in Europe and America catering to the masculine market.

toilinet, toilinette a cloth of silk or cotton warp with wool filling, closely woven in plain or loom-figured material for waistcoats.

tom-bons full, wrapped loose pantaloons of white cotton worn by the Moslem Afghan men and women. They are full around the waist and hips, tapering down gradually to a snug fit at the ankles.

tondor lace a Danish lace of drawnwork and embroidery, sometimes with a fine cordonet, of the seventeenth and eighteenth centuries.

tongs an American Colonial term for work breeches or overalls made of coarse cotton or linen. Also, the first long breeches for boys of the period about 1820.

tonneau silhouette a skirt much like the earlier peg-top model in shape and as short-lived, circa 1914.

tonsure the shaving of the crown of the head leaving a circular fringe of hair, first practiced by monks. By the seventh century, it was a rite denoting admission to the clerical state.

tonsure wig see *wig, tonsure.*

tontarra see *beret.*

top boot see *boot, top.*

top hat see *hat, top.*

topaz a semi-precious stone of aluminum phiosilicate, the characteristic yellow color varying from pale yellow to deep orange, occasionally blue, rarely pink, red. A yellow variety of quartz is known as Oriental topaz or yellow sapphire.

topcoat coat worn over a suit, according to season. see *overcoat, great coat.*

topee, topi of Hindu name and new in the 1860's, first worn by the British Army in India. Made from pith cork of the Indian spongewood tree, it is very light in weight, covered with white cotton and lined with green cloth. It is insulated against the hot sun and impervious to air and water.

tops and drops old English for earrings with ear catches and pendants.

toque originally a round full cap of soft material, gathered into a headband and often decorated with a small plume. In present usage, a small round brimless woman's hat, suggestive of the original shape.

toque, Spanish see *Spanish toque.*

toquilla the straw of a genuine Panama hat. see *jipijapa; hat, Panama.*

torchon lace also known as Beggar's, Peasant's and Bavarian lace. A bobbin lace of heavy linen or cotton thread; the coarse pattern is used in fancy work and the fine for costume. see *Bavarian lace.*

torero Spanish bullfighter, see illustration.

torque a neck or arm band, usually of gold or perhaps bronze, worn by the ancient Gauls, Britons and Germans, a spirally twisted bar of gold bent into a hoop with an opening, the ends of which were fashioned into knobs or serpents' heads. Taken as spoils by the Romans, torques were awarded to the soldiers for valorous deeds.

torsade a gold or silver fringe which edged the shoulder pads or military epaulettes designating an officer's grade. It was also used on hats.

tortoise shell the large scales of the carapace, or shield, of a species of seaturtle beautifully mottled and semitransparent. Used in the making of jewelry and luxury accessories such as eyeglass frames, cigar and cigarette cases, Spanish combs, etc., and imitated in plastic.

tote bag essentially a handbag based on the paper shopping bag, with deep straight sides and strong handles; open at the top. The shopping bag originated during World War II when, for lack of delivery service, shoppers carried their purchases home. Shops furnished strong paper bags with cord handles, which were universally popular. Eventually these bags were colored and decorated, serving as an advertising medium for the store.

toupee, masculine a small patch of false hair to cover a bald spot. A small wig of the eighteenth century, with a curl or top knot at the crown of the head.

tourmaline, turmaline a semi-precious stone, a complex silicate and magnesium with varying quantities of other minerals. Color may vary from black, brown or yellow to red, green or colorless.

tournure French for bustle. see *bustle.*

tovaglio (Italian), **bavolet** (French) names of the European peasant bonnet with a deep ruffle at the back of the neck. It was known in the eighteenth century as a Paris fashion and called Fanchon. see *bavolet.*

tow yarn spun from an inferior flax, used for sheetings. Tow cloth was an old-time linen homespun.

tower headdress a tall coiffure of the seventeenth and eighteenth centuries. see *fontange.*

toyo a cellophane-coated rice-paper straw made in Formosa, Okinawa and Japan. It is shiny and smooth and resembles panama.

tracing wheel a small steel wheel with teeth and a handle used for marking off seams, tucks and joinings for sewing.

trademark, trade-mark name meaning the name or symbol of a manufactured product which is legally protected by registration.

train the trailing back section of a formal gown, attached in back to the shoulders or the waist. In the medieval period, women's skirts and, very often, men's cloaks were long, touching the floor in folds and sometimes trailing behind. In the fourteenth century the length of the train was regulated according to the wearer's rank. In Louis XIV's day, trains reached exaggerated lengths for ceremonial use. They were fastened at shoulders or waist and unhooked and put aside after the ceremony. Trains grew still longer in Louis XV's reign and were copied by Napoleon, luxuriously embroidered. The beautiful ermine-trimmed velvet robes survive in the traditional coronation attire of Great Britain. Trains continue to be worn for fashionable weddings and affairs of state but less often than in the past.

trank the oblong leather piece marked with a glove pattern from which the glove is cut.

transfer pattern a design for embroidery. A carbon drawing may be transferred by a hot iron, or a perforated design may be transferred by rubbing chalk through the perforations.

transformation any small hairpiece used to change the wearer's hairstyle.

transparencies gowns of sheer lawn or muslin painted with bouquets of colored flowers and worn over an undergown of bright colored moiré satin. Transparencies were also of gold or lace tissue worn over figured brocades. 1660's.

trapeze line In 1958, Yves Saint Laurent, protégé of and successor to Dior, was acclaimed for his Trapeze Line which evolved into the A-Line. The A-Line later became the Tent Shape in coat and dress.

trapunto a kind of quilting worked between two pieces of fabric in which the design is stitched flat and then stuffed with cotton batting in sections, in this manner filling in each part of the design separately.

trembling cap-gold and silver cord net with pearls-Italian-16th C.

trembling cap of gold or silver cord net banded with pearls. Italian, late sixteenth century; a conical cap with a long tail like a chaperon.

trench coat worn by British officers, WWI-of water-proofed cotton gabardine-adopted by civilians

trench coat topcoat of British officers in World War I. Of processed gabardine with an extra processed lining, it was used also by U.S. officers in World War II. The original model had reinforced shoulder flaps and gun flaps. After the war it was copied for civilian use by both sexes, soon becoming a contemporary classic.

trencher cap same as *mortarboard.*

tressure, tressour medieval terms for caul, reticulated or netted headdress of the fourteenth and fifteenth centuries.

trews a Celtic garment of breeches and hose knitted in one piece. Close-fitting and worn under kilts by Highlanders and Irishmen.

tricolette a knitted fabric made of rayon, silk or cotton and resembling jersey cloth. Used for women's clothing.

tricot see *jersey.*

tricotine see *cavalry twill.*

tricorne see *cocked hat, androsmane; continental; Kevenhuller.*

Trigère, Pauline see *couture, haute.*

Trilby-a soft felt hat, beaver-like-Tyrolese style-feather wings-1908

trilby a soft felt hat in Alpine shape with a plush-like texture resembling beaver. First decade of the twentieth century.

tripe a fabric of velvet weave but not silk, now known as velveteen.

trollopée a loose, flowing gown of the Watteau period (1715–1723), open in front and sometimes drawn up in back. It was worn as a morning dress and also called a flying gown.

trolly or **trolley lace** as English bobbin lace; its pattern consists of flowers, sprays, dots and squares outlined with a heavy thread.

tropical worsted summer wear woolens of lightweight mixtures in two or single-ply yarns in warp and filling. For men's and women's suitings, twentieth century.

trotcozy a Scottish shoulder covering or small cape with cowl hood used when walking.

trotteur French for a plain tailored woman's outfit with sturdy shoes for walking in town or country, from the French trotter, to trot. Twentieth century.

trouser skirt see *skirt, harem.*

trousers, trowsers of Oriental origin, worn by barbarians, as distinguished from the Greeks and Romans. The Britons then wore braccae which were made of checkered cloth. During the Roman domination, the Britons adopted Roman dress while the Scots and Irish retained their trousers, called truis. The word "trousers" appears first in the reign of Henry VIII of England. The substitution of full-length breeches for knee breeches dates from the French Revolution. Those who wore long breeches were patriots or "sans culottes," meaning without knee breeches, to distinguish them from the aristocrat. Eventually, with the addition of a jacket, the ensemble evolved into the habit or suit of the nineteenth century. Both trousers and black satin knee breeches remained the style for evening, breeches being full dress for many British and European officials. see *sans-culottes.* Trousers or long breeches of the early nineteenth century ended halfway between calf and ankle with side buttons and loops. Made tight-fitting, they were of stockinette, buckskin and finely striped cotton. The most popular cloth was buff or yellow nankeen imported from China. Until the 1850's trousers were very tight, with the strap under the boot, lasting into the 1860's. The fall front closure gave way to a center-front fastening and side pockets became general. The early attempt to crease trousers down center front of leg did not succeed. The Prince of Wales, later Edward VII, upon his visit to America in 1860, wore creases front, back and sides of the legs. Creases became general by the 1890's, having been introduced by army officers. Cuffs on trousers appeared at the turn of the century, the result of Englishmen turning up their trousers on rainy days in the muddy paddock.

trousers, bridge see *pantalons à pont.*

trousers, peg-top see *peg-top trousers.*

trousers, sailor until the 1950's, made with a front fall and bell bottoms; now tailored in civilian fashion.

trousseau the personal outfit for a bride, her clothes, jewelry, household linens, etc.

troussoire see *chatelaine.*

truncated the top of a cone cut off or squared, as a hat with its crown top flattened.

trunk hose short, puffed breeches attached to the long stockings or tights which were in fashion from 1575 to 1600. Trunk hose and codpiece were secured to the doublet by points or lacings. From 1560 on, trunk hose were usually slashed or paned, revealing a full, padded lining of contrasting colored silk. see *slashing.*

trunks a man's piece of atheletic apparel, a tight-fitting, knitted or jersey garment. It has an elastic waistband and covers the body from waist to thighs. Worn from the late nineteenth century and used for track sports and swimming.

tsaruchia contemporary, sturdy, peaked-toed shoes worn by royal guardsmen (evzones) in Greece. Black leather with red or blue pompons.

T-shirt a short term for tennis or sports shirt, of knitted lightweight cotton or wool with crew or V-neck and usually white. It may be sleeveless or have short or long sleeves. May also have a "mock" turtle neck.

T-strap on a woman's shoe, a strap along the instep which joins an ankle strap at right angles, making a "T."

tubbeck or **tupak** the tubular dress of Burmese men and women. Long, straight yardage of cotton or silk is wrapped round the body to form a straight silhouette, over which is worn a short, simple white cotton jacket.

tuck a fold of fabric stitched in place. see *dart.*

tucker a guimpe-like yoke of lace or embroidered fabric worn to fill in above a low-cut bodice, seventeenth and eighteenth centuries.

tuft similar to short, upturned tassel.

tuftaffata, tuftaffaty a heavy silk taffeta of early English and New England days. Also a "taffaty" fashionable in the Elizabethan period and the seventeenth century. It was a taffeta woven with velvet, chenille or rasied-pile stripes and was used for doublets, jerkins, gowns and petticoats.

tuke, tewke a canvas of the fifteenth and sixteenth centuries.

trunk hose and doublet covered with cutwork, embroidery and galloon-silk hose and ribbon garters-English-1567

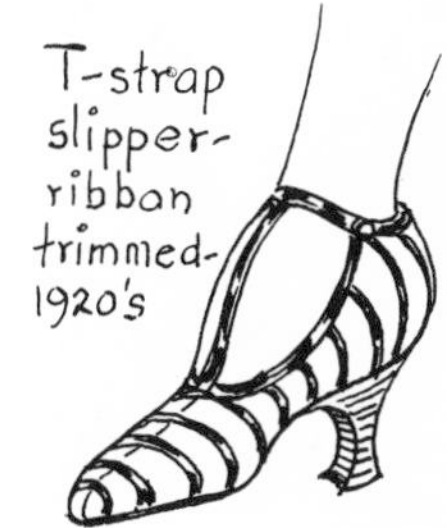

T-strap slipper-ribbon trimmed-1920's

tulle a very fine net or gauze of silk or cotton, first made in Nottingham, England, in 1768 on a stocking machine, wrongly supposed to have originated in France. It was made with a loosely woven tricot stitch which unraveled. Despite its poor quality, it became popular for the fashionable headdress and the huge mobcap of the period and also was inexpensive. Modern tulle is a very fine net, usually silk, and used chiefly for veiling. It was used in the 1950's for evening gowns.

tunic a short garment worn by ancient Greeks and Romans. In modern woman's dress, a tunic is of shorter length than the basic skirt over which it is worn. A hip-length blouse; any undress jacket worn by British soldiers; the tight-fitting jacket of the British guardsman.

tunica see *tunicle.*

tunicle a close-fitting vestment or tunic worn by a bishop under the dalmatic.

tupu ornamental jewelry worn by the Araucanian Indian women of Chile. A piece of silver work about ten inches long by four inches wide consisting of three heavy chains attached to a shield which fastens a cloak. From the chains hang a pendant carrying many silver coins.

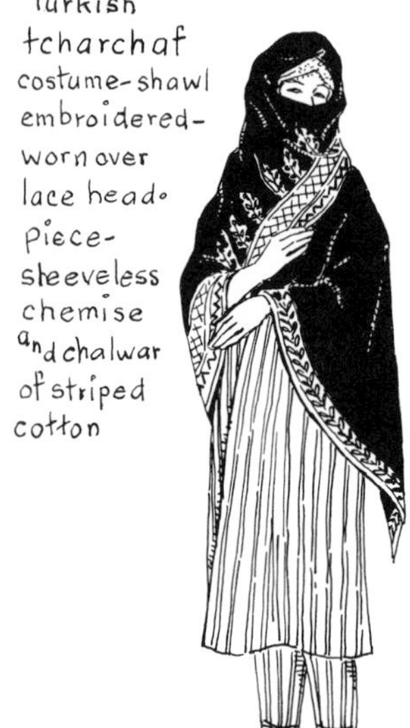

tuque a Canadian sportscap, a knitted stocking type made pointed at both ends and turned one end into the other, a doubly warm headpiece.

turban a particular style of headdress worn by men of the Mohammedan faith, of obscure Oriental origin. A scarf of fine linen, cotton or silk folded around the head. "Dulband" was its Persian name, meaning a sash. In centuries past, it was considered an offence in Mohammedan countries for an unbeliever to wear the turban.

turban, knitted a knitted band about four inches wide, shaped around the head by invisible stitches. Designed by Agnés of Paris in the 1920's for the bobbed head. The turban continued to be a smart headpiece for women.

turkey red cotton cloth and embroidery cotton dyed a brilliant, durable red, imported from Turkey. Popular in the late nineteenth century, and widely used in the peasant embroidery of the period.

turkey-back silhouette a ladies' short coat fashionable in the 1860's. A little below hip length, it hung fairly straight in front but flared out in back from the neck over the bustle.

Turkish dress see illustrations; *chalwar; kusak.*

Turkish embroidery of gold, silver and silk thread, done in conventional designs and native stitches. It was worked on both sides, eliminating a "wrong side." Used for garments.

Turkish point lace, oyah a lace made with crochet needle and colored silk in an intricate flower design in relief.

The turban
"desert turban" with mameluke point-hues of red-French-1803
velvet turban-Titus coiffure-Directoire-1790's
turban à la Rachel-white satin-gold spangles-aigrette-French-1833
gauze turban-chin strap-aigrette-French-1797
turban of pleated gauze with spangles and band-French-1803
turban of tulle, pearls, jewels and aigrette-American-1790's
turban-pale gray satin-Balenciaga-1944
turban-white satin with mameluke point and pearl fringe-French-1806
velvet turban with aigrette and jewels-French-1790's

The turban

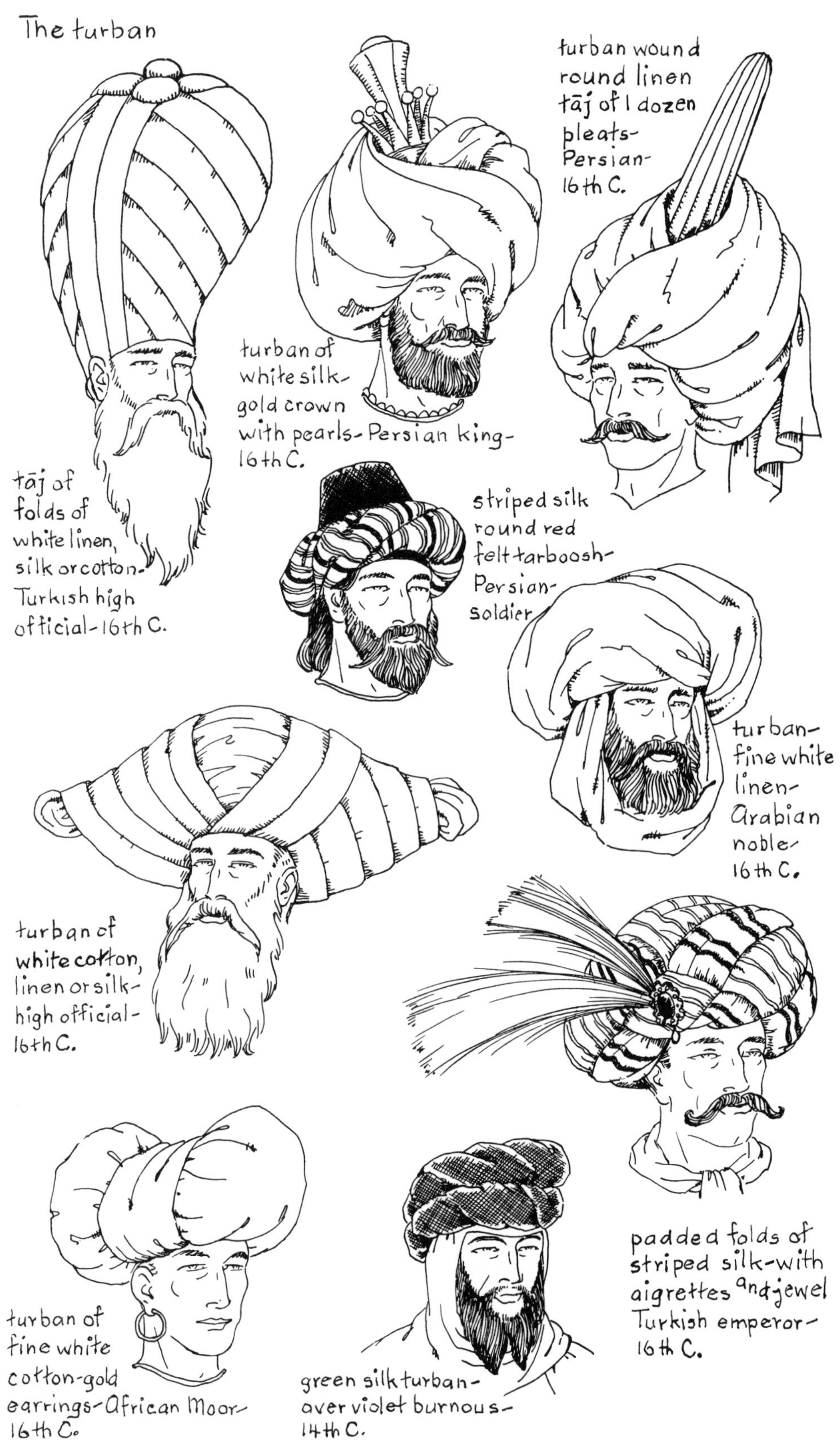

taj of folds of white linen, silk or cotton-Turkish high official-16th C.
turban of white silk-gold crown with pearls-Persian king-16th C.
turban wound round linen taj of 1 dozen pleats-Persian-16th C.
striped silk round red felt tarboosh-Persian-soldier
turban-fine white linen-Arabian noble-16th C.
turban of white cotton, linen or silk-high official-16th C.
padded folds of striped silk-with aigrettes and jewel Turkish emperor-16th C.
turban of fine white cotton-gold earrings-African Moor-16th C.
green silk turban-over violet burnous-14th C.

Turkish toweling, terry cloth, Moorish cloth cotton or linen woven with raised loops on both sides. Very absorbent and used chiefly for masculine and feminine bath robes, towels and wash cloths. It was first made in England in 1848, but ignored by the British. A merchant sold the goods in Turkey, where the natives used it for the draped turban. Years later, the British accepted the toweling as a British import.

turquoise an opaque gem stone, color ranging from deep blue to pale bluish-green. The name comes from the old French name for Turkey, the best examples of the stone coming from the Near East.

turret a crownless white linen toque worn in the twelfth century with chin-band or barbette. Worn sometimes over the wimple, flowing hair, or coiffure dressed in a chignon at the nape.

turtle the growing scarcity and costliness of alligator skins for shoes and bags created a demand in the 1960's for sea turtle skins. Turtle markings are larger than alligators', the skins softer, but turtle accessories can be produced for a lower selling price. Having hard or soft shell, there are two hundred species of both the land and sea reptiles. Recently skins have come from the Caribbean Sea, the best from the coasts of Mexico and Honduras. Only the skin of the legs is usable.

turtle neck masculine, feminine, knitted, or jersey sweater with a long, straight, tubelike collar which is rolled down to the height desired, with no front opening. A standing, knitted collar was new in the 1960's.

tuscan a yellow straw in lacy designs from Tuscany, Italy; made from the tops of bleached wheat stalks. Used for hats.

tussah, tusseh, tussore, tusser, tussur a type of silk which includes pongee and shantung. A very strong silk woven from the tussah silkworm of India, bred on the jujube tree. Usually in natural fawn color because it does not always dye well. Popular for dresses and men's and women's summer suits.

tutulus Etruscan; originally the headdress of braids worn by the flamen or pagan priest and his wife, the braids built up in conical shape. Eventually the conical shape evolved into a pointed cap with an olive twig on top tied by a fillet of wool.

tuxedo American name for the dinner jacket, the design improvised by American millionaires living in Tuxedo Park, N.Y., who wished a less formal and more comfortable dress for small dinners. A short coat of black or midnight blue worsted with rolling silk collar, worn with a black silk waistcoat and trousers with braid side seam. In the late 1920's, a double-breasted dinner jacket made the waistcoat unnecessary. see *dinner jacket; black tie.*

tuxedo collar see *collar, tuxedo.*

tuxedo-dinner coat or "black tie"-semi-formal evening dress-black or midnight blue cloth-contemporary

turret cap of white linen attached to coif-hair in a net-French and German-13th C.

tutulus-shaped felt hat-ringlets over forehead and curls in back-Etruscan man

tutulas headdress of braids-jeweled fillet-back hair in curls—Etruscan man

tweed, Donegal a handscoured, homespun tweed, originally made by Donegal Irish peasants on hand looms. Also, loosely woven tweeds of Yorkshire yarns dyed and finished in Donegal. Today, mostly machine-made, with the slubs woven in. Used for suits, topcoats and sportswear.

tweed, Harris see *Harris tweed.*

tweed, Scotch a coarse or soft woolen fabric, usually rough-surfaced, in plain or twill weave. Made in plaids, checks or mixtures and first produced in Scotland by weavers on the Tweed River.

Twentieth Century costume see illustrations, pages 355–379.

twill or **diagonal weave** the strongest of all weaves, having a distinct diagonal line from selvedge to selvedge. Wool twills include serge and gabardine; cotton twills, denim and coutil or ticking.

twill, cavalry see *cavalry twill.*

twill, middy see *middy twill.*

twill, Poiret see *Poiret twill.*

twist a thread of firmly twisted silk used for making buttonholes and tailored ornaments.

twists a trade term for woolen and worsted cloths woven of yarns of two colors twisted together, producing a mottled effect in the pattern.

Tyrian purple a reddish-blue or bluish-red dye formerly obtained from mollusks native to the coast of Israel, where Tyre is situated. The color was famous throughout the ancient world and is often referred to in classical literature.

Tyrolean, Tyrolese dress still worn today in the Tyrol, a province of western Austria in the Alps, bordered by Ger-
(*continued on page 380*)

Tyrol-Gray cloth jacket, bright green trim, braces, jacket and belt-black leather breeches, red trim, black felt hat with feather-woolen socks-Austrian

Tyrol-black velvet over white blouse-black cotton skirt-printed cotton apron-felt hat with plumes-red socks-Austrian

Tyrol-white blouse-red bodice and skirt-black velvet cap of beads and flowers-jewel belt and ribbons-Italian

Tyrol-Mountain Maid with brandy cask-black velvet bodice and skirt-pink silk shawl fringed-pink apron-black felt hat with pink cord, tassel and flowers-Bavarian

Tyrol guide-leather suit-jacket dull red-breeches darker-waistcoat, dark green-brown cap-feather panache-gray socks-black shoes-Bavarian

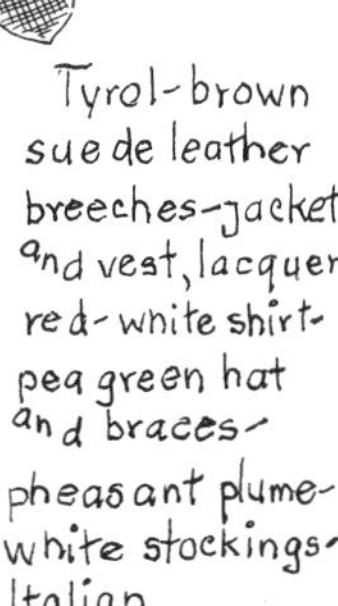

Tyrol-brown suede leather breeches-jacket and vest, lacquer red-white shirt-pea green hat and braces-pheasant plume-white stockings-Italian

Twentieth Century
bathing dress-
1900-1930
Annette Kellerman's
swim suit-black
knitted cotton
maillot and tights-
1909
dress, bloomers,
black lisle
stockings and
corset-black or
navy mohair-
black and white
trimming-
1900
bathing corset
and brassière
of rubber
sheeting-
1915
knitted black
wool maillot
over shorts-
colored trim-
rolled black
silk stockings-
canvas shoes-
1924
black taffeta dress
and bloomers-
black and white
checked trimming-
heavy black
silk stockings-
black linen
buskins-
1915
knitted swim suit-
white wool with
navy blue polka
dots-navy trim
and shorts-
1928

Twentieth Century-
corsetry-
1900-1910
in center-
garter belt for
"straight front"-
often worn over
corset-
satin
front•laced
corset-
closed back-
1904
satin brocade
with lace
and ribbon-
back•
lacing-
1901
straighter
and longer
lines-
polka dot
fabric-
1906
front•laced
corset
fastened to
side of front-
1904
multi•colored
striped ribbon-
back lacing-
1905
whaleboned
brassière-
adjustable
shoulder straps-
1905

Twentieth Century-
lingerie-
1900-1910
"French drawers"-
fitted hip band-
closed crotch-
side-buttoned
chemise-
batiste, lace
and ribbon-
1902
combination
corset-cover
and "umbrella
drawers"-
circular
pattern-
1904
combination
corset-cover
and petticoat-
batiste, lace,
tucks, ribbon
threaded
through
entre-deux-
1902
knitted
union suit-
drawstring at
neck and arms-
cotton, wool,
or silk
nightgown
of nainsook-
entre-deux with
ribbon,
embroidery
and lace-
1905
gored and
tailored
taffeta
petticoat
of the period-
dust ruffle
at hem
"bosom
amplifier"-
cambric, lace,
beading and
ribbon-
1906
nightgown-
batiste with
white
embroidery
and tucks-
1909

Twentieth Century-
negligee-
1900-1910
Japanese kimono-
interlined silk
crêpe-embroidery-
padded hem
1909
dressing
sacque-
white lawn
with lace-
box pleats-
1901
pajamas-
pongee-
embroidery
and frogs-
1902
"robe de chambre"-
violet dotted
cream flannel-
violet silk
foulard-
collar and
cuffs, tucked
nainsook
1902
kimono of
striped
and plain
wash silk-
1907
matinée of
silk mull-
picot edging-
beading with
ribbon-
1904

Twentieth Century-
corsetry-
1910-1920
back-lacing-
mercerized
batiste-
elastic
gussets-
1912
sueded
tricot
and lace-
1912
well-boned
for the
heavy figure-
white coutil-
lace and ribbon
1911
brocaded
satin girdle
buttoned
in front-
1914
pink satin
with elastic
waistline-
low front
lacing-
1913
front lacing-
mercerized
brocade-
lace
edging-
1918
brassière-
mounted on
flesh colored
chiffon-
elastic
slipover-
snap front
closure-
low side
lacing-
1913
girdle of
suede cloth-
satin panels
front and
back-elastic
waistline-
1915
brassière-
all-over
lace
lined
with net-
ribbon band-
elastic straps-
1913
brassière of
tucked lawn
and embroidery-
1914

Twentieth Century-lingerie-1910-1920
umbrella drawers-nainsook with embroidery and ribbon bowknots-1912
petticoat-wash silk-deep lace flounce-beading and ribbon-1912
combination corset-cover and knickerbockers-nainsook, lace edging, beading and ribbon-1913
the classic ensemble-vest and knickers of glove silk-pale tints-1918
combination corset-cover and drawers-batiste, lace, embroidery, beading and ribbon-1913
"envelope chemise"-crepe de Chine with lace, beading and ribbon-1918
chemise-flesh colored crepe georgette-dark blue satin and embroidery-1919
princess slip-white batiste-lace insertion, edging and deep flounce-beading with ribbon-1913

Twentieth Century-
negligée and
sleepwear
1910-1920
matinée of
crepe de chine-
tucks and lace-
1912
pajamas
of cotton,
wool or
wash silk-
1918
nightgown-
batiste and
cluny lace
with ribbon-
1913
negligée-satin
or velvet-crepe
georgette-
tassels-
self
ornament-
1918
pajama
lounge
suit-print
and plain
silk-coat,
trousers
and blouse-
1919
handmade
Philippine
nightgown-
white cotton
embroidery
on white
nainsook
traveling and
night robe of
striped silk-
1919

Twentieth Century-
corsetry-
1920-1930
evening brassière-flesh colored satin-concealed boning-shirred ribbon trim-1920
slip-on girdle of elastic tricot laced at the sides-brassière of black Chantilly threaded with gold-1925
evening corset hooked in front-silk tricotine with lace-back belt of elastic-1920
foundation garment of elastic tricot-two front bones 1928
slip-on garter belt-brocade with elastic back panel-1927
maternity girdle-satin with front panel of elastic tricot-snap closure-side lacings-1927
foundation garment of brocade, lace and elastic tricot-1929
corset-girdle-brocade and elastic tricot-embroidered motif-1929

Twentieth Century-
lingerie-
1920-1930
nightgown-
shell pink
crepe de Chine-
yoke and belt
of bias
chiffon folds-
1921
backless brassière-
pink satin-chiffon
roses-elastic
belt-1921
batiste
brassière-
lace and white
embroidery-
1921
"dance set"
brassière
and pantie-
pink glove silk-
appliqué blue
and peach-
1927
nightgown-
sheer yellow
voile and
Alençon
lace-
1929
the slip of
bias cut
silk crepe,
chiffon or
ninon-
1925
envelope chemise
with pockets-
glove silk
and lace-
1927
for general wear-
vest and knickers
of glove silk
in pale colors
pajama of
white glove silk-
appliquéd with
black and green chiffon-
1927

Twentieth Century-
negligée-
1920-1930
negligée of two
shades of chiffon-
slashed chasuble
over slip with
pleated skirt-
1922
negligée of
satin meteor
with frills
and corsage of
crepe georgette-
1921
negligée of
zenana cloth
and marabou-
1922
negligée tied to
one side-yellow
crepe de Chine-
ecru Alençon
lace-
1925
tea or dinner
pajamas of
satin with lapels
and appliqué
of lamé-
1926

Twentieth Century-
bathing dress-
1930 - 1954
knitted
red woolen
maillot-
1931
ballerina suit-
blue and white
striped rayon
jersey-white
trunks-
1940
halter-neck
maillot of
knitted
black wool-
1945
knitted wool
suit-purple
with white
and cerise
stripe-
1941
the "bikini"-
jacquard
linen-yellow
and orange-
1948
black wool jersey
suit with
sleeves-gilt hooks
and eyes-gilt
balls on cord-
1953
brown wool
jersey bloomer
suit with
white trimming-
1953
hooded
maillot of
black wool jersey-
1954

Twentieth Century-
corsetry-
1930-1940
knit foundation
of Lastex and
Bemberg-
"uplift" style-
1934
step-in girdle
of Lastex the
two-way stretch
woven fabric-
1932
all-in-one-
satin, elastic
and lace-
detachable crotch
shield-zippered
back-
1931
foundation
of satin ribbon
and net-
1933
Lastex step-in
pantie girdle-
detachable
garters-
1935
step-in girdle of
batiste and elastic-
zipper closure-
1934
step-in
corset of
pink satin-
featherboning-
zippered back-
lace brassière-
1939
strapless
brassière-
uplift bosom-
lace with
featherboning-
hooked front
closure-
1938
the French, back-laced,
side-zippered corset
which "did not take"
1939
step-in
satin corset-
side zippered
closure-front
lacing-
1939

Twentieth Century-
1930-1940
lingerie
hand-embroidered
satin slip-inserted
pleated chiffon-
1931
circular-cut
panties-silk
with lace
inserts-net
bandeau-
1931
tailored
combination.
vest, brassière
and bloomers
of glove silk-
1930
nightgown-
diagonally cut-
blue and
pink crepe-
1932
slip of
white handkerchief
linen with
eyelet embroidery-
threaded with
ribbon-
1939
nightgown-
fine white cotton-
tucks and edging-
sash ribbon in slot-
1938

Twentieth Century-
negligée-
1930-1940
hostess gown-
green and
silver lamé-
1936
full-length robe of
quilted calico-
lined and
piped with
contrasting
color-
1930's and '40's
pink robe-knitted
yarn or ribbon-
crepe lined-
satin trimming
and sash-
1937
hostess
pajamas-
gold brocade
coat with
black satin
trousers
and trim-
1936
gown and
coat of
sheer gray
voile-
1937
boudoir jacket-
cream satin-
ecru Alençon
lace collar-
1938

Twentieth Century-
1940-1954-
chemise, slip and
petticoat
white cotton
petticoat-
white cotton
embroidery-
1947
half-slip-
black taffeta-
pleated net
with ribbon
stripes-1949
chemise slip-
black or colored-
crepe, silk or
chiffon-lace-
pleated frills-
1949
half-slip-
permanently
pleated nylon net-
1950
the
crinoline-
stiffened
net and
featherboning-
1951
full slip-
nylon
tricot and
lace-black
and pale colors-
1952
petticoat of
tulle over taffeta-
boned Lastex
midriff-1954
crinoline
for evening
or wedding-
plastic frame-
1952
petticoat of
taffeta over
organdy-ribbon
through beading-
1954

Twentieth Century-
corsetry-
1940-1954
all•in•one-
basque
silhouette-
Lastex and
satin weave-
hips of
Lastex and
net weave-
lace cups-
1940
uplift and
diaphragm
control-
Lastex satin
and lace-
1944
uplift and
plunging
neckline-
plush•covered
wire-black
lace-
1945
tight•waisted
corselette-
high bosom-
black satin-
1947
quêpière
or waist
cincher -
boned nylon-
front lacing-
uplift, strapless
"bra"-lace
with boning-
1947
corselette-
flattened uplift
and long diaphragm
control of the
Renaissance-
Paris-1954
tight•waisted
girdle of
Lastex
and satin-
lace motifs-
1948
black girdle-
elasticized
nylon lace-
ruffle over
crotch shield-
1954
corselette-
half•brassière-
tight waist-
embroidered
marquisette
and satin-
long garters-
1952

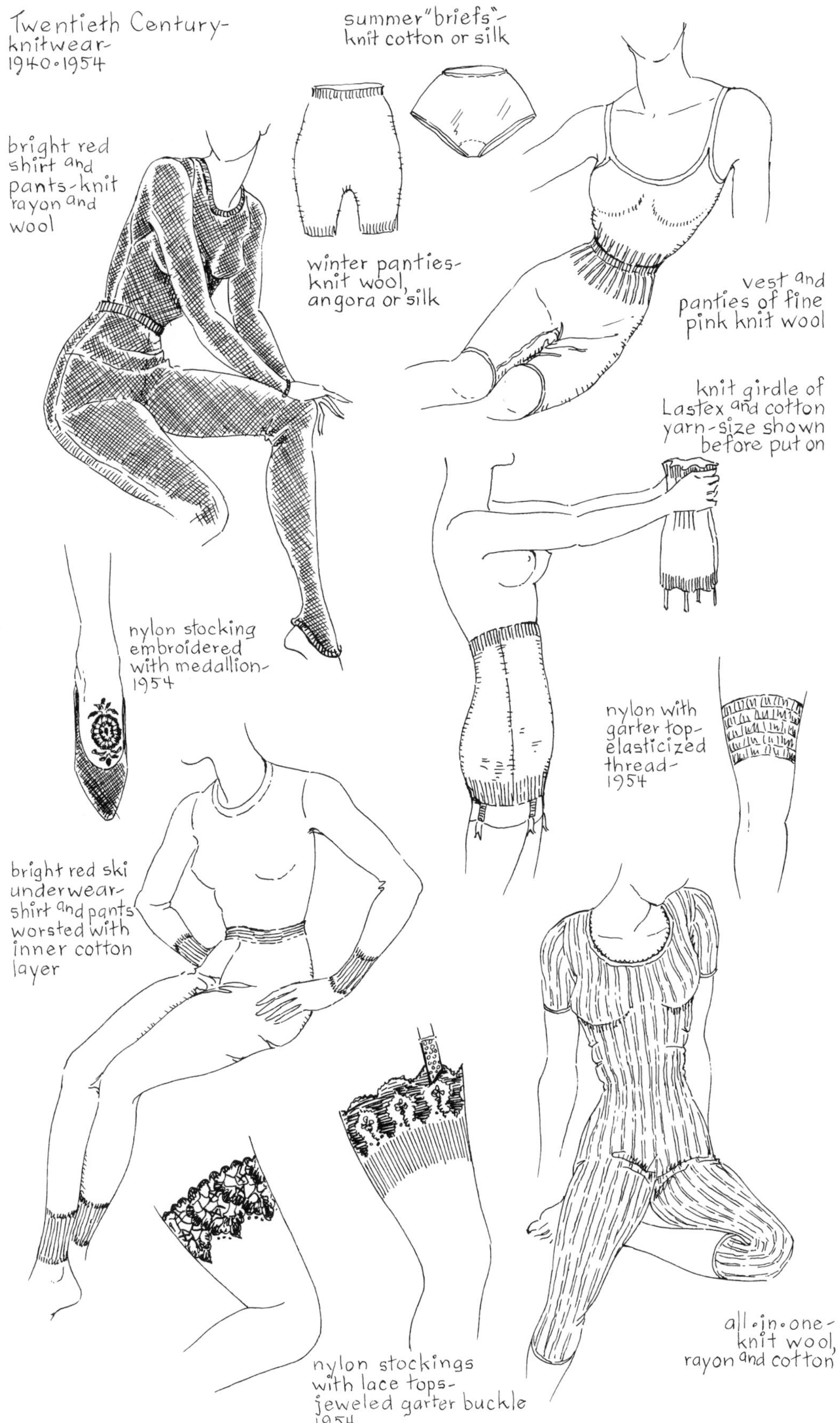
Twentieth Century-
knitwear-
1940-1954
summer "briefs"-
knit cotton or silk
bright red
shirt and
pants-knit
rayon and
wool
winter panties-
knit wool,
angora or silk
vest and
panties of fine
pink knit wool
knit girdle of
Lastex and cotton
yarn-size shown
before put on
nylon stocking
embroidered
with medallion-
1954
nylon with
garter top-
elasticized
thread-
1954
bright red ski
underwear-
shirt and pants
worsted with
inner cotton
layer
all-in-one-
knit wool,
rayon and cotton
nylon stockings
with lace tops-
jeweled garter buckle
1954

Twentieth Century-
negligée-
1940 · 1954
lounge suit-
quilted calico
jacket- black
velveteen trim
and trousers-
1947
hostess coat-
black silk jersey
combined with
aqua and coral-
1947
breakfast
cape of pink
chiffon and lace-
1948
Empire negligée-
voluminous
gray taffeta-
1948
negligée-
rose georgette-
yoke outlined
with appliquéd
lace motifs-
1948
tied bed
jacket-
pink or white
nylon fleece-
net puffings-
Valenciennes
lace-
1950
peignoir of
white or pale blue
albatross-
flowered ribbon-
1952

Twentieth Century-
sleepwear-
1940-1954
"shortie" nightdress-
white, pink or blue
cotton-drawstring
neck-1946
pajamas of
crêpe, satin
or silk jersey-
1946
mandarin sleep
coat-white nylon
jacquard-pale
piping and frogs-
1948
nightdress-
pale blue
nylon and
lace-bloused
back-
1952
nightgown-
white georgette
and lace-
ribbon sash
in slot-
1948
pajamas-
cotton flannel-
striped and
solid color-
1953
sleep
separates-
coat and
skirt of
nylon tricot
and lace-
1953
shirtcoat-
white cotton-
embroidery
and tucks-
1954

Twentieth Century-
bathing togs
heavy ribbed
knitted wool-
changeable
red and black-
top and trunks-
1st decade
heavy knit
red wool-
one-piece with
attached skirt-
2nd decade
two-piece-
woolen jersey-
navy blue
and white-red
striped trunks-
white web belt-
1920's
elastic knit
swim trunks
in vivid colors-
1950's
two-piece-
woolen jersey-
white top-
navy blue trunks-
white web belt-
1930's
boxer shorts
of printed
linen-shirred
elasticized belt-
terry cloth coat-
1940's and 1950's

Twentieth Century-
Ageless Footwear
alpargata-
hemp sandal-
black leather
ties-
Spanish
peasant
leather
boot and
sandal-thong
ties-colored
stitchery and
appliqué-
Polish
woman
cowboy boot-stirrup
heel-colored
inlay and
stitching-
Western U.S.
mukluk-sealskin
with fur inside-
thong or cotton
ties-
Eskimo
Chinese boy's fur shoe-
felt sole-link buttons-
Central
Asia
leather-red or blue pompon-
highland troops
and shepherds-
Greek
knob
sandal or
wooden clog-
India
laptis of birch
bark-Russian
peasant
woman's
red babouche
or mule-
Near East
mule of the
Occidental
mode
carbatine-most primitive
shoe-one
piece
rawhide-
Italian
peasant
woman's
beaded
deerskin
moccasin
N.A. Indian
fur anklet-
Zulu chief-
Africa
tabi (sock) and
gēta (clog)-
Japanese
huarache sandal-
wood with
leather
insole-
braid
edge-
metal
loops-
leather thongs-
Mexican
palm leaf
sandal-
Mexican Indian
Roman woman's
modish sandal-
white calf
skin-star
ornament
sabot-wooden sole-
leather
uppers-
Portuguese
peasant
Guatemalan
Indian sandal-
leather-
dark blue
counter
Moslem shoe of red
morocco-
peaked toe
Moslem
shoes-mules or babouches-
red morocco-turned back
counter-gold
stitchery-yellow
morocco-colored
design
modern calfskin
version of the
Highland rawhide
cuaran
or
brogue-
origin
of
the
modern
ghillie-
Scotch
18th C. pump-black
patent leather or calf-
silver buckle-dress
shoe of many
European
national
costumes
zapatilla-wooden clog-
cotton upper-
bright colored-
Philippine
espadrille-
colored cloth
with braided hemp
sole-Spanish
white buckskin
boot-moccasin-
Taos and
Santa Clara
Indian women
southwestern
U.S.
highlow-black
kid or
suede-
bright
green
laces-
Polish
peasant
bride
kamik-
dyed
hairless
sealskin-
blue with red
and white
skin appliqué-
colored
stitchery-
Greenland
sabot worn by
peasants of France,
Holland and
Belgium-
all wood
or wood
and leather-
carving
yellow morocco boot-
red piping and
pompon-Turkish woman's

Twentieth Century-
masculine
sundries
high fold
collar-
striped silk
scarf-1910
low fold
collar-
brocaded
silk scarf-
1910
dress shirt-
stiff bosom
plain or
piqué-wing
collar-
bow tie
matching
bosom-
pearl
studs-
1910
dress
waistcoat-
dull black
or white silk-
poke collar-
1912
attached collar
buttoned down-
white oxford-
1920's
cloth day vest-
double-breasted-
1920
striped
collar-band
shirt-collar
separate-
1910
pleated
dress shirt-
batiste or silk-
matching tie and
cummerbund-
black or maroon silk-from 1930's
pleated
dress shirt-
piqué, batiste,
voile or silk-
from 1940's
cotton
sports
shirt and
shorts-
1939
sports shirt
of varied
fabric and
weave-1945
short-sleeved
sports shirt-
silk or cotton
in brilliant
color-
1939
figured silk
waistcoat
for country
wear-
1953
pin collar-
small knot
in scarf-
most of
period

Twentieth Century-
sleepwear and
negligée
dressing gown-
cloth, silk or
velveteen-
whole
period
sleepcoat-
mercerized
cotton or
pongee-frog
fastenings-
1920's
nightshirt-
muslin
or cotton
flannel-
1st decade
sleepcoat-
cotton or
silk-1950's
"separates"-
long and short
sleeves and
breeches-
blue, gray,
maize and
wine cotton-
1953
striped
broadcloth
pajamas-
whole period
knitted pajamas for
winter wear-navy blue-
blue and white trim-
1950's
nightshirt-
cotton
broadcloth-
1950's

Twentieth Century-
underwear
union suit-
knitted cotton
or wool-ankle
or knee-length-
1st decade
two-piece white
cotton top and
drawers-
2nd decade
one-piece
white cotton
combination-
1920's
buttonless
combination-
white
crossbar
dimity-
1920's
two-piece
cotton mesh,
broadcloth
or pongee-
pale colors-
1930's
knitted
tee-shirt-
plaid cotton
boxer
shorts-
1950's
knitted
cotton
skeleton
shirt and
briefs-
1950's
tee-shirt and
drawers-
knitted wool-
white for general
wear-bright
red for skiing-
1950's

midi-length-black and white striped voile over bras and shorts-1964
nun's dress-"mini-medieval"-black hood white band and cowl-black jumper with shorts-1968
maxi length
sheer, lacy pantyhose-1960's
bridal gown-silk linen with Cluny lace-wimple headdress-lace-edged apron-1964
mini-length shirtdress of voile with embroidery and buckled belt-1960's
Sassoon's geometric hair-do ending in a point at the nape-1966
plaid jacket over plain mini skirt-taffeta turban-1960's
mini-skirt suit and cap-Tattersall cloth-Courrèges boots-black and white leather-1960's
mini-dress of wool jersey-large felt hat-Gernreich 1960's
beach dress-silk brass and bikini-dotted voile scarf-scarf-1960's
pantsuit of plaid wool-large felt hat-Tiffeau-1960's
plaid cloth Scotch riding cap-1960's

many, Switzerland and Italy. Costume details vary from district to district, but in general men, women and children wear the white linen blouse. Men wear a jacket and short cloth or leather breeches held up by wide embroidered cloth braces. Both sexes wear embroidered cloth waistcoats and knitted woolen hose, very often white. Colorful bands border the feminine full skirt and a large white apron usually covers it. Black leather boots are worn and black leather low shoes have heavy, flat soles, a large silver buckle frequently adorns the feminine low shoe. Hats of felt or straw are wide-brimmed and usually dressed with a barnyard feather or brush.

tyubetevka a pillbox type of hat with flat or peaked crown ornamented with varicolored embroidery. It is known as the Uzbek cap and is popular all over Central Asia and Russia.

tzute rectangles of hand-loomed woolen fabric, usually orange, with stripes in red and black, worn by Tzutuhil Indians of western Guatemala. The pieces are carried as handwork and are tied into turban, wide sash, rebozo, shoulder scarf, blanket, etc.

tyubetevka-
known as "Uzbek
cap"-popular over
Central Asia and
Russia-of felt,
ribbon and embroidery-
worn by men and
women

U

udones full-length stockings of cut and sewn cloth worn by the early Christian clergy and Roman citizens. Those for the priestly class were made of white linen and later of silk. The Udo (singular) fitted over the foot to above the knee. Udones, (plural of udo) were a regular part of European dress from the fifth to the eleventh centuries. Chausse to the Normans, heuse to the Germans, and hose to the Saxons.

ulster a heavy overcoat originally worn by men and women in Ulster, northern Ireland. A long, loose-fitting coat, usually double-breasted, with a full- or half-belt. The coat was formerly made of Ulster frieze. Worn in the U.S. in the first and second decades, twentieth century.

underwear-"underpinings" of a lady of the turn of the 20th C.—chemise of white nainsook, lace and ribbon—corset of brocaded pink coutil

ultramarine the word meaning "from beyond the sea." In medieval times, a costly pigment for painting made by pulverizing lapis lazuli; a deep blue of high saturation and low brilliance.

umbrella from umbraculum, Latin. Babylonians, Assyrians, Greeks, Etruscans and Romans made use of the umbrella, which dates far back into antiquity. A Chinese legend notes that it was invented by the Chinese in the eleventh century B.C., and had twenty-eight ribs. It was widely used for rain in the Orient and the Near East, where it was made of leather. In the Middle Ages, it was adopted by the Catholic Church as a symbol of dignity and power. Falling into disuse, it survived in Portugal, was taken up in Italy and called an "umbrella," and then in France became a woman's fashion, with the name of "parapluie." 1787 is the first date of manufacture in England. The first umbrellas shipped to America came from India to Baltimore in 1772 and were considered feminine accessories. see *sunshades, parasols;* illustrations next page.

underdrawers see *drawers.*

underfur the soft, thick fur underlying the long, coarse guard hairs of a furbearing animal.

underpinnings a name for feminine lingerie.

underproper the wire frame which supported the starched ruff worn in the sixteenth and seventeenth centuries. see *supportasse.*

undershirt the masculine body garment of knitted white lisle or wool

Ulster-heavy, long, loose, double-breasted overcoat-model shown-American-1912

Umbrella

ancient Greek
Babylonian and Assyrian
silk umbrella late 17th C.
silk tilting parasol-about 18 inches diameter-1795
silk tilting parasol-1796
silk with galloon and gauze frill-18th C
silk umbrella-ivory and ebany handle-1813
parasol of pale blue silk with fringe-1813
parasol of red and blue striped silk-red ribbon-1880's

worn under the outer muslin, linen or silk shirt.

undervest a feminine sleeveless body garment of knitted lisle or silk worn under the corset in the nineteenth and early twentieth centuries.

underwear, feminine see *lingerie.*

underwear, masculine consists of skeleton shirt and trunks of cotton, wool or nylon.

undress, military the prescribed uniform for all ordinary occasions.

undressed kid see *kid, undressed.*

Ungaro, Emmanuel see *couture haute.*

uniform prescribed dress of certain style and color for members of a certain society, school or organization, such as a military unit.

union suit a knitted undergarment combining shirt and drawers in one piece. Of wool for winter warmth and lisle or rayon for summer. Made ankle- and wrist-lengths before the use of central heating. Today, used principally for skiing.

unpressed pleats see *pleats, unpressed.*

unprime furs see *furs, unprime.*

unwoven cloth see *felt cloth.*

uparnā a scarf worn as a shawl or veil by Hindu and Mohammedan men and women in India. Of muslin or silk woven with gold or silver threads.

uplift a brassière built to lift and hold the breasts; some are built to hold firm and flatten.

uraeus the symbol of Egyptian sovereignty, a representation of the sacred asp worn by ancient kings and queens. It was attached to the crown in the center of the forehead.

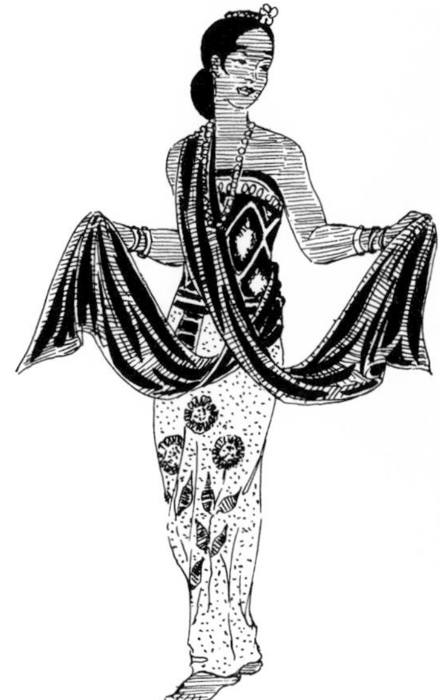

uparnā—same as dopaṭṭa—Indian scarf worn by both sexes—of silk or muslin with gold or silver threads

Uraeus—sacred asp and goddess of Lower Egypt—vulture, goddess of Upper Egypt worn by Egyptian king

uraeus—sacred asp and goddess of Lower Egypt, of silver and enamel in conventionalized style

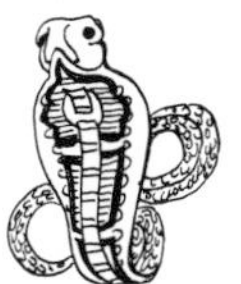

uraeus—goddess of Lower Egypt—worn by a queen of Egypt

V

vair fur of the Russian or Siberian squirrel, a precious fur sewn in alternating gray and white pieces and worn by only kings, nobles and prelates. Medieval.

val lace see *valenciennes lace.*

valence a linen cover which the medieval knight wore on his helmet.

valencia a strong vesting material, figured or striped, of faille or cotton warp with worsted weft. Used principally for livery waistcoats.

Valenciennes or **Val lace** real lace made of linen or cotton thread. A fine bobbin lace in which the thread forms the ground and motifs, without cordonnet, on open and regular mesh. Used on handkerchiefs, baby's wear and fine lingerie. Excellent machine-made imitations are widely used. Commonly known as Val lace, and much used for dresses, blouses lingerie and hats, nineteenth and twentieth centuries.

Valentina see *couture, haute.*

Valentino see *couture, haute.*

vallancey, vallancy a large wig of the seventeenth century which shaded a gentleman's face.

vamp front of the shoe, that part of the shoe upper consisting of instep and toe.

vampy, vampay see *scogger.*

Van Dyck collar see *falling band.*

Van Dyck style the seventeenth century fashions made familiar by the portraits painted by Anthony Van Dyck, court painter to Charles I. see *cavalier.*

vanity case usually a small dressy bag or box for evening use in which the lady carries powder, lipstick and rouge, and other articles. see *compact, vanity case.*

vareuse from the French for the undervest or shirt worn by sailors for messy work; a term formerly used in the southern United States.

vasquine see *basquine.*

vat-dyed When fabric is steeped in vat dye and exposed to the air, the dye is reformed by oxidation and precipitated into the fiber, becoming fast to sun and water.

veal calf see *calf, veal.*

vegetable dye dye obtained from plants, i.e. not mineral or synthetic.

vegetable fibers those which originate from plants such as flax, cotton, jute, ramie and kapok.

vegetable flannel a flannel made of fine wool, of German manufacture.

vegetable hair a fibrous substance prepared from the long moss in southern United States. Used for padding, packing, etc.

vegetable horsehair a stuffing and padding of fiber from the European dwarf fan palm.

vegetable ivory the fruit of a tropical palm in South America. When growing, the nut is soft and creamy, but hardens and resembles animal ivory. Used almost entirely for buttons. see *ivory nut.*

vegetable silk a fibrous material obtained from the coating of seeds of a Brazilian tree. Used for stuffing and padding.

veil The veil has come down from the ancient cradle of civilization in the valley of Euphrates and Tigris. It is most time-honored and meaningful of costume accessories in feminine dress, and a part of as many religions as it has been of fashion. For thousands of years it has stood for bondage, humility, modesty, holiness, marriage, mourning or beauty. In Biblical times, Hebrew women wore veils of gauze as a status mark. In the Christian Church, Paul, apostle to the Gentiles, reproved women for appearing in church with uncovered heads. The feminine veil of the East was worn long before 622 A.D., the beginning of Mohammedanism and it was the adoption of the Moslem religion that carried the veil to Egypt. Though the veil continues to be worn, it is slowly disappearing in the Arab countries. A decree of Turkey in 1928 stated that the long veil worn for centuries was no longer mandatory. In the Empire and Victorian periods, veils were floating wisps of tulle or lace attached to hat or bonnet. In the last decade of the nineteenth century the taut face veil appeared, often sprinkled with chenille dots and tied over bonnet or hat. The veil more or less disappeared at the end of World War I. The short face veil in nose length survived, tied with black velvet ties to keep the hatless coiffure in order, but it has lost much of its former allure.

veil, bridal The Greek bride wore a sheer Tyrian veil, white or colored, woven of wool or linen. It was attached to the back of her headdress or tiara, which was ornamented with pearls. A veil of yellow or saffron was worn by the Roman pagan bride, while that of the Christian bride was white or purple. In the Middle Ages, a bride's headdress was either a sheer white wimple or a tiny skullcap of pearls. The white veil is not again mentioned until the late eighteenth century when a machine for making tulle was invented in Notthingham, England in 1768. It manufactured net and lace wide enough to be used for veils and shawls. The first American bride to wear a veil is said to have been the adopted daughter of George Washington, Nellie Custis.

veil, empress demi-veil a nose length veil worn with a tiny hat in Watteau style, early 1860's, named for the Empress Eugénie.

veil, gremial see *gremial veil.*

veil, motoring a long, wide chiffon veil worn at the turn of the twentieth century in the early days of automobiles. It was a necessary protection against dust, since most cars were of touring or open style and many roads unpaved. Emerald green was considered the most effective protection for the complexion.

veil, mourning a custom of centuries that varied with different countries. The European custom called for all-black outer dress for men and women. The women, especially widows, wore a long, black, heavy crêpe veil for one year. Deep mourning was on the wane by the begin-

Lace veil-corded silk bonnet French-1806
cap of velvet or felt with frontlet and veil-French-15th C.
Bridal veil-lace net-hair dressed in Apolla's knot-shell hair pins-French-1831
capote or poke bonnet-sati with straw visor and lace veil French-1801
bridal headdress-white satin band lace fans in back with jeweled broach-1914
navy blue felt with wings and face veil-1918
fedora or Alpine hat with face veil worn bicycling-1890's
short, circular bridal veil of smoke blue tulle with a pair of birds-1937
black straw with Venetian lace, ostrich and veil-French-1904
black straw sailor-silk puggree-harem veil with chiffon hem-New York-1918
doll hat-pink roses and aster-pink veil-French-1940
black velvet-plumes black and royal blue-dotted veil-French-1893
formal black silk hunting hat-chenille veil-1930's
navy blue sailor cap with floating veil-New York-1910
black felt bowler worn with tailored suit-coarse black mesh veil-1936
lace veil tied over a velvet toque-1920
saucer hat of white felt with black trim and dotted veil-1892

ning of the twentieth century and today has all but disappeared.

Velásquez, Diego de court painter to Philip IV of Spain. Like his contemporary, Van Dyck, he portrayed the current fashions so memorably that the style is associated with his name. He recorded the broad bell-shaped hoop flattened back and front and the slimming, long-pointed corset topped by the ruff, known today as the Infanta style, and the elegance of black for both sexes.

velcro trade name of a nonmetallic, over-lapping fastener consisting of two strips of fabric faced with tiny nylon hooks which, when pressed together, hold fast. To undo, the strips are simply pulled apart. Invented by Georges de Mestral, a Swiss. First used, early 1960's on "cover-ups" in beauty salons.

veldschoen a South African Dutch shoe of untanned hide made without nails, and insole stitched to the uppers; similar to some American Indian footwear.

veldt coat a sports jacket similar to the Norfolk and worn for golf and hunting.

vellum originally a thin calf or lamb gut prepared for use as parchment. Now, fine-grained lamb, kid or calfskin prepared for the same purpose. A vegetable composition is made to resemble vellum. Used in lace-making and embroidery patterns.

vellum cloth made for the tracing of designs. A linen or cotton fabric, thin and sized on one side.

velours, beau a calfskin used for gloves which has been worked, rubbed and brushed until it resembles velvet.

veloutine a merino fabric corded and having a velvety surface.

velvet or **velours** originally made in India and imported by Genoa and Venice. It became a fabric of great luxury. In the sixteenth century, the manufacture of velvet developed in Florence, Milan and Genoa and in Lyons, France; and eventually in Germany and Holland. Velours is the French word for velvet, while the English "velours" applies to a thick-bodied, close-napped, soft type of cloth with a face finish. This latter is used for coats and felt hats, upholstery and drapery fabrics.

velvet, bagheera a fine piece-dyed velvet, crush-resistant because of the uncut pile.

velvet, chiffon or **wedding ring** a soft, luxurious velvet so fine that a width of it may be drawn through a wedding ring.

velvet, cut a background of chiffon, georgette or voile with a brocaded velvet pattern. Closer-woven than transparent velvet.

velvet, Lyons a rich stiff velvet with a back of silk, linen, cotton or rayon and a short, erect pile. Used for dresses but especially for hats.

velvet, nacré a changeable-colored velvet made with the back of one color and the pile of another, producing an iridescent effect.

velvet, panne woven like a plain velvet but with the pile pressed flat in one direction, giving a smooth, lustrous finish.

velvet, stamped a velvet with an allover crushed pattern stamped on the pile by hot dies.

velvet, tartan see *tartan velvet.*

velvet, transparent in printed designs and solid colors and made with a rayon pile on a silk or rayon back. A soft, sheer, easily draped, lightweight velvet.

velvet, uncut a fabric woven like velvet but with the loop warp left cut.

velveteen a cotton velvet with short, close pile. Used for wearing apparel both feminine and masculine, especially sports clothes. see *tripe.*

velveret a velvet with a cotton back.

venerable hood see *French hood.*

Venetian cotton cloth in twill or satin weave with glossy texture. Used for skirts, linings, masquerade and bathing costumes.

Venetian cloth woolen cloth of fine texture woven either with a nap or diagonal twill. Used for dresses and skirts of medium weight.

Venetian embroidery see *Roman cut work.*

Venetian lace many styles of laces made in Venice such as reticella, drawn work, cut work, flat work, raised point, guipure needlepoint.

Venetians full short breeches like knickerbockers, tied below the knees; worn in the sixteenth and seventeenth centuries.

verdigris a color named after a greenish-blue pigment, drug or deposit that forms on copper, brass or bronze surfaces. Verdigris is sometimes called peacock or Spanish green.

verdingale see *farthingale.*

vermilion a brilliant red like the dye from the cochineal insect; a color varying from crimson to nearly orange.

Verona serge a cotton and wool worsted, thin and woven with a twill.

vertugadin see *farthingale.*

vest see *waistcoat.*

vest, skeleton see *skeleton vest.*

vestee feminine, dicky which resembles a waistcoat, usually without armscyes or back. The fabric usually contrasts in color and/or texture with that of the garment.

vestings fabrics intended for men's scarfs, vests and trimmings, such as bird's-eye linen, silk piqué, Persian patterned and corded silks.

vestments garments and accessories of ecclesiastical attire. see *alb; chasuble; dalmatic; amice; cassock; surplice; stole; tippet; tunkle; maniple; chimere; rochet.*

Vicara trade name of a fiber made from protein of corn. Vicara has a soft, luxurious texture like cashmere and good draping quality.

vichy a cotton dress fabric woven of two threads of different colors.

vici kid see *kid, vici.*

Victorian bonnets of mid-nineteenth century, with ribbons tied under the chin, which were prim and dainty, and especially flattering to most women.

victorine fur tippet or pelerine of the early nineteenth century.

vicuña a wild ruminant animal of the Andes, smaller than the guanaco, living in herds from Ecuador to Bolivia. Allied to the llama and alpaca. The animal is becoming scarce because it is much hunted for its soft wool and fur. Vicuña is the finest, softest and costliest of the wool-type fabrics. Used for overcoatings, suitings and fine sweaters.

Vietnam a 1960's style worn by young women, a simple, straight, frock like tunic of black silk with long tight sleeves, a standing collar and a narrow belt; the skirt length between knee and ankle with fitted pantalets showing below.

Vietnamese costume basically Chinese. see *cai-ao; caiquan; sinhs.*

vigogne yarn a cotton yarn made up with about twenty per cent wool or wool waste.

vigoureuse, vigoureux a worsted cloth with a mixture effect in coloring produced by printing the warp before weaving.

vinyl a trademarked, American man-made couturière fabric introduced in 1965. Chiefly for waterproofed capes, coats and suits, and boots, belts and drapes well. It takes dye and print in brilliant colors; for skirts, hats and tote bags. Available in transparent finish and by the yard for home dressmakers. Patterns include tattersalls, stripes and dots as well as solid colors.

Vionnet, Madeleine see *couture, haute.*

virgin wool newly sheared wool which has not been used. Trade mark adopted, Products Labeling Act of 1929.

viscacha a rodent allied to the Chinchilla family, a cross between chinchilla and opossum. From Argentina, it is a poor fur, commonly used in Europe for linings and trimmings, little used in the United States.

Trademark of quality-tested pure Virgin Wool

Vietnamese tunic or cai-co-plum-colored satin with embroidered gold Chinese motifs-trousers of white linen-black silk cap

Vietnamese woman with wicker carrying pole-white cotton jacket-black skirt called sinhs-straw hat with white cotton top

Vietnamese tunic or oudai of printed sky-blue silk-pantaloons black silk or velvet-large straw hat

viscose wood pulp and cotton linters which, by a series of treatments in manufacture, are converted into rayon filaments and thence into a widely used fabric.

visor, vizor, vizard in armor, the upper front piece of a helmet which was movable and could be raised to show the face. In modern usage, the projecting forepiece of a cap to protect the eyes from the sun.

viyella the trade name for a modern twill-woven part-wool dress flannel in many weights, widths and fine colors. It is widely used for masculine, feminine and children's wear. Made in England.

voile a fine, plain, transparent cloth of cotton, silk, rayon or wool. A crisp fabric of great strength for its weight. see *indestructible voile.*

volant French for flounce or ruffle. see *flounce; ruffle.*

volet or **cointoise** a scalloped pennant attached to the helmet of a chevalier in a tournament of the Middle Ages. Also, a short flowing veil attached to a woman's headdress of the same period. see *cointise; quintise.*

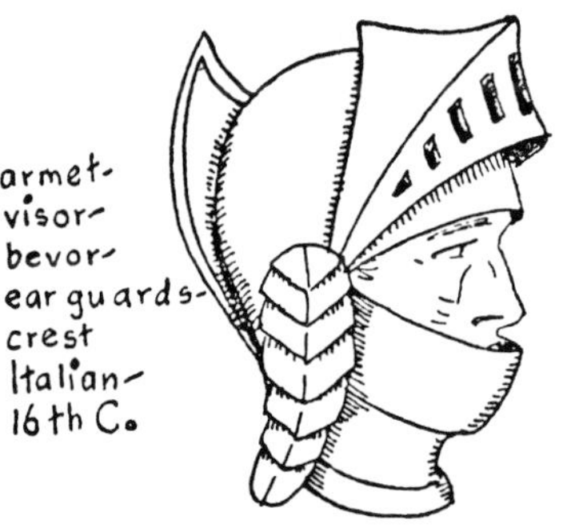

W

wadding any mass of soft fibrous stuff used to pad, stuff or shape clothing.

wadmal, wadmol, wadmel a woolen stuff, often coarse and hairy. Formerly used for stout warm clothes and blankets in the British Isles and Scandinavia.

waffenrock German for a quilted tunic, doublet or tabard worn with armor. Wambais is another German name for the garment. see *mandilion; tabard.*

waffle cloth, waffle piqué, honeycomb cloth a fabric with a honeycomb weave. Used for women's and children's apparel, dresses and coats. In white, used for men's evening ties, shirt fronts and waistcoats.

waist a garment which clothes the body from neck to waist, a bodice or blouse.

waist cincher, waist liner, waist pincher a foundation girdle introduced for wear with Dior's New Look of 1947. Short above and below the waistline, it was made of rayon satin, cotton lace and power net and lightly boned to produce the tiny waist. see *guepière.*

waistcoat, vest in men's wear, a continuation of the doublet of the Middle Ages. A sleeveless but lined body jacket, waist-length, and worn between jacket and dress shirt. Made single- or double-breasted, of contrasting color or fabric or matching the suit cloth. A backless waistcoat appeared in the 1950's for summer wear. It consisted of two front pieces buttoned center front. Two narrow belt pieces, attached to the sides, buckled in back; the fronts also joined by a narrow neckband in back. see *gilet.*

wale rib or ridges as in corduroy, piqué or any twilled fabric. "Wide wale" in corduroy is about a quarter inch wide.

walking coat it resembled the cutaway coat in design but was a bit shorter and had pocket flaps on the hips. It varied in being quite often made of fancy suitings. see *frock coat; English coat; Prince Albert.*

walking shoe a sturdy, comfortable, leather shoe with medium or low heel.

walking stick see *cane.*

wallaby any of the smaller and medium-sized kangaroos from Australia but tanned in the United States. An excellent shoe leather, close-grained and fine, yet tough. see *kangaroo.*

wallachian or **walachian embroidery** a colorful piece of handwork executed in solid buttonhole stitch.

wallaroo see *kangaroo.*

wallet a flat folding purse in which is carried bills and coins, personal documents such as driving license and credit and membership cards. *A Dictionary of Men's Wear,* published 1908, W. H. Baker, says the wallet is for carrying bank notes lengthwise and billets d'amour.

wambais, wammus a man's jacket quilted with flax or tow. More recently, chiefly in the southern United States, a heavy, loosely knitted cardigan with leather belt.

wampum an Algonquin word for beads and strings of beads made from hard clam and whelk shells found along the coast. The original word (meaning white) was shortened by the European settlers. Beads and wampum belts became a medium of exchange between Indians and settlers.

warp the threads that extend lengthwise in a loom and which are crossed by the weft or filling.

warp lace a lace worked on a net in which only the warp threads are visible. Used for glass curtaining.

warp-printed usually silks, wherein the warp threads are printed with the pattern or design before weaving, the weft threads being of neutral or plain color, producing a blurred effect.

wash and wear a fabric treated with wrinkle-resistant properties which makes the laundered garment wearable with little or no ironing. "Wash and wear" and "drip dry" are synonymous terms for such fabrics which have been available since about 1955.

wasp waist - old blue velvet and black - separate capelet - mink muff and bands - black velvet hat with blue and black ostrich - French - 1893

wasp waist or **hourglass silhouette** of the 1890's and early 1900's, produced by a corset heavily boned with steel and whalebone. An eighteen-inch waist was the most desired and admired measurement.

watch The first pocket watch was the invention of a locksmith of Nuremberg in the fifteenth century. It was egg-shaped and called a "Nuremberg live egg." A watch presented to Queen Elizabeth I is described as an armlet of gold with rubies and diamonds containing a "clock." It was really the first wrist watch but had only an hour hand; the minute hand was invented in the seventeenth century. The first thin watches appeared in 1776 and machine-made watches in 1838. A watch on a pin was worn by the Gibson Girl in 1907, and the modern wrist watch appeared in 1914. In the late nineteenth and twentieth centuries, ladies' watches were also worn on necklace chains or on long chains with the watch tucked into a belt pocket. The wrist watch attached to a buckled leather strap was developed for the convenience of the soldier in World War I. Women also adopted the leather wrist strap, but for dress, exquisitely small watches, plain or jeweled, were worn attached to black ribbon or jeweled bands.

waterfall coiffure, tiny hat of rose taffeta with ribbon rosettes - French - 1860's

watch cap see *cap, watch.*

watch, chatelaine see *chatelaine watch.*

watch, hunting-case a man's pocket watch with both dial and back covered; the dial covering, on a spring hinge, could be snapped shut to protect the glass from breakage. With the development of plastic unbreakable crystals, this style was given up. A smaller version was worn by ladies in the late nineteenth and early twentieth centuries, suspended from the neck on a long chain and tucked into the belt. The hunter wrist watch for ladies, mid-twentieth century, has a decorative snap lid, generally jeweled.

watch, repeater a man's watch of the nineteenth century with a chime which struck the hours. Pressing a spring made the hour chime repeat. This obviated the necessity of lighting a candle or lamp in order to tell the time in the middle of the night.

water repellent describes a water-resistant cloth or garment which permits a breathing through the cloth and is more comfortable to wear than a waterproofed finish. Though resistant, it is not impervious to water.

watered silk see *moiré.*

waterfall a headdress of the 1860's with the hair cascading from a knot on the top of the head to the nape of the neck.

waterproof a waterproof fabric is a cloth completely sealed against moisture.

waterproofing various processes by which fabrics and leather are rendered impervious to water.

Watteau bonnet a style featured in the paintings of the French painter Jean-Antoine Watteau (1684–1721). Of straw or felt with ostrich plumes and velvet ribbon. French, 1770's.

Watteau gown the principal style of the French Regency (1715–1723) as pictured by the painter Jean-Antoine Watteau. A loose sack or dress worn over a tight bodice and very full underskirt. The gown had loose folds falling from the shoulders in back, becoming part of the skirt. The neck in front was low and the stomacher ornamented with ribbon. In the 1730's, the Watteau gown became the robe à la française with six box pleats stitched to the back and ending in a train. By 1770 this loose gown was formal dress for court functions. The robe volant or "flying gown" was a variation of the Watteau pleats, the style lasting to the 1770's.

Watteau mantilla of flowered silk held to the figure by a cord or ribbon; A velvet hood lined with satin.

Watteau pleats see *pleats, Watteau.*

Watteau sacque an at-home costume of a hip-length blouse open in front over a stomacher, with pleats falling from the neck in back. Worn over several petticoats. Eighteenth century.

wearing apparel a general term for all clothing.

weasel any of the small slender-bodied animals of the weasel family. see *ermine; marten; mink; sable; skunk; stoat; wolverine.*

weather skirt see *safeguard.*

weaving in its simplest form, the art of making cloth on a frame; a process in which one makes a piece of cloth by interlacing two yarns or strands of threads at right angles. In the third century A.D. Syrian weavers in Byzantium developed the weaving of patterned fabrics by the use of shuttles.

webbing narrow strips of elasticized woven material which are used for garters and suspenders.

wedding gown White appears to have become customary for brides during the First Empire (1799–1815) when the tiny jackets and long coats were of rich dark colors but the dress invariably white. For well over a century white has prevailed, of heavy silk, velvet or lustrous satin with a full-length lace or tulle veil. By the mid-twentieth century, customs became less rigid and a bride might wear a gown of less conventional style and perhaps a shoulder-length headdress of tulle. see *bridal dress.*

wedding ring see *ring, wedding.*

wedge or **platform sole** of wood or leather for sports shoes with heel and sole in one layer and piece, flat on the ground from heel to toe. Fashionable in the 1940's. First worn in ancient Greek drama and called the "tragic kothornos."

wedgie after Wedgies, a trademark; a wedge-heeled shoe.

weeds garments, especially mourning attire. A black band on a man's hat or sleeve, mourning clothes or a widow's black veil. see *mourning.*

weft the threads that cross the warp from selvedge to selvedge. see *warp.*

weighted silk see *silk, weighted.*

weighting, loading a process of adding body and weight to a fabric, especially silk yarn which loses weight when boiled to free it of natural gums. Sizing may also be applied to linen or cotton. see *sizing.*

Weitz, John see *couture, haute.*

Wellington boot see *boot, Wellington.*

Wellington half-boot see *half-boot, Wellington.*

Welsh flannel fine hand-woven cloth from the wool of sheep of the Welsh mountains.

welt a cord, fold, etc., sewn to an edge or border to strengthen or trim.

West of England cloth woolen cloths of fine reputation from the textile centers of Bradford, Huddersfield, Leeds, etc., extra fine worsteds, broadcloths, etc.

whalebone a horny substance from the upper jaw of the baleen whale. It has served as a stiffening in costume since the Middle Ages. It was used to shape the long, peaked toes of footwear; the tall, pointed feminine hennin; the plumes of helmets and many other items. Finally, in the sixteenth century, whalebone replaced iron and steel for stays and busks of corsets and the peasecod-belly of the gentleman's doublet. Today it is obtained chiefly from the bowhead of Greenland, home of the Arctic whale, but it is scarce, as is the use of bones in today's feminine underpinings.

whang leather a Scotch term for leather thongs, lacings and straps.

whipcord a diagonal twill-woven fabric of hard-twisted yarns. Usually in solid colors as Oxford gray, tan and white. Used for sportswear and military uniforms.

whisk see *gallila.*

whiskers see *beards.*

white the color of pure snow, reflecting all the rays of the spectrum combined.

white bob wig see *wig, white bob.*

white coat see *seal, baby.*

white fox see *fox, white.*

white tie the popular term for men's formal evening dress of black tailcoat, white waistcoat and white tie, as opposed to "black tie" which is for informal evening use.

whitney see *witney.*

wide-awake hat another name for the Quaker's hat, a low-crowned, broad-brimmed hat.

widow's peak a widow's bonnet with a peak dipping over the forehead; also, a coiffure with a point of hair in the middle of the forehead. see *attifet bonnet; coiffure.*

wig a covering of interwoven human hair or synthetic fiber shaped to the head to hide a deficiency of natural hair.

wig, Adonis a popular hairpiece in the early eighteenth century. It was fashioned of white or gray hair.

wig, bag a powdered wig with ends tied in a black silk bag to keep powder off the coat, the bag also worn while growing hair. Pigeon's wings often accompanied the bag over ear and cheek.

wig, barrister's wig see *wig, full-bottomed; professional.*

wig block a wooden block, round on top, used for making and dressing wigs.

wig, bob a short wig of the eighteenth century worn on ordinary occasions, and for negligée by men and boys. The curled, bushy, usually white wig was a favorite with the clergy and was worn by the Quakers.

wig, campaign worn in service and traveling. It had a curled toupee over the front of the head, pigeon's wings over the ears and the back hair in a black silk bag. Late seventeenth and early eighteenth centuries.

wig, full-bottomed a wig with high peaks worn from 1750 through the first two decades of the nineteenth century. "Corners" of hair were inserted in concealed parts to shape its contour. The full-bottomed wig was especially favored by elderly and professional men. English and American barristers wore it to the late eighteenth century, and it has been retained to the present by the British as part of official and professional dress. A smaller wig remains part of the uniform of the coachmen of the British sovereign.

wig, hedgehog style the natural hair was cut short on the top of the head and at the sides, the back hair tied in the black silk bag. 1785.

wig, pigeon's wings wig with two curled puffs, one over each ear, eighteenth century.

wig powder pure white powder, appearing in 1703, to cover the wig. Snow-white was most fashionable, gray next, and least fashionable was the brown wig dusted with brown powder. The height of the powder vogue was from 1760 to 1776. Favored colors were grayish pink, blue and violet scented with violet, chypre and pulverized starch.

wig, Spanish hair is the most desirable hair for present-day wigs. Spanish hair is long, black, soft and shiny and easy to process. Spain is the leading exporter of hairpieces and wigs, amounting to over 25,000 pounds a year, as of the 1960's.

wig, tie or **tye** hair simply drawn back and tied with a black silk ribbon.

wig, tonsure the gray wig of the French abbot, made with the tonsure. Eighteenth century.

"wide-awake" Quaker hat of beaver with ribbon and buckle–1780's

Wigs
full-bottomed wig-two points-French and English-judiciary
powdered pigtail wig with pigeons' wings-1731
full-bottomed black wig-English-1670
full-bottomed-white wig-English and American judges-18th C.
Ramillies wig-ribbon bows and solitaire-English cavalry-1740's
solitaire-gray powdered tie-wig with toupet-English-1730's
powdered wig with toupet, puffs and cadogun-English-1774
hedgehog style, wig or natural-French-1785
powdered bag wig-with pigeons' wings-silk bag and ribbon-1728
powdered bob wig-English and French-18th C
gray wig with tonsure-French abbé
white bob wig-cleric American-18-th C.

Wigs - Falls

wig and jeweled circlet- Egyptian Queen- 2033 B.C.

wig of short tube-like curls-Egyptian-2560-2420 B.C.

Cypriote curls-toupee of spiral curls-Greek

Cypriote curls in toupee form- Roman-1st C. A.D.

coiffure à la Zazzera-silk wig- usually yellow- Italian-circa 1475

natural hair with falls-one pendant-three dressed in rolls

coiffure à la Japonaise- natural hair with added falls and floral piece

falls dressed over bobbed hair

falls dressed over short hair

wimple and gorget of sheer lawn-jeweled velvet band or crown-German-13 th C.

chinband, wimple and brim in white linen on a red toque-French-13th C.

witch's costume-black cloth and white muslin-black felt hat over lingerie cap-laced bodice

wig, toupee a curled toupee over the front of the head. see *campaign wig.*

wig, white bob the white wig of elderly, clerical and professional men. American, last quarter eighteenth century.

wigan a cotton fabric, canvas-like, used to stiffen garments. from Wigan, England.

wigs, Queen Elizabeth's Queen Elizabeth I, who had as many as eighty wigs at one time, is supposed to have worn them over a shaved head. Her favorite colors were red and saffron, though she had blond hair as a young woman. By way of compliment, her ladies dyed their locks red. Her wigs were dressed with jewels, pearls and feathers. Mary, Queen of Scots, whose wigs came from France, when in prison changed her wig every other day and wore one to the executioner's block.

wild silk see *silk, wild.*

wildcat see *lynx.*

willow a straw of woven esparto grass and cotton and similar to esparterie. Used instead of buckram for higher-priced hats.

wimple a headkerchief worn in the twelfth and thirteenth centuries, square, rectangular or circular in shape, placed on top of the head and hanging to the shoulders. Known also as the headrail. It was held in place by a fillet of metal, or by a crown if worn by a lady of rank. Of fine white linen, often in colors, especially saffron yellow. After centuries of being worn by court ladies, it remained the headdress of women in general. As often as not, it was worn with a chinband.

wincey, winsey a cloth usually with cotton or linen warp and wool filling, either plain or twilled. Used especially for warm shirts, skirts and pajamas.

windblown bob the hair clipped short, simulating a windblown coif.

windbreaker a sports jacket made of leather or heavy woolen cloth with interlining or quilting, resistant to wind.

windclothes made especially for Arctic exploration and therefore of windproof materials.

Windsor cap see *cap, Windsor.*

Windsor knot see *collar, Windsor.*

wing collar see *collar, wing.*

wings puffs marking the junction of the sleeve and shoulder, a fashion of the second half of the sixteenth century.

winkle-picker in England the name for a shoe with a sharply pointed toe, fashionable the first half of the twentieth century. The term comes from a small sharp pick used when eating periwinkles, a kind of mussel.

Winterhalter another term for the crinoline period, named after the elegant portraits painted by Franz Xavier Winterhalter (1805–1873). He was a German portrait and court painter who lived in Paris from 1834 to 1870.

witch's costume a modern fancy dress imitation of the seventeenth century countrywoman's dress, featuring a steeple hat with narrow brim and a scarlet cloak. The second half of the seventeenth century was the period of most intense witch persecution in England and the American Colonies.

witch's hat as it is known today, a tall, peaked or steeple-crowned hat with a wide brim. Of black felt wool or black beaver, the hat was worn by Puritan women over a white linen or lawn cap in the seventeenth century.

witney, whitney a sturdy woolen cloth, heavy and coarse, made in Witney, England, in the eighteenth century. It was used for coats and breeches. Also, a soft overcoat and blanket cloth resembling chinchilla, the surface tufted in transverse ridges.

witzchoura a feminine redingote, about 1808; a long, Empire cloak, fur-lined, of Russian origin. The same style was copied in percale for summer wear, without fur.

wolf a doglike mammal found in the forested regions of North America, Europe, Asia and Africa. The most valuable for the fur trade comes from northern sections. There are two distinct species, the large gray timber or Canadian arctic, and the small red wolf called prairie or coyote.

wolf, coyote the Mexican name for a small species of wolf from western United States and Canada, known in the fur trade as western wolf. Cheaper than wolf and used for popular priced coats.

wolverine a bearlike animal, largest of the weasel family. It is found in the northern regions of America, Russia, Siberia and Scandinavia. The fur is durable, warm and deep, with long top hair. It is the only fur which does not frost, and therefore was worn by the Eskimos and used as fringe and trimming by the Indians. Used as trimming in the fur trade, expensive because of limited quantity.

wombat see *kangaroo.*

wooden shoes see *shoes, wooden.*

wool a natural fiber obtained from sheep which accounts for most of the wool used in clothing. Specialty fibers or wool from other animals are alpaca, camel's hair, cashmere, llama, mohair and angora goat. Not until a late period did the Egyptians wear any wool and then only for cloaks. Egyptian sheep had coarse, greasy, dark wool, the fleecy type of the Mediterranean world. The art of weaving wool was attained early in ancient times by many different peoples. When Alexander the Great, in the fourth century, invaded India, the natives were found wearing woven woolen shawls of great beauty. The Greeks learned to process and weave wool from the Egyptians, the Romans from the Greeks and by way of Rome, the knowledge passed to the Occidental world. Though the early weaving loom was a seemingly crude instrument, it is said that the fineness of texture produced using it has not been excelled to our day. In the twelfth century, the English King Henry II imported Flemish weavers into England and established weavers' guilds. He granted to the City of London the exclusive privilege of exporting woolen cloth. For many centuries the manufacture of woolen cloth was a household industry. Not until the late nineteenth century were all the processes grouped together in one building. see *shoddy; virgin wool; woolen; worsted.*

wool, Australian see *Australian wool.*

wool batiste an all-wool fabric, fine and lightweight, thinner than challis. Used for dresses and negligées.

wool, brushed see *brushed wool.*

wool crepe a lightweight woolen fabric with crepy texture of various weights and surface effects. Used for suits, dresses, blouses, etc.

woolens woolen fabrics are made of shorter fibers than worsteds. The yarns are soft, loosely twisted and usually have a slightly fuzzy texture as in tweeds, coatings, and meltons.

worsted a woolen fabric made of yarn which is smooth and compact and has been evenly combed, producing a long-wearing cloth such as serge or gabardine. Its name is derived from Worstead, a

witzchoura, a pelisse or fur-lined coat—velvet with astrakan lining and chinchilla trim—1818

timber wolf—length 48 inches—tail 16 inches

wolverine—3 to 3½ feet long—tail 6 inches

village in England, once the center of the woolen industry.

worsted yarn a smooth-surfaced yarn spun from long-stapled pure wool fibers combed so that the fibers lay parallel to each other in weaving. The yarns are loosely twisted for knitting.

Worth, Charles Frederick An Englishman who came to Paris before he was twenty years of age. He became a famous couturier, and in 1858 founded the House of Worth. He was the first to exhibit his creations on living mannequins. The Empress Eugénie and most European royalty were his patrons. For thirty years he was the arbiter of Paris fashions.

wraparound see *skirt, wraparound.*

wrapper a loose dressing robe.

wrapper an informal house gown of the late nineteenth and early twentieth centuries, usually with ruffled neck, sleeves and hem. Fastened in front and held to the figure with a tie belt or left to hang loose. Made of a great variety of fabrics, either plain or trimmed with lace or other decoration.

wraprascal a long, loose greatcoat of the eighteenth century used for riding by both sexes. Buttoned with large metal buttons and sometimes caped. see *Joseph* or *Josie.*

wreath masculine, a crown or chaplet of intertwined leaves, especially laurel leaves, worn in antiquity as a sign of honor. Feminine, a garland of intertwined flowers for the Queen of May or for a bride.

wristlet a bracelet, an ornamental ribbon; a strap to hold a watch; knitted worsted bands as protection against cold, all worn on the wrist. see *muffetees.*

wylie coat Scotch name for a nightdress consisting of undervest and petticoat. Worn by women and children.

bathing suit and wrap-around skirt of print cotton—brown on black—Greta Plattry—1956

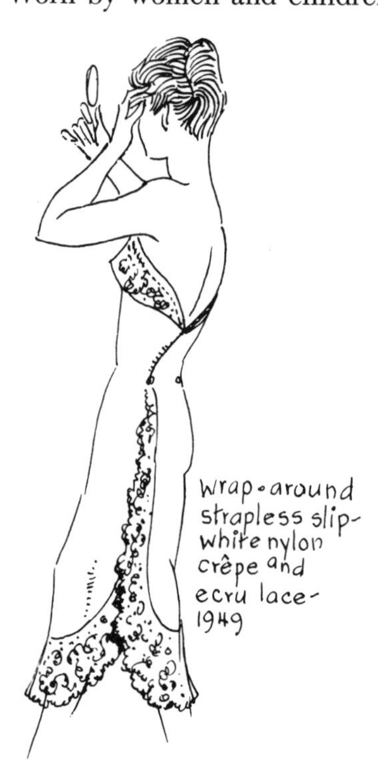

wrap-around strapless slip—white nylon crêpe and ecru lace—1949

Y

yachting A lady's yachting costume in the late nineteenth and early twentieth centuries usually consisted of white flannel or heavy linen skirt worn with shirtwaist with stiff collar and bow tie. The jacket had full-puffed sleeves above the tight forearms. A mannish peaked cap completed the outfit. see *boating wear.*

yak lace a coarse English bobbin lace made in Northampton from Yak wool.

yard measure the English and American linear measure established in the reign of Henry II (1154–1189) by the length of the king's arm. Formerly equal to the Scotch ell. Now, the standard thirty-six inch yard.

yarmulke, yarmelke the Jewish skullcap to be worn at all times with general dress by Orthodox Jews. Also a cap worn in reverence when reading the Torah.

yarn fibers or **filaments** used for knitting or weaving after being twisted or laid in a continuous thread.

yarn, fingering see *fingering yarn.*

yashmak, yashmac a long, narrow face screen that all Mohammedan women once wore. It has slits for the eyes, covered with strips of lace. A narrow piece of ivory, silver or gold supports the veil over the nose. It is tied by strings in back of the head. Another form of yashmak was a little black "awning" that shielded the face. Sloping down from the forehead, it was a square of black horsehair. The wearing of the yashmak, along with the enveloping haik, is a custom centuries old among peoples of the East and Europeans living under Moorish domination. In the twentieth century cloak and veil are slowly being discarded. see *jellaba; haik; litham; maharmah.*

yarmulke-skullcap supposed to be worn at all times by Orthodox Jewry

yashmak of black horsehair with silk shawl draped over a tarboosh-Turkish

yellow one of the three primary colors with blue and red; yellow mixed with blue gives the secondary color green and mixed with red the secondary color orange. Yellow plus green gives the tertiary color yellow-green, yellow plus orange the tertiary color yellow-orange. Light yellows are lemon, straw and primrose; dark yellows are cadmium and gold.

Yugoslavian embroidery stitchery worked in brightly colored yarns with various stitches, principally cross-stitch, double purl-stitch and slanting satin stitch. Done on coarse linen.

Z

zamarra-zamarro- the Spanish shepherd's goatskin coat-cloth sleeves

zamarra, zamarro a sheepskin coat worn chiefly by Spanish shepherds.

zarape see *serape.*

zenana the name for the harem or seraglio, formerly the women's quarters in an East Indian or Persian house from where women are, or were, secluded. Also the name of a lightweight striped fabric, the stripes simulating quilting. Of silk or flannel and used for lingerie or negligée garments.

zephyr a sweater or loose-knit construction made of a silky, tight-twist yarn.

zephyr gingham a plain-woven gingham with a fine, soft finish done in a variety of colors and patterns such as plaids, stripes and checks.

zephyr yarn an embroidery and knitting yarn of a fine, soft woolen or worsted.

zibelline a thick, lustrous woolen cloth with a long, silky nap brushed in one direction. Used for women's cloaks and capes.

zibet, zibetha a relative of the civet cat of Africa which inhabits India, China and the Malay Peninsular. Its stripes are more numerous and regular, and it yields a scent similar to that of the civet. see *civet, civetta.*

zigzag a line composed of even, short, sharp turns or angles. Also, an overall pattern of such lines in a cloth or braid.

zipper the mechanical slide fastener first manufactured in the 1920's and perfected in the 1930's. Used to fasten dresses, foundation garments, or wherever a trim, concealed closure is needed.

zircon, jargoon a mineral whose transparent varieties are used as gems; red, brownish yellow, blue, various greens and colorless. From Ceylon come smoky, pale yellow varieties, "jargon" or jargoon. Called the "poor man's diamonds."

zona wide bands of cloth or soft leather worn by ancient Greek and Roman women over the breasts and around the hips; a wide leather belt that the Greek centurion wore under his cuirass; a hip girdle or a stomach band of wool, or heavy linen or chamoised leather.

zona belt an outer belt or girdle that Jews and Christians in the Levant were formerly obliged to wear to distinguish them from the Moslems.

zori the national Japanese shoe fashioned in many styles of straw, felt and wood. Sometimes the masculine sandal is slightly elevated by a low, broad heel, but the feminine shoe is always flat.

Zouave jacket a bolero style of jacket with rounded corners, of deep, blue Arabian cloth, no collar, no buttons, but gold braid ornamentation and worn with full red cloth pantaloons. Uniform of the Zouave regiment originally formed of Kabyles of Algiers. Many Frenchmen joined the body of infantrymen and in 1838, it became a French unit and fought in the Franco-Prussian War, 1870–1871.

Zouave jacket of Arab blue cloth with red braid-red cloth pantaloons-red cap with blue tassel-1838

The uniform was copied by some independent companies of the U.S. Army in the Civil War and was also copied in feminine fashions of the 1870's.

zucchetto a skullcap. see *cap, calotte.*

zukin a Japanese scarf or challis to protect the coiffure, should a headcovering be needed, as in winter; the traditional protection against the sun is the parasol.

zucchetto-skullcap worn by Roman Catholic ecclesiastics

BIBLIOGRAPHY

ACCESSORIES OF DRESS—Lester and Oerke—Manuel Arts Press, Peoria, Illinois—1940

ALBUM OF AMERICAN HISTORY—James Truslow Adams—4 vols. Charles Scribner's Sons, New York, 1944–1948

AMERICAN INDIAN—Oliver La Farge—Crown Publishers, New York, 1936.

APPAREL ARTS—Anniversary Issue, 1936—Esquire, Inc., New York

BOBBINS OF BELGIUM—Charlotte Kellog—Funk and Wagnalls Co., New York, 1920

BOOK OF COSTUME—by a Lady of Rank (Mary Margaret Stanley Edgerton, Countess of Wilton) Henry Colburn, London, 1847

BRITISH COSTUME DURING XIX CENTURIES—MRS. CHARLES H. ASHDOWN—Thomas Nelson and Sons, Ltd., 1910

CLANS and TARTANS of SCOTLAND—Robert Bain—Collins, London and Glasgow

CLOTHES—James Laver—Horizon Press, Inc., New York, 1953

COSMETICS AND ADORNMENT—Max Wykes-Joyce, Philosophical Library, New York, 1961

COSTUMES ANCIENS et MODERNES—Cesare Vecellio—Firmin Didot Frères et Fils, Paris, 1859

COSTUME IN ENGLAND—F. W. Fairholt, F.S.A.—2 vols. C. Bell and Sons Ltd., London, 1846—1910–1916

COSTUME THROUGHOUT THE AGES—Mary Evans, A.M.—J. B. Lippincott and Co., Philadelphia, 1930

COSTUMES AND FASHIONS IN OLD NEW ENGLAND—Alice Morse Earle—Charles Scribner's Sons, New York, 1893

DICTIONARY OF THE AMERICAN INDIAN—John L. Stoutenburgh Jr.—Philosophical Library, New York, 1960

DICTIONARY OF MEN'S WEAR—William Henry Baker—Britton Printing Co., Cleveland, Ohio, 1908

DICTIONARY OF TEXTILE TERMS—Dan River Mills Inc.—Danville, Virginia, 1960

DICTIONNAIRE DU COSTUME—Maurice Leloir—Librairie Gründ, Paris, 1951

DIE MODE—Mittel Alter, XVI, XVII, XVIII jahrhundert—Max von Boehn—Munich, 1919, 1925, 1925, 1928—4 vols.

DRESSMAKERS OF FRANCE—Picken and Miller—Harper and Brothers, New York, 1956

EARLY AMERICAN COSTUME—Warwick and Pitz—Century Co., New York, 1929

ENCYCLOPAEDIA BRITANNICA—11th Edition, New York, 1911

ENCYCLOPEDIA OF COSTUME—James Robinson Planché—London, 1876

ENCYCLOPEDIA—NEW STANDARD—Funk and Wagnalls—New York and London, 1937

ENCYCLOPEDIA OF EGYPTIAN CIVILIZATION—translated from the French—Georges Posener-Tudor Publishing Co., New York

ENGLISH COSTUME—Dion Clayton Calthrop—Adam and Charles Black, London, 1907

EVERYDAY LIFE IN ROMAN BRITAIN—Marjorie and C. H. B. Quennell—B. T. Batsford Ltd., London, 1924

EVERYDAY LIFE IN ANGLO-SAXON, VIKING AND NORMAN TIMES—Marjorie and C. H. B. Quennell—B. T. Batsford Ltd., London, 1926

FABRIC FACTS—Fairchild Publications, Inc., New York, 1965

FIELDBOOK OF NATURAL HISTORY—E. Lawrence Palmer—McGraw Hill Book Co. Inc., New York, Toronto, 1949

FASHIONS FOR MEN—Editors of Esquire Magazine—Harper and Row, New York, 1966

FUR—A PRACTICAL TREATISE—Max Bachrach—Prentice-Hall Inc., New York, 1936–1937–1946–1947

HERITAGE OF COTTON—M. D. C. Crawford—Fairchild Publications Inc., New York, 1948

HISTORY OF AMERICAN COSTUME—1607–1870—Elizabeth McClellan—Tudor Publishing Co., New York, 1942

HISTORIC COSTUME FOR THE STAGE—Lucy Barton—Walter H. Baker Co., Boston, 1938

HISTOIRE DE LA DENTELLE—Madame Bury Palliser—Librairie de Firmin, Didot et Cie, Paris, 1892

HISTOIRE DU COSTUME EN FRANCE—J. Quicherat—Librairie Hachette et Cie, Paris, 1875

HISTORY OF CORSETS—M. D. C. Crawford and E. Guernsey—Fairchild Publications Inc., New York, 1951

HISTORY OF COSTUME—Carl Kohler—George G. Harrap and Co. Ltd., London, 1928

HISTORY OF HOSIERY—Milton N. Grass—Fairchild Publications Co. Inc., New York, 1955

HISTORY OF LINGERIE—M. D. C. and E. G. Crawford—Fairchild Publications Inc., 1952

HISTORY OF UNDERCLOTHES—G. Willet and Phillie Cunnington—Michael Joseph, Ltd., London, 1951

INDIANS—Editors of American Heritage—American Heritage Publishing Co. 1961

INDIANS OF THE AMERICAS—National Geographic Society—Washington, D.C., 1955

INDIANS OF AMERICA—Lillian Davids Fazzani—Whitman Publishing Co., Racine, Wisc., 1935

INDIAN COSTUMES OF THE UNITED STATES—Clark Wissler—American Museum of Natural History—Doubleday, Doran and Co. Inc., New York, 1940

INDIANS, NORTH AMERICAN—George Catlin—2 vols.—George Grant, Edinburgh, 1926

LANGUAGE OF FASHION—Mary Brooks Picken—J. J. Little and Ives Co. New York, 1932

LAROUSSE UNIVERSAL—2 vols.—Librairie Larousse, Paris, 1922

LE CORSET DANS L'ART ET LES MOEURS DU XIII AU XX SIÈCLES—F. Libron et H. Clouzot, Paris, 1933

LA COSTUME CHEZ LES PEUPLES ANCIENS ET MODERNES—Fr. Hottenroth

LE COSTUME HISTORIQUE—M. A. Racinet—Firmin Didot et Cie., Paris, 1888—6 vols.

LOVE OF A GLOVE—C. Coddy Collins—Fairchild Publications Inc., New York, 1945

MALE AND FEMALE COSTUME; From the Notebooks of BEAU BRUMMEL—Eleanor Parker—Doubleday, Doran and Co., New York, 1932

MANUEL OF LACE—Jeannette E. Pethebridge—Cassell and Co. Ltd.—London, 1931

MODES AND MANNERS OF THE XIX CENTURY—Dr. Oscar Fischel and Max Von Boehn—4 vols.—J. M. Dent and Co., London—E. P. Dutton Co., New York—1909-1909-1909-1927

PAGEANT OF HATS ANCIENT AND MODERN—Ruth Edgar Kilgour—Robert M. McBride and Co., New York, 1958

POCKET TEXTILE DICTIONARY—Kogos Publications Co., New York, 1962

REMEMBER WHEN—Allen Churchill—Golden Press, Inc., New York, 1967

SHORT HISTORY OF COSTUME AND ARMOUR—Kelley and Schwabe—B. T. Batsford Ltd., London, 1931

TASTE AND FASHION—James Laver—George G. Harrap and Co. Ltd., London, 1948

TASTE IN AMERICA—Ishbel Ross—Thomas Y. Crowell Company, New York, 1967

THE ART OF ENGLISH COSTUME—C. Willet Cunnington—Collins, London, 1948

THE BEAUTIFUL PEOPLE—Marylin Bender—Coward—McCann, Inc., New York, 1967

THE DANDY—BRUMMELL TO BEERBOHM—Ellen Moers—Viking Press, Inc., New York, 1960

THE REGIONAL COSTUMES OF SPAIN—Isabel de Palencia—Madrid, 1926

THE ROMANCE OF LACE—Mary Eirwen Jones—Spring Books, London

THE STORY OF LACE AND EMBROIDERY—David E. Schwab—Fairchild Publications, Inc., New York, 1951

THE STORY OF LINEN—WILLIAM F. LEGGETT—Chemical Publishing Co., New York, 1945

THE WONDERFUL WORLD OF CLOTHES—U.S. Committee for Unicef—Robert Hall Clothes, Inc., 1965

THE WORLD AND ITS PEOPLES—Greystone Press, New York—1960's

THIS IS FASHION—Elizabeth Burris-Meyers—Harper and Brothers, New York, 1943

TOOLS AND TOYS OF STITCHERY—Gertrude Whiting—Columbia University Press, New York, 1928

TWO CENTURIES OF COSTUME IN AMERICA—Alice Morse Earle—The Macmillan Co., New York, 1903

WEBSTER'S NEW INTERNATIONAL DICTIONARY—G. and C. Merriam Co., Springfield, Mass., 1937

WEBSTER'S BIOGRAPHICAL DICTIONARY—C. and G. Merriam Co., Springfield, Mass., 1953

PERIODICALS—

CIBA REVIEW—Basle, Switzerland

FAIRCHILD PUBLICATIONS, Inc., New York

GENTLEMEN'S QUARTERLY, Esquire, Inc., New York

HARPER'S BAZAAR, New York

THE METROPOLITAN MUSEUM OF ART—Bulletins—New York

THE NATIONAL GEOGRAPHIC MAGAZINE—Washington, D.C.

THE NEW YORK TIMES, New York

TIME MAGAZINE Inc., New York

VOGUE MAGAZINE, New York